From **LEO ROSTEN'S**
TREASURY OF JEWISH QUOTATIONS:

❋ "When a father helps a son, both smile; when a son must help his father, both cry."

❋ "Those who do not help others need doctors to help them."

❋ "Safeguarding a girl in love is harder than guarding a sackful of fleas."

Read 4,349 more in the pages that follow.

"Life is a dream for the wise, a game for the fool, a comedy for the rich, a tragedy for the poor."
SHOLEM ALEICHEM

"The pursuit of knowledge for its own sake, an almost fanatical love of justice, and the desire for personal independence—these are the features of Jewish tradition which make me thank my stars that I belong to it."
ALBERT EINSTEIN,
The World as I See It

LEO ROSTEN'S
TREASURY
OF
JEWISH
QUOTATIONS

BANTAM BOOKS
TORONTO · NEW YORK · LONDON

LEO ROSTEN'S TREASURY OF JEWISH QUOTATIONS
*A Bantam Book / published by arrangement with
the author*

PRINTING HISTORY
McGraw Hill edition published November 1972
2nd printing ....December 1972
3rd printing ....March 1973
Bantam edition / November 1977

*All translations from the Hebrew/Aramaic texts used for this
anthology—whether the Torah, the Talmud, collections of midrashim, memoirs, essays, letters, poems, autobiographies—were
made by Rabbis Solomon D. Goldfarb, Aaron Kriegel and Jay
Rovner; and all translations were freely rephrased in English
by Leo Rosten. Translations for Yiddish sources were made by
Mr. Rosten, Rabbi Goldfarb and various consultants.*

*Bantam Books are published by Bantam Books, Inc. Its trade-
mark, consisting of the words "Bantam Books" and the por-
trayal of a bantam, is registered in the United States Patent
Office and in other countries. Marca Registrada. Bantam
Books, Inc., 666 Fifth Avenue, New York, New York 10019.*

PRINTED IN THE UNITED STATES OF AMERICA

TO
the scholars, rabbis, poets, philosophers
and plain men of good sense
from whose words, quoted in these pages,
I have learned so much.

Contents

THE STORY
OF
THIS BOOK

"I have tried to include only those sayings that will make you laugh, smile, or think."

LEO ROSTEN

"*I never met a man in whom I failed to recognize some quality superior to myself; if he was older, I said he has done more good than I; if he was younger, I said he has sinned less; if richer, I said he has given more to charity; if poorer, I said he has suffered more; if wiser, I paid honor to his wisdom; if not wiser, I judged his faults less severely. Take this to heart, my son.*"

The Testament of
Judah ben

Jehiel Asher (1250–1327)

How the Obsession Began

I started this book when I was six years old. I did not, of course, know that I was becoming an anthologist, nor that I would spend fifty-eight years collecting gems—verbal gems of wit, insight and wisdom, particularly those used and loved by Jews.

I was raised by a mother and father who simply leaped at the chance to utter a folk saying, in Yiddish, in the day-by-day rearing of their children. And so proverbs, epigrams, maxims, *vitsn* of every conceivable sort were woven into the fabric of my daily life. No aspect of my conduct escaped comment or instruction, chastisement or praise—through an adage. Had I forgotten a chore? Torn my shirt? Not finished my milk? . . . Was I protesting too much? Excusing too long? Explaining too little? . . . Had I arrived too late? Left too early? Neglected my homework? . . . Was I guilty of insufficient consideration to a widow, an old man, a beggar, a clerk? Not helped a neighbor, hurried the grocer, ignored a greeting, fudged on a promise? . . . Was I being stubborn, jealous, willful, vain? Would Mr. Becker think me unfriendly or Mrs. Feibush unkind, Joey Tiven insensitive or Molly Shulman unjust?

For even the possibility of having committed some breach of decorum, I heard a mighty precept that might teach me—heir of all the ages—how better to conquer my thoughtlessness, guard my tongue, refine my conduct, so that I might one day be worthy to be called a *mentsh*. My tender age, the normal distractions of youth, innocent impulsiveness—all received short shrift from my mother, a lady of indomitable will, who sought perfection and discounted my explanations (God forbid they should be *excuses*) for the errors of my boyish ways.

So it was through the proverbs and parables of the Jews that I was introduced to the kingdoms of ethics, reason, psychology, philosophy. The words of ancient sages and scholars poured into my ears—to teach me the imperatives of honor, the ingredients of manners, the dimensions of duty, guilt, shame, self-respect . . . I tell you, as I look back on it now, the building of the Pyramids involved no greater complexities of analysis and choice than accompanied the simple business of living out one day in what I can only call the ethical furnace of my home.

Now, the maxims I heard from my mother and father were, of course, not original with them: they were folk sayings—heard from his or her father, who had heard it from his or her mother, who had heard it from his or her uncle, who was quoting a friend who was only repeating what some rabbi had told him a sage, quoted in the Talmud as "speaking for" another seer, had once said.*[1]

And *that* patriarch, had my parents known it, was interpreting Hillel or Rabban Gamaliel, who was repeating an adage first heard in Judea or Babylon or Alexandria—and *that* aphorism, for all anyone knows, had been refurbished by some twelfth-century scholar in Cordova or some sixteenth-century mystic in Safed, some eighteenth-century rabbi in Vilna or some twentieth-century *hasid* in Dubno or Berdichev or Brooklyn.

And there was another bottomless well of folk wisdom that gushed sweet waters into our Chicago home. Each night, as soon as we finished dinner (we called it "supper"), my father would open the *Daily Forward* ("Forvits" is how it is rendered in Yiddish). How he loved that journal! It served as chronicle, town crier, telephone, movies, radio, television, almanac, encyclopedia—all in one. The news was a daily bazaar of human deeds and follies; a circus of the singular, the fanciful, the brutal, the grotesque; a recessional of the wonders and crimes, the glories and horrors the race of man each day created.

My father would spread the *Forvits* across the table under the gas lamps, and would proceed to read; and as he read he would mumble and cluck and sigh, muttering astonishment or approval, marveling over this miracle or deploring that disaster. The most noteworthy items he read aloud to my mother and me; and so, even as a boy, I

---

* Numbered references are identified or expanded at the end of this Preface, pp. 71–76.

apprehended snatches of meaning from the reports about the movers and shakers of the world: breadlines in Warsaw, maneuvers off Jutland, a *brouhaha* in Washington, a small pogrom in Rumania, a large one in the Ukraine . . . To all these reverberations of the great world in our warm little kitchen my father counterpointed his own commentary—admiration or dismay or disgust, eloquent grunts or scoffing snorts, an epiphany of "Mnh!" and "Mnyeh!"s, shocked "Oy!"s, affirmative "Ai-ai-ai!"s, cynical "Hoo-hah!"s—all replaced, as his Americanization proceeded, with ungreenhornish "My!"s and "Imagine!"s, "Fakers!" or (in outraged regression) *"Paskudnyaks!"*

When the reading of the news was completed, my father turned to the *"Bintl Brief"* ("Bundle of Letters"), the "agony column" of Letters to the Editor that was a veritable Vanity Fair: and now I heard about raffish boarders making advances to respectable young landladies; consumptive men forced to live on the pittances of in-laws; Socialist seamstresses who lamented their swains' indifference to the Class Struggle; sad tales of lost children, abandoned sweethearts, greedy relatives, heartless sons, unforeseen pregnancies—every conceivable experience that cast fate's harsh shadow across unprepared lives. The *Bintl Brief* threw onto the public stage of print the high hopes and brave dreams, the aching disillusionments and small miseries of life in this shimmering New World to which the immigrant hordes had come.

The letters to the *Forward* often asked for advice: "Should I marry him?" "Is such a woman to be trusted?" "Will capitalism change only through revolution?" "How can a mother's heart bear such shame?" "Does a business partner need a *written* promise?" And the editor, famed Abe Cahan, often answered the questions himself, in consoling, indignant, or magisterial words. Many of the letters, and more of the answers, contained Jewish folk sayings, which my father read or improved ("Sleep faster: we need the pillows"), and the adages sank roots in my mind:

"When you're hungry, sing; when you're hurt, laugh."
"When a father helps a son, both laugh; when a son helps his father, both cry."
" 'For instance' is not proof."
"It's better to be embarrassed than ashamed."
"Safeguarding a girl in love is harder than guarding a sackful of fleas."

"A man is not honest just because he had no chance to steal."

"Dear God: let us not suffer all that we may be able to endure."

"A fool measures water with a sieve."

"A saloon can't corrupt a good man, and a synagogue can't reform a bad one."

"Little children don't let you sleep; big children won't let you live."

"He only lies twice a year—in summer and in winter."

After the daily, delicious heartthrobs of the *Bintl Brief* came the climax to each night's vicarious dramas: the reading of a short story—a tale by Cahan himself, or by I. J. Singer, the great Sholem Asch, or the incomparable Sholem Aleichem. My father read very well; he had a faultless sense of comic timing and significant pauses; he was a marvelous mimic. And those stories held me in thrall.

To this day, I remember the textures, if not the plots, of the tales these as-yet-unheralded writers spun out: about an impending *shidakh* or a calamitous purchase, an encounter with an anti-Semite or an uneasy deposit in that novel institution (likely to swindle its depositors at any moment) known as a Bank (the deposit was promptly withdrawn). Sages and salesmen, yearning widows and shameless philanderers; overworked men, undernourished wives; the dreamy, the lazy, the successful, the *shlemiels*; men burning with idealism, men soured by life; the favors and fevers of love sought, love lost, love gained, love not requited; *shtetl* customs and American foibles; *brises*, betrothals, betrayals, Bar Mitzvahs; the pleasure of wine in a *gleyzele*, the danger of *schnapps* in a glass; children who flourished, children who perished; the laugh in the doorway, the cry in the night—I can hear them all again, faint old music as from a calliope, playing its accompaniment to the kaleidoscope of characters that turns in my memory.

And here, too, in the tales told by fine writers, lay a cornucopia of folk sayings they knew or witticisms they coined. It was from Sholem Aleichem, if I am right, that I first learned:

"To a marriage, walk; to a divorce, run."

"Gossip is nature's telephone."

"April Fool: a joke repeated 365 times a year."

"A bachelor is a man who comes to work each morning from a different direction."

"The girl who can't dance says the band can't keep time."

"When a poor Jew eats a chicken, one of them is sick."

I do not think we can ever recover the freshness of childhood; yet our minds are populated by people from the past. In my memory, none move more merrily, more vividly, in more magical measure, than the characters in those stories my father read to me when both I and he—*olevasholem*—were so very young.

* * *

I was lucky to be an immigrant child, and to grow up in a bilingual world; nothing so sharpens the ear to the subtleties that differentiate words as constantly shuttling between two vocabularies. A language, in Walter Nash's phrase, is "a palisade of verbal custom."

> In language I make . . . effigies and create ikons. In words, whispering, stumbling words, in the litter and ceaseless drift of words, is my searching for my own identity . . . and the articulation that will go on, at the heart of all experience, till at last all burdens are laid down and I need no more words, not even amen and good night.[2]

And as I grew older, it was from storekeepers or soapbox orators, at meetings of the Workmen's Circle or on picnics of Chicago's Lodzer colony, that I heard more and still more scintillating sayings:

"When a young man marries, he divorces his mother."

"Out of snow, you can't make cheesecake."

"The man who marries for money will earn it."

"A rabbi whose congregation doesn't want to run him out of town isn't a rabbi; and a rabbi whose congregation does run him out of town isn't a man."

"When you go to a restaurant, choose a table near a waiter."

The folk sayings were only sardonic or scathing: some stopped my heart:

"I felt sorry for myself because I had no shoes—until I met a man who had no feet."

"The rich have heirs, not children."

"Pity was invented by the weak."

"When you add to the truth, you subtract from it."

"No one is as deaf as the man who will not listen."

* * *

The adages I heard struck me, even in my puberty, as much more than little homilies. They were illuminations, electrifying flashes of perception and perspicuity. And, perhaps because I dimly dreamed of someday being a writer, they struck me as masterpieces of precision: the use of small words to teach huge truths. Even the homeliest folk saying impressed me as having a certain beauty; for there *is* beauty—or, at least, elegance—in the economy and pungency with which a simple saying can convey a profound verity.

Words must surely be counted among the most powerful drugs man ever invented. In my adolescence, I became an absolute nut about aphorisms. I collected epigrams the way some boys collect stamps. For years, obsessed with a fear of forgetting anything, I wrote down every *bon mot* I read or heard. My pockets became filing cases for tersities of wisdom (scribbled on scraps of paper, backs of envelopes, margins torn from newspapers), a hodgepodge of verbal wonders—from O. O. McIntyre or Will Rogers to "Kin" Hubbard and the true masters: Mark Twain, G. K. Chesterton, Oscar Wilde, Bernard Shaw, H. L. Mencken (the most neglected humorist in American letters). In a spree of affluence, I bought a 4-by-6-inch card catalogue, and packets of lined cards, and blank index guides on which to write my categories: "Fate . . . Lust . . . Honor . . . Folly . . ."—and so began to systematize my own precious Bartlett.

I devoured any anthology that offered the cream of the jests of Bacon, Montaigne, Sydney Smith, La Rochefoucauld. I still remember my rapture on discovering Ambrose Bierce's *Devil's Dictionary*, or my jubilation in collected quotations of Epictetus, Marcus Aurelius, Balthasar Gracian, Heinrich Heine. I reveled in admiration over the genius that could marshal words, metaphors, irony, paradox with so much originality, to achieve such deft insight. In a way, I honed my mind on the whetstones of epigrams. I came to suspect, long before I encountered Sigmund Freud, that witticisms are "strategems to evade the censors of the self," that "comedy is a complex masquerade [and] murder oft peeps through the masks of our wit," that "humor is the messenger of truths that churn behind the camouflage of levity."[3]

And then, with the audacity of the young, I turned aphorist myself, selling an article to the *New Republic*, entitled: "Political Lexicon"; it was a twenty-four-year-old's broadside, dripping cynicism, against the stupid, heartless, hypocritical System. One line will give you the flavor:

> *Rules of War:* The rules, solemnly observed by sovereign nations, which make it illegal to hit below the toes.

I was, of course, too young to *know* very much: to distinguish grievances from truth; to suspect the sardonic, which is so attractive to youth, and respect the expedient, which enrages the impatient.

I now tried to distinguish adages from apothegms from aphorisms. What makes an epigram different from a precept or proverb, a folk saying from a maxim? I cannot say that I did much more than tone up my semantic muscles in this foredoomed exercise; but I did begin to think of folk sayings as proverbs' homely brothers—and of both as packaged common sense. An adage, I decided, is sober, an aphorism arresting, but an epigram must tickle the ribs. Proverbs deal with universals; epigrams deal with anything. An adage may be trite; an aphorism is no aphorism if it is. Proverbs are encapsulated experience; epigrams are flashes of fun. Proverbs are the primers we inherit from the past; epigrams are often new, young, in vogue—and may pass out of use. Epigrams, I concluded, are displays of wit traceable to a known man, often more clever than true, prized more by intellectuals than by the masses.

It may amuse you to know that I was so lost in my obsession that I visualized aphorisms as dressed in silk, epigrams as bedecked with sequins, proverbs as wrapped in fur. Folk sayings, obviously, ran around in honest homespun.

* * *

It occurred to me that witticisms achieve the greatest longevity of a writer's output. How few of us have read a page by the authors of lines we remember with that special gratitude we accord the wickedly apposite.

"If triangles had a God, He would have three sides."

"The doctor who treats himself has a fool for a doctor—and a fool for a patient."

"No one forgets where he buried the hatchet."

"Conscience is the inner voice that tells us that someone is watching."

"An idealist is one who, upon observing that a rose smells better than a cabbage, concludes that it will also make better soup."[4]

* * *

The more I read, down the years, the more I found myself plumbing beneath and beyond the surfaces of wit. I came to see that the sayings of a people reflect its particular history, values, and sensibilities; that any people, whether nation, tribe, or sect, possesses a distinctive style of thought, special patterns of esteem or scorn, characteristic reflexes of affection and contempt and moral outrage —and all these are mirrored in the adages men prize.

Yet the more I studied proverbs, the more I found certain common themes running through all of them: whatever a people's experience or ethos or faith, men ultimately voice the bitter conclusion that life is unjust, fate blind, fortune heartless. And I began to understand that all men, whether Zulu or Christian or Jew, desperately try, through the reiterated sorcery of words, to fortify their faith in a passionate necessity to believe that virtue *will* be rewarded, that evil will be punished, that truth will somehow triumph in the end.

The Bonus of Bernstein

I went to study in London in 1934, and in that glorious hodgepodge of villages nestling around the Thames I discovered secondhand-book stores such as I had never dreamed of before. There were thousands of them, crammed from floor to ceiling, spilling their frayed bodies across sagging shelves, indoor counters and outdoor bins. The shops stood like noble beggars—near the British Museum, off Russell Square, in alien Soho; but most of them were crowded along Charing Cross Road, unshaved cheek by untidy jowl, and overflowed into the lanes and alleyways that web off that paradise for bibliophiles. Foyles, bulging out the seams of four high buildings, was but the

largest athenaeum: St. Martin's Lane, which is not a lane
but a traffic jam, shimmered with frumpy shops for anti-
quarians, faddists, collectors of anything ever written on
Aztec gold or Battersea boxes; the empires of Assyria,
China, Islam; the art of Mogul miniatures or Mithraic
amulets; the politics of Sparta, Solon, Suleiman, Samarkand.

How many hypnotized hours I spent in those dusty
dungeons, reading as much as browsing, and browsing
much more than buying (I was living on $1.50 a day), I
cannot remember. One day, my eye, traveling along a
decrepit shelf, fell upon a thick, greenish volume whose
title, in shining gilt, was *Jüdische Sprichwörter und Redensarten*. I took the book down. The text was Yiddish, on the
right-hand pages, with Roman-letter phonetic renditions
on the left; and the pages were numbered "backwards,"
as Hebrew books are, starting from what would be the end
of an English volume.

The volume was a collection of folk sayings compiled
by one Ignaz Bernstein. I glanced through the pages idly,
then with excitement—for not only did I recognize a great
many old friends from home: I read quiddities I had never
heard before. (Many were totally incomprehensible, for
they contained Russian, Polish, Lithuanian words, or "inside" phrases of Galitizianer Jews.)

Once or twice a week, after that, I went back to the shelf
in that stall in that shop (could it have been in Cecil
Court?) where Ignaz Bernstein's work mutely rested. I
would plunge into its pages, scribbling notes; and when I
returned to the Commons Room of the London School of
Economics, I would with assumed aplomb toss off verbal
firecrackers—to friends, an opponent at the chess table,
the usual covey of kibitzers: "There's a Yiddish folk saying that goes . . ."

How I longed to buy Bernstein! But how could I? The
volume was selling for 15 shillings, I think—a fearful sum
for my budget. But my yearnings grew, my continued
pirating made me feel guilty, and the desiccated Scrooge
who owned the book store was giving me glances that
increased in nastiness with each visit. It all made me covet
Ignaz Bernstein as I coveted few books before or since.

One day I noticed something on the title page: my heart
leaped. Bernstein's work had been published the very year
of my birth—and in Warsaw, which is but seventy miles
from Lodz, where I was born. I felt like Saul on his way to

Damascus. Had destiny drawn me to this seedy shop in a
sunless lane in a far-off land? The subject, the place of
publication, the date, even the author's initials, "I.B."
(which the madness of desire made me moan "*Ich bin*": "I
am")—were these not magical omens? I swiftly figured
that if I cut down on three breakfasts, skipped four lunches,
say, and trimmed the costs of three dinners . . . I handed
fifteen precious shillings to the startled owner and hurried
back to my digs in Brunswick Square.

Every night thereafter, when the long days' studies were
completed, I rewarded myself with a dip into Bernstein,
reading the Yiddish, slogging through the phonetic explications of idioms I could not fathom, lost in a remote
yet vaguely familiar world of *shtetl* sayings and rustic
adages . . .

Then tragedy struck. Bernstein disappeared. I searched
through my skimble-skamble of notes, papers, journals,
textbooks, books borrowed from the library or the student
on the floor above. But I could not find Bernstein. I
searched again, quickly, with no success, then reassured
myself by thinking he would turn up tomorrow—perhaps
under my bed, in the closet, fallen behind the bookcase.
But I was wrong. He did not. Bernstein had really disappeared! Where, when, by whose hand? Lost? Stolen?
Thrown out by the harpy widow (of a *pukka sahib* slain
in "Indja") to whom I paid rent? Committed to the "dust
bin" by my slovenly char? To be sold to some bookseller
in Bloomsbury or on voracious Charing Cross Road? To
end in a dump in Bethnal Green or as kindling for some
fireplace in Chelsea? Oh, God! (Nay, *Gotenyu!*)

On and off, during the years that followed, I would think
of *Jüdische Sprichwörter und Redensarten:* but I never ran
across another copy—not in London or New York or
Hollywood. I wrote to several book dealers on Fourth
Avenue, and to bookfinding services; but the months passed,
year in, year out, and the pain wore off and in time I
became too deeply involved in work and Washington to
take up the chase again.

It is a strange thing, wholly mystifying to (and inexplicable by) me that it was not until thirty years later,
as I was finishing the present anthology, that I suddenly
remembered Ignaz Bernstein again. I phoned a librarian
friend and asked if he knew of Bernstein's compendium.
He told me the book had just been reprinted—in Old-

sheim, Germany—and suggested I try certain booksellers on the Lower East Side. Need I say how swiftly I phoned them? The first had never heard of Bernstein; the second offered to order the book ("You should have it in eight weeks"); but the third dealer whispered, "I have a copy . . . quite expensive, I'm afraid . . . oh, not the new edition; the old 1908 . . ." I did not let him finish. "Are you sure? Will you check? Please." In a moment I heard the miraculous truth, and within an hour, dear Ignaz Bernstein, published in 1908, was in my hands once more.

The first thing I did, naturally, was turn to the flyleaf. Could fortune be so kind as to have resurrected the very volume I had owned in Brunswick Square over three decades ago? Alas: no signature, in my handwriting or any one else's, was inscribed on the olive-green paper.

Whose copy of Bernstein I now own I shall never know. But how grateful I am to whoever it was who bought it, received it, stole it, lost it, or sold it so that it could once more become mine! I still find many of its local locutions odd, many of its nouns and names furiously incomprehensible, many of its provincial idioms impenetrable; yet I treasure the more durable of those old, all-but-forgotten pearls, some of which I added to my final draft of the volume you hold in your hands.

The Power of Proverbs

But let us return to the theme of this preface. My love of proverbs was in no way unusual. The truth is this: Men quote proverbs "the better to express *themselves*." Adages are the wit of the inarticulate. Proverbs are the gospel of the poor. Folk sayings are the college of the masses.

More important: Proverbs are what a people—any people—believe, cherish, and teach their young. They are those gleanings of knowledge and experience with which the dead dower each generation of the living. Shakespeare has a phrasing that runs: "We patch grief with proverbs." I think we do more than that. We patch our ignorance and our impotence with them, too.

Proverbs clarify our thinking, crystallize our hopes, assuage our immense anxiety about the immensities of what we do not, unaided, understand. They flash light into places where reason falters for lack of it. Indeed, the proverb is often reason laid bare, argument stripped of fat, complexity clarified beyond misinterpretation.

You may retort that proverbs often contradict one another (as any reader of anthologies, including this one, soon discovers). The sagacity that advises us to look before we leap promptly warns us that if we hesitate we are lost; that absence makes the heart grow fonder, but out of sight, out of mind. What can one believe? Simply that life is full of contradictions, that proverbs reflect and express them, and that many apothegms are more witty than true. Examples:

"Honest men marry soon, wise men not at all." Well, now, was Solomon not wise? Are wise men never honest? Are no bachelors fools? Do no thieves marry young?

"He who does not rise early never does a day's work." This is an agrarian cliché: Do watchmen perform no service? Do no scholars or poets or composers work far into the night?

"Not to advance is to retreat." Really? Not to advance may be to escape disaster. Advance—or retreat—when and *why*? The Charge of the Light Brigade was insanity, pure and simpleminded, as Cecil Woodham-Smith's superb retelling shows us.[5]

"There is no wisdom like silence." How can you judge what is not said? Are mutes then paragons of wisdom?

But I should not press the case: a foolish consistency, "the hobgoblin of little minds," is secondary. Folk sayings are born singly; they are not *designed* for consistency: they are not, indeed, designed at all: they occur. So I have tried to make this compendium not an assemblage of the consistent or the undebatable, but a collection of insights that are often not on speaking terms with one another. What they add up to, because of their very flouting of consistency, is a treasury of precepts which can extricate a man from any predicament. (That is a Hindu saying.)

Proverbs, said Emerson, are "the sanctuary of our intuitions." But they are more: they are the precious distillation of what man has *learned* from centuries of experience. Aristotle considered apothegms the product of intellectual maturity and, recognizing their enormous power, declared it "unbecoming" for the young to utter maxims![6]

"Respect [these] discoveries of the wise," the author of *Ecclesiasticus* tells us, "for of them shalt thou learn instruction." Yet it is much more than instruction that we receive from "the discoveries of the wise": it is insight—and delight, pleasure in the precision of phrasing, the music of alliteration, the felicity of verbal counterpoint and balanced construction, all orchestrated by that special genius that can popularize the profound.

Proverbs and the Jews

That the ancient Hebrews set great store by proverbs scarcely needs to be said: consider how lavishly they are strewn through the Old Testament, or were presented separately—in the Book of Proverbs, the books of the prophets, "wisdom literature"*—the Apocrypha.[7]

The Talmud, that monumental compendium of 1200 years of dialectics (from the 5th century before, to the 8th century of, the Christian Era) and commentaries, discussion and debate on the Torah (the first five books of the Old Testament) and the post-Biblical sages, is an inexhaustible treasure trove of pithy sagacities (in Aramaic) on every conceivable aspect of faith, life, law, man, virtue, evil, customs, morals and mores.[8] The names of over 2,000 rabbi-teachers appear in the Talmud; so far as I know, no one has counted the apothegms.[9]

It is wise to remember that proverbs preceded printing by thousands and thousands of years: it was by oral transmission that the meat and marrow of wisdom circulated among the tribes of man. Collections of sayings (first handwritten, which few men could afford, and later printed) were very popular with the Jewish masses.

The so-called "wisdom literature" was rooted in and flowered from popular wisdom; the scholars and poets who collected folk sayings often improved upon them—but their origins remain the masses. Proverbs are an

---

* "Wisdom literature" is the overall term used to designate the Book of Proverbs, Ecclesiastes, certain Psalms, and the Apocrypha: Ecclesiasticus, the Wisdom of Solomon, IV Maccabees.

"international genre"—with separate classes for verbal instruction and moral exhortation. ("Happy is the man who . . ." straddles both.) Sayings are still used as pedagogy by primitive (preliterate) groups, and were more formally employed by the ancient Chinese, Hindus, Persians, Egyptians to train civil servants. As early as King Solomon, the Hebrews used oral precepts for vocational training—and to educate an elite, a new class, the officials of the ancient state of Israel. Religious/moralistic sayings spread among the Israelites to transmit the essence of monotheism, of "Yahwistic piety," and as exhortations to obey the Law. Proverbs disseminated not only elementary knowledge and skills, but a whole code of morals, a system of ethics, a set of sanctions for a new way of life.[10]

The lucidity and vitality of proverbs made them priceless for instruction; and the rabbis preferred to teach orally rather than from written texts. They feared that if repeated disputations about the meaning of Holy Scripture were written, they would attain undesirable authority. Worse, once a judicial interpretation is written down (the scholars of Judaism reasoned) men tend to feel that what is written is superior to what is told. Above all, the rabbis wanted to preserve a direct, lively, intimate rapport with their students. The Talmud told them: "Prayer should not be recited as if a man is reading from a document."

The rabbis, seeking to keep their audiences alert (during a discussion, no less than a sermon), would often toss Greek, Latin, Arabic, Persian words into their exposition: this was sure to excite interest and provoke questioning.[11] The Haggadah (see Guide Note D, below), an enormous repository of folklore, fables, parables, allegories, witticisms, is studded with foreign words and phrases—which are then explained. The preachers of Judaism found a folk saying more effective than a sermon, in the same way that a scalpel is more precise than a club. "Epigrams stab to the heart."[12]

The marvelous sayings of Jesus ben Sirach (*Ecclesiasticus*) and the matchless *Pirke Abot* ("Saying of the Fathers"), which embraced six centuries of Jewish wisdom and wit (from the third century before, to the third century after, the Christian Era), were and are among the most beloved of Jewish books. In the Middle Ages, Jewish thinkers and psalmists published literally thousands of different collections of Talmudic and folk wisdom.[13] And in each new generation, new teachers, prophets, poets, philosophers, legalists and local wits, some famous, some obscure, kept adding (or embellishing) sayings and profundities to the unclosed treasury of Jewish thought: Rashi's classic commentaries, Bahya ibn Paquda's *Duties of the Heart*, Maimonides' majestic code, Judah Ha-Levi's noble *Kuzari*, the mystical revelations of the *Zohar*.

In the eighteenth and nineteenth centuries, an immense treasure of aphorisms poured into Jewish thought from the hasidim of Eastern Europe, who preached religious ecstasy and glorified saintly souls. The hasidim were rabbis (often not formally ordained), mystics, holy men, whose every rumination was seized upon by disciples: "Our hasid is wiser than your hasid" was a refrain that encouraged the competitive production of aphorisms.[14]

In the nineteenth and twentieth centuries, new men of letters invigorated the old tradition: Chaim Bialik, the leading poet in the renaissance of Hebrew, published a huge *Sefer Ha-Agadah* (in collaboration with Ravnitzki) and a smaller "assemblage" of apothegms. Nathan Stutchkoff's *Der Oytser fun der Yidisher Sprakh* ("Thesaurus— or Treasure—of the Yiddish Language") is a cornucopia of folklore and folk sayings. My hero Ignaz Bernstein has preserved for history almost four thousand *vitsn*. A short, excellent culling of proverbs from the Talmud was published in 1900 by one Madison C. Peters, who seems to have drawn heavily on preceding anthologies and translations.[15]

In recent years, American publishers have given us English translations of Mendele Mocher Seforim, Sholem Aleichem, the remarkable aphorist "The Chofetz Chaim" (Rabbi Israel Meir Kahan), Hebrew poets from Spain, post-Biblical writers and philosophers—to say nothing of miscellaneous collections, in English, of Jewish proverbs compiled by Lewis Browne, Joseph L. Baron, Hanan Ayalti, Fred Kogos, et alia.

* * *

A lovely passage in Midrash* (*Canticles*, 1b) runs:

---

* For descriptions of Midrash, Mishnah, Talmud, see the Guide Notes, pp. 61–71.

Scorn not the *mashal* [proverb], for through it thou mayest gain a firm hold upon the Law, like a king who lost a piece of gold [and] by means of a wick, which is worth but a trifle, was able to find it again.

"A firm hold upon the Law . . ." History inflicted such a succession of catastrophes on the Jews, from Babylon to Buchenwald, that special utility became attached to what was not destructible. Proverbs are portable. Wisdom takes up no room. Adages were the one Jewish treasure no Pilate could plunder, no inquisitor burn, no Cossack loot, no Nazi defile or destroy. Proverbs were the jewels concealed in Jewish minds.

The voluminous output of sayings, ironies, insights and paradoxes flowed from the Jews' untiring exercise of analytic intelligence, their training in introspection, their need to be astute observers (i.e., to anticipate the acts of tyrants or bullies or brigands)—and their literacy.

When the overwhelming majority of mankind was illiterate, it was hard to find a Jewish lad over six who could not read and write. Most adult male Jews handled at least *three* languages: Hebrew in synagogues and "houses of study," Yiddish at home, and—to—Gentiles the language of the land in which they lived. My father, a workingman denied the equivalent of a high-school education, handled Yiddish, Hebrew, Polish and English. . . . Jews were linguists of necessity.[16]

A dominant proportion of the sayings in this volume deal with man's behavior, and cast a dazzling light on man's inner drives and moral dilemmas. Many Jewish folk sayings—about sex, dreams, pride, lust—seem fresher than Freud, though they may be older than King David. Yet this should not surprise us; for if a people hold themselves responsible to God for their every thought, if their teachers persuade them that their fate for all eternity depends on how they live, you may expect them to become intensely self-aware, self-examining, and self-critical. Psychology begins in introspection; philosophy begins in asking "Why?," "How?," "To what end?"

The Pedigree of Proverbs

I must add that the sayings loved and repeated by the Jews were not limited to what only their ancestors had created. Historians, archaeologists, philologists and ethnologists have so expanded and enriched our knowledge of the past that we now know how polyphonic was the life and growth of cultures, and how remarkable are the similarities of legend and myth in widely separated portions of our globe. (This is no new idea: Josephus, after recounting the story of Moses and the Red Sea, reminds us that Alexander the Great was also said to have marched his forces through a parting, by God's will, of the Pamphylian Sea.)

Since the Israelites lived within the teeming interplay of cultures that made up the civilization of the Middle East, they were long exposed to Hittite, Phoenician, Chaldean, and Arabic wisdom; then to Greek philosophy, the lore of Persia and the fables of Hindus; then to the writings of the Romans and the thought of Muslims and Moors.[17] And after the Jews were expelled from Spain, they came into close contact with French, Dutch, Italian, German, English, Rumanian, Polish, Russian (indeed all Slavonic) culture, as we shall see.

The enrichment which migrations and persecutions (as a by-product) conferred on Judaic thought and cosmopolitanism is impossible to appraise. What is clear (and rarely remarked upon) is that the children of Israel *had* to become anthropologists. It should not surprise us that Hebrew proverbs incorporated the wisdom of many other peoples: the *degree* to which such sayings and folklore filtered into the consciousness of the Jews is beyond measure. "A drowning man does not care about getting wet" is an Arabic saying—but the same idea is echoed in various forms in various tongues. The same is certainly true of "Penny wise, pound foolish," or "If you seek honey, expect bee stings"—which was cited long ago by al-Mutanabbi, an Arab who must have been quoting the greatest of proverbists: Anonymous.

What all this adds up to is this: the parentage of a folk saying is often as difficult to determine as the posthumous location of "Abraham's bosom." Of the eighty-two fables we attribute to Aesop, for instance, only one, according to Aristotle (*Rhetoric*, II), can safely be called original. Aesop, a slave in Samos, collected and transcribed the animalized lore of countless centuries—and a hodgepodge of peoples. How memorable is Thackeray's summation:

> The tales were told ages before Aesop; and asses under lions' manes roared in Hebrew; and sly foxes flattered in Etruscan; and wolves in sheep's clothing gnashed their teeth in Sanskrit, no doubt.[18]

I think you will be surprised by the number of aphorisms attributed to other sources or persons that are to be found in the Talmud, which often alludes to popular sayings and often clinches an argument, for one or another technical point of law, by citing a piece of folk wisdom.[19]

> "Give every man the benefit of the doubt."
> "Look at the contents, not at the bottle."
> "Don't threaten a child: either punish or forgive him."
> "A dream uninterpreted is like a letter unopened."
> "It is better to die on your feet than live on your knees."
> "Experience is the name we give our mistakes."
> "In our dreams, it is not we who sin—but the dream."
> "All is well that ends well."

I hope all this will impress you as much as I was impressed when, in my salad days, reading John Wycliffe's preface to his translation of the Bible, I learned that he had undertaken the awesome labor because he felt the Bible is meant "for the government of the people, by the people, and for the people."

*   *   *

Last year in London I purchased a dish towel on which I found block-printed:

> "Little dogs make the most noise."
> "No one needs help to get into trouble."
> "An obedient wife commands her man."
> "Idle young men become unhappy old men."

Are not these lovely sayings characteristically "Jewish"? They certainly are; but they happen to come from the storehouse of horse sense of the Maoris of New Zealand.

But the following, surely, are Jewish in style, mood, and substance:

> "A nation's treasure is its scholars."
> "Don't open a shop unless you like to smile."
> "With virtue, you can't be entirely poor;
>   without virtue, you can't really be rich."
> "Deep doubts, deep wisdom; small doubts,
>   little wisdom."

But they are old Chinese proverbs.

Are there, then, any special qualities, any singular psychology or philosophical stance, which distinguish the proverbs of Jews from those of other people? I think so; and I think you will think so, too, if you scan the pages of the anthology that follows.

At this point, however, let me explore one important aspect of the role which proverbs have played in Jewish life—a role which has not, in my judgment, been sufficiently emphasized.

Proverbs and Jewish Women

Jewish boys would begin to study Hebrew as early as the age of three, and very rarely (unless mentally deficient) remained illiterate past the age of six. On his first day in the *cheder*, the elementary Hebrew school, the little boy's parents would take him to the *melamed* (teacher) and would stand over the child as the letters of the Hebrew alphabet were pointed to and pronounced: "*Aleph . . . beyz . . . gimel . . .*" Sometimes the letters would be printed on a slate and coated with honey, for the young scholar to lick off as he repeated the sounds; sometimes the mother would have popped cookies, shaped in the form of Hebrew letters, into the little scholar's mouth before he was taken to the *cheder*; sometimes the mother would reward the boy with a honey-cookie, shaped in the form of the letter the lad pronounced, as soon as he uttered the name; sometimes the mother or *melamed* would place a drop of honey on the child's tongue, asking, "How does that taste?" "Sweet," the boy would of course reply. "The study of Torah," the *melamed* or mother would reply, "is sweeter." And at the end of the child's first lesson, his mother would enfold him, with a shawl or veil, and utter a prayer that her son "fulfill his life with years of study [Torah], marriage and good deeds."[20]

Every Jewish male over thirteen hurried to the synagogue to pray at least three times a day: in the morning (*shahrith*), in the afternoon (*minhah*), after sundown (*maarib*).

> The synagogue, from its inception, was a place for both prayer and study, and the distinction between the two is exceedingly difficult to draw. . . . Study and prayer, or (better) study-prayer, was the most potent mortar in Jewish life. It was the linchpin in a Jew's self-esteem. It lent meaning and purpose to the most difficult and desperate of existences. It illuminated life. It ennobled, inspired, redeemed. It admitted even the humblest Jew to the company of sages, prophets, scholars, saints.[21]

Now, learning in *groups* and discussion in groups were especially favored; the Talmud (*Berakoth*, 63) says: "Learning is achieved only in company." So:

> Virtually all of male Jewry participated in a perpetual seminar. Even the cobblers. Even the tailors. The drivers and diggers, farmhands and carpenters. The peddlers and beggars and shopkeepers. . . . They were all arguers, dialecticians, amateur theologians.[22]

And in the *Beth Midrash* ("house of study") every Jew sat "like [an] intellectual magnate. . . . When a problem came up, there was immediately a host of people pouring out opinions, arguments, quotations. . . . The stomachs were empty, the homes barren, but the minds were crammed with the riches of the Torah."[23] One may learn a good deal about Jewish life by remembering that it was customary for Jews, when they met or whiled away an hour, to ask one another: "*Zug mir a shtikl Torah*" ("Tell me a piece of Torah"). Then discussion—fervent, contentious, casuistic, all-absorbing—was launched.

The point I now want to stress is this: when a Jew came home, he would tell his wife what "portion" of Torah he had read or discussed or heard discussed; what maxim from Akiba or the Saadia Gaon, what fresh explications of a man's duty to his parents, children, brothers, sisters, the old, the sick, the poor; what revelations of the Messiah's coming, or the nature of immortality, or the rewards in the "world-to-come" for the bitter travails of this life on earth.

Such majestic mysteries, conveyed to a mother or wife or child, required prodigious simplification—not only because they are themselves saturated in complexity, but because even the discussions of Jewish laymen were extremely technical, cloaked in theological conundrums, flecked with such a profusion of split hairs that they torment ordinary reason. (Anyone who has plowed through a page of Talmud will know what I mean.)

And no device proved more useful to the Jewish husband, in imparting quick summaries, than—proverbs, parables, folk sayings. The meaning of a metaphor in Genesis or a parable in the Haggadah; the reduction of a logical dilemma to a nutshell; the rendition of Rabbi Meir's paradox or Yitskhok the Tailor's question—all were borne down that verbal stream in which the core of the sacred teachings, and their embroidering by prophets and scholars, moved from the temple of God through the houses of study into the streets and home to the kitchens.

In this endless process, it was folk sayings that made the hallowed homely, the sacred secular, the lofty cozy. And since Yiddish was the language through which Eastern European Jewish mothers could participate in the savoring of Talmudic law and lore, Yiddish was the language they used to transmit the great tradition to their children.

So it was that I, like any other Jewish boy, heard—from my mother or father or uncle—some bit of wit or wisdom or wonder, coined twenty centuries ago, which lay within the forbidding forests of the Talmud, or which (I would discover forty years later) was a saying of Rab Ashi or some disciple of some illustrious sage who had adorned one or another school of thought in some academy in Jerusalem or Babylon.

A word about Yiddish is in order.

Detour: Yiddish

The journeyings of the Jews presented them with the necessity of learning the languages of the territories through which they wandered, or the provinces in which—for a week or a decade or a century—they were permitted to settle. In order to live, to work or trade or raise their sustenance, Jews had to become at least bilingual (they carried Hebrew with them, of course).

The ancient rabbis and scholars knew Greek and Latin. As groups of Jews moved eastward into the Middle and Far East, they picked up new languages—in what is now Turkey, Persia, India, even China.

During the first century before the Christian era, Jewish settlements were established in Greece and along the entire Eastern Mediterranean from Asia Minor to Alexandria. In succeeding migrations, Jews moved into the Crimea and the Balkans. When the Eastern Catholic successors to Constantine launched their savage persecutions, Jews were driven farther up into the Ukraine, up the Volga, into Kiev and places under the hegemony of barbaric Slavs. (Rabbinical letters allude to Jews whose native tongue had become Russian, and who read the Torah in Russian.) When the Tartar hordes overran the Russian steppes and decimated the Ukraine, Jewish (and Slavic) survivors fled into the Carpathians, up into Poland and Lithuania and provinces of Muscovite Russia. (Early Polish coins contain Hebrew lettering, and suggest that Polish rulers authorized Jews to mint their money.) A Jewish community settled in Vienna in the eighth or ninth century.

In migrations *westward* from Palestine and Egypt, Jews settled in Rome, along the Mediterranean, in Germany (Jewish groups accompanied the Romans into Teutonic regions as early as the fourth century), in Spain and France. In the Middle Ages, merchant Jews criss-crossed Europe, some settling in various localities.

The Crusades inflicted hideous catastrophes on Jews all along the Crusaders' routes, driving them from the Rhineland and the Danube deeper into Central Europe, Bohemia, the Balkans and the territories from which, in time, a Polish suzerainty was formed. In the thirteenth century, when the Jews were brutally expelled from France and England (as, in the fifteenth, they were hounded out of Spain and Portugal), masses of Jews wandered back into North Africa, Egypt, Palestine; or into the Netherlands, Germany, Italy, *mittel-Europa*.

Now, in each of these historic convulsions, the Jews learned new parlances. Jews learned Arabic, Dutch, several Slavic tongues, and languages born of Latin: Italian, Spanish, Portuguese, French.

The odd story of a new tongue, Yiddish, begins (so far as recent scholarship has reconstructed it) in the tenth and eleventh centuries, when Jews from Northern France came down the Rhineland, where they picked up the Germanic dialects of places in which they sank roots: Cologne, Trier, Coblenz, Mainz. Jews who filtered farther eastward learned the regional parlance of Frankfurt, Wurzburg, Stuttgart. So grew up a vernacular, Judaeo-German, that was to become the foundation of Yiddish (the name comes from the German *Jüdisch*). And when Jews were invited (!) to come to reside in Poland, to form an economic class between ignorant peasants and indolent noblemen, they brought Hebrew and German with them. It was in the settlements of Middle and Eastern Europe—in Galicia, Hungary, Rumania, the Ukraine, Poland, Russia, Lithuania—that, after the seventeenth century, an unique Jewish language flowered and a novel literature grew up.

Yiddish, let me emphasize, was scorned by the rabbis and detested by the intellectuals of Judaism—especially by German Jews, to whom Yiddish was "a loathsome jargon," "vulgar," "piggish." Jewish intellectuals preferred the established languages of Europe, languages with a "proper" vocabulary, an accepted grammar, a dignified history and literature. But the Jewish masses clung to their beloved vernacular, and embroidered and enriched it *ad libitum*. . . . Hebrew, after all, was "God's tongue," far too sacred to be demeaned by earthly, earthy uses. More and more, Yiddish became the workaday tongue for everyday life, for sharing the vicissitudes of daily and domestic affairs. Eastern European Jews were often trilingual; and Yiddish became the vehicle for irreverent folk sayings which Hebrew could not countenance, and homely anecdotes Hebrew would not trifle with.

There is no slang, for instance, in Hebrew; in Yiddish, slang was invented, embraced, relished and embellished with gusto. Hebrew possessed no colloquial words for genital organs; Yiddish showed no hesitation in coining explicit words, vulgar or euphemistic, for the instruments of sex and the rondos of copulation.

And so Yiddish, "the Robin Hood of languages," has practiced the most buoyant banditry among the words of every land in which its practitioners wandered. In the course of twenty-four hours, a son of Judah, speaking Yiddish today, may, without being aware of it, raid over two dozen other languages.*

I always marvel over how ingenious Yiddish became in developing a vocabulary of psychological insight; how fertile in discovering nuances for the observation of man and society; how resourceful in perfecting words to describe the marvelous gallery of human character types; ** above all, how perceptive in understanding that baffling interplay of comedy, tragedy, fantasy, and farce that is human life. I am not unaware of the risks one runs in generalizing, but surely there is good reason to call German ponderous, French lean and logical, Italian lyrical, Russian melancholy, Arabic flowery, English powerful. And Yiddish?

Steeped in sentiment, it is sluiced with sarcasm. It loves the ruminative, because it rests on a rueful past; it favors paradox, because it knows that only paradox can do justice to the injustices of life; it adores irony, because the only way the Jews could retain their sanity was to view a dreadful world with sardonic eyes.[24]

What does all this have to do with proverbs and folk sayings? A very great deal. Maurice Samuel tells us:

The Yiddish masses were strangers to earthy joys that lightened the lives of their . . . neighbors. Their consola-

---

* For example: Hebrew (*mezuza*), English (*donton* = "downtown"), Aramaic (*alevay*), Russian (*kishke*), Polish (*pisk*), Ukrainian (*paskudnyak*), Rumanian (*gridzhe*), Czech (*nebish*), Ukrainian (*blints*), Italian (*yente*), French (*davn*), Spanish (*Schnaiur*, a name derived from *señor*), Turkish (*kave*).

** Examples: *nudnik, nebbech, shlepper, shlump, shmendrick, shlemiel, Kuni Lemmel, tummler, kibitz, gonif, shnuk, Moyshe Kapoyr, kochleffel, platkemacher, shtunk, yachneh, Khaim* (or *Chaim*) *Yonkel, bulbenik, plosher, etcetera* (which is not Yiddish).

tions were to a large extent [those] of the imagination, and therefore their language, besides serving a normal need, had an esoteric function unimaginable to their neighbors. All languages have their peculiarities and impenetrable privacies. . . . The spirit of Yiddish sets it apart from contiguous langauges. The difficulty of translating Yiddish . . . lies less in the absence of corresponding vocabularies than in the Jewish-Yiddish conception of the meaning of life and the destiny of the people.[25]

All this is by way of prelude to saying that Jewish proverbs, like Jewish life, are freighted with emotion, laden with ornate metaphors and purple exaggerations, glutinous benedictions and fearsome maledictions:

"May the cholera seize him!"
"May his insides sound like a music box!"
"May all his teeth fall out, save one" (so that he may
   have a permanent toothache).
"I would like to treat him like a treasure—bury him in
   the ground with loving care."

The folk sayings in this volume are drawn from Yiddish and Hebrew (the former often translated from Hebrew), and Yiddish is "a tongue that never takes its tongue out of its cheek. . . . In its innermost heart, Yiddish swings from shmaltz to derision."[26]

It is the proverbs and folk sayings which enrich that language, and which do indeed have a unique flavor, that I collected for over fifty years. Then arose a perplexing question: how best translate them?

The Torments of Translation

Every language spoken by man (there are over 2,800) is combed with uniqueness. Human languages are as different as peas in a pod (if you examine them under a microscope). What human tongues have in common is only purpose: the use of words to try to describe, understand and communicate the measureless sensations of existence, the swarm of impressions on the self, the marvelous symbolic productions of the human mind, the infinite fantasies of the imagination, the divine and the wretched parameters of the human condition:

> Of all man's marvelous inventions, language is surely the most amazing. It is the *sine qua non* of man's estate; it distinguishes him from his animal cousins; it permits experience to be accumulated and transmitted; it makes abstract thought—generalization, discrimination, analysis, hypothesis—possible. Without language, there could be nothing remotely like science or technology: no poetry or physics; no transistor or computer; no laser, maser, zipper or Hollandaise sauce. . . .
>
> The Bible says, "In the beginning was the word." If that means anything, it means that language existed *before* man. . . . The great Rabbi Akiba's disciples took it for granted that an alphabet existed before God created the world. I have no way of proving this, but there is no way of disproving it either."[27]

A language is a *Weltanschauung*. Even languages very close in origin, history and structure develop surprising differences. The English "conscience" is not the same as the French *conscience* (which means "consciousness" or "conscientiousness"). German had no word for "bully" until the twentieth century (a mordant comment on Teutonic values) and can only render the Englishman's idea of "fair play" as " '*fair*' *Spielen*." If this be true of tongues so close to each other in birth, so laden with cognates, so cross-fertilized by usage and literature, how much more does it intrude when one tries to translate Yiddish or Hebrew into English?

Translation is not simply a matter of dexterity in transferring synonyms. Translation does not contend with words, but with meanings. To translate is to decode: to transpose one mode of thinking, feeling, fearing, appraising, into the word patterns of another. No language can be separated from its historical skeleton, its psychological skin, or its sociological garments. Languages are acculturated verbalizations of experience and thought.

Christian missionaries in the Orient, for instance, were sorely perplexed because Chinese had neither a word for "word" nor a word for, or an idea of, "sin." (The closest was *tsui*, which meant "crime"). And in Africa or Polynesia, the Christian messengers of the Lord found bewildering difficulty in trying to communicate the idea of

God—i.e., one supreme deity—to people mystified by such an impoverished theology. In language, which is a system of "culturally ordained categories," each of us "builds the house of his consciousness."[28]

One of the translators at the United Nations tells us that when an English or American speaker says, "I assume," interpreters render that in French as "I deduce" and in Russian as "I consider."[29]

It is hard for us truly to believe that each culture teaches its people what to say about what that culture has taught them to think, feel, see, or even hear. The pioneering studies of Edward Sapir (whom I was fortunate to know) and Benjamin Lee Whorf have forced us to consider the surprising degree to which our sensations, our thoughts, even our actions, are influenced by the particular system of sounds and symbols we inherit. We all tend to assume that we are experiencing the real world, "but in many cases we are free only to experience the possibilities and limitations of grammar."[30]

For instance: Do you think dogs go "*woof-woof*," "*bow-wow*" or "*arf-arf*"? In English prose, they bark that way. But in German, dogs go "*wau-wau*," in Chinese "*wang-wang*," in Vietnamese "*gau-gau*," and in Japanese "*wan-wan*." In Yiddish, dogs go "*how-how*," and there is a saying: "The dog who barks '*ho-ho*' is not dangerous, but the one who growls '*how-how*' is." (I cannot help wondering how a Laplander or Litvak would translate "going to the dogs.")

In German, frogs are said to croak "*quak-quak*," which would confuse an American duck. Scottish roosters would surely be flabbergasted to learn that French roosters go "*cocorico*" (at least in French novels). As for Arabian donkeys, which Arabian writers tell us go "*ham-ham*," I quail to think of what they would think if they learned that in Rumanian it is dogs that go "*ham-ham*." I leave it to zoologists to decide whether, perhaps, different breeds make different sounds.

Any sensible American will tell you that scissors go "*snip-snip*," "*snip-snap*," or "*snap-snap*." But to a Greek, believe it or not, scissors go "*kritz-kritz*." And to a Chinese, scissors hiss "*su-su*." As for Spaniards, Italians, and Portuguese, their scissors retain as marked a national identity as any other, being written respectively as "*ri-ri*," "*kri-kri*," and "*terre-terre*."[31]

All this may disturb your comforting assumption that in onomatopoeia, at least, there is universal agreement; that everyone, whether Choctaw or Irish or Cypriot, produces the same oral renditions of and for the same heard sounds; that different languages must employ the same vocalizations for objectively uniform acoustics.

But the notion that onomatopoeia crosses the frontiers of language rests on the misconception that verbal allusions accurately mirror "real" sounds: they do not; they record and reflect those sounds our culture has instructed us to hear, or predisposed us *not* to hear. A German child is taught to hear the buzzing of a bee not as "*bzz-bzz*" (which English bees do, apparently in order to validate our word "buzzing") but as "*sum-sum*." If you will repeat "*sum-sum*" for a while, you may come to prefer it to "*bzz-bzz*"—or you may, in the interest of world peace, henceforth describe all bees as going "*bzz-bzz sum-sum*."

Do you think that in every society men grow so angry they "see red"? Well, "our classification of the spectrum into . . . red, orange, yellow, green, blue and violet is culturally arbitrary, and persons in other cultures divide the spectrum quite differently. Perception itself is an aspect of human *behavior*."[32]

Optical recordings often express learned ways of seeing and inferring. I once wrote: "We see things as *we* are, not as they are." Professor E. H. Gombrich tells us that ancient artists drew eyelashes on the lower lids of horses' eyes (the drawing *they* had seen and studied showed eyelashes on horses' lower lids); but lower eyelashes do not happen to exist on real, undrawn horses. . . . As Degas once blurted: "Drawing is not what one sees, but what others must be made to see."

Have I wandered from proverbs and translation? Only to illustrate, I hope, how complicated simple things become if we examine them with care. The mere change of sound, in translating, can alter the sensual glow and hum of the original. I commend to you Bernard Berenson's appraisal of critics: They break a watch into its parts, to hear how it ticks. Changing one word's *position* can alter meaning dramatically: "What is harder than getting a pregnant elephant in a Volkswagen? Getting an elephant pregnant in a Volkswagen."

The most tormenting aspect of translation is this: What is idiomatic in one tongue is idiotic in another. Think for a moment of what happens if a translator of English does not realize that "Tell it to Sweeney" is a rebuff, not a request; that "a Northern Spy" may have been an undercover agent for Ulysses S. Grant—or only a variety of apple; that Occam never used his razor for shaving, any more than Cleopatra used her needle for sewing; that "Jack-in-the-pulpit" does not mean the preacher's name is Jack; that "behind the 8-ball" is gibberish in nine tenths of the world; and that when athletes engage in a "rhubarb" they do not sit down to eat the stuff.

It gives me the greatest pleasure to inform you that Russian physicists believe that the first nuclear atomic pile in history was constructed in a pumpkin field—that being their natural translation of "squash court," the site in the concrete bowels of the stadium ("Stagg Field") of the University of Chicago.

As for poetry, I can do no better than give you Chaim Bialik's despairing dictum: "Reading poetry in translation is like kissing a woman through a veil."

*   *   *

I cannot help feeling that where a translator, however fine a scholar, is not a writer, translation starts under a deadly handicap. For if a writer is anything he is one who is sensitive to words, who loves their texture, their nuances, their conceptual echoes and overtones. An empathy for language—which is to say, a refined and heightened awareness of words—is simply a *sine qua non* (how do you say that in English?) for translators. The man who hears not the beat of a word, much less a sentence, or who is indifferent to simile and metaphor, or who does not savor parallel construction, or who is word-blind and cadence-deaf, is bound to butcher his task. A seventeenth-century man of letters, John Denham, bristled:

> Such is our pride, our folly and our fate
> That only those who cannot write, translate.

The Bill of Rights composed by the 1971 International Conference on Literary Translation reads:

The translator's chief obligation is to create the work in a new language with the appropriate music and the utmost response to the silences of the original.[33]

As an admirer of the manifesto, I wish that its writers had said "another," not "a new," language: translators are surely not obliged to invent a tongue from scratch.

"A good translation," said Benedetto Croce, "is a work of art."

The Importance (and Misdemeanors) of Translation

Not until I was immersed in this work did a perfectly obvious thought occur to me: how monumental a role translators have played in human history. Indeed, what we know of history, or of the lore, legends and literature of other peoples, is almost entirely a product of translators. Except for scholars who are multilingual, education itself, for most of us, is rooted in translated works. How many of us have read Thucydides in Greek? Or tackled Livy in Latin? Or, for that matter, savored Dante, Cervantes, Goethe, Tolstoy, in the original? As Miles Smith of Oxford wrote in 1611, in a preface to the King James Version of the Bible:

> Translation it is that openeth the window, to let in the light; that breaketh the shell, that we may eat the kernel; that putteth aside the curtaine, that we may looke into the most Holy place. . . .

The entire web of our culture is interlaced with translations; interpreters may properly be called the carriers of civilization, and its true cross-fertilizers. Take the great books of Greek philosophy, science, geography, astronomy, medicine. The words of Euclid, Aristotle, Aristarchus of Samos (who held that the earth revolves on its own axis, and moves around the sun), Plato, Galen, and later Ptolemy, were (except for a small band of scholars) unknown to the Europeans of the twelfth and thirteenth centuries, until those words were translated into Latin—from Arabic, into which tongue they had been rendered from Syriac, into which language they had been translated from the Greek. These Latin texts, thrice removed from the original, flowed into Europe's monasteries and universities to transform the late medieval world. The first complete translation of Plato into Latin was not made until 1482.[34]

Plutarch and Suetonius provided kings and princes with political lessons from their predecessors. It was from translations of Machiavelli that one or another Anglo-Saxon, Nordic or Slavic ruler learned stratagems of statecraft, power politics, diplomacy. It was from translations of Castiglione that Europe's royal courts learned the rudiments of manners. And the poets of the Renaissance, like the playwrights of Elizabethan England, were profoundly influenced by their reading of translated classics; Ben Jonson tells us that Shakespeare "had small Latin and less Greek," yet Shakespeare based six plays on Greek history, and six of his greatest on Roman.[35]

Suppose I make the point another way: Had translations *not* been made, would Homer, Vergil, Erasmus, Montaigne, be recognized outside of our universities? Were translations forbidden what would you or I know of Sumeria or Confucius, Carthage or Copernicus or Montezuma? Of the Mongol hordes or the Moghul dynasts? Of life in medieval Kyoto? Of the Crusades—or Dostoevski? Of what happened this morning in Peking, Moscow, Tokyo, Berlin?

*   *   *

But what we do know about history, through translations, is pitted with astonishing errors because of translation. (The Italians say, "*Traduttore traditori*": translators are traitors.) Take a simple example: Do our history books tell us that Greek tyrants were not tyrannical? They should: for among the ancient Greeks a tyrant (*tyrannos*) was simply one who had seized power; many Greek "tyrants" were liberal, popular and far from tyrannical.

Now take a more important body of errors in translation, if one contemplates the consequences: the Bible. I first became aware of the farrago of boners in English translations of Holy Scripture when I spent a year studying comparative religion in the Divinity School of the University of Chicago. (Mind you, I had not the slightest intention of becoming a divine, divine though the idea may sound; I was simply fascinated by the varieties of men's faith, the psychology of belief, the anatomy of man's accumulated knowledge about gods and God.) It was no small revelation, to me, to learn such simple but startling facts as these: That the Bible (from the Greek *biblia*) is a collection of "little books"; that these books were not written at one time, and not by one man, but by a good many men across a stretch of at least 1,300 years (if you date the earliest parts of the Old Testament prior to 1,200 before the Christian Era, and the last of the New Testament post-100); that the holy books were gathered together, in far from systematic fashion, down the centuries—according to the haphazard judgment of religious leaders, rabbis, kings, preachers, priests; that the Bible was not even called "Bible" until the fourteenth century—and not "Holy" until 1568; that the immortal King James Version (1611) was the *third* English translation authorized; that the Wycliffe Bible (c. 1388) was branded heresy; that Tyndale's great translation of 1525* so fixed the English style and mood that all later versions "must be looked upon as revisions . . . not independent translations";[36] that from 1611 to 1697 the New Testament was revised seven different times; that a revised Revised Version appeared in 1885, and at least twenty variant translations have appeared since then.[37]

At the University, I met Professor Edgar J. Goodspeed, who had completed his "American" (that is what he named it) translation of the New Testament. I was simply astounded to learn how many solemnly printed passages in the Old and New Testaments were questionable, misleading, or downright *wrong*, when compared with the earliest Hebrew/Aramaic/Greek manuscripts. "Candles" and "candlesticks," for instance, are historical impossibilities (torches or oil lamps were what the Hebrews used); "the Three Wise Men" were not wise men at all: they were

---

* Tyndale's story is as fascinating as it was tragic. He started to translate the New Testament, but found such hostility to this in England that he went to Germany. A Church injunction stopped him in Cologne; he fled to Worms. Copies of his translation reached England in 1526, and were denounced and suppressed by the bishops. Cardinal Wolsey sent an order to have Tyndale arrested in Worms. Tyndale worked in a hideaway and published his translation of the Pentateuch in 1520. His defenses of the Reformation were denounced by Thomas Môre; his criticism of Henry VIII's divorce incurred the monarch's wrath. Wolsey's agents captured Tyndale in Antwerp, where he was correcting some translations; he was tried for heresy, condemned, and strangled at the stake. Then, on orders of Emperor Charles V, his body was burned. . . .

I tell this story at length to suggest the perils which translators sometimes confronted.

astrologers or soothsayers (the rendering of the Greek *magoi* or the Latin *magi* as "wise men" is just false). "Servant" in the Bible often means "slave" (slavery was rife in the ancient world); and to "add one cubit unto his stature" (Matthew 6 : 27) is a bit ludicrous, since a cubit is about 18 inches.

The King James version uses a late sixteenth century idiom (already somewhat archaic by the time that great Bible was printed[38]) that lends glory to the text—and discombobulating ambiguity: What on earth is meant by "Ye are not straitened in us"? Or "We do you to wit of the grace of God"? Or take the misleading references to money: a "penny" was not a trifle to the Hebrews; it was the going rate for twelve hard hours of work. Or take the fallacious impressions of time: "the third hour" leads a modern reader to think that what is meant is 3 A.M. or 3 P.M.; but what "the third hour" meant was the third hour after dawn: i.e., 8 or 9 in the morning.

In many unhappy cases, the original meaning of a word is precisely *opposite* the meaning we derive from it in the translation by King James's reverent scholars. The phrase "by and by" meant, to the Hebrews, not "in a little while," but "immediately." And to the King Jamesians, so apparently simple a word as "comprehend" signified not "comprehension," as we today assume, but "overcoming an obstacle."[39]

Of greater consequence are the startling changes in the translations of gospel recently made, and jointly agreed upon, by committees of scholars themselves Protestant, Catholic, Jewish. Let me mention a few:

(1) "In the beginning God created the heaven and the earth" is now rendered, in several modern translations, as: "When God began to create the heaven and the earth." (Obviously, God existed before He created anything.)

(2) The Third Commandment now reads: "Thou shalt not swear falsely by the name of the Lord your God; for the Lord will not clear one *who swears falsely* by "His name" (my italics). The change is of cardinal importance; for in the new translations man is commanded to avoid *perjury*, not profanity (as the King James "take the name of the Lord in vain" seemed to signify).

(3) The Israelites, fleeing from their pursuers, did not cross the Red Sea. They were nowhere near the Red Sea at the time. What the Israelites cross, in modern translations,

is the "Sea of Reeds" or "The Sea of Bulrushes," either of which is accurate English for the Hebrew *Yam Suf* of the ancient texts.[40] (I wish I could say the error made was tantamount to mistaking "Reed Sea" for "Red Sea"—an instantly plausible and visual mistake.) The change to "Sea of Reeds" offers us a crutch for credibility; after all, the rushes in a marsh part more readily, without divine intervention, than the waters of a sea. (But how were the pursuing Egyptians drowned?)

(4) The most historic change, surely, has been made in Isaiah 7 : 14 (and therefore in Matthew 1:22–21, which quotes Isaiah 7 : 14). The King James Bible, as do portions of the bibles in over 1,431 different translations, recounts how Isaiah promised Hezekiah (a king of the Jews who was defending himself against two enemy armies) that his aggressors will be destroyed:

> Therefore the Lord himself shall give you a sign; Behold, a virgin shall conceive, and bear a son . . .

But new translations render this passage as:

> Therefore the Lord himself shall give you a sign: A young woman is with child, and she will bear a son . . .

The word Isaiah used was *almah*, which in Hebrew does not mean "virgin," but "young woman." (The Hebrew word for "virgin" is *betulah*.) Isaiah used the word he meant, which Greek and Latin translators later misinterpreted. (I hasten to add that faith in the Virgin Birth does not depend simply on how one translates this passage.)

Since my student days, over a dozen excellent new translations of the Bible have appeared, many of them inspired by the dramatic discovery of ancient documents that predate all earlier manuscripts (the most famous and significant, of course, are the Dead Sea Scrolls). And the new translations agree on the corrections I have sketched above.[41]

Before you vent too much wrath on errant scribes and scholars, or their modern correctors, let us consider with clarity the pitfalls and phantoms that make any translator's life a misery: Let us return to some special problems Yiddish presents to the translator.

On Translating Yiddish

To translate, we have seen, is to recreate portions of a culture in words which are comprehensible to someone to whom that culture is unknown or but thinly comprehended. To translate Yiddish is to translate a certain style of life, a construct of apperceptions, a system of values, intricate subtleties of thinking and feeling which are imbedded in the language of Eastern European Jews and their descendants.

To translate Yiddish into English is quite different from translating, say, French into Italian: for a common religion (Christianity), equalities of statehood, shared political ideas and whilom sovereigns—all these endow English, French, Italian, German, Spanish, with a common (or close) inventory of experience, common codes of etiquette, common models of masculinity or ideals of femininity, assumptions about salvation, hunting, drinking, passions—all of which are worlds removed from Jewish experience and ideology. The translator of Yiddish is therefore compelled to build cultural-psychological bridges across chasms that do not separate other peoples from one another—or do not separate them so widely.

Many Yiddish words and phrases are exasperatingly difficult to translate—at least, to my finicky satisfaction. To render Yiddish (or German or French) word-by-word would be to produce such barbarisms as "It grows a pain," or "It comes a child." And I'm afraid there are only pallid equivalents in English for a whole symphony of vivid and delectable Yiddish words. Consider these hallowed few:

> *chutspa:* monumental gall, colossal effrontery;
> *mishpokhe:* a family unit that embraces relatives far, near, remote, and numerous;
> *kvel:* a beaming pride in a child's achievements, or an unworthy (but ever-so-pleasurable) gloating over an enemy's humiliation;
> *kvetsh:* a chronic griper-complainer-drip-sourpuss;
> *tchotchke* or *tsatske:* a toy, a trinket; but also a mistress, a playgirl, a pretty, brainless young thing—whether wife or girlfriend;

paskudnyak: a gross, greedy, contemptible man or woman;
shlemiel: a simpleton in spades, a maladroit pipsqueak; a
   butter-fingered bumpkin: "A *shlemiel* falls on his back
   and breaks his nose";
shlimazl: a born loser, a football to fate, a man who buys
   a suit with two pairs of pants and promptly burns a hole
   in the jacket;
zaftik: juicy; but a *zaftik* woman is inviting to the touch
   and seductive to the glands.[42]

Or take the Slavic particle *zhe,* which is used in Yiddish
to add a note of needling, in impatience or accusation, to
the commonplace. If you want to say, "For heaven's sake,
when will you be ready?" you say *"Venzhe vest di zayn
greyt?"* ("When already will you be ready?") If you want
to end a conversation with a courteous but unmistakable
hint, you say *"Zayt zhe mir gezunt,"* which Englishes
abominably as "Be already to me well . . ." but means:
"go already—in good health."

And if Yiddish words can perplex a translator, consider
how their arrangement can derange their substance:

   "He should live so long" is not an amiable hope but a
creamy curse.
   "From this he makes a *living*?" is not a question; it is a
put-down.
   "*This* I need?" is a contemptuous rejection of what it
appears to be asking, for it means, "Of all the things in the
world I do *not* need, this leads the list."
   "Do you want it to sing, too?" when asked of a customer who returns a canary merely because it is mute,
turns a reasonable expectation upside down, and thus
means: "How carping of you to expect this beautiful bird,
which has so splendid an array of nonvocal attributes, to
sing, *too.*"

When Yiddish phrases or idioms are to be translated,
the difficulties become magnified yet further. A translator
who renders *"Vus makhst du?"* as "What are you making?"
is absolutely right—*if* the question is being asked of a
relative or friend (*du*) who is standing over an anvil; but
the translation is cockamamy nonsense if the speaker is
greeting someone—for *"Vus makhst du?"* only means
"How are you?"

The unwary reader of the Yiddish phrase *"Hak nisht
(or nit) kayn tschainik,"* translating the words literally as

"Don't knock a teapot" (it *means* "Don't yak, yak, *yak* so much"), will be as deluded as the inexpert translator of the Polish phrase "He is underpinned with a child" who does not know it means "In every man, a child is hidden."

To render the Yiddish *broyges* as "angry" is to destroy the distinctions between *broyges*, *beyz* and *onkast*: To be *broyges* is to be "on the outs with"; a man who is "*broyges*" is not on speaking terms with you. In the bygone Bronx, "*broyges*" was cleverly, if inelegantly, translated "mad on," as in this indignant declaration, heard on Tremont Avenue: "Invite her to my party? Never! I'm mad on her."

* * *

The most crushing ripostes, the most taunting acerbities, bloom and thrive in Yiddish, which seems limitless in devices that sow seeds of sarcasm in the soil of ordinary discourse: Let me expand on this point, which I sketched out, in briefer form, in the *Joys of Yiddish*:

(1) *Emphasis by translating a predicate adjective:*
"Funny, he isn't."
("He isn't funny" is not funny; but "Funny, he isn't," is—for it means "There are many things you can say about him, even fine, flattering things, but the one thing you can *not* say is that he is funny.")

(2) *Demolition of a virtue through repetition with a prefatory "shm-":*
"Good-shmood, he eats like a horse."

(3) *Emphasizing a defect by repeating a word with the "shm"-gambit:*
"Fat-shmat, she has to dance the Watusi."

(4) *Stressing an asset through "shm"-prefaced reiteration.*
"Poor-shmoor, he'd give his shirt to a beggar."

(5) *Dismissing an idea out-of-hand by framing it as a question:*
"I should invite him to my son's *Bar Mitzvah?*"
(When a question is framed "I should . . . ?" instead of "Should I . . . ?" you may be pretty sure you are being told, not asked.)

(6) *Sarcasm via the addition to a straightforward sentence of "only," "just" or "merely":* this transforms the forthright into the murderous:

"Why did he leave her? She only tried to poison him—once a week."

"She was an angel about the divorce; she just wanted his seven gold teeth."

"We were merely three hours late—on a two-hour flight."

(7) *Inferential aspersion through innocent interrogation:*
   "Already he's not satisfied?"
   "For *that* you blame me?"
   "For that you *blame* me?"

(8) *Scathing disdain by placing the object before the subject:*
   "*Thanks* she expected for arriving so late?"

(9) *Maximizing indignation by repeating a question in the exact form in which it was asked.* In this ploy, my using Question B as a reply to your Question A (B being identical to A) indicates that the answer to your question is so obvious that its use by you constituted an affront to me that is best erased by umbrage via echo. Note three exquisite variations:

I

Q. "Did you send flowers to the hospital?"
A. "Did I send flowers to the hospital?"
   (Meaning: "How can you insult me by doubting it?")

II

Q. "Did you send flowers to the hospital?"
A. "Did I send flowers to the hospital!"
   (This converts a boorish question into an aggrieved affirmation, meaning, "I practically bought out the florist's shop.")

III

Q. "Did you send flowers to the hospital?"
A. "Did I send flowers to the hospital?!"
   (Meaning: "How could any decent human being *not* send flowers to the hospital?")

(10) *Imputing stupidity through sardonic reprise:*
   Q. "Would you like some cheesecake?"
   A. "Would I like some cheesecake?"
   (Shorthand for, "Who in his right mind would not jump at the chance to eat some cheesecake?")

(11) *Rejection by repetition in which ridicule is implied:*
   Q. "Will you take twenty dollars for it?"
   A. "Will *I* take twenty dollars for it?"
   (This expresses incredulity at so ridiculous an offer.)

(12) *Noble forbearance by repeating a question without comment on it:*
Q. "Will you take twenty dollars for it?"
A. (*sighing*) "Will I take twenty dollars for it?"
(This calls attention to my reasonable character—despite your cheap offer.)

(13) *Tactical acquiescence without binding acceptance:*
Q. "Will you take fifty dollars for it?"
A. "Will I take fifty dollars for it?"
(This hedges too-prompt acceptance, which might lead you to wonder whether you had been too generous.)

(14) *Underlining asininity by holding up a mirror to it:*
Q. "Don't you want to get well and spend the winter in Palm Beach?"
A. "No, I don't want to get well and spend the winter in Palm Beach."

(15) *Underlining asininity by holding a contrary mirror before it:*
Q. "How would you like a free week in the Virgin Islands?"
A. "I'd rather rent a basement in a home for the aged."

(16) *Contempt by concurrence:*
Q. "But won't you die if they don't operate?"
A. "Yes, I'll die if they don't operate."
(Meaning, "Only an idiot asks such a question.")

(17) *Deflation by magnified concurrence:*
Q. "A bird in the hand is worth two in the bush, so accept the offer."
A. "Any bird in the hand is worth two in the bush!"
(Meaning: "In that case I should accept any offer.")

(18) *Scorn through stressing on word:*
"Her he *loves*?"
(This casts doubt on the sanity of the lover.)

(19) *Criticism by stressing another word in the same sentence.*
"*Her* he loves?"
(This suggests that the loved one lacks any semblance of those qualities that might make a sane man love her.)

(20) *Relieving guilt by linking a curse to instant but only nominal cancellation:*

"May darkness invade his eyes, God forbid!"
"May a fire rage in his bowels, let God prevent that!"
"May God avoid driving her crazy with shingles!"

But I must not strain your patience by extending mine. (For the difficulties of translating Hebrew, see Appendix II.)

On Translating Proverbs

In translating proverbs and folk sayings, insensitivity to the cadences of a culture, no less than the overtones and resonances of its language, can prove fatal. If euphony is expelled from an epigram, its very heart is stilled; if alliteration is abolished, the playfulness of a saying may be destroyed; if mushiness replaces succinctness, an aphorism becomes a banality. Earnest but inept translators can turn a bit of wisdom into a pile of nonsense.

Take this line, exactly as I found it, attributed to "the Talmud":

Bad matches beget good children.

On the face of it, the sentence struck me as absurd. Why? (1) If bad marriages produce good children, then what kind of offspring do good marriages produce? (2) Do *both* bad and good marriages beget good children? (3) Is the happiness or integrity of a marriage irrelevant to the character of the offspring? (4) How could one of the Talmudic sages, who were exceptionally rigorous in reasoning, let pass so many-forked a proposition?

I brought my problem to one of my experts, who traced the sentence to its source and translated the passage in which it appeared. Then I reduced the passage, which contained involutions which need not detain us, to:

Even a bad marriage can beget good children.

I have the greatest sympathy for immigrants who had to learn English, a most difficult and perverse tongue, in their adulthood; but just as my sympathy turns sour when a tone-deaf fiddler plays Mozart, my patience runs out when an inveterate bungler commits a translation.*

Many English translations of Yiddish folk sayings simply boggle the mind; others offend the ear; and some are so insipid that they turn wit into waffles. Do you think my judgment harsh? Then come with me through a rogue's gallery of semantic misdemeanors I found in one or another place:

(1) "Worms eat you when dead . . ." I regret to tell you I never knew a dead worm who could eat.

(2) "Regard the speech, not the speaker." Does "regard" mean look at, respect, appraise, think about, be fond of? The irritating confusion is easily removed:

> "Judge the speech, not the speaker."

(3) Even immortal Hillel cries to be rescued from translators, one of whom quotes him:

> "Who does not increase, decreases." What Hillel *meant*, I submit, was: "The man who does not grow [in knowledge], grows smaller."

(4) "What the eyes don't see the heart will not hurt." This abortion confuses the coronary with the myopic. Should it not read: "What the eyes don't see, the heart won't feel"?

(5) One earnest Yiddishist translated a saying into: "What's straight talk to your face is falsehood when spoken behind your back." "Straight talk" is ungainly, and its antonym is not "falsehood" (straight talk can be erroneous, and truth can be oblique); and is falsehood false only when "spoken"? The triple excrescense is readily remedied:

> "What is candor to your face is slander behind your back." (My rhyming of "candor" and "slander" is an unexpected bonus.)

(6) A scholar I need not name quotes a *midrash:* "Is then evil good? Yes; for . . ." I could not believe this translation to be accurate. How could the rabbis, so ferocious in their indictment of "the Evil Impulse," possibly call Evil "good"? I guessed that the original passage might

---

* One translatotr of Yiddish regularly renders *fraylikh* as "laugh" (it means "cheerful"), *beyz* as "wicked" (in contexts which dictate "angry"), "too much" as the English for a *sakh* (which means "much" or "a lot," but *not* "too much"), and *vill redn* into "has a lot to say" (it can only mean "wants to talk").

mean that the Evil Impulse may sometimes *serve* the good
—which is as far a cry from being good as being sick is
from being sickening. I discussed this (evil, not sickness)
with my experts on Talmud and my guess turned out to be
correct.

(7) Is not English massacred in "You must not take an
offense on anything a fool does"? The sentence has a dis-
located spine. The adage can be phrased briskly: "Never
be offended by a fool."

(8) Or take this well-known folk-saying: "On their
gravestones, all Jews are good men." What the saying
means is ironic: "In their epitaphs, all men are good." You
may decide for yourself whether "epitaph" is more exact
than "gravestones."

(9) "Those who want people to think they are wise,
agree with them." Here is a stew of pronouns gone mis-
referent: who are "they"? I prefer to rephrase the thought
this way:

"If you want people to think you wise, agree with everyone."

(10) I cannot believe that anyone with a sense of style
will prefer: "What a deaf man does not hear, he figures out
for himself," to "The deaf imagine what they cannot hear."
Thank you.

(11) "Who is a hero? He who keeps down a retort."
Well, "keeps down" is un-English; and a *vits* is not a
retort. Another translator (Keeps Down's brother) crip-
ples the same saying as: "Who is a hero? He who does
not make a witticism." Well, ordinarily, "witticism" is *vits*
in English; but *vitsn* come in various flavors, some pleasant,
some sour, some joyous, some bitter. The saying is most
effective, I think, in these words:

"Who is a hero? He who represses a wisecrack."

(12) "A lock is good only for an honest man." But
what in the world did the translator mean by "good"? Did
he think a lock works well only on the door of an honest
man? Did he believe locks are prejudiced against crooks?
The original lends itself to transplanting that will preserve
a shrewd observation:

"Locks keep out only the honest."

(13) "*Az men maynt, genart men zikh*" has been translated as: "To assume is to be deceived." This is grossly
inaccurate; the epigram should read:

"To assume is to deceive one's self."

Deception is as different from self-deception as trust is from delusion.

(14) "There is no barber that cuts his hair." Once I stopped shuddering over that "that," I had no qualms about changing the saying to:

"No barber cuts his own hair."

(15) "He is a giant who has many dwarfs about him." Not bad, I suppose; but my discontent is eased by re-writing:

"That man is a giant who is surrounded by dwarfs."

After all, you can have a good many dwarfs "about" and yet be leagues (as dwarfs go) away from being surrounded by them.

By now you no doubt suspect how therapeutic I found it to rewrite those translators who bury bright sayings in the mausoleums of their prose.

The last word is Proust's: "When I read another writer, I set my inner metronome to his rhythm."

How My Translations Were Made

Lest you credit me with linguistic powers I do not pretend to command, I hasten to tell you that my only reading of Aramaic, Hebrew, or Arabic sources has been in translations, a great number of which have, happily, been showered upon us within the past fifty years.[43]

Most of the sayings in this book *have been freshly translated from either Yiddish, Hebrew, or English* (which peculiarity I explain below). I checked my own translations of Yiddish folk sayings with Rabbi Solomon D. Goldfarb, who worked with me for many months, producing translations of Hebrew works (from the Talmud, post-Biblical philosophers, ancient theologians, medieval poets) which I then rephrased—condensed or expanded, decorated or denuded—into that English formulation I considered most accurate, which means most harmonious or pointed, lofty or impish, noble or sardonic or paradoxical. Where amiable differences arose, I took advantage of the independent judgment of scholars at the Jewish Theological Seminary. On technical problems in linguistics and philology, I tapped the multilingual abilities of Dr. Felix Kaufmann.

I alone must take responsibility for each sentence, and therefore each interpretation, in the pages that follow. If, on one or another point, you take exception to my rendition, I can only say that I have tried to be faithful to the meaning, not just the wording, of each proverb; and I sought to strengthen, or enliven that meaning by the English into which I reworded it. What I have tried to do is recreate aspects of the life and life-style of the Jewish people, through their sayings. This means that I have tried to retrieve the substance and flavor of ideas which are often phrased in such archaic language, or concealed within such esoteric contexts, that their meaning is incomprehensible to modern readers (except those who have been immersed in the Talmud, Jewish customs, lore and law).

Above, I used the odd phrase "translated from English." What I mean by this is that in a lifetime of reading and socializing, I collected thousands of Yiddish and Hebrew apothegms—in English. When I assembled all my notes to compile this anthology, I read my hoard with a fresh eye— and a sinking heart. I realized that I simply had to rephrase or jettison and replace much of the English. The labor this involved is too painful to describe. Suffice it to say that I was often driven to translate the English of an epigram back into Yiddish—and the Yiddish back into clearer, deeper, or (I trust) wittier English.

Speaking of English suggests that a short side-excursion may help non-Jews understand what often makes them wince: the emotional flamboyance of some of their best friends.

A Word to Non-Jews

Since a language is a vehicle for a culture, it contains within itself that invisible scale of proportions which (along with a thousand other subtleties) the culture assigns to the expression of emotions. Compare the ethos of the Jews in this respect with, say, that of the English.

Englishmen prize privacy; Jews prize intimacy. The

English dislike displaying their feelings; Jews think feelings are meant to be verbalized.

Englishmen understate the serious ("The riot was a bit of a mess") and overstate the trivial ("What a *frightfully* amusing hat!"); Jews tend to inflate what is important ("That will blacken his name for all time!") and pooh-pooh what is not cataclysmic ("Stroke-shmoke, he can still wink with one eye!").

The English repress uneasiness; Jews feed it banquets of nourishment. An Englishman treats a disaster as unfortunate; a Jew thinks a hangnail an injustice.

The English are embarrassed by confidences; Jews are let down by "coldness."

The English place a premium on the concealment of emotion (in a crisis, John Bull does "fly into a calm"); they voice a deep conviction as if it were a tentative opinion; they are made uncomfortable by a raised voice or a trickled tear; they disapprove of the dogmatic—and all of this puzzles people (besides Jews) who were steeped in other modalities of affect.

Where Egypt wails, England blinks. Where Hindu women tear their hair, English women study their nails. An Italian explodes invective; an Englishman sniffs "Really?" When the Russians thunder "*Averyone* knows . . ." the English demur "But I should think that . . ." Where Americans cry, "It's terrific!" Englishmen concede, "Rather impressive." And where Englishmen murmur "What a pity," Jews cry "What a disaster!"

These differences in what anthropologists call "character structure" are crucial to anyone who tries to understand values which are foreign to his own, or comprehend conduct which departs from his ingrained expectations. Jews may strike Anglo-Saxons as verbose and melodramatic because Jews are early taught (as I was) to feel an *obligation* to respond to the misfortunes of others with visible, audible sympathy—so that no one can possibly fail to recognize the depth and sensitivity of one's compassion. To Jews, emotions are not meant to be nursed in private: they are meant to be dramatized and displayed—so that they can be *shared*. What is sweeter than a tearful or gleeful *shmus:* a juicy exchange of feelings or frustrations, dreams and experience? Not to do this, O Albion, is to lack "true feeling," to be blinded by selfish preoccupations, to fail in one's duty as a man.

I suppose that whereas a psychiatrist regards "empathy" as feeling for others, a Jew considers empathy heartless if it does not give equal time to himself. It is not that Jews (or Greeks or Arabs) are genetically maudlin, and wallow in wailing and hyperbole; they have just been taught that it is healthier to express than repress; that one must help those in stress by echoing their lamentations (which reduces their burden); that to embroider your own emotions is an obligation to your fellow men—who are entitled to participate in your miseries, no less than your triumphs, as you are in theirs.

The English think "a stiff upper lip" is a sign of courage; Mediterranean people judge a "stiff upper lip" to be *inappropriate* (why should suffering cast doubt on courage?) —since eyes filled with tears, and eloquent expressions of consolation, can give so much comfort to those, stricken by fate, who have been raised, too, to expect men to be *simpático*, to act decently, to be *sympatish* conveyors of "feeling-with."

But delicate gradations of tact lie beneath these surfaces of deportment. At a funeral, a Jew is expected to keen and wail and weep, but during *shiva*, the seven days of mourning at home, he comes to pay his respects and offers no greeting at all! For he must be (or appear to be) so deeply plunged in grief, so compassionate to the bereaved, that speech is beyond his powers.

After long, precious immersion in three cultures, accustomed from my crib on to gales of laughter and epiphanies of disaster, I have come to the conclusion that Americans treat "neurotic" as a synonym for "nuts"; that Englishmen think "neurotic" an adjective applicable to foreigners; and that Jews consider "neurotic" a synonym for "human."

Cosmetic Devices That May Interest Linguists and Grammarians

Let me set down some of the cosmetic devices I have employed in translating certain adages, in an effort to free them from their imprisonment within the linguistic amber of the past:

(1) I drop the charming but archaic "thou" and "thee," except when the Lord is addressed. (I think He will approve.)

(2) I often replace Biblical with modern usage: e.g., changing "potsherd" to "shard," or "Disclose not" to "Don't tell."

(3) I rewrite Biblical phrases muddled in translations: "Like clouds with wind . . ." is literal—and clumsy; I think it more graceful to say, "Like wind-blown clouds . . ."

(4) Semitic languages employ circuitous syntax ("With a spoon, you can't empty the ocean"); I mete out mercy to my readers by enlisting English style ("You can't empty the seas with a spoon").

(5) Where Talmudic terms may mislead the contemporary reader, I change the phrasing; for instance, rabbinical debates are studded with "Evil Impulse"; I try to make clear whether evil, instinct, or evil impulse is intended: they *are* different in this post-Freudian world.

(6) Jewish proverbs are laden with allusions utterly foreign to gentiles: *shadchen, hasidim, Baal-Shem, golem, yikhes, Kuni Lemmel.* (To read Mendele Mocher Seforim or Sholem Aleichem is to enter a museum of humorous references and similes—often erudite, often parodied, sometimes accurate, sometimes intentionally garbled.) I explain such references, wherever possible, in the text itself, or radically recast the saying.

(7) "Sage" appears often in old proverbs, to mean a sage, scholar, prophet, rabbi, or even necromancer: I use the word most suitable in English diction.

(8) Old sayings are full of the pronoun "one": "What one would have, he does not possess; what one possesses, he does not care for." I reword such sentences: "What a man wants, he does not have; what he possesses, he does not prize."

Note the effect obtained by the change from "one" to "a man," "would have" to "wants," and "care for" to "prize."

(9) Old sayings are often phrased, in English, in the Hebrew-Aramaic style of Biblical times: "Drive forth" I change to "drive out" ("forth" suggests merely motion, "out" registers disapproval). Similarly, "The good" is momentarily puzzling, for it may refer to either virtue or the virtuous; I use "the good man" for the latter.

(10) In many instances, I add a noun, or change a substantive to an adjective, to make the text more explicit;

thus, I prefer "the righteous man" to "the righteous" where the verb is singular, and use "the righteous" for a group.

(11) To insure clarity, I often change the passive voice to the active, or an adjective to a clause. Example: "A beaten dog should not be shown a cane" may be describing a dog who is beaten or defeated or depressed; such uncertainty is excluded in: "Don't show a cane to a dog who has been beaten."

(12) I sometimes change intransitive verbs to transitive: "One who is envious of . . ." is inferior, to my mind, to "The man who envies . . ."

(13) I sharpen or simplify wherever meaning can be strengthened: Maimonides' *Guide to the Perplexed*, I, 31 is often given in English as: "We naturally like whatever is familiar, and dislike whatever is strange." I prefer to make this: "By nature we like the familiar and dislike the strange."

(14) I try to refurbish such diction as: "What's easy to utter may be hard to carry." I felt no guilt in making this: "What's easy to say may be hard to bear."

(15) Wherever possible, I try to heighten accuracy: "Who does not please his parents will have sons who don't obey," I change to: "The man who disobeys his father will have disobedient sons." The congruence of "man . . . father . . . sons" (instead of "who . . . parents . . . sons"), and the counterpointing of "disobeys" and "disobedient," tighten the muscle to the thought.

(16) I sometimes *join* sentences whose ideas gain in power from union: "He gives little who gives with a frown. He gives much who gives little with a smile" is enriched by combination and, therefore, immediate contrast: "The man who gives little with a smile gives more than the man who gives much with a frown."

(17) I see no excuse for perpetuating abominable diction: "Better experience an injustice than do one." "Experience" makes the reader hesitate (is it a noun or a verb?); the lazy "do" should not march by the side of the mighty "injustice"; injustices sound more unjust when "committed" than when "done"; and surely "experience" is less eloquent than "suffer." So I frame this memorable injunction: "It is better to suffer an injustice than to commit one."

(18) Wherever possible, I seek to abolish ambiguity: "As you put a fence around your vineyard, so . . ." There is

no way of knowing what that "as" means until the reader reaches the "so." Is the following not clearer: "Just as you build a fence around your vineyard, so . . ."?

(19) In a few cases, I combine two folk sayings to emphasize the ironic intention of each: "All brides are beautiful" and "All dead men are pious." I placed each of these, as a separate saying, in its appropriate category in the anthology, but added a new, combined aphorism: "All brides are beautiful, and all dead men look pious."

Few men reject a free bonus.

Who Is Left Out?

There is a gallimaufry of witticisms by Jews from Heinrich Heine to Groucho Marx that I have not included,* because their quips, however funny or memorable, are not folk sayings or proverbs or maxims. Where I *have* included the words of a modern writer (Sholem Aleichem, or Rabbi Israel Meir Kahan, "The Chofetz Chaim") it is because they are clearly in the tradition of Jewish thought.

I have included some sayings of recent paternity because any jury would agree that they are "Jewish" in content and ambience:

"When you go to a restaurant, take a seat near a waiter."

That tidbit might well have been uttered in Beersheba, Barcelona, or Bialystok.

* * *

Thus endeth my Preface to the Reader, may you live in good health unto 120! The reason "120" is used by Jews in exchanging felicities, is that that is the age at which Moses died. One exuberant gentleman I knew used to say, "May you live until 121!"—and when asked why, replied, "Because I wouldn't want you to die suddenly."

LEO ROSTEN

May 20, 1972
New York, New York

---

* With two exceptions, for Heine, too haunting to be excluded; see GOD and OLD AGE in the collection.

Acknowledgments

I extend deep thanks to Rabbi Solomon D. Goldfarb; his vast knowledge of the Talmud and the sprawling *corpus* of rabbinical literature, his capacity for identifying obscure quotations or tracing them to their source, and his friendly encouragement during many difficult stretches of my labors were true *mitzvahs*.

For help on countless technical problems, I owe thanks to my patient friend Professor Seymour Siegel of the Jewish Theological Seminary. For valuable comments on anthropological aspects of the Preface, I am grateful to Dr. Margaret Mead. For a battery of invaluable editorial/historical/philological suggestions, I thank my multilingual colleague, the memory expert of the Chaos Club, Dr. Felix Kaufmann. The staff of the New York Public Library were unfailingly helpful; their expertise merits the gratitude of any author.

In the final stage of preparing the manuscript, I was helped with Talmudic and rabbinical verifications by Rabbis Aaron Kriegel, Jay Rovner, and Leslie Friedman, all of whom are a credit to their Seminary, whose librarian, Dr. Menahem Schmelzer, enriched my source materials with many recommendations. Other research aid was conscientiously executed by Angelika Wolff. Gale Picard provided tireless assistance in organizing the collocation. Froso Calise's equanimity and efficiency were a boon. Rita Callahan supplied secretarial first-aid on many crucial occasions.

Many friends answered my many inquiries, to give me nuggets of Jewish wit I had not heard or read before. My mother and Mr. and Mrs. George Echt followed the finest principles of *mishpokhe* by surveying their memories and circle of acquaintances to give me dozens of delightful folk sayings, plus a hundred more from their acquaintances in the rabbinate. Abe Altrovitz of the Minneapolis *Star* sent me columns in which he had published adages submitted by his readers. At least 250 owners of *The Joys of Yiddish* wrote me sayings they had heard from their parents—who came from Bucharest, Johannesburg, Frankfurt, Budapest, Rio de Janeiro, Lisbon, Tokyo.

My wife, as always, deserves a bouquet for allowing our house to be transformed into a research factory, and for amiably suffering, for so long, a husband possessed and obsessed by an enterprise that often seemed to have no end. Many good friends gave me asylum when I feared I was ready for one.

LEO ROSTEN

HELPFUL HINTS
TO THE
READER

What Proverbs/Folk Sayings
Are Included?

I have not included many proverbs (from the Old Testament or the Apocrypha) because they are so familiar that they have come to be hackneyed through overusage. What I *have* tried to include in this anthology are only those Jewish sayings that will make you laugh or smile or think. Since this is an emphatically personal compendium, I have excluded any saying that did not make *me* smile or laugh or think.

On Arrangement

I first intended to arrange the quotations, within a category, according to their pungency, risibility, or surprise—placing the funniest or more striking sayings at the beginning, and the longer, legalistic sayings at the end. In this, I followed the advice in the Talmud which tells us that a teacher should begin a lesson with something amusing. It is lamentable that so few teachers know this, and that those who do are often elephantine in their levity.

In the end, however, the material seemed to fall best into the following order: folk sayings; quotations from the Torah, the Talmud and rabbinical literature; selections from individual aphorists.

I salvaged my original intention by calling the reader's attention to my favorites—I just could not restrain myself—by using a special symbol (❋, which printers charmingly call a "fleuron").

On Repetitions

(1) You will find some sayings repeated—that is, appearing in different wordings in different places, under different topic categories. This is intentional, not accidental. I repeat entries in different sections because:

    (a) content sometimes embraces more than one category: e.g.,

        "To a drunkard, no liquor is bad; to a merchant, no money is tainted; to a lecher, no woman is ugly."

        This saying clamors for inclusion under DRUNKARDS, BUSINESS, MONEY, LUST.

    (b) it seemed advisable to give those readers who will use this anthology as a reference work a maximum number of places in which to find an adage;

    (c) some adages are so good that they deserve to be repeated;

    (d) who is hurt?

(2) You will sometimes find different versions of the same saying. This is also intentional. Example:

    "Small children disturb your sleep;
        big children disturb your life."
    "Little children won't let you sleep;
        big children won't let you rest."
    "Little children don't let you sleep,
        and big children won't let you live."

Each has its own distinctive thrust. To choose one and omit two others would be to exclude varying insights on the same theme.

Sources and Attributions of the Authors Quoted

(1) The largest number of adages in this collection are not credited to a given book or person because they are folk sayings.

(2) Wherever possible, I cite the name of the scholar, rabbi, philosopher or poet whom I quote; but please remember that in the Talmud a sage often uses a popular saying to buttress his point; he did not necessarily coin the proverb—though it is sometimes attributed to him.

(3) Exact attribution becomes particularly difficult because the names of 2,000 scholars appear in the Talmud, and many are quoting other rabbis or sources, and many names are identical: for instance, I have noted some 25 Simeons, 20 Joses, 14 Eleazar/Eliezers. To be sure, many names are further identified (e.g., Simeon the Just, Simeon ben Lakish, Simeon of Teman; or Eleazar of Modi'im, Eliezer ben Eliezer bar Kappara); but hasty quoters often drop a place-name or patronym which tells us which Simeon or Eleazar is being quoted. By my count, in the index to the Talmud, "Rab," for instance, appears 1,330 times; "Abaya" 1,225 . . . but who can be certain when either was quoting? And how many times does one or another great teacher say, "As our people know . . ." Therefore:

(4) It is sometimes impossible to guarantee the originality of a line: to be sure that an apothegm in the *Pirke Abot* ("Sayings of the Fathers"), say, or in an eleventh-century poem by Ibn Gabirol was invented there, fresh and new; for the scholar may have been echoing a folk saying, the poet quoting or paraphrasing. And a humorist like "Mendele" (Mocher Seforim) or Sholem Aleichem loved to repeat (or deliberately butcher) a saying well-known to his readers. Where an aphorism *is* credited to an individual, in this anthology, it is because the weight of evidence or expert opinion strongly confirms his paternity.

(5) A large number of quotations come or are adapted from the Talmud; these are more specifically identified

(contrary to much contrary and irritating practice) by book, tractate and page number.

(6) All editions and translations of the Talmud preserve the same pagination, which was established by its first printer, Daniel Bomberg (who was not a Jew), in Venice, early in the sixteenth century. My references can be verified in the English translation published by the Soncino Press (London, 1935–1952). But I should caution the reader that my quotations often do not coincide *verbatim* with the Soncino text—for I found many of my quotations, during decades of readings, in one or another of Heaven-knows-how-many essays and books; or the particular passage may have been translated for me from the Hebrew Talmud by Dr. S. D. Goldfarb—and was then sharpened, shortened, polished or reworded by me, according to my own judgment about style, pungence or context. I defend the license of translators as strongly as that of poets.

(7) In the BIBLIOGRAPHY, I have listed the more important printed sources read or consulted. I hope I need not again stress that a very great number of the sayings in these pages I *heard* (see ACKNOWLEDGMENTS) from my parents, relatives, friends, rabbis, colleagues in seminars I was privileged to attend for six years at the Jewish Theological Seminary, or received from readers of *The Joys of Yiddish.*

GUIDE NOTES
ON
TORAH
AND
TALMUD

A. The Torah:

1. English and Hebrew Nomenclature

The Torah (from Hebrew, "doctrine" or "teachings") refers to the first five books of the Old Testament, called "the books of Moses" by Jews[44] and the Pentateuch in Greek and English:

Genesis: Greek for "origin" or "creation"; in Hebrew, this book is called *Bereshith*, from *Be-Reshith*: "In the beginning" (originally, the name was *Sefer Maaseh Bereshith*: "Book of Creation").

Exodus: Greek for "road out"; in Hebrew, the book is named after its opening word, *Shemot*: "Names."

Leviticus: Late Latin for the Greek *Leutikos*; in Hebrew, this book is known as *Vayyikra* or *Va-Yikra*, the opening word: "And He called." (This book was once called *Torat Kohanim*, "the priestly code.")

Numbers: Known in Hebrew as *Bemidbar*, from *Be-Midbar*: "In the wilderness."

Deuteronomy: Known in Hebrew as *Dvarim* ("Words"), after the second word of the text (the first word means "These are the . . ."); this book was also called *Mishneh Torah*, "Repetition of the Law," from which came the Greek *Deuteronomion*.

2. Torah: Larger Meaning

In general discourse, "Torah" can mean not only the first five books of the Old Testament, but also:

(1) The actual Scroll, containing the five books of Moses, hand-written on parchment (kept in the "ark," in a synagogue or temple, behind the high altar), from which specified readings are publicly given on the Sabbath, on Mondays and Thursdays, and during festivals.

(2) The divine teachings of the Lord.

(3) The Old Testament as a whole.

(4) All Jewish Law, including the oral tradition of Judaic religion and moral precepts.

(5) Living in accordance with the teachings of Judaism; "to live Torah," "to live by Torah," "to practice Torah," mean to practice Judaism's prescriptions about faith, compassion, study, and duty to one's fellow man.

B. The Talmud

1) WHICH TALMUD?

Wherever "Talmud" is cited in the anthology of quotations, the standard Talmud (Babylonian) is meant; **when the less-frequently used Jerusalem Talmud is cited, the attribution is worded "Talmud J."**

The great Palestinian and the Babylonian academies produced separate Talmuds: the *Talmud Yerushalmi* (of Jerusalem), which was compiled and collated around the fifth century; and the *Talmud Babli* (Babylonian), written in Aramaic and Hebrew, about a century later. When we speak of the Talmud today, *we generally refer to the Babylonian Talmud:* it had a much greater influence on Jewish law and life; the Jerusalem text, which is shorter and incomplete, was not preserved *in toto*; the Babylonian Talmud contains about 2,500,000 words, more than three times the number in the Jerusalem Talmud.

The English translation of the Babylonian Talmud was published in 35 volumes and in 12 volumes (which do not include all the voluminous commentaries) by Soncino Press, London, from 1935 to 1952.

Page numbering is identical in all editions and translations of the Talmud; "62b," for instance, was the reverse side of the original sheet, "62a"; this form has been preserved down the centuries.

2) WHAT IS THE TALMUD?

The Talmud is not the Bible. It is not the Old Testament. It is not "a" book.

The best way to think of the Talmud is as the minutes of a symposium on religion, law, philosophy, ethics, that lasted without interruption (but with constantly changing scholars and authorities) for 1,200 years, from the fifth century before, to the eighth century after, the Christian Era, "when [the Babylonian Talmud] was substantially in its present state."[45] (The name "Talmud" was first used in the middle of the eighth century; it comes from Hebrew *lamad*, "study," or *limed*, "teach.")

The Talmud is a monumental compendium of 63 *massekhet* (books) that record this 1,200 year-long seminar of oral analysis, debates, commentaries, commentaries *upon* commentaries of the Torah (the first five books of the Old Testament) by over 2,000 scholar-rabbis who devoted their lives to interpreting "the Law" so that its majestic teaching could be applied to religious rites and obligations in countless new, everyday problems.

The Talmud is a work of immense size, intricate structure, multifarious topics, enmazed subtleties, archaic dilemmas, mind-boggling feats of intellectual skill—and casuistries that exasperate the modern mentality. (One is tempted to scorn the dialectical acrobatics, the sophistry and hair-splittings; but in all fairness one should remember that the rabbis were steeped in an intellectual tradition not unique to them, but shared by apostles of scholasticism in other fields and faiths; for all were imprisoned within ironbound suppositions and "sacred" rules of explication; rare was the mind blessed, in those distant days, with the kind of critical/historical capacity that would liberate intellectual operations.)

I know of no work remotely the Talmud's equivalent: so universal in scope; so profound in its explorations of the nature of wisdom, virtue, truth, morals, ethics, laws; and often so quaint, parochial, and superstitious.

The discussions in the Talmud range from astronomy to urination, from the structure of the cosmos to the planting of Egyptian beans, from God's purposes to man's tragedies ("A man who crosses a river behind a woman will be excluded from the world-to-come"—because she will have to lift her skirts and he will be struck by unchaste thoughts).

The Talmud encompasses everything from religion to metaphysics, history, medicine, epistemology, pedagogy, hygiene, etc. It revolves around the enduring central ques-

tions that characterize the human condition: the nature of
God, the purpose of life, the meaning of truth, the mystery
of death, the duties of man, the hopes of a hereafter, the
forms of punishment for evil and rewards for virtue.

The Talmud is, in one sense, the university in which
every Jew for centuries studied and in which he was
trained.

3) WHAT THE TALMUD IS NOT

The Talmud does not offer Jews a codified or consistent
system of belief (though the scholars weave threads of
unity within its complex whole).

The Talmud is not a legal code, though it bursts with
cases, arguments, ecclesiastical decisions. (For "the code,"
see *Shulhan Aruk* in the GLOSSARY.)

The Talmud is not a history, though it is crammed with
invaluable information about the ancients.

It is not a treatise on philosophy, though it is a philosopher's treasure—and nightmare.

> The Talmud . . . was not only a book of philosophy or
> devotion, it was a reservoir of national life; it was the
> faithful mirror of the civilization of Babylon and Judea;
> at the same time it was a magical phantasmagoria of all
> the wild dreams, the fables, the legends, the scraps of sci-
> ence . . . the reveries, the audacious theories discovered by
> the Wandering Jew in his endless travels. Every generation
> of Judaism had accumulated its facts and fancies there.[46]

The Talmud is not a book of ethics, though it is unique
in the richness and range of its discourses on moral
problems.

It is not a text in anthropology, though it contains invaluable data on folklore, customs, mores, superstitions,
early cosmologies.

The Talmud is—the Talmud.

> Say what you will of the Judaism of the Middle Ages; call
> it narrow; deride it as superstitious . . . [but] for sweetness
> and spirituality of life, the Jew of the Ghetto, the Jew of
> the Middle Ages, the Jew under the yoke of the Talmud,
> challenges the world.[47]

4) THE NAMES OF THE TALMUD'S SIX ORDERS (BOOKS) *

1. ZERAIM ("Seeds," or the laws of agriculture)
2. MO'ED ("Festivals, set feasts")
3. NASHIM ("Women")
4. NEZIKIN ("Damages": civil and criminal law)
5. KIDDUSHIN ("Sacred or Hallowed Things")
6. TOHOROTH ("Cleannesses" or "ritual purity")

---

* Soncino Press, London, (12 vols.) 1936 to 1952.

5) THE NAMES OF THE 63 TRACTATES

Relevant ones are identified by name in the GLOSSARY.

6) "THE MINOR TRACTATES OF THE TALMUD"

(more properly "The Minor Tractates added to the Talmud") :

ABOTH D' RABBI NATHAN; SOFERIM; SEMAHOTH; KALLAH; KALLAH RABBATI; DEREKH ERETZ RABBAH; DEREKH ERETS ZUTA; PEREK HASHALOM; GERIM; KUTHIM; ABADIM; SEFER TORAH; TEPHILLIN; ZIZITH; MEZUZAH.

These have been translated into English.[48]

C. The Mishnah

The original six "orders" of legal material, arranged by topics, which are the base of the Talmud, are called the Mishnah (from a Hebrew root meaning "to review" or "to repeat" [learning], a collection of interpretations of Biblical passages and laws as they were applied to social conditions in Palestine between the fifth century before, and the second century of, the Christian Era.

These laws included ecclesiastical court decisions, regulations on ritual, ethical teachings, etc. They were originally transmitted by rabbis orally, so as not to impair the sanctity of the written Law: i.e., the Torah. The Mishnah is the collocated "Oral Law." What often confuses laymen (like me) is that "Mishnah" is used to mean either the six fundamental orders of the Talmud, or a particular paragraph or interpretation of the text, or for a collection of earlier teachings: "The Mishnah of Rabbi Meir," "The Mishnah of Rabbi Akiba," etc.

The Mishnah was written in simple Hebrew (with some loan-words from Aramaic, Greek, and Latin), and was authoritatively redacted or edited by Judah ha-Nasi ("the Prince"), around the year 200. The first printed edition appeared in 1492, in Naples, published by Soncino.

A Mishnah opens the six "orders" (*Sedarim*) and sixty-three tractates (*Massekhot*) of the Talmud (see above). Each of the Mishnah's sixty-three tractates is divided into chapters (*Perakim*), of which there are 523; each chapter is set forth in paragraphs.

The Mishnah is not the work of any one man, school, or time; nor were its contents new. The Mishnah was the end result of four to six centuries of analysis and teaching in Palestine.

The work had its origins after the return of the Hebrews to Judea from their Babylonian exile (537 B.C.E.), when the scholars of the Great Assembly, the Jews' religious and legislative body, established basic rules for the interpretation of Jewish law. The scribes (*Sopherim*) were official copyist/teachers; later sages (*Tannaim*) continued to interpret Biblical laws, in the context of changing historical, political, social conditions.

Hillel made one of the earliest attempts to codify the vast and entangled body of oral teachings, but no one knows what became of that enterprise. Akiba performed the pioneer work of collecting and classifying oral decisions and precedents into a *Mishnah* or "review" and Akiba's work was continued and completed by Judah ha-Nasi, also known simply as "Rabbi," who declared the canon closed around the year 200.*

The Mishnah thus serves as the central commentary used in both the Babylonian and Jerusalem Talmuds.

The Mishnah was such a formidable achievement that it was accepted by the rabbis as *the* authority in interpret-

---

* For biographical vignettes of these and other scholars, see BIOGRAPHIES, Appendix III.

ing the Old Testament, and was elevated to a station which only the Torah could supersede.

The Mishnah has been translated into English, with prodigious scholarship and footnotes, by Dr. Herbert Danby (Canon of St. George's Cathedral, Jerusalem), Oxford University Press, London, 1933.

I am fond of an old rumination:

> The Mishnah begins with an open *mem* and ends with a closed *mem*—to teach us that when a man begins to study, he believes all the mansions of knowledge are open to him; but when he finishes, he discovers how much knowledge is still behind doors closed to him.[49]

D. The Midrash and Haggada

From the time of Ezra (the fifth century before the Christian Era), a group of scholars known as *Sopherim* (scribes) were "skilled in the laws of Moses." These men were teachers of "the Oral Law," as derived from the Torah.

The effort to "investigate" Scripture, in order to find its true meaning and implications, was known as *Midrash* (from *darash*, the Hebrew for "investigate"). The *midrashim* are efforts to "penetrate" a text and illuminate its inner spirit.*

The first *midrashim* were strictly legal in nature, and are known as *halaka*. At the same time, a different kind of Midrash was growing: colloquial and moralistic, not juridical: this was the Midrash *Haggada* (from the Hebrew: "to tell").

The Haggada presents its lessons in informal, sometimes homely, often imaginative, amusing and poetic ways—as a roving commentary on and about those portions of Scripture which are not the Law, but which are anecdotal,

---

* Four types of interpretation of the holy Torah were devised: *pshat*, the simple, literal meaning; *remez*, hints of meaning, or clues to content; *drush*, homily exposition of a text; and *sod*, the secret, mystical, esoteric meaning contained beneath the surface of a word or passage. But the sacred texts remain indisputable; in the Talmud, *Shabbat* (63a), the rabbis ruled: "Nothing can supersede the *plain* meaning of the text" [my italics].

legendary, or folklore. From the Midrash Haggada come many of the moral lessons the rabbis used to inspire Jews to greater piety and virtue. From haggadic parts of the Talmud (about a third of its contents) one can glean a marvelous harvest of historical and medical data, wonderful legends and unforgettable anecdotes.

The Haggada is often a collection of sermons, delivered on the afternoons of the Sabbath, when Jews gathered to hear Scripture taught, explained and discussed.

The earliest haggadic *midrashim* were collections of sayings, lyrical verses, moralisms, by the most revered rabbis. Called the *Pirke Abot*, or "Sayings of the Fathers," this is the most popular, most beloved and most quoted work in rabbinical literature. (You will find more than a hundred passages from *Pirke Abot* in the present collection.)

The Midrash was written in Hebrew, with occasional passages in Aramaic. A volume of the Midrash often bears the name of the book of the Bible under discussion.

Midrash Rabbah ("Great Midrash") is a misnomer; it consists of ten books: one for each volume of the Pentateuch (Torah) and one for each of the five "scrolls" (Song of Songs, Ruth, Lamentations, Ecclesiastes, Esther). The names of some other volumes of Midrash are: *Mekilta*, *Sifre*, *Sifra*, *Pesikta de Rab Kahana*, *Tanhuma*. (For each, see the GLOSSARY.)

A set of strict rules (hermeneutics) was agreed upon by the rabbis—regulations which defined and delimited the ways in which Scripture could be interpreted in order to provide new rulings or to justify new teachings. The seven rules established by the great Hillel, plus forty-five by two later scholars, remain the authoritative guidelines of Biblical exegesis in Judaism. (Incidentally, one of the things that upset the rabbinical authorities about Jesus of Nazareth was the fact that he expounded the Law without attention to these principles, offering teachings on his own authority; the Jews could not concede that Jesus was the Messiah,[50] even though many of them respected and supported Jesus' noble teachings.)

Until the seventh century, scholars continued to make additions, albeit minor, to the Talmud. These men were called *Seboraim* ("reasoners"). Until the twelfth century, rabbis continued to write their commentaries—as works of Midrash.

The whole process of interpreting Holy Scripture, to make it relevant to changing life, to keep it fresh as a source of inspiration, authority and faith, continued in the period known as the Talmudic or Rabbinic era.

The total body of teachings contained in the Talmud, Midrash and Responsa (see F, below) is known as Rabbinical Judaism.

E. The Gemara

The second division of the Talmud is the *Gemara* (from the Aramaic "completion"), or commentaries upon the Mishnah. (The language of the Gemara is Aramaic, but contains a great deal of Hebrew.)

There are two Gemaras: one is the work of the Palestinian schools, and was edited around the year 380 in Tiberias. The other Gemara, the work of the Babylonian School, is much larger and more widely known, and is included when the word "Talmud" is used. This Gemara was edited around the year 500 by Rabbi Ashi and his disciple Rabbi José, and is usually published with the commentary of the celebrated sage Rashi.* It contains further comments which are called *Tosephoth*, the work of French and German scholars in the twelfth to the fourteenth centuries.

Note: The Gemaras of both the Palestinian and the Babylonian Talmuds do not represent a complete commentary on the complete Mishnah. Large sections are missing from both Gemaras.

F. The Responsa

The widely dispersed communities of Jews often needed authoritative rulings on a thousand and one aspects of life not explicitly covered in the Torah. During the Babylonian exile, letters were sent to great

---

* For more information on these and other scholars, see BIOGRAPHIES in Appendix III.

scholars asking for their interpretations of, and rulings on, the Law to be followed. The scholars' replies, known as *responsa*, were of critical importance in preserving and adapting Judaism to new political and social pressures.

Over 500,000 *responsa*, published in over 1,000 compilations, have been found, from such illustrious scholars as Alfasi, Rashi, Maimonides, the *tosephists* of France and Germany in the twelfth to the fourteenth centuries, Joseph Caro, who assembled the great *Shulhan Aruk* (Set Table) of regulatory laws, and others.

Another aspect of the importance of *responsa* correspondence is worth mentioning. During many periods, the reading or study of the Talmud was forbidden to Jews by hostile sovereignties. (In 1242, the Church, in Paris, ordered all Talmudic literature to be burned: twenty-four cartloads vanished in the flames; in 1553, a huge number of volumes were destroyed in Rome; in 1757, thousands of Talmud volumes were burned in Poland, by order of a bishop; and the depredations of the Nazis in Germany, Austria, and conquered parts of Poland and Russia need not be detailed.) In these tragic and critical times, the *responsa* were a means of circumventing the prohibitions.

The *responsa* remain priceless repositories of contemporary data on the intellectual life, historical events, social conditions, philosophical disputations, etc., of all the places in which Jews lived, or to which they traveled. *Responsa* are still being written—e.g., to answer questions concerning, say, the times of prayer, which will surely need reinterpretation in the age of space travel.

Here are some striking examples:

May *challa* [braided bread, for the Sabbath] be sliced by the bakery's machine?

May a rabbi officiate at a wedding where the groom is under a psychiatrist's care, trying to be cured of impotence?

May a physician hasten the end of the sufferings of a patient with terminal cancer—where the family agrees, and one of the doctors, the patient's own son, concurs with the others, who recommend the withdrawal of intravenous fluids?

May a man wear a toupee during a religious service?

What can be decided, by Jewish Law, about operations to change a male to a female, or vice versa? (The surgery sterilizes the person.)

What are the religious implications in a case where a Jew's heart stops beating, but is restarted in open-heart surgery?

May a Jewish officer wear his sword, as part of his full-dress uniform, during a wedding ceremony?

Our hospital has one mechanical-kidney machine. How should a Jewish doctor decide which patient to save, among all who need it?

Can Jewish Law protect the operator of a television station who has done a worthy public-service job from another Jewish operator who has applied for an F.C.C. license—to replace the first operator? Is this unfair competition?[51]

Reference Notes

1. Example: "Rabbi Bizna ben Zabda said in the name of Rabbi Akiba who had heard it from Rabbi Panda who had it from Rabbi Nahum who had had it from Rabbi Biryam who was reporting the words of a certain elder—and who was that? Rabbi Bana'ah . . ." Talmud, *Berakoth*, 55b, Soncino, London and New York, 1948.

2. Walter Nash, *Our Experience of Language*, Batsford, London, 1971, p. 192.

3. Leo Rosten, *Rome Wasn't Burned in a Day: The Mischief of Language*, Introduction, Doubleday, New York, 1972.

4. These epigrams were coined by, respectively, Voltaire, William Osler, "Kin" Hubbard, H. L. Mencken, and Mencken again.

5. Cecil Woodham-Smith, *The Reason Why*, Constable, London, 1953.

6. Aristotle, *Rhetoric*, II, any edition.

7. The Apocrypha and Pseudepigrapha are not in the formal, closed canon, produced from the time of the Second Temple (about 538 B.C.E.) to the defeat of Bar Kochba's rebellion against the Romans (135 C.E.). See *Apocrypha* in the GLOSSARY. An excellent work is R. Travers Herford, *Talmud and Apocrypha*, KTAV, New York, 1970.

8. The span of time covered by the Talmud is the subject of considerable difference of opinion among experts (I am certainly not one). The "orthodox," often dogmatic figure for the number of years encompassed by the Talmud is 600. But if one remembers that the Old Testament is the "source" for, and subject matter of, Talmud, this would extend the time period to "about ten centuries." (See the Introduction to *The New English Bible*, Oxford University Press and Cambridge University Press, London and New York, 1961, 1970.) The most recent researches of Rabbi Louis Finkelstein, Chancellor emeritus of the Jewish Theological Seminary, supports the startling judgment that many passages in the *Mishnah* (see Guide Note C, pp. 65–67) and other rabbinical works were written *before* or during the Babylonian exile—that is to say, six or more centuries prior to what has, until recently, been the consensus of the experts. This justifies my "1200 years" figure. (See Louis Finkelstein, *New Light from the Prophets*, Basic Books, New York, 1969, pp. 1–13).

9. Aramaic was the Semitic language spoken, millennia ago, around the Tigris and Euphrates rivers. During their exile in Babylonia, the Hebrews adopted Aramaic as their language. For a scholarly survey of proverbs in the Bible, Apocrypha, and Talmud, see *The Jewish Encyclopedia*, Vol. X, KTAV Publishing House, New York (no date cited), pp. 226–231, where several hundred Aramaic sayings and "Judaeo-German" (i.e., Yiddish) proverbs are included.

10. William McKane, *Proverbs: A New Approach*, SCM Press, London, 1970, pp. 6–17.

11. See Samuel Rapaport, *A Treasury of the Midrash*, KTAV, New York, 1968, p. 5.

12. Alexander Smith, in *Dreamthorp: A Book of Essays Written in the Country*, J. E. Tilton Co., Boston, 1864; reprinted, Peter Pauper Press, Mount Vernon, New York, 1947.

13. Collections of proverbs were numerous and popular among Jews for many centuries: Rabbi Hai Gaon's *Musar ha-Sekhel* ("The Ethics of Wisdom"), Samuel ha-Nagid's *Ben Mishle*, Moses ibn Ezra's *Tarshish*, and a good many works translated from Arabic (in which many Hebrew poets and scholars framed their

words): Ibn Gabirol's great *Mibhar ha-Peninim* ("Choice of Pearls") and *Tikun Midot ha-Nefesh* ("The Improvement of the Qualities of the Soul"), Abraham ben Hasdai's *Ben ha-Melekh ve-ha-Nazir* (a story of the Buddha), *Mahberot Immanuel* ("The Compositions of Immanuel of Rome") etc. Many of the originals, especially those in Arabic, were lost for centuries; many have been found and reprinted within the last hundred years.

14. The hasidim produced many remarkable folk-sages, most notably Nachman of Bratslav ("The Bratslaver") whose brilliant sayings were published as *Sefer ha-Midot*. Leaders of the *Haskalah* ("Enlightenment") movement which waged ideological warfare against the "medievalist" hasidim, collected the apothegms of *their* brightest minds (e.g., the *Sefer ha-Midot* of Solomon Rubin).

15. Ludwig Seligman (*Parabeln, Legenden und Gedanken aus dem Talmud*), Emanuel Deutsch (*The Talmud*), Rabbi Henry Cohen (*Talmudic Sayings*), Leopold Dukes (*Rabbinische Blumenlese*), and others.

16. Leo Rosten, *Joys of Yiddish*, McGraw-Hill, New York, 1968, p. xx.

17. The amount of legend, custom, and demonology that is common to the people of the Old Testament and other peoples (whether Masai tribes or Polynesian clans) has been thoroughly documented by James Frazer (*Folklore in the Old Testament*) and greatly expanded by Theodor H. Gaster (*Myth, Legend and Custom in the Old Testament*). And as I write these words, a book just published in England lies before me: Professor William McKane's *Proverbs: A New Approach* (S.C.M. Press, London, 1970), a *tour de force* of cross-analysis of the old sayings of Assyria, Babylon, and Egypt.

18. William Thackeray, *The Newcomes* (any edition).

19. Evidence for prior collections of folk sayings is found in the Talmud: *Baba Kamma* (92b, 93a) and *Yebamoth* (118b): see the *Babylonian Talmud* (12 vols.), translated into English by various authors, edited by I. Epstein, Soncino Press, London, 1935–1952.

20. For a survey of educational practices among Jews, see Simon Greenberg, "Jewish Educational Institutions," in *The Jews: Their History, Culture and Religion,*

        edited by Louis Finkelstein, Vol. II, third edition,
        Harper, 1960.

21. *Joys of Yiddish, op. cit.*, p. 39.

22. *Ibid.*, pp. 41–42.

23. A. J. Heschel, *The Earth Is the Lord's*, Abelard-
    Schuman, New York, 1964, p. 46.

24. *Joys of Yiddish, op. cit.*, p. viii.

25. Maurice Samuel, *In Praise of Yiddish*, Cowles, New
    York, 1971, pp. 14–15.

26. *Joys of Yiddish, op. cit.*, p. xviii.

27. This quotation combines a passage from *Joys of Yid-
    dish* with my article, "Is It Greek to You, Too?" *Look*,
    February 7, 1967, p. 8.

28. See John L. Mish, in *The World of Translation*, P.E.N.
    Conference, New York, 1970, pp. 241–47. The defini-
    tion of language is from Walter Nash, *op. cit.*, p. 252.

29. Peter T. White, "The Interpreter: Linguist Plus Diplo-
    mat," *The New York Times Magazine*, November 6,
    1955.

30. Walter Nash, *op. cit.*, p. 18. I have been greatly in-
    fluenced by Edward Sapir's ideas and by his classic
    Language, Harcourt Brace, New York, 1921; by
    Richard Lee Whorf, *Language, Thought, and Reality*,
    ed. John B. Carroll, M.I.T. Press, Cambridge, Mass.
    1956; by H. N. Shenton, E. Sapir, and O. Jesperson,
    International Communication, London, 1931. Readers
    interested in variant positions may peruse the work
    in linguistics of Roman Jakobson, C. K. Ogden and
    I. A. Richards, Leonard Bloomfield, Harry Hoijer, and
    Noam Chomsky. For a Roman Catholic exposition,
    see David Crystal, *Linguistics, Language and Religion*,
    Burns and Oates, London, 1965.

31. For all of these animal sounds, see Helmut Braem's
    delightful and illuminating chapter, "Languages Are
    Common Yet Unique," in *The World of Translation*,
    op. cit., pp. 121–134.

32. M. H. Segall, D. Campbell and M. J. Herskovits, in
    The Influence of Culture on Visual Perception, Bobbs-
    Merrill, 1966, pp. 37, 213.

33. Quoted in *The World of Translation, op. cit.*, p. 8.

34. See Lewis Galantière, "An Ancient Art," in *Transla-
    tor: An Occasional Publication*, P.E.N., New York,
    Vol. 1, No. 1, May 1963, pp. 5–6.

35. See Gilbert Highet, *The Classical Tradition*, Oxford University Press, 1949, pp. 196, 217.

36. See A. F. Polland, *Records of the English Bible*, Oxford University Press, 1911.

37. For data to support the various items, see the relevant entries in *Dictionary of the Bible*, edited by James Hastings, revised edition edited by Frederick C. Grant and H. H. Rowley, Scribner's, New York, 1963; *Peake's Commentary on the Bible*, edited by Matthew Block and H. H. Rowley, Nelson, London, 1967; the *New Standard Jewish Encyclopedia*, edited by Cecil Roth and Geoffrey Wigoder, Doubleday, New York, 1966; Frederick C. Grant, *The Gospels: Their Origin and Their Growth*, Faber and Faber, London, 1957; and other standard sources on the Bible, its history, recent discoveries, and alterations.

38. Donald Ebor, Chairman of the Joint Committee for *The New English Bible*, Oxford & Cambridge University Presses, London, 1970, p. v.

39. See various footnotes in *The Goodspeed Parallel New Testament: The American Translation and the King James Version*, University of Chicago Press, 1943; for Old Testament data see *The Cambridge History of the Bible*, Vol. I: *From the Beginnings to Jerome*, edited by P. R. Ackroyd and C. F. Evans, Cambridge University Press, London, 1970, and the introductions to *The New English Bible, with the Apocrypha*, Oxford and Cambridge University Presses, 1970.

40. *Ibid.* Also see *The Torah: A new translation of the Holy Scriptures according to the Masoretic text*, Jewish Publication Society of America, Philadelphia, 1967. A summary of the changes made will be found in *New York Times*, October 12, 1962, p. 1 ff.

41. See the Bibles cited above, plus *The Anchor Bible*, edited by William F. Albright, Doubleday, 1958; *The New American Bible*, translated by Members of the Catholic Biblical Association of America (carrying the imprimatur of Patrick Cardinal O'Boyle, Archbishop of Washington), P. J. Kennedy & Sons, New York and Collier-Macmillan, London, 1970; *The Jerusalem Bible* (based on *La Bible de Jérusalem*, Paris*), Darton, Longman & Todd, London, 1966, 1968.

42. The insatiable reader can find these and 400 other words explained and illustrated, in depth, in *The Joys of Yiddish, op. cit.*

43. I cite particularly the Soncino Press (London), whose English translation of the entire Talmud is an historic achievement (one can only regret that the English prose of the scholars is so often turgid); the Jewish Publication Society of Philadelphia, which has translated the Torah and many invaluable post-Biblical works into English; the presses of Yale, Oxford, and Cambridge universities; in New York, Schocken Books, YIVO (Yiddish Scientific Institute), the KTAV Publishing Company, Phillip Feldheim, Bloch Publishers, Hermon Press, and others.

44. Although the Torah has for centuries been regarded as the hallowed transcription of God's words by Moses (even though they describe his death), recent Biblical scholarship has disclosed such variations in style, gaps in sequence, and differences in modes of narration that it is difficult "to ascribe the whole group [of five books] to a single author; four distinct literary 'traditions' can be identified and found side by side in the Pentateuch." From *The Jerusalem Bible*, Reader's Edition, *op. cit.*, p. 3.

45. *New Standard Jewish Encyclopedia*, ed. Cecil Roth and Geoffrey Wigoder, Doubleday, 1970, p. 1830.

46. A. Mary Robinson, "Social Life in France in the Fourteenth Century," *Fortnightly Review*, vol. 57, 1892. Quoted in *Essays in Jewish Booklore*, KTAV Publishing House, New York, 1971.

47. E. G. Hirsch, in *A Book of Jewish Thoughts*, ed. H. H. Hertz, Oxford, London, 1920, p. 10.

48. *Minor Tractates of the Talmud* (2 vols.), Soncino Press, London 1965.

49. *Peer le Yesharim*, 16.

50. For a more detailed analysis of the nature of the Messiah, in Jewish theology and history, see the Headnote for MESSIAH in the present collection, p. 363. For an exceptional study of Jesus, see Morton Scott Enslin, *The Prophet from Nazareth*, Schocken Books, New York, 1968.

51. Adapted from Solomon B. Freehof, *Modern Reform Responsa*, Hebrew Union College Press (no city given), 1971.

A Note on the Names
of Authors Cited

1. You will often encounter names with the following elements cited in the present dictionary of quotations:
   ABBA: Hebrew for "father (of)"
   BAR: Aramaic for "son (of)"
   BEN: Hebrew for "son (of)"
   IBN: Arabic for "son (of)"
2. When "i" is tacked on to a Hebrew surname, it means "son of."
3. The names of "orders" of the Talmud, the Minor Tractates added to the Talmud, the Apocrypha, collections of Mishnah or Midrashim, etc., are discussed in the GLOSSARY.
4. Where the name of the author of a quotation is followed by "Rabbi" or "Rebbe" (as in "The Sassover Rabbi" or "The Lubliner Rebbe") it implies the author was hasidic (see GLOSSARY).
5. "Rabban," a variant of "rabbi," was used in ancient times to honor outstanding scholars, and was used particularly for high priests of the Sanhedrin, the supreme ecclesiastical court of the Jews (it disappeared near the end of the fourth century).
6. I have held to a minimum the use of those affectionate acronyms Jews devised for famous sages: *Rambam*, for Maimonides (from *R*abbi *M*oshe *b*en *M*aimon), etc. The most important of these acronyms are defined in the GLOSSARY.
7. Those few Hebrew/Yiddish words or names which are not immediately explained, within the quotations themselves, are defined in the GLOSSARY.

I rashly decided to write a biographical vignette for each of the men to whom more than one quotation in my dictionary is attributed (see BIOGRAPHIES, Appendix III). I did that because it exasperates me to run across the name of an author, in an anthology, about whom I can learn more only by consulting a dozen reference works—often without success: for some names are variously spelled; pseudonyms are often not identified; some names do not appear in standard sources; and, alas, so on. The obstacles encountered, the time consumed, the pitfalls dug by earlier investigators, sometimes appear to be the work of demonic forces. Let me illustrate:

(1) The story of Rabbi Meir, the second-century collator of Mishnah, must be sifted out from twenty-four other "Meirs" listed in the admirably thorough *Jewish Encyclopedia* of 1904.

(2) The often-quoted "Ibn Ezra" may be Moses or Abraham (ben Meir)—both eleventh-twelfth century Spanish-Jewish scholars; and Moses is Moses ben Jacob Ka-Sallah, or, as he is known in Arabic literature, Abu Harun Musa.

(3) "Ha-Nakdan" *may* be traced back to Berechiah ben Natronai, or Berechya ben Berechiah ben Natronai, or Berechya ben Natronai, or Benedict le Pointeur ("the punctuator").

(4) "Falaquera," a distinguished Spanish-Jewish philosopher-translator of the thirteenth century, sometimes appears as Palquera, or Shem Tob Palquera, or Ibn Falaquera.

(5) The immortal Ibn Paquda, eleventh-twelfth century philosopher and *dayan* (ecclesiastical judge), author of the classic *Duties of the Heart*, may first be met under Bahya ibn Pakuda, or "Bachya the Saint," or Bachya ben Joseph ibn Pakuda.

It both relieved and amused me to discover that such vexations do not die with time. Try, for instance, to find out who Malcolm de Chazal is (or was): he coined some of the wittiest epigrams in the *Viking Book of Aphorisms*, edited by W. H. Auden and Louis Kronenberger, who cannily offer no dates or biographical data. (Chazal, so far as I can discover, is a hermitlike postmaster in a small town in a southern province of France.)

ANTHOLOGY
OF
JEWISH
QUOTATIONS

"*Certainly the heroism of the defenders of every other creed fades into insignificance before this martyr people, who for thirteen centuries confronted all the evils that the fiercest fanaticism could devise, enduring obloquy and spoliation, the violation of the dearest ties and the infliction of the most hideous sufferings, rather than abandon their faith.*"

W. E. H. Lecky,
Spirit of Rationalism,
vol. II, p. 270.

A

(Use of the fleuron [✳] denotes that a quotation is a favorite of the author's.)

ABILITY
See: CAPABILITY

ABSOLUTISM
✳ If you insist too long that you're right, you're wrong.
See also: GOVERNMENT, LAW, POLITICS

ABSTINENCE
He who denies himself (a little) wine is a sinner; how much more so, then, is the man who denies himself too many things.   TALMUD: *Nedarim*, 10a

Are not enough things prohibited you in the Law? Must you prohibit yourself still others?
                           TALMUD J.: *Nedarim*, 41

The man who causes himself pain by not enjoying what is not sinful may be called a sinner. TALMUD: *Nazir*, 19a

Those who abstain are physicians of faith and healers of souls.   BAHYA IBN PAQUDA, *Duties of the Heart*

See also: ASCETICS/ASCETICISM, EXCESS, FASTING, GLUTTONY, TEMPERANCE

ABUSE
The man who hears himself abused and remains silent will be spared many other abuses. TALMUD: *Sanhedrin*, 7a

See also: GOSSIP, LIARS/LIES

ADAM

Note. Genesis tells us that God created man from *adamah* ("dust of the ground"). In the Talmud (*Sanhedrin*, 38a, b), the revered Rab says that Adam's head was made of earth ·from the Holy Land, his body from the soil of Babylonia, his limbs from the earth of other lands.

The curious *Sybilline Oracles** (3 : 24–26), written by unknown Greek, Jewish, and Christian hands, incorporating six centuries of polyglot legends, offers us the charming theory that Adam's name consists of the first letters of four Hellenistic words which encompass the world: "A" for *anatole* (east), "D" for *dysis* (west), "A" for *arktos* (north), "M" for *mesembria* (south).

The rabbis thought Adam "of an extreme beauty and brightness, like the sun" (Talmud: *Baba Bathra*, 58a), soon clothed in garments made of light, not animal skins (*Genesis Rabbah*, 20). As we all know, Adam grievously sinned and so was deprived of all glory, and "the light of the world was robbed of its brightness, which will not return until the Messiah comes." (*Zohar*)

—L.R.

❊ God saw that heaven and earth were jealous of each other, so He created man out of earth—and his soul out of heaven.

Adam would never have taken a wife if he hadn't been put to sleep first.

Adam invented writing.   —A legend

❊ Why did God create only one man? So that no one could say virtue and vice are hereditary.

TALMUD: *Sanhedrin*, 4a

When a man uses a die to stamp out coins, they all come out alike; but God stamped all men with the die of Adam, yet each is different: So everyone has a right to say, "For my sake was the world created."

TALMUD: *Sanhedrin*, 4 : 5

Why did God create Adam alone? In order to teach us that whoever destroys a single life is as guilty as though he

---

* Translated from the Greek by H. N. Bate, Society for the Promotion of Christian Knowledge, London, 1937.

had destroyed the entire world; and that whoever saves
one life, earns as much merit as though he had saved the
entire world. TALMUD, J.: *Sanhedrin*, 4 : 5

❋ Why did God create but one man? So that no one of his
descendants should be able to say, "My father is better
than your father." TALMUD: *Sanhedrin*, 37a

Why was man created a solitary human being, without a
companion? So that it could never be said that some
races are better than others. TALMUD: *Sanhedrin*, 37a

God acted as Adam's best man. TALMUD: *Berakoth*, 61a

When Adam first saw the sun go down, and beheld an ever-
deepening gloom enfold the world, he was possessed by
terror. And God took pity and endowed Adam with
divine intuition: to take two stones—one named Darkness, the other The Shadow of Death—and rub them
hard against each other, and in that way discover fire.
And when Adam did this, he exclaimed, "Blessed be the
Creator of Light!" TALMUD

When the pious reproach Adam, who is seated at the gates,
for having sinned and brought death to them, Adam
answers: "I died with only one sin, but you committed
many; because of them, not me, have you died."
Tanhuma Hukkat, 16

Adam was the first to enter Hades.
Sibylline Oracles, 1 : 81

Adam sits at the gates, weeping for the multitude of souls
who pass through the wide gate to receive their punishment, and filled with joy for the virtuous few who enter
the narrow gate to receive their reward.
The Testament of Abraham

Adam's dust was collected from all parts of the world.
RABBI MEIR in TALMUD: *Sanhedrin*, 38a

If God really loved Man, would He have created Adam?

See also: ADAM'S RIB, ANCESTORS, EVE, GOD AND MAN, MAN

ADAM'S RIB

Note. The Old Testament's story of the creation of the first
woman from the first man's rib is far from being unique.

Similar tales are found among Polynesians, Burmese, Siberian Tatars, the Yuki and Salinan Indians of California, etc. . . . Such fables will enchant anyone who reads Frazer's *Golden Bough*, but elementary courses in anthropology suggest that these myths may simply be echoes of Biblical accounts told to the natives' grandfathers by Christian missionaries.* (See CONVERTS.)

—L.R.

ADULTERY

There is no worse adultery than that of the woman who, while making love with her husband, thinks of another man.   MIDRASH: *Tanhuma*

See also: DIVORCE, MARRIAGE, MEN AND WOMEN

ADVERSITY

Adversity is the best college.

Uphill, we always climb with caution; downhill, we dash carefree.

Even life's smoothest path is studded with stones.

See also: CONFLICT, HAPPINESS, LIFE: ITS ADVERSITY, MISFORTUNE, QUARRELS

ADVICE

❋ Love can't take advice, and lovers won't.

A good saying at the right moment is like a piece of bread during a famine.

Sweet words won't warm you, but sweet thoughts will.

❋ Teach your tongue to say "I do not know," lest you invent something.   TALMUD: *Berakoth,* 4a

Set a fence around your words.

HILLEL in TALMUD: *Niddah,* 3b

* For a dizzying succession of data, see Theodor H. Gaster, *Myth, Legend and Custom in the Old Testament,* Harper & Row, New York, 1969, pp. 21, 330–31; and in V. Lauternari's intriguing *The Religions of the Oppressed,* Macgibbon & Kee, London, 1963, and Knopf, New York, 1963, *passim.*

Who is this that darkeneth counsel by words without knowledge?   *Book of Job*, 38 : 2

ADVICE: EXAMPLES OF

❅ When you're hungry, sing; when you're hurt, laugh.

❅ If you're going to do something wrong, at least enjoy it.

❅ Never consult a woman about her rival, a coward about
   a war, or a merchant about a bargain.

Words should be weighed, not counted.

If you can't bite, don't show your teeth.

❅ In a restaurant, choose a table near a waiter.

If you want to be a barber, practice on someone else's
   beard.

If you eat your bagel, you'll have nothing left but the hole.

❅ If things aren't the way you like, like them the way they
   are.

You can't fill a sack that's full of holes.

❅ It is better to be embarrassed than ashamed.

Don't pat your stomach while the fish is still in the pond.

❅ What you can do, do; what you have, hold; what you
   know, keep to yourself.

If you know, tell; if you can, do; if you have, hold on to it.

❅ For a long, happy life, breathe through your nose and
   keep your mouth shut.

❅ He who has butter on his head should not walk in the
   sun.

If you sit home, you won't wear out your shoes.

❅ When you flee from fire, you may run into water.

If a dog barks, go in; if a bitch barks, stay out.

❅ Don't offer pearls to men who deal in onions.

Don't ask questions about fairy tales.

❅ The man who bends his back shouldn't complain if it's
   beaten.

Don't hitch a horse and an ox to the same wagon.

✻ Only a genius or a fool rushes into print.

Better ask ten times than get lost once.

Don't feed your horse too much too often: he'll become rebellious.

✻ Better be ridiculed than shamed.

Treat him like a rabbi and watch him like a thief.

Because of the thorns, don't uproot the garden.

✻ Don't worry about what may happen tomorrow; just correct what you spoiled yesterday.

Hire a helper and do it yourself.

If you don't run so far, the way back will be shorter.
MIDRASH: Ecclesiastes Rabbah, 11 : 9

Give every man the benefit of the doubt.
Sayings of the Fathers, 1 : 7

Be pliable—like a reed, not rigid—like a cedar.
TALMUD: Ta'anith, 20b

Be obscure, that you may endure.
TALMUD: Sanhedrin, 14a

See also: GOSSIP, KNOWLEDGE, SILENCE, TALK, WISDOM, WORDS

AGE

✻ Two things grow weaker with the years: teeth and memory.

The man who wants to know everything gets old fast.

✻ If you don't want to get old, hang yourself while young.

A man can be gray at the sideburns and silly in the head.

✻ Gray hair is a sign of age, not wisdom.

To lose years is far worse than to lose dollars.

At seventy, a man is as he was at seven.

Fortunate are those who actually enjoy old age.

Three kinds of people grow old before their time: those who raise chickens for a living; those who give orders but are not obeyed; and those who live on an upper floor.

The old who are not wise should not be called venerable.

TALMUD: *Yebamoth*, 80b

Four things make a man age prematurely: fear, anger, children, and a bad-tempered wife.

MIDRASH: *Tanhuma*

AGNOSTICS

See: FAITH, GOD: COMPLAINTS ABOUT, HEREAFTER, PRAYER: IRONIC COMMENTS ON, RELIGION, SKEPTICISM, VIRTUE

ALIMONY

Note. In the first century before the Christian Era, Jewish wives began to receive a specified and secure sum, in case of a husband's death or a divorce, from the husband's estate. The *ketubah* ("marriage settlement contract") granted a wife a legal lien on her husband's estate; and by rabbinical laws, a wife was not permitted to release her husband from this obligation. (This protected women from the amorous chicanery of men who might seek financial concessions before committing themselves to matrimony.)

Orthodox Jews still maintain the form and guarantees of the *ketubah*.

—L.R.

See: FAMILY, MARRIAGE, MEN and WOMEN, WIVES

ALTRUISM

The world goes on only because of those who disregard their own existence.   TALMUD: *Hullin*, 89a

See also: COMPASSION, GOOD DEEDS, HELP, PITY, SELFISHNESS

AMBITION

❋ The Jew who can't be a cobbler dreams of being a professor.

If you don't climb too high, you won't have far to fall.

If you look up to the heights, hold your hat.

❋ Eggs want to be smarter than hens.

Man strives and God laughs.

A human being must either climb up or climb down.

> TALMUD: *Erubin*, 21a

Fire rises—and goes out; water descends—and is not lost.
> Berechiah ben Natronai, ha-Nakdan, *Fox Fables*

Man's obsession to add to his wealth and honor is the chief
source of his misery.

> MAIMONIDES: *Guide to the Perplexed*, 3 : 39

Ambition is bondage.

> IBN GABIROL, *Choice of Pearls*

See also: CONTENTMENT, HAPPINESS

ANCESTORS

Note. Jews accord special honor (*koved*) to a man or
woman because of the notable merits, virtue, good deeds,
or learning of his or her ancestors. The commandment
to "honor thy father and mother" carries power in
Jewish thought second only to that accorded the
Almighty.

Affluent Jews would try to marry their daughters to
young men of illustrious intellectual background, however poor; and for their sons they sought scholars'
daughters as brides. (See headnotes for FAMILY and
SCHOLARS.)

> —L.R.

God prefers your deeds to your ancestors' virtues.

> MIDRASH: *Genesis Rabbah*, 74

See also: ADAM, CHILDREN, FAMILY, FATHERS, HONOR,
MOTHERS

ANGELS

❋ The virtue of angels is that they cannot deteriorate; their
flaw is that they cannot improve. Man's flaw is that he
can deteriorate; and his virtue is that he can improve.

> —Hasidic saying

❋ There was a time when angels walked the earth; today, they are not found even in heaven.

Two angels always accompany everyone—and they testify for or against him.   TALMUD: *Ta'anith*, 11a

True dreams come from angels; false dreams come from demons.

adapted from TALMUD: *Berakoth*, 55b

Those who pray in Aramaic will get no aid from the angels: angels do not understand Aramaic.

TALMUD: *Shabbath*, 12b

Man was made a little lower than the angels.

adapted from *Book of Psalms*, 8 : 5

Through intelligence and knowledge man comes to resemble the character of the angels.

adapted from IBN GABIROL

Man is not an angel, whose reasoning works perfectly.

JOSEPH CASPI, *Yore Deah*

Angels do not eat; they merely appear to be eating; hence we learn a man should not turn aside from local custom.

Rashi, *Commentaries on the Pentateuch, Genesis*

See also: GOD, HEAVEN, HELL, HEREAFTER, SAGES, SATAN

ANGER

Because you're angry at the rabbi, why refuse to say "*Amen!*" to the prayer?

Anger is a fool.

A boiling kettle overflows.

Whoever is consumed by rage hears no thunder and sees no lightning.

❋ Never try to pacify someone at the height of his rage.

An angry man is unfit to pray.   NACHMAN OF BRATSLAV

He who curbs his wrath merits forgiveness for his sins.

When you give vent to your feelings, anger leaves you.

Anger and temper shorten our years.

Anger in a house is like a worm in a plant.

All Hell rules over the man who is angry.

TALMUD: *Nedarim*, 22a

When a sage is angry, he is no longer a sage.

TALMUD: *Pesahim*, 66a

✳ Never anger a heathen, a snake, or a pupil.

TALMUD: *Pesahim*, 113a

Observe people when they are angry, for it is then that their
true nature is revealed.   *Zohar*

A gentle answer turns away wrath; but harsh words stir up
anger.   *Book of Proverbs*

✳ Anger begins with madness and ends in regret.

HASDAI, *Ben ha-Melekh ve-ha-Nazir*
(The King's son and the Nazirite)

Smoking a pipe helps mellow our anger.

THE LUBLINER RABBI

See also: CONTENTMENT, HATE, HEALTH, PASSION, PEACE,
TEMPER

ANIMALS

Note. The wry, dry, percipient adages that follow deal,
nominally, with the animal kingdom; but each cocks a
sidelong glance at Man: his nature, his dilemmas, his
propensities for obtuseness, folly, and paralogic. Jews are
not unique in this, of course: fairy tales and folk epics
and nursery rhymes have always employed the majesty
of the lion or the cunning of the fox, the gluttony of the
pig or the helplessness of the lamb, as devices for communicating comments about the lords of creation.

Aesop's *Fables* are, of course, the most famous of
parables. And a long line of continuity can be traced
from Aesop to Rudyard Kipling's *Jungle Books* to the
altogether unique genius of Walt Disney. Such a line
would run through the folk tales of India or Araby, the
matchless anecdotes of the Chinese, the rich Brahman
bestiary of the *Panchatantra* (written in Sanskrit). You
will find fables in Herodotus, and in Horace's *Satires*.
Perhaps the shrewdest fabulist since Aesop was Jean de
La Fontaine. And Gotthold Lessing, who disliked the
cynical French tales, created new ones in German.

All these mythical stories about animals are designed

to teach, to moralize, to make sharp and sometimes sardonic observations on the conduct and character of Man. So are the Jewish witticisms I cite below.

—L.R.

❃ If a horse had anything to say, he would speak up.

Animals have long tongues, but they can't say a blessing.

Even a flea can bite.

The goat is God's creature, too—but why must he stink?

If you set geese among oats, they'll starve to death.

The dog who follows you is devoted—to the crumbs he expects.

❃ The camel wanted horns—so they took away his ears.

No one is as poor as a dog, or as rich as a pig.

An ox doesn't know his own strength.

You can't get fur from the hide of a dog.

If a horse realized how small a man is, it would trample him at once.

Birds only come down where there are seeds to pick.

Gazelles are the animals most loved by God . . . because a gazelle harms no one, and never disturbs the peace.

MIDRASH: *Midrash Samuel*, 9

If you throw a bone to a dog, he will lick even the dust on your feet.   *Zohar*

Don't show a beaten dog a cane.

See also: CHARACTER, CLEANLINESS, GREED, SAFETY, SURVIVAL

ANTI-SEMITISM

Note. The Jews are not hated because they have evil qualities; evil qualities are sought for in them, because they are hated.

MAX NORDAU

What was their crime? Only that they were born. . . . That is why the Portuguese burnt them.

VOLTAIRE, *Sermon du Rabi Akib'*

The study of the history of Europe teaches [this]
lesson: the nations which dealt fairly with the Jew
have prospered; the nations that tortured and oppressed him wrote out their own curse.

OLIVE SCHREINER

The literature on anti-Semitism is immense, fascinating,
partisan, vicious, horrifying, and as complex as any subject
so steeped in demagoguery, psychopathology, xenophobia,
superstition, paranoia, and poisonous prejudice must be.
For two recent interesting excursions into this realm, see
Arland Ussher's *The Magic People: An Irishman Appraises
the Jews* (Devin-Adair, New York, 1951) and Jean-Paul
Sartre, *Anti-Semite and Jew* (Schocken, New York, 1965).

—L.R.

God told Moses to accept His holy mission—but be prepared for beatings and curses.

The happiness of Jews is never entirely free from fear.

❋ Dear God, if you really loved the Jews why did you
make them "the chosen people"?

When a Jew is right, he is beaten twice as hard.

❋ Calamity may be blind, but it has a remarkable talent
for locating Jews.

Why are there so many Hamans, but only one Purim?
[Haman tried to exterminate all the Jews in Persia; Purim
is the festival that commemorates Esther's success in foil-
ing Haman.]

Whatever can happen to all Jews will happen to one Jew.

Misfortune favors Jews; fortune greets them last.

One day, a Jew passed the imperial train and saluted the
Emperor Hadrian, who waxed furious: "You, a Jew,
dare to greet the Emperor! You shall pay for this with
your life!" Later that day, another Jew passed the Emperor and did not greet him. "A Jew dares pass a Roman
Emperor without saluting?" Hadrian exclaimed. "You
shall be killed!" To his puzzled courtiers, Hadrian explained, "I hate Jews, so I use any excuse to destroy
them."   —adapted from TALMUD

To be a Jew means to be ready to be a martyr.
> MIDRASH: *Exodus Rabbah*, 42 : 9

The sufferings of the Jews in one year could not be recorded even if all the seas were full of ink, and all the
reeds were pens, and all men were set to work writing the
story.   —adapted from MIDRASH: *Megillath Ta'anith*

See also: HATE, HOSTILITY, INQUISITION, INTOLERANCE,
JEWS, PERSECUTION, POGROMS, PREJUDICE

ANXIETY

✻ Only one type of worry is correct: to worry because you
worry too much.

Riches bring anxiety: wisdom gives peace of mind.
> IBN GABIROL

See also: CONSCIENCE, LIFE, SUFFERING, TROUBLE, WORRY

APOSTATES ·

See: PROSELYTES

APPEARANCE

If velvet and silk hang in your closet, you can step out in
rags.

At night, all cows look black.

✻ A homely patch is prettier than a beautiful hole.

It is the worm that lures the fish, not the fisherman and not
the rod.

Not everyone at whom dogs bark is a thief.

A man looks to you the way you look at him.

When you have a new coat hanging on the wall, your old
one doesn't feel ashamed.

Men see what we wear, not what we eat.

The man who lives in a house did not necessarily build it.

✻ A goat has a beard—but that doesn't make him a rabbi.

Don't look at the pitcher, but at its contents: for a new pitcher may be full of old wine, and an old pitcher may be empty.   *Sayings of the Fathers*, 4 : 20

✴ If you judge by beards and girth, goats are the wisest creatures on earth.   JOSEPH SOLOMON DELMEDIGO

See also: CONDUCT, DECEIT, DECORUM, DRESS, FACE, ILLUSION

ARBITRATION

Arbitration is justice blended with charity.
                                    NACHMAN OF BRATSLAV

See also: COMPROMISE, LAW

ARGUMENT

✴ The man with an unimpressive argument rattles off many of them.

One strong point is worth ten weak ones.

✴ If you protest long enough that you're right, you're wrong.

A woman will argue even with the Angel of Death.

He who seeks the truth must listen to his opponent.
                        ISAAC SAMUEL REGGIO, *Torah and Philosophy*

See also: CAUSE AND EFFECT, LAW, PROOF, QUARRELS, TALK

ARROGANCE

✴ The man who praises himself will shame himself.

The man who despises little things will gradually fail.

Arrogance is a kingdom—without a crown.
                                TALMUD: *Sanhedrin*, 105a

✴ When you turn proud, remember that a flea preceded you in the order of divine creation.
                                TOSEPHTA: *Sanhedrin*

How great some men would be, were they not arrogant.
                        TALMUD: *Kallah Rabbathi*, 3

The unrepentant go to Hell, the shamefaced to Eden.
                              Sayings of the Fathers, 5 : 20

Chutzpa [arrogance, gall] prevails even in heaven.
                              TALMUD: *Sanhedrin*, 205a

See also: CONCEIT, HUMILITY, PRIDE

ASCETICS/ASCETICISM

Those who are spiritually healthy, yet become ascetics, will
    become morally ill.   MAIMONIDES, *Mishneh Torah*

The Torah tells us to follow the path of moderation . . .
    not to dwell in the wilderness, nor in the mountains, nor
    to don hair garments, nor to afflict the body.
                   MAIMONIDES, *Mishneh Torah*, Deut 3 : 1

See also: ABSTINENCE, FASTING, GLUTTONY

ASHKENAZIM

See: GLOSSARY

ASTROLOGY

Note. The ancient Hebrews, like the Babylonians, Egyptians, and Greeks, were impressed by astrology. In the Bible, the Hebrew word *mazel* referred to a planet or a constellation of the zodiac, and the word was invoked when "fate" was involved. Later, Talmudic sages sternly warned the Jews to eschew soothsaying and diviners. Perplexed believing Jews had a hard time knowing what to think; The Bible, after all, talks of the "signs of heaven"—Jeremiah, for instance, and Isaiah. But the Midrash teaches: "The Holy One forbade astrology in Israel"; and it is said that God made Abraham "a prophet, not an astrologer." The great Maimonides called astrology "a disease, not a science."

Nonetheless, Jews continue to utter "*Mazl tov!*" The supernatural or divinational aspects are forgotten (just as "God be with you" became "good-bye"), and *mazel* has become simply "luck," "*Mazl tov!*", "Congratulations."

                                                    —L.R.

Do not believe the astrologers . . . our Torah [holds] that a man's conduct is in his own hands, that no external compulsion prevents a man from being virtuous or vicious—except as he may be so constituted, by nature, and finds it easy or hard to do a certain thing. But that a man must do, or refrain from doing, something [because of the stars] is entirely untrue. . . . Astrology is a disease, not a science.

MAIMONIDES, *Hilhoth Tshuvah* (Laws of Repentance)

So it is with all astrologers (says the Talmud): they see something but do not understand what they see.

RASHI, *Commentaries on the Pentateuch, Numbers*

See also: DESTINY, FATE

ATHEISTS

True faith needs no evidence.

❋ Don't ask questions of God: He may say, "If you're so anxious for answers come up here."

Many who say they don't believe in God, ask His mercy.

❋ Few sailors are atheists, for they are in daily peril.

The fool has said in his heart, "There is no God."

Book of Psalms, 14 : 1

See also: FAITH, GOD, SKEPTICISM

AUTHORITY

Note. Political scientists have always seemed to me to underestimate the enormous impact on secular authority of the Hebrew concept of monotheism—and the historic line which monotheism drew to limit the legitimacy and power of the temporal. Ancient monarchs—in Assyria, China, Egypt, Central America, the Hellenic world— were omnipotent; their authority was unchallengeable. The law was the King's Law, and his subjects had no separate, higher, moral or philosophical authority through which to question or resist royal power. The monarch was beholden to no one, "owed" nothing to the people, and could change or ignore laws to suit the royal whim.

But among the Hebrews, the king became subordinate to, and an agent of, God—who alone deserved unquestioning obedience. No king of Israel could dream of "divine rights," or sacrifices to *him* (as Persian, Babylonian, Sumerian, Roman, Incan kings did). One historic consequence of monotheism lay in the fact that any monarch was held responsible to God (who, presumably, had chosen him). A king or queen was commissioned, as it were, to protect the people's *rights*, the property and integrity of those over whom he reigned. The Jews clung to the idea of "limited monarchy"—a concept that was inconceivable to many of the emperors and conquerors under whose hegemony they fell.

—L.R.

No office can dignify a man, but many a man dignifies his office.

When people who have led hard lives are given authority, they are harsher than tyrants.

Alas for the possession of that authority that buries its possessor!　　　　　　　　　　　　　SAADIA GAON

The man who cannot control himself becomes absurd when he wants to rule over others.　　　　ISAAC ARAMA

See also: DEMOCRACY, GOVERNMENT, INFLUENCE, LAW, POLITICS, POWER

B

BACHELORS

Note. Great social pressure was exerted, in a Jewish community, for every young man to get married—and while young. An unmarried male was looked upon as insensitive to his duty, even something of a sinner. He was evading the responsibility to "multiply," as God commanded; to perpetuate life itself; to honor the solemn debt that attends the gift of having been born; to provide himself with a *Kaddish* to mourn his death and honor his name.

A man who remained unmarried after the age of twenty was considered unblessed, living without joy, derelict in his duty to Jewry—for who knew what learned sons, what marvelous *talmide khakhomin* ("disciples of the wise"), he might have sired?

Yet paradoxically, as in so many other matters, Jews remarked on the sagacity of bachelors by poking fun at those deluded by the illusion of marital bliss.

—L.R.

❋ Bachelor: A man who comes to work each morning from a different direction.

A cow can't be a butcher, nor can a bachelor be a matchmaker.

❋ When a bachelor dies, girls are avenged.

Man is not even called man until he is united with woman.
                                                    Zohar

When a bachelor reaches twenty and is still unmarried, the Holy One says, "Let him rot!"
                                    TALMUD: *Kiddushin*, 29b

Unmarried teachers are as arrogant as kings, but their minds are like those of children.
                                    —adapted from MIDRASH

See also: MARRIAGE

BAD

See: EVIL, VIRTUE, WICKED/WICKEDNESS

BAPTISM

Note. "This was the time of Nicholas I. Some of these 'soldiers of Nicholas,' as they were called, were taken as [Jewish] boys of seven or eight—snatched from their mothers' laps. They were carried to distant villages . . . and turned over to some peasant, who used them like slaves. . . . No two were ever left together, and they were given false names . . . entirely cut off from their

own world. And then the lonely child was turned over
to the priests, and he was flogged and starved and terri-
fied . . . but still refused to be baptized. . . . After he
entered the army, he was bribed with promises of pro-
motions and honors . . . and endured the cruellest
discipline [but would not agree to be baptized].

"When he was discharged, at the age of forty, he was
a broken man, without a home, without a clue to his
origin, and he spent the rest of his life wandering among
Jewish settlements, searching for his family, hiding the
scars of torture under his rags, begging his way from
door to door.

"There were men in our town whose faces made you
old in a minute. They had served Nicholas I, and come
back, unbaptized." Mary Antin, *The Promised Land*,
Heinemann, London, 1911.*

BARBARIANS

Whoever helps or caters to a barbarian causes the exile of
his children.

See also: GOVERNMENT

BASTARDS

Note. You must bear with some careful distinctions here.
What we call "illegitimate" is not quite bastardy, in
Jewish law and tradition. A *mamzer* (bastard), in rabbinical law, is a child born of an adulterous or incestuous
union. But if the father of the child can be identified, the
child is not, technically, a *mamzer*. He is, alas, a *mamzer*
if his paternity is uncertain or unprovable.

But note this: Under Talmudic law, the Jewish community is solemnly obligated to pay for the feeding,
clothing, and education of such children. Apart from
the compassion for the mother and the innocent child,
the social value of this custom should be noted: many
a bastard turned out to be a scholar, or a success through

---

* For an historical account of child martydoms, see Simon Dubnow,
History of the Jews in Russia and Poland, J. P. S. A., 1918, Vol. II, pp.
18–29.

whom Judaism benefited. Indeed, there is a well-known saying that a *mamzer* who is a *talmid khokhem* ("disciple of the wise"), one of the wisest of the wise, is preferable to a high priest who is ignorant. And one of the affectionate terms Jews use about an especially bright, articulate, or ingenious person is, "Oh, what a *mamzer!*"

Mamzeyrim (plural) were not allowed to marry non-*mamzeyrim*; they were expected and encouraged to marry other *mamzeyrim*—otherwise their offspring were classified as not legitimate. This Orthodox religious dictum is being strongly protested in Israel today. On November 9, 1971, a National Bastard Day dramatized the wide opposition to the rabbinate's "monopoly" of rituals and rights in marriage. A bill has been introduced into the Israeli parliament (Knesset) to institute civil marriages—which would ignore the "legitimacy" of those seeking to wed.

Conservative and Reform rabbis strongly support this. After all, the Talmud tells us that in the world to come all the *mamzeyrim* will appear and the blessed Messiah will himself take up their cause. I trust they will receive restitution for the stigma, sufferings, or injustices that befell them, innocent souls, in this world below. (I also think that the way things are going these days among the rebellious, "emancipated" young, this issue may become as academic as their conduct, on or off campuses, is unacademic.)

—L.R.

Blood never turns into water.

A learned bastard stands higher than an ignorant high priest.   MIDRASH: *Numbers Rabbah* 6 : 1

No one has the gall of a bastard.
                    MIDRASH: *Haneelam*, Genesis, 118

Most bastards have a just complaint.
                    TALMUD J.: *Kiddushin*, 4 : 11

A fool is worse than a bastard—if the bastard is wise.
                    TALMUD J.: *Kiddushin*, 4 : 11

❈ If there were fewer swine, there would be fewer bastards.

See also: FAMILY, SONS

BEAUTY

✳ It is good to look at the fair—and live with the wise.

What good is beauty without luck?

Too beautiful is sometimes a fault.

A pretty face costs money.

How many lament their looks, and how few lament their brains!

Better a little with beauty than much without it.

✳ It is not that that which is beautiful pleases us, but that that which pleases us is called beautiful.

The beautiful is not dear; but the dear is beautiful.

Beauty fades, but a good name endures.
                            APOCRYPHA, *Ahikar*, 2 : 49

A beautiful ornament looks best on a beautiful woman.
                            TALMUD J.: *Nedarim*

Charms are deceptive, and beauty is a breath; but a woman who reveres the Lord will be praised.
                            Book of Proverbs

Do not look too long on the beauty that belongs to someone else.   BEN SIRACH, *Ecclesiasticus*

See also: CHARACTER, NATURE, VIRTUE

BEGGARS/BEGGING

It is better to strip a carcass of its hide than to beg.

A beggar does more for an alms-giver than the alms-giver does for the beggar.

Better be a servant in a temple for heathens than accept alms.   TALMUD J.: *Berakoth*, 9

✳ I have tasted everything, and found nothing as bitter as begging.   IBN GABIROL, *Choice of Pearls*

See also: BORROWERS/BORROWING, CHARITY, GOOD DEEDS, THE POOR/POOR MEN

BENEVOLENCE

See: CHARITY, GOOD DEEDS, KINDNESS

BETRAYAL

If you betray your cause, you support the other's.

See also: TREACHERY

BIBLE

Note. "The whole drama of mankind is contained in this, the Book of Books . . . Mahomet, I think, called the Jews the 'People of the Book.' That Book is their country. Within its boundaries they live and enjoy inalienable citizenship and cannot be dislodged. . . . Around them, nations rose and disappeared; states flourished, decayed, vanished; revolutions raged across the world. But the Jews sat poring over this Book, oblivious to the wild chase of time that rushed over their heads."

HEINRICH HEINE

"There is not a verse [of the Bible], not a word, but is thick-studded with human emotion."

WALT WHITMAN

See: GOD, ISRAEL, TORAH; also see Preface; and GUIDE NOTE A, p. 61.

BIRTH

The world is new to us every morning—this is God's gift; and every man should believe he is reborn each day.

BAAL SHEM TOV

BITTERNESS

✳ All sentences that start with "God forbid" describe what is possible.

Every man knows his own bitterness,
And in his joy no stranger can share.

Book of Proverbs 14 : 10

See also: ENVY, JEALOUSY

BLAME

Better pray for yourself than blame someone else.

When a fool does something wrong, he blames others; the
seeker of wisdom who does wrong blames himself; but
the wise man blames neither himself nor others, for he
is pious.   IBN GABIROL, *Choice of Pearls*

See also: CONSCIENCE, GUILT, WISDOM

BLIND

The blind like to hear tales of wonder.

BOASTERS

Note. Our ancestors, Jew and non-Jew alike, were fearful
that man's boastings, his very success might offend some
god—and boomerang into disaster. An envious or jealous
mortal could cast an evil spell on another's luck or health.
    Among Jews, *keyn eyn-oreh* ("no evil eye") is a
magical phrase uttered to: (a) ward off the evil eye; (b)
protect a child or loved one; (c) show that one's praises
are not contaminated by envy. Jews have a long tradition
of scorn for the vainglorious.

                                              —L.R.

He who has a wide mouth has a narrow heart.

❉ One coin in a bottle rattles; the bottle filled with coins
makes no sound.   TALMUD: *Baba Mezi'a*, 85b

Barren trees make more noise than fruit-bearing trees. . . .
They ask fruit-bearing trees: "Why don't you make any
noise?"—to which the trees reply, "Our fruits are sufficient advertisement."
                    MIDRASH: *Genesis Rabbah*, 16 : 3

Burning thorns crackle, as if to say, "We too are wood!"
            MIDRASH: *Ecclesiastes Rabbah*, 7 : 6

More smoke than roast.   —Rabbinic saying

Like wind-blown clouds that bring no rain is he who boasts
of gifts he does not give.   *Book of Proverbs*

Don't boast about tomorrow; you don't know what one day
can bring.   adapted from *Book of Proverbs*, 27 : 1

❋ Both the boaster and the fool don't know the proper time for silence.   BEN SIRACH, *Ecclesiasticus* 20 : 6

He who advertises his name, loses it.
                    HILLEL in *Sayings of the Fathers*, 1 : 14

See also: ARROGANCE, CONCEIT, FOOLS, PRIDE, VANITY.

BOOKS

Note. I have always loved the idea of those pious Jews who envisaged "the world to come" as an immense library, where all the truly good books written by man would be available to the righteous dead. In the *Sefer Hasidim* ("Book of the Pious"), there is an enchanting folk tale about books being placed on tables in cemeteries, so that the souls of the dead would be able to read and study, should they want to, as they did in life. One Sabbath eve a group of gentiles passed a Jewish cemetery, and to their astonishment beheld an old Jew seated at a table near his grave, lost in thought, his head propped on one hand as the other turned the pages of a book. . . .

To an extent unequalled among other sections of humanity, Jews have been interested in books. . . . (The Jew) copied books. He owned books. He patronized literature. He was interested in intellectual life and . . . movements. Even in the most soul-destroying period of oppression, it might be assumed that almost every ghetto Jew, however humble his circumstances and however lowly his calling, was likely to have his modest library. A book was not to him, as to his neighbor, an object of veneration, of mystery, of distrust. It was sheer necessity of everyday life.*
                                                        CECIL ROTH

Jewish literature is crammed with references to the nobility of books. In the fifth century before the Christian Era, Nehemiah, Governor of Judah for the Persian King Artaxerxes I, "founding a library, gathered the acts of the kings, and of the prophets, and of David, and the epistles of the kings concerning holy gifts." (II Maccabees, 2 : 13)
By tradition, books were treated by Jews as special, treasured objects: when they grew old or frayed, it was

---

* In *Essays on Jewish Booklore*, KTAV, New York, 1971, p. 179.

thought sacrilegious to throw them out; old books were placed in a synagogue's attic; when space ran out, books were solemnly buried, in a ceremony fit for the burial of a saint. Even books the Jews hated were never burned, but were called "apocryphal" or "outside," and were locked away or hidden.

Rabbinical literature is full of admonitions about the solemn duty of a Jew to lend books to others, even enemies (so that learning will be increased); of the obligation of every community of Jews to build a library; of meticulous advice about the binding, airing, care, and preservation of books and manuscripts. Along with the *mitzvah* attached to the ransom of enslaved Jews, was one for Jews who bought back books which had been captured by brigands, pirates, or the robbers of synagogues. Thousands of prized Talmuds and rabbinical writings, stolen from Jews, were bought back—by them, or other Jews.

But not all: we must remember the vast number of books that were destroyed forever. After the expulsion from Spain, thousands of Jews fled to Lisbon; the authorities there soon issued a decree that anyone owning a Hebrew book would be put to death. In Venice, in 1553, in "the Bitter Month," officials burned Talmuds and thousands of other volumes. So did the Romans, who ransacked all Jewish homes and burned their books in the Campo dei Fiori. . . . Countless precious Hebrew manuscripts and incunabula before the year 1500 no longer exist. Indeed, the complete text of the Babylonian Talmud has survived in only one ancient manuscript! (See headnote: VANDALISM).

My own boyhood was gloriously enriched by an eccentric classmate, "Potch," who stored 300 beautiful volumes in my bedroom closet. He claimed that the books—all new, in fresh cartons—were presents, but I soon learned they had been stolen. . . . What delicious hours, for all the moral qualms I suffered, were mine! (If you care to explore this conflict between conscience and bibliomania, consult *People I Have Loved, Known, or Admired*, McGraw-Hill, New York, 1970, pp. 121–30.)

—L.R.

❉ If you drop gold and books, pick up the books first, then the gold.

❊ The Archangel Metatron, the librarian of heaven, brings
new books to the Holy One, who then presents them to
the Academy on High, for careful study.   —A legend

❊ Whenever the shelves in the Library of Heaven were
entirely full, and a new, worthy book appeared, all the
books in the celestial collection pressed themselves closer
together, and made room.   —A legend

Of the making of books, there is no end.

Ecclesiastes, 12

❊ Those who consider a thing proved simply because it is
in print are fools.

MAIMONIDES, *Letter to Yemenite Jews*

Every author should weigh his work and ask, "Will humanity gain any benefit from it?"

NACHMAN OF BRATSLAV

Whoever is able to write a book and does not, is as if he has
lost a child.   NACHMAN OF BRATSLAV

Not by chance are son and book named in Latin by the
same word: *liber*.

JOSEPH SOLOMON DELMEDIGO, *Noblot Hokhmah*
("Notes of Wisdom")

My pen is my harp and my lyre; my library is my garden
and my orchard.   JUDAH HA-LEVI

❊ A man's wisdom extends only as far as his books, and a
man should sell all he may possess to buy books. For as
our sages said: "He who increases books, increases
wisdom."   JUDAH CAMPANTON

❊ Books should be placed in stately array near the dead,
so that the souls of the righteous may in death study as
they did on earth.

—Judah of Regensburg, *Sefer Hasidim*
("Book of Saints")

❊ Should a man face straitened circumstances, he should
first sell his gold and jewels, then his house and estate,
but not—until the very end, when he has nothing left—
his library.

—Judah of Regensburg, *Sefer Hasidim*
("Book of Saints")

A book should not be used as a missile, a shield, or an
object for punishment.   JUDAH OF REGENSBURG

❊ If you have one son who does not like to lend his books,
and another son who does, leave your library to the
second, even if he is the younger
                              JUDAH OF REGENSBURG

❊ You must not refuse to lend a book even to an enemy,
for the cause of learning will suffer.
            —a pious Jew, quoted by JUDAH OF REGENSBURG

Never use a pen or a tablet as a bookmark [for you may injure the book].   JUDAH OF REGENSBURG

Never refuse to lend books to anyone who cannot afford to
purchase them, but lend books only to those who can be
trusted to return them.   IBN TIBBON

Cover your bookcases with rugs or linens of fine quality;
preserve them from dampness and mice and injury; for
it is your books that are your true treasure.
                                      IBN TIBBON

Handle books with respect: never put a book underneath
paper when you line the paper for writing.
                                      IBN TIBBON

Make books your companions; let your bookshelves be your
gardens: bask in their beauty, gather their fruit, pluck
their roses, take their spices and myrrh. And when your
soul be weary, change from garden to garden, and from
prospect to prospect.   IBN TIBBON

❊ My book is like my beloved; does a man lend his beloved
to others?   MOSES BEN ABRAHAM DARI

❊ Those who refuse to lend their books . . . shall be fined.
        —minutes of the Latvian Jewish Community Council,
                                              1736

When a man travels and finds books which are not known
in his hometown, it is his duty to buy them, rather than
anything else, and bring the books back home with him.
            —Judah of Regensburg, *Sefer Hasidim*
                                ("Book of Saints")

❊ Three possessions should you prize: a field, a friend, and
a book.   HAI GAON

❊ Lend books to the poor before you lend them to the rich.
                                    JUDAH THE PIOUS

Read only brief or systematic books, one at a time, and books beautifully written, on fine paper and attractively bound. Read in an attractive room, and from time to time let your eyes gaze upon beautiful objects so that you will come to love what you read.
                        PROFIAT DURAN, *"Maaseh Ephod"*
                                    (a Hebrew grammar)

❊ It is a man's duty to keep an eye on the honor of his books. . . . If you keep a box of books in your bedroom, place it at the head, not at the foot, of your bed . . .
                                    JUDAH THE PIOUS

See also: KNOWLEDGE, LEARNING, SCHOLARSHIP, STUDY, TRUTH, WISDOM

BOORS

A boor does not fear sin, and a vulgar man cannot be a saint.   HILLEL in *Sayings of the Fathers*, 2 : 5

See also: CONDUCT, DECORUM, SENSITIVITY

BORE

❊ When a bore leaves the room, you feel as if someone came in.

See also: FOOL, NEBECH, SHLEMIEL.

BOREDOM

We get tired even of *kneydlekh* [dumplings].

Let things get worse—just so they're different!

See also: EXCESS, IDLENESS, MODERATION

BORROWERS/BORROWING

Note. The use of borrowed money is a *sine qua non* of economic growth; yet lending for interest was long hobbled (see Deuteronomy 23 : 20) by simplistic laws, theological taboos, and moral opprobrium—which is often sanctimonious self-indulgence, and seems endemic to man.

Roman law held that a debt is personal, so promissory notes could not be transferred and could not become claims against an estate. In Germany, a debt died when a creditor died. Even in England, up to the middle of the nineteenth century, some debts were not transferrable. But the Talmud ruled that for Jews all debts must be honored—even after a debtor or creditor dies; the Talmudists understood the importance of the negotiable—yet they, too, wrestled with what economists now consider unproductive misconceptions about "usury." The Talmud developed remarkably modern rules governing property, trade, contracts, insurance—but forbade any Jew to accept "excessive" interest in loans; it was left to the rabbis to determine "equitable" rates.

In the year 1200, Maimonides saw that economic growth required that money be used, by being lent, and said that charging interest was neither usurious nor wicked, but served a salutary economic function.

Popes and kings, noblemen and entrepreneurs, long enlisted or preempted the aid of Jews to finance the building of cathedrals, palaces, estates—in this way transferring the medieval sin of "usury" to those outside the Christian fold, souls so doomed to perdition that added transgressions did not matter. Thus the Jews were forced to become moneylenders, and often royal treasurers; and then—but for the rest, see the headnotes for LENDING, MONEY, and USURY.

—L.R.

✻ If you laugh when you borrow, you'll cry when you pay.

The biggest worriers can't pay the smallest debts.

Borrow, and you'll sorrow.

✻ Borrowing, like scratching, is only good for a while.

He who need not borrow lives without worry.

You can't borrow money on the basis of "I would" or "I should."

The man who habitually borrows is not fit to be a judge.
　　　　　　　　　　　TALMUD: *Kethuboth*, 105b

✴ The man who greets his creditors too warmly is guilty of usury in words.

           —adapted from Talmud: *Baba Mezi'a*, 75b

✴ The borrower is the servant of the lender.

           Book of Proverbs, 28 : 1

The borrower is liable for any accident [to the thing he borrows].

      RASHI, *Commentaries on the Pentateuch, Exodus*

See also: BEGGARS/BEGGING, BUSINESS, CREDITORS, LENDING

BRAINS

✴ Prejudice is a blindness in the brain.

✴ If you harden your heart with pride, you soften your brain with it, too.

✴ God looks first into our hearts, then at our brains.

The tongue is the messenger of the brain.

✴ Many complain of their looks, but who complains about his brains?

See also: INTELLECT, INTELLIGENCE, REASON, WISDOM

BRIBERY

If you don't bribe, you won't ride.

✴ It is surprising how many spots on the character are removed by a solution of gold.

When bribery increased, the span of life decreased.

           TALMUD: *Sotah*, 47b

If a man, even one wise in Torah, takes a bribe, his mind will ultimately become confused; what he has learned will be forgotten.

      RASHI, *Commentaries on the Pentateuch, Exodus*

If you grease the wheels, you can ride.

           SHOLEM ALEICHEM

See also: CONSCIENCE, HONOR

BRIDES

Note. Every Jewish bride, however poor, wore a wedding gown and had a trousseau: a collection in even the poorest Jewish community insured that. Wedding guests were obligated to praise the bride and extol her beauties. It was traditional for the groom to give the bride a simple ring (the rabbis wanted to minimize differences between the wealthy and the poor), and for the bride to give the groom a new *talis* (prayer shawl).

❋ All brides are beautiful—and all corpses look pious.

The bride with beautiful eyes need not worry about her figure.

A groom and a bride have glass eyes. [They see no faults in each other.]

When the groom is desired, the bride needs no words.

Three kinds of mortals need to be protected from others: a patient, a groom, and a bride.

TALMUD: *Berakoth*, 54b

Every bride is beautiful.

BET (school of) HILLEL in TALMUD: *Kethuboth*, 17a

See also: GIRLS, IRONY: EXAMPLES, MARRIAGE, WEDDINGS

BROTHERS

Whoever seeks a faultless brother will have to remain brotherless.

❋ If my brother steals, it is the thief who is hanged—not my brother.

A brother turned enemy is an enemy for life.

A brother helped by a brother is like a fortified city.

Book of Proverbs

A friend is friendly at all times.
But a brother is born for adversity.   *Book of Proverbs*

Honor your father and mother, and include your oldest brother.   TALMUD: *Kethuboth*, 103a

If you do not give to your poor brother, in the end you will
   have to receive from him.   *Sifre—Deuteronomy*, 116

See also: DUTY, FAMILY

BURIAL

The deceased rich once were buried in ornate caskets, and
   the poor in cheap coffins; so the rabbis have decreed that
   all who die, however rich or poor, be buried in plain
   caskets.   TALMUD: *Mo'ed Katan*, 27a

Walk reverently in a cemetery, lest the dead say: Tomorrow
   they will join us, yet today they mock us!
                                          TALMUD: *Berakoth*, 18a

See also: DEATH, THE HEREAFTER

BUSINESS

Note. Anyone tempted to jump to uncomplimentary conclusions (after reading the number of sayings Jews bandy
   about concerning trade, business, commerce) might remember that for centuries Jews were forbidden to own
   land, or farm it, or enter a profession, or enroll in a
   college.

   The supposed "natural shrewdness" of Jews as busi-
   nessmen has never impressed me; my early years in
   Chicago were spent among Jews who were conspicuously
   unaffluent. I thought of Jews as laborers, artisans, crafts-
   men: our streets were lined with little shops—grocers,
   tailors, barbers, bakers, butchers, shoemakers—and but
   one small bank in ten large blocks.

   When I lived in England, I was surprised by the dry
   acerbic comments of the English anent the "native cunning" of the Welsh, the "hunger-for-money" of the
   Scots, the "instinctive cleverness" of the Irish. And when
   I traveled through Vermont and New Hampshire I came
   to know what "shrewd Yankee" really means: parsimony, thrift, and a shrewdness for which Jews are
   customarily belabored.

   As a peripheral comment, it is Italy that gave English
   most of its business vocabulary: "bank . . . credit . . .
   net . . . account . . . debit . . ." et cetera.

If you invest in a fever, your profit is a disease.

❊ When you send a fool to market, the merchants rejoice.

Trade may make you a king but it robs you of leisure.

The dough must be bad, indeed, if the baker admits it.

❊ The saloonkeeper may love the drunkard, but will he let him marry his daughter?

Make one sale, and already some call you a merchant.

❊ I trust you completely, but please send cash.

It's easier to get into something [business] than to get out of it.

When you are the only buyer, buy; when other buyers are present, act uninterested.

Don't open a shop unless you know how to smile.

The best broker is cash.

❊ If you invest a needle, you won't win more than a needle.

A nearby penny is worth a distant dollar.

❊ Entrances are wide; exits are narrow.

Business is not brotherhood.

Better a steady dime than a rare dollar.

You don't make big fortunes by peddling little things in the street.

The man who studies can't conduct a business; and a businessman can't devote enough time to study.

Hasty purchases are not good.

False scales are an abomination to the Lord;
But a just weight is his delight. *Book of Proverbs* 11 : 1

"It is nothing, it is nothing," says the buyer; but when he leaves, he boasts.

—adapted from *Book of Proverbs*, 14

While the sand is yet on your feet, sell.

TALMUD: *Pesahim*, 113a

Better a small profit at home than a large one from abroad.

TALMUD: *Pesahim*, 113a

❊ The pot that belongs to partners is neither hot nor cold.
                                              TALMUD: *Erubin*, 3a

Three possess a certain charm: a place to its occupants, a
woman to her husband, and a bargain to the customer.
                                              TALMUD: *Sotah*, 47a

In business, everything depends on aid from heaven.
                                              TALMUD: *Megillah*, 6b

Fifty productive men are better than two hundred who are
not.   TALMUD J.: *Pe'ah*, 8 : 8

This is the manner of merchants: first they show the poor
stuff and then they show the best.
        RASHI, *Commentaries on the Pentateuch, Numbers*

As a peg stays between the joinings of stones, so sin [greed]
intrudes between buyer and seller.
                          BEN SIRACH, *Ecclesiasticus*, 27 : 2

A man's drive for profit should be prompted by the desire
to give charity.   NACHMAN OF BRATSLAV

See also: GAMBLING, GOLD, LENDING, MONEY, THRIFT, USURY

C

CABALA

Note. "The pupils of the Ari ["the holy lion"],* of blessed
   memory, once asked him why he had never written a
   book on the Kabbalah. He replied that it was impossible,
   because the moment he plunged into a subject a veritable
   torrent of thoughts overwhelmed him, one subject leading him irresistibly to another and another and another.
   Even when he speaks to his disciples, said the Ari, he
   must exert strenuous effort to keep his thoughts to one
   subject."**
                          —adapted from a collection by S. Y. AGNON

See GLOSSARY: CABALA, ZOHAR

---

* Rabbi Isaac ben Solomon Luria (*q.v.*), BIOGRAPHIES, p. 550.
** *Essays on Jewish Booklore*, KTAV, New York, 1942–1971.

CANTORS

Note. The cantor (*khazn*) is the professional singer who sings long passages of the liturgy—not as a chant or in a singsong (as the laity do) but with truly virtuoso singing, especially in the sweet falsettoes. Emotion is expressed with intensity; the cantor speaks for the worshippers (he is known as *shaleah tsibur*, or "emissary of the congregation") in expressing the emotions embedded in the sacred texts.

The cantor has come to be regarded as a simple man —even a simpleton: hence the many jokes and gibes at his expense. It is even libeled that *khazn* is an acronym formed from the first letters of "*Khazonim zaynen naronim*": "Cantors are fools."

For more than ten centuries, no music was heard in a synagogue; but as Catholic and Protestant religious services grew more and more opulent, Jewish worshippers, too, sought musical enrichment. Toward the end of the Renaissance, in a radical departure from tradition, congregations began to employ professional cantors; in Eastern Europe, the idea was anathema. In time, the special bravura style of rendering prayer won over even the fundamentalists.

—L.R.

All cantors are fools, but not all fools are cantors.

❋ Any Jew can be a cantor, except that at this moment he happens to be hoarse.

One man is an expert on folklore, another on brushes, but everyone is an expert on cantors.

A *khazn* without a voice is like a sheep without wool.

When a *khazn* knows no Hebrew, he is called a cantor.

❋ A cantor is a fool: he stands on a platform but thinks he's on a pedestal. IBN ZABARA, *Book of Delight*, ch. 5

See also: PRAYER, RABBIS, WORSHIP

CAPABILITY

❋ Corn can't grow on the ceiling.

If you can't do what you want, do what you can.

You can't make a beaver hat out of a pig's tail.

You can't make ten when even one doesn't exist.

A nut tree will not grow apples.

No cloth is so fine that moths are unable to eat it.

Though his tongue be long, an ox can't blow the shophar [the ram's horn blown in the synagogue during the High Holy Days; it symbolizes how God reprieved Abraham by allowing him to sacrifice a ram instead of Isaac, his son].

The flute which makes sweet music for princes is not appreciated by weavers.   TALMUD: *Yoma*, 20 : 2

Even an angel can't do two things at the same time.
               MIDRASH: *Genesis Rabbah*, 50 : 2

See also: INTELLIGENCE, REASON

CAPITAL PUNISHMENT

"In those old, wild, barbarous days, when neither life nor the death of anyone counted for anything, Rabbi Akiba openly condemned capital punishment, a practice today recognized as highly uncivilized."   LEO TOLSTOY

See COURTS, JUDGES, LAW

CAUSE AND EFFECT

If you don't eat garlic, you won't smell.

❋ If cats wore gloves, they would catch no mice.

❋ If you eat your bagel, you'll have nothing left but the hole.

If you're busy with tar, your hands will get dirty.

When one link snaps, the whole chain collapses.

❋ If everyone sweeps in front of his door, the whole city will be clean.

Ropes drawn too taut break.

Storms pass, but their driftwood remains.

❋ When one blind man leads another, both fall into the pit.

If the shepherd is lame and the goats are swift, there will
be an accounting at the gate.

Can fire be near tow and not singe it?
TALMUD: Sanhedrin, 37a

The pace of the ass depends on the amount of feed he gets.
TALMUD: Shabbath, 51b

❋ The hole, not the mouse, is the thief.
TALMUD: Gittin, 45a

They have sown the wind, and they shall reap the whirlwind.   Book of Hosea, 8 : 7

From a tiny spark comes a great conflagration.
BEN SIRACH, Ecclesiasticus, 11 : 32

See also: ARGUMENT, CIRCUMSTANCES, ENDS AND MEANS,
FORGETTING

CAUTION

❋ Caution at first is better than tears at last.

Don't let go of a lion in your grip; he will devour you.

❋ Better measure ten times and cut once, instead of measuring once and cutting ten times.

Never expose yourself unnecessarily to danger: A miracle
may not save you . . . and if it does, it will be deducted
from your store of luck—or merit.
TALMUD: Shabbath, 32a

Caution should not be overcautious.
BAHYA IBN PAQUDA, Duties of the Heart

Don't be like the bird that sees the grain but not the trap.
JUDAH IBN TIBBON, A Father's Admonition

See also: FORESIGHT, HASTE, JUDGMENT, PRUDENCE

CENSORSHIP

Note. The Talmud (*Sanhedrin* 100b) lists the immortal
sayings of Ecclesiasticus (Jesus ben Sirach) as one of the
"forbidden" books—that is, a work "outside" the canon.
But Ecclesiasticus was greatly loved by Jews, widely
quoted by rabbis, and swiftly translated from Hebrew

into Aramaic (the language of the Israelites in Babylon, and in Palestine in 180 when Ben Sirach wrote his masterpiece).

According to each one's bent, the rabbis periodically responded to "secular" books with alarm, anger, or warnings to the laity. Their motives were pure enough (what censor's are not?): They were determined to keep the religious and intellectual life of their Jewish communities pure, unpolluted by reading that might disturb faith with agnostic, heretical, Greek or Christian thought —or by secular science. By "secular" the rabbis meant books about philosophy, poetic celebrations of paganism or pantheism, the classics of Greece and Rome, works in sciences that appeared to threaten the Talmud's cosmology.

Maimonides' *Guide for the Perplexed* (1190), which asserted that Judaism rested on reason and could be comprehended best on Aristotelian principles, created a furor in the learned circles of Europe. The book was much admired by Muslim and Christian thinkers (Aquinas, Leibniz), but fervently opposed by rabbis, who, in 1305, forbade Jews to read philosophical works of this kind until they were twenty-five. Those under twenty-five who disregarded the ban, designed to last fifty years, were threatened with anathematization. (In the eighteenth and nineteenth centuries, Maimonides' work became "the Bible of the enlightened.")

Other important Jewish writers who were taboo, at one time or another, include Levi ben Gershon, Isaac ben Moses Arama, the cabalists, hasidim, Reformists, the Baal Shem. See BIOGRAPHIES in the present volume.

—L.R.

See BOOKS, EROTICA, READING, STUDY

CERTAINTY

If there is room for question, something is wrong.

Better a small certainty than a large doubt.

If you insist you're right long enough, you'll be wrong.

Between "sure" and "perhaps," "sure" prevails.

TALMUD: *Kethuboth*, 12b

✳ Don't rely on If and Perhaps.
> BACHYA IBN PAQUDA, *Duties of the Heart*

There is no certainty without some doubt.
> ELIAS LEVITA, *Tishbi*

Those who grieve over the doubtful will rejoice over the sure.
> MOSES IBN EZRA, *Shirat Yisrael*

See also: CONTEXT, JUDGMENT, **LAW,** PRUDENCE

CHARACTER

✳ Saloons can't corrupt good men, and synagogues can't reform bad ones.

Spots on the character can be removed—with a little gold.

✳ It is better to have nobility of character than nobility of birth.

A giant is very tall even though he stands in a well.

Better a crooked foot than a crooked mind.

Every innkeeper praises his beer.

It *may* be that you will find an honest saloonkeeper, or a shepherd who is a thief.

What's in a man is sure to come out, one way or another.

Spit in a whore's face and she'll say, "It's raining."

✳ If the light is crooked, the shadow is crooked.

The cloak of a saint may cover the character of a scoundrel.

The man who is not good for himself is not good for others.

Should a peasant become a king, he still would not take the basket off his head.

Rub him with honey and he'll still smell of tar.

To accept an excuse shows a good character.

He enjoys giving so much that he hopes others will be in need, so that he may help them.

✳ To drunkards, no liquor is bad; to merchants, no money is tainted; to lechers, no woman is ugly.

❀ He is the kind of man who first prepares the bandage, then inflicts the wound.   TALMUD: *Megillah*, 13a

❀ What a man wants, he does not have; what he has, he does not prize.

There are three types of "doers": If a man says, "I shall do it soon," his character is poor; if he says, "I am ready to do it," his character is average; if he says, "I am doing it," his character is praiseworthy.

—Hasidic saying

God decides what shall befall a man, but not whether he shall be righteous or wicked.   TALMUD: *Niddah*, 16b

❀ You can know a man by three signs: his tips, his tippling, and his temper. —adapted from the TALMUD

There are four types among men:
The ordinary one says: "What is mine is mine, and what is yours is yours."

The queer one says: "What is mine is yours, and what is yours is mine."

The saintly one says: "What is mine is yours, and what is yours is yours."

The wicked one says: "What is mine is mine, and what is yours is mine."

Sayings of the Fathers, 5 : 16

Like garden, like gardener. TALMUD J.: *Sanhedrin*, 2 : 6

As the breath of the potter, so the shape of the vessel.

Zohar

Remember the virtues you lack and the faults you have; forget the good you did and the wrong you received.

Orhot Tsadikim ("Ways of the Saints")

In this world, one who is a dog can become a lion, and one who is a lion can become a dog.

MIDRASH: *Ruth Rabbah*, 3 : 2

❀ Character is tested through three things: business, wine, and conversation.   *Abot de Rabbi Nathan*, ch. 31

As is its fuel, so will be the fire.

BEN SIRACH, *Ecclesiasticus*, 28 : 10

Watching for other people's blemishes prevents me from investigating my own—which task is more urgent.
                    BAHYA IBN PAQUDA, *Duties of the Heart*

Moral conduct is a preparation for intellectual progress: only that man whose character is pure, calm and steadfast can reach correct conceptions.
                    MAIMONIDES, *Guide to the Perplexed*, I : 34

The man who keeps silent in the face of abuse is a true Hasid.   NACHMAN OF BRATSLAV

See also: ANIMALS, DISCIPLINE, HONESTY, MAN

CHARACTER ILLUSTRATED VIA ANIMALS

A dog without teeth is no longer a dog.

One recognizes the chick by its pecking.

The dog who barks "ho-ho" is not dangerous; the one who growls "how-how" is.

You can deck a pig in palms, but he will still act like a pig.

You can't make an arrow out of a pig's tail.

What, besides beef, can you expect from an ox?

❋ An eagle doesn't catch flies.

Let a dog on your bench and he'll jump to your table.

A lion should not weep in the presence of a fox.

❋ The goat has a beard, but still is no rabbi.

CHARACTER OF THINGS

Three things grow overnight: profit, rent, and daughters.

Though a castle totter, it is still called a castle; should a dunghill be built to the sky, it is still a dunghill.

❋ Said the cat: "If I had eyes of silver and ears of gold, I still would not stop stealing."   APOCRYPHA: *Ahikar*

See also: EVIL, HONESTY, HONOR, MAN, VIRTUE

CHARITY

Note. The Judaic admonition to be righteous, compassionate and, above all, help one's fellow man is called *tsedakah—"righteousness." This is the closest word for "charity" in Hebrew or Yiddish*; for Jews never separated charity from duty—that is, from moral and religious obligation. Deuteronomy (15:11) says, "For the poor shall never cease out of the land; therefore I command thee, saying, thou shalt open thine hand wide unto thy brother . . ."

Jews are forbidden to turn away anyone who asks for help. The poor and needy must, moreover, be spared embarrassment. Every Jewish community contained a hostel attached to the synagogue, for travelers or itinerants. Jews place great stress on helping the poor, the sick, the handicapped—and refugees, who have always been a part of the history of Jews.

Every community had a special fund for the needy; every holiday includes philanthropic activities; every home once contained little boxes into which coins for various charities were dropped. Every Jewish child was taught early in life to feel a duty to help those who needed help. Orphans were supported by communal funds. Fatherless or poor girls received a wedding gown, trousseau, and dowry from the community. The penniless received free burial. And even paupers were obligated to contribute nominal sums to the community fund.

All these obligations, incidentally, were superseded by the duty to ransom Jewish captives or slaves. A moving account of this side of the Jewish experience was written by Cecil Roth in the chapter, "A Community of Slaves," in *Personalities and Events in Jewish History*.

Maimonides analyzed and rated the different forms of *tsedakah*. The highest form, he said, is to help someone to help himself; after that, to help a man anonymously and secretly—so that the benefactor does not know whom he helps, and the benefactee does not know (so cannot feel obligated to) the one who helped him. I have never heard an improvement upon this.

—L.R.

✳ The longest road in the world is the one that leads from your pocket.

❋ If charity cost nothing, the world would be full of philanthropists.

To steal for charity is still stealing.

Charity is also a habit.

A sick person should be asked; a healthy one—given.

He is a philanthropist—with other people's money.

His charity stops at his pocketbook.

He who gives, lives; he who does not give, does not.

❋ Lend before witnesses, but give without them.

Rather give charity to a cripple than to a needy scholar.

The best charity is good will.

A man gives little if he gives much with a frown; he gives
  much if he gives little with a smile.

If you won't give to Jacob you will have to give to Esau.

Charity is the very salt of riches.
                              TALMUD: *Kethuboth*, 66b

The man who refuses to live within his means, but seeks to
  be supported by charity, must not be helped.
                              TALMUD: *Kethuboth*, 67b

We should be grateful for the presence of rogues among the
  poor; for if not for them, we would sin each time we
  ignored an appeal for alms. TALMUD: *Kethuboth*, 68a

To shut one's eye to charity is like worshipping idols.
                              TALMUD: *Kethuboth*, 68b

❋ The greatest charity is to enable the poor to earn a living.
                              TALMUD: *Shabbath*, 63a

Charity knows neither race nor creed.
                              TALMUD: *Gittin*, 61a

[When a rabbi saw a man give a penny to a beggar in
  public:] "Better had you given him nothing than put him
  to shame."   TALMUD: *Hagigah*, 5a

He who gives alms in secret is greater than Moses.
                              TALMUD: *Baba Bathra*, 9b

Whoever gives the poor money is blessed sixfold; whoever does it with a kind word is blessed sevenfold.

TALMUD: *Baba Bathra*, 9b

Better be a servant in a heathen temple than take alms.

TALMUD J.: *Berakoth*, 9

When the year has been prosperous, people become more brotherly.   MIDRASH: *Genesis Rabbah*, 89 : 4

As a torch is not diminished though it kindles a million candles, so will he not lose who gives to a good cause.

MIDRASH: *Exodus Rabbah*, 30 : 3

Better is he who gives little to charity—from money honestly earned, than he who gives much—from money acquired by fraud.   MIDRASH: *Ecclesiastes Rabbah*, 4

He who closes his ear against the cry of the poor will himself one day call and not be heard.

—adapted from *Book of Proverbs*

He who lengthens the life of a poor man [through charity] will have his own life lengthened when his time to die comes.   *Zohar*

There are three kinds of almsgivers: the one who gives, but does not want others to give; the one who gives and wants others to give; the one who neither gives nor wants others to give.   *Sayings of the Fathers*, 5 : 19

Do not harden your heart against your poor brother; if you do not give to him, you will, in the end, have to receive from him.   *Sifre—Deuteronomy*, 116

✳ The door which is not opened for a beggar will open for a doctor.   *Pesikta Rabati*, 42b

Man is worthy of being called Man only if he is charitable.

Yalkut Ruveni

There is a kind of charity which is pernicious: that of the man who gives alms to an adulterer, or to a glutton, or to a drunkard ... or who supplies weapons to murderers ... or who gives food to robbers.   *Sefer Hasidim*

To give everything to religion is not piety but folly: it impoverishes a man so that he must come to depend on charity. We need show no compassion for such a man,

for he belongs to those described by the sages as "pious
fools who destroy the world."

> MAIMONIDES, *Mishneh Torah*: 8 : 13

❉ The sages would sometimes tie money in a cloth bag and
throw it behind their backs for poor men to pick up, so
that the poor should not feel shame.

> MAIMONIDES, *Mishneh Torah*, 10 : 1—14

The great sages used to go about throwing money through
the doors of the poor [and hurrying away, not to be
seen]: this is virtuous.

> MAIMONIDES, *Mishneh Torah*, 10 : 1—14

❉ If a poor man asks for alms, and you have nothing to
give, console him with words; for it is forbidden to
chastise a poor man or raise your voice against him,
since his heart is broken.

> MAIMONIDES, *Mishneh Torah*, 10 : 1—14

Poor men, required to give to charity, may fulfill their
obligations by exchanging alms.

> JOSEPH CARO, *Shulhan Aruk*

No man is ever impoverished by giving alms, nor is harm
ever caused by it.   JOSEPH CARO, *Shulhan Aruk*

He who refuses aid which he has the power to give is ac-
countable to justice.   JOSEPHUS, *Against Apion*, II, 27

A poor but humble man who gives nothing to charity is
preferable to a rich but haughty man who does.

> NACHMAN OF BRATSLAV

❉ Charity cures heartaches.   NACHMAN OF BRATSLAV

A *mitzvah* [good deed] that costs money is worth more than
one that costs nothing.   NACHMAN OF BRATSLAV

Always help the persecuted.   NACHMAN OF BRATSLAV

Before reciting his prayers, a man should give to charity.

> NACHMAN OF BRATSLAV

Charity with a smile shows the donor's character.

> NACHMAN OF BRATSLAV

Even the poor should give some token of charity.

> NACHMAN OF BRATSLAV

He gives twice who gives quickly.
> LEONE DA MODENA, *Tsemah Tsadik*

Don't use the chutzpa of a beggar as an excuse for not helping him.   RABBI SHMELKE OF NICKELSBURG

❋ Men are always close—to their pockets.
> SHOLEM ALEICHEM

See also: COMPASSION, DUTY, GENEROSITY, GOOD DEEDS & TAKING, KINDNESS, MERCY, OBLIGATION, PITY, RESPONSIBILITY

CHARM

Two things can't be bought: charm and luck.

❋ The charming don't have to be beautiful.

Charm surpasses beauty.

A little charm does no harm.

Charm can't be bought at the grocer's.

If you open a shop, stock up on charm.

See also: BEAUTY, DECORUM

CHASTITY

❋ Jews have no nunneries.

CHEAP

❋ What's cheap is expensive.

Cheap *borsht* (beet soup) is a blessing to the toothless.

To the poor, *borsht* (beet soup) tastes as good as caviar to the rich.

If you can't afford the expensive, be grateful for the cheap.

The cheapest man can be very generous—with the money of others.

See also: BUSINESS, JUDGMENT, VALUE

CHILDREN

Little children, little troubles; big children, big troubles.

❋ Little children won't let you sleep; big children won't let you live.

The *nakhes* [pleasures] we get from children are far more precious than gold.

Children bring joy, children bring sorrows.

Little children don't let you chew, and with big ones you can't afford the new.

Each child brings his own blessing into the world.

You can tell a Jew by how he treats his children.

Whom God would punish, he sends bad children.

Children—and money—form a happy world.

❋ One father can support ten children, but ten children seem unable to support one father.

Children are like grass: some blossom and some fade.

A boy, a blessing; a girl, a worry.

A child's tears move the heavens themselves.

❋ If you're a child at twenty, you're a jackass at twenty-one.

If the world will ever be redeemed, it will be through the virtues of children.

Even a child is known by his deeds.

A mother's blow never disables a child.

❋ A child's simple sense is a kind of wisdom.

For children, we tear the world apart.

The apple doesn't fall far from the tree.

Sometimes a dog is more loyal than a child.

❋ A little child is a pig; a big child is a wolf.

Don't gossip about the children of others while yours are still growing up.

Your child may be a robber, yet you dance at his wedding.

❊ Five fingers on one hand—yet no two are alike.

One [child] is not enough.

It is better not to have had children than to bury them.

Those who marry for money will have unworthy children.

❊ Take care of the children of the poor, for they will be
the ones who advance knowledge.
TALMUD: Nedarim, 81a

A child is a staff for the hand—and a hoe for the grave.
TALMUD: Yebamoth, 65b

❊ Every child tends to exaggerate its own importance.
TALMUD: Sukkah, 21a

No kids, no wethers; no wethers, no sheep . . . No children,
no adults; no adults, no sages.
MIDRASH: Genesis Rabbah, 42 : 3

Don't fret over married children; they will take care of
themselves.   NACHMAN OF BRATSLAV

We each have the kind of children we deserve.
NACHMAN OF BRATSLAV

❊ Children without a childhood are tragic.
MENDELE MOCHER SEFARIM

❊ It is better that children cry than that their fathers cry.

See also: ANCESTORS, DAUGHTERS, FAMILY, FATHERS,
MOTHERS, SONS

CHILDREN: ON BEGETTING THEM

Of children and glasses, one never has too many. [Both are
fragile.]

A man without children is like a piece of wood which,
though kindled, does not light—or give off light.

He who begets a fool does it to his sorrow;
And the father of a dolt will have no joy of him.
Book of Proverbs

Let not the fear of bad offspring deter you from having
children; you must do your duty and God will do what
pleases Him.   TALMUD: *Berakoth*, 10a

Not to beget children is to impair the divine image.
          MIDRASH: *Genesis Rabbah*, 34 : 14

CHILDREN: ON TEACHING THEM

He who does not bring up his son to some honest calling
brings him up to be a thief.

Don't limit a child to your own learning, for he was born
in another time.   —Rabbinic saying

✻ If you teach your children in their youth, they won't
have to teach you in your old age.   —Hasidic saying

We learn best what our heart prepares us to learn.
          TALMUD: *'Abodah Zarah*, 19a

If you don't teach the ox to plow when he is young, it will
be difficult to teach him when he is grown.
          MIDRASH: *Midrash Proverbs*, 22

Teach a child good manners during babyhood.
          NACHMAN OF BRATSLAV

CHILDREN: ON RAISING THEM

It is easier to have children than raise them.

Train a child in the way he should take,
And when he is old, he will not depart from it.
          Book of Proverbs 22 : 6

It is important for a growing child to be given things he can
break: Rabbah often bought imperfect earthenware for
his little ones to smash, should they want to.
          TALMUD: *Yomah*, 78b

Never promise something to a child and not give it to him,
because in that way he learns to lie.
          TALMUD: *Sukkah*, 46b

When the chicks of a hen are young, she gathers them to
her; when they are grown, she drives them away.
          MIDRASH: *Leviticus Rabbah*, 25 : 5

Love your children equally, even though the favored disappoint you and the neglected make you happy.

BERECHIAH BEN NATRONAI HA-NAKDAN, *Fox Fables*

❋ The man who disobeys his father will have disobedient sons.

Wherever children are learning, there dwells the Divine Presence.

At five, your son is your master; at ten, your slave; at fifteen, your double; and after that, he is your friend or foe—depending on how you raised him.

The man who spares the rod hates his son.

—adapted from *Book of Proverbs*, 13 : 24

Play no favorites: when Joseph got a many-colored coat, his brothers came to hate him.

MIDRASH: *Genesis Rabbah*, 84 : 8

❋ If you don't respect your parents, your child will not respect you.

MAIMONIDES, *Guide to the Perplexed*, 3 : 9

See also: DISCIPLINE, KNOWLEDGE, LEARNING, PIETY

CHILDREN: ON PUNISHING THEM

❋ If you must beat a child, use a string.

TALMUD: *Baba Bathra*, 21a

Don't threaten a child: Either punish him or forgive him.

TALMUD

The rod of correction creates wisdom; but a child left to himself brings disgrace to his mother.

Book of Proverbs

The branch sprung from violence has no tender twig.

BEN SIRACH, *Ecclesiasticus*, 40 : 15

A mother's curse roots up the young plant.

BEN SIRACH, *Ecclesiasticus*, 3 : 9

Gold must be hammered, and sometimes a child must be beaten.   *Alphabet of Ben Sirach*, 4

❋ When a father is quick-tempered, his children are confused.   NACHMAN OF BRATSLAV

A strict master will not have understanding sons.

NACHMAN OF BRATSLAV

CHILDREN: AND PARENTS

❊ It is better that a child should cry than its parents.

❊ About his children, every parent is blind.

❊ The rich don't have children: they have heirs.

❊ One father can support ten children; but ten children don't seem to be able to support one father.

❊ Parents once taught their children to talk; today children teach their parents to be quiet.

Pity the child who has been banished from his father's table.

It is better not to live than to be dependent on your children.

❊ The talk of the child in the street is that of his father or mother at home.

Though parents have a dozen children, each is the only one.

Crooked parents can produce straight children.

Any finger hurts as much as any other. [All children are equally loved.]

To its parents, no child is superfluous.

The follies of children are termites to their fathers' possessions.

A father loves his children; but they love their children.
                              TALMUD: *Sotah*, 49a

As my fathers planted for me, so do I plant for my children.
                              TALMUD: *Ta'anith*, 23a

It is normal for a child to fear his father more than his mother; it is normal for a child to love his mother more than his father.
          RASHI, *Commentaries on the Pentateuch, Exodus*

See also: FAMILY, FATHERS, MOTHERS

CHILDREN: GRANDCHILDREN

❊ When you have a grandchild, you have two children.

Grandchildren are like children.
                              TALMUD: *Yebamoth*, 62b

A man appreciates the love of his grandchildren more than the love of his children. *Zohar*

See also: FAMILY, FATHERS, MOTHERS

CHUTZPA

❊ After murdering his father and mother, he asked the court to be merciful because he was an orphan.

While beating you up, he cries, "Help! Help!"

See: ARROGANCE

CIRCUMSTANCES

There's no need to light a lamp at noon.

❊ The same sun bleaches linen and blackens gypsies.

A little coin in a large jar makes a great noise.

❊ If things are not as you like, like them as they are.

❊ Entrances are wide, but exits are narrow.

When an old man takes a young wife, he gets young and she gets old.

A cat and a rat will make peace over a carcass.

❊ A thief takes one path; his pursuers confront ten.

❊ What is bread for one is death for another.

A heavy load [of bread] is no burden.

When the wet leaves [on a tree] burn, what can the dry ones say?

When the light goes out, the mice dance.

❊ When a teacher fights with his wife, it's tough on his students.

At the seashore, thornbushes are veritable fir trees.
TALMUD: *Pesahim*, 4a

❊ The man who makes arrows is often slain by one of them.
TALMUD: *Pesahim*, 28a

If the victim is fat enough, a cat and a weasel feast together. TALMUD: *Sanhedrin*, 105a

If a man goes into a tannery, the smell does not leave him all day, even though he bought nothing.

Abot de Rabbi Nathan, 11 : 14b

Silence is not commendable in the presence of absurdities; wrath is, when voiced over sin. IBN GABIROL

See also: ADVICE, ANIMALS, CAUSE AND EFFECT, COMPROMISE, CONTENTMENT, CONTEXT, COOPERATION, DEPENDENCY, ENDS AND MEANS, INFLUENCE, WISDOM

CIVILIZATION

Note. "In the infancy of civilization, when our island was as savage as New Guinea, when letters and arts were still unknown to Athens, when scarcely a thatched hut stood on what was afterwards the site of Rome, this condemned people (Jews) had fenced cities and cedar palaces, their splendid Temple, their fleets of merchant ships, their schools of sacred learning, their great statesmen and soldiers, their natural philosophers, their historians, and their poets. What nation ever contended more manfully against overwhelming odds for its independence and religion? What nation ever, in its last agonies, gave such signal proofs of what may be accomplished by a brave despair?"*

THOMAS BABINGTON MACAULAY

"The Roman *patria* applied only to the city of Rome. . . . The ancient Greeks concentrated their colonization on localities abutting great bodies of water. The ancient Hebrews followed the changing centers of civilization. Ensconced at first around the shores of the Euphrates and the Tigris, they pulled up stakes and journeyed to the Nile when it became the hub of civilization. For a long period they settled in Egypt, but the magnetic, gravitational 'pull' of onmarching civilization . . . again attracted them into its orbit, propelling them into centers that had been established along the eastern shores of the Mediterrean."**

ALAN STEINBACH

See BOOKS, COMMUNITY, GOVERNMENT, HISTORY, ISRAEL, LAW, POLITICS

---

* *Essay and Speech on Jewish Disabilities*, Jewish Historical Society of England, London, 1910.

** *Essays on Jewish Booklore*, KTAV, New York, 1971, p. xviii. For interesting essays on this and related themes, see Cecil Roth, *The Jewish Contribution to Civilization*, Macmillan, London, 1938.

CLEANLINESS

Note. Talmudic deliberations contain the most extraordinary, detailed, "modern" prescriptions about personal cleanliness, which is considered an obligation to the body God gave man. Christians often remarked on the unusual emphasis Jews placed upon cleanliness and hygiene; some medieval commentators said this amounted to a "cult of purity." Such a "cult" was of immense value in keeping Jewish families healthier than they might otherwise have been. Every Jewish community was required by Talmudic law to maintain a public bathhouse. Bathing could only have helped fortify a sense of self-respect. This seems all the more significant, I think, if one considers the differences in hygiene and sanitation that existed between Jewish and other communities in the Middle East.

—L.R.

✳ Poverty comes from God, but dirt does not.

A scholar with one spot on his garments deserves the worst.
TALMUD: *Shabbath,* 114a

"Cleanliness is next to godliness," it is said. Carefulness leads to cleanliness, cleanliness to purity, purity to humility, humility to saintliness, saintliness to fear of sin, fear of sin to holiness, and holiness to immortality.
TALMUD

See also: ANIMALS, CLOTHING, CONDUCT, DECORUM, POVERTY, SCHOLARS

CLOTHES/CLOTHING

Fools see men's clothes; wise men see men's spirits.

Our clothes conceal our blemishes.

A homely patch is more beautiful than a beautiful hole.

✳ The clothes of other people do not warm us.

In your town, your reputation counts; in another, your clothes do.   TALMUD: *Shabboth,* 14b

The man who does not respect clothes will not benefit from them.   TALMUD: *Berakoth,* 62a

Man's honor [dignity] accompanies his dress.
MIDRASH: *Exodus Rabbah*

The dress of a wise man must be free of stains; he should
not wear the apparel of princes, to attract attention, nor
the raiment of paupers, which incurs disrespect.
MAIMONIDES, *Mishneh Torah*, 5 : 7–13

Eat less and dress better.   —adapted from IBN TIBBON

See also: CONDUCT, DECORUM, STATUS

CLUMSY MEN

He can't even tie the tail of a cat.

If he were to fall on his back he would break his jaw.

See also: SHLEMIELS, SHLIMAZLS

COMFORT

It breaks no law to be comfortable.

The change from trouble to comfort gives us more pleasure
than uninterrupted comfort does.
MAIMONIDES, *Guide to the Perplexed*, 3 : 24

See also: COMPASSION

COMMANDMENT

Live by the commandments; do not die by them.
TALMUD: *Sanhedrin*, 74a

Six hundred and thirteen commandments were given to
Moses: 365 negative, corresponding to the days of the
year, and 248 positive, corresponding to the number of
joints in the human body.   TALMUD: *Makkoth*, 23b

A commandment is to the Torah what a lamp is to the sun.
MIDRASH: *Psalms*, 17 : 7

See also: LAW

COMMON SENSE

❊ No barber cuts his own hair.

A thread is always found on a tailor.

❊ A meowing cat won't catch a mouse.

Just to look costs nothing.

You can catch flies better with honey than with vinegar.

The scholar who sets forth to look for a bride would be well advised to take an ignorant but sensible man along.

❋ Some scholars have the sense of donkeys: they only carry a lot of books.
                                    —adapted from BAHYA IBN PAQUDA,
                                    Duties of the Heart

See also: CIRCUMSTANCE, JUDGMENT, REASON, WISDOM

COMMUNITY

The man who avoids society is inclined to wickedness.

If fire strikes the wet, what chance have the dry?

Nine rabbis cannot make a *minyan*, but ten shoemakers can. [To "make a minyan" means to constitute a quorum of ten for prayers or other religious services.]

❋ When the sheep are sheared, the lambs tremble.

Let us be like the lines that lead to the center of a circle—uniting there, and not like parallel lines, which never join.   —Hasidic saying

A community is too heavy for any man to carry alone.

The wolf will grab the sheep that strays from the flock.
                                    MOSES IBN EZRA, *Shirat Yisrael*

See also: GOVERNMENT, LAW, POLITICS, PUBLIC WELFARE

COMPANIONS

❋ If you lie with dogs, you rise with fleas.

With men, as with apples, one rotten spoils the others.

We need comrades—both for joy and for sorrow.

Give me comradeship, or give me death.
                                    TALMUD: *Ta'anith*, 23a

❋ How can a jar and a kettle associate happily when, whichever is struck, the same one is always smashed?
                                    BEN SIRACH, *Ecclesiasticus*, 13 : 2

When one of my friends died, one of my limbs perished.
IBN GABIROL

A companion who tells you your faults is better than a
companion who hands you a gold coin.
IBN GABIROL

See also: DEVIL, FRIENDS/FRIENDSHIP

COMPASSION

Note. Rakhmones, which in Yiddish usage means "pity" or
"compassion," is a quintessential word that lies at the
heart of Jewish thought. All of Judaism's philosophy,
ethics, ethos, learning, education, are saturated with a
sense of, and a heightened sensitivity to, the primacy and
nobility of *rakhmones.*

God is often called the God of Mercy and Compassion
(*Adonai El Rahum ve-Hanun*). The writings of the ancient prophets are permeated with appeals for *rahamim,*
which is considered a divine attribute.

Rakhmones is not found in the Bible; *rahamim* is—in
an unforgettable way: The Lord decided that a world
governed by justice alone would be impossible; for human beings to endure requires that compassion (*rahamim*) be added.

Women's Liberation Movementeers may be interested
to know that the Hebrew root *rehem means* "a mother's
womb," and that the rabbis said that men and women
should give others the same love that a mother feels for
the issue of her womb.

—L.R.

One heart is mirror to another.

❋ Some men can't even spare a sigh.

When a man has compassion for others, God has compassion for him.   TALMUD: *Bezah,* 32a

The man who begs aid for his comrade, while himself in
need, is answered first.   TALMUD: *Baba Kamma,* 92a

❋ When the Egyptians were drowning in the Red Sea, the
angels in heaven began to break forth in songs of jubilation, but the Holy One, blessed be He, silenced them:
"My creatures are perishing—and ye are ready to sing!"
—adapted from TALMUD

Never beat or inflict pain on any animal, beast, bird, or insect.   *Sefer Hasidim*

❊ Can you ask a cruel man's advice about compassion?
                          BEN SIRACH, *Ecclesiasticus*, 37

If one is cruel to himself, how can we expect him to be compassionate with others?
                          HASDAI, *Ben ha-Melekh, ve-Ha-Nazir*

Whoever fails to visit a sick, friendless person is as if he shed his blood.   AKIBA in TALMUD: *Nedarim*, 40a

Where there is no compassion, crime increases.
                          NACHMAN OF BRATSLAV

❊ If we do not help a man in trouble, it is as if we caused the trouble.   NACHMAN OF BRATSLAV

Toothaches afflict those who have no compassion for animals.   NACHMAN OF BRATSLAV

See also: ALTRUISM, FORGIVENESS, GENTILES, GOD, GRATITUDE, GRIEF, HEART, HEAVEN, HELP, KINDNESS, MERCY, PITY, SENSITIVITY

COMPLAINT

❊ Dear God: I know you will provide, but why don't you provide *until* you provide?

If you're not in pain, why are you moaning?

The bad wheel usually creaks the most. (The least deserving make the most noise.)

Don't grumble; it may lead to other sins.
                          Derekh Erets Zuta

See also: CONTENTMENT, ENVY, GREED, HAPPINESS, JEALOUSY

COMPROMISE

A mountain cannot meet with a mountain, but one man can meet with another.

The profits of compromise are nothing compared to its losses.   "THE CHOFETZ CHAIM"

See also: ARBITRATION, CIRCUMSTANCES, COOPERATION, DE-
MOCRACY, GOVERNMENT, LAW, TALK

CONCEIT

Money leads to conceit, and conceit to sin.

❋ The *khokhem* [wise man] who parades his knowledge is
worth less than the stupid man who, ashamed, hides his
ignorance.

No one is as ugly as the man who is conceited.

❋ If you harden your heart with pride, you soften your
brain with it, too.

Conceit and poverty make a wretched combination.

If a man always praises himself, it tells us that he knows
nothing.   *Zohar*

❋ The conceited man is not a sinner but a fool.
                                   "THE CHOFETZ CHAIM"

See also: ARROGANCE, MONEY, PRIDE, VANITY

CONDUCT

Don't be too sweet, lest you be eaten up; don't be too bitter,
lest you be spewed out.

The spittle a man throws upward falls back on his own face.
                        MIDRASH: *Ecclesiastes Rabbah*, 7 : 9

If you have paid a fine in court, sing and walk away.
                              TALMUD: *Baba Kamma*, 7

When you see a man stronger than you, rise.
                              APOCRYPHA: *Ahikar*, 2 : 61

The way a man walks tells us whether he is wise or foolish,
learned or ignorant.
                        MAIMONIDES: *Mishneh Torah*, 5 : 7–13

See also: APPEARANCES, BOORS, CHARM, CLEANLINESS, CLOTH-
ING, COURTESY, DECORUM, MANNERS, STATUS

CONFESSION

If we were to recount all our sins, we would never complete
the list. Therefore, we use the alphabetical form: The

alphabet has a beginning and an end. The [Yom Kippur] confessional is in the plural because every Jew is responsible for all other Jews.   SEYMOUR SIEGEL

See also: GOD *and* MAN, REPENTANCE, SALVATION, SIN

CONFIDENCE

The man who has confidence in himself gains the confidence of others.   —Hasidic saying

Don't be too sure of yourself till the day you die.
          HILLEL in *Sayings of the Fathers*, 2 : 5

See also: JUDGMENT, SELF-ESTEEM

CONFLICT

✱ The cat loves fish—but doesn't want to wet her paws.

See also: COMPROMISE, FORESIGHT, PRUDENCE

CONFORMITY

The man who follows the gait of others will sway from side to side.

✱ If you want people to think you wise, just agree with them.

Where many go, no grass will grow.

Had not a great man praised you, I might have objected to what you say.

When one dog barks, he easily finds others to bark with him.
          MIDRASH: *Exodus Rabbah*, 31 : 9

If you meet a lion, roar; if you meet a donkey, bray.
                              FALAQUERA

To accept tradition without examining it, with intelligence and judgment, is like the blind blindly following others.
          Bahya ibn Paquda, *Duties of the Heart*

See also: INDIVIDUALITY, MASSES, POPULARITY

CONSCIENCE

❋ You can wash your hands, but not your conscience.

A guilty conscience is a snake in the heart.

Only the things you do can leave a clear conscience.

❋ Be the master of your will, and the slave of your conscience. —Hasidic saying

The pangs of conscience are better than floggings.
TALMUD: *Berakoth*, 7a

What restrains beasts from doing harm is something external—a bridle or a bit; but man's restraints lie within himself. MAIMONIDES *Commentary on the Mishnah*

See also: DECEIT, DISCIPLE, DUTY, FALSEHOOD, FRAUD, GUILT, LIES, SIN

CONSIDERATION (FOR OTHERS)

❋ Don't drain your well as long as others may need water.

Too courteous is discourteous.

Never address a slave as "slave," for the very name is contemptible.

When you come to a new city, follow its customs.

Don't taunt your neighbor for your own blemishes.
TALMUD: *Baba Mezi'a*, 59b

The family servant should eat after the meal is over; but if especially good meat or old wine is served, he should receive his portion immediately, so that he be spared the pain of waiting. TALMUD: *Kethuboth*, 61a

Never wait until a shy employee asks for his wages; pay him before he asks. GERSONIDES

❋ Among those who stand, do not sit; among those who sit, do not stand. Among those who laugh, do not weep; among those who weep, do not laugh.
Hillel in *Tosefta Berakoth*, 2

Never rebuke a man in such a way as to shame him in public.
RASHI, *Commentaries on the Pentateuch, Leviticus*

CONSOLATION

An apt utterance is a joy to a man, and a word in season—
how good is it!   *Book of Proverbs*, 15 : 23

CONTENTMENT

Why seek honey when sugar is so sweet?

❋ To pursue happiness is to flee from contentment.

Three things soften a man's heart: a pleasant melody, a
pleasant scene, and a fragrant odor.
                              TALMUD: *Berakoth*, 57b

Two things never come together—contentment and envy.
                                          IBN GABIROL

The worst bondage is exile from peace of mind.
                                      THE BELZER RABBI

CONTEXT

All colors look alike in the dark.

❋ A heavy rain may be good for the fields but is bad for
the roads.

Near golden wagons you will find golden nails.

The man who has not tasted the bitter does not know what
the sweet is.

There is no quality so deplorable but that it sometimes
serves a use, and no quality so praiseworthy but that it
sometimes is lamentable: Silence is a commendable trait,
but it is detestable when preserved while listening to
absurdities; wrath is reprehensible, but if expressed over
transgressions, it is praiseworthy.   IBN GABIROL

CONVERTS

Note. By tradition, rabbis are obliged to try to dissuade non-Jews from formal conversion. (This may have originated as an effort to test the intensity of the desire to be converted.) A long period of study and training in Judaism's practices and principles of faith is mandatory, and discourages those swayed by transient impulse. Converts are accorded complete equality of status under Jewish law: The one legal (halakic) taboo is against a rabbi's marrying a woman proselyte.

The history of conversion to Judaism is worth sketching. Converts to Judaism have been known since the days recorded in the Bible (e.g., Ruth) and there were a considerable number of proselytes to Judaism during the aggressive Hasmonean (or Hashmonai) dynasty in Judea, in the second century. Some very great rabbis were thought to be descended from proselytes (e.g., Akiba).

Some Talmudists held that one reason God dispersed the Jews was to spread the True Faith and make converts everywhere.

Converts continued to adopt Judaism in modest numbers during the Middle Ages, despite the fact that it was a capital offense carrying gruesome, fatal penalties. In the eighth century, the Khazar tribes of southern Russia turned Jewish. (See Judah ha-Levi, in BIOGRAPHIES.) Some converts came to Judaism from the ranks of the Catholic clergy: French, English, German, Dutch. Proselytes from Islam were not uncommon, nor later from the Protestant ranks. Russian peasants in the nineteenth century were caught up in the "Sabbotnik" (a Judaistic) movement. Balkan and Italian converts emigrated to the state of Israel after 1948.

My favorite story in the proselytic zone involves one Te-Ua, a Maori, converted to the Anglican faith, early in the nineteenth century, who then started a local Israelite cult that sang hymns in a blissful mélange of Hebrew, Greek, English, and German. He became known as "Tiu" ("Jew"), and his faith was so potent that he declared himself the Moses of his people and proclaimed New Zealand the new Canaan.*

---

* See Theodor H. Gaster, *op. cit.*, pp. 330–31. Also see Vittorio Lauternari's fascinating *Religions of the Oppressed* (tr. Lisa Sergio), Macgibbon and Kee, London, 1963; Knopf, New York, 1963.

In the United States, there has been a noticeable increase in the number of proselytes to Judaism, because of
the growing number of mixed marriages, in which the
majority of the grooms are Jewish and the brides
gentile.*

—L.R.

The true convert is dearer to God than the Israelites, for
had not the Israelites seen the thunder and lightning on
Mount Sinai, the shaking mountain and blaring trumpets,
they might not have accepted holy Torah. But the
proselyte who saw none of these has opened his heart to
the Holy One. Who can be dearer to God?

MIDRASH: *Tanhuma*

When anyone says he wants to become a convert, the rabbis
(should) ask: "Why? Do you not know the Israelites are
hounded and persecuted?" If the answer is, "Yes, I
know, and want only to be worthy," the rabbis should
accept him.

TALMUD: *Yebamoth,* 47a

See also: FAITH, ISRAEL, PROSELYTES, RELIGION

COOPERATION

We fall down by ourselves, but it takes a friendly hand to
lift us up.

If a moron holds a cow by the ears, a clever man can milk
her.

See also: CAUSE and EFFECT, CIRCUMSTANCES, COMPROMISE,
HELPING

COUNSEL

It is better to ask the way ten times than take the wrong
road once.

If you ask, you won't err.

Many come for counsel, but not all are helped by it.

For want of counsel, a people will fall;
But safety lies in a wealth of counselors.

Book of Proverbs, 11 : 14

---

* *New Standard Jewish Encyclopedia,* op. cit., p. 1570.

Before trouble comes, obtain advice; after it comes, advice
    is useless.   IBN ZABARA, *Book of Delight*, ch. 2

❈ The best of animals needs a whip, the purest of women
    a husband, the cleverest of men advice.   IBN GABIROL

See also: ADVICE, FORESIGHT, JUDGMENT

COURAGE

❈ When there is no money, half is gone; when there is no
    courage, all is gone.

He who has nothing to lose can try anything.

Nerve succeeds.

He who does not dare, will not get his share.

❈ Don't consult a coward about war.

To lose courage is worse than to lose an army.

See also: COWARDICE, ENDURANCE, FORTITUDE, HONOR, OP-
    TIMISM, VALOR

COURTESY

Too much courtesy is a discourtesy.

The most courteous man is one who bears with the discour-
    teous.

See also: CONDUCT, CONSIDERATION, DECORUM, MANNERS

COURTS

❈ Where there is room for question, something is wrong.

Justice delayed is worse than injustice.

From litigation you can never recover your losses.

❈ An oath [in court] is worthless if it affirms the impos-
    sible: for instance, that you saw a camel fly.
                                    TALMUD: *Shebuoth*, 29a

Silence [in a court] may be equivalent to confession.
                                    TALMUD: *Yebamoth*, 87b

A man may not accuse himself of a crime.
                                    TALMUD: *Yebamoth*, 25b

No man can be declared guilty in his absence [from the courtroom].   TALMUD: *Kethuboth*, 11a

A benefit may be conferred, but not a disability imposed, on a man in his absence.   TALMUD: *Erubin*, 7 : 11

❊ When a court has pronounced a sentence of death, its members [judges] should taste nothing for the rest of that day.   TALMUD: *Sanhedrin*, 63a

If your cloak is taken from you by a court of law, sing a song and go your way. [You are saved from theft.]
          —adapted from TALMUD: *Sanhedrin*, 7a

See also: EVIDENCE, JUDGES, JUSTICE, LAW

COURTSHIP

❊ One man gets caressed for a pinch, another gets slapped.

It costs nothing to make sweet promises.

Love makes us blind, deaf, and dumb.

The right mate comes with the first date.

Those who can't love, flatter.

Flattery is a device for theft.

If you want the daughter, flatter the mother.

Before a rooster approaches a hen, he promises her: "Come to me and I shall give you a gown of many colors." But afterwards he says, "May I lose the comb on my head if I have the means to buy such a thing."
          TALMUD: *Erubin*, 100b

It is natural for a man to woo a woman, not for a woman to woo a man, for it is the loser who seeks what he lost [the rib].   TALMUD: *Niddah*, 31b

See also: DECEIT, DECORUM, FLATTERY, LOVE, MARRIAGE

COWARDS, COWARDICE

❊ There is no cure for cowardice.

If you have nothing to lose, at least be brave.

❊ Never consult a woman about her rival, nor a coward about war.

When you lose all your money, you have lost half, but when you lose courage you have lost all.

You'd be surprised by how often nerve succeeds.

If you have no choice, you lose nothing by being brave.

Soldiers grow brave after eating.

Don't enter the forest if you fear leaves.

If you carry a lantern, you will not fear the darkness.

See also: COURAGE, FEAR, HONOR, VALOR

CREDITORS

❊ No man shows impatience with his creditors.

Fear pays no debts.

Lending makes enemies.

If you are owed money by a man who is unable to repay it, do not keep crossing his path.
TALMUD: *Baba Mezi'a*, 75b

Better eat vegetables and fear no creditors, than eat duck and hide from them.   TALMUD: *Pesahim*, 114a

See also: BORROWERS, DEBT, LENDING, MONEY

CRITICISM

The man who can't bear to hear a word of criticism will have to hear many.

It is easier to negate than to affirm.

❊ It's easier to find faults in others than virtues in oneself.

Reprove not a scorner, lest he hate you; reprove a wise man, and he will love you.   *Book of Proverbs*, 9 : 8

A rebuke sinks deeper into a man of intelligence than a hundred lashes into a fool. *Book of Proverbs*, 17 : 10

❊ He who winks makes trouble; he who openly reproves makes peace.   *Book of Proverbs*, 16 : 7

Wheat needs grinding, and men need correction.

> TALMUD: *Abodah Zarah*, 44a

In honoring, we begin with the most prominent; in censuring, we begin with the least important.

> TALMUD: *Berakoth*, 61a

A man's mind is hidden in his writings; criticism brings it to light.   IBN GABIROL, *Choice of Pearls*

Include yourself in any reproof.

> NACHMAN OF BRATSLAV

He who cannot accept reproof cannot become great.

> NACHMAN OF BRATSLAV

A man can detect a speck in another's hair, but can't see the flies on his own nose.

> MENDELE MOCHER SEFORIM

See also: EGOTISM, FLATTERY, GREAT MEN, INTELLIGENCE, WISE MEN, WRITING

CRUCIFIXION

Note. "Your madness goes so far as to say that we [Jews] are scattered because our fathers condemned to death Him whom you worship. O ye pious tigers, ye fanatical panthers, who . . . have no better way of supporting your sect than by executioners, can you not see that it was only the Romans who condemned Him? We [Jews] had not at that time the right to inflict death; we were governed by Quirinus, Varus, Pilate. No crucifixion was ever practised among us. Not a single trace of that form of punishment is to be found. Stop punishing a whole nation for an event for which it cannot be responsible. Would it be just to burn the Pope and all the Monsignori in Rome because the first Romans ravished the Sabines and pillaged the Samnites? Amen."

> VOLTAIRE, *Sermon du Rabin Akib.*

See: ANTI-SEMITISM, INTOLERANCE, JEWS, PERSECUTION, POGROMS, PREJUDICE

CRUELTY

Even the mercy of the wicked is cruel.

❉ He is the kind of man who first prepares the bandage, then inflicts the wound.   TALMUD: *Megillah*, 13a

It is cruel not to forgive one who begs for forgiveness.
          RASHI, *Commentaries on the Pentateuch, Numbers*

See also: CONSCIENCE, COMPASSION, GOOD DEEDS, KINDNESS, SIN, VIRTUE

CURSES

Note. Anglo-Saxons may well marvel over the opulent repertoire of curses available to the peoples in Mideastern cultures, where oral maledictions are a sort of popular art form.

Among Jews, swearing is rare but cursing is common; let me explain. By "swearing" I mean the venting of frustration or anger in obscene phrases directed at no one in particular; by "cursing" I mean the invocation of calamity (pain, injury, death) upon someone—hoping that God, though not directly asked to do so (indeed, usually asked *not* to), will direct his wrath upon the one cursed and in the form requested. For example: "*Damn* this hammer!" is swearing; "May he be buried in the ground and bake bagels, God forbid" is cursing.

One reason why ornamental cursing gives pleasure to Jews is that since fighting was so despised, *verbalized* hostility came to be correspondingly prized. Consider: If you break my jaw, you have merely demonstrated the power of your muscle—which an animal, ignoramus or barbarian can do. If, instead, you hurl a juicy excretion at me, you act like a man, not a beast; you use the wits God gave you—instead of fists, feet, teeth, claws or fangs.

How much sweeter than a blow is the malediction: "May all your teeth fall out—except one!" (Why "except one?" So that you will retain the capacity to be afflicted by toothaches.)

Robert Graves, I think, observed that the more lurid a curse, the less poison it carries; and Maurice Samuel, in his charming *In Praise of Yiddish*, characterizes the

flamboyance of Oriental curses as "arabesques of affliction and gratification [that] dizzy the mind."

The elaboration of Jewish curses reaches staggering
heights of picturesqueness: "May his intestines sound
like a music box"; "May he own a hundred houses, and
in each a hundred rooms, and in each room a hundred
beds; and may he go from bed to bed in search of one
moment's sleep!"

I, for one, am awed by such ingenuity in the catharsis
of disaffection.

—L.R.

✱ I would like to treat him like a treasure: bury him with
care and affection.

✱ God grant him so much breath that he should always be
able to ask what the weather is like—outside.

May God send a fool to help him.

✱ May his stomach churn like a music box.

May his navel turn dizzy.

May a *kazarnya* [armory] fall on his head!

May he grow sick from his satisfactions.

✱ May his buttocks drop off!

Let bunions grow on his bunions, and on his carbuncles—
boils.

May he get sick—and remember it.

May I dance over his corpse and spit prune pits into his
eyes.

✱ May he own five ships of gold—all wrecked.

May a child be named after him soon. [Ashkenazic Jews
were forbidden to name a child after a living person.]

If he had twice as much sense he would be an idiot.

Don't wish him even on his enemies.

May all his teeth fall out—except one [so he can have a
toothache].

May a flood pour over him.

May a thunderbolt find his head.

Like a beet should he grow—with his head in the earth.

A *shvarts* [dark] year upon him!

❋ Let onions grow in his navel.

May he have to crawl on all fours.

He should swell up like ten mountains.

May his name return without his body.

May cramps parade through his bowels.

May delirium guide even his words.

May he need a prescription.

Let him lie in the earth and bake bagels.

May he spend all he has on physicians.

May he beat his head against the wall.

May he be seized by the cholera.

May he be seized by a nine-year convulsion.

May prolonged nausea overcome him.

BUT REMEMBER, PLEASE:

A curse does not arrive as fast as a telegram. [Don't take curses too seriously.]

Like a sparrow flitting, a swallow fluttering,
The curse that is groundless will not reach home.
Book of Proverbs, 26 : 2

A curse uttered by a sage will be fulfilled, even if it was undeserved.   TALMUD: *Berakoth*, 56a

CUSTOMS

Old tunes can be found for many a new song.

❋ Customs are more powerful than laws.
TALMUD: *Yebamoth*, 61a

See how the people act, and that is the law.
TALMUD: *Berakoth*, 45a

When you come to a city, follow its customs.

> MIDRASH: *Exodus Rabbah*, 47

Some of the roads most used lead nowhere.

See also: COMMUNITY, HABIT, LAW, TRADITION

CYNICISM

If you want men to like you, agree with them.

> —Hasidic saying

❋ The Torah spread light, but it is money that gives warmth.

D

DANGER

I have escaped with the skin of my teeth.

> *Book of Job*, 19 : 20

See also: ADVERSITY, SUFFERING, TROUBLE

DAUGHTERS

❋ What the daughter does, the mother did.

The man who marries off a daughter doesn't regret the dowry.

He who seeks the daughter flatters the mother.

❋ A good daughter makes a good daughter-in-law.

Fill your house with guests and you'll marry off your daughter.

A married daughter is like a piece of bread—cut off.

To marry off a daughter is like removing a hump from your back.

A daughter is a treasure—and a cause of sleeplessness.
BEN SIRACH, *Ecclesiasticus*, 42 : 9

Some daughters are more precious than sons.
RABBI HAI GAON

A beautiful daughter is worth—half her dowry.
SHOLEM ALEICHEM

It is hard to raise sons; and much harder to raise daughters.
SHOLEM ALEICHEM

See also: FAMILY, FATHERS, GIRLS, MOTHERS, WOMEN

DAUGHTERS-IN-LAW

❊ A daughter-in-law is always a bit of a mother-in-law.

One can talk to a daughter, yet mean the daughter-in-law.

The daughter is scolded, but the daughter-in-law is meant.

A daughter-in-law can no more live under the same roof with her mother-in-law than a goat can live in the same barn with a tiger.

See also: FAMILY, MOTHERS-IN-LAW, SONS-IN-LAW, WOMEN

DEATH

Note. Judaic law forbids display or ostentation at a funeral. The rabbis instituted simple burial rites to enforce the idea of "democracy in death," so that no family, however poor, would be shamed by the simplicity of coffin or shroud.

The prayer for the dead is called the *Kaddish*, which extols God, but contains not a single reference to death or mourning. Sholem Aleichem has left us this delightful memory of the *Kaddish* he and his five brothers recited in mourning for their mother:

You should have heard us deliver that *Kaddish!* A pleasure! All our relatives beamed with pride, and strangers envied us. One of our relatives . . . exclaimed, 'When a woman has six sons like that to say *Kaddish* after her, she will surely go straight to paradise. Either that or the world is coming to an end!'*

---

* Quoted in Maurice Samuel, *The World of Sholom Aleichem*, p. 37.

On the anniversary of a death, a memorial candle or lamp is lighted in the home, and another in the synagogue, to burn from sunset to sunset. A burning light is connected with the idea of immortality—perhaps as suggested in Proverbs (20 : 27): "The spirit of man is the candle of the Lord . . ."

It is considered both a *mitzvah* and a duty to attend a funeral. In a small community, everyone was expected to attend—except the teacher (*melamed*), who was enjoined not to interrupt instructing the children, unless a saintly sage or relative had died. At Orthodox funerals, collectors for charity pass among the mourners.

Note to attorneys: Jewish law does not contain the idea of a "legal death"—i.e., a period of time, say seven years, after which a court can declare someone "officially" dead for legal purposes. Changes are being made in Israel and America to allow for missing-in-action cases.

—L.R.

When you start thinking of death, you are no longer certain of life.

❋ Dying while you are young is a great boon in your old age.

❋ It's astonishing how important a man becomes when he dies.

How odd is death: the old often survive the young.

Every man knows he will die, but no man wants to believe it.

❋ All corpses look pious.

As long as one limb moves, men reject the grave.

Death may be free—but it costs a life.

❋ For dying, you always have plenty of time.

Bread and death: everything revolves around them.

We are never late for two occasions: marrying and dying.

It is better not to have had children than to bury them.

Better a noble death than a wretched life.

Death does not knock on the door.

Is there a bad mother, or a good death?

From a cemetery, you cannot "take back."

Better ten times sick than once dead.

❋ The death of the rich is smelled far away.

Better ten times ruined than dead once.

Life is only loaned to man; death is the creditor—who one day will claim it.

All corpses' faces look alike.

❋ To die, you don't need a calendar.

While men live, the whole world is too small—once dead, the grave is large enough.

❋ The road to a cemetery is paved with suffering.

The homeliest life is better than the prettiest death.

When Elijah is the coachman, you travel fast.

No one knows who will see tomorrow.

No man dies before his time.

❋ An old woman, visiting a cemetery, addressed the graves: "How peacefully you sleep, good souls! Still, if you don't mind, I would rather not join you."

Even the best horse, when dead, is only a carcass.

Up to seventy, we learn wisdom—then we die fools.

Death is merely moving from one home to another.
THE KOTZKER RABBI

It is better to go to a house of mourning than to a house of feasting.   *Ecclesiastes*, 2

[When dust returns to dust] the spirit shall return to God, who gave it.   *Ecclesiastes*, 7

The world, which was made for us, abides; but we, for whom it was made, depart.
APOCRYPHA: *II Baruch*, 14 : 5

Love is as strong as death.   *Song of Solomon*, 8 : 6

✻ In death, two worlds meet with a kiss: the world going out and the future coming in.

TALMUD J.: *Yebamoth*, 57a

The dead don't feel the scalpel. TALMUD: *Shabbath*, 13b

When a sage dies, all men should mourn.

TALMUD: *Shabbath*, 105b

No man dies with even half his desires fulfilled.

Don't question God: He may say, "If you're so anxious for answers, come up here."

The death of a woman is felt by no one so keenly as by her husband.   TALMUD: *Sanhedrin*, 22

Sleep is a sixtieth of death.   TALMUD, *Berakoth*, 57b

When you take leave of the dead, say not "Go to peace," but "Go in peace."   TALMUD, *Berakoth*, 64a

✻ In a harbor, two ships sailed: one setting forth on a voyage, the other coming home to port. Everyone cheered the ship going out, but the ship sailing in was scarcely noticed. And a wise man said: "Do not rejoice over a ship that is setting out to sea, for you cannot know what storms it may encounter, what fearful dangers it may have to endure. But rejoice rather over a ship that has safely reached port, and brings home all its passengers in peace."

And this is the way of the world: when a child is born, all rejoice; when a man or woman dies, all weep. We should do the opposite. No one can tell what trials and travails await a child; but when a mortal dies in peace, we should rejoice, for he has completed his long journey, and is leaving this world with the imperishable crown of a good name.

—adapted from the TALMUD

When Death summons a man to appear before his Creator, three friends are his: The first, whom he loves most, is money, but money cannot accompany him one step; his second friend is relatives, but they can only accompany him to the grave, and cannot defend him before the Judge. It is his third friend, whom he does not highly esteem, his good deeds, who can go with him, and can appear before the King, and can obtain his acquittal.

TALMUD

It is nobler to visit a house of mourning than a house of
  feasting.   *Ecclesiastes*, 2

When the time comes for an accounting of man's deeds, it
  is too late to do anything about them.
                          MIDRASH: *Genesis Rabbah*, 84 : 12

❋ Man enters the world with closed hands, as if to say,
  "The world is mine"; he leaves with open hands, as if to
  say, "I take nothing with me."
                       MIDRASH: *Ecclesiastes Rabbah*, 5 : 14

The world weeps when a fruit tree is cut down.
                                              Yalkut Ruveni

On the day of his death, a man feels he has lived but a
  single day.   *Zohar*

"When my time comes to die," said the frog, "I go down
  to the sea, there to be swallowed by one of its creatures;
  thus even my death is a deed of kindness."
                                            Yalkut Shimoni

Fear not death, for it is your destiny.
                          BEN SIRACH, *Ecclesiasticus*, 41 : 3

What is it that troubles you? Death? Who lives forever?
                                          SAMUEL HA-NAGID

❋ Death, the terror of the rich, is the desire of the poor.
                       IBN ZABARA, *Book of Delight*, 7 : 25

What is the cause of death? Life.
    —adapted from IBN ZABARA, *Book of Delight*, 7 : 27

A short life with wisdom is better than a long life without it.
                       MOSES IBN EZRA, *Shirat Yisrael*, 119

God gave us the blessed hope of immortality, through
  which we may console ourselves for the vanity of life,
  and overcome the fear of death.   JEDAIA BEN BEDERSI

See also: ANGELS, BREAD, BURIAL, DESTINY, FAILURE, FU-
  TURE, GOD, THE HEREAFTER, LAZY, LIFE, LIFE and DEATH,
  MAN, RESURRECTION, SUICIDE, WEALTH, WIDOW

DEATH: ANGEL OF DEATH

To summon Death's Angel, send a lazy messenger.

❋ Don't try to swap jokes with the Angel of Death.

The Angel of Death doesn't look at calendars.

The Angel of Death always manages to find an excuse.

❋ It is the Angel of Death who nourishes our synagogues, for if not for the *Kaddish* [prayer for the dead] how many men would attend them?

The Angel of Death may slaughter—but he is always right.

Death's Angel won't let you take money along.

The Angel of Death does not care whether a dead man has a shroud.

❋ If the rich could hire the poor to die for them, the poor would make a very good living.

The Angel of Death has many eyes.

Both the doctor and the Angel of Death kill—but the doctor charges a fee for it.   IBN ZABARA, *Book of Delight*

DEBT

❋ Tears pay no debts.

You can't pay a debt with your pedigree.

You can't pay debts without regrets.

The greatest of worries won't pay the smallest of debts.

Never take the clothes of a woman or a child in repayment of a debt.   —adapted from *Exodus*, 22 : 25–6

It is better to eat herbs and fear no creditors, than eat meat and have to hide from them. TALMUD: *Pesahim*, 114a

The man who does not pay his debts but gives alms commits robbery.   *Sefer Hasidim*

Better go to sleep without supper than get up in debt.
         JUDAH IBN TIBBON, *A Father's Admonition*

See also: BORROWING, CREDITORS, LENDING, TEARS

DECEIT

If his word was a bridge, men would be afraid to cross it.

It's not hard to deceive people—once.

He who deceives me lets shame fall upon him; if he deceives me twice, let shame fall on me.

❋ From afar you fool people; nearby, you fool only yourself.

Like a madman who hurls deadly firebrands is the man who deceives his neighbors and says, "Was I not joking?"
                                    Book of Proverbs, 26 : 19

The kiss of an enemy is full of deceit.
                        adapted from *Book of Proverbs*, 27 : 6

Deception in words is worse than deception in money.
                                    TALMUD: *Baba Mezi'a*, 58

See also: APPEARANCES, CONSCIENCE, COURTSHIP, FALSEHOOD, FLATTERY, FRAUD, FRIENDS/FRIENDSHIP, FRIENDS: FALSE FRIENDS, IDEAS, LIARS/LIES, SELF-DECEPTION

DECORUM

When the guest coughs, he needs a spoon.

❋ Better be embarrassed than ashamed.

Never address a slave as "slave" for to do so is to humiliate him.

A rabbi's daughter is not allowed to do what a bathkeeper's daughter is.

Don't humiliate a beggar by giving him alms in a way that attracts attention.

Before taking leave, one should not finish an ordinary conversation with idle talk, but with some comment on halaka [law]. —adapted from TALMUD, *Berakoth*, 31a

For a well-bred man, a little is adequate.
                        BEN SIRACH: *Ecclesiasticus*, 31 : 19

When your neighbor is in trouble, abstain from visible pleasures.   GERSONIDES

Among those who stand, do not sit; among those who sit, do not stand; among those who laugh, do not weep; among those who weep, do not laugh.
                                    HILLEL in *Tosefta Berakoth*, 2

The wise man should not walk with a haughty expression;
nor should he walk with a slow gait, like a woman; or
run about like a madman; or stoop like a hunchback; he
should gaze downward, as though in prayer, and walk
like a man preoccupied.

MAIMONIDES, *Mishneh Torah*, 5 : 7–13

See also: APPEARANCES, BOORS, CHARM, CLEANLINESS,
CLOTHING, CONDUCT, CONSIDERATION, COURTESY, HONOR/
HONORS, MANNERS

DEEDS

If a man does despicable deeds, let him not depend upon
the merits of his parents.

Deeds are male, words female.

They say to fruit-bearing trees, "Why do you not make any
noise?" and the trees reply, "Our fruits are sufficient
advertisement."   MIDRASH: *Genesis Rabbah*, 16 : 3

Whether Jew or Gentile, man or woman, rich or poor—it
is according to deeds that God's Presence descends.

MIDRASH: *Eliahu Rabbah*, 8

❋ What is hateful to you, do not to your fellow man: that
is the whole Law; all the rest is interpretation.

HILLEL in TALMUD: *Shabbath*, 31b

Nothing accomplishes nothing.   BAHYA IBN PAQUDA

The intention is the foundation of the deed.

MOSES IBN EZRA, *Shirat Yisrael*, p. 141

See also: BOASTING, CONDUCT, GOOD DEEDS, TALK, VIRTUE

DEMOCRACY

The many (people) have more wisdom than the few.

In the multitude of counsellors there is safety.

Book of Proverbs, 11 : 14

We must not appoint a leader over the community without
first consulting the people.   TALMUD: *Berakoth*, 55a

❋ Happy is the time where the great listen to the small, for in such a generation the small will listen to the great.
TALMUD: *Rosh Hashanah*, 25b

❋ The Torah can be interpreted in forty-nine different ways; and God instructed Moses, "Decide according to the majority." TALMUD J.: *Sanhedrin*, 4 : 2

See also: EQUALITY, GOVERNMENT, LAW, MASSES, POLITICS

DEMONS

A demon is at home with demons.

The world is full of demons; at least drive them out of yourself.

Obsessions are worse than diseases.

False dreams are the works of demons.

See also: DEVIL, DISEASE, EVIL, HELL, SATAN, SIN, VIRTUE

DEPENDENCY

The fruit should pray for the welfare of the leaves.

❋ If the hunter can't shoot, his hound goes hungry, too.

See also: CAUSE AND EFFECT, CIRCUMSTANCES, DEPENDENCE

DESIRE

No man leaves this world with even half of his desires satisfied.

Desire confuses the senses.

Desire can blind the wise.

Desires are the net of folly.
MOSES IBN EZRA, *Shirat Yisrael*

The greatest misers with money are the biggest spendthrifts with desires. MOSES IBN EZRA, *Shirat Yisrael*

The man who is not careful about obeying the law against stealing will be less careful about the law against covet-

ing; whatever his eyes see, his heart will desire—and
with a longing that can never be satisfied.

LEONE DA MODENA

See also: ENVY, GREED, JEALOUSY, LUST, SIN

DESPAIR

❋ A drowning man will grab even the point of a sword.

You can't drive away the darkness with sticks or weapons.
The only way is to light a candle and the darkness will
disappear by itself. Our candle is the Torah.

"THE CHOFETZ CHAIM"

See also: HOPE, PESSIMISM, RESIGNATION, SUFFERING, TORAH

DESTINY

❋ The man who is destined to drown will drown in a glass
of water.

God is our father, destiny our step-father.

What can't be avoided can be welcomed.

Weep for the man who knows not his good fortune, and
laugh for him who knows not his destiny.

TALMUD: *Sanhedrin*, 103a

See also: ASTROLOGY, DEATH, FATE, FORTUNE, HEREAFTER,
LUCK

DETERMINATION

The hardest rock will yield to those who drill with determination.

Where men truly wish to go, there their feet will manage
to take them.   TALMUD: *Sukkah*, 53a

See also: PERSEVERANCE, WILL

DEVIL

Note. Though Jewish theology and literature are rife with
references to the Evil One, Jews seem to have no concept quite as anthropomorphic as the Devil. The idea of

Satan (in Job) is the closest Jews came to a physical image of the incarnation of evil, a cunning and maleficent tempter; the rabbis, instead, preferred to refer to "the Evil Impulse." (See headnote for EVIL).

—L.R.

If you live with a devil, you become a devil.

A man who looks better than the Devil is promptly called handsome.

✱ The moment you sit down to a really big meal, the Devil sends you a guest.

Should the Devil [Evil Impulse] say: "Sin—God will forgive you," don't believe him. TALMUD: *Hagigah*, 16a

Satan is especially active at the time of danger.
RASHI, *Commentaries on the Pentateuch, Genesis*

See also: COMPANIONS, DEMONS, EVIL, HELL, IMPULSE, SATAN, SIN, VIRTUE

DIASPORA

Note. "History relates very few measures that produced so vast an amount of calamity. In three short months, all unconverted Jews were obliged, under pain of death, to abandon the Spanish soil. Multitudes, falling into the hands of the pirates who swarmed around the coast, were plundered of all they possessed and reduced to slavery; multitudes died of famine or of plague, or were murdered or tortured with horrible cruelty by the African savages. About 80,000 (Jews) took refuge in Portugal, relying on the promise of the king. Spanish priests lashed the Portuguese into fury, and the king was persuaded to issue an edict which threw even that of Isabella into the shade. All the adult Jews were banished from Portugal; but first all their children below the age of fourteen were taken from them to be educated as Christians. Then, indeed, the cup of bitterness was filled to the brim. The serene fortitude with which the exiled people had borne so many and such grievous calamities gave way, and was replaced by the wildest paroxysms of despair. When at last, childless and broken-hearted, they sought to leave the land, they found that the ships had been purposely detained, and the allotted time having expired, they were reduced to slavery and baptized by force. A great peal of rejoicing filled the Peninsula, and proclaimed that the triumph of the Spanish priests was complete."

—W. E. H. LECKY,
History of Rationalism in Europe, vol. II

"The Greeks, I hear, would weep when a babe was born, and rejoice when an old man died; it seemed fitting to cry for the newborn, since he is entering the valley of weeping; and it is fitting to rejoice for the dead, since they have gone to the final place of rest. But Jews ought to weep when they are born and when they die and in the days between. They suffer the sorrows and evils of exile; their enemies seek every occasion to harm or humiliate them. . . . I grieve for them not because they are Jews, but because they are poor, powerless and lowly. We Jews have no other kingdom except that which the Lord of all the Universe gave us. He said to Isaiah: " 'I will look on him who is poor and contrite in spirit.' "

—adapted from SOLOMON IBN VERGA,
Shebet Yehuda, 29

See: HEREAFTER, ISRAEL, JEWS, PERSECUTION, SABBATH; and GLOSSARY: DIASPORA

DISCIPLES

There are four kinds of disciples: Quick to learn, but quick to forget: in him the gift is canceled by the failing; slow to learn, but slow to forget: in him the failing is canceled by the gift; quick to learn and slow to forget: his is a fortunate lot; slow to learn and quick to forget: his is an evil plight.   *Sayings of the Fathers*, 5 : 18

See also: PROSELYTES, SCHOLARS, STUDY

DISCIPLINE

Good men need no discipline, and bad men are beyond its help.

The man who spares the rod hates his son.

Book of Proverbs, 13 : 24

Don't make a fence that is more important [expensive] than
   what is fenced in.   MIDRASH: *Genesis Rabbah*, 19 : 3

See also: CHARACTER, CHILDREN, CONSCIENCE, TEMPER

DISCRETION

As a jewel of gold in a swine's snout, so is a pretty woman
   who is without discretion.   *Book of Proverbs*, 11 : 22

❋ Your friend has a friend, and your friend's friend has a
   friend [so be discreet].   TALMUD: *Kethuboth*, 109b

Don't say "Hang this up for me" to one from a family
   where there was a hanging.
                           TALMUD: *Baba Mezi'a*, 59b

Never shame a man by rebuking him in public.
         Rashi, *Commentaries on the Pentateuch, Leviticus*

When you speak at night lower your voice; when you speak
   by day, look around first.
                           IBN GABIROL, *Choice of Pearls*

The fewer a man's words, the fewer his mistakes.
                           IBN GABIROL, *Choice of Pearls*

See also: CONSIDERATION, JUDGMENT, MANNERS, PRUDENCE,
   TACT

DISEASE

❋ An *aynredenish* [obsession] is worse than a disease.

Don't tell a sick man to get up, or a healthy one to lie down.

If you're not in pain, don't cry "Oy!"

❋ No matter where you place a sick man, he's still in pain.

Sometimes the remedy is worse than the ailment.

❋ When there's a cure, it was only half a disease.

Melancholy creates diseases—which happiness cures.

Envy is a disease that gnaws at the soul.

The door closed to good deeds opens to disease.

God sends cures for diseases.

Poverty in a home is worse than fifty plagues.
                              TALMUD: *Baba Bathra*, 116a

For one sick, six things are good: to sneeze, to perspire, to
open the bowels, to emit semen, to sleep, and to dream.
                    —adapted from TALMUD, *Berakoth*, 57b

The fox does not get sick from breathing the dust of his
own den.   —adapted from TALMUD: *Kethuboth*, 71b

✻ The words of Torah heal the soul, not the body.
                              MAIMONIDES, *Mishneh Torah*

The idle man, even if he has all he needs, will end in weakness, insanity and disease.   SAADIA GAON

It is a serious disease to worry over what has not occurred.
                              IBN GABIROL

See also: DOCTORS, HEALTH, MEDICINE, PAIN, SICKNESS,
SUFFERING.

DISHONESTY

✻ When a crook kisses you, count your teeth.

What he says he doesn't mean, and what he means he
doesn't say.

One crook can't fool another.

He who does not take care of the property of another is
dishonest.   TALMUD: *Baba Mezi'a*, 24a

See also: DECEIT, HONESTY, LIARS/LIES, THIEVES

DIVORCE

Note. As with the status of women in Jewish life, so the
conditions of divorce are often misinterpreted by those
who read and run. Ancient texts are quoted by those
ignorant of the subsequent profound changes in rabbinical decisions, and in actual practice among Jews.
    The Torah gives a husband the right to divorce his
wife—but *not*, as is sometimes assumed, easily or arbitrarily. Divorce was regarded as a calamity, a blow to

the integrity of the home, a defeat for the perpetuation
of the community. The Talmudic rabbis, following the
prophet Malachi, who condemned divorce, said that
"the very altar sheds tears" for the man who divorces
his wife (Sanhedrin, 22).

The marriage contract (*ketubah*), from very early
times, protected a Jewish wife from her husband's hasty,
selfish, or capricious desire for an abrogation of the
marriage. Alimony, totally unknown in the Biblical era,
was begun to help Jewish women in the first century
before the Christian Era. Since the year 1000, a religious
(as distinguished from a civil) divorce terminates a
marriage among Orthodox Jews *only if both husband
and wife agree to it*—and if the civil courts grant a civil
divorce. (Reform rabbis do not ask for a religious divorce, in addition to a civil divorce, before a husband or
wife may remarry.)

Down the ages, Jewish laws on divorce have been
modified in favor of the wife. The denigration of European women in the Middle Ages found no counterpart
in Jewish mores—where, indeed, the status of women
was heightened. Maimonides declared that if a husband
was not satisfying his wife's conjugal rights, or was re-
pulsive to her, she could win a divorce. "A woman," said
Maimonides, "is not like a captive, compelled to consort
with a man against her will."

In general, divorce is discouraged—in whatever branch
of Judaism; rabbis are bound by their office to try to
exhaust every possibility for reconciliation. Where it is
unmistakable that domestic discords cannot be healed,
that marital harmony and love have died, divorce is
permitted.

A useful summary of Jewish attitudes to, and laws
about, divorce will be found in *Jews and Divorce* (edited
by Jacob Fried, KTAV Publishing House, New York,
1968). —L.R.

Each day they decide to divorce, but each night they head
for bed.

If a woman can't make a *kugl* [noodle or potato pudding],
divorce her.

❊ When a divorced man marries a divorced woman, four
go to bed. TALMUD: *Pesahim*, 112a

❊ A man should not marry a woman with the mental reservation that, after all, he can divorce her.

TALMUD: *Yebamoth*, 37b

❊ Tears fall on God's altar for whoever divorces his first wife.   TALMUD: *Gittin*, 90a

See also: ADULTERY, MARRIAGE, MEN AND WOMEN, WIVES

DOCTORS

❊ Don't ask the doctor; ask the patient.

A new doctor has one blind eye. [The family doctor knows you better.]

Don't live in a town where there are no doctors.

The greatest doctor is time.

Doctors and gravediggers are partners.

The door that is closed to good deeds opens up for doctors.

A great doctor works with an angel at his side.

All physicians, even good ones, will end in Hell.*

Doctors can cure anything except poverty.

❊ No physician can cure a prejudice, which is a blindness in the mind.

❊ Where there is no wine, drugs are useful.

TALMUD: *Baba Bathra*, 58b

A physician who takes no fee is worth no fee.

TALMUD: *Baba Kamma*, 85a

Pay homage to the physician before you need him.

MIDRASH: *Exodus Rabbah*, 21 : 7

See also: DISEASE, HEALTH, MEDICINE

DOWRY

Sell even the Holy Scrolls to make sure that a poor girl has a dowry.

Beauty is half the dowry.

---

* I do not understand why.—L.R.

You can't get a scholar without a dowry.

The more defects a girl has, the larger the dowry she needs.

See also: DAUGHTERS, MARRIAGE, OBLIGATION

DREAMS

Note. Man sleeps. Man dreams. No matter what his creed or race, culture or time. In ancient Gaza or medieval Japan, modern Iceland or (certainly) Beverly Hills. Whether cave man, Confucian, Inca—or space man heading for the moon.

Men dream in joy or terror, or in phantasmagoria of wonders not seen on land or sea. No people has ever been indifferent to the mystery and magic of dreams. No people has failed to convert them into omens, prophecies, divinations.

The Old Testament assigned great importance to dreams, which were thought to be one way in which the Almighty (blessed be He) makes known His wishes—especially to the prophets: thus, the revelations to Joseph and Daniel, and the dreams Yahweh sent non-Jews: Pharaoh, in the Book of Genesis, and Balaam, in the Book of Numbers.

Jews, traditionally, believe that the soul returns to God each night and is returned, by God's blessing, upon awakening; the lovely prayer said upon awakening thanks the Lord "for returning my soul unto me." The ancient Egyptians thought that dreams foretell the future. The Greeks held that dreams cure sickness. The Romans prayed to Mercury before retiring, asking the god to send them good visions. Natives of the Fiji Islands, like a thousand other groupings of mankind, believe that their souls leave their bodies in a dream. The Iroquois regarded dreams as supernatural commands, which had to be executed.

Calpurnia's dream might have saved Caesar and changed the world. Constantine's apparition of a luminous cross, inscribed *In hoc signo vinces*, drove him to march against Maxentius at Saxa Rubra, and the dreamer entered Rome in triumph, behind a purple banner on which was emblazoned what he said he had beheld: a Greek *Chi* and *Rho*, the first two letters of "Christos." Many a historian has speculated on what turns our history would have made had not Constantine lifted a small, harassed faith onto the very throne of imperial power, made Christianity the state religion, and sent Roman legions to the Bosphorus, to build a new Jerusalem there . . . all because of a dream.

Long before Sigmund Freud, this immortal passage was written:

Every man appears to have certain instincts, but in some men these passions are controlled by reason and, the nobler desires prevailing over them, the instincts are either wholly supressed or reduced in strength. I mean particularly those desires which are awake when the taming power of the personality is asleep. For it is in sleep that the wild beast in our nature rears up and walks about naked. And there is no conceivable folly or shame or crime, however unnatural, not excepting incest or parricide, of which such a nature may not be guilty. In all of us, even in good men, there is a latent wild beast, who peers out in sleep.

The author was Plato.

I find it surprising that except for Joseph and Daniel, no one in the Old Testament *interpreted* a dream. This singular gap was remedied in the Talmud, where one of the longest haggadic sequences, with no digressions, sought to analyze dreams (*Berakoth:* 55b–57a). The interpretations are often quaint, often cryptic, often saturated in superstition. One smiles over the fanciful meanings read into dreamed elephants, asses, horses, snakes; or the solemn adjudication that if in Palestine you dream you are naked that is a sign of virtue, but if in Babylon, it reveals a failure to perform enough good deeds.

Yet, some rabbinical insights about the kingdom of sleep are astonishing. It is these, and the charming folk sayings Jews made up about the phantoms of the night, I now give you.

—L.R.

❋ In sleep, it is not we who sin—but our dreams.

Only in dreams are carrots as big as bears.

❋ The dumplings in a dream are not dumplings, but dreams.

A dream is a fool—for it is sleep that is the master.

Ask for three things: a good wife, a good year, a good dream.

❊ Thieves have easy jobs, but bad dreams.

We can make the dream more important than the night.

In dreams, fools get rich easily.

What good is a sweet dream if the dawn is cold?

A fool dreams foolish dreams.

In bed, thoughts come into your mind so that you may know the thoughts of your heart.
> —adapted from the *Book of Daniel*, 2 : 20–30

I [God] do speak . . . in a dream.
> *Book of Numbers*, 12 : 6

❊ During the night [dream], a man's soul testifies as to what he did during the day. *Zohar*

❊ A dream not interpreted is like a letter not read—so what harm can it do?
> —adapted from TALMUD: *Berakoth*, 55b

Just as wheat cannot be without some straw, so no dream is without some nonsense. TALMUD: *Berakoth*, 55a

❊ Men see in their dreams only that which is suggested by their own thoughts. TALMUD: *Berakoth*, 55a

Any dream is better than that of being hungry.
> —adapted from TALMUD: *Berakoth*, 55a

Neither a happy dream nor a bad one is ever entirely fulfilled. —adapted from TALMUD: *Berakoth*, 55a

All dreams "follow the mouth"—i.e., the interpretation; hence, are fulfilled.
> —adapted from TALMUD: *Berakoth*, 55b

The sadness of a bad dream, like the pleasures of a good one, are sufficient [they need not be fulfilled].
> —adapted from TALMUD: *Berakoth*, 55b

If you have a dream which makes you sad, have it interpreted—in the presence of three others.
> —adapted from TALMUD, *Berakoth*, 55b

When a dream speaks truth, it is through an angel; when a
dream speaks falsely, it is through a demon.

> RABA, in TALMUD: *Berakoth*, 55b

There are twenty-four dream interpreters in Jerusalem—
and each gives a different interpretation.

> —adapted from TALMUD, *Berakoth*, 55b

To those who paid him, Bar Hedya interpreted a dream
favorably; to those who did not, he interpreted a dream
unfavorably. —adapted from TALMUD: *Berakoth*, 56a

If one dreams of intercourse with one's mother, it means
he can expect to get understanding—for it is written,
"Yea, thou wilt call understanding 'mother.'"

> TALMUD: *Berakoth*, 57a (the quotation is
> adapted from the *Book of Proverbs*, 2 : 3)

If one dreams of intercourse with his sister, he can expect
to gain wisdom, for it has been written: "Say to wisdom,
thou art my sister."

> TALMUD, *Berakoth*, 57a (the quotation is from
> *Book of Proverbs*, 7 : 4)

If you see King David in a dream, you may hope for piety;
if you see King Solomon, you may hope for wisdom; if
you see King Ahab, fear for punishment.

> TALMUD: *Berakoth*, 57b

If, in a dream, you see the Book of Psalms, you may hope
to gain piety; if you see the Book of Proverbs, you may
hope to gain wisdom; if you see the Book of Job, fear
punishment. TALMUD: *Berakoth*, 57b

O Lord: as Thou turned the curse of Balaam into a blessing, so turn all my dreams into something good.

> in the Siddur (prayer book) recited between
> benedictions in some congregations

There is reality in any dream—except a dream during a
fast. —adapted from *Shulhan Aruk*

Dreams lift up fools. BEN SIRACH, *Ecclesiasticus*, 34 : 1

A good man has a bad dream to urge him to repentance; a
bad man has a good dream to give him some reward in
this world.

> —adapted from RASHI, Commentary on *Berakoth*

Three kinds of dreams are fulfilled: the dream of early
  morning, a friend's dream about you, and the dream that
  is interpreted within the dream. To which some add: the
  dream which is repeated.
                    RABBI JOHANAN, in TALMUD: *Berakoth*, 55a

The joy a blind man gets from a dream nullifies itself.
                    —adapted from RABBI JOSEPH in TALMUD:
                                              Berakoth, 55a

A bad dream can be worse than a flogging.
      adapted from RABBI HISDA in TALMUD: *Berakoth*, 55a

A part of a dream may be fulfilled, but never the whole.
                    —adapted from RABBI HISDA in TALMUD:
                                              Berakoth, 55a

See also: FOOLS, ILLUSION, SLEEP

DRESS

Eat according to your means, but dress above them.

❋ Men greet you according to your dress; they say good-
  bye according to your sense [wisdom].

See also: APPEARANCE, CONDUCT, DECORUM, ILLUSION,
  VANITY

DRUNKARDS

Note. Jewish drunkards are exceedingly rare (even pro-
portionately, in these bibulous times), and the souse is
almost unknown in Jewish literature. Yet drinking is not
foreign to Jewish culture. A Jewish child may be introduced to a sip of wine at an early age, and the blessing
over wine sanctifies each Sabbath. The goodness of wine
is often mentioned in the Bible; and many Biblical metaphors use wine as an allusion to prosperity and good
times. The Talmud holds that drinking wine in moderation "unfolds a man's brain," and some *hasidim* said a
teetotaler cannot possess great wisdom.

The rabbis believed that wine possessed curative prop-
erties: "Wine is the greatest of all medicines." "Where
wine is lacking, drugs are necessary," Rabbi Huna said.
"Wine helps to open the heart to reasoning." But the

sages always stressed moderation in drinking, as in everything else—except study.

Jews have a certain contempt for anyone who loses
control of his faculties, or acts in an uncouth, "bestial"
manner.

. . . drunkards were rarely seen among Jews. When night
came and a man wanted to pass away time, he did not
hasten to a tavern to take a drink, but went to pore over a
book or joined a group which—either with or without a
teacher—revered books. . . . Physically worn out by their
day's toil, they sat over open volumes, playing the austere
music of the Talmud . . . or the sweet melodies of . . .
piety of the ancient sages.*

Drinking, if not drunkenness, has clearly increased
among American Jews; I do *not* attribute this to the delightful injunction in the Talmud: "When a man faces
his Maker, he will also have to account for those pleasures of life he failed to enjoy."

Traditional Jewish pride in sobriety is eloquently expressed by Israel Zangwill, in his classic *Children of the
Ghetto**:*

On thousands of squalid homes the light of Sinai shone. . . .
The Ghetto welcomed the Sabbath Bride with proud sound
and humble feast. . . . All around, their neighbors sought
distraction in the public-houses, and their tipsy bellowings
resounded through the streets. . . . Here and there the
voice of a beaten woman rose on the air. But no Son of
the Convenant was among the [drunken] revellers or the
wife-beaters. The Jews remained a chosen race, a peculiar
people, faulty enough, but redeemed at least from the
grosser vices—a little human islet won from the waters of
animalism by the genius of ancient engineers.   —L.R.

❀ When one man tells you you're drunk, hesitate; when
two tell you, think it over; when three tell you—lie down.

The tongue of the drunk reveals what is on the minds of the
sober.

❀ It's better to be dead drunk than dead hungry.

----

* A. J. Heschel, *The Earth Is the Lord's*, Abelard-Schuman, New York,
1964, p. 45.
** Jewish Publication Society, 1892.

When drink enters, judgment leaves.

❋ When a drunkard has no whiskey, he talks of whiskey.

❋ A saloonkeeper may love a drunkard—but won't let him marry his daughter.

❋ A drunkard can't help harming someone.

❋ Drunkenness exiles a man from his family.

The workman who is a drunkard will never get rich.

They reel to and fro, and stagger like drunken men, and are at their wit's end.   *Book of Psalms*, 107 : 27

Wine is a mocker, strong drink a brawler; none who reels under them is wise.   *The Book of Proverbs*, 20 : 1

A drunkard cannot plead his case.
                                   NACHMAN OF BRATSLAV

A teetotaler is rarely wise.   THE KORETSER RABBI

See also: FOOD AND DRINK, LIQUOR, TEMPERANCE, WINE

DUTY

A scholar profanes the Name of God if he does not pay the butcher at once.
                    —adapted from TALMUD: *Yomah*, 86a

When Rabbi Ammi's hour to die came, he wept bitterly; and his nephew asked, "But why do you weep? Is there any Torah you have not learned and taught? Is there any kindness you have not practiced? And you never accepted public office, or sat in judgment on others." The Rabbi replied: "That is why I weep: I was given the ability to establish justice, but never carried it out."
                    MIDRASH: *Tanhuma on Mishpatim*

When a man knows any evidence in favor of a defendant, he is not free to keep silent, for in doing so he may become responsible for the defendant's death.
                    MIDRASH: *Sifre Kedoshim*, 19

Man should perform his duties to his fellow men even as to God.   MISHNAH: *Shekalim*

Those who warn the wicked are saved from blame, even if the warning goes unheeded.   *Zohar*

A man should remember three things: that he has only one day to live; that he has only the page before him to study; and that he is the only Jew on whom the survival of Torah depends.   "THE CHOFETZ CHAIM"

See also: CHARITY, EVIDENCE, GOOD DEEDS, LAW, OBLIGATION, RESPONSIBILITY, STUDY

E

EARS

Ears have flaps, to cover them when slander is uttered.

❋ Ears are the doors to the heart.

❋ Your ears belong to yourself, but your tongue is heard by others.

Even a road has ears.   MIDRASH: *Leviticus Rabbah*, 32

If the ear is stuffed, what use is the [warning] bell?
                    IBN GABIROL, *Choice of Pearls*

Ears are the gates to the mind.
                    MOSES IBN EZRA, *Shirat Yisrael*

The ear is more useful than the eye for knowledge.
                                        GERONDI

See also: FACE, LEARNING, SLANDER

EATING AND DRINKING

(*See:* FOOD)

EDEN

See HEAVEN, PARADISE

EDUCATION

"In an unlettered world, when even kings could not sign their names, they had already developed a system of universal education, so that an illiterate Jew was, even in the Dark Ages, a contradiction in terms."*

CECIL ROTH

Note. It is remarkable how powerful and pervasive the role of education became among Jews, wherever they lived. Jews felt that knowledge about God's Torah must be perpetuated—and depended on the amount of learning transmitted to the young; hence every Jewish community provided an education—no matter how poor the community or how lowly the young scholar. Rabbinical authority even forbade a Jew to reside in any village that had no teacher of Hebrew for the young.

Jewish boys began studying as early as the age of three. They would study six to ten hours a day, six days a week. Many received their Hebrew education in a room (*cheder*) in the home of a *melamed* (teacher); in the larger (*Talmud Torah*) schools, there were several rooms and more than one teacher. These schools customarily were supported by the community and charged no tuition. A student of Abelard wrote:

> Christians educate their sons . . . for gain. . . . A Jew, however poor, had he ten sons would put them all to letters, not for gain . . . but to the understanding of God's laws; and not only his sons, but his daughters.**

Centuries before "adult education" courses were instituted, such education was common in Jewish communities as an obligation of religion. Each morning before going to work, and each evening after work, Jews gathered—in the synagogue, or outside its entrance, or in the House of Study attached—for communal study and colloquia on the Torah, Talmud, the work of great sages and scholars, the on-going, never-interrupted interpretations of the Law.

The Jews' extreme emphasis on education was expressed not only in the most intense effort to educate one's sons, but in the longing for a son-in-law who would be a scholar. This was considered a great honor. It was quite common for a family, as part of a girl's dowry, to pledge the support of the young couple for a number of years. The son-in-law

---

* In *Essays in Jewish Booklore*, KTAV, New York, 1971, p. 179.
** *Great Jewish Personalities in Ancient and Medieval Times*, edited by Simon Novick, B'nai Brith Publishers, New York, p. 240.

often would move into his in-laws' home, there to receive free room and board, and devote himself solely to Talmudic studies.

In Eastern Europe, many women supported their husbands for a lifetime so that the men need never do anything but study Talmud, frequent the Bet Midrash ("house of study") and the synagogue, and thus add to Israel's glory and the Jews' hopes of salvation from the miseries of life on earth.   —L.R.

❃ In time, even a bear can be taught to dance.

If the student is good, so is the teacher.

❃ To educate fools is folly.
                            —adapted from *Book of Proverbs*, 16 : 11

A village without a school should be abolished.
                                        TALMUD: *Shabbath*, 119a

The very world rests on the breath of children in the schoolhouse.   TALMUD: *Shabbath*, 119b

Educating a fool is putting him in chains.
            —adapted from BEN SIRACH, *Ecclesiasticus*, 21 : 19

The education of children must never be interrupted, even to rebuild the Temple.   TALMUD: *Shabbath*, 119b

Six things are not fit for an educated man: to walk in the street perfumed, to walk alone at night, to wear worn shoes, to dally with a woman too long in the street, to sit at table with illiterate men, to arrive late at the synagogue.   TALMUD: *Berakoth*, 43b

If you don't teach the ox to plow when he's young, it will be difficult to teach him when he is grown.
                                MIDRASH: *Midrash Mishle*, 22

Don't poke fun at an uneducated man: you may mock your own ancestors.   BEN SIRACH, *Ecclesiasticus*, 8 : 4

See also: LEARNING, SCHOLARS, SCHOLARSHIP, STUDY, TEACHERS

EFFORT

When you must, you can.

❃ Peeling an egg does not put it into your mouth.

Roasted doves don't fly into your mouth unaided.

If you sweep the whole house, you will find everything.

See also: DETERMINATION, LAZINESS

EGOTISM

❋ He thinks he can hear a flea cough and a roach sneeze.

❋ There is no one more lonely than those who love only themselves.

They are madly in love, he with himself, she with herself.

Egotists always grumble, for egotism can never be satisfied.

I cannot be the judge in the case of a student of the Law, because I love him as myself—and no one can see a fault in himself.
                              RAB ASHI in TALMUD: *Shabbath*, 119a

There is more hope for a fool than for a man wise in his own eyes.   *Book of Proverbs*, 29 : 20

Man cannot see anything to his own disadvantage.
                              TALMUD: *Shabbath* 119a

See also: CONCEIT, PRIDE, SELF-CENTEREDNESS, SELF-ESTEEM, SELFISHNESS, VANITY

EMOTIONS

Every heart has its own secrets.

Secrets are betrayed by the face.

An orphan eats much, an unhappy heart talks much.

❋ Sugar in the mouth won't help bitterness in the heart.

When the eyes don't see, the heart won't feel.

Feelings that don't show on the face lie on the heart.

One heart sympathizes with another.

❋ When the heart is full, the eyes overflow.
                              SHOLEM ALEICHEM

See also: GRIEF, HEART, PASSION, SORROW, SUFFERING

ENDS AND MEANS

❋ You can't chew with someone else's teeth.

Without a hand, you can't make a fist.

He who has bread will find a knife.

❋ Those who want to beat a dog always find a stick.

Every pot finds its cover.

To cite the end is no justification of the means.
                                    —adapted from TALMUD

The man who needs the fire must fan it.
                                MIDRASH: *Samuel Rabbah*, 9

See also: CAUSE AND EFFECT, CIRCUMSTANCES, CONTEXT

ENDURANCE

(*See:* FORTITUDE)

ENEMY

Only one God—but so many enemies.

No enemy can do a man as much harm as he does himself.

A tongue is a dangerous enemy.

Enemies don't come free, you must pay for them.

❋ "Rejoice not at thine enemy's fall"—but don't rush to pick him up either.

When you get a slap, you get an enemy, too.

❋ A friend you have to buy; enemies you get for nothing.

❋ Whether rabbi or street cleaner, everyone has enemies.

Better a good enemy than a bad friend.

Be careful when your enemy speaks honey.

It's easy to get an enemy, but hard to find a friend.

❋ It is better that my enemy see good in me than that I see bad in him.

Who is a hero? He who turns an enemy into a friend.
                                Abot de Rabbi Nathan, ch. 23

Peace after enmity is sweeter than sweetness.

If your enemy is hungry, give him bread; if he is thirsty, give him water. *Book of Proverbs*, 25 : 21

Sincere are the words of a friend;
But deceitful are the kisses of an enemy.
Book of Proverbs, 27 : 6

The kisses of an enemy are deceitful.
Book of Proverbs, 27 : 6

Oh, that mine adversary had written a book!
Book of Job, 31 : 35

If two men claim your help and one is your enemy, help him first. TALMUD: *Baba Mezi'a*, 32b

Dogs in a kennel snarl at each other; but when a wolf comes along, they become allies.
TALMUD: *Sanhedrin*, 105a

An enemy is not hidden in adversity.
BEN SIRACH, *Ecclesiasticus:* 12.8

❋ Every type of enmity contains the possibility of being cured, except that of the man who hates you out of envy.
IBN GABIROL, *Choice of Pearls*

A needle's eye is not too narrow for two lovers, but the whole world is not wide enough for two enemies.
IBN GABIROL, *Choice of Pearls*

Every man's enemy is under his own ribs . . .
BAHYA IBN PAQUDA, *Duties of the Heart*

One enemy is one too many. ASHER BEN JEHIEL

See also: ENVY, FRIENDS/FRIENDSHIP; FRIENDSHIP: FALSE FRIENDS, HATE, JEALOUSY, LONELINESS, QUARRELS, WAR

ENVY

❋ Don't count the teeth in someone else's mouth.

❋ He is less upset by his poverty than by your wealth.

❋ Envy turns into hate.

An envious man grows lean over the fatness of his neighbor.

That place seems good where we are not.

Envy destroys contentment.

Another man's tidbit always smells sweet.

Envy is like a disease—it consumes the soul.

A man envies everyone, except the accomplishments of his son or his pupil.

How appetizing is the fish on the other man's table.

Envy, cupidity and ambition drive a man from the world.
> *Sayings of the Fathers*, 4 : 30

Without envy, the world could not abide, for then no one would marry or build a house.
> MIDRASH: *Genesis Rabbah*, 9 : 9

Your revenge over the man who envies you is how he responds to your good fortune. . . . No one hurts himself more: his mourning is ceaseless, his soul grieves, his intellect deteriorates, his heart is in turmoil. Such a man is only cheered up by the misfortune of others.
IBN GABIROL, *Choice of Pearls* (my paraphrase—L.R.)

All types of hatred are curable except that which flows from envy.   IBN GABIROL, *Choice of Pearls*

No man can be called wise unless he possesses three qualities: never to scorn one, less learned, who seeks knowledge; never to envy someone richer; and never to accept a fee for his learning.   IBN GABIROL

❋ Envy is hatred without a cure.
BAHYA BEN ASHER, *Kad ha-Kemah*

❋ Don't envy a sinner: you don't know what awaits him.
—adapted from BEN SIRACH, *Ecclesiasticus*, 9 : 11

The man who covets is guilty of robbery in thought.
NACHMAN OF BRATSLAV

See also: BITTERNESS, CIRCUMSTANCES, COMPLAINT, DESIRE, ENEMY, GRATITUDE, GREED, HATE, HEALTH, JEALOUSY, UTILITY

EQUALITY

Nine rabbis can't make a minyan [quorum for prayers] but ten cobblers can.

In the public baths, all men are equal.

❋ The masses aren't asses.

Be sure you have the support of your equals before you challenge your superiors.

The rich and the poor meet face to face, for the Lord is the creator of them both.　　*Book of Proverbs*, 22 : 2

Before the Eternal One, the highest of men and the lowliest of men are equal.　　MENDEL OF VITEBSK

See also: DEMOCRACY, GOVERNMENT, LAW, MASSES, POLITICS, POWER, STATUS

EROTICA

Note. In the literature of the Jews, erotic material rarely appeared—and where it did, the books were swiftly locked away and their reading banned. The *Shulhan Aruk* of Joseph Caro chastises Immanuel of Rome (*q.v.*) for his lusty verses in his *Mahbarot* ("Compositions"); other rabbis, fearing its "immoral" potentialities, urged publishers and copyists not to disseminate such morally offensive works.

More important than the occasional condemnation of erotica (most of which reads like *Rebecca of Sunnybrook Farm*, compared to our contemporary writings) was the rabbis' fear of, and hostility to, "secular" writings: *i.e.,* books on philosophy, logic, science, the Greeks, the Romans. See headnote: CENSORSHIP

—L.R.

See LUST, PASSION, SEX

ERROR

❋ The man who answers speedily errs speedily.

❋ Experience is our name for accumulated errors.

Error that comes from lack of study is a sin.
　　　　　　　　　　　　Rabbinical maxim

Once error creeps in, it stays.
　　　　　　　　TALMUD: *Baba Bathra*, 21a

God forgets those who reject proof that they are wrong.
                                        NACHMAN OF BRATSLAV

❊ Men make mistakes not because they think they know
  when they do not know, but because they think others
  do not know.   SHOLEM ALEICHEM

See also: KNOWLEDGE, LEARNING, REASON, SIN, TRUTH

EVE

Note. Considering the unprecedented brouhaha Eve let
  loose in the world, it is surprising how small a role she
  is actually allotted in Genesis: "little more than a per-
  sonification of human life, which is perpetuated by
  woman."*

  The first reference to Adam's mate, in the Masoretic
  text (Genesis, 2 : 23), calls her *ishah* (translated as
  "woman") because she was taken from *ish* ("man"). Not
  until Genesis, 3 : 20, does Adam break free from the
  generic "woman" or "wife" to coin a name for his mate:
  havah, "because she was the mother of all the living
  [*hai*]."**

  Now, eyewitness (or earwitness) testimony about the
  naming of Eve is, alas, lacking. And lest you think I flirt
  with blasphemy, let me enlist the authority of the *Encyclopedia of the Jewish Religion,* which disposes of Eve
  in nine crisp lines, informing us that modern Bible
  scholars treat the story of Eve as a traditional fable
  conceived by primitive peoples to explain the origin of
  mankind, the reason for menstruation and labor pains,
  and the subordinate position of women in the world:
  "The rabbis did not propound a doctrine of original

---

  * *Dictionary of the Bible,* ed. J. Hastings, F. C. Grant and H. H.
Rowley, Scribners, New York, 1963, p. 277.
  ** *The Torah: The Five Books of Moses, a new translation according to
the Masoretic text,* J.P.S.A., Philadelphia, 1962. But *havah* is a nettlesome
word to philologists, who say it was not strictly Hebrew in origin; and its
alleged sonic resemblance to *ha-ra* ("evil") offers other scholars a porten-
tous, if fragile, linkage between the name of woman and the conception of
sin. Further titillation lies in the observation that it bears a resemblance to
an Arabic word for serpent. (See *Dictionary of the Bible, op. cit.,* pp.
266–67, and *Encyclopedia of the Jewish Religion,* ed. Werblowsky and
Wigoder, Holt, Rinehart, Winston, Israel, 1965, p. 136).

sin, and the taint of Eve's sin was in any case removed
by the Israelites' acceptance of the Law."*

I, for one, have always wanted to know more about
Eve's legendary predecessor, Lilith (*q.v.*). However you
feel about either, it is hard not to admire the astute
answer Gamaliel's daughter gave to a sacrilegious king,
in the last entry below.

—L.R.

❋ Adam would never have had Eve had God not put him
to sleep first.

"If you know everything," said the cynic to the sage, "tell
me what Eve did whenever Adam came home?"
"She counted his ribs," said the sage.

Adam's last will and testament read: "Don't believe Eve's
version."

The King said to Rabbi Gamaliel: "Your God is a thief,
for He put Adam to sleep, then stole one of his ribs!"
At this, the Rabbi's daughter cried out, "Police! Police!"
"What happened?" asked the King.
"A thief stole into my house," she replied, "and took my
silver pitcher—and left a gold one in its place."
The King said: "If only such a thief would come to me!"
To which Gamaliel's daughter replied, "Then why do you
mock our God? He took one rib from Adam only to
enrich him with Eve."
—adapted from TALMUD: *Sanhedrin*, 39a

See also: ADAM, ADAM'S RIB, ANCESTORS, GOD, LILITH, MEN
and WOMEN, MARRIAGE, SERPENT, SIN, WIVES

EVIDENCE

❋ No answer is a type of answer.

❋ To assume is to fool one's self.

❋ The drunkard smells of whiskey—but so does the bartender.

Where there's a flame there must be a fire; and there is no
smoke except from fire.

---

* *Encyclopedia of the Jewish Religion, op. cit.,* p. 136.

❋ Half an answer also tells you something.

❋ You don't have to see the lion if you see his lair.

A man's death-trap may be between his cheeks [his words or testimony].

When all people cry "Crazy!" believe them.

❋ If one man says, "You're a donkey," don't mind; if two say so, be worried; if three say so, get a saddle.
—adapted from MIDRASH: *Genesis Rabbah*, 45 : 10

A man should be able to classify everything he believes, so that he can say: "This I believe because it is handed down from the Prophets; this I believe from the evidence of my senses; and this I believe from reason." Whoever believes anything that does not fall within these three categories, to him apply the saying: "The thoughtless believeth every word." (Proverbs 14 : 15)
MAIMONIDES, *Responsa II*, 25a

See also: ERROR, JUDGES, LAW, LOGIC, REASON, TRUTH

EVIL

Note. Since God is just, observing Jews hold, He will not treat the wicked and the virtuous in the same way: the former will be punished, the latter rewarded. But the rabbis sought to avoid a morality based on expedience. They stressed that personal reward is not a proper reason for either faith, virtue, or righteousness. It is the love of God, fidelity to His commandments, the endless performance of good deeds, that must govern men's lives. (Moses said this in Deuteronomy, and the prophets, elders and rabbis echoed it down the centuries.)

Now, this attitude presented many difficulties in a world where the evil often do flourish, and where the good and innocent do suffer and perish—as Job's three friends and Jeremiah complained, asking for God's explanation. There was none. "It is not in our power," said Rabbi Jannai and a hundred seers since him, "to explain the prosperity of the wicked—or the sufferings of the righteous." But Jews continued to try to explain, and to complain, and clung to faith in ultimate justice— in heaven, if not on earth.

—L.R.

God is everywhere, even in evil thoughts.

❋ Evil is a two-edged sword.

❋ If there were fewer swine, there would be fewer bastards.

The good is remembered; the bad is felt.

It is easier to abandon evil traits today than tomorrow.
Hasidic saying

The Evil Impulse springs up in children not at five or six—
but at ten, and from there on.   Rabbinical saying

The righteous man studies what he should answer,
But the mouth of the wicked pours out evil.
Book of Proverbs, 15 : 28

He who returns evil for good—evil will never depart from
his house.   *Book of Proverbs*, 17 : 13

Say not, "I will repay evil." Wait for the Lord to help you.
Book of Proverbs, 20 : 22

Both right and wrong are the work of our hands.
APOCRYPHA: *Psalms of Solomon*, 9 : 4

The greater the man the greater his potential for evil, too.
TALMUD: *Sukkah*, 52a

The Evil Will lures man in this world, then testifies against
him in the world to come   TALMUD: *Sukkah*, 52a

God created the Evil Impulse, but He also created its anti-
dote, the Torah.   TALMUD: *Kiddushin*, 30b

When the righteous man departs, evil enters.
TALMUD: *Sanhedrin*, 113b

❋ Evil is sweet in the beginning but bitter in the end.
TALMUD J.: *Shabbath*, 14 : 3

Israel argues, "Even though we sin, and Thou art angry,
Thou shouldst not forsake us: for if the potter makes a
jug and leaves a pebble in the clay, is it not inevitable
that the jug should leak? Thou didst create in us from
our childhood the Evil Inclination, therefore we beseech
thee, cause the inclination to pass away so that we may
do Thy will." And God replies, "I shall do so—in the
world to come."   MIDRASH: *Exodus Rabbah*, 46 : 4

Does the Evil Impulse ever serve good? Yes, for if not for the Evil Impulse, no man would build a house, nor marry a wife, nor beget children, nor engage in trade.

MIDRASH: *Ecclesiastes Rabbah*, 3 : 11

❋ The Evil Urge begins as a guest and proceeds like the host.   MIDRASH: *Genesis Rabbah*, 22 : 6

Don't court evil, and evil won't come to you.

MIDRASH: *Genesis Rabbah*, 22 : 8

We must expect that even in the millennium, evil will be weakened, but not totally extinguished.   *Zohar*

He is called a man who masters his evil desires.   *Zohar*

He who returns evil for evil acts wrongly; he should be patient, and let God help him.   *Zohar*

When the Evil Impulse comes to you, it is like iron still cold: If you do not drive it out, it becomes molten—as if transformed by fire.   *Zohar*

The Evil Impulse is like a cake of yeast: placed in one spot, it ferments throughout.   *Zohar*

❋ The world was created for the sake of those who are ashamed to do evil.   Introduction to *Tikune Zohar*

Keep three things in mind and you will escape the toils of wickedness: Know whence you came, whither you are going, and before Whom you will have to give a strict account.   *Sayings of the Fathers*, 3 : 1

Feel no sadness because of evil thoughts: it only strengthens them.   NACHMAN OF BRATSLAV

See also: GOD, GOOD AND EVIL, GOOD MEN, HABIT, HEREAFTER, SATAN, SIN, WICKEDNESS

EXCELLENCE

Excellence comes from men's rivalry with each other.

—adapted from *Ecclesiastes*, 4 : 40

See also: CHARACTER, SCHOLARS, WISE MEN

EXCESS

❊ Where there is too much, something is missing.

He who is everywhere is nowhere.

Too much means left over.

Three things are good in a little measure, and bad in large: yeast, salt, and hesitation. TALMUD: *Berakoth*, 34a

Food prepared by two cooks is neither hot nor cold.
TALMUD: *Erubin*, 3a

Too much oil will quench the wick. *Psalms*

Lamps are more often extinguished by too much oil than by too little. TESTAMENT OF JUDAH ASHERI

Fast so that you may condemn excess. Do not believe that much eating and drinking make the body grow, or enlarge the understanding; the reverse is true.
MAIMONIDES, *Responsa II*, 39a

Too much good food is worse than too little bad food.
FALAQUERA, *Sefer ha-Mevakesh*

Nothing is more precious than light, yet too much of it is blinding. JOSEPH DELMEDIGO

See also: ABSTINENCE, BOREDOM, FASTING, FOOD, GLUTTONY, HEALTH, JUDGMENT, MODERATION

EXCUSES

Oh Lord, give me an excuse!

Gluttons find ample excuses for gorging.

❊ Girls who can't dance say the musicians can't keep time.

❊ Ten excuses are less persuasive than one.

Not to answer is one kind of answer.

Don't do what you'll have to find an excuse for.

❊ To be cheated once is understandable; to be cheated thrice is inexcusable.

❊ Fools always find an excuse for their folly.

❋ If you measure before you cut, you'll avoid the need for excuses.

Don't repent so much—just don't sin so often.

❋ The guilty make excuses before they are accused.

❋ There is no excuse for not helping someone when you can.

EXPERIENCE

❋ Experience is the name people give their mistakes.

❋ Some of the most well-trodden roads lead nowhere.

❋ The man who has been bitten by a snake is afraid of a piece of rope.

❋ You can't run past the moon.

If you lie on the ground, you can't fall.

❋ Once a man has been burned by the hot, he blows on the cool.

❋ A thread is always found on a tailor.

The sun shines brighter after it rains.

No one can know where the shoe pinches except the one who walks in it.

Where there is honey, there are flies.

❋ The best preacher is the human heart; the best teacher is time; the best book is the world; the best friend is God.

On black earth, the best corn grows. [Simple folk often have the best hearts.]

Only the one who eats the dish knows how it tastes.
                          MIDRASH: *Deuteronomy Rabbah*

Without experience there can be little wisdom.
                          BEN SIRACH, *Ecclesiasticus*

Only those accustomed to the sun can endure its glare.
                          JUDAH ARYEH MOSCATO

No dog is smarter than one who has been beaten.
                          SHOLEM ALEICHEM

See also: FEAR, HABIT, LEARNING

EXPERTS

❋ Those who can't sing can still be experts on singing.

See also: EXPERIENCE, JUDGMENT

EYES

One eye has more faith than two.

Truth is in the eyes; lies stay behind them.

The eye is small, yet it sees the whole world.

❋ The eye does not see as well as the heart.

❋ Even those with big eyes do not see their own faults.

The eye and heart are spies for the body: the eyes see, the heart covets—and the body commits the sin.
RASHI, *Commentaries on the Pentateuch, Numbers*

What has been created that is worse than the eye? It sheds tears on every face.
—adapted from BEN SIRACH, *Ecclesiasticus*, 31 : 13

For learning, the eye is less useful than the ear.
—adapted from GERONDI

See also: FACE, TRUTH, VANITY

FACE

❋ The worst informer is the face.

The face will betray a secret.

Troubles that don't show on your face lie on your heart.

He who shuts his eyes is hatching some scheme;
He who tightens his lips is planning some mischief.
Book of Proverbs, 17 : 20

The face of one man is as different from the face of another
as the thought of one from another.
                                    TALMUD: *Berakoth*, 58a

Looks explain words.
            —adapted from MOSES IBN EZRA, *Shirat Yisrael*

✻ An ugly face is the best guardian of a woman's virtue.
                            IMMANUEL OF ROME, *Mahberot*

See also: APPEARANCE, EARS, EYES

FAITH

✻ I know the Lord will help—but help me, Lord, *until* you
help.

Most sailors are religious: daily peril makes them so.

Truth is in your prayerbook.

✻ What God does is best—probably.

Faith is shown in charity.

True faith needs neither evidence nor research.

If a thousand hasidim [pious men] gathered around a block
of wood, it, too, could work miracles.

✻ God requires no synagogue—except in the heart.
                                        Hasidic saying

The true proselyte is dearer to God than the Israelites were
at Mount Sinai: for had not the Israelites seen the thunder and lightning, the quaking mountain and the sounding trumpets, they would not have accepted the Torah;
but the true proselyte, who saw none of these things, has
surrendered to the Holy One. Can anyone be dearer to
God?   MIDRASH: *Tanhuma*

✻ If the Greek gods steal, by whom shall their faithful
swear?   APOCRYPHA: *Ahikar*, 8 : 22

Rivers full of water don't freeze as quickly as rivers with
little water. [The deeply learned will not "grow cold" to
faith, as the superficially learned may.]   *Zohar*

God conceals Himself from our minds, but reveals Himself
to our hearts.   —adapted from *Zohar*

❋ With faith, there are no questions; without faith, there
are no answers.   "The Chofetz Chaim"

A man should believe in God through faith, not because of
miracles.   Nachman of Bratslav

Man must not rely on pure reason; he must mix faith with
it.   Nachman of Bratslav

Better a superstitious believer than a rational unbeliever.
                                        Nachman of Bratslav

Faith is not only in the heart; it should be put into words.
                                        Nachman of Bratslav

See also: FASTING, GOD, HERETICS, HOLINESS, MIRACLES,
PRAYER, REASON, RELIGION, TRUTH

FALSEHOOD

God created everything except falsehood.

Half-truths are falsehoods.

Young liars turn into old thieves.

If you deal in falsehoods, perfect your memory.

❋ Flattery grows into falsehood.

See also: DECEIT, FRAUD, HONESTY, LIARS/LIES, TRUTH

FAME

See: GLORY, GREAT MEN, HONOR, REPUTATION

FAMILY

Note. Pride of lineage is strong among Jews, but *yikhes*
refers to more than pedigree, for *yikhes* must be earned
as well as inherited. The crucial ingredients of *yikhes*
are: learning, virtue, philanthropy, service to the community. One who does not live up to his family's past
record swiftly "loses" his *yikhes*. The highest *yikhes*
attaches to the man of learning.

Wealth or success never confer such *yikhes* on a
family or its descendants as comes from the respect
accorded knowledge. "All Jews are *mishpokhe*" means

that Jews are one family: a common heritage, common obligations, common values. The state of Israel accepts, without exception, Jewish immigrants of the widest, sharpest cultural difference.

—L.R.

Blood never turns into water.

✻ There are no praises and no blessings for those who are ashamed of their families.

✻ A successful man's family always provides him with at least one *nukhshleper* [sycophant].

Measure your *mishpokhe* [relatives] not in length but in width.

A little hurt from one of your kin is worse than a big hurt from a stranger.

✻ Before you marry a girl, study her brothers.

A nobleman worries about his horses and dogs, a Jew worries about his wife and children.

There are three partners in any man: God, his father, and his mother.

Look for the good, not the evil, in the conduct of members of the family.

Better a morsel of dry bread, with peace, than a house full of feasting, with strife.   *Book of Proverbs,* 17 : 1

An advantage over a kinsman is the worst kind of disadvantage.   APOCRYPHA II, *Maccabees,* 5 : 6

See also: ANCESTORS, BASTARDS, BROTHERS, CHILDREN, DAUGHTERS, DAUGHTERS-IN-LAW, FATHERS, MOTHERS, MOTHERS-IN-LAW, PARENTS, SONS, WIVES

FASTING

It's good to fast—with a chicken leg and a bottle of wine.

✻ Our rabbi is so poor that if he didn't fast every Monday and Thursday, he'd starve to death.

It is good to fast—when the table is covered with fish.

Fasting is more effective than charity, for the latter is done
   with money, but the former can be done only by one's
   own person.   TALMUD: *Berakoth*, 32b

Do not fast in excess. [It weakens the capacity to perform
   good deeds.]   TALMUD: *Ta'anith*, 11a

See also: ABSTINENCE, ASCETICS/ASCETICISM, EXCESS,
   FAITH, FOOD and DRINK, WINE

FATE

❋ When things don't get better, don't worry—they may get
   worse.

❋ The man fated to drown will drown in a glass of water.

God is a father, fate is a stepfather.

What you can't avoid—welcome.

Even the biggest ball of twine unwinds.

There are two types of men: One who is first-rate, and fate
   made him last; the other who should be last, and fate put
   him first.   MOSES IBN EZRA, *Shirat Yisrael*

The man who ascribes things to accident sees a bird's nest
   and thinks it has no special purpose.
                              BAHYA BEN ASHER, *Kad ha-Kemah*

See also: ASTROLOGY, DEATH, DESTINY, FORTUNE, FUTURE,
   LUCK

FATHERS

❋ When a father helps a son, both smile; when a son must
   help his father, both cry.

One may tell the truth—even to one's father.

It is better that the child cry than the father.

Fathers are always trying to make their sons good Jews;
   when will they try to be good Jews instead of leaving
   the task to their sons?

A father should be treated like a king.

A child should not sit in the place his father habitually uses.

❋ If in anger you push your wife or child away with one hand, let the other bring them back to your heart.

No man in the world loves one more than one's father.

It is better to beg for bread than be dependent on your son.

Children's children are the crown of old men;
And fathers are the pride of their children.
Book of Proverbs, 17 : 6

The only time a son should disobey his father is if the father orders him to commit a sin.   TALMUD, *Yebamoth*, 5b

Whoever teaches his son teaches not only his son but also his son's son—and so on to the end of generations.
TALMUD: *Kiddushin*, 30a

Should a father tell his son to throw gold into the sea, the son should obey.   TALMUD: *Kiddushin*, 32a

❋ Even a rabbi should rise [in the presence of his pupils] when his father enters.
—adapted from TALMUD: *Horayat*, 13b

He who raises a child is to be called its father, not the man who only gave it birth.
MIDRASH: *Exodus Rabbah*, 46 : 5

A father suffers for the troubles of his son.
Midrash Sekhel Tov

It is because Esau respected his father that his descendants rule the world.   *Zohar*

Our sages recommended that a father should spend less than his means on food, up to his means on dress, and beyond his means for his wife and children.
MAIMONIDES: *Mishneh Torah*, Deot V

A man's father is his king.   *Pirke de Rabbi Eliezer*, 39

When a father is quick to lose his temper, his sons are fools.
NACHMAN OF BRATSLAV

When a father complains that his son has taken to evil ways, what should he do? Love him more than ever.
BAAL SHEM TOV

See also: ANCESTORS, CHILDREN, DAUGHTERS, FAMILY, MOTHERS, PARENTS, SONS, WIVES

FEAR

❋ When you have no choice, don't be afraid.

❋ The man afraid of leaves should not enter a forest.

❋ When the sheep are shorn, the lambs tremble.

❋ Fear is the father of hate.

If a man carries his own lantern, he need not fear darkness.
Hasidic saying

❋ Fear only two: God, and the man who has no fear of
God. Hasidic saying

❋ Fear the man who fears you. Hasidio saying

Obeying out of love is better than obeying out of fear.
RASHI, Commentaries in the Pentateuch, Deuteronomy

Whoever fears the Lord is afraid of nothing.
BEN SIRACH, Ecclesiasticus, 34 : 14

If you come near a king, you come near a lion:
Others will fear you, but your fear will be great, too.
HAI GAON, Musar Haskel

See also: COURAGE, COWARDS, EXPERIENCE, GOD, RESIGNA-
TION

FEELINGS

See: EMOTIONS

FIGHTING

❋ When a miller fights a chimneysweep, the miller gets
black and the chimneysweep gets white.

See also: HATE, QUARRELS, VIOLENCE, WAR

FLATTERY

❋ If you can't love, learn how to flatter.

To flatter is to steal.

Flattery must lead to falsehoods.

A lying tongue brings destruction to itself; and a flattering mouth works its own ruin.   *Book of Proverbs*, 26 : 28

He who reproves men will get more thanks in the end than he who flatters them.   *Book of Proverbs*, 28 : 23

A man may flatter his wife for the sake of peace; his creditor, to get an extension; and his teacher, to get special attention.   *Otsar Midrashim*

Flattery leads to vulgarity; the flatterer is despised.
                                    NACHMAN OF BRATSLAV

❀ Flattery is unavoidable, needed by all men, so I may as well become a rabbi.   THE RUPSHITZER RABBI

Flattery is permissible only to promote peace.
                                    THE KORETSER RABBI

See also: CRITICISM, DECEIT, LIARS/LIES, PRAISE

FOLKLORE

See: ADVICE, CIRCUMSTANCES, CUSTOMS, LAW, WISDOM

FOLLY

❀ Of what use is wisdom, when folly reigns?

❀ What's left over from the thief is spent on the fortune teller.

A stranger's folly produces laughter; your own creates shame.

❀ It's folly to try to run past the moon.

Any man who understands his own foolishnesses is already a little wise.

❀ A fool who wants to hang himself grabs a knife.

Wisdom may increase with the years, but so does folly.

Man does not commit a sin unless he is possessed by folly.
                                    TALMUD: *Sotah*, 3a

See also: EGOTISM, FOOLS, IGNORANCE, ILLOGIC, INTELLI-GENCE, MAN, NONSENSE, WISDOM/WISE MEN

FOOD AND DRINK

Note. Eating and drinking, to the ancient Hebrews, involved grave religious obligations and reinforced the idea of the Jews as a people "set apart," chosen by the Lord as "Mine . . ." (Leviticus). Strict dietary laws were believed to strengthen the dedication of a Jew to his role as one of God's instruments for the redemption of mankind.

Genesis 9 : 4 forbade the consuming of animal blood to all the seed of Noah. Moses, in Leviticus and Deuteronomy, forbade Jews to eat internal fat or suet, carrion, or the carcass of any animal that has died instead of having been slain in the ritual manner. The Talmud says forbidden foods "pollute the body and the soul." (Paul, in Acts 21 : 25, asked Christians to shun the blood of meat and the meat of strangled animals.)

For over 2000 years rabbis developed and refined an elaborate code of regulations concerning food. The ritualistic details became so minute that a major part of the rabbis' expertise lay in their mastery of the rules: what is proscribed and what permitted; when one food or another is allowed; how food must be prepared, how cooked, etc. An authorized slaughterer of animals, the *shokhet*, was and is still supervised by rabbis.

Whatever it was that originally prompted the taboo on pork was fortunate, for pork is the carrier of the parasites of trichinosis. Similarly, hepatitis has been traced to contaminated clams, which (even uncontaminated) are taboo to observing Jews.

Food taboos are quite common, of course, among the races of man: Egyptians ate no cow, bull, or cat (which were deities); Babylonians ate no birds of prey; Muslims are forbidden to eat pig—as are Borneans, Laplanders, Navajos or the Yakuts of Turkey. In many parts of Polynesia, the eel is taboo. Iranians will eat no scaleless or finless *pisces.* I could exhaust you with a more exhaustive catalogue of culinary taboos.

For a clear, simple explanation of the *kosher* laws, see Samuel H. Dresner, *The Jewish Dietary Laws: Their Meaning for Our Time*, including Seymour Siegel, *A Guide to Observance*, Burning Bush Press, New York, 1959.

—L.R.

FOOD

❋ How just is our Lord: The rich He gives food—and the poor He gives appetite.

A man can forget absolutely everything—except to eat.

What is the proper time to eat? If rich, when you will; if poor, when you can.

Borsht and bread make your cheeks red.

❋ One man has no appetite for his food, while another has no food for his appetite.

Meat, not hay, makes the lion roar.

Only from your own table can you go away full.

Meat without salt is fit only for dogs.

At other people's parties, one eats heartily.

Anyone who eats in the street is like a dog.

If you eat pudding on the Sabbath, you'll be full all week.

❋ Soldiers become much smarter after eating.

More people die from overeating than from undernourishment.   TALMUD: *Shabbath*, 33a

❋ Miracles do occur, but they rarely provide food.
                                        TALMUD: *Shabbath*, 53b

Food is better than drink up to the age of forty; after forty, drink is better.   TALMUD: *Shabbath*, 152a

If you have a fine meal, enjoy it in a good light.
                                        TALMUD: *Yomah*, 74b

❋ Feed your animals before you sit down to eat.
                                        TALMUD: *Berakoth*, 40a

Man can live without spices, but not without wheat.
                                        MIDRASH: *Psalms*, 2 : 16

Consider your table as a table before the Lord: Chew well and hurry not.   *Zohar*

Too much good food does more harm than too little bad food.   FALAQUERA, *Sefer ha-Mevakesh*

❋ Man eats to live; he does not live to eat.
                              ABRAHAM IBN EZRA, *Yesod Mora*

Food to a man is like oil to a lamp: If it has much, it
  shines, if too little, it is quenched; yet a lamp is sooner
  extinguished by too much oil than by too little.
                              The Testament of Judah Asheri

Eat sparingly and lengthen your life.
                              THE KORETSER RABBI

A man should eat slowly, properly, even if he eats alone.
                              NACHMAN OF BRATSLAV

Don't dance before you eat.   SHOLEM ALEICHEM

See also: EXCESS, GLUTTONY, MODERATION

FOOD: EATING AND DRINKING

❋ "For dust thou art, and unto dust shalt thou return"—
  in between, can a little drink hurt?

The rich eat when they want, the poor when they can.

Snatch and eat, snatch and drink, for this world is like a
  wedding.   TALMUD: *Erubin*, 54a

❋ Eat a third, drink a third, and leave a third of your
  stomach empty; then, should anger seize you, there will
  be room for its rage.
                              —adapted from TALMUD: *Gittin*, 70a

If a man eats and drinks only to satisfy himself, that is not
  praiseworthy: He should eat and drink to preserve life,
  in order to serve his Creator.
                              JOSEPH CARO, *Shulhan Aruk*

You cannot pursue knowledge without eating and drinking;
  if men engaged only in the pursuit of knowledge, the
  human species would die out.   SAADIA GAON

To eat and drink much does not enlarge the understanding;
  the opposite is achieved.
                              —adapted from MAIMONIDES, *Responsa* II : 39a

See also: DRUNKARDS, EXCESS, GLUTTONY, TEMPERANCE,
  WINE

FOOLS

❋ A fool can ask more questions in an hour than ten wise men can answer in a year.

❋ That fools are fond of sweets is a discovery of the wise.

❋ A fool who wants to hang himself grabs a knife.

When a fool goes to market, the merchants rejoice.

❋ A fool has to figure out how to find a notch in a saw.

One fool can buy more than ten wise men can sell.

Never show a fool half-completed work.

Don't ask a fool a question—or give him an explanation.

A fool needs many shoes.

❋ Drunkards sober up, but fools remain fools.

God protects fools—who else?

If he were not my fool, I'd be laughing, too.

A fool forgets the first blow by the time you raise the stick for the second.

❋ A fool measures water with a sieve.

❋ If you send a fool to close the shutters, he'll close them all over town.

When a fool laughs, he raises his voice.

Were you to grind him up in a mortar, he'd say you were after the pepper.

❋ If a fool says nothing, you can't tell whether he's a fool or a sage.

❋ Whatever is on a fool's mind is on his tongue.

❋ Don't approach a goat from the front, a horse from the back, or a fool from any side.

When the Messiah comes, all the sick will be healed—but fools will stay fools.

The biggest cripple of all is the fool.

Fools need not be sown; they sprout by themselves.

Fools don't get gray.

Fools search always for yesterday.

There is no remedy for a fool.

❋ Why is it that fools generally have pretty wives?

Fools don't seem to age.

❋ You can educate a fool but you can't make him think.

A dead man is mourned for seven days, a fool is mourned for a lifetime.

God gave fools hands and feet—and let them run.

❋ Foolishness sometimes succeeds, but it is still foolishness.

Every village has its idiot.

❋ A fool if rich is treated like a lord.

A fool is a fool forever.

We laugh at strange fools, but are ashamed of our own.

❋ In a fool, the tongue is superfluous.

The worst fool is clever for himself.

From a fool, what do you get? Trouble.

You can tell an ass by his long ears, a fool by his long tongue.

❋ A fool can be an expert—on other fools.

❋ When you praise a fool, you water his folly.

Even a fool sometimes says something clever.

One fool makes many fools.

If all men were fools, they wouldn't be known as fools.

You'll find sense in a fool when you see an ass mount a ladder.

A half-fool may be a real sage.

A fool can't be questioned—or explained.

Fools, like weeds, flourish without rain.

If you keep quiet, you're half a fool; if you talk, you're a whole fool.

Dare not do business with fools.

❊ Only a fool or a genius rushes into print.

❊ The biggest foolishness of the fool is this: he thinks he's
   smart.

To try to be smarter than everybody is the greatest foolishness.

A fool is his own informer.

The world is a pleasant place—for fools.

He who has little in his head, must have plenty in his feet.
   [Fools run fast.]

❊ A fool complains of the cold in July.

Never be offended by a fool.

The only thing you can do with idiots and thorns is get rid
   of them.

❊ The fools who sing all summer weep all winter.

The wicked can't conceal his wickedness, nor the fool his
   folly.

Who is a fool? He who sleeps in a cemetery.
                                    TALMUD: *Hagigah*, 3b

The world is in the hands of fools.
                                    TALMUD: *Sanhedrin*, 46b

A fool is worse than a bastard—if the bastard is wise.
                                    TALMUD J.: *Kiddushin*, 4 : 11

The pious fool sees a child drowning and says, "As soon as
   I take off my phylacteries, I'll save him"; while he does
   so, the child drowns.   TALMUD J.: *Sotah*, 3 : 4

A fool considers his ways right.
                                    Book of Proverbs, 12 : 15

Understanding is a wellspring of life unto him that hath it:
   but the instruction of fools is folly.
                                    Book of Proverbs, 16 : 11

Of what use is money in the hand of a fool:
To buy wisdom, when he has no sense?
                                    Book of Proverbs, 17 : 16

When a fool holds his tongue, he too is thought clever.
                                    Book of Proverbs, 17 : 28

A whip for the horse, a bridle for the ass, and a rod for the back of fools.   *Book of Proverbs*, 26 : 3

Answer not a fool according to his folly, lest you become like him.   *Book of Proverbs*, 26 : 4

Like a stick brandished by a drunkard is a parable in the mouth of fools.   *Book of Proverbs*, 26 : 9

As a dog returns to his vomit, a fool repeats his folly.
                Book of Proverbs, 26 : 11

A stone is heavy, and sand is weighty; but a fool's vexation is heavier than both.   *Book of Proverbs*, 27 : 3

He cuts off his feet who sends a message by a fool.
                Book of Proverbs, 26 : 6

Better be met by a bear robbed of her cubs than by a fool in his folly.   *Book of Proverbs*, 17 : 12

A fool thinks everyone else is a fool.
                MIDRASH: *Ecclesiastes Rabbah*, 10

A parable from a fool is worthless, because he tells it at the wrong time.   BEN SIRACH, *Ecclesiasticus*, 20 : 20

The head of a fool is like a broken dish; it will not hold knowledge.   BEN SIRACH, *Ecclesiasticus*, 21 : 14

❊ The talk of a fool is like a heavy pack on a journey.
                BEN SIRACH, *Ecclesiasticus*, 21 : 16

To a fool, wisdom is like a ruined house.
                BEN SIRACH, *Ecclesiasticus*, 21 : 18

To the fool, instruction is chains on his feet.
                BEN SIRACH, *Ecclesiasticus*, 21 : 19

❊ Teaching a fool is like gluing a broken pot.
                BEN SIRACH, *Ecclesiasticus*, 22 : 7

The love of a fool is only a transient whim.
                RABBENU TAM

It is easier to tolerate a whole fool than a half-fool—that is, a fool who tries to act clever.
                IBN GABIROL, *Choice of Pearls*

Beware of the fool who is pious.
                IBN GABIROL, *Choice of Pearls*

Man does not live in peace, except for fools: they love tranquillity. MOSES CHEFETZ, *Mlehet Mahshevet*

When a fool talks, he grinds much and produces little.
    SHOLEM ALEICHEM

FOOLS AND WISE MEN

A fool says what he knows, a sage knows what he says.

❊ Two kinds of men are always embarrassed: a fool among wise men, and a wise man among fools.

❊ When a wise man talks to a fool, two fools are conversing.

What embitters the wise cheers up the foolish.

With the wise, the older the wiser; with the ignorant, the older the more foolish.

❊ A blow from a sage is better than a kiss from a fool.

What one fool can spoil, ten sages can't fix.

❊ If a fool keeps his mouth shut, he sounds like a sage.

A fool can throw a stone into a well—and a hundred wise men can't recover it.

One fool can ask more questions than ten wise men can answer.

When a fool holds a cow by the horns, a wise man can milk her.

The fool who, ashamed, hides his ignorance is better than the *khokhem* [wise man] who parades his wisdom.

Better to be in Gehenna [Hell] with a wise man than in *Gan Eden* [Paradise] with a fool.

A fool takes two steps where a wise man takes none.

The wise man eats to live; the fool lives to eat.

It is better to lose to a wise man than win from a fool.

Better a fool who has traveled than a wise man who remained home.

A fool loses, a smart man finds.

The wise man conceals his intelligence; the fool reveals his foolishness.

Of what use is wisdom when folly reigns?

He who walks with wise men will become smart; but the companion of fools will smart for it.
> —adapted from *Book of Proverbs*, 13 : 20

A fool's ways are right in his own eyes, but a wise man listens to advice.
> —adapted from *Book of Proverbs*, 12 : 15

✶ Give the wise a wink, the fool a fist.
> MIDRASH: *Midrash Proverbs*

A fool laughs, but a wise man smiles.
> BEN SIRACH, *Ecclesiasticus*, 21 : 20

✶ The wise reports what he saw, the fool what he heard.
> HASDAI, *Ben ha-Melekh ve-ha-Nazir*

Wise man are pleased when they discover truth, fools when they discover falsehood.
> IBN GABIROL, *Choice of Pearls*

Man is wise only while he searches for wisdom; if he thinks he has found it, he is a fool.
> IBN GABIROL, *Choice of Pearls*

See also: FOLLY, ILLOGIC, ILLUSION, MAN: HUMAN TYPES, NEBEKH, SHLEMIELS, WISDOM, WISE MEN

FORESIGHT

Better ask the way ten times than get lost once.

✶ The man who lives without a plan will die without a shroud.

Fortune is more powerful than foresight.

✶ If you sing all summer, you'll weep in winter.

✶ When you go to a restaurant, choose a table near a waiter.

Better an egg today than a chicken tomorrow.

Don't throw away the dirty before you have the clean.

❁ Better measure ten times before you cut, or you may
have to cut ten times before you measure.

Don't throw stones into the well from which you drink.

Woe to him who makes a door before he has a house, or
builds a gate and has no yard.
                                            TALMUD: *Shabbath*, 31b

If you don't plow in summer, what will you eat in winter?
                                            MIDRASH: *Midrash Proverbs*

❁ A wealthy Jew fell sick; and when near death he asked
a scribe to write his last will and testament, dictating
these clauses: "To the faithful slave who brings this
document and all my wealth, I leave all my property.
To my only son, in Judea, I leave any one thing he may
choose out of all my possessions." The slave returned
with all the wealth of his dead master and showed the
will to a rabbi, who said to the Jew's son: "If your
father had left everything to you, the slave would have
fled with the wealth; now he has brought everything
safely to you, and you may choose *him*, according to the
will: for all the property of a slave belongs to his master."
                      —adapted from MIDRASH: *Tanhuma Bereshit*

Before a wise man ventures into a pit, he lowers a ladder—
so that he can climb out.
                                            SAMUEL HA-NAGID, *Ben Mishle*

❁ Plan for this world as if you expect to live forever; but
plan for the hereafter as if you expect to die tomorrow.
                                            IBN GABIROL, *Choice of Pearls*

See also: CAUSE AND EFFECT, CAUTION, CONFLICT, FORTUNE,
JUDGMENT, LUCK, MISFORTUNE, PRUDENCE

FORGETTING

❁ Men can forget anything—except when to eat.

What is learned in one's youth is not easily forgotten.

❁ Memory and teeth grow weaker with time.

If not for our ability to forget, we would never be free from
grief.
                                            —adapted from BAHYA IBN PAQUDA,
                                                  Duties of the Heart, 2 : 5

In two years, a man can forget what it took him twenty to
learn.   *Abot de Rabbi Nathan*, 24 : 6

See also: CAUSE AND EFFECT, LEARNING, MEMORY

FORGIVENESS

Those who want to be forgiven must learn to forgive.

✲ If you take revenge, you will regret it; if you forgive,
you will rejoice.

Regard as enormous the little wrong you did to others, and
as trifling the great wrong done to you.
                    TALMUD: *Derekh Erets Zuta* I : 29

One who is begged for forgiveness should not be so cruel
as not to forgive.
        RASHI, *Commentaries on the Pentateuch, Numbers*

Forgive the man who has done you ill, and give to the man
who has refused you.   SAADIA GAON

Learn to receive blows, and to forgive those who insult you.
                        Abot de Rabbi Nathan, 41

See also: COMPASSION, GOD, GOOD DEEDS, JUDGMENT, JUS-
TICE

FORTITUDE

✲ When you have no choice, at least be brave.

✲ Pray that you will never have to suffer all that you are
able to endure.

Fortitude is enlarged by food.

The man who cannot survive bad times will not see good
times.   Hasidic saying

If you carry your own lantern, you will endure the dark.
                                    Hasidic saying

See also: COURAGE, ENDURANCE, FREEDOM, STRENGTH, VALOR

FORTUNE

When fortune calls, quick!—offer her a chair.

One ounce of fortune is worth a pound of forecast.

❋ From fortune to misfortune is but the span of a hand; but from misfortune to fortune is an immensity.

When thieves fall out, the peasant keeps his cow.

Fortune is a wheel that turns with great speed.

❋ The fortune of this world is like a wheel with two buckets: the full becomes empty and the empty becomes full.

❋ The man who does not rely on fortune postpones misfortune.   TALMUD: *Berakoth*, 64a

Show not your power in a time of might, for fortune is given to flight.   IBN GABIROL, *Choice of Pearls*

See also: FATE, FUTURE, GAMBLING, GOLD, HAPPINESS, LUCK, MISFORTUNE, POWER

FRAUD

Fraud with words is worse than with money.

You may defraud others, from a distance; but close up, you defraud yourself.

It's not hard to cheat successfully—once.

Bread won by fraud tastes sweet to a man;
But afterwards his mouth will be filled with gravel.
                                        Book of Proverbs, 20 : 17

See also: CONSCIENCE, DECEIT, FALSEHOOD, LAW, LIARS/LIES, SIN

FREEDOM

❋ Thought is a universe of freedom.

❋ A slave is a free man if he is content with his lot; a free man is a slave if he seeks more than that.

To be too proud is to be in a prison.

❋ The only free man is the one who studies Torah.
                                        Sayings of the Fathers, 6 : 2

Freedom is the world of joy.   NACHMAN OF BRATSLAV

To be immobile is to be in chains.

Moses ibn Ezra, *Shirat Yisrael*

See also: DEMOCRACY, EQUALITY, GOVERNMENT, LAW, MASSES, PRISON, POLITICS, POWER

FRIENDS/FRIENDSHIP

❊ If you can't help a friend with money, at least give a *krekhts* [sigh].

❊ The man who seeks a faultless friend will remain friendless.

One enemy is too many; and a hundred friends are not enough.

❊ It's not good to be alone—even in Paradise.

❊ One's best friend is in the mirror.

Descend a step in taking a wife; ascend a step in choosing a friend.

A big blow from a stranger hurts less than a small blow from a friend.

❊ The man who has no money to lend friends makes no enemies.

Better one old friend than two new ones.

A friend you get for nothing, an enemy you have to pay for.

Men become like those they associate with.

Old friends, like old wine, don't lose their flavor.

Better one friend with a dish of food than a hundred with a gripe.

❊ We all remain better friends—at a slight distance.

With a glass of wine, you can find many friends.

It's good to eat with a friend, but not from one plate.

❊ Your friend has a friend—so tell him no secrets.

Friendship is stronger than kinship.

❊ If your friend is honey, don't lick him up altogether.

Many crowd the gate of abundance but even friends pass the door of misery.

One is none. [It is better to have others than be alone.]

✳ Man can eat alone, but not work alone.

You can't patch up a torn friendship.

Sometimes a good friend is better than a brother.

✳ The man who thinks he can live without others is mistaken; the one who thinks others can't live without him is even more deluded.   Hasidic saying

If two logs are dry and one is wet, the kindling of the two will kindle the wet one, too.

TALMUD: *Sanhedrin*, 93b

✳ My friend is he who will tell me my faults, in private.
IBN GABIROL, *Choice of Pearls*

A man without friends is like a left hand without a right.
IBN GABIROL, *Choice of Pearls*

Do not give your love to a friend all at once.
IBN GABIROL, *Choice of Pearls*

The meek becomes known in anger, the hero in war, and a friend in time of need.

IBN GABIROL, *Choice of Pearls*

There are three types of friends: those like food, without which you can't live; those like medicine, which you need occasionally; and those like an illness, which you never want.   IBN GABIROL

Were I to break off with friends who sin, I would be friendless.   —adapted from IBN GABIROL

A good friend is a tower of strength; to find one is to find a treasure.   BEN SIRACH: *Ecclesiasticus*, 6 : 14

✳ Question a friend: perhaps he did not say what you think, or if he did, so that he will not say it again.
BEN SIRACH: *Ecclesiasticus*, 19 : 14

Do not condemn your friend: you do not know what you would have done in his place.

HILLEL, in *Sayings of the Fathers*, 2 : 5

It is better to have a friend in the market place than gold
in the coffer.   LEONE DA MODENA

❋ Your best friend is the one who is a friend without
expecting anything.   LEONE DA MODENA

A man has three friends: his sons, his wealth, and his good
deeds.   *Pirke de Rabbi Eliezer*, 34

Friendship: one heart in two bodies.
                     IBN ZABARA, *Book of Delight*, ch. 7

A real friend feels no need to excuse himself for some
failing.   THE LUBLINER RABBI

To pull a friend out of the mire, don't hesitate to get dirty.
                                           BAAL SHEM TOV

See also: DECEIT, ENEMY, FALSE FRIENDS, FAMILY; HATE,
NEIGHBORS, WEALTH

FRIENDS: FALSE FRIENDS

❋ The good fellow to everyone is a good friend to no one.

Some friends remain friends only up to the pocket.

❋ The man who takes offense for no reason gets friendly
for no reason.

When you have a pretty wife, you are a bad friend.

A false friend is worse than a dog.

The man who puts a friend to public shame is as guilty as a
murderer.

❋ False friends are like migratory birds; they fly away in
cold weather.   Hasidic saying

People treat each other in a friendly fashion—when times
are good.   MIDRASH: *Genesis Rabbah*, 9 : 5

Stay away from your enemies, but guard yourself against
friends.   BEN SIRACH: *Ecclesiasticus*, 6 : 13

See also: DECEIT, ENEMY, FAMILY

FUNCTION

See: CAUSE AND EFFECT, UTILITY

FUTURE

✻ Yesterday is your past; today is your future—because your tomorrow is unknown.

See also: DEATH, FATE, FORTUNE, HEREAFTER, LIFE

G

GAMBLING

Sick men need not be gamblers, but congenital gamblers are sick.

✻ Gamblers show no mercy when gambling.

Gambling is an obsession.

✻ Those who don't rely on luck lessen their bad luck.

See also: BUSINESS, FORTUNE, LUCK, MONEY, SIN

GEHENNA

See: HELL

GENEROSITY

✻ The man who gives little with a smile gives more than the man who gives much with a frown.

✻ Give with a warm hand, not a cold one [i.e., in your will].

The generous man will be enriched;
And he who waters will himself be watered.

Book of Proverbs, 11 : 25

Be grateful to your benefactors, even though their generosity is not without self-interest: to gain status, or a place in the world to come.

—adapted from BAHYA IBN PAQUDA

The truly wise are as liberal with their wisdom as clouds
are with their rain.   MOSES IBN EZRA, *Shirat Israel*

See also: CHARITY, GOOD DEEDS, GRATITUDE, PHILANTHROPY

GENTILES

Note. We must be careful not to confuse the Jews' use of
the word "goy" ("gentile") with the word "Christian."
Very often, a Jewish proverb meant to criticize *heathens*
has been translated as if it is anti-Christian. The barbs
of the Jews about *goyim* were often directed against
pagans, not Christians; against barbarians, not Greeks;
against those who practiced savagery, idolatry, licentious
rites. Many folk-sayings about *goyim* preceded Christianity.

An old rabbinical saying goes: "The righteous of all
nations will share in the world to come." The great
Rashi reminded Jews that "Gentiles of the present age
are not heathens." The *Sefer Hasidim* ("Book of the
Pious") says: "If a Jew attempts to kill a non-Jew, help
the non-Jew."

Respect for others, woven into the values of plural-
ism, forms an old and integral part of Jewish tradition.
The rabbis taught: "Whether Jew or gentile, man or
woman, rich or poor—according to a man's deeds does
God's Presence rest on him."

The highest traditional contempt of Jews is reserved
for those who are cruel, uncivilized, or unlearned; those
who hurt, torment, exploit, or kill others.

Yet it would be dishonest to deny that relentless persecution, century after century, in nation after nation, has
left Jews a legacy of bitter sayings: *"Dos ken nor a goy"*
("That only a *goy* is capable of doing"); *"A goy blaybt
a goy"* ("A gentile remains a gentile," or, less literally,
"What did you expect: once an anti-Semite, always an
anti-Semite").

Experience is a bitter teacher, and it made many
Jews feel that gentiles are not always gentle.

—L.R.

Gentiles aren't used to Jewish troubles.

God says: "Both the gentiles and the Israelites are My

handiwork: Can I let the former perish on account of the latter?"   TALMUD: *Sanhedrin*, 98b

The Jew is urged to aid gentiles in administering the affairs of his community.   TALMUD J.: *Gittin*, 5 : 9

If a non-Jew blesses you, respond "Amen," for it is written: "Thou shalt be blessed by all peoples."

TALMUD J.: *Berakoth*, 8b

For a Jew to cheat a gentile is worse than to cheat a Jew, for in addition to breaking the moral law, it brings Jews into contempt.   TALMUD, *Baba Kama*, 113b

✽ If you permit your tongue to speak evil of gentiles, it will end by speaking evil of Israelites.

MIDRASH: *Deuteronomy Rabbah*, 6 : 3

See also: COMPASSION, DUTY, JEWS

GIRLS

Note. The position of the girl in the family, the assumptions of what her duties and future duties as a wife would be, the physiological determinants and limits of female work, menstruation, pregnancy, breast feeding, the care of babies, the subordinate social status of girls—all these show great similarity in most of the cultures and tribes of antiquity. Farming, stock tending, nomadic life, the division of labor that automatically assigned cooking, feeding, the care of the young to the female (and hunting, heavy labor, war, defense, etc., to the male)—all these, despite some conspicuous exceptions, explain a good deal about the status of women in religious hierarchies, in pre-industrial society, in medieval court circles, in the working and middle classes produced in post-agrarian societies.

But the particular rights and protections given Jewish girls (female orphans, e.g., were required by law to be helped before males—so that girls would never be forced to beg) are too often misconstrued by historians, and can only be understood in the context of those facts and laws of Jewish life that governed family relations. For a brief description of this background, see the headnote for WOMEN.

—L.R.

A baby girl is a good omen.

✱ The girl who can't dance says the band can't keep time.

✱ An ugly girl hates the mirror.

If everybody looks for a pretty bride, what happens to the ugly girls?

✱ It is easier to guard a sack of fleas than a girl in love.

✱ Homely girls are easily seduced.

Jews have no nunneries.

With nets you catch birds, with presents—girls.

✱ When a girl has no other virtues, a freckle can be considered one.

A maiden is like velvet—fondle her.

It is not wise to borrow from a poor man—or kiss an ugly girl.

All girls lap up sweet words.

Girls should marry before boys do, for the shame of a woman is greater than the shame of a man.
                              TALMUD: *Kethuboth*, 67b

Help the girl orphan before the boy orphan; the boy may beg, but not the girl.
                —adapted from TALMUD: *Kethuboth*, 67b

Little girl, don't be so sweet—lest you be consumed.
                              Yemenite proverb

Go understand a girl: she can't wait for the wedding, yet weeps on the way to the canopy.
                              SHOLEM ALEICHEM

See also: DAUGHTERS, MEN AND WOMEN

GIVING AND TAKING

The man who likes to take does not like to give.

✱ Lend before witnesses, but give without them.

If you put something in, there is something to take out.

If you are given, take; if someone else takes, cry "Help!"

Let not your hand be stretched out to take, and withdrawn
at the time of giving back.

BEN SIRACH: *Ecclesiasticus*, 4 : 31

See also: CHARITY, GENEROSITY, GREED, JEALOUSY, PHILAN-
THROPY

GLORY

Too much glory can be half disgrace.

Honor is more precious than glory.

❋ Any man surrounded by dwarfs looks like a giant.

Glory avoids those who chase after it, and is endowed on
many who did not try to pursue it.

❋ Good men need no monuments: their acts remain their
shrines.   —adapted from *Mishneh Shekalim*, 5 : 2

See also: HONOR AND HONORS

GLUTTONY

The eye is small, but can devour all.

❋ Those who have wide mouths have narrow hearts.

One beggar can't be at two fairs.

One man can't eat with two mouths.

The glutton for cake often loses the bread.

What a fat belly cost, I wish I had; what a fat belly does, I
wish on my enemies.

Gluttons dig their graves with their teeth.

The man who increases his flesh increases food for the
worms.

Sayings of the Fathers, 2 : 8

If you feel driven to eat, get up in the middle of a meal—
and stop.   BEN SIRACH: *Ecclesiasticus*, 31 : 21

The glutton is like a dog who is never satiated; he becomes
disgusting to everyone and, being subject to diarrhea, his
body becomes like a sieve . . .   SAADIA GAON

Heavy eating is worse than daggers.   JUDAH BEN ASHER

More men die from overeating than undernourishment.

NACHMAN OF BRATSLAV

See also: EXCESS, FOOD, GREED, WINE

GOD

Note. The following tale is to be found in the *Baba Mezi'a* tractate of the Jerusalem Talmud:

When a certain rabbi went to Rome, he chanced to find a jeweled bracelet that belonged to the Empress. An official crier went about proclaiming: "Whoever returns the Empress's bracelet within thirty days shall receive a reward; but if it be found upon him after thirty days—his head will be cut off."

The rabbi returned the bracelet on the thirty-first day. The Empress asked him: "Did you not hear my proclamation?"

"Yes," answered the rabbi.

"Then why did you not return the jewel within the thirty days?"

"In order," said the rabbi, "that you should not say that I feared you; I returned it because I fear God."

Whereupon the Empress said, "Blessed be the God of the Jews."

—L.R.

See GOD and MAN, GOD: WHERE DOTH HE RESIDE?, GOD: HIS POWER, GOD: COMPLAINTS ABOUT, GOD: IN HIS BEHALF

GOD'S NAME

Note. Four Hebrew letters, YHVH (which appear 6,823 times in the Old Testament), form the Hebrew name for God: *Adonai* is a substitute for these sacred letters. *Adonai* is never pronounced by pious Jews except during solemn prayer, and with head covered. When God is mentioned in ordinary discourse, a devout Jew changes even the substitute names: instead of "*Adonai*" he says "*Adoshem*"; when saying "*Elohim*" he makes it "*Elokhim*." Orthodox Jews, writing or printing the name of the Lord, omit the vowel, to make G-d.

We do not know how YHVH was pronounced by the ancients: There are no vowel letters in Hebrew; vowel *sounds* are indicated by diacritical marks (dots, dashes). Today, YHVH is rendered vocally as "Yahveh." ("Jehovah," which first appeared in Christian texts in 1516, is simply incorrect—based on a German papal scribe's reading of YHVH with the diacritical marks meant for *Adonai*, which had been added in the margins of a scroll, as aids to pronunciation; so YHVH became, in transliterated Latin, YeHoVaH.) The King James version of the Bible usually translates YHVH as "Lord."

—L.R.

GOD AND MAN

❋ Truth rests with God alone—and a little with me.

When God does a favor, He doesn't boast about it.

Before God, weep; before people, laugh.

The rainbow is a sign that God has forgiven us.

❋ God is closest to those whose hearts are broken.

Man reaches God through truth.

No one ever lost anything to God.

When God gives bread, men provide butter.

❋ God waits long, but He pays with interest.

We get life from God, but make a living from men.

Dear God: Save me from having but one shirt, one eye, or one child.

Of God's purpose, one should not ask questions.

❋ God punishes; it is man who takes revenge.

About tomorrow, let God worry.

Man needs woman, woman needs man, and both need God.

❋ Some don't believe in God, yet ask His mercy.

God sends the remedy before the disease.

God punishes with one hand—but blesses with the other.

❋ Don't try to bargain with the Lord.

We don't know what to thank God for.

He who gave us teeth will give us bread.

It is better to receive from God by the spoonful than from man by the bushel.

What God does not choose to give, you cannot take.

God has no riches of his own; it's what he takes from one that he gives to another.

The spirit of God is pleased with one whom the spirit of man finds pleasing.

When we are young, God forgives our stumblings; when we mature, God weighs our works; when we grow old, God waits—for our repentance.

❋ Oh God: Spare us what we can learn to endure.

❋ Oh, Lord, give me a good excuse.

There is no mediator between God's children and God.
TALMUD J.: *Berakoth*, 9 : 1

Keep me as the apple of Thine eye, and hide me under the shadow of Thy wings. *Book of Psalms*, 17 : 8

God loves these three: the one who does not get angry; the one who does not get drunk; and the one who does not insist upon his privileges. TALMUD: *Pesahim*, 113a

Lord of the world, rather a bitter olive given by Thee than sweets provided by man. TALMUD: *Sanhedrin*, 108b

❋ To love God truly, you must first love man. And if anyone tells you that he loves God but does not love his fellow man, he is lying. Hasidic saying

His glory is on me—and mine on Him. *Hymn of Glory*

A broken and contrite heart, Oh God, [do] not despise.
Book of Psalms, 51 : 17

He who hears himself cursed and remains silent becomes a partner of God—for does not the Lord hear nations blame Him, yet remain silent.
MIDRASH: *Psalms*, 86 : 1

❋ If God really loved man, would He have created him?

Who displeases man displeases God.
Sayings of the Fathers, 3 : 10

❋ If the [Greek] gods steal, by whom shall their believers swear?   APOCRYPHA: *Ahikar*, 8 : 22

Lord, be Thou neither against us nor for us!
                    BAR KOCHBA, before going into battle;
                    in TALMUD J.: *Ta'anith*, 4 : 6

He who flees from God flees into himself.   PHILO

❋ God: Make an opening for me no wider than a needle's eye, and I will open for you a gate through which armies can pass.   *Pesikta de Rabbi Kahana*

God gave man the power to reason, which makes man capable of perfection.
            MAIMONIDES, *Guide to the Perplexed*, I : 2

Reason is the mediator between God and man.
        ABRAHAM IBN EZRA, *Commentary to Pentateuch*

Man was created to serve God and to cleave to Him, not to accumulate wealth and erect buildings which he must leave behind.   IBN EZRA, *Yesod Mora*

As man acts, God reacts.   BAAL SHEM TOV

I don't want to know why I suffer, but whether it is for Thy sake.   THE BERDICHEVER RABBI

It is my desire to do God's will, not that God do my will.
                    THE GERER RABBI

When young, remember that service to the Lord is like food—best when fresh; and when old, remember that service to God is like wine—best when old.
                    THE KOBRINER RABBI

Don't ask God for what you think is good; ask Him for what he thinks is good for you.
                    "THE CHOFETZ CHAIM"

❋ God will forgive me: *c'est son métier* ["it's his business"].   HEINRICH HEINE

See also: HELL, HEREAFTER, HEREDITY, HERETICS, HOLINESS, MARRIAGE, WOMEN

GOD:—WHERE DOTH HE RESIDE?

God said: Wherever you find the mark of a man's foot, there I am revealed to you.

❋ The favorite place of God is in the heart of man.

Have not I commanded thee: Be strong and of good courage; be not affrighted, neither be thou dismayed: for the Lord thy God is with thee whithersoever thou goest.   *Book of Joshua*, I : 9

Oh burning bush: Not because you are tall, but because you are lowly, did God reveal Himself in you.
                                    TALMUD: *Shabbath*, 67a

❋ God conceals himself from man's mind, but reveals himself to his heart.   *Zohar*

Thou art far, farther than the heaven of heavens, and near, nearer than my body is to me.
                      BAHYA BEN ASHER, *Kad ha-Kemah*

❋ A house testifies that there was a builder, a dress that there was a weaver, a door that there was a carpenter; so our World by its existence proclaims its Creator, God.
—adapted from RABBI AKIBA, *Midrash Temura*, ch. 3

GOD: HIS POWER

He who took care of the parents will also provide for the children.

❋ God is not kind to those who are not kind to others.

❋ Were God to will it, a broom would shoot.

Only God can judge.

Man drives, but it is God who holds the reins.

If God doesn't approve, a fly doesn't move.

God gives nothing for nothing.

❋ Man makes plans; God changes them.

God does not bargain, nor does He change.

Whom God would punish, he sends bad children.

God sends the frost according to the clothes.

❋ Rome's Hebrew elders were asked, "If your God takes no pleasure in the worship of idols, why does He not destroy them?" The Hebrews replied, "If men worshipped what the world does not need, God would have destroyed them; but men worship the sun, the moon, the stars, the planets; is God then to destroy His world because of the fools?"

The Roman replied, "Then He ought to destroy the things the world does not need, and leave the others." To which the Hebrew elders said, "Then the worshippers of the stars, sun, and moon would be strengthened in their idolatry, for they would say, 'Behold, these verily are true gods, for they have not been destroyed.' "
—adapted from TALMUD: *'Abodah Zarah*, 54b

Everything is in God's hands, except the fear of God.
TALMUD: *Berakoth*, 32b

❈ When we appear before His Throne, God will not ask, "Have you believed in God?" but "Have you dealt honorably with your fellow men?"
—adapted from TALMUD: *Shabbath*, 3a

God is long-suffering, but He collects His due.
TALMUD J.: *Ta'anith*, 2 : 1

❈ Wherever you find man's footprints, there God was before you.   *Mekilta to Exodus*, 17 : 6

A day in the mind of God is like a millennium in the reckoning of man.   *Book of Psalms*, 90 : 4

The ways of man are pure in his own eyes; but the Lord weighs the motives.   *Book of Proverbs*, 16 : 2

❈ God left unfinished the north corner of the world, saying: "Whoever claims to be a god, let him complete that."   *Pirke de Rabbi Eliezer*, ch. 3

God is everywhere, even in evil thoughts.
THE KORETSER RABBI

GOD: COMPLAINTS ABOUT

Note. One of the most interesting, surprising, and (to me) endearing aspects of the attitude of Jews to the Lord is the candor of their complaints about Him: grievances phrased with such tact, felicity, irony or wit that they manage to stop just this side of the sacrilegious.

To be both pious and critical, loving and sardonic, fearful and unafraid, respectful and indignant, represents a most delicate and sophisticated feat.

I think that the complaints against the Lord are managed without guilt, which is the most remarkable aspect of all, because believing Jews hold that:

(a) God made a covenant with the Hebrews, according to the Holy Torah;

(b) a contract requires responsible performance from both sides, however vast the disparity in the status, virtue or power of the contracting parties;

(c) reciprocal responsibility justifies a complaint by either party about the imperfect conduct or non-performance of the other;

(d) the relation between a Jew and the Lord is one-to-one, since the entire structure of the Jewish faith rests on the assertion, in the Talmud, that there are no mediators, no intermediaries, between God and man (rabbis are not agents of the Lord);

(e) since Jews hold that God gave each man a Conscience, by which to decide for himself whether to observe His commandments or not; and Reason, through which to analyze everything under the sun; and Free Will, which contains the capacity to err, sin or blaspheme (and take the consequences), Jews simply exercise these God-given gifts to the full;

(f) the Lord of the Universe is surely far too great, kind, just and all-knowing to mind little man's efforts to lighten life's burdens by the play and pleasure of levity, for—

(g) it would be a humorless, therefore imperfect, God who did not understand the preciousness of laughter in a world so laden with suffering and tragedy.

What I am trying to explain may come down to the simple fact that a robust people, if not their solemn pedants, simply take it for granted that God has a sense of humor, too. How else could He put up with *His* problems?

—L.R.

❋ Dear God, You help strangers, so why not me?

❋ "Thou hast chosen us from among all the nations"—but why did you have to pick on the Jews?

God will provide—but if only He would provide *until* He provides.

❋ If God lived on earth, people would knock out all His windows.

❊ Don't question God, for He may reply: "If you're so anxious for answers, come up here."

O, Lord: glance down from heaven and take a good look at Your world.

Don't play games with God—first, because you shouldn't; second, because He won't let you.

❊ Dear God, help me get up: I can fall down by myself.

God loves the poor, but He helps the rich.

❊ What God does is best—probably.

Whom God loves, He punishes.

Man thinks, and God laughs.

Father in heaven, You don't have to raise me up, but don't throw me down.

God pays well, but He is often in arrears.

❊ God, if you don't help me, I'll ask my uncle in America.

GOD: COMPLAINTS IN HIS BEHALF

❊ Men fear the gallows more than God.

If only Man were worth as much as God can give.

There is only one God—and so many enemies.

God made Man in three stages: when he is young, God forgives his stumblings; when he is man, God weighs his purpose; when he grows old, God waits until he repents.

If men thanked God for good things, they wouldn't have time to complain about the bad.

There is no room for God in the man who is full of himself.
                                                    Hasidic saying

God decides what a man shall be, and what shall befall him, but not whether he shall be righteous or wicked.
                                        TALMUD: *Niddah* 16b

❊ An old man was invited into Abraham's tent, but Abraham learned that the man was a fire worshipper and turned him out. That night, God appeared to Abraham, and said, "I have borne with that fool for

seventy years; could you not have endured him for one
brief night?"

—Old story, attributed to *Poor Richard's Almanack*,
which credits no earlier source

Because the prophets had to speak in a language understood by the masses, they said He is a jealous and aveng-
ing God.   JOSEPH ALBO, *Sefer Ikarim*, 2 : 4

Men are wrong to think that outside of the Bible nothing
persuades belief in the Eternal; many other proofs of
God exist . . .   SAADIA GAON

Don't ask God to change the laws of nature for you.
                              NACHMAN OF BRATSLAV

See also: ADAM, FAITH, GOOD DEEDS, HEREAFTER, PIETY,
PRAYER, SABBATH, SATAN, VIRTUE, WORSHIP

GOLD

✳ The age of gold was the age when gold did not rule.

Gold has a dirty father (the earth) but is honored everywhere.

Gold shines—even in mud.

✳ The key of gold opens all doors.

A little gold can lighten up your world.

Gold is attracted to gold.

Gossip is silenced with gold.

Gold confers authority.

Gold can't accompany a man to heaven.

The love of gold leads to madness.

See also: BUSINESS, FORTUNE, GREED, MONEY, RICHES,
WEALTH

GOOD

Note. "Love thy neighbor as thyself" comes from Leviticus
(19 : 18). This so-called Golden Rule is basic to Judaism;
it is extensively cited in Rabbinical literature; it is
found in the sayings of Ben Sirach (*Ecclesiasticus*), in

the Testament of the Twelve Patriots, in Tobit; it is in
Philo, in Josephus, and, of course, is told of Hillel, who
said: "What is hateful to thee, do not unto others: that
is the whole Law—all the rest is commentary." (See
headnotes for GOOD DEEDS, VIRTUE.)

—L.R.

❋ Too good is bad for you.

The man who is far from his good is near his harm.

Whether you do little or much, let it be out of good intentions.   TALMUD: *Shebu'oth*, 15b

The Evil Impulse serves goodness, for if not for the Evil
Impulse no man would marry or beget children, or engage in trade.
—adapted from MIDRASH: *Ecclesiastes Rabbah*, 3 : 11

See also: EVIL, GOOD DEEDS, GOOD AND EVIL, GOOD MEN,
SELFISHNESS, SIN, VIRTUE

GOOD DEEDS

Note. Kiddush ha-Shem is the cardinal conception that men
become sanctified by following God's commandments
and in so doing "sanctify His name." In Leviticus (22 :
32), the Lord says: "I will be hallowed among the children of Israel; I am the Lord which hallows you." (The
opposite of *Kiddush ha-Shem* is *Hillul ha-Shem*, "the
profaning of God's name.")

Kiddush ha-Shem involves the idea that any generous,
altruistic deed honors all Jews, for the Jews are "a
kingdom of priests," and each Jew must bear a responsibility to act in such a way as to honor all Jewry.

As a case of true *Kiddush ha-Shem*, the Talmud cites
the case of a Jew's returning to an Arab, from whom
he had purchased a camel, a jewel he had found around
the camel's neck, saying: "I bought a camel, not a gem."
And the Arab cried, "Blessed be the God of Israel."

—L.R.

A good deed has many claimants.

❋ Troubles no one wants to steal from you; good deeds
no one can.

❋ The man who comforts a pretty young widow does not only mean to perform a good deed.

The beggar does more good for the giver than the giver does for the beggar.

❋ He who has fed strangers may have fed angels.

That man deserves the highest honors who does not ask for them, but performs worthy deeds.

If a man intends to perform a good deed but is prevented from doing so, he is to be treated as though he has done it.

TALMUD: *Kiddushin*, 40a

Happy is he who performs a good deed: for he may tip the scales for himself and the world.

TALMUD: *Kiddushin*, 40 : 2

The one who causes a good deed to be performed is as meritorious as the one who performs it.

TALMUD: *Sanhedrin*, 99b

❋ The beginning and the end (of Torah) is the performance of lovingkindness.   TALMUD: *Sotah*, 14a

❋ The whole value of a benevolent deed lies in the love that inspires it.   TALMUD: *Sukkah*, 49b

Good deeds are better than creeds.
—adapted from *Sayings of the Fathers*

Deeds of kindness weigh as much as all the commandments.   TALMUD J.: *Pe'ah*, 1 : 1

He who does not himself do good cannot depend on his father's works and merits.

MIDRASH: *Midrash Psalms*, 1 : 64

The door that is closed to a good deed will open to a doctor.   MIDRASH: *Song of Songs Rabbah*, 6 : 1

❋ Happy is the man whose deeds are greater than his learning.   MIDRASH: *Eliyahu Rabbah*, 17

Be like a helmsman—on the lookout for good deeds.
MIDRASH: *Leviticus Rabbah*, 21 : 4

❋ It is better to visit a house of mourning than a house of feasting.   *Ecclesiastes*, 2

The man whose good deeds exceed his wisdom is like a tree with few branches and many roots: all the raging winds will not move him.

Sayings of the Fathers, 3 : 17

The reward of a *mitzvah?* Another *mitzvah.*
—adapted from *Sayings of the Fathers*

One *mitzvah* [good deed] leads to another, just as one *averah* [sin] leads to another.

Sayings of the Fathers, 4 : 5

Whoever performs one good action gains an advocate, whoever commits a sin procures an accuser.

Sayings of the Fathers, 4 : 15

❋ That good deed is most meritorious of which no one knows.   —adapted from MAIMONIDES

❋ Naked a man comes into the world, and naked he leaves it; after all his toil, he carries away nothing—except the deeds he leaves behind.   —adapted from RASHI

To revive a man is no slight thing.

NACHMAN OF BRATSLAV

A man's good deeds are used by the Lord as seeds for planting trees in the Garden of Eden: thus, each man creates his own Paradise.   THE MEZERITZER RABBI

Let a good man do good deeds with the same zeal that the evil man does bad ones.   THE BELZER RABBI

❋ Good deeds bring a man immortality.

THE SASSOVOR RABBI

When Akaybya was on his death-bed, his son asked, "Father, commend me to your friends."
"No, my son," said Akaybya, "I shall not."
"Have you found anything unworthy in me?" asked the son.
"No, my son. But it is your deeds that can bring you close to men, and your deeds can drive you from them."
—adapted from ELEAZAR ROKEACH

See also: ALTRUISM, CHARITY, DUTY, EVIL, FORGIVENESS, GENEROSITY, GOD, GOOD, GOOD AND EVIL, GOOD MEN, GRATITUDE, GRIEF, GUILT, HEART, HEAVEN, HELP, HEREAFTER, HEREDITY, HOLINESS, JEALOUSY, SELFISHNESS, SIN

GOOD AND EVIL

Good and a little is better than bad and a lot.

✻ Better the bad of the good [men] than the good of the bad [ones].

It is better to see good than to hear bad.

Both good and evil are the work of our own hands.
                    APOCRYPHA: *Psalms of Solomon*, 9 : 4

The potter does not test cracked vessels, because to tap them even once is to break them; but he does test good vessels, because no matter how many times he taps them they do not break; so God tests not the wicked but the righteous.   MIDRASH: *Genesis Rabbah*, 32 : 3

There is no good without some evil in its midst.
                    MIDRASH: *Genesis Rabbah*, 68 : 10

The path of goodness begins in a thicket of thorns, but soon emerges into an open plain; the way of evil begins as a plain, but soon runs into thorns.
                    Sifre Deuteronomy, 11 : 6

✻ Man is lucky that during childhood he cannot tell good from evil, for if he had mature powers of perception he would die of grief.
                    BAHYA IBN PAQUDA, *Duties of the Heart*

See not evil in others and good in yourself, but the good in the other and the failings in yourself.
                    THE BERDICHEVER RABBI

See also: EVIL, GOD, GOOD, GOOD MEN, JEALOUSY, SELFISH-NESS, SIN, VIRTUE

GOOD MEN

He is a good man, but his dog won't let you near him.

Good men need no recommendation, and bad men it won't help.

✻ Where the good pay, the bad demand.

Be on the best of terms with all men, including the heathen: you may be beloved above and well liked below.
                    TALMUD: *Berakoth*, 17a

When the good die, they live (in the example they provide).   TALMUD: *Berakoth*, 18b

Good men promise little and perform much; wicked men promise much and perform nothing.
                            TALMUD: *Nedarim*, 21b

The man who asks mercy for another while both are in peril will be answered first.
                            TALMUD: *Baba Kamma*, 92a

To a fool it is like sport to do wrong; but is it hateful to a man of sense.   *Book of Proverbs*, 10 : 23

We cannot understand either the prosperity of the evil or the sufferings of the virtuous.
                            Sayings of the Father, 4 : 21

Good men are hard to provoke and easy to calm.
                  —adapted from *Sayings of the Fathers*, 5 : 17

Good men need no monuments: their deeds are their shrines.   *Mishne Shekalim*, 5 : 2

I dislike the man who is like snow: at first white and pure; later muddy and soiled.   THE RIZINER RABBI

❋ As between a pious man and a clever man, the pious one is superior; as between a pious man and a kind man, the kind man is superior.   THE KORETSER RABBI

In freezing weather, one man keeps warm by donning a coat, the other by heating his house; the first is selfish, the second is humane.   THE KOTZKER RABBI

❋ I don't like the good man who preens himself on his goodness.   THE LUBLINER RABBI

The man who has led a good life will find many allies.
                            NACHMAN OF BRATSLAV

See also: EVIL, GOOD, GOOD DEEDS, GOOD AND EVIL, HEATHEN, HEREAFTER, PIETY, SIN, VIRTUE

GOSSIP

❋ What's easy to say may be hard to bear.

What you don't see with your eyes, don't invent with your mouth.

❋ The tongue has no bones—so it's loose.

❋ If you want to find out what's happening in your house, talk to your neighbors.

It's easier to hear a secret than to keep it.

❋ A tongue can be a dangerous weapon.

You can't close *all* the mouths on earth.

❋ Loose tongues are worse than wicked hands.

Our ears often don't hear what our mouths say.

❋ Your ears belong to yourself; your tongue is heard by others.

Send [only] your ears into the streets.

If you don't open your mouth, no flies will get in.

When people keep gossiping about something, it may be true.

❋ Those who think of themselves don't gossip about others.

Run from gossip as you would run from ghosts.

Gossip is the most common of human habits and causes the most trouble.

People eat and drink together, yet pierce each other with the sword of their tongues.   TALMUD: *Yomah*, 9b

Gossip comes from peddlers—and vermin from rags.
                              TALMUD: *Berakoth*, 51b

Man's fingers are shaped like nails, so that he can put them in his ears when ugly words reach them.
                              TALMUD: *Kethuboth*, 5a

Your friend has a friend, and your friend's friend has a friend [so be discreet].
                    —adapted from TALMUD: *Kethuboth*, 109b

❋ Gossipers start with praise and end with derogation.
                    MIDRASH: *Tanhuma Shelah*, 9

❋ Even if all of a slander is not believed, half of it is.
                    MIDRASH: *Genesis Rabbah*, 56 : 4

The whisperer separates friends.
                    Book of Proverbs 16 : 28

What your eyes have seen
Report not hastily to the mob.   *Book of Proverbs*

He who overlooks an offense promotes good will;
He who repeats a tale separates friends.
                                        Book of Proverbs 17 : 9

Where there is no wood, a fire goes out;
And where there is no whisperer, a quarrel dies down.
                                        Book of Proverbs 26 : 20

From a man's mouth you can tell what he is.   *Zohar*

Men's eyes and ears don't always depend on will power;
    but a man's tongue always is subject to his will.

                                                        Zohar

You enclose your vineyard with thorns: put doors and bolts
    on your mouth.   BEN SIRACH: *Ecclesiasticus*, 28 : 24

❊ Gossip: nature's telephone.   SHOLEM ALEICHEM

See also: CRITICISM, FOOLS, LIES/LIARS, RUMOR, SCANDAL,
    SECRETS, SLANDER, TALK

GOVERNMENT

Note. Ancient Israel created a commonwealth (1200–586
    before the Christian Era) that is rather remarkable in
    the history of man's political institutions. The political
    theory imbedded in Deuteronomy and Leviticus (much
    neglected by students of political science) gave the
    Hebrews the basis for a state with a "built-in" constitu-
    tion in which certain rights of the people enjoyed
    priority, and in which the *duties* of a ruler to his people
    were delineated with as great force as were his powers or
    privileges.

    Dr. J. H. Hertz compares the stable, undespotic king-
doms of Israel to the 158 quarreling, jealous, fratricidal
states of ancient Greece: "The Greeks displayed to the
full that fatal vice of factiousness which imbues politics
with fanaticism, and proscribes opponents by massacre
or exile."

    Nietzsche called the Greeks "political fools" because
every political experiment they tried failed; and portions
of the Greek population were oppressed whether a city-
state was built on a theory of republic, aristocracy,

oligopoly, democracy, or some other. By contrast to Greece, Egypt, or the despotisms of the East, Israel's theocratic state was stable, unified, and uniquely democratic.

—L.R.

A fool in office is an ass tied to the sun.

Co-rulers become over-rulers.

Sages are superior to kings.

❋ Don't live in a city run by scholars.
AKIBA in TALMUD: *Pesahim*, 112a

❋ Fish die out of water; men die without law and order.
TALMUD: *'Abodah Zarah*, 4a

The real guardians of a state are the teachers.
TALMUD J.: *Hagigah*, 1 : 7

The power of great men can be used for evil no less than good. —adapted from TALMUD: *Sukkah*, 52a

Safety lies in the counsel of multitudes.
Book of Proverbs, 24 : 6

Where there is no vision, the people perish.
Book of Proverbs, 29 : 18

❋ Pray for political stability, for if not for fear of the government men would swallow each other alive.
Sayings of the Fathers, 3 : 1

Do not place trust in princes. *Book of Psalms*, 146 : 3

What kind of man is fit to govern? Either a sage given power, or a king who seeks wisdom. IBN GABIROL

A government can fall because of one injustice.
"THE CHOFETZ CHAIM"

See also: AUTHORITY, BARBARIANS, COMMUNITY, COMPROMISE, DEMOCRACY, EQUALITY, FREEDOM, LAW, POLITICS, POWER

GRAMMAR

Grammar is to speech what salt is to food.
IBN EZRA, *Shirat Yisrael*

God created grammar according to the principles of nature.
—adapted from ABRAVANEL

See also: LANGUAGE, SPEECH, WORDS

GRATITUDE

We never know all we should be grateful to God for.

It was for my good that my cow broke her leg.

Be grateful to the beggar: he gave you the chance to do good.

❋ If a Jew breaks his leg, he thanks God that he did not break both legs; if he breaks both legs, he thanks God he did not break his neck.

Rab declared: "We give thanks unto Thee, oh Lord our God, because we are able to give thanks."

TALMUD: *Sotah,* 48

See also: CHARITY, COMPASSION, ENVY, GOOD DEEDS, GENEROSITY, INGRATITUDE, JEALOUSY, PRAYER

GREAT MEN

❋ The man who is surrounded by dwarfs looks like a giant.

If a great man says something that seems illogical, don't laugh; try to understand it.   TALMUD: *Berakoth,* 19b

The greater the man, the greater his potential for evil (no less than good).   TALMUD: *Sukkah,* 52a

As long as light comes from the great, the light of the lesser is unseen; once the light of the great disappears, the light of the lesser shines.

MIDRASH: *Deuteronomy Rabbah,* 5

Little sins are great when great men commit them.
—adapted from ABRAHAM IBN EZRA
Commentary to Genesis, 32 : 9

The man who can't accept criticism can't become great.

NACHMAN OF BRATSLAV

See also: CRITICISM, GOOD MEN, POWER, SAGES, WISE MEN

GREED

Men are always close—to their pockets.

❋ The eye is small, but devours all.

❋ If eyes did not see, hands would not take.

If you look for cake, you'll lose your bread.

What is grabbed will be lost.

Don't desire what you can't acquire.

❋ When the paupers start dancing, the musicians stop playing.

Show a dog a finger, and he wants your whole hand.

A handful does not satisfy a lion.
TALMUD: *Berakoth*, 3b

When the camel demanded horns, they cut off his ears.
TALMUD: *Sanhedrin*, 106a

Some men begin with a pitcher and end with a barrel.
TALMUD: *Baba Kamma*, 27a

If you grasp too much, you cannot hold it; when you take a little, you can.   TALMUD: *Rosh Hashanah*, 4b

Those who increase their flesh only increase food for the worms.   *Sayings of the Fathers*, 2 : 8

The man who loves silver won't remain satisfied with silver.
SAADIA GAON

More die from overeating than from undereating.
NACHMAN OF BRATSLAV

See also: ANIMALS, COMPLAINT, CIRCUMSTANCES, DESIRE, GIVING AND TAKING, GLUTTONY, GOLD, HEALTH, JEALOUSY, SELFISHNESS, SIN

GRIEF

❋ All things grow with time—except grief.

Grief may affect one's words the way wine would.

❋ God is closest to those with broken hearts.

To grieve alone is to suffer most.

Outer garments can hide inner grief.

The deeper the grief, the less words can express it.

No man should be held responsible for the words he utters
in his grief.   TALMUD: *Baba Bathra*, 16a

✻ The man who offers sympathy to someone bereaved a
year ago is like a doctor who asks a man who has broken
a leg to break it again—so that the doctor can mend it
to show his skill.   TALMUD: *Mo'ed Katan*, 21b

Don't try to console a man while the corpse is still in the
house.   *Sayings of the Fathers*, 4 : 25

Bereavement is like a wheel that goes around the world.
       RASHI, *Commentaries on the Pentateuch: Genesis*

Everything that grows begins small and becomes big; but
grief starts big and becomes small—and disappears.
                                                IBN GABIROL, *Ethics*

✻ Children, luckily, can't tell good from evil; if they did,
they would die of grief.
                              —adapted from BAHYA IBN PAQUDA,
                                                Duties of the Heart

✻ If we could not forget, we would never be free from
grief.
                              —adapted from BAHYA IBN PAQUDA,
                                                Duties of the Heart

See also: COMPASSION, CONSIDERATION, EMOTION, GOOD
DEEDS, GROWTH, HEART, SUFFERING, TEARS

GROOMS

Three kinds need to be protected from others: a patient,
a bride, and a groom.   TALMUD: *Berakoth*, 54b

See: BACHELORS, MARRIAGE, WEDDING, WIVES

GROWTH

The man who does not grow grows smaller.
                                          —adapted from HILLEL
                                  in *Sayings of the Fathers*, 1 : 14

Be not in a hurry, like the almond, first to blossom and last
to ripen. Be rather like the mulberry, last to blossom
and first to ripen.   APOCRYPHA: *Ahikar*, 2 : 7

See also: GRIEF, KNOWLEDGE, LEARNING, POWER

GUESTS

❉ Guests, like fish, begin to smell on the third day.

A guest for a day can see quite a way.

❉ We are delighted with a good guest the minute he arrives—and with a bad one, the minute he leaves.

❉ Who is the most despicable of guests? The one who
brings another guest along.

A guest is like rain: too long is a nuisance.

❉ The first day, a guest is fed roast chicken; the second
day, eggs; the third day, beans.

A woman recognizes the character of a guest sooner than
her husband does.   TALMUD: *Berakoth*, 10

See also: HOSPITALITY

GUILT

If you don't steal, you won't feel guilty.

A guilty man runs when no one is chasing him.

The guilty are uneasy [self-conscious].

❉ If you do something wrong, at least enjoy it.

On the thief's head, the hat burns. [For years, I was puzzled by this. Why a hat? Why does it burn? Does a thief
feel as *if* a hat is burning on his head? . . . The Yiddish-
ists I consulted were as baffled as I; but I found the
explanation in a charming story in Ignaz Bernstein's
Jüdische Sprichwörter und Redensarten: It seems that
during a country fair, an old Jew put his broad-brimmed
hat down for a moment to wipe his brow; when he
reached for his hat, it was gone. He looked around
anxiously and, to his dismay, saw a sea of hats similar
to his own. What to do? In a stroke of insight that deserves the immortality he unwittingly acquired, the old

Jew cried out: "Look! Look! The hat on the thief's head is on fire!" At once, one man swept his hat off his head and betrayed his larceny.]

Silence may be equivalent to confession.
TALMUD: Yebamoth, 87b

✳ The guilty man who denies his guilt doubles it.
TALMUD

Guilt has its home among fools.   <i>Book of Proverbs</i>

A broom sweeps clean, and itself becomes soiled; cleanse yourself of those offenses of which you may be guilty.
BAAL SHEM TOV

See also: BLAME, CONSCIENCE, GOOD DEEDS, HEREAFTER, INNOCENCE, LAW, LIARS/LIES, SHAME, TRUTH, VIRTUE

H

HABIT

A dog without teeth still gobbles at a bone.

✳ When a habit begins to cost money, it's called a hobby.

If you always drink vinegar, you don't know there's anything sweeter.

The most common habit is gossip—and it causes the most trouble.

✳ Sins repeated seem permitted.
—adapted from TALMUD: Yomah, 86b

Men cling to the opinions of habit.
MAIMONDES, Guide to the Perplexed, I : 31

Those who live near a waterfall are not disturbed by its roar.   JUDAH ARYEH MOSCATO

It is harder to break evil habits than to split rocks.
THE RIZINER RABBI

See also: CONTENTMENT, CUSTOM, EVIL, EXPERIENCE, TRADITION

HAPPINESS

A heavy purse makes a light heart.

Not every heart that gives forth laughter is happy.

Those who are happy despite poverty can prevail against anything.

❊ From happiness to sorrow takes a moment; from sorrow to happiness takes years.

Melancholy creates nervous ailments; cheerfulness cures them.

Happiness vanishes when envy appears.

❊ While we pursue happiness, we flee from contentment.
Hasidic saying

Three things make a man happy: a good home, a good wife, and good enough possessions.
—adapted from TALMUD: *Berakoth*, 57b

Happy is he who knows his place and stands in his own place. TALMUD

The miserable man is unhappy every day; but the cheerful man enjoys a constant feast.
Book of Proverbs 15 : 15

Bright eyes gladden the heart;
Good news fattens the bones. *Book of Proverbs* 15 : 30

One day's happiness makes a man forget his misfortune; and one day's misfortune makes him forget his past happiness. BEN SIRACH: *Ecclesiasticus*, 11 : 25

When someone tells me he is making a living "but it wouldn't hurt if things were a little better," I ask, "How do you know it wouldn't?" "THE CHOFETZ CHAIM"

See also: ADVERSITY, AMBITION, CONTENTMENT, FAITH, FORTUNE, HOME, JOY, LIFE, LUCK, TORAH, WIVES

HASTE

❊ The only thing speed is good for is catching flies.

No good comes from hurrying.

If you measure fast, you'll cut ten times; if you measure slowly, you need cut but once.

Quickly got, quickly lost.

❋ Sleep faster: we need the pillows.

See also: CAUTION, FORESIGHT, SENSE

HATE

Where you are loved, go rarely; where you are hated, go
  never.

Hatred usually joins lies.

❋ Hatred is the fruit of fear.

❋ The hatred that comes from envy lasts.

❋ If you are fair, your fairness will destroy your hate.

A man should hate only his own shortcomings.

To hate a man is as if to hate God.

Hate ruins the savor of food and the peace of sleep.

Hate is like a channel made by water: it widens continually.   TALMUD: *Sanhedrin*, 7a

Hate is like a plank of a bridge: once put in place, it stays
  there.   TALMUD: *Sanhedrin*, 7a

Hatred for insufficient reason is the greatest of sins.
                                    TALMUD: *Yomah*, 9b

The Holy Temple was destroyed because of baseless hatred.
                                    TALMUD: *Yomah*, 9b

The hatred of other men destroys your own world.
                            Sayings of the Fathers, 2 : 15

Better a dish of herbs, where love is,
Than a fatted ox served with hatred.
                            Book of Proverbs, 15 : 17

Righteous lips cover up hatred.
                            Book of Proverbs 10 : 18

If you will remember the end of all things, you will cease
  hating.   BEN SIRACH: *Ecclesiasticus*, 25 : 6

The man who talks rashly [in railing speech] is hated.
        —adapted from BEN SIRACH, *Ecclesiasticus*, 9 : 18

❋ People usually hate what they do not understand.
                              MOSES IBN EZRA, *Shirat Yisrael*

❋ Love blinds us to faults, but hatred blinds us to virtues.
                              IBN EZRA, *Shirat Yisrael*

❋ A man who hates men is hated by them.
                              IBN GABIROL, *Choice of Pearls*

The man who sows hatred reaps remorse.
                              IBN GABIROL, *Choice of Pearls*

Unfounded hate only multiplies quarrels.
                              NACHMAN OF BRATSLAV

See also: ANGER, ENVY, FRIENDS/FRIENDSHIP, FIGHTING,
HOSTILITY, LOVE, REMORSE, VIRTUE

HEALTH

Too much is unhealthy.

❋ Your health comes first — you can always hang yourself later.

What a fat belly cost, I wish I had; what it does, I wish on
my enemies.

True, God sends us colds—but according to our clothes
[were you dressed warmly enough?].

Don't put a healthy head on a sick pillow.

❋ When the head is a fool, the body is in trouble.

A great doctor does not work alone; a great angel is always
at his side.

Worms eat you when you're dead; worries eat you up when
you're alive.

The man who takes as good care of himself as he does
his livestock won't get sick.

❋ What soap is for the body, tears are for the soul.

If you chew well with your teeth, you'll feel it in your
toes.   TALMUD: *Shabbath*, 152a

Three things drain a man's health: worry, travel, and sin.
                              TALMUD: *Gittin*, 70a

A fox does not die from breathing the dust of his own
den.   TALMUD: *Kethuboth*, 71b

Eat a third and drink a third, but leave the remaining third
of your stomach empty: for then, if anger overtakes
you, there will be room for your rage.
                                    TALMUD: *Gittin*, 70a

Six things are good omens for the sick: sneezing, perspir-
ing, open bowels, emission of semen, sleep—and a
dream.   TALMUD: *Berakoth*, 57b

The science of medicine is authorized by God Himself.
                                    TALMUD: *Berakoth*, 60a

The purpose of maintaining the body in good health is to
[make it possible for you to] acquire wisdom.
         MAIMONIDES: *Commentaries on the Mishnah*, v

See also: ANGER, DISEASE, DOCTORS, ENVY, EXCESS, GREED,
JEALOUSY, MEDICINE, MODERATION, SUFFERING

HEART

❋ A stab in the heart leaves a hole.

❋ God is closest to those with broken hearts.

❋ The heart sees better than the eye.

Trouble tears the heart in two.

❋ Pearls around the neck may be like stones upon the
heart.

❋ A heavy purse makes a light heart.

The heart is small yet embraces the world.

❋ The eye reveals what the heart would say.

When the heart is full, it is the eyes that overflow.

A man's heart is a lock, but even a lock can be opened
with the right key.

❋ God looks at a man's heart before He looks at a man's
brains.

The heart is a half-prophet.

❋ The culture of the heart is greater than the culture of the mind.

The heart of man and the bottom of the sea are unfathomable.

When you pour your heart out, it feels lighter.

God knows that the best synagogue is the human heart.
Hasidic saying

Man can see his reflection in water only when he bends down close to it; and the heart of man, too, must lean down to the heart of his fellow; then it will see itself within his heart.
Hasidic saying

If you want to endure this world, equip yourself with a heart that can withstand suffering.
MIDRASH: *Leviticus Rabbah,* 30

❋ The heart can ennoble any calling: A kind jailer may exceed the saintly in true merit, and a jester may be first in the kingdom of heaven, if they have diminished the sadness of human lives. RABBI BAROKA in TALMUD

❋ Any wound is better than a wound in the heart.
BEN SIRACH, *Ecclesiasticus,* 25 : 13

The tongue is the pen of the heart.
BAHYA IBN PAQUDA, *Duties of the Heart*

Words that come from the heart enter the heart.
MOSES IBN EZRA, *Shirat Yisrael*

❋ Man is a holy Temple, and his heart is the holy of holies. JONATHAN EIBESCHUTZ, *Yaarot Dvash*

See also: COMPASSION, CONSIDERATION, EMOTION, GOOD DEEDS, INTELLIGENCE, REASON

HEATHEN

The heathen is your neighbor, your brother; and to wrong him is a sin. MIDRASH: *Tana de Rabbi Eliyahu,* 284

See also: BARBARIANS, GOOD MEN, JEWS, LOVE, NEIGHBORS, SIN, VIRTUE

HEAVEN

Note. Very orthodox Jews are persuaded that there is a literal heaven. (Cabalists claimed there were two, one on earth and one "in the highest.") *Gan Eden,* "the garden of Eden," is a synonym for the Paradise to come. The Talmud lists seven heavens. (The recurrence of seven as a favored, virtuous, lucky or magical number is, of course, familiar to students of history, philosophy, and the mythology of peoples around the globe: e.g., the Seven Against Thebes, the Seven Deadly Sins, the Seven Gifts of the Spirit, the Japanese Seven Gods of Luck, the Seven Years of Tannhäuser, the Seven Virtues, the Arabs' Seven Viziers, etc. The ancient Hebrew scribes had Seven Names for God, out of the many by which He was called, which required especial care in copying—and during the Middle Ages, the Lord was sometimes referred to as "The Seven.")

Rab, the great savant, said Paradise would entail no eating, drinking, business, envy, hatred, ambition—or cohabitation: the righteous would simply sit around, crowns on their heads, basking in the blazing glory of the Divine Presence. Of this concept, Maimonides dryly noted: "To believe so is to be a schoolboy, who expects nuts and sweetmeats as compensation for his studies. Celestial pleasures can neither be measured nor comprehended by a mortal being, any more than a blind man can distinguish colors, or the deaf appreciate music."

—L.R.

❋ It is worse to be in heaven with a fool than in hell with a sage.

The smallest grass on earth has its guiding star in heaven.

❋ A special place is reserved in Heaven for those who can weep, but not pray.

❋ In Heaven, they do not grant half-favors.
                                    TALMUD: *Yomah,* 69b

❋ There are halls in heaven that open only to the voice of song.   *Zohar*

Better an hour of happiness in heaven, than a lifetime of pleasure on earth.   *Sayings of the Fathers,* 4 : 22

A clown may be first in the kingdom of heaven, if he has helped lessen the sadness of human life.

RABBI BAROKA in TALMUD

See also: GOOD DEEDS, HELL, HEREAFTER, PARADISE, VIRTUE

HELL

Note. Gehenna, the word derived from the Hebrew *gehi-nom* ("hell"), comes from the name of that accursed "valley of the sons of Hinnon" where child sacrifices were made to the idol Moloch. Talmudic literature is unclear about the literal location for a literal Hell to which the wicked shall be sent after death. Except for the very orthodox, and pious clusters of hasidim, Jews do not, I believe, think very much about a fiery abode of unremitting torments for those who were sinners on earth. I must add that Jews are equally ambiguous, or allegorical, about Paradise: its location, daily routines, and unimaginable bliss. (See headnote for HEAVEN.)

—L.R.

❊ Hell is not so bad as the road to it.

One path leads to Paradise, but a thousand lead to Hell.

In Hell you can buy an ox for a penny, but what man there has one?

In Hell, the wicked, too, rest on the Sabbath.

Isaiah asked the Lord, "What must a man do to be saved from Hell?" And the Lord said: "Let him give charity, sharing his bread with the poor, giving money to the scribes and the students; let him not behave arrogantly to his fellow men; let him steep himself in the Torah and in its commandments; let him live by humility; let him not speak in puffed-up spirit. Whoever has these qualities will inherit the future life."

—adapted from MIDRASH: *Pesikta Rabbah,* 198a

The unrepentant go to Hell, the shamed to Eden.

Sayings of the Fathers, 5 : 20

A man's enemy cannot harm him as much as he can harm himself; for his enemy cannot cast a man into Gehenna, as he does himself.   SAADIA GAON

There is no hell like an evil woman [wife].   IBN ZABARA

See also: GOD, HEAVEN, HEREAFTER, SATAN, SIN

HELP

❀ Those who do not help others need doctors to help them.

To help a stranger may be to help an angel.

The man who helps others with no desire for praise deserves the highest of honors.

To help a fellow man may be to tip the scales (of God's reckoning) for the entire world.
           —adapted from TALMUD: *Kiddushin*, 40 : 2

If you do not help a man with his troubles, it is equivalent to bringing troubles to him.   NACHMAN OF BRATSLAV

❀ Always help those who are being persecuted.
                              NACHMAN OF BRATSLAV

See also: ALTRUISM, COMPASSION, CONSIDERATION, COOPERATION, GOOD DEEDS, SERVICE, VIRTUE

HEREAFTER

The scoffer, the liar, the hypocrite, and the slandered can have no share in the future world.

The man who has a son in this world does not feel lonely in the world to come.

❀ The world is like an inn, the world to come like home.
                              TALMUD: *Mo'ed Katan*, 9b

Men who are just, whatever their nation, will be rewarded in the world to come.   TALMUD: *Sanhedrin*, 105a

❀ When a man appears before the Throne of Judgment, the first question he will be asked is not "Have you believed in God?" or "Have you prayed and observed the ritual?"—but "Have you dealt honorably with your fellow man?"   TALMUD: *Shabbath*, 31a

In the hereafter, men will be called to account for depriving themselves of the good things the world offered.
                                        TALMUD J.: *Kiddushin*, end

A bastard can have a place in the world to come.
                                        MIDRASH: *Ecclesiastes Rabbah*

A man must not rely on the virtues of his ancestors: if he does not do good in this world, he cannot fall back on the merit of his fathers, for in the time to come no man will eat off his father's works, but only of his own.
                                        MIDRASH: *Midrash Psalms*, 146 : 3

This world is no more than the vestibule of the world to come, so prepare in life to enter the hereafter.
                                        Sayings of the Fathers, 4 : 16

When a man departs from this world, neither silver nor gold nor jewels accompany him—only Torah, and his good deeds.
                                        Sayings of the Fathers, 6 : 9

❊ Conquerors here are conquered in the hereafter.
                                        Sefer Hasidim

The prosperity that the wicked enjoy here is a measure of the rewards that the righteous will receive in the hereafter.   MIDRASH: *Midrash Psalms*, 37 : 3

We must expect that even in the millennium, though evil will be weakened—it will not be entirely destroyed.
                                        Zohar

In the world to come, there will be neither famine nor war, jealousy nor strife: Prosperity will be everywhere, and the sole task will be to know the Lord. And then men will know things that are now hidden; and they will attain all of that knowledge of the Holy Creator that is within the capacity of mortals.
                                        MAIMONIDES: *Mishneh Torah*, end

❊ Plan for this world as if you hope to live forever; but plan for the hereafter as if you expect to die tomorrow.
                                        IBN GABIROL, *Choice of Pearls*

See also: BASTARDS, DEATH, EVIL, FATE, FUTURE, GOD: COMPLAINTS ABOUT, GOOD DEEDS, GOOD MEN, GUILT, HEAVEN, HELL, RESURRECTION, SIN, VIRTUE

HEREDITY

You need luck to inherit brains.

Don't take credit for what you inherited.

It is not for us to ask why God made some men smart and some men stupid.

A fool is not responsible for the brain he was given.

To do good is better than to inherit intelligence.

The worm in horseradish who thinks he's in heaven is only expressing the worm's capacity for imagination.

What environment can do, heredity cannot do.

MIDRASH: *Tanhuma, Vayetze* 13

See also: ANCESTORS, DEEDS, FAMILY, GOD: COMPLAINTS ABOUT

HERETICS

❋ The heretic has closed his heart, not his mind.

Sailors are not heretics: they live in daily peril.

When he was warned about his associations with a known heretic Rabbi Meir answered, "I enjoy the sweetness of fruit, but throw away the rind."

TALMUD: *Hagigah,* 15b

All Israelites have a share in the future world [except] he who says there is no resurrection, he who says the Law has not been given by God, and an *apikoros* [heretic].

Mishnah

❋ If all the ancient sacred writings had been preserved, some would be found to be heretical.

NACHMAN OF BRATSLAV

See also: APOSTATES, FAITH, GOD: COMPLAINTS ABOUT, RELIGION

HEROES

Note. "The castle [at York, in 1190] had sufficient strength for [the Jews'] defence . . . but the cruel multitude . . . felt such a desire of slaughtering those they intended to despoil, that . . . the attacks continued, till at length the Jews perceived they could hold out no longer. . . .

"When the Jewish council was assembled, the *Haham* [Rabbi] rose and addressed them . . . 'Men of Israel! . . . Death is before our eyes; and we have only to choose an honourable and easy one. If we fall into the hands of our enemies, which we cannot escape, our death will be ignominious and cruel. It is therefore my advice that we elude their tortures; that we ourselves should be our own executioners; that we voluntarily surrender our lives to our Creator. God seems to call for us; let us not be unworthy of that call.' Having said this, the old man sat down and wept.

"The assembly was divided in its opinions. Again the Rabbin rose . . . "My children, since we are not unanimous in our opinions, let those who do not approve of my advice depart from this assembly.' Some departed, but the greater number . . . now employed themselves in consuming their valuables by fire; and every man, fearful of trusting to the timid and irresolute hand of the women, first destroyed his wife and children, and then himself . . .

"All this was transacted in the depth of the night. In the morning the walls of [York] castle were seen wrapt in flames, and only a few . . . beings, unworthy of the sword, were viewed on the battlements, pointing to their extinct brethren. When they opened the gates of the castle, these men verified the prediction of their late Rabbin; for the multitude, bursting through the solitary courts, found themselves defrauded of their hopes, and in a moment avenged themselves on the feeble wretches who knew not how to die with honor."
—Isaac d'Israeli, *Curiosities of Literature,* 1793, vol. 2

See INQUISITION, INTOLERANCE, MARTYRS, PERSECUTION, POGROMS

No man is a hero to his *mishpokhe* [relatives].

Who is a hero? He who suppresses a wisecrack.

The soldiers fight—and the kings are called heroes.

The greatest hero is the man who turns his enemy into a friend.   *Abot de Rabbi Nathan,* 23

See also: COURAGE, ENEMY, GLORY, GREAT MEN, HONOR/ HONORS, WAR

HISTORY

Note. "We are so old that in our history everything has happened and nothing new can occur."   MAX NORDAU

"Jewish history is a history of martyrdom and learning."
HEINRICH GRAETZ

Many pens are broken, and seas of ink consumed, to describe things that never happened.
MIDRASH: *Tanhuma*

The Jews are God's stake in human history.
A. J. HESCHEL

See ISRAEL, JEWS

HOLIDAY

❋ After a holiday, only debts and dirty dishes remain.

HOLINESS

If you sanctify yourself a little, you are sanctified much.
TALMUD: *Yomah,* 39a

We may add to the sacred from the profane.
TALMUD: *Yomah,* 81b

In holy matters, we may promote, but not demote.
TALMUD: *Shabbath,* 21b

There are sparks of holiness in everything; they constitute our spirituality.   THE MEZERITZER RABBI

See also: FAITH, GOD: COMPLAINTS ABOUT, GOOD DEEDS, PIETY, SAINTS, VIRTUE

HOME

Note. The Jewish home is considered a temple, sanctified by God. Each Friday the poorest domicile is scrubbed from stem to stern for the eve and celebration of the holy Sabbath. To call a Jewish woman "a real *baleboste*" means to honor her as a true homemaker.

—L.R.

Things can be good anywhere, but they're even better at home.

There is no greater honor than to stay at home.

❋ Pity the home where everyone is the head.

A man who never leaves his home is like a man who spends his life in prison.

Woe to the house that serves to carry the load of a whole family's quarrels.

Anger in a home is like rottenness in fruit.
TALMUD: *Sotah*, 3b

Immorality in a home is like a worm in fruit.
TALMUD: *Sotah*, 3b

First build a home, then marry.   TALMUD: *Sotah*, 44a

❋ Home? The wife.   TALMUD: *Yomah*, 2a

❋ In his home, even a weaver is a ruler.
TALMUD: *Megillah*, 12b

Dine on onions, but have a home; reduce your food and add to your dwelling.   TALMUD: *Pesahim*, 114a

Like a bird that strays from her nest
Is a man who strays from his home.
Book of Proverbs, 27 : 8

Let your house be an assembling place for the wise: Powder yourself in the dust of their feet, and drink in their words with zest.   *Sayings of the Fathers*, 1 : 4

❋ In his own home, every man is king.
Abot de Rabbi Nathan, 28

The man who builds his home with the wealth of others builds his own grave.
BEN SIRACH: *Ecclesiasticus*, 21 : 9

The trip is never too hard, if you know you're going home.
"THE CHOFETZ CHAIM"

See also: CHILDREN AND PARENTS, HUSBANDS, MARRIAGE, MEN AND WOMEN, WIVES

HOMELAND

There is a divine covenant in everyone's heart: to love his native soil—despite its climate.
MIDRASH: *Genesis Rabbah*, 34 : 15

Some men long more for their homeland than for their
food.   MOSES IBN EZRA, *Shirat Yisrael*

See also: ISRAEL

HONESTY

❋ A man is not honest just because he has had no chance
to steal.

❋ Locks keep out only the honest.

It is not the rich who pay; it is the honest.

❋ An honest slap is better than a false kiss.

If you walk straight, you won't fall.

Treasures unjustly acquired are of no avail;
But honesty saves from death.
                                   Book of Proverbs, 10 : 2

See also: CHARACTER, DISHONESTY, FALSEHOOD, LAW, LIARS/
LIES, SINCERITY, THIEVES

HONOR AND HONORS

Note. The more learned or influential a Jew, the greater
is his responsibility to serve as an example of rectitude.
The concept of common *noblesse oblige* (if you will
pardon the oxymoron) is strong in Jewish life, but Judaic
aristocracy entails not pedigree (which is prized) but
knowledge plus morality plus good deeds.

The most honored figure in the life and culture of
traditional Jewry was the *talmid khokhem*: the scholar
of scholars, one of the rare, spiritual sages fit to be
called "a disciple of the wise," one of those who might
contribute to the awesome accumulated thought and
ruminations known as "the sea of the Talmud." (See
headnote for SCHOLARS.)

—L.R.

Honors are like a shadow: the harder you chase them, the
further they run from you.

❋ Honor is measured by the one who gives it, not by the
one who receives it.

Your honor is dearer than your money.

✿ It is better to die on your feet than to live on your knees.

Faith pulls us to Heaven, honor pulls us to earth.

To pledge yourself is to sell yourself.

The man who does good and does not pursue *koved* [honors], him will *koved* overtake.

Flee from an insult, but don't hurry after honors.

The man who gives with a smile is more honorable than the man who gives with a wince.

Who is honored? He who honors Mankind.

It is more honorable to help a cripple than a scholar.

No labor, however humble, dishonors a man.
> TALMUD: *Nedarim*, 49b

✿ All men should rise when a sage passes.
> TALMUD: *Kiddushin*, 33a

The place does not honor the man; the man honors the place. TALMUD: *Ta'anith*, 21b

Like snow in summer, or rain in harvest,
Honor is unseasonable for a fool.
> *Book of Proverbs*, 26 : 1

The crown of a good name is greater than the crown of learning. *Sayings of the Fathers*, 3 : 13

It is better to be a footstool to a king than a king of fools.
> BERECHIAH BEN NATRONAI, HA-NAKDAN, *Fox Fables*

✿ I am below what people say, and above what they think.
> MOSES IBN EZRA, *Shirat Yisrael*

See also: ANCESTORS, COURAGE, DECORUM, GLORY, HEROES, MONEY, REPUTATION, RICHES, SHAME, VALOR, WEALTH

HOPE

✿ It is good to hope, but bad to depend on it.

✿ Hoping and waiting turn wise men into fools.

✿ Too much hope can drive you crazy.

The longer the wait, the greater the disappointment.

The grave is already open, yet man still hopes.

As long as a man breathes he should not lose hope.

TALMUD J.: *Berakoth*, 9 : 1

Hope deferred makes the heart sick;
But desire fulfilled is a tree of life.

Book of Proverbs, 13 : 12

Number me the days that are not yet come, gather me the raindrops that are scattered, make me the withered flowers to bloom again.

APOCRYPHA: *II Esdras*, 5 : 36

Hope is a liar.   SHOLEM ALEICHEM

HOSPITALITY

Note. Great stress was placed on hospitality, a prime good deed, among Jews. Every synagogue had a hostel, attached or near to it, for wayfarers. The food offered to a guest had to be as abundant as possible, even if (as was often true) a family had to "go without" for many a day to come. *Hakhnosesorkhim*, a recurrent Hebrew phrase for hospitality, was considered Abraham's salient virtue—and is in the liturgy recited each morning. The Passover service emphasizes this, too.

The head of a Jewish household usually tried to bring a stranger home from the synagogue to share the Sabbath dinner. A Jewish stranger in a community on a Friday night was fairly certain to receive an invitation to "come home and make *shabbes* with us."

—L.R.

Hospitality is one form of worship.

❊ He who has fed a stranger may have fed an angel.

Men like guests more than women do.

TALMUD: *Baba Mezi'a*, 97a

Hospitality to strangers shows reverence for the name of the Lord.   TALMUD: *Shabbath*, 127a

To welcome a fellow man is to welcome the *Shekhinah* [Divine Presence].

MIDRASH: *Mekilta to Exodus*, 18 : 12

Welcome everyone—with joy.
> *Sayings of the Fathers,* I : 15

See also: CHARITY, COMPASSION, DUTY, GUESTS, OBLIGATION

HOSTILITY

❋ Hostility is like an itch: the more you scratch, the more it itches.

❋ Hostility is like the plank of a bridge: the longer it endures, the firmer it becomes.

Hostility ruins sleep.

Hostility is like a stream: once it opens a path, it swiftly widens.

❋ Never try to pacify a man at the height of his hostility.

Hostility blinds you to others' virtues.

The hostile man engenders hostility against himself.

❋ Hostility makes an easy alliance with lies.

Hostility comes from fear.

The hostility that is rooted in envy lasts.

In time, hostility becomes hate.

Hostility is curable—unless it rests on envy.
> —adapted from IBN GABIROL, *Choice of Pearls*

❋ The world goes on because of those who close their lips when they meet hostility from others.
> NACHMAN OF BRATSLAV

❋ I conquered my hostility by putting it away until the day I might need it.   THE KORETSER RABBI

See also: ANGER, CRITICISM, HATE, MAN, QUARRELS, PEACE

HUMILITY

❋ Too humble is half proud.

The fruits of humility are love and peace.

Just as water leaves a high place to travel to a low one, so do the words of Torah find a resting place only in the man of humble spirit.   TALMUD: *Ta'anith*, 7a

The larger cluster of grapes hangs down lower than the smaller; so is it among Israel: the greater the man, the humbler he is.   MIDRASH: *Leviticus Rabbah*, 36 : 2

It is better to be humble with the lowly
Then to share spoils with the proud.
                              Book of Proverbs, 16 : 19

❊ Humble yourself here, and you won't be humbled hereafter.   MIDRASH: *Exodus Rabbah*, 30 : 19

Be not like a large door, which lets in the wind, or like a small door, which makes the worthy stoop; be rather like the threshold, which all men are able to cross.
                              Tana de Rabbi Eliyahu, 193

The bashful go to Paradise; the brazen go to Purgatory.
                              Sayings of the Fathers, 5 : 31

Be very humble, for man's destiny is the worm.
                              Sayings of the Fathers, 4 : 4

❊ The summit of intelligence is reached in humility.
                              IBN GABIROL, *Choice of Pearls*

❊ The green shoots of humility are love.
                              IBN GABIROL, *Choice of Pearls*

I find humility a greater help to me than all my fellow men.
                              IBN GABIROL, *Choice of Pearls*

Wisdom begets humility   ABRAHAM IBN EZRA

❊ A sage said: "I never met a man in whom I failed to recognize something superior to myself: if he was older, I said he has done more good than I; if younger, I said I have sinned more; if richer, I said he has been more charitable; if poorer, I said he has suffered more; if wiser, I honored his wisdom; and if not wiser, I judged his faults lighter."   *The Testament of Judah Asheri*

❊ The man who acts humble in order to win praise is guilty of the lowest form of pride.
                              NACHMAN OF BRATSLAV

See also: ARROGANCE, CONCEIT, LOVE, MODESTY, PRIDE, RIGHTEOUSNESS, TORAH, WISDOM

HUNGER

❋ When you're hungry, sing; when you're hurt, laugh.

❋ Those who are sated don't believe those who are hungry.

When the stomach is empty, so is the brain.

Lazy? Hungry.

The stomach has no windows.

❋ When hunger comes through the door, love flees through the window.

Hunger is an insistent landlord.

An empty stomach cannot tolerate anything.

❋ You die of hunger only during a famine.

❋ When a Jew is hungry, he sings; when a nobleman is hungry, he whistles; when a peasant is hungry, he beats up his wife.

Love and hunger can't live together.

A hungry man can have sixty toothaches while a well-fed one smacks his lips.   TALMUD: *Baba Kamma*, 92b

He who is sated with food disdains the honeycomb;
But to the hungry man every bitter thing is sweet.
Book of Proverbs, 27 : 7

The workman's appetite works for him,
For his hunger urges him on. *Book of Proverbs*, 16 : 26

Don't approach a hungry man for a favor: before his meal he is like a voracious animal; after it, like a contented lamb.   SHOLEM ALEICHEM

See also: POOR MEN, POVERTY

HUSBANDS

❋ When a man is too good for this world, it's too bad for his wife.

❋ The man who marries for money earns it.

It is better for a woman to have one husband, though he be useless, than ten wealthy children.

✳ An old man who marries a young wife grows younger—
but she grows older.

A faithless husband makes a faithless wife.
                                    TALMUD: *Sotah*, 10a

A man should not become the husband of a pregnant
woman or divorcee until her child is born.
                                    TALMUD: *Yebamoth*, 36b

✳ A henpecked husband can't get relief in a court.
                                    TALMUD: *Baba Mezi'a*, 75b

See also: DIVORCE, MARRIAGE, MEN AND WOMEN, WIVES

HYPOCRISY

An insincere kiss is worse than an honest blow.

If you want to be considered smart, just agree with everyone.

The hypocrite will never see God's face.
                                    TALMUD: *Sotah*, 42a

There are four classes of men who cannot see the Holy
Spirit: mockers, hypocrites, slanderers, and liars.
                                    MIDRASH: *Midrash Psalms*, 101 : 7

An idolater worships one object, but there is no limit to the
number of men whom the hypocrite will worship.
                                    BAHYA IBN PAQUDA, *Duties of the Heart*

✳ Beware the man who has two faces—and two hearts.
                                    MOSES IBN EZRA, *Shirat Yisrael*

See also: GOSSIP, LIARS/LIES, SLANDER

I

IDEALS

If I do not acquire ideals in my youth, when will I? Not
in old age.   MAIMONIDES

Everyone is dedicated to that which he desires and chooses.
SAMUEL HA-NAGID

A generation in which human ideals do not improve must
perish.   THE KORETSER RABBI

See also: ALTRUISM, COMPASSION, SELFISHNESS

IDEAS

Those on the other side of a fence have different ideas.

✻ Corrupt ideas are worse than corrupt money.

Fooling people with words is more contemptible than
cheating them out of money.

See also: CUSTOM, INTELLIGENCE, JUDGMENT, REASON

IDLENESS

✻ The hardest work of all is to do nothing.

Idlers get busy when other men sleep.

Rip and sew, but don't stay idle.

Through slothfulness the rafters sink in, and through
idleness of hands the house leaks.
Ecclesiastes, 10 : 18

The sluggard will not plow in autumn;
So in harvest he seeks a crop in vain.
Book of Proverbs, 20 : 4

As vinegar to the teeth, and smoke to the eyes,
So is the sluggard to those who send him on an errand.
Book of Proverbs, 10 : 26

✻ Whoever does no work will suffer all his life.
MAIMONIDES: *Mishneh Torah,* Deot 4

Man dies of idleness—and boredom.
Abot de Rabbi Nathan, 11

✻ The idle man, even a king, ends in weakness, sickness,
or madness.   —adapted from SAADIA GAON

See also: BOREDOM, BUSINESS, CHARITY, SHIRKERS, THRIFT,
WORK

IDOLATRY

Roman pagan to a rabbi: "Your God abominates idolatry; why then does He not destroy the idols?"

"Would you have God destroy the sun and moon because of the foolish people who worship them?"

TALMUD: *Abodah Zarah*, 54b

See also: FAITH, GOD, HYPOCRISY/HYPOCRITES

IGNORANCE

Note. An *am ha-arets* (from the Hebrew: "people of the soil") is described in the Talmud as one who does not respect the Law, and by Maimonides as "a boor in whom is neither learning nor moral virtue." Rabbi Nathan ben Joseph called an *am ha-arets* "one who has children and does not educate them . . ."

—L.R.

✳ Only the ignorant are really poor.

✳ The greatest luck of an *am ha-arets* [ignoramus] is this: he doesn't know that he doesn't know.

Beware of those whose ignorance is joined with piety.

✳ When a scholar seeks a bride, he should take an ignoramus along to advise him.

✳ Even a blind hen sometimes finds a grain.

Wise men, grown older, grow wiser; ignorant men, grown older, grow more foolish.

For the ignorant, old age is winter; for the learned, old age is the harvest.   Hasidic saying

The man who hides his ignorance is better than the *khakhem* (wise man) who parades his wisdom.

The ignorant think less clearly as they grow older; scholars think more clearly as they age.

TALMUD: *Kinnin*, 3 : end

The ignorant cannot really be pious.

Sayings of the Fathers, 2 : 5

Do not say, "I will love the learned and hate the ignorant"; love them both.

—adapted from *Abot de Rabbi Nathan*, 16

❋ He who refuses to learn deserves extinction.
                    HILLEL in *Sayings of the Fathers*

Don't make fun of the ignorant: you may be maligning
    your ancestry.   BEN SIRACH, *Ecclesiasticus*, 8 : 4

See also: ADVICE, FOOLS, ILLOGIC, NEBEKH, SHLEMIELS,
    STUPIDITY

ILLOGIC

❋ A deaf man heard a mute tell him how a blind man saw
    a cripple run—on water.

Sleep faster, we need the pillows.

Beating your wife with the paddle won't make the sheets
    white.

Food is cooked in a pot, but the plate gets the praise.

See also: FOLLY, FOOLS, NONSENSE, SENSE, STUPIDITY

ILLUSION

❋ A worm in a jar of horseradish thinks he's in Paradise.

A mirror fools no one except the homely.

❋ Illusions are comforting; just don't act upon them.

Some things smell sweet and taste bitter.

❋ He's half a millionaire: he has the air, but not the
    million.

❋ We always think that others are enjoying themselves.

Illusions drive men mad.

See also: ADVICE, FOLLY, IMAGINATION, REALITY, SENSE

IMAGINATION

❋ The deaf imagine what they cannot hear.

Things can be imagined more quickly than they can be
    achieved.

See also: ILLUSION, REALITY, SENSE

IMMORALITY

Men hate moralists, without being immoral.

Immorality in a house is like a worm in a plant.
                                        TALMUD: *Sotah*, 3b

See also: GOOD, GOOD AND EVIL, HONESTY, HONOR/HONORS,
SIN, VIRTUE

IMMORTALITY

✻ The good die but live on, in the example they provided.
            —adapted from TALMUD: *Berakoth*, 18b

Whoever lives by Torah, good deeds, humility and the fear
of God will be saved from eternal doom.
                        MIDRASH: *Pesikta Rabbati*, 198a

Live as if you expect to live forever, but plan as if you expect to enter the hereafter tomorrow.
                        IBN GABIROL, *Choice of Pearls*

God, the Source of Life, endowed us with the blessed hope
of immortality, so that we can console ourselves over the
vanity of life, and contend with the dread of death.
                                        JEDAIA BEN BEDERSI

See also: DEATH, ETERNITY, HEREAFTER, PARADISE, SALVA-
TION, SOUL

IMPUDENCE

✻ Impudence [*chutzpa*] is sovereignty without a crown.
                        TALMUD: *Sanhedrin*, 105a

See also: ARROGANCE, CONCEIT, HUMILITY, VANITY

IMPULSE

See: MAN, PASSION, TEMPER

INDEPENDENCE

Better independent than humiliated.

Better a pushcart with your own money than a store with
someone else's.

Rather than become dependent, do work even if it is
beneath you.   TALMUD: *Pesahim*, 113a

See also: CHARITY, DEPENDENCE, HONOR, POWER, SELF-
ESTEEM, VIRTUE

INDIVIDUALITY

❋ If I am like someone else, who will be like me?

Not all horses enjoy the same thing.

Rabbi Zusya said, before his death: "In the world-to-come
I shall not be asked: 'Why were you not Moses?' but
'Why were you not Zusya?' "   Hasidic saying

❋ Some prefer vinegar and some prefer wine.
                                TALMUD: *Kiddushin*, 48b

Even one ear of corn is not exactly like another.
                                TALMUD: *Sanhedrin*, 4 : 9

The Creator made all men different in features, intelligence,
and voice, in order to promote honesty and chastity.
            RABBI MEIR in TOSEPHTA: *Sanhedrin*, 8 : 6

Men's features are not alike; nor are their opinions.
              MAIMONIDES: *Mishneh Torah*, Deot 1

See also: ADAM, INDEPENDENCE, MAN, and individual character traits

INDUSTRIOUSNESS

He who comes first grinds first.

He who needs the fire must fan it.   *Midrash Samuel*

If a man does not plow in the summer, what will he eat
in the winter?   *Midrash Proverbs*

He who tills his ground will have plenty of food;
But he who follows empty pursuit lacks sense.
                            Book of Proverbs, 12 : 11

See also: DETERMINATION, EFFORT, WILL, WORK

INEVITABILITY

❉ The stone fell on the pitcher? Woe to the pitcher. The pitcher fell on the stone? Woe to the pitcher.

MIDRASH: *Esther Rabbah*, 7 : 10

See also: CAUSE AND EFFECT, CONSEQUENCES, REALITY

INFLUENCE

One egg can whiten a whole bowl of borsht.

To be in the company of a wise man is like going into a perfumery: you may not buy a thing, but the sweet scent will cling to you for a day.

Abot de Rabbi Nathan, 11 : 14b

See also: AUTHORITY, CAUSE AND EFFECT, CONSEQUENCES, POWER

INFORMER

An informer should be hanged by his tongue.

See also: LIARS, SLANDER

INGENUITY

❉ Some things are clever only the first time.

An impudent young Pole put both hands behind his back and challenged a rabbi in this way: "Your attention! I hold a little bird in one of my hands. Guess which one. If you guess right, I'll let the bird go free; if you guess wrong, I'll strangle it, and its death will be on your head! . . . What does your precious Talmud tell Jews about a dilemma such as this?"

The rabbi studied the young man dolorously, then sighed: "Our Talmud tells us that the awful choice between life and death—is in your hands."

Hasidic story

See also: LOGIC, REASON, RESOURCEFULNESS

INGRATITUDE

When he was a puppy I fed him, and when he became a dog he bit me.

❋ If you give people nuts, you'll get shells thrown at you.
Yemenite proverb

See also: CHARITY, GRATITUDE, GREED

INHERITANCE

❋ If you come for the legacy you may have to pay for
the funeral.

The richest inheritance can become a burden.

Dowries and legacies bring no luck.

Dogs fight over a bone, and mourners over a will.

To dissipate your inheritance, wear white linen, use glass,
or be an absentee employer.   TALMUD: *Hullin*, 84b

See also: LUCK

INIQUITY

All iniquity is like a two-edged sword;
A blow from it cannot be healed.
BEN SIRACH, *Ecclesiasticus*, 21 : 3

See also: EVIL, SIN

INJUSTICE

The best morsels are given to the worst dogs.

Better suffer an injustice than commit one.

See also: EVIL, HONOR, JUSTICE, LAW, SIN

INNOCENCE

❋ God looks into our hearts before he looks into our
minds.

Innocence goes with peacefulness.

Don't try to identify the Tree of Knowledge: you may cast
suspicion on one innocent.
MIDRASH: *Genesis Rabbah*, 15 : 7

See also: CHILDREN, GOOD DEEDS, GUILT, MAN, VIRTUE

INQUISITION

Note. "Would you believe that as the flames were consuming these innocent victims, the inquisitors . . . were chanting our prayers? These pitiless monsters invoked the God of mercy and kindness and pardon while committing the most atrocious, barbarous crime, acting in a way which demons in their rage would not use against brother demons."

—VOLTAIRE, *Sermon du Rabin Akib*

"In 1390 . . . the Catholics of Seville being excited by the eloquence of a great preacher . . . attacked the Jews' quarter, and murdered 4,000 Jews. . . . About a year later, similar scenes took place at Valentia, Cordova, Burgos, Toledo, Barcelona . . . the Inquisition was established [and] numbers of converted Jews were massacred. Others, who had been baptized during past explosions of popular fury, fled to the Moors, to practise their religious rites, and at last, after a desperate resistance, were captured and burnt alive."

W. E. H. LECKY, *Rationalism in Europe*, 1865, chap. 6

See: ANTI-SEMITISM, INTOLERANCE, PERSECUTION, POGROMS, PREJUDICE

INSANITY

The *entire* world isn't crazy.

❋ There is no man without his own kind of *meshugas* (craziness).

Even the man who has everything dare not stay idle, for the idle man, be he even a king, will end in weakness, sickness, or insanity.   —adapted from SAADIA GAON

See also: DISEASE, ILLOGIC, ILLUSION, NONSENSE, REASON

INSIGHT

In sleep, thoughts come to your mind to reveal the thoughts of your heart.

—adapted from the *Book of Daniel*, 2 : 29–30

Where there is no knowledge there can be no insight, and where there is no insight there can be no knowledge.

Sayings of the Fathers, 3 : 2

The beginning of wisdom is to desire it.
> IBN GABIROL, *Choice of Pearls*

See also: INTELLIGENCE, REASON, SENSE, UNDERSTANDING

INTELLECT

❋ Man's best companion is his intellect; his worst enemy is his lust.

The man who wishes to attain human perfection should study Logic first, next Mathematics, then Physics, and lastly Metaphysics.
> MAIMONIDES, *Guide to the Perplexed*, I

Intellect is the dividing line between man and beast: it masters natural impulses and subdues passions.
> IBN GABIROL: *Choice of Pearls*

There is no [genuine] distinction except in the intellect.
> HAYYIM VITAL

Intellect is a man's guard; without it he is like an infant.
> THE KORETSER RABBI

See also: INTELLIGENCE, PASSION, REASON, UNDERSTANDING

INTELLIGENCE

❋ When brains are needed, muscles won't help.

❋ Any man can count his own teeth.

Of what use are gray hairs, when the brains are still green?

❋ Eggs may be smarter than hens, but they rot faster.

We don't need intelligence to have luck, but we do need luck to have intelligence.

Borrowed brains are of no use.

❋ Silence is the only good substitute for intelligence.

As face reflects face in water,
So the mind of Man reflects Man.
> *Book of Proverbs*, 27 : 19

The senseless man pours contempt on his neighbor;
But the intelligent man keeps silent.
> *Book of Proverbs*, 11 : 12

The spiritual perfection of man consists in his becoming an intelligent being—one who knows all that he is capable of learning. And such knowledge is obtained not by virtue or piety, but through inquiry and research.
MAIMONIDES: *Guide to the Perplexed*, 3

❊ *Seykhl* [good sense] is a gift, but intelligence is an acquisition. IBN GABIROL

Sweet of voice, but short of brains.
IMMANUEL OF ROME, *Mahberot*

Brains to the lazy are like a torch to the blind—a useless burden. BEDERSI, *Behinat ha-Olam*

See also: IGNORANCE, INTELLECT, INSIGHT, KNOWLEDGE, REASON, STUPIDITY, UNDERSTANDING

INTOLERANCE

Note. "Insulted, plundered, hated, and despised by all Christian nations, banished from England by Edward I, and from France by Charles VI, they found in the Spanish Moors . . . a special sympathy for a race whose pure monotheism formed a marked contrast to the scarcely disguised polytheism of the Spanish. . . . Jewish learning and Jewish genius contributed very largely to that bright but transient civilization which radiated from Toledo and Cordova, and exercised so salutary an influence upon the behalf of Europe. But when, in an ill-omened hour, the Cross supplanted the Crescent on the heights of the Alhambra, this solitary refuge was destroyed, the last gleam of tolerance vanished from Spain, and the expulsion of the Jews was determined."
—W. E. H. Lecky,
Rationalism in Europe, 1865, chapter 6.

❊ No one is as deaf as the man who will not listen.

See also: ANTI-SEMITISM, INQUISITION, JEWS, PERSECUTION, PREJUDICE

IRONY: EXAMPLES

Any man can count his own teeth.

Too bad: The bride is too beautiful.

There are two involved in feasting on a chicken: me and the chicken.

❊ The fool who shuts up sounds like a sage.

❊ The daughters of the rich are always beautiful.

A pretty thanks—to your navel. [Thanks for nothing.]

One father manages to support ten children; but ten children don't seem to be able to support one father.

The can of a tinsmith is full of holes, and the shoemaker goes barefoot.

Even the unlucky need luck.

A Litvak is so clever that he repents *before* he sins.

Men become more brotherly during prosperity.

❊ A broken clock is still better than one that goes wrong: at least it is right twice a day.

It's worth as much as a blown-out egg.

The world would burst with philanthropists—if giving cost nothing.

❊ He is a good man—according to his epitaph.

❊ All corpses look pious.

Many men are generous—with other people's money.

❊ God gave me such a good brain that in one minute I can worry more than others do in a year.

Miracles do happen—but they rarely provide food.

To judge according to beards or girth is to conclude that goats are the wisest creatures on earth.
> —adapted from JOSEPH SOLOMON DELMEDIGO

See also: ADAGES, ADVICE, SARCASM

IRRATIONALITY

See: FOLLY, ILLOGIC, ILLUSION, REASON

ISRAEL

Note. Since the exile of the Jews to Babylonia, Zion or Israel has continued the idea of a reunited Jewish people returned to their homeland. "By the rivers of Babylon, there we sat down, yea, we wept when we remembered Zion" (Psalm 137). Wherever they lived, when Jews prayed they turned in the direction of Jerusalem.

Erets Yisroel ("the land of Israel") is the believing Jews' "Promised Land," promised by God to Abraham's descendants, the kingdom of David and Solomon, the land in which Holy Jerusalem was built, the land where the Messiah will appear.

—L.R.

✳ Whatever will happen to all Israel will happen to Mr. Israel.

Burial in Israel is like burial under the altar of the Temple.
TALMUD: *Kethuboth*, 11a

Israel has no *mazel* [lucky star], because it is under God's direct protection.   TALMUD: *Shabbath*, 156a

Israel is shielded and lifted by its precepts as a dove by its wings.   TALMUD: *Shabbath*, 130a

The community is Israel's rampart.
TALMUD: *Baba Bathra*, 7a

Israel is like a vine: the people are the branches, the unlearned the leaves, and the learned are the fruit.
TALMUD: *Hullin*, 92a

Israel is like a vine: trodden underfoot; but some time later its wine is placed on the table of a king. So, Israel, at first oppressed, will eventually come to greatness.
TALMUD: *Nedarim*, 49b

As everyone treads on dust, so does every nation tread on Israel; but dust lasts longer than metal, and so shall Israel outlast the others.
MIDRASH: *Genesis Rabbah*, 41 : 9

✳ Why is Israel like a dove? Other birds, when tired, rest on a branch; but when the dove tires, she rests one wing and flies with the other.
MIDRASH: *Genesis Rabbah*, 39 : 10

God told Moses and Aaron: "Accept my mission, but be prepared for stones and curses."
MIDRASH: *Exodus Rabbah*, 7

Myrtle is sweet to the one who smells it, but bitter to the one who bites it; so Israel brings prosperity to those who grant it kindness, and depression to those who afflict it with evil.   MIDRASH: *Esther Rabbah*, 6 : 5

Why is Israel like sand? As in the sand you dig a pit, and in the evening find it filled up, so is it with Israel.
　　　　　　　　　　—adapted from MIDRASH: *Pesikta*

Sand mixed in bread injures the teeth: so will those who persecute Israel suffer for it.
　　　　　　　　　　—adapted from MIDRASH: *Pesikta*

✳ When trouble comes into the world, Israel feels it first: when good comes, Israel feels it first, too.
　　　　　　　　MIDRASH: *Lamentations Rabbah*, 2 : 3

The death of a sage is worse for Israel than the death of a king; for a sage cannot be replaced, but all Israel is eligible to succeed a king.   —adapted from MIDRASH

Why is Israel like a worm? Because the worm's sole strength lies in its mouth. So is it with Israel [for it has the power of prayer].   *Zohar*

✳ A tent cannot stand without pegs and cord, and Israel cannot stand without scholars. *Seder Eliyahu Rabbah*

✳ Living in Israel is itself an atonement for one's sins.
　　　　　　　　RABBI MEIR in *Sifre—Deuteronomy*

Among the nations Israel is like the heart amidst the organs of the body: both the sickest and the healthiest of all.
　　　　　　　　JUDAH HA-LEVI, *Kuzari*, ch. 2

✳ The real slavery in Egypt was this: the Israelites learned to endure it.   SIMCHA BUNIM

As sand is moved from place to place without a sound, so Israel is exiled from place to place without complaint.
　　SAMUEL BUBER, *Introduction to Tanhuma*, 134

See also: JEWS, SABBATH, SCHOLARS

J

JEALOUSY

❋ Love may be blind, but jealousy sees too much.

❋ We anger God with our sins, and men with our virtues.

The jealousy [competition] of scribes helps increase wisdom.
TALMUD: *Baba Bathra*, 21a

Jealousy in the heart makes the bones rot.
Book of Proverbs, 14 : 30

Wrath is ruthless, and anger a torrent;
But before jealousy who can stand?
Book of Proverbs, 27 : 4

Jealousy is as cruel as the grave. *Song of Solomon*, 8 : 6

❋ The man who loves without jealousy does not truly love.
Zohar

See also: ENVY, LOVE, SUSPICION

JERUSALEM

Note. Jerusalem was established because of administrative
and military necessities: the great city, like the monarchy,
was *not* an aspect of the early life and dreams of ancient
Israel. Urban life was a challenge of no small proportions in the religious tradition of Israel, until then a
semi-nomadic and agricultural people.

David captured Jebus/Jerusalem in the 11th century
before the Christian Era and made the city the center of
a united Israel. He moved the holy Ark of the Covenant
to his new capital—which became the head of an empire that, at its apogee, stretched from the Red Sea to
the Euphrates.

In the Diaspora, Jews all over the world looked towards, and dreamed of, Jerusalem as the spiritual heart
of Judaism and the symbolic capital of Jewry.

L.R.

"The Assyrians burnt it and deported its population;
the Romans slew a million of its inhabitants, razed it to
the ground, passed the ploughshare over it, and strewed
its furrows with salt; Hadrian banished its very name
from the lips of men, changed it to 'Aelia Capitolina,'
and prohibited any Jew from entering its precincts on
pain of death. Persians and Arabs, Barbarians and
Crusaders and Turks, took it and retook it, ravaged it
and burnt it; and yet, marvellous to relate, it ever rises
from its ashes to renewed life and glory."
        —J. H. HERTZ, at the Thanksgiving service for
        the capture of Jerusalem by British forces, 1917.

To dwell in the Holy Land tends to prevent sin.
                        TALMUD: *Kethuboth*, 111a

Jerusalem was destroyed because its children did not attend
    school.   TALMUD: *Shabbath*, 119b

See: ISRAEL

JEWS

Note. What is a Jew? Morris N. Kertzer's lucid answer, in
    a book bearing that question as its title,* takes up 207
    pages. One can list a bibliography of staggering length on
    the topic. A refreshing lucidity distinguishes the following
    passage from Dr. Morris Adler:

Jews do not constitute a church but a people. One of the
reasons the modern Jew finds it difficult to define his
identity is that the English language offers no term to
suggest the complex of ethnic, national, cultural and religious elements that constitute the collective life of the
Jew. The irreligious Jew is not read out of the community.
Affiliation . . . is not a matter of creed. The religion of the
Jew embraces areas that modern man would call secular.
There is no instance, in the Western world, of an ethnic
group whose religion emerged out of its own history . . .
the word church does not fit the Jewish situation.**

I sometimes remember Mark Twain's words:

---

* *What Is A Jew?*, World Publishing Co., New York, 1953.
** *The World of the Talmud*, B'nai Brith Hillel Foundations, 1958, p.
124.

The Jew made a marvelous fight in this world, in all the ages; and has done it with his hands tied behind him. The Egyptian, the Babylonian, and the Persian rose, filled the planet with sound and splendor, then faded to dream stuff and passed away. The Greek and the Roman followed, and made a vast noise, and they are gone. Other peoples have sprung up and held their torch high for a time, but it burned out, and they sit in twilight now, or have vanished. The Jew . . . is now what he always was—exhibiting no decadence, no infirmities of age . . . no slowing of his energies, no dulling of his alert and aggressive mind.*

Allow me one final, arresting quotation, from Heine:

I see now that the Greeks were only handsome youths, whilst the Jews were always men—powerful, indomitable men—who have fought and suffered on every battlefield of human thought.**

—L.R.

❋ When a Jewish farmer eats a chicken, one of them is sick.

❋ The Jew who can't be a cobbler dreams of becoming a professor.

❋ Jews are just like everyone else—only more so.

Better a Jew without a beard than a beard without a Jew.

❋ If a Jew breaks a leg, he thanks God he did not break both legs; if he breaks both legs, he thanks God he did not break his neck.

The joy of Jews is never free of anxiety.

A Jew is always short one day. ["If I only had one more day."]

❋ When a Jew is hungry, he sings; when a peasant is hungry, he beats his wife.

The nobleman thinks of his horse and dog; the Jew thinks of his wife and child.

❋ "Thou hast chosen us from among all the nations"—but why did You have to pick on the Jews?

---

* "Concerning the Jews," *Harper's Monthly*, September 1899.
** In *A Book of Jewish Thoughts*, ed. J. H. Hertz, Oxford, London, 1920, p. 66.

❀ When trouble comes, Jews feel it first; when fortune smiles, Jews feel it last.

❀ Every Jew has his own brand of madness.

A Jew on a desert island will build two synagogues—so that he will have one he does not want to go to.

Gentiles aren't used to Jewish troubles.

❀ A nation that persecutes Jews cannot last long.

Tie my four limbs, but throw me among my own.

Jewish wealth is like a March snow.

Misfortune seldom misses a Jew.

A Jew answers a question with a question.

If a Jew be right, he is beaten all the more.

One is not doomed among Jews.

❀ Whoever renounces idol worship may be called a Jew.
                              TALMUD: *Megillah*, 13a

Poverty is the ornament of the Jews.
                              TALMUD: *Hagigah*, 9b

A Jew is prohibited from deceiving even a worshipper of idols.   TALMUD: *Baba Kamma*, 113b

"They are my servants" [Lev., 25 : 55]—not servants' servants.   TALMUD: *Baba Mezi'a*, 10a

What is permitted one Jew is permitted another.
                              TALMUD: *Bezah*, 25a

If a group of Jews on a long journey are overtaken by barbarians who say, "Give us one of your number, or we shall kill you all," let all be slain: for no Israelite may deliberately be delivered to barbarians.
                              TALMUD: *Sanhedrin*, 84a

❀ We (Jews) must not appoint a leader in any community without first consulting the people.
                              TALMUD: *Berakoth*, 55a

There are three impudent creatures: among beasts, the dog; among birds, the cock; among people, Israel. But Rabbi Ammi added: "Do not consider this as blame; it is praise, for to be a Jew means to be ready to be martyred."   MIDRASH: *Exodus Rabbah*, 42 : 9

Is a Jew an alien anywhere? Wherever he goes, his God is
with him.   MIDRASH: *Deuteronomy Rabbah*, 2 : 16

❊ If all the seas were ink, and all the reeds pens, and all
the people scribes, it would not be enough to record all
the misfortunes of the Jews in a single year.
                                MIDRASH: *Megillath Ta'anith*

Ye shall be a peculiar treasure unto me among all peoples.
                                Book of Exodus, 19 : 5

God found the Jews as one finds grapes in the desert.
                                Book of Hosea, 9 : 10

A true Jew is distinguished by three characteristics: sympathy, modesty, benevolence.
                                Sayings of the Fathers, 5 : 22

No Jew, however learned and pious, may consider himself
one whit better than a fellow Jew, however ignorant or
irreligious.   *Simcha Bunim*

The best weapons of a Jew are his prayers.
                                NACHMAN OF BRATSLAV

The real "Jewish Question" is this: From what can a Jew
earn a living?   SHOLEM ALEICHEM

Though Pesach [Passover] comes but once a year, Jews ask
questions all year long. [The Passover feast features "the
four questions," usually asked by the youngest son.]
                                SHOLEM ALEICHEM

❊ We are God's stake in human history. A. J. HESCHEL

It is no challenge to die like a Jew; the true challenge is to
live like a Jew.   "THE CHOFETZ CHAIM"

See also: ISRAEL, PERSECUTION, REFUGEES, SABBATH, SYNA-
GOGUE

JOY

Joy finds its completion in success.
                                IMMANUEL OF ROME, *Mahberot*

A man's joy is greatest when his family is with him.
                                EPHRAIM LUNTSHITZ, *Keli Yakar*

Joy and sadness are as close as day and night.

HAYYIM OF VOLOZHIN

See also: CONTENTMENT, FAMILY, HAPPINESS, PIETY, PLEASURES

JUDAISM

Note. It has been said that whereas the core of Christianity is the figure of Jesus, the core of Judaism is the Law—as set forth in the Torah, the Oral Tradition, the Talmud. It was a Christian scholar who made this interesting distinction: Christianity is a religion built around an ideal person; Judaism is a religion of ideals.

Not even Moses is considered divine by Jews; nor is he worshipped; nor is he sanctified. There is one passage in the Talmud, indeed, in which the learned agree that the patriarch Ezra was entirely virtuous—virtuous enough to receive the holy tablets on Mount Sinai from the Lord, but that Moses happened to precede him. In the Book of Nehemiah (8 : 8) we are told that at a great convocation of the Jews, after their return from slavery in Babylonia (in the middle of the fifth century before the Christian Era), Ezra read the Torah before the Jews and "they read in the book, in the law of God, distinctly; and they gave the sense and caused them to understand the reading." What Ezra had decided to do was translate the laws of God into ordinances (Ezra, 7 : 10), so that the Holy Torah would be *applied*, given the authority of Law—which was continually to be increased by close study and interpretation. The word "*Midrash*," which means "interpretations," comes from the root of the word Ezra himself employed as "to seek": *lidrosh*, which can also be translated as "to interpret."

So began the long tradition and practice of teachers, scholars, rabbis, sages, interpreting and teaching the Law. (See GUIDENOTES for Talmud, Mishnah, Midrash).

—L.R.

See: JEWS, RELIGION, TORAH

JUDGES

Note. Every Jewish community in Europe usually had its own civil court (*Beth Din*), presided over by a chief rabbi or a *dayan*. (In rabbinic literature, *dayan* means either "sage" or "rabbinical judge"; every *dayan* was a rabbi, but only a rare rabbi was a *dayan*.) These Jewish courts dealt with religious and local (Jewish community) problems, and with those disputes (marriage, divorce, legacies, debts) in which the disputants sought advice or arbitration. These courts had no legal authority: Jews came to them voluntarily and accepted their judgments. The first question asked of litigants was: "Do you wish law or arbitration?"

When a dispute involved formal litigation, at least three rabbi-judges were required to sit on the bench of the *Beth Din*. In the Middle Ages, special "guild" courts governed different trades and occupations. In Israel today, these courts are official: they operate in the office of the central Rabbinate; they have exclusive jurisdiction over certain areas: legal status, marriage, inheritances, etc.   —L.R.

✻ Don't blame the judge for the law.

When a judge sits in judgment over a fellow man, he should feel as if a sword is pointed at his own heart.
                                   TALMUD: *Sanhedrin*, 8a

✻ Two scholars who dislike each other may not sit together as judges.   TALMUD: *Sanhedrin*, 29a

Judgment delayed is judgment voided.
                                   TALMUD: *Sanhedrin*, 95a

No man can be declared guilty in his absence.
                                   TALMUD: *Kethuboth*, 11a

A habitual borrower is unfit to be a judge.
                                   TALMUD: *Kethuboth*, 105b

As Rabbi Samuel was boarding a ferry, a man rushed up to help him; the rabbi asked why he was so attentive, and the man said, "Because I have a lawsuit that will come up in your court." To which Rabbi Samuel replied, "Then I am forbidden to be your judge."
                                   TALMUD: *Kethuboth*, 105b

✻ I cannot try the case of one of my students, because I love him as myself, and no one can see a fault in himself.   TALMUD: *Shabbath*, 119a

❋ A judge who has drunk a quart of wine may not sit in judgment: He will condemn the innocent and acquit the guilty.   MIDRASH: *Leviticus Rabbah*, 1 : 4, 8

❋ If there be no officer to enforce the law, what power do judges possess?   MIDRASH: *Tanhuma, Shofetim*

He who passes judgment on fools is himself judged a fool.
MIDRASH

The judge who knows other judges have erred, but agrees because he does not want to shame them, will end in Gehenna.   *Sefer Hasidim*

Don't sue a judge, for he will have it his way.
BEN SIRACH, *Ecclesiasticus*, 8 : 14

Just as you listen to the poor man, listen to the rich man, for it is written, "Ye shall not favor persons in judgment."   *Abot de Rabbi Nathan*, 20 : 22a

❋ The rabbis said about capital cases: "We decide by a majority of one for acquittal, but only by a majority of at least two for conviction."
RASHI, *Commentaries on the Pentateuch, Exodus*

See also: COURTS, EVIDENCE, JUSTICE, LAW, REASON

JUDGMENT

Before you start up a ladder, count the rungs.

❋ A chicken in the hand is better than an eagle in the sky.

❋ When shnaps [liquor] goes in, judgment goes out.

Ask advice wherever you will, but act according to your own judgment.

❋ Don't try to fill a sack that's full of holes.

It is better to measure ten times and cut once, than measure once and cut ten times.

❋ Judge a man not by the words of his mother, but from the comments of his neighbors.   TALMUD

Judge a man only by his own deeds and words; the opinions of others can be false.   TALMUD

It is better to have one bird in a cage than a hundred in the air.   MIDRASH: *Ecclesiastes Rabbah*, 4 : 6

If you come too close to fire, you get burnt; if you stray too
far, you'll be cold; the art [of judgment] is to find the
right distance.   *Mekilta on Jethro*

Judge every man charitably.
                              Sayings of the Fathers, 1 : 6

The man who accepts tradition without applying his own
intelligence and judgment is like a blind man following
others.   BAHYA IBN PAQUDA, *Duties of the Heart*

❄ If you can't have what you want, want what you can
have.   IBN GABIROL, *Improvement of Character*

See also: ABILITY, FORESIGHT, PRUDENCE, REALITY, SENSE

JUSTICE

The just way is always the right way.

Justice delayed is worse than injustice.

Give every man the benefit of the doubt.
                              Sayings of the Fathers, 1 : 7

The Roman Emperor Antoninus once said to Rabbi Judah
the Prince, "On the Day of Judgment, Soul and Body
will stand before the Heavenly Judge, and the Body will
say, 'It is the Soul, not I, who sinned; for without the
Soul, I am as lifeless as a stone.' And the Soul will say,
'How canst Thou impute sin to me? It is the body that
dragged me down.' . . . What say you to that?"
    Answered Rabbi Judah: "A king once had a garden
of wonderful fruits and put two men to guard over it—
a blind man and a lame man. One day, the lame man
said, 'I see some luscious fruit, but cannot reach it.' 'Then
get on my back,' said the blind man. 'I can carry you
there, then you stand on my shoulder and we shall both
enjoy plenteous fruit.' When the king discovered the
fruit gone, he haled both men before him. The lame
one said, 'I could not have been the thief: I cannot
walk!' And the blind man said, '*I* could not have been
the thief; I cannot see a thing!' But the king was very
wise and asked the lame man to climb on the shoulders
of the blind man—and sentenced them both. In the same
way, your Majesty, will the Divine Judge of the Universe mete out judgment—to body and soul together."
                              —adapted from TALMUD

Abraham said to God: "If you want the world to exist
you cannot insist upon complete justice; if it is complete justice you want, the world cannot endure."
                    MIDRASH: *Genesis Rabbah*, 49 : 20

Don't try to identify the Tree of Knowledge: Heaven
forbid that we cast suspicion on any [innocent] tree!
                    MIDRASH: *Genesis Rabbah*, 15 : 7

When Rabbi Ammi's hour to die came, he wept bitterly;
and his nephew asked, "But why do you weep? Is there
any Torah you have not learned and taught? Is there
any kindness you have not practiced? And you never
accepted public office, or sat in judgment on others." The
rabbi replied: "That is why I weep: I was given the
ability to extend justice, but never carried it out."
—adapted from MIDRASH: *Tanhuma on Mishpatim*

If you see wicked men perverting justice, do not say:
"Since they are many, I must follow after them."
           RASHI, *Commentaries on the Pentateuch, Exodus*

To arbitrate is to temper justice with charity.
                           NACHMAN OF BRATSLAV

See also: GOOD, RIGHTEOUSNESS, VIRTUE

K

KILLING

Whoever destroys a single life is as guilty as though he had
destroyed the entire world; and whoever rescues a single
life earns as much merit as though he had rescued the
entire world.   TALMUD: *Sanhedrin*, 37 : a

Someone came before Raba and said: "The mayor of my
town has told me, 'Go and kill so and so; if you do not,
I will have you killed.'
   Raba said to him: "Let him kill you. Do you think
your blood is redder than another man's? Perhaps his
blood is redder than yours."
                           TALMUD: *Sanhedrin*, 72b

If a man kills a thief, it is not murder, since a thief is like one who has been dead from the beginning.

RASHI, *Commentaries on the Pentateuch, Exodus*

See also: ADAM, COMPASSION, GOOD DEEDS, KINDNESS, TORAH, VIRTUE

KINDNESS

Kindness is the beginning and the end of the Law.

A kindness is remembered, a meanness is felt.

Kindness is better than piety.

❋ God is not kind to those who are not kind.

Kindness is even greater than charity.

A kind word is better than a handout.

One should feed his animals before sitting down to table.

TALMUD: *Gittin*, 62a

The highest form of wisdom is kindness.

TALMUD: *Berakoth*, 17a

Where there is no truth, there is no kindness.

NACHMAN OF BRATSLAV

See also: ALTRUISM, CHARITY, COMPASSION, CONSIDERATION, GOOD DEEDS, PIETY, VIRTUE

KNOWLEDGE

With knowledge, one is nowhere lost.

Knowledge is the best merchandise.

❋ Some men study so much they don't have time to know.

❋ To know a trade is to own a kingdom.

❋ Every new answer raises a new question.

A man is greater than the knowledge he acquired.

The head of a fool is like a broken dish: it will not hold knowledge.

Those who know much age fast.

❋ It is better to know nothing than to learn nothing.

❁ A light for one is a light for a hundred.
                              TALMUD: *Shabbath*, 122a

❁ If thou hast acquired knowledge, what canst thou lack?
  If thou lackest knowledge, what hast thou acquired?
                              MIDRASH: *Leviticus Rabbah*, 1

❁ Man enters the world with a whimper and exits with a
  cry: for he enters the world without knowledge, and
  leaves it without knowledge.
                              MIDRASH: *Ecclesiastes Rabbah*, 5

When wine comes in, knowledge goes out.
                              MIDRASH: *Tanhuma Yashan on Leviticus*, 7

❁ Knowledge is a hoard from which nothing can be lost.
                                              IBN GABIROL

He who increases knowledge, increases sorrow.
                                          Ecclesiastes, 1 : 18

❁ When one's deeds are greater than one's knowledge,
  knowledge is effective; but when one's knowledge is
  greater than one's deeds, the knowledge is futile.
                              Sayings of the Fathers, 3 : 14

❁ Knowledge should have no other purpose than to know
  what is true.   —adapted from MAIMONIDES

❁ Through intelligence, man achieves . . . knowledge and
  comes to . . . bear a resemblance to the character of the
  angels.   IBN GABIROL

Knowledge: A little light expels much darkness.
                     BAHYA IBN PAQUDA, *Duties of the Heart*

The man of knowledge who has no fear of sin is like a
carpenter without tools.   *Abot de Rabbi Nathan*

❁ Knowledge that is paid for will be longer remembered.
                                  NACHMAN OF BRATSLAV

See also: EDUCATION, FOOLS, GOOD DEEDS, INTELLIGENCE,
LEARNING, STUDY, TORAH, WISDOM

KOSHER

See: FOOD AND DRINK

L

LABOR

See: WORK

LANGUAGE

God created language—and man according to its principles.

ABRAVANEL

❋ A language is a dialect that has an army and a navy.

MAX WEINREICH

See also: EDUCATION, KNOWLEDGE, LEARNING, SCHOLARS, STUDY, TRANSLATION

LAUGHTER

❋ Not every heart that laughs is cheerful.

❋ Too much laughter can deaden the mind.

❋ Laughter is heard further than weeping.

We laugh alone and we weep alone.

Man should not fill his mouth only with laughter in this world.　　　—adapted from TALMUD: *Berakoth*, 30b

A fool raises his voice when he laughs, but a wise man smiles quietly.　　BEN SIRACH, *Ecclesiasticus*, 21 : 20

See also: CONTENTMENT, PLEASURE, SUFFERING, TEARS

LAW

Note. When the rabbis and philosophers of Judaism used "the Law" or "Torah," a complicated concept was involved. For the Law includes the Written Law, in the five books of Moses, and the "traditions of the elders" or "the Oral Law"—that is, the practices and beliefs developed around, or attached to, the Written Law. There is yet a third meaning: that of a spirit or connection between Written and Oral Law that unifies the two into one all-encompassing body of faith, principles, and precepts for living.

"The Law," i.e., the Torah, offered no explicit suggestion as to the way many juridical conflicts could be resolved. It was the rabbis and scholars, in their extraordinary discussions, who found answers to countless problems. They interpreted the Law by reinterpreting the Torah's text. (See guidenotes: TALMUD, MISHNAH, MIDRASH.) It takes no expert to present a hundred passages from the Torah or the Talmud that present uncertainty or inconsistency or imprecision (see, for instance, the headnote on SABBATH).

In countries where Jews were forced to live apart from the general population, the government often granted judicial authority (in cases involving only Jews) to rabbinical judges (*dayanim*).

The Talmud is full of explicit and impressive instructions for the administration of justice: A judge may not listen to the arguments of one litigant in the absence of the other; equality before the law is so underscored that preference must not be shown even to the learned; the first question put to litigants was: "Do you wish law or arbitration?" (See headnote for JUDGES.) The legal sophistication and modernity of many legal passages in the Talmud would impress any historian of jurisprudence.   —L.R.

❋ Without law, civilization dies.

❋ A new king makes new laws, but new laws cause new transgressions.

❋ The beginning and the end of the Law [Torah] is kindness.

Don't use the conduct of a fool as precedent.
                                    TALMUD: *Shabbath*, 104a

Anyone through whom another man has been falsely punished will be barred from Heaven's gates.
                                    TALMUD: *Shabbath*, 149a

The law of the land is the law of the Jew.
                                    TALMUD: *Baba Bathra*, 113a

To break an oral agreement which is not legally binding
is morally wrong.   TALMUD: *Baba Mezi'a*, 44a

❋ Only such decrees should be issued which the majority
of a community can endure.
                            MIDRASH: *Midrash Psalms*

❋ If there be no officer to enforce the law, what power
do judges have?   MIDRASH: *Tanhuma, Shofetim*

The falling of rain is an event greater than the giving of
the Law, since the Law is for Israel, but rain is for the
whole world.   MIDRASH: *Midrash Psalms*, 117

The Law forbids revenge.
          —adapted from *Abot de Rabbi Nathan*

❋ What is hateful to you, do not to your fellow: that is
the whole Law; all the rest is interpretation.
                            HILLEL in TALMUD: *Shabbath*, 31a

See also: COURTS, EVIDENCE, JUDGES, JUSTICE, TORAH

LAW AND ORDER

❋ Fish die when they are out of water, and people die
without law and order. TALMUD: *'Abodah Zarah*, 4a

See how the people act, and that is the Law.
                            TALMUD: *Berakoth*, 45a

❋ Just as it is forbidden to permit that which is prohibited, so it is forbidden to prohibit that which should
be permitted.   TALMUD J.: *Terumoth*, 5 : 3

If there be no officer to enforce the Law, of what avail is
the judge?   MIDRASH: *Tanhuma*, Shofetim

See also: COURTS, EVIDENCE, JUDGES, JUSTICE

LAZINESS

❋ The man who looks for easy work always goes to bed
tired.

A lazy messenger finds many excuses.

The lazy dance while others slave.

One's the type who chops the wood, the other's the type who does the grunting.

The hardest work in the world is doing nothing.

As vinegar to the teeth, and as smoke to the eyes, so is the sluggard to those who send him on an errand.
                              Book of Proverbs, 10 : 26

A lazy man is like a stone covered with rot: men flee from the stench.   BEN SIRACH, *Ecclesiasticus* 22 : 1

Rest has value only after toil; rest without toil is not rest, but indolence; so the sluggard never attains the rest for which he craves.   SAADIA GAON

❊ Brains to the lazy are like a torch to the blind—a useless burden.   BEDERSI, *Behinat ha-Olam*

See also: IDLENESS, SELFISHNESS, SHIRKERS, SIN, WORK

LEADERS/LEADERSHIP

Beware of the chief seat, because it shifts.

He who has a co-ruler has an over-ruler.

Woe to the ship whose captain has been lost.
                              TALMUD: *Baba Bathra*, 91b

A man is led the way he wishes to follow.
                              TALMUD: *Makkoth*, 10b

The body follows the head.   TALMUD: *Erubin*, 41a

❊ Too many captains will sink a ship.   TALMUD

The serpent was dragged into a ditch, into fire, and amidst thorns, when its head followed its tail!
                    MIDRASH: *Deuteronomy Rabbah*, 1 : 10

When the shepherd blunders, his flock blunders after him.
                    MIDRASH: *Pirke de Rabbi Eliezer*, 42

❊ A wise man is a greater asset to a nation than a king.
                              MAIMONIDES

❊ A king is like fire, necessary when far, scorching when near.   IBN GABIROL

The man most fit for high station is not the man who demands it.   MOSES IBN EZRA, *Shirat Yisrael*

A little sin is big when a big man commits it.
                    —adapted from ABRAHAM IBN EZRA,
                        Commentary to Genesis, 32 : 9

A leader must not think God chose him because he is great:
Does a peg in the wall, on which the king hangs his crown, boast that its beauty attracted the king's attention?   MOSES OF KOBRYN

When a man is able to take abuse with a smile, he is worthy to become a leader.   NACHMAN OF BRATSLAV

A place becomes known far and wide if it is the home of a great man.   THE ROPSHITZER RABBI

See also: AUTHORITY, GOVERNMENT, GREAT MEN, LAW, POWER

LEARNING

Note. "Learning was for two thousand years the sole claim to distinction recognized by Israel. 'The scholar,' says the Talmud, 'takes precedence over the king.' Israel remained faithful to this precept throughout all her humiliations. Whenever, in Christian or Moslem lands, a hostile hand closed her schools, the rabbis crossed the seas to reopen their academies in a distant country. Like the legendary Wandering Jew, the flickering torch of Jewish scholarship passed from East to West, from North to South, changing every two or three hundred years from one country to another.

"Whenever a royal edict commanded them to leave the country in which their fathers had been buried and their sons born, the treasure Jews were most anxious to carry away with them was their books. Among all the *autos-da-fé* which the daughter of Zion has had to witness, none has cost her such bitter tears as those flames which, during the Middle Ages, greedily consumed the scrolls of the Talmud."

                    —A. LEROY BEAULIEU, *Israel Among the Nations*,
                Heinemann, New York, 1893

See headnote: BOOKS

✱ The man who lacks learning lacks everything.

Learning is a lifelong occupation.

✻ The man who understands least asks the most questions.

✻ First learn; then teach.

Learning requires a talent for sitting.

Don't act the philosopher before you have learned enough to be one.

You can get more water from one deep well than from ten shallow ones.

In time, even a bear can learn to dance.

✻ He who seeks to know everything grows old quickly.

Whoever tries to profit from learning will be punished.

It is worse to learn nothing than to know nothing.

If you go into many houses, you are sure to carry something out [learn something].

Where there is learning there is wisdom.

Don't look for more honor than your learning merits.
Rabbinical saying

✻ For the ignorant, old age is winter; for the learned, it is the harvest.　　　　　　　　Hasidic saying

Learning is more important than action—when it leads to action.　　　　　　　　TALMUD: *Megillah*, 26

✻ Once an error is learned, it is hard to unlearn.
TALMUD: *Baba Bathra*, 21a

Learning advances from the rivalry of scholars.
TALMUD: *Baba Bathra*, 21a

If you are a man of the sword, you can't claim to be a man of the book; and if you are a man of the book, you will not be a man of the sword.
TALMUD: *'Abodah Zarah*, 17b

✻ Much have I learned from my teachers, more from my colleagues, but most from my students.
TALMUD: *Ta'anith*, 7b

If you understand the why and wherefore of what you learn, you do not forget it quickly.
TALMUD J.: *Berakoth*, 5 : 1

A man should not say, "I will love the learned and hate the unlearned"; he should say, "I will love them all."
Abot de Rabbi Nathan, 16

❋ A learned bastard stands higher than an ignorant High Priest.   MIDRASH: *Numbers Rabbah*, 6 : 1

Do not say: I will learn when I will have leisure; you may never have it.   *Sayings of the Fathers*, 2 : 5

Learning is not obtained by the bashful.
Sayings of the Fathers, 2 : 6

Warm yourself at the fire of the learned, but beware of their glowing coals, lest you get scorched. [Don't delve too deeply into profundities you may not understand; you may draw the wrong conclusions.]
Sayings of the Fathers, 2 : 14

❋ Learning is one thing that can't be bequeathed.
—adapted from *Sayings of the Fathers*, 2 : 16

The crown of learning is not so great as the crown of a good name.   *Sayings of the Fathers*, 3 : 13

Do not make learning into a crown to flaunt, nor into a spade with which to dig [for money].
Sayings of the Fathers, 4 : 5

❋ Move to a place where there is learning; you can't expect learning to move to you.
Sayings of the Fathers, 4 : 20

What you learn as a child is like ink on fresh paper; what you learn when old is like ink on used paper.
—adapted from *Sayings of the Fathers*, 4 : 27

He who learns from the immature is like the man who eats unripe grapes and drinks fresh wine; he who learns from the old is like the man who eats ripe grapes and drinks old wine.   *Sayings of the Fathers*, 4 : 28

He who possesses both learning and piety is like an artist with all his tools at hand.
JOHANAN BEN ZAKKAI in *Abot de Rabbi Nathan*, 22

He who does not increase knowledge diminishes it; and he who refuses to learn deserves extinction.

HILLEL in *Sayings of the Fathers* (*Note:* It was not uncommon for the sages to stress the importance of a duty by exaggerating the punishment for its nonperformance. —L.R.)

✻ A man should have no purpose in learning except this: to learn wisdom itself.   MAIMONIDES

A man should never stop learning, even on his last day.
                                             MAIMONIDES

✻ For learning, the ear is more useful than the eye.
                                               GERONDI

✻ The learning for which you pay will be remembered longer.   NACHMAN OF BRATSLAV

See also: IGNORANCE, ISRAEL, KNOWLEDGE, LOGIC, PIETY, REASON, TRUTH, VIRTUE

LENDING

Note. Lending money for interest was expressly forbidden in Deuteronomy (23 : 20 ff.) between "brother and brother"—whether Jew to Jew (or, as interpreted later by Catholic Church fathers) between Christian and Christian. But Deuteronomy goes on to say (28 : 12) that it is a blessing to lend to a needy nation—and a blessing not to need to borrow.

For the curious and tragic story of the Jews' role as moneylenders and their reputation as "usurers," see the headnote for USURY. Jews were often forced into moneylending—barred from all other trades, crafts, occupations, or professions—then were taxed prohibitively. Jews were often ordered to administer a king's or prince's moneylending—to shield the noble from the Catholic sin of usury. Jews were drafted to raise money for the building of cathedrals, palaces, armies, crusades.

The economically invaluable services performed, through the lending of money, did not spare the Jews from paying a terrible price for the function they were persuaded, forced, or seduced into serving: In Strasbourg, in 1349:

On Saturday—St. Valentine's Day—they burnt the Jews on a wooden platform in their cemetery. There were about two thousand people of them. . . . And everything that was owed to the Jews was cancelled, and the Jews had to surrender all pledges and notes that they had taken for debts. . . . The money was indeed the thing that killed the Jews. If . . . the feudal lords had not been in debt to them, they would not have been burnt.

JACOB R. MARCUS. *The Jew in the Medieval World, A Source Book: 315–1791;* Atheneum, New York, p. 47.

See also headnotes for BORROWING, MONEY, USURY.

　　　　　　　　　　　　　　　　　　　　—L.R.

❊ If you lend money, you buy enemies.

❊ If you lend someone money and he avoids you, you've gotten off cheap.

Lend before witnesses, but give without them.

❊ Interest grows without rain.

A long loan is still not a gift.

❊ If you have received a plow or a pillow as collateral for a loan, return the plow each morning and the pillow each night.　　　　　　　TALMUD: *Baba Mezi'a,* 114b

He who gives pledges for a stranger will suffer; but he who hates giving pledges is secure.　　　*Book of Proverbs*

❊ The interest on borrowed money is like the bite of a snake.

　　　RASHI, *Commentaries on the Pentateuch, Exodus*

❊ Don't lend to a man stronger than you; and if you do, act as though you had lost it.

　　　　　　BEN SIRACH, *Ecclesiastes,* 8 : 12

See also: BORROWING, DEBT, MONEY

LETTERS

A letter is like a body, its meaning like a soul.

❊ A letter not opened is like a dream not interpreted.

LIARS/LIES

❋ He only lies twice a year: in summer and in winter.

❋ A liar is like a mute: neither tells the truth.

You may go a long way through lies—but not back.

❋ The clever liar gives no details.

❋ A half-truth is a whole lie.

❋ A liar believes no one else.

❋ What he says he doesn't mean, and what he means he doesn't say.

❋ Hostility makes easy alliances with lies.

❋ Liars need good memories.

A lie one must not tell, and some truths you should not tell.

❋ You mustn't tell a lie, but you're not bound to always tell the truth.

❋ Truth may walk about naked; but lies should be clothed.

A liar tells his story so often that he begins to believe it himself.

❋ Sometimes truth is the safest lie.

Better say "I don't know" than lie.

❋ Truth shows in the eyes; lies stay behind them.

When young, a liar; when older, a thief.

With a story or a lie, only children can be rocked to sleep.

A lie has no feet [no leg to stand on].
                              TALMUD: *Shabbath*, 104a

Lordly words are not fitting for a fool; much less are lying words for a lord   *Book of Proverbs*, 17 : 7

I said in my haste, "All men are liars."
                              Book of Psalms, 116 : 11

❋ If you wish to strengthen a lie, mix a little truth in with it.   *Zohar*

Lies are forbidden—unless uttered to make peace.
Baraita Perek ha-Shalom

Since dishonor is habitual with a liar, his shame attends him continually.   BEN SIRACH, *Ecclesiasticus*, 20 : 26

❉ Do not think a thing proved because it is in a book; the liar, who deceives men with his tongue, does not hesitate to deceive them with his pen.
MAIMONIDES, *Epistle to the Yemenites*

The man who intends to lie seeks witnesses from far away.
JUDAH ASHERI

❉ To some men, lying is a profession.
MOSES HAYYIM LUZZATTO, *The Path of the Upright*

❉ A man who can't lie can't be a marriage broker.
MENDELE MOCHER SEFORIM

He who has no confidence utters falsehoods, and he who utters falsehoods has no confidence.
NACHMAN OF BRATSLAV

Lies are usually caused by an undue fear of men.
NACHMAN OF BRATSLAV

❉ For thirteen years, I taught my tongue not to tell a lie; and for the next thirteen, I taught it to tell the truth.
THE KORETZER RABBI

See also: HONOR, HYPOCRISY/HYPOCRITES, SIN, TRUTH

LIBERTY

See: AUTHORITY, DEMOCRACY, EQUALITY, FREEDOM, GOVERNMENT, INDEPENDENCE, LAW, MASSES, POLITICS, POWER

LIFE

❉ Life is a dream—but please don't wake me.

Life is with people.

❉ A man should go on living—if only to satisfy his curiosity.

Youth is the one thing that never returns.

❋ Ever since dying came into fashion, life hasn't been safe.

❋ Life is the greatest of bargains: we get it for nothing.

Life is not what men want, but what God decrees.

Life is bitter as bile—but without bile, no man can live.

In this life, luck won't help you unless you cooperate.

❋ It's a short way from happiness to sorrow, but a long way from sorrow to happiness.

What you fall into you can fall out of.

Not all the time is life bad—or good.

❋ When life isn't the way you like, like it the way it is.

❋ Pray that you will never have to bear all that you are able to endure.

Worse we never need, and better has no limits.

What's new at sea? They're catching fish.

If things don't get better, they may get worse.

❋ If you sing before you get out of bed, you'll cry before you go to sleep.

What you don't get you can't lose.

❋ In life, each of us must sometime play the fool.

We all bring a hearty appetite to other people's parties.

❋ We do not live on joy, nor die of sorrow.

Neither good nor bad lasts forever.

We long remember the good—and longer the bad.

It is better to live in joy than die in sorrow.

❋ All life ends in weeping.

If you live long enough, you'll see everything.

One man wants to live but can't, another can but doesn't want to.

Three types of men lead lives that are not worth living: he who is too ready to rage; he who is too soft-hearted; and he who is too fastidious.   TALMUD: *Pesahim*, 113a

Don't worry about tomorrow: who knows what may befall
you this day?   TALMUD: *Yebamoth*, 63b

❋ All beginnings are difficult.   *Mekilta on Jethro*

If there were this life only, nothing could be more bitter.
                    APOCRYPHA: *II Baruch*, 21 : 13

Our days are scrolls: write on them what you want to be
remembered for.
                    BAHYA IBN PAQUDA, *Duties of the Heart*

❋ Mobility is one of God's wonders.
                    BAHYA IBN PAQUDA, *Duties of the Heart*

A long life without wisdom is worse than a short life with it.
    —adapted from MOSES IBN EZRA, *Shirat Yisrael*, 119

One can learn much about life from a checker game: surrender one to take two; don't make two moves at one
time; move up, not down; and when you reach the top,
you may move as you like.   THE TSUPENSTER RABBI

❋ Life is a dream for the wise, a game for the fool, a
comedy for the rich, a tragedy for the poor.
                    SHOLEM ALEICHEM

See also: HAPPINESS, HEAVEN, HELL, SUFFERING, VIRTUE

LIFE: Cynical Comments on

❋ The only thing you get free in this life is garbage.

When a man has it too easy, he starts sliding on ice.

Wise men walk, while fools ride.

There will be mud in front of my door, too, one day.

❋ When there's a wind, garbage flies high.

It's easy to poke a fire with someone else's hand.

The more flesh, the more worms.
                    HILLEL in *Sayings of the Fathers*

❋ April Fool: A joke repeated 365 times a year.
                    SHOLEM ALEICHEM

❋ Life is a blister on top of a tumor, and a boil on top of
that.   SHOLEM ALEICHEM

LIFE: Rueful or Resigned Comments on

Even the greatest swimmer can drown.

❋ So many hymns—and so few noodles.

In this world, there are more *shokhtim* [slaughterers] than chickens.

All of life is a war.

The fees for circumcision, confirmation, wedding, burial— all come due too soon.

The provision is scant, and the road is long.
                                    TALMUD: *Kethuboth*

Not everyone who rejoices today will rejoice tomorrow.
                              MIDRASH: *Tanhuma* (Shmini)

The road through life is like the edge of a blade, with the nether-world on either side.   THE SASSOVER RABBI

See also: DEATH, IRONY: EXAMPLES, RESIGNATION

LIFE: The Purpose of

❋ There are three lives that are no lives: he who lives off others, he who is ruled by his wife, he whose body is racked by pain. (And some say, he who has only one shirt!)   TALMUD: *Bezah*, 32b

The Golden Mean is to love this world, to do good in life, and to aspire to the world to come.   SAADIA GAON

Many say a man should try to lengthen his life, asking, "What profit is there after death?" . . . Yet men who spend their days in pleasure do not live long. And those who increase their days also increase their anxiety, their vexation, their guilt, and their sins.   SAADIA GAON

See also: GOOD DEEDS, HAPPINESS, HEAVEN, HEREAFTER, SOUL, SUFFERING, VIRTUE

LIFE AND DEATH

We all know when we set forth; but we none of us know when we'll return.

Ask not that all troubles cease, for when troubles end, so does life.

Hurry and eat, hurry and drink, for this world is like a wedding feast from which we must soon depart.

TALMUD: *Erubin*, 54a

Birth and death are like ships: why do we rejoice over a ship setting out on a journey [birth] when we know not what she may encounter on the seas? We should rejoice when the ship returns safely to port [death].

—adapted from *Midrash Tanhuma:* Vayakel, I

❊ "Life is a passing shadow," says Scripture. The shadow of a tower or a tree? No: the shadow of a bird—for when a bird flies away, there is neither shadow nor bird.

MIDRASH: *Genesis Rabbah*, 80

❊ We rejoice over a birth and mourn over a death. But we should not. For when a man is born, who knows what he will do or how he will end? But when a man dies, we may rejoice—if he left a good name and this world is in peace.

—adapted from MIDRASH: *Tanhuma on Exodus*

❊ A man who lost his brother was asked, "What was the cause of his death?" and replied, "Life."

IBN ZABARA, *Book of Delight*, 7 : 27

❊ Life is a terrible disease—cured only by death.

HAI GAON, *Musar Haskel*

Heaven is wonderful, but getting there is most of the fun.

"THE CHOFETZ CHAIM"

Why is a man sad when at the end of his life he leaves for his true home in heaven?   "THE CHOFETZ CHAIM"

❊ It is no challenge to die like a Jew; the real challenge is to live like a Jew.   "THE CHOFETZ CHAIM"

See also: DEATH, HEREAFTER, TROUBLES

LIGHT

Light is especially appreciated after the dark.

HASDAI, *Ben ha-Melekh ve-ha-Nazir*

The light of a candle is useful when it precedes you; it is useless when it trails behind.

BAHYA BEN ASHER, *Kad ha-Kemah*

See also: CAUSE AND EFFECT, CIRCUMSTANCES, KNOWLEDGE

LILITH

Note. Lilith, "the demon of the night," was the Assyrian siren mentioned by Isaiah (34 : 14) and described in the Talmud as having wings (*Niddah*, 24b). In old rabbinical tradition, Lilith flew about in the night, with her long tresses streaming like a demonic owl, and snatched up babies. She sometimes masqueraded as a serpent. *And* she preceded Eve as Adam's wife! More recondite lore fancied the idea that Lilith had been Satan's paramour before she latched on to Adam in unholy wedlock.

Jewish cabalists spoke of Lilith as the epitome of lust, temptation, illicit sex; and many believed that all demons and evil spirits were the children of Lilith, who had forced Adam into the conjugal performance that produced them. . . . So forceful and fearful was this legend that, in Eastern Europe, Jewish mothers used amulets to protect their newly born from Lilith, who (everyone knew) was driven by a monstrous obsession to kill each of Adam's descendants—as soon as they entered the world.*

The Lilith legend obliged those who believed it to believe that Eve was created by God only *after* Lilith, tired of Adam, harshly dropped him and refused to come back to his desolate arms. (In Greek mythology, Lamia, a Lybian queen, deflowered by Zeus himself, had her children killed by jealous Hera, then sought the same infanticidal revenge Lilith practiced. Lamia was sometimes serpentine and bisexual.) *See* EVE. —L.R.

LIQUOR

Liquor may muddle the head—but troubles take it off altogether.

Whiskey makes men brawl.

❋ A little brandy warms you in winter and cools you in summer.

The judge who has drunk too much is not fit to judge.

---

* *New Standard Jewish Encyclopedia, op. cit.,* p. 1226.

The teacher who has had too much to drink is not fit to teach.

Liquor's tongue reveals what is on the mind.

❋ When whiskey enters, judgment flees.

The drunkard who has no whiskey talks of whiskey.

Men sotted with liquor cannot help harming somebody.

❋ Teetotalers are rarely wise.

Liquor can make a man an exile from his own family.

See also: ABSTINENCE, DRUNKARDS, WINE

LOGIC

❋ "For instance" is not proof.

To jump to a conclusion is to by-pass the process of proof.

Every "why" has a "therefore."

❋ Lust is the enemy of logic.

Logic opens a universe of freedom.

Out of snow you can't make cheesecake.

A bachelor matchmaker, a spinster grandmother—these cannot be.

We cannot learn everything from general principles: there may be exceptions.   TALMUD: *Kiddushin,* 34a

See also: ILLOGIC, PREJUDICE, REASON

LONELINESS

Loneliness eats into the soul.

It's better to be bored than lonely.

❋ Even in Paradise, it's not good to be alone.

❋ If you seek a faultless friend, you will remain friendless.

A son in this world prevents loneliness in the world to come.

A man can eat alone, but not work alone.

The man who thinks he can live without others is mistaken; the man who thinks others can't live without him is more mistaken.   Hasidic saying

If I were to cut myself off from those of my brethren who sin, I would be alone.   —adapted from IBN GABIROL

In everyone's heart stirs a great homesickness.
                                   RABBI SEYMOUR SIEGEL

See also: FAMILY, FRIENDS, HEREAFTER

LOVE

❋ Three things can't be hidden: coughing, poverty, and love.

Love, like butter, is better with bread.

❋ Love may be blind, but jealousy sees too much.

Love is sweet—but better with bread.

❋ Love me a little less, but longer.

❋ To love mankind is easy; to love man is hard.

To promise and to love cost no money.

If you don't love me don't kiss me.

❋ Where love is, no room is too small.

Who loves you scolds you.

You can't love God without first loving Man.

Love which never reproves is not love.

❋ One drop of love can create a sea of tears.

Those who tease you love you.

Love can't be forced.

Love destroys one's mental equilibrium.

Light love, heavy consequences.

For a little love, you can pay your whole life.

When love is strong, a man and woman can make their bed on a sword's blade; when love is weak, a bed of sixty cubits is not wide enough.
                               TALMUD: *Sanhedrin*, 7a

A woman prefers poverty with love to riches without love.
—adapted from TALMUD

Love and hatred exaggerate. —adapted from TALMUD

Love is the greatest pleasure open to man.
Seder de Rabbi Eliahu Rabbah

Love is as strong as death. *Song of Solomon*, 8 : 6

Hatred stirs up strife; but love draws a veil over all transgressions.
Book of Proverbs, 10 : 12

"Love your neighbor as yourself" is the great principle of the Torah.
MIDRASH: *Torath Kohanim on Leviticus*, 19

To obey out of love is better than to obey out of fear.
RASHI, *Commentaries on the Pentateuch, Deuteronomy*

A cheerful face makes for love. *Orhot Tsadikim*

What you love for yourself, love also for your fellow man.
FALAQUERA, *Sefer ha-Mevakesh*

❋ A fool's love is but a transient whim.
RABBENU TAM

He who truly loves another can read his thoughts.
THE KORETSER RABBI

Don't believe in the love of the one who cast his burdens upon you but denied you his favor.
IBN GABIROL, *Choice of Pearls*

All love has reality, except the love of the stupid.
IBN GABIROL

Love renders one blind and deaf.   IBN GABIROL

❋ Of what use is love, if you have no one to love?
IMMANUEL OF ROME, *Mahberot*

❋ Love turns one person into two; and two into one.
ISAAC ABRAVANEL

See also: COMPASSION, COURTSHIP, HATE, KINDNESS, LUST

LUCK

❋ When a man has luck, even his ox calves.

When Luck enters, give him a seat!

❋ If you have luck, you don't have to be smart.

❋ An ounce of luck is better than a pound of gold.

❋ You don't need intelligence to have luck, but you do need luck to have intelligence.

Too good is bad for you.

❋ God is a father, luck a stepfather.

❋ To have luck without sense is like carrying a sack full of holes.

Those with luck hit the bull's-eye without taking aim.

❋ Even the unlucky need luck.

Luck can't be bought at the grocer's.

❋ The man who runs after good luck runs away from good peace.

Sometimes a piece of bad luck can come in handy.

❋ It takes no brains to be lucky.

Beauty is better with luck.

If you don't depend on good luck you will postpone bad luck.

Coins are round: sometimes they roll to you, sometimes to others.

If you have bread and butter, your luck is good.

❋ Whenever you can, hang around the lucky.

Luck always finds a welcome.

The bright world is darkened by bad luck.

With luck's help, cleverness can succeed.

❋ From luck to misfortune is only a step; but from misfortune to luck is a long way.

❋ Luck doesn't help those who won't cooperate.

❋ Luck makes men think you smart, because luck makes you rich.

❋ To have bad luck, one still must have luck.

Without luck nothing happens right.

The first winner is the last loser.

Everything depends on *mazl* [luck].

If you don't depend on luck, you will postpone bad luck.
                    —adapted from TALMUD: *Berakoth*, 64a

Weep for the man who does not know his good fortune.
                              TALMUD: *Sanhedrin*, 103a

If a man becomes sick, he should not tell anyone on the day, lest he have bad luck; but he may reveal his illness after that.   —adapted from TALMUD, *Berakoth*, 55b

❋ Need makes people better; luck makes them worse.
                                        Hasidic saying

See also: FORTUNE, INTELLIGENCE, RICHES

LUFTMENSH

A *luftmensh* [someone with his head in the clouds] is always searching for yesterday.

The *luftmensh* takes a bath and forgets to wash his face.

When a *luftmensh* goes to the market, all the merchants smile.

God protects the *luftmensh;* who else can?

The *luftmensh* does not seem to age.

See also: FOLLY, ILLOGIC, ILLUSION, MAN: HUMAN TYPES, NEBEKH, SHLEMIEL

LUST

Lust is like rot in the bones.

A lecherous old man is intolerable.
                              TALMUD: *Pesahim*, 113b

❋ Lust and reason are enemies   IBN GABIROL

Lust is pursued by foolish men because of the immediacy of
its delight . . . they ignore the suffering and wretched-
ness that follow in its train.   **IBN GABIROL**

Poverty cannot disgrace the wise, nor can lust enslave them.
                                   —adapted from **IBN GABIROL**

❋ Lust should be stifled, for it cannot lead to truth.
                           MOSES IBN EZRA, *Shirat Yisrael*

See also: DESIRE, ENVY, GREED, JEALOUSY, PASSION, SEX,
SIN, SUFFERING

LUXURY

The spendings of the rich feed more mouths than their
philanthropies do.

❋ We would all live in luxury, if we didn't have to eat.

When luxuries grow, so do necessities.

See also: EXCESS, RICHES, VANITY, WEALTH

M

MAN

❋ Some people are like new shoes: the cheaper they are,
the louder they squeak.

❋ Man comes into the world with an *Oy!* and leaves with
a *Gevalt!*

Only man was endowed with shame.

❋ If Man is but another animal species, why has no other
species produced even one Darwin?

If God really loved Man, would He have created us?

❋ It is easier to know ten countries than one man.

❋ Every man has his own *meshugas* [craziness].

Every man is blind—to himself.

A man is what he is, not what he used to be.

❋ A man is, alas, only a man—and sometimes not even that.

All virtues in one man are nowhere to be found.

Man has two eyes, two ears, but only one mouth.

❋ To love mankind is easy; to love man is hard.

Don't pity him who is a man; pity him who is not a man.

❋ He is mediocre—not close to wise, and not far from foolish.

❋ A man is weaker than a straw and stronger than iron.

To love God, you must first love Man.

❋ Animals have long tongues and can't speak; men have short tongues and dare not.

Man is not like any other single creature; but he is like all of them collectively.

❋ A man is a man because he is a man.

To displease men is to displease God.
                    —adapted from *Sayings of the Fathers*, 3 : 10

Man is endowed by nature with two eyes: one to see his neighbors' virtues, the other to see his own faults.
                                        Hasidic saying

In everyone there is something precious, found in no one else; so honor each man for what is hidden within him— for what he alone has, and none of his fellows.
                                        Hasidic saying

❋ Man is closest to himself.   TALMUD: *Yebamoth*, 25

It would have been better if man had not been created; but since he *has* been created, let him examine his works.
                                        TALMUD: *Erubin*, 13b

❋ Why was man created on the last day? So that he can be told when pride takes hold of him: God created the gnat before thee.   TALMUD: *Sanhedrin*, 37a

Even one ear of corn is not exactly like another.

TALMUD J.: *Sanhedrin*, 4 : 8

Men fall only in order to rise. *Zohar*

One is really not a man until he reaches the age of twenty-
five. *Yalkut Shimoni*

Man is like a trumpet that produces a tone if blown into;
If the blower leaves, it can produce no sound.

Derekh Tsedek

At one, man is a king, adored by all; at two, he is like a
pig, wallowing in dirt; at ten, he skips like a goat; at
twenty, he neighs like a horse; married, he works like an
ass; when a father, he snarls like a dog; and when old,
he dodders like an ape.

MIDRASH: *Ecclesiastes Rabbah*, 1 : 2

Man was made a little lower than the angels.

—adapted from *Book of Psalms*, 8 : 5

❊ Where there are no men, try to be a man.

Sayings of the Fathers, 2 : 6

A man is a world in miniature.

Abot de Rabbi Nathan, 36

One man is equivalent to all creation.

Abot de Rabbi Nathan

The power of reasoning, with which God endowed man,
makes man capable of perfection.

MAIMONIDES, *Guide to the Perplexed*, 1 : 2

There is no such thing as two men exactly alike—nor two
thoughts.   MAIMONIDES (*probably adapted from*
TALMUD J.: *Berakoth*, 809)

After God created language, He made man—according to
its principles.   ABRAVANEL

This world is like a house: the sky a ceiling, the earth a
carpet, the stars lamps . . . and man is its master.

BAHYA IBN PAQUDA, *Duties of the Heart*

There is no one who never stumbled.   SAMUEL HA-NAGID

We must always hold the reins of the animal within us.

"THE CHOFETZ CHAIM"

Man is a miracle.   THE KORETSER RABBI

If a man is covered with a blanket, he feels warmer: not so
a stone.   THE RIZINER RABBI

MAN: IRONIC OBSERVATIONS ON

All brides are beautiful—and all dead men are pious.

❋ Man has large eyes—but cannot see his own faults.

The peasant will cling to his basket even if a crown is
placed on his head.

❋ The *badkhn* [wedding jester] makes everyone cheerful;
only he is in misery.

❋ The man who blows the foam off his glass is not really
thirsty.   TALMUD: *Sanhedrin*, 100b

Men are like weasels: they hoard and know not for what
purpose.   TALMUD J.: *Sabbath*, 14 : 1

MAN: PSYCHOLOGY OF

❋ To a drunkard, no liquor is bad; to a merchant, no
money is tainted; to a lecher, no woman is ugly.

❋ A man's worst enemy can't wish for him what he can
think up himself.

❋ Man's nature changes every seven years.

❋ One man likes sour cream, the other prayer.

What men want, they do not have; what they have, they
do not prize.

The world is full of troubles, but each man feels only his
own.

To know a man you must ride in the same cart with him.

Man worries over the loss of his possessions, not over the
loss of his years; but his possessions cannot help him,
and his years will never return.   Rabbinical saying

❋ A man shows his character by three things: his tipping,
his tippling, and his temper.

                    TALMUD: *Erubin*, 65b

❋ Like fish, like men: the greater swallow the smaller.
TALMUD: *'Abodah Zarah*, 4a

In the morning Man says, "Would that it were evening!"
and in the evening Man says, "Would that it were morning!"   —adapted from *Deuteronomy*, 28 : 67

❋ Pallor is a sign of anger, talk is a sign of folly, and self-praise is a sign of ignorance.   *Zohar*

❋ By nature we like the familiar and dislike the strange.
MAIMONIDES: *Guide for the Perplexed*, I : 31

Men like the opinions to which they have been accustomed
from their youth; they defend them, and shun contrary
views: and this is one of the things that prevents men
from finding truth, for they cling to the opinions of habit.
MAIMONIDES: *Guide for the Perplexed*, I : 31

❋ How can you expect me to be perfect . . . when I am
full of contradictions?
MOSES IBN EZRA, *Shirat Yisrael*

❋ Man regrets the past, is anxious about the present, and
is concerned for the future.
Ha-Penini, *Behinat Olam*, 13

MAN AND HIS FELLOW MEN

If men knew what one thought of the other, they would
kill each other.

We anger God by our sins and people by our virtues.

❋ Artists seldom like each other.

For God, have fear; with men, be on guard.

❋ The man who believes he can live without others is mistaken; and the man who thinks others can't live without
him is more mistaken.   Hasidic saying

Dear God, bless me so that I don't need people.
—adapted from the grace after meals

Three kinds of mortals need to be protected from others:
a patient, a groom, and a bride.
TALMUD: *Berakoth*, 54b

Condemn no man and consider nothing impossible, for there is no man who does not have his hour.

Sayings of the Fathers, 4 : 6

Don't rely on the broken reed of human support.

ASHER BEN JEHIEL

MAN: HUMAN TYPES

✱ He is the kind of man who first prepares the bandage, then inflicts the wound.   TALMUD: *Megillah*, 13a

Four kinds of men are intolerable: an arrogant poor man, a deceitful rich man, a lecherous old man, and the head of a synagogue who lords it over his congregation.

TALMUD: *Pesahim*, 113b

Four types of men may be thought of as dead: the poor, the blind, the leprous, and the childless.

TALMUD: *'Abodah Zarah*, 5a

✱ Who is wise? He who can learn from every man.
Who is strong? He who can control his passions.
Who is rich? He who is content with his lot.
Whom do men honor? He who honors his fellow men.

BEN ZOMA in *Sayings of the Fathers*, 4 : 1

There are four types among men:
  The ordinary one says: "What is mine is mine, and what is yours is yours."
  The queer one says: "What is mine is yours, and what is yours is mine."
  The saintly one says: "What is mine is yours, and what is yours is yours."
  The wicked one says: "What is mine is mine, and what is yours is also mine."   *Sayings of the Fathers*, 5 : 16

✱ There are four types of temperaments: easy to provoke and easy to calm—here the fault is canceled by the virtue; hard to provoke, but hard to calm—here the virtue is canceled by the fault; hard to provoke, and easy to calm—this is the temperament of a good man; easy to provoke, but hard to calm—this is the temperament of the wicked.   *Sayings of the Fathers*, 5 : 17

The bashful man cannot learn, the ill-tempered man cannot teach, and the one who preoccupies himself with
worldly affairs cannot impart wisdom.

> HILLEL in *Sayings of the Fathers*, 2 : 6

❋ There are four types of men in this world:
The man who knows, and knows that he knows: he is
wise, so consult him.

The man who knows, but doesn't know that he knows:
help him not forget what he knows.

The man who knows not, and knows that he knows not:
teach him.

Finally, there is the man who knows not but pretends
that he knows: he is a fool, so avoid him.

> IBN GABIROL, *Choice of Pearls*

A pretty maiden, a cup of wine, a beautiful garden, the
song of a bird, the murmur of a book—these are for the
lover, the lonely, the poor, the sick.

> ABRAHAM IBN EZRA, *Yesod Mora*

MAN AND GOD

❋ O, Lord—glance down from heaven and take a real look
at Your world.

❋ When God wants to break a man's heart, he gives him a
lot of sense.

Man is in bondage to his impulses—and to his Creator.

There are three partners in man: God, his father, and his
mother.   TALMUD: *Kiddushin*, 30b

Four types of men will never see God's face: the scoffer,
the liar, the slanderer, and the hypocrite.

> TALMUD: *Sotah*, 42a

Man was created last for a reason: If he is worthy, he will
find all nature at his service; if he is unworthy, he will
find all nature arrayed against him.

> THE KORETSER RABBI

See also: ADAM, CHARACTER, FAMILY, GOD, LIFE, MEN AND
WOMEN, OLD AGE, PRIDE, VANITY, YOUNG AND OLD

MANNERS

✸ Good manners will open any door.

Don't push yourself where you shouldn't be.

You may look, but not stare.

Without study, there are no good manners.

Don't taunt your neighbor for your own blemish.
                                    TALMUD: *Baba Mezi'a*, 59b

In a house where someone was hanged, don't say, "Hang
this up for me."
                    —adapted from TALMUD, *Baba Mezi'a*, 59b

A woman will uncover her neighbor's pots in order to see
what's cooking.   TOSEPHTA, *Taharoth*, 8

✸ At the table of the great, don't gulp.
                            BEN SIRACH, *Ecclesiasticus*, 31 : 12

There is no truer index to intelligence than the way one acts
at the table.   IBN GABIROL, *Choice of Pearls*

✸ The test of good manners is to be patient with bad ones.
                                                    IBN GABIROL

Say not to your neighbor, "Dine at my house for I dined at
yours"; it sounds like usury.
                    —adapted from MAIMONIDES, *Mishneh Torah*

See also: ANGER, BOASTING, CONSIDERATION, DECORUM,
LAUGHTER, SENSITIVITY, TEMPER, THOUGHTFULNESS

MARRIAGE

Note. The first positive commandment of the Bible is the
one that enjoins man to "Be fruitful, and multiply"
(Genesis, 1 : 28). The Hebrews looked favorably upon
early marriage: the Talmud set eighteen as the proper
age; some rabbis encouraged marriage as early as fourteen. A rabbi or formal religious service may be waived,
by Talmudic dictum, under certain conditions. A Jew
on a desert isle, it is fondly related, once wed himself to
a woman—and made Heaven and Earth witnesses: "I
call upon Heaven and Earth to witness that I consecrate
you as my wife, according to the laws of Moses and of
Israel."

    The idea of marriage as holy and mystical, and of God

as participating in it, has created charming legends. It is said that when souls are created in heaven, an angel cries: "This boy for that girl!" Marriage *reunites* the male and female aspects of one soul, the *Zohar* tells us.

Arranging marriages was considered a sacred matter: The union of two souls, and the agreement to have children and raise them as Jews, was part of Israel's obligation in its compact with God. (Commentaries in the Talmudic tractate *Baba Kamma* deal with the role of the matchmaker in perpetuating the existence of Israel itself.)

God is considered the supreme *shadkhn* (matchmaker): there is an old legend that forty days before a Jewish child is born, its mate is selected in Heaven. The professional *shadkhn* performed an important social function, gathering information about eligible mates in far-removed villages, trying to match family standing and pedigree, weighing individual qualities that might strengthen compatibility, etc.

Our modern aversion to the idea of arranged marriages is, of course, a post–eighteenth-century attitude: it did not occur to earlier generations of Jews or their contemporaries that "love and marriage" go together.

Elaborate premarital "arrangements" were once required. A dowry (*nadn*) was, of course, part of every Orthodox nuptial contract. Presents of value were exchanged in advance between bride and groom: the latter usually gave his betrothed a prayer book (*siddur*), a veil, a fine comb, a sash, a ring. The bride-to-be gave her betrothed a prayer shawl (*talis*), a gold or silver chain, even a watch.

Jewish folk sayings on marriage are like those of almost every other people, a mishmash of delightful contradictions: they exalt it, deride it, praise it, scorn it, revere it, and poke fun at its victims.   —L.R.

❋ When a young man marries, he divorces his mother.

❋ Even a bad match can beget good children.

❋ The man who marries for money earns it.

Early to rise and early to wed does no harm.

❋ By day they fight, but bed at night.

❋ Jews have no nunneries.

Husband and wife are one flesh, but have different purses.

When there is peace in the house, even morsels of food will be enough.

A third person may not interfere between two who sleep on the same pillow.

He who is without a wife dwells without blessing, life, joy, help, good, and peace—and without defense against temptation.   TALMUD: *Yebamoth,* 62b

Whosoever remains unmarried does not deserve to be called a man.   TALMUD: *Yebamoth,* 63a

❋ More than man desires to marry, woman desires to be married.   TALMUD: *Yebamoth,* 113a

When a man marries, his sins decrease.

TALMUD: *Kiddushin,* 29b

If you must sell everything . . . marry your daughter to a scholar.   TALMUD: *Pesahim,* 49b

Forty days before the creation of a child, a voice proclaims in heaven: "So-and-so's daughter for so-and-so's son!"   TALMUD: *Sotah,* 2a

❋ The female [child] should be married first, for the shame of a woman is greater than the shame of a man.
TALMUD: *Kethuboth,* 67b

❋ It was the custom [in ancient Judea] to plant a cedar tree when a boy was born, and to plant a pine when a girl was born; and when they were married, the canopy was made of branches woven from both trees.

TALMUD: *Gittin,* 57a

Before a young man marries, his love goes to his parents; after he marries, it goes to his wife.

Pirke de Rabbi Eliezer

Without a hedge the vineyard is laid waste; without a wife, a man is a homeless wanderer; and who trusts an armed band of vagabonds?   BEN SIRACH, *Ecclesiasticus*

❋ When a soul is sent down from heaven, it contains both male and female characteristics; the male elements enter the boy baby, the female the girl baby; and if they be worthy, God reunites them, in marriage.   *Zohar*

See also: BACHELORS, COURTSHIP, DAUGHTERS, DIVORCE, DOWRY, FATHERS, LOVE, MEN AND WOMEN, MOTHERS, SONS, WIVES

MARRIAGE AND GOD

❋ God sits above and makes matches below.

Between husband and wife only God should judge.

❋ The Holy Spirit can rest only upon a married man, for an unmarried man is but half a man, and the Holy Spirit does not rest on what is imperfect.

Rabbinical saying

God creates new worlds constantly—by causing marriages to take place.   *Zohar*

If husband and wife are worthy, the Holy Presence abides with them; if not, fire consumes them.

RABBI AKIBA in TALMUD: *Sotah*, 17a

See also: BACHELORS, DIVORCE, FAMILY, GOD, HUSBANDS, LIFE, LOVE, MEN AND WOMEN, SEX

MARRIAGE: CYNICAL COMMENTS ON

❋ A man may ride on a coach, but a woman rides on her apron.

For dying or marrying, there's always time.

After the wedding it's too late to have regrets.

The ceremony lasts an hour, but the troubles last a lifetime.

Marry fast and get stuck for good.

❋ It is as hard to arrange a good marriage as it was to divide the Red Sea.   TALMUD: *Sotah*, 2a

Many a married man hoards—for the future husband of his wife.   IBN GABIROL, *Choice of Pearls*

Honeymoon for a month, trouble for life.

HASDAI, *Ben ha-Melekh ve-ha-Nazir*

A man enters the *khupe* [marriage canopy] living, and comes out a corpse.   SHOLEM ALEICHEM

See also: ADVICE, COURTSHIP, DIVORCE, HUSBANDS, MEN AND WOMEN, WIVES

MARRIAGE: ADMONITIONS, ADVICE, AND LEGALITIES

Marriage is made in Heaven; but second marriages are arranged by people.

❊ Better break the engagement than the marriage.

❊ When an old man takes a young wife, the man becomes young and the woman old.

Those who marry while they have no secure livelihood are fools.

A man should not marry a pregnant widow or divorcee until her child is born.   TALMUD: *Yebamoth*, 36b

The children of the man who married for money will turn out to be a curse to him.   TALMUD: *Yebamoth*, 37a

A man should not marry a woman with the mental reservation that, after all, he may divorce her.
    TALMUD: *Yebamoth*, 37b

❊ A henpecked husband gets no relief in court.
    TALMUD: *Baba Mezi'a*, 75b

The old and the young should not be joined in marriage, lest both the peace and the purity of marriage be destroyed.   TALMUD: *Sanhedrin*, 76a

No marriage contract is made without a quarrel.
    TALMUD: *Shabbath*, 130a

Now that the Roman Government seeks to prevent the circumcision of our sons, should we ordain that no one marry and beget children? No, for then the descendants of Abraham would die out.
    TALMUD: *Baba Bathra*, 60b

See also: BACHELORS, CHILDREN, DIVORCE, FAMILY, HUSBANDS, LOVE, MEN AND WOMEN, WIVES

MARTYRS

Note. Being a martyr is the highest form of *Kiddush ha-Shem* ("sanctification of God's Name")—that is, enduring torture and accepting death because of faith in God, or to prevent a desecration of God's name. The idea of martyrdom as the ultimate testimonial to one's faith in God seems to have arisen, as a mass phenomenon, during the Jewish wars against Hellenization.

—L.R.

See HEROES, INQUISITION, PERSECUTION, POGROMS

MASSES

The masses aren't asses.

The masses are fools.

The public is a clod.

Public safety comes from consulting the multitude.
              —adapted from *Book of Proverbs*, 11 : 14

❋ When I see no way of teaching a truth except by pleasing one intelligent man and offending ten thousand fools, I address myself to the one, and ignore the censure of the multitude.
     MAIMONIDES, *Guide to the Perplexed*, Introduction

See also: DEMOCRACY, FAME, GLORY, HONOR, PEOPLE, POLITICS, POWER, REPUTATION, STATUS

MEDICINE

Words are like medicine: measure them with care; an overdose can hurt.

Doors closed to good deeds open to disease.

Love is the best medicine.

Don't judge a doctor; poll his patients.

❋ No medicines heal sick souls.

❋ Some medicine does in a week what no medicine does in seven days.

See also: DISEASE, DOCTORS, HEALTH, MODERATION

MEEKNESS

✻ Too meek is half-proud. Better be humble with the meek than share spoils with the proud.
                    —adapted from *Book of Proverbs*, 16 : 19

There is a type of meekness that brings a man to Gehenna: For instance, the judge who knows that other judges made an error, but says, "Shall I put them to shame?" . . . Or the man who hears a congregation speak falsely and says, "Who am I to correct them?" . . . There is a kind of humility which is not righteousness.

Sefer Hasidim

See also: HUMILITY, LAW, MODESTY, PRIDE, SELF-ESTEEM

MELANCHOLY

✻ It is hard to repent of the sin of melancholy—for, in doing so, we fall into a deeper melancholy, realizing we have sinned.   THE BERSHIDER RABBI

See also: CONSCIENCE, DISEASE, SADNESS, SORROW, SUFFERING

MEMORY

✻ Two things get weaker with time: your teeth and your memory.

✻ What's good, we remember; what's bad, we feel.

Habitual liars need a powerful memory.

✻ Men can forget anything—except when to eat.

There is a difference between learning one's lesson a hundred times and learning it a hundred and one times.
                    TALMUD: *Hagigah*, 9b

See also: FORGETTING, LEARNING, LIARS/LIES, LOGIC, REASON

MEN AND WOMEN

✻ Men should take care not to make women weep, for God counts their tears.

A man may ride on a coach; but a woman rides on her apron.

Man's brains are his jewels; woman's jewels are her brains.

Rather talk to a woman and think of God than talk to God and think of a woman.

Women persuade men to good as well as to evil, but they always persuade.

Should a male and a female orphan need to be supported, let the female take precedence, for a boy can beg, but a girl must not.   TALMUD: *Kethuboth*, 67a

It is easier to appease a male than a female—because the first man was created out of dust, which is soft, but the first woman was created out of bone, which is hard.
                                        TALMUD: *Niddah*, 31b

A man likes visitors; not so a woman.
                                        TALMUD: *Baba Mezi'a*, 97a

Man and woman are one body and soul.
                    —adapted from TALMUD: *Menahoth*, 93a

Women want to be married more than men do.
                    —adapted from TALMUD: *Yebamoth*, 113a

Females should be married before males, for the shame of a woman is greater than that of a man.
                                        TALMUD: *Kethuboth*, 67b

❉ The ideal man has the strength of a man and the compassion of a woman.   *Zohar*

Parsimony, soft-heartedness, and naïveté are vices in a man—but virtues in a woman.
                    HASDAI, *Ben ha-Melekh ve-ha-Nazir*

A man without a wife is a homeless wanderer.
                                        BEN SIRACH, *Ecclesiasticus*

Elderly men who are popular with young women usually lack wisdom.   NACHMAN OF BRATSLAV

❉ A man is young if a girl can make him happy or unhappy; he enters middle age when a woman can make him happy but not unhappy; he becomes old when a woman can make him neither happy nor unhappy.
                                        MORITZ ROSENTHAL

See also: COURTSHIP, GOD, LOVE, MARRIAGE

MEN AND WOMEN: CYNICAL COMMENTS ON

❋ Man searches for a mate and finds his own rib.

Pray to God to preserve you from bad women, and preserve yourself from the good ones.

❋ "If you know everything," said the cynic to the *tsadik* [holy man], "tell me: What did Eve do whenever Adam came home?"

> "She counted his ribs," said the *tsadik*.

❋ Adam's last testament read: "Don't believe Eve."

If a male dog barks, enter; if a female dog barks, depart.
> TALMUD: *Erubin*, 86a

At the time of the Golden Calf, the women refused to use their golden ornaments for idolatry; so today they rule over their husbands.   *Yalkut Ruveni*

MERCY

❋ The mercy of the wicked is cruel.
> *Book of Proverbs*, 12 : 10

See also: COMPASSION, GOOD DEEDS, KINDNESS, PIETY, POWER, RIGHTEOUSNESS

MESSIAH

Note. The history and different connotations of "Messiah" deserve careful explanation. The word comes from Hebrew: *ha-mashiah:* "the anointed." The Hebrew *mashiah* in Greek became *messias;* in translation, *christos;* hence, *messias* = messiah; *christos* = Christ—and each denotes "the anointed one."

In the Old Testament, *meshiah* was the title given to kings ("God's anointed") and priests, who were initiated by being anointed with sacred oil. Later, *meshiah* meant a prophet, or anyone with a special mission from God. Then *meshiah* came to mean the awaited Deliverer of the Jews from their bondage and oppression, who will restore the kingdom of Israel. Finally, *meshiah* stood for the Savior who will make the world of men acknowledge God's sovereignty, and will thus usher in the Day of Judgment.

English translations of the Bible tend to separate the idea of "the anointed" from the "Messiah"—the first being used for the living, the second for the expected. But the Jewish concept should be approached historically. The Old Testament uses the term *meshiah* or anointed king for Saul, David, Zedekiah, and Cyrus of Persia, who was no Hebrew.

King David established the dynastic principle among the Hebrews. And from this developed the idea that some man, blessed by God, would come from the House of David to end Israel's tribulations, enforce justice, and establish peace. As a spiritual leader, the Messiah would establish a messianic age—on earth, be it noted—which the prophets Isaiah and Micah foretold. And in the new Age of Righteousness, all of mankind would be redeemed.

Jews thus distinguished the earthly Messiah from a heavenly Messiah: the earthly Messiah, Deliverer of the Jews, would be a man born of the line of David; but the heavenly Messiah lives in Heaven "under the wings of the Lord" (Enoch, 39) and existed before even the sun and the stars were created. The idea of a *divine* "Son of Man" was not understood by Jews in the later Christian sense.

The doctrine of the Messiah has been one of the most powerful elements in the history of Judaism. Whenever catastrophes—epidemics, starvation, pogroms, wars, expulsions, or any of the torments visited upon the Jews—seemed unendurable, the faithful looked once more into their holy books for some hopeful, hidden sign, some new revelation, some miraculous harbinger of deliverance. Pious mystics, astrologers, cabalists, and, later, some hasidim even predicted the exact time when the Messiah would usher in the Kingdom of God. (So did Christian Millenarians throughout the Middle East, Europe, and England.)

The Romans feared messianic predictions for political reasons, considering them an incitement to, or a camouflage for, rebellion against Rome's rule; and messianic movements often did lead to political militancy.

Whenever an empire under which Jews suffered crumbled—the Persian, the Byzantine, the Roman—the messianic fervors were intensified. A memorable statement on this tragic-hopeful theme is that of Professor Hugh

Trevor-Roper: ". . . when Popes and Kings allied themselves with the blind prejudices of the Church and the mob, such patronage availed the Jews no more than the Moriscos of Spain or the Huguenots of France. Whither then were the persecuted remnant to turn for relief? Whither indeed but to that stock refuge of the oppressed: mysticism, the Messiah, the Millennium. As the defeated humanists of Spain sank into private ecstasies, as the *marabout* on his African dunghill promises a Mahdi to the dejected bedouin, as the Anabaptists of the seventeenth century manipulated their Scriptural logarithms to hasten the Apocalypse, so also the Jews of the Dispersion deviated into mystical heresies, counted the days to the Millennium, or discovered the Messiah."*

Messianic ideas opposed the sense of resignation, the passive acceptance of Israel's fate on earth that, some Jews felt, was encouraged by Talmudic law. A group called *Neturei Karta*, who today live in Israel, refuse to recognize Israel as an independent state, because they maintain that such a holy sovereignty could only have been established by the *meshiah*—and the *meshiah* has, clearly, not yet arrived.

—L.R.

When the Messiah comes, all the sick will be healed—but fools will remain fools.

See also: HEREAFTER, MIRACLES, PARADISE, SALVATION

MILLENNIUM

In the Millennium we must expect Evil to be diminished, but not abolished. *Zohar*

See: GOD, HEAVEN, HEREAFTER, PARADISE, SALVATION

MIND

❊ God looks into our hearts before he looks into our minds.

The mind of each man is as unique as his face.
—adapted from TALMUD: *Berakoth*, 58a

* *Historical Essays*, Macmillan, London, 1963, pp. 148–49.

Man's mind is the Holy of Holies, and to admit evil
thoughts is like setting up an idol in the Temple.
                                THE BERDICHEVER RABBI

See also: EMOTIONS, INTELLECT, INTELLIGENCE, LOGIC, REA-
SON, SOUL

MIRACLES

Note. The prophet Elijah is the leading miracles man in
Jewish folklore. He is credited with saving the sick, rescuing the doomed, and countless miraculous deeds. A
special symbolic place in ceremonials (the Passover
Seder, circumcision) is reserved for Elijah and his ever-
hoped-for appearance on earth. For it is Elijah who will
return to this world, blowing his horn, to signal the
Messiah's appearance and the day of Redemption.
   I should remind you that according to Scripture this
once-fierce but since-beloved prophet never died: he
was transported directly to heaven, within a whirlwind
and on a flaming chariot.

                                               —L.R.

If God willed it, brooms would shoot.

❊ You think it a miracle if God does the will of your
rabbi; we think it a miracle if our rabbi does God's will.

If a thousand pious men gathered around a log, it, too,
could work miracles.

Miracles don't happen every day.
                                TALMUD: *Pesahim,* 50b

Miracles do occur—but they rarely provide food.
                                TALMUD: *Shabbath,* 53b

❊ Hope for a miracle—but don't depend on one.
                        —adapted from TALMUD: *Megillah,* 7b

❊ A miracle cannot prove that which is impossible; it is
useful only as a confirmation of what is possible.
                        MAIMONIDES, *Guide to the Perplexed,* 3

Believe in God through faith, and not because of miracles.
                                NACHMAN OF BRATSLAV

See also: FATE, FORTUNE, GOD, ILLUSION, LUCK, REASON,
SKEPTICISM

MISERS

❋ Misers worship an idol.

A miser's moneybags are a bed for mice.

A miser is worse than a pauper.

Even the birds in the air despise a miser.

A miserly man is like a fattened ox: he will give of his fat only when he has been deprived of his life.

Some men are like weasels; they hoard and know not its purpose.   TALMUD J.: *Sabbath*, 14 : 1

Seeking charity from a miser is like fishing in the desert.
IBN GABIROL, *Choice of Pearls*

❋ The greatest miser with money is the biggest spend-thrift with desires.   MOSES IBN EZRA, *Shirat Yisrael*

Miserliness is an expensive habit.
"THE CHOFETZ CHAIM"

A miserly man and a fat cow are useful only after death.
SHOLEM ALEICHEM

See also: CHARITY, MONEY, THRIFT, WEALTH

MISERY

Many crowd the gate of abundance, but neither brother nor friend enters the door of misery.

See also: CONSCIENCE, DUTY, GOOD DEEDS, MELANCHOLY, REPENTANCE, REVENGE, SORROW, SUFFERING

MISFORTUNE

❋ Other men's misfortunes are not hard to bear.

The fear of a misfortune is worse than the misfortune.

A boil isn't so bad—on someone else's neck.

Nothing is so bad but that some good may not come of it.

The bitterest misfortune can be concealed with a smile.

❋ If the house has fallen, woe to the windows.

Whether the stone falls on the pot, or the pot on the stone, woe to the pot!   SIMEON BEN JOSE BEN LAKUNIA in
MIDRASH: *Esther Rabbah*, 7 : 10

One day's happiness makes misfortune forgotten, and one day's misfortune makes a man forget past happiness.
BEN SIRACH, *Ecclesiasticus*, 11 : 25

To imagine that no misfortune will befall you is like wishing not to live at all, for misfortunes are a necessary part of this transient world.   IBN GABIROL

See also: FACE, FATE, FORTUNE, HAPPINESS, LUCK, POVERTY, SORROW, SUFFERING

MISOGYNIST

See: HATE, MAN

MITZVAHS

Note. A *mitzvah* ("commandment") means an act meritorious in God's eyes, a truly virtuous, kind, compassionate deed. I think that *"mitzvah"* is encountered second only to "Torah" in the vocabulary of Judaism. There are 613 (!) separate *mitzvoth*: 248 are positive, 365 negative. The rabbis often used the phrase *simha shel mitzvah* ("the joy of fulfilling a pious act") to drive home the notion that good deeds which are performed out of a sense of duty are not as meaningful as those performed out of the pure desire to do good. Judaic ethics rest on the idea of performing good deeds—as a mandatory obligation or (better) as a volunteered expression of the desire to do good. Israel Zangwill called *mitzvoth* "the sacred sociology of the Jews.

—L.R.

See: CHARITY, COMPASSION, GOOD DEEDS, MAN, VIRTUE

MOCKERY

See: SARCASM, SELF-MOCKERY

MODERATION

You'll suffer more from overeating than from undereating.

Three things are good in small quantities and bad in large: yeast, salt, and hesitation.   TALMUD: *Berakoth*, 34a

✳ There are eight things of which a little is good and much is bad: travel, mating, wealth, work, wine, sleep, spiced drinks, and medicine.   TALMUD: *Gittin*, 70a

Too much sitting aggravates hemorrhoids; too much standing hurts the heart; too much walking hurts the eyes; so divide your time between the three.

TALMUD: *Kethuboth*, 111b

The Torah may be likened to two paths, one of fire, the other of snow. Turn in one direction, and you die of heat: turn to the other and you die of the cold. What should you do? Walk in the middle.

TALMUD: *Hagigah*, 2 : 1

See also: ASCETICS/ASCETICISM, ENVY, EXCESS, GLUTTONY, GREED

MODESTY

✳ Too much modesty is half-conceit.

When pride comes, scorn comes; but with the modest is wisdom.   *Book of Proverbs*, 11 : 2

Modesty is the noblest of all ornaments.

ELEAZAR ROKEACH

MONEY

Note. "It is in the nature of man to long for wealth," says the *Shulhan Aruk* (the "prepared table," or Code of Jewish Law). This was published (1564-65) long before Adam Smith. Jewish law and attitudes to moneylending, interest, and usury (which, I'll wager, are quite different from what you may think) are sketched in the headnotes for BORROWING, LENDING, and USURY.

—L.R.

Gold has a dirty father [the earth] yet is everywhere esteemed.

❀ If you have money, men think you are wise, handsome, and able to sing like a bird.

❀ The man who thinks that anything can be accomplished by money is likely to do anything for money.

❀ Shrouds have no pockets.

To be without money is a great mistake.

Bad neighbors count a man's income, not his expenses.

No dollar is a bastard.

Money really adds no more to the wise than clothes can to the beautiful.

❀ It isn't that a full purse is so good; it's that an empty one is so bad.

It's not that money makes everything good; it's that no money makes everything rotten.

A purse without money is only a piece of leather.

Money can buy anything—except sense.

❀ To have money is not always so *Ai-yi-yi*, but not to have it is *Oy-oy-oy*!

Money can marry off even a grandmother.

❀ If you can't help out with a little money, at least give a sympathetic groan.

❀ A heavy purse is light to carry.

❀ If you have no money, attend no auctions.

When you bribe, you ride.

When the purse is full the stomach is still.

Money is a soap that removes the worst stains.

❀ Some people are slaves—to gold and silver.

❀ Money helps Man like reality.

Money without children is riches without savor.

❀ If you sow money, you reap fools.

A golden key [money] opens all doors.

❀ You can silence gossip if coins tinkle in your pocket.

Money in the pocket means peace in the house.

The world rests on three things: Money, money, and money.

The Torah gives light, but warmth comes from money.

A good income cures most ills.

❋ It's easier to make money than to keep it.

To have money is good; to have control of money is still better.

With money, you can do everything.

❋ Without money, this world is not fit to live in.

A little money lights up my world—like the sun.

Better a steady dime than a rare dollar.

Money goes to money.

He who has money has authority.

The love of money leads to idolatry and causes those who have it to fall into madness.

When Death summons a man to appear before his Maker, money, which man most loves, cannot go with him.

TALMUD

There's no money for provisions, but there is for waste.

TALMUD: *Hagigah*, 5a

All the parts of the body depend on the heart, and the heart depends on the purse.

TALMUD J.: *Terumoth*, 8

See also: BUSINESS, FOOLS, FORTUNE, GREED, MISERS, RICHES, THRIFT, WEALTH

MONOTHEISM

Note. However the history of man is written in the future, one thing seems to me certain: the Hebrew concept of monotheism represented a most profound *intellectual*, no less than religious, revolution:

　(1) It freed men from a fearful subordination to the forces of nature, by positing a loving (or punishing)

supranatural cosmic power; the idea of one God emancipated men from their terror of many evil demons,
supernatural apparitions, fiendish hobgoblins, animistic
cacodemons, etc.

(2) Monotheism fused *religion and morality*: ethical
conduct became a duty to the deity; morality now par-
took of the divine.

(3) The love of God was a novel and immense contribution (the Hebrews' predecessors and contemporaries
feared, placated, or made sacrifices to a gallery of gods
who were unloving, willful, vain, jealous, angry, petulant
—in short, oddly undivine; the *Iliad* is a marvelous
chronicle of the curious intramural feuds that raged on
lofty Olympus).

(4) The concept of One God ultimately became a
stimulus to *science* (even though the rabbis were opposed
to the secular and the scientific), because it suggested a
unitary, consistent pattern within which everything in
nature functioned. Monotheism offered the idea of order,
consistency, and meaning in the universe—all waiting for
man to explore and understand.

(5) The idea of One God contained within itself the
concept of a central cause, a prime reason for things;
and the searches for that reason, whether in the analysis
of sacred writings or experimental ventures or the cool
observation of physical phenomena, became a systematic
enterprise. For once cosmic unity is accepted, universal
consistencies, regularities, and interrelations follow; and
each new discovery adds weight to the view that behind
all of the multifarious, mystifying phenomena of the
world, there is one final and consistent set of principles.
(I am by no means downgrading the surpassing brilliance
of polytheistic Greece.)

Von Humboldt shrewdly observed that the love of nature, to say nothing of the sympathetic study of it, could
only begin after superfluous pagan gods had been removed from man's intellectual apparatus. And Einstein,
in one of his most famous asides about quantum physics,
said that he could not believe that God "threw dice"—
i.e., that the laws of the universe are random.

See quotations: GOD.

—L.R.

MORALS

"One lesson, and only one, history may be said to repeat
with distinctness, that the world is built somehow on
moral foundations; that in the long run it is well with the
good; in the long run it is ill with the wicked. But this is
no science; it is no more than the old doctrine taught
long ago by the Hebrew prophets."
            —J. A. Froude, in *A Book of Jewish Thoughts,*
            ed. J. H. Hertz, Oxford, London, 1920, p. 151.

I take comfort from this noble quotation, and only wish
that "the long run" were not so long.

                                                    —L.R.

❋ The world hates two types: the informer and the
moralist.

See also: EVIL, GOOD, GOSSIP, LIARS/LIES, LUST, SEX, SIN,
SLANDER, TRUTH

MOTHERS

❋ God could not be everywhere, so he created mothers.

A child without a mother is like a door without a knob.

❋ A mother has glass eyes [she cannot see her children's
faults].

❋ A mother understands what a child does not say.

❋ One mother achieves more than a hundred teachers.

A mother is a veil: she hides her children's failings.

❋ The warmest bed of all is Mother's.

❋ When a young man marries, he divorces his mother.

Mothers have big aprons—to cover the faults of their
children.

The best fork is Mother's hand.

There is no such thing as a bad mother.

Many a young foal's skin served as a saddle on its mother's
back.

Hearing the approaching step of his mother, Rab Joseph
would say: "I must stand up, for the *Shekhinah* [Holy
Spirit] enters."   TALMUD: *Kiddushin*, 31 : 2

The life of the mother takes priority over the unborn child.
                          MISHNAH: *Ohalot*, 7 : 6

A foolish son is grief to his mother.
                          Book of Proverbs, 10 : 1

A modest woman has good children.
                          NACHMAN OF BRATSLAV

See also: CHILDREN, DAUGHTERS, FAMILY, HUSBANDS, MAR-
RIAGE, PARENTS, SONS, WIDOWS, WIVES

MOTHERS-IN-LAW

If you're angry with your mother-in-law, you yell at her
daughter.

A mother-in-law and a daughter-in-law in one house are
like two cats in a bag.

The mother-in-law and the daughter-in-law should not ride
in the same cart.

✾ Adam was the luckiest man: he had no mother-in-law.
                          SHOLEM ALEICHEM

See also: DAUGHTERS-IN-LAW, SONS-IN-LAW

MOURNING

Note. The sages of the Talmud instruct Jews not to mourn
too long, too deeply, or self-accusingly. They prescribe
the protocol of grief: three days of weeping, followed
by four days of eulogy of the departed. The seven-day
shiva period is followed by a thirty-day period (*shlo-
shim*) of lesser mourning, and an eleven-month period
during which the mourner recites the Kaddish (prayer
for the dead) twice daily. The deceased is remembered
each year on the anniversary of his death.
                                          —L.R.

It is better to go to a house of mourning than to a house of
feasting.   *Ecclesiastes*, 7 : 2

❊ When a sage dies, all men should mourn, for they are
his kinsmen.   TALMUD: *Shabbath*, 105b

See also: DEATH, GOOD DEEDS, SUFFERING

MURDER

See: KILLING

MYSTICISM

See: ASTROLOGY, FOLLY

N

NATURE

God used the principles of nature to create language, and
the principles of language to create Man.
                                                ABRAVANEL

When the first man saw the first little blade of grass, he felt
sorry for it—and the first rains fell.

Not a handful of rain descends from above without the
earth sending up two handfuls of moisture to meet it.
                        MIDRASH: *Genesis Rabbah*, 13 : 13

Don't ask the Lord to change the laws of nature for you.
                                    NACHMAN OF BRATSLAV

If Man is worthy, all nature will be at his service; if Man
is not worthy, all nature will join against him.
                            —adapted from THE KORETSER RABBI

See also: GOD, WORLD

NEBEKH (NEBBECH)

Note. In the vocabulary of character-types, woven out of
pity, candor and insight, *nebekh* stands (along with
*nudnick, shlemiel, shlimazl, shnuk, shmendrick, yold,
Chaim Yankel, shlepper*) in that pantheon of special

Yiddish words coined to describe the ineffectuals of this world. (For definitions, see Glossary; for longer descriptions, illustrations, and stories about each, see *The Joys of Yiddish, op. cit.*)

"*Nebekh*" is both a noun and an interjection. As a noun, it means an innocuous nonentity, a helpless, hapless soul—first cousin to a *shlemiel* (*q.v.*). But whereas one may dislike a *shlemiel* it is hard to feel anything but sympathy for a *nebekh*.

As an interjection, *nebekh means* "alas . . . too bad . . . unfortunately . . ." expressing affectionate dismay, regret, or commiseration. Hence the irony of the story of the Jew in Berlin who said he would be the happiest man in the world if he could only be sitting on a bench with a friend and exclaim, "Look who's there! It's, *nebekh*, Hitler."

—L.R.

A *nebekh* (alas) is only a man—and sometimes not even that.

❋ When a *nebekh* leaves the room, you feel as if someone came in.

Better ten enemies than one *nebekh*.

A *nebekh* talks as if whispering secrets to mice.

A *shlemiel* is always knocking things off a table, and the *nebekh* always picks them up.

❋ When a *shlemiel* trips, he knocks down a *shlimazl*; and a *nebekh* repairs the *shlimazl's* glasses.

See also: FOOLS, SHLEMIEL, SHLIMAZL

NECESSITY

When there is no meat, one must pick the bones.

❋ If things aren't the way you like, like them the way they are.

Necessity can break iron.

When a wave approaches, bend your head.

—adapted from AKIBA, in TALMUD: *Yebamoth*, 121 : a

See also: ADVERSITY, DESTINY, FATE, LIFE, RESIGNATION

NEIGHBORS

✻ Love they neighbor, even when he plays the trombone.

You can judge a man better by the comments of his neighbor than by the praises of his mother.

Before you buy a house, investigate the neighbors.

If you mix with the neighbors, you'll learn what's going on in your own house.

Better a neighbor near at hand than a brother far away.
Book of Proverbs, 27 : 10

An envious neighbor counts your income, not your expenses. *Yalkut Shimoni, Deuteronomy*

See also: ENVY, FRIENDS

NITPICKERS

The fault-finder will complain that the bride is too pretty.

He's the type of man who wonders whether a flea has a *pupik* [naval].

NONSENSE: EXAMPLES OF

✻ Sleep faster, we need the pillows.

Let's go to town tomorrow, if we're alive; if not, let's go on Wednesday.

✻ The best tailor among all the cobblers is Jacob the baker.

There's nothing so nonsensical that it hasn't been written (or printed).

✻ A mute told a deaf man how a blind man saw a cripple run on water.

If my aunt had wheels, she would be a carriage.

If a grandmother had a beard, she'd be a grandfather.

See also: FOLLY, FOOLS, ILLOGIC, IRONY: EXAMPLES OF, PARADOXES: EXAMPLES OF, SHLEMIEL

O

OBLIGATION

❊ If you give food to a small child, you must tell its mother. TALMUD: *Shabbath*, 10b

He who eats of another's bread is afraid to look at him.
TALMUD J.: *Orlah*, 1 : 3

No man may buy a beast, an animal, or a bird until he has provided food for it. TALMUD J.: *Yebamoth*, 15 : 3

I did not find the world desolate when I entered it; my fathers planted for me before I was born: so do I plant for those who will come after me.

TALMUD J.: *Ta'anith*, 23a

See also: CHARITY, CONSCIENCE, DUTY, GOOD DEEDS, HONOR, RESPONSIBILITY, VOWS

OCCUPATION

See: BUSINESS, SKILL, TRADE, WORK

OLD AGE

❊ Gray hair is worthless if the brain is still green.

Fortunate are those who enjoy old age.

❊ If you don't want to get old, hang yourself while young.

Though old people dye their hair, the roots remain white.

❊ When asked how he had lived to so long and happy an old age, a rabbi replied: "I have never been angry with my family; I have never envied men greater than I; and I never gloated over anyone's downfall."

The new may be true, but the old is gold.

For the ignorant, old age is as winter; for the learned, it is
a harvest.   Hasidic saying

Men worry over the loss of their possessions, not over the
loss of their years—which never return.
                                                    Rabbinical saying

An old man in the house is a burden; but an old woman in
the house is a treasure.   TALMUD: *'Arakin*, 19a

Respect an old man who has lost his learning: remember
that the fragments of the Tablets broken by Moses were
preserved alongside the new.   TALMUD: *Berakoth*, 8b

The ignorant think less clearly as they age; the wise more
clearly as they grow older.   TALMUD: *Kinnin* 3 : end

❋ To learn from the young is to eat unripe fruit and drink
new wine; to learn from the old is to eat ripe fruit and
drink old wine.
         —adapted from *Sayings of the Fathers*, 4 : 28

Just because I am old, do not forget me, do not neglect me.
                                            Standard Prayer Book

Do not dishonor the old: we shall all be numbered among
them.   BEN SIRACH, *Ecclesiasticus*, 8 : 6

To honor an old man one should not sit in his place or contradict his words.
         RASHI, *Commentaries on the Pentateuch, Leviticus*

The longest beards and fattest bellies are found in goats, but
that does not make them the wisest creatures on earth.
         —adapted from JOSEPH SOLOMON DELMENDIGO

❋ The prosperity of a country can be seen simply in how
it treats its old people.   NACHMAN OF BRATSLAV

Suggested inscription for a Hebrew Home for the Aged:
"They suffer from the three worst ailments of mankind:
they are sick, they are old, and they are Jews."
                                            HEINRICH HEINE

See also: AGE, LEARNING, WISDOM, YOUNG AND OLD, YOUTH

OPINION

❋ If men knew what one thought of another, they would
kill each other.

If everybody says so, believe them.

How long halt ye between two opinions? I Kings, 18 : 21

Moses made agreement between the members of a community a part of religion.   JOSEPHUS

❋ Men like the opinions to which they have become accustomed . . . and this prevents them from finding truth, for they cling to the opinions of habit.
      MAIMONIDES, *Guide to the Perplexed*, I : 31

See also: EVIDENCE, REASON, TRUTH

OPTIMISM

❋ Let's go to the circus tomorrow, if—God willing—we're alive; and if not, let's go Tuesday.

When things are not as you like, like them as they are.

Better is he who shows a smiling countenance then he who offers milk.   TALMUD: *Kethuboth*, 111b

When the going seems rough, look at the jewels you're carrying.   "THE CHOFETZ CHAIM"

See also: COURAGE, HOPE, LUCK, SHLEMIEL

ORPHAN

When an orphan grieves, no one sees it; when he rejoices, the whole world does.

❋ A *chutzpanik* is a man who, having killed his mother and father, asks the court for mercy because he is an orphan.

One who adopts an orphan is as if he begot him.
                    TALMUD: *Megillah*, 13a

Between male and female orphans, provide first for the female: the male may beg, but not the female.
                    TALMUD: *Kethuboth*, 67b

See also: CHILDREN, FAMILY, PARENTS

P

PAIN

❋ The greatest pains are those you can't tell others.

❋ A toothache makes you forget a headache.

❋ Not to have felt pain is not to have been human.

Any ache but heartache; any pain but in the head.
                                        TALMUD: *Berakoth*, 11a

See also: DISEASE, HEALTH, SUFFERING

PARABLES

Let not a simple parable seem trivial in your eyes, for
    through it you acquire an insight into the complex law.
                        MIDRASH: *Song of Songs Rabbah*, 1 : 8

A parable from a fool is worthless because he tells it at the
    wrong time.   BEN SIRACH, *Ecclesiasticus*, 20 : 20

See also: ADVICE, EDUCATION, PEDAGOGY, TEACHING

PARADISE

❋ Even in Paradise, it's miserable to be alone.

Better to be in Hell with a wise man than in Paradise with
    a fool.

One day Alexander the Great came to the gate of Paradise and knocked, and the guardian angel asked, "Who
is there?"
    "Alexander."
    "Which Alexander?" asked the angel.
    "*The* Alexander!" thundered the Conqueror. "Alexander
the Great, Conqueror of the world!"
    "He is not known here," said the angel. "He cannot
enter; for this is the Lord's gate and only the righteous may
enter here."

Alexander demanded proof that this was indeed the heavenly gate. And a fragment of a human skull was thrown out to him, with these words: "Weigh it."

So Alexander took it to his Wise Men, who fetched a pair of scales and placed the bone in one, while Alexander placed gold and silver in the other. But the small bone outweighed them all. . . . More and more silver and gold were piled into the scale, until Alexander's great crown and all of his jewels were there—but they all flew upwards, like feathers.

Then one of the Wise Men placed a few grains of dust on the skull, and now that side of the scale flew up: for the bone had surrounded the eye, and nothing will satisfy man's eye until it is covered by the dust of the grave.

> —adapted from TALMUD

✻ Those who feel true shame go to Eden.

> *Sayings of the Fathers*, 5 : 20

My thoughts form an Eden in my heart.

> JUDAH HA-LEVI, *Kuzari*

God uses a man's good deeds as seeds to plant trees in Paradise: in this way every man creates his own Paradise.   THE MEZERITZER RABBI

See also: GOD, HEAVEN, HEREAFTER, WORLD TO COME

PARADOXES: EXAMPLES OF

Black earth gives white bread.

Better do nothing than make nothing.

When a miller fights with a chimneysweeper, the miller gets black and the sweeper turns white.

✻ Where there's too much, something is missing.

Too good is bad for one.

✻ If you go a little slower, you'll arrive a little sooner.

Going backwards [in the wrong direction] is still a form of travel.

✻ A one-eyed man sees more of you than you, with two eyes, see of him.

The worst libel can be the truth.

❋ Gold, like children, must sometimes be beaten.
                                        Alphabet of Ben Sira, 4

The only whole heart is the one that has been broken.
                                        "THE CHOFETZ CHAIM"

The longer the blind live, the more they see.
                                        SHOLEM ALEICHEM

See also: ILLOGIC, IRONY: EXAMPLES OF, LOGIC, REASON

PARENTS

A child should treat his parents as though they were his king
   and queen.

Those who are ashamed of their parents can win neither
   blessings nor praises.

❋ Not to teach your son to work is like teaching him to
   steal.   TALMUD: *Kiddushin*, 29a

The child honors his mother more than his father because
   his mother affects him by her words—so God set the
   honoring of the father before the honoring of the
   mother; and the child fears his father more than his
   mother, because it is the father who teaches him Torah—
   so God set the fearing of the mother before the fearing
   of the father.   TALMUD: *Kiddushin*, 31 : a

❋ Let us be grateful to our parents: had they not been
   tempted, we would not be here.
                                        TALMUD: *'Abodah Zarah*, 5a

Honor your father and mother, even as you honor God;
   for all three were partners in your creation.   *Zohar*

He who does not support needy parents bears evil testimony
   against himself.   *Tana de Ben Eliahu*

To "fear" one's parents means not to sit in their place, not
   to speak in their stead, and not to contradict them.
      RASHI, *Commentaries in the Pentateuch, Leviticus*

❋ The man who disobeys his parents will have disobedient
   sons.   NACHMAN OF BRATSLAV

The troubles parents take for their children are inspired by
   a form of selfishness: to be proud of their achievements.

PARTNERS

The pot that belongs to partners is neither hot nor cold.

PASSION

Passion is a master.

A tranquil mind is health for the body; but passion is like rot in the bones.

Man is in bondage to his passions—and his Creator.

Passion leads to prejudice, not reason.

When passion burns within you, remember that it was given to you for good purposes.   Hasidic saying

The pursuit of passion becomes boring.   Hasidic saying

At first, man's passions are like a cobweb's thread; at last, they become like thickest cord   TALMUD: *Sukkah*, 52a

❋ Our passions are like travelers: at first they make a brief stay; then they are like guests, who visit often; and then they turn into tyrants, who hold us in their power.
                              TALMUD: *Sukkah*, 52b

Men make a harness for their beasts; how much more should they fashion a harness for their passions.
                     —adapted from TALMUD J.: *Sanhedrin*

❋ Who is strong? The man who can control his passions.
          BEN ZOMA in *Sayings of the Fathers*, 4 : 1

It is easier for an apathetic man to be stirred to enjoyment than for a man burning with passion to curb his lusts.
                     MAIMONIDES: *Eight Chapters*, IV

All passions contain an element of sadness.
                     —adapted from JONATHAN EIBESCHUTZ,
                                   Yaarot Devash

PASSOVER

See GLOSSARY: PESACH

PATIENCE

To be patient can be better than being rich.

You can drain a whole brook, or drill through the hardest granite, if only you have enough patience.

See also: HOPE, OPTIMISM, PERSEVERANCE, RESIGNATION

PATRIOTISM

✳ If not for patriotism, barren lands would be deserted.

See also: ISRAEL, POLITICS, WARS

PAUPER

✳ To welcome a pauper come only two: a cold wind and a snapping dog.

The pauper who arrives in a town does no favor to the local poor.

✳ Rejoice, pauper: dirt is cheap.

Paupers at least have good waistlines.

✳ One good thing about being a pauper: you save on laundry.

God protects paupers—from committing expensive sins.

Paupers are cold in summer and hot in winter.

✳ The ignorant are the true paupers.

✳ Paupers serve God's purpose: they make it possible for the rich to perform good deeds.

✳ God is pleased when a pauper finds a treasure—and returns it.

God is happy when one pauper scratches another's back.

Paupers need no guards, and fear no thieves.

See also: CHARITY, GOOD DEEDS, PHILANTHROPY, THE POOR/ POOR MEN, POVERTY, WEALTH

PEACE

Better a bad peace than a good war.

Peace is to man what yeast is to dough.

Three things can't live together in peace: wives, dogs, and chickens.

❊ For the sake of peace one may lie, but peace itself should never be a lie.

❊ When you quarrel, do it in such a way that you can make up.

Peace: the wisp of straw which binds the sheaf of blessings.

Peace is important, for God's name is *Shalom* [peace].
MIDRASH: *Exodus*, 9

The Holy Scripture was given to mankind in order to establish peace. MIDRASH: *Tanhuma, Jethro*

Talmidei hakhamim [saintly wise men] strengthen peace in the world. *Standard Prayer Book*

Rabban Simeon ben Gamaliel had said: "The world rests on three things: On justice, on truth, on peace." Said Rabbi Mona: "But these three are one and the same: for if there is justice, there is truth, and if there is truth, there is peace." *Perek ha-Shalom*

A peace which comes from fear and not from the heart is the opposite of peace. GERSONIDES

❊ Where there is no peace, prayers are not heard.
NACHMAN OF BRATSLAV

❊ Whenever a treaty of peace is signed, God is present.
NACHMAN OF BRATSLAV

Work for peace within your family, then in your street, then within the community. THE BERSHIDER RABBI

Better an insincere peace than a sincere quarrel.
THE LUBLINER RABBI

See also: CRITICISM, FAMILY, FEAR, MARRIAGE, POLITICS, QUARRELS, WARS

PEDAGOGY

❊ Open your discourse with a jest, and let your hearers laugh a little; then become serious.

TALMUD: *Shabbath*, 30b

If there are more than twenty-five children in an elementary class, appoint an assistant.

TALMUD: *Baba Bathra*, 21a

A teacher who has drunk a quart of wine may not teach.

MIDRASH: *Leviticus Rabbah*, 1 : 4

To teach what is error is transgression.

—adapted from *Sayings of the Fathers*, 4 : 13

The ill-tempered cannot teach.

HILLEL, in *Sayings of the Fathers*, 2 : 6

Unmarried teachers have childish minds.

—adapted from MIDRASH

❊ Of what use is wisdom that is not taught?

—adapted from BEN SIRACH, *Ecclesiasticus*, 20 : 30

See also: EDUCATION, LEARNING, STUDY, TEACHERS

PEOPLE

❊ When people who have led hard lives are given authority, they are harder than tyrants.

Where there is no vision, the people perish.

Book of Proverbs, 29 : 18

❊ The voice of the people is as the Voice of God.

MIDRASH SAMUEL on *Pirke Abot*

See also: DEMOCRACY, FREEDOM, GOVERNMENT, LAW, MAN, MASSES, POLITICS, POWER

PERFECTION

There's no such thing as a perfect thing.

❊ Perfection is an obsession.

The perfect man has a man's strength and a woman's compassion.   *Zohar*

Man is capable of perfection—because of the power of reasoning, which God gave him.

MAIMONIDES, *Guide to the Perplexed*, I : 2

To seek perfection, in property or health or character, is not a worthy human goal; nor is it a proper cause of pride and glory for man; the knowledge of God is [the only] true wisdom, and the sole perfection man should seek.

—adapted from MAIMONIDES, *Guide to the Perplexed*

A faultless man is possible only in a faultless world.

HASDAI, *Ben ha-Melekh ve-ha-Nazir*

See also: CHARACTER, GOD, GOOD, WISDOM

PERSECUTION

Note. The story of the persecution of the Jews, one of the more harrowing aspects of Western history, need not be recapitulated here. ("Oh Lord," runs one folk saying, "do not inflict upon us all that we may be able to endure.") One passage, of literally thousands one may read in history books, lingers in my mind:

Thus were the Jews burnt at Strasbourg, and in the same year in all the cities of the Rhine, whether Free Cities or Imperial Cities or cities belonging to the lords. In some towns they burnt the Jews after a trial, in others, without a trial. In some cities the Jews themselves set fire to their houses and cremated themselves. It was decided in Strasbourg that no Jew should enter the city for a hundred years, but . . . the Jews [were allowed to come] back to Strasbourg, in the year 1368 after the birth of our Lord. Jacob R. Marcus, *The Jew in the Medieval World, A Source Book: 315–1791*, Atheneum, New York, 1969 p. 47.

❀ It is better to be persecuted than to persecute others.

Persecutors are blind, and no medicine can cure them.

There are so many Hamans, but only one Purim. [Purim, "the Feast of Lots," commemorates the rescuing of the Jews of Persia from Haman's plot to exterminate them.]

God loves the persecuted, and hates the persecutors.

Pesikta Rabbati, 193b

The prayers of the oppressed and the poor are the first to reach the highest heaven.   IMMANUEL OF ROME

See also: ISRAEL, POWER, PREJUDICE

PERSEVERANCE

❋ Quiet waters wash down cliffs.

A tree can't be felled with one stroke.

Even the hardest granite yields to the drilling of those who persevere.

The man who persists in knocking will succeed in entering.
                    MOSES IBN EZRA, *Shirat Yisrael*

❋ A man can transform faults into virtues if he but perseveres.   THE MAGGID OF DUBNO

See also: DETERMINATION, ENDURANCE, WILL

PESSIMISM

❋ If things don't get better, wait—they'll get worse.

❋ All sentences that start with "God forbid" describe what is possible.

Remember: every uphill has its downhill.

Buttered bread always falls on its face.

❋ You don't want to get old? Hang yourself while young.

Expect nothing and you'll never be disappointed.

Even great swimmers drown.

So many prayers—and so few noodles.

❋ If you have it easy, you'll slide on life's ice.

The only thing you get free is garbage.

Each of us must sometimes play the fool.

❋ All life ends in weeping.

What doesn't get better can get worse.

What's new at sea? They're catching fish.

Don't worry about tomorrow; who knows what will befall you today?   TALMUD: *Yebamoth*, 63b

❅ April Fool is a joke—repeated 365 times a year.
                                        SHOLEM ALEICHEM

See also: DESPAIR, HAPPINESS, HOPE, ILLUSION, OPTIMISM

PETULANCE

❅ Because he hates the cantor he doesn't say "Amen!" to
the prayer.

❅ The proud are petulant, and the petulant are foolish.

See also: CHARACTER, ILLOGIC, MAN: HUMAN TYPES, STUB-
BORNNESS

PHILANTHROPY

❅ The poor profit more from the luxuries of the rich than
from their philanthropy.

If you don't open your door to the poor, you will open it
for the doctor.

❅ To give little with a smile is better than giving much
with a frown.

The promise of the generous is a gift; the gift of the miser
is a promise.   IBN GABIROL, *Choice of Pearls*

See also: CHARITY, DUTY, GOOD DEEDS, LUXURY

PHILOLOGY

Note. "It must also be admitted that little attention was paid
to philology, so that the great Talmudist often mistook a
Greek word for an Aramaic, and, *horribile dictu*, sometimes would not even be able to distinguish Aramaic
from Hebrew. But while a little grammar would certainly have been of some use to the mediaeval scholar,
a larger portion thereof would as little have made him a
Talmudist as it has succeeded in the case of the modern
grammarians and philologians."
            —LOUIS GINZBERG in *Students, Scholars and Saints*,
                    Jewish Publication Society of America, 1928,
                                            pp. 72–73.

See LANGUAGE, WORDS

PHILOSOPHERS/PHILOSOPHY

❋ Philosophy is the road to knowledge, and knowledge is the road to freedom.

Philosophers without experience tend to be silly.

If all men were philosophers, the social order would be destroyed and the human race exterminated: men need many material things to survive.

MAIMONIDES: *Eight Chapters*

See also: REALISM, REASON, SAGES, SCHOLARS, STUDY, TALMUD, TORAH, WISDOM, WISE MEN

PHYLACTERIES

See GLOSSARY: TEFILLIN, p. 623

PHYSICIANS

See: DISEASE, DOCTORS, HEALTH, PREJUDICE, SICKNESS, SOUL

PIETY

❋ Better be good than pious.

A pious man walks in light and is not afraid to walk alone; the impious man walks in darkness and is anxious for company.

It does not matter whether a man does much or little, if only he directs his heart to Heaven.

TALMUD: *Berakoth*, 17a

Those who, in their dreams, see the Book of Psalms may hope to gain piety.

—adapted from TALMUD, *Berakoth*, 57b

Do not act toward the Lord as other people act toward their gods: honoring them when times are good, but cursing them when disaster strikes. Israel should praise the Lord no matter whether He brings good times or evil.

Mekhilta to Exodus, 20 : 30

❋ Without wisdom there is no piety, without piety there is no wisdom.

Sayings of the Fathers, 3 : 21

Beware the pious who are fools.

—adapted from IBN GABIROL, *Choice of Pearls*

❊ What I want to know is not why I suffer, but only whether I suffer for Thy sake.

THE BERDICHEVER RABBI

❊ I am in constant fear lest I may become too wise to remain pious.   THE KORETSER RABBI

The pious man is better than the clever man.

THE KORETSER RABBI

See also: FAITH, GOD, GOOD, ISRAEL, RELIGION, VIRTUE, WISDOM

PITY

"It was part of the spirit of Prophecy to be dumb-founded at human ferocity. . . . In the presence of the iniquities of the world, the heart of the Prophets bled . . . and their cry of indignation re-echoed the wrath of the Deity. Greece and Rome had their rich and poor, just as Israel had in the days of Jeroboam II; and the various classes continued to slaughter one another for centuries; but no voice of justice and pity arose from the fierce tumult. . . . The words of the Prophets have more vitality at the present time, and answer better to the needs of modern souls, than all the plastic masterpieces of antiquity."
—JAMES DARMSTESTER, quoted in *The Pentateuch and Haftorahs*, ed. by Dr. J. H. Hertz, Soncino Edition, second edition, London: 1970, p. 930.

Better be cursed than pitied.

The greatest pity of all is deserved by a very poor woman in childbirth. [Where will food come from?]

❊ Pity was invented by the weak.

MENDELE MOCHER SEFORIM

See also: COMPASSION, CONSIDERATION, EMOTIONS, GOD, MAN: HUMAN TYPES

PLEASURE

❊ If you're going to eat ham, at least let it be juicy.

❊ Perpetual pleasure is no pleasure.   Hasidic saying

When a man faces his Maker, he will have to account for
those [God-given] pleasures of life which he failed to
enjoy.   TALMUD J.: *Kiddushin,* end

The lover of pleasure will come to want; the lover of wine
and oil will not grow rich.   *Book of Proverbs,* 21 : 17

The man who pursues pleasure cannot control his life.
                                              SAMUEL HA-NAGID

❀ Those who spend their days in pleasure don't live long.
                                              SAADIA GAON

❀ All pleasures contain an element of sadness.
                          JONATHAN EIBESCHUTZ, *Yaarot Devash*

You may reach a compromise between evil and good by
enjoying legitimate bodily pleasures—and serving God
at the same time.   THE MEZERITZER RABBI

POGROMS

Note. "When Richard I ["The Lion-Hearted"] ascended the
throne, the Jews, to conciliate the Royal protection,
brought their tributes. Many . . . appearing at West-
minster, the Court and the mob imagined that they had
leagued to bewitch His Majesty. A rumor spread rapidly
through the city that in honor of the festival the Jews
were to be massacred. The populace, at once eager of
royalty and riot, pillaged and burnt their houses and
murdered the devoted Jews. The people of York soon
gathered to imitate the people of London."
                          —ISAAC D'ISRAELI. *Curiosities of Literature,*
                                              London, 1793.

"The central feature of this year's report [1906, American Jewish Year Book] is the table of massacres of Jews
in Russia, during the period whose entrance and exit are
guarded by Kishineff and Bialystok as bloodstained sen-
tinels. The figures frightfully arrayed are so heart-rending
that one is impelled to apologize for perpetuating them.
It would be a wanton harassment of the feelings, were it
not a document to stimulate Israel to self-help, and
gentiles to self-introspection."
                          Quoted in *Of Making Many Books,*
                                      edited by Joshua Block,
                                      J.P.S.A., 1953, p. 83.

See: ANTI-SEMITISM, ISRAEL, JEWS, PERSECUTION, PREJU-
DICE

POLITICS

A fool in office is like an ass tied to the sun.

❋ One is a lie, two are lies, but three lies becomes politics.

He who has a co-ruler has an over-ruler.

❋ Fish die out of water, and people die without law and
order.   TALMUD: *'Abodah* ZARAH, 4a

Safety lies in the counsel of the multitudes.
                    —adapted from *Book of Proverbs*, 11 : 14

❋ Sages are more important than kings, for if a sage dies,
who can replace him? When a king dies, all Israel is
eligible to succeed him.   —adapted from MIDRASH

When a person is appointed an official among men, he is
considered a man evil in Heaven.
                    —adapted from *Mishnah Adoyoth*, 5 : 6

Woe to high position, for it takes the fear of Heaven from
him who occupies it.   *Midrash ha-Gadol*

❋ Kings may be judges of the earth, but wise men are the
judges of kings.   IBN GABIROL

A king is like fire—necessary when far, but scorching when
near.   IBN GABIROL

The man who can take abuse with a smile is fit to become a
leader.   NACHMAN OF BRATSLAV

See also: DEMOCRACY, FREEDOM, GOVERNMENT, LAW,
MASSES, POWER, STATUS

THE POOR/POOR MEN

Note. A Jewish community in Eastern Europe had at least
one *shnorer* (beggar), and often a platoon. The *shnorer*
was not a run-of-the-mill mendicant, but a professional
man; for many *shnorers* considered they had a tacit
license from the Lord and were in fact, doing His bidding: after all, were they not helping Jews discharge the
solemn obligation to help the poor? Beggars made it
possible for a Jew to accumulate *mitzvahs* (good deeds);

and any man who served as an agent for the performance of *mitzvahs* was part of God's marvelous scheme for improving the human race. The *shnorer* often read a good deal, could quote Talmud with confidence, was a synagogue "regular," and took part in discussions of Torah and Talmud on an equal footing with his benefactors.

—L.R.

✻ It's no disgrace to be poor—which is the only good thing you can say about it.

✻ It's no disgrace to be poor, but it's no honor, either.

Rejoice, pauper: dirt is cheap.

When you cook with straw, the food is raw.

✻ When a poor man gets to eat a chicken, one of them is sick.

✻ If you're poor, remember: at least it's good for the waistline.

Only the ignorant are truly poor.

✻ Those who have nothing are always ready to share it with others.

You don't need teeth to eat borsht.

If you have no linen, at least you save on laundry.

When you have no butter for your bread, it is not yet real poverty.

✻ A full bag is heavy to carry, but an empty one is heavier.

✻ The heaviest weight in the world is an empty pocket.

Love not sleep, lest you come to poverty; keep your eyes open, and you will have plenty of food.

Book of Proverbs, 20 : 13

THE POOR: IRONIC COMMENTS ON

✻ The poor have it hard only twice a year: in the summer and in the winter.

God really does help the poor: He protects them from committing expensive sins.

Poor men don't develop pot bellies.

❋ The poor are always liberal.

The poor fear no thieves.

The Talmud tells us that a fine dwelling, fine clothes, and a beautiful wife broaden a man's understanding: I need all the understanding I can get—to serve God as He deserves.

A poor man is happy when he loses something—and finds it again.

Poor men need no guards.

A poor man can be tempted by a slice of bread.

No one is so miserable as the poor man who is invited to two weddings for the same day.

❋ For what does a poor man blow his whistle? For nothing, since he owns nothing but a whistle.

The poor are cold in summer and hot in winter.

❋ The poor child's shoes grow with his feet.

To the poor, bread is more useful than air.

❋ When a poor man makes a wedding, his dog gets the shivers!

It is easy to offend a poor man.

The poor man is like a sack full of holes.

The poor man also wants to live.

Poor is to rich as crooked is to straight.

The poor are like hunchbacks: they carry what they have on their backs.

A poor man may eat meat and wine yet feel bitterness in his heart.

❋ Things are never as good with money as they are bad without it.

❋ Poor relatives are distant relatives.

To the poor, life is bitter—and death more so.

An ox for a penny! But what if you don't have the penny?

Those without shoes recall the comfort in their father's home.

Bad luck chases after the poor.
                                        TALMUD: *Baba Kamma*, 92a

The poor are likened to the dead.
                                        TALMUD: *Nedarim*, 76

❉ No one is so poor as he who is ignorant.
                                        TALMUD: *Nedarim*, 41a

You can't compare the man who has bread with the man who has not.   TALMUD: *Yomah*, 18b

Just as you listen to a poor man, listen to one rich: for it is written, "Ye shall not favor persons in judging them."
                                        Abot de Rabbi Nathan, 20 : 22a

Who despises small things shall become poor.
                                        BEN SIRACH, *Ecclesiasticus*, 19 : 1

No one is as poor as the man who worries about poverty.
                                        IBN GABIROL, *Choice of Pearls*

I have succeeded in half my prayer for the poor: the poor are willing to accept gifts—if the rich offer them.
                                        THE ROPSHITZER RABBI

God must hate the poor, else why did He make them poor?
                                        SHOLEM ALEICHEM

THE POOR: IN DEFENSE OF

❉ Whoever steals from a poor man steals from God.

He who laughs at the poor will become a laughingstock.

❉ Honor the sons of the poor for they give science its splendor.

Take heed of the poor, for they produce learning.
                                        TALMUD: *Nedarim*, 81a

He who mocks the poor insults his Maker; he who rejoices at their calamity will not go unpunished.
                                        Book of Proverbs, 17 : 5

The prayers of the poor are heard by God before the
prayers of all others.   *Zohar*

He who lengthens the life of a poor man will have his own
life lengthened when his time comes.   *Zohar*

Despise no man: pearls [of wisdom] may be found in a poor
man's tunic.   Eliezer ben Isaac, *Orhot Hayim*

God is the poor man's advocate.   "THE CHOFETZ CHAIM"

Beware of discourtesy to the poor: The Lord stands near
them.   THE SLONIMER RABBI

POOR MEN AND RICH MEN

✻ If the rich could hire others to die for them, the poor
would make a very nice living.

✻ The rich man carries his God in his pocket, the poor
man—in his heart.

God loves the poor but helps the rich.

The poor man thinks, the rich man laughs.

A cheap rich man is worse than a pauper.

Before the fat man grows lean, the lean man wastes away.

The rich eat the meat; the poor eat the bones.

Poverty runs after the poor, and wealth runs after the rich.

✻ Though a rich man's fortune goes down and a poor
man's up, they still do not end up even.

Poor and rich lie in the earth as equals; only on earth are
the rich better off.

A rich man's wealth is his fortress; the ruin of the poor is
their poverty.   *Book of Proverbs*, 10 : 15

✻ The rich swell up with pride, the poor from hunger.
                                    SHOLEM ALEICHEM

See also: CHARITY, FATE, FORTUNE, GOOD DEEDS, LUCK,
MONEY, PAUPERS, POVERTY, SUFFERING, STATUS, WEALTH,
WISDOM

POPULARITY

✳ Woe to the one nobody likes, but beware of the one everyone likes.

If you want to be popular, ask people questions.

To please others always costs a lot.

Those who try to please everyone will die before their time.

✳ When I see no way of teaching a truth save one that will please one intelligent man but will offend ten thousand fools, I address myself to the one and ignore the censure of the thousands.

MAIMONIDES, *Guide for the Perplexed* (Introduction)

See also: FAME, GLORY, HONOR, REPUTATION, STATUS, TEACHING

POSSESSIONS

If possessions are near at hand, their owner consumes them; if possessions are at a distance, they consume him.

See also: AMBITION, BUSINESS, HAPPINESS, RICHES, STATUS, WEALTH

POVERTY

Note. I think historians would agree that the Hebrews of old brought a new conception of poverty and the poor to Western civilization: They subordinated money/property rights to moral and compassionate obligations.

We might remember that the glorious Greeks did not especially pity or respect the poor, the weak, the humble. (We need but recall the chilling candor of the dialogue, recounted in Thucydides, between the Melians and the Athenians, who had besieged the island of Melos, then slaughtered or enslaved every soul thereon.) The noble Romans, powerfully motivated for the public weal, so deeply respected property that they held poverty to be deserved; concern for the poor was considered proper for slaves, perhaps, but not for Roman freemen. (True enough, those who served the republic, though poor, were honored.) Those who could not pay their debts were imprisoned, or sold into slavery, or simply slain.

Seneca "recoiled in horror" from the poor; Vergil praises one of his heroes for feeling no sympathy for the starving; and some Romans wrote that it was *cruel* to feed the hungry, because that would only prolong lives of insupportable misery.

Now: In the Jewish Commonwealth (it preceded the Greek and Roman empires), the poor occupied a peculiarly secure place; the community was legally bound to feed, clothe, educate, and protect them. Orphans, widows, poor brides-to-be; the sick, the old, the handicapped; wayfarers, mendicants, mental defectives—all were automatically aided by communal funds. Jewish ownership of property was not absolute (tithing held a superior claim).

Above all, the idea of a freeing Messiah, the Redemption, total equality for the virtuous in a world-to-come—all this promised the poorest and lowliest Israelite ultimate justice, supreme dignity, and priceless favor in the eyes of God. These ideas, incorporated into Christianity, dramatically transformed the world. (See headnote for CHARITY.)

—L.R.

✻ Poverty shows first on the face.

Poverty is no disgrace, but it's no great honor, either.

✻ Doctors have a cure for everything but poverty.

Poverty and laziness are brothers.

Those who are happy despite poverty can prevail against everything.

✻ Conceit and poverty make a poor combination.

When the poor move, poverty moves right along with them.

✻ You can often hide poverty with a needle and a brush.

When bread runs out, strife knocks at the door.

✻ The wife wails and the dog whines and the child cries and poverty howls.

Poverty's head is very hard.

✻ Poverty in a home is worse than fifty plagues.

TALMUD: *Baba Bathra*, 116a

Poverty is the ornament of the Jews.

> TALMUD: *Hagigah*, 9b

❋ Poverty makes handsome women ugly.
> —adapted from TALMUD: *Nedarim*, 66b

Put all other sufferings in one side of the scale, and poverty
in the other, and poverty would be heavier.

> MIDRASH: *Exodus Rabbah*, 31 : 12

Nothing is more painful than poverty.

> MIDRASH: *Exodus Rabbah*, 31 : 12

In all labor there is profit; but mere talk leads only to
penury. 　　　　　　　　　*Book of Proverbs*, 14 : 23

Wise men who are poor are all too often ignored.

> *Book of Ecclesiastes*, 9 : 16

He who fulfills the Torah amidst poverty will fulfill it
amidst wealth; he who neglects Torah amidst wealth will
come to neglect it amidst poverty.

> *Sayings of the Fathers*, 4 : 9

❋ Poverty was created to give the rich an opportunity for
charity. 　　　　　　　　　ANAV, *Maalot ha-Midot*

See also: CHARITY, GOOD DEEDS, LEARNING, THE POOR/POOR
MEN, STATUS, VIRTUE, WORK, WISDOM

POWER

❋ Two dogs can kill a lion.

The man with an ax delivers the whacks.

Money is power.

A stick in the hand is better than a tongue in the mouth.

❋ Henchmen are worse than their masters.

He who shares power has an over-ruler.

You can't move a mountain with a splinter.

The master is kind—but in his hand is a whip.

As among fish, so among men: the larger swallow the
smaller. 　　　　　　　　TALMUD: *'Abodah Zarah*, 4a

If a fox becomes king, bow. 　　TALMUD: *Megillah*, 16b

Iron axes can break iron.   TALMUD: *Sanhedrin*, 96b

❋ The obscure endure.
                    —adapted from TALMUD: *Sanhedrin*, 14a

❋ Where there are no officers to enforce the law, of what
  avail are judges?   MIDRASH: *Tanhuma, Shofetim*

A farmer puts the yoke on his strong ox, not his weak one.
                    MIDRASH: *Genesis Rabbah*, 32 : 3

❋ A sage takes precedence over a king.
                    —adapted from *Mishnah*

Can you draw out the Leviathan with a hook?
                    Book of Job, 41 : 1

Put not your trust in princes.   *Book of Psalms*, 146 : 3

Gain authority for the purpose of acting as judge of what
  is right, of supporting the poor, of delivering the oppressed from the oppressor, of removing the spoiler, and
  of driving off those who are perverse, for it is written:
  "Behold, a king shall reign in righteousness" (Isaiah,
  32 : 1).   SAADIA GAON

Don't rely on the friendship of a king—if his minister is
  your enemy; but if you are friends with the minister,
  fear not the king.   IBN GABIROL

❋ A tiny fly can choke a big man.
                    IBN GABIROL, *Choice of Pearls*

Kings are judges, but sages judge kings.
                    —adapted from IBN GABIROL

❋ A giant feels the sting of a bee.
                    IMMANUEL OF ROME

To work for another is like taking honey from a bee: accompanied by a sting.   THE ROPSHITZER RABBI

See also: AUTHORITY, GOVERNMENT, POLITICS, STRENGTH,
WEAKNESS

PRAISE

A little praise may be uttered in a man's presence; too much
  praise should not be uttered in his presence; but all of
  his praises may be sung in his absence.
                    —adapted from TALMUD: *Erubin*, 18b

✻ To eat too much honey is not good; therefore be sparing of your compliments. *Book of Proverbs*, 25 : 27

Just as a smelter is for silver, and a furnace for gold, so a
man is tested by what he praises.
Book of Proverbs, 17 : 3

Let another man praise you, not your own mouth—
A stranger, and not your own lips.
Book of Proverbs, 27 : 2

Only a part of a man's praise should be recounted in his
presence; but in his absence all of his good qualities
may be told.
RASHI, *Commentaries on the Pentateuch, Genesis*

See also: DECORUM, FLATTERY, PRIDE

PRAYER

Note. For some 3000 years, Jews retained a most vivid
sense of being part of one uninterrupted prayer to, and
dialogue with, the Lord. Chapters of the five books of
the Torah ("the Books of Moses") are read in the
synagogues, week by week; and when on the festival of
Simhat Torah ("the day of rejoicing in the Law"), the
final words of Deuteronomy are read—to be allowed to
read it is a signal honor given to a learned member of
the congregation—the congregation breaks into an excited "*Khazak, khazak, venit khazak!*" ("Be strong, be
strong, and gather new strength!")—and at once the
year-long cycle of readings is begun anew, with the first
verse of Genesis.

By tradition, pious Jews pray at least thrice a day
(but see below): *shaharith*, in the morning; *minhah*, in
the afternoon; *maareb*, in the evening. Ten male Jews are
required for a religious service. Solitary prayer is certainly laudable, but the pious hold that whenever ten
males assemble for worship or study, God's Presence
dwells among them.

To strictly religious Jews, the ceremonial demands
for prayer are very heavy, however deeply the faithful
rejoice in them. *Brokhes* (prayers) are recited upon
arising, before retiring, before and after every meal,
while washing one's hands (which must be done as soon
as one gets out of bed, and before praying, and before

eating), upon returning from a journey, recovering from an illness, seeing the new moon, donning a new garment, seeing a great scholar or sage, *et cetera*.

The Silent Devotion, a prayer of nineteen benedictions, is offered three times daily by Orthodox (and many Conservative) Jews, but four times on the Sabbath (and two other days) and five times on Yom Kippur. Recited or chanted while standing, this devotion involves three central thoughts: Wisdom, Learning, Immortality. It offers a hope for the welfare of the supplicant, his family, and the community at large; and it thanks the Lord for His blessings.

A devout Jew will not read from the Torah, or study Talmud, or pronounce the name of God unless his head is covered; the truly Orthodox *never* leave their heads uncovered by hat or *yarmlke* (skull-caplet). No rabbinical edict I can uncover directs Jews to cover their heads while praying, though Exodus did prescribe head-covering for the Temple priests.

Reform Jews think that in the Western world it is more appropriate to bare one's head as a sign of respect. Conservative Jews retort that baring the head imitates non-Jewish custom: Christians bare their heads in church since Paul (Saul of Tarsus) wrote that any who covered his head while "praying or prophesying . . . dishonoureth his head." (I have always believed Saul was overreacting against his early training.)

Orthodox and Conservative Jews wear a prayer shawl (*tallith;* "*talis*" in Yiddish) and phylacteries (*tephillin*) when praying—except on the Sabbath. Reform Jews do not wear phylacteries.

The *tallith* is striped at the ends, across its width—usually in black. (This may signify mourning over the destruction of the Temple.) In America, most Jews fold the *tallith*, which is made of silk, and wear it rather like a long scarf. But Orthodox Jews use a voluminous, robelike *tallith*, and during the most solemn portions of prayer place part of the shawl over their heads—to shut out anything that might diminish the intensity of their concentration.

They say that when God finished the world, He asked one of the angels if anything was lacking on land or sea, in the air or in heaven. The angel answered that although everything was perfect, only one thing was wanting on

earth—speech, to praise God's works. The Lord approved
the angel's words, and soon there appeared the race of
man. This is an ancient story, and in its spirit I say: "It is
God's work to benefit men, and His creatures' work to
thank Him."   —PHILO

For the very close connection between prayer and study,
in Jewish life, see my headnote for STUDY. See also
SIDDUR.   —L.R.

✳ When I pray, I pray quickly, because I am talking to
God; but when I read the Torah, I read slowly, because
God is talking to me.

Prayer without devotion [conviction] is like the body without a soul.

God does not listen to the prayers of the proud.

The prayer goes up and the blessing comes down.

✳ Nine saints do not make a *minyan* [quorum for prayer]
but one ordinary man can—by joining them.

Oh Lord of the Universe: please take a real look at Your
world!

A place is reserved in Heaven for those who weep, but
cannot pray.

Prayers are heard best at night.

✳ Better pray for yourself than curse another.

✳ Prayer is the service of the heart.
                                TALMUD: *Ta'anith*, 2 : 1

Rab declared, "We give thanks unto Thee oh Lord, our
God, because we are able to give thanks."
                                TALMUD: *Sotah*, 48

Don't stop praying even when the knife is placed against
your neck.   TALMUD, *Berakoth*, 9a

Give, oh Lord, each one his bread, each body what it needs.
                                TALMUD: *Berakoth*, 29b

✳ Even when the gates of Heaven are closed to prayer,
they are open to tears.   TALMUD: *Berakoth*, 32a

✳ Pray only in a room with windows [to remember the
world outside].   TALMUD: *Berakoth*, 34b

❋ He who prays for his neighbor will be heard for himself.
                              TALMUD: *Baba Kamma*, 92b

The pious man waits an hour before praying, and concen-
    trates his thoughts upon the Lord; even if a king greets
    him, he should not answer; and even if a snake winds
    around his head, the pious supplicant should not in-
    terrupt his prayer.
                        —adapted from TALMUD, *Berakoth*, 30b

The gates of prayer are sometimes closed, but the gates of
    repentance are forever open.
                    MIDRASH: *Deuteronomy Rabbah*, 2 : 7

❋ The prayers of the poor are heard by God ahead of all
    others.   *Zohar*

❋ It is the prayers of the poor and the oppressed that reach
    the highest heavens.   IMMANUEL OF ROME

Do not hurry when you leave a place of worship.
                              JOSEPH CARO, *Shulhan Aruk*

The prayer of a sick person is more effective than any-
    one else's, and is answered first.
        RASHI, *Commentaries on the Pentateuch, Genesis*

❋ You don't have to pray loudly; just direct your heart
    to heaven.   RABBI CHIA

He who prays without knowing what he prays does not
    pray.   MAIMON BEN JOSEPH, *Letter of Consolation*

O God, I stand before Thee, knowing all my deficiencies,
    and overwhelmed by Thy majesty. . . . Thou knowest
    what is for my good. If I recite my wants, it is not to
    remind Thee of them, but that I may better understand
    how great is my dependence upon Thee. . . . Oh, Lord,
    my heart is not haughty, nor are mine eyes lofty.
                              BAHYA IBN PAQUDA

Gold and silver are purified through fire; if you feel no
    sense of improvement after praying, either you are made
    of base metal, or your prayer lacked heat.
                              THE KORETSER RABBI

I love to pray at sunrise—before the world becomes pol-
    luted with vanity and hatred.   THE KORETSER RABBI

Unless we believe that God renews creation every day, our prayers grow habitual and tedious.

BAAL SHEM TOV

Don't petition God to change natural laws for your sake.

THE SASSOVER RABBI

There is a very high rung only one man in a generation can reach: that of having learned all wisdom, then praying like a child.   MENDEL OF RYMANOV

Prayers truly from the heart open all the doors in Heaven.

NACHMAN OF BRATSLAV

The shophar [the ram's horn sounded on the High Holy Days] is a prayer without words.   SAUL LIEBERMAN

PRAYER: IRONIC COMMENTS ON

❋ If prayer did any good, they'd be hiring men to pray.

No one gets slapped for saying "Amen!"

❋ And now, dear God, farewell: I am going to America.

Praying can do no harm.   TALMUD J.: *Berakoth*, I : I

See also: AGNOSTICS, FAITH, GOD, HEAVEN, HEREAFTER, PIETY, PRIDE, REPENTANCE, STUDY, WORSHIP

PREJUDICE

❋ No physician can cure the blind in mind.

Prejudice joins hate to fear.

Prejudice is a sickness in the brain.

Prejudice is reason's enemy.

❋ Passion and prejudice are allies.

See also: HATE, JUDGMENT, OPINION, PASSION, REASON

PRIDE

❋ Pride is a mask for faults.

❋ If you harden your heart with pride, you will soften your brain with it, too.

❋ Pride is a prison.

Pride ends on the dunghill.

You may deal in rags yet dress in silks.

Nothing is more dangerous for a poor man than pride.

The proud man thinks, "Wherever I sit is the front."

❋ The proud are petulant, and the petulant are foolish.

God does not listen to the prayers of the proud.

The proud man is disturbed by the slightest wind.

A proud man is not loved even in his own house.
TALMUD: *Baba Bathra*, 98a

Concerning the man of pride, God has said: "I and he cannot abide together." TALMUD: *Sotah*, 5

Absalom was proud of his hair, and was therefore hanged by his hair. TALMUD: *Sotah*, 9b

❋ If you must hang, choose a high tree.
—adapted from TALMUD: *Pesahim*, 112a

❋ If ever man becomes proud, let him remember that a flea preceded him in the divine order of creation!
TOSEFTA: *Sanhedrin*, 8 : 8

A proud man never praises anyone. *Zohar*

❋ King Solomon put a tiny ant in his palm and asked: "Is there anyone in the world greater than I?"
"Yes," answered the ant, "I am, since God sent you to carry me." *Midrash Vayosha*

When pride cometh, then cometh shame: but with the lowly is wisdom. *Book of Proverbs*, 11 : 2

❋ It ill becomes a lion to weep in the presence of a fox.
Tanna de Be Elijah, 17

❋ Pride is the reservoir of sin.
BEN SIRACH, *Ecclesiasticus*, 10 : 13

❋ He who believes he has not sinned carries pride within himself, and that is worse than sin.
BAHYA IBN PAQUDA, *Duties of the Heart*

The proud man cannot humble himself to learn wisdom.
SAADIA GAON

❊ The man who acts humble in order to win praise is guilty of the lowest form of pride.

NACHMAN OF BRATSLAV

The Torah itself becomes coarse in the mouth of a man of pride.   NACHMAN OF BRATSLAV

❊ The conceited man is not a sinner but a fool.

"THE CHOFETZ CHAIM"

See also: ARROGANCE, CONCEIT, HUMILITY, MEEKNESS, VANITY

PRISON

Envy is a prison.

The proud live in their own prison.

Ignorance is a prison.

Fools do not know what a prison they live in.

The greedy are imprisoned for life.

❊ Prisoners are free if content with their state; free men who seek more than their lot are prisoners to desire.

Immobility is a prison.

See also: FREEDOM, LIBERTY

PROGRESS

Progress is slow, setbacks are swift.

MOSES IBN EZRA, *Shirat Yisrael*

See also: ADVICE, AMBITION, EFFORT, WEALTH

PROMISES

See DUTY, GOOD MEN, RESPONSIBILITY, VOWS

PROOF

❊ "For instance" is not proof.

❊ To give an example only gives an example.

❋ A truth, established by proof, does not gain in force
from the support of scholars; nor does truth lose its
certainty because of popular dissent.
        MAIMONIDES, *Guide to the Perplexed*, Intro. II

❋ Do not regard a thing as proved because you find it in
books; for the liar who deceives men with his tongue will
not hesitate to deceive them with his pen.
        MAIMONIDES, *Letter to the Yemenite Jews*

Those who believe a thing proved because it is in writing
are fools.   MAIMONIDES, *Letter to the Yemenite Jews*

❋ A miracle cannot prove what is impossible; it is only
useful to confirm what is possible.
        MAIMONIDES, *Guide to the Perplexed*, III

❋ God will forget the man who stubbornly rejects proof
that he is wrong.   NACHMAN OF BRATSLAV

See also: EVIDENCE, ILLOGIC, LAW, LOGIC, REASON, TRUTH

PROPERTY

❋ It is better to be a rich tenant than a poor landlord.

See also: BUSINESS, POSSESSIONS, RICH MEN, WEALTH

PROPHETS

Leave it to the people; if they are not prophets, they are
the sons of prophets.   TALMUD: *Pesahim*, 66a

Sages rank higher than prophets, for the power of prophecy
does not abide with a man every moment, but the power
of wisdom does.   *Zohar*

See also: ISRAEL, RABBIS, SAGES, WISE MEN

PROPRIETY

Never accept a present from a thief.

❋ In a house of the hanged, ask no one to hang up your
coat.

Too much courtesy is offensive.

Among those who laugh, do not weep; among those who
weep, do not laugh.   HILLEL in *Tosephta Berakoth*

See also: CONDUCT, CONSIDERATION, DECORUM, MANNERS,
TACT

PROSELYTES

Note. Jews distinguished forced apostates from Judaism
(*anusim*) from those who join another faith of their own
volition (*meshumadim*). The most famous and important of Jewish *anusim,* of course, were the *marranos*
of Spain.   —L.R.

A convert is neither a Jew nor a gentile.

If anyone desires to become a proselyte, the rabbis ask
him: "Why? Do you not know that the Israelites are
harried, hounded, persecuted?" If he says, "I know, if
only I would be worthy," they receive him without
further argument.   TALMUD: *Yebamoth,* 47a

During a great famine, King Monobaz, a convert to Judaism, unlocked his ancestral treasures and distributed
them among the poor. His ministers rebuked him: "Your
fathers amassed these treasures, and you squander
them."

"No," said the king. "They collected earthly treasures,
but I preserve heavenly treasures. Their treasures could
be stolen; mine are beyond mortal reach. Their treasures
were barren; mine will bear fruit for time without end.
They preserved money; I have preserved lives. Their
treasures are of this world; mine are for eternity."
                                      —adapted from TALMUD

The true proselyte is dearer to God than the Israelites were
at Mount Sinai: for had not the Israelites seen the
thunder and lightning, the quaking mountain and the
sounding trumpets, they would not have accepted the
Torah; but the true proselyte, who saw none of these
things, has surrendered to the Holy One. Can anyone
be dearer to God?   MIDRASH: *Tanhuma*

See also: CONVERTS, FAITH, ISRAEL, RELIGION

PROVERBS

Acquaint yourself with the proverbs of the wise, for by them shalt thou be instructed.

Had I not lifted the shard, would you have found the pearl? [Used to praise a maxim.]

TALMUD: *Yebamoth*, 92 : 2

If you want to know the Creator, study proverbs [Haggadah]. MIDRASH: *Sifre—Ekev*, 45

A proverb has three characteristics: few words, good sense, and a fine image. MOSES IBN EZRA, *Shirat Yisrael*

A proverb without wisdom is like a body without a foot. MOSES IBN EZRA, *Shirat Yisrael*

See also: ADVICE, WISDOM

PRUDENCE

❋ Don't sell the hide of a bear that's still in the woods.

The man who rents one garden will eat birds, but the man who rents many gardens—the birds will eat him. [To attempt too much is to lose all.]

Whoever moves into a run-down house is preparing a grave for himself.

Better a chicken in the hand than an eagle in the sky.

If you fight a wave, it overpowers you; let it roll over you.

Better a little pumpkin in your hand than a big one in the field. TALMUD: *Sukkah*, 56b

A man should not hide all his money in one corner. MIDRASH: *Genesis Rabbah*, 76 : 3

❋ Don't run too far; you will have to return the same distance. MIDRASH: *Ecclesiastes Rabbah*, 11 : 9

The simple man trusts everything; the sensible man pays heed to his steps. *Book of Proverbs*, 14 : 15

❋ As long as I do not utter a word, I am its master; once I utter it, I am its slave.
—adapted from IBN GABIROL

Fortune often attends flight.
>   —adapted from IBN GABIROL, *Choice of Pearls*

See also: FORESIGHT, JUDGMENT, SENSE

PUBLIC

It's bitter and bad when the public is wrong.

The voice of the people is as the Voice of God.
>   *Midrash Samuel on Abot*

See also: DEMOCRACY, GOVERNMENT, LAW, MASSES, OPINION, POLITICS

PUBLIC WELFARE

If a man is not by temperament a scholar, he should devote his time to public affairs and the public welfare.
>   MIDRASH: *Leviticus Rabbah*, 25

See also: AUTHORITY, DUTY, POLITICS

PUNISHMENT

❋ We forget blows, but not words.

When a calf kicks, it's time to punish the cow.

❋ The worst punishment is a sleepless night.

If my brother steals, it is the thief—not my brother—who is hanged.

Scolding doesn't help; a stick does.

❋ To punish a pupil, use nothing harder than a shoelace.
>   TALMUD: *Baba Bathra*, 21a

Anyone through whom a man has been incorrectly punished will be barred from Heaven.
>   TALMUD: *Shabbath*, 149a

If, in a dream, you see a Book of Job, fear punishment.
>   TALMUD: *Berakoth*, 57b

A soothing tongue is a tree of life; but wild words break the spirit.   *Book of Proverbs*, 15 : 4

He who associates with sinners, even if he does not imitate them, shares in their punishment.
>   *Abot de Rabbi Nathan*, 30

❊ A court which executes a man once every seventy years may be called destructive.   Eliezer ben Azariah

Does the Law really intend that the man who tore out another's eye should have his own eye torn out? Some men are weaker than others; and perhaps the guilty one, being weaker, would die as a result of the punishment.

What the Torah says is "An eye for an eye," *not* "A life for an eye." . . . It is impossible to inflict on a second man exactly the same wound as was suffered by the first, for the first wound was not measured as to length, depth, and width. If we observe the ruling: "As he did, so shall it be done to him," the injury would have to be exactly the same, neither more nor less.

RABBI HANANEL

See also: JUDGES, JUSTICE, REVENGE

PURPOSE

Even a tree needs a function and searches for a task.

Everything is good—in its time.
adapted from *Ecclesiastes*, 3 : 1–8

There is no man who has not his hour, and no thing that has not its place.   *Sayings of the Fathers*, 4 : 3

See also: CAUSE AND EFFECT, CIRCUMSTANCES, GOD AND MAN

QUARRELS

❊ Quarrels are the weapons of the weak.

❊ Be sure you have the support of your equals before you challenge your superiors.

When two quarrel, a third grabs the hat.

❊ A quarrel is like an itch: the more you scratch, the more it itches.

When the maids quarrel, the master learns about the pilferage.

❋ A quarrel begins with a pitcher and ends with a barrel.

Spread the table and the quarrel will end.

The first quarrel is the best quarrel.

Gossip can estrange the closest friends.

Quarrel (if you must) with someone above you.

Don't interfere in an argument between lovers—or kin.

❋ When you quarrel, quarrel in such a way that you can make up.

Strife is like the plank in a bridge: the longer it endures, the firmer it becomes.

Strife is like water going through a crevice: the wider the crevice, the stronger the flow.

Discord is like a leak in a cistern: drop by drop, the water escapes.

❋ When two men quarrel, the one who yields first displays the nobler nature.   TALMUD: *Kethuboth*, 71b

A quarrel is like a stream of water: once it opens a way, it becomes a wide path.   TALMUD: *Sanhedrin*, 7a

❋ When men quarrel, even God's anger does not frighten them.   *Zohar*

Do not quarrel with a powerful man, or you may fall into his hands.   BEN SIRACH, *Ecclesiasticus*, 8 : 1

❋ Don't quarrel with a loud man.
                     BEN SIRACH, *Ecclesiasticus*, 8 : 3

❋ The world stands firm because of those who close their lips during a quarrel.   NACHMAN OF BRATSLAV

A quarrelsome man deserves no honors.
                                       NACHMAN OF BRATSLAV

The greater a man's wisdom the more will he avoid quarrels.
                                       NACHMAN OF BRATSLAV

❋ Better an insincere peace than a sincere quarrel.
                                       THE LUBLINER RABBI

See also: CONTENTMENT, HATRED, PEACE, WAR

R

RABBIS

Note. "Rabbi" means "my teacher." The rabbi (in Yiddish, *rebbe*) is not a priest or minister, in the Christian sense. He is not an intermediary between God and man; nor is he a spiritual arbiter; nor does he exercise any formal religious authority over others; nor does he enjoy hierarchical status. I know that all this is difficult to believe. But the fact is that a rabbi's influence rests on his learning, his character, his personal qualities. Formal ordination, although it has ancient roots (Numbers, 27 : 18, 19) did not even become institutionalized until modern times; a rabbi may be ordained by another rabbi.

The rabbi *rarely leads religious services*: the *hazzan* (cantor) usually does; but any respected, learned layman may be asked to take the pulpit. Only in modern times, incidentally, did rabbis become Sabbath preachers.

The first rabbis were not professional priests at all, but men respected by the community for their superior character and learning. They exercised moral leadership, and acted as judges or counselors, simply because they were recognized to be worthy of teaching and leading. Jewish scholars established the precept that no man should use the Torah as a "spade" with which to dig for wealth. The great names of the Talmud are the names of workmen-scholars: Hillel was a woodchopper; Shammai, a surveyor; Ishmael, a tanner; Abba Hoshaiah, a launderer.

The very title of "rabbi," given to those who taught in the academies, was not used until the beginning of the Christian Era. Ordination (*smikhah:* "the laying on of hands") could, by rabbinical law, be performed only in Israel and by a member of the Sanhedrin. The Romans forbade the ordination of rabbis, under punishment of death. Ordination thus ended in the fourth century of the Christian Era, along with the political and economic decline of Jewry in Palestine. Formal ordination seems to have disappeared, for in the twelfth century Maimonides raised the possibility of renewing ordination—through an assembly of all the rabbis in Palestine, who would give one of their number the power to ordain others.

Such attempts at restoring ordination failed until the institution of modern ordination, which is made official by a certificate (not a license) called *hatarat horaah*, which means "permission to teach" (!), and usually includes the phrase "*Yoreh, yoreh, yadin, yadin*," which is translatable as "He may indeed judge and give a decision." Ordination confers no sacerdotal powers: the teaching, as authority, extended only to rituals and dietary laws, and the judging only to civil cases.

Modern ordination can be said to have begun in Germany during the fourteenth century, with Rabbi Meir ha-Levi of Vienna. In the fifteenth century, the practice spread to Italy and Poland.

Traditionally, a rabbi is a teacher of Torah (in the broad sense: the Bible, Talmud, and later rabbinic works) and seeks to apply it to daily life. Jewish scholars were expected to share their knowledge with the less learned, and their insights with the less astute. They were expected to instruct, to spread enlightenment, to elevate the moral and religious life of the Jewish community.

What does a rabbi *do*? He performs the ceremonials that attend birth, confirmation, marriage, death; he interprets the tenets of Judaism; he oversees instruction in synagogue or temple; he offers comfort and consolation; he visits hospitals; he counsels families; he tries to "guide the perplexed."

All this may explain the curious mixtures of reverence, amusement, impertinence, and even scorn contained in the sayings Jews love to exchange about the rabbinical community.   —L.R.

✴ A rabbi whose congregation does not want to drive him out of town isn't a rabbi; and a rabbi they do drive out isn't a man.

Influence with the *rebetsn* [rabbi's wife] is better than with the rabbi.

The moment you ask a rabbi a simple question, he starts to give you a complicated answer.

Every rabbi's wife is a magician: how else can she raise a family on his salary?

✻ Our rabbi is so poor that if he didn't fast every Monday and Thursday, he'd starve to death.

✻ If you quarrel with the rabbi, make peace with the bartender.

✻ A goat has a beard—but that doesn't make him a rabbi.

The crown of a good name is greater than the crown of priesthood.   *Sayings of the Fathers*, 3 : 13

RABBIS: IRONIC COMMENTS ON

It's good to be important, for then the rabbi delivers your funeral eulogy in person.

You think it a miracle if God does the will of your rabbi; we deem it a miracle if our rabbi does God's will.

It is wiser to deal with a local thief than a strange rabbi.

Since flattery is unavoidable, and a universal necessity, I may as well become a rabbi.   THE ROPSHITZER RABBI

✻ It was hard for Satan alone to mislead the whole world, so he appointed rabbis in different localities.
                              NACHMAN OF BRATSLAV

Unless you can play baseball, you'll never get to be a rabbi in America.   SOLOMON SCHECHTER

See also: PIETY, SCHOLARS, STUDY, TORAH, WISDOM

RANSOM

Note. The number of sayings and legal rulings that deal with ransom seem surprising only if we forget Jewish experience throughout history. An Egyptian satrap, a Roman sheriff, an Arabian brigand, a Bulgarian adventurer or drunken Cossack would kidnap a Jewish worthy, or a group of pilgrims, then blackmail the Jewish community for ransom. The alternatives pictured were not pleasant to contemplate.

    And so Jewish community funds—for the needy, the old, the sick; for orphans, widows, the halt and the blind; for free burials, free clothes, dowries for poor maidens

—contained a high-priority fund, until quite late into the Middle Ages, called *Pidyon Shebuyim*, a fund set aside for the ransoming of Jews. All other obligations were made secondary to that of freeing Jewish captives. (See Cecil Roth's "A Community of Slaves," in his *Personalities and Events in Jewish History*, pp. 112–35.)
—L.R.

Captives should not be ransomed at exorbitant costs—for the safety of society: otherwise, our enemies will exert every effort to capture victims. But a man may ransom himself at any price.   TALMUD: *Gittin*, 45b

Ransom a captive before you feed the poor. No act of charity is greater: and money collected for any purpose whatsoever may be used as ransom—even if collected to build a synagogue.   JOSEPH CARO, *Shulhan Aruk*

Every moment delayed in ransoming a captive is like shedding his blood.   JOSEPH CARO, *Shulhan Aruk*

See also: CHARITY, FREEDOM, SLAVERY

REALISM

❊ Out of snow, you can't make cheesecake.

If you chop wood, chips will fall.

❊ You can't put "Thank you" in your pocket.

❊ If you can't endure the bad, you won't live long enough to enjoy the good.

❊ The man who does not make a choice makes a choice.

When two play, one must win and one must lose.

❊ When the wind blows, garbage flies.

You can't pull two hides off one ox.

❊ A chicken can't be slaughtered without blood being shed.

There are bones without meat, but no meat without bones.

One log won't even warm the fireplace.

Another man's cloak won't keep you warm.

❋ There is no cloth so fine that moths are unable to eat it.

A carpenter without tools is no carpenter.
MIDRASH: *Exodus Rabbah*, 40 : 1

See also: CAUSE AND EFFECT, CIRCUMSTANCES

REASON

Note. Judaism rests on the assumption that piety can be buttressed by reason but not without faith; that God gave men reason—to use; that God gave men the freedom to choose, and the capacity to live good lives or bad lives.

The rabbis held that reason is not enough for man: that the problems of life cannot be solved without faith. In this, they differed from many philosophers of Greece. The Jews, according to one Greek commentator, were "a people of creative skepticism." —L.R.

A principle illustrated by an example only produces an example.

❋ "For instance" is not proof.

When Man reasons, God laughs.

To make an assumption is to fool yourself.

❋ Reason lives in the universe of freedom.

Passion is the friend of prejudice, not reason.

❋ The man who does not make a choice makes a choice.

Lust and reason are enemies.

God conceals himself from our reason, but reveals Himself to our hearts. —adapted from *Zohar*

Reason is the mediating angel between God and man.
ABRAHAM IBN EZRA, *Commentary to Pentateuch*

❋ Man is not an angel, whose reason always works perfectly, nor is he a mule whose reason works not at all.
JOSEPH BEN ABBA MARI CASPI, *Yoreh Deah*

It is the power of reasoning [*seykhl*] with which God endowed man that renders man capable of perfection.
MAIMONIDES: *Guide to the Perplexed*, 1 : 2

See also: BRAINS, FAITH, INTELLECT, INTELLIGENCE, LOGIC

RECONCILIATION

A reconciliation that does not explain that error lay on
both sides is not a true reconciliation.
                            MIDRASH: *Genesis Rabbah*, 54 : 3

See also: COMPROMISE, PEACE, QUARRELS

REDEMPTION

Redemption, like a livelihood, must be earned each day.
                            MIDRASH: *Genesis Rabbah*, 20 : 9

See also: HEREAFTER, SABBATH, SALVATION, VIRTUE

REFUGEES

If you change houses, you need only change your shirt; if
you change lands, you change your whole life.

The refugee is like a plant without soil or water.
                            MOSES IBN EZRA, *Shirat Yisrael*

See also: ISRAEL, JEWS, PATRIOTISM, PERSECUTION

REGRET

❋ You may regret telling the truth.

No one has a monopoly on regret.

❋ We regret more what we say than what we don't say.

See also: HOPE, REMORSE

RELATIVITY

❋ The big you have seems small, the small you have not
seems big.   TALMUD: Berakoth, 33b

If there are no small ones, there will be no big ones.
                            TALMUD J.: *Sanhedrin*, 10

When the home is in flames, one does not worry over the
broken windows.   HILLEL ZEITLIN

See also: CIRCUMSTANCES, ENVY, GREED

RELIGION

Moses did not make religion a part of virtue: but he declared other virtues to be a part of religion—I mean

justice, and fortitude, and temperance, and a universal agreement of the members of the community with one another.　　　　　　　　　　　　　　　　JOSEPHUS

See also: FAITH, GOD, ISRAEL, PIETY, SABBATH, TORAH, VIRTUE, WISDOM

REMORSE

❀ Never mind the remorse; just don't do what causes it.

Revenge begets remorse.

See: CONSCIENCE, DUTY, GOOD DEEDS, REPENTANCE, REVENGE, SUFFERING

REPENTANCE

❀ Rob not and repent not.

❀ A Litvak is so clever that he repents *before* he sins.

❀ When the sin is sweet, repentance is not so bitter.

The ways of repentance are no less hidden than the ways of sin.

The tears of repentance are not shed in vain.

Repentance is a key that opens any lock.

❀ When we are young, God forgives our stumblings; when we mature, He weighs our words; and when we grow old, He waits—for our repentance.

If only one man repents for his sins, the whole world is pardoned.

Repentance prolongs a man's life.
　　　　　　　　　　　　　TALMUD: *Yomah*, 86b

One must not say to a man who has repented [and changed his way of life], "Remember your former transgressions."
　　　　　　　　　　　　　TALMUD: *Baba Mezi'a*, 58b

Consider every day your last and you will always be ready —with good deeds and repentance.
　　　　　　　　　　　　　TALMUD: *Shabbath*, 153a

Don't criticize a wicked man who abandons his wickedness —and repents.　　　　MIDRASH: *Proverbs*, 6 : 30

✳ The gates of prayer are sometimes open, sometimes closed; but the gates of repentance are open forever.
                        MIDRASH: *Deuteronomy Rabbah*, 2 : 7

The Lord will accept repentance for everything except giving another man a bad name.
                        —adapted from *Zohar*

Just as the ocean is always open, even so are the gates of repentance.   *Yalkut Tehilim*, 789

Repent the day *before* you die [which means every day, for who knows the day of his death].
                        RABBI ELIEZER in *Sayings of the Fathers*, 2 : 10

It is not easy to repent of the sin of melancholy: for when a man begins to repent of it, he falls into a deeper melancholy, realizing he has sinned.
                        THE BERSHIDER RABBI

See also: CONSCIENCE, GUILT, HEREAFTER, PRAYER, SIN

REPRISALS

The dog who is struck by a stone bites—another dog. [The oppressed turn upon the more oppressed.]   *Zohar*

See also: RETRIBUTION, REVENGE

REPUTATION

You can rub him with honey and he'll still smell of tar.

In your town, it is your name that counts; in another, your clothes.   TALMUD: *Shabbath*, 145

✳ No tombstones need be erected on the graves of the righteous; their deeds are their monuments.
                        TALMUD, *Pesahim*, 119a

Happy is the man who leaves a good name.
                        TALMUD: *Berakoth*, 17a

What is a profanation of the Name? For example, if a scholar does not pay the butcher at once. [It sets a bad example.]   TALMUD: *Yomah*, 86a

✳ Even if all of a slander is not believed, half of it is.
                        MIDRASH: *Genesis Rabbah*, 56 : 4

Every man has three names: one his father and mother gave him, one others call him, and one he earns himself.
MIDRASH: *Ecclesiastes Rabbah*, 7 : 1

Beauty wanes, but a name endures.
APOCRYPHA: *Ahikar*, 2 : 49

The Lord will accept repentance for all sins, except one: giving a man a bad name. —adapted from *Zohar*

A good name is more desirable than great riches, a good reputation than silver and gold.
Book of Proverbs, 22 : 1

He who earns a good name acquired it for his own good.
Sayings of the Fathers, 2 : 7

There are three crowns: the crown of learning, the crown of priesthood, the crown of royalty; but greater than any of these is the crown of a good name.
Sayings of the Fathers, 4 : 13

He who advertises his name, loses it.
HILLEL in *Sayings of the Fathers*, 1 : 13

❋ What you think of others tell us what they think of you.
MOSES IBN EZRA, *Shirat Yisrael*

A place becomes known far and wide because it is the home of a great man. THE ROPSHITZER RABBI

See also: FAME, GOOD DEEDS, HONOR, SELF-ESTEEM, SLANDER

RESIGNATION

Note. The story is told of a rabbi who lost every one of his thirteen sons, and in his terrible grief said to their mother, who could not be consoled: "But our sons have not died in vain. Think of it: when great misfortune strikes other men, they will remember ours, and recall that *we* lost thirteen sons; and perhaps they will not be angry with—blessed be His name!—the Lord."

—L.R.

❋ All utterances prefaced with "God forbid" are possible.

So it goes: one man has a purse, but another has the money.

Fowl become inured to the killings.

❊ If things aren't the way you like, then like them the way they are.

❊ It will do about as much good as bleeding [cupping] a corpse.

Let him whose cloak a court of law has taken sing his song and go his way. [He was saved from theft.]
                                    TALMUD: *Sanhedrin*, 7a

When a fox has his hour, bow to him.
                                    TALMUD: *Megillah*, 16

To cry over the past is to offer a vain prayer.
                                    MISHNAH: *Berakoth*, 9 : 3

He who tries to resist the wave is swept away, but he who bends before it abides.
                                    MIDRASH: *Genesis Rabbah*, 44 : 15

❊ To each wave that approached me, I bent my head.
                                    RABBI AKIBA in TALMUD: *Yebamoth*, 121a

See also: ADVERSITY, CIRCUMSTANCES, HOPE, LIFE, OPTIMISM, PESSIMISM, REALISM

RESPONSIBILITY

If each one sweeps in front of his own door the whole street is clean.

When the shepherd is lame and the goats are fleet, there will be an accounting at the gate of the fold.

❊ Hold no man responsible for what he says in his grief.
                                    TALMUD, *Baba Bathra*, 16a

A man should not fast excessively (it weakens a man for good deeds).   TALMUD: *Ta'anith*, 11a

To deal with a deaf-mute, an idiot, or a minor is bad, for you are liable (responsible) and they are not.
                                    MISHNAH: *Baba Kamma*, 8 : 4

The man who warns the wicked, even if his warning goes unheeded, has saved himself from blame.   *Zohar*

See also: CAUSE AND EFFECT, CONSCIENCE, CHARITY, DUTY, OBLIGATION

RESOURCEFULNESS

✴ When things are scarcer than you wish, a herring will have to serve as a fish.

When you can't go over, go under.

What you don't have in your head, you have in your feet.

See also: EFFORT, ENDURANCE, INGENUITY

REST

No rest is worth having unless it follows work.

SAADIA GAON

A man's body grows sluggish through too much rest; his stomach gets inflated, and disease is created in the lower parts: sciatica, gout, even elephantiasis. Even if a man has all he needs, he dare not stay idle, for the idle man will end in weakness, insanity, and sickness; and this truth applies even to a king or ruler.   SAADIA GAON

The only truly desirable rest is the rest to be enjoyed in the world-to-come.   SAADIA GAON

Only if a man knows himself, and has no illusion about himself, and understands every existing thing in relation to itself, will he find real rest [of mind].

MAIMONIDES, *Eight Chapters*, 5

Just as the body becomes exhausted by hard labor and is reinvigorated by rest, so the mind needs its weariness relieved by rest.   MAIMONIDES, *Eight Chapters*, 5

See also: CONTENTMENT, HEALTH, WORK

RESURRECTION

Note. The earliest portions of the Bible are vague about the concept of resurrection; the Book of Daniel mentions it ($12 : 2$); but Isaiah gave the idea potent, poetical form—as a prophecy to all of hard-pressed Israel: "The dead shall live, the bodies shall arise. . . . Awake and sing, ye who dwell in the dust." Later, the prophet Ezekiel, in Babylon, proclaimed: "Behold, I will open your graves, and cause you to come out of them, O my people."

The Pharisees, after the Exile (during the time of the Second Temple), adopted a belief in the resurrection: i.e., that the dead would literally rise from their graves at "the end of days." The Sadducees did not accept this concept. In *Ecclesiasticus* (second century B.C.E.), Jesus ben Sirach, an aristocrat and a Sadducee, tartly wrote:

> "When the dead is at rest
> Let his memory rest!"

But the Sadducee view did not prevail, for it was from the ranks of the plainer folk that the Pharisees and, later, most rabbinical scholars came.

Christianity and Islam, of course, adopted resurrection as an integral aspect of their creeds. The Talmud accepts resurrection as a basic, sacred tenet of Judaic faith. The rabbinical tradition agreed that the redemption of man is not possible, nor divine reward and punishment, nor immortality of the soul, without that physical resurrection, followed by a reunion of bodies with their souls, which the Messiah's coming will effect. The power of these ideas to Jewry for thousands of years was of incalculable importance in holding their world-dispersed community together, and in convincing them that divine justice would be meted out.

For centuries, all of the prayers in the liturgy of Judaism specifically mentioned the resurrection (the second paragraph of the *Amidah*, the part of the prayer recited when standing) and the *Shmona Esra* (the Eighteen—now Nineteen—Benedictions). The daily prayers of observing Jews still contain this passage in the second of these benedictions ". . . You revive the dead with great mercy [and] keep faith with them who lie in the dust. . . . Blessed art Thou, O Lord, who revivest the dead."

But one must always remember that religious ideas were never embalmed beyond changeability in Judaism; Jewish faith underwent constant analysis, exegesis, criticism; every aspect of belief and the Law was debated throughout centuries of disputation—both scholarly and lay. Maimonides, who sometimes departed from traditional rabbinical judgments (and was roundly denounced for it), placed resurrection among his majestic *Thirteen Articles of Faith*. But the dogma of bodily resurrection continued to bother many sages and scholars, who conceived of the world-to-come, of eschatology and perfection, in terms of supernal, eternal bliss of the *soul*.

Orthodox Jews continued to interpret resurrection literally—differing only as to whether it would include all of mankind, only the deserving righteous, or only Jews. Any disbelief in, or skepticism about, the physical actuality of resurrection was condemned by the Orthodox as heresy; and in the end resurrection was held to be the reward of "all the righteous of all nations."

Reform Judaism does not accept bodily revival and refusion with the soul; the Reform liturgy has expunged earlier, Orthodox phrasings. Many Reform scholars point out that the concept of physical resurrection is a carry-over from primitive experience, agrarian societies, pagan fertility cults, Egyptian and Babylonian myths, the mystic religions of the East—and that such a conception should have no place in modern Judaic faith and worship. Among Conservative Jews (who stand midway between the Orthodox and the Reformed), the doctrine of the resurrection has been blended into the larger, comforting precept of the soul's immortality— without bodily attendance or reinforcement. "Eternal Life" has become the phrase adopted in the prayer books of Conservative and Reform Jews instead of "resurrection."

Most modern Jews, I suspect, do not ponder much over whether the coming of the Messiah or salvation, immortality or the world-to-come, are to be taken literally, but are inclined to regard them with ancient, symbolic affection, with a sense of historical respect and continuity, as affirmations of a larger, more important concept—the faith in One omnipotent, compassionate, and forgiving God.   —L.R.

Those who sleep in the dust shall awake.

> *Daniel*, 12 : 2

The dead shall live, the bodies shall arise.

> *Isaiah*, 26 : 19

❊ Awake and sing, ye who dwell in the dust.

> *Isaiah*, 26 : 19

I will open your graves, my people, and cause you to come
out of them.   *Ezekiel*, 37 : 12

The righteous man has hope in his death.
                                Book of Proverbs, 14 : 32

Death is when two worlds meet with a kiss: this world
going out, the future coming in.
                                TALMUD J.: *Yebamoth*, 57a

Man is born to die; the dead will live again.
                                Sayings of the Fathers, 4 : 22

❋ Death is merely moving—from one home to another:
and if we are wise, we will make the latter the more
beautiful.   THE KOTZKER RABBI

I am going out one door, and shall go through another.
                                BAAL SHEM TOV

See also: DEATH, HEREAFTER, IMMORTALITY, PARADISE

RETRIBUTION

❋ God waits long, but he pays with interest.

As you brew, so shall you drink.

Those who sow the wind shall reap the whirlwind.
                                Book of Hosea, 8 : 7

He who digs a pit will fall into it, and he who rolls a stone,
it will come back upon him.
                                Book of Proverbs, 26 : 27

He who can hire a poor worker but does not, shortens the
worker's life, and his own life will be shortened, too.
                                Zohar

Because you drowned others, you were drowned, and those
who drowned you shall be drowned, too.
                                HILLEL in *Sayings of the Fathers*, 2 : 6

See also: ADVICE, CAUSE AND EFFECT, FORGIVENESS, GOD,
REVENGE

REVELATION

Only through what is disclosed can man learn what is un-
disclosed.   LEOPOLD ZUNZ

See also: HEAVEN, HEREAFTER, REASON, RESURRECTION

REVENGE

Note. All the ancient religions of the Middle East contained *lex talionis*, "the law of retaliation." "Thou shalt give life for life, eye for eye, tooth for tooth, hand for hand, foot for foot" (Exodus 21 : 23–24). But many who venerated the Torah's teachings on lovingkindness, and the loving and forgiving of neighbors, wondered whether this passage could mean what it seems to mean; in the quotations that follow, you will find rabbinical interpretation of the "eye for eye" injunction. Note especially the remarkable passage by Rabbi Hananel.

—L.R.

God punishes, men take revenge.

❋ Revenge begets remorse and remorse begets misery.

The smallest revenge will poison the soul.

Revenge is half consolation.

❋ Blood that has been shed does not rest.

If you take revenge, you will regret it; if you forgive, you will rejoice.

Who takes vengeance destroys his own house.

Thou shalt not avenge.   *Leviticus*, 19 : 18

Say not, "I will pay back evil." Wait for the Lord to help you.   *Book of Proverbs*, 20 : 22

If a man says "I will not lend you my shovel because you refused to lend me your scythe," that is revenge—which the Law forbids.   *Abot de Rabbi Nathan*

Does the Law really intend that the man who tore out another's eye should have his own eye torn out? Some men are weaker than others; and perhaps the guilty one, being weaker, would die as a result of the punishment.

What the Torah says is "An eye for an eye," *not* "A life for an eye." . . . It is impossible to inflict on a second man exactly the same wound as was suffered by the first, for the first wound was not measured as to length, depth, and width. If we observe the ruling: "As he did, so shall it be done to him," the injury would have to be exactly the same, neither more nor less.

RABBI HANANEL

See also: CONSCIENCE, FORGIVENESS, RETALIATION, RETRIBUTION

REVOLUTION

✻ One unjust act can cause a revolution.

Revolution is the right of slaves.
                H. Leivick (Leivick Halpern), in *The Golem*

See also: GOVERNMENT, POLITICS, POWER, SLAVERY

RICHES/RICH MEN

The wise know the value of riches, but the rich do not
  know the pleasures of wisdom.

The rich eat when they want to, the poor when they can.

He heapeth up riches, and knoweth not who shall gather
  them.   *Book of Psalms*, 39 : 6

A good name is worth more than great riches.
                              Book of Proverbs, 22 : 1

✻ Listen to the rich no less than the poor, for it is written:
  "Ye shall not favor persons in judging them."
                      Abot de Rabbi Nathan, 20 : 22a

See also: POOR MEN AND RICH MEN, WEALTH

RIGHTEOUSNESS

✻ The righteous man who says he is righteous—is not
  righteous.

✻ What is just is always right.

The righteous man gives a little more than a scale indicates.
                      TALMUD: *Baba Bathra*, 7b

The righteous promise little and perform much; the wicked
  promise much and perform not even a little.
                      TALMUD: *Baba Mezi'a*, 87a

Gray hairs are a glorious crown which is won by a righteous
  life.   *Book of Proverbs*, 16 : 31

Better a little with righteousness than great revenues with
  injustice.   *Book of Proverbs*, 16 : 8

As the whirlwind passes, so the wicked man vanishes;
But the righteous one is rooted forever.
                              Book of Proverbs, 10 : 25

The wicked man earns illusive wages;
But he who sows righteousness has a true reward.
                              Book of Proverbs, 11 : 18

A righteous man cares for his beast;
But the mercy of the wicked is cruel.
                              Book of Proverbs, 12 : 10

Righteousness delivereth from death.
                              Book of Proverbs, 10 : 2

If a man has two cows, one strong and one weak, he lays
    the yoke upon the strong: God does the same with the
    righteous.   MIDRASH: *Genesis Rabbah*, 32 : 3

It is beyond our power to explain the prosperity of the
    wicked or the troubles of the righteous.
                              Sayings of the Fathers, 3 : 16

See also: EVIL, GOOD, GOD, HEAVEN, HEREAFTER, PIETY,
    PRAYER

RIVALRY

Superior work is what results from a man's rivalry with
    his neighbor.   MIDRASH: *Ecclesiastes Rabbah*, 3 : 11

ROBBERS/ROBBERY

❋ A scholar is not a robber, and a robber is not a scholar.
                              TALMUD: *'Abodah Zarah*, 176

See also: THIEVES

RUMOR

❋ Tongues are more dangerous than swords, for tongues
    can hurt from afar.

❋ When in doubt, shut up.

To repeat what you have not seen is to increase what you
    only heard.

If there were no listeners there would be no rumors.

❋ If you hear your neighbor died, believe it; but if you
    hear he became rich, don't believe it.

✴ What you see and hear, you cannot help; but what you
say depends on you alone.   —adapted from *Zohar*

The man who rails is feared, and he who talks rashly is
hated.

                    —adapted from BEN SIRACH, *Ecclesiasticus*, 9 : 18

See also: GOSSIP, SCANDAL, SECRETS, SLANDER, TALK

S

SABBATH

Note. The Torah's laws governing the Sabbath presented
considerable difficulties to Jews in the conduct of daily
life. Should a physician go to attend a dying man on the
Sabbath? Should the injunction against handling money
on the Sabbath be waived so that ransom might be paid
to save the life of a captive? The male child is supposed
to be circumcised on the eighth day after birth, but if
the eighth day falls on the Sabbath, during which no
work of any kind is permitted ("whosoever doeth any
work therein shall be put to death"—*Exodus*, 35 : 2),
and if "no man [should] go out of his place on the
seventh day" (*Exodus*, 16 : 29)—then what was to be
done about circumcision? Or how could Jews defend
themselves against, say, the Romans—who, knowing of
the Sabbatical injunction, attacked Jews on the holy day?

In these, and a thousand comparable problems, the
oral interpretation and amplification of rabbi-scholars
made it possible for the Jews to hold to the letter of the
Law—by reinterpreting what the letters might mean.
(See Guide Notes for TORAH, TALMUD, MISHNAH, MID-
RASH, and GEMARA.)

Shabbes (the Sabbath) is called "the Queen of the
week," "the Bride." In however bitter a time and place,
the Sabbath, to Jews, was the miraculous time when even
the lowliest or poorest felt himself in kingly communion
with the Almighty, favored by God's special concern:

"It is a sign between me and the children of Israel!" (Exodus, 31 : 17).

Each Sabbath, down the generations, in every land in which they have lived, Jews have scrubbed every nook of their dwelling, bathed themselves with care, donned fresh garments, laid out their best linens, glasses, utensils: for *shabbes* brought—each week, throughout a lifetime—a sense of personal splendor, cleanliness, devotion, exaltation. The old rabbis believed that the *neshoma yesera* ("extra soul") descends each Friday when the sun sets. *Shabbes* was redolent with intimations of divinity, the hint of angels, visions of heaven, all the blessed on golden thrones under the sparkling stars. ("Our house was filled with the odor of burning wax, blessed spices," writes Isaac Bashevis Singer, "and with an atmosphere of wonder and miracles.")

What did the Jews do on *shabbes*? They prayed—and studied; they read; they enjoyed sleep—the special Sabbath sleep of bliss; they discussed the Torah and the Talmud. Moses had enjoined them, and Philo, "[to] assemble . . . on these seventh days . . . in a respectful and orderly manner . . . [to] hear the laws read [and explained] so that none should be ignorant of them."

Considered historically, the idea of a workless seventh day was revolutionary. (The Fourth Commandment ordains Sabbath for beasts of burden no less than men.) The Greeks and Romans scorned it. Seneca called the Hebrews "this most outrageous people [who] lose almost a seventh part of their life in inactivity." Juvenal jeered at those Roman Christians "to whom every seventh day is idle." Horace and Martial thought the idea foolish, conducive to laziness.

Every Sabbath morning a portion of the Five Books of Moses is read in the synagogue, together with a reading from the Prophets, so that the Torah is completed in one year—and the cycle is promptly begun again. In their homes, all summer, fathers and grandfathers traditionally engaged the children in discussions —of the *Sayings of the Fathers* or portions of the Mishnah that discuss ethical problems. How can one appraise the consequences of a people, young and old, spending one day a week, year after year, generation after generation, in such seminars on religion, morals, ethics, responsibility?

Once, when some Falasha Jews were being tortured, and were goaded to name their savior, they cried: "The savior of the Jews is the Sabbath!" Of which England's Rabbi Hertz wrote: "They spoke wiser then they knew."

—L.R.

❋ On the Sabbath, the wicked in Hell, too, rest.

The savior of the Jews is the Sabbath.
Saying of the Falasha Jews

Remember the Sabbath day, to keep it holy. Six days shalt thou labor, and do all thy work: But the seventh day is the Sabbath of the Lord, thy God.
the Fourth Commandment, *Exodus*, 20 : 8–10

The Sabbath was delivered unto you, and not you unto the Sabbath.   TALMUD: *Yomah*, 25b

The Sabbath was given for the study of the Torah.
TALMUD: *Pesikta Rabbati*, 22

❋ The Sabbath was given for pleasure [of the scholars].
Pesikta Rabbati, 22

Shabbes (the Sabbath) is the Queen of the week.
TALMUD, *Shabbath*, 119a

[The Sabbath] is a sign between me and the children of Israel.   *Exodus* 31 : 17

Some rules governing the Sabbath are as scantily supported [in Scripture] as mountains hanging by a hair.
MISHNAH: *Hagigah*, 1 : 8

The Jews, in bondage in Egypt, possessed scrolls, in which they reveled every Sabbath. These promised them that God would redeem them because they rested on the Sabbath.   MIDRASH: *Exodus Rabbah*, 5

Blessed art Thou, O Lord . . . who has commanded us to kindle the Sabbath light.   *Standard Prayer Book*

More than the Jews kept the Sabbath did the Sabbath [observance] keep the Jews [alive].   AHAD HA-AM

See also: REDEMPTION, RESURRECTION

SADNESS

A pretty garment can conceal a sad heart.

❋ The deeper the sadness, the less tongue it possesses.

❋ "And it came to pass" usually introduces a tale of sadness. TALMUD: *Megillah*, 10b

Laughter may come from an aching heart. All pleasure contains an element of sadness.
JONATHAN EIBESCHUTZ, *Yaarot Devash*

See also: HAPPINESS, MELANCHOLY, MISFORTUNE, PLEASURES, SUFFERING

SAFETY

❋ The wolf does not fear the dog, but his bark.

He who can cringe creeps forward.

❋ It is worse to live on your knees than die on your feet.

If two are traveling in a desert, and only one has a canteen of water, if both drink, both will die, but if only one drinks he will survive; the son of Patura thought: "It is better that both should drink and die, rather than that one should witness his companion's death." Rabbi Akiba thought, " 'That your brother may live with you' implies that your life takes precedence over his life." [At least one life is saved.] TALMUD: *Baba Mazi'a*, 62a

If all men were philosophers, the social order would be destroyed and the human race exterminated: men need many material things to survive.
MAIMONIDES: *Eight Chapters*

The fox feels safe only as long as the leopard has others to prey on. IBN ZABARA, *Book of Delight*

See also: AUTHORITY, LAW AND ORDER, POLITICS, POWER, STRENGTH

SAGES

Note. Anyone who has read the first five books of the Old Testament (the Torah) may sympathize with the problems that confronted the ancient "book men"—the sages,

rabbis, philosophers—who set out to clarify and enforce
God's edicts among the Hebrew people. After all, the
Torah is held to come directly from God; it is God's
word; it can be neither denied, corrected, nor evaded.
(See headnote: TORAH.)

The Torah contains injunctions and commandments
from On High. But much that is in the Five Books of
Moses is obscure in meaning; much is metaphorical;
much is in the form of parables the exact meaning of
which was not easily agreed upon. Much of the Torah
is worded in so generalized a form that the absence of
details represents an absence of the procedures to be
followed in observing the Law. And the Torah is not
free of contradictions: some laws are given more than
once, in different form—for reasons never explained
in the Torah itself.

Changing problems and crises of the most dreadful
nature simply demanded that certain injunctions be
reinterpreted so that Israel might live. (See, for instance,
the headnotes for REVENGE, SABBATH.) This presented no
easy problem. See the Guide Notes: TALMUD, MISHNAH,
GEMARA, MIDRASH, and headnote for SCHOLARS.

—L.R.

✻ They are our sages because we are their fools.

A complete fool is better than a half-sage.

✻ After the death of Rabbi Moshe, Rabbi Mendel of
Kotzk asked one of his disciples: "What was most important to your sage?" The disciple thought, and replied: "Whatever he happened to be doing at the
moment."   Hasidic story

Some men are stupid: they stand up to honor a Holy
Scroll, but do not rise to honor a sage.
                          TALMUD: *Makkoth*, 22b

✻ When a sage dies, all men should mourn, for they are
his kinsmen.   TALMUD: *Shabbath*, 105b

Just as a small log may set fire to a large one, so do
smaller scholars sharpen the wits of sages.
                          TALMUD: *Ta'anith*, 7a

The curses of a sage even when not deserved will come to
pass.   TALMUD, *Berakoth*, 56a

To see a sage die is like seeing a holy scroll burn: "On such a day, I fast," said Rabbi Abbabu.

TALMUD J.: *Mo'ed Katan*, 3

❊ A sage takes precedence over a king, for if a sage dies, we have no one like him, but if a king dies all Israel is eligible to succeed him.

—adapted from the MIDRASH

Sages rank higher than prophets, for the power of prophecy does not abide with a man every moment, but the power of wisdom does.   *Zohar*

See also: KNOWLEDGE, POLITICS, SCHOLARS, WISDOM, WISE MEN

SAINTS

Note. A venerable legend of the Jews concerns the *Lamed-Vov Tsadikim* ("the Thirty-Six Saints"), living men who do not know they are saints but perform such surpassing deeds of kindness and compassion that God allows the world to go on because of them. Not only does each of the Thirty-Six not know how saintly and sainted he is, no one else can ever identify him, either. A member of the Thirty-Six Saints may be a pauper, a cobbler, a hem-stitcher, a seer. A *Lamed-Vov* discloses his identity only in very dire emergencies: When Jews are in mortal peril, one of the *Tsadikim* may swoop in to do God's bidding—suddenly, magically—then will vanish as inexplicably as he appeared.

This idea of doing good for the sake of goodness alone, without intention of reward or recognition or simple gratitude from the one benefited, played a central role in the ethical pantheon erected by generations of rabbinical philosophers. The less self-serving a good deed, the less known or publicized, the less one receives praise or credit or reward, the nobler it is: After all, *God* knows, and must cherish most the pure of heart.

—L.R.

❊ Bad men do well in this world, saints in the next.

❊ If charity cost no money, and favors represented no inconvenience, the world would be bursting with saints.

A vulgar man cannot be a saint.

HILLEL in *Sayings of the Fathers*, 2 : 5

See also: ANGELS, IRONIES, RIGHTEOUSNESS, VIRTUE

SALVATION

Note. There is no satisfactory way of translating the word/
concept of "salvation" into Hebrew or Yiddish, for in
Jewish thought salvation has simply meant the deserved
reward of those who "live Torah," fulfill the commandments, perform the *mitzvahs* of good deeds, kindness,
compassion, help to one's fellow men—those mortals, in
short, who exemplify true piety and virtue by the way
they live on earth.

Jews do not believe that a man inherits the guilt of
Adam's Fall, nor that man is born in, with, or out of sin.
They hold that personal salvation is achieved by personal
conduct. Every man, Jew or not, is believed to be responsible for, and capable of, attaining his own salvation: each can approach God in his own fashion, without
a mediating rabbi, priest or minister.

The writings of the rabbis reflect an abiding realism,
I think, about the nature of man's nature: his passions,
irrationalities, vanity, willfulness, propensity of evil; but
rabbinical writings stress man's power to choose, to
act, to overcome his baser impulses. Moreover, man is
held to have been created incomplete by God's intention,
precisely so that men may themselves cooperate in virtue
—thus completing God's work. (See headnote for SIN.)

—L.R.

Whoever lives by Torah, good deeds, humility, and the
fear of Heaven, will be saved from doom.
                    MIDRASH: *Pesikta Rabbati*, 198a

See also: HEAVEN, HEREAFTER, ISRAEL, JEWS, REPENTANCE,
RESURRECTION, SIN, TORAH, VIRTUE

SARCASM: EXAMPLES OF

✸ Eggs want to be smarter than hens.

The world is beautiful, shining, bright, and easy—but for
whom?

✸ When a *nebbekh* leaves a room, it feels as if someone
came in.

✸ To avoid all sorrows, just cut off your head.

A hearty thanks—to your navel.

⁂ A crow flies high—and perches on a pig.

Let God worry about tomorrow—who will give me a loan today?

It's about as much help as throwing a bean at a wall.

⁂ Things are going beautifully for me—as they do for a saint in this world.

The rabbi finishes the wine only to make his disciples happy.

⁂ He acts rich: he owns a whole head of cabbage.

To be a millionaire, he'll sell you the shirt off his back.

See also: ANIMALS, IRONY, PARADOXES, SCHOLARS: AMUSED COMMENTS ON

SATAN

⁂ Satan seduces us in this world, and accuses us in the next.   TALMUD: *Sukkah,* 52b

Satan's torment was worse than Job's. He was like a servant told to break a cask without spilling the wine.
                      TALMUD: *Baba Bathra,* 16b

When a man is in danger, Satan presses charges against him.   MIDRASH: *Genesis Rabbah,* 91

⁂ If Satan says, "Sin—for the Lord will forgive you," don't do it.   —adapted from TALMUD: *Hagigah,* 16a

Satan brought curses on the world through his cleverness.
                                         Zohar

Like iron, out of which man can fashion whatever tools he needs when he heats it in the forge, so Satan can be subdued to the service of God, if tempered by the Torah, which is like fire.   *Abot de Rabbi Natham,* 16

It was hard for Satan alone to mislead the world, so he appointed rabbis in different places.
                              NACHMAN OF BRATSLAV

You can't trust Satan: he tries to persuade you not to go to the synagogue on a cold morning; and when you do go, he follows you there.   THE KORETSER RABBI

See also: DEMON, DEVIL, EVIL, HELL, SIN, TORAH, VIRTUE; and headnotes for DEVIL, EVIL

SCANDAL

Why were our fingers made flexible? So that we may stop our ears with them when evil [scandal] is being spoken.
                                    TALMUD: *Kethuboth, 5*

See also: GOSSIP, RUMOR, SLANDER, TALK

SCHOLARS

Note. To study, for Jews, was "to come under the wings of the Divine Presence." Atop the Jewish pyramid of respect, unchallenged, stands the scholar—not the ruler, the prince, the millionaire, the rabbi. (A rabbi can, of course, be a great scholar; but scholars were more respected than rabbis.)

A Jewish mother customarily sang a lullaby of hope that her little son might become not rich or successful, but learned and wise—a *talmid khokhem* ("disciple of the wise," "expert on Talmud"). A student was considered a great matrimonial catch—and families offered dowries or outright support to them during their years at a *yeshiva* (college). High honor was accorded the family in which a daughter married a scholar. "If you must, sell everything [to] marry your daughter to a scholar," comes from the Talmud (*Pesahim,* 49b).

Penurious students were supported by the community. Some students walked "from the banks of the Danube to the banks of the Seine, (defying) hunger and cold, to drink in the words of some far-famed master" (Louis Ginzberg, in *Students, Scholars and Saints,* J.P.S.A., 1928). Those who came from far distances were lodged with local families. It was considered an act of piety to feed a *yeshiva bocher,* many of whom went from home to home, eating and sleeping in a different place each night.

In the old country, before a boy entered a *cheder* (school) he was carried into the synagogue by his father or *melamed* (teacher), and sometimes placed in front of the *bimah* (pulpit) to face the entire congregation; and sometimes the Scroll of the Torah was unrolled and

the Ten Commandments were read aloud, addressed to
the boy directly, reenacting the scene on Mount Sinai.

On his first day in *cheder*, the boy's mother and father
would stand over him as the teacher pointed to the
letters of the alphabet. As the lad repeated the names of
the letters, his mother might give him a cookie, shaped in
the form of that letter. Sometimes, honey would be put
on the slate, so that the child should lick it—to learn
that "learning is sweet." At the end of this first lesson,
the mother would enfold the boy and pray that her son
"fulfill his life with years of Torah study, marriage, and
good deeds."

The scholar was expected to be immaculate in clothes
and person; indifferent to physical comforts or material
rewards; gentle in manner; sensitive to others. He had
to combine scholarship with rectitude. Indeed, these
virtues were assumed to go hand in hand: those who
study are virtuous, and those who *know* will not do
evil. See headnotes for SCHOLARSHIP, STUDENTS, STATUS.

—L.R.

✻ The table that has fed no scholars is not blessed.

A scholar can't conduct a business.

✻ The fate of Israel depends on its scholars.

The scholar who has abandoned the study of Torah is like
a bird that has abandoned its nest.
                              TALMUD: *Hagigah*, 9b

✻ Just as the kernel of a nut is not despised, even though
the shell be marred, so it is with [the appearance of] a
scholar.   TALMUD: *Hagigah*, 15b

He who has learning but does not fear God cannot enter
Heaven.   TALMUD: *Shabbath*, 31a

A scholar with a spot on his garments deserves the worst.
                              TALMUD: *Shabbath*, 114a

✻ If you must, sell everything and marry your daughter
to a scholar.   TALMUD: *Pesahim*, 49b

A scholar who is the son of a scholar is modest; but a
scholar who is the son of an ignoramus trumpets his
knowledge abroad.   TALMUD: *Baba Mezi'a*, 85b

❉ A scholar is not a robber, and a robber is not a scholar.
TALMUD: *'Aboda Zarah*, 17b

❉ The ignorant think less clearly as they grow older, but scholars think more clearly with the years.
TALMUD: *Kinnin*, 3 : end

To treat a scholar to wine is like offering a libation to God.
TALMUD: *Yomah*, 71a

A scholar should be like a bottle which lets in no wind; like a deep garden bed which retains its moisture; like a pitch-coated jug which preserves its wine; and like a sponge which absorbs everything.
TALMUD: *Derekh Erets*, 1 : 2

To partake of a meal at which a great scholar is present is to feast upon the refulgence of the Divine Presence.
TALMUD: *Berakoth*, 64a

❉ A scholar who is not as unyielding as iron is no scholar.
TALMUD: *Taanith*, 4a

The man who is not a scholar by temperament should devote his time to public affairs.
MIDRASH: *Leviticus Rabbah*, 25

A scholar who is a bastard [*mamzer*] is preferable to a high priest who is ignorant.
MIDRASH, *Numbers Rabbah*, 6

❉ Just as a tent cannot stand without pegs and cords, so Israel cannot stand without scholars.
Seder Eliyahu Rabbah

The "bite" of the learned is like the bite of a fox, their sting is like a scorpion's, their hiss like a serpent's: all their words are like coals of fire. [A scholar's words are not to be taken lightly.]
Sayings of the Fathers, 2 : 10

❉ There are four types [of students]: the sponge, the funnel, the strainer, and the sifter: The sponge soaks up everything; the funnel takes in at one ear but lets out at the other; the strainer lets pass the wine and retains the lees; and the sifter holds back the coarse flour and collects the fine.
Sayings of the Fathers, 5 : 15

It is imperative that most men work in [physically] productive occupations, so that the few who devote them-

selves entirely to learning may have their wants provided;
in this way, the human race goes on, and knowledge is
enriched.
MAIMONIDES, *Commentary on Mishnah, Introduction*

When you help scholars, you gain a share in their learning.
NACHMAN OF BRATSLAV

SCHOLARS: AMUSED COMMENTS

The most important thing a scholar needs is a small appetite.

❋ Some scholars study so much that they don't leave
themselves time to think.

❋ When a scholar sets out to look for a bride, he should
take an ignoramus along to advise him.

Every scholar has his own peculiarities [eccentricities].

❋ When a scholar makes a mistake it is a big one.

❋ The scholar [lost in his thoughts] does not see that borsht
is red.

I have been rewarded for what I interpreted—and for
what I left uninterpreted.   TALMUD: *Pesahim*, 22b

How does an uneducated man regard a scholar? At first,
like a golden ladle; if he talks with him, like a silver
ladle; and if the scholar is his beneficiary, like an
earthen spoon.   TALMUD: *Sanhedrin*, 52b

❋ Some scholars are both wise and handsome—and would
be still wiser were they less handsome.   TALMUD

A carcass is better than a scholar without common sense.
MIDRASH: *Leviticus Rabbah*, 1 : 15

A scholar without sensibility is less than an ant.
MIDRASH: *Leviticus Rabbah*, 1 : 15

❋ Some scholars are like camels loaded with silk: neither
the silk nor the camel is of any use to the other.
ABRAHAM IBN EZRA, *Yesod Mora*

❋ Some scholars are like donkeys: they only carry a lot
of books.   BAHYA IBN PAQUDA, *Duties of the Heart*

See also: EDUCATION, ISRAEL, KNOWLEDGE, LEARNING,
SABBATH, STATUS, STUDY, TORAH, WISDOM

SCHOLARSHIP

Note. It is most revealing that relatively few of the students at a *yeshiva* (college) in Eastern Europe received
(or wanted) a rabbinical degree. The primary purpose
of the *yeshiva* was not to produce rabbis, but Jews well-
versed in the Talmud: learned men, disciplined in their
thinking, who would dedicate themselves to live according to the Torah and spend their lives studying the
ever-discussable Talmud.

May I repeat a quotation from W. E. H. Lecky, the
Irish historian, who summarized the Jewish ethos in the
following passage?

While those around them were grovelling in the darkness of besotted ignorance . . . enthralled by countless
superstitions in which all love of enquiry and all
search for truth were abandoned, the Jews were still
pursuing the path of knowledge, amassing learning,
and stimulating progress with the same unflinching
constancy that they manifested in their faith. *The
Rise and Influence of Rationalism in Europe,* Vol. II,
3d edition; Appleton, New York, 1906, p. 271.

—L.R.

See: ISRAEL, KNOWLEDGE, LEARNING, SCHOLARS, STUDY,
TRUTH, WISDOM

SCIENCE

Note. Until the tenth century, there is almost nothing in
the literature of the Jews that approximates science or
scientific analysis. The marvels of nature excited awe and
a veneration of the wonders God had created on earth.
Within the Talmud's system of discourse, its exegetical
debates and sophistical distinctions, there was no place
for science as we know it. The rabbis set their faces
against secular knowledge (as did Catholic authorities).
Professor Charles Singer points out that although many
Greek names are found in the Talmud, not one Greek
scientist is included; even Aristotle is not mentioned.
Maimonides incurred great hostility, for his writings
and range approached scientific method. (See BIOG-
RAPHIES.)

Yet the Jewish passion for literacy, for learning, for
scholarship, the support given any student of promise,

the emphasis on study, analysis, reasoning, argument, the profound veneration of knowledge—all these were bound to break through the insulating walls of traditional Talmudic authority.

It was through Arabic thought and Islam, via the Sephardic Spanish intellectuals, that science came to the Jews. Many medieval rabbis became accomplished in mathematics, for instance, or astronomy, medicine, Hellenic philosophy. (See BIOGRAPHIES.)

For the past four centuries, the contribution of Jewish scientists (physicists, mathematicians, biologists, chemists, physiologists, philosophers, economists, etc.) has surely been remarkable; as of 1971, sixty Jews have won Nobel Prizes (first awarded in 1901).

I think that the old tradition of Judaism is neatly symbolized in this anecdote: An agnostic Jew smiled, "But Darwin has proved that man is only another animal"; to which a rabbi responded, "Then why has not a single breed of animal ever produced a Darwin?"

—L.R.

❉ The sons of the poor give science its splendor.

Science, though it seems to waste Torah, actually confirms and clarifies it.   THE KORETSER RABBI

See also: INTELLECT, INTELLIGENCE, KNOWLEDGE, SCHOLARS, STUDY, TRUTH, WISDOM

SCRIPTURE

Where there is Scripture, there is wisdom.

A passage from Scripture can yield many meanings, just as a hammer splits one rock into many fragments.
                TALMUD: *Sanhedrin*, 34a

See also: GOD, TORAH, TRUTH, WISDOM

SECRETS

❉ What three know is no longer a secret.

If you tell your secret to three, ten will know it.

Secrets are easier heard than kept.

❉ Your friend has a friend: don't tell him.

To be in on a secret is no blessing.

❋ The tongue has no bones, so it's very loose.

❋ Don't tell a secret in a field of mounds.

Don't tell a secret even to an ape.

❋ When wine goes in, secrets come out.

It is easy to get a fool to reveal a secret.

Fools and children cannot keep secrets.

The secrets of men are as different as their faces.
—adapted from TALMUD, *Berakoth*, 58a

If you never repeat what you are told, you will fare none
the worse.   BEN SIRACH, *Ecclesiasticus*, 19 : 9

❋ What you hide from an enemy don't tell a friend.
IBN GABIROL, *Choice of Pearls*

A sage when asked, "How do you hide a secret?" answered,
"I make my heart its grave."   IBN GABIROL

❋ Your secret is your prisoner; once you reveal it, you
become its slave.   IBN GABIROL

See also: ADAGES, GOSSIP, SILENCE, SLANDER, TALK

SECURITY

A man who does not own a piece of land is not a complete
[secure] man.   TALMUD: *Yebamoth*, 63a

See also: MONEY, POWER, SAFETY, STRENGTH, SURVIVAL

SELF

If I shall be like him, who will be like me?

The hen hears the rooster's sermon—and searches for its
own kernel of corn.

To flee from God is to flee into the self.
—adapted from PHILO

❋ If I am not for myself, who will be for me? And if I
am only for myself, what am I? And if not now—when?
HILLEL in *Sayings of the Fathers*, 1 : 14

If I am here, all is here; and if I am not here, who is here?
                    HILLEL in TALMUD: *Sukkah*, 53a

The I is the soul, which endures.
                                        NACHMAN OF BRATSLAV

See also: CHARACTER, HONOR, INDIVIDUALITY, MAN, SELF-
    ESTEEM, SELFISHNESS

SELF-CENTEREDNESS

❋ When you sit in a hot bath, the whole city feels warm.

In a mirror, everyone sees his best friend.

See: EGOTISM

SELF-DECEPTION

❋ To assume is to fool oneself.

❋ At a distance, you fool others; close, you fool yourself.

The girl who can't dance tells herself the orchestra can't
    keep time.

Our ears often do not hear what our tongues utter.

He acts like a man of means because he owns a head of
    cabbage.

The wisest of men can fool himself.

❋ Those who chase happiness run away from contentment.
                                        Hasidic saying

See also: CHARACTER, CONCEIT, EGOTISM, FOLLY, REASON,
    VANITY

SELF-ESTEEM

❋ The sun will set without your help.

❋ The girl who can't dance says the orchestra can't keep
    time.

If you lose your self-respect, you also lose the respect of
    others.

It is better to be alone than demeaned.

Three things enlarge a man's spirit [self-esteem]: a beautiful home, a beautiful wife, and beautiful garb.

TALMUD, *Berakoth*, 57b

Don't crave to sit at the table of kings: your own table is better than theirs; and so is your crown.

Sayings of the Fathers, 6 : 5

Don't let your wife, your son, or your friend dominate you.

BEN SIRACH, *Ecclesiasticus*, 33 : 20

Eat less and dress better.

—adapted from IBN TIBBON

See also: CONCEIT, CHARACTER, EGOTISM, HONOR, VANITY

SELF-IMPROVEMENT

"Do better," a peasant said to Rabbi Bunim, when he purchased some item. This became Rabbi Bunim's motto: "Do better."

If a man makes a harness for his beast, how much more should he fashion a harness for his impulses—which prompt him to lead a good or evil life.

TALMUD J.: *Sanhedrin*

It is not enough to appeal to a man to improve his ways; help him do so.   THE KORETSER RABBI

See also: AMBITION, GROWTH, INTELLIGENCE, SELF-ESTEEM, STUDY, WISDOM

SELF-KNOWLEDGE

❊ "Barking dogs don't bite," but they don't know it.

SHOLEM ALEICHEM

See also: ANIMALS, MAN

SELF-MOCKERY

❊ One of life's greatest mysteries is how the boy who wasn't good enough to marry your daughter can be the father of the smartest grandchild in the world.

❊ If a suit doesn't fit, it may be because you have grown smaller.   "THE CHOFETZ CHAIM"

SELF-PITY

I felt sorry for myself, because I had no shoes—until I met a man who had no feet.

See also: EGOTISM, MAN: HUMAN TYPES

SELFISHNESS

❋ When the streets are muddy, shoemakers rejoice.

He loves everyone—from a distance.

❋ Better a grape for me than two figs for thee.

To hoard is worse than to steal.

❋ A man who offers sympathy to someone bereaved a year ago is like a doctor who asks a man who has broken a leg to break it again—so that the doctor can show his skill.   TALMUD: *Mo'ed Katan*, 21b

See also: ALTRUISM, CHARITY, EGOTISM, GOOD DEEDS, KINDNESS, SYMPATHY

SENSE (SEYKHL)

❋ When the Lord wants to break a man's heart, he gives him *seykhl* [good sense].

You can't live with someone else's *seykhl* [brain].

Seykhl has free will.

❋ Some things are clever only the first time.

To have luck but no sense is like carrying a sock full of holes.

The angel who mediates between man and God is *seykhl*.
                                        ABRAHAM IBN EZRA

With *seykhl*, you have everything; without *seykhl*, life is a desert.   SAMUEL HA-NAGID

Seykhl is the very root of wisdom.   SAMUEL HA-NAGID

Man's best gift is his *seykhl*.   MOSES IBN EZRA

❋ When *seykhl* is crooked, who can repair it?
                                        GERONDI

A man of good sense guards his tongue and attends to his
   own affairs.   IBN GABIROL

Lost *seykhl* can't be recovered.   IBN GABIROL

See also: FOLLY, FORESIGHT, INTELLIGENCE, JUDGMENT,
REALISM, WISDOM, PRUDENCE

SENSITIVITY

When a student knows that his teacher is able to answer
   him, he may ask a question; otherwise, he should not.
                     TALMUD: *Hullin*, 6a

Address another man in the language he understands; do
   not use literary speech with the uneducated, nor vulgarity with the learned.   *Zohar*

See also: COMPASSION, CONSIDERATION, DECORUM, MAN-
NERS, SPEECH

SENTIMENT

Note. The attitude of Jews to the expression of sentiment
is as un–Anglo-Saxon as is that of Italians or Hindus.
(See Author's Preface: "A Word to Non-Jews.") Jews
do not regard "a stiff upper lip" as a sign of superior
character: they expect emotions to be expressed, shared
with (and therefore enjoyed by) others. To an Englishman, Jews no doubt seem maudlin, for they do love
heightened effect, hyperbole, *shmaltz*; and they do rush
to identify with the suffering or troubles of others; and
they do not think it "unmanly" to weep or carry on at
funerals.

   Second generation Jews (in England and the United
States) learned to restrain their readiness to laugh, cry,
moan, or gloat. The Waspicization of behavior has led
to a marked toning-down of visible and audible emotional levels. Such deprivation may find special rewards
in the Jewish sayings in these pages.   —L.R.

The gift is not as nice as the sentiment.

❋ Sweet words can't warm you; sweet thoughts can.

See also: COMPASSION, CONSIDERATION, DECORUM, GIVING,
KINDNESS, MANNERS, SENSITIVITY

SEPHARDIM

See GLOSSARY

SERPENT

Note. Many and wondrous are the tales men have spun about serpents, perhaps because the snake sloughs off its skin, apparently rejuvenating itself—thus achieving immortality. The Mesopotamian goddess of life, for instance, was "the divine serpent, lady of life."*

Among the Jews, the reptile symbolized wisdom and even smacked of sanctity: the divine sign of Moses' mission was his staff's turning into a snake (Exodus, 4 : 2–4). The serpent was also believed to possess singular medicinal powers; Moses, you remember, fashioned a snake out of brass to cure the Israelites in the wilderness.

In the Bible, the serpent was not condemned to crawl on its belly until after it had persuaded Eve to eat the apple on the Tree of Knowledge (in Greek mythology, a serpent guarded the golden apples in the Garden of the Hesperides) and Jews were thereafter forbidden to eat reptilian fare (Leviticus, 19 : 26). One of the miraculous aspects of the Great Temple in Jerusalem, said the rabbis, was the fact that the snakes within its capacious precincts never bit a human being (*Pirke Abot*, 5 : 8).

An ancient Brahmin fable recounts that the Lord of the Universe sent an immense snake down to earth, which gave birth to ten thousand others—which became "sins in the hearts of men."

—L.R.

See EVE

SERVANTS

The servant is often nobler than the master.

The new [servant] may be true, but the old is gold.

See also: AUTHORITY, CONSIDERATION, SENSITIVITY, STATUS

---

* See Theodor H. Gaster, *op. cit.*, pp. 338–39.

SERVICE

❋ A candle lights others, and consumes itself.

See also: CHARITY, COOPERATION, HELP

SEX

Note. The most important single comment one can make
about the attitude of Jews to sex, I think, is that Jews
consider sexual appetites normal, God-given, not sinful,
morally satisfiable within marriage. Judaism raises no
serious problems about the "evil," "impurity," or car-
nality of the body: Man's body is holy, being God's
creation, God's gift, God's design. How, then, can man's
divinely endowed needs and functions—if moderately,
properly expressed, in marriage—be tinged with sin?
Sex is treated with surprising ease and "modernity" in
rabbinical thinking: Body and soul form a unity; neither
is purer or wickeder than the other; when a mortal commits a sin the soul is as responsible as the body.

Rabbinical decisions on cohabitation, marriage, divorce, often anticipate modern psychology and sex
hygiene. Chastity was enjoined as a premarital duty:
early marriages were therefore encouraged; girls were
not scorned for not marrying, if they so decided; cohabitation was considered laudable (especially on the
eve of the Sabbath), since it would produce children.
Modesty is prized, as in all other aspects of human
conduct. Moderation in sex is considered sensible. The
avoidance of temptation is stressed. Illicit sex was held
sinful, as was promiscuity; prostitution was totally re-
jected. Under Biblical law, sodomy was a crime; but
female homosexuality, though held to be abhorrent and
scandalous, was not punishable.

Under rabbinical law, a husband and wife are not permitted to come into close physical contact, much less
cohabit, throughout the time of her menstruation, or for
seven days afterward. On the seventh day, the wife is
required to take a bath in running water, or in a bath
expressly built for that purpose: a *mikve*.

A community of Jews was strictly obligated to maintain a community bathhouse. The rules and regulations
governing the *mikve* are quite detailed; in fact, a whole
section of the Mishnah explores this subject. Today, only

very religious Jewish women observe the *mikve* custom
—or attend a bathhouse for *mikves* such as were found
in profusion in Europe and on the Lower East Side.

—L.R.

❈ If you're going to do something wrong, at least enjoy it.

Man has a small organ; the more he feeds it the more it
needs—and vice versa.   TALMUD: *Sukkah*, 52

Man's shame is between his legs, a fool's between his
cheeks.   MOSES IBN EZRA, *Shirat Yisrael*

See also: LOVE, LUST, MARRIAGE, MEN AND WOMEN, PAS-
SION, WOMEN

SHADKHN

Note. Because of the great importance Jews attached to
marriage, as a sacred obligation to God and a necessity
for the survival of Israel, the institution of the *shadkhn*,
the professional matchmaker and marriage broker, grew
up—and thrived. Unmarried girls were a pain in the
heart of the Jewish community, no less than her parents;
bachelors were considered selfish shirkers of their responsibility to "go forth and multiply."

A *shadkhn* would enter in his record of marriageable
males or females a careful list of the scholars, teachers,
rabbis, in the family background. The more the learning,
the higher the *yikhes* (honor) and the greater the
DOWRY (*q.v.*). Successful Jews sought to marry their
daughters to promising scholars, not potential rich men.
The *shadkhonim* performed a most valuable function in
matching marital possibilities, effecting meetings between young men and women who would not otherwise
know each other, for they often lived in different villages,
and at remote distances. (See headnotes for BACHELORS,
MARRIAGE, SCHOLARS.)   —L.R.

See MARRIAGE

SHAME

❈ Only man was endowed with shame.

Better pain in your heart than shame on your face.

❋ Better be ridiculed than shamed.

He who has no shame before the world has no fear before God.

There is always hope for the man who is capable of being ashamed.   TALMUD: *Nedarim*, 20a

❋ To shame a man in public is like shedding his blood.
                                   TALMUD: *Baba Mezi'a*, 68b

Shame not others and you will not be shamed by them.
                                   TALMUD: *Mo'ed Katan*, 9b

It is better for a man to cast himself into an oven than to shame a comrade in public.   TALMUD: *Berakoth*, 43b

The man who commits a transgression, and is filled with shame, has his sins forgiven.   TALMUD: *Berakoth*, 12b

There is a great difference between the man who feels shame in his soul and the man who is ashamed only before his fellow man.   TALMUD: *Ta'anith*, 15a

Shame is an iron fence against sin.   *Orhot Tsadikim*

Many precepts of the Torah are fulfilled not because of piety but only out of shame.
                        —adapted from BAHYA IBN PAQUDA

Be ashamed before God as you are before His creatures.
                        HASDAI, *Ben ha-Melekh ve-ha-Nazir*

Since dishonor is habitual with a liar, he is continually attended by shame.
                        BEN SIRACH, *Ecclesiasticus*, 20 : 26

An undeserved title brings more shame than honor.
                                   "THE CHOFETZ CHAIM"

See also: ADVICE, CHARITY, PIETY, REPENTANCE, SIN/SIN-NERS, SOUL

SHIRKERS

He who is slack at his work is brother to him who destroys.
                                   Book of Proverbs, 18 : 9

The sleeping cat doesn't catch a rat.

ABRAHAM IBN EZRA, Shirim

See also: ADVICE, AMBITION, COOPERATION, HELP, LAZINESS, SUCCESS, WORK

SHLEMIEL

Note. Who knows where this delectable word originated? Perhaps from Adelbert von Chamisso's 1814 classic, *Peter Schlemihls Wunderbare Geschichte* (a fable in which Peter sold his soul to Satan—and lost his shadow); or from the name of the leader of the tribe of Simeon, one Shlumiel, who (according to Numbers, 2) always lost his battles while other Hebrew generals were winning theirs; or (possibly) as a variant of *shlimazl.* In any case, a *shlemiel,* though closely related to a *shlimazl* (*q.v.*), is more precisely a simpleton, a gull, a pipsqueak; clumsy, submissive, uncomplaining, naive; a Caspar Milquetoast writ large—and in Yiddish.

—L.R.

❋ The *shlemiel* falls on his back and breaks his nose.

❋ When a *shlemiel* takes a bath, he forgets to wash his face.

When a *shlemiel* kills a rooster, it hops; when he winds up a clock, it stops.

❋ A *shlemiel* wonders if a flea has a navel.

When a *shlemiel* scalds his tongue on hot (soup), he then blows on the cold.

When he falls on straw, the *shlemiel* hits a stone.

SHOLEM ALEICHEM

See also: ADVICE, FOOLS, LUCK, MISFORTUNE, NEBBEKH, SHLIMAZL

SHLIMAZL

Note. The word comes from the German *schlimm* ("bad") and the Hebrew *mazl* ("luck"), but a *shlimazl* is thought of as more than simply unlucky. He is the chronic loser, patsy, fall-guy, pigeon. I use these slang words because *shlimazl* is only one of many vivid words, coined in Yiddish, to find a wryly affectionate description for psychological types. A *shlimazl* may also be characterized in psychiatric nomenclature as one predisposed to be victimized, one "accident prone." So *shlimazl* conveys the idea of one doomed (innocently) to fail *and* (perhaps) masochistically inclined to cooperate with the inequitable fates.

❋ If a *shlimazl* [luckless one] sold umbrellas, it would stop raining; if he sold candles, the sun would never set; and if he made coffins, people would stop dying.

❋ A *shlimazl* buys a suit with two pair of pants and promptly burns a hole in the jacket.

When a *shlimazl* sells an umbrella, the sun comes out.

❋ A *shlemiel* is always spilling hot soup—down the neck of a *shlimazl*.

Only *shlimazls* believe in *mazl* (luck).

When a *shlimazl* winds a clock, it stops.

When it rains gold, it is the fate of the *shlimazl* to be under a roof.

See also: FATE, FORTUNE, LUCK, MISFORTUNE, NEBBECH, SHLEMIEL

SHOFAR (SHOPHAR)

The Shofar (ram's horn blown in the Synagogue during Rosh Hashanah and Yom Kippur) has a profound meaning. It says: "Awake, ye sleepers, and ponder your deeds. Remember your Creator, and return to Him in penitence. Be not among those who miss reality in their pursuit of shadows, and waste their years in a quest for vain things. Look to your souls. Examine your acts. Forsake evil, all of its ways and thoughts, so that God may have mercy on you."   MAIMONIDES

The shofar is a prayer without words.

SAUL LIEBERMAN

See GLOSSARY: PESACH

SICKNESS

The prayers of the sick are more effective than the prayers of others, and are answered first.

RASHI, *Commentaries on the Pentateuch, Genesis*

See also: DISEASE, DOCTORS, HEALTH, MEDICINE

SIDDUR

Note. The *Siddur*, which is the collected "order" of prayers, is the most widely used single book in Judaism. It is curious that although prayers are found in the Torah, in the Prophets (Abraham, Hannah, Jonah) and in the Book of Psalms, Jewish prayers were not formally collected until the year 500 of the Christian Era. Why? Because the rabbinical tradition forbade writing down the Oral Law—which included prayers. The Talmud contains the *meditations* of individual sages and saints, and is crowded with discussions of prayer which fashioned rules and ordinances anent praying. Psalms (55 : 18) alludes to "evening, morning and noon" prayers; Daniel faced Jerusalem and "kneeled . . . thrice a day and prayed" (Daniel 6 : 11).

The exact time when formal prayers were instituted among Jews remains obscure. Communal praying may have grown up simply as a substitute for Temple sacrifices. In Babylon, prayer surely served to preserve and intensify religious fidelity. The early *siddurim* included comments on customs, law, religious services, etc. The most famous *siddurim* are the early ones of Rabbi Amram Gaon of Sura (875), Saadia Gaon, Maimonides (for the Sephardic rite), Rashi, Rabbi Simcha (which established Ashkenazic rites).

Today's *Siddur* is an anthology of 4000 years of prayers, poems, liturgical hymns—kept up to date: a prayer for the state of Israel was introduced in 1948. See PRAYER.

—L.R.

SIGH

✳ If you can't give money, at least give a sympathetic sigh.

A sigh can break a man in two. TALMUD: *Berakoth*, 58b

See also: EMOTION, FEELINGS, SUFFERING

SILENCE

❊ Eloquent silence often is better than eloquent speech.

Silence is the fence that encloses wisdom; but mere silence is not wisdom.

❊ The man who is silent tells us something.

❊ Speech is difficult, but who can keep quiet?

If a word be worth one shekel, silence is worth two.
TALMUD: Megillah, 18a

For many afflictions, silence is the best remedy.
TALMUD: Megillah, 18a

Silence (may be) equivalent to admission.
TALMUD: Yebamoth, 87b

If silence is good for the wise, how much better it is for fools.   TALMUD: Pesahim, 98b

❊ Press your lips together: don't be in a hurry to answer.
TALMUD: 'Abodah Zarah, 35a

❊ Silence is restful: it rests the heart, the lungs, the larynx, the tongue, the lips—and the mouth.   Zohar

❊ I grew up among wise men and learned that nothing is better than silence.   Sayings of the Fathers, 1 : 17

Silence protects wisdom.
AKIBA in Sayings of the Fathers, 3 : 19

Where words abound, sin will not be wanting; but he who holds his tongue acts wisely.
Book of Proverbs, 10 : 19

❊ One [kind of] man remains silent because he has nothing to say; another keeps silent because he knows it is the time for it.   BEN SIRACH, Ecclesiasticus, 20 : 6

Both a boaster and a fool miss the fitting time for silence.
BEN SIRACH, Ecclesiasticus, 20 : 6

❊ I am better able to retract what I did not say than what I did.   IBN GABIROL

You may regret your silence once, but you will regret your speech twice.   IBN GABIROL

Guard your tongue as you treasure your wealth.

IBN GABIROL

❋ Man was given two ears and one tongue, so that he may listen more than speak.

HASDAI, Ben ha-Melekh ve-ha-Nazir

Unless you speak wisely, keep silent.

IMMANUEL OF ROME

See also: BOASTING, FOOLS, GOSSIP, LIARS, SLANDER, TALK, TRUTH, WISDOM, WISE MEN

SIN/SINNERS

Note. Judaism defines two types of sin: against God, and against other men. A sin against the Deity is expiated by direct confession (a rabbi cannot serve as intermediary), true remorse, and "a return to God." But a sin against man must be "absolved" by a direct plea for forgiveness from the one sinned against: God will not forgive such sins, although he punishes them.

Judaism contains no concept of Original Sin, or inherited guilt, or the innate shame or impurity of man's flesh.

See headnote for YOM KIPPUR.   —L.R.

❋ No man suffers for another's sins: he has enough of his own.

❋ If not for fear, sinning would be sweet.

Never mind the remorse; just don't commit the sin.

Sin takes money, too.

The knowledge of Scripture is no obstacle to sin.

❋ A Litvak is so clever that he repents *before* he sins.

As long as a man does not sin, he is feared; as soon as he sins, he is afraid.

❋ When the sin is sweet, repentance is not so bitter.

❋ A sin repeated seems permitted.

TALMUD: Yomah, 86b

It is better to sin out of good intentions than to conform with evil [greedy] intent.   TALMUD: <i>Nazir</i>, 23b

Whoever can pray on behalf of his neighbor and fails to do
so is [called] a sinner.   TALMUD: *Berakoth*, 12b

Three things sap a man's strength: worry, travel, and sin.
                                   TALMUD: *Gittin*, 70a

Man does not commit a sin unless he is possessed by folly.
                                   TALMUD: *Sotah*, 3a

Wives save us from sin.   TALMUD: *Yebamoth*, 63b

Tremble before committing a minor sin, for it may lead you
to a major one.   TALMUD: *Derekh Erets*, 1 : 26

Whoever destroys any useful thing is guilty of a sin.
                                   TALMUD: *Sabbath*, 105

Leave them alone: let men sin unwittingly rather than
willfully.   TALMUD: *Shabbath*, 148b

✤ If the Evil Impulse says: "Sin—God will forgive you,"
don't heed it.   TALMUD: *Hagigah*, 16a

Sinners should not be excluded as unworthy of joining their
fellow Jews in prayer; frankincense of an offensive odor
was included in the incense used in the holy Temple.
                                   TALMUD: *Kerithoth*, 6b

✤ The eye and the heart are sin's agents.
                                   TALMUD J.: *Berakoth*, 1

A sinner is like a man who sees open manacles—and puts
his hands in them.   TALMUD J.: *Nedarim*, 9 : 1

✤ Sin is sweet in the beginning, but bitter in the end.
                                   TALMUD J.: *Shabbath*, 14 : 3

It is better to be called a fool all of one's days than to sin
for one hour.   MISHNAH: *Edoyoth*, 5 : 10

To make another man sin is worse than to kill him; for it
is to doom him not only in this world but in the next.
                                   MIDRASH: *Numbers Rabbah*, 21

From the moment a man thinks about committing a sin,
he is faithless to God.
                                   MIDRASH: *Leviticus Rabbah*, 8 : 5

The biggest sinner is the one who regrets his previous goodness.   *Zohar*

❋ A little sin is big when a big man commits it.
ABRAHAM IBN EZRA, *Commentary to Genesis*, 32 : 9

It is wise to work as well as study Torah, for between the two, you will forget to sin.
Sayings of the Fathers, 2 : 2

Consider three things, and you will avoid sin: Above you is an all-seeing eye, an all-hearing ear, and a record of all your acts. *Sayings of the Fathers*, 3 : 1

Righteousness exalts a nation—but sin is a people's ruin.
Book of Proverbs, 14 : 34

❋ The man who has knowledge but no fear of sin is like a carpenter without tools. *Abot de Rabbi Nathan*

Don't kindle the coals of a sinner: you may be scorched by the flame of his fire.
BEN SIRACH, *Ecclesiasticus*, 8 : 10

Do not envy a sinner: you don't know what disaster awaits him. BEN SIRACH, *Ecclesiasticus*, 9 : 11

❋ Pride is the reservoir of sin.
BEN SIRACH, *Ecclesiasticus*, 10 : 13

Sin destroys the soul of man.
BEN SIRACH, *Ecclesiasticus*, 21 : 2

Run from sin as from a snake; if you approach, it will bite you. BEN SIRACH, *Ecclesiasticus*, 21 : 2

The path of sinners is paved smooth, but at its end lies the pit of Hell. BEN SIRACH, *Ecclesiasticus*, 21 : 10

Whoever thinks he has not sinned carries great pride within himself and that is worse than sin.
BAHYA IBN PAQUDA, *Duties of the Heart*

At first, sin is like a spider's web; but in the end, it is like the cable of a ship.
RABBI AKIBA in MIDRASH: *Genesis Rabbah*, 22 : 6

Let man love man and mercy win, From Thy grace, not his sin! IBN GABIROL, *Choice of Pearls*

❋ Beware of the pious fool, and the wise sinner.
IBN GABIROL, *Choice of Pearls*

✻ Were I to cut myself off from my brethren because of their sins, I would be alone.   IBN GABIROL

We are like mice: one man eats the cheese and all men are blamed.   IBN VERGA, *Shebet Yehuda*

We should not tempt even an honest man to sin, much less a thief, for that is like putting fire next to tow.
          MARTIN BUBER, MIDRASH: *Tanhuma*, 26b

There is a type of sinner who does evil with a policy, guided by an "ism." "I am no ordinary thief or murderer," he says, "I am a communist and I believe in communism." But sinning with a policy, says the Torah, is unforgivable.   "THE CHOFETZ CHAIM"

See also: EVIL, FEAR, GOD, GOOD, HEREAFTER, PUNISHMENT, PIETY, RETRIBUTION, SHAME, SUFFERING, VIRTUE

SINCERITY

✻ Better an insincere "Good morning" than a sincere "Go to hell."

It is the eye that says what the heart means.

✻ An honest slap is better than a dishonest kiss.

Words that come from the heart enter the heart.
          MOSES IBN EZRA, *Shirat Yisrael*

See also: ALTRUISM, GOOD, HONESTY, HONOR, TREACHERY, TRUTH, VIRTUE

SKEPTICISM

The reddest apple can contain a worm.

If God will provide, why doesn't He?

An example is not proof; it is only an example.

What was written and is believed is not thereby proved true.

✻ Once a miracle happens, it shows it's not a miracle.

Why is it that miracles don't provide food?

✻ An act of reason is a miracle.

✻ Rather a skeptic than a fool.

✻ People who say "For instance" do not prove anything—except "for instance."

✻ The Torah does not tell us to believe what is absurd.
JOSEPH AEBO, *Sefer ha-Ikarim*

See also: ADVICE, EVIDENCE, IRONIES, LOGIC, PROOF, REALISM, REASON, SUSPICION

SKILL

To have a skill is to be free from anxiety.

To know a trade is to own a kingdom.

A trade is a shield against poverty.

✻ Nothing is difficult—if you only know how.

That house is blessed where the man has a trade.

✻ It is not good to have too many trades: many trades, few blessings.

✻ A man at work is the equal of the most learned.

Good tools are half an artisan.

A handicraft honors those who engage in it.
TALMUD: *Nedarim*, 49b

Master a trade, and God will provide.
MIDRASH: *Ecclesiastes Rabbah*, 6

✻ Together with the study of Torah, learn a trade.
MIDRASH: *Ecclesiastes Rabbah*, 9

The man who has a trade is like a woman who has a husband, or a vineyard which has a fence.
MIDRASH: *Ecclesiastes Rabbah*, 10 : 6

✻ A carpenter without tools is not a carpenter.
MIDRASH: *Exodus Rabbah*, 40 : 1

To have a trade is to have a fence: it protects you against trespassers.
Tosephta: Kiddushin, 1 : 11

A famine may last seven years, yet passes the artisan's gate.
RABBI RABA, TALMUD: *Sanhedrin*, 29a

The master craftsman does everything himself; the fool hires a passer-by.
Book of Proverbs

See also: BUSINESS, WORK

SLANDER

❋ The tongue is a dangerous enemy.

❋ What is candor to your face is slander behind your back.

An angry tongue is worse than a wicked hand.

❋ If there were no listeners, there would be no backbiters.

❋ It is better to speak good of yourself than bad about others.

Whoever slanders a fellow man denies God.

❋ Some men are prone to steal, but all men seem prone to slander.

If you think of yourself, you will not speak badly of others.

❋ The slanderer, like the liar and the hypocrite, will find no place in the world to come.

❋ The man who slanders hurts three people: the man slandered, the man to whom the slander is uttered—and himself.   TALMUD: 'Arakin, 15b

❋ It is a duty to say what should be heard, and a duty not to say what should not be heard.
                                    TALMUD: Yebamoth, 65b

A good man who speaks evil is like a palace next to a tannery: one defect destroys all the grandeur.
                                    TALMUD: Shabbath, 56b

❋ Slander is in the same category with murder.
                                    TALMUD J.: Pe'ah, 1

❋ Slander is worse than weapons; for weapons hurt from near, slander from afar.   TALMUD J.: Pe'ah, 1 : 1

Hot coals, cooled on the outside, cool within; but slander, cooled outwardly, does not cool inside.
                                    TALMUD J.: Pe'ah, 1 : 1

❋ Even if all of a slander is not believed, half of it is.
                                    MIDRASH: Genesis Rabbah, 56 : 4

When Rabban Gamaliel told his servant to buy the best meat in the market, the slave brought home a tongue. The next day Rabban Gamaliel asked him to buy the worst thing in the market and again the servant brought

home a tongue, wisely saying, "There is nothing better
than a good tongue, and nothing worse than an evil one."
                          MIDRASH: *Leviticus Rabbah*, 33

Scripture says, "Cursed art thou [serpent] above all creatures," because the serpent uttered slander.
                              MIDRASH: *Tanhuma*, 24a

If others speak ill of you, let the worst they say seem a
trifle; if you speak ill of others, let the trivial seem
enormous.   *Sifre*, 89b

❊ God will accept repentance for all sins except one:
giving another man a bad name.   *Zohar*

A fickle man sows discord, and a whisperer separates
friends.   *Book of Proverbs*, 16 : 28

Righteous lips cover up hatred; but he who lets out slander
is a fool.   *Book of Proverbs*, 10 : 18

❊ For thirteen years I taught my tongue not to tell a lie;
for the next thirteen, I taught it to tell the truth.
                              THE KORETSER RABBI

See also: FOOLS, GOSSIP, HYPOCRITES, LIES/LIARS, TRUTH,
VIRTUE

SLAVERY

Note.
The Jews, hunted out of Spain in 1492, were in turn
cruelly expelled from Portugal. Some took refuge on the
African coast. Eighty years later the descendants of the
men who had committed or allowed these enormities were
defeated in Africa, whither they had been led by their
king, Dom Sebastian. Those who were not slain were
offered as slaves at Fez to the descendants of the Jewish
exiles from Portugal. "The humbled Portuguese nobles,"
the historian narrates, "were comforted when their pur-
chasers proved to be Jews, for they knew that they had
humane hearts."   —Morris Joseph, *Judaism as Creed
                                        and Life*, 1891.

Wars, captivity, slavery, ransom, selling human bodies
—are as old as mankind. The most enlightened Greeks
held slaves to be but "animated tools" (the phrase is
Aristotle's) who had no rights whatsoever. (In Athens,
the ratio of slaves to freemen was about 5 to 1.) To the

Romans, defeat clearly justified enslavement, as it did to the Assyrians, Aztecs, Chaldeans, Egyptians, Persians, Chinese, *et alia*.

The attitude of the ancient Hebrews takes on particular significance in an historical context: they purchased Canaanite (non-Hebrew) "servants" from neighboring tribes or peoples—and these slaves became proselytes: the males being circumcised, the females made subject to Jewish laws regarding women, diet, hygiene, marriage, etc. The Hebrew master was admonished by Torah not to be brutal to his "servants" (the word in Scripture often used for slaves)—not to be either unkind or unjust.

In Israel itself, there were no slave markets. The forcible capture, enslavement, or sale of a human was a criminal offense. The Hebrews were obligated to give any fugitive slave asylum, and not to surrender him or her to his owners; and a fugitive who reached Palestine was accorded full legal freedom.

A Hebrew could sell his or her own services to another Hebrew, for six years. Many did so—in order to live, in order to pay their debts, out of a desire to be assured of a home, protection, etc. After the six-year period, the male servant-slave was released. A female servant-slave (if she had not become wed to her owner or his son) could not be sold; she had to be redeemed by her own family. All Hebrew slaves, including those who chose to remain with their masters after their six-year servitude, were legally freed in "the year of Jubilee" (*Leviticus* 25 : 40). Jewish masters and slaves were often on "family" terms; many slaves inherited property, or were accepted as the husbands or wives of their master's children. (All these conditions of servitude became impossible or irrelevant after the Babylonian Exile.)

Centuries later, the Talmud instructs masters to treat their slaves as equals (*Kiddushin* 20): "You should not eat white bread, and he black; you should not drink old wine, and he new; you should not sleep on a feather bed, and he on straw." The master's feet could be washed by a disciple, a student, or his son—but not by his slave (*Mekilta*, a midrashic tract, on Exodus 21 : 2).

Small wonder that it was said that "he who gets a Hebrew as a slave gets a master."

—L.R.

❋ A man can have nothing worse over him than another man.

❋ A slave should never be addressed as "slave," for the very name is contemptible.

To be immobile is to be in chains.
                              MOSES IBN EZRA: *Shirat Yisrael*

❋ Ransom a captive before you feed the poor: no act of charity is greater.   JOSEPH CARO, *Shulhan Aruk*

Every moment of delay in ransoming a captive is like shedding his blood.   JOSEPH CARO, *Shulhan Aruk*

Revolution is the right of slaves.
                    H. LEIVICK (LEIVICK HALPERN) in *The Golem*

See also: FREEDOM, INDEPENDENCE, POWER

SLEEP

❋ Sleep is the best doctor.

❋ The one-eyed need sleep, too.

Less sleep, more living.

No punishment is worse than a night without sleep.

❋ Sleep is a thief.

Sleep faster, we need the pillows.

When you go to sleep on an empty stomach, you count the beams on the ceiling.

Sleeping is one-sixtieth part of death.
                              TALMUD: *Berakoth*, 57b

He who reaps in the summer acts wisely; he who sleeps during harvest acts shamefully.
                              Book of Proverbs, 10 : 5

If a man can't learn without napping at noon, let him nap —but not too long.   JOSEPH CARO

Even in a brief sleep, do not be intent on your pleasure, but on restoring your body to serve God.
                    —adapted from JOSEPH CARO, *Shulhan Aruk*

See also: DREAMS, HEALTH, MEDICINE

SNAKES

See SERPENT

SOCIETY

See: COMMUNITY, GOVERNMENT, ISRAEL, LAW, MAN, POLI-
TICS, SAFETY

SOLDIERS

Soldiers are braver after eating.

Soldiers do the fighting and generals are called heroes.

If one soldier knew what the other [enemy] thinks, there
would be no wars.

Better be a dog in peace than a soldier at war.

Those who hate the smell of powder should not go to war.

Men of the sword can't claim to be men of the Book.

TALMUD: 'Abodah Zarah, 17b

See also: COURAGE, VIOLENCE, WAR

SONS

Note. Apart from the preference for sons found in any
primitive, agricultural, or nomadic society (as workers,
warriors, defenders, and perpetuators of the tribe),
Jewry considered a son their *"Kaddish"—i.e.,* the reciter
of that prayer for a dead parent which helps the departed
soul find peace. Jewish couples who had no sons would
adopt an orphan to serve as their *Kaddish.*

The *bar mitzvah* ("son of the commandment" or
"man of duty") is a ceremony, *not* a confirmation. It is
held in a synagogue or temple when a thirteen-year-old
Jewish boy reaches the status, and assumes the duties,
of a "man." The *bar mitzvah* signifies that a young male
is now a "man of duty," committed to lifelong religious
and ethical obligations. He can now be counted as an
adult in the *minyan* of ten males required before religious services can begin, and he can be called to the
pulpit to recite a passage from the Torah.

The *bar mitzvah* ceremony is not an ancient one; it did not exist until the fourteenth century; and it is not a sacrament, nor a sacramental rite, for Orthodox Jews consider Jewishness something that does not require confirmation.

Ancient rabbinical sources hold that after his thirteenth birthday, a Jewish boy is responsible for observing the 613 (!) holy commandments. With all due respect to the elders, I feel obliged to record my wonder whether a careful accounting of this is kept, even in heaven.

—L.R.

To strike a grown son is to drive him to sin.

May you live to introduce your son to Torah, to marriage, and to good deeds. (Traditional blessing which is part of the circumcision ceremony.)

✻ Even if a man is a rabbi, when his father enters, the son must rise [in the presence of his pupils].
TALMUD: *Horayot*, 13b

✻ The only time a son should disobey his father is when [if] the father orders him to commit a sin.
TALMUD: *Yebamoth*, 5b

A son is his father's foot.   TALMUD: *Erubin*, 70b

Should a father order his son to throw gold into the sea, the son should obey.   TALMUD: *Kiddushin*, 32a

✻ One father can support ten sons, but ten sons seem unable to support one father.

There are four types of sons: the wise, the simple, the wicked—and the one who does not yet know how to ask questions.   *Mekilta* to *Exodus*, 13 : 14
(in the Haggada for Passover)

He who spares the rod hates his son.
Book of Proverbs, 13 : 24

A wise son makes a glad father;
But a foolish son is a grief to his mother.
Book of Proverbs, 10 : 1

A father is to be treated as a king.
Pirke de Rabbi Eliezer, 39

A bad son is like a sixth finger; to cut it off hurts, and to leave it is to be beset with a blemish.

IMMANUEL OF ROME

At five your son is your master, at ten your slave, at fifteen your double; after that, he is your friend or your enemy, depending on how he was raised.

HASDAI, *Ben ha-Melekh ve-ha-Nazir*

See also: CHILDREN, EDUCATION, FAMILY, FATHERS, ISRAEL, LEARNING, MOTHERS, PARENTS, SCHOLARS, SONS-IN-LAW

SONS-IN-LAW

❋ One of life's greatest mysteries is how the boy who wasn't good enough to marry your daughter can be the father of the smallest grandchild in the world.

Lighter than bran [worthless] is a son-in-law who lives in the house of his father-in-law.

TALMUD: *Baba Bathra*, 98b

He who lives in his mother-in-law's house for thirty days deserves a flogging.   TALMUD: *Kiddushin*, 12b

See also: DAUGHTERS-IN-LAW, MARRIAGE, MOTHERS-IN-LAW, PARENTS

SORROWS

No one knows the sorrow of another.

Sorrows thin our bones.

❋ The deeper the sorrow, the less voice it has.

Cut off the head and you'll end the sorrow.

Sorrows create ailments; happiness cures them.

One man can carry more sorrows than ten horses could bear.

The man who increases knowledge increases sorrow.

Ecclesiastes, 1 : 18

See also: MISFORTUNE, SUFFERING, TEARS

SOUL

Note. In the Talmud it is said that God created individual souls—when He created the world. When a child is born, his or her preassigned *neshomeh* (spirit) joins the body. But the Talmud nowhere mentions transmigration of the soul—i.e., its leaving the body after death. Many rabbis considered such stuff superstition—and a denial of monotheism. Yet mystics and ordinary folk clung to the idea. (The "mystery religions" of the East—in Persia, India, Egypt, among Greek cults—are full of transmigratory souls, who inhabit the bodies of mortals or animals.)

No precise distinction existed between body and soul until rabbinical (i.e., post-Biblical) days, when the Hebrew *neshomeh* came to mean that aspect of man that is spiritual, noncorporeal—and immortal. (The Jews were influenced in these metaphysical niceties by Greek thought.)

In the Middle Ages, Jewish cabalists were attracted to the idea of souls wandering around, as punishment, to atone for their sins; the concept (*galuth*) even filtered into an explanation for the dispersion of Jews from the Holy Land; and prayers referred to this as God's punishment "for our sins." In Orthodox Judaism, the idea of resurrection is important; the conception of bodily resurrection is linked to the immortality of the soul.

—L.R.

❋ Those who find a difference between soul and body have neither.

The body is a sponge; the soul is an abyss.

What soap is to the body, tears are to the soul.

❋ The smallest revenge poisons the soul.

A blind man lifted up a lame man to rob the King's orchard, and could not escape either complicity or punishment: in the same way, the soul and the body will be reunited for judgment.   MIDRASH, *Leviticus Rabbah*, 4 : 5

Is not the soul a guest in the body?
                    MIDRASH: *Leviticus Rabbah*, 32

My soul was also on Mount Sinai.
                    MIDRASH: *Exodus Rabbah*, 28 : 4

❋ When a soul is sent down from Heaven, it contains both male and female elements: the male part enters the male child, the female enters the female; and if they are worthy, God reunites them in marriage.   *Zohar*

❋ The soul is the Lord's candle.

Book of Proverbs, 20 : 27

(When dust returns to the earth), the spirit shall return to God, who gave it.   *Ecclesiastes*, 12 : 7

The man who injures the soul of another injures his own.

APOCRYPHA: *II Enoch*

Wisdom is to the soul as food is to the body.

ABRAHAM IBN EZRA

I have stilled and quieted my soul, and like a babe with his mother, my soul is now with me like a weaned child.

BAHYA IBN PAQUDA

Upon death, the soul goes out of one door and enters another.   —adapted from BAAL SHEM TOV

See also: GOD AND MAN, HEALTH, HEAVEN, HELL, HEREAFTER, RESURRECTION

SPEECH

❋ If a horse had anything to say, he would speak up.

The heart of fools is in their mouth; the mouth of the wise is in their heart.

All the world is on the tip of the tongue.

Had I been on Sinai, I would have asked God for two mouths: one for ordinary speech, and one for Torah; but now I think that since the world is ruined by man's one mouth, how much worse would it be if he had two!

TALMUD J.: *Berakoth*, 1 : 2

Let thine ears [too] hear what thy mouth speaketh.

TALMUD J.: *Berakoth*, 2 : 4

From a man's mouth you can tell who he is.   *Zohar*

A soothing tongue is a tree of life.

Book of Proverbs, 15 : 4

The mouth of the righteous is a fountain of life;
But the mouth of the wicked is filled with violence.
Book of Proverbs, 10 : 11

❀ What is lofty can be said in any language, and what is
mean should be said in none.   MAIMONIDES

❀ The tongue is the heart's pen and the mind's messenger.
          BAHYA IBN PAQUDA, *Duties of the Heart*

Consider the speech, not the speaker.
          CASPI, *Commentary on Yoreh Deah*

The worst of men is he whose tongue is mightier than his
mind.   MOSES IBN EZRA, *Shirat Yisrael*

❀ Man's chief superiority over animals is his power of
speech; if he abuses it, he is no higher than they.
          THE SASSOVER RABBI

❀ If a horse with four legs can sometimes stumble, how
much more can a man with only one tongue.
          SHOLEM ALEICHEM

See also: GOSSIP, GRAMMAR, LIARS, SENSITIVITY, SLANDER,
TALK, WORDS

SPIRIT

A broken spirit is hard to heal.

❀ Loneliness breaks the spirit.

When you have no choice, mobilize the spirit of courage.

See also: MAN, SOUL, SUFFERING

STATUS

Note. The most respected members of a Jewish community
were pious scholars (see headnote: SCHOLARS) and laymen called *balbatim*. These leaders possessed outstanding
character and reliability: the vulgar, however rich; the
ill-mannered, however successful; the nonrespecters of
learning, however flourishing—there were not *balbatish*,
and were not accorded the deference and esteem enjoyed by *balbatim*.

—L.R.

❀ Not everyone on the dais is distinguished.

❀ He is a *shammes* [guard] in a pickle factory. [Low man on anyone's totem pole.]

Be a servant to noblemen rather than chief of the vulgar.

❀ Food is cooked in a pot, but people praise the plate.

Better a footstool for a king than a king of fools.

The servant of a king is something of a king.

❀ A sage takes precedence over a king.
> —adapted from MISHNAH

❀ When a sage enters, all men should rise (unless they are at work).   TALMUD: *Kiddushin*, 33a

Before I was elected to the court, I would have thrown to the lions anyone who said, "Become a candidate"; afterwards, I would throw boiling water on anyone who suggested I resign.   TALMUD: *Menahoth*, 109

❀ If you must hang, choose a high tree.
> —adapted from TALMUD: *Pesahim*, 112a

❀ God loves those who do not insist upon their privileges.
> —adapted from TALMUD: *Pesahim*, 113a

Better a man of low rank who works for his living than one who puts on airs but has nothing to eat.
> *Book of Proverbs*

Burning thorns make much noise, as if to say: "We, too, are wood."   MIDRASH: *Ecclesiastes Rabbah*, 7

Rather be the tail among lions than the head among foxes.
> *Sayings of the Fathers*, 4 : 15

Don't crave to sit at the table of a king; your own table is better—and so is your crown.
> *Sayings of the Fathers*, 6 : 5

The sons of sages are not always sages—so that no one can think Torah is inherited, and so that the sages' sons do not hold themselves superior to others.
> —adapted from *Sayings of the Fathers*, 2 : 12

See also: ANCESTORS, CHARACTER, FAME, GOD, HONOR, HUMILITY, MONEY, POLITICS, POVERTY, POWER, RICHES, SAGES, TORAH

STRANGERS

Note.
"Love the stranger and the sojourner," Moses commands, "because you have been strangers in the land of Egypt." And this was said in those remote, savage times when the chief ambition of races and nations consisted in crushing and enslaving one another.
                                        —Leo Tolstoy

❋ A big blow from a stranger hurts less than a small blow from a friend.

He who has fed strangers may have fed angels [as did Abraham].

❋ The troubles of a stranger aren't worth an onion.

❋ A stranger's folly creates laughter; your own folly produces shame.

Respect a stranger, but suspect the stranger.

It is hard to eat bread at a stranger's table.
                                        TALMUD: *Bezah*, 32

How shall we sing the Lord's song in a strange land?
                                        Book of Psalms, 137 : 4

See also: CHARITY, DUTY, GOOD DEEDS, FRIENDS, KINDNESS, NEIGHBORS

STRENGTH

Separate reeds are weak and easily broken; but bound together they are strong and hard to tear apart [like Israel's unity].   MIDRASH: *Tanhuma, Nizavim*: 1

See also: ENDURANCE, ENERGY, POWER, WEAKNESS

STUBBORNNESS

❋ There is no cure for stubborness.

❋ Some men go from Heaven to Hell out of sheer stubbornness.

❋ Stubbornness is a disease.

He who stiffens his neck against many reproofs will suddenly be broken beyond repair.

Book of Proverbs, 29 : 2

God forgets the man who stubbornly rejects proof that he is wrong.   NACHMAN OF BRATSLAV

See also: ARGUMENT, BOASTING, CONCEIT, ERROR, SELFISHNESS

STUDENTS

What sacrifices was he not ready to bring, the Jewish youth who trudged afoot from the banks of the Danube to the banks of the Seine, bidding defiance to hunger and cold, only to drink in the words of some far-famed master! How he would wander about, a restless wayfarer, for half a year, across ditches and mountains and among brigands on his journey from Cologne to Venice for the sake of the Talmud explanations to be had from an Italian scholar?
—Louis Ginzberg, in *Students, Scholars and Saints*. The Jewish Publication Society of America, 1928, pp. 68–69.

See EDUCATION, KNOWLEDGE, LEARNING, SCHOLARS, STUDY, TEACHERS

STUDY

Note.

Centuries before the modern idea of adult education was evolved, Jews regarded it as a religious duty to band themselves together for study every morning before the labors of the day began, and every evening when the ghetto gates closed them off from association with the outside world.
—Cecil Roth. In *Essays on Jewish Booklore*, KTAV, New York, 1971, p. 179.

The tradition of study, the reverence for ideas, the inculcated passion to analyze and *know* has led many Jews, since the Middle Ages, to distinguish themselves in secular literature, secular philosophy, medicine, law, science. But the intellectual tradition began in faith—and was long hostile to the secular.

The Jews structured an entire culture around the core of prayer and study—and the latter flowed out of the former, as a co-equal part of man's sacred obligations. In studying or discussing Torah or Talmud, the pious Jew believed he was actually earning "a portion of bliss." So male Jews were always reading—even in markets, at country fairs, while "minding the store." Itinerant Jews —peddlers, salesmen—usually carried some part of the Talmud, Mishnah, or some collection of Midrashim, to read while away from home, to fulfill the "appointment" they had pledged.

The synagogue, from its inception (around 586 before the Christian Era, when Nebuchadnezzar drove the Jews into exile), was a place for both prayer and study (some experts say) and became the mortar of Jewish society, the carrier of cultural continuity, the motor that constantly regenerated the Jews' sense of identity. Prayer-and-study lent hope and meaning to poverty, persecution, perpetual insecurity, and repeated banishments. Study-prayer illuminated the hardest life, compensated for the harshest adversities, gave life a sense of purpose, admitted the humblest Jew to the company of prophets, sages, and saints. There was a certain ecstasy in the singsong verbalization of Talmud which a passer-by would hear issuing from a synagogue, a *Bet Midrash*, a Talmud Torah (school)—or a Jew's home.

The *shul*, the Yiddish word for "school," which the synagogue was called, was the capital, the center, the forum of Jewish communal life. Day and night men sat, read, prayed, studied, discoursed, debated there. Many synagogues never closed their doors. A pious Jew began and ended each day there. Men would drift from group to group in the *shul*, between prayers, listening with one ear to catch a word from those reciting or arguing.

The Talmud holds that God Himself goes from one *Bet Midrash* to another, and made it mandatory for Jews to build a *shul* as soon as a community contained ten males (a *minyan*)—and to support ten *batlanim* if need be: i.e., men who do no work but devote all their time to prayer-and-study, for the good of all Israel.

It was considered best to study in groups, because true learning could only be achieved, the Talmud said (*Berakoth*, 63), in group study. So virtually all of Jewry participated in a perpetual seminar on Torah and Talmud—which means a perpetual seminar on the most complex aspects of faith, metaphysics, truth, morals, duties, epistemology, etc. Every boy past the age of six (except for mental deficients) could read and write. They all became exegetes, dialecticians, amateur theologians. And *their* descendants enriched the knowledge, the technology, and the science of the West in proportions far greater than their number. (See headnote for SCHOLARS.)   —L.R.

✳ When I pray, I pray swiftly, because I am talking to God; when I study, I read slowly, because God is talking to me.

✳ Some men study so much, they don't have time to know.

Prayer without study is like a soul without a body.

✳ A scholar can't conduct a business; and a merchant has not enough time to study.

✳ Jerusalem was destroyed because the children did not attend school.   TALMUD: *Shabbath*, 119b

He who studies but does not repeat his lessons is as one who plants but does not enjoy the fruit.
                                        TALMUD: *Sanhedrin*, 90

Blessed were our ancestors, for their discipline was such that they were punished for falling asleep during their studies.   TALMUD: *Tamid*, 28a

Study is worth as much as ritual sacrifice.
                        —adapted from TALMUD: *Menahoth*, 110a

✳ The chief thing is not to study but to do.
                                Sayings of the Fathers, 1 : 17

Don't say, "I shall study when I find the time," because you may never find time.
                        HILLEL in *Sayings of the Fathers*, 2 : 4

If there is no bread there is no study [so support the students].   *Sayings of the Fathers*, 3 : 17

Do not neglect study because of your pleasures, or even for your occupation.   —attributed to MAIMONIDES

If a man can't learn without sleeping at noon, let him sleep —but not too long.   JOSEPH CARO

I weep because I can study God's law no more.
                                        A blind rabbi

Happy is the man who devotes his time to study, and he who resists temptation.   THE SLONIMER RABBI

See also: CHILDREN, EDUCATION, LEARNING, PEDAGOGY, TEACHERS

STUPIDITY

❋ Approach a goat from the back, a horse from the front, and a stupid man from no direction whatsoever.

❋ Some are so stupid they must search for a notch in a saw.

Don't ask the stupid a question, and don't give them an explanation.

Drunkards can sober up, but the stupid remain stupid.

❋ Why don't the stupid turn gray?

❋ No cure exists for stupidity.

❋ The stupid do not even understand stupidity.

To praise the stupid is to nourish their stupidity.

❋ Educating the stupid does not teach them how to be smart.

To the stupid, this world is very pleasant.

When the smart talk to the stupid, both act like fools.

You confront lions and ask of foxes?!
                              TALMUD J.: *Shebi'it*, 9 : 4

On the lips of a sensible man wisdom is found;
But a man without sense needs a rod for his back.
                              Book of Proverbs, 10 : 13

❋ Some scholars are like donkeys: they only carry a lot of books.   BAHYA IBN PAQUDA, *Duties of the Heart*

Sweet of voice but short of brains.
                              IMMANUEL OF ROME

See also: COMMON SENSE, FOOLS, INTELLIGENCE, SCHOLARS, SENSE, WISDOM

SUCCESS

❋ The door to success has two signs PUSH—and PULL.

Failures are the pillars of success.

❋ Success is intoxicating—even without wine.

Even to fall from a fine horse is worthwhile.

You won't get ahead by keeping quiet.

See also: BUSINESS, EFFORT, ENDURANCE, LUCK, PERSIS-
TENCE, RICHES, WEALTH

SUFFERING

Note. Suffering is man's lot in a world where God's purposes are never wholly revealed; and the rabbinical
philosophers were driven to conclude that suffering
serves divine purposes: it purifies, it teaches, it is itself
an agency of God's plan. Virtue, besides, is divine—
and its own reward to mortals who practice it and are
transmogrified by its grace. The noblest comment on
this is, oddly, "secular": Maimonides' statement that
to do right and avoid evil, whatever the suffering, is to
be a man, for each man owes it to his humanness to seek
to purify his desires and perfect his conduct.

—L.R.

No man knows another's sorrows.

❋ A stab in the heart leaves a hole.

God is closest to those with broken hearts.

The one who suffers alone suffers most.

One man can bear more than ten oxen can carry.

❋ From happiness to suffering is a step; from suffering to
happiness seems an eternity.

Suffering creates nervous ailments; happiness cures them.

Things are going very well for me—as they do for a saint
in this world.

Suffering can also make one laugh.

Suffering [sorrow] makes bones thin.

From happiness to misery is a short step; from misery to happiness is quite a way.

If you cut off the head, you'll abolish the pain.

❋ The deeper the sorrow, the less tongue it has.

Garments conceal the suffering underneath.

The paths to a cemetery are paved with suffering.

❋ The stars in heaven weep with him who weeps at night.
                                    TALMUD: *Sanhedrin*, 104

❋ "And it came to pass" usually introduces a tale of woe.
                                    TALMUD: *Megillah*, 10b

Not to know suffering means not to be a man.
                                    MIDRASH: *Genesis Rabbah*, 92

❋ If you want to live in this world, equip yourself with a heart that can endure suffering.
                                    MIDRASH: *Leviticus Rabbah*, 30

❋ We can understand neither the suffering of the good nor the prosperity of the wicked.
                    —adapted from *Sayings of the Fathers*, 4 : 21

Even in laughter the heart may be aching, and the end of joy may be sorrow.   *Book of Proverbs*, 14 : 13

Like one who drops vinegar upon a wound is he who sings songs to a sorrowing heart.
                                    Book of Proverbs, 25 : 20

Suffering is precious, for it is a divine covenant.
                                    Mekilta, 20 : 20

❋ One day's happiness makes us forget suffering, and one day's suffering makes us forget all our past happiness.
            —adapted from BEN SIRACH, *Ecclesiasticus*, 11 : 25

❋ Any wound is better than a wound in the heart.
                    BEN SIRACH, *Ecclesiasticus*, 25 : 13

What I want to know is not why I suffer, but whether I suffer for Thy sake.   THE BERDICHEVER RABBI

❋ The only whole heart is a broken one.
                                    "THE CHOFETZ CHAIM"

A lack of accomplishment is the greatest suffering.
"THE CHOFETZ CHAIM"

See also: EMOTIONS, ENDURANCE, HAPPINESS, HEALTH, LAUGHTER, PAIN, SORROW, TEARS

SUICIDE

Note. Suicide is a crime, like murder, in traditional Judaism; and suicides were denied proper mourning burial rites. Yet the rabbis realized that many (if not most) of those who took their lives were mentally sick—and not responsible for their deeds, hence could not rightly be condemned. Unless a suicide was clearly unbalanced of mind, the body was buried in a special place at one side of a cemetery.

Samson and Saul committed suicide, as did the whole garrison at Masada, in 73, to escape capture by the Romans—all 960 Zealots, under Eleazar ben Jair, men, women, and children perished in one mass destruction. In England, in 1190, the Jews besieged in York castle exterminated themselves, except for a few. (See Isaac d' Israeli's moving account, in the headnote to HEROES, above.) The sacred prohibition of suicide was waived, in these and many other historic disasters, and in the eyes of Jews those driven to suicide, under such hopeless circumstances, became heroes, legends of courage and resolute faith.

The number of Jews who have committed suicide to escape torture, incineration, forcible conversion, slavery or slaughter is simply uncountable. The toll of self-destruction in Austria, Czechoslovakia, Germany, Poland, France and all the places on which the horrors of Nazi rule fell—no one dare estimate the number.

—L.R.

He who commits suicide bit by bit, day by day, has lost both this world and the next one.

Suicide is more reprehensible than homicide [the latter may have justification].
The Testament of Judah Asheri

The man who puts his talents to selfish uses commits spiritual suicide. —adapted from HILLEL in
Sayings of the Fathers, 1 : 13

See also: KILLING, SIN, VIOLENCE

SUPERSTITION

Note.

> Say what you will of the Judaism of the Middle Ages; call
> it narrow; deride it as superstitious . . . [but] for sweetness
> and spirituality of life, the Jew of the Ghetto, the Jew of
> the Middle Ages, the Jew under the yoke of the Talmud,
> challenges the world.
> —E. G. Hirsch, in *A Book of Jewish Thoughts*. Ed. J. H.
> Hertz, Oxford, London, 1920, p. 10.

Where there are many women there is much superstition.

An unbeliever went into a synagogue, stared at the Ark,
the Scrolls, the Eternal Light, and declaimed: "These
are just superstitions! If I'm wrong, let God correct me."
And a great voice came down from Heaven, saying "You're
right."

See also: ASTROLOGY, BELIEF, FOLLY, ILLUSION, LUCK,
MIRACLES, MYSTICISM, REASON

SURVIVAL

❋ To endure, be obscure.

See also: SAFETY

SUSPENSE

The suspense is often worse than the ordeal.

SUSPICION

❋ Respect the stranger—and remain suspicious.

Man is not suspected of a deed unless he did it—at least
partially; or thought of doing it; or saw others doing it
and enjoyed it.   TALMUD: *Mo'ed Katan*, 18

If you bring suspicion on yourself, don't condemn anyone
who thinks ill of you.   IBN GABIROL

See also: EVIDENCE, GUILT, JEALOUSY, JUDGES, LAW

SYMPATHY

❋ If you can't help, at least make a sound of sympathy.

A man devoid of sympathy is not a man but a monster.

❋ Sympathy doesn't provide food, but it makes hunger more endurable.

The capacity to sympathize raises man above the animals.

Sympathy is a little medicine to soothe the ache in another's heart.

See also: COMPASSION, CONSIDERATION, GOOD DEEDS, GRIEF

SYNAGOGUE

Note. See headnote for STUDY.   —L.R.

❋ If there were only two Jews left in the world, one would summon the other to the synagogue—and he would go.

A Jew on a desert island will build two synagogues—so that there is always one he does not want to go to.

❋ Two Jews on an island will build three synagogues— one for each, and the third neither wants to attend.

The best synagogue is the heart.

See headnote for STUDY, and entries under FAITH, PIETY, PRAYER, WORSHIP

T

TACT

❋ Better one word in time than two ill-timed.

If someone in a man's family was hanged, don't say, "Hang this up for me."   TALMUD: *Baba Mezi'a,* 59b

When a student knows that his teacher is able to answer him, he may ask a question; otherwise, he should not.
                                         TALMUD: *Hullin,* 6a

❋ Where wisdom enters, subtlety accompanies it.
                                         TALMUD: *Sotah,* 21b

Don't rebuke your fellow in such a way as to shame him in
    public.
            RASHI, *Commentaries on the Pentateuch, Leviticus*

A word without thought is like a foot without muscles.
            MOSES IBN EZRA, *Selected Poems*, 92

See also: CONSIDERATION, DECORUM, MANNERS, SENSITIVITY

TALK

The heart does not mean everything the tongue utters.

❋ Those who talk a lot usually talk about themselves.

❋ If you have nothing to say, say nothing.

❋ Speech is hard, but who can keep quiet?

An embittered heart talks much.

The tongue is more dangerous than a dagger.

❋ All mutes have a great deal to say.

What's said should not be barked: talking is not barking.

On the tips of tongues the fate of the world rests.

Women are nine times more talkative than men.

One word too many serves no purpose.

Your friend has a friend: don't tell.

❋ Shoemakers talk about their lasts, sailors about their
    sails.

To have no tongue is like having no [warning] bell.

❋ A tongue can be a dangerous enemy; so can yours—to
    yourself no less than to others.

❋ In good times it's good to talk: in bad times, not to.

The less you talk, the healthier.

Talk is a shekel; silence is two.   TALMUD: *Megillah*, 18a

Before you take leave of a friend, offer some serious com-
    ment [in philosophy or law] so that he will remember you
    thereby.   —adapted from TALMUD, *Berakoth*, 31a

My tongue is the pen of a ready writer.
Book of Psalms, 45 : 1

A man of learning spares his words.
Book of Proverbs, 17 : 27

❋ If you talk too much, you'll say what you didn't intend
to.   —adapted from *Book of Proverbs*

In all labor there is profit; but mere talk leads only to
poverty.   *Book of Proverbs*, 14 : 23

Where words abound, sin will not be wanting.
Book of Proverbs, 10 : 19

Our eyes and ears do not always depend upon our will
power, but a man's tongue does.   *Zohar*

What is the sign of a foolish man? He talks too much.
Zohar

❋ If you talk too much, you talk nonsense.
MAAMAR MORDECAI

It is better to abstain from talking than from eating.
Rosh Hagivah

❋ As long as words are in your mouth, you are their lord;
once you utter them, you are their slave.
IBN GABIROL, *Choice of Pearls*, 33

A man's ear belongs to himself; his tongue belongs to
others.   IBN GABIROL

❋ You may regret your silence once, but you will regret
your talk twice.   IBN GABIROL

❋ The mouth is a door, and should be kept closed.
BAHYA BEN ASHER, *Kad ha-Kemah*

Men detest the man who talks too much.
BEN SIRACH, *Ecclesiasticus*, 20 : 8

The tongue is the mind's messenger.
BAHYA IBN PAQUDA, *Duties of the Heart*

❋ Why did God give man two ears and one mouth? So
that he will hear more and talk less.
—adapted from HASDAI

The chief superiority of man over animals lies in his power
of speech; but if we speak folly, we are no better than
animals.   THE SASSOVER RABBI

But how can you say, "It was *only* talk, so no harm was
done?" Were this true, then your prayers, and your
words of kindness, would be a waste of breath.

NACHMAN OF BRATSLAV

✳ Gossip is nature's telephone.   SHOLEM ALEICHEM

See also: ARGUMENT, FOOLS, GOSSIP, SILENCE, SLANDER,
SPEECH, WORDS

TALMUD

Note.
Even the Bible itself did not come so close to the daily life
of the Ghetto as the Talmud and the Mishna. The Bible
was a thing eternal, apart, unchanging. The Talmud was a
daily companion, living, breathing, contemporary, with a
hundred remedies for a hundred needs. A nation persecuted, lives through time of stress rather by its commentaries than by its Scriptures. In the Ghetto the Talmud was
a door into the ideal, always open.
—A. Mary F. Robinson, "Social Life in France in the
Fourteenth Century," *Fortnightly Review*, vol. 57, 1892.

For a description and history of the Talmud, see
GUIDE NOTE B (pp. 62–65).
R. Travers Herford, distinguished student of the Talmud, has observed that the rabbi-teachers took the
Judaism of the prophets, and "brought it to bear upon
the lives of the people in a way and to an extent which
the prophets had never been able to accomplish." It is not
far from the truth to say that if it had not been for the
rabbis, the prophets might have been forgotten.
The reason that the Talmud grew as it did is that it
was the work of rabbis, generation after generation, to
try to adapt the Law, the Torah, to new problems and
the transformed realities which Jews faced—in captivity
or in freedom, as rulers or ruled, as men and women
and parents, or as subjects of the Romans or Catholic
sovereigns, Muslim Spain or the brutal hegemony of
the tsars. (See headnote for RABBIS.)   —L.R.

To know one virtue is greater than to know all of the
Talmud.

See also: JEWS, LAW, RABBIS, STUDY, TORAH

TAXES

Taxes grow without rain.

See also: GOVERNMENT, POLITICS

TEACHERS: I

❋ First learn; then teach.

He who teaches a child is as if he had created it.
                                    TALMUD: *Sanhedrin*, 19b

Whoever teaches his son also teaches his son's son—and
so on to the end of man's generations.
                                    TALMUD: *Kiddushin*, 30a

The calf wants to suckle, but even more does the cow want
to give suck. [The teacher may need to teach more than
his pupils need to learn.]   TALMUD: *Pesahim*, 112a

❋ God said: You must teach, as I taught, without a fee.
                                    TALMUD: *Nedarim*, 37a

In teaching, do not favor the children of the rich—and
teach the children of the poor without compensation.
                                    TALMUD: *Ta' anith*, 24a

The bad teacher's words fall on his pupils like harsh rain;
the good teacher's, as gently as the dew.
                                    TALMUD: *Ta'anith*, 7a

Blessed is the son who studies with his father, and blessed
is the father who teaches his son.   TALMUD

The man from whom people learn must be especially strict
with himself.   —adapted from TALMUD: *Bezah*, 2 : 6

A teacher who has drunk a quart of wine may not teach.
                                    MIDRASH: *Leviticus Rabbah*, 1 : 4

A pupil receives but a fifth of the reward that accrues to
the teacher.   MIDRASH: *Song of Songs Rabbah*

Be very careful in teaching, for an error in teaching is
tantamount to a willful transgression.
                                    Sayings of the Fathers, 4 : 13

❋ The ill-tempered cannot teach.
                                    HILLEL in *Sayings of the Fathers*, 2 : 6

When I see no way of teaching a truth but one that will please one intelligent man but will offend ten thousand fools, I address myself to the one, and ignore the censure of the thousands.

MAIMONIDES: *Guide to the Perplexed, Introduction*

❉ In seeking knowledge, the first step is silence, the second listening, the third remembering, the fourth practicing, and the fifth—teaching others.   IBN GABIROL

TEACHERS: II, CRITICAL COMMENTS ON

One mother can achieve more than a hundred teachers.

❉ When a teacher fights with his wife, it's tough on his students.

The man who can't even tie a cat's tail can become a *melamed* [teacher of elementary subjects].

The man who learns but does not teach is like a myrtle in the desert: no one profits from it.

TALMUD: *Rosh Hashanah*, 23a

Unmarried teachers are as arrogant as kings, but their minds are like those of children.

—adapted from MIDRASH

Hidden wisdom and concealed treasure—of what use is either?   BEN SIRACH, *Ecclesiasticus*, 20 : 30

He who has not studied enough and teaches imperfect knowledge is to be treated as if he has sinned intentionally.

MAIMONIDES: *Guide to the Perplexed, Introduction III*

See also: LEARNING, PEDAGOGY, RABBIS, SCHOLARS, STUDY, WISE MEN

TEARS

❉ When we laugh, everyone sees it; when we weep, no one does.

❉ What soap is for the body, tears are for the soul.

❉ Caution at first is better than tears at last.

❉ There is a special place in Heaven set aside for those who can weep, but cannot pray.

❋ Laughter is heard further than weeping.

All of life ends in tears.

❋ Ink dries fast; tears do not.

When you pour your heart out [in tears] it feels lighter.

❋ What good is the golden urn that is full of tears?

The gates to our tears are never locked.   *Zohar*

See also: LAUGHTER, LIFE, SORROW, SUFFERING

TEPHILLIN

See GLOSSARY:TEPHILLIN, pp. 623–624

TEMPER

❋ A man who can't control his temper is like a city without defenses.

You can tell a man by his tipping—and his temper.

A forbearing man is better than a warrior; and he who rules his temper is better than one who takes a city.
                                        Book of Proverbs, 16 : 32

He who spares his words has true wisdom; and he who holds his temper is a man of sense.
                                        Book of Proverbs, 17 : 27

If a man cannot control his temper, how much less can he control others?   —adapted from IBN GABIROL

See also: ANGER, IMPULSE, PASSIONS

TEMPERANCE

It's healthier to undereat than overeat.

To the extremist, there is no midway between extremes.

Man, who can make a harness for his beast, should make one for his appetites.   TALMUD J.: *Sanhedrin*, 10 : 1

Temperance enlarges understanding.
                —adapted from MAIMONIDES, *Responsa* II : 39a

See also: EXCESS, FOOD: EATING AND DRINKING, GLUTTONY, MODERATION, PRUDENCE, TORAH, WINE

TEMPTATION

✳ If girls were not pretty, men would completely ignore temptation.

✳ In a maiden, temptation sleeps; in a wife, it's wide awake.

A man without a wife has no defense against temptation.
—adapted from TALMUD: *Yebamoth*, 63a

Never put yourself in temptation's path; for even King David could not resist it.   TALMUD: *Sanhedrin*, 107a

✳ Be grateful to your parents; had they not been tempted, you wouldn't be here.
—adapted from TALMUD: *'Abodah Zorah*, 5a

✳ The most effective defense against temptation is this: Shut your eyes.   IBN GABIROL, *Choice of Pearls*

✳ Temptation laughs at the fool who takes it seriously.
"THE CHOFETZ CHAIM"

See also: LUST, MEN AND WOMEN, PASSION, VIRTUE

THEFT

See: THIEF/THIEVES

THIEF/THIEVES

✳ A man is not honest simply because he had no chance to steal.

✳ Not only did he break the commandment not to steal, he stole the Bible.

A thief has long hands and short pockets.

When thieves fight, the peasant keeps his cow.

A thief has an easy job but bad dreams.

✳ When a crook kisses you, count your teeth.

A thief has to be clever.

Minor thieves are hanged; major thieves are thanked.

A thief takes one path, but his pursuers confront ten.

✳ It's hard to rob a thief.

❋ Never accept a present from a thief.

❋ If my brother steals, what they hang is not my brother but the thief [in him].

If you need a thief badly enough, cut him from the gallows.

Don't steal and you won't have to repent.

When servants quarrel, masters learn about the pilferage.

❋ If you steal from a thief, you taste of thieving.

Don't mention the gallows in the presence of a thief.

To hoard is worse than to steal.

Stolen waters are sweet, and bread eaten in secret is pleasant.   *Book of Proverbs*, 9 : 17

For a Jew to cheat a Gentile is worse than cheating a Jew; for in addition to violating the moral law, it brings Jews into contempt.   TALMUD: *Baba Kamma*, 113b

You can't protect yourself against a thief in your own home.

❋ It is not the mouse but the hole that's the thief.
                                    TALMUD: *Gittin*, 45a

To rob one's fellow of a penny may be as bad as robbing him of his life.   TALMUD: *Baba Kamma*, 119a

Not to teach your son a trade is like teaching him to steal.
                                    TALMUD: *Kiddushin*, 29a

Do not steal your property back from a thief, lest you seem a thief yourself.   TALMUD J.: *Sanhedrin*, 8 : 3

The thief who finds no chance to steal considers himself law-abiding.

                    —adapted from TALMUD: *Sanhedrin*, 22a

❋ "What most encourages theft?" asked a teacher.
    "Hunger," replied one pupil.
    "Envy," said another.
    "Extravagance," said a third.
    But a fourth student answered best: "Those who buy stolen goods."
                    —adapted from MIDRASH: *Leviticus Rabbah*, 6 : 2

The man who steals men's confidence is the worst of thieves.   MIDRASH: *Mekilta Mishpatim*

All thievery depends upon a receiver.
>> MIDRASH: *Leviticus Rabbah*, 6

To kill a thief is not murder, for a thief is like one who has
been dead from the beginning.
>> RASHI, *Commentaries on the Pentateuch, Exodus*

A thief invokes God's aid while breaking into a house.
>> IMMANUEL OF ROME

A thief is better than a liar, but they are both doomed.
>> BEN SIRACH, *Ecclesiasticus*, 20 : 25

See also: DECEIT, HONESTY

THOUGHT

✻ Thought is a universe of freedom.

✻ My thoughts form an Eden in my heart.
>> JUDAH HA-LEVI, *Kuzari*

Dive into the sea of thought, and find there pearls beyond
price.   MOSES IBN EZRA, *Shirat Yisrael*

Thought serves as a mirror: it shows us the ugliness and the
beauty within.   MOSES IBN EZRA, *Shirat Yisrael*

Words are but the shell; meditation is the kernel.
>> BAHYA IBN PAQUDA, *Choice of Pearls*

✻ Thinking is more precious than all five senses.
>> NACHMAN OF BRATSLAV

Those who are pure of heart find new thoughts whenever
they meditate.   NACHMAN OF BRATSLAV

Thought is nobler than words, because it guides them.
>> THE MEZERITZER RABBI

See also: INTELLECT, KNOWLEDGE, LOGIC, REASON, STUDY

THRIFT

✻ If you eat your bagel, you'll have nothing left but the
hole.

It is easier to earn than to save.

Those who don't save pennies don't have dollars.

Don't throw away a shirt because of one worn place in a
corner.

❋ The thriftiest with money are the most spendthrift with
desires.   MOSES IBN EZRA, *Shirat Yisrael*

See also: BORROWING, EXTRAVAGANCE, FORESIGHT, LEND-
ING, MONEY

TIME

❋ In time even a bear can learn to dance.

Time can transform everything.

❋ Time brings wounds and time heals wounds.

Yesterday is your past; today is your future—for your
tomorrow has yet to be known.

The greatest of doctors is time.

With time, fowl get used to the killing.

❋ "And if not now, when?" asked Hillel. When will the
"now" be? The now that is now, this moment, never
existed before—from the time the world was created;
and this moment will never exist again. Formerly there
was another "now," and later there will be another
"now," and every "now" has its own special import and
function.   Hasidic saying

Snow begins pure white but turns into slush, and all beauty
will in time change into corrupted matter.
                                                    Sefer Hasidim

There is a time to love, and a time to hate.
                                              Ecclesiastes, 3 : 8

Though a plague last seven years, no one dies before his
time.   ASHI in TALMUD: *Sanhedrin*, 29a

Time is of short duration and flies away swifter than the
shades of evening. We are like the child who grasps a
sunbeam in his hand, and when he opens it finds it
empty, to his amazement, and all the brightness gone.
                                              JEDAIAH ben BEDERSI

People say "Time is money" but I say "Money is time," for
every luxury costs so many precious hours of your life.
                                              "THE CHOFETZ CHAIM"

See also: DESTINY, FATE, FORTUNE

TOLERANCE

✸ When three men cry "You're crazy!" the fourth should say "Bim bom." [This can mean either "Confirm the verdict," or "Give them the answer they want—what harm will it do?"]

See also: COMPASSION, CONSENSUS, KINDNESS, OPINION, PREJUDICE

TORAH

Note. The word "Torah" (Hebrew: "doctrine" or "teaching") has several significant meanings in the usage of that sacred word by Jews.

(1) Technically, Torah refers to the Pentateuch, or "the Five Books of Moses" (Genesis, Exodus, Leviticus, Numbers, and Deuteronomy).

(2) In another sense, "the Torah" designates the actual scroll, containing the Five Books of Moses, handwritten on parchment, from which readings are publicly annunciated in the synagogue on the Sabbath festivals, Mondays and Thursdays.

(3) In a general sense, Torah is all of Jewish law and religious studies. (Torah *she-bealpeh* refers to the oral teachings of the rabbis, as contrasted to Torah *shehbiksav*, the written teachings.)

(4) In the largest usage, Torah means Judaism—as a religion, a philosophy, a commitment, a set of values: hence the phrases to "live," "live by," or "practice" Torah.

For the rabbinical interpretations that were needed to enforce the Torah's laws and moral edicts, see the Guide Notes for TALMUD, MISHNAH, MIDRASH, GEMARA (pp. 62–69), and see the entries under COURTS, JUDGES, LAW.

When scholars approached the Torah, ordinary rules of textual analysis were excluded: obviously, no rabbi, however wise, could dismiss an unclear or contradictory passage by saying that the Author of the Holy Book was unclear, uncertain, or wrong.

The rabbis held that ambiguities or contradictions in the sacred text were the result of insufficient knowledge, insufficient study, insufficient understanding. How could these be overcome? By continuing, rigorous reexamination and reanalysis of the text—for meanings beneath

the surface, for significance disguised by language, for
precepts concealed within old words and old phrases.

The laws which grew to govern the ways in which the
Torah could be interpreted forbade the reading *into* any
passage of something that was not actually (or infer-
entially) apparent. Rules of interpretation (hermeneutics) were refined to protect the sanctity of the holy
Torah and to give authority to particular explications
of that text. As Morris Adler puts it, the work of rabbinical scholars "was a work of discovery, not of innova-
tion. They saw themselves . . . as interpreters, not
legislators." (*The World of The Talmud, op. cit.,* p 25.)

—L.R.

Torah is the best of wares [possessions, merchandise].

✳ The Torah lives—even in a hovel, up to its neck in dirt.

The Torah begins with acts of loving and ends with kindness; it begins with God clothing Adam and Eve, and
ends with God burying Moses.   TALMUD: *Sotah,* 14a

✳ The beginning and end of Torah is performing acts of
loving-kindness.   TALMUD: *Sotah,* 14a

The words of the Torah abide with him who regards himself as nothing.   TALMUD: *Sotah,* 21b

The Torah may be likened to two paths, one of fire, the
other of snow. Turn in one direction, and you die of
heat; turn to the other and you die of the cold. What
should you do? Walk in the middle.

TALMUD: Hagigah, 2 : 1

✳ God weeps over anyone who could have occupied himself with Torah and did not.   TALMUD: *Hagigah,* 5 : 2

Even an idolator who studies Torah is like the high priest.

TALMUD: Baba Kamma, 38a

The study of Torah outweighs all sacrifices.

TALMUD: Menahoth, 110a

The words of the Torah are compared to water, wine, and
milk (Isaiah 55 : 1), because just as these are kept only
in the simplest of vessels, so the Holy Words are preserved in the humblest of men.

TALMUD: Ta'anith, 7a

The Torah can be interpreted in forty-nine different ways, and God instructed Moses, "Decide according to the majority."
TALMUD J.: *Sanhedrin*, 4 : 2

The Torah says: "If thou forsakest me for one day I shall forsake thee for two days."
TALMUD J.: *Berakoth*, end

There is no end [no bottom] to Torah.
—adapted from *Book of Job*, 11 : 9

Wine cannot stay sweet in gold and silver vessels, but only in cheap earthenware; in the same way, the words of the Torah will keep only with the man who makes himself lowly.
Sifre—Deuteronomy, Ekeb, 48

❋ Like wine, the Torah pleases the heart and improves with age.
MIDRASH: *Sifre—Deuteronomy*, 48

❋ He who loves Torah is never satiated.
MIDRASH, *Deuteronomy Rabbah*, 7

When two men sit together and fail to discuss Torah—lo! there is the seat of the scornful. But when two men do discuss Torah, the Holy Spirit rests on them.
Sayings of the Fathers, 3 : 2

One should not make an ax of the Torah.
Sayings of the Fathers, 4 : 5

Where there is no Torah there is no good conduct, and where there is no good conduct there can be no Torah.
Sayings of the Fathers, 3 : 17

❋ Where there is no food there can be no Torah; but where there is no Torah, there will be no food.
Sayings of the Fathers, 3 : 17

He who honors the Torah is honored by mankind.
Sayings of the Fathers, 4 : 6

He who fulfills the Torah amidst his poverty will in the end fulfill it amidst wealth; he who neglects the Torah amidst wealth will in the end neglect it amidst poverty.
Sayings of the Fathers, 4 : 9

❋ The only free man is he who engages in the study of Torah.
Sayings of the Fathers, 6 : 2

You want me to teach you the whole Torah? This is its
basic principle: What is hateful to yourself do not do to
your fellow man. If you want no one to harm you, do
not harm him; if you want no one to take what is yours,
do not take from him what is his.

Abot de Rabbi Nathan, 27a

✤ The man who studies the Torah in his old age is like an
old man who has married a young woman.

Abot de Rabbi Nathan, ch. 23

What is hateful to thee, never do to thy fellow man: that
is the entire Torah; all the rest is commentary.

HILLEL in TALMUD: *Shabbath,* 31a

The more Torah, the more life.

HILLEL in *Sayings of the Fathers,* 2 : 7

✤ The Torah does not tell us to believe absurdities.

JOSEPH ALBO, *Sefer ha-Ikarim*

The Torah is our life and the length of our days. While
loving and studying the Torah, we may be in great
danger from our enemies; but if we gave up our studying, we should disappear and be no more.

AKIBA in TALMUD

Torah should lead to good deeds, not only to faith, not
only good intentions.

ELIJAH DELMEDIGO, *Behinat ha-Dat*

How long are we required to study Torah? Until the day
of our death . . . Some of Israel's wisest men were
woodchoppers, other drawers of water, some even blind
men—and all of them studied Torah day and night.

MAIMONIDES, *Mishneh Torah*

The words of Torah heal the soul, not the body.

MAIMONIDES: *Mishneh Torah*

✤ The Torah is truth, and the purpose of knowing it is to
live by it.   MAIMONIDES

✤ Men who see Torah collapsing should have their eyes
examined.   "THE CHAIM CHOFETZ"

✤ Every living soul is a letter of the Torah.

NATHAN OF NEMIROV

❋ There are seventy ways of studying Torah; one is in silence.   THE TCHARKOVER RABBI

See also: FAITH, GOD, PIETY, SABBATH, SCHOLARSHIP, STUDY, RELIGION, TRUTH, VIRTUE, WISDOM

TRADE

A trade is a kingdom.

To know a trade is to own a mine.

See also: BUSINESS, WORK; for OCCUPATIONS, see SKILL

TRADITION

Tradition protects the Torah [the Law].
                          Sayings of the Fathers, 3 : 13

The man who accepts tradition without examining it with his own intelligence and judgment, is like a blind man led by others. BAHYA IBN PAQUDA, *Duties of the Heart*

See also: CONFORMITY, CONSENSUS, INTELLECT, SKEPTICISM

TRANSGRESSION

❋ New laws cause new transgressions.

If a man thrice guards himself against transgression, God guards him against it thereafter.
                          TALMUD J.: *Kiddushin*, 1

❋ Transgression is forgiven by shame.
                  —adapted from TALMUD: *Berakoth*, 12b

If the man who walks in the ways of the Lord accidentally transgresses, then every creature—below and above him —helps to conceal it.   *Zohar*

❋ The heart and the eyes are like spies for the body: the eye sees, the heart covets, and the body commits the transgression.
          RASHI, *Commentaries on the Pentateuch*, Numbers

❋ A silk thread begins as the weakest of things, the mucus of a worm; yet how strong it becomes when entwined

many times! . . . So it is with transgressions: they grow
strong with repetition.
                    BAHYA IBN PAQUDA, *Duties of the Heart*

See also: EVIL, FAITH, LAW, PIETY, SIN, TEMPTATION

TRANSLATION

Reading poetry in translation is like kissing a woman
    through a veil.   —adapted from CHAIM BIALIK

TRAVEL

The fool who traveled is better off than the wise man who
    stayed home.

❋ No matter what happens, travel gives you a story to tell.

Travel leads to three things: it diminishes the marital rela-
    tionship, it decreases wealth, and it lessens one's fame.
                    RASHI, *Commentary on Genesis* (Abraham)

See also: CIRCUMSTANCES, EXPERIENCE, LIFE

TREACHERY

❋ Those who betray their cause support the other's.

The side that breaks a truce during a war will lose.
                    NACHMAN OF BRATSLAV

Trees are cut down by their own kind. [Ax handles are
    made of wood.]

See also: DECEIT, HYPOCRISY, LIARS

TROUBLE

❋ Troubles are drawn to wetness—to tears and to brandy.

❋ Troubles that don't show on the face lie on the heart.

It's easier to endure trouble with soup than without soup.

❋ Chopped liver is better than chopped troubles.
[*Gehokte tsores*—"chopped troubles"—is a popular way of
    saying troubles compounded.]

Nothing causes more trouble than the tongue.

❋ Bygone troubles are a pleasure to discuss.

Man should remember: Not all trouble comes from Heaven.

We do not live on joys, or die of troubles.

❋ Though the world is full of trouble, each man feels only his own.

Troubles are to man what rust is to iron.

❋ Ask not that all troubles end, for when troubles end, life ends, too.

The longer the life, the more the troubles.

Man grows accustomed to troubles.

❋ Trouble tears the heart apart.

Troubles are as common as wood, but they can't heat up the oven.

Every day brings its own troubles.

The world is big, its troubles still bigger.

Trouble is a thorn in the heart.

Troubles bind people together.

Troubles don't come alone.

Man is born unto trouble, as the sparks fly upward.
                                        Book of Job, 5 : 7

The man who knows that deterioration is the rule of life won't take his troubles too seriously.   FALAQUERA

❋ Little troubles are really not so bad—for someone else.
                                        SHOLEM ALEICHEM

See also: CONTENTMENT, HAPPINESS, HOPE, JOY, LIFE, PAIN, SUFFERING, WORRY

TRUST

❋ He who lives on trust is lost.

Trust not in yourself until the day of your death [because you may undo your good deeds].
            HILLEL in *Sayings of the Fathers*, 2 : 4

See also: FAITH, GOD, LIFE, PIETY, SKEPTICISM

TRUTH

❋ The truth never dies—but it lives a wretched life.

❋ Truth rests with God alone—and a little with me.

❋ When you tell the truth you don't have to remember what you said.

If you add to truth, you enter the domain of lies.

❋ Truth is heavy, so few men carry it.

❋ Truth is neither alive nor dead: it just aggravates itself all the time.

Man finds God through truth.

Truth shows in the eyes; lies stay behind the eyes.

Nothing is more harmful to a new truth than an old error.

Ultimately, truth rises, like oil on water.

❋ Many love truth, but not many speak it.

Half a truth is a whole lie.

A lie one must not say; and some truths you should not tell.

❋ The worst libel can be the truth.

❋ Truth creeps; lies race.

Lust cannot lead to truth.

Truth may walk around naked; but lies should be clothed.

Children and fools tell the truth.

A joke is a half-truth.

Heaven and earth have sworn that nothing shall remain lost [i.e., the truth].

❋ The truth lights, but money warms.

You may regret having told the truth.

Truth can be the greatest deceiver.

If you are proved right, you achieve little; but if you are proved wrong, you gain much—for you learn the right.

Truth is its own witness.

Passion and truth are enemies.

Better the ugly truth than a beautiful lie.

God loves the truth.

Everyone boasts of the truth, but few [none] have it

❋ The truth has every charm—but is very shy.

A hint can hurt more than the truth.

Truth wears many faces.

Death reveals the truth.

❋ When you add to the truth, you subtract from it.
TALMUD: Sanhedrin, 29a

Truth is God's seal.   TALMUD, Shabbath, 54

Truth, justice and peace are one.
—adapted from Perek ha-Shalom

At times even liars speak the truth.
MOSES IBN EZRA, Shirat Yisrael

A truth, established by proof, does not gain in force from
the support of scholars; nor does it lose its certainty because of popular dissent.
MAIMONIDES, Guide to the Perplexed, Intro. II

❋ No other purpose should be attached to truth than that
you should know what is true.   MAIMONIDES

❋ A truth does not become greater by repetition.
MAIMONIDES

Men cling to the opinions to which they are accustomed
from youth; this prevents them from finding the truth,
for they cleave to the opinions of habit.
MAIMONIDES: Guide to the Perplexed, I : 31

The Torah is truth, and the purpose of knowing it is to live
by it.   MAIMONIDES

Truth should be neither cowardly nor bashful.
JOSEPH BEN CASPI, Sefer ha-Mussar

❋ Truth is not nullified because unbelievers deny it.
SAADIA GAON

❋ Hope and fear are not proper tests of truth.
MOSES MENDELSSOHN

❊ Truth has a halo.   SAMUEL HA-NAGID, *Ben Mishle*

The truth hurts like a thorn, at first; but in the end it blossoms like a rose.   SAMUEL HA-NAGID, *Ben Mishle*

❊ Perfection demands of us not so much the capacity to tell good from evil, as truth from falsehood.
                    FALAQUERA, *Commentary on [Maimonides']*
                              Guide to the Perplexed.

Truth is the very seal of life.
                    JONATHAN EIBESCHUTZ, *Yaaroth Dvash*

Victory cannot tolerate truth.   NACHMAN OF BRATSLAV

Where there is no truth there is no grace.
                              NACHMAN OF BRATSLAV

❊ For thirteen years, I taught my tongue not to tell a lie; for the next thirteen years I taught it to tell the truth.
                              THE KORETSER RABBI

Everything can be imitated, except truth; for imitated truth is no longer truth.   THE KOTZKER RABBI

See also: DECEIT, GOSSIP, LIES, PROOF, SLANDER, TALK, VIRTUE

U

UGLINESS

There is no one so ugly as the man who is satisfied with himself.   Hasidic saying

See also: ARROGANCE, BEAUTY, CONCEIT, SELF-ESTEEM, VANITY

UNDERSTANDING

❊ The heart sees better than the eye.

The man who has understanding has everything.

The wise man hears one word—but understands two.

The less a man understands, the happier he is.

❋ You can look into someone else's eyes, but not into someone else's heart.

Many see, but few understand.

❋ Carry your own lantern and you need not fear the dark.

The Talmud tells us that a fine home, fine clothes, and a good wife will broaden a man's understanding: I need all the understanding I can, to serve God as He deserves.
Hasidic saying

Wisdom is with aged men, and understanding in length of days. *Book of Job*, 12 : 12

How much better is wisdom than gold, and understanding than silver. —adapted from *Book of Proverbs*, 22 : 1

The discourse of a fool is like a burden on a journey; but pleasure comes from the lips of a man of understanding.
BEN SIRACH, *Ecclesiasticus*, 21 : 16

Whoring and wine remove understanding. SAADIA GAON

The more a man understands, the more is expected of him.
"THE CHOFETZ CHAIM"

❋ The longer a blind man lives, the more he sees.
SHOLEM ALEICHEM

See also: COMPASSION, HEART, INSIGHT, INTELLIGENCE, KINDNESS, KNOWLEDGE, PROOF, REASON

UNHAPPINESS

See: EMOTIONS, FATE, FORTUNE, HEALTH, LUCK, MISFORTUNE, SORROW, SUFFERING

UNIVERSE

The universe is always unfinished . . . It calls for our continuous labor and unceasing renewal—for we are partners of the Creator. SIMCHA BUNIM

See also: ETERNITY, GOD, HEAVEN, HEREAFTER, NATURE, WORLD

USURY

Note. Deuteronomy (23 : 20) forbids lending money at interest, "between brother and brother," but rabbinical modifications in the Talmud, which laid down some remarkably sophisticated guides to economic activity, forbade Jews from taking "excessive" interest; rabbis were responsible for advising what was fair to both lender and borrower. Maimonides said that lending money at interest was necessary and beneficial: an economy grows for the benefit of all.

To economists, the medieval Christian Church gravely erred in considering banking "usurious," no matter how proper or acceptable the interest rate charged. How, except through borrowing money, could men buy tools, seed, livestock? Pay taxes? Recover from drought, accident, disease?

Kings and barons and the clergy often built palaces and churches by raising money from Jews, who were then reviled for "usury." The Church considered it a sin to accept interest; but since Jews were doomed to perdition anyway, it let them take on one more sin. Barred from the land, and often from trade and crafts as well, the Jews in medieval Europe were often forbidden to earn a living *except* through moneylending.

Most of the interest earned on money was then taken from the Jews—via exorbitant taxes. In time, the lending of money became a state monopoly—which Jews were compelled to administer for the royal purse. And whenever Jews were forced out of banking/investment/moneylending, interest rates ("usury") everywhere *rose*. Several popes denounced Christian moneylenders for their "heartless" rates; seventeenth-century monarchs asked Jews to lend them money so as to break the monopoly interest rates being charged by Christian bankers; Pitt enlisted the aid of English Jews against English financiers, whose high interest rates were "strangling" the Treasury.

In the nineteenth and twentieth centuries, the anti-Semitism that had once forced Jews into banking operated to bar them from the inner circles of the financial-social elite.

See also headnotes for BORROWING, LENDING, MONEY.

—L.R.

❋ Usury is one form of murder.

The man who does not lend money on interest, either to Jew or Gentile, walks with honor.

TALMUD: *Makkoth*, 24a

The testimony of a usurer is not valid in a court of justice.

TALMUD: *Sanhedrin*, 24b

❋ A man who is careful to greet his creditors warmly is guilty of usury in words.   TALMUD: *Baba Mezi'a*, 75b

Consider the folly of the usurer: were a man to call him a scoundrel, he would fight him; yet he takes pen and ink and in the presence of witnesses gravely writes himself down as a scoundrel and a denier of God's word.

TALMUD: *Baba Mezi'a*, 71a

Usury, like the bite of a poisonous snake, looks small, but its effects are deadly.   MIDRASH: *Exodus Rabbah*, 31

The usurer has no fear of God . . . for God says, "He who lives on usury in this world shall not inhabit the world to come."   MIDRASH: *Exodus Rabbah*, 31 : 6

See also: BORROWING, BUSINESS, MONEY, LENDING

UTILITY

❋ An ugly patch is nicer than a beautiful hole.

❋ As long as a cow can be milked, it is not slaughtered.

A tree serves no use until it is chopped into wood.

New brooms sweep cleaner.

The animals whose meat we eat, and from whose hide we get shoes . . . are more useful than most of our fellow men.   MOSES IBN EZRA: *Shirat Yisrael*

See also: CAUSE AND EFFECT, FUNCTION, VALUE

V

VALOR

Valor means persevering in the right, and mastering your desires, until you feel that to die in the best way is better than to live in the worst.   IBN GABIROL

See also: COURAGE, ENDURANCE, FORTITUDE, HONOR

VALUE

It is worth as much as a blown-out egg.

Pearls are not sold along with vegetables.

A pearl remains a pearl anywhere: and if lost, it is lost only to its owner.   TALMUD: *Megillah*, 15a

If you achieve wisdom, what do you lack; and if you lack wisdom, what do you have?

MIDRASH: *Leviticus Rabbah*, 1

✢ Verbal disparagement does not diminish the value of silks.   SAADIA GAON

See also: CIRCUMSTANCE, GOOD DEEDS, KINDNESS, KNOWLEDGE, LEARNING, MONEY, WISDOM

VANDALISM

Note. As far back as the time of Syrian King Antiochus IV (175–163 B.C.E.), the Scrolls of the Torah were ripped to pieces and burned. The destruction of the Second Temple of course consumed priceless manuscripts. In 1242, the religious authorities of Paris burned no less than twenty-four cartloads of Talmuds and Talmudic manuscripts. In 1288, the city of Troyes burned ten Jewish martyrs—and their libraries. Pope Clement IV proclaimed in a bull that Talmuds be confiscated by the Church and destroyed by pious monks. England burned

Jewish books in 1299. Pope Benedict XIII in 1415,
Emperor Maximilian in 1510; a Bishop Dembowski in
the eighteenth century—each ordered the destruction of
Hebrew books and manuscripts. As for the holocaust
of the Nazis, in Germany, Austria, Czechoslovakia,
Poland, Denmark, Holland, Norway, the Ukraine: it is
safe to say that every Jewish home contained books . . .
                                                    —L.R.

See headnotes: BOOKS, INQUISITION, JEWS, LEARNING,
POGROMS.

VANITY

True, "All is vanity"—but who can get along without it?

❋ Many complain of their looks, but no one complains of
his brains.

❋ If you want to see your best friend, look in the mirror.

A mirror can be the greatest deceiver.

❋ Even the man with big eyes does not see his own failings.

No man is as ugly as the man who is self-satisfied.
                                             Hasidic saying

Absalom was vain about his hair, therefore was he hanged
by his hair.   TALMUD: *Sotah*, 9b

A giant in your eyes may be a dwarf in ours.
                       MIDRASH: *Genesis Rabbah*, 65

There is no room for God in the man who is filled with
himself.   BAAL SHEM TOV

See also: APPEARANCE, ARROGANCE, CONCEIT, FLATTERY,
MAN, PRAISE

VENGEANCE

See: RETALIATION, RETRIBUTION, REVENGE

VICE

❋ God created only one man so that no one could call
virtue or vice hereditary.   TALMUD: *Sanhedrin*, 38a

The wise man turns vices into virtues, but the fool turns virtues into vices.   *Orhot Tsadikim*

Each virtue in its extreme becomes a vice.
                    JOSEPH BEN HANAN EZOBI, *Karaiat Kesef*

✴ If you hide your vices, hide your virtues, too.
            —adapted from IBN ZABARA, *Book of Delight*

See also: EVIL, GOOD, LUST, PASSION, SIN, VIRTUE

VIOLENCE

Violence in a house is like a worm in fruit.

If the Book, then no sword; if the sword, then no Book.
                        TALMUD: *'Abodah Zarah*, 17b

See also: ANGER, ARROGANCE, LIFE, MAN, QUARRELS, REASON, WAR

VIRTUE

✴ God first looks at a man's heart, then at his mind.

A saloon won't harm a good man, a synagogue won't help a bad one.

No man possesses all virtues.

✴ We anger God with our sins, and men with our virtues.

·To know all of the Talmud is a great thing; to learn one virtue is greater.

✴ Not in your ancestry, nor in your inheritance, but in your self seek holiness.

✴ Why did God create only one man? So that virtue and vice would not be called hereditary.
                        TALMUD: *Sanhedrin*, 38a

✴ The heart of virtue is good intentions.
                        TALMUD: *Megillah*, 20a

The man who thinks wisdom is more important than virtue will lose his wisdom.   *Sayings of the Fathers*, 3 : 5

If you conceal your vices, conceal your virtues.
                        IBN ZABARA, *Book of Delight*

The little that is pure is much; the much that is impure is little. BAHYA IBN PAQUDA, *Choice of Pearls*

❋ Man's finest virtue is that of which he is unaware.
MOSES IBN EZRA, *Shirat Yisrael*

An ugly face is the only effective guardian of a woman's virtue. IMMANUEL OF ROME, *Mahberot*

❋ The man who is pure of heart will find new thoughts whenever he meditates. NACHMAN OF BRATSLAV

A man can transform a fault into a virtue, if he only perseveres. THE MAGGID OF DUBNO

Be not entirely offended by one who seeks to harm you: he may have virtues you do not possess.
THE SASSOVER RABBI

I don't like those who are "pure as snow"—for snow is not long white and pure, but soon turns muddy and soiled.
—adapted from THE RIZINER RABBI

See also: COMPASSION, EVIL, GOOD, HUMILITY, INNOCENCE, KINDNESS, MAN, SIN

VISION

Your old men shall dream dreams, your young men shall see visions. *Book of Joel*, 2 : 28

Where there is no vision, the people shall perish.
Book of Proverbs, 29 : 18

See also: DREAMS, FORESIGHT, IMAGINATION, LEADERS, POWER, WISDOM

VISITING

❋ Guests, like fish, begin to smell on the third day.

The woman sees the guests' faults before the man does.

Visiting is like rain: prayed for when absent, but tiresome when overdone. IBN GABIROL, *Choice of Pearls*

See also: GUESTS, HOSPITALITY

VOWS

Note. Judaism attaches the most solemn, weighty importance to the fulfillment of personal promises. Jews are required by the law to fulfill every vow, even if that entails extreme sacrifices.

Consider the text of Kol Nidre, the prayer that ushers in the holiest day of the year, Yom Kippur, "the Day of Atonement." The invocation is not a paean to God—it is a legal document (in Aramaic, not Hebrew), which is recited three times, with awesome solemnity, as the Torah Scroll is held aloft before the congregation:

"Kol Nidre [all vows], obligations, oaths, anathemas, be they called *konam* or *konas* or by any other name, which we may vow or swear or pledge . . . from this Day of Atonement until the next . . . we do repent. May they be deemed to be forgiven, absolved, annulled, or void— and made of no effect. They shall not bind us nor have power over us [and] the vows shall not be considered vows nor the obligations obligatory, nor the oaths oaths."

If the latter part seems confusing, remember that Jews were often not allowed to swear by their God, while in a court; and in Kol Nidre they were referring to oaths they were often brutally forced to take, under the most humiliating circumstances (wearing thorns, kneeling, standing on a pig-skin, teetering on a three-legged stool from which one peg had been removed, etc.). Kol Nidre also absolved Jews (they hoped) from the conversions to Catholicism they had been tortured into undergoing.

The rabbis made it clear that Kol Nidre's appeal for dispensation applied only to vows involving the vower, and did not affect his duty toward others. Vows of conscience, directed to God, were differentiated from promises made to men: the former could be remitted, but not the latter.   —L.R.

Vows are a fence for abstinence.
        RABBI AKIBA in *Sayings of the Fathers*, 3 : 13

See also: DUTY, FAITH, OBLIGATION, PIETY

VULGARITY

To parade one's learning or one's virtues is vulgar.

Better be a servant to a nobleman than a captain of the vulgar.

Don't use vulgarity with men of learning.   *Zohar*

See also: CONSIDERATION, DECORUM, MANNERS, SAINTS, TACT, VIRTUE, WISDOM

WAR

❋ A small war may cause a large chaos.

If one soldier knew what the other [enemy] soldier thinks, there would be no war.

One word can start a war.

It is better to be a dog in peacetime than a soldier in war.

Don't consult a merchant about a bargain, or a coward about war.

❋ If you can't stand the smell of gunpowder, don't go to war.

❋ Even on the threshold of war, we [Jews] are bidden to begin in no other way than with peace, for it is written: "When you draw near a city to fight, first offer it peace."
                              MIDRASH: *Leviticus Rabbah*, 9

When men war, even God's anger does not frighten them.
                                                      Zohar

See also: ANGER, FIGHTING, PEACE, QUARRELING, VIOLENCE

WEAKNESS

❋ Quarrels are the weapons of the weak.

❋ When a cow falls, everyone sharpens his knife.

Separate reeds are weak and easily broken; when bound together, they are hard to tear apart.

MIDRASH: *Tanhuma Nizavim*, 1

See also: COMPASSION, POWER, STRENGTH, WEAKNESS

WEALTH: I

✻ We would all be rich—if we didn't have to eat.

✻ The rich have heirs, not children.

✻ A poor man's roast and a rich man's death are smelled far away.

What good is a silver urn if it is full of tears?

✻ Sad is the man who has nothing but money.

✻ Pearls around the neck [may represent] stones upon the heart.

Better be a rich tenant than a poor landlord.

While a rich man sleeps, his profits increase.

A heavy purse makes a light heart.

✻ Wherever there is too much, something is lacking.

✻ When a wallet grows, so do necessities.

A lazy hand brings poverty; but the hand of the diligent brings wealth.   *Book of Proverbs*, 12 : 24

Some people are chained—to gold and silver.
TALMUD: *Shabbath*, 54a

Not everyone is privileged to enjoy two tables [wealth and wisdom].   TALMUD: *Berakoth*, 5b

Gold and silver, precious jewels and pearls are left behind when God calls you.   *Sayings of the Fathers*, 6 : 9

Who is really rich? The man who is satisfied with his share.   *Sayings of the Fathers*, 4 : 1

✻When told of a man who had acquired great wealth, a sage replied, "Has he also acquired the days in which to spend it?"   IBN GABIROL, *Choice of Pearls*

❊ When a man's wealth diminishes, even his children don't accept his opinion.

❊ The more money you have, the harder it is to part with it.   "THE CHOFETZ CHAIM"

WEALTH: II—IRONIC COMMENTS ON

❊ If you rub elbows with a rich man, you'll rub a hole in your sleeve.

❊ What a fat belly cost, I wish I had; what it's worth, I wish on my enemies.

❊ To be a millionaire, he'd be glad to sell you the shirt off his back.

If you steal enough eggs, you, too, can become rich.

❊ Rich people are wise, handsome—and sing like angels.

❊ The rich may go down and the poor up—but they still don't end up even.

❊ The rich are often thin and the poor are often fat.

A rich man, though foolish, is treated like a lord.

You can live like a lord and die like a fool.

See also: CONTENTMENT, HAPPINESS, LAZINESS, MONEY, POVERTY, RICH MEN, TORAH

WEAPONS

Words are weapons.

❊ When you are weaponless at least act brave.

The tongue is the most dangerous of weapons.

Slander is worse than weapons, for weapons hurt from near, but slander hurts from afar.   TALMUD J.: *Pe'ah*, I : I

See also: GOSSIP, RUMORS, SLANDER, WAR

WEDDINGS

Note. Wedding customs among Jews varied greatly throughout the world. In ancient Greece, a Jewish bride and groom wore garlands and wreaths; in Roman times,

Jews used lighted torches. Jews in Germany once married only under a full moon, Jews in Spain only under a new moon.

The custom of the groom's breaking a glass (after the rabbi has pronounced his benediction) has many interpretations: some say it commemorates the destruction of the Temple. The Talmud counsels Jews to remember that all happiness is transient; that Jews must never forget the sufferings of their ancestors; that a thoughtful father once was so disturbed by the frivolity of the guests at his son's wedding that "he broke a fine glass . . . and they became sad."

Orthodox Jews "celebrate" the couple for seven days (following the Bible's account of the festivities after the marriage of Jacob and Leah). Teachers used to adjourn classes to join a wedding party, with their students: it was a *mitzvah* to participate in the happiness of a bride and groom.   —L.R.

If you dance at every wedding, you'll weep at every funeral.

❋ To a wedding, walk, to a divorce, run.

SHOLEM ALEICHEM

See also: DIVORCE, MARRIAGE

WICKED/WICKEDNESS

❋ The wicked do well in this world, the saints in the next.

The good pay, the bad demand.

When the wicked are in power, crime increases.

❋ A good man needs no recommendation; a bad one, it won't help.

A word helps a good man; but even a stick can't help the wicked.

❋ The mercy of the wicked is cruel.

Book of Proverbs, 12 : 10

The tongue of the righteous is choice silver;
The mind of the wicked is of little worth.

Book of Proverbs, 10 : 20

He who walks honestly walks safely;
He who walks crookedly will be found out.

Book of Proverbs, 10 : 9

He who seeks good will win forever;
But he who aims at the harmful will bring it upon himself.

Book of Proverbs, 11 : 27

The righteous promise little and perform much; the wicked
promise much and perform not even a little.

TALMUD: *Baba Mezi'a*, 87a

Seven pits lie open before the good man—and he escapes:
only one lies before the wicked man—and he falls into it.

TALMUD: *Sanhedrin*, 7a

When they are in trouble, the wicked repent; once the
trouble is over, they return to their evil ways.

MIDRASH: *Tanhuma*, Exodus

✻ It is forbidden to pray that a wicked man die: Had
Terah died while he worshiped idols, Abraham [his son]
would not have come into the world.

Midrash ha-Neelam

It is beyond man's power to explain the prosperity of the
wicked, or the troubles of the good.

Sayings of the Fathers, 3 : 16

The wicked are easy to provoke and hard to calm.

—adapted from *Sayings of the Fathers*, 5 : 17

The good die young, so that they may not degenerate; but
the wicked live on so that they may repent, or produce
virtuous progeny.   *Zohar*

✻ The quintessence of wickedness is foolishness.

"THE CHOFETZ CHAIM"

✻ I love more the wicked man who is aware of his wickedness, than the good man who preens himself on his goodness.   THE LUBLINER RABBI

See also: EVIL, GOOD, SIN, TRANSGRESSION, VIRTUE

WIDOWS

Note. In the Torah, a widow is given legal protection
(Exodus 22 : 21 and Deuteronomy 27 : 19). Her prop-

erty cannot be taken from her by creditors; she cannot be denied any sum stipulated in her marriage contract; she must be supported by her husband's heirs, if destitute. Later rabbinical decrees further ruled that a bride could not in her marriage contract surrender the lien which her claim (on her dead husband's estate) represented.

See also headnote for WOMEN.   —L.R.

❋ Better a young widow than an old maid.

❋ A widow with a golden roof is still a widow.

The man who comforts a beautiful young widow does not only intend to perform a good deed.

Do not take in pawn a widow's possessions—even if she be rich.

See also: DEATH, MARRIAGE, WIVES

WIFE

See WIVES

WILL

Man is in bondage to his impulses—and his creator.

❋ Our eyes and ears are not subject to our will—but our tongues are.   —adapted from *Zohar*

Skill is nil without will.

IBN TIBBON, *A Father's Admonition*

See also: EFFORT, ENDURANCE, SKILL

WINE

Wine helps open the heart to reason.

❋ When wine goes in, secrets come out.

Better old wine than old strength.

Wine is the greatest medicine.

Rabbi Meir said: "The tree of which Adam ate was a vine; wine brings sorrows to man."

TALMUD: *Sanhedrin,* 70a

❋ Where there is no wine, drugs are necessary.
TALMUD: *Baba Bathra*, 58b

The judge who has drunk a quart of wine may not sit in judgment, for he will condemn the innocent and acquit the guilty.   MIDRASH: *Leviticus Rabbah*, 1 : 4, 8

Wine is an unreliable messenger! I sent it down to my stomach, and it went up to my head!
AL-HARIZI, *Tahkemoni*

Wine, though bitter, sweetens all bitterness.
MOSES IBN EZRA, *Selected Poems*

❋ The Talmud declares that wine, in moderation, unfolds a man's brain: A teetotaler rarely possesses great wisdom.   THE KORETSER RABBI

See also: DRUNKARDS, HEALTH, REASON

WISDOM

Note. In Jewish thought, wisdom is not simply the fruit of intelligence, scholarship, or knowledge; wisdom is held to involve basic attributes of character and conduct toward one's fellow men. The highest *khakhmah* (wisdom) lies in being learned *and* righteous *and* spreading lovingkindness.   —L.R.

If a man does not try to reach wisdom, wisdom will not come to him.

❋ Wisdom is better than piety.

With wisdom alone, don't go to market.

❋ Of what use is wisdom when folly reigns?

Wisdom not acted upon is like a tree without fruit.

Wisdom is gentle.

❋ Wisdom is a tree whose fruit is virtue.
Rabbinical saying

Teach us [to] apply our hearts unto wisdom.
Book of Psalms, 90 : 12

The wisdom of the poor is despised.
Book of Ecclesiastes, 9 : 16

If, in a dream, you see the Book of Proverbs, you may
hope to gain wisdom.   TALMUD, *Berakoth*, 57b

Wisdom is more precious than pearls.
                              Book of Proverbs, 3 : 15

Where wisdom enters, subtlety comes along.
                              TALMUD: *Sotah*, 21b

❋ The jealousy [competition] of scribes helps increase
wisdom.   TALMUD: *Baba Bathra*, 21a

Wisdom, like wine, keeps best in a plain vessel.
                              —adapted from TALMUD

❋ Without experience there is little wisdom.
                              BEN SIRACH, *Ecclesiasticus*

Wisdom is the consciousness of self.
          MAIMONIDES, *Guide for the Perplexed*, 1

To seek perfection in property or health or character is not
a worthy goal, nor a proper cause of pride and glory;
the knowledge of God is true wisdom, and is the only
perfection man should seek.
          MAIMONIDES, *Guide for the Perplexed*, 3 : 53

Wisdom must not be pursued with any ulterior motive: to
obtain honors, or to gain money, or to improve one's
material state by the study of Torah.
                              MAIMONIDES, *Mishneh Torah*

Wisdom, like gold ore, is mixed with stones and dust.
                              MOSES IBN EZRA, *Shirat Yisrael*

Wisdom is like fire: a little enlightens, much of it can burn.
                              MOSES IBN EZRA, *Shirat Yisrael*

In seeking wisdom, the first step is silence, the second listening, the third remembering, the fourth practicing, the
fifth—teaching others.   IBN GABIROL

Wealth brings anxiety, but wisdom leads to peace of mind.
                              IBN GABIROL

❋ Wisdom is a hoard from which nothing is lost.
                              IBN GABIROL

❋ The beginning of wisdom is to desire it.
                              IBN GABIROL, *Choice of Pearls*

To seek wisdom when old is like making a mark in the
sand; to seek wisdom when young is like hammering an
inscription on stone.   —adapted from IBN GABIROL

Wisdom is to the soul as food is to the body.
ABRAHAM IBN EZRA

Wisdom is God's power in action; for without it, everything is but theory.   THE MEZERITZER RABBI

❋ Wisdom is God's raiment.   THE MEZERITZER RABBI

Old men who are popular with young women usually lack
wisdom.   NACHMAN OF BRATSLAV

WISDOM: WISE MEN/THE WISE

Note. A *khokhem* is one who possesses or displays *khakhma*
(wisdom); he need not be an intellectual; many a butcher
or barber was known as a *khokhem*, and the early sages
almost invariably toiled in humble occupations.

The wisest of the wise was the *talmid khokhem*, "the
disciple of the wise," the lifelong student of Torah and
Talmud. No formal agency could make one a *talmid
khokhem*. The title came via recognition from peers. As
a young scholar demonstrated greater and greater
sagacity, deeper insight, nobler humility—he began to
be called a *khokhem*. The *talmid khokhem* remained a
student throughout his life, be it noted. The Jews exempted many a *talmid khokhem* from paying communal taxes, not only because *khakomim* were notori-
ously poor, but because Jews wanted them to spend
every moment in Talmud study. A *khokhem* studied for
the community, as it were, and for its welfare: for
learning, and the study of Torah, were noted by the
Lord Himself. So the Talmud scholar was supported by
the community and by his wife, whom the community
accorded great respect because her labors enabled her
husband to study without being distracted by concern for
mundane wherewithal. (See headnotes for SCHOLARS,
LEARNING.)   —L.R.

❋ The wise man hears one word—and understands two.

Wisdom increases with the years, but so does folly.

The wise know the value of riches, but the rich do not
know the pleasures of wisdom.

❋ Some wise men are handsome; and they would be more wise had they been less handsome.

❋ If you want to be considered smart, agree with everyone.

The wisest man can fool himself.

To recognize your folly is the first step towards wisdom.

❋ That fools love sweets was a discovery of the wise.

❋ A wise man lowers a ladder before he jumps into a pit.

The wise man who parades his wisdom is worse than the fool who, ashamed, conceals his ignorance.

When a wise man makes a mistake, it's a whopper.

❋ Wise men report what they have seen, fools what they have heard.

It is good to look at the fair but live with the wise.

A fool sees a man's clothes; a wise man sees a man's spirit.

The man who understands his foolishnesses is wise.

Old men who marry young women usually lack wisdom.

❋ The wise measure ten times before cutting once; fools cut ten times before measuring once.

God grants wisdom only to those who can be wise.

Silence is a fence enclosing wisdom; but silence alone is not wisdom.

Money adds no more to the wise than clothes do to the beautiful.

Say unto wisdom, "Thou art my sister."
                                        Book of Proverbs, 7 : 4

❋ When a wise man is angry, he is no longer wise.
                                        TALMUD, *Pesahim*, 66a

The wise do not rest either in this world or in the world to come [for they always strive for greater wisdom].
                        —adapted from TALMUD: *Berakoth*, 64a

Wisdom is with aged men, and understanding in length of days.   *Book of Job*, 12 : 12

The man who thinks wisdom is greater than virtue will lose his wisdom.   *Sayings of the Fathers*, 3 : 5

The wise man is he who can learn from every man.
Sayings of the Fathers, 4 : 1

Make your home an assembling place for the wise, and
drink their words with zeal.
Sayings of the Fathers, 1 : 4

If you acquire wisdom, what do you lack; if you lack
wisdom, what do you have?
MIDRASH: *Leviticus Rabbah*, 1

To be in the company of a wise man is like going into a
perfumery; you may buy nothing, but the scent will
cling to you for a day.
Abot de Rabbi Nathan, 11 : 14b

Man is wise only while searching for wisdom; when he
thinks he has found it, he is a fool.
IBN GABIROL, *Choice of Pearls*

The wise man blames neither himself nor others, for he
is pious.   IBN GABIROL, *Choice of Pearls*

❋ A wise man's question contains half the answer.
IBN GABIROL, *Choice of Pearls*

Poverty cannot disgrace the wise man, nor can lust enslave
him.   IBN GABIROL

❋ The wise are pleased when they discover truths; fools are
pleased when they discover falsehoods.
—adapted from IBN GABIROL

Kings may be judges of the earth, but wise men are the
judges of kings.   IBN GABIROL

No man is wise unless he possesses three qualities: never to
scorn one less learned who seeks wisdom; never to envy
someone who is richer; and never to accept a fee for his
learning.   IBN GABIROL

The sage is wise because he spent more on oil [on lamps to
read by] than others spent on wine.
—adapted from IBN GABIROL

❋ A wise man is a greater asset to a nation than a king.
MAIMONIDES

A short life with wisdom is better than a long life without
it.   MOSES IBN EZRA, *Shirat Yisrael*, 119

The truly wise man is as liberal with his wisdom as clouds are with their rains.   MOSES IBN EZRA, *Shirat Israel*

Wisdom is the light in man.   MOSES CORDOVERO

Wine and women: they put wise men on guard.
                                        BEN SIRACH, *Ecclesiasticus*

If you judge men by their beards and their girth, then goats are the wisest creatures on earth.
                                        JOSEPH SOLOMON DELMEDIGO

Everyone is wise—in his own eyes.

                                        BARUCH SPINOZA

If you cling to wisdom, you cannot cling to [impure] desires.   THE MEZERITZER RABBI

I am in constant fear lest I become too wise to remain pious.
                                        THE KORETSER RABBI

See also: AGE, FOOLS, GOD, KNOWLEDGE, LEARNING, PIETY, SAGES, TORAH, TRUTH

WITNESSES

Four eyes see more than two.

✳ Lend before witnesses, but give without them.

The man who intends to lie will look for witnesses from afar.   JUDAH ASHERI

See also: ADAGES, EVIDENCE, LAW, LIARS/LIES

WIVES: I

Note. Despite many "antifeminist" aspects of Judaism, wives enjoyed rights rarely accorded their non-Jewish sisterhood. Jewish Law forbade wife-beating, and Jewish courts could punish and even anathematize a wife-beater.

The code of law (Shulhan Aruk) forbade a husband from being "unduly familiar" with his wife, or injuring her dignity, or (Heaven forfend!) beating or selling her. Further, a husband was enjoined not to cohabit with his wife "unless she desires it" (!) and was "certainly forbidden to force her," or to have intercourse if she hated him, or said she did not want his attention, or was intoxicated, or was asleep. A husband was forbidden to cohabit with his wife if she had decided he wanted to divorce her. He was commanded not to deny his wife's "conjugal rights" and to satisfy her if he saw her "primping and coquetting, even if it is not the appointed time."

One of the most interesting Rabbinical decrees declared that a new husband must not leave his town, even to serve in the army, for the first year of marriage—"in order that he may rejoice with her."

For the singularly advanced conceptions of Divorce among the Hebrews, see that category. And for the high status of women in Judaism, see the long headnote for WOMEN.   —L.B.

✳ Give your ear to all, your hand to your friends, but your lips only to your wife.

Old maids make devoted wives.

✳ The man who is too good for the world is no good to his wife.

A gentle girl makes a dove of a wife.

A maiden should pretty herself for the boys she may meet; a wife should be pretty for her husband.

✳ When the wife is fat, the loaves she bakes are round.

Why is it that fools have pretty wives?

Between a husband and wife only God can judge.

It does no harm to listen to one's own wife.

A shrewish wife can, alas, be right.

A little table, a little bench—oh, to be a *balebuste* [housewife].

✳ It is better to have an ugly wife for one's self than a beautiful wife for others.

An old maid who gets married becomes a young wife.

If you love your wife, you love her family, too.

✳ When a young girl marries an old man, he gets younger but she gets older.

If you're faithful to your wife, you have a healthy body.

House and wealth are inherited from our fathers;
But a sensible wife is a gift from the Lord.
Book of Proverbs, 19 : 14

❋ Love your wife as you love yourself—and honor her
more.   TALMUD: *Yebamoth*, 62 : b

A beautiful wife makes for happiness and her husband's
days are doubled.   TALMUD: *Yebamoth*, 63b

❋ Wives save men from sin.   TALMUD: *Yebamoth*, 63b

❋ When a young man's wife dies, the altar of God is
draped in mourning.   TALMUD: *Sanhedrin*, 22a

There is a substitute for everything except the wife of
your youth.   TALMUD: *Sanhedrin*, 22a

❋ Home is the wife.   TALMUD: *Yomah*, 2a

❋ A man without a wife is not perfect [complete].
                                  TALMUD: *Yomah*, 12a

❋ Tears fall on God's altar for whoever divorces his first
wife.   TALMUD: *Gittin*, 90a

Husband and wife are like one flesh.
                                  TALMUD: *Menahoth*, 93b

Three things broaden a man's mind: an attractive house,
attractive furniture, and an attractive wife.
                                  TALMUD: *Berakoth*, 57b

A beautiful wife enlarges a man's spirit.
                —adapted from TALMUD: *Berakoth*, 57b

Be careful to honor your wife, for blessing enters the house
only because of the wife. TALMUD: *Baba Mezi'a*, 59a

❋ Thy wife is short, so bend down and consult her.
                                  TALMUD: *Baba Mezi'a*, 59a

❋ I never call my wife "wife": I call her "home"—for it
is she who makes my home.
                —adapted from TALMUD: *Shabbath*, 118b

Man is not even called man until he is united with woman.
                                                Zohar

❋ Before you take a wife, study her brothers.
                    RABBI RABA, TALMUD: *Baba Bathra*, 110a

A man without a wife is a homeless wanderer.
                              BEN SIRACH, *Ecclesiasticus*

❋ Better your wife's kisses than those of your neighbor's
  wife.   SHOLEM ALEICHEM

WIVES: CRITICAL COMMENTS

❋ If you give the bear a wife, he will stop dancing.

❋ A wife is a bit of a dove and a bit of a devil.

Pretty faces don't produce good wives.

The first wife pulls the wagon; the second wife rides on the
  seat.

A wife can make a man a master—or a slave.

❋ When the wife wears the pants, the husband washes the
  floor.

When the wife wears the pants, the husband rocks the child.

❋ Where the wife is a slob, the cat is a glutton.

A man's wife has scarcely stopped living before another
  woman is ready to take her place.

❋ Some men get along with their wives like stonemasons
  with their stone.

A young wife is like a bird: she should be kept in a cage.

❋ A short wife can have a big mouth.

If a wife wants her husband to stay home, she should talk
  less and clean more.

A second wife is like a wooden leg.

A shrewish wife is a scourge.

❋ A heavy rain chases you into the house; a mean wife
  chases you out.

The wife of a righteous man is herself righteous; and the
  wife of a murderer is as he is.

"Rebbe, since you know all things, tell us what did Eve do
   whenever Adam returned home late?"
"She counted his ribs."   Hasidic story

It is better to live in a corner of the roof, than share a large
   house with a quarrelsome wife.
                          Book of Proverbs, 21 : 9

A foolish son is his father's ruin; and a quarrelsome wife is
   like a constant drip.   *Book of Proverbs*, 10 : 9

A good wife is a crown to her husband; but one who acts
   shamefully is like rot in his bones.
                          Book of Proverbs, 12 : 4

Hell awaits the man who always follows the advice of his
   wife.   TALMUD: *Baba Mezi'a*, 59a

❋ A bad wife is like a dreary, rainy day.
                          TALMUD: *Yebamoth*, 63

The woman who does not adorn herself for her husband
   deserves the worst.   HAI GAON

How can an intelligent man test himself? By enduring the
   company of a bad wife.   IBN GABIROL

A bad wife is like a wolf: she may change her hair but not
   her nature.   IBN GABIROL

See also: DIVORCE, GIRLS, HUSBANDS, LOVE, MARRIAGE, MEN
   AND WOMEN, WOMEN

WOMEN

Note. There are so many misconceptions about the status
   of women in Judaism that I trust you will forgive a
   lengthy headnote for this category. Start with the Bible:
   the mother is placed on equal footing with the father in
   the Ten Commandments; Miriam is acclaimed one of
   the emancipators of the Israelites from the Egyptians
   (Micah, 6 : 4); Deborah was a leader in the war of independence; the praises of women and mothers are sung
   and resung in Proverbs.
      The loftiest word in Hebrew is held to be *rahamanut:*
   "mercy, compassion;" literally, the word means "mother
   love." An old Jewish saying goes "God could not be
   everywhere, so he created mothers."

The rabbis often said that women are superior to men
—in chastity, compassion, and piety. "Man is not even
called man until he is united with woman," says the
Zohar. "The ideal man has the strength of a man and
the compassion of a woman."

The infrequency of infidelity or divorce among Jews is
well-known. It is no small thing that the Talmud tells
Jewish men: "Love your wife as yourself, and honor her
more than yourself. . . . Cause no woman to weep, for
God counts her tears. . . . Israel was redeemed because
of the virtue of its women." "God's blessing does not
descend upon the unmarried man—for he is imperfect"
is an old rabbinical saying; the Talmud (*Yebamoth*,
63a) says: "The man who remains unmarried does not
deserve to be called a man."

Each week of each year, on the eve of the Sabbath,
Jewish women for centuries have been "Queens of the
Sabbath," and their husbands sang a tribute, *Eshes Hayil*
("A Woman of Valor"):

> Strength and honor are her clothing . . .
> She openeth her mouth with wisdom . . .
> Her children arise up, and call her
>   blessed; her husband also, and he
>   praiseth her.

The mother lights the candles and offers a benediction:
and in this she becomes a priestess of the Lord.

Or consider this: "Between a male and female orphan,
provide first for the female: the male may beg, but not
the female" (Talmud, *Kethuboth* 67b).

Perhaps the simplest illustration of the advantages
enjoyed by Jewish women is the rarity of wife-beating—
a custom much practiced and admired in the ethos of
peoples among whom the Jews lived. Wife-beating—in
Europe no less than the Middle East—was very common;
many tribes, town statutes, even Catholic canon law,
expressly made it legal. In England, wives were legally
beaten into the late fifteenth century—and *sold* throughout the nineteenth (read Hardy's *The Mayor of Caster-
bridge*) and into the twentieth. In the Middle East,
Africa, and Eastern Europe, a man's right to beat his
wife was as natural as rain.

But very early, Jewish Law ordered the *Beth Din* to
punish any wife-beater; and, if need be, to anathematize

him; if necessary, to force him to give his wife a divorce
—maintaining her full legal, monetary compensation.
An old folk saying goes: "When a Jew is hungry, he
sings; when a nobleman is hungry, he whistles; when a
peasant is hungry, he beats his wife."

Other legal protections the Jews give to women are
notable: by rabbinical law, a man was required to marry
a girl he had seduced, and was never permitted to
divorce her. Jewish husbands were forbidden to use
their wives as unwilling sexual receptacles. Maimonides
said that a woman is not a slave "compelled to consort
with a man against her will," and declared that, if a
husband did not satisfy his wife's conjugal rights, she
could divorce him. Jewish women were legally protected
against desertion or capricious divorce; and they could
obtain a divorce where a marriage had become intolerable: Jewish women were not forced to endure husbands
who were drunkards, gamblers, libertines.

Alimony was given to Jewish women long, long before that institution was widespread in the west. Widows
were specially protected and supported. Women's property rights under Jewish law were considerably superior
to those of other nations; "in respect to possessing an
independent estate, the Jewish wife was in a position far
superior to that of English wives before the enactment
of recent legislation" (Israel Abrahams).

Jewish women ran their households with a degree of
independence unknown to their contemporaries; they
managed the household budget, carried on financial trans-
actions outside the home, and were frequently given
community funds to dispense or invest according to
their discretion.

It is in the *educating* of females that the Jews displayed all-too-familiar masculine bias. Jewish girls' education was, for centuries, far inferior to that given
Jewish boys. But it is not true that Jewish females were
barred from education. As early as 1475, a Talmud
Torah (school) for girls existed in the Jewish settlement
in Rome; and periodically, through history, travelers and
commentators remarked on the fact that, compared to
non-Jewish females, very few Jewish women were
illiterate. (See Cecil Roth's essay in *The Jewish Library:
Woman*, edited by Leo Jung, Soncino Press, London,
1970.)

Jewish women were expected to make it possible for Jewish males to study Torah—by raising, feeding, sheltering, healing, even supporting them. The women of Israel were held responsible for the basic moral supervision and training of children; they were indoctrinated to indoctrinate the young with a love of study, learning, and obligation to others. Women were not required to study Torah, as men were—although the Mishnah (*Nedarim*, 4) advises instruction in Scripture for both boys and girls, and Judah the Pious declared: "Everyone should know the Divine Law and commandments; youths . . . in Hebrew; women and girls . . . in their mother tongue."

The most widely read work in Yiddish literature is the *Tseno-Ureno* ("Go Out and See") by Jacob ben Isaac Ashkenazi (1550–1628). It was directed to Jewish women, and became a sort of woman's Bible. Ostensibly a translation of the Pentateuch, the *haphtarahs*, and the Five Scrolls, the *Tseno-Ureno* is a charming mosaic of legend, allegory and ethical observations. It became the chief source of Jewish knowledge for generations of mothers who, Sabbath after Sabbath, absorbed its cabala-flavored philosophy of life. In an important sense, this book reflected the triumph of individual interpretation over literal translation, the prominence of the woman's role in everyday Jewish life, and the emphasis of Polish ritual over that of the more worldly Germanic Jews. It overshadowed all previous works in Yiddish, and it affected the life of Ashkenazic Jews more deeply and more lastingly than any other.

Isaac Yanover wrote an unpretentious "home book" for women, in the sixteenth century, that became immensely popular in Eastern and Central Europe: the *Teitsh-Chumash*, an engaging array of material from the Bible and Talmud, and from folklore, humor, allegories, superstitions and legends. In its pages, Jewish women found their devotional guide, their ethical counselor, their household almanac on every conceivable problem from dress and dancing to prayer and behavior.

The status of Jewish women has changed dramatically, needless to say, in the last century. They have taken on greater and greater prominence in trade unions, politics, community organizations. The transformation of the female's status is obvious if one but thinks of Israel,

where the Prime Minister is a woman and where women
receive equal educational opportunities, the right to vote,
etc. (See also headnotes on DIVORCE, FAMILY, WIDOWS,
WIVES.)   —L.R.

WOMAN/WOMEN: I

* God did not create woman from man's head, that he
  should command her; nor from his feet, that she should
  be his slave; but from his side, that she should be
  nearest his heart.

                              as the source adapted from TALMUD

A woman may wear pearls around her neck, though she
have stones on her heart.

Culture in a woman is worth more than gold.

* Women persuade men to do good as well as to do evil
  —but they always persuade them.

Don't deny a pregnant woman's wish.

Women don't blame the tailor when he sews their shrouds.

* A woman of sixty, like a girl of six, will run at the
  sound of wedding music.

* Blessed art Thou, oh Lord, who hast made me according to Thy will.   Morning prayer

A woman is a better appraiser of guests than a man is.
                              TALMUD, *Berakoth*, 10b

* The death of a woman is felt by no one so much as her
  husband.   TALMUD: *Sanhedrin*, 22

* A woman prefers poverty with love to riches without
  love.   —adapted from MISHNAH: *Sotah*, 3 : 4

Everything derives from woman.
                              MIDRASH: *Genesis Rabbah*, 17

Alexander the Great came to a city inhabited by women,
to make war on them, but they said: "If you kill us,
people will say:
    'He conquered women;' and if we kill you, they will
    say:
    'What a king: Women killed him!' "
        Then Alexander said: "Bring me bread; I am
        hungry."

But they brought him a loaf of gold.

"Can I eat gold?" asked Alexander angrily.

The women answered: "If you wanted bread, was none in your kingdom? Did you have to march to so far a place?"

So Alexander departed, having inscribed on the gates of their city: "I, Alexander, was a madman, to come to Africa to be taught by women."

— adapted from MIDRASH: *Tanhuma Buber*

❊ After they were divorced, the man married a bad woman, and she made him bad; the woman married a bad man, and she made him good; this proves that all depends upon the woman.

MIDRASH: *Genesis Rabbah*, 17 : 7

The ideal man has a man's strength and the compassion of a woman.   *Zohar*

If a man and a woman ask for food or clothing, always give the woman preference.   JOSEPH CARO, *Shulhan Aruk*

A woman is like a garden.   *Pirke de Rabbi Eliezer*, 1

❊ Be careful not to make women weep, for God counts their tears.   TALMUD: *Baba Mezi'a*, 59a

❊ A woman can be evaluated by her cooking, her dressing — and her husband.   SHOLEM ALEICHEM

WOMEN: NEGATIVE COMMENTS ON

❊ When a woman dies, people find out how many children she had.

❊ Where there are many women there is much superstition.

Women are nine times more talkative than men.

❊ A woman can argue even with the Angel of Death.

❊ May God protect you from bad women: protect yourself against good ones.

A woman, it is said, has long hair and short sense.

❊ Test gold with fire, and a woman with gold.

Where there are many women there is much superstition.

The best horse needs a whip; the wisest man, advice; the most chaste woman—a man.

A woman who turns into a witch is worse than a woman who was born one.

✻ There is a key for every door, and one for every woman.   TALMUD: *Berakoth*, 45b

God cursed woman, but all men pursue her.
                              TALMUD: *Yomah*, 75a

A woman will uncover her neighbor's pots to know what's cooking.   TOSEPH, *Taharoth*, 8

✻ Hell can lie between the lashes of a beautiful woman's eyes.   *Sefer ha-Hinukh*

Like a golden ring in the snout of a sow is a beautiful woman lacking in taste.   *Book of Proverbs*, 11 : 22

A contentious woman is like a continual dripping on a rainy day.
                    —adapted from *Book of Proverbs*, 27 : 15

✻ There is no hell like an evil woman [wife].
                                              IBN ZABARA

Don't associate with a woman singer; you may be captured by her wiles.   BEN SIRACH, *Ecclesiasticus*, 9 : 4

I would rather dwell with a lion or serpent than with an evil woman.   BEN SIRACH, *Ecclesiasticus*, 25 : 16

✻ Wine and women put wise men on guard.
                              BEN SIRACH, *Ecclesiasticus*

✻ An ugly face is the only effective guardian of a woman's virtue.   IMMANUEL OF ROME, *Mahberot*

✻ A woman's tears are a form of bribery.
                                      THE SHATZOVER RABBI

✻ Women? You suffer before you get them, while you have them, and after you lose them.
                                          SHOLEM ALEICHEM

See also: DOMESTICITY, EVE, GIRLS, GOD, HAPPINESS, HOME, MARRIAGE, MEN AND WOMEN, WIVES

WORDS

❋ Words should be weighed, not counted.

❋ You can forget a blow, but not a word.

A slap disappears; a word does not.

One word can start a war.

A word is like an arrow: in a hurry.

❋ Words are like medicine: they should be measured with care, for an overdose may hurt.

❋ Like a bee, a word may have honey in its sting.

Learned men spare words.

Fools love to use words.

Pleasant words are as a honeycomb, sweet to the soul, and health to the bones.   *Book of Proverbs*, 1 : 24

Who . . . darkens counsel by words without knowledge?
                              Book of Job, 38 : 2

Like apples of gold in a setting of carved silver is a word that is aptly spoken.   *Book of Proverbs*, 25 : 11

❋ A soothing tongue is a tree of life; but wild words break the spirit.   *Book of Proverbs*, 15 : 4

An apt utterance is a joy to a man, and a word in season— how good is it!   *Book of Proverbs*, 15 : 23

The instruments of both life and death are contained within the power of the tongue.
                              Book of Proverbs, 18 : 21

One word can be canceled by another.
                              TALMUD: *Gittin*, 32b

❋ The righteous need no tombstones; their words are their monuments.   TALMUD: *Pesahim*, 119a

Words are the guide to acts: the mouth makes the first move.   LEONE DA MODENA, *Tsemah Tsadik*

❋ Looks explain words.
          —adapted from MOSES IBN EZRA, *Shirat Yisrael*

❋ Words are like bodies; meanings are like souls.
    MOSES IBN EZRA, *Commentary on Exodus*, 20 : 1

As the length of a tree's branches depend on its roots, so right words depend on a man's good sense.
    IBN GABIROL, *Poems*

❋ If I do not utter a word, I am its master; once I utter it, I am its slave.   —adapted from IBN GABIROL

❋ You may regret your silence once, but you will regret your words often.   —adapted from IBN GABIROL

Words are the shell; meditation is the kernel.
    BAHYA IBN PAQUDA, *Choice of Pearls*

A word without thought is like a foot without muscles.
    MOSES IBN EZRA, *Selected Poems*, 92

❋ Thought is better than words, because it guides them.
    THE MEZERITZER RABBI

A kind word is no substitute for a piece of herring or a bag of oats.   SHOLEM ALEICHEM

See also: ARGUMENT, CRITICISM, FOOLS, GOSSIP, SLANDER, TALK, WISDOM, WISDOM: WISE MEN/THE WISE

WORK

❋ The hardest work is being idle.

Bread does not come from flour alone.

❋ Work is easy—for those who like to work.

❋ When a furrier is out of work, he too is cold.

The cobbler who sticks to his job keeps his pot full.

❋ Men at work are not obliged to stand up when a sage passes by. [Other men are.] TALMUD: *Kiddushin*, 33a

❋ Not to teach your son to work is like teaching him to steal.   TALMUD: *Kiddushin*, 29a

If you are told, "I toiled [in study] and I didn't get," believe it not; if told, "I didn't toil and I got," believe it not; but if told, "I toiled and I got," believe it.
    TALMUD: *Megillah*, 6b

No labor, however humble, dishonors man.

TALMUD: *Nedarim*, 49b

❋ To earn a living can be as hard as to part the Red Sea.

TALMUD: *Pesahim*, 118a

The workman's rights always take precedence over those of his employer.   TALMUD: *Baba Mezi'a*, 77a

Weeds spring up and thrive; but to get wheat, how much toil we must endure!

MIDRASH: *Genesis Rabbah*, 45 : 4

Superior work results from a man's rivalry with his neighbor.   MIDRASH: *Ecclesiastes Rabbah*, 3 : 11

The man who works is blessed.

MIDRASH: *Psalms*, 23

It is wise to work as well as study Torah: between the two, you will forget to sin.   *Sayings of the Fathers*, 2 : 2

❋ A man can die if he has nothing to do.

Abot de Rabbi Nathan, 11 : 23a

It is imperative that most men engage in productive occupations, so that the few men who devote themselves entirely to learning may have their wants provided; for in this way, the human race goes on—while knowledge is enriched.

MAIMONIDES, *Commentary on Mishnah, Introduction*

❋ To work for another man is often like taking honey from a bee: accompanied by a sting.

THE ROPSHITZER RABBI

See also: LAZINESS, POVERTY, SKILLS, THRIFT, TRADE

WORLD

❋ The world is beautiful, shining bright, and easy—but for whom?

❋ This world is a dream—but please don't wake me up.

❋ O, Lord of the Universe—please take a real look at Your world!

❋ God has said: "Do not corrupt My world; for if you do, who will set it right after you?"

✱ We can have both heaven and hell in this world.

The world is God's looking-glass.

This world can be changed neither by cursing nor by laughing.

✱ If all men pulled in one direction, the world would keel over.

The world is a collection of cogs: each depends on the other.

✱ The entire world is not crazy.

Without money, this world is not fit to live in.

God created a world that is full of many little worlds.

✱ So it goes in this world: one man has the purse, the other the money.

✱ The world itself rests upon the breath of the children in our schools.   TALMUD: *Shabbath*, 119b

✱ The world is in the hands of fools.

TALMUD: *Sanhedrin*, 46b

Hurry and eat, hurry and drink, for this world is like a wedding feast from which we must soon depart.

TALMUD: *Erubin*, 54a

The world is like a ladder: one man goes up while another goes down.   MIDRASH: *Tanhuma, Numbers*, 49

God created many worlds and destroyed many worlds before he created this one of heaven and earth.

MIDRASH: *Genesis Rabbah*

✱ Rabban Simeon ben Gamaliel had said: "The world rests on three things: On justice, on truth, on peace." Said Rabbi Mona: "But these three are one and the same: for if there is justice, there is truth, and if there is truth, there is peace."   *Perek ha-Shalom*

✱ This world was created for those who are ashamed to do evil.   Introduction to *Tikune Zohar*

This world is like a house: the sky is a ceiling, the earth a carpet, the stars lamps . . . and man is its master.

BAHYA IBN PAQUDA, *Duties of the Heart*

This world is like a fair: people gather for a while, then part. BAHYA IBN PAQUDA, *Duties of the Heart*

❋ A faultless man is possible only in a faultless world.
HASDAI, *Ben ha-Melekh ve-ha-Nazir*

The world is a tree, and man is its fruit. IBN GABIROL

❋ Just as a house testifies to a builder, a dress to a weaver, a door to a carpenter, so the world proclaims its creator, God. RABBI AKIBA, *Midrash Temura*, chapter 3

The man who despises this world is a hero: only a weakling honors it. MOSES IBN EZRA, *Shirat Yisrael*

❋ Just as your hand, held before the eye, can hide the tallest mountain, so this small earthly life keeps us from seeing the vast radiance that fills the core of the universe.
NACHMAN OF BRATSLAV

The world is a tempestuous sea, immense in its depth and its breadth, and time is a frail bridge built over it—its beginning fastened with those cords of chaos that preceded existence, but the end is eternal bliss, lighted by God's countenance. JEDAIA BEN BEDERSI

❋ The world is new to us every morning—that is God's gift, and a man should believe he is reborn each day.
BAAL SHEM TOV

See also: GOD, HEAVEN, HEREAFTER, NATURE

WORLD-TO-COME

Note. The idea of the immortality of the soul served to reconcile man to the sufferings and injustices of this world, which Job, Jeremiah, Ecclesiastes, so eloquently protested. And the Hebrew masses, from the time of the Maccabees, nourished their hopes and salved their sorrows by the retention of faith in a world to come— in which the good will at last be rewarded.

The pious Jew spent an enormous amount of his time in prayer and study (of Torah and Talmud) in order to earn "a portion of bliss" in the eternal hereafter.

—L.R.

This world was created for the wicked; the world-to-come for the righteous.
—adapted from RAB in TALMUD, *Berakoth*, 61b

See: HEREAFTER, IMMORTALITY, RESURRECTION

WORRY

✴ It is better to have ten worries than one.

The greatest of worries can't pay the smallest of debts.

A horse has a huge head, so let him worry.

✴ Worms eat you when you're dead; worries eat you up alive.

✴ The good Lord gave me a brain that works so fast that in one moment I can worry as much as it would take others a whole year to achieve.

Noblemen worry about their horse and dogs; Jews worry about their wife and children.

✴ Only one kind of worry is proper: to worry because you worry so much.

Worry saps a man's strength.   TALMUD: *Gittin*, 70a

✴ Don't worry about tomorrow; who knows what will befall you today?   TALMUD: *Yebamoth*, 63b

✴ It is a serious disease to worry over what has not occurred.   IBN GABIROL

Why should you be anxious about a world that is not yours?   THE SASSOVER RABBI

See also: ANXIETY, CONSCIENCE, MAN, MELANCHOLY, MISFORTUNE, TROUBLES

WORSHIP

Note. There is an old, delightful story that "the three pillars" of Judaism, *Torah* (learning), *Avodah* (worship), and *Gemilus hasadim* (kind deeds) came before God; and they cried that with the dispersion of the Jewish people they would be forgotten. "Not so," answered the Lord. "I shall tell the Jews to build synagogues. The rabbi will teach them Torah; the cantor will lead them in Avodah."

"But how will *I* be remembered?" asked Kind Deeds.

"Ah," said the Lord, "during the service, each Jew will turn toward his neighbor and offer him a pinch from his snuffbox."

                                                —L.R.

Could we fill the seas with ink
And use each blade of grass as quill,
And were all the world of parchment
And was every man a scribe:
To write the love of God
Would drain the seas dry,
And the scroll would reach from sky to sky.

                                    MEIR BEN ISAAC NEHORAI

The best worship is silence and hope.   IBN GABIROL

See also: PIETY, PRAYER, SYNAGOGUES

Y

YOM KIPPUR

Note. It long was the custom for Jews on the eve of Yom
   Kippur, the last of the annual ten days of penitence, to
   hurry to all whom they had offended or been unfriendly
   —to beg their pardon. Families would solemnly assemble
   to ask forgiveness of one another for any slights or
   selfish acts they might have committed in the preceding
   year. All this was done so that one might enter upon Yom
   Kippur with a clean conscience.

   On Yom Kippur, observing Jews confess their sins
   collectively—for on that awesome day, say the pious, all
   men stand before the Lord for His judgment. The confession, which is repeated several times during the day,
   involves a cataloguing of no fewer than fifty-six (!)
   categories of sin: "For the sin we have committed before
   Thee by [stating one of fifty-six varieties], oh God of
   Forgiveness, forgive us, pardon us, grant us remission."
   Note that the confession of guilt is recited as a collective
   "we," not as an individual "I." On Yom Kippur, Jews
   "share" one another's transgressions—plus a feeling of
   general responsibility for the misdeeds of mankind.

                                                    —L.R.

The Yom Kippur liturgy has many occasions for confession. There are the great confessionals, *Ashamnu* and

Al Chet. The confessional has two interesting characteristics: First, it is in alphabetical order, and, second, it is in the plural. For if we were to recount all our sins, we would never complete the list; therefore, we use the alphabetical form, for the alphabet has a beginning and an end. The confessional is in the plural because all Jews are responsible for all other Jews.

SEYMOUR SIEGEL

❉ The *Shofar* [the ram's horn sounded on the High Holy Days] is a prayer without words.   SAUL LIEBERMAN

See also: CONFESSION, ISRAEL, JEWS, SINS

YOUNG AND OLD

❉ Old boys become young men.

❉ If you don't want to get old, hang yourself while young.

What you become accustomed to do in your youth, you do in your old age.

❉ When an old man takes a young wife, he gets young and she gets old.

Young trees bend; old trees break.

Youth is a crown of roses, but old age is a crown of willows.

What the old chew, the young spit out.

The old often survive the young.

When one is young, God forgives his stumblings; when one is a man, God weighs his works; when one grows old, God waits for his repentance.

❉ Wise men, when older, grow wiser; ignorant men, when older, become more foolish.

❉ The old maid who marries becomes a young wife.

At even, a boy skips like a goat; at seventy, a man dodders like an ape.

The glory of the young is their strength: the beauty of the old is their gray hair.   *Book of Proverbs,* 20 : 29

If old men tell you "throw down" and young men tell you "build up," throw down and do not build up, because

destruction, by the old, is construction, and construction,
by the young, is [often] destruction.

TALMUD: *Megillah*, 31a

❋ Old camels often carry young hides [as cargo].

TALMUD: *Sanhedrin*, 52a

When you learn as a child, it is like ink on fresh paper;
when you learn as an old man, it is like ink on used
paper.   *Sayings of the Fathers*, 4 : 27

❋ To seek wisdom in old age is like a mark in the sand;
to seek wisdom in youth is like an inscription on stone.

IBN GABIROL

Old men who are popular with young women usually lack
wisdom.   NACHMAN OF BRATSLAV

See also: ADVICE, AGE, LIFE, MAN, YOUTH, WISDOM

YOUTH

❋ Trees bend only when young.

Youth is a wreath of roses.

When cucumbers are young, you can tell whether they will
grow into good food.

❋ Youth is one thing that never returns.

If I do not acquire ideals when young, when will I? Not
when I am old.   MAIMONIDES

See also: AGE, LIFE, YOUNG AND OLD

APPENDICES

I. On the English Spelling of Hebrew and Yiddish Words*

Every translator must decide what English letters to use in spelling certain Hebrew/Yiddish words. For the reader's convenience I offer the alternative spellings of words, names, and books, as they may be found in other English works. Problems arise with:

(1) English "t" or "s" to end a word (*Bet* or *Bes*); if indicating the Hebrew spelling and pronunciation of a Hebrew word, I use the "t," but in rendering the Yiddish pronunciation of a Hebrew loan-word, one is obliged to use the "s."

(2) English "b" or "v" (e.g., *Baba* or *Bava*); I prefer the "b."**

(3) English "a" or "ah" to end a word (*Zara* or *Zarah*); I follow the usage of the author I am quoting.

(4) English "t" or "th" to end a word (*Berakot* or *Berakoth*); I prefer the "t," but in quoting I follow the form used by the author of the quotation.

(5) "Ch" or "h" or "kh" or "h" for the back-of-the-throat fricatives (approximated by the *ch* of the German *ach* or the Scottish *loch*); although the use of "h" or "ch" in English is increasing, I retain the "ch" at the beginning of a word *if* it is one that many readers of English have already become familiar with (*chutzpa, cheder,*

---

* For a fuller explanation and historical background, see my *The Joys of Yiddish, op. cit.,* pp. xxiv–xxviii, and pp. 514–15.
** Hermann L. Strack's authoritative *Introduction to the Talmud and Midrash* uses "b"; so does the Soncino Press edition of the *Babylonian Talmud* and the *Minor Tractates of the Talmud;* so does Herbert Danby's monumental *The Mishnah. The New Standard Jewish Encyclopedia,* edited by Cecil Roth, uses the "v", as do many contemporary writers (*e.g.,* E. J. Lipman, *The Mishnah*).

Chaim). I use "kh" rather than "h" in the middle or at the end of a word, to insure it will be pronounced, e.g. *mishpokhe, nebekh*. But note:

(6) I spell "hasid," "hasidic," "hasidim" with an "h" (not a "ch") because that is becoming standard practice in Jewish source materials; I suppose the reader who cannot manage the guttural *kh* sound, or who would pronounce "chasid" with the "ch" of "Chinese," comes closer to the comprehensible (orally) in uttering "hasid" with the "h" of "house" than with the "ch" of "choose."

(7) "Z" or "tz" or "ts" to begin a word (e.g., *zaddik*) which is pronounced "ts"; I prefer the "ts," to discourage the readers' use of the "z" sound, as in "zebra."

(8) Hebrew, Arabic, or Aramaic names are often rendered in English with an apostrophe, inverted apostrophe, hyphen, space, or successive capital letters; I prefer to use the space or hyphen, but follow the form used by the author or editor being quoted.

In all of the above, the lack of consistency, which I regret, is both necessary and expedient.

Some of these "rules" represent a reversal from those I followed in *The Joys of Yiddish*; in making the changes, I was simply bowing to the growing consensus among linguists about how Hebrew/Yiddish orthography should be standardized.

II. On Translating Hebrew

Compared with Yiddish, Hebrew* is wholly alien to, and remote from, the languages of the Indo-European family—which were the tongues of nearly all immigrants from the Old World to the New. Those languages are often cousins, sometimes siblings, so millions of new Americans could swiftly learn that, say, "book" or "house" were the English versions of the German/Yiddish *buch* or *Haus* or *hoiz*. This was impossible with Hebrew, where "book" is *sepher* and "house" is *bet*. Hebrew found no cognates in English.

Nor is vocabulary the decisive point; Hebrew changes words according to their function; and the order in which Hebrew sets words, to frame a sentence, so differs from English that even expert translators often moan over their difficulties.

The Hebrew which has been translated for this anthology is almost entirely ancient or medieval. This means that the very tone and stance of the content differ from today's ways of thinking and writing. The wisdom imbedded in Hebrew aphorisms is rooted in, and tied to, the Law; the philosophical sayings mediate, as it were, between the Law and the people. Every word (or even syllable) of a Hebrew sentence may possess an internal association with some principle of the Law. Translation simply cannot preserve all these linkages and echoes.

In contrast, *Yiddish* folk sayings, though often rooted in

---

* The word "Hebrew" possibly stemmed from *ibri*, or *ivri*, which denoted "one from the other side" (of the Jordan). What language was spoken by the people whose history is recorded in the Old Testament? The Old Testament tells us only "the lip of Canaan" and "Judaic." The word "Hebrew," to describe the original language of the Old Testament, does not occur until around 130 of the Christian era—in a Greek translation of the work of Jesus ben Sirach.

a Talmudic insight, branch out exuberantly and take their shape and meaning from the earthy experience of the masses.

More specifically: Hebrew texts originally contained no vowels: rabbis added diacritical marks (in the margins) above or below a consonant to signal its pronunciation. (These vowel signs followed different patterns, so different scholars resolved the resulting ambiguities in different ways until a uniform system was adopted, in Tiberias, in the fifth–sixth century of the Christian era.) *

In Hebrew, as in certain other languages, like Hopi, tenses as we know them in English do not exist; instead, there are "aspects of tense" (one for processes, one for endings). Masculine and feminine gender change blithely. The singular is freely used to represent the collective. Letters such as *tof* and *shin* were often used interchangeably. Because there are no relative pronouns in Hebrew, possessive adjectives change their endings—say, where dependent clauses appear without benefit of an introductory conjunction.

Nor is this all: A Hebrew sentence often runs verb-subject-object ("Plucked he daisies"), or entirely omits a verb: "To her a child" means "She bore a child."

Hebrew employs many connectives, but especially uses the letter *vov*—added as a conjunction; the combination is often translated as "and." But it can also mean "however . . . but . . . when . . . because . . . despite . . . accordingly . . . yet . . . thereupon . . ." etc.

The editors of the new translation of the Torah for the Jewish Publication Society of America (1962) say that to render the particle *waw* as "and," which was customary in old translations, "is to misrepresent the Hebrew rather than to be faithful to it" (p. iii).

---

* Hindu priests faced the same problem when the popular pronunciation of their oldest hymns (in Vedic Sanskrit) began to diverge from the esoteric norm; this was a special problem because the faith required that rites employ exact chanting pronunciation, to be effective. Worse, whereas altered vocalizations represented a "corruption" of faith in the mystery religions, as in Greece, changes in the sound of Hindu texts were tantamount to sacrilege. So the Hindu priests, like the ancient Hebrew priests, were obliged to write down standard phonetic signs, to avoid the capriciousness of orally transmitted, memorized but unwritten pronunciations. (See David Crystal, *Linguistics, Language and Religion*, Burns and Oates, London, 1965, p. 20.)

Hebrew sentences which contain *vov* were often given a *causal* content in English which is not justified by the Hebrew. To illustrate:

"He went into the garden and wept"

can also mean

"He went into the garden because he was weeping"

or

"He went into the garden after he wept"

or

"He went into the garden and, because of that, wept"

or

"Even though he went into the garden, he wept."

So I have changed "and" to whichever connective best conveys the meaning of the original text. For instance:

"Sin is sweet in the beginning and bitter in the end"

takes on greater force, I think, as

"Sin is sweet in the beginning *but* bitter in the end."

Before indignant experts rush in to remind me that "the original" of one or another Hebrew text is far better than the one from which I quote a passage, let me confess that for the sake of clarity or impact: (a) I have adapted or paraphrased as often as I have quoted; (b) I often use translations from Hebrew that were made specifically for me; (c) "original texts" may sound impressive, but they often turn out to be woefully deficient in accuracy or completeness.

Professor Benzion Halper, who edited the excellent anthology *Post-Biblical Hebrew Literature*, cautions us to remember that the old scribes themselves often used abbreviations, dropped occasional letters at the end of occasional words, and that individual words are not clearly divided, one from another, in old Hebrew manuscripts.

"Even the most careful manuscript or edition contains erroneous readings, and the most slovenly work sometimes preserves correct passages. . . . In a vast number of cases . . . the texts are hopelessly corrupt . . . the manuscripts and editions offer no aid [and] I was obliged to resort to emendations."*

---

* Benzion Halper, *Post-Biblical Hebrew Literature*, Jewish Publication Society of America, Philadelphia, 1921, pp. xi–xii.

Puns were popular among the Hebrews, and prophecy via puns will be found in Micah, Isaiah, Jeremiah, just as they were in the Greek oracles, among the vestal virgins of Rome, and in Arabic fables.* But puns are rarely preserved in translation, and where tried are pitifully tortured.

---

* *Jewish Encyclopedia, op. cit.,* vol. 10, p. 227. Professor Theodor H. Gaster holds that Micah's lovely "Tell it not in Gath" rose from the phonetic similarity of "Gath" and the Hebrew word for "tell" (*ta-gidhu-u*); Isaiah deliberately called the city of Dibon "*Dimon*," which would be filled with blood, for which the Hebrew is "*dam*"; when Ezekiel says Gilgal "will be driven into exile" he is playing on *Gilgal* and *galah*, the Hebrew word for "exile." See Gaster, *Myth, Legend and Custom in the Old Testament,* Harper and Row, New York, 1969, pp. 657–58.

III. Biographical Vignettes of the Authors Quoted

I have tried in these vignettes to give the reader a succinct account of the life and teachings of the leading rabbis/philosophers/scholars/poets who are named, in the preceding pages, as authors of individual quotations.

The profusion of Jewish scholars and philosophers called "rabbi" should be understood in its historical context. "Rabbi" means "my teacher," not "priest" or any version of a mediator between God and man. The title "rabbi" was not used until the beginning of the Christian Era.

Formal ordination, incidentally, ended in the fourth century and was not resumed until the fourteenth (see Headnote for RABBIS). And since formal ordination, by tradition, could only be performed in Palestine, and by a member of the Sanhedrin (which disappeared before the end of the fourth century), Jewish medieval scholars, Talmudists, philosophers, were called "rabbi," by their disciples or correspondents or laymen, as a tribute to their learning —not because of any ecclesiastical status or office. Jewish communities often conferred the title of "rabbi" on scholars or saintly wise men who had no diplomas of formal ordination—nor were they expected to have.

—L.R.

NOTE. Readers may wish to remember that, *"ben," "bar"* and *"ibn"* mean "son of" (respectively, in Hebrew, Aramaic, Arabic); that *"abba"* is Hebrew for "father of"; that when "i" ends a Hebrew name it means "son of."

Where "ibn" appears within a name, I do not capitalize it; when it appears as the initial word (e.g., "Ibn Tibbon"), I do.

ABRAVANEL (ABARBANEL, ABRABANEL), ISAAC A. (*1437–1508*)

Descended from an illustrious family of Spanish Jews, Abravanel, born in Lisbon, was a philosopher, scholar, and statesman who served Alfonso V of Portugal as treasurer and adviser. He was forced to flee to Spain, on charges of conspiracy, in 1483. He entered the court service of Ferdinand and Isabella. The 1492 decree expelling Jews from Spain (unless they converted to Catholicism) drove him to Italy, where he entered the service of King Ferdinand of Naples as diplomatic adviser. When the French took Naples, Abravanel went to Sicily, then Corfu, finally to Venice, where he served as a diplomatic negotiator for the government. He died in Venice in 1508.

Abravanel's copious, lucid writings include a commentary on the Bible (which influenced seventeenth- and eighteenth-century Christian exegesis), and religious writings that stressed belief in divine revelation and the Messiah. Sometimes called "the last Jewish Aristotelian," Abravanel was anti-Maimonidean; but what is confusing about him is his alternating defense of and attack upon rationalism and secular philosophy. His writings were important during the Messianic movements that swept Jewry (and Christian millenarian sects) in the sixteenth and seventeenth centuries.

AHAD (ACHAD) HA-AM (*"One of the People"*): pen-name of *ASHER GINZBERG*. (*1856–1927*)

A brilliant essayist, editor, and polemicist, of great influence in the late nineteenth and early twentieth centuries, Ginzberg was born in the Ukraine, settled in Odessa, and began to write essays critical of Theodor Herzl's "political" Zionism; for these he used the pseudonym "One of the People." He criticized the colonization of Palestine, which he visited several times; he advocated a revival of Judaism via "spiritual Zionism" for which a Jewish state in Palestine would be but a beginning. He was active in the negotiations that led to the Balfour Declaration (1917) that committed England to the establishment of a Jewish "national home" in Palestine. In 1922, he moved to Tel Aviv. There he published his memoirs and correspondence (six volumes), which are invaluable as documentation in the history of modern Jewish politics and literature.

AKIBA (AKIVA): *AKIBA BEN JOSEPH*. (*40–135*)

The greatest Biblical scholar of his day, a true giant in the history of Judaism, Akiba was one of the *Tannaim* (a teacher during the period between Hillel's death and the generation after Judah ha-Nasi). He is often called "the father of Rabbinical Judaism." He single-handedly collected, collated, and arranged the entire body of "Oral Law" according to subject matter. This collection of the individual *halakot* served as the basis for the Mishnah. He also definitively fixed the canon of the Old Testament. (He opposed including *Ecclesiasticus*, which he admired.)

Akiba's was a work of incalculable importance, considering the disorganized and confused state of *halakot* (logical support for, and amplifications of, *halaka*). Akiba was driven by a desire to correct misinterpretations of Torah which resulted from the inaccuracies of Greek translations and were affecting the Jewish community. He developed a system of analysis that assigned every word, letter, or symbol of the Torah some specific significance, usable in rabbinical decisions. He insisted that the wording of the Torah was entirely different from all other books.

The brilliance of Akiba's work effected many changes in Jewish law, customs, and social life (e.g. he changed prevailing attitudes to women, slavery, intermarriage— all in a liberal direction). There is not an aspect of the Judaic conception of God, heaven, the origin of man, freedom of will, eschatology, ethics, justice that was not profoundly affected by Akiba.

All this is the more astonishing if we consider that Akiba was virtually uneducated until he was forty, and for years was an *am ha-arets* (ignorant man) who detested the "pedantry" of the rabbis. Born in Lydda, Palestine, Akiba was a shepherd who, with a large family dependent upon him, enrolled at forty in the academy headed by Eliezer ben Hyrcanos). After thirteen years of study, he became a teacher, then established his own school in Bene Berak, near Jaffa. Akiba's academy, said to have had 24,000 students, produced some of the greatest *Tannaim* of the second century (Eleazer ben Shammai, Rabbi Meir, Simeon ben Yohai) and an immense number of followers and disciples.

Rabbi Akiba was a man of spotless character, vast kindness, great humility; his teachings stressed modesty and scorned anyone "who esteems himself for his knowledge." He traveled widely among the Jewish communities in and outside Palestine. He considered the greatest precept of Judaism to be: "Thou shalt love thy neighbor as thyself" (Leviticus, 19), yet turned nationalist in politics. He hailed Bar Kochba (*q.v.*) as the Messiah, and supported the Jewish revolt against Roman rule. When the Roman authorities forbade the teaching of Torah, Akiba publicly ignored it. He was imprisoned, then condemned to death, in Caesarea, by one of Hadrian's officials.

Akiba was flayed alive. As the skin was raked from his living body, he recited his *Shema* (the Hebrew prayer that begins "Hear, O Israel, The Lord our God, The Lord is One"); he was asked how he could endure such pain, and whether he was some sort of magician. Akiba replied: "No, but I rejoice at this chance to love my God 'with all my life,' having until now only been able to serve him 'with all my means.'" That scene has become part of Jewish tradition: The association of the *Shema* with Akiba's death has made the prayer a common death-bed affirmation of faith.

ALBO, JOSEPH. (*c. 1380–c. 1435*)

Spanish religious philosopher, a disciple of Hasdai Crescas, the Crown Rabbi of Aragon. Albo participated in the famous "Disputation of Tortosa" (1414) between Christians and Jews. His *Sefer ha-Ikkarim* ("Book of Principles") is an outstanding statement of medieval Jewish philosophy and faith, concerned with those questions of the Messiah and salvation with which Christian theologians were challenging Judaism. Albo distinguished between secular, natural, and Divine law—and assigned sacred primacy to the third. Like many medieval philosophers, he tried to use reason and experience as guides to finding God's will, and ended by stressing faith, revelation, and miracles.

ALFASI, ISAAC BEN JACOB; *also known as ISAAC BEN JACOB HA-KOHEN. Acronym: "Rif." (1013–1103)*

This illustrious scholar-judge was called "Alfasi" ("man of Fez") because he came from Fez and taught there until he was driven to Cordoba, Spain, at the age of seventy-five. He attracted many disciples (among them, Maimonides' future teacher) and composed distinguished *responsa* from North Africa and Spain. He concentrated on the study of the Talmud and collected its legal data and judgments in the *Sefer ha-Halakhot* ("Book of Legal Decisions"), colloquially called *Alfas*. This massive work, the most authoritative text on Talmud until Maimonides superseded it, was so important (during the period when the reading, study, or discussion of the Talmud was prohibited by secular authorities) that it was called "the little Talmud." Alfasi omitted all Haggadic material. In cases of conflict between the Babylonian and Jerusalem Talmuds, he chose to follow the former. The *Sefer ha-Halakhot* inspired a great many commentaries and critical analysis. Alfasi was greatly admired by Maimonides, who, in his *Commentary on the Mishnah,* called Alfasi's juridical decisions "unassailable" (except for a handful). Alfasi died at ninety; on his gravestone is inscribed:

"... the angels of God approached thee
And wrote the Torah on the tablets of thy heart ..."

"AL-HARIZI": JUDAH BEN SOLOMON BEN HOPHNI; *also known as "ALHARIZI." (c. 1170–c. 1235)*

"Al-Harizi," born in Spain, is one of the leading lights and poets of medieval Hebrew literature. He used an informal humorous style, typical of medieval Arabic and Hebrew literature, traveled widely, and wrote about a great variety of subjects. He was the author of *Takhemoni* ("Apothecary"), which consists of fifty *makamot,* or narratives in rhymed prose—an Arabic literary form which he introduced into Hebrew literature. He translated many books from Arabic into Hebrew, including Maimonides' *Guide for the Perplexed.*

ANAV (ANAU, ANAW), JEHIEL BEN JEKUTHIEL:
Hebrew name: Min Ha-Anavim. (Thirteenth century)
This family, presumably settled in Rome by the emperor

Titus, and known in Italian as Piatelli or Mansi, produced many scholars, physicians and poets. Jehiel Ben Jekuthiel was an author, poet, and copyist of sacred texts. He wrote a liturgical poem to commemorate the burning of the synagogue in Rome in 1268. His most popular work is *Maalot ha-Midot* ("The Merit of the Rules").

ARAMA, ISAAC: ISAAC BEN MOSES ARAMA. (*c. 1420–1494*)

Born in Spain (probably in Zamora, where he was head of a rabbinical academy), he served as rabbi in Tarragona, in Fraga, in Calatayud. He sought to counteract the effects of the Christian sermons which the Jews in Spain were compelled to attend. The 1492 decree, expelling all Jews from Spain, drove him to Naples, where he worked and where he finally died.

His major efforts were devoted to refuting philosophers who emphasized Judaism's philosophical, rather than theological, content, or who denied the special nature of God's revelation to the Jews. His best-known book is *Akedat Yitshak* ("The Offering [or "Binding"] of Isaac"): a tract on the relationship between theology and philosophy.

ASHER BEN JEHIEL (JECHIEL); *also known as HA-ASHER and ASHERI (both meaning "the Asherite"), or by the acronym "the RoSH" (from "Rabbenu Asher"). (1250–1327). Do not confuse him with Judah ben Asher (q.v.), his son, or Jacob, his brother.*

Asher ben Jehiel was born in Germany, lived in southern France, then went to Toledo, where he became a rabbi. A leading student of Rabbi Meir of Rothenburg, he followed his teacher's absolute opposition to "liberal" interpretations of Talmud. Asher violently opposed all but Talmudic thought, held religion and philosophy to be incompatible, and hewed to the theological conservatism dominating German Jewry. He fought the influence of Maimonides and even tried to persuade the Toledo synod to forbid Jews to read Greek, Latin, or Islamic books. His influence weakened the contemporary movement in which Jewish students and scholars were acquainting themselves with the classics, secular literature, and works in science.

Asher's abstracts of *halakot* (Talmudic laws), which deliberately excluded the Haggadic (non-legalistic) aspects and debate, are attributed in most editions of the Talmud to "Rabbenu Asher"—from which comes the acronym "Rosh." The rabbinical *decisions* which he himself handed down were separately collected and published (by his son Jacob) as *Piske ha-Rosh.* Asher's *responsa* (answers to questions on Judaic law) provide rich, first-hand information about Jews in Spain in the first decades of the fourteenth century.

ASHI: *RAB ASHI. (c. 352–c. 427)*

The *Rab* ("master") tells us Ashi was a very great rabbi; in fact, he was the leader of the academy at Sura for over fifty years—and chief editor of the Babylonian Talmud, which he arranged, collated, and edited (with the assistance, in so monumental a task, of many scholars and students). He collected all the interpretations of the Mishnah which had been handed down in Babylonian rabbinical academies—to compose the Gemara (*see Glossary*). The Gemara incorporated into the Babylonian Talmud the pertinent discussions of the *Amoraim* (Jewish lecturer–scholar–law-givers in Palestine and Babylon).

Ashi's phenomenal erudition and rigorous judgment make him one of the cardinal figures in all Talmudic thought. He revived Sura as a center of rabbinical thought, and reconstructed both the academy and the synagogue so that their physical splendor became legendary.

"BAAL SHEM TOV (TOB)" *or "BA'AL SHEM-TOV"* ("*Master of the Good Name*") *or "the BeSHT"* (*the acronym*): *ISRAEL BEN ELIEZER. (1700–1760)*

The founder of the remarkable Hasidic movement; a revered, immensely influential, legendary figure, credited with many miraculous cures. *"Baal Shem"* was the name given to men of saintly deportment whom Eastern European Jews believed to possess magical powers (presumably attained through recondite manipulations of the letters that form God's Name), men chosen by the Lord Himself for divine purposes.

Israel ben Eliezer was the most important of these "holy men," a Polish Jew, a *melamed* (teacher of chil-

dren), a lime-burner turned evangelist. He was a visionary who preached simple sermons in an ecstatic, "God-
possessed" style. He traveled about spreading a simple
gospel: "Love God, love Torah, love Man." He urged
his faithful to celebrate the Lord by enjoying life—in
song, laughter, spontaneous dancing, ecstatic states, un-
restrained evidence of adoration of the Holy One. All of
this infuriated orthodox rabbis and scandalized tradi-
tionalists.

Eliezer was a gifted aphorist who scoffed at the
learned, whom he called sterile pedants: "They spend so
much time studying Talmud they have no time to think
about God." The Lord, said Eliezer, is served by deeds
and joy, by living out the precepts of the Torah—*not*
by obsessive reading and academic preoccupations with
texts.

The Baal Shem's adoring disciples grew until they
numbered some 10,000 semi-frenzied souls; their sanctified leader, branded a mountebank or a heretic by the
rabbis of Poland and Galicia, was formally excommunicated by the illustrious Gaon of Vilna, who banned all
of Eliezer's teachings. But Eliezer's influence continued
to grow, for

the Besht said to the poor and the ignorant: God is in
everything, including man. Every man, therefore, is good,
and even a sinner can approach God with devotion. It
does not matter that a simple Jew is unlearned—honest
prayer is as important as erudition. . . . Man must enjoy
human passions, not repress them or run from them. . . .
An entire culture within the culture of the *shtetl* grew up
around the liberating visions of the *Baal Shem Tov*—and
ended, as movements begun by simple men often do, in
a cult."*

The Baal Shem "rejuvenated" Jewry, says Professor
A. J. Heschel; for through Rabbi Israel ben Eliezer Jews
"fell in love with the Lord and felt such yearning for
God that it was unbearable. . . . In the days of Moses,
Israel had a revelation of God; in the days of the Baal
Shem, God had a revelation of Israel."**

* *Joys of Yiddish*, p. 24.
** A. J. Heschel, *The Earth Is the Lord's,* Abelard-Schuman, New York,
1964, pp. 76–98.

Eliezer never wrote down his sermons, parables and sayings. They were included in the various works of his disciples, especially in the publications (about twenty years after the Besht's death) of Jacob Joseph of Polonya. They constitute a remarkable body of homely acumen, exalted aspiration, and touching phrasing.

The Baal Shem carried on the cabalistic teachings of Isaac ben Solomon Luria (*q.v.*), sometimes known as "Ari," whose teachings were posthumously presented in the writings of a disciple, Hayyim Vital (*q.v.*).

BACHYA (BAHYA) BEN ASHER: *full name BACHYA BEN ASHER IBN HALAWA.* (*d. 1340*)

He was born in Saragossa and was a student of Solomon ben Adret, but was more influenced by the works of Ben Adret's teacher, Nachmanides (*q.v.*), whose example Bahya followed in using the cabala as a basis for interpreting scripture. His best known work is a commentary on the Pentateuch. He also wrote *Kad ha-Kemah* ("The Jug of Flour"), an ethical work based on cabalistic concepts.

BAHUR. *See LEVITA, ELIJAH.*

BAR KOCHBA or BAR COCHBA or BAR KOKHBA (*Hebrew: "Son of the Star"*); *the popular name for SIMEON BAR (or BEN) KOSIBA or COZIBA.* (*d. 135 of the Christian Era*)

For centuries, the heroic figure of Bar Kochba has been a part of Jewish folklore, but "more myth than man." Scholars and historians possessed scanty data about "the Second Revolt" of the Jews against the Roman oppressors of Jerusalem. But the Dead Sea caves yielded a priceless cache of letters, 1800 years old, which have authenticated Bar Kochba, his warriors, his successes against the Roman legions, his brief restoration of a Jewish state.

A great revolutionary leader, Bar Kochba claimed to be the Messiah, descended from David, and led the revolt against Hadrian in 132. The revered Rabbi Akiba became his shieldbearer, and acclaimed him the Messiah, but others disputed this overly optimistic view. The ultra-orthodox called Bar Kosiba "Bar Coziba" ("son of deceit") because he once cried, before going into battle: "O Lord, don't help us—and don't spoil it for us!"

Bar Kochba captured Jerusalem, proclaimed a new Jewish state, and held off large, superior Roman armies for over three years. In 135, a Roman counterattack, commanded by Julius Severus, defeated Bar Kochba's forces in their last stronghold, Betar, where Bar Kochba was slain. Records of the time say that 985 villages were destroyed and that 580,000 Jews died in the long fighting (apart from the thousands who perished of hunger and disease).

Rather little is known of Bar Kochba's personal life and characteristics; the anecdotes about him in the Talmud picture him as daring, impetuous, and autocratic —attributes confirmed by the testimony of the letters recently found near the Dead Sea. (See Yigael Yadin, *Bar-Kokhba*, Random House, New York, 1971.)

"THE BELZER RABBI": *SHALOM BEN ELEAZAR*. (*19th cent.*)

Little has been published in English, so far as I can discover, about this hasid who lived in the Galician town of Belz for fifty years, from about 1816 to 1856, and there "founded a hasidic dynasty"; his office passed down to his son, grandson, and great-grandson. Like most hasidic rabbis, his sayings were transmitted orally and recorded by later disciples. Sayings and anecdotes concerning the Belzer Rabbi have appeared in a number of hasidic works: *Dober Sholom* is a collection devoted mainly to him; a recent biography, *Ha-Rab mi-Belz* ("The Rabbi from Belz"), was published in Israel.

BENJAMIN BEN JONAN, OF TUDELA (*BENJAMIN OF TUDELA*). (*Twelfth century*)

This celebrated rabbi, merchant, traveler-memoirist was the first European to describe the Far East—as far, that is, as the borders of China. He lived in Tudela, northern Spain, and between 1160 and 1165 set forth from Saragossa on journeys from which he did not return for seven or eight (some say thirteen) years. He kept clear, carefully detailed notes, from which his travelogue was compiled (by another hand) in 1543. It was translated into Latin, German, French, Dutch, English (in 1625). Benjamin visited almost 300 different places—from France and Italy to Corfu, Greece, Palestine, Turkey, Syria, Egypt, Iraq, and Sicily. He was at one time believed to have entered China, before Marco Polo, but present experts doubt that he went beyond India and Ceylon.

His travel book, *Masaot shel Rabi Binyamin*, contains invaluable data and astute observations on the politics, commerce, geography, and customs of the places he visited—plus the information he collected, in his travels, about places to which he never went. Like all travelers in those days, he made many errors and accepted some tall stories. But his descriptions of Constantinople or Genoa or Alexandria, his observations on Greeks, Turks, Druzes, his comments on officials of the Byzantine court, the Baghdad caliphate—all have proved to be accurate and are invaluable to historians.

Benjamin was especially interested in the communities of Jews, wherever he went, and his accounts of medieval Jewish life are among the best and richest available; they testify to a far-ranging curiosity about everything from schools and synagogues to civil status and occupations. He collected statistical data on the number of Jews in various places—among the first numerical facts gathered on Jewish populations. He catalogued Jewish trades and tradesmen (silk, dyeing, glass-making, ship-building, etc.). He described special Jewish sects in Cyprus, Damascus, Caesarea, etc. His story of David Alroy (Menachim ben Solomon), a famous false messiah of Mesopotamia, is the principal source of our information on that colorful, learned, dubious character who led a messianic movement that began among the "Mountain Jews" of Persia.

The appendix to Benjamin of Tudela's book contains unusual information he had gathered about places and people he did not visit: Slavic lands, the Jews in Germany, northern France. A sample of Benjamin's travelogue is included in *Jewish Travellers*, edited by Elkan N. Adler (Hermon Press, 1966, pp. 38–63); the full text was translated and critically examined by Marcus Nathan Adler, London, H. Froude, 1907 (out of print, alas).

BEN NATRONAI. *See BERECHIAH BEN NATRONAI, HA-NAKDAN.*

BEN SIRACH, JESUS, or JESHUA BEN ELEAZAR BEN SIRA or SIMEON BEN SIRACH; *his Hebrew name, SIMEON, was given in Greek as JESUS or JESHUA. (fl. around 180 before the Christian Era)*

He is the author of the immortal *Ecclesiasticus* (also known as the *Book of Proverbs* or *Sayings of Jesus ben Sirach*) which was composed around 180 B.C., was translated into Greek in 132 B.C. by his grandson, and was subsequently included as a major part of the Apocrypha.

A remarkable lyrical poet and a brilliant aphorist, Ben Sirach belonged to an elite group of scholars and scribes in Jerusalem. He was a renowned teacher in his own school. His work belongs to the "Wisdom Literature" of the Hebrews, in which the recounting of proverbs, parable and fables played an important role. Ben Sirach modestly said he was a "grape-gatherer," but he embroiders earlier proverbs with much beauty and originality. He was a worldly man, widely traveled, forever inspired and enthralled by the services in the Temple. His poetic apothegms contain striking, shrewd, pragmatic observations on man's nature, good and evil, wisdom, free will, parents, children, even commerce.

It is fascinating to note that even though the Talmud (Sanhedrin: 100b) lists Ben Sirach as one of the forbidden books, "outside" the canon, the rabbis often quoted him, and his book was translated from Hebrew into Aramaic—which was the vernacular of Hebrews in Palestine in that time. So well known was Ben Sirach that many of his proverbs, when quoted, simply began "It has been written" or "It is said"—the formal phrase used to introduce sayings from the Old Testament.

He tried to demonstrate the superiority of Judaism over Hellenistic thought, but shows the influence of the latter. (For instance, he considers earthly wisdom part of the Law, the wise virtuous, the foolish wicked— whereas preceding philosophers of Judaism sharply separated divine from human wisdom.)

Ben Sirach's original Hebrew text, which took the Book of Proverbs as its model, was lost in the late tenth century. In 1896, many manuscripts were discovered in the *genizah* ("hiding place") of the Fostat (Cairo)

Synagogue; it was from these and later discoveries (over 100,000 leaves) that Ben Sirach's great work was reconstructed, by Professor Solomon Schechter. In the Masada excavations (1964) under Yigael Yagin, five more chapters were unearthed. But no single manuscript to this day contains the complete Hebrew text of that masterpiece, *Ecclesiasticus*.

BEN ZOMA, SIMEON. (*fl. early 2nd cent. of the Christian Era*)

A famous *Tanna* (teacher) and mystic, famed and acclaimed for his erudition. It was said: "Whoever sees Ben Zoma in his dream is assured of scholarship." Only a few of his written paragraphs have come down to us (most of what we know comes from the disciples who quoted him), but they are enough to indicate his skill and fecundity as an aphorist. It is believed that his theosophical ventures into "the garden of esoteric knowledge" caused Ben Zoma finally to display signs of mental aberration.

"THE BERDICHEVER RABBI": *LEVI ISAAC OF BERDICHEV, or LEVI ISAAC BEN MEIR.* (*1740–1809*)

This chasidic luminary led congregations in Pinsk and Berdichev (or Berdychev) in the Ukraine, and wrote a compilation of ethical sayings. His prayers, Yiddish poems, and songs were widely loved; his Hebrew work *Kedushat Levi* ("The Holiness of Levi;" "The Holy Prayer of Rabbi Levi"), a commentary on the Pentateuch, is considered a classic of hasidic literature. Many legends surround his name and life.

BERECHIAH BEN NATRONAI, HA-NAKDAN (*"the Translator" or "Punctuator"*); *also known as Berechya ben Natronai, and Benedict le Pointeur* (*"Punctuator"*). (*Twelfth–thirteenth century*)

Berechiah, a scribe-punctuator of Bible texts, was a leading writer of fables. He lived in France and England, knew Latin, French and (perhaps) English as well as Hebrew, and is best known for his very popular *Mishle Shualim* ("*Fox Tales*"). This charming collection of 119 folk stories leaned heavily on Aesop, though it includes fables from Hebrew, the Talmud, Midrash—plus many tales Berechiah probably invented. The stories are neatly

satirical, offering moral homilies about animals and in-
sects and even the Leviathan which depict quite human
foibles and failings. Berechiah achieved delightful comic
effects through his allusions to Hebraic sayings and
Talmudic passages, having a dog or wolf, say, calmly
quote a well-known passage from one of the Prophets.
In the original, the prose is rhymed—which suffers
greatly, I am told, in translation. (Incidentally, the Fox
does not appear in every story, as one would expect
from the book's title: Berechiah was simply using the
Talmud's generic name, "fox tales," for fables of any
sort.)

"THE BERSHIDER RABBI": *RAPHAEL (RAFAEL) OF BERSHID or BERSHAD.* (*d. 1816*)

All I can find out about "The Bershider" is that he was a
disciple of "The Koretser Rabbi" (*q.v.*). Like many
hasidic rabbis, he wrote little or nothing, but is remembered through the sagacities, uttered to his flock,
that were widely repeated and carried down the oral
stream of attributions.

THE "BESHT." See *BAAL SHEM TOV*.

BET HILLEL (*"School of Hillel"*).

"BET HILLEL" and "BET SHAMMAI" were the con-
tending schools of *Tannaim* (teachers) during the first
century of the Christian era. They differed sharply in
their approach to, and decisions on, several hundred
cases. We are told that the clash of philosophical prem-
ises almost led to a small civil war among the Jews; but
it should be remembered that philosophical differences
often were enmeshed with political disagreements—
especially about rebellion against Roman rule. The school
of Shammai represented an ultra-nationalistic political
position.

In general, the school of Shammai held the more conservative position, and the Hillelites what may be called
the liberal, humanistic view. But in some cases, the
positions were reversed; sometimes one faction would
adopt the analytic method and conclusions of the other.
The doctrines of the School of Hillel eventually pre-
vailed in most cases involving Jewish law. One legend
holds that a proclamation supporting the Hillel school

was issued by a BAT KOL, "divine voice," from heaven itself. Such advocacy was difficult to contest.

BIALIK, CHAIM NACHMAN, *or HAYYIM NAHMAN BIALIK.* (*1873–1934*)

A great Hebrew poet, a commanding figure in modern Jewish literature, and a central force in twentieth-century Judaic culture. Born in Russia, Bialik moved to Berlin and founded several publishing houses. He became Chairman of the *Vaad ha-Lashon* ("Hebrew Language Council") in Tel Aviv, where he went to live in 1924. Bialik was a spearhead in reviving and modernizing Hebrew—as writer, publisher, editor, translator, anthologist. He translated Shakespeare, Cervantes, *The Dybbuk*, and *William Tell* into Hebrew.

He wrote many exquisite poems and stories, a classic anthology of Midrashic literature (with Y. H. Rabnitsky), and edited the poems of Moses ibn Ezra and Solomon ibn Gabirol. He was a discerning anthologist of Jewish folk tales and played an important role on the board of editors of The Hebrew Technical Dictionary (1929).

"THE BRATSLAVER RABBI". *See NACHMAN OF BRATSLAV.*

BUBER, MARTIN (*1878–1965*)

One of the great philosopher-theologians of the modern era, Martin Buber was born in Vienna, raised in Lvov, Poland, studied at German universities, was profoundly influenced by hasidic thought, and envisioned religion as a continuing dialogue between God and man: In this, he exercised a profound and enduring influence on Christian theology.

Buber edited the Zionist journal *Die Welt* ("The World") and founded the so-called "democratic faction" of the Zionist movement. With Franz Rosenzweig, he made a German translation of the Bible. Buber served as Professor of the Philosophy of Jewish Religion and Ethics at the University of Frankfurt. He settled in Jerusalem in 1938, and became Professor of the Sociology of Religion at the Hebrew University. He was a strong advocate of *rapprochement* between Jews and Arabs.

His best known works, in English, are *Tales of the Chasidim* (or *Hasidim*), *I and Thou*, *Between Man and Man*, *The Prophetic Faith*.

BUBER, SOLOMON (*1827–1906*)

Grandfather of Martin Buber, Solomon Buber was a scholar of Talmud who earned his livelihood as a businessman in Lvov, Poland. He discovered important ancient *midrashim* in obscure manuscripts and published them with comprehensive notes. Buber wrote many essays on the history of the Polish Jews, and edited medieval masterworks by Rashi (*q.v.*), Saadia Gaon (*q.v.*), and others.

BUNIM (BUNAM), SIMCHA: *SIMCHA BUNAN (BUNAM) BUNEHART; also known as "the Cosmopolitan Rebbe."* (*1765–1827*)

This exceptional rationalist, the son of a *maggid* (itinerant teacher-preacher), disciple of such seers as Rabbi Moses Leib of Sassov (*q.v.*), followed the advice of Rabbi Israel of Kozienice, and went to work as the representative of an industrialist. He led a rich, secular life, abandoning his hasidic clothes and enjoying the Polish and German theater. Then he became a factor in lumber, then a chemist. But his interest in Talmud and hasidism did not die; each night, he closed his apothecary shop and consulted "the Jew of Bunim Pzysha," Rabbi Jacob Isaac; and when that worthy soul died, Bunim succeeded him as rabbi.

Bunim emphasized Maimonides and Judah ben Low ben Bezalel of Prague—against those who were following the Baal Shem (*q.v.*). Bunim placed little faith in cabalism—and none in popularly touted "miracles." Indeed, his scorn for "the cult of the *tsadik* [saint]" was expressed in a dry epigram: "A fur hat and an illustrious father do not make a *tsadik*."

Bunim went blind, accepting this fate philosophically: "What is good for me to see, I see—with 'the inner light.' That which would not be good for me to see, I do not wish to see at all." Rabbi Bunim was a prolific producer of parables which are quoted to this day; they explain the admiration he has continued to enjoy.

CARO (KARO), JOSEPH: *or JOSEPH BEN EPHRAIM CARO. Not to be confused with at least eight other rabbis or historians, in Poland, Germany, Russia, Turkey, who bear the distinguished family name of Caro.* (*1488– 1575*)

Joseph Caro was the last of the great codifiers of the rabbinical laws and interpretations of the Law. His *Shulhan Arukh* ("The Prepared Table"), published in 1564, is still accepted in orthodox circles as the final code of authority on Judaic law, ethics, and ritual.

Caro was born in either Portugal or Spain and went to Turkey with his parents. He became strongly interested in mysticism, though not (oddly enough) in the cabala; and he even yearned for a martyr's fate "to sanctify God's sacred Name." (In this, he was influenced by Solomon Molcho, a Portuguese-Spanish convert to Judaism.) Caro had many dreams, which he called revelations from a divine mentor who was the Mishnah personified.

He emigrated to Palestine, after several years in Salonica and Constantinople. In Safed, under Jacob Berab, who ordained him, Caro founded his own *yeshiva.* His *Bet Yosef* ("House of Joseph"), an extraordinary commentary and analysis of Talmudic and post-Talmudic literature from which the *Shulhan Aruk* was digested, brought him tremendous prestige—and an authority such as had not honored any Jewish intellectual since Maimonides. Rabbis wrote to him from Italy and France for his judgment on complex cases—despite recurring discontent with his messianic strain.

He alleged that he was being made privy to great secrets confided to him by an angel. But his codifications of Judaic Law show no signs of his mystical predilections. And the sheer range and detail of his "Table" can only elicit admiration; he instructs the reader in such matters as Thoughts While Shampooing Hair; Tatooing and Depilation; Can Interest Be Taken on Loans?; The Taboo on Excessive Displays of Excessive Grief; Promises and Vows and Oaths, etc.

The historic *Shulhan Aruk* survived violent attacks from the rabbis of Poland and the influential Solomon Luria; the Ashkenazic rabbis thought that the Sephardim, of whom Caro was of course one, were prone to introduce "dangerous" innovations in ritual and liturgy. The hostility to the *Shulhan Aruk* raged for a century after its appearance, but in the middle of the seventeenth century the classic began to be accepted by even Polish Talmudists.

Some authorities consider Caro too rigid and his Judaism, therefore, "a strait-jacket." But no one questions his massive scholarship or his achievement in reconciling Sephardic and Ashkenazic religious practices.

CASPI, JOSEPH BEN ABBA MARI. *Not to be confused with his namesake, Joseph Caspi ben Shalom of the sixteenth century.* (*c. 1280–c. 1340*)

Born and raised in the south of France, Caspi (which stands for "made of silver," a surname derived from his birthplace, Largentière) traveled widely in France, Spain, and Egypt. His Provençal name was Don Bonafous de Largentera.

A philosopher and grammarian, he was greatly influenced by Aristotle and Averroes, whose teachings he found entirely consonant with Judaism: This did not endear him to medieval rabbis. Many of Caspi's works (he was a prolific author) were lost; his most important two books are commentaries on Maimonides' *Guide for the Perplexed*. Strict Talmudists reprove Caspi for his belief that the universe is eternal—*i.e.*, was not made by God.

CHAIM OF VOLOZHIN. *See HAYYIM BEN ISAAC.*

CHIA, RABBI. *See HIYYA.*

"CHOFETZ CHAIM" or HAPHETZ HAYYIM ("He who desires life"); *also called RABBI HACOHEN. ISRAEL MEIR KAHAN.* (*1838–1933*)

A formidable rabbi, one of the most respected leaders of Ashkenazic Jewry, "The Chofetz Chaim" told and invented hundreds of homely folk stories, each with a moral designed to underline a total preoccupation with Torah and service to the Almighty.

His pen-name comes from a story in the Talmud ('Abodah Zarah, 19b): Rabbi Alexandrai stretches out his hands to the people and asks: "Who wants life?" As they flocked to him, Rabbi Alexandrai told them to re-

read King David's words [34th Psalm]: "Who is the man who desires life, and wants to enjoy happiness for many days? Keep your tongue from evil and your lips from deceit. Avoid evil and do good; seek peace and pursue it."

A bearded, formidable figure, Rabbi Hacohen wrote a considerable number of books—mostly meant for laymen: as guides to living; to reinforce piety, prayer, purity of devotion, the sanctity of the family, one's primary duty to God; or to discourage gossip, encourage charity; or to lift the hearts of Jewish soldiers drafted into foreign armies, or to comfort Jews lonely in far-off lands.

All of his tales and writings were permeated by absolute fundamentalism, unswerving orthodoxy, insistence on every jot and tittle of gospel truth.

One story illustrates this patriarch's acting-out of one of the 613 *mitzvahs:* A thief stole a parcel from the rabbi's person and shot away—and "Chofetz Chaim" ran after him, frantically yelling, "I forgive you! I forgive you!"

He died at the age of ninety-five.

CORDOVERO, MOSES BEN JACOB; *also known as RAMAK or REMAK.* (1522–1570)

Moses Cordovero, rabbi of Safed, came from a Spanish Jewish family, no doubt from Cordoba's illustrious colony of Jews. He studied under the great Caro (*q.v.*) and proceeded to explore the cabala and its mysteries. Extremely competent in Arabic philosophy as well as Judaic thought, Cordovero became a leader of the mystical school in Safed. His expositions of the fundamentals of cabalistic theology (divine emanations, the Names of God, hidden significances attributed to letters of the Hebrew alphabet, etc.) won him great renown. Cordovero echoed Aristotle's ideas that the thinking of the Lord must be different, in kind, from human modalities of reason—that in divine thinking, the thought and the material objects thought of, are inseparable, one, absolute. Spinoza probably read Cordovero with profit: their conceptions of God are strikingly similar. *Pardes Rimonim* ("Orchard of Pomengrates") is the work by which Cordovero is best remembered.

DELMEDIGO, ELIJAH: *ELIJAH CRETENSIS BEN MOSES ABBA DELMEDIGO. Do not confuse with Joseph Solomon ben Elijah Delmedigo (q.v.). (1460–1497)*

Delmedigo (from the Italian "del Medico") is the name of a famous Jewish family of scholars and physicians who emigrated from Germany to Crete, in the late fourteenth century, and were rabbis on that island for generations.

Elijah ben Moses was born in Candia, as a child showed unusual intellect, and in his early twenties was invited to head a Talmudic school in Padua. His Latin was elegant. He held chairs in philosophy at the universities of Padua, Venice, Perugia and Florence. (Pico della Mirandola, the great Renaissance humanist, was one of his students—and was to translate the *Zohar* into Latin.)

Elijah Delmedigo became one of the stars in the brilliant galaxy of talent in Florence. He expounded the theories of Maimonides and Averroes, whose work he translated, and wrote learned commentaries on Plato and Aristotle. In Judaic matters, he attacked cabala ("an intellectual swamp"), upheld the *halakic* portions of Talmud as divine, but said the Haggadic portions could claim no sanction higher than that of mortal judgments. Jealousies, intrigues, and a quarrel with the rabbi of Padua, who distrusted Delmedigo's secular writings and disliked his staunch independence in religion, drove Delmedigo to return to Crete. He taught philosophy there. His reputation grew so great that upon his death "crowds of learned Christians, clad in mourning" attended his funeral.

His best-known book, an effort to separate philosophy and religion, is *Behinat ha-Dat* ("Examination of Religion"), from which the quotations in the present anthology were taken.

DELMEDIGO, JOSEPH SOLOMON BEN ELIJAH; *also known by the acronym YaSHaR (from JOSEPH SOLOMON ROFE). Do not confuse with Elijah ben Moses Delmedigo (q.v.). (1591–1655)*

Born in Candia, Crete, of the distinguished Jewish Italian family of physicians and scholars, Joseph Solomon Delmedigo, son of the rabbi of Candia, entered the

University of Padua when fifteen, and specialized in mathematics and astronomy. He was a physician, philosopher, mathematician, Talmudic scholar, and astronomer (he studied under Galileo). He often visited Leone da Modena (*q.v.*) in Venice, and was influenced by that ingenious, erratic figure.

Delmedigo's somewhat secular views made life in Crete difficult for him; he went to Cairo, to find books to add to his library; and there met Karaite Jews—and wrote a book on mechanics. In Turkey, he studied the cabala. Then he visited or worked in Germany, Holland, Bohemia, Poland (he was personal physician to Prince Radziwill, in Vilna); was for a time a teacher of Sephardic Jews and a rabbi in Hamburg and Amsterdam; served as town physician of Frankfort; and settled in Prague, in 1648, where he lived until his death.

Joseph Delmedigo's reputation was marred by the fact that he defended the Cabala publicly but scoffed at it in private. For all his piety and erudition, he won a reputation for insincerity; I think he feared being accused of heresy.

But he was a far-ranging intelligence, of notable versatility and outstanding scholarship. He wrote on logic, chemistry, geometry, harmony, ancient science, astronomy, metaphysics, optics. He translated Hippocrates' Latin aphorisms into Hebrew, and some of Philo's and Abravanel's writings. His *Sefer Elim* ("Book of Elim," an allusion to Exodus, 15 : 27) answers twelve questions in science, gives seventy paradoxes in mathematics, and is a collection of various writings.

EIBESCHUTZ, JONATHAN (*EYBESHITZ, EYBE-SCHITZ, EYBENSCHUTZ*). (*c. 1690–1764*)

Born in Cracow, Eibeschutz became one of the leading scholars and Talmudists of his time. He presided over a *yeshiva* in Prague and became the chief rabbi of Metz, Germany. He was an authority on the cabala. Some thought him a follower of the legendary, notorious Sabbatai (or Shabbetai) Zvi (or Zvei or Zevi), "the Messiah of Izmir," one of the more amazing mystics and mountebanks of the seventeenth century. (See my *Joys of Yiddish*, pp. 503–7).

ELEAZAR (ELIEZER) HA-KAPPAR; *not to be confused with his son, Bar Kappara.* (*Second century*)

This fourth-generation *Tanna* is quoted several times in the Mishnah (*Aboth*, 4, 21–22). His lucid exhortations on peace, virtue, envy, ambition, evil, and the judgment of God are cited in the *Pirke d'Rabbi Nathan* (xxiv, 4), in *Derekh Erets Zuta* (9, 1), and in *Sifre Be-Midbar* ("Sifre on the Book of Numbers").

Authorities caution us that Eleazar's son, Bar Kappara, may have coined some of the precepts attributed to his father. Bar Kappara collected *The Mishnah of Bar Kappara*. He was a brilliant maker of fables and conversationalist, and headed an academy near Lydda (Lod).

ELEAZAR BEN JUDAH of WORMS: *also known as ELEAZAR ROKEACH (ROKEAH).* (*c. 1160 or 1176–1238*)

This Talmudic scholar, a native of Mayence, and a rabbi in Worms, was descended from the famous Kalonymus family. In 1196, two Crusaders broke into his home and murdered his wife and two daughters (and possibly his son, too) before his eyes.

Eleazar ben Judah was immensely erudite, studied astronomy and, as a liturgist, wrote over fifty psalms and dirges. Absorbed in cabala, he stressed the confession of sin and its heartfelt repentance. He popularized an haggadic mysticism that was to be profoundly influential among the Ashkenazim. In 1233, he participated in the historic Synod of Mayence, which produced a body of important Judaic enactments.

Eleazar published many treatises: on the unity of God, gematria, confession, mystical ruminations about different passages of Torah and the psalms, commentaries on the prayers of other Talmudists (*e.g.,* Delmedigo), on the different names of God, on angels, on seventy-three "Gates [chapters] to the Torah." But it is his exquisite ethical sayings, which echo the style of the prophets, that are most remembered. His best-known work (1505) is *Sefer ha-Rokeakh* ("The Book of the Dealer in Spices"), from which he came to be known as Eleazar Rokeach.

ELIEZER BEN ISAAC, HA-GADOL: *also called ELIE-ZER GAON, "ELIEZER THE GREAT."* (*Eleventh century*)

A famous German rabbi, often quoted by no less than Rashi (*q.v.*), Eliezer ha-Gadol was believed by some to be the author of *Orhot Hayim* ("Paths of Life"); but this work is now credited to Eliezer ben Hyrcanos (or Hyrcanus), *q.v.*, in the *Jewish Encyclopedia* (vol. v, p. 115). Eliezer ha-Gadol may be the author of a penitential prayer, "*Elohai Baser Ameka*" ("My God, fortify your people"), which very orthodox Jews recite in the *Yom Kippur Katan* ("Minor Days of Atonement") prayers/fasts before the new moon.

ELIEZER, ISRAEL BEN. *See "BAAL SHEM TOV."*

EZOBI, JOSEPH BEN HANAN (*Thirteenth century*)

A poet who lived in Perpignan, Ezobi wrote liturgical passages about the Feast of Pentecost and Jewish martyrs under Hadrian. His most important poem was *Kararat Kesef* ("Bowl of Silver"), which advised his son on how to live and study—warning him against Greek thought and urging him to read Talmud and study Maimonides. *Kararat Kesef* has been translated into English by I. Freedman (*Jewish Quarterly Review*, vol. viii, p. 535).

FALAQUERA (PALQUERA), SHEM-TOV BEN JOSEPH; *also known as SHEM TOB PALQUERA, or IBN FALAQUERA.* (*1225–c. 1290*)

This Spanish philosopher-poet-translator came from a distinguished family of Jews in Toledo. His life and personal characteristics remain virtually unknown. From his treatises on religion, philosophy, psychology, metaphysics, it is clear the Falaquera was extremely knowledgeable about Plato, Aristotle, Greek and Arabic philosophy. He made Hebrew translations and scholarly abridgments of Averroes and Avicenna. His works embrace a very wide range, from dreams and the nature of body and soul to the compatibility of Torah with secular science. He defended Maimonides and urged Jewish scholars to study the great Greek thinkers. He even attempted a prose-poetic summation of all human knowledge. It is no wonder he was called "*Shem Tob*" (Good Name).

GABIROL. *See IBN GABIROL.*

"THE GERER RABBI": *ISAAC MEIR BEN ISRAEL ALTER* (*of Rothenburg*); *also known as "The Old Gerer Rabbi" and "Hiddushe ha-Rim."* (*1799–1866*)

This rabbi, one of the leading Talmudists of Poland, was so esteemed that forty years after his death his followers were said to number over 100,000. At the age of seventeen, he had written extensive notes for several tractates of the Talmud; they are known as *Hiddushe ha-Rim* ("New Interpretation of Rabbi Isaac Meir").

GERONDI, JONAH BEN ABRAHAM: *or GERONDI "THE PIOUS." Not to be confused with Gersonides* (*q.v.*). (*d. 1263*)

Jonah ben Abraham Gerondi, called "the Pious," headed the important Toledo *yeshiva* (rabbinical college). He was a cousin of Nachmanides (*q.v.*), wrote ethical treatises, and produced commentaries on the Talmud that influenced later scholars. Gerondi, incidentally, was the surname given to families from Gerona (or Gerunda) in Catalonia, an important Jewish community from the eleventh century until the expulsion of the Jews in 1492.

GERSONIDES: LEVI BEN GERSON (GERSHON); *also known by the acronym "RaLBaG;" as Leon de Bagnols; and* (*in Latin*) *Magister Leo Hebraeus.* (*1288–1344*)

Very little is known about the life of this remarkable French Jewish philosopher, physician, Talmudist, scholar, mathematician and astronomer. He was a master of the works of Aristotle and Averroes, wrote important books on geometry (he is said to have laid the foundations of modern trigonometry), invented a nautical device called "Jacob's Staff," and improved the *camera oscura*. His writing on astronomy criticized Ptolemaic assumptions. He is said to have been the last Jewish Aristotelian. His views were severely criticized by Hasdai Crescas, the Spanish Jewish philosopher who was Crown Rabbi of Aragon(and whose disciple was Joseph Albo, *q.v.*).

Gersonides' chief work, insofar as this anthology is concerned, was *Milhamot Adonai* ("Wars of the Lord").

GINZBERG ASHER. *See "AHAD HA-AM."*

HA-ASHERI. *See ASHER BEN JEHIEL.*

HA-GADOL. *See ELIEZER BEN ISAAC, HA-GADOL.*

HAI GAON: *or HAI (Gaon means "Eminence").* (939–1038)

The *geonim* (plural of *gaon*) were the intellectual leaders of the Jewish community in Babylon from the sixth to the eleventh century. They led the studies of the academies in Sura, Nehardea, and Pumbedita, and exercised great judicial-legal-temporal power among Jews everywhere.

Hai, son of an influential *gaon*, was the last *gaon* of Pumbedita. He was appointed head of the ecclesiastical court, the *Bet Din*, in 998. Hai made his academy the leading center of Jewish scholarship; students from all of Europe and Asia flocked to Pumbedita. Theologians and rabbis often wrote to Hai, whose responses interpreting the Law were accepted as definitive. He wrote learned commentaries (in Arabic) on Torah and Talmud until his death, past the age of ninety-nine.

HA-KAPPAR, ELEAZAR. *See ELEAZAR HA-KAPPAR.*

HA-LEVI, AARON OF BARCELONA. (*c. 1300*)

The author, probably, of *Sefer ha-Hinukh* (*Hinnukh*), "the Book of Education," a classic which enumerates and analyzes the 613 divine precepts. The text was early translated into Latin and into French.

HA-LEVI, JUDAH: *JUDAH BEN SAMUEL HA-LEVI, or JEHUDA HALEVI or HA-LEVI. Do not confuse ha-Levi with the French writers, Elie or Joseph Halevy.* (*c. 1075–1141*)

By profession a physician ("We heal Babylon, but it cannot be healed," he said), ha-Levi, a Spanish Jew born in Toledo, won a reputation as a poet-philosopher. A master of Arabic, he introduced Arabic forms and meter into Hebrew verse. His *Zionides* ("Songs of Zion") are lovely, lyrical expressions of the Jews' longings to return to the holy land. He used much symbolism in his poetry and included many quotations from the Bible and rabbinical literature. His "sacred" poems were so beautiful that they became part of many Jewish liturgies.

Ha-Levi's most important work was *The Kuzari* (or *Ha-Kuzari*)—written (1130–1140) in Arabic, just before ha-Levi left Spain. The title alludes to a discussion between a rabbi and a king of the Khazars, a Turkish or Finnish sect settled along the lower Volga. (The king was converted to Judaism, according to legend—400 years before ha-Levi began his masterwork.) *The Kuzari* is a long defense of, and sustained argument for, the faith of the Jews. The subtitle, "An Argument for the Faith of Israel," tells us this was a defense of a severely harassed religious group, caught within the struggle of Catholics and Muslims for the domination of Spain—and Holy Palestine (where the Crusaders appeared to have doomed Israel to extinction). Ha-Levi often used the dialogue form, reminiscent of Plato, in his account of the debate between the Khazars and "the Rabbi." Translated into Hebrew by Judah ibn Tibbon (*q.v.*), *The Kuzari* exercised a world-wide influence on Jews: it is considered a classic in the literature of Judaism. It has been translated into English (Schocken Books, 1964), and the introduction by Henry Slonimsky is well worth reading.

HA-LEVI, JUDAH HASID. *See JUDAH the PIOUS.*

"HA-NAKDAN." *See BERECHIAH BEN NATRONAI, HA-NAKDAN. (Third century)*

It was said of this great Babylonian halakist (expert on the Law) that he could recite the entire body of rabbinical Law from memory. He was a scribe, a disciple of Rab (Abba Arika), and his name is found often in the Talmud (in both the Babylonian and Jerusalem texts) because he taught many scholars the tradition and responsibilities of the scribe.

"HA-PENINI." *See BEDERSI, JEDAIAH BEN.*

HAPHETZ HAYYIM. *See "CHOFETZ CHAIM."*

HASDAI, ABRAHAM BEN SAMUEL HA-LEVI, or IBN HASDAI. *(fl. first part of thirteenth century)*

This Barcelona Jew, supporter of Maimonides and a vigorous polemicist in his behalf, translated many works into Hebrew from Arabic; some classic Arabic works became known only through Hasdai's translations. He translated Maimonides' famous *Letter to Yemen* from Arabic into Hebrew. He wrote in an elegant style.

His story of the Buddha *(Ben ha-Melekh ve-ha-Nazir)*, taken from Arabic sources (themselves translated from Indian or Persian, and probably embellished by Hasdai), played an important part in acquainting Western Europe with Buddhism.

HAYYIM BEN ISAAC, OF VOLOCHIN; *also known as* CHAYIM OF VOLOZHIN. *(1749–1821)*

A leading Lithuanian Talmudic scholar, a student of the great Vilna Gaon, Chayim ben Isaac founded a *yeshiva* (rabbinical academy) in Volozhin, in 1802. He was extremely influential, amongst the Jews of Lithuania, in opposing both the hasidic and Haskalah (enlightenment) movements.

HILLEL. *(flourished first century of the Christian Era)*

Called "the Elder," *(ha-Zakan)* and the leader of the Pharisees, Hillel was a peerless scholar, teacher, judge, legalist, unsurpassed in intellect and influence, renowned for the saintliness of his character and conduct. He stressed humility, charity, love, fear of God, and—above all—love of one's fellowmen and a passion for peace. He is credited with the Golden Rule, albeit in reverse form, saying to a non-believer: "What is hateful to thee, do not unto thy fellow man. That is the whole Law: all the rest is commentary." (Jesus was certainly influenced by many anecdotes told about Hillel; and Paul, the evangelist, was a pupil of Hillel's grandson, Gamaliel.)

Details of Hillel's early life are scant. Born in Babylonia, he is nowhere called, as was common practice, "Hillel, son of [his father's name]." Some held him to be descended from David. In the days of King Herod, Hillel, suffering great hardships, received a Doctor of Laws degree in Jerusalem. There he worked for about forty

years. Many Jews drew parallels between the life of
Moses and the life of Hillel; both presumably died at the
age of 120. Hillel's descendants led Judaism in Palestine
for five centuries.

Legend holds that Hillel became the head of the Sanhedrin (the highest ecclesiastical court of the Jews).
He did create the basic seven rules of hermeneutics used
to determine the full meaning of passages, prescriptions
and laws in the Old Testament, and the prestige of his
name was so potent that it often endowed his interpretations of the Law with the status of decrees. Hillel's
"school" (called *Bet Hillel*, "the School of Hillel") came
to prevail over the contrary interpretations of Shammai,
his colleague and opponent, and "the Shammai school."
It is a curious tribute to Hillel's wisdom and character
that the profound respect and affection he enjoyed among
Jews was never embroidered (as other sages' names
were) with legends about putative wizardry, miraculous
cures, or necromantic capacities.

Hillel's many marvelous sayings are preserved in the
Babylonian Talmud, partly in Hebrew and partly in
Aramaic (at that time the language of the masses). His
style is lucid and epigrammatic; his thought is permeated by singular compassion and an almost mystical
consciousness of God; his emphasis on brotherly love
and peace were basic formative elements in the gospel of
Christianity. His conceptions of duty, honor, righteousness, learning are unsurpassed for simplicity of phrasing
and nobility of substance: "If I am not for myself, who
is for me? And if I am only for myself, what am I? And
if not now—when?" He must surely be ranked among
the wisest and noblest men in human history.

HIYYA (CHIA) BAR ABBA: *called HIYYA RABBAH,
the Great, or HIYYA THE ELDER, to distinguish him
from Rabbi Hiyya bar Abba (bar-Wa, bar-Ba)—whose
biography follows this one. (second century of the
Christian Era)*

Often quoted in the literature of the Haggadah, Hiyya was
the author of many important, conservative legal decisions (*halakot*), and was highly regarded in Babylon
as a physician. He edited several historic *halakot* that had
not been included in the Mishnah (*Baraitot de Rabi
Hiya, Mishnayot Gedolot, Mishnah de Rabi Hiya*), and

exerted great influence in founding rabbinical schools and furthering the practices of learning.

HIYYA (CHIA), RABBI: *HIYYA BAR ABBA; also known as HIYYA BAR WA or HIYYA BAR BA. Not to be confused with the elder, Rabbah Hiyya—above. (End of third century of the Christian Era)*

He is referred to, in the Palestinian/Babylonian Talmuds, as Rabbi Hiyya, Hiyya bar-Ba, Hiyya bar-Wa. A native of Babylon, descended from priestly Amoraim (scholar-teachers), he went at an early age to Palestine, where he became a disciple of Rabbi Johanan. He became a master, so acknowledged of *halaka* (Law). He recited the words of the masters with such fidelity that his renditions were preferred to all others for accuracy and reliability. He was so fanatical about the sanctity of Oral law that he castigated those who sought to write down his own profound commentaries—but it was, nonetheless, sensibly done.

IBN EZRA, ABRAHAM BEN MEIR; *also known as ABEN EZRA. (1092–1167)*

A scholar and poet, Ibn Ezra lived in Spain until he was fifty-one, then traveled widely in France, Italy, England and (possibly) Palestine. He wrote many poems, both secular and sacred, and produced a great many Hebrew aphorisms and paradoxes. His interpretations of the Law were exceptionally sophisticated in textual and linguistic analysis. He wrote several works on astrology, a commentary on Exodus, and translated many Arabic works in Hebrew.

IBN EZRA, MOSES BEN JACOB *(known in Arabic as ABU HARUN MUSA). Do not confuse with Solomon ben Moses ibn Ezra. (1055–after 1135)*

Born in Granada, of a great Spanish Jewish family, he fled after the Amoravides, a Muslim sect, captured that town. He was a distinguished linguist, a melancholy poet, a philosopher of acumen, close to Judah ha-Levi (*q.v.*) who said "Moses ibn Ezra draws pearls from the wells of thoughts." After his flight from Granada, he endured much suffering. He wrote in Arabic and in Hebrew: many religious and secular poems, a book on rhetoric, another on poetry which includes valuable material on

Hebrew poetry and the history of poetry in Spain, and a philosophical treatise on Neo-Platonism. He included many aphorisms in his writings.

Moses ibn Ezra is an acknowledged master of Hebrew and Arabic; his *Tarshish* (1210 lines) and *"Anak"* are vivid secular excursions into beauty, wine, love, the countryside, friends, love-sickness, misfortune and death. Yet a current of gravity ran through all of his work, even where the subject is gay, even frivolous.

IBN FALAQUERA. *See FALAQUERA.*

IBN GABIROL: *SOLOMON BEN JUDAH IBN GABIROL (GEBIROL); also known as ABU AYYUB SULAIMAN IBN YAHYA IBN JABIRUL. (c. 1021–about 1058)*

Born in Saragossa, orphaned, sickly—for the rest, little is known of the early years of this immortal medieval poet and essayist. He began to write poetry at sixteen, greatly influenced by mystical literature, earlier Spanish Hebrew poetry, and Sufism, a Muslim sect.

Ibn Gabirol wrote many cheerful verses, celebrating love and drinking; many intensely introspective, gloomy poems; and many noble, lyrical works that exalt humility, submission to God, and a spiritual yearning for the redemption of man: many of the latter became part of Jewish liturgy. His great *Keter Malkhut* ("Crown of Kinship with the Divine") was a lofty tribute to the Lord—and a revelation of Ibn Gabirol's sense of insignificance in the cosmos. Several of his neo-Platonic treatises, written in Arabic and translated into Latin, influenced the Catholic scholastics and—later—Spinoza. His most important philosophical treatise is *Tikun Midot ha-Nefesh* ("The Improvement of the Moral Qualities").

His work was not collected until the nineteenth century, and was not published *in toto* until 1924–32 (by Chaim Bialik and Y. Ravnitsky). He is one of the poets most loved by readers of Hebrew, and is one of the aphorists most often quoted in this anthology.

IBN HASDAI. *See HASDAI.*

IBN PAQUDA (PAKUDA), BAHYA BEN JOSEPH; *or BACHYA IBN PAQUDA; sometimes called "the Saint".* (c. 1050–c. 1120)

A *dayan* (ecclesiastical judge) in Saragossa, Ibn Paquda
was a philosopher-theologian about whose life very little
is known. But his influence on Jewish moralists and
mystics has been enormous, chiefly because of his masterpiece *Hovot ha-Levavot* (*"The Duties of the Heart"*),
perhaps the first Jewish systematic treatise on ethics.

Bahya divided the duties of man into those which
are physical (and visible) and those which are spiritual
—including faith, compassion for others, the avoidance of jealousy, hostility, vengefulness. He tried, as he
said in his preface, to synthesize for the first time "the
duties of the mind and the duties of the heart." The work
is simple in style, natural in phrasing and feeling, employs charming parables, and directs personal appeals
(for which he gently apologizes) to the reader.

Duties of the Heart was written in Arabic, translated
into Hebrew and Ladino and Yiddish, bridging the
Sephardic and Ashkenazic worlds with equal popularity.
Bahya ibn Paquda became so beloved by the Jewish
masses that he was dubbed "the Saint." The book was
gracefully translated into English by Moses Hyamson.

Ibn Paquda said that self-examination, asceticism,
humility and love of God are as important as observing
the commandments. He was greatly influenced by Saadia
Gaon (*q.v.*), and quotes Aristotle and Muhammed (after
all, the sages had said that many a wise man is to be
found among the gentiles). Bahya is quoted on many
topics in the present anthology.

IBN TIBBON, JUDAH BEN SAUL; *or JUDAH IBN
TIBBON.* (*c. 1120–d. sometime after 1190*)
Not to be confused with others, contemporary and later,
whose patronym is "Ibn Tibbon": namely Abraham,
Jacob ben Machir, Judah ben Moses, Moses, Moses ben
Isaac, Samuel, Samuel ben Judah. The family of Spanish
Jewish scholars were translators and commentators of
great importance in the history of Hebrew literature.

Judah ben Saul ibn Tibbon was a physician, born in
Granada, from which he was driven in 1150 to settle in
Lunel, in southern France. He translated Arabic works
by Spanish Jews into Hebrew—most notably Saadia
Gaon, Bahya ibn Paquda, and Judah ha-Levi. Ibn
Tibbon has been criticized for taking excessive poetic
license in these translations, but praised for his ingenuity

in concocting Hebrew terms for technical concepts in philosophy. Perhaps his own best-known work (not translation) was his "ethical will" to his son, Samuel: a paternal, moralistic guide to duty and faith—with careful advice about the preservation of manuscripts.

IBN VERGA, JUDAH (JOSEPH). (*Fifteenth to sixteenth century*)

The *Jewish Encyclopedia* and the *New Standard Jewish Encyclopedia* differ on identifying Ibn Verga. Sources also differ about whether one Solomon ibn Verga was the son of Judah (or Joseph); Judah is presumed by some students to have been Solomon's grandfather; and some scholars cite a second Joseph ibn Verga—of Avlona, Spain. (I'm sorry if all this confuses you; it does me.)

Judah ibn Verga was an historian, astronomer and rabbi who left Seville in 1492, at the time of the catastrophic (to Spain no less than to Jewry) expulsion. He went to Lisbon, where he suffered martyrdom. He wrote *Shevet Yehudah* ("The Rod of Judah")—a title also used in Italy by Solomon ibn Verga, who had also fled Spain.

IBN ZABARA, JOSEPH BEN MEIR. (*c. 1140–c. 1200*)

A physician in Barcelona and a Spanish Hebrew poet, Ibn Zabara's *Sefer Shaashuim* ("Book of Delight") contains many delightful parables and anecdotes, in rhymed verses, and is a treasury of folk lore—which he said he had collected during his extensive travels. He has been translated into English, beautifully, by the late Professor Moses Hadas of Columbia University.

"IMMANUEL of Rome": *IMMANUEL BEN SOLOMON; also known as IMMANUEL BEN SOLOMON BEN JEKUTHIEL, or as the Italian poet MANOELLO GIUDEO.* (*1260–c. 1328*)

A poet and teacher, Immanuel traveled widely through his native Italy. He wrote many philosophical commentaries on the Old Testament, but only a portion were ever published. His vast body of poetry contains majestic hymns—and surprisingly candid erotica.

He is believed to have been the first poet to introduce the form of the sonnet into Hebrew literature. He also wrote an "imitation" of Dante. His *Mahberot Immanuel* ("Compositions of Immanuel"), which is the work quoted in the present anthology, was a collection of miscellaneous writings and verse on the model of Al-Harizi's *Tahkemoni*, proscribed by some Italian rabbis because of its occasionally earthy content. He worked in the rhymed prose (interspersed with poetic excursions) structure known as *makamot*.

ISRAEL BEN ELIEZER. *See "BAAL SHEM TOV."*

JABIRUL. *See IBN GABIROL.*

JEDAIA BEN BEDERSI; *also known as JEDAIAH of BEZIERS; pen-name "HA-PENINI" ("Dispenser of Pearls"). (c. 1270–c. 1340)*
Physician, philosopher, poet, from a well-known family in Beziers (south France), Bedersi was an advocate of philosophical inquiry. He wrote many books, the best known, reprinted in over eighty editions, being *Behinat Olam* ("Examination of the World"). His poetry includes a 1,000-word prayer in which each word begins with the letter *aleph*(A).

JOSEPHUS: *FLAVIUS JOSEPHUS; his Hebrew name was Yoseph ben Mattityahu ha-Cohen. (c. 38–c. 100)*
Josephus came from a distinguished priestly family in Palestine, was a political scientist of distinction, and became the Jewish military commander in Galilee, which the Romans attacked in the year 67. He was captured and became a turncoat, in the eyes of Jewish patriots, when he urged the Jews to end their rebellion. He even accompanied Vespasian and Titus to the siege of Jerusalem, and there tried to persuade the Jews to make peace.

Josephus is, of course, a leading authority on the events in the rebellion of the Jews against Roman rule, but historians question his objectivity: His historical writings defend his own role in the hostilities and try to justify his integrity—both as a Jewish patriot and an advocate of the Roman position. His *Autobiography* denied the charges of Justus of Tiberius, who attacked Josephus as the prime "cause" of the Jewish wars. Josephus' *The Jewish War* and *The Antiquities of the*

Jews cover the history of the Jews from the first century before the Christian Era through the wars against Roman government from 66–79 of the Christian Era. His *Contra Apion* is an eloquent, if apologetic, answer to Apion's nasty anti-Semitic charges. (Apion, an Alexandrian historian, was part of a delegation to the emperor Caligula that opposed the delegation of Jews led by Philo.)

In sum: Josephus is a gifted historian, writer and polemicist. His politics may be criticized for an expediency that testified to poor character—or may be defended as the sagacity of a political realist who had the courage to offend popular opinion and bring calumny upon his name.

JUDAH BEN ASHER; *also known as* JUDAH ASHERI. *Do not confuse with his brother Jacob, author of* Arbah Turim, *a famous codification of Talmudic decisions.* (*1270–1349*)

Son of the great Talmudist Asher ben Jehiel (*q.v.*), "the Rosh," Judah ben Asher was born in Germany, went to Spain at the age of thirteen, returned to Germany and again to Spain—to arrange for his father's settlement in Toledo as rabbi. Upon his father's death, he became rabbi of Toledo's Jewish community. He was greatly esteemed for his firmness in Talmudic discussions. His eloquent "ethical will," translated as the *Testament of Judah Asheri*, is quoted in the present anthology.

"JUDAH the PIOUS," JUDAH HASID HA-LEVI. *Do not confuse with Judah ha-Levi.* (*1638–1700*)

A cabalist, born in Podolia, the Ukraine, Judah headed a sect which practiced hasidic rites, praying in visible and audible ecstasies, emphasizing man's sinfulness, the necessity for true penitence, and the imminence of the Messiah and the redemption of the world.

Judah's reputation as a *tsadik* and oracle spread so wide that he made a pilgrimage to Palestine with no less than 1,500 ardent disciples. It was an ill-fated journey, many dying or being killed long before they reached the Holy Land (1700). And Judah himself perished only a few days after reaching his goal. His followers, treated as believers in "the false Messiah," Sabbetai (or Shabbatai) Zvi (or Zevi), were so vigorously persecuted, by those who feared and hated the Sabbetaian movement, that they straggled back to Russia and Poland.

Judah the Pious is known for his charming parables and sayings, which have been orally transmitted for several hundred years.

KAHAN, ISRAEL MEIR. *See "CHOFETZ CHAIM."*

KARO. *See CARO.*

"THE KORETSER RABBI": *PHINEAS BEN ABRAHAM OF KORETS. (1726–1791)*

A Lithuanian Chasidic rabbi, he departed from his traditional Judaic education after coming under the influence of the Baal Shem Tov (*q.v.*). He opposed *pilpul* (casuistic) methods of exegesis. He preached a simple gospel of humility and veneration of the Lord.

"The KOTZKER RABBI": *MENAHEM MENDEL OF KOTZK; full name Menahem Mendel Heilprin—later Morgenstern. (1787–1859)*

A brother-in-law of "the Gerer Rabbi" (*q.v.*), Menahem Mendel Heilprin supported the 1830 revolution of the Poles against the Czars and, to evade capture and punishment, changed his name to Morgenstern. He was a formidable, if not ferocious, character whose acolytes often hid under their tables to escape the wrath of his censure. He spent the last two decades of his life in total isolation—in the study of his home. None of his writings survive: he destroyed them all—whether out of misguided piety, excessive humility, or anxiety about their possible misinterpretation, I do not know. His shrewd, tart sayings were orally transmitted, and printed in 19th and 20th century books.

KRANZ, JACOB BEN WOLF. *See "The Maggid of Dubno."*

LEONE DA MODENA, "LEON of MODENA," LEONE MODENA: *LEON JUDAH ARYEH. (1571–1648)*

This brilliant, erratic figure, was a rabbi, a superb preacher, an inexhaustible writer, a poet, a compulsive gambler, a theater director, a sophisticate who headed a gambling syndicate in the ghetto of Venice and moved in the loftiest circles of Venetian society. Leone's sermons were so eloquent that Catholics and members of the nobility attended them; his fame as a teacher attracted many aristocratic students from France, including an archbishop. His personal life and multifarious activities are the stuff of picaresque fiction.

He was born in Venice, the scion of a distinguished family of Jews (his grandfather had been knighted by Charles V). A child prodigy, he knew the classics, mathematics, much natural history. He wrote a tract *against* gambling (before he was fourteen) that was good enough to go into Latin, German, French translations, and into that Judaeo-German vernacular that would become Yiddish. He became a hopelessly addicted gambler, which he blamed, with great poise, on astrological influences. At one time or another, he practiced no less than twenty-six professions; he squandered his income at the gaming tables and suffered many tragedies in his private life. (One of his sons was killed in a brawl; another went to Brazil and disappeared; Leone's wife was insane for years.)

The Venetian rabbinate tried to excommunicate Leone for his gambling, but his brilliant moralistic essay of defense persuaded them that they were acting arbitrarily—and contrary to Talmudic Law.

This gifted fantast published an enormous number of tracts, treatises, poems and books—in Hebrew and Italian, including a collection of 400 of his sermons, a system of mnemonics, commentaries on the Pentateuch, translations of Ecclesiastes, a collection of Hebrew poems, "enigmas and remedies," moral maxims, prayers, abridgements of the Passover Haggadah, a primer on the technical terminology of logic, etc. His work is not distinguished by profundity. But his autobiography (one of the very early autobiographies to be written in Hebrew) and his vivid, voluminous letters provide an extraordinary and truly invaluable picture of Venice in its golden seventeenth century, and the life of the Jews during that period.

LEVITA, ELIAS, or ELIJAH BAHUR, ELIJAH MEDAKDEK, ELIJAH TISHIBI: *ELIJAH BEN ASHER HA-LEVI ASHKENAZA.* (*1468–1549*)

He was born in Neustadt, Germany and died in Venice. In Rome he was supported, with his family, by a Cardinal, to whom he gave lessons in Hebrew in exchange for lessons in Greek. He spent thirteen years in the palace, writing the works which won him a wide reputation. When Rome was sacked in 1537, Elijah was driven out, back to Venice. One of his students now was the French ambassador, later a Bishop, who subsidized Levita's great concordance of the Masoretic texts, *Sefer ha-Zikhronot* ("Book of Remembrance"). It took him twenty years to complete.

Elijah was important as lexicographer and grammarian; his writings on the Hebrew language are considered models of methodology. He propounded the unpopular theory that the "vocalizations" in Bible texts were post-Talmudic. He wrote a lexicon to the Talmud, *Tishbi* ("The Tishbeite"), and the first known dictionary of Yiddish-Hebrew, plus two novels in Italian verse, and Hebrew poems. He translated into Yiddish many works —especially the extraordinary *Bovo Bukh*, an Italian romance (based on an English cycle by one Bevis of Hampton) that played an enormous role in the education of Jewish women. (See my *Joys of Yiddish*, pp. 46–7).

"THE LUBLINER RABBI": *JACOB ISAAC HORO-WITZ, "The Lubliner." (1745–1815)*

Known as "the seer of Lublin," acclaimed for his purity and clairvoyance, "The Lubliner" (also called "Our holy rabbi") was a hasid possessed by a conviction that he was personally struggling against the agents of the Evil Impulse. For seven years, he literally shielded his eyes against the possibility of seeing anything unworthy or tempting. He was obsessed by a fear of falling into sin and even feared his own powers as a preacher and *tsadik* ("holy man").

His gospel emphasized joyousness in worship and humility in conduct. He attacked affluent Jews for their vainglory, and won a large following among the poor of Lublin, Poland—especially after he proclaimed that the sufferings of the Napoleonic wars were a sign of the imminent coming of the Messiah. He wrote three books, of which *Divre Emet* ("Words of Truth") was of particular interest to the present anthology.

LURIA, ISAAC BEN SOLOMON: *known as "ARI" (Hebrew: "the holy lion," also an abbreviation for "Ashkenazi"). Do not confuse him with such notables as Berman Ashkenazi, Bezalel Ashkenazi, Jacob Ashkenazi, Solomon Ashkenazi (all sixteenth-century Talmudists or authors) and Tzevi (Zevi) Ashkenazi. (1534–1572)*

"Ari" came from Jerusalem, was educated in Egypt, and achieved fame in Safed, where he taught and won fame by identifying certain ancient graves. He greatly impressed the community by his saintliness, asceticism, and explorations of mysticism. Countless legends of miracles, during his life and afterwards, have been woven around "Ari"—not least because of his self-proclaimed familiarity with supernatural familiars. His teachings were extremely influential, reviving and invigorating earlier cabalistic trends in Judaism.

The pupils of the Ari ("the holy lion"), of blessed memory, once asked him why he had never written a book on the Kabbalah. He replied that it was impossible, because the moment he plunged into a subject a veritable torrent of thoughts overwhelmed him, one subject leading him irresistibly to another and another and another. Even when he speaks to his disciples, said the Ari, he must exert strenuous effort to keep his thoughts to one subject.*

Luria's lectures and ideas were written down after his death, by Hayyim Vital (*q.v.*): *Ets Hayim* ("Tree of Life"), *Sefer ha-Gilgulim* ("Book of Wheels") and *Peri Ets Hayim* ("Fruit of the Tree of Life").

LUZZATTO, MOSES HAYYIM: *(often abbreviated into the acronym "RaMHal"). (1707–1747)*

Poet, mystic, probably paranoid (he thought Biblical figures were dictating secrets to him, and sometimes was persuaded he was the Messiah), Luzzatto was born in Padua of a wealthy family. He was educated in Latin and several other languages, was an indefatigable reader of Talmud, and grew especially attracted to its cabalistic, metaphysical portions. He wrote at least 150 poetic

---

* Adapted from a collection by S. Y. Agnon, in *Essays on Jewish Booklore*, KTAV, New York, p. 171.

psalms, hymns, poems, and a drama about Samson. His Hebrew was so pure, his style so Biblical, that some thought his psalms were rediscovered Biblical text; this caused considerable annoyance among the elders, who held Luzzatto to be presumptuous in modeling his poems on the Bible.

To his disciples, Luzzatto often confided mysteries and revelations which, he believed, Biblical heroes were communicating to him. His reputation as a cabalist spread through and beyond Italy, but he was severely denounced by Venetian and German rabbis, who (remembering the harm done by Shabbatai Zvi), persuaded him to renounce his teachings of the cabala. His works were thereupon locked in a stout casket. Luzzatto was given the official title of rabbi, but later was pressed into leaving for Amsterdam. He died in Palestine.

His most enduring work is *Mesillat Yesharim* ("The Way of the Righteous"), a work on ethics of great beauty, undoubtedly a classic, read and studied to this day, and admirably translated into English by Mordecai M. Kaplan.

"THE MAGGID OF DUBNO": *JACOB BEN WOLF KRANZ*. (1740–1804)

One of the most impressive preachers of his time, the Maggid ("preacher-teacher") of Dubno traveled throughout Poland and Galicia. The many parables and aphorisms with which he brightened his sermons were collected and published after his death.

"THE MAGGID OF MEZERITZ": *DOB BAER OF MEZHIRICH or DOB BAER OF MEZERITZ; known also as "the Preacher* [Maggid] *of Mezeritz" or "the Mezeritzer".* (1710–1772)

Originally a simple folk preacher or *maggid*, never ordained as a rabbi, Dob Baer was greatly influenced by the mystical teachings of Solomon Luria. He lived an ascetic life, fasted much, "prayed with copious tears and self-abasement," and succumbed to the charismatic influence of the Baal Shem (*q.v.*), whom he went to meet in person; after that worthy's death, "the Mezeritzer" became the leader of the hasidic movement. He was believed to be a worker of miracles. He appeared in public only on the Sabbath, clothed in white. He was singularly effective in attracting not only simple folk to "vulgar" hasidic practices of ecstatic veneration, but influenced younger rabbis, scholars, and cabalists as well. Indeed, virtually all of the hasidic rabbis or preachers of the next generation were his acolytes and became his emissaries. Hasidim spread throughout Poland, Lithuania, Galicia, the Ukraine.

"The Mezeritzer" established the idea that the *tsadik* ("holy" or "righteous man") is more than a pious, virtuous figure—he is a holy intermediary between the Lord and the Jews. His teachings were entirely oral; he wrote neither sermons, essays, nor books. His sayings were published by one of his disciples, Rabbi Solomon ben Abraham of Lutsk, who freely admitted that he did not himself understand many of the great hasid's more mystical sayings.

MAIMON (MAIMUM) BEN JOSEPH. *Not to be confused with MAIMONIDES, (q.v.), who was his son, Moses; nor with Solomon Maimon, Lithuanian Jewish philosopher of the eighteenth century. (c. 1110–1165)*

Maimon ben Joseph was a scholar of Cordoba (or Cordova), Spain, where he was a *dayan* ("rabbinical judge"). He fled Cordoba in 1148 with his family, wandered about Spain for twelve years, emigrated to Fez, North Africa, and eventually moved to Egypt (his son Moses having written an article that incurred official suspicion; see Maimonides). He wrote a commentary, in Arabic, on the Pentateuch, and on many aspects of Judaic religious rites. The most important surviving work of Maimon ben Joseph's is a letter of consolation (long attributed to his son): *Igeret ha-Shemad* ("The Epistle of Conversion"—from Judaism to other religions). This eloquent affirmation was addressed to those Jews who had been subjected to so much persecution, suffering and exile that their faith was shaken, faltering, or renounced.

MAIMONIDES: *MOSES BEN MAIMON; also known by the acronym "RaMBaM," for Rabbi Moses ben Maimon. (1135–1204)*

One of the commanding minds in Jewish history, Maimonides (known in Arabic literature as "Abu Imran Musa ben Maimum ibn Abd Allah") has been called "the second Moses." He was born in Cordoba (Cordova);

was first educated by his father, Maimon ben Joseph (*q.v.*) in rabbinical fashion; and was then placed to study with Arabic masters. At an early age, Maimonides was introduced to almost every branch of learning then known.

The Maimon family fled Cordoba (which fell into the hands of a fanatical Muslim sect, the Almohades), wandered through Spain for twelve years, and then moved to Fez, where they passed for a time as Muslims. But young Maimonides' writings (on reason and faith) attracted the attention of the authorities when an informer accused him of having defected from Islam (!). Only the help of a friendly Arabic poet-theologian saved Maimonides from execution. The family swiftly left Fez for Accra, then Jerusalem, and then (since Jerusalem was still possessed by passions pro and con the Crusaders) settled in Fostat (Cairo).

Now Maimonides studied to become a physician (he thought it unseemly to earn his living by writing about religion). He became personal physician to the vizier of Saladin, through whom he attended the royal family, and administered the affairs of the Jews of Cairo, who acknowledged him as their leader.

Scholarly writings—in philosophy, jurisprudence, Talmudic law, astronomy, medicine—poured from his pen. He always thought the medical knowledge of his day superficial and empirically dubious, but he wrote on many medical subjects, including a treatise on sexual intercourse; and he made a notable collection of medical axioms. His medical writings and opinions were used extensively (in Latin translation) in the universities of Europe for four centuries.

By 1158, Maimonides had produced several works on technical logic, his classic catalogue of the 613 Talmudic precepts, a commentary on the Mishnah, and his *Thirteen Articles of Faith*—all in Arabic. His insightful *Epistle to Yemen* (1172), responding to questions written to him from that south Arabian community of Jews (where many were being forced to convert, and others were beginning to follow one or another false Messiah), made so profound an impression that many Yemenite congregations included the name "our teacher Moses" in their *Kaddish* ("prayer for the dead").

From 1170 to 1180 he worked on *Mishneh Torah*

("Repetition of the Law"), a massive fourteen-volume Hebrew codification and compendium of the entire *halaka* (the legal part of the Talmud and later literature). Contemporary critics railed that Maimonides was trying to make his own laws, was not citing his rabbinical authorities, and was, in effect, trying to supplant the Talmud—a view made easier because in the introduction Maimonides said readers could now consult his book on any aspect of the Law, without laborious reading in other texts. (He also promised to publish a revised edition, with references, but never found the time to do so.) The *Mishneh Torah* remains unsurpassed for range, detail, depth, and systematic coordination of the Babylonian and the Jerusalem Talmuds, the Midrash, and the decisions of the *gaoim*. It was a staggering feat of erudition and energy.

In 1190, Maimonides wrote his most famous book, in Arabic, *Dalalat al-Ha'irin* ("*Guide of the Perplexed*"*), which set forth the faith of Judaism in a lucid, powerfully reasoned structure and tried to synthesize philosophy and religion. Maimonides, though thoroughly steeped in neo-Platonic and Aristotelian ideas, opposed many of Aristotle's arguments about the creation of the universe, the nature of God, prophecy, etc. He considered "the perfect man," one who contemplates the divine as a philosopher but remains animated, as a man, by passionate love of the Lord. The *Guide for the Perplexed* made a very strong impression on Muslim and Christian thinkers, especially on Aquinas and Leibnitz. Maimonides insisted that Judaism rested on reason; he even asserted that Judaism could be thoroughly comprehended only on Aristotelian principles: to worship or to have faith on other grounds, Maimonides held, was a form of idolatry. This created a furore, understandably, among the learned and anti-secular Jews of Europe. In 1305, the reading of philosophical works of Maimonides' sort was forbidden to Jews until they were twenty-five years old; excommunication was threatened to any under twenty-five who did so.

During the Haskalah (Jewish Enlightenment) move-

---

* This classic is also called "Guide to the Perplexed" and "Guide for the Perplexed."

ment of 1750–1880, Maimonides again became the spearhead of anti-traditionalist positions and the authority for Jewish rationalist emphases; his great *Guide* was called "The Bible of the *Maskilim*" ("enlightened ones"), and has remained so to this day.

MEIR, RABBI: *also known as MEIR BA'AL HA-NES* *("Meir the Miracle Worker"); his original name may* *have been "ME'-ASHA," according to the Babylonian* *Talmud; he is also known, in Aramaic, as "Nehorai."* *Not to be confused with twenty-four other "Meirs" listed* *in the* Jewish Encyclopedia. *(fl. second century of the* *Christian Era)*

The commanding importance of the great Rabbi Meir is demonstrated by the fact that his Mishnah became the basis for the larger Mishnah of Judah ha-Nasi, the ultimate authority in Judaic law. Rabbi Meir was one of the most brilliant of the Tannaim (teachers of the first two centuries, named in the Mishnah, beginning after the death of Hillel and concluding with the generation that followed Judah ha-Nasi). "Meir" means "one who enlightens"; and the Talmud states that the name was *given* him because he taught the Law so profoundly to the wisest men of his day, "opening their eyes" to the deepest meanings and subtleties of *halaka* ("law").

Meir's origins are uncertain. He was born somewhere in Asia Minor. (He is believed, in legend, to have been descended from the emperor Nero and converted to Judaism after Nero's fall.) He became a student of Akiba and Ishmael, and was a member of the Sanhedrin after the savage persecution launched by Hadrian.

Meir was thoroughly at home in Greek and Latin, traveled widely, and enlivened his lectures with memorable fables, aphorisms and parables. (These, and many stories of his sufferings, generosity and ingenuity, are often mentioned in midrashic literature.) He was a man of great modesty and a champion of peace (he stayed clear of Bar-Kochba's rebellion). It may be said that he hated only ignorance. He coined a great many aphorisms, repeated to this day ("When in Rome, do as the Romans do"). His wife was a noted scholar, too.

Rabbi Meir was an exegete and dialectician of phenomenal power: The Talmud says he could present 150 reasons for declaring something ritually clean, under the Law—and 150 proving the reverse. Indeed, some of his rulings did not become laws because the rabbis could not tell, so thorough and dazzling were his explications, which of two opposing views he himself preferred.

So revered was Rabbi Meir's name among religious Jews that in Poland and Russia, special little boxes for alms bore the name: *"Meir Baal ha-Nes Pushke."* (For the meaning of *pushke* or *pishke* see my *Joys of Yiddish*, pp. 301–2.)

MENAHEM MENDEL, OF VITEBSK: *"MENDEL OF VITEBSK."* (*1730–1788*)

A hasidic rabbi who, in 1777, left Russia for Palestine with over 300 devout and devoted followers. They settled first in Safed, then in Tiberias. Mendel of Vitebsk was admired for the metaphysical aspects of his teachings.

"MENDEL OF RYMANOV"; *MENAHEM MENDEL "OF RYMANOV." Not to be confused with other rabbis named Mendel, who are identified with other place-names.* (*b. ?–d. 1815*)

Rabbi "Mendel of Rymanov" was a hasid whose sermons and orthodoxy attracted thousands of Jews to his little town in Galicia. He was a strict traditionalist who insisted on the preservation of the smallest rites observed by Jews throughout the centuries. He declared that the Messiah would appear during (or soon after) the Napoleonic wars of his time. His prophecy has not been fulfilled.

"MENDELE MOCHER SEFORIM" (*"Mendele the Book-Seller"*): SOLOMON (SHALOM) JACOB ABRAMOWITCH. (*c. 1836–1917*)

If any one man can be called the founder of Yiddish literature, it is "Mendele Mocher Seforim." Sholem Aleichem aptly dubbed him the "Grandfather" of Yiddish letters.

Born in Russia in 1836, Abramowitch studied in a *yeshiva*, but soon began to write poetry and articles for Hebrew journals. He wrote the first short story, in the modern sense, published in Hebrew. Then he applied his talents to the uses of Yiddish as a literary vehicle. His satirical stories and adaptations, his astute and ironic delineations of the conflicts between the orthodox elders and the rising generation of Jews, brought him criticism so severe that he moved to Zhitomir on the Ukrainian border. He translated the Psalms into Yiddish and wrote extensively on the life of the Jews in Russia, on the savagery of pogroms, on the nature of anti-Semitism. With Bialik and Ravnitsky, he translated the Pentateuch into Yiddish.

Abramowitch perfected a modern, literary Hebrew which opened new vistas to Jewish authors; and it was he who made Yiddish an authentic, energetic literary tongue. His best-known work is the *Travels of Benjamin III*, which is immensely popular with the Jewish masses and a classic of humor and characterization. Among his other writings are *In the Days of the Storm, The Little Man,* and *Fishke the Lame.*

MENDELSSOHN, MOSES: *or "MOSES DESSAU," as he signed his name; or by the acronym "RaMBeMaN."* (*1729–1786*)

He is sometimes called "the third Moses" (Maimonides being the second) and is the central figure around whom and because of whom a new era in Judaism began. The most important representative of the Jews in Germany, the leading figure of the Enlightenment, a distinguished philosopher, Moses Mendelssohn's erudition and character achieved such standing in Germany that the city of Berlin exempted him from paying taxes. He was a passionate exponent of civil rights and an eloquent expositor of Judaism as a religion and a philosophy. His intervention stopped or prevented the legal discrimination and oppression that threatened Jews in Dresden and in Switzerland.

Mendelssohn, born in Dessau, was a poor young man; after many hardships, he became a tutor, a book-keeper, and, at last, a successful businessman. He first came to prominence with a letter that defended the Jews against savage critics of Gotthold Lessing's play, *Die Jüden*, a plea for tolerance written by a non-Jew. Mendelssohn became the model for Lessing's famous drama, *Nathan the Wise.*

At home in German, Hebrew, Latin, French, and English, Mendelssohn won the Academy of Science (Berlin) prize for an essay on metaphysics—no small feat if we know that one of his rival entrants was

Immanuel Kant. Mendelssohn annotated Ecclesiastes, translated the Pentateuch and the Psalms into German, and wrote a brilliant analysis of Maimonides' book on logic. His *Phädon*, a discourse on immortality, won him the extraordinary sobriquet: "the German Socrates."

MOSCATO, JUDAH ARYEH (LEONE). (*Sixteenth century; d. before 1594*)

Rabbi, poet, philosopher, student of ancient civilizations, Moscato was born near Ancona, Italy, and fled to Mantua (after Pope Paul IV expelled the Jews from the pontifical states), where he became chief rabbi. He was a typical scholar of the Renaissance, well-versed in Latin and Greek literature. He was a great admirer of Maimonides, and a student and exponent of the cabala. He wrote the first important book (published posthumously) about Judah ha-Levi's (*q.v.*) *The Kuzari*. He held that the civilizations of Egypt, Greece and Rome were predominantly the products of Judaic thought.

MOSES, JACOB BEN. *See "RABBENU TAM."*

MOSES OF KOBRYN. (*d. 1858*)

The town of Kobryn, in Grodno province, Russia, contained a Jewish colony as far back as the sixteenth century, and a *yeshiva*, of over 400 students, that produced many rabbis of repute. Moses of Kobryn was a hasidic rabbi—which is all I can find out about him.

"NACHMANIDES" (NAHMANIDES); *MOSES BEN NAHMAN; acronym RaMBaN; in Spanish he was known as Bonastruc de Portas. (1194–c. 1270)*

In 1263, when Rabbi Nachman of Gerona was sixty-nine, King James I of Aragon summoned him to the court in Barcelona—to defend Judaism in a disputation with the Dominican Fra Pablo (Paul) Christiani, a fulminating apostate from Judaism. The confrontation took place before an illustrious audience of ecclesiastical officials, court dignitaries, and prominent Jews.

Rabbi Nachman asked for freedom of speech (and immunity from its consequences), which the King graciously granted. Nachman's later account of this dramatic meeting attests to his knowledge, his equanimity (he had already debated the fanatical, rather ignorant Fra

Pablo in Gerona), his good humor—and his courage, for he did not hesitate to preach a sermon, on the following Sabbath, against the King's conversionist efforts. Nachman even dared question the King on a cardinal article of Christian faith: the miraculous conception of Jesus.

So effective was Nachman's reasoning, scholarship and character that King James rebuked Fra Pablo, congratulated the rabbi, and even gave him a parting gift. But the publication of the text of the debate was too much: Catalonians accused Nachmanides of blaspheming their faith, burned his pamphlet in public, and—despite King James' promise—brought the old rabbi to trial. He was exiled from Spain. After three years of wandering about (he was a physician as well as a rabbi), he settled in Palestine, in 1267. One of his letters states there were only two Jewish families in post-Crusade Jerusalem!

Nachmanides established a synagogue and a *yeshiva* in Jerusalem, corresponded widely, delivered sermons, and wrote a popular commentary on the books of the Torah. He also wrote poetry and books about the Law, in which he tried to reconcile rational and cabalistic interpretations of the Pentateuch. It is worth noting how many medieval intellectuals, theologians, mystics, and preachers wrestled with the same problem.

"NACHMAN OF BRATSLAV": *NACHMAN BEN SIMCHA OF BRATSLAV; known as "the Bratslaver."* (1770–1811)

A leading hasidic rabbi, founder of the sect called "the Bratslaver hasidim," Nachman was born in Poland—a grandson of the famous Baal Shem Tov (*q.v.*). He was an ardent cabalist and ascetic who won acclaim in Palestine, where he traveled for study, then returned to Poland. His teachings emphasized self-abnegation, penitence and fasting. He held the Evil Impulse (*yezer hara*) to be necessary, because it makes possible man's perfection.

Nachman won a huge following: because of the power of his personality, his fervent sermons, his ingenious parables and his countless aphorisms. His followers were criticized and, in some cases, excommunicated—on the ground that Nachman was a follower of Shabbetai Zvi,

"the Baal Shem," and the notorious charlatan, Jacob
Frank, a sybarite who held that redemption could be
achieved via impurity of conduct. Nachman's sermons
and sayings were published after his death by a disciple,
Nathan ben Naphtali Herz of Nemirov. His profound
and epigrammatic observations on man, life, God, the
hereafter insure his immortality.

NATHAN, OF NEMIROV (NEMROV): *NATHAN BEN NAPHTALI HERZ (HIRZ)*. (*d. 1830*)

Rabbi Nathan of Nemirov appears in this anthology chiefly
because he acted as Boswell to his Dr. Johnson: Rabbi
Nachman of Bratslav (*q.v.*)—whose sermons, parables,
and sayings he recorded. Nathan wrote these, and many
of Nachman's stories, in Yiddish. He describes the
particular sermon or occasion that caused Rabbi Nachman to make up a given story. Rabbi Nathan opened his
own printing press in 1821, to print Hebrew works he
had transcribed or edited: collections of prayers, legal
rulings, treatises on morals, the *Shulhan Aruk* ("Set
Table"), etc.

NEHORAI. *See MEIR, RABBI.*

PALQUERA, SHEM TOB. *See FALAQUERA.*

PAQDA or PAQUDA. *See IBN PAQUDA.*

PHILO: *PHILO JUDAEUS*. (*c. 20 before the Christian Era–died after 40 of the Christian Era*)

We know little about the particular events of his life,
except that he was born in Alexandria and was a member
of the delegation of Jews sent to Rome, in 40 of the
Christian Era, to seek Caligula's protection against the
anti-Semitic activities of Alexandrian Greeks.

Philo was a philosopher and a philosopher of science,
who produced many works in metaphysics, theology,
ethics, epistemology, natural science. As an observer-
historian, he has left us vivid descriptions of the persecutions of Flaccus, governor of Egypt; and he recorded
the story of the Jewish deputation to Caligula in Rome
and the controversy there.

Philo was more familiar with Greek philosophy than
with Judaism (he seems to have had little formal edu-

cation in Judaic theology or law). It was long believed
that he knew no Hebrew (he read the Greek translation
of the Old Testament); yet he wrote interesting etymo-
logical expositions of Hebrew names. Interestingly
enough, he held the Old Testament to be the basic
source and sole measure of truth—whether in religion
or in science.

Despite his emphasis on human brotherhood, wisdom,
and the purest devotion to God, Philo was never influential in Judaic thought, during his time or later; but his
role in the origins of Christianity was immense. He wrote
extensively on the nature of God and man, reason and
the soul, his thinking heavily permeated with the ideas
of Plato and the Stoics. He held that perfection can be
achieved only through a renunciation of the sensuous
and "the soul's irrational" propensities, and that true
wisdom is possible only in the mastery of philosophy,
which in its highest stages makes it possible to see the
divine—even God Himself.

Philo was the deepest thinker produced within that
branch of Judaism that was Hellenistic. The Palestinian
Jews soon shed Greek philosophical influences in theology; but the new religion that sprang up around Jesus
of Nazareth, propelled by the titanic evangelism of Paul
of Tarsus, was enormously affected by Philo's doctrines.

RABA: RABA JOSEPH BEN HAMA (*280–352*)

This famous Babylonian Amora ("interpreter," "explainer")
headed the Rabbinical academy at Mahoza—at that
time the only one in Babylon. He became renowned as
an authority on *halaka* (Law) and Haggadah (inter-
pretative ethics, legends, etc.) He was admired by the
mother of the Persian king (Sapoo II), became very
wealthy, and was praised for many philanthropies to
the non-Jewish poor.

RAB ASHI. *See ASHI.*

RABBAH: RABBAH BAR BEN HANAH. *Do not con-*
fuse with Midrash Rabbah. See Glossary. (dates un-
known)

A third-generation Amora ("scholar" of the third–sixth
century), he was the grand-nephew of Hiyya (or Chia)
the First, who had also been called "Rabbah"—a title

reserved for academy heads. Rabbah Bar Ben Hanah was famous for his florid accounts of his many travels. He has been fondly dubbed "the Jewish Sinbad."

RABBAN. *See ZAKKAI, JOHANAN BEN.*

"RABBENU TAM" (*"Our perfect Master"*): *JACOB BEN MEIR TAM.* (*c. 1100–1171*)

Acclaimed "Our perfect Master," Jacob ben Meir Tam was the greatest authority on Talmud among the Jews of France and Germany, the most eminent Tosaphist. (*Tosophot,* Hebrew for "addenda," refers to exegetical notes on Talmud made, from the twelfth to the fourteenth centuries, by rabbinical scholars in Germany and France, which criticized Rashi's monumental commentary and used supplementary discussions for the explication of law.) The Talmud contains both the Tosaphists' revisions of Rashi and Rashi's exegesis itself. This bears particular meaning for "Rabbenu Tam"—whose mother was Rashi's daughter—and whose older brother was the illustrious Samuel ben Meir, known as "RaSHBaM."

Jacob ben Meir Tam headed a rabbinical academy in Ramerupt, where his home was wrecked by French crusaders; he was almost killed by their blows. He became the leading rabbinical figure of his time and won the official protection of the King of France. He attended the assembly of French rabbis in Troyes who decreed that thereafter all disputes between Jews be settled in Jewish courts.

His major work is *Sefer ha-Yasher* ("Book of the Straight Path"), which contains thirty treatises on the Talmud plus his written responses to questions of rabbinical law and ritual. (Present editions are said to contain only a portion of Tam's original, plus material not certain to be his.) Rabbenu Tam sought, as he wrote, "to reconcile the [differing] traditions of the text [of Talmud] with the original . . ." He inveighed against expository innovations: "My grandfather [Rashi] made one correction, and [my brother] Samuel made twenty more . . ." He particularly opposed the use of texts where erasures or new entries occurred.

As French and German Jews developed more harmonious relations with their neighbors, it was necessary to find religious support for newer ways of living in a Christian world. Rabbenu Tam tried to be realistic about changes, and often defended contemporary departures from old ritual—*if* he could but find a Talmudic justification for them. He particularly permitted changes in dietary practices, marriage ceremonies, and the formation of a *minyan* (quorum). His influence among later rabbis was greater than that of even Maimonides. He and Rashi are sometimes called "the two highest mountains" in European Judaism.

"RASHI": *acronym for RABBI SHLOMO BEN ISAAC; SOLOMON YITSHAKI ("son of Isaac" is indicated by the "i" at the end of Yitshak); or SOLOMON BAR ISAAC.* (*1040–1105*)

This illustrious scholar, whose lucid commentaries on the Bible and the Babylonian Talmud made the latter "an open book," is the giant on whose work Nachmanides and Abraham ben Ezra based their historic interpretations of the Torah. The first book ever printed in Hebrew (in Reggio, Italy, in 1475) was Rashi's *Commentary on the Pentateuch*.

Many legends once surrounded his name, his fame, his life, and his work. He was born in Troyes, France, studied in the Rhineland with various teachers, and returned to establish a school in Troyes. But Rashi earned his living not by using his immense knowledge as a "spade" for a livelihood (an activity frowned upon in rabbinic tradition) but by working in his vineyard. His academy produced many notable scholars and disciples. Despite popularly believed stories, he did not travel throughout Europe and Asia—nor did he meet Maimonides. But he met many foreign luminaries in Troyes, a thriving commercial center.

Rashi's scholarship was unsurpassed, his style lucid, his approach to any problem brisk and direct. His reasoning was a model for all who followed him. He was thoroughly familiar with existing methodologies of textual analysis—Palestinian, Babylonian, Italian, and Ashkenazic. His commentary on the whole of Talmud, liberally lightened by many *midrashim*, is a monument in Judaic thinking, and a *tour de force* of analytic skill. He established revised, parallel texts, based on early manuscripts, the oral tradition, and the research of contemporaries. He was exceptionally gifted in defining theological and philosophical terms, in clarifying difficult or unusual phrasings, and in providing linkages between different, differing passages in the Torah or Talmud. He cut through complexities and quibblings with the confidence—and the bluntness—of a true master. His judgment was as balanced as his reasoning was clear.

He was a master of style, combining grace with precision. His mixing of Hebrew, Aramaic, and French (he used 3,000 words in the vernacular) still provide philologists with an invaluable source for medieval usages. Despite legend, Rashi seems to have known no Latin or Greek—which makes his achievement all the greater: his exegetical brilliance is his own, not beholden to scholarly works in those languages.

Rashi had three daughters, who married pupils of his —and his family and descendants became important disseminators of Rabbinical learning. When the Jews were expelled from France (Hebrew books were burned in Paris in 1240) and later from Spain, "the Bible and the Talmud, with the commentaries of Rashi, were their inseparable companions . . . often their supreme as well as their only solace, and the chief bond of their religious unity" (Morris Liber, in *Jewish Encyclopedia*, KTAV, New York [no date], vol. 10, p. 328).

The importance of Rashi's contributions to an understanding of the Pentateuch is seen in the fact that Christian scholars translated his work into Latin, German and other languages, and often cited him as an authority. Rashi's insistence on clarity and common sense led him to make drawings of many objects he described; he incorporated these drawings into his explications of Torah and Talmud—but they were omitted by hidebound copyists, so that Rashi's phrases "like this" were followed by blank spaces in the texts.

Through the writings of Nicolas de Lyre (or Lyra), a French monk, Martin Luther was greatly influenced by Rashi's work. The King James translators of the Bible made constant use of Rashi's commentaries.

It is no exaggeration to say that Rashi is the most widely quoted authority in Judaic scholarship. He was dubbed "Parshandata," which means "the interpreter of the Torah." His pellucid observations on Hebrew were said by experts to revive and reveal the truest nature of that ancient tongue. In fact, many scholars refined their Hebrew grammar and syntax by studying Rashi.

Countless editions of his commentaries have been published; laymen (such as I) who have not studied him in the original will find a valuable, simplified introduction to Rashi's work in the translation and selections by Chaim Pearl (Norton & Co., New York, 1970). Modern texts of this great rabbi's work sometimes combine Old French (for which his eleventh-century manuscripts are an invaluable source), Hebrew and Yiddish. No body of commentary on Torah or Talmud remains more popular with the laity, and more widely used by theologians.

REGGIO, ISAAC SAMUEL: *also known by the acronym "YaSHaR." Not to be confused with his father, Abraham or Vita ben Azriel Reggio; or Issachar Ezekiel Reggio; or Leone Reggio. (1784–1855)*

Born in Austria, of Italian-Jewish ancestry, Isaac Samuel Reggio was a mathematician who became interested in the study of Talmud after his professorship (in geography and history) was revoked by Austrian anti-Semitic legislation. He translated the Pentateuch into clear, simple Italian, studied the cabala (to which, unlike his father, he developed a strong aversion), became a follower of Moses Mendelssohn, and was a leading figure in the Haskalah (Enlightenment) in Northern Italy. His critical commentaries on Torah drew strong negative reactions from German scholars.

In Venice, he published an appeal for a Jewish seminary, which was established in Padua and for which Reggio devised the curriculum—which included the study, by rabbinical students, of Western and classical philosophy. Reggio opposed hair-splitting parades of dexterity in exegesis. He wrote many books, hoping to join modern thought and science to Judaic scholarship. He held that most of the ordinances in the Talmud were the product of the Pharisees, and should not be considered observances of perpetual, unchanging validity.

"THE RIZINER" or "THE RIZINER RABBI" (REBBE):
ISRAEL OF RUZHIN. (1797–1851)
A famous hasidic rabbi and *tsadik* ("holy or righteous
man"), "the Riziner" succeeded his father in the presti-
gious post. He regarded himself, as did many of the
leading hasidim, as a sort of sovereign, a messenger of
the Messiah, who deserved to live in considerable
luxury. His piety, wisdom, and aphoristic skills made his
reputation; his sayings, cherished and lovingly repeated
by his flock, have come down to us.

"THE ROPSHITZER RABBI": *NAFTALI (NAPHTALI)
OF ROPSHITZ (ROPCZYCE). (1760–1827)*
Books about the hasidim give us almost no facts about the
life and works of "the Ropshitzer." He won a reputation as a wit, no less than a hasid and a learned student
of Talmud. He voiced strong views against Napoleon
and his conquests in Eastern Europe.

"THE ROSH." See *ASHER BEN JEHIEL.*

SAADIA GAON: *SAADYAH BEN JOSEPH; also known
as SAADYAN ("Saadiah" may be the Hebrew equivalent of the Arabic name "Sa'id"). (882–942)*
A *gaon* was a leading scholar, in Babylon, during the "post-
Talmudic" era (sixth to eleventh centuries). The *geonim*
were the eminences who led the three great Rabbinical
academies (at Sura, Nehardea, and Pumbedita); their
secular authority over Jews everywhere was very great.

Saadia ben Joseph was the Gaon of Sura, so admired
that after his death the academy was closed—for over
forty years. His intellectual and philosophical range
astounded his colleagues. He is the father of the scientific
study of the Hebrew language and Biblical texts. He
brought Arabic and Muslim thinking into Judaic thought,
and wrote many scientific papers: most have disappeared, but are known through references to them by
contemporaries, disciples and other scholars.

He was born in Dilaz, in upper Egypt; almost nothing
is known of his youth. (His detractors said he was not
born a Jew, but Saadia stressed his lineage as being
noble, of the family of Shelah, the son of Judah.) By
the time he was twenty, Saadia had completed a great

Hebrew dictionary, *Agron.* He wrote polemical attacks
against the Karaites and other heretical sects, strongly
defending traditional Judaism. He left Egypt for Palestine, then Babylon. Appointed to a post in Sura, the first
"foreigner" to be a *gaon,* he pursued his duties with
stupendous energy and found himself involved in bitter
intramural disputes that ended with reciprocal excom-
munications.

He wrote widely on philology, law, philosophy, lexi-
cography, and liturgy. He translated most of the Bible
into Arabic, appending his commentary in Arabic. (He
seems to have planned this translation for Muslims as
well as Jews). His best-known philosophical work is
Amanat wa-i 'Tiqadat ("Beliefs and Opinions") which
was translated from Arabic into Hebrew by Judah ibn
Tibbon (*q.v.*), and into English, in 1948, by S. Rosenblatt.

SAMUEL HA-NAGID (*"The Chief" or "Prince"*):
*SAMUEL HA-LEVI BEN JOSEPH IBN NAGRELA
or NAGDELA.* (*993–1056*)

He was born in Cordoba (or Cordova), was educated in
rabbinical literature, and learned Latin, Arabic and
Berber. Driven out of Cordoba by the Berber conqueror, Suleiman, Samuel emigrated to Malaga, where
his penury forced him into selling spices. His skill in
Arabic, and the beauty of his calligraphy, won the attention of the Vizier in Granada, who found "the Levite"
so astute a diplomatist that he made him his chief
counsellor.

Samuel became the beloved chief or *Nagid* of the
Jewish community in Granada, serving as both chief
rabbi and liaison to the Muslim court. The Vizier's successor, Habus (or Habbus), placed Samuel in charge of
all diplomatic and military matters. After Habus' brother
became king, Samuel acted, in effect, as head of state,
and was privately called "king of Granada."

He was a gentle, modest man, interested in furthering
knowledge, and most bountiful in his benefactions. (He
purchased enormous numbers of books for scholars who
could not afford them.) He was the patron of many
Spanish Jewish writers and poets, notably Solomon ibn
Gabirol (*q.v.*). Moses ibn Ezra (*q.v.*) wrote that Samuel
ha-Nagid "raised the kingdom of science from its low-

liness, and the star of knowledge [in Spain] once more shone forth." Samuel had so many admirers among Muslim scholars and state officials that he remained Vizier, despite conspiracies against his authority, and was succeeded in that high office by his son.

Few of his writings have survived. He wrote an introduction to the Talmud printed in all standard editions, poetical works in the manner of Psalms and Ecclesiastes, and a large number of undistinguished poems. (There was a saying: ". . . as cold as the songs of Samuel the Levite.") What has been preserved, fortunately, is a portion of his collection of maxims, *Ben Mishle*; from this book come those aphorisms credited to him in this anthology.

"THE SASSOVER RABBI": *MOSES LEIB OF SASSOV* (*SASOB*); *also known as Rabbi Moshe Yehuda Leib of Sassov.* (*1745–1807*)

The rabbi of Sassov or Sasov, in Tsarist Russia, Rabbi Moses Leib was affectionately dubbed "the father of widows and orphans." He was tireless in his efforts to raise money for the poor and the bereaved, and to ransom Jews held as hostages.

SCHECHTER, SOLOMON. (*1850–1915*)

A major leader of Conservative (as distinguished from Orthodox and Reform) Judaism, president of the Jewish Theological Seminary in New York, Solomon Schechter was born in Rumania, studied in Vienna and Berlin, and lectured on Talmud in Cambridge, England. His identification of a long-lost Hebrew manuscript of *Ecclesiasticus*, discovered in Cairo in 1896, and his subsequent analyses of the contents of that *genizah* ("hiding place") won him a world-wide reputation among Biblical scholars. His three-volume *Studies in Judaism* is outstanding. He also edited texts of historical importance (*Abot de Rabbi Nathan*) and contributed major interpretations of Judaism.

"THE SHATZOVER RABBI": *ABRAHAM SACHA-TZOURER or ABRAHAM OF SOCHASZEW; known as "The Tzaddik of Sochochov"* (*or Sochaszew*). (*1839–1910*)

He came from very poor beginnings and as a rabbi was

helped each week by the fifteen rubles Rabbi Isaac Meir
Alter sent him. He became the son-in-law of "the
Kotzker Rabbi" (*q.v.*), was known as "the holy man of
Sochochov," and was the head of the hasidic court in
his town. His *yeshiva* attracted (and produced) many
gifted scholars; his personal following, doing homage to
their illustrious *tsadik*, was very large. His two works
on *halaka* were used in some Lithuanian seminaries as
"companion texts" in the study of Talmud and post-
Talmudic rabbinical literature.

"SHMELKE (SCHMELKE) OF NICKELSBURG": *SAMUEL (or SHMELKE) OF NICHELSBURG*. (*1726–1778*)

A disciple of Dob Baer, "the Meritzer Rebbe" (*q.v.*),
Shmelke was an ordained rabbi whose scholarship was
so great that he won the special favor of the great
Elijah Gaon (*q.v.*) of Vilna. He was the teacher of "the
Lubliner . . . the seer of Lublin" (*q.v.*), served as rabbi
in several communities, and was the brother of Rabbi
Phineas of Frankfurt.

SHOLEM (SHOLOM) ALEICHEM: *pen-name of SHALOM (or SOLOMON) RABINOVITZ*. (*1859–1916*)

There is but one Sholem Aleichem, although the phrase,
which means "Peace Unto You," is the conventional
salutation among Jews, heard whenever Jews meet—or
part (when they say *Aleykhem sholem:* "and unto you,
peace"). In Hebrew, *sholem* is pronounced *sha-lóm*, in
Yiddish *shó-lem*.

Sholem Aleichem, often called "the Mark Twain of
Yiddish literature," is the best-known, most beloved and
most influential Yiddish writer of the twentieth century.
He is a master of humor, characterization and sheer
narrative enchantment. His style is limpid, his characters
matchless; his mixture of compassion, irony and rueful-
ness is a delight. He never tried for "big" effects or
pretentious works. His work has the quality of conversation—and has achieved the status of folklore. He
is, *par excellence*, the master of the re-creation of life
in the *shtetl*.

The sensationally successful *Fiddler on the Roof* is
based on one of Sholem Aleichem's characters: Tevye,
the milkman (and his wife and five daughters); but those

who think well of this amiable play would be astonished by the greater range, humor, and universality of the character types Sholem Aleichem created. Translations of this great artist are, alas, never quite satisfactory. (Isaac Bashevis Singer attributes this, in part, to the difficulties of translating Sholem Aleichem's mischievous mingling of accurate and deliberately bowdlerized Biblical or Hebrew sayings, whose humor depends on a knowledge of what is being satirized; and, in part, to the fact that it takes a humorist to translate humor.) For a superb re-creation of Sholem Aleichem's unique people and locales, one can do no better than read Maurice Samuel's classic, *The World of Sholom Aleichem* (Schocken paperback, 1965). Translations of interest: *Inside Kasrilevke*, translated by Isidore Goldstick and others (Schocken paperback, 1968); *The Adventures of Menahem-Mendel*, translated by Tamara Kahana (Putnam, 1969); *Old Country Tales*, translated by Curt Leviant (Putnam, 1966); and *Stories and Satires*, translated by Curt Leviant (Thomas Yoseloff, 1963).

Shalom (or Solomon) Rabinovitz was born in Russia in 1859. In Kiev, he wrote stories, novels and essays, in Hebrew and Russian; but he came into his own when shaping and adorning Yiddish as a vehicle for narration. He subsidized an annual, *Di Yiddishe Folksbibliotek*, in which he published and encouraged a whole generation of writers in Yiddish. His greatest works were written in New York, where he lived for a decade until his death in 1916. His writings about the life of Jewish immigrants in the *goldene medine* of America are unmatched for reportage, understanding and impish humor.

SIMEON BEN JOSE BEN LAKUNIA (or LEKONYA).
(Fourth century)
A *Tanna* "of the fourth generation," brother-in-law of Eleazar ben Simeon (*q.v.*), most of Ben Lakunia's commentaries on *halaka* have not survived. The two sayings attributed to him in this anthology may be sentences he quoted from then-current folk sayings.

"THE SLONIMER RABBI": *AVRUM (ABRAHAM) OF SLONIM.* (*1804–1883*)
A disciple of "the Kobriner," Rabbi Moshe of Kobryn, Rabbi Avrum founded "the Slonim dynasty" of *tsadikim*

("holy men"). He wrote many letters to his disciples in Palestine. His *Yesod ha-Avodah* ("The Principle of Service"), published in 1892, is of great importance in the history of the hasidic movement: It virtually canonized the role of the *tsadik* as the core of religious activity in a Jewish community. Avrum drew heavily on parables and illustrative anecdotes from history and everyday living; quoted lavishly from the Babylonian and Jerusalem Talmuds, from the mystical Zohar, from Maimonides, etc. He wrote midrashic homilies on Exodus: notably *Beer Avraham* ("The Well of Abraham"); and of special interest is his collection of letters, *Hesed le-Avraham* ("The Grace of Abraham"), which, because of its cabalistic views on creation and Judaism, was not published until after his death. He feared it would be misinterpreted or would serve to mislead the naïve or the immature.

SPINOZA (DE SPINOZA or ESPINOSA), BARUCH (or BENEDICT). (*1632–1677*)

"Spinoza" comes from the name of a town, Espinosa, near Burgos. Spinoza's grandfather and father had escaped to Holland and were leaders of the Jewish Sephardic community there. Spinoza received his training in a *yeshiva* in Amsterdam, and went on to learn Latin, mathematics, physics, astronomy, chemistry, and medicine. Thoroughly acquainted with Aquinas and scholasticism, he was influenced by Jewish medieval and renaissance philosophers, especially Maimonides (*q.v.*), and Hasdai Crescas.

What was decisive in Spinoza's thinking was his discovery of Descartes; the idea that reason, not tradition or texts, should govern philosophy made so great an impression on him that he was suspected of heresy in the Jewish community, and was "called up to the Law." In 1656 he was formally excommunicated (he was twenty-three)—after an interrogation, to parts of which he answered that according to Holy Scripture angels were phantoms, that the soul is mortal, that God has "extension" or body. . . . (The excommunication—rescinded centuries after his death—was based not only on Spinoza's heresies, but on the fears of the Jews that Dutch freedom might not be elastic enough to countenance Spinoza's views, and that the Jewish community would be made to suffer for them.)

Spinoza moved outside of Amsterdam and became part of a Mennonite circle whose doctrines were similar to those of Quakers. He became a lens-grinder, an optician, a tutor of philosophy, Latin and Hebrew. In Leyden, he began his *Ethics* (written in Dutch and published posthumously), a great exposition of pantheism. His *Tractatus Theologico-Politicus*, published anonymously, exposed contradictions in the Bible and made incisive distinctions between piety and reason, faith and truth. It created a furore and was proscribed in many parts of Holland; but it is the foundation of all modern Bible criticism. Spinoza was consulted, by letters, by the leading intellectuals and scientists of his time. His influence on Leibniz, who visited him, was tremendous.

He was a gentle man, exceptionally calm, kindly, philosophical. In spirit, he remained isolated from both Judaism and Christianity. His use of Euclidean methods; his opposition to the authority of rabbis or priests, synagogue or church; his insistence that the state guarantee freedom of thought in religion, no less than politics; his belief that nothing is "supernatural" or outside of nature; his view that God is an infinite substance "causing" itself—or Himself—all made a profound impression on thinkers of the seventeenth and eighteenth centuries.

He held that true freedom lies in the power and purity of the intellect, and that happiness is achieved through the *intellectual* (not mystical or traditional or non-reasoning) love of God. He remains one of the truly seminal names in philosophy, theology, ethics, and political theory.

"THE TCHARKOVER RABBI": *ZEVI HIRSCH HA-LEVI HURWITZ (d. 1758)*

A great Talmudist, "the Tcharkover" was the rabbi most respected by the Baal Shem (*q.v.*). He was the father of Shmelke of Nickelsburg.

TIBBON. *See IBN TIBBON.*

"THE TSUPENSTER RABBI": *NAHUM TSUPENSTER. (d. 1868)*

I can find little about this hasidic rabbi who was (probably) the same as the one known as "Nahum of Stepinesht." He was a faithful follower and disciple of "the Riziner

Rabbi" (*q.v.*); his sayings were repeated by his admirers and descendants.

VERGA. *See IBN VERGA.*

VITAL, HAYYIM. *Not to be confused with JOSEPH, MOSES, SAMUEL BEN HAYYIM, or DAVID BEN SOLOMON VITAL.* (*1543–1620*)

Hayyim Vital, descended from a famous family of southern Italian Jewish scholars, was born in Safed. His life is surrounded by legends of his powers as a worker of miracles. He was a mystic and cabalist who sometimes claimed his soul was the soul of the Messiah.

Vital was a disciple of Isaac Luria. In Damascus, where he worked from 1590 on, he mastered Lurianic *cabala* and preached the imminent appearance of the Messiah. His *Ets Hayim* ("Tree of Life") was published without his permission (his notes, locked in a strongbox, were taken therefrom by his brother and another disciple). This work was important in spreading Luria's esoteric mysticism throughout Jewish communities in the Middle East and Europe. He wrote essays on repentance, holiness, the future world, the transmigration of the soul, and cabalistic interpretations of various passages from the Bible.

WEINREICH, MAX. (*1894–1969*)

A scholar-editor pioneer in the world of Yiddish, its history, linguistics, literature, and folklore; he was one of the founders of *YIVO* (Yiddish Scientific Institute) in Vilna, and became Professor in City College of New York.

YOM-TOB LIPPMANN. *See Zunz, Leopold.*

ZABARA. *See IBN ZABARA.*

ZAKKAI, JOHANAN BEN: titled *"Rabban"* (*"our master"*). (*First century of the Christian Era*)

Leader of the Pharisees, disciple of and successor to Hillel, founder of the great *yeshiva* at Jabneh (or Yabneb), Johanan ben Zakkai was called "Rabban" to emphasize his eminence over other rabbi-scholars. His rulings on questions of law were usually accepted against their Sadducee alternatives. His sayings, in Haggadah, are still famous. He included many proverbs and fables in his writings. It is said that Hillel, just before his death, named Johanan, his youngest pupil, to succeed him, calling him "the father of coming generations."

Ben Zakkai's reestablishment of the academy of Jabneh was of immense importance, for it continued the Judaic tradition despite the end of services in the Temple, where religious activity had centered. Jabneh replaced Jerusalem as the seat of the Sanhedrin. Johanan was an important secular leader of the Palestinian Jews, a tower of strength, despite his age, in keeping Judaism alive and in purifying it, as it were, from "the Temple cult." Among his students was Akiba, who became the intellectual giant of Jewry in the next generation.

ZEITLIN, HILLEL (*1872–1943*)

This writer-philosopher is considered the leading exponent of hasidic thought in recent Yiddish literature. He was born in Russia, was an ardent Zionist, and initially wrote his works in Hebrew. In Vilna, he began to publish in Yiddish. He strongly opposed assimilationist and secular trends in Jewish life. He perished in the holocaust of the Warsaw ghetto.

ZOMA. *See BEN ZOMA, SIMEON.*

ZUNZ, LEOPOLD: *also known by his Hebrew name YOM-TOB LIPPMANN.* (*1794–1886*)

Philologist, historian and scholar, Zunz (from "Zons," the name of a town on the Rhine) is called "the founder of the science of Judaism" (*"Jüdische Wissenschaft"*)—*i.e.*, the systematic study of Judaica. He revealed the widespread inaccuracies of books, written by non-Jews, about Judaism. Zunz pioneered modern Judaica research in historic works on rabbinical literature, homiletics, Jewish names, the history of the liturgy, medieval hymns and poems, Jewish contributions to science, studies of the Torah, etc.

His *Gottesdienstliche Vorträge der Juden* (Lectures for Jewish Religious Services) is often called the most influential single book about Judaism of the nineteenth century. The preface attacked the authorities of Germany for their failure to give Jews full citizenship, for excluding research about Judaism from government

patronage, etc. So powerful was the preface, a plea for
the return of the sermon into German synagogues, that
the authorities suppressed it. Zunz exercised a tremendous influence on the growth of Reform Judaism.

IV. Glossary

'ABADIM. A Minor Tractate added to the Talmud.

ABBA. Aramaic word for "father," "my father." In Babylonia, *Abba* became fused to the "r" of "*Rab*," to become "Rabba" or "Raba"; in Palestine, this was shortened to "Ba"/"Va."

'ABODAH ZARAH. Hebrew: "idolatry." The eighth tractate in NEZIKIN, fourth order of the Talmud.

ABOT DE RABBI NATHAN. A Minor Tractate added to the Talmud. There are two versions of *Abot de Rabbi Nathan*; one · has forty-one chapters, the other forty-eight; they stem from the times of the *Tannaim*.

ABOTH (ABOT, AVOTH, AVOT). Hebrew: "the fathers." The ninth tractate in NEZIKIN, *ibid. Aboth*, the only tractate without argument or debate, is also known as *Pirke Abot*, "Sayings of the Fathers." See *Av* and *Pirke Abot*. (Scholars consider *"Abot de Rabbi Nathan,"* above, to be a commentary to *Pirke Abot*.)

ADAM. Hebrew: "man." The Biblical name for the first man. Genesis, II : 7 says God created a man of *adamah* ("earth" or "dust of the ground").

ADDITIONS TO DANIEL. A book in the Apocrypha.

ADDITIONS TO ESTHER. A book in the Apocrypha.

ADONAI. Hebrew: "My Lord." The sacred title of God; usually translated as "Lord" in English. *Adonai* is plural in form (*Adoni* is the singular), but Hebrew, like many Western languages, uses the plural for the singular in formal or reverential situations.

ADOSHEM. From Hebrew *ha-shem*: "the name." The name of God used in ordinary discourse, not in formal religious services, instead of *Adonai*.

AGGADAH. See HAGGADAH.

AKEDAT YITSHAK (pronounced yits-*hok*). Hebrew: "The binding of Isaac." Also the title of a book by Isaac Arama (*q.v.*). The title refers to Abraham's attempt to sacrifice Isaac on Mount Moriah.

ALAV HA-SHALOM (*aleha ha-shalom:* feminine). Hebrew: literally, "On him (or her) peace." The phrase used automatically when referring to someone who is dead—as, in English, one says "of blessed memory," or "May he rest in peace."

ALIYAH (plural ALIOT). Hebrew: "going up . . . ascent." (1) A spiritual pilgrimage, usually to Jerusalem. (2) The honor of being called to the pulpit during a synagogue service, or to recite the blessings before and after the reading of a section of the Torah. (3) Migration to the State of Israel.

AM HA-ARETS. Hebrew: literally, "people of the soil." An ignoramus, an unlettered, uneducated boor. (In Biblical times, these Israelites were drifting away from Judaism, and marrying outside the faith.) The Talmud describes an *am ha-arets* as one who does not respect the Law and the rabbis. Maimonides defined him as "a boor in whom is neither learning nor moral virtue." Rabbi Nathan ben Joseph called an *am ha-arets* "one who has children and does not educate them. . . ."

AMIDAH. Hebrew: "standing." The principal prayer of Jews, usually: *Shemona Esra*, or the Eighteen Benedictions, recited while standing.

AMORA (plural AMORAIM). From Aramaic and Hebrew: *amar*; "speak." Scholar-teacher-lecturers who lived chiefly between 200 and 500, and whose opinions are cited in the GEMARA (*q.v.*). An *amora* often explained to an audience in popular language (usually Aramaic) what an erudite scholar lectured about.

APOCRYPHA. Greek: "hidden," "obscure." Works not in the canon of Jewish sacred writings, though clearly kin. The books of Ecclesiasticus, Judith, Tobit, Esdras, Maccabees I and II, Daniel, Wisdom of Solomon. (Greek translations of the Apocrypha included other books, such as the story of Susanna). These works were written during the period of the Second Temple and following its destruction and the rebellion led by Bar Kochba (*q.v.*). Some of these "post-Biblical" books were incorporated into the Septuagint, canonized by the Roman Catholic Church. Other books outside the canon are in the PSEUDEPIGRAPHA (*q.v.*), which also includes works by unknown and probably invented authors.

The books of the Apocrypha, although written by and for Jews, were preserved by the Christian Church; in the Middle Ages they were virtually unknown to rabbis and Jewish scholars. (An authoritative work on this subject is R. Travers Herford's *Talmud and Apocrypha*, KTAV Publishing House, New York, 1970.)

'ARAKIN. Hebrew: "Vows . . . evaluating." The fifth tractate in KODASHIM, the fifth order of the Talmud.

ARAMAIC. The language used by most Jews during the Babylonian Exile (536 B.C.E.). The Gemara and first translations of the Bible were written in Aramaic, the *lingua franca* of the Middle Eastern world.

ARI. Popular name for Isaac Luria, "the Ashkenazi" or "the Lion." (See BIOGRAPHIES.)

ASHKENAZI. From *Ashkenaz:* Hebrew for "Germany." A Jew or Jewish tradition in, or from, Central and Eastern Europe; contrasted with Sephardi or Sefardi (*q.v.*)—Spanish or South European Jewry; the name once used for a kingdom in ancient Armenia. The name Ashkenazim has been applied, since the sixteenth century, to the Jews of central and Eastern Europe— ancestors of the vast majority of Jews in the United States (the first Jewish immigrants to America were Sephardim).

Ashkenazim and Sephardim are the two main branches of Jewry. The Sephardic Jews lived in, or come from, Africa, Portugal, Spain, and southern France, and some

in the Orient. The Ashkenazim moved from northern
France to Germanic cities along the Rhine, then to
Central and Eastern Europe, where they found settle-
ments of Jews who had emigrated, long before, from
Babylon and Palestine.

Medieval rabbis dubbed Germany *"Ashkenaz"* after
a passage in Jeremiah (51 : 27), and decided that, after
the Flood, one of Noah's great-grandsons, named Ashkenaz, had settled in Germany.

The Ashkenazim followed the religious practices and
traditions of the rabbi-scholars of Palestine; the Sephardim continued and elaborated the practices and traditions of Jews in Babylonia.

Ashkenazic Jews are distinguished from Sephardic
Jews in their style of thought, their pronunciation of
Hebrew, aspects of their liturgy, many customs, food
habits, ceremonials. YIDDISH is the Ashkenazic language—and universe: the vernacular of Sephardic Jews
is Ladino, a dialect of Spanish.

The Ashkenazim created a distinctive civilization—in
a Yiddish literature that Sephardic Jews could not understand—about a kind of person the Sephardim had never
seen, celebrating passions and visions Sephardim could
comprehend only by an effort. It was in the Ashkenazic
world that *Yiddishkeit* ("Jewishness") reached its golden
age. The culture of Ashkenazim is markedly different
from that of Sephardim (see SHTETL). At the core of
Sephardic thought, wrote Abraham Menes, lay the
question: "What must a Jew know?" At the heart of
Ashkenazic life, stirred the challenge: "What must a
Jew do?" (For more details see my *Joys of Yiddish*,
pp. 19–20, 460–461.)

You may hear it said that the Sephardim were the
aristocrats of Judaism, the deepest philosophers, the
first Jewish mathematicians and astronomers, the van-
guard of rationalism, enlightenment, and critical inquiry.
In this context, the words of the late Professor Louis
Ginzberg (in *Students, Scholars and Saints*, J.P.S.A.,
1928, p. 64.) are particularly pointed:

Modern historians [praise] the well-ordered studies of the
Sefardim, and [censure] the topsy-turvy methods in vogue
among the Ashkenazim, which embarked a ten-year-old
lad on the "sea of the Talmud" and kept him there until
he became a master navigator. [But] is it not startling to

find that since the time of Rabbi Joseph Caro (d. 1575) the Sefardim cannot show a single name in the realm of the Talmud comparable with the distinguished scholars of Poland? . . . There must have been method in the methodlessness of the Polish Jew.

AV (plural: AVOT). Hebrew: "father." (1) A teacher of Mishnah who helped establish the methods of legal interpretation. These important scholar-legalists were called *Tannaim* (*q.v.*). They lived during the last 200–250 years before, and the first two centuries of, the Christian Era. (2) The ethical precepts and aphorisms of these teachers, as recorded in *Pirke Abot* (*q.v.*). (3) In the Bible, the *avot* are Abraham, Isaac, and Jacob.

BAAL SHEM. Hebrew: "Master of (God's) Name." The name given a holy man, healer, saintly magic-worker, especially in Eastern Europe. See Baal Shem Tov (Israel ben Eliezer), in BIOGRAPHIES.

BABA (BAVA). Hebrew: "gate" (see following three entries).

BABA BATHRA. Hebrew: "the last gate." The third tractate in NEZIKIN, the fourth order of the Talmud dealing with civil law.

BABA KAMMA. Hebrew: "the first gate." The first tractate in NEZIKIN, *ibid*.

BABA METZI'A. Hebrew: "the middle gate." The second tractate in NEZIKIN, *ibid*.

BABYLONIAN TALMUD. See Guide Note B, pp. 62–65.

BAMIDBAR. The oldest name for *Numbers*, the fourth book of the Pentateuch (the five books of Moses), which describes the numbering of the Israelites; later *Bamidbar* was replaced by the fourth word in the opening sentence, *Be-Midbar*, "In the Wilderness."

BAR. Aramaic for Hebrew word "ben," denoting membership in a class, usually meaning "son" or "son of."

BARAITHA. Hebrew: "that which is external." A Tannaitic teaching, not included in the official *Mishnah*.

BARUCH. A book of the Apocrypha of the Old Testament.

BAVA. See BABA.

BEKOROTH. Hebrew: "first born . . . firstlings." The fourth tractate in KODASHIM, the fifth order of the Talmud.

BEL AND THE DRAGON. A book in the Apocrypha.

BE-MIDBAR. See BAMIDBAR.

BEN. Hebrew: "son" or "son of."

BERAKOTH. Hebrew: "blessings . . . benedictions." The first tractate in ZERAIM, the first order of the Talmud.

BERESHITH (BE-RESHIT). Hebrew: "In the beginning." (1) The Hebrew name for the First Book of Moses, originally, "Book of Creation," rendered into Greek by *Genesis*, "origin," because it gives an account of the creation of the world and the beginnings of life. *Bereshith* is the first Hebrew word in its opening sentence. (2) *Bereshith* is also the name of the first of the fifty-four weekly Torah readings (*Sedrahs*) on Sabbath mornings. (3) *Shabbath Bereshith* can also refer to any ordinary Sabbath.

"BESHT." The acronym for Baal Shem Tov. (See *BIOGRAPHIES*.)

BETH DIN. Hebrew: "house of law." A Jewish court. Three main levels of Jewish courts existed during the Mishnaic period: one with three judges, one with twenty-three judges, and the great Sanhedrin—of seventy-one. After 425 C.E., only courts of three, five, or seven judges continued to function.

BEZAH. Hebrew: "[an] egg." The seventh tractate in MO'ED, second order of the Talmud; the tractate is also known as *YOM TOV*.

BIBLE. From Greek: *biblia*, "little books." The Hebrew Bible, "the sacred canonical books," originally structured as twenty-four books, divided into three sections: *Torah, Neviim, Ketuvim* (i.e., "Torah, Prophets, Hagiographa").

See Guide Notes, TORAH, TALMUD, MISHNAH, MIDRASH, GEMARA, pp. 61–69.

BIKKURIM. Hebrew: "first fruits." The eleventh and last tractate in ZERAIM, the first order of the Talmud.

CABALA (CABBALAH, KABBALAH). Hebrew: "tradition." A mystical system based upon the permutations of numerical values assigned to letters of the Hebrew alphabet, and believed in this way to reveal "hidden" meanings to words and phrases. Feats of divination, numerology, and esoteric thought became influential among Jews during the Middle Ages. The *Zohar* (*q.v.*), probably written in the thirteenth century (translated into Latin 200 years later by Pico della Mirandola), made cabalism a movement of considerable consequence.

Originally, cabalism meant the Oral Tradition; in the twelfth century, Jewish mystics asserted that there was an unbroken link between their ideas and those of ancient days. God was known to the cabalists as *En Sof* (Infinite One); His existence was made known through ten *sefirot,* or "divine emanations."

The cabalists held that reason alone could never penetrate the exalted, mystical experience involved in their perception of God's mysteries. Occult formulae and numerological acrobatics went into the cabalists' efforts to comprehend God's will, and many a prediction excitedly hailed the imminent appearance of the Messiah and the Day of Judgment. Some cabalists mortified the flesh; others set themselves prodigious tasks of fasting, penitence, prayer—to atone for evil, purge the soul of sin, redeem the spirit. The center of cabalistic teaching in the sixteenth century was Safed, Palestine, which was the seat of a sizable community of mystics. Isaac Luria (see BIOGRAPHIES) was the outstanding cabalist (known as the "Ari"—the "Lion"), a visionary who claimed to speak with the Prophet Elijah, presided over fervent disciples to whom he expounded arcane invocations containing many secret, "hidden Names" of God, upon which the faithful were exhorted to meditate. Esoteric and minatory rituals were ordained over every conceivable interpretation of passages from the Torah or the names of prophets.

(NOTE: It is not so hard to understand why mystical doctrines attracted Jews, in the later Middle Ages, given the poverty and abiding terror under which they lived. Many devout souls became convinced they would be delivered from their terrible tribulations only by the Messiah. What, except the miraculous, was there to place hope in? See Hugh Trevor-Roper's brilliant analytic description, in *Historical Essays,* Harper and Row, New York, 1957, 1966, pp. 146 ff.)

CHACHEM. See HAKHAM.

CHANNUKAH. See HANUKKAH.

CHASID (CHASSID). See HASID.

CHEDER (HEDER). Hebrew: "room." The room or school where boys learned/learn elementary Hebrew. The *cheder* was often the free school for boys who could not afford to attend a YESHIVA (*q.v.*).

CHUTSPA. Hebrew: "insolence." Gall, brazen effrontery, indescribable presumption-plus-arrogance. The classic definition of *chutspa* is this: *Chutspa* is that quality enshrined in a man who, having killed his mother and father, throws himself on the mercy of the court because he is an orphan.

COHEN. See KOHEN.

DARKE TSEDEK. Hebrew: "Paths of Justice." A book of homilies by Zachariah Mendel of Yeroslav.

DEMAI. Hebrew: "doubtful crops . . . produce not certainly tithed." The third tractate in ZERAIM, the first order of the Talmud.

DEREKH ERETS. Hebrew: "the way of the land . . . local customs and courtesies." The title of two minor tractates appended to the Talmud. See below.

DEREKH ERETS RABAH (RABBAH) (*rabah:* Hebrew: "large.") A collection published in translation in the Soncino edition of the *Minor Tractates of the Talmud;* it emphasizes rules of decorum, modesty, manners— through stories of the lives of the Sages.

Technically, the minor tractates are not "of the Talmud" but are appended to it.

DEREKH ERETS TSUTA (*tsuta:* "small") Published in the minor tractates "of" the Talmud; a collection of

ethical teachings, plus the praising of peace, with advice
to the learned about their religious and teaching duties.
Although printed after DEREKH ERETS RABBAH,
there is no substantive progression from the one to the
other.

DEUTERONOMY. The Greek name for the fifth book
of the Torah. See Guide Note: TORAH (pp. 61–62)
and DVARIM, below.

DEUTERONOMY RABBAH. See Guide Notes A and C
(pp. 61–62, 65–67).

DEVARIM. See DVARIM, below.

DIASPORA. Greek: "dispersion"; in Hebrew, *galuth:*
"exile." Literally, the dispersion of Jews from the holy
land, and their settlement in other lands; but the word
carries profound overtones of recurrent persecutions,
misery, and tragic expulsion from one land after another,
sometimes after centuries of residence. Since the sixth
century B.C.E., when the ancient kingdom of Judah was
conquered and the Babylonians effected forcible deporta-
tions (to what is now Iraq), Jews have lived "in exile."
(I use quotation marks because of the great number of
Jews who elected not to return to live in Palestine, or
to the State of Israel.) Jewish colonies thrived all
through the Middle East and along the northern coast
of Africa. The conquests of Alexander the Great and
the Romans tended to unify the culture of Mediterranean
and Middle Eastern people; but political/religious repres-
sion drove Jewish groups into the Balkans, into Italy,
Spain, France, the Rhineland, the Netherlands, England.

During the Middle Ages, fanatical harassments drove
Jews more and more into Eastern Europe—Poland, the
Ukraine, Turkey. In the nineteenth and twentieth centuries, drastic discrimination, poverty, and pogroms
made the Jews leave "the Pale" of Russia and Poland,
and many settlements in Austria, Rumania, Hungary—
for England, the United States, South America, South
Africa, Australia, and Palestine.

DVARIM. Hebrew: "words." The name of the fifth book
of the Torah, from the opening phrase in the Hebrew
text; but the oldest name, contained within the book
itself, was *"Mishneh Torah"*: "The Repetition of the

Torah." Greek-speaking Jews translated this as *deuteros nomos* or *Deuteronomion*, i.e., "Second Law." This title was given in the Latin Bible as *Deuteronomium* and then, in English versions, as Deuteronomy.

'EDUYYOTH (EDUYOTH, EDUYYOT, EDYOT). Hebrew: "testimonies," (collection of *mishneot*). The seventh tractate in NEZIKIN, the fourth order of the Mishnah, known as *Behirta* ("chosen") in the Talmud. The tractate covers proceedings of the high court in Javneh; but the same materials appear in other tractates.

ELOHIM. A generic name for God, used among many ancient peoples in the Near East. In the Hebrew Bible, *Elohim* is one of the names of God most frequently used—along, and sometimes combined, with YHVH (*q.v.*). Medieval Jewish philosophers maintained that *Elohim* refers to that aspect of God found in nature.

EPISTLE OF JEREMY. A book in the Apocrypha (*q.v.*).

'ERUBIN (ERUVIN). Hebrew: "Sabbath travel regulations . . . the fusion of Sabbath limits." The second tractate in MO'ED, the second order of the Talmud; it embraces many regulations concerning the Sabbath. (Some authorities consider *Erubin* to be a continuation of *Shabbat*, the first tractate in MO'ED.)

ESDRAS. Two books in the Apocrypha (*q.v.*), usually attributed to the prophet Ezra. The books are called Esdras III and IV because Ezra I and II are ascribed to Ezra and Nehemiah.

ESTHER. A book (*Megillat[h] Esther*) in the Bible (*q.v.*), probably written around 330 B.C.E.; it describes the role of Esther, wife of Ahasuerus, in saving the Jews of Persia from extermination. See PURIM, below. The name "Esther" ("star") is the Persian or Babylonian form of *Hadassah*. See MEGILLAH.

ETS HAYIM. Hebrew: "tree of life." (1) The wooden sticks around which a Torah scroll is rolled; the words come from a verse in the Book of Proverbs; "It [Torah] is a tree of life to them who hold it." (2) The name of a book presenting the ideas of Isaac Luria. (See BIOGRAPHIES.)

EXODUS. Greek: "road out." The second book of the Torah, called in Hebrew *Shmot* ("Names") after its opening word. See Guide Note A, (pp. 61–62).

EXODUS RABBAH. A midrashic commentary on Exodus in the Midrash. See Guide Note D, (pp. 67–69).

GALUTH. Hebrew: "exile." In Yiddish, pronounced *goles*. See DIASPORA.

GAN EDEN. Hebrew: "paradise . . . Garden of Eden." "God planted a garden eastward, in Eden," says Genesis. Popular tradition placed Eden between the Tigris and Euphrates rivers. The Talmudists and cabalists were persuaded that there were two gardens of Eden: the luxuriant garden on earth; and the one in the heavens, the eternal abode of the righteous after death. When a mortal dies, his or her good deeds are weighed against bad deeds. See GEHENNA.

GAON. Hebrew: "genius," "pride," or "excellency" (plural: *geonim*). (1) The head of a Talmudic academy. (2) A rabbi whose learning was so great that he was given the honorary title of *gaon*. (3) A scholar-genius. The title *gaon* was held by the heads of the Talmudic academies of Babylonia from 589 to 1040, then fell into disuse; it was revived and applied to a rabbi of exceptional learning or an authority unquestioned by world Jewry. The *geonim* ruled on religious questions; questions were sent them from all parts of the Diaspora; they provided *responsa* (*q.v.*).

GEHENNA. Greek for the Hebrew: "Gehinnon . . . the valley of Hinnom." (1) The name of a valley, southwest of Jerusalem, where human sacrifice was practiced. (2) The name of the place where the wicked will abide, after death, to expiate their misdeeds. One description in the Talmud pictures Gehenna as a dark place, filled with everlasting fire and sulfurous fumes. ("Purgatory" is nowhere named in the Bible; this name entered official Roman Catholic Church usage in the thirteenth century; back in the third century, Origen had said that souls wait in a fearful place to be "purged of evil" so they may enter the Kingdom of Heaven undefiled. The Church of England has scorned Purgatory as "grounded upon no warranty of Scripture, but rather repugnant to the Word of God." See Gustav Davidson's learned and unique *A Dictionary of Angels*, Free Press, 1967.)

GEMARA. Hebrew: "completion" or "learning." The discussion—lengthy, discursive, difficult, and still often charming—of the *Mishnah*, which together with it constitutes the Talmud. See Guide Notes D and E: GEMARA (pp. 67–69).

GEMATRIA. From Greek: *gamma*, the third letter in the alphabet, and *tria*, "three." In Hebrew, the letters of the alphabet also served the ancients as numbers: *aleph* = 1, *bet* = 2, etc. Each letter, hence each word or phrase, possessed a numerical "value." Mystics converted numerical values into supposed keys to the meanings of passages in the holy texts, to reveal a new meaning or resolve an old ambiguity. Example: The Hebrew word for "pregnancy," *herayon*, has a numerical value of 271, which is "the total number of days a woman carries a child." The manipulation of numbers became a popular mode of Biblical and Talmudic interpretation during the Middle Ages. Many scholars employed *gematria* in the hope of discovering the exact date on which the Messiah would arrive. So far, the Messiah has not confirmed the researches and expectations of the gematriasts.

GENESIS. The Greek name for the first book of the Torah; in Hebrew: "Bereshith" or "*Be-Reshit*." See Guide Note A: TORAH (pp. 61–62).

GENESIS RABBAH. A book in the Midrash (see Guide Note E: p. 69), containing 100 passages from Genesis which are extensively interpreted.

GITTIN (GITIN). Aramaic: "divorces . . . bills of divorce." The fifth tractate in NASHIM, the third order of the Talmud; its nine chapters discuss Judaic laws of divorce.

GOLEM. Hebrew: "yet-unformed thing." A robot, a simpleton, a clod. (For legends and dramas, see my *Joys of Yiddish*, pp. 137–38.)

HAGGADAH. Hebrew: "tale" or "narration." (1) The narrative, read aloud at the Passover *seder*, which recounts the story of Israel's bondage in, and flight from, Egypt; the material comes from many sources, and contains prayers, psalms, hymns, and songs for the children. (2) The vast, colorful repository of allegories, historical episodes, folklore, prayers, parables, witticisms, anecdotes about martyrs, saints, sages, etc., found in the Talmud, very popular with Jewish people. Also called Aggadah. See Guide Note D (pp. 67–69). (*The Passover Anthology*, by Philip Goodman, J.P.S.A., 1961, is an invaluable and comprehensive collection of material about every aspect of Passover.)

HAGIGAH. Hebrew: "festival sacrifice . . . the festal offerings." The twelfth tractate in MO'ED, the second order of the Talmud.

HAGIOGRAPHA. Greek: "holy writings;" in Hebrew, *ketuvim:* "writings." The third/final part of the Old Testament, which follows the Prophets and consists of twelve books: the five "Scrolls" (*megilloth*) read in the synagogue on special days (Ruth, the Song of Songs, Lamentations, Ecclesiastes, Esther) and Psalms, Proverbs, Job, Daniel, Ezra-Nehemiah, Chronicles I and II.

HAKHAM. Hebrew: "wise man"; "one who exemplifies or practices *hakhmah*." (See below.)

HAKHMAH. Hebrew: "wisdom." (1) The divine spirit of Wisdom which, according to the Midrash, preceded the creation of the world. (2) Wisdom, profundity, astuteness. (3) The total reservoir of rabbinical knowledge. (4) Wisdom handed down by tradition and impossible to learn by experiment. (5) Cabalistic knowledge.

HALAKA (HALAKHA, HALACHA). Hebrew: "guidance" or "step." (1) The legalistic parts of the Talmud as distinguished from the ethical, poetic, allegorical, anecdotal materials known as the *Haggadah*). (2) The decisions of the rabbis on disputes about ritual, obligations, duties. (3) The Law that governs devout Jewry's conduct in religious-ethical-social matters. (4) The accumulated jurisprudence of Judaism—without Biblical citations. *Halaka* encompasses all the laws to which observing Jews are bound. But the rabbis did not "create" *Halaka*; they interpreted, clarified, and codified legal teachings, constantly adapting them to changed historical and social circumstances. Many rabbis believed the source of all Law was the Revelation at Sinai.

HALITSAH (Hebrew: "taking off"). The ceremony, described in Deuteronomy 25 : 5–10, in which a childless widow releases her brother-in-law from the ancient requirement to marry her.

HALLAH. Hebrew: "dough offering." (1) The ninth tractate in ZERAIM, the first order of the Talmud. (2) The braided white bread, glazed with egg white, which is a Sabbath delicacy. Orthodox Jews place two *challahs* (*challa, challeh,*—many spellings) on the table on the eve of Sabbath, uncut until after the blessing. (This perpetuates the memory of the Temple in Jerusalem, where two rows of bread were set before the altar.)

HAMAN: See PURIM.

HA-NAGID. See NAGID.

HANUKKAH (CHANNUKA, HANNUKAH). Hebrew: "The Feast of Dedication," more colloquially known as "The Feast of Lights." One of the less solemn Jewish festivals, this eight-day holiday falls on the 25th of the Hebrew month of Kislev and continues into the month of Tevet (in December, according to our calendar). Hanukkah commemorates the historic victory of the Jewish Maccabees over Syrian despots (167 before the Christian Era), a fight for religious freedom that rescued Judaism from annihilation. The Apocrypha tells the story (Maccabees I and II). The rebellion, led by a priest, Mattathias, and his son, Judah the Maccabee ("the Hammer"), continued for three years against the armies of Antiochus IV, who wanted to turn the Hebrews to Greek polytheism. Antiochus desecrated the great Temple, ordered the Jews to build shrines for idols and to stop circumcising male babies.

Guerrilla groups of Jews, equipped with primitive weapons, fought the Seleucid soldiers—and won a surprising victory at Emmaus. They returned to Jerusalem and set about restoring the burned Temple. On the twenty-fifth day of the Hebrew month of Kislev, in 165 B.C.E., Judah the Maccabee rededicated Zion's Temple—lighting the eternal light.

Each Hanukkah, Jews around the world light candles for eight days—one the first evening, adding one light each night on a nine-branched menorah. The ninth candle, called the *shames* (servant), stands apart from the rest and is used to light the others; this is interpreted to show that one can give love and light to others without losing any part of one's own radiance. (*Hannukah*, edited by Emily Solis Cohen, Jr., J.P.S.A., 1965, is a comprehensive and invaluable collection covering every aspect of "the Feast of Lights.")

HAPHTARAH (HAPHTORAH, HAFTORAH). Hebrew: "end . . . conclusion." A chapter from the Prophets, read in the synagogue on Sabbaths and festivals after the reading from the Torah. When the Romans prohibited the Torah reading, a common evasion was to read a *haphtarah* containing a reference to the appropriate part of the Torah.

HASID (CHASID, HASSID). Hebrew: "pious," "pious one." (1) A most pious man. (2) A follower of the Hasidic philosophy and way of life (a disciple of a great rabbi). In the days of Roman rule, the Hasidim were militant Pharisees. But the term usually refers to the extraordinary Hasidic movement of the seventeenth–eighteenth centuries which raced through Jewish communities of eastern and central Europe. This movement was founded by Israel ben Eliezer (called "the Baal Shem Tov"—see BIOGRAPHIES), who preached a folk gospel that had enormous appeal to small-town Jews, because it opposed the rabbinical emphasis on formal learning and scholastic casuistry. Israel ben Eliezer extolled simple faith, joyous worship, everyday pleasures; God requires no synagogues, except "in the heart." Prayers should be spontaneous, personal, happy. The Hasidim danced and clapped hands while singing the Lord's praises. Hasidic rabbis, often not ordained, preached with delightful parables, anecdotes and folk sayings. They angered many of Jewry's rabbinical establishment. The Gaon of Vilna, head of the rabbinical academy, formally anathematized the Hasidim.

A Hasidic leader was treated by his followers with greater awe than Jews customarily gave a rabbi. Disciples repeated a Hasid's every phrase, imitated his every gesture. Hasidism's leaders became known as *tsadikim* (*q.v.*)—seers, near-saints, prophets believed to possess supernatural powers. The title *tsadik* even became hereditary. Hasidism still has passionate adherents, in small, lively enclaves in Israel, South America and the United States.

HASMONEAN: See MACCABEE.

HEBREW. From the Hebrew root *ivri*, which may originally have meant "one from the other side of the river [Jordan]." To be exact, "Hebrew" should be applied only to Israelites and Judeans before the Babylonian Exile (586 B.C.E.); after that date, the name "Jew" (from "Judah") became accepted.

HERMENEUTICS. From Greek: "interpretation;" the Hebrew is *midot* ("rules" or "measurements"). Hermeneutics is the system of rules that govern the linguistic/exegetical ways by which a word, phrase, or passage of sacred writings may be interpreted. These rules were first set down by Hillel (see BIOGRAPHIES) in seven principles, dealing with permissible and nonpermissible inference, deduction, limitations on textual particulars/generalizations. Rabbi Ishmael enumerated thirteen rules; Rabbi Eliezer ben Rabbi Yose ha-Galili enumerated three (but the latter appear only in post-Talmudic literature). Other curious methodologies for hermeneutics were emphasized later: e.g., *gematria* (*q.v.*) and *notarikon*, which treated some words as abbreviations for larger phrasings. (See Akiba in BIOGRAPHIES.)

HORAYOTH. Hebrew: "decisions . . . instructions." The tenth tractate in NEZIKIN, the fourth order of the Talmud. The tractate discusses legal errors committed by the Sanhedrin (*q.v.*) or by a high priest.

HULLIN. Hebrew: "unconsecrated animals . . . animals killed for food." The third tractate in KODASHIM, the fifth order of the Talmud, which sets forth the ritual and techniques to be followed in slaughtering animals.

IBN. Arabic for "son [of];" *ibn* became "*ben*" or "*bin*" when used between the proper names of father-and-son.

ISRAEL. Hebrew: "Champion of God." (1) Precisionists used "Israel" only to name the people of the Northern Kingdom, where the so-called "Ten Tribes of Israel" dwelt. (2) The name of the state created on May 14,

1948. (3) Jewry as a whole. (4) Popular Jewish first name.

JERUSALEM TALMUD. Hebrew: *"Talmud Yerushalmi."* See Guide Note B: TALMUD (pp. 62–65).

JESUS. See Guide Note D: MIDRASH (p. 67–69).

JESUS BEN SIRACH. See BIOGRAPHIES: *BEN SIRACH.*

JUDITH. A book in the Apocrypha; it describes a siege in Samaria and the beheading of Holofernes, the Assyrian general, by the pulchritudinous Judith. The book was written in Hebrew, but has survived only in a Greek translation. Many experts regard the text as unreliable.

KABALA (KABBALA). See CABALA.

KADDISH. Aramaic: *Kodosh*, "holy." In Hebrew: "consecration." (1) A prayer glorifying God's name, recited at the close of synagogue prayers. (2) The mourner's prayer. (3) A son, called affectionately *"my Kaddish."*
     The *Kaddish* was originally a doxology, recited after completing a reading from the Bible or a religious lesson from the Mishnah, that glorifies God's name, affirms faith in the establishment of His Kingdom, and expresses hope for peace. The language of the prayer is Aramaic, which was spoken by the Jews in their Babylonian exile and during the days of the Second Temple or Commonwealth. In time, a belief grew that the praises of God in the *Kaddish* would help the souls of the dead find lasting peace; and the prayer became known as the Mourner's Prayer (even though it contains no reference to death). The *Kaddish* is recited at the grave, and, for varying months after a death, by the children, parents, siblings of the deceased, then each year on the anniversary of death (*Yortsayt*). There are five separate *kaddish* forms: the short, the whole, the mourners', the rabbinical, and the "kaddish of renewal," which is given at the grave. The *kaddish* is recited only when a *minyan* (*q.v.*) attends. Females may recite the *kaddish* in Conservative and Reform services.

KALLAH. Hebrew: "bride." (1) A bride. (2) One of the Minor Tractates, containing material on marital relations. *KALLAH* is now included in virtually all editions of the Talmud.

KALLAH RABBATHI. A larger tractate of *KALLAH* (see above), in the Minor Tractates.

KARET (KARETH). Hebrew: "excision." A punishment for sin—not ordered by a *Beth Din* (ecclesiastical court) but divinely imposed, presumably, through an "accident," disease, sudden death, etc. Such punishment presumably cut the offender from a place in the world-to-come.

KEDUSHAH (plural: *kedushot*). Hebrew: "sanctification." (1) This is a form of doxology contained in the repetition of the *Amidah* (*q.v.*). (2) The name of the third of the Eighteen/Nineteen Benedictions. (3) Noun, meaning "holiness."

KELIM. Hebrew: "utensils" or "vessels." The first tractate in TOHOROTH (TOHOROT), the sixth order of the Talmud, which deals with ritual laws on the purification of glass, earthenware, and metal utensils.

KERITHOTH. Hebrew: "divine punishment . . . extirpation." The seventh tractate in KODASHIM, the fifth order of the Talmud; it deals with *karet* (see above).

KETUBAH (KETTUBAH). Hebrew: "written document." The traditional, marriage contract, specifying the wife's legal rights in the estate, if her husband dies or divorces her.

KETHUBOTH (KETUBBOT). Hebrew: "marriage contracts . . ." The second tractate in NASHIM, the third order of the Talmud; it deals with monetary aspects of divorce or widowhood, and the reciprocal duties of husbands and wives.

KIDDUSH. Hebrew: "sanctification." (Do not confuse with *Kaddish*, above.) The prayer and benediction that celebrates the Sabbath and Jewish holy days. The father of the family recites Genesis 2:1–3, which tells how God rested on the seventh day and made it holy. Two *brokhes* (blessings) follow: praising God for having created wine; thanking Him for having created the Sabbath "as a memorial of the Creation" and "in remembrance of the departure from Egypt." Some Jews

recite the *Kiddush* without wine (and without the blessing for wine), using the *challe* loaf instead (thousands
of Jews were too poor to afford wine every Friday).
The *Kiddush* ceremony predates the Christian Communion and Eucharist; the first Christians adapted the
ritual of a communion (or "love feast") that was used
among the sect of Jews called Essenes.

KIDDUSH HA-SHEM. Hebrew: "sanctification of God's
Name." (1) Hebrew term for martyrdom. (2) Righteous
acts performed in public. (3) Doing more than is required in order to praise God before Gentiles.

KIDDUSHIN. Hebrew: "sanctifications" or "betrothals,"
"marriage rites." (1) The Jewish rite of marriage. (2)
The seventh tractate in NASHIM, the third order of the
Talmud; it deals with prohibited and permitted engage-
ments, specifying legal regulations.

KIL'AYIM. Hebrew: "diverse kinds." The fourth tractate
in ZERAIM, the first order of the Talmud; it discusses
prohibited "minglings" of animals, seeds, fabrics.

KINNIN. Hebrew: "bird nests . . . bird offerings." The
eleventh (last) tractate in KODASHIM, the fifth order
of the Talmud; it deals with regulations concerning
Leviticus 5 and 12:8, on offerings after the birth of a
child; the tractate discusses the pairs of birds, "two
turtles or two young pigeons," which were made obligatory as offerings to expiate certain offenses—and certain
unclean conditions.

KLEE YAKAR. Hebrew: "beloved vessel." A commentary
on the Torah by Rabbi Ephraim Lunchitz (Luntshitz),
in the seventeenth century. Lunchitz was head of the
yeshiva in Lvov and chief rabbi of Prague.

KODASHIM. Hebrew: "sacred" or "hallowed things."
The fifth order of the Talmud. It contains eleven tractates
on ritual, sacrifices, slaughtering.

KOHELETH. Hebrew: meaning uncertain, but probably
a name; the Greek, chosen by Jerome, is best rendered
as "collector of wise sayings for teaching." A part of the
HAGIOGRAPHA which expounds gloomy ideas about
life, faith, reason, oppression. The authorship ("Koheleth, son of David," whom the rabbis took to be Solo-

mon) prevented the rabbis from banning this great lyrical, pessimistic masterpiece, which is today read in synagogues during the Feast of Tabernacles. Contemporary experts on the Bible consider Koheleth a pseudonym and date the book somewhere around the third century before the Christian Era.

KOHELETH RABBAH. The Midrash on the Book of Ecclesiastes, included in the Midrash Rabbah and dated by scholars as a post-Talmudic work.

KOHEN (COHEN). Hebrew: "priest." Before the Exodus, the head of every Israelite family was a consecrated, priestly mediator between God and man; and the first-born male possessed authority as legatee of his father's estate. After the Exodus, the tribe of Levi was selected as the priesthood, in place of sons in general—partly because of the traumatic experience of the Golden Calf episodes; and the descendants of Aaron (Moses' brother), were made responsible for supervising laws of hygiene, instruction in the laws, maintaining the Tabernacle, etc. To estop a priesthood from achieving *political* hegemony, the tribe of Levi was not allotted land in Israel; they lived on tithes, portions of sacrifices, and land apportioned from other tribes. (One must admire the political foresight and sophistication this entailed.)

There were seven grades of priesthood (see Exodus, 30:22–33 and Deuteronomy 20:2–12) from the High Priest (*kohen gadol*) to deputies, war-priests, Temple treasurers, ordinary *kohens*.

The Kohens hold a special status in Orthodox Jewry to this day; they are the first called up to read from the Torah; they may not marry divorcees; they must not go to cemeteries (except for nearest blood relations), etc.

KOL NIDRE. Aramaic: "all vows." This plaintive prayer (in Aramaic) ushers in the holiest of days, Yom Kippur (*q.v.*); it is uttered, just before sunset, by the cantor—three times, first softly, then louder, the congregation reciting it softly along with him. Throughout, the Torah scroll is held aloft by three men. The melody is exceptionally moving, and seems to recapitulate the history of Jewish suffering and persecutions. (Beethoven placed part of *Kol Nidre* in his *Quartet in C# Minor*; Tolstoy characterized the prayer as an "echo of the martyrdom of a grief-stricken nation.") But the words of *Kol Nidre* are severely legalistic:

Kol Nidre [all vows], obligations, oaths, anathemas, be they called *konam* or *konas* or by any other name, which we may vow or swear or pledge . . . from this Day of Atonement until the next . . . we do repent. May they be deemed to be forgiven, absolved, annulled or void—and made of no effect. They shall not bind us nor have power over us [and] the vows shall not be considered vows, nor the obligations obligatory, nor the oaths oaths.

Kol Nidre was originally regarded with contempt by rabbi/scholars. It was Rabbi Yehudai the Gaon, an eighth-century sage of Babylonia, who introduced *Kol Nidre* into the synagogues. For the special importance which Jews attach to promises, see Headnote: VOWS in the collected quotations of this volume, which explains why certain vows "shall not be considered vows" and why certain oaths (forced out of Jews by threat and torture) were not to be treated as legitimate or binding.

KOSHER. Hebrew: *kasher:* "fit." The rabbinical regulations which govern the dietary laws of observing Jews, based on the tractate *Hullin* (*q.v.*) and the second part of the *Shulhan Aruk* (*q.v.*). See FOOD AND DRINK in the collected quotations.

KUNI LEMMEL. German: *Lümmel*, "bumpkin." A yokel, a Simple Simon. (For the subtle and ironic differences between a *Kuni Lemmel* and a *shlemiel*, a *nebekh*, a *Chaim Yankel, et alia*, see *The Joys of Yiddish*.)

KUTHIM (KUTIM). One of the Minor Tractates added to the Talmud, it discusses the relations between Jews, Samaritans (*Kuthim* was the Talmudic name for Samaritans and any who did not accept the Oral Law) and non-Jews. In censored editions of the Talmud, *Kuthim* was used to replace various appellations for non-Jews, and vice versa.

KUZARI. A classic, written in Arabic, variously called *Kitab al-Khazari, The Kuzari, Ha-Kuzari,* by Judah ha-

Levi, recounting the discussions 400 years earlier between a rabbi and the king of the Khazars, a Tatar people on the lower Volga, which ended with the king's conversion to Judaism. See BIOGRAPHIES: *HA-LEVI*.

LEVITICUS. Greek: *Leuitikos*; late Latin: *Leviticus*: "book of the Levites"; in Hebrew: *Va-Yikra*, after the opening word of this third book of the Pentateuch. Leviticus is also known as *Torat(h) Kohanim* ("the priestly code" or "laws of the priests") for it contains much of the Mosaic law concerning priests, sacrifices, and ritual purity. Scholars differ on the dating of parts of Leviticus: some hold it to be a collection of isolated works and commandments, some think it preceded the Exile; parts clearly seem traceable to the Sinai period. See Guide Note A: The Torah, (pp. 61–62).

LEVITICUS RABBAH. (Complete title: Midrash Leviticus Rabbah.) The third book in the Midrash Rabbah (see below): one of the earliest *midrashim* (fifth–sixth century). It consists of thirty-seven chapters concerning the weekly readings from Leviticus, the third book of the Torah—at a time when these readings covered a triennial cycle.

LOSHN-KODOSH. Yiddish from Hebrew: "sacred language." The language of the Torah. Yiddish is called *mama-loshn* ("mother tongue"; see below.)

MAALOT HA-MIDOT. Hebrew: "The merit of the rules." See *ANAV*, in BIOGRAPHIES.

MAAMAR MORDECAI. Hebrew: "Mordecai's essay (or sermons)."

MA'ASER SHENI. Hebrew: "second tithe." The eighth tractate in ZERAIM, the first order of the Talmud; it consists of five chapters on tithes in Jerusalem.

MACCABEES. Derivation unknown. (1) The Maccabees (or Hasmoneans), a dynasty of priests, founded by Mattathias, called *Hasmonai*—possibly after an ancestor, or after the place mentioned in the Book of Joshua (15:27). Mattathias's five sons, of whom Judah the Maccabee was the oldest, led the revolt of the Jews in Palestine against the Syrian autocrat Antiochus Epiph-

anes (75–164 B.C.E.). (2) Four individual books in the
Apocrypha; that is:

Maccabees I; describes the Hasmonean family's history—from Antiochus, who made martyrs of seven
children (called Maccabees by later Christians) who
refused to perform idolatrous rites; their mother, Hannah
(Salome), is honored in many shrines throughout the
Christian world. The original Hebrew text of the book
has been lost; the Greek translation survived in the
Septuagint.

Maccabees II; written probably in the second century
B.C.E., describes the Hasmonean uprising, and revolves
around the extraordinary story of Judah the Maccabee;
this account apparently is a shortened version of a
Greek work, written by one Jason of Cyrene.

Maccabees III; written in Greek, describes the persecutions of Ptolemy IV (Philopator) and the miraculous
deliverance of the Temple. (Some authorities believe
the data referred to Caligula's persecutions in Egypt.)

Maccabees IV; an eloquent philosophical work ex-
tolling reason, as against passions. Clearly influenced by
the philosophy of the Stoics, the book was written in
Greek by a Jew, sometime in the last century before,
or the first century of, the Christian Era; its only connection with "Maccabees" is that the author quotes II
Maccabees from time to time.

MAGEN (MOGEN) DAVID. Hebrew: "Shield of David."
The 6-pointed Star of David, symbol of Israel; no one
is sure why, how, or when it became a symbol of Jewry.
The Zionist Congress adopted it in 1897. No reference
to the *Magen David* is found in rabbinical writings until
the thirteenth century; and the first explicitly Jewish
association did not occur until the seventeenth.

MAGID. Hebrew: "teacher" or "preacher" (plural: *magidim*). A teacher/preacher, usually itinerant. The *magid*
played a significant role in Jewish communities in
Eastern Europe in the eighteenth and nineteenth centuries. A shabbily clothed "country preacher," he wandered about, on foot or by cart, from *shtetl* to *shtetl*.
Note that the *rabbis* were not expected to preach sermons; they were occupied with study, teaching, interpreting the law, stimulating discussion of the Torah. In
earlier times, a *darshan* ("expounder") was paid to de-

liver sermons in the synagogue on Sabbath afternoons; the *darshan* was also a learned man, a rabbi, whose preachings were in Hebrew, erudite, often pedantic.

The *magidim* came to play a cherished role among the poor laity; the *magid* generally used Yiddish, was informal in his sermons, and lived off contributions. Some *magidim* were orators of the fire-and-brimstone school, but the most beloved were homey types, mixing jokes and parables into their sermons. The lore of Ashkenazic Jews was vastly enriched by the delightful fables and moralistic tales circulated by the *magidim*.

MAKKOTH. Hebrew: "punishment by flogging." The fifth tractate in NEZIKIN, the fourth order of the Talmud; it deals with lashings, perjury, and places of refuge for persons guilty of involuntary manslaughter (*shogegim*).

MAMA-LOSHN. Yiddish: "mother language" or "mother tongue." (1) The colloquial name for Yiddish. Since the holy books were in Hebrew, and generally only Jewish males were taught to read Hebrew, Yiddish became "the mother's tongue" in Eastern European Jewish homes. Yiddish derives from the German brought by medieval German Jews into Poland, mixed with words from Hebrew and Eastern European tongues. Yiddish is incomprehensible to Sephardic Jews, whose vernacular, Ladino, is derived from Spanish. (2) Candid, truthful talk: "Let's talk *mama-loshn*" means "Get down to brass tacks."

MARRANO. Spanish: "pig." (Derivations other than Spanish are sometimes suggested.) The contemptuous name used by Spanish and Portuguese Catholics, five hundred years ago, for Jews converted by force—who remained "secret Jews." Popes Clement VI, Boniface IX, Nicholas V opposed such persecutions and expressly forbade forcible or threat-induced conversions; but the Church in Spain, Portugal, France, Mexico carried on an effective Inquisition. In Spain, many Marranos rose to positions of great influence: ". . . the majority of distinguished Spanish families married into newly converted Christian families."* One family came to include

---

* Paul Borchsenius, *History of the Jews*, Vol. III, Simon & Schuster, 1966, pp. 212–213.

a minister of finance in Navarre, a vice-chancellor of Aragon, a speaker of the *Cortes* (Parliament), a bishop, a judge of the high court. In the fifteenth century, Spain burned "new Christians," and pious fanatics devised hideous tortures. Torquemada, the Chief Inquisitor, persuaded Isabella and Ferdinand to expel all Jews. Between 150,000 and 500,000, including many at the very heart and mind-center of Spanish culture, were driven out; about 100,000 found their first sanctuary in Portugal (whence they were later expelled); a few thousand went to Italy, to North Africa cities, and some roamed as far as Poland and Turkey. Spain never recovered from the disastrous excision. Marranos founded important Jewish communities in Amsterdam and London.*

MASORAH. Hebrew: "tradition" (but this translation is uncertain). (1) The traditional readings of the text of the Hebrew Bible. (2) The traditions governing the writing, reading, spelling of words and phrases in the Bible.

MASSEROT (MA'ASEROT, MASSEROTH). Hebrew: "tithes." A tractate in ZERAIM, the first order of the Talmud.

MAVIN (MAYVIN). Hebrew: "understanding." Yiddish for a true expert, a seasoned judge of quality, a connoisseur.

MEGILLAH. Hebrew: "scroll, roll volume . . ." (plural: *megilloth*). (1) The Scroll of Esther, which is read in synagogues during Purim (*q.v.*). (2) The tenth tractate in MO'ED, the second order of the Mishnah, which describes the time and manner of the public reading of the Scroll of Esther during the feast of Purim, and also discusses the public reading of other portions of Scripture. There are five *megilloth* in the Bible: The Song of Songs, the Book of Ruth, Lamentations, Ecclesiastes, and Esther. (3) In popular usage, anything very long, verbose, a rigmarole. (The Book of Esther wanders in interminable details.)

---

* See Professor Cecil Roth's *History of the Marranos*, third edition, Oxford, 1959; also B. Netanyahu, "The Marranos of Spain," in *Proceedings of the American Academy for Jewish Research*, XXXI, 1963.

MEKILTA (MEKHILTA). Aramaic: "measure" or "rule"; Hebrew, *midah*: "rules by which to interpret." The *Mekilta* is an ancient collection of both halakic and haggadic *midrashim* (first and second centuries B.C.E.) on some thirteen chapters of Exodus, from the School of Rabbi Ishmael; it is often called *Rabbi Ishmael's Mekilta* (*Mekilta d' Rabbi ›Yishmael*), or *Mekilta*, or simply "M." Another *Mekilta* has been discovered: that of Rabbi Shimon (Simeon) ben Yohai.

MELAMED (plural: *melamdim*). Hebrew: "teacher." A teacher—of elementary Hebrew. *Melamdim* were an impecunious lot, teaching by rote and repetition; a Jew who had no other way of making a living, or who had failed, would often become a *melamed*.

MENAHOTH (MENAHOT). Hebrew: "flour offerings . . . meal offerings." The second tractate in KODASHIM, the fifth order of the Talmud. It discusses the preparation of meals and bread.

MENTSH (MENCH). Yiddish, from German: "person." An upright, honorable person; someone of consequence; someone to admire and emulate. Jewish children often hear the admonition: "Behave like a *mentsh!*" or "Be a *mentsh!*" The key to being "a real *mentsh*" is—character: rectitude, dignity, a sense of what is right, the fulfillment of ethical obligations.

MESHUGE. Hebrew: "crazy." Insane, eccentric, obsessed, absurd; such a man is a *meshugener*; such a woman is a *meshugene*.

MESILLAT YESHARIM. "The Way of the Righteous." (See Moses Hayyim Luzzatto in BIOGRAPHIES.)

MESSIAH. See Headnote: MESSIAH (p. 322).

MEZUZA. Hebrew: "doorpost." (1) One of the seven Minor Tractates added to the Talmud; it contains only two chapters on how *mezuzot* should be copied, written, or applied. (2) The little oblong container affixed to the right doorjamb of an observing Jew's home. The *mezuza* consecrates the home as a temple. An Orthodox Jew touches his fingers to his lips, then to the *mezuza*, each time he enters or leaves his home. Inside the *mezuza* is a tiny rolled-up parchment on which are verses from

Deuteronomy 6:4–9, 11:13–21, beginning with, "Hear, O Israel, the Lord our God is one." Inscribed passages contain the command to "love the Lord your God . . . with all your heart and soul," and includes the reminder that God's laws are to be observed away from, as well as at, home.

MIDRASH. Hebrew: "exposition . . . homily." See Guide Note D, (pp. 67–69).

MIDRASH CANTICLES RABBAH: Canticles: from Latin: "chant." The Song of Songs (in Hebrew, *Shir ha-Shirim*). The first of the five scrolls included in the Hagiographa (*q.v.*). The Midrash on Canticles is part of the Midrash Rabbah (see below).

MIDRASH DEUTERONOMY RABBAH. In Hebrew: *Dvarim Rabbah*. A homiletic, nonlegalistic Midrash on Deuteronomy. (See Midrash Rabbah, below).

MIDRASH EXODUS RABBAH. In Hebrew: *Shemoth Rabbah*. The part of the Midrash Rabbah that deals with the book of Exodus.

MIDRASH GENESIS RABBAH. In Hebrew: *Bereshith Rabbah*. The portion of the Midrash Rabbah that interprets, or homiletically expounds, the Book of Genesis.

MIDRASH HAGGADAH (AGADAH). (1) The homiletic (folklore, fables, parables, theological speculations) portions of the Midrash, as contrasted to the legalistic. (See HAGGADAH and HALAKA.) (2) A compendium of rabbinical interpretations of the first five books of the Old Testament (the Torah) edited from manuscripts by Solomon Buber, who dates these *midrashim* as having been composed in the sixteenth century. Midrashic materials form a literature stretching over a thousand years.

MIDRASH HALAKA. The legalistic portions of the Midrash, as contrasted with the Midrash Haggada (*q.v.*), which contains folklore, parables, ethical allegories—from which rabbinical rulings and laws were often derived. (See Guide Note D, pp. 67–69).

MIDRASH LAMENTATIONS RABBAH. In Hebrew: *Ekhah Rabbat* (h). The Midrash on the third of the five *megilloth* or scrolls; part of the Midrash Rabbah (see below).

MIDRASH LEVITICUS RABBAH. In Hebrew: *Va-yikra Rabbah.* See Midrash Rabbah (below) and Guide Notes B, D and E (pp. 62–65, 67–69, 69).

MIDRASH NUMBERS RABBAH. In Hebrew: *Be-Midbar* ("in the wilderness") *Rabbah.* The Midrash on the Book of Numbers, included in the Midrash Rabbah (see below) and Guide Notes B and E (pp. 62–65, 69).

MIDRASH RABBAH. This title is actually a misnomer for:

(1) The collection of *midrashim* ("commentaries" or "investigations") on the Torah and the five *megilloth* (Song of Songs, Ruth, Lamentations, Ecclesiastes, Esther). The unapt title *Midrash Rabbah* grew out of a set of complicated facts: Genesis begins with *Be-Reshit* or *Bereshith* ("In the beginning"); the Midrash for Genesis became identified as *Bereshith Rabbah*—("Bereshith: the Great Work"); and "*Rabbah*" began to be tacked on to all the other collections of midrashic materials, such as those on the *megilloth* mentioned above.

(2) The Midrash named after a rabbi who collected *midrashim*; "rabbi" in Aramaic is "*rabbah.*"

The entire *Midrash Rabbah* was translated into English by H. Freedman and Maurice Simon, published in London in 1939.

MIKVE (MIKVAH). Yiddish from Hebrew: "ritual bath . . . immersion pool." The bath, prescribed by ritual, which religious Jewish women take (a) at the end of their menstrual period, (b) before being married, (c) after bearing a child. The woman recites a benediction while in the water. A community of Jews was obligated by rabbinical law to maintain a community *mikve.* The regulations governing the *mikve* are quite detailed and are set forth in the sixth tractate of TOHOROTH.

MILHAMOT HA-SHEM. Hebrew: "Wars of the Lord." A book by Gersonides (see BIOGRAPHIES).

MINOR TRACTATES OF THE TALMUD. (See Guide Note B 6, p. 65). The use of "of" is inexact; the Minor Tractates are appendages to, and not all accepted parts of, the Talmud.

MINYAN (MINYON). Hebrew: "number" or "counting." The ten male Jews required for religious services. No congregational rites can begin "until we have a *minyan*"; to have ten men is to have a "synagogue." (In certain special circumstances, exceptions to a *minyan* are permitted for a wedding, circumcision, etc.)

Solitary prayer is laudable, but a *minyan* possesses special merit to the observant, who have held from antiquity that when ten male Jews assemble for study or worship, God's Presence (*Shekhinah*) dwells among them. The Lord said He would spare Sodom if ten truly righteous men could be discovered there. And since God exempted Joshua and Caleb from His castigation of the spies who returned from Canaan, a congregation is twelve minus two—or ten (Numbers, 14:22–38), according to Mishnah.

MISHLE. Hebrew: "proverbs." This is the name in Hebrew for the Book of Proverbs.

MISHLE SHUALIM. Hebrew: "Fox Tales." (See Ha-Nakdan in BIOGRAPHIES.)

MISHNAH (MISHNA): See Guide Note C (pp. 65–67).

MISHNEH TORAH. Hebrew: "repetition of the Law". (1) The book of Deuteronomy. (2) The great codification of Jewish laws by Maimonides (see BIOGRAPHIES).

MISHPOKHE (MESHPOCHE). Hebrew: "relatives . . . extended family." The closest synonym in English is "clan." See *Joys of Yiddish.*

MITZVAH (plural *mitzvot*). Hebrew: "commandment." (1) Commandment; divine commandment. (2) A meritorious act, a "good work," a truly virtuous, kind, ethical deed.

Mitzvah is second only to *Torah* in the vocabulary of Judaism. *Mitzvot* are of various kinds: those of positive performance (e.g., caring for the widow and orphan), and those of negative resolve (e.g., not accepting a bribe); those between man and God (fasting on *Yom Kippur*) and those between man and man (paying a servant promptly).

Mitzvot are regarded as profound obligations, but

must be performed not from a sense of duty but with "a joyous heart." There are 613 separate *mitzvot* listed in the *Sefer Mitzvot Gadol*, of which 248 are positive and 365 negative. Maimonides listed all the *mitzvot* in his *Book of the Mitzvot*; he remarked that the man who performed only one of the 613 deserved salvation—*if* he did so not to win credit, but entirely for its own sake. The potential number of *mitzvot* is endless. Israel Zangwill called *mitzvot* the Jews' "sacred sociology."

MO'ED. Hebrew: "set feast." The second order of the Talmud, dealing with festivals, fasts and the Sabbath.

MO'ED KATAN. Hebrew: "minor festival days." The eleventh tractate in MO'ED, the second order of the Talmud.

MOGEN DAVID. See MAGEN DAVID.

MOISHE KAPOYR. Yiddish for one who must do things backwards, who persists in being contrary and contradictory. For a longer description see *Joys of Yiddish.*

MOREH NEVUHIM. Hebrew: "Guide for the Perplexed." The philosophical classic by Maimonides (see BIOGRAPHIES). In English, the title is often given as "guide of . . ." or "guide to . . ."

NAGID (HA-NAGID). Hebrew: "leader, prince." This word appeared in Muslim and some Christian countries in the Middle Ages as the title, recognized by the state, for a head of a Jewish community. (Compare "Nasi.")

NASHIM. Hebrew: "women." The third order of the Talmud; seven tractates on betrothals, weddings, marital vows, husbands and wives, Levirate marriages, divorces.

NASI. Hebrew: "prince." (1) The president of the Sanhedrin. (2) Today, the title of the president of the State of Israel.

NAZIR. Hebrew: "a Nazirite," from *nazar*, "to dedicate (oneself)." The fourth tractate in NASHIM, the third order of the Talmud; nine chapters on Nazirite vows as prescribed in the Bible (Numbers 6:1–21). These vows have virtually disappeared. The Nazirites were ascetics who eschewed wine or intoxicants, did not cut their hair, and avoided contact with even a relative's corpse. Samson and Samuel were Nazirites.

NEDARIM. Hebrew: "vows." The third tractate in NASHIM, the third order of the Mishnah.

NEVIIM. Hebrew: "Prophets," which became the name for "the Prophetic Books." The *neviim rishonim* ("the former [first] prophets") are the books of Joshua, Judges, Samuel, Kings—which relate the history of the Israelites from their time in Canaan to the destruction of the First Temple (586 B.C.E.), covering both Hebrew kingdoms: Israel and Judah. The *neviim aharonim* ("later prophets") are Isaiah, Jeremiah and Ezekiel. The other twelve or "Minor Later Prophets" are sometimes grouped together as one book, *The Minor Prophets,* in English; or as *T're Asar* ("The Twelve") in Hebrew.

NEZIKIN. Hebrew: "damages . . . civil and criminal law." The fourth order of the Talmud; ten tractates which govern oaths, court damages, criminal law. NEZIKIN contains the great and beloved collection of ethical sayings, *Pirke Abot* (*q.v.*), "The Sayings of the Fathers."

NUMBERS. See Guide Note B (pp. 62–65).

NUMBERS RABBAH. The Midrash on the Book of Numbers (see above); the Midrash Numbers Rabbah.

OLEVASHOLEM. Yiddish form of ALAV HA-SHOLOM, above.

ORHOT HAYIM. Hebrew: "Paths of Life." The name of an important book by Eliezer ben Isaac ha-Gadol (See BIOGRAPHIES).

ORHOT TSADIKIM. Hebrew: "The Ways of the Righteous."

OTSAR. Hebrew: "treasure . . . treasure trove."

OTSAR MIDRASHIM. A collection of 200 midrashim, annotated by David Eisenstein.

PASSOVER. See PESACH.

PE'AH. Hebrew: "gleanings . . . corner . . . edge of the field." The second tractate in ZERAIM, the first order of the Talmud. The produce of the corners of a field had to be left for the poor; no maximum area or amount was specified. *Peot* (Yiddish: *peyes*) refers to the "corner" curled earlocks worn by Hasidic and other very orthodox Jews, in conformity with Leviticus 19 : 27.

PERAKIM: See Guide Note B (pp. 62–65).

PEREK. Hebrew: "chapter." This is also a common name for *Sayings of the Fathers*.

PEREK HA-SHALOM. Hebrew: "Chapter of Homilies on Peace." One of the Minor Tractates attached to the Talmud.

PESACH. Hebrew: *Pessah*: "passover," "sparing." The Passover holiday and celebration, one of the most cherished of Jewish holidays, the Festival of Freedom. It lasts eight days (seven in Israel) and commemorates Israel's deliverance from enslavement in Egypt over 3200 years ago, as recounted in Exodus. (To be exact, the "passing over" of the houses of Hebrews, during the plague Exodus describes [12:13] as afflicting the first-born, refers to the sacrifice, on the eve of the Exodus, of a lamb.) Hence, *pesach* means the first day of the "Feast of the Unleavened Bread."

On the first and second nights of Passover (Israeli Jews and Reform Jews celebrate only the first), a family *seder* is held. This combination of banquet and religious service is the highlight of the holiday—and, to many, of the year. Nothing containing leavening, or which has come in contact with a leavening agent, may be used during the festival; special china and utensils are used during the Passover week. On the table are matzos (unleavened bread), a reminder of the haste in which the Israelites left Egypt, without waiting for their bread to rise; bitter herbs, marking the bitterness of slavery; an egg and bone, symbolic of the offerings brought to the Temple; *haroset*, a mixture of chopped nuts, apples, cinnamon, and wine, representing the clay from which the Israelites made bricks while in slavery. Each setting has a wineglass, including the one placed for Elijah. The father half-reclines at the head of the table, propped up on pillows or on a sofa; this dramatizes freedom and ease. Guests are customarily invited.

Following the *Kiddush*, the grandfather, father, or oldest son opens the *seder* with a prayer in Aramaic:

This is the bread of affliction that our fathers ate in the
land of Egypt. All who are hungry, let them come and eat;
all who are needy, let them come and celebrate Passover
with us. Now we are here: next year may we be in Israel.
Now we are slaves: in the year ahead may we be free men.

This prayer was probably composed shortly after the
Romans crushed Judea, in the year 70, and the Jews
went into *galut*—exile. The Haggadah, the narrative
read at the *seder*, includes rabbinical comments, hymns,
prayers, four stylized questions and answers—the whole
constituting a ceremony of celebration and praise to the
Lord.

PESAHIM. Hebrew: "Paschal lambs; feast of Passover."
The third tractate in MO'ED, the second order of the
Talmud; ten chapters describe the Passover rites.

PESHAT. Hebrew: "the literal meaning." The simplest
interpretation of any passage in Holy Scriptures; distinguished from *derash*, which is an exhortation or moral
read into a passage; *remez*, a tenuous allusion; and *sod*,
an arcane or mystical meaning.

PESIKTA. Hebrew: "section."

PESIKTA d'RAB KAHANA. A collection of thirty-one
homilies about holidays, festivals, and Sabbaths—dating
back to the seventh century. The work was ingeniously
reconstructed by Leopold Zunz (see BIOGRAPHIES)
and has been newly edited by Professor Bernard Mandel-
baum.

PESIKTA RABBAH. Homilies included in the MIDRASH
RABBAH. (See above.)

PESIKTA RABBATI. A collection of forty-seven homilies
about festivals and special occasions, compiled (apparently) in Palestine around the seventh century; translated
into English in 1968 (by W. G. Braude.) Often catalogued as *Midrash Pesikta Rabbati*.

PIRKE. Hebrew: "chapters of . . ."

PIRKE ABOT (AVOT). Hebrew: "Sayings of the Fathers."
An ethical tractate included in the Mishnah, in the order
NEZIKIN, and immensely popular among Jews. It con-
tains profound sayings of rabbis across six centuries—

from the third century before, to the third century after, the Christian Era. *Pirke Abot* is part of the liturgy: Sephardic Jews recite it at home each Sabbath between *Pesach* (*q.v.*) and Pentecost; Askenazic Jews every summer Sabbath day from Passover to Rosh Hashana. Countless commentaries on, and translations of, this beautiful, aphoristic work have been published.

PIRKE ABOT (AVOTH) DE RABBI NATHAN. A later, larger edition of *Pirke Abot*; translated into English by Judah Goldin (Yale University, 1955).

PIRKE HA-ROSH: See ASHER BEN YEHIEL in BIOGRAPHIES.

PRAYER OF AZARIAH AND SONG OF THE THREE CHILDREN. In the Apocrypha (*q.v.*).

PRAYER OF MANASSES. In the Apocrypha (*q.v.*).

PSEUDEPIGRAPHA. Greek: "falsely ascribed title." Apocalyptic and eschatological writings, not accepted in the Biblical canon; the best known are the Psalms of Solomon, the Testament of the Twelve Patriarchs, the Apocalypse of Baruch, the Ascension of Isaiah, the Book of Enoch. Scholars firmly differ on which writings belong in the Pseudepigrapha and which in the Apocrypha. Pseudepigrapha were known only in translations until the discovery of the Dead Sea Scrolls, where originals were found. See APOCRYPHA.

PURIM. Hebrew: *pur*: "lot." The Feast of Lots, which commemorates the rescue of the Jews of Persia from Haman's plot to exterminate them (5th century B.C.E.). Lots had been drawn by Haman, first Minister to King Ahasuerus (possibly Artaxerxes II), to set the date on which the Jews would be slaughtered. A miraculous deliverance was effected by beautiful Queen Esther and Mordecai, her uncle and guardian. Haman ended on the gallows he had erected to dispatch Mordecai. The story is told in the Book of Esther. Since the Middle Ages, an enemy of the Jewish people has been known as a "Haman."

In synagogues and temples, the *Megillah* (Scroll of Esther) is read on the eve and morning of Purim. Whenever the name of Haman is uttered, the children set up a racket of jeers, and spin ratchety noisemakers.

In some communities, Haman's name is written upon the soles of one's shoes, so that the name may literally be wiped out. Among the customs associated with Purim are the sending of gifts (food and money) to the poor, and the exchanging of gifts with friends. The symbolic food of Purim is the *hamntash*, a three-cornered sweet pastry filled with prunes or poppy seeds.

Purim is not a truly religious holiday and, like Channukah, is not universally treated as such: e.g., work, business, secular life is not greatly altered in most, but not all, Jewish communities.

RAB: With Samuel, the first of the Babylonian *Amoraim* (*q.v.*), active between 220 and 250.

RABA: A great Babylonian *Amora*; he lived in the first half of the fourth century.

RABBA (RABBAH). (1) The title usually indicating Rabbah bar Nahmani (third–fourth century), the great Babylonian *Amora*, head of the academy at Pumbedita. (2) The title also given Rabbah Bar Ben Hanah (third–fourth century), the Palestinian rabbi-traveler known as "the Jewish Sinbad."

RABBAN. Hebrew: "our master." (1) A form of "rabbi," a title higher than "rabbi," accorded to four outstanding scholars of early Mishnaic times: Gamaliel I and II, Simeon ben Gamaliel, and Johanan ben Zakkai. (2) The president of the Sanhedrin.

RABBENU. Hebrew: "our master," "our teacher." Moses is called "Moishe Rabbenu."

RABBENU TAM. Hebrew: "our perfect master." The title given Jacob ben Moses, twelfth-century *Tosephist*. (See BIOGRAPHIES.)

RABBI. Hebrew: "my teacher." A title of respect adopted by the Hebrews in Palestine during the first century of the Christian Era; it became the form by which ordained members of the Sanhedrin (*q.v.*) were addressed. In Babylon, scholar-authorities were called *Rav*: "master." In time, "rabbi" came to signify the religious leader in a synagogue or temple.

RALBAG. The acronym for Rabbi Levi ben Gershon (see BIOGRAPHIES).

RAMBAM. The acronym for Maimonides (Moses ben Maimon; see BIOGRAPHIES).

RAMBAN. The acronym for Moses ben Nahman; see BIOGRAPHIES.

RAMHAL. The acronym for Moses Hayyim Luzzato; see BIOGRAPHIES.

RASH. See ROSH.

RASHBAM. The acronym for Samuel ben Meir; see BIOGRAPHIES.

RASHI. The acronym for the great Rabbi Solomon Yitzhaki; see "Rashi," in BIOGRAPHIES.

RAV. "Master." The Babylonian form of "rabbi."

RESPONSA. In Hebrew: *sheelot u-teshuvot,* "questions and answers." The replies written by authoritative scholars in answer to letters inquiring about a thousand-and-one aspects of Jewish Law, Torah, and Talmud. More than 500,000 *responsa,* appearing in over 1,000 compilations, have been published. (Disciples of the rabbis made copies of their masters' correspondence.) Many manuscripts (in Hebrew and Arabic) were discovered in 1896–1897 in the *Genizah* ("hiding place," where religious literature—which is never thrown away —is deposited) of a synagogue in Cairo.

The *responsa* form of communication is mentioned in the Talmud (*Sanhedrin,* 11b and 29a) and the Jerusalem Talmud (Talmud J.: *Kedoshin,* 82 : 12). *Responsa* began in Babylonia, with the *geonim's* juridical replies to questions; they encouraged correspondence as a way of preserving bonds with distant communities. From the twelfth to the fifteenth century, the problems Jews faced in adjusting to new political, social, and economic vicissitudes required that rabbinical authorities reinterpret the Law; innumerable problems were encountered which had not been covered in the Talmud and are not to be found in the Torah. The influence of *responsa* is seen in the correspondence of such luminaries as Alfasi, Rashi, Maimonides, the Tosephists, Rabbi Meir of Rothenberg, and Joseph Caro, who assembled the comprehensive *Shulhan Aruk* (*q.v.*). The *responsa* of various great scholars proved invaluable

during times when the reading of the Talmud was proscribed by hostile political authorities.

In addition to describing the life and religious problems of Jews in the widespread communities of the
Diaspora, the *responsa* contain invaluable data on historical events, social conditions, intellectual life, and
philosophical/theological schools of thought. *Responsa*
are still being written: for some striking examples, see
Guide Note F (pp. 69–70).

RIF. The acronym for Rabbi Isaac Ben Jacob Alfasi (1013–
1103) of Fez; see BIOGRAPHIES.

RIM. The acronym for Rabbi Isaac Meir; see BIOGRA-
PHIES.

ROSH. The acronym for Rabbenu Asher; see BIOGRA-
PHIES.

ROSH HASHANAH (ROSH HA-SHANAH). Hebrew:
"The head of the year . . . New Year Observance . . .
Feast of the New Year." (1) The eighth tractate in
MO'ED, the second order of the Talmud, on the new
Moon's celebration, the prayers for the holy day, etc.
(2) The commemoration of the birthday of—the world;
according to the rabbis, in the Talmud and Midrash.

Rosh Hashana, like all Jewish holy days, is determined by the lunar calendar: it falls in late September
or early October and opens the Ten Days of Penitence
(the Days of Awe), which end with Yom Kippur (*q.v.*).
During these ten days of prayer, all mankind presumably pass before God, who looks into their deeds and
hearts.

On Rosh Hashana, the *shophar* (ram's horn) is blown
several times: first to celebrate God's kingship; secondly,
to stress the role of the individual; third, to remind the
congregation of all the events associated with the blowing of the ram's horn. (In ancient Judea, the ram's horn
was used to send signals from one mountain to another.)
In the Talmud, one rabbi ventures the reassuring comment that the blowing of the *shophar* helps to confuse
Satan and his hosts.

Rosh Hashana is a happy time; families gather from
everywhere for the holiday and feast; bread or apple is
dipped in honey to symbolize a hoped-for "sweetness"
in the year ahead. The traditional Rosh Hashanah greet-

ing is "*Le-shana tova tikasevu,*" "May you be inscribed for a good year." Orthodox and Conservative Jews observe two days of Rosh Hashanah; Reform Jews celebrate only one.

ROV. See RABBI.

SABORAIM. (SEBORAIM). See TANNA, and Guide Note D (pp. 67–69).

SACHEL. See SEYKHL.

SANHEDRIN. From Greek: *synedrion:* "assembly." (1) "The High Court . . . the Sanhedrin." (2) Fourth tractate in NEZIKIN, the fourth order of the Mishnah; it deals with legal aspects of the courts, judicial procedure, criminal law—and lists the sins for which one will be excluded from the world-to-come. (3) The seventy elders, plus a Patriarch or President (Nasi), who sat in the Temple in Jerusalem as a combination of Supreme Court and College of Cardinals, ruling on theological, ethical, civil, and political matters. After the year 70, when the Temple was destroyed, the Sanhedrin met in Yavneh; tradition assigns further meeting places, the last being Tiberias, where the Sanhedrin was outlawed, in 425, by the Roman authorities.

Modern scholars think there must have been two Sanhedrins: one of aristocrats and priests, the other a court of Pharisees who attended to matters of ritual, the calendar, etc. After the year 425, the Sanhedrin's functions were replaced by those of the *Beth Din* (*q.v.*). After the State of Israel was founded in 1948, a movement tried to revive the Sanhedrin, but this was not achieved because of constitutional problems.

SEDER. Hebrew: "order." (1) An order of the Talmud. (2) The Passover feast. See PESACH.

SEFARDI. See SEPHARDI.

SEFER (SEPHER). Hebrew: "book."

SEFER ELIM: "Book of Elim." See Delmedigo, Joseph Solomon, in BIOGRAPHIES.

SEFER HA-GILGULIM. "Book of Transmigrations") or "Metamorphoses"). See Isaac Luria, in BIOGRAPHIES.

SEFER HA-HINUKH. Hebrew: "Book of education." A classic of the thirteenth century, by Rabbi Aaron ha-Levi of Barcelona (see BIOGRAPHIES).

SEFER HASIDIM. Hebrew: "Book of the Pious" or "Saintly." Written by Rabbi Yehuda he-Hasid of Regensburg in the thirteenth century, this famous work on ethics has appeared in an early, long, unorganized text, and as a later, briefer, more orderly presentation. The *Sefer Hasidim* may be the work of more than one author; some authorities attribute it to the great Judah he-Hasid ("the Pious"), a major force in medieval Jewry. The work is a mirror of medieval Judaic thought, containing folklore, anecdotes, legends, a great deal of demonology and superstition—and aphorisms, quoted in the present anthology, about everything from praying to paying Taxes; the respect due to parents and the seductive perils of secular writings; the sin of slander and the proper attitude to non-Jews; the raising of children and the virtues of modesty.

SEFER HA-YASHAR. Hebrew: "Book of Yashar" or "Book of the Straight Way." See Rabbenu Tam in BIOGRAPHIES.

SEFER IKARIM (HA-IKKARIM). Hebrew: "Book of Principles." See Joseph Albo in BIOGRAPHIES.

SEFER SHAASHUIM. Hebrew: "Book of Delights." See Ibn Zabara in BIOGRAPHIES.

SEFER TORAH. Hebrew: "Book of the Torah." (1) A Book in the Minor Tractates added to the Talmud. (2) The Scroll containing the Five Books of Moses, kept in the Ark at the front of a synagogue or temple. Readings from the *Sefer Torah* are made in synagogues or temples each Sabbath and festival, on Mondays, Thursdays and fast days. The Scroll is of parchment, hand-lettered, in Hebrew; in Ashkenezic communities it is covered with a mantle of silk or velvet, often adorned with a breastplate and crown of silver.

SEFIRAH (SEFIRAT[H] HA-OMER). Hebrew: "counting." The forty-nine-day period that begins with the second day of Passover (when the *omer*, a sheaf of new barley, was traditionally brought to the Temple in Jerusalem as an offering) and ends on Shevuoth, the feast of the first-fruit harvest. The "omer is counted" during daily prayers, followed by the recitation of Psalm 67. The forty-nine days of *Sefirah* have become a period of mourning because of the misfortunes which, tradition holds, the Jews suffered during this period: the persecutions under Roman rule, the martyrdom of Rabbi Akiba, the slaughter of Jews by the Crusaders. The famous revolt of the Warsaw Ghetto against Nazi troops occurred during *Sefirah*.

SEMAHOT. Hebrew: "joyous occasions"—but this is a euphemism for *Evel Rabati* (*Rabbati*): "Great [tractate on] mourning." A book in the Minor Tractates added to the Talmud.

SEPHARDI (plural, SEPHARDIM). Hebrew: *"Sepharad,"* the name found in Obadiah (9:20), which early medieval rabbis identified as Spain. Spanish and Portuguese Jews, and the descendants of the Jews of Spain, Portugal, and the Middle East. The Sephardic tradition, culture, liturgy, etc., differ in many important ways from those of the Ashkenazim (*q.v.*) of Eastern Europe. The Sephardim were beholden to the Babylonian tradition (as were the Jews in all places on the Mediterranean); the Ashkenazim followed the rabbi-scholars of Palestine.

Sephardic Judaism was elitist, intellectual, and dominated Jewish culture from around 600 until the expulsion of the Jews from Spain at the end of the fifteenth century. It was a sophisticated blend of Talmudic thought, Greek philosophy, Aristotelianism, science (as it then existed), and the ideas of Averroës, the great Islamic scholar whom medieval Christians were forbidden, by formal Church prohibition, to read. Sephardic scholars and rabbis were acquainted with Latin, Spanish, French, and they broadened Judaic thought with knowledge from geometry, algebra, astronomy, medicine, metaphysics, music, mechanics.

Sephardic Jews rose to positions of considerable eminence in Spain, Portugal, North Africa—as physicians, philosophers, poets, financiers, diplomats, advisers to kings and courts. The Sephardic Jews wrote mostly in Arabic, even when writing about Torah and Talmud.

When the Sephardic Jews were expelled from the Iberian countries, they moved on to settle along the coastline of the Mediterranean (they soon dominated the culture and religious practices of Jewish communities in North Africa and the Middle East), and to Holland and England—and their colonies.

The Sephardim were sophisticates, enlightened, cosmopolitan; the Ashkenazim (who lived under very harsh Russian, Polish, Austrian rulers, confined to the Pale, excluded from owning land or entering a profession, subjected to repeated pillaging and ghastly pogroms) were peasants, peddlers, proletarians, fundamentalist in faith, steeped in poverty, bound to orthodox tradition, filled with fervent Messianic dreams, and hostile to secular knowledge (partly because education in Christian countries was clerical, therefore not available to and for Jews). Professor Louis Ginzberg remarks: "For the Sefardim, learning was a matter of sentiment; for the Polish Jew, it was an intellectual occupation."*

Today, Sephardic designates any Jews following Sephardic rites, whether from Spanish ancestry or not. Middle Eastern, North African and Oriental Jews are Sephardic.

Communities of Sephardic Jews are today found throughout Asia Minor, in Israel, Turkey, Greece, and in England, Holland, Latin America and the United States (Sephardim were the first Jewish immigrants). Sephardic Jews claim that their liturgy stems from the academies of Babylonia; Ashkenazim follow the Palestinian ritual. The vernacular used by Old World Sephardic Jews, as opposed to the Yiddish (Judeo-German) of Ashkenazic Jews, is Ladino, a form of Spanish.

SEYKHL. Yiddish from Hebrew: "understanding." Native good sense, common sense, judgment.

SHABBATH (SHABBAT). Hebrew: "rest . . . cessation from labor . . . Sabbath." (1) The first tractate in MO'ED, the second order of the Talmud; twenty-four chapters on the rules governing the Sabbath. (2) The Sabbath, which became more than a weekly respite from servitude, labor, anxiety. *Shabbes* (Yiddish for *"Shabbat"*) is called "the Queen of the Week," "the Bride." In however bitter a time and place, the Shabbath was

---

* *Students, Scholars and Saints*, J.P.S.A., 1928, p. 64.

the miraculous day when even the lowliest, poorest Jew could feel himself in kingly communion with the Almighty, favored by God's special concern: "It is a sign between me and the children of Israel" (Exodus, 31: 17). To "make Shabbes" means to be festive.

The Mishnah sets forth a sizable number of Sabbath prohibitions: baking, plowing, writing, carrying, even tying a knot. On the Sabbath, Jews prayed—and studied; they read; they discussed Torah and Talmud. A rabbi or elder read the laws, to "expound them point by point, until the late afternoon, when [all] depart, having gained knowledge . . . and an advance in piety" (Philo). Every Sabbath morning, a portion of the Torah is read in the synagogue, together with a reading from the Prophets; the entire Torah cycle is completed each year.

On the six Sabbaths between Passover and Shevuoth (Pentecost) and Rosh Hashanah (among the Ashkenazim), fathers and grandfathers would traditionally engage their children, at home, in discussions of the *Sayings of the Fathers* (*Pirke Abot*) or portions of the Mishnah. Cultural historians may appraise the magnitude of the consequences of an entire people, young and old, spending one day a week, year after year, century after century, in a seminar on morals, ethics, responsibility, reason, faith.

Jews try to invite a stranger, traveler, student, or poor man to share the *shabbes* meal. This serves to make Jews everywhere feel part of one universal fellowship.

Shabbes ends after sundown Saturday, with a home religious service called *Habdalah*, the "separation" of the Sabbath from week days.

SHALOM (SHOLEM, SHOLOM). From the Hebrew root meaning "whole . . . entire . . . peace." (1) Peace. (2) The greeting and leave-taking word or phrase used by Jews—*Shalom aleykhem* ("peace unto you") being responded to by *Aleykhem shalom* ("and to you, peace"). In Yiddish, "*shalóm*" is pronounced "*shólem*."

SHAS. Hebrew initials for *Shishah Sedarim:* "the six orders" of the Mishnah, which form the foundation of the Talmud. When Catholic censorship in the sixteenth century outlawed the use of the word "Talmud," Jews used *Shas* instead.

SHEKEL (plural: SHKOLIM). Hebrew: "coin," "weight." (1) A coin. (2) Money. The *shekel* was the most important silver coin in Biblical times.

SHEMA. Hebrew: "hear." The opening word of Deuteronomy: 6, 4: "Hear, O Israel, the Lord our God, the Lord is one . . ." This has become the name of three selections from the Bible (beginning with Deuteronomy: 6:4–9, and containing 11:13–21, Numbers: 15:37–41) which are recited morning and evening, every day, as dictated in Deuteronomy: 6:7 . . . "You shall speak of them . . . when you lie down and when you rise up."

SHEVET YEHUDAH. Hebrew: "The Rod of Judah"; see Ibn Verga, Judah, in BIOGRAPHIES.

SHEBI'IT. Hebrew: "the Seventh Year." The fifth tractate in ZERAIM, the first order of the Talmud; ten chapters deal with sabbatical years, debts, and legal documents.

SHIDUKH (SHIDDACH). Hebrew, from Aramaic: *shidukha*: "marital match." (1) An arranged marriage; a "match" or betrothal. (2) Talmudic term for premarital discussions between the parents of those to be betrothed.

SHIRAT YISRAEL. Hebrew: "The Poetry of Israel."

SHIR HA-SHIRIM. Hebrew: "The Song of Songs."

SHMOT. Hebrew: originally *Sefer Y'Ziat Mizraim:* "the Book of the Going out of Egypt." At an early date, this book of the Torah was known by its opening phrase, *Ve-Eleh Shmot* ("And these are the names"). Its English designation is Exodus, the name used in the Septuagint. See Guide Note A (pp. 61–62).

SHOPHAR. Hebrew: "trumpet," "horn"; specifically "ram's horn." The ram's horn (usually 10 to 12 inches long), blown in the synagogue during Rosh Hashanah and Yom Kippur, which reminds the pious how Abraham, offering Isaac in sacrifice, was reprieved when God said Abraham could sacrifice a ram instead. The man who blows the *shophar* must be of blameless character; in some traditions, the elaborate ritual adds up to about one hundred *tekiot* (arrangements of *shophar* sounds) for *Yom Kippur*. The *shophar* was used in ancient Palestine to signal danger, call for defense, announce a holiday, call together convocations. In Israel today the *shophar* is used on high official occasions. See YOM KIPPUR.

SHULHAN ARUK (SHULCHAN ARUKH). Hebrew: "set table." The title of a most influential and popular compilation of rabbinic laws that regulate the practice of Judaism; written by Joseph Caro (Karo) in 1555; see BIOGRAPHIES.

SIBYLLINE ORACLES. A series of prophecies, in Greek hexameter verse, combining pagan, Hebrew, and Christian legends from the second century before, to the fourth century after, the Christian Era. The text attacks Israel's oppressors, especially Rome, projects the history of the peoples around the Mediterranean, and predicts wars and catastrophes that will precede the Messiah's coming and the redemption of mankind.

SIDDUR. Hebrew: "arrangement," "order." The daily and Sabbath prayer book. It contains the three daily services, the Sabbath prayers, *Sayings of the Fathers*, and special readings. The *Siddur* is based on a compilation made during the ninth century in an academy in Babylonia. Additions and emendations have since been inserted and communities have developed different liturgies. The first printed *Siddur* appeared in 1486—thirty years after the Gutenberg Bible; its colophon reads: "Here is completed the sacred work for the special *minhag* (ritual) of the Holy Congregation of Rome, according to the order arranged by an expert."

Sephardic Jews refer to the "*tephillah*," and not the "*siddur*."

SIDRA. Aramaic: "order." That part of the Pentateuch which is read in the synagogue each Sabbath. The reading of the entire Torah consumes one year, and is promptly begun again, on the same day the final passage is read.

SIFRA (SIPHRA). Aramaic: "the book." (Do not confuse with *Sifre*, below.) A legal commentary or *midrash* on the book of Leviticus; also called *Torat Kohanim* ("the law of the priests") or *Sifra de-Ve-Rav* ("the book of the School of Rav"). It is the work of Rabbi Akiba's academy and expounds the position of Rabbi Judah, one of Akiba's students.

SIFRE. Aramaic: "the book." A Tannaitic commentary on the books of Numbers and Deuteronomy—the former *halakic*, the latter *haggadic*. This book is the work of Rabbi Ishmael's school—opposed to Rabbi Akiba's on many points.

SIMHAT (SIMCHAT) TORAH. Hebrew: "the day of rejoicing in the law." A festival, observed on the ninth and final day of SUCCOTH (in Israel, on the eighth night), which honors the Torah; a gay occasion, with feasting and dancing. The last chapters of Deuteronomy are read—and immediately the congregation cries, "*Chazak, chazak, venit chazak!*" ("Be strong, be strong, and let us summon new strength!" And then the first chapter of Genesis is begun, to show that the Torah has neither beginning nor end. The holy scrolls are removed from the synagogue's Ark on the eve of Simhat Torah and each male in the congregation takes his turn carrying them; the congregation sings; the men carrying the Torah scrolls "dance."

SIRACH (SIRAH, SIRA), JESUS BEN; see BIOGRAPHIES.

SOPHER (SOFER); plural: SOPHERIM or SOFERIM. Hebrew: "scribe." In the kingdom of Judea, the scribe held the highest office. Scribes transcribed the Scrolls of the Law and wrote all legal documents. The scribe was the community's leading scholar; rabbis were not called scribes; but in time, scribes were replaced as teachers and scholars by rabbis. (See RABBI). The *Sopherim* developed many regulations from Scripture: on prayer, feasts, liturgy. They also changed Hebrew texts (in 18 places), to minimize references to God which they considered anthropomorphic. Their efforts to make the Torah *the* authority served to reduce the powers of the priests, who inherited their position. Torah no longer remained the esoteric monopoly of a caste. This revolutionized Judaism, opening the study of the Law to philosophers and teachers, "democratizing" the mysteries which, in ancient religions, were jealously guarded by hereditary priesthoods. The *Sopherim* were Sadducees; the *Tannaim* were Pharisees.

Note: The word "scribes," for *Sopherim,* developed unfortunate associations; in the New Testament, "scribes" is often used as a synonym for hypocrites. To be both accurate and just, *Sopherim* should be translated as "men of the book."

SOPHERIM (SOFERIM). Hebrew: "men of the book"; plural of *sopher* (*sofer*). (1) The scribes. (2) A book in the Minor Tractates added to the Talmud.

SOTAH. Hebrew: "Wife who has erred . . . suspected adultress." (1) The fifth tractate in NASHIM, the third order of the Talmud. (2) A wife suspected of adultery, who undergoes the ordeal of "the bitter waters" (Numbers 5:12–31).

SUCCOTH (SUKKOTH). Hebrew: "booths." The Feast of Tabernacles (or Booths), the holiday that starts on the fifth day after Yom Kippur (*q.v.*) and is celebrated for nine days by the Orthodox, and for eight days in Israel and among Reform Jews. Throughout the week, a pious family eats its meals in a *sukkah* (booth) set up out of doors, roofed with branches and decorated with flowers and fruit. The booth, intended to look temporary, represents the hastily erected dwellings Jews used during the forty years of wandering in the wilderness. ". . . your generations may know that I made the children of Israel to dwell in booths, when I brought them out of the land of Egypt." (Leviticus 23:43). Philo considered the *sukkah* a democratic institution because there all Jews, rich or poor, dwell in a primitive shelter.

Hoshanah Rabbah, "the great Hosanna," is observed on the seventh day by a procession around the synagogue; the men carry palm and willow branches, and the entire congregation chants verses praising God and requesting His saving powers.

SUKKAH. Hebrew: "booth." The sixth tractate in MO'ED, the second order of the Talmud, whose five chapters present laws about the Feast of Tabernacles (see above).

SUSANNA. A book in the APOCRYPHA.

TA'ANITH (TAANIT): Hebrew: "fast . . . first day of fasting." The ninth tractate in MO'ED, the second order of the Mishnah; it deals with fasting, droughts, petitions to God for rain.

TABERNACLES, FEAST OF. See SUCCOTH.

TAHKEMONI. Fifty narratives, in rhymed prose, written by Judah al-Harizi; see BIOGRAPHIES. The *Tahkemoni* describes the experiences in many places to which the author had traveled, or the tales he heard there. *Tahkemoni* is sometimes translated as "Apothecary" (e.g., *New Standard Jewish Encyclopedia, op. cit.,* p. 73.)

TALLITH (TALIT, TALIS). Hebrew: "covering." The prayer shawl used by Jewish males, according to some practices at their Bar Mitzvah, to others, upon marriage and at morning prayers. The *tallith katan,* a smaller garment, is worn by very orthodox Jews under their shirts, at all times. The Torah tells Jewish males to wear a garment fringed at the four corners. The fringes are called *zizith* (*q.v.*).

The *tallith* reminds a Jew of his bond and duty to God. At one time, the *tallith* was a gown or cloak worn in public; but because of repeated humiliations, the rabbis decreed that it be used in the synagogue or at home, during prayer services. Black or blue bands cross the prayer shawl, to memorialize the destruction of the Temple and mourn it forever. An observing Jew gives his son a *tallith* on the latter's Bar Mitzvah; his bride or parents-in-law may give him one for his wedding; and he is buried in a shroud with his *tallith.*

TALMID HAKHAM (CHACHEM). Hebrew: "wise in study"; more exactly, "a disciple of the wise." One who is greatly learned in Talmud. The *talmid hakham* represented the ideal man, highest in the Jewish hierarchy of respect.

TALMUD. See Guide Note B (pp. 62–65).

TALMUD TORAH. Hebrew: "Study of Torah." (1) One of the cardinal concepts and values of Judaism: religious study and lifelong dedication to it. (2) A Hebrew school which, in the United States, offered a daily two-hour Hebrew session, after the public schools closed, and classes on Sunday morning; Talmud Torahs have greatly declined in number, many of their activities having been absorbed into the synagogue and temple.

TAMID. Hebrew: "daily sacrifice . . . the daily or perpetual offering." (1) The ninth tractate in KODASHIM, the fifth order of the Talmud. (2) The burnt-offering, each morning and afternoon in the Temple, as described in Numbers 28:1–8.

TANAKH. Hebrew: "the Bible." The name constructed from the first letters of the Hebrew names for the three major sections of the Bible: *Torah, Neviim* (Prophets), and *Ketuvim* (Writings or Hagiographa).

TANHUMA or TANHUMA RABBAH: The Midrash of Rabbi Tanhuma bar Abba, a fourth-century Palestinian scholar, who wrote many *midrashim* and advanced the forms of homiletics.

TANNA (plural: TANNAIM). Aramaic: "one who teaches by repetition." The name for the Talmudic scholars whose work was recorded in the Mishnah. The *Tannaim* are distinguished from the *Sopherim* (*q.v.*) in that the *Tannaim* were Pharisees, the *Sopherim*, Sadducees. After the destruction of the Second Temple (70), the Tannaim became the leaders "of such Jewish life as survived." When written forms of the Law were prohibited by political authorities, the Tannaim became "living libraries." Judaism may be said to be the product of the Tannaim; their Mishnah is the central Judaic authority. Rabbis identified with the Gemara are called *Amoraim* (*q.v.*); later commentators are called *Saboraim,* or "opinion expressers."

TARGUM. Aramaic, from Assyrian: "interpretation or translation in another language." The Aramaic translation of the Bible. The practice of public oral Aramaic translation of the passages read from the Torah probably began around the time of Ezra. (See Talmud: *Megillah,* 3a.)

TARSHISH. See Moses Ibn Ezra, in BIOGRAPHIES.

TEBUL YOM (TEVUL YOM). Hebrew: "he who has bathed that day." The tenth tractate in TOHOROTH, the sixth order of the Talmud.

TEFILLAH. Hebrew: "a prayer." (1) The Amidah (*q.v.*). (2) One of the *Tefillin.* (3) The Sephardic name for a prayer book.

TEFILLIN (TEPHILLIN). Aramaic: "attachments." (1) A "pseudo-Talmudic" small treatise in the Minor Tractates. (2) Phylacteries (from the Greek *phylakterion:* "protection" or "fortress"; see Matthew 23:5): two tiny boxes, containing portions of the Torah inscribed on parchment, that are affixed to the head and left arm while praying during morning services, except on Sabbath and festivals.

The custom of donning *tefillin* is derived from the injunction in Exodus 13:16 and in Deuteronomy 6:8, etc. The process of putting on *tefillin* is elaborate, and carefully prescribed: the *Shulhan Aruk* (*q.v.*) lists 160 (!) details.

TEMURAH. Hebrew: "exchanges"; "the substituted offering." The sixth tractate in KODASHIM, the fifth order of the Talmud.

TERUMOTH. Hebrew: "heave-offerings." The sixth tractate in ZERAIM, the first order of the Talmud.

TISHA BOV (TISHA B'AV, TISHA B'AB). Hebrew: "the ninth day of the month *Ab* (or *Av*)." The day of fasting and mourning that commemorates the destruction of both the First and the Second Temples in Jerusalem. (The Babylonians razed the first Temple in 586 B.C.E.; the Romans destroyed the second in the year 70.) Reform Jews do not observe this day of communal lamentation, known as "the blackest day in the Jewish calendar" —which has added post-Temple disasters, catastrophes, and horrors: the slaughter of Bar Kochba's followers in 138; Hadrian's leveling of Jerusalem; the death of Rabbi Akiba and nine other martyrs; the Crusades and their unholy massacres, rapes and depredations; England's expulsion of the Jews in 1290; Spain's expulsion of the Jews in 1492, etc.

Tisha Bov usually falls in August, and climaxes nine days of mourning, during which meat is not eaten, marriages not performed, smiles or laughter forbidden to the orthodox. Those who enter the synagogue do not greet one another; they sit on the floor or on low benches; a black curtain is draped over the Ark; one flickering light barely illuminates the synagogue. The Book of Lamentations is recited by the cantor in a low, depressing chant. (In Sephardic communities, the Book of Job is also read.) Poems of immense sadness (some date

from the Middle Ages) are intoned; but the service ends
on a note of hope, with the reading of Judah ha-Levi's
Zionide.

TISHBI. "The Tishbeite." Lexicon to the Talmud by Elijah
Levita (see BIOGRAPHIES.)

TOBIT. A book in the Apocrypha. It includes a version
of the Golden Rule. It is found in Greek, Latin, Syrian,
and Aramaic; no early Hebrew manuscript exists. It tells
the story of Tobias, sent to Persia, who marries Sarah
(whose previous seven husbands had been killed on their
wedding nights by the infatuated demon Ashmedai);
the marriage was effected only with the help of the
Archangel Raphael. Tobias was a most pious man,
exiled with the Ten Tribes, who was blind—until Raphael, the angel, restored his sight. The Book of Tobit
was put together around the second to first centuries
B.C.E.

TOHOROTH. Hebrew "cleanliness." (1) The ritualistic
regulations of cleanliness of body and foods. (2) The
sixth order of the Mishnah, consisting of 12 tractates.
(3) The name of the fifth tractate of the order of the
Talmud (Mishnah) of the same name, with ten chapters
dealing with presunset prohibitions on uncleanliness.

TORAH. See Guide Note B (pp. 62–65).

TOSEFOTH (TOSEPHOT): See Guide Note E (p. 69).

TOSEPHTA (TOSEFTA). A supplement-commentary on
the Mishnah, from compendia written by Rabbi Hiyya
(Chia) bar Abba (see BIOGRAPHIES) and Hashaiah
(third and fourth century), or by one of Akiba's disciples,
Rabbi Nehemiah. It contains six orders; some paragraphs, called *Baraitot,* are versions of paragraphs from
Mishnah, others follow passages from Talmud, and
others seem independent of major sources.

TOV. Hebrew: "good."

TSADIK (plural: TSADIKIM). Hebrew: "righteous man."
A term of respect for particularly pious, learned, saintly
elders. The Talmud tells us that it is the virtues of
thirty-six *tsadikim,* in each generation, that keep the
world going. (See Headnote: SAINTS.) The idealiza-

tion of the *tsadikim* was a central aspect of Hasidism (*q.v.*) and led to attributions of miracles, mystical powers, and divine revelation.

The hasidic *tsadik* was considered a blessed intermediary between God and man; his advice was treasured and followed; his words were virtually sanctified by disciples. In time, the title became hereditary, and Eastern European "dynasties" have been carried over into the United States, Israel, etc.

TSORES (TSOURIS). Yiddish from Hebrew *tsarah*: "trouble." Troubles, woes, worries. The singular is *tsore* or *tsure*. Especially aggravating adversities are called *gekokhte* (chopped-up) *tsores*.

VAV. The sixth letter of the Hebrew alphabet, pronounced "v".

VA-YIKRA (VAYIKRA). Hebrew word: "And He called." This opens Leviticus (once known as *Torat Kohanim*, "the code of priests"). "Leviticus" is a Latin word, derived from the Greek *leutikos* in the Septuagint.

VITSN. Yiddish: "witticisms, wisecracks."

WISDOM LITERATURE. The books of Proverbs, Job, Ecclesiastes, Psalms—plus "apocryphal" writings: The Wisdom of Solomon, Ecclesiasticus by Jesus ben Sirach (see BIOGRAPHIES), and Maccabees. See APOCRYPHA.

WISDOM OF SOLOMON. The book, attributed to King Solomon eulogizing wisdom and virtue. Originally written in Greek, probably by a Hebrew from Alexandria, its date is uncertain. It is in the Apocrypha.

YADAYIM (YADAIM). Hebrew: "hands." The eleventh tractate in TOHOROTH: it roams from the cleanliness of hands to problems of wisdom literature (see above), Hebrew and Aramaic, the Sadducees and Pharisees.

YAROT DEVASH: a collection of sermons of Rabbi Jonathan Eibeshutz (see BIOGRAPHIES).

YAHVEH. See YHVH.

YALKUT SHIMONI. The most comprehensive of Midrashic collections; attributed to Rabbi Simeon ha-Darshan of Frankfurt (thirteenth century).

YEBAMOTH (YEVAMOT). Hebrew: "brother's wife, sister-in-law." The first tractate in NASHIM, the third order of the Talmud; it deals with childless widows whom their brothers-in-law must marry, according to Deuteronomy 25:5, or "release" through a ceremony (*halitsah*) described in Deuteronomy 25:7–10. The Sephardim upheld obligatory marriage; the Ashkenazim preferred and adopted *halitsah*.

YESHIVA. Hebrew: "seat." (1) A rabbinical college or seminary. (2) In the United States, a Hebrew day school in which both religious and secular subjects are studied. The *yeshiva* was an outgrowth of the *Beth Midrash*, the "house of study" in every Jewish community.

One of the earliest *yeshivot* was established in Palestine, at Javneh, by Rabbi Johanan ben Zakkai (see BIOGRAPHIES). After the destruction of Jerusalem, the Sanhedrin moved to Javneh; the academy attracted scholars and became the seat of Jewish scholarship. During the Talmudic period, *yeshivot*, established elsewhere in Palestine and Babylonia, were the creative source of Jewish theology, law and moral guidance.

From the tenth century on, *yeshivot* were formed wherever Jews migrated: North Africa, Italy, Spain, France, Germany, England, Holland—but especially in Ashkenazic centers in Eastern Europe. The *yeshiva* was for centuries not simply a religious school, but the college for general education.

YESHIVA BOCHER. Hebrew: *bahur:* "young man"; hence, a young man who is a student at a *yeshiva* (see above); hence a scholarly, unworldly type, whether attending a *yeshiva* or not.

YETSER (YEZER) HA-RA. Hebrew: "the Evil Impulse (or Inclination)." Often used in Talmudic literature to signify sexual desires, as well as other "sinful" propensities.

YETSER (YEZER) HA-TOV. Hebrew: "the Good Impulse (or Inclination)."

YHVH. The "Tetragrammaton," the four letters representing the most sacred name of the God of Israel, pronounced only by the High Priest of antiquity, on Yom Kippur, when he entered "the sanctuary of the Holy of Holies" to seek forgiveness for himself and his people.

But no one really knows how YHVH was pronounced; probably as "Yahveh." ("Jehovah" is the erroneous transliteration of a German papal scribe in 1516). In prayer, the name of God is pronounced *Adonai*. In other circumstances, a variety of names have evolved, according to the aspect of the Lord intended: His power, His compassion, His wrath, etc. Maimonides lists these names-by-attribute as seven: YHVH, *El, Eloha, Elohim, Elohai, Shaddai,* YHVH *Tsevaot.* But other names are used by Jews: *Boreh Olam* (Creator of the World), *El Elion* (Most High One), En Sof (Infinite One), etc.

YIDDISH. From the German: *"jüdisch:"* "Jewish." The vernacular of East European Jews; sixteenth-century Middle High German at its base, with 15–20% Hebrew words and names, and an equal or greater amount of loan-words from Slavic tongues. Today, Yiddish contains many adapted English words and phrases. (For the distinctive characteristics of this delight-laden tongue, see my *"Joys of Yiddish,"* McGraw-Hill, 1968; Pocket Book edition, 1970.)

YIKHES. Yiddish, from the Hebrew *yihus:* "pedigree . . . ancestry." Family prestige, which must be retained and deserved through virtue, learning, good deeds, charity.

YISROEL (YISRAEL). Hebrew: "Israel." (1) The land of Israel (*Erets Yisroel*). (2) The people of Israel. (3) The name assumed by Jacob after he fought the Angel of the Lord (Genesis 32:29). (4) The collective name for the twelve tribes who left Egypt and settled in Canaan. (5) The name of the Northern Kingdom of Israel (933–722 prior to the Christian Era), formed when ten tribes seceded, after the death of King Solomon. (6) The name of the State of Israel (*Medinat Yisroel*). In Jewish literature, *Yisroel* is used interchangeably with "Jew" and "Hebrew."

YIZKOR. Hebrew: "May [God] remember." Memorial service for the dead, held in a synagogue or temple. *Yizkor* is the shortened name for the memorial service, *Ha-Zkarat Neshamot,* "Remembrance of Souls," recited on the eighth day of Pesach, the second day of *Shevuoth,* the eighth day of Succoth, and on Yom Kippur. Deceased ancestors and parents, "the crown of our head and glory," are extolled. Private prayers are then made in memory of close relatives; those reciting *Yizkor* pledge themselves to perform "acts of charity and goodness." The service continues with a congregational prayer, *El Maleh Rahamim*, which petitions God to grant peace and eternal life to the departed souls. Part of the *Yizkor* service is a memorial to martyrs of all generations.

YOMA. Aramaic: "the day"; Hebrew: "*Yom ha-Kippurim*:" "the Day of Atonement." The fifth tractate of Mo'ed, the second order of the Mishnah, which describes the Yom Kippur services, fast, atonement and repentance.

YOM KIPPUR. Hebrew: "Day of Atonement." (Some scholars trace *kippur* to the Babylonian word for "purge," "wipe off.") The last of the annual Ten Days of Penitence; one of the two high Holy Days of the Jewish calendar; the day which has the strongest hold on Jewish conscience. Rosh Hashanah marks the first of the Days of Penitence (*Yamim Noraim*), when, say the Orthodox, all men stand before God for judgment; but His decision is made on the last of the Ten Days: Yom Kippur. The synagogue service begins just before nightfall the evening before Yom Kippur. The cantor stands before the Ark; on each side stands an honored member of the congregation, carrying a large Scroll of the Torah. The three men act as spokesmen for the congregation and recite:

With the . . . permission of the Lord, blessed be He, and this sacred congregation, we declare it lawful to pray with those who have transgressed.

This is thrice repeated; then the cantor intones Kol Nidre (*q.v.*). Prayers continue from the next morning until after sunset. Since purity of conscience is the theme of the day, the curtain of the Ark is white; the rabbi and cantor wear white robes; many men in the congregation wear white skull-caps (*yarmlkes*) and white robes.

Confession, repeated several times during the day, involves a cataloguing of fifty-six categories of sin. Tradition-observing Jews repeat: "For the sin we have committed before Thee by (stating one of the fifty-six varieties), O God of forgiveness, forgive us, pardon us, grant us remission," and beat their breasts. The confession is recited as a collective "we," not an individual "I." Jews "share" each other's transgressions—plus general responsibility for the misdeeds of mankind. Yom Kippur ends with the blowing of the *shophar*.

YOREH DEAH. See Joseph Caro, in BIOGRAPHIES.

YORTSAYT (JOHRTZEIT). Yiddish (from German): "anniversary." The observances to commemorate the death of someone in the family: with an annual prayer, the lighting of a ceremonial candle, etc. Orthodox Jews fast all day.

Yortsayt is the one Jewish religious ceremony for which no Hebrew name is exactly equivalent.

ZABIM (ZAVIM). Hebrew: "those who suffer from bodily discharges [flux]." The ninth tractate of TOHOROTH, the sixth order of the Mishnah.

ZADDIK. See TSADIK.

ZEBAHIM. Hebrew: "animal sacrifices . . . animal offerings." The first tractate in KODASHIM, the fifth order of the Talmud; in the Tosephta (see above) it is called *Korbanoth* ("sacrifices").

ZERAIM. Hebrew: "seeds." The first order of the Talmud, pertaining to laws of prayer and minute details of laws governing agriculture.

ZIONIDES: "Songs of Zion." See Judah ha-Levi, in BIOGRAPHIES.

ZIZITH (Yiddish: Tsitsis). Hebrew: "fringes." The fringes at the corners of the prayer shawl (*tallith*)—or the *tallit katan*—the short garment worn by Orthodox males under their shirt or vest. See TALLITH, above.

ZOHAR. From the Hebrew: *Sefer ha-Zohar:* "Book of Splendor." The most important book of the cabalistic movement; probably written in the thirteenth century; believed to have been written/assembled by the Spanish rabbi Moses (Moshe) de Leon—who deliberately attributed the work to a second-century rabbi, Simeon ben Yohai.

The *Zohar*, nominally a commentary on the Torah, is a fantastic compendium of superstitions, mysticism, folklore, and numerology to reveal hidden meanings in the Bible: abstruse codes, dreams, symbols; cryptic excursions into demonology (and angelology); ways of exorcising devils; the transmigration of souls. (It should be noted that such preoccupations were common to the Christian world of that time, as well.) The *Zohar* is especially beholden to a "science of numbers" (see GEMATRIA, above): a numerical value is assigned each Hebrew letter and a text from the Bible is arranged vertically, backwards, diagonally, upside down, in a triangle, a palindrome, an acrostic, etc.

The *Zohar* also contains wonderful folk stories, ethical dicta, and moving prayers. The book exerted an enormous influence on large sectors of Jewry, particularly the hasidim (*q.v.*). Rabbis often warned Jews not to court mental dangers by too-deep immersion in the *Zohar*. Among Yemenite Jews, the Zohar is what the Talmud is to Ashkenazic Jews.

V. Selected Bibliography

My son, make your books your companions. Let your shelves be your treasure grounds and gardens. When you are weary, change from garden to garden. Your desire will renew itself, and your soul will be filled with delight.

JUDAH IBN TIBBON (c. 1120–1190)

1. Books and Articles Published in English

In this Bibliography, the following abbreviations are used:

H.E.W.   *Hebrew Ethical Wills*, 2 vols., Jewish Publication Society, 1948

J.P.S.A.   Jewish Publication Society of America.

P.B.H.L.   *Post-Biblical Hebrew Literature*, B. Halper, ed., 2 vols., Jewish Publication Society of America, Philadephia, 1921

ABRAVANEL, ISAAC. "The Advantages of a Republic Over a Monarchy," in *P.B.H.L.*

ADLER, MORRIS. *The World of the Talmud*, Schocken Books, New York, 1963

HA-AM, AHAD (Asher Ginzburg). *Essays, Letters, Memoirs*, tr. L. Simon, Oxford, East and West Library, London, 1946
——. *Selected Essays*, tr. and ed. Leon Simon, J.P.S.A., 1962

ALBO, JOSEPH. *Sefer ha-Ikkarim* (1428), tr. I. Husik, J.P.S.A., 1929
——. "*The Various Ranks of Prophecy*," in P.B.H.L.

AL-HARIZI, JUDAH BEN SOLOMON, "Seven Young Men Discuss the Merits of the Various Virtues," in *P.B.H.L.*

The Apocrypha and Pseudepigrapha of the Old Testament in English, ed. R. H. Charles, Oxford University Press, London, 1968

JUDAH BEN ASHER. "Ethical and Moral Admonitions," in *P.B.H.L.*
——. "The Testament of Judah Asheri," in *H.E.W.*

BAAL SHEM, ISRAEL. "In Defiance of Despondence," in *H.E.W.*

BAR HIYYA, ABRAHAM, HA-NASI. *The Meditation of the Sad Soul*, tr. Geoffrey Wigoder, Schocken Books, New York, 1969

BARON, SALO. *A Social and Religious History of the Jews*, vol. II, Columbia University Press, New York, 1937, pp. 215–321

JEDAIA BEN-BEDERSI. "The Nothingness of Man and His Pursuits," *P.B.H.L.*

BENJAMIN OF TUDELA. "Description of Jerusalem and Its Surroundings," in *P.B.H.L.*

BEN SIRACH, JESUS. "In Praise of the High Priest Simeon, the Son of Johanan," in *P.B.H.L.*

——. "Wisdom Is a Source of Happiness," in *P.B.H.L.*

BICKERMAN, ELIAS. *From Ezra to the Last of the Maccabees: Foundations of Post-Biblical Judaism*, paperback, Schocken Books, New York, 1968

BIRNBAUM, PHILIP. *Jewish Concepts*, Hebrew Publishing Co., New York, 1964

——, editor. *A Treasury of Judaism*, Hebrew Publishing Co., New York, 1962

BLAU, JOSEPH L. *The Story of Jewish Philosophy*, Random House, New York, 1962

Book of Delight, tr. Israel Abrahams, J.P.S.A., 1912.

A Book of Jewish Thoughts, arr. by Joseph Herman Hertz, Bloch Publishing, New York, 1954

BORCHSENIUS, PAUL. *The History of the Jews* (5 vols.), Simon and Schuster, New York, 1965

BUBER, MARTIN. *The Legend of the Baal-Shem*, tr. by Maurice Friedman, paperback, Schocken Books, New York, 1969

——. *Tales of the Hasidim: Early Masters*, paperback, Schocken Books, New York, 1961

Cambridge History of the Bible (vol. I): *From the Beginning to Jerome*, eds. P. R. Ackroyd and C. F. Evans, Cambridge University Press, London and New York, 1970

CHAJES, Z. H. *The Student's Guide Through the Talmud*, tr. and ed. Jacob Shachter, Phillip Feldheim, Inc., New York, 1960

COHEN, REVEREND A. *Jewish Proverbs*, John Murray, London, 1911

——. *Everyman's Talmud*, Dutton, New York, 1949

COHEN, I. *Parallel Proverbs*, Dvir, Tel Aviv, 1954

"Deuteronomy Rabbah (MIDRASH)." *Midrash Rabbah* (vol. VII), tr. J. Rabbinowitz, Soncino Press, London, 1961

Dictionary of the Bible, ed. James Hastings, Scribner's, New York, 1963

Ecclesiastes. The Holy Scriptures, according to the Masoretic text, J.P.S.A., 1917, 1945, 1955

"Ecclesiastes Rabbah (MIDRASH)." *Midrash Rabbah* (vol. VIII), tr. by A. Cohen, Soncino Press, London, 1961

ELEAZAR OF MAYENCE. "The Ideals of an Average Jew," in *H.E.W.*

ELIJAH GAON (of Vilna). "Letter of Elijah (Gaon) of Wilna," in *H.E.W.*

The Encyclopedia of the Jewish Religion, eds. R. J. Zwi Werblosky and Geoffrey Wigoder, Holt, Rinehart, Winston, New York, 1966

Ethics of the Fathers, ed. and tr. Joseph Herman Hertz, in *The Daily Prayer Book*, Bloch Publishing Company, 1957

The Ethics of the Talmud: Sayings of the Fathers: Pirke Aboth, ed. and tr. R. Travers Herford, paperback, Schocken Books, New York, 1962

"Exodus Rabbah (MIDRASH)." *Midrash Rabbah* (vol. III), tr. S. M. Lehrman, Soncino Press, London, 1961

The Fathers According to Rabbi Nathan, tr. Judah Goldin, Yale University Press, New Haven, Connecticut, 1955

FINKELSTEIN, LOUIS. *New Light from the Prophets*, Vallentine, Mitchell, London, 1969

FLEG, EDMOND. *The Jewish Anthology*, tr. Maurice Samuel, Harcourt, Brace, New York, 1925

FRENKEL, RABBI ISSER. *Men of Distinction* (vol. I), Sinai Publishing, Tel Aviv, Israel, 1967

GANZFRIED, RABBI SOLOMON. *Code of Jewish Law*, tr. Hyman E. Goldin, Hebrew Publishing Company, New York, 1961

GASTER, THEODOR H. *Myth, Legend and Custom in the Old Testament*, Harper and Row, New York, 1969

"Genesis Rabbah (MIDRASH)." *Midrash Rabbah*, 2 vols., tr. H. Freedman, Soncino Press, London, 1961

GERONDI, JONAH. *The Gates of Redemption*, tr. Shraga Silverstein, Phillip Feldheim, New York, 1967

GINZBERG, LOUIS. *Legends of the Bible*, J.P.S.A., 1909, 1968

——. *On Jewish Law and Lore*, paperback, Atheneum, New York, 1970

——. *Students, Scholars and Saints*, J.P.S.A., 1945

Give Us Life: Mesholim and Masterwords of the Chofetz Chaim, coll. and ed. Mendel Weinbach, Feldheim Publishers, Jerusalem, New York, 1969

GLATZER, NAHUM N. *Hillel the Elder: the Emergence of Classical Judaism*, Schocken paperback, New York, 1970

GLUSTROM, SIMON. *The Language of Judaism*, Jonathan David, New York, 1966

GOODMAN, PHILIP, editor. *Essays on Jewish Booklore*, KTAV, New York, 1971

GRAETZ, HEINRICH. *History of the Jews* (vol. VI), J.P.S.A., 1949

GRAYZEL, SOLOMON. *A History of the Jews*, J.P.S.A., 1968

Great Ages and Ideas of the Jewish People, ed. Leo Schwarz, Random House, New York, 1956

The Great Jewish Books and Their Influence on History (3 vols.), eds. Samuel Caplan and Harold U. Ribalow, Horizon Press, New York, 1952

HA-LEVI, JUDAH. *The Kuzari*, tr. Hartwig Hirschfeld, paperback, Schocken Books, New York, 1964; also *Book of Kuzari*, tr. Hartwig Hirschfeld, Pardes Publishing House, Inc., New York, 1946

——. *Selected Poems*, tr. Nina Salaman, J.P.S.A., 1924

Hammer on the Rock: A Midrash Reader, ed. Nahum N. Glatzer, tr. Jacob Sloan, Schocken Books, New York, 1948

The Hasidic Anthology: Tales and Teachings of the Hasidim, tr. and compiler, Louis I. Newman, paperback, Schocken Books, New York, 1963

Hebrew Ethical Wills (vols. I and II), ed. Israel Abrahams, J.P.S.A., 1926, third impression, 1948

Hebrew Poems from Spain, tr. David Goldstein, Schocken Books, New York, 1966

Hebrew Proverbs and Their Origin, compiled by Lazar Blankstein, ed. Samuel Ashkenazi, Riryath-Sepher Ltd., Jerusalem, 1964 (several languages)

HERFORD, R. TRAVERS. *Talmud and Apocrypha*, KTAV, New York, 1970

HESCHEL, ABRAHAM J. *The Earth Is the Lord's*, Abelard-Schuman, New York, 1964

HIRSCH, SAMSON RAPHAEL. *The Nineteen Letters of Ben Uziel*, tr. B. Drachman, Funk & Wagnalls, New York, 1899

HORODEZKY, S. A. *Leaders of Hasidism*, Hasefer Agency for Literature, London, 1928

HURWITZ, SIMON. *The Responsa of Solomon Luria* (*Maharshal*), Bloch Publishers, New York, 1938

HUSIK, ISAAC. *A History of Mediaeval Jewish Philosophy*, Macmillan, New York, 1916

IBN AL-FAYYUMI, NATHANAEL. *The Bustan Al-Ukul*, ed. and tr. David Levine, Columbia University Press (reprint, AMS Press, Inc., New York, 1966)

IBN EZRA, ABRAHAM BEN MEIR. "Plaintive Song," in *P.B.H.L.*

IBN EZRA, MOSES BEN JACOB. "Dirge on the Death of His Brother," in *P.B.H.L.*; "Poem Addressed to One of His Noblest Friends," p. 101.

IBN GABIROL, SOLOMON. *Choice of Pearls* (*Mibhar ha-Peninim*), tr. B. H. Ascher, London, 1895

——. *Improvement of the Moral Qualities*, tr. S. S. Wise, Columbia University Press, New York 1902; reprinted, AMS Press, New York, 1966.

——. *The Kingly Crown*, tr. Bernard Lewis, Vallentine, Mitchell, London, 1961

——. *Selected Religious Poems of Solomon Ibn Gabirol*, tr. Israel Zangwill, ed. Israel Davidson, J.P.S.A., 1923

IBN PAQUDA, BAHYA. *Duties of the Heart* (2 vols.), tr. Moses Hyamson, Phillip Feldheim, Inc., Jerusalem and New York, 1970

——. "Pious Reflections and Admonitions to the Soul," in *P.B.H.L.*

IBN TIBBON, JUDAH. "A Father's Admonition," in *H.E.W.*

——. "Why the Jewish Religion Does Not Especially Encourage Asceticism," in *P.B.H.L.*

IBN TIBBON, SAMUEL BEN JUDAH. "On the Limitations of Man's Intellect," in *P.B.H.L.*

IBN ZABARA, JOSEPH BEN MEIR. *The Book of Delight*, tr. Moses Hadas, Columbia University Press, New York, 1932, paperback, 1962

——. "Jacob the Broker and the Necklace," in *P.B.H.L.*

IMMANUEL OF ROME. "The Poet Visits Paradise," in *P.B.H.L.*

——. *Tophet and Eden*, tr. H. Gollancz, University of London Press, Ltd., London, 1921

The Jewish Encyclopedia: A Descriptive Record of the History, Religion, Literature, and Customs of the Jewish People from the Earliest Times (12 vols.), ed. Isidore Singer, Funk & Wagnalls, 1901–1951, KTAV Publishing House reprint (no date)

The Jewish Library (vol. III), "Woman," ed. Leo Jung, Soncino Press, London and New York, 1970

A Jewish Reader: In Time and Eternity, ed. Nahum N. Glatzer, paperback, Schocken Books, New York, 1961

The Jews: Their History, Culture and Religion (2 vols.), ed. Louis Finkelstein, Harper, New York, 1960

Josephus: The Jewish War, tr. G. A. Williamson, Penguin Books, London, revised edition, 1970

KLAPHOLTZ, YISROEL. *Tales of the Baal Shem Tov*, Feldheim, Jerusalem-New York, 1970

KOGOS, FRED. *1001 Yiddish Proverbs*

Language of Faith: A Selection from the Most Expressive Jewish Prayers (original text and new English verse), Schocken Books, New York, 1947, 1967

LIBER, MAURICE. *Rashi*, tr. Adele Szold, Hermon Press, New York, 1970, (first edition: J.P.S.A., 1906)

LIPSCHITZ, MAX A. *The Faith of a Hassid;* Jonathan David, New York, 1967

LUZZATTO, MOSES HAYYIM. *Mesillat Yesharim:* "The Path of the Upright," tr. Mordecai M. Kaplan, J.P.S.A., 1966

MAIMON, SOLOMON. *Solomon Maimon: An Autobiography*, tr. J. C. Murray, London, 1888 (Schocken Books, New York, 1947, ed. M. Hadas)

Maimonides: His Wisdom for Our Time, ed. and tr. Gilbert Rosenthal, Funk & Wagnalls, 1969

MAIMONIDES, MOSES. *The Eight Chapters of Maimonides on Ethics*, tr. J. I. Gorfinkle, Columbia University Press, New York, 1912

—— *Guide for the Perplexed*, tr. M. Friedlander, George Routledge & Sons, London, 1904 (2nd Edition)

———— *Iggeret Teman* ("Epistle to Yemen") ed. A. S. Halkin, tr. B. Cohen, New York, 1952

MARCUS, JACOB R. *The Jew in the Medieval World: A Source Book: 315–1791*, Temple Book, Atheneum, New York, 1969

MCKANE, WILLIAM. *Proverbs: A New Approach*, SCM Press, London, 1970

Memoirs of My People: Jewish Self-Portraits from the 11th to the 20th Centuries, ed. Leo W. Schwarz, paperback, Schocken Books, New York, 1963

Midrash Rabbah (vol. X), tr. and ed., Harry Freedman and Maurice Simon, Soncino Press, London, 1961

The Minor Tractates of the Talmud (2 vols.), tr. A. Cohen, Soncino Press, London, 1965

MINTZ, JEROME. *Legends of the Hasidim*, University of Chicago, 1968

The Mishnah, tr. Herbert Danby, Oxford University Press, London, 1933

The Mishnah, tr. and selected by Eugene J. Lipman, Norton, New York, 1970

MOORE, GEORGE FOOTE. *Judaism in the First Centuries of the Christian Era: The Age of the Tannaim* (vol. III), Cambridge, Mass., 1927–1930

NASH, WALTER. *Our Experience of Language*, B. T. Batsford, London, 1971

NEWMAN, LOUIS I. *Maggidim and Hasidim: Their Wisdom*, Bloch Publishers, New York, 1962

Orchot Zadikkim ("The Ways of the Righteous"), ed. and tr. Seymour Cohen, Phillip Feldheim, Inc., Jerusalem and New York, 1969

Peake's Commentary on the Bible, ed. Matthew Black and H. H. Rowley, Nelson, London, 1962, reprinted 1967

The Pentateuch and Haftorahs (with Hebrew Text, English Translation and Commentary), ed. J. H. Hertz, Soncino Press, London, second edition, 1960

The Pharisees, ed. R. Travers Herford, Macmillan, New York, 1924

Pirke d' Rabbi Eliezer, tr. Gerald Friedlander, Hermon Press, New York, 1916

Post-Biblical Hebrew Literature: An Anthology, tr. and selected by B. Halper, J.P.S.A., 1921

PRINZ, JOACHIM. *Popes from the Ghetto: A View of Medieval Christendom*, first paperback edition, Schocken Books, 1968

PRITCHARD, JAMES B., editor. *The Ancient Near East*, Princeton University Press, 1969

A Rabbinic Anthology, eds. C. G. Montefiore and H. Loewe, J.P.S.A., 1960

RABINOWICZ, HARRY M. *The World of Hasidism*, Vallentine, Mitchell, London, 1970

RABINOWITSCH, DR. WOLF ZEEV. *Lithuanian Chasidism*, Vallentine, Mitchell, London, 1970

RAPAPORT, SAMUEL. *Tales and Maxims from the Midrash*, KTAV, New York, 1968

——. *A Treasury of the Midrash*, KTAV, New York, 1968

RASHI. *Commentaries on the Pentateuch*, tr. and selected by Chaim Pearl, Norton, New York, 1970

The Rest Is Commentary, ed. Nahum N. Glatzer, Beacon Press, Boston, 1961

ROSTEN, LEO. *The Joys of Yiddish*, McGraw-Hill, New York, 1968, paperback Pocket Books, 1970

ROTH, CECIL. *A History of the Jews: From Earliest Times through the Six Day War*, Schocken Books, New York, revised edition, 1970

—— *The Jewish Contribution to Civilization*, Macmillan, London, 1938

—— *Personalities and Events in Jewish History*, J.P.S.A., 1953

Saadia Gaon: The Book of Beliefs and Opinions, tr. Samuel Rosenblatt, Yale University Press, New Haven, 1948

SAMUEL, MAURICE. *In Praise of Yiddish*, Cowles, New York, 1971

Sayings of the Jewish Fathers, Comprising Pirque Aboth in Hebrew and English, ed. Charles Taylor, KTAV, New York, 1969

SCHECHTER, SOLOMON. *Studies in Judaism*, Meridian Books, Cleveland and New York, 1958

"Shulhan Aruk of Rabbi Karo," in *Anthology of Medieval Hebrew Literature*, ed. Louis Feinberg, The Burning Bush Press, New York, 1961

The Standard Hebrew Prayer Book (The Siddur), the Rabbinical Assembly of America, and the United Synagogue of America, New York, 1960

The Standard Jewish Encyclopedia, ed. Cecil Roth, Doubleday, Garden City, New York, 1966, new revised edition, Cecil Roth and Geoffrey Wigoder, Doubleday, 1970

STRACK, HERMANN L. *Introduction to the Talmud and Midrash*, J.P.S.A., Philadelphia, 1931 (paperback, Temple Book, Atheneum, New York, 1969)

The Sybilline Oracles, tr. in blank verse by Milton Tovey, Hunt and Eaton, New York, 1890

Talmud: The Babylonian Talmud (12 vols.), ed. I. Epstein, Soncino Press, London, 1936

Talmud: Seven Minor Treatises (Sefer Torah, Mezuza, Tefillin, Zizith, Abadim, Kutim, Gerim, and Soferim II), ed. M. Higger, Bloch, New York, 1930

TAUBENHAUS, G. *Echoes of Wisdom*, Haedrich & Sons, Brooklyn, 1900

Three Jewish Philosophers: Philo, ed. Hans Lewy; Saadia Gaon, "Book of Doctrines and Beliefs," ed. Alexander Altman; Judah ha-Levi, "Kuzari," ed. Isaak Heineman, J.P.S.A. (reprint, Atheneum, New York, 1969)

The Torah: A New Translation of the Holy Scriptures According to the Masoretic Text, J.P.S.A., 1962

Tosefta, ed. M. S. Zuckermandel, Bamberger & Wahrmann, Jerusalem, 1937

Tractate Avoth: Ethics of the Fathers, tr. Philip Blackman, Judaica Press, New York, 1964

TRATTNER, ERNEST R. *Understanding the Talmud,* Nelson, New York, 1955

A Treasury of Jewish Quotations, ed. Joseph L. Baron

Universal Jewish Encyclopedia, ed. Isaac Landman, The Universal Jewish Encyclopedia, Inc., New York, 1943

VERMES, G. *The Dead Sea Scrolls in English,* Penguin Books, Harmondsworth, England, 1968

The Wisdom of Israel, ed. Lewis Browne, Random House, New York, 1945

Wit and Wisdom of the Talmud, ed. Madison C. Peters, Baker and Taylor, New York, 1900

The World of Translation: Papers Delivered at the Conference on Literary Translation under the Auspices of P.E.N., American Center (no publisher cited), 1971

Yiddish Proverbs, ed. Hanan J. Ayalti

ZBOROWSKI, M., and E. HERZOG. *Life Is With People: The Culture of the Shtetl,* paperback, Schocken, New York, 1962

The Zohar, tr. Harry Sperling and Maurice Simon, Soncino Press, London, 1949

Zohar: The Book of Splendor, ed. Gershon G. Scholem, paperback, Schocken, New York, 1963

2. Books Published in Yiddish Only

BERNSTEIN, IGNAZ. *Jüdische Sprichwörter und Redensarten* ("Jewish Proverbs and Sayings"), printed by Josef Fischer, Warsaw, 1908, reprinted by Georg Olms, Hildesheim, Germany, 1969

JEUSZOHN, B. *Fun Untser Alten Oytser* ("From our old treasure"), Moshe Justman, (8 vols.) Warsaw, 1932–1938

LAZEROV, JUDAH LOEB. *Encyclopedia of Jewish Wit,* Pardes, New York, 1928

MEKLER, DAVID LOUIS. *Fun Rebins Hawf* ("From the Rabbi's Store of Knowledge"), Jewish Book Publishing Co., New York, 1931

Or Olam ("Light of the World"), A. Kahana, Warsaw, 1928

Peyer Yisroel ("Glory of Israel"), S. Freund, Prezemysl, 1925

RAWNITZKI. JOSHUA CHAIM. *Yidishe Vitsn* ("Jewish Wit"), 2
vols., Sklarsky, New York, 1950

Sipurey Besht ("Collection of the Besht"; author unknown),
A. J. Kleiman, Piotrkov, 1911

STUTCHKOFF, NAHUM. *Der Oytser fun der Yidisher Shprakh*
("The Treasury-Thesaurus of the Yiddish Language"),
Yiddish Scientific Institute-YIVO, New York, 1950

WISSEON, M. A. *Khokhma un Harifut* ("Wisdom and Witticisms"), published by the author, Vienna, 1927

3. Books Published in Hebrew Only

For books in Hebrew only: Wherever possible, I cite the
place and date of publication, and the name of the publisher or
"printer"; the *edition* named is the one used by Dr. Solomon
D. Goldfarb in his research assistance; since many of the books
listed are quite old (collections of essays, sermons, tales, interpretations of the law, legends), they have often been reprinted.
A short description of the more important Hebrew books referred to in the preceding pages will be found in the GLOSSARY.

NOTE: The publishing centers for Hebrew and Yiddish books
(until the twentieth century) were located in Eastern Europe.
Books about the life or teachings of a famous hasid or *tsadik*
appeared in the locality in which they were active: Vilna,
Koretz, Warsaw, Prezemysl, etc. Experts on hasidic literature
(Buber, Kahana, Horodetzky) edited and compiled much of
the hasidic material.

AHAD HA-AM. *Al-Parashat Derakhim* ("At the Crossroads"),
Jüdischer Verlag, Berlin, 1920

AL-HARIZI, JUDAH. *Tahkemoni* (possibly "The Apothecary" or
"The Wise One"), ed. Max Emmanuel Stern, printed by
Edlen von Schmidt und Holzwarth, Vienna, 1854

ARAMA, ISAAC (ISAAC BEN MOSES). *Akedat Yitshak* ("The
Binding of Isaac"): Sermons on the weekly sections of the
Torah and of the five Megilloth; V. Kittseer, Pressburg,
1849

——. *Mishalim* ("Proverbs"), printed by L. Schnauss, Leipzig,
1859

ATAR, HAYIM IBN. *Or Ha-Hayim* ("The Light of Life"), printed
by Gershon Madpis, Zolkiew, 1858

BAAL SHEM, ISRAEL. *Midrash Ribash Tov* ("Midrash of the
Good Rabbi Israel Ben Eliezer"), printed by Marton
Abraham, Kecskemet, 1927

BAHYA BEN ASHER (BACHYA). *Kad Hakemah* ("Jug of Flour"),
in *Kitvei Rabenu Bahya* ("Collected Writings of Rabbenu
Bahya"), ed. Charles B. Chavel, Mosad Harab Kook,
Jerusalem, 1969

BERECHIAH BEN NATRONAI, HA-NAKDAN. *Fuchsfabeln* (*Mishle
Shualim:* "Fox Fables"), Erich Reiss Verlag, Berlin, 1921

BIALIK, CHAIM, and J. RAVNITZKY. *Sefer Ha-Agadah* ("Book of the Narrations"), Dvir Co. Ltd., Tel Aviv, 1936

COHEN, AARON (AARON BEN ZEBI HIRSCH HA-KOHEN OF OPATOW). *Keter Shem Tov Ha-Shalem* ("The Complete Crown of the Good Name"), Lvov, 1864

CORDOVERO, (MOSES BEN YAKOV) MOSES. *Pardes Rimonim* ("Orchard of Pomegranates"), Amsterdam, 1708; Munkacz, 1905–1906, Harav Mordecai Ati, Jerusalem, 1961–1962

DARKHE TSEDEK ("Paths of Justice"), Zechariah Mendel of Yeroslav; Honigson's, London, 1958

DAVIDSON, ISRAEL. *Otsar ha-Mishalim ve-ha Pitgamin* ("Thesaurus of Proverbs and Parables" from medieval Jewish Literature), Mosad Harav Kook, Jerusalem, 1956–1957

DELMEDIGO, ELIJAH. *Behinat ha-Dat* ("Examination of Religion"), printed by Anton Edlen von Schmid, Vienna, 1833

EIBESCHUTZ, JONATHAN. *Yaarot Dvash* ("Honeycombs with Honey"): A Collection of Hebrew Sermons, Lemberg 1858 edition, printed by M. F. Poremba

ELIEZER BEN HYRCANOS. *Pirke de Rabbi Eliezer* ("Ethics of Rabbi Eliezer"), Vilna, 1838 (photocopy of Warsaw 1852 edition, O.M. Pblg., New York, 1946)

EPHRAIM SOLOMON BEN AARON OF LENCZYCZA (LUNTSHITZ). *Klee Yakar* ("Beloved Vessel"): Commentaries on the Pentateuch, Amsterdam, 1709, 1767, Zolkiew, 1799

FALAQUERA, SHEM-TOB BEN JOSEPH. *Reshit Hakhmah* ("The Beginning of Wisdom"), Fafelever, Berlin, 1902

———. *Sefer Ha-Mevakesh* ("Book of the Seeker"), Traklin, Warsaw, 1924

———. *Sefer Ha-Nefesh* ("Book of the Soul"), printed by Alexander Gins, Warsaw, 1864

HA-LAHMI, DAVID. *Hochmei Yisrael* ("The Wise Men of Israel"), A. Zioni, Tel Aviv, 1957

HALEVI, AARON (authorship disputed). *Sefer ha-Hinukh* ("Book of Education"), Eshkol, Jerusalem, 1958

HASDAI, ABRAHAM BEN SAMUEL, HA-LEVI. *Ben ha-Melekh ve-ha-Nazir* ("The Son of the King and the Hermit"), Mosad Harav Kook, Zhitomir, 1850, Tel Aviv, 1950

HAYYIM BEN ISAAC, OF VOLOZHIN. *Sheelot u-Teshuvot Hut ha-Meshulah* ("Questions and Answers"): "The Triple Braided Reply", J. C. Metz, Vilna, 1882

HORODETZKY, SAMUEL A. *Ha-Hasidut ve-ha-Hasidim* ("Hasidism and the Hasids"), 4 vols., Dvir, Berlin, 1922–1928

IBN EZRA, MOSES. *Shirat Israel* ("The Poetry of Israel"), in Arabic and Hebrew, tr. Al Muhadonah wal Mudhakarah, Styble, Leipzig, 1924

IBN GABIROL, SOLOMON BEN JUDAH. *Keter Malkhut* ("Crown of Kingship"), Mosad Harav Kook, Jerusalem, 1950

JUDAH BEN SAMUEL HE-HASID. *Sefer Hasidim* ("Book of the

Pious"), ed. J. Wistinetzki, 2nd edition, Frankfurt a/M, M.A. Wahrmann, 1924

MAIMONIDES, MOSES. *Teshuvot ha-Rambam* ("*Responsa* of Rambam"), ed. Alfred Freimann, Mekirze Niramim, Jerusalem, 1934

Mekhilta de Rabbi Simeon ben Yohai, ed. David Hoffman, Jüdisch-Literarische Gesellschaft, Frankfurt a/M, 1905

Midrash Agadah, ed. Solomon Buber, Vienna, 1894, Madah, New York, 1959–1960

Midrash: Agadat Bereshit, ed. Solomon Buber, Vilna, 1902 (2nd edition, 1925, Menorah, New York, 1959)

Midrash Rabah, ed. Romm, Vilna, 1878

Midrash Tanaim (in Hebrew and German), ed. David Hoffman, Nord-Ost, Berlin, 1913

Midrash Tehilim ("*Shoher Tov*": "Seeker of the Good"), ed. Solomon Buber, photo-offset edition, Vilna, 1891

Midrash Yalkut Shimoni ("Collection of Simeon"—homilies on the Midrash), collected by Simon ha-Darshan (also known as Simeon Kara, Berrl Lorje, and Leib Matfe), Zolkiew, 1858

Midrash Zuta ("Small Midrash"), ed. Solomon Buber, printed by H. Itzkowski, Berlin, 1894, photo-offset: Vilna, 1925, Tel Aviv, 1963–1964

Mishle Yisrael ("Proverbs of Israel"), ed. Meyer Waxman, printed in Jerusalem, 1933

NACHMAN OF BRATSLAV. *Torat Rabi Nahman* ("The teachings of Rabbi Nachman"), ed. S. Horodetzki, Deviv, Berlin, 1923

Otsar Midrashim (a "treasury" of two hundred *midrashim*, annotated), ed. J. D. Eisenstein, The Editor, New York, 1915

Otsar Midrashim ("Treasury of *Midrashim*"), ed. Adolf Jellinek, Vienna, 1883

Pesikta Rabati (Midrashic collection of discourses for the festivals and the special Sabbaths), edited in 1880 by Meir Freidman (no publisher cited; probably the press of Y. Kaiser)

Pesikta Zutarta: Lekah Tov ("Good Teaching"), Midrashic commentary on the Torah and the *Hamesh Megillot*, by Rabbi Tobias ben Eliezer, ha-Gadol, Prague, 1725

REGGIO, ISAAC SAMUEL. *Torah ve-ha-Filosofia* ("Torah and Philosophy"), printed by Anton Edlen von Schmid, Vienna, 1828

SCHARFSTEIN, ZVI. *Otsar Ha-Ravonot ve-ha-Piteamim* ("Lexicon of Ideas and Epigrams"): quotations from classical and modern Hebrew literature, 3 vols., Jabneh, Tel Aviv, 1966

VITAL, HAYYIM. *Ets Hayim* ("Tree of Life"), Korets, 1819

4. Books Published in German Only

FURMAN, ISRAEL. *Jüdische Sprichwörter und Redensarten* ("Jewish Proverbs and Sayings"), Menorah, Tel Aviv, 1968

LIPPERHEIDE, WILHELM. *Sprichwörterbuch* ("Book of Proverbs"), 3rd edition, Dorner, Berlin, 1934

Midrash Tanaim (in Hebrew and German), ed. David Hoffman, Nord-Ost, Berlin, 1913

INDEX

ABOUT THE AUTHOR

LEO ROSTEN, a writer of remarkable versatility and intellectual range, is the creator of the immortal *H*Y*M*A*N   K*A*P*L*A*N*, *Captain Newman*, *The Joys of Yiddish* and many other books. His name has often appeared on the movie screen and his pioneering studies of Hollywood and Washington correspondents are considered social-science classics.

A Ph.D. from the University of Chicago, Mr. Rosten studied at the London School of Economics and has taught at several American universities, as well as having served the U.S. Government as deputy director of the Office of War Information. His writings have won for him several distinguished citations.

Here are the Books that Explore the Jewish Heritage–Past and Present.

Fiction

☐	**Exodus** Leon Uris	11090	$2.25
☐	**The Heart Is Half A Prophet** Ruth Goldstein	10701	$1.95
☐	**Last of the Just** Andre Schwarz-Bart	10469	$1.95
☐	**Mila 18** Leon Uris	10802	$1.95
☐	**The Wall**	2569	$2.25

Non-Fiction

☐	**Questions & Answers About Arabs and Jews** Ira Hirschmann	11199	$1.95
☐	**A Bag of Marbles** Joseph Joffo	6407	$1.75
☐	**The New Bantam-Meggido Hebrew & English Dictionary** Levenston & Sivan	2094	$1.95
☐	**The Essential Talmud** A. Steinsaltz	10199	$2.95
☐	**A Kabbalah for the Modern World** Gonzalez-Wippler	6410	$1.95
☐	**Treasury of Jewish Quotations** Leo Rosten	10877	$2.95
☐	**The War Against The Jews** Dawidowicz	2504	$2.50

Bantam Book Catalog

Here's your up-to-the-minute listing of every book currently available from Bantam.

This easy-to-use catalog is divided into categories and contains over 1400 titles by your favorite authors.

So don't delay—take advantage of this special opportunity to increase your reading pleasure.

Just send us your name and address and 25¢ (to help defray postage and handling costs).

MESSE NOIRE

DU MÊME AUTEUR

Les Adieux à l'Empire, France-Empire, 2006.
Le Détective de Freud, éditions De Borée, 2010.
Casanova et la femme sans visage. Une enquête du commissaire aux morts étranges, Actes Sud, 2012 ; Babel noir nº 82.
Messe noire. Une enquête du commissaire aux morts étranges (prix Historia du roman policier 2013), Actes Sud, 2013.
Tuez qui vous voulez ! Une enquête du commissaire aux morts étranges, Actes Sud, 2014.

© ACTES SUD, 2013
ISBN 978-2-330-02698-1

OLIVIER BARDE-CABUÇON

MESSE NOIRE

UNE ENQUÊTE DU COMMISSAIRE
AUX MORTS ÉTRANGES

roman

BABEL NOIR

À ma mère qui m'a donné le goût de l'histoire.

La nuit tombe, mais les taches ne partent pas.

ILSE AICHINGER

I

FEUX FOLLETS
ET AUTRES DIABLERIES

Une cloche sonna dans le lointain. Le crépuscule avait enveloppé le cimetière d'un fin voile noir, estompant les formes des pierres tombales et des stèles. Une pluie fine et glacée murmurait doucement, détrempant le sol des allées. Le moine effleura le visage de l'homme du bout des doigts et se releva lentement.

— On dirait qu'il est mort de peur…

— Il y a de quoi, murmura le sergent du guet en tendant le bras pour désigner les feux multicolores qui semblaient flotter en l'air dans le lointain.

En ce mois de décembre 1759, le Paris de la mort s'étalait sous leurs yeux. Plus qu'un regroupement de tombes, le cimetière était un immense parc au relief tourmenté et à la végétation abondante. Une large allée bordée d'arbres dépareillés menait jusqu'à une petite colline dévorée par la mousse et peuplée d'ombres spectrales. Là-bas, des flammèches jaunâtres ou vermillon tourbillonnaient au-dessus des tombes. Le son de la cloche expira. Un vent lourd grondait rageusement. Près de là, on entendit un chien hurler à la mort.

— Il faut aller voir, dit le moine d'une voix basse.

— Ce sont là diableries, protesta l'autre. Moi et les archers du guet, nous ne bougerons pas de là !

— J'irai seul alors. Faites-moi donner une lanterne.

11

Le sergent du guet le considéra avec attention. Sous la capuche de son interlocuteur, on discernait des yeux noirs et vifs, brillants d'intelligence et d'humanité. Son regard reflétait une curiosité attentive pour le monde qui l'entourait. Le moine devait avoir une cinquantaine d'années. Un faisceau de minces rides sillonnait son front comme autant de signes de perplexité ou de curiosité intellectuelle. Les traits de son visage étaient fins et un mince filet de barbe, à peine argentée par endroits, soulignait la courbe aristocratique de son menton.

— Ne devriez-vous pas attendre le commissaire aux morts étranges ? demanda avec nervosité le sergent du guet. On peut affronter seul les hommes mais pas les esprits malins ou les âmes en peine…

— Cela suffit, répondit fermement le moine, j'y vais. Je ne crains rien en ce bas monde, moi !

Il s'empara de la lanterne tendue par un archer du guet et ajouta comme pour lui-même :

— Ni dans l'autre d'ailleurs !

Ses hommes tremblants regroupés autour de lui, le sergent du guet regarda l'énigmatique moine s'éloigner dans la nuit noire. Il avait entendu au sujet du collaborateur du commissaire aux morts étranges, chargé d'élucider les meurtres les plus mystérieux de Paris, autant de choses détestables que merveilleuses : hérésie, duel, dépeçage de cadavres mais aussi une science infinie puisant dans les textes les plus anciens… Silencieusement, il se signa.

Le pauvre halo de lumière de sa lanterne tremblotait devant le moine, dérobant au passage des impressions fugitives de désolation. Autour de lui, lierre, ronces et mauvaises herbes tapissaient les tombes aux pieds d'anges brisés. Une poignante impression de

12

solitude et d'abandon émanait de ces lieux. Le froid se faisait plus mordant à mesure que la nuit tombait. Il gravit d'un pas prudent des escaliers rongés par la moisissure et arriva au sommet d'un monticule. Les flammèches colorées étaient autant de feuilles au vent. Certaines d'entre elles s'éteignaient au bout de quelques secondes seulement mais il en naissait aussitôt d'autres, bleu pâle, rouges ou jaunes... Le moine les contempla avec ravissement.

— C'est magnifique, chuchota-t-il.

Il fit quelques pas afin de poser sa lanterne sur une tombe et mieux jouir du spectacle.

— Ah! dit-il en se figeant.

Une rigole de sang s'était formée au pied de la stèle et un coq égorgé gisait sur la pierre tombale.

— Cette escapade nocturne commence à devenir intéressante, dit-il en se parlant à lui-même comme il en avait pris l'habitude en prison par le passé. Ainsi, on sacrifie au diable! Pour ma part, je préférerais sacrifier à Bacchus, dieu de l'ivresse, ou à Vénus, déesse de l'amour. Enfin, chacun ses goûts!

En s'accroupissant, il découvrit un cierge de cire noire à moitié consumé.

— Messe noire et évocation satanique, fit une voix grave derrière lui.

Le moine se retourna. Tout absorbé par sa découverte, il n'avait pas entendu arriver Volnay, le commissaire aux morts étranges, vêtu d'une veste à col à revers et enveloppé dans un long frac anglais. Âgé de vingt-cinq ans environ, grand, mince de hanches et carré d'épaules, il avait une figure agréable, encadrée de cheveux noirs longs retenus en arrière par un ruban de taffetas noir plié en forme de fleur. Son nez était court et droit, sa mâchoire bien dessinée mais son maintien restait sombre et sévère. La lueur de sa lanterne s'accrochait à son visage, jetant des reflets dorés sur la cicatrice qui courait au coin de son œil droit jusqu'à la tempe.

— Messe noire et feux follets, mon fils, compléta gaiement le moine en désignant les tourbillons colorés qui s'agitaient autour d'eux. Newton en a parlé dans un de ses traités et les compare à des vapeurs s'élevant des eaux putréfiées, *ignis mentes*, les esprits du feu…

Son père, le moine, aimait à étaler sa science. Stoïque, Volnay attendit la suite.

— Dans notre cas, je dirai que la décomposition des cadavres libère parfois des gaz qui s'enflamment spontanément au contact de l'air. Lorsqu'il y a du vent comme ce soir, le commun des mortels croit voir Jack à la lanterne en personne !

Il eut un ricanement légèrement condescendant.

— Les paysans ont un certain sens pratique. Ils plantent une aiguille par terre pour forcer les feux follets à passer à travers le chas, leur laissant ainsi le temps de s'enfuir. Tout le monde sait en effet qu'il est aussi difficile pour un feu follet de passer par le chas d'une aiguille que pour un riche d'entrer au paradis !

— Laissons les feux follets pour l'instant, décréta froidement le commissaire aux morts étranges, même si le gardien du cimetière en est mort de peur.

Il s'éloigna, sa lanterne à la main comme une âme perdue. Dans la terre humide, ses bottes émettaient un chuintement mouillé. Le vent faisait battre les pans de son frac derrière lui.

— Mon fils, rétorqua le moine en haussant la voix, je doute qu'un gardien de cimetière meure pour quelques feux follets ou coq noir. Il a dû se passer autre chose…

14

— Quoi ?

— Je l'ignore pour l'instant. Je ne suis pas un policier, moi ! Je suis un chercheur de sens !

Volnay promena sa lanterne à travers les tombes, évitant soigneusement les flammèches.

— Elles ne brûlent pas, mon fils ! s'exclama le moine. Que cherches-tu ?

— Des tombes profanées par les célébrants de cette messe noire. Le contact à l'air libre des cadavres expliquerait l'apparition de ce phénomène… Non, je ne vois rien à part quelques croix renversées. Peut-être que l'apparition des feux follets a mis en fuite nos célébrants avant qu'ils n'aient le temps d'achever…

Au loin, les hurlements lugubres du chien reprirent. Dans ceux-ci s'exprimait quelque chose de primitif mais d'incroyablement humain qui glaçait le sang comme s'ils révélaient une véritable souffrance. Le moine tapa du pied par terre pour se réchauffer. L'humidité commençait à le saisir. Il leva la tête vers le ciel et écarta théâtralement les bras.

— Oh vous Seigneur qui faites si peu pour nous d'ordinaire, aidez-nous à comprendre ce mystère !

— Ne blasphème pas ! cria sèchement le policier qui s'était éloigné à portée de voix.

Le moine rit, les yeux fermés sous la caresse de la pluie.

— Quel dommage que tout soit détrempé, remarqua-t-il. Nous aurions pu lire quelques traces sur cette tombe. D'habitude, c'est une jeune vierge qui s'étend nue sur la pierre, un crucifix au milieu des seins, tête en bas, et une hostie consacrée entre les cuisses…

— Elle est là, fit une voix basse.

Le moine sursauta avant de reconnaître l'intonation déformée de Volnay. Celui-ci s'était immobilisé sous un arbre, face à une croix brisée. Pataugeant dans la terre humide, le moine s'empressa de le rejoindre.

— Comme tu viens de la décrire, ajouta le policier du même ton rauque. À un détail près : la malheureuse enfant a été étranglée.

La victime se trouvait étendue sur la tombe, les bras en croix, offerte à la pluie. Elle était très belle et très jeune, sa peau pâle et glacée et ses lèvres bleues de froid. Le moine se pencha sur elle et, d'un geste doux, lui ferma les yeux.

— On a tué un ange, murmura-t-il accablé.

Il serra les poings, la rage crispait ses traits.

— On nous rabâche que le bien est à l'origine et le but de chaque être? On nous trompe : l'homme n'a aucune mesure pour infliger du mal à autrui !

Sa colère enfla encore.

— Siècle de fous, de malades et de pervers où l'ignorance crasse le dispute à l'infamie! Elle ne doit pas avoir treize ans !

Le commissaire aux morts étranges balaya les environs du regard. Il ne portait pas de chapeau et le vent jouait avec ses cheveux d'un noir de corbeau, portés longs et sans poudre. Il concentra de nouveau son attention sur le moine. Plus son père vieillissait et plus il devenait sensible à la mort ou à la perte d'un être plus jeune que lui.

— Remets-toi de ton émotion, lui dit-il doucement, nous avons à trouver les coupables de cette folie.

Le moine acquiesça.

— Je n'ai après tout rien contre Jésus-Christ, chuchota-t-il. S'il existe, qu'il reçoive près de lui cette pauvre âme désemparée.

Il se releva.

— Ne bouge pas ! ordonna le commissaire aux morts étranges. Nous sommes sur la scène d'un crime. Ici se concentrent tous les indices dont nous avons besoin. Si nous n'y prenons garde l'enquête sera compromise avant même d'avoir commencé.

Il parlait avec sévérité et sur un ton sans appel.

— Commençons par protéger nos indices. La pluie ne nous aide pas mais au moins sommes-nous seuls sur les lieux et personne ne viendra piétiner et tout gâcher. Convenons d'abord de repérer les traces de nos pas pour les neutraliser et d'emprunter de nouveau celles-ci dans tous nos déplacements.

Dans le ciel, les étoiles semblaient figées par le froid. Sous cette pâle lumière, ils établirent de concert leurs repères puis le commissaire aux morts étranges reprit :

— Les indices sont là, sous nos yeux : un cadavre, une hostie, un crucifix, des empreintes de pas. Il nous faut faire parler tout cela ! J'ai besoin d'en savoir plus sur le rituel de la messe noire.

Le moine lui jeta un regard vide puis un éclair de lucidité éclaira la prunelle de ses yeux alors que son cerveau recommençait à fonctionner normalement.

— Comme tu le sais, expliqua-t-il d'une voix lasse, la messe noire est un culte rendu à Satan en parodiant la messe. Tout y est donc inversé : le corps d'une femme nue sert d'autel, les cierges sont noirs au lieu d'être blancs. Il ne s'agit pas d'une célébration mais d'un simulacre dénaturé, une profanation… Il existe beaucoup de rituels de messe noire. Un prêtre défroqué ou renégat, des hosties consacrées, une vierge et une prostituée, un crucifix ou un calice rempli de vin ou de l'eau d'un puits où l'on a jeté le corps d'un enfant non baptisé…

Il s'interrompit un instant, le regard dans le vague.

— Au premier coup de onze heures, la messe est dite à l'envers et se termine au douzième coup de minuit.

— Il n'est pas minuit, remarqua Volnay, ils ont dû être interrompus…

— Il faut dire que, pour plus de résultat, la messe est souvent dite trois fois.

— Diable !

— Normalement, continua le moine d'un ton morne, le prêtre dit la messe et la prostituée la sert. Des fragments de messe sont récités à l'envers et le mot *mal* remplace le mot *bien*, *Satan* celui de *Dieu*. La prostituée donne la communion, aspergeant de vin la poitrine de la jeune vierge et plaçant l'hostie pour la souiller dans le… euh… dans l'antre sacré de la jeune fille.

Il se tut.

— Bien, dit pensivement le commissaire aux morts étranges. Cela me permet de comprendre la configuration de la scène. C'est curieux, on a tracé comme une croix dans le sol.

Le moine hocha la tête.

— Celui qui dit la messe fait le signe de croix du pied gauche sur le sol. Je te l'ai dit : tout est inversé.

— Cela signifie donc que l'officiant se tenait ici. À côté de lui, une femme car la terre est nettement moins tassée et l'empreinte plus petite. Les autres sont en face… Je dirais deux… non, trois personnes. Je vais en prendre la mesure.

Il déplia une ficelle et prit les mesures en faisant un nœud pour le début et la fin de chaque empreinte.

— Encore une empreinte de femme, fit-il d'un ton glacial. Trois hommes et deux femmes…

Il fronça les sourcils.

— Avant de savoir, il faut supposer. Nous aurions donc deux célébrants de la messe, trois spectateurs et… une victime à sacrifier.

Le moine se mit à genoux près du corps sans vie. Un instant, bizarrement, le commissaire aux morts étranges crut qu'il allait prier mais déjà les doigts fins et déliés du moine couraient le long du cadavre, soulevant bras et avant-bras, examinant les coudes.

— Des traces d'étranglement peu marquées autour du cou, pas de geste de défense occasionnant des blessures, pas de contusion sur les avant-bras, dit-il, mais je dois l'examiner à la lumière et sans cette maudite pluie glacée.

— Abrite-moi, fit Volnay. J'ai besoin de dessiner la scène du crime sans être trempé.

Le moine s'exécuta et, d'un pan de sa soutane, abrita le papier et le fusain de son fils qui se mit à dessiner avec habileté sur son genou.

— Voilà, fit le commissaire aux morts étranges au bout d'un moment. Je ferai le portrait de la jeune morte une fois son corps à l'abri.

Avec précaution, il fit quelques pas vers les feux follets qui semblaient maintenant s'évanouir dans la nuit et s'arrêta près de la tombe où il avait au départ rejoint le moine. Il reporta son attention sur le coq égorgé.

— Pourquoi avoir sacrifié ce coq sur une tombe éloignée ?

Il se tourna vers le moine mais celui-ci semblait ne pas avoir entendu.

— Père ?! insista Volnay.

Le moine tressaillit car rares étaient les moments où son fils prononçait ce mot qui remuait son cœur. "Père", c'était un peu comme si son cœur était un instrument de musique et que l'on en pinçait une corde.

Je vieillis et je deviens sensible, se dit-il.

Mais il n'en pensait pas un mot.

— Oui, mon fils ?

— As-tu entendu ma question ?

— Non, mon fils.

Volnay la répéta et le moine haussa les épaules.

— Je n'en ai pas la moindre idée.

Le commissaire aux morts étranges le considéra d'un air intrigué. Jamais, il n'avait vu son père aussi peu concentré sur la scène d'un crime.

— Y a-t-il quelque chose que tu veuilles me dire ?

— Oui, dit le moine.

Ses pupilles semblèrent se remplir d'une eau trouble.

— Lorsque nous trouverons ces meurtriers, faisons en sorte qu'ils soient longuement torturés avant d'être brûlés et dépecés.

Le commissaire aux morts étranges fronça les sourcils. Tout cela ne ressemblait pas à son père, farouche opposant de la peine de mort comme de la torture. Il regarda à nouveau la jeune victime à qui le moine avait fermé les yeux avec tant de douceur et demanda :

— La connais-tu ?

Le moine résidait tout comme son fils sur la rive gauche de la Seine, dans une petite impasse discrète, à quelques pas de la rue Saint-Jacques.

Lui et Volnay descendirent le corps de la carriole qu'un archer du guet reconduisit à l'écurie d'une auberge non loin de là. Le policier proposa son aide au moine mais celui-ci tint à porter seul la jeune fille dans ses bras. Il le fit comme s'il s'agissait d'une gamine endormie qu'il ne souhaitait surtout pas réveiller. À un moment, la tête enfantine roula sur sa poitrine. Le cœur du moine se serra et il cligna brièvement les yeux. La pluie avait dessiné comme des larmes sur son visage. Il réajusta brièvement sa prise, sous le regard inquiet de son fils. Un grand froid envahit ce dernier lorsque son père déclara :

— Il nous faut vite l'amener chez moi pour qu'elle puisse se réchauffer.

Sans répondre, Volnay lui ouvrit la porte. Après avoir descendu un escalier raide, ils longèrent avec leur fardeau un long couloir sombre pour se retrouver face à une double porte en fer. Ils déposèrent le corps par terre et le moine tourna une clé dans la serrure. Le policier entra à sa suite dans une profonde cave voûtée aux murs de pierre. Celle-ci recelait un incroyable laboratoire regorgeant de creusets, d'alambics, de cornues et de fourneaux, froids ou ronflants. Il était bientôt minuit. Les deux hommes s'appliquèrent à allumer minutieusement les torches accrochées au mur avant de s'occuper du lustre couronné de bougies. Ensuite, sans un mot, ils soulevèrent à nouveau la jeune fille pour la déposer avec respect sur une table en pierre que le moine recouvrit préalablement d'une couverture. Le cœur du commissaire aux morts étranges se serra lorsque le moine parla doucement au cadavre.

— Ah ma jeune amie, cela me soulève le cœur que d'avoir à procéder ainsi mais il faut me pardonner : c'est pour trouver ceux qui vous ont causé tant de mal.

Il se pencha pour examiner l'hymen de la jeune fille. Le commissaire aux morts étranges s'agita, mal à l'aise. C'était la première fois qu'il entendait le moine parler à un cadavre qu'il examinait. La connaissait-il ? Pourtant, à la question posée, son père avait répondu négativement.

— Elle est vierge, dit froidement le moine en se relevant. Au moins ces chacals ne l'ont pas souillée !

Encore une fois, ce ton rageur éveilla la curiosité de Volnay. Jamais il n'avait vu son père trahir une émotion en examinant un cadavre.

— Une enfant d'une douzaine d'années, répéta doucement le policier comme pour lui-même. Une vierge, une prostituée et un prêtre renégat…

Une mèche de cheveux blonds et soyeux barrait le front de la jeune fille, le moine la remit doucement en place.

— On dirait de l'or filé, s'émerveilla-t-il.

Il ouvrit les doigts et laissa glisser ses cheveux entre ses doigts.

— Peux-tu poursuivre ? demanda doucement son fils.

Tout en marmonnant, le moine entreprit avec une loupe l'examen du corps, étudiant avec attention les genoux, les coudes, les bras et avant-bras. Puis, il souleva avec prudence la nuque, écartant les cheveux à la recherche de contusions ou d'une bosse.

Finalement, il se tourna vers Volnay.

— La pluie gâte les indices tandis que le froid pétrifie le corps et nous prive de précieux renseignements, notamment sur l'heure de sa mort. C'est pour cela que j'étais pressé de la ramener au chaud. Je ne relève ni plaie, ni bosse, ni ecchymose sur le corps. Elle n'a pas lutté pour se défendre et ne s'est pas débattue. Même un mouton se démène et bêle devant l'autel où on l'immole. Pourquoi n'a-t-elle pas réagi ?

— Elle était consentante à cette mascarade et ne se doutait pas de la suite ? hasarda le commissaire aux morts étranges.

Perplexe, le moine se gratta la barbe.

— Quand même, nous sommes en décembre et le froid est mordant. Qui supporterait de se coucher ainsi nue sur une dalle glacée ?

Il poursuivit son examen du corps.

— Peux-tu avancer ta lanterne ? Là ! C'est étrange, les marques autour de son cou sont à peine visibles, pas suffisantes pour la priver d'air. Elle est peut-être morte de peur ou de froid…

— Tu me diras cela après l'autopsie, fit Volnay conciliant.

Son père lui jeta un regard sec.

— Il n'est pas question que j'ouvre cette pauvre enfant !

Le policier prit un air soucieux que l'autre ignora. Le moine recula d'un pas et contempla songeusement le corps.

— Instinctivement, dit-il, elle aurait dû tenter de se protéger et on devrait trouver des entailles sur ses mains ou ses avant-bras. Mais non, il n'y a même pas de marque autour de la bouche pour l'empêcher de crier.

— Ses dents sont bien soignées, remarqua le commissaire aux morts étranges en lui écartant légèrement les lèvres. Il en va de même pour ses mains. Elle n'est pas du peuple…

— Que connais-tu du peuple ? grogna le moine.

Le policier ne répondit pas. Il contemplait la jeune morte. Séchés par une serviette, ses cheveux blonds apparaissaient lisses et clairs. D'une main tranquille, il ébouriffa la chevelure sous l'œil agacé du moine.

— On dirait qu'on lui a coupé plusieurs mèches.

— Foutre du pape ! jura son père. Je ne l'avais pas remarqué !

Pour se rattraper, il entreprit de comparer chaque mèche l'une après l'autre.

— Tu as raison et je doute qu'elle se soit taillé cela elle-même.

Le moine plissa les yeux comme pour mieux réfléchir.

— Elle s'allonge nue, les bras en croix, en plein mois de décembre sur une dalle glacée et humide puis présente son cou au bourreau !

Il secoua la tête.

— À moins que…

Le moine commença à s'agiter.

— Mais oui, sacrebleu, c'est bien sûr ! Que n'y ai-je pensé plus tôt ?

— Penser à quoi ? s'impatienta le commissaire aux morts étranges.

— J'ai mon idée mais il est trop tôt pour en parler, maugréa son père. Et j'ai besoin de ne pas être dérangé tout le temps…

— Tu es d'une humeur détestable, fit Volnay. Je te laisse et je rentre me coucher !

— Bonne idée, la nuit porte conseil à qui sait l'entendre !

Après avoir raccompagné son fils et fermé soigneusement la porte derrière lui, le moine redescendit dans son laboratoire. Il entreprit alors d'examiner la bouche de la petite victime. À l'aide d'un mouchoir, il récolta sous sa langue un peu de jus laiteux et collant. Il le renifla avec suspicion.

— C'était donc cela, murmura-t-il satisfait. On l'a droguée…

Volnay sortit de l'impasse, goûtant à la beauté silencieuse des rues enneigées la nuit. À peu de pas de là, il se retrouva face à un chien au pelage tout crasseux.

Ses yeux noirs, étrangement humains, brillaient d'intelligence. L'animal geignit, ouvrit la bouche en rejetant la tête en arrière comme pour hurler mais, au lieu de cela, poussa une plainte triste, presque un gémissement. Volnay s'approcha lentement de lui et, s'assurant qu'il ne montrait pas les crocs, le flatta un instant.

— Nous sommes-nous déjà rencontrés quelque part mon ami à quatre pattes ? lui demanda-t-il gravement.

Puis il sourit, gratta une dernière fois le chien derrière les oreilles avant de regagner son domicile à peu de distance de là. Ses bottes battaient le pavé avec assurance mais, le regard aux aguets, il scrutait les zones d'ombre, la main sur la poignée de son épée.

Pour le commissaire aux morts étranges, la nuit n'était pas plus une tranquille parenthèse qu'un instant de repos. Les crimes les plus abominables se commettaient aux heures les plus noires et, au petit matin, les décrotteurs de Paris ramassaient les cadavres. La nuit semblait placer Paris hors de tout droit et de toute morale.

Des rires joyeux fusèrent de l'obscurité. Volnay dressa l'oreille puis hocha lentement la tête. Du jour de l'Épiphanie à la veille du mercredi des Cendres, régnait le temps de Carnaval. Avant que ne lui succèdent l'austérité du Carême et Pâques, symbole de renouveau, qui anéantirait les péchés et les ténèbres de l'hiver, Carnaval permettait à tous de renier sa spiritualité et de laisser libre cours à ses instincts bassement matériels. Déguisements et masques gommaient les classes sociales et les différences entre êtres humains, donnant à ceux-ci l'occasion de s'oublier dans une identité précaire qui laissait débrider les instincts et parler les sens.

La police du royaume n'appréciait guère cette période où l'ordre royal même était remis en question.

Elle donnait lieu à de nombreuses rixes, violences et paillardises. Les valets volaient leurs maîtres et débauchaient leurs maîtresses. Les archers du guet et le clergé étaient insultés. La farce tournait parfois au drame. Aussi, une ordonnance de police de 1746 interdisait désormais aux personnes masquées de porter bâtons et épées ou d'en faire porter par leurs laquais. Une autre ordonnance, de 1742, défendait d'entrer de force dans les lieux où se jouait de la musique, de violenter les traiteurs, leurs femmes et enfants et de contraindre les violons à jouer toute la nuit. C'était un moyen sûr pour lutter contre le tapage nocturne en temps de Carnaval.

Seulement voilà, ce n'était pas le temps de Carnaval ! Malgré tout, il rencontrait souvent, depuis le début de décembre, ce genre de groupes. Une fois le soleil couché, à l'approche de Noël, une étrange exaltation semblait saisir la ville.

Bientôt, le commissaire aux morts étranges aperçut la lueur d'un flambeau porté par un jeune homme avec un masque en papier au nez démesurément allongé. Il annonçait un groupe joyeux d'une douzaine de jeunes gens. Les filles dansaient une sorte de farandole tandis que les garçons chantaient des couplets obscènes. En découvrant Volnay seul, ils eurent une exclamation collective d'heureuse surprise puis, satisfaits, se dirigèrent vers lui pour le tourmenter ou le détrousser. Le commissaire aux morts étranges eut un sourire froid et dégaina à moitié son épée. Le groupe marqua un temps d'arrêt puis reprit sa direction initiale. Manifestement, on trouvait plus facile d'humilier un bourgeois esseulé qu'un homme armé et décidé. Volnay se recula pour les laisser passer à deux mètres de lui. Des quolibets fusèrent et certaines jeunes filles lui tendirent leur croupe de manière suggestive en chantant :

Enfile, enfile, enfile, l'aiguille de Paris !

L'une d'elles, à la silhouette grande et élancée, quitta alors le groupe et vint s'accrocher à son bras. Elle portait le masque de la mort.

— Viens danser avec la mort et goûter à ses baisers !

Elle joignit la parole à l'acte et l'embrassa à pleine bouche avant de s'enfuir en riant pour rejoindre les autres. Volnay resta un moment immobile, le cœur battant dans le noir. Puis, il reprit sa marche comme si de rien n'était. Derrière lui, le chien, qui s'était immobilisé, reprit une marche prudente à sa suite.

II

AFFAIRE D'ÉTAT
ET AUTRES DIABLERIES

Une lueur pâle filtrait à travers les tentures, s'aventurant jusqu'aux reliures dorées des livres qui ornaient tout un pan de mur.

— Debout! Debout!

Volnay ouvrit un œil et puis un autre. Son regard tomba sur la pie qui tournait et retournait dans sa cage dans un grand bruissement d'ailes. Parée d'une longue queue étagée, elle arborait avec fierté un plumage noir aux reflets violacés sur la poitrine et la tête, blanc au niveau du ventre, des flancs et à la base des ailes, verdâtre sur la queue.

— Debout! répéta-t-elle.

Encore tout ensommeillé, Volnay la fixa stupidement. Il s'était endormi à sa table de travail en tentant de récapituler les maigres indices en sa possession : un prêtre renégat, une prostituée, une jeune vierge étranglée et trois spectateurs. Ah oui, il y avait aussi un gardien de cimetière mort de peur et des feux follets!

Ses pensées le ramenèrent à son père. Il se frotta le visage avec la paume de ses mains et, faute d'interlocuteur à qui se confier, dit à la pie :

— Je ne l'ai jamais vu comme cela. Voici bientôt trois ans que je travaille avec lui sans qu'il laisse transparaître la moindre émotion devant un cadavre. De la compassion certes mais pas d'émotion…

Il secoua la tête, continuant son monologue comme pour se convaincre.

— C'est avant tout un homme de science et de raison, je le sais depuis l'enfance même s'il a peu passé de temps avec moi pendant celle-ci…

Il eut un sourire amer.

— Mon père préférait la compagnie des philosophes ou des alchimistes à la mienne. Un enfant, ça n'est pas assez intelligent pour soutenir une conversation sur les systèmes politiques à travers le temps ou les théories de M. Newton sur les corps en mouvement…

La pie resta silencieuse mais son regard noir semblait lire en lui. Volnay continua, comme encouragé de ne pas être interrompu.

— Et voilà qu'aujourd'hui, c'est un peu comme si, en tuant cette pauvre enfant, on venait de lui briser le cœur. Je ne comprends pas…

— Comprends pas, répéta la pie bavarde. Comprends pas !

Il était tombé sur Paris un froid à rompre les os. La ville semblait se recroqueviller sur elle-même comme une vieille femme transie. Pourtant, des artisans travaillaient bien avant l'aube à la porte de leur boutique. Ils se retournèrent avec curiosité à la vue de la carriole conduite par le moine, escortée de deux exempts de police. Il avait neigé peu avant l'aube. Le cheval allait au pas, posant avec précaution ses sabots dans cette neige fraîche.

Une fois arrivé dans son impasse, le moine sauta de la carriole avec agilité.

— Allez, dépêchez-vous de m'amener ce cadavre à l'intérieur ! D'habitude on me les apporte de nuit. Mes voisins vont encore dire du mal de moi !

Les deux exempts obtempérèrent sans un mot. Ils craignaient presque autant le moine que son supérieur, le taciturne commissaire aux morts étranges. Le premier posa le pied sur une plaque de verglas et chuta lourdement. Le second descendit plus prudemment. Ensemble, ils se penchèrent pour saisir le cadavre enveloppé dans une couverture et, d'une démarche pataude, encombrés par leur pesant fardeau, ils suivirent le moine.

Une fois les exempts congédiés, le moine contempla le corps du gardien du cimetière en se frottant les mains de plaisir.

— À nous deux, mon gaillard ! déclara-t-il. Je sens que tu as beaucoup de choses à me dire ! J'en donnerais la queue de mon chat à couper, quoique je n'aie pas de chat…

Une mince couche de givre étincelait dans la cour sous le soleil du matin. En sortant de chez lui, Volnay cligna des yeux, ébloui. L'acacia dressé face à sa maison était recouvert de cristaux de glace. Le commissaire aux morts étranges inspira à pleins poumons l'air froid et de minces filets de vapeur s'exhalèrent de ses lèvres. Un bref jappement le fit sursauter. C'était le chien de la veille.

— Tu es encore là, toi ?

L'animal l'observa avec une expression d'intelligence quasi humaine avant d'agiter joyeusement la queue comme s'il le reconnaissait. Volnay chercha dans sa poche le quignon de pain qu'il y avait glissé avant de sortir et le lui lança. L'animal s'en saisit et se hâta de déguerpir avec son butin.

Le policier quitta la cour minuscule devant sa maison pour en gagner une seconde un peu plus grande puis une troisième, de brique et de pierre, avec en son centre un puits à margelle. Celle-ci donnait sur le passage pavé, bordé de bornes chasse-roues par lequel la rue de la Porte-de-l'Arbalète menait à la rue Saint-Jacques.

Les ruelles, les allées et les portes cochères tenant de lieux d'aisances pour une grande partie de la population, la neige était par endroits souillée d'excréments. Heureusement, la pureté de l'air glacé chassait la puanteur qui habitait nombre de quartiers aux beaux jours. C'était l'avantage de l'hiver, l'été la ville puait plus fort qu'une porcherie.

Volnay se dirigea vers l'auberge dans laquelle il laissait habituellement son cheval. Ensuite, au pas prudent de sa monture, il prit la direction du cimetière de la veille, croisant les garçons limonadiers qui se répandaient dans les rues pour apporter cafés ou bavaroises dans les garnis. Arrivé au cimetière, le commissaire aux morts étranges gravit le monticule habillé d'un blanc manteau immaculé. La neige recouvrait désormais d'un voile de pureté ces lieux blasphémés dans la nuit. L'air lui piquait les poumons de mille aiguilles glacées. Une gaze légère semblait s'étirer pour envelopper les tombes d'un voile laiteux. Un début de brume sans doute. Il fallait faire vite. Il hâta le pas.

Conformément à ses instructions, un archer du guet se trouvait en faction sur une pierre tombale, à distance du lieu du crime afin de ne pas piétiner les éventuels indices. Il avait relayé deux heures auparavant un de ses compagnons d'infortune et battait de la semelle pour se réchauffer, les lèvres bleuies par le froid. Personne n'était venu, assura-t-il, et il avait évité de marcher ailleurs que sur la plate-bande qu'on avait assignée à la première sentinelle. Les empreintes de pas sur la glace pouvaient d'ailleurs en attester.

Le commissaire aux morts étranges le remercia et l'autorisa à rentrer à sa caserne. Ce qui devait être préservé l'avait été et, pour le reste, il préférait rester seul.

Avec méthode, il quadrilla les rangées de tombes à la recherche de traces suspectes mais la neige tombée dans la nuit avait tout recouvert si quelque chose lui avait échappé la veille. Le commissaire aux morts étranges s'arrêta pour réfléchir. Il pensa au gardien du cimetière. Si la venue de l'homme avait dérangé la cérémonie, acteurs et spectateurs de la messe noire se seraient empressés de quitter les lieux. Mais par où ? L'entrée du cimetière risquait d'être surveillée alors…

Il chercha des yeux un escalier qui redescendrait de la colline de l'autre côté. Il le trouva et suivit ensuite une allée qui le mena jusqu'à une porte couverte de rouille et protégée par des broussailles. Il lui sembla que certaines avaient été foulées aux pieds. Il déblaya doucement la neige près de la porte et découvrit ce qu'il cherchait : l'empreinte d'un pied enfoncé. Ce devait être la personne qui s'était arc-boutée pour tirer la porte à elle. Il sortit d'une de ses poches son rouleau à ficelle et compara l'empreinte avec ses mesures. Elle correspondait parfaitement à celle d'un des spectateurs de la messe noire !

Il entreprit de déblayer toute la neige alentour mais ne trouva pas d'autres empreintes. Alors, il examina minutieusement les broussailles. Au bout d'une longue recherche, son obstination fut récompensée par la découverte d'un fil de laine rouge accroché à des ronces. Il le récupéra soigneusement et s'empressa de le ranger à l'abri dans sa bourse à indices.

Lorsqu'il revint à l'entrée du cimetière, le sergent du guet l'attendait comme on le lui avait ordonné la veille. Son teint était blême et il respirait à grand-peine. Face à lui, l'œil sévère et les joues pâles, le commissaire aux morts étranges le toisa d'un air ni aimable, ni affable.

— Sachez tout d'abord que je n'ai pas apprécié que vous ayez laissé mon assistant s'aventurer seul dans ce cimetière en pleine nuit. Maintenant, répondez à mes questions. Qui vous a appelé ?

Le commissaire aux morts étranges avait beau ne pas avoir plus de vingt-cinq ans, il en imposait tant par son autorité personnelle que par celle de sa fonction. Aussi, l'autre se hâta de lui répondre.

— Les assistants du gardien du cimetière. Ce sont eux qui ont trouvé celui-ci mort de saisissement.

— Où cela ? Soyez précis, je vous prie !

— En haut du monticule. Ils se sont empressés de le ramener à l'entrée du cimetière et de nous alerter. Ils étaient de plus terrifiés par les feux…

— Ils ne sont donc restés là-bas que quelques instants ?

— Oui, ils me l'ont confirmé.

— Cela a donc laissé tout le temps aux participants de la messe noire, si ce sont eux que le gardien a surpris, pour s'enfuir.

— Et jamais nous ne les retrouverons, soupira le sergent du guet.

— Détrompez-vous, le reprit sèchement Volnay, ils ont laissé derrière eux assez d'indices pour que je leur remette un jour la main dessus !

Les rayons du soleil au zénith se réfléchissaient sur la neige dans un scintillement aveuglant lorsque le moine pénétra dans la ruelle de l'Or. C'était une longue voie étroite bordée de maisons à un ou deux étages. Une population mystérieuse et discrète la peuplait : marchands d'onguents, spirites, exorcistes, alchimistes, astrologues, sorcières ou nécromanciens…

Non moins fugace était le passage des personnes qui leur rendaient visite, de la mégère qui souhaitait nouer l'aiguillette de son bourgeois au grand seigneur de la cour en quête d'un peu plus de pouvoir et d'argent. On pénétrait dans ces maisons selon des codes établis. Leurs caves profondes recelaient maints instruments de laboratoire ou symboles d'autres temps. Des cérémonies secrètes s'y déroulaient parfois pour évoquer des esprits disparus. On se pressait chez un tel pour y bénéficier de philtres favorisant l'amour ou chez un autre pour s'y faire lire l'avenir à travers la fumée d'une tête d'âne en train de brûler. Ici, les chercheurs de trésor évoquaient les âmes du purgatoire pour les aider à localiser l'or enterré, là on vendait des flûtes enchantées ou des runes. À l'inverse des rues de Paris, personne ne criait ou parlait fort, tout se déroulait de manière silencieuse et furtive.

Derrière les carreaux recouverts de givre, le moine sentit le poids des regards des curieux habitants de la ruelle de l'Or. Un homme le bouscula, son manteau déformé par des objets qu'il dissimulait dessous, contre sa poitrine.

— Formules magiques, philtres, amulettes, matériel pour envoûtement et talismans de protection, lui glissa-t-il, êtes-vous intéressé ?

— Non.

— Poudre magique pour vous soutenir dans l'effort de faire plaisir aux femmes ? insista l'autre.

Le moine secoua la tête en souriant.

— Merci, pour cela j'ai déjà tout ce qu'il faut sur moi !

Sans hésiter, il se dirigea vers une maison qui semblait rentrer sous terre et, après avoir frappé un rythme convenu, entra. Dans la semi-pénombre, il cligna des yeux pour accommoder. Il se trouvait au-dessus d'un escalier qui le conduisit par deux révolutions symétriques dans une cave voûtée au sol jonché de tapis épais et de coussins colorés. Au fond de celle-ci, près d'une cheminée où crépitait une belle flambée, se dressait une silhouette frêle couverte de la tête aux pieds d'un voile blanc, les bras croisés sur la poitrine. Ses cheveux semblaient de fil d'argent et ses yeux verts ornés de longs cils rappelaient la couleur des fonds marins.

— Vous revoilà, fit une voix féminine. Il y a bien longtemps que je n'ai eu l'honneur de votre visite.

— Un mois et une semaine, précisa le moine. Je le sais car lorsque vous m'honorez d'un sourire, je suis le plus heureux des hommes, ma belle Dame de l'Eau.

— Incorrigible flatteur ! Allons approchez près du feu et dites-moi ce que vous avez en tête. Il y a des années, vous me visitiez pour des raisons personnelles mais aujourd'hui je sais bien qu'il n'en est plus de même. Cette bure a quelque peu éteint votre sensibilité !

Il s'approcha d'elle, les yeux pétillants.

— Vous vouliez sans doute parler de ma sensualité ? Rassurez-vous, elle n'est pas complètement étouffée !

La Dame de l'Eau eut un haussement d'épaules impuissant et son rire frais emplit la pièce.

— Ces galanteries ne sont hélas plus de mon âge, vous avez trop tardé à vous déclarer !

Le moine hocha gravement la tête.

— C'est bien moi : je fais tout à contretemps ! Effectivement, je suis ici pour une raison précise. Avez-vous entendu parler de résurgence du culte satanique ?

Elle lui jeta un doux regard de reproche.

— Pourquoi parler de résurgence ? Ce culte a existé de tout temps. Le diable est le grand négateur de la puissance divine et il se trouvera toujours des gens pour dénier celle-ci.

Le moine approuva et déclama d'un ton sentencieux :

— "Ils donnent au diable leur âme immortelle puis le baisent au cul tenant des chandelles ardentes en leurs mains. Ils crachent sur la croix, en dépit de Jésus-Christ et de la Sainte-Trinité avant de tourner leur cul vers le ciel, en dépit de Dieu."

La Dame de l'Eau eut un rire indulgent.

— À qui pensez-vous, mon ami ?

— Ma chère, je pense à des gens qui n'hésitent pas à tuer…

— Des nourrissons comme du temps de la Voisin ?

— Non, de jeunes vierges.

Le regard de la dame s'assombrit.

— Voilà qui est bien nouveau quoique je ne sois pas surprise.

Elle eut un moment d'hésitation et ajouta d'une voix basse :

— En fait, rien de ce qui est mauvais dans la nature humaine ne me surprend plus aujourd'hui.

Le moine approuva sombrement avant de reprendre ses questions.

— Avez-vous remarqué dans la ruelle de l'Or des gens cherchant cierges noirs, coqs à sacrifier ou hosties consacrées ?

La Dame de l'Eau réfléchit.

— Comme vous le savez, répondit-elle prudemment, il existe deux types de magie : la noire et la blanche. La magie blanche a vocation à soulager les maux de l'humanité et la magie noire à contenter des intérêts personnels. Dans nos campagnes, on trouve encore nombre de mages capables d'influer sur l'ordre de la nature pour faire pourrir les moissons sur pied, tarir les vaches ou empêcher les fruits de mûrir. Dans la ruelle de l'Or, nous comptons autant de personnes qui vendent les articles nécessaires à la magie blanche qu'à la magie noire. Cependant, aucun n'est assez fou ou démoniaque pour commercer des hosties consacrées. Nous évitons ici toute magie qui a recours aux démons et tout pacte diabolique même si quelques nécromanciens évoquent les morts.

D'un geste circulaire, la Dame de l'Eau désigna tout ce qui se trouvait à l'extérieur.

— Voyez-vous, nous formons ici une sorte de communauté avec, comme partout, de bons et de mauvais éléments. Cependant, même ces derniers ne supporteraient pas d'être exposés au danger de ce type de cérémonie. C'est la roue assurée et toute la ruelle de l'Or rasée et brûlée. Non, jamais notre communauté n'accepterait que de telles pratiques se développent ici.

— Et les envoûteurs ?

— Asservir la volonté d'autrui ou la détruire est le propre de l'homme, qu'il soit envoûteur ou pas.

— C'est vrai qu'on peut être roi de France et envoûteur, approuva le moine. Mais, sans nous lancer dans des considérations politiques, certains ont-ils ici pignon sur rue ?

— Oh, la demande d'envoûtement a toujours été très forte, c'est un marché d'avenir ! Élixirs, charmes et philtres d'amour, poupées ensorcelées pour réduire ses ennemis, nouage d'aiguillette pour maris infidèles, potions pour modérer le trop grand désir de l'action de Vénus chez la femme… ce sont là pratiques courantes et, à vrai dire, le principal fonds de commerce de la ruelle de l'Or avec la divination et la lecture de l'avenir. De plus le commerce de l'envoûtement alimente celui des leveurs de maléfices et génère un autre marché : celui de la protection contre l'envoûtement : amulettes, talismans… On vend de quoi se protéger contre les maléfices que l'on a vendus, ainsi l'équilibre est préservé !

— Un peu comme des marchands d'armes qui en vendraient à chaque camp qui s'affronte. C'est la loi de l'équilibre revue et corrigée par les charlatans !

— Oui, cependant, attention ! Parfois, fausse est la magie, vrai est le magicien !

Elle contempla songeusement le feu.

— Tout ce que désirent les gens est d'avoir ce qu'ils ne possèdent pas. De manière extravagante, c'est toujours ceux qui ont le plus qui souhaitent en posséder plus encore. Si l'on veut définir le rôle de la ruelle de l'Or, il est simple : leur faire croire que cela est possible.

Le moine soupira.

— Magie d'appropriation…

Il se campa près du feu, tendant ses mains à réchauffer aux flammes.

— Notre commissaire aux morts étranges est expert et savant en beaucoup de choses mais pas en magie noire, confia-t-il. Je n'aime pas notre mission. Elle va nous mener dans des lieux ignobles et je ne sais même pas vers quoi orienter notre enquête.

La Dame de l'Eau se joignit à lui auprès de l'âtre pour contempler d'un air pensif les bûches enflammées.

— Tout comme vous, votre fils s'adapte aux situations les plus complexes.

C'était une des très rares personnes à connaître leur lien de parenté mais le moine avait foi en elle comme en lui-même.

— Mon fils est trop rigide, maugréa le moine. Je crois qu'il s'est construit en opposition à moi.

— C'est souvent le cas avec les enfants, dit-elle doucement, mais parfois cela leur passe…

Le moine hocha la tête. Ses pensées semblaient affleurer jusque dans ses yeux. On y lisait une douleur muette.

— Il est tout ce que j'ai sur cette maudite terre mais le sait-il?

— Le lui avez-vous dit?

— Il ne m'en offre pas l'occasion…

— Provoquez celle-ci!

Face au silence épais de son compagnon, la Dame de l'Eau fit diversion.

— Pour en revenir à notre premier sujet, sabbat, messes noires ou rituels d'envoûtement, vous trouverez toujours un point commun entre eux : l'acte de copulation!

Un éclair joyeux traversa le regard du moine.

— Je vois très bien ce que vous voulez dire!

Elle le gronda gentiment.

— Vous êtes insupportable!

S'approchant d'un bassin de marbre au milieu de la pièce, elle effleura de la paume la surface de l'eau et dit :

— Mon art à moi est véritable, vous le savez. Ma magie est celle de la nature. Tout ce qui est en haut est comme ce qui est en bas pour faire miracle d'une seule chose…

Le moine se pencha et plissa les yeux devant les rides qui parcouraient le bassin.

— L'eau est un miroir, continua la Dame de l'Eau. Et qui sait en interroger la surface trouvera un signe ou une réponse à ses questions…

L'autre resta immobile avant de soupirer :

— Le charme de l'eau n'opère plus sur moi. J'ai vieilli et perdu la clé des rêves. Je vais avoir besoin d'autre chose…

Sa compagne arqua délicatement un sourcil.

— Mon ami, vous faites trop de cas des plantes.

— Sans elles, je ne dormirai plus depuis longtemps ! J'ai accumulé tant de cauchemars en moi !

Il battit l'air des mains comme pour chasser cette dernière remarque et reprit :

— À propos, avez-vous entendu parler de certaines drogues qui plongent les gens dans une sorte de léthargie bienheureuse ?

— C'est-à-dire ?

— Je cherche quelqu'un qui vend des plantes hallucinantes, celles qui rendent fou ou donnent des visions merveilleuses, procurant félicité et grande satisfaction…

— De quel genre ?

— Du genre qui ne donne pas envie de revenir car l'illusion de la réalité est bien plus plaisante que la réalité elle-même.

— Il suffit de dormir pour cela, remarqua-t-elle.

— Certes, certes mais tous les savetiers ne rêvent pas qu'ils sont roi. Il est des va-nu-pieds qui rêvent chaque nuit qu'ils sont va-nu-pieds !

Elle sourit.

— Vous avez raison, comme d'habitude ! Enfin, pour en revenir à votre question, je vais vous indiquer deux maisons dans la ruelle où vous trouverez de telles choses. La première est celle d'une rebouteuse et guérisseuse. C'est plutôt une bonne créature et les plantes n'ont pas de secret pour elle. Vous y trouverez des fleurs de pavot…

— *Papaver somniferum*, approuva le moine. J'y ai pensé un moment.

— Il existe aussi l'herbe-aux-sommes, la jusquiame noire.

— *Hyoscyamus niger*, elle est très toxique mais soulage les maux de dents. Toutefois, l'utilisation combinée de certaines plantes peut conduire à une transe ou un sommeil léthargique.

La Dame de l'Eau approuva de la tête.

— La seconde personne est un Grec, marchand de potions. On dit qu'il a commerce avec l'Orient.

— Oh, s'exclama le moine, c'est lui que j'irai visiter le premier.

— Attention car il est fier et ombrageux. Ne vous présentez pas à lui comme policier mais plutôt comme acheteur.

— Je vais suivre vos conseils de ce pas, ils m'ont toujours clairement montré la voie !

— J'aime votre esprit et la gaieté de celui-ci, dit-elle.

— Vous avez toujours été très indulgente avec moi, ma chère amie…

Il prit congé de la dame, baisa galamment sa main et sortit.

Dans les couloirs du Châtelet, le commissaire aux morts étranges croisa procureurs, huissiers et greffiers tout de noir vêtus, sinistres corbeaux le jaugeant du regard avant de mieux le condamner. Un maroquin sous le bras, jouant les importants, ils le bousculèrent sans un mot d'excuse. Tous participaient d'une manière ou d'une autre à tisser cet écheveau inextricable de lois, coutumes et jurisprudence édictées selon les caprices des gouvernants et de leurs serviteurs en noir. Ici on vous réprimandait pour le vol d'une grappe de raisin, là on vous envoyait aux galères pour le même délit.

S'il ne travaillait plus au Châtelet depuis sa nomination comme lieutenant général de police, Sartine y conservait un bureau. Sa nouvelle fonction était complexe car, outre la police au sens strict, il avait également en charge les bonnes mœurs, la santé, la religion, l'approvisionnement des vivres, la voirie, la réglementation des domestiques et des manœuvres. La surveillance du prix du pain lui causait le plus de soucis car à celui-ci pouvaient être attachées bien des révoltes du peuple par le passé. Il gérait également les sciences et les arts mais cette dernière fonction se contractait surtout dans la police du livre! Quant à la gestion de la pauvreté qui relevait de ses services, elle se résumait principalement à envoyer les mendiants en prison.

Volnay entra donc dans une grande pièce au sol froid jonché de tapis précieux et aux murs recouverts de tapisserie de prix. Malgré l'heure matinale, des flambeaux éclairaient les lieux. Le lieutenant général de police aimait à scruter les traits de ses visiteurs. Sous les mèches bouclées de sa perruque blanchie de poudre de riz et son front haut et dégarni, son regard était autoritaire et incisif. Il portait un habit de velours jaune tissé de motifs floraux avec des boutons revêtus de fil d'argent et des volants de manche en dentelle aux fuseaux.

— Ah, chevalier de Volnay ! Vous arrivez bien ! Au rapport, vite !

Habitué à la sécheresse de son supérieur, Volnay obtempéra.

— Cinq personnes se trouvaient sur les lieux du crime, expliqua-t-il d'un ton neutre. D'après les empreintes, je déduis que trois hommes et deux femmes étaient présents en plus de la victime.

— Ah oui, vos méthodes nouvelles… maugréa Sartine.

Il pianota nerveusement des doigts sur son bureau, un meuble au bois précieux, décoré d'appliques en bronze doré.

— Deux de ces personnes semblaient officier, reprit Volnay impassible. Vous savez ce que l'on dit pour la célébration des messes noires…

— Oui, l'interrompit Sartine avec brusquerie. Un prêtre renégat et une prostituée donnent la communion sous les deux espèces. Le célébrant abaisse l'hostie noire, au lieu de l'élever, avant de la souiller en la plaçant dans le sexe de la jeune vierge. Ensuite il la déchiquette pour faire souffrir le Christ dans sa propre chair. Quant au vin, je n'ose vous dire ce qu'il est réellement !

Le commissaire aux morts étranges hocha la tête. Il n'avait jamais douté que Sartine connaisse ses classiques.

— La sixième personne est la victime, ajouta le commissaire aux morts étranges. Une jeune fille d'une douzaine d'années. Je vous en ai apporté un croquis.

Sartine le prit du bout des doigts comme s'il s'attendait à trouver quelque chose d'horrible et regarda le croquis avec attention. Une lueur de surprise sembla traverser son regard.

— Une bien jolie enfant, murmura-t-il.

Une seconde, Volnay crut qu'un sourire attendri venait d'adoucir la physionomie froide de son interlocuteur mais, l'instant d'après, il ne retrouva plus que le masque impassible du lieutenant général de police. Celui-ci lui rendit le dessin, avec regret semblait-il, puis se ravisa.

— Je le garde, vous en avez d'autres, j'imagine.

— Certes…

Volnay savait que Sartine, comme tant de personnes puissantes, dirigeait de loin. Le simple fait qu'il conservât le portrait de la victime d'un meurtre était en soi une chose étonnante. Que se passait-il?

— Chevalier de Volnay, reprit son supérieur d'un ton compassé, vous n'êtes pas sans vous rappeler l'affaire des messes noires pendant le règne du prédécesseur de notre bon roi?

— Oui, la favorite de Louis XIV, la Montespan, employait la femme la Voisin dans de misérables cérémonies pour conserver les faveurs du roi…

— Comme vous y allez! Il n'a jamais rien été prouvé à l'encontre de Mme de Montespan! s'exclama le lieutenant général de police.

— Et pour cause! Le roi brûla personnellement les documents du procès et vous seul devez être dépositaire des notes du lieutenant de police de l'époque, M. de La Reynie.

Le teint de Sartine, d'habitude vieil ivoire, passa au cramoisi.

— Esprit frondeur! Votre insolence n'a donc pas de limites, prenez garde!

Le commissaire aux morts étranges ne broncha point. Son supérieur savait se montrer cassant et le rabaisser si besoin. Il tenait de temps à autre à rappeler l'importance de ses fonctions et la distance qui le séparait du commun des mortels. Ce genre de manifestation d'autorité glissait sur Volnay comme la pluie sur la montagne.

M. de Sartine fit quelques pas dans la pièce pour se calmer et entreprit de réajuster sa perruque.

— Reprenons les faits, fit-il en plissant les yeux, car il y a bien deux affaires distinctes : celle de la marquise de Brinvilliers et celle de la femme la Voisin. En 1672, Godin de Sainte-Croix, un officier en demi-solde perclus de dettes, meurt. Lors de l'inventaire après décès, on découvre un coffret plein de fioles remplies d'arsenic et une cassette de documents édifiants. Sa maîtresse, la marquise de Brinvilliers, y reconnaît avoir empoisonné à l'arsenic son propre père et ses deux frères, manquant de peu son mari légitime, tout cela pour s'approprier leur héritage. La cassette découverte, la marquise de Brinvilliers se réfugie à Londres puis à Liège dans un couvent. En 1673, La Chaussée, le valet de Godin de Sainte-Croix, est reconnu coupable de crimes et condamné à être rompu vif.

Sartine sortit une blague à tabac de sa poche et cala une prise dans le creux de son pouce écarté avant de renifler profondément. La reniflade terminée, il éternua, se moucha et poursuivit d'un ton satisfait.

— Au mois de mars de l'année 1676, François Desgrez, le plus fin limier du lieutenant général de police, La Reynie, se déguise en prêtre pour pénétrer dans ce couvent, arrêter la marquise et la ramener en France pour la faire écrouer à la Conciergerie.

Une grimace crispa le bas de son visage.

— L'enquête se poursuit pendant plusieurs années et La Reynie remonte patiemment le réseau des deux amants, s'épouvantant de ce qu'il découvre. Après un long procès, la marquise de Brinvilliers est exécutée. La police arrête de nombreuses personnes, dont la femme la Voisin, fournisseuse de poisons et jeteuse de maléfices. L'identité de certains de ses clients est tout bonnement stupéfiante…

Mme de Montespan, ancienne favorite du roi et mère de ses enfants, le maréchal de Luxembourg, Racine, des nièces de Mazarin, la duchesse de Bouillon, la comtesse de Polignac, la comtesse de Soissons, Mme de Vivonne, belle-sœur de Mme de Montespan, et les femmes de chambre de celles-ci… compléta en silence Volnay.

— Les révélations des accusés mettant en cause des personnes de haute naissance, un tribunal spécial est créé : la Chambre ardente, acheva Sartine d'une voix sourde. La Reynie fait arrêter trois cent soixante personnes dont cent dix sont jugées. On en pend ou brûle trente-six et les autres finissent leurs jours en prison ou aux galères. La Voisin est brûlée vive en place de Grève le 22 février de l'année 1680. La cour de Louis XIV est éclaboussée par cette affaire.

Surtout la cour, se dit Volnay qui, cette fois, évita d'exprimer sa pensée. S'il provoquait souvent ses supérieurs, il savait toutefois s'arrêter à temps. La liberté de pensée n'était guère prisée par les autorités.

— Il y a autre chose, reprit Sartine soudain très grave. À toutes les accusations d'empoisonnement, s'ajoutent celles de meurtres d'enfants par des prêtres débauchés lors de ces messes noires.

Il déglutit.

— Volnay, dit-il d'un pressant, il ne faut pas que cela se reproduise !

— Peut-être serait-il intéressant que je relise les notes du lieutenant de La Reynie, risqua le jeune homme.

— Pourquoi donc ?

Le commissaire aux morts étranges haussa légèrement les épaules.

— Pour comprendre ce qui peut pousser des gens à ce type de cérémonies, à savoir comment tout cela arrive, par quels réseaux on passe…

Sartine secoua la tête, catégorique.

— Après avoir relu toutes les pièces de l'affaire des Poisons, Louis XIV décida que celle-ci devait rester dans un *éternel oubli*. Il fit brûler en 1709 tous les registres, procès-verbaux et rapports de police. Il ne reste plus rien.

— Si ! La mémoire, la mémoire collective. Celle-là, rien ne peut l'effacer.

Sartine haussa un sourcil.

— C'est pour cela qu'il nous faut très rapidement résoudre cette affaire. Je ne tiens pas à passer les dix prochaines années de ma vie à instruire une nouvelle affaire des Poisons !

— Nous n'en sommes pas là, remarqua calmement le commissaire aux morts étranges. Il n'y a aucun poison dans cette affaire. J'ai simplement à retrouver cinq meurtriers qui ont étranglé une jeune fille après un simulacre de messe chrétienne.

— Une seule de ces personnes l'a étranglée, non ? fit remarquer Sartine.

Il arpentait la pièce d'une démarche nerveuse. De temps en temps, ses doigts trituraient sa perruque comme pour se rassurer.

— Et les autres sont ses complices, termina Volnay d'un ton glacial. Elles ne valent pas mieux que lui.

— Oui, sans doute. Enfin peut-être… L'affaire est plus grave que vous ne le pensez. Les archers du guet n'ont pas tenu leur langue, ils seront punis mais le mal

48

est fait. Déjà la rumeur se répand dans tout Paris et vous savez à ce que l'on pense…

— L'affaire Montespan…

— L'affaire la Voisin! le corrigea vivement Sartine. Mais tout ceci est du passé, un passé terrible qu'il faut oublier. Depuis que j'ai acheté ma charge dans la police au service du roi, je n'ai jamais été confronté à ce type d'affaire. Aucun rapport quelconque de police ne m'informe de tels actes. Il convient de clore rapidement cette enquête avant que la rumeur ne s'étende à toute l'Europe que Paris voit une résurgence du culte satanique. Je compte sur vous et votre père pour mener cette affaire à bien et avec la plus grande discrétion possible.

Il sortit sa blague à tabac puis, semblant se rappeler qu'il venait déjà de priser, se ravisa.

— La rumeur, Volnay, la rumeur… Elle est légère au départ, elle s'envole puis elle devient une opinion : l'opinion publique.

Il fit une pause.

— Nous ne demandons pas au peuple d'avoir une opinion, vous en êtes conscient, Volnay?

— De plus en plus, monsieur!

Néanmoins, pensa Volnay, *Versailles décline et c'est désormais à Paris que naît l'opinion. Un jour, nous vous pendrons vous et les vôtres!*

Sartine réajusta sa perruque.

— Je suis au courant de tout ce qui se dit dans la capitale du royaume. Des officiers de police en tenue civile fréquentent les auberges, les tavernes, les marchés ou les parvis des églises après la messe. Ils écoutent et notent tout ce qu'ils entendent. Je lis avec attention tous leurs rapports dont je rends compte au roi une fois par semaine.

Volnay hocha sombrement la tête. Il savait que, chaque mardi matin, Sartine racontait au roi tous les mauvais propos qui se tenaient dans Paris contre lui, sa cour, le pape ou simplement l'autorité. On appelait cela le mardi des grenouilles et le roi s'amusait surtout à entendre les ragots sur les gens de sa cour ou de son Église ; apprendre qu'un tel commettait le péché de Sodome et de bougrerie ou que telle marquise couchait avec ses domestiques le mettait en joie.

— Eh bien, reprit Sartine en haussant le ton, vous serez heureux d'apprendre que l'on parle de messes noires ! C'est même devenu le sujet préféré de conversation des Parisiens !

Il alla à son bureau, ouvrit un tiroir et s'empara d'une bourse qu'il lança à Volnay.

— Alors faites vite ! Voici pour délier les langues si besoin et couvrir vos frais. Tenez-moi au courant personnellement et directement. Pas de papier qui traîne ou de rapport. Vous viendrez me voir régulièrement.

D'un geste sec, il congédia le commissaire aux morts étranges. Avant de sortir, Volnay se retourna. Sartine lui avait déjà tourné le dos et, debout devant son bureau, contemplait pensivement le portrait de la jeune fille.

Après son rendez-vous avec Sartine, Volnay demeura quelques heures au Châtelet pour lire les rapports du guet pour les nuits précédentes. Il s'intéressa également aux violations de sépultures. Après une après-midi ainsi passée à la lumière des chandelles, il rentra chez lui, les yeux rougis par la lecture. La nuit tombait et les artisans commençaient à fermer leurs échoppes. Des lumières brillaient derrière les carreaux des cafés.

Ouvriers et manœuvres quittaient chantiers et ateliers pour regagner leur pauvre grabat. D'autres se glissaient dans les cabarets pour y fumer une dernière pipe et s'abrutir d'alcool. Lorsque Volnay poussa la porte de sa demeure, ce fut pour découvrir le moine s'entretenant en latin avec la pie.

— *A bove ante, ab asino retro, a morionem undique caveto*. "Prends garde au bœuf par-devant, à l'âne par-derrière, à l'imbécile par tous les côtés!"

— C'est un conseil que je suivrais!

— J'aimerais que ton oiseau parle plusieurs langues, expliqua son père en se retournant.

— Cela lui servira certainement beaucoup dans la vie! répondit sans rire son fils.

Le policier remarqua que le moine était passé de l'affliction à une gaieté surfaite. Cela ne le rassura pas.

— J'espère que tu as quelque chose de décent à boire, fit le moine, car j'ai à te parler.

— Toi, tu as découvert quelque chose, fit Volnay en souriant.

Le moine eut une petite mimique victorieuse.

— Diable, je n'en suis pas très fier mais hier nous avons oublié un cadavre.

— Quoi?! Une seconde victime?

— Le gardien du cimetière…

— Oh, c'est vrai, reconnut le policier. De ce point de vue-là…

Le moine balaya l'objection d'un revers de main.

— Pas d'excuse. Nous étions sur une scène de crime et nous nous sommes préoccupés d'une seule victime, éliminant d'emblée l'autre de l'acte criminel. Nous avons sauté aux conclusions en ce qui la concerne. On nous dit qu'elle est morte de peur. Comme un âne je répète qu'elle doit être morte de peur et au total on n'examine pas son corps ! *Errare humanum est ! Perseverare diabolicum !*

Le moine s'amusa à lancer quelques graines à la pie en murmurant doucement :

— Vilain roi, vilain roi…

— Vilain roi, répéta la pie d'une voix aux intonations vaguement humaines.

— On te pendra… On te pendra…

— Vas-tu m'expliquer ? s'agaça le commissaire aux morts étranges.

Son père se retourna vivement, un sourire radieux aux lèvres.

— Mon cher fils, j'ai l'honneur de t'annoncer que le sieur Fontaine, ci-devant gardien de cimetière, n'est pas mort de saisissement. On l'a tout simplement étouffé sans laisser de traces extérieures.

Il s'approcha du feu qui flambait joyeusement pour s'y chauffer les mains. L'hiver restait froid et la température dans la maison basse.

— J'ai noté des signes d'hémorragie à la tête et à la poitrine, reprit-il. Des bleus sur sa poitrine semblent démontrer qu'un homme de forte corpulence, voire plusieurs, s'est assis sur lui. On lui a maintenu les poignets contre le sol. Le dos de ceux-ci en est presque ensanglanté. Je relève également une bosse derrière la tête qu'il a dû se faire en se cognant tandis qu'on le suffoquait en appuyant sans doute un manteau ou une couverture sur sa bouche et ses narines. On a bien évité de l'étrangler afin de ne pas laisser de marques autour de son cou.

Il prit un air modeste et s'empara du tisonnier pour retourner une bûche trop grosse.

— Ce n'est pas tout ! fit-il triomphalement en se redressant.

Son fils soupira.

— Eh bien?

— Tu te rappelles que je ne m'expliquais pas que cette jeune fille se soit laissé étendre nue sur une tombe glacée sans un geste de défense. J'ai retrouvé dans sa bouche les restes d'un jus laiteux et collant. Il s'agit à ma connaissance d'une drogue qui provoque une espèce d'heureuse somnolence, un sentiment profond de bien-être et de satisfaction. Voilà pourquoi elle s'est laissé mener comme un mouton au sacrifice. Cette drogue est coûteuse car elle provient d'une plante qui se cultive dans des contrées d'Asie. Le vendeur en est un Grec de la ruelle de l'Or que j'ai visité ce matin et qui m'en a très obligeamment vendu une fiole. L'homme est peu bavard. J'y retournerai avec toi pour le persuader de nous parler de ses clients!

Il conclut modestement :

— Tu vois que j'ai progressé en peu de temps de manière spectaculaire! Et toi, de ton côté? s'enquit-il innocemment.

Volnay le rejoignit près du feu et leva ses mains. Même protégés par des gants de laine, ses doigts étaient gourds et raides.

— Notre bon M. de Sartine m'a fait tout un couplet sur l'affaire des Poisons, dit-il d'un ton détaché.

— Gens peureux, gens puissants! Sartine a peur, tout simplement. Autant la sorcellerie est campagnarde, autant les messes noires se sont développées dans des milieux très aisés quand ce n'est pas au sein même de la cour comme dans l'affaire de la Brinvilliers.

— Tu n'étais pas né, remarqua sans rire le commissaire aux morts étranges.

Le moine se retourna vivement vers lui.

— Oh, cela remonte peut-être à Louis XIV mais nous continuons encore à en parler dans le cercle des philosophes. Les lumières de notre siècle sont loin d'avoir chassé toutes les ombres. Nous aimons à prendre en exemple cette affaire comme de tout ce qui nous fait le plus horreur.

Il sautilla sur place, ravi de pouvoir commencer son exposé.

— La marquise de Brinvilliers, par ailleurs jolie et intelligente femme, est arrêtée après la découverte chez son amant d'une cassette remplie de documents compromettants. Ces documents, dont l'amant se sert pour faire chanter sa maîtresse, démontrent que la belle marquise a aidé son père et ses frères à avaler leur langue afin de s'approprier leurs biens. Son mari a réchappé de justesse au poison mais quelques servantes qui en savaient trop n'ont pas eu cette chance !

— Père, nous en avons déjà parlé avec Sartine !

Le moine se planta devant la cage à oiseau et entreprit de lisser d'un doigt le plumage noir aux reflets métalliques de la pie.

— Et ce n'est pas tout ! continua-t-il comme s'il n'avait rien entendu. La très charitable marquise de Brinvilliers apporte vins et confitures aux malades dans les hôpitaux. Malheureusement, après ses passages le taux de mortalité croît à une vitesse stupéfiante. C'est que notre belle empoisonneuse teste ses produits sur les malades avant de les utiliser sur les bien portants ! Ah ! L'expérimentation des potions médicinales, voilà un sujet intéressant…

Une fois lancé, le moine était intarissable. Volnay s'assit donc en silence pour écouter la suite.

— L'exécution de la Brinvilliers en 1676 n'est que le prélude à quelque chose de bien plus grave. Travaillée par le bourreau, la marquise révèle beaucoup de choses. Le lieutenant de police de l'époque, La Reynie, dispose alors d'assez d'informations pour remonter les filières. Il se rend compte avec effarement que des milliers de personnes de toute condition s'adonnent dans Paris au poison ou aux messes noires et à l'envoûtement. Même le roi est effrayé de découvrir autant de noirceur sous son règne.

Le moine s'interrompit pour caresser amoureusement les plumes de la pie et lui murmurer qu'elle était le plus bel oiseau du monde.

— En 1679, reprend-il, l'enquête rebondit avec l'arrestation d'une certaine Marie Bosse qui aurait fourni des poisons à certaines épouses de membres du Parlement souhaitant se débarrasser de leur mari.

— Et voilà que Marie Bosse dénonce la femme d'un mercier-joaillier, dame Catherine Monvoisin, dite la Voisin, intervint Volnay toujours pressé d'arriver aux faits plutôt que de supporter les interminables digressions de son père.

Le policier ajouta une bûche dans le feu, ce qui provoqua une gerbe d'étincelles.

— Et La Reynie continue avec zèle son enquête qui l'amène dans le milieu des messes noires…

Son père fit mine de se boucher le nez et se hâta de reprendre l'histoire à son compte.

— Cela sent mauvais à la cour ! La marquise de Brinvilliers avait prévenu : *S'il pleut sur moi, il dégouttera sur beaucoup de monde !* Or, un proche de Colbert a été mis en cause par la Brinvilliers et d'autres sont accusés par la Voisin. Louvois, ministre de la Guerre et attaché à la perte d'un Colbert successivement affaibli par cette affaire, la faillite de la Compagnie des Indes occidentales et par la liaison du roi avec la marquise de Maintenon, mène de son côté une enquête secrète pour le compte du roi.

Il plissa le front et le frotta du plat de la main comme s'il voulait stimuler sa mémoire.

— Après l'exécution de sa mère, reprit-il, la fille de la Voisin met en cause la favorite du roi en disgrâce, Mme de Montespan. On raconte qu'elle commerce avec la Voisin pour obtenir des poudres lui permettant de lui ramener les faveurs du roi mais aussi pour empoisonner des rivales.

À cet instant du récit, le moine se plaignit de la soif et, lui connaissant cette manie, Volnay déboucha prestement une bouteille d'un vin de Bourgogne.

— Ah, du vin de Givry ! Le préféré de feu le bon roi Henri IV si tant est qu'un roi puisse être bon ce qui n'est pas dans la nature de cette fonction !

Il s'interrompit pour boire une rasade et claqua des doigts pour ramener à lui une attention pourtant déjà tout acquise.

— Dans le bel hôtel particulier de la Voisin, on découvre une drôle de sacristie et, dans sa cave, des milliers d'ossements d'enfants. Soumise à la question, la Voisin va tout avouer. Elle fabrique et vend des poisons à base d'arsenic et de bave de crapaud ! On surnomme ce mélange, pilé dans un mortier et saupoudré dans les plats, *la poudre de succession* tant on l'emploie pour hâter le trépas de ses proches ! Tu veux hériter d'un parent en trop bonne santé ? Un peu de poudre et hop l'argent est dans le sac !

À ce moment on cogna brutalement contre la porte. Le commissaire aux morts étranges sursauta légèrement. Les visites étaient rares sinon inexistantes depuis le départ de Casanova et Chiara de Paris au printemps. Le policier alla ouvrir. Un souffle glacé se rua à l'intérieur. Volnay cligna des yeux car la lumière du jour était faible dans la petite cour. Il se trouvait devant deux personnages qui portaient un loup sur le visage et faillit leur refermer la porte au nez tant l'avait agacé l'incident de la nuit dernière avec la jeune femme au masque de mort. La perruque sur la tête de l'homme retint toutefois son attention et il s'effaça devant eux.

— Vous ici ?

Sartine eut un bref ricanement et ôta son masque.

— Allez savoir pourquoi, cette année, tout le monde se masque à l'approche de Noël. C'est étrange mais bien pratique pour se déplacer discrètement. Me voilà donc !

— Lorsque l'on parle du diable, marmonna le moine en se levant machinalement.

Le lieutenant général de police lui jeta un regard peu amène mais l'autre ne s'en soucia guère. Il venait d'apercevoir une forme délicieusement féminine sur le pas de la porte et guettait le moment où l'inconnue allait tomber le masque. Elle le fit d'un geste charmant, révélant un visage à la beauté sauvage et au regard assuré. Elle était presque aussi grande que le commissaire aux morts étranges et de longs cheveux fins, d'un brun aux reflets roux, ruisselaient dans son dos. Elle portait des boucles d'oreilles en forme de croissant et à ses poignets des bracelets d'or tintaient à chacun de ses gestes. Sous des cils longs et fournis, d'immenses yeux verts, mouchetés de jaune, brillaient d'une lueur surnaturelle.

Son regard balaya la pièce qui servait à la fois de salon, bureau et salle à manger, s'attardant au passage sur les étagères de livres reliés, aux couvertures cloutées et aux reliures gaufrées, qui s'élançaient à l'assaut des murs.

— Laissez-moi vous présenter Mlle Hélène de Troie, fit Sartine.

Hélène de Troie ? Le commissaire aux morts étranges et son père échangèrent sans mot dire un regard entendu. Sartine avait décidé de se moquer d'eux ouvertement. Le moine s'inclina toutefois avec la galanterie d'un grand seigneur devant la jeune femme. Même le lieutenant général de police semblait enchanté d'être aussi bien accompagné. Seul le commissaire aux morts étranges ne marqua ni surprise ni intérêt. Son visage s'était figé en un masque de pierre, indéchiffrable. À l'intérieur, ses pensées prenaient toutefois une tournure vertigineuse. Jamais encore Sartine n'avait mis un pied en sa demeure et il fallait un événement exceptionnel pour que cela arrivât. Qui plus est, tout s'était décidé très vite puisque Sartine, rencontré vers midi le jour même, ne lui avait pas fait part de sa prochaine visite.

Le moine s'empressa de débarrasser la visiteuse de son manteau et l'invita à s'asseoir près du feu. Elle portait une robe de velours rouge à l'anglaise, fermée sur le devant, la jupe montée par fronçage et couturée selon une ligne remontant sur les hanches vers la taille, les pans relevés dans les poches latérales de la robe et drapés dans le dos. Un habit pour quelqu'un intéressé par plus de liberté de mouvement.

— Votre enquête sur la messe noire devrait être difficile, vous allez avoir besoin d'aide, décréta solennellement Sartine.

Son visage vint s'orner d'un méchant sourire. Aussitôt Volnay redouta la suite.

— Et j'ai décidé de vous en procurer !

Il fit un vaste geste en direction d'Hélène de Troie.

— Mademoiselle vous accompagnera dans vos recherches et vous sera d'un précieux secours. Vous n'imaginez pas tout ce dont elle est capable !

Le moine se leva et s'inclina de nouveau devant elle, lui baisant cette fois la main avec ravissement.

— Monsieur de Sartine, vous vous trompez, je ne l'imagine que trop bien !

La jeune femme le remercia du compliment, si c'en était un, d'un sourire distant.

— Cela signifie-t-il que mademoiselle va nous accompagner durant toute notre enquête ? demanda le commissaire aux morts étranges toujours impassible.

Sartine prit un air réjoui.

— Vous avez tout à fait saisi ma pensée !

— Il n'en est pas question, décréta Volnay d'un ton égal. Je mène seul mes enquêtes avec mon... avec mon assistant.

En dehors de Sartine qui savait tout, comme il se doit, le commissaire aux morts étranges évitait en public de révéler que ce savant, jadis condamné au bûcher et qui pour y échapper portait désormais la bure, était son père. Le lieutenant général de police jeta un bref coup d'œil au moine qui contemplait le plafond avec insistance comme s'il souhaitait se faire oublier. De fait, l'entrée de Sartine semblait l'avoir plongé dans de graves tourments, certes tempérés par l'entrée de sa charmante escorte féminine.

— Vous ne menez pas une enquête ordinaire, fit le lieutenant général de police qui n'aimait pas qu'on remette en question ses décisions. Une messe noire s'est déroulée dans un lieu public, un cimetière ! Et cela s'est terminé par deux meurtres !

— Il n'y a pas de meurtre que nous ne sachions élucider seuls, répliqua Volnay d'une voix tranchante. Et je ne vois pas ce qu'une personne comme mademoiselle pourrait bien nous apporter.

Il s'inclina sèchement vers cette dernière et ajouta :

— Cela dit sans vouloir vous offenser, mademoiselle.

Machinalement, les deux hommes en face d'elle s'étaient approchés tandis que Sartine se reculait. Le plus jeune semblait soupçonneux, le plus âgé admiratif. Sous ses longs cils noirs, la jeune femme observa le commissaire aux morts étranges à la dérobée. Sa mise sobre était impeccable, ses bottes noires rutilaient et son gilet entrouvert sur le haut laissait blouser une écharpe de batiste. La minceur de Volnay, la force tranquille qui se dégageait de lui et la finesse des traits de son visage attiraient le regard des femmes. Toutefois, il était aussitôt arrêté par la froideur qui lui servait de bouclier pour se protéger des autres. Au contraire, le moine adoptait une attitude ouverte et ses yeux reflétaient une sagesse infinie.

— Vous ne m'offensez pas, dit-elle, j'ai déjà entendu bien pire.

Elle allongea négligemment une jambe et l'on devina aussitôt sous le tissu la courbure parfaite de celle-ci.

— Maintenant, je crois en Dieu, murmura le moine extasié.

Sans s'émouvoir de la remarque, Hélène lui adressa un léger sourire. À la couleur des flammes, la couleur de ses yeux avait encore changé et évoquait maintenant celle d'une prairie brûlée par l'été.

— Heureux d'entendre ça ! marmonna Sartine. Mieux vaux tard que jamais !

Il considéra le moine avec un brin d'hostilité.

— Je vous aurais plutôt cru tenté par le culte du diable !

Volnay tressaillit, l'allusion était claire. La jeune femme resta impassible mais toute son attention était concentrée sur la réponse à venir du moine. Celui-ci ne déçut pas son public.

— Contrairement aux courtisans de Versailles, fit-il froidement, je n'ai aucune attirance pour un culte qui me forcerait à baiser le cul d'autrui !

Sartine sembla prêt à exploser mais le rire frais d'Hélène s'éleva dans la pièce, dissipant toutes les tensions.

— Vous êtes tel que je l'imaginais, conclut-elle.

— Et pire encore, conclut sèchement Sartine en revêtant de nouveau son masque.

Il fit quelques pas vers la porte.

— Je vous laisse, mademoiselle. Quant à vous, messieurs, vous devrez l'écouter, répondre à toutes ses questions et la laisser vous accompagner partout où elle le désirera. Si vous ne le faites pas, je vous dessaisirai de cette enquête ! Suis-je clair ?

Il les considéra d'un air hautain. Le moine ne dit rien mais un éclair brilla dans ses yeux calmes. Volnay s'empressa d'acquiescer pour éviter un esclandre.

— Nous ferons comme vous le désirez.

Sartine parut surpris de cette reddition soudaine. Il considéra un instant le commissaire aux morts étranges d'un air soupçonneux puis tourna les talons, non sans avoir galamment salué la jeune femme. Une bourrasque glacée accompagna sa sortie. Le moine poussa un juron. Dans sa morgue, Sartine n'avait pas refermé la porte. Le commissaire aux morts étranges alla s'appuyer au battant puis se retourna et marcha lentement vers Hélène. La jeune femme le considérait, une expression énigmatique sur le visage.

— Si jeune et déjà la confiance du lieutenant général de police, murmura-t-il songeusement. Est-il possible de vous demander en quoi consistent vos fonctions auprès de M. de Sartine ?

Il se tenait parfaitement droit devant Hélène qui ne le quittait pas du regard. Ils se jaugèrent en silence.

La jeune femme eut une moue amusée.

— Bien sûr que non !

Volnay fronça les sourcils.

— Peut-être pourriez-vous alors nous aider en remettant la main sur les notes de M. de La Reynie lors de l'affaire la Voisin ?

— Pourquoi donc ? La Chambre ardente qui jugea de ces affaires fut dissoute il y a bien longtemps...

— Certes, insista le commissaire aux morts étranges, mais il est intéressant pour nous de bien connaître le sujet et savoir comment s'organisaient ces messes noires, qui elles réunissaient, comment elles se déroulaient...

Hélène hocha lentement la tête. Une mèche de ses cheveux fins tomba sur ses yeux sans qu'elle prenne la peine de l'ôter.

— Je comprends. Ce qui vous intéresse est surtout le mode opératoire. On dit que la Voisin n'était pas seulement empoisonneuse mais faiseuse d'anges. Elle utilisait le petit corps des nourrissons pour en extraire le sang, le foie et le cœur pour ses mixtures...

Le moine la contempla avec curiosité.

— Vous savez bien des choses pour une personne de votre âge.

— J'ai passé ma journée à parcourir les notes du lieutenant La Reynie, répondit-elle très naturellement !

Le moine échangea avec le commissaire un nouveau regard entendu. Qui donc dans le royaume pouvait se targuer d'avoir lu les notes de La Reynie ? Cela confirmait également que Sartine redoutait bien une nouvelle affaire...

— Ceux qui servent la messe, reprit Hélène en dardant sur eux son regard, le font pour l'argent. Ceux qui y assistent sont souvent en disgrâce et recherchent un retour de faveur de leur monarque. Vous savez comment sont les courtisans : ils ne vivent et respirent que pour être vus du roi. Seule sa lumière les éclaire. Seul son soleil les réchauffe.

— Les courtisans sont des ignares, marmonna le moine, ils ne savent que deux choses : l'heure du lever du roi et l'heure de son coucher !

Hélène le gratifia d'un sourire charmeur.

— Dites-moi, mademoiselle, demanda froidement Volnay. Êtes-vous informée de choses que M. de Sartine n'ait pas daigné porter à notre connaissance ?

La jeune femme arqua délicatement un sourcil, semblant peser sa réponse à l'aide d'une toile d'araignée.

— À ma connaissance, non, répondit-elle enfin d'un ton neutre. Ceci dit, il est tout à fait possible que le lieutenant général de police ait omis de me faire part de certaines données du problème s'il les juge confidentielles…

Le commissaire aux morts étranges daigna enfin lui accorder un hochement de tête approbateur.

— Et peut-on savoir quelles sont les compétences que le lieutenant général de police Sartine vous prête ?

— Eh bien…

Elle s'interrompit pour réfléchir.

— Je sais monter à cheval, tirer au pistolet, me battre à l'épée et à la dague. Je m'intéresse aux mathématiques, je connais le nom de toutes les étoiles dans le ciel. Je parle également anglais, italien, allemand, latin, grec et araméen…

Le moine haussa un sourcil intéressé et la complimenta.

— C'est très bien, mademoiselle.

— Ce n'est pas tout…

— Oui ? fit-il.

— Je suis un peu sorcière !

Il y eut un silence stupéfait puis le moine partit d'un grand éclat de rire.

— J'adore, j'adore !

Volnay fit un pas en avant.

— Où avez-vous appris tout cela ? On n'apprend guère ces choses-là aux jeunes filles.

Le moine intervint.

— Étiez-vous au couvent pour apprendre ces langues ? À celui de la Madeleine de Traisnel par exemple ?

Hélène eut un rire moqueur.

— C'est un couvent à la mode mais on n'y forme que des coquettes. Est-ce que je leur ressemble donc ? Danser, chanter et jouer de l'épinette, voilà ce que l'on apprend à ces charmantes cervelles d'oiseau, soit dit, monsieur, sans vouloir offenser votre pie !

La jeune femme fit une pause songeuse.

— On ne veut pas que les femmes apprennent, on leur enseigne simplement comment avoir l'air de tout savoir sans rien connaître. Des serins, voilà ce qu'on en fait, des serins dans une cage.

Elle se tourna vers Volnay pour ajouter du même ton :

— Soit dit, monsieur, toujours sans vouloir offenser votre oiseau en cage !

Et, comme pour se faire pardonner, elle se leva pour aller lisser les plumes de la pie qui se mit à jacasser bruyamment. Le père et le fils s'entreregardèrent. En quelques minutes, Hélène venait de faire exploser la condition féminine soumise de leur siècle et reculer les limites de la pensée.

Elle ressemble à Chiara, faillit dire le moine mais il se retint justement pour ne pas raviver le chagrin d'amour de son fils. Chiara avait regagné ses terres de Toscane depuis six mois et, si son fils en recevait des nouvelles, il ne lui en parlait pas.

— Si l'on en revient à l'affaire des Poisons, poursuivit Hélène d'un ton soigneusement neutre, il est clair que Louis XIV ne pouvait se permettre de voir sa favorite, la Montespan, accusée de tels crimes. La crainte du scandale était trop forte. Et puis, il lui aurait été humiliant de reconnaître ainsi s'être autant trompé sur le compte de sa maîtresse. Par orgueil, il ne l'a même pas disgraciée et se comporta comme si elle était innocente de tout, continuant à lui rendre visite chaque jour pour donner le change.

— J'ignore si au cours de ces entrevues, ce bon Roi-Soleil lui parlait des nourrissons égorgés pendant les messes noires, grommela le moine.

Le commissaire aux morts étranges jeta un bref coup d'œil à la jeune femme, elle ne semblait pas désarçonnée ni surprise de la tournure de cette conversation. Le policier jugea toutefois bon de clore cette discussion qui pouvait s'avérer dangereuse devant une inconnue.

— Louis XIV comprit le danger de toutes ces révélations et se hâta d'ordonner la clôture de la procédure, dit-il. Grâce à cela, la majorité des suspects ou accusés s'en sortit à bon compte.

— Les rois sont sans morale et sans viscères, conclut le moine.

Hélène le considéra longuement et avec intérêt. Le commissaire aux morts étranges frémit. Le moine parlait trop et disait à n'importe qui ce qu'il pensait. Certains allaient en prison pour de telles paroles et il ne se passait pas une semaine sans que Volnay ne tremble pour son père. Comme si elle avait compris l'inquiétude du commissaire aux morts étranges, la jeune femme se tourna vers lui.

— Rassurez-vous, je ne suis pas ici pour vous espionner et rapporter vos paroles à M. de Sartine. Je suis là pour vous aider.

Elle se pencha vers le moine.

— Je suppose que le cadavre de la jeune morte est dans votre cave ?

Il hocha lentement la tête sans la quitter des yeux.

— Je voudrais la voir.

— J'ai fait des dessins d'elle, ils sont très ressemblants, intervint le commissaire aux morts étranges.

Hélène ne releva même pas.

— Rien ne remplace un visage que l'on voit en face et il ne faut pas trop attendre, non ?

Le moine pâlit légèrement.

— Est-ce bien utile ?

Elle se raidit.

— Je pense que ma requête n'a rien d'exagéré. Vous m'avez accepté dans votre enquête devant M. de Sartine. Respectez-en les conditions et tout ira bien. Écartez-vous-en d'un pas et il vous en cuira !

III

LE MOINE, LA FEMME
ET AUTRES DIABLERIES

Les derniers lambeaux de jour disparaissaient lorsque le moine et la jeune femme arrivèrent rue de la Lanterne, pataugeant dans une bouillasse froide qui macula de traces grises les jolies bottes couleur crème d'Hélène. La bise transformait l'air en mille aiguilles acérées. Ils s'engouffrèrent en toute hâte dans l'impasse du Loup-Pendu.

— J'ai emménagé là récemment, expliqua le moine, pour me rapprocher de mon... du commissaire aux morts étranges. Cela facilite la vie et puis je dispose ici d'une double cave très fraîche et servie par deux escaliers dont l'un donne directement dans ma chambre. C'est d'un pratique ! Enfin, je peux conserver plusieurs jours dans ces caves les cadavres dans de bonnes conditions.

Sortant son trousseau de clés, il introduisit la plus grosse dans la serrure de la porte. Celle-ci était en chêne, épaisse et cloutée, renforcée d'acier. Une porte difficile à enfoncer, jugea Hélène. Le propriétaire des lieux était de toute évidence soit prudent, soit méfiant, l'un n'empêchant d'ailleurs pas l'autre.

Les restes d'un feu agonisaient dans une vaste cheminée de marbre rouge du Languedoc. Le moine raviva les flammes et alluma suffisamment de chandelles pour chasser la pénombre de la pièce. Les rideaux de serge cramoisie étaient tirés. Près du feu, une belle table à écrire en palissandre, recouverte de papiers, trahissait le goût du propriétaire des lieux pour la plume. Au mur, des tableaux sur toile ou des estampes sous verre reproduisaient des sujets galants plaisamment exécutés. Bergers et bergères s'y livraient au délicieux jeu de l'aveu des sentiments mais, parfois, des personnages aux allures de courtisans affichaient plus nettement leurs désirs en semblant réclamer leur dû à leurs compagnes. Une tapisserie en chiné flambé couvrait le mur au nord et une bordure de bois doré surmontait la porte d'une pièce attenante, qui devait être la chambre. Au sud, se trouvait une cuisine où les plantes aromatiques grimpaient jusqu'aux casseroles de cuivre.

Tout indiquait l'aisance, un goût pour le beau et une certaine légèreté. Les yeux d'Hélène glissèrent sur un tableau représentant un groupe de jeunes gens égarés dans un parc boisé. Selon l'humeur de celui qui le contemplait, il invitait soit à la gaieté, soit à la mélancolie. Un couple d'amoureux s'en allait au hasard d'une allée, bras dessus, bras dessous, gracieux et fragile à la fois. Le regard dur et attentif d'un homme tout de noir vêtu les suivait. D'autres personnes venaient peupler le tableau de leur jeunesse et de leur insouciance. Mais, à bien y regarder, les têtes penchées, les regards en biais et les corps tendus semblaient signaler les tensions exacerbées de relations amoureuses complexes. Hélène remarqua alors que, dans ce tableau, tout était fait pour cacher le véritable sujet de celui-ci. Sur un tapis d'herbe verte, un jeune homme s'emparait de la main d'une adolescente à la nuque exquise. La posture du buste de celle-ci dénotait un mouvement de recul mais il se pouvait bien que ce retrait ne fût que feint car la main de son compagnon n'enserrait guère sa taille élancée. Un instant, elle crut saisir dans le profil du jeune homme qui guidait sa compagne les traits du moine moins âgé.

La jeune femme s'attarda devant le tableau mais le moine ne semblait pas désireux de commenter cette peinture. Il entraîna la visiteuse à sa suite jusque dans la seconde cave et souleva la lourde couverture qui la recouvrait.

— Voici donc notre jeune morte, fit Hélène d'un ton détaché une fois devant le cadavre. C'est étrange, on dirait qu'elle dort…

Elle l'examina avec curiosité mais sans s'en approcher et se retourna vers le moine.

— Que faites-vous avec les corps que l'on vous amène ?

Le moine haussa un sourcil.

— Que voulez-vous donc que j'en fasse ? J'examine la température et la couleur du corps, la rigidité ou la flexibilité des membres, l'état des yeux et de la mâchoire, l'enflure, la bouffissure, l'engorgement des voies, l'état des sphincters, les taches, les ecchymoses, les plaies, les ulcères, les fractures, luxations, hernies, chutes, écoulement du sang et autres liquides de la bouche du nez ou des oreilles, voire de l'anus et du vagin…

Il avait une voix chaude aux accents calmes et cultivés, un ton aux nuances élégantes. Devant elle, il débordait d'une vie insolente. Elle l'écoutait avec attention, une lueur d'admiration dans le regard. Le moine s'en aperçut et conclut modestement mais théâtralement :

— En bref, je regarde tout ce qui peut paraître s'éloigner d'un état normal et régulier.

Inclinant la tête, elle le récompensa d'un sourire éclatant.

— J'admire votre science nouvelle, fit-elle.

Le moine se rengorgea.

— Ce n'est rien, j'ai toujours été en avance sur mon époque mais je n'ai guère de mérite à cela car elle est en retard sur tout !

Un rire cristallin jaillit de la gorge d'Hélène. Elle balaya la pièce du regard et s'approcha d'une table d'expérience dans la première cave.

— Oh, qu'est-ce que ceci ? Quel étrange appareil !

— Il s'agit d'un microscope composé, il a été inventé en 1590 par Zacharias Jansen. La version que vous voyez est plus évoluée et doit beaucoup aux travaux de Robert Hooke au siècle dernier. Ces combinaisons complexes de lentilles, soigneusement polies, permettent un agrandissement jusqu'à trois cents fois la taille initiale mais je pense que l'on peut faire mieux !

— Trois cents fois ! Comment est-ce possible ?

— Grâce à la science… Cela me permet d'étudier tous les indices trouvés sur une scène de crime.

— Et qu'examinez-vous aujourd'hui ?

Le moine se mordit les lèvres. Il s'agissait du fil de laine découvert ce matin même par son fils sur les lieux du crime.

— Une expérience que je mène sur les tissus, répondit-il avec aplomb. Mais ceci est peu de chose. Donnez-moi votre main !

Elle le regarda droit dans les yeux puis se déganta avec lenteur. Le moine frissonna intérieurement. En ôtant son gant, Hélène donnait l'impression de retirer un vêtement. Enfin, elle lui tendit une main souple et tiède, aux doigts longs et déliés. Le moine retira le fil de laine et attira l'index de la jeune femme à sa place.

— Mettez votre œil à cette extrémité. Vous voyez les sillons imprimés sur le bout de vos doigts. Voilà, c'est encore mieux qu'une empreinte de pas ! Je travaille à produire une substance qui permette de relever les empreintes laissées par les doigts sur les lieux du crime. Une fois un suspect arrêté, je pourrai ainsi lui prendre une empreinte en mettant son doigt dans de l'encre puis sur un papier ou simplement sur une plaque de verre comme celle-ci. Ensuite, je comparerai les deux empreintes.

— Admirable ! Encore faut-il que vous attrapiez le bon suspect !

— Pas forcément, songez que je peux aussi innocenter celui-ci ! Tenez, regardez !

Il s'empara d'une petite plaque en verre et y posa son index qu'il pressa fortement.

— Faites de même.

Hélène s'exécuta non sans hésitation.

— Parfait !

Il plaça la plaquette de verre à la place du morceau d'étoffe.

— Maintenant regardez…

Elle colla l'œil à la lunette et poussa une brève exclamation de surprise.

— Oh, comme c'est intéressant ! Elles sont très différentes et donc…

— Vous avez bien deviné. L'empreinte de nos doigts révèle nos identités. Un jour, sur les lieux de crime, on relèvera ces empreintes pour les comparer à toutes celles des criminels que l'on possède déjà !

— Vous êtes décidément très savant, fit-elle.

Le moine dissimula sa satisfaction derrière un grognement modeste.

— Une seule chose m'inquiète : il faudra beaucoup de plaquettes de verre et bien les étiqueter !

La jeune femme lui décocha un regard irrésistible.

— Vous trouverez bien un moyen…

Il hocha la tête.

— Sûrement, mais dans une prochaine vie ! Les chats en ont bien sept. Pourquoi le moine n'en aurait-il pas deux ou trois ?

À nouveau, Hélène reprit sa marche dans le laboratoire. Du fait de la présence des cadavres, le moine avait éteint la plupart des fourneaux mais certains recélaient encore bien des merveilles en train de cuire.

— M. de Sartine prétend que vous recherchez le secret de l'immortelle jeunesse…

— Comme tout le monde, mademoiselle, comme tout le monde…

— Si vous le trouvez, faites-moi signe, cela m'intéresse !

— Je vous ferai un prix d'ami !

Hélène s'immobilisa devant une masse qui révélait les contours d'un corps humain. Le moine fronça les sourcils. Sous la toile qui le recouvrait, se trouvait le cadavre du gardien de cimetière.

— Qui avez-vous donc là ? demanda-t-elle négligemment.

— Oh, un de mes paroissiens de passage, répondit-il sans rire. Je fais chambre d'hôte parfois…

Tout sourire s'effaça du visage de la jeune femme.

— Ne serait-ce pas plutôt le corps du gardien de cimetière que vous avez fait enlever à l'aube en sa demeure, l'arrachant à sa veuve éplorée, avec deux exempts du Châtelet ?

Ah diable, pensa le moine, *il faut que j'arrête de sous-estimer cette jeune dame sous prétexte qu'elle est jolie !*

— Si fait, mademoiselle, si fait…

— Et qu'avez-vous découvert ?

Elle s'était approchée du corps et sa main effleurait le drap qui le recouvrait.

— Mort de peur, dit rapidement le moine.

D'un coup sec, elle arracha le drap et se pencha sur l'homme.

— Moi, je dirais plutôt mort congestionné, fit-elle calmement.

— Vraiment?

Le moine s'était approché.

— Oh, vous avez raison, fit-il en se penchant à son tour, j'ai dû mal regarder dans la pénombre!

Le visage attentif d'Hélène se trouvait à quelques centimètres du sien, au-dessus du cadavre. D'un coup son parfum l'envahit. Il exhalait les senteurs de bien des choses oubliées comme la sensualité de l'ambre, la mélancolie de la rose, la fraîcheur de la fougère… Sans modifier sa position, la jeune femme se tourna lentement vers lui.

— Et si nous faisions la paix pour vraiment travailler ensemble? fit-elle en articulant chaque syllabe.

Il la considéra, fasciné par les paillettes dorées qui s'agitaient dans ses prunelles.

— J'en serais ravi, répondit-il rapidement. Cet homme a été étouffé.

Elle hocha la tête.

— Il a dû surprendre les célébrants de la messe noire…

— Sans doute et ceux-ci ont pensé à l'étouffer plutôt que l'étrangler afin de ne pas laisser de marques! Surprenant, non?!

— Ils ont beaucoup de sang-froid.

— Il en faut pour tuer une enfant!

Un courant d'air glacé entra par une lucarne et balaya la pièce. Il sentit la jeune femme frissonner.

— Vous allez prendre la mort ici, dit le moine d'un ton paternel. Montons, je vais vous préparer une boisson chaude. Nous deviserons ensuite plus confortablement.

Un sourire mutin passa sur les traits d'Hélène.

— Et de quoi allons-nous parler, monsieur l'érudit?

Le moine rabattit d'un geste sec le drap.

— De vous, voyons!

Quelques instants plus tard, il s'effaça pour la laisser entrer dans la pièce qui lui servait à la fois de salon et de cuisine. Elle passa devant lui en l'effleurant. Le même parfum chaud d'herbes et de fleurs sauvages émanait d'elle, rehaussé par l'ambre gris. Sans fébrilité, le moine en huma l'arôme avec reconnaissance comme on respire un bouquet fraîchement cueilli.

Hélène fit le tour de la pièce, s'attardant au passage devant le clavecin dont ses doigts effleurèrent les touches.

— Savez-vous jouer? demanda-t-elle.

Le visage du moine se ferma.

— Non, il appartenait à ma femme avant sa mort.

— Oh, je vous demande pardon.

— Elle jouait divinement, continua-t-il comme s'il n'avait pas entendu. Elle chantait aussi. Un ange n'aurait pas chanté mieux qu'elle.

Il y eut un silence profond que le moine rompit le premier.

— On gèle ici, je vais rallumer le feu.

Habilement, il raviva le foyer jusqu'à ce qu'une langue de flamme vînt lécher les bûches sèches rajoutées. Puis il approcha de la cheminée un grand fauteuil aux coussins rembourrés et moelleux.

— Prenez place, je vous en prie.

Elle s'assit avec un soupir d'aise puis contempla ses pieds d'un air désolé.

— J'ai marché dans la neige et mes pieds sont trempés, se plaignit-elle. Mes bottes étaient trop fines. Voulez-vous bien m'aider à les retirer?

Le moine acquiesça gravement et mit un genou à terre. Sans hésiter, elle lui tendit un pied botté en le regardant droit dans les yeux. Les doigts du moine flânèrent un instant, caressant le cuir mouillé.

— Il faudrait les huiler, remarqua-t-il d'un ton neutre.

Il tira lentement, surpris par la douceur inattendue du cuir et la facilité avec laquelle le pied glissa hors de la botte. Une cheville gainée de soie apparut. Le moine la tint un instant entre ses mains avant de poser délicatement le pied à terre.

La jeune femme lui tendit alors de manière très naturelle son autre pied botté. Le moine cilla brièvement et renouvela l'opération mais cette fois il garda quelques secondes de plus la cheville légère de la jeune femme comme pour mieux en examiner les contours fragiles.

Hélène resta immobile et silencieuse mais un frisson la parcourut. Le moine se releva et fit un pas en arrière. S'il était troublé, il se gardait de le montrer.

— Il vous faut ingurgiter quelque chose de chaud et de consistant tout à la fois car je suppose que vous n'avez pas soupé.

— Vous supposez bien.

— Je vais d'abord vous chercher une couverture.

Il revint bientôt avec une étoffe de laine. La jeune femme se pelotonna sur les coussins réchauffés par les flammes et s'enroula sans mot dire dans la couverture, ne laissant dépasser que ses pieds posés près de l'âtre de la cheminée. Le moine s'émut devant ce tableau mais n'en oublia pas pour autant de poser les interrogations qui l'agitaient.

— Je me pose beaucoup de questions depuis la venue de Sartine. Que le lieutenant général de police s'intéresse assez à cette affaire pour nous dépêcher un de ses plus précieux agents révèle qu'il est effrayé.

— C'est bien essayé mais qui vous dit que je suis un de ses plus précieux agents ? rétorqua-t-elle. Enfin, toujours est-il que Sartine craint une résurgence du culte satanique.

— Sartine raisonne juste et carré comme une flûte, se moqua le moine, et il n'ose éternuer de peur de péter !

— Que voulez-vous dire par là ?

— Sartine est prudent, dans cette affaire, il n'y va que d'une fesse…

— Il m'a prévenue contre vous…

— Vous m'en direz tant !

Un silence puis le moine demanda avec un brin de dureté dans la voix :

— Mais pourquoi me le dites-vous ?

La jeune femme se leva et, ses pieds chaussés de bas, glissa sans bruit vers le feu.

— M. de Sartine dit ce qu'il veut et moi je me fais mon opinion par moi-même. Comme vous, monsieur, je n'ai ni dieu, ni maître, ni tribun.

Un sourire éclaira son visage et elle poursuivit :

— "Faute de savoir ce qui est écrit là-haut, on ne sait ni ce qu'on veut, ni ce qu'on fait et on suit sa fantaisie qu'on appelle raison ou sa raison qui n'est souvent qu'une dangereuse fantaisie qui tourne tantôt bien, tantôt mal…"

Le moine applaudit chaleureusement.

— Diderot ! Vous choisissez bien vos auteurs !

Il se dirigea vers un coin de la cuisine garni de plantes séchées : feuilles de laurier, bouquets de thym ou de persil, sauge, cerfeuil ou ciboule. Rangés en colonnes conquérantes sur les étagères, les bocaux recélaient des trésors aromatiques : poivre, mélisse, clous de girofle, cannelle ou coriandre. D'un panier d'osier dépassaient quelques légumes un peu ratatinés. Il en choisit plusieurs avec soin puis décrocha du mur une casserole de cuivre

— Voyez, fit-il en versant délicatement le vin de Bourgogne, c'est un plat simple, mais délicieux. Après avoir fait revenir ces choux rouges avec du bouillon, deux quartiers de pomme de reinette séchée et un oignon, je rajoute un verre de vin rouge par chou.

Avec un sourire un peu forcé, il ajouta :

— C'est un plat de pauvre mais je l'ai moi-même été trop souvent et ma soif de liberté fait que je terminerai certainement ma vie dans cette condition.

— Vous êtes pourtant d'une haute lignée, remarqua-t-elle négligemment.

Le moine tressaillit légèrement.

— Vous êtes décidément bien renseignée et bien surprenante car vous ne me cachez rien de ce que vous savez.

— Pourquoi en serait-il autrement ?

— Parce que vous travaillez pour Sartine et que c'est un fourbe.

— Vous ne devriez pas toujours dire ce que vous pensez, lui reprocha-t-elle d'un ton doux. Cela a déjà causé votre malheur par le passé…

— Ce n'est pas ma façon de penser qui a fait mon malheur, rétorqua-t-il, mais la façon de penser des autres.

— Certes.

— Tenez, par exemple, un jour j'écrivis dans un de mes livres : *Je crois en moi, le reste, je vérifie.* Cela parut comme une attaque contre Dieu et l'Église.

J'aurais dû écrire pour être tranquille : *Je crois en Dieu, le reste, je vérifie !*

Pendant qu'ils parlaient, le moine s'affairait comme à son habitude et un parfum délicieux se répandit dans la maison. Il avait rajouté deux bûches dans la cheminée et un feu d'enfer crépitait mais le froid était tel dehors que la température était encore très basse dans la maison.

— Voilà, c'est prêt. Je vous l'apporte.

Silencieusement, ils savourèrent le met puis la jeune femme soupira.

— Il est tard, il me faut rentrer dormir si je veux vous accompagner demain dans votre enquête.

— C'est la pleine nuit, protesta le moine. Les rues ne sont pas sûres. Nous passerons chez le chevalier de Volnay et nous vous escorterons jusque chez vous.

— C'est bien aimable à vous mais je ne crains pas les rues de Paris la nuit.

— Je n'aime guère cette mode actuelle des masques, remarqua le moine, une jolie femme comme vous, seule de surcroît, sera immanquablement importunée par de jeunes gens ivres. Je refuse de vous laisser aller seule.

Elle le fixa un long instant.

— Eh bien soit, j'attendrai le jour ici. Ce fauteuil et cette étoffe sont très confortables. Remettez quelques bûches dans l'âtre et je passerai une nuit merveilleuse.

— Je peux vous proposer un lit dans ma chambre, je prendrai le fauteuil.

— Le fauteuil me convient, fit-elle d'un ton définitif.

Le moine sembla réfléchir.

— Je vais vous préparer une tisane pour vous délasser, fit-il enfin. Je possède le secret des herbes qui détendent les nerfs.

Des guirlandes d'herbes aromatiques et odorantes pendaient du plafond comme les tresses de la chevelure d'une fée. Il en sélectionna quelques-unes avec précaution et les mit à infuser.

Étrangement, quelques minutes après l'avoir bue, la voix d'Hélène se fit plus faible puis elle ferma les yeux. Le moine la contempla à la lumière vacillante de l'âtre. Une douce lassitude semblait la saisir à la chaleur des flammes. Le moine attendit encore quelques instants avant qu'elle ne s'endorme puis se leva.

— Allons, au travail ! murmura-t-il pour lui-même.

Et il se mit à la fouiller.

Assis en silence sur un tabouret, le moine contemplait Hélène endormie. Son air oscillait entre le doute et l'attendrissement, admirant les traits purs du visage, les longs cils noirs et sa chevelure qui alternait d'une mèche à l'autre entre le brun et le roux. La jeune femme ne dormait pas paisiblement. Son sommeil était agité et ses lèvres s'entrouvraient parfois pour laisser échapper des mots inaudibles mais qui semblaient exprimer la peur et le désarroi. Intrigué, le moine se penchait alors pour écouter mais n'y entendait rien comme si elle parlait en dormant dans une langue qui lui était inconnue même si les consonances appartenaient sans doute aux pays d'au-delà de la mer.

À cet instant, un souffle glacé glissa entre ses chevilles et la réveilla. Elle ouvrit un œil. Le commissaire aux morts étranges refermait la porte derrière lui.

— Que se passe-t-il ? demanda-t-elle d'une voix ensommeillée.

— C'est le petit matin, dit calmement Volnay.

Il dissimulait sa surprise. Pourquoi la jeune femme avait-elle passé la nuit ici?

Comme le froid avait envahi la pièce, il s'accroupit près de la cheminée. Les braises luisaient faiblement, quelqu'un avait manifestement alimenté le feu pendant la nuit. Il jeta un regard soupçonneux au moine immobile sur son tabouret et entreprit de tisonner avant de rajouter une bûche. Lorsque les flammes claires s'élevèrent, il se redressa et tendit ses mains au-dessus de l'âtre pour se réchauffer.

— Avez-vous un peu d'eau pour ma toilette? demanda Hélène en quittant son fauteuil.

Elle réajusta autour d'elle les plis froissés de sa robe.

— Je vais vous en apporter dans ma chambre après l'avoir tiédie, répondit galamment le moine en se levant.

La cheminée était garnie de crochets et d'une crémaillère. Il versa dans celle-ci un broc d'eau.

— Cela sera bientôt prêt, lança-t-il avec enthousiasme.

Son fils leva les yeux au ciel avant de se plonger dans la contemplation des flammes. Il ne s'en tira que lorsque l'eau fut chaude et la porte de la chambre refermée derrière Hélène. Alors, le moine se glissa près de lui.

— Hier soir, chuchota-t-il, je lui ai donné une tisane de mon invention. Elle s'est endormie comme un bébé et j'ai pu la fouiller sans la réveiller.

— Oh!

À l'évidence, le procédé choquait le commissaire aux morts étranges.

— Ne t'inquiète pas, précisa le moine en se méprenant, c'était en tout bien tout honneur. Je n'ai pas l'intention de lui montrer mon goupillon!

— Je l'espère bien, fit sèchement son fils, quoique je ne comprenne pas le pourquoi de cet acte.

Son père se permit un sourire amusé.

— Une jeune femme d'une beauté sauvage est introduite par Sartine dans notre duo d'enquêteurs. Te jugeant imperméable à sa séduction, elle s'en prend à moi. Tu aurais vu la manière dont elle m'a demandé de la déchausser !

— Elle t'a demandé de la déchausser ?! s'exclama Volnay.

— Oui, sous prétexte d'avoir les pieds mouillés. Bref, des regards de braise, des compliments... j'ai beau avoir ma vanité, j'ai l'âge que j'ai et je sais pertinemment que cette jeune beauté veut avant tout assujettir son pouvoir sur moi. Pourquoi ? Eh bien je pensais le découvrir en fouillant ses affaires.

— Et tu n'as rien trouvé, conclut froidement Volnay.

— Rien à part une amulette qu'elle porte au cou et une dague bien aiguisée ! L'amulette est une pierre de bénédiction, appelée *abraxas*, très prisée en Égypte ou en Perse. Tout cela n'est pas normal ! Et que dire de ce pied mignon qu'elle m'a fourré dans les mains...

— Calme-toi, dit froidement son fils. Elle n'a pas la moitié de ton âge.

— Mais elle n'est pas moitié moins savante que moi ! Elle a dit à un moment qu'elle parlait araméen.

— Et alors ? fit son fils qui ne voyait pas le rapport.

— L'araméen était une langue apparentée à l'hébreu, celle des tribus nomades de la Chaldée, avant de s'imposer comme la langue administrative de l'Empire babylonien puis de l'Empire perse jusqu'en Égypte. Elle avait supplanté l'hébreu en Israël avant Jésus-Christ, lequel Jésus prêchait également en araméen.

Il se tut un instant et chuchota comme pour lui-même :

— Mais qui parle encore l'araméen de nos jours ?

Ses épaules se voûtèrent légèrement. Il se pencha en avant comme pour prêcher mais en fait il se parlait à lui-même. Longtemps seul en prison, le moine avait pris cette habitude de confronter ses opinions à haute voix avec quelque double de lui-même qu'il se créait. Il sembla ainsi avoir oublié la présence de son fils pourtant attentif.

— En dormant, elle parlait dans une langue qui m'est inconnue mais dont les racines me semblent familières. Or seul notre non-conscient s'exprime lorsque l'on dort. Cela signifierait-il qu'elle parlait dans sa langue natale ?

— Quel est ce non-conscient dont tu parles ? demanda Volnay.

Les yeux du moine pétillèrent de malice.

— Oh, c'est une théorie à moi qui m'écarte quelque peu de mon cher Aristote ! Lorsque nous sommes éveillés, notre conscience l'est également, tu es d'accord ? Et lorsque nous dormons elle ne l'est plus. Or nos rêves sont toujours riches de sens. Conclusion : nous possédons une conscience non éveillée en nous !

Le commissaire aux morts étranges haussa légèrement les épaules.

— C'est une théorie intéressante mais ce n'est pas dans le sommeil que je mène mes enquêtes.

— Tu as tort, l'activité de veille de l'esprit alors que notre corps est inerte pourrait te surprendre ! Et qui pourrait diriger cette veille, sinon notre cerveau ? Un cerveau alors débarrassé de toutes nos petites limites et du pitoyable carcan de nos règles… Rends-toi compte que le sommeil est le seul moment de notre vie où nous n'avons de compte à rendre ni à notre conscience, ni à notre raison. Le rêve est alors comme un enfant que ses parents ne surveillent plus !

Ses yeux étincelaient et il en sautillait sur place d'excitation.

— Bref, reprit le moine en voyant le désintérêt de son fils, je pense que la nuit, l'esprit d'Hélène la ramène à une époque de son enfance. Cela ne t'arrive jamais ?

Volnay pâlit imperceptiblement.

— Je n'ai pas le temps de rêver, moi ! répondit-il sévèrement. Et je n'en ai pas plus pour découvrir qui est cette femme. C'est une espionne de Sartine et nous n'avons pas d'autre choix que de l'associer à notre enquête puisque telle est la volonté du lieutenant général de police ! De toute façon, si elle n'était pas là, Sartine nous ferait suivre et espionner par ses mouches. Au moins, nous aurons moins de monde sur nos talons !

Il s'interrompit car la porte de la chambre venait de s'ouvrir et la jeune femme réapparut. Si elle avait entendu leur conversation, elle n'en laissait rien paraître.

— Avez-vous du nouveau ? s'enquit-elle.

— Oui, répondit froidement le commissaire aux morts étranges. J'ai demandé que les procureurs et les commissaires de quartier me signalent toutes les disparitions de jeunes filles dans la semaine qui a précédé le meurtre. J'ai ainsi appris à l'aube qu'il y avait eu trois disparitions. Couvrez-vous chaudement, nous sortons ! Notre victime est peut-être l'une d'elles !

IV

JEUNES FILLES DISPARUES
ET AUTRES DIABLERIES

Dehors, le froid les saisit de plein fouet. Le moine battit des bras pour se réchauffer et tomba en arrêt devant le chien.

— Bonjour toi !

Volnay le rejoignit.

— Ce chien me suit depuis hier. Il est vrai que je lui ai donné à manger…

Hélène lui jeta un regard surpris. Le moine s'en aperçut et rit.

— Eh oui, fit-il, notre commissaire aux morts étranges n'est pas aussi insensible qu'il veut bien le laisser paraître !

La ville ne se déclinait plus qu'aux couleurs blanches et grises de l'hiver. Dans le ciel bas, les fumées des cheminées se tordaient au-dessus des toits comme de gigantesques serpents cherchant à étrangler leurs proies. Ils commencèrent par l'adresse la plus proche et remontèrent la rue de Saint-Yon pour gagner la rue Saint-Jacques peuplée d'échoppes de libraires, de graveurs et de marchands d'estampes. La proximité de la Sorbonne avait conduit ces professions ainsi que de nombreux imprimeurs à s'y installer.

La neige semblait avoir enveloppé les rues d'une ouate feutrée. Seuls résonnaient dans l'air froid le carillon des cloches des églises environnantes et les jurons des voituriers. Ils passèrent devant l'échoppe d'un écrivain public qui tenta de leur vendre une lettre d'amour pour cinq sous puis devant l'étal odorant d'une marchande de beignets.

— Gare dessous ! cria une voix au-dessus d'eux.

Ils évitèrent de justesse le contenu du seau d'excréments destiné à évacuer les besoins de toute une maisonnée. Bientôt, Volnay désigna la devanture d'une librairie.

— Ce doit être celle-ci car il est indiqué dans le rapport de police qu'elle se trouve entre deux échoppes de graveur.

Le commissaire aux morts étranges poussa la porte. Il régnait dans la boutique une ambiance studieuse, presque austère. Les rayons étaient garnis de livres soigneusement rangés. Même le comptoir en était encombré. Une paire de bésicles sur le nez, un homme vint à leur rencontre. Son regard se porta sur le moine qui, pour lutter contre le froid, avait passé sur ses épaules une peau de loup. Cela lui donnait avec sa bure un air étrange, presque sauvage, même s'il gardait aux lèvres un sourire aimable.

Le libraire s'exprimait dans un langage très châtié et avec un brin de suffisance. La communauté des libraires et des imprimeurs se réduisait à quelques centaines de membres. Pour y entrer, on devait suivre des études classiques, certifiées par le recteur, et réussir un examen professionnel devant un jury de la chambre royale et syndicale, rue du Foin-Saint-Jacques. Attachées à l'université, ces professions en étaient d'autant plus considérées. Le commissaire aux morts étranges lui présenta sans succès le portrait de la jeune fille morte dans le cimetière et ils quittèrent le pauvre père désemparé.

Hiver comme été, toute une foule d'oisifs, de rentiers ou de domestiques se pressait en course dans tout Paris. La ville regroupait six cent mille âmes et amenait de France ou d'Europe tous ceux attirés par ce qui brillait. Dans les rues commerçantes, le parcours devenait éprouvant au milieu de la foule et sur le sol gelé. Un jeune voiturier avec une charrette à bras leur proposa de prendre la jeune femme. Volnay et son père se mirent donc à marcher de part et d'autre du véhicule qui creusait deux sillons noirs dans la neige fraîche.

Un monde équivoque et bigarré se pressait autour d'eux. Les voix aigres des crieurs perçaient parfois le brouhaha de la foule. À travers celle-ci, des porteurs d'eau se faufilaient avec adresse sans perdre une goutte de leur précieux liquide. Les vinettiers vendaient leur piquette à la pinte et les coupeurs de bourse les frôlaient dangereusement. Le moine en attrapa un, la main dans la poche de son fils.

— Le cou te démange à ce point que tu veux être pendu, grommela-t-il au mécréant, ou bien as-tu simplement besoin de te faire allonger la colonne ?

Il le repoussa brutalement et l'autre s'empressa de déguerpir. De sa voiture, Hélène avait suivi la scène avec attention.

— Quel curieux policier que celui qui laisse s'enfuir les voleurs, se moqua-t-elle.

— Je ne suis pas chargé de serrer ceux qui volent pour manger, répondit froidement le commissaire aux morts étranges.

Le moine intervint avec philosophie.

— Voyez-vous, jeune dame, le problème de ce royaume est que ses ressources sont grandes mais ses bénéficiaires peu nombreux !

Et il ajouta sans rire :

— Nous en tenons compte dans nos interventions !

Ils poursuivirent leur chemin en se protégeant des jets de déjection sous les étages en saillie de maisons biscornues. Le nom de certains endroits témoignait à lui seul de l'état de saleté dans lequel ceux-ci se trouvaient : rue Merdière, Pipi, Merderon… En chemin, le moine tira plusieurs fois sa bourse pour des enfants ou des femmes, gueux comme des rats d'église, qui mendiaient. Hélène lui en fit compliment.

— Ce n'est rien, répondit-il modestement, c'est l'argent de Sartine !

— Il est bien employé mais il ne suffira pas.

Le moine s'arrêta de marcher.

— Peu importe, mademoiselle. Je porte un amour fraternel à toutes les classes de la société et plus particulièrement à celles qui souffrent.

Ils se rangèrent pour laisser passer un convoi funèbre au corbillard timbré aux armes d'une grande maison. Les chevaux caparaçonnés de noir et de moire d'argent marchaient d'un pas lourd et pesant, suivi de carrosses drapés de voiles sombres. Les passants se signèrent. Une femme cria parce qu'on lui écrasait les pieds. On crut qu'il s'agissait d'un vol à la tire et il y eut de dangereux mouvements de foule car, instinctivement, celle-ci se pressait alors aux trousses du voleur jusqu'à l'attraper. On appelait cela les arrestations *à la clameur publique*.

Le voiturier les tira de cet embarras en empruntant une petite rue moins fréquentée, seulement peuplée de badauds frileux ou de poissonniers qui hurlaient pour avertir les gens de l'arrivée de leur marchandise. Sur les marches gelées des églises dormaient ou mouraient de pauvres hères.

Dans une pierre dure incorporée à la façade de la première et dernière maison de chaque rue étaient gravés le nom de celle-ci et le numéro du quartier. Mais aucune maison ne possédait de numéro propre et le commissaire aux morts étranges questionnait les passants et se guidait par rapport aux indications soigneusement notées par le greffier : enseignes de commerçants ou d'auberges, églises, fresque, statue… Volnay connaissait un huissier qui avait ainsi erré une journée entière avant de trouver sa destination.

Arrivés devant la menuiserie recherchée, ils congédièrent le voiturier après rétribution et entrèrent dans une cour de terre battue entourée de maisons hautes qui la privait presque entièrement de lumière. Des monceaux de planches de bois l'encombraient. Quelques enfants sales et dépenaillés jouaient avec des clous à même la terre gelée. Sabots aux pieds, une femme au visage grêlé s'employait à faire sa lessive dans une auge, les doigts gourds de froid. Sourcils et barbe gris, vêtu d'un habit râpé et de bas rapetassés, le menuisier vint leur parler mais le croquis le laissa indifférent.

— Ce n'est pas elle, fit-il d'un ton bourru. Je ne risque d'ailleurs pas de la revoir si elle a rejoint son coquin de Pierre que je lui défendais de fréquenter. Si elle revient, elle recevra du bâton comme elle n'en a encore jamais reçu !

Le moine et son fils échangèrent un regard entendu puis tournèrent les talons, suivi de la jeune femme. Dans leur dos ils entendirent un compagnon jurer et le menuisier s'écrier :

— Tu es à l'amende de vingt sols !

Toujours attentionné, le moine offrit galamment son bras à Hélène pour l'aider à marcher sur le sol glissant même si ses assises semblaient aussi sûres que les siennes.

— Le père de la troisième disparue est un astrologue, déclara le commissaire aux morts étranges. Il loge rue des Canettes, paroisse Saint-Sulpice.

— Alors, nous n'avons qu'à nous fier à notre bonne étoile pour parvenir chez lui ! remarqua malicieusement le moine.

— Pas vraiment, selon mes indications, sa maison se situe entre une boutique de perruquier et celle d'un marchand chapelier.

Le ciel virait au noir et les maisons en encorbellement, avec un étage supérieur débordant sur l'étage inférieur, obscurcissaient encore plus la rue. Il leur fallut s'en remettre aux indications bourrues des riverains jusqu'à ce qu'ils pensent être arrivés à destination.

C'était une maison aux murs de pierre noircis par le temps, avec un étage et une curieuse tourelle accolée qui la surplombait. Ils montèrent une demi-douzaine de marches pour accéder à l'entrée. Après qu'ils eurent frappé à une lourde porte cloutée, une grosse servante au visage revêche vint leur ouvrir. Le commissaire aux morts étranges se présenta et on les introduisit dans un hall mal éclairé par une étroite fenêtre. À leur gauche on devinait la cuisine et à droite un salon de réception. La servante bâilla puis se signa quatre fois avec son pouce devant la bouche pour empêcher que le diable n'y entre.

— Il est dans son maudit cabinet, en haut de la tourelle comme à son habitude, maugréa-t-elle. Je vous laisse y monter car mon genou me fait mal !

Lorsqu'elle eut le dos tourné, le moine remarqua gaiement qu'elle avait les hanches et le derrière si large qu'ils semblaient renforcés sur la culasse.

L'escalier était raide et les marches rendues glissantes par l'humidité qui imprégnait les lieux. À plusieurs reprises, Hélène trébucha et, chacun à leur tour, le père et le fils qui l'encadraient la retinrent de justesse, l'un avec empressement, l'autre avec agacement. Ils se retrouvèrent devant une porte en fer, fermée à clé. Le commissaire aux morts étranges frappa vigoureusement.

— Monsieur, ouvrez-nous, je vous prie ! Je suis le chevalier de Volnay, commissaire du Châtelet !

Ils tendirent l'oreille mais n'entendirent rien. Le policier allait cogner de nouveau lorsque le bruit d'une clé dans la serrure l'arrêta. Un visage tout chiffonné apparut à hauteur de son épaule. Le crâne entièrement chauve ressemblait à un œuf trop longtemps couvé. Les yeux de l'homme étaient profondément enfoncés dans leur orbite et une poche gonflée comme une pêche ornait chaque dessous de paupière. Il leur jeta un regard hagard.

— Monsieur ! Vous venez pour ma fille ? Je suis si inquiet…

Ils entrèrent prudemment. La pièce était ronde et éclairée par une grande fenêtre dans le toit. Une tenture défraîchie mettait en scène des personnages mythologiques et réchauffait quelque peu les murs de pierre. Volnay la considéra attentivement. La scène représentait Héraclès bébé tétant la déesse Héra avec tant de force qu'elle en avait mal et le repoussait. Un jet de lait venait alors éclabousser le ciel, formant la Voie lactée.

Le feu qui brûlait dans une petite cheminée ne parvenait pas à assainir la pièce glaciale si bien qu'un nuage de vapeur se formait à leurs lèvres lorsqu'ils respiraient.

— Est-ce votre fille que j'ai représentée sur ce croquis ? questionna le commissaire aux morts étranges en sortant celui-ci de sa besace.

Un hurlement de douleur lui répondit.

— Elle est morte, c'est cela ? Ma pauvre Sophia est morte ?

— C'est bien elle, murmura lugubrement le moine.

L'astrologue était tombé à genoux et se labourait le visage de désespoir. Hélène le prit doucement par les épaules et, aidé par le policier, le releva. Ils le firent asseoir devant son bureau, attendant que l'homme se calme. Alors, chose étrange à voir, Hélène le saisit dans ses bras et le tint longuement serré contre elle alors qu'il pleurait. Lorsque cela fut terminé, elle s'écarta doucement de lui. L'homme ravala ses sanglots et hoqueta :

— Les astres me l'avaient annoncé mais je ne voulais pas le croire.

— Les astres ? demanda le moine soudain curieux.

— Le jour de sa disparition, son thème était désastreux. J'ai tout de suite compris qu'un grand malheur allait arriver.

Volnay parla enfin et le son de sa voix était si grave que tout le monde l'écouta attentivement.

— Quand a-t-elle disparu ?

L'astrologue renifla.

— Hier, en début d'après-midi. Nous l'avons attendue jusqu'au soir puis je suis allé prévenir le guet.

— Quelqu'un a-t-il vu quelque chose ?

— Non, personne. Elle était assise sur l'escalier comme elle aimait le faire et puis, l'instant d'après, elle n'y était plus…

Le visage du commissaire aux morts étranges était fermé mais son regard brillait d'une détermination farouche.

— Monsieur, je vous assure que je n'aurai pas de repos avant de retrouver le meurtrier de votre fille.

L'autre ne répondit rien. Il contemplait ses chaussures avec le plus profond désespoir. Pendant ce temps, Hélène s'était approchée du bureau sur lequel, à côté d'un livre sur l'Apocalypse, s'étalait une carte colorée. Elle se pencha pour la regarder.

— Monsieur, ne serait-ce pas la carte de la constellation du Crabe?

L'astrologue renifla encore et leva la tête.

— Oui… oui!

Il se releva et la rejoignit d'un pas mal assuré. De ses longues mains maigres et jaunâtres, il balaya la carte.

— À l'ouest, vous trouvez la constellation du Lion et à l'est celle des Gémeaux. Dans les récits des Grecs anciens, on raconte qu'Hercule écrasa du talon le crabe qui osait lui pincer l'orteil alors qu'il combattait l'Hydre!

— Dans les civilisations mésopotamiennes, remarqua la jeune femme, on dit que le Crabe représente la porte que traversent les âmes ayant séjourné dans les étoiles afin de renaître sous la forme humaine.

— C'est juste, madame, c'est juste, murmura l'astrologue étonné par sa science.

Les yeux du moine s'étrécirent. Si les connaissances exprimées par Hélène le ravissaient, elles ne l'en intriguaient que plus encore.

— En quoi consiste votre travail? demanda Volnay.

L'autre frotta vigoureusement ses yeux rougis. Le commissaire aux morts étranges remarqua à un de ses doigts une chevalière sertie d'un énorme et magnifique rubis.

— Les étoiles nous parlent, fit l'astrologue. Les planètes influencent nos actes, nos rêves même…

Les yeux du moine brillèrent de curiosité.

— Comment cela?

L'astrologue le considéra avec attention, dérangé par la bure de son interlocuteur, vêtement qui ne prédisposait pas à l'écoute de son sujet.

— La lune, les planètes et leurs conjonctions exercent une fascination sur nos vies tout comme sur nos rêves. Ainsi Mercure nous poursuit dans la recherche de nos plaisirs matériels tandis que Saturne engendre des rêves de mort…

Il considéra d'un œil soudain terne la tapisserie en face de lui.

— Oui, sombres sont les rêves de Saturne qui nous entraînent dans les recoins les plus obscurs et au bord de profonds précipices pour écouter les chants de la mort…

— Les étoiles prédisposent, remarqua le moine. Elles ne déterminent pas. L'homme conserve son libre arbitre!

— Vous vous trompez, s'écria l'astrologue, les astres influencent nos pensées comme nos actes.

— Pas du tout, rétorqua le moine, l'homme sage commande à ses étoiles. Le fou leur obéit.

Son regard tomba sur un papier couvert de signes et de chiffres.

— Qu'est-ce que ceci? demanda le moine. À qui appartient ce thème astral?

L'astrologue se troubla.

— À quelqu'un du quartier, répondit-il d'une voix tendue.

Sous le regard insondable du commissaire aux morts étranges, il fit disparaître le thème sous un monceau d'autres papiers.

— D'où observez-vous les étoiles? s'enquit le moine avec curiosité.

— Je vais vous montrer.

L'astrologue emprunta une échelle qui donnait sur une petite plate-forme éclairée par une grande lucarne. Sur celle-ci était fixée une lunette.

— Voici un bel engin, apprécia le moine.

Après avoir jeté un dernier regard au bureau de l'astrologue, son fils les rejoignit sans bruit mais demeura sur le dernier barreau de l'échelle car la plate-forme était trop étroite pour les accueillir tous les trois. M. Marly caressa amoureusement la lunette. Il semblait avoir oublié la mort de sa fille.

— "En tant que mortel, je sais que je suis né un jour, mais quand mon regard suit la course circulaire des innombrables étoiles, mes pieds ne touchent plus terre ; j'implore Zeus de me régaler d'ambroisie, la nourriture des dieux."

— Ptolémée… murmura le moine en reconnaissant l'auteur.

Perché sur son échelle, Volnay se sentit ridicule et entreprit de redescendre à reculons en prenant garde de ne pas se rompre le cou. Il fut accueilli au sol par le regard ironique d'Hélène. Sans se soucier d'elle, il gagna à pas rapides la table de l'astrologue et souleva les papiers pour examiner le thème astral que leur hôte s'était trop vite empressé de dissimuler. Ceci effectué, il remit soigneusement tout en ordre. Un instant, ses doigts hésitèrent au-dessus du livre de l'Apocalypse comme si quelque chose l'y attirait. Et puis, sa main retomba à ses côtés et, sans répondre à l'interrogation muette d'Hélène, il retourna au pied de l'échelle. Là-haut, son père discutait à bâtons rompus avec l'astrologue, citant Platon pour qui la contemplation de la voûte étoilée amenait l'homme à mettre son âme en harmonie avec l'ordre divin.

— Pourriez-vous redescendre ? demanda sèchement le policier.

Au-dessus de lui, les deux hommes se turent et puis le moine commença à descendre avec agilité.

— Sais-tu que ce sont les Babyloniens qui ont inventé l'astrologie ? demanda-t-il à son fils en touchant terre.

— Ce sont eux qui ont eu l'idée les premiers d'une table d'interprétation des qualités données à chacun des astres, s'empressa d'ajouter l'astrologue à mi-chemin sur l'échelle.

Il mit pied à terre avec une grâce pataude et continua :

— Car il faut comprendre à un instant précis la correspondance entre la position des astres et les événements qui se déroulent sur terre.

À cet instant, le commissaire aux morts étranges reprit la parole pour questionner l'astrologue sur les habitudes de sa fille et ses connaissances. Lorsqu'il eut terminé, il dit :

— Monsieur, nous repasserons dans une heure. Il faudra nous suivre pour reconnaître formellement le corps de votre fille. En attendant, pouvons-nous examiner sa chambre pour les besoins de notre enquête ?

Le pauvre père les contempla d'un air vide puis un éclair de compréhension traversa son regard et il hocha finalement la tête.

— Ma servante va vous y conduire.

Le commissaire aux morts étranges fit un signe discret à ses compagnons et ils se retirèrent. Au bas de l'escalier, ils trouvèrent la femme qui semblait les attendre.

— Quelque chose ne va pas ? demanda-t-elle d'un air méfiant.

— Veuillez nous montrer la chambre de Sophia, s'il vous plaît, fit le commissaire aux morts étranges d'un ton sans appel.

La chambre était étroite, meublée d'un lit bas, d'une table qui servait à la fois pour le travail et pour la toilette et d'un grand coffre pour ses effets personnels. Près du lit, sur un chevet, se trouvait une chandelle à moitié consumée. Le commissaire aux morts étranges l'alluma car la pièce était très faiblement éclairée par une minuscule fenêtre sans rideau qui donnait sur une cour murée au-dessus de laquelle le ciel semblait peser comme un couvercle gris.

Le policier fit un tour rapide mais professionnel du lieu, promenant un doigt sur une étagère pour remarquer :

— Pas un brin de poussière…

Il se mit à genoux pour examiner dessous le lit puis se releva et, soulevant le matelas de laine, le palpa d'une main experte.

— Le lit est propre et bien aéré. On ne peut rien dire de l'hygiène de cette jeune fille, ou de sa servante.

De son côté, le moine examinait des livres soigneusement rangés sur l'étagère, quelques-uns à reliure pleine de veau, la tranche marbrée à l'éponge mais la plupart de la Bibliothèque bleue, ces livres imprimés à peu de frais, seulement protégés d'une couverture de papier bleu et racontant contes et légendes ou aventures épiques.

— Au vu de leur état, constata-t-il, elle les a lus et relus des dizaines ou des centaines de fois pour s'évader de ces quatre murs gris…

Il en feuilleta quelques-uns et eut un imperceptible mouvement de surprise avant de reposer le livre qu'il

tenait en main comme si de rien n'était. Hélène observait de son côté les deux hommes sans rien dire. Le
commissaire aux morts étranges examina la table. Il y
avait là un broc d'eau pour la toilette, un peigne, une
plume avec son encrier et quelques papiers.

— Des pages d'écriture en latin… des exercices de
conjugaison. Rien de signifiant mais c'était quelqu'un
d'instruit.

Lui et le moine fouillèrent ensuite le coffre, y trouvant quelques effets simples et sans coquetterie. La
fouille exécutée, le policier appela la servante.

— Regardez le coffre puis la chambre et dites-moi
s'il manque quelque chose en dehors des vêtements
que votre jeune maîtresse portait.

— Il lui est arrivé quelque chose? demanda la femme d'un ton revêche.

Elle ne paraissait guère émue.

— Étiez-vous attachée à cet enfant?

L'autre haussa les épaules.

— Je sers ici depuis trois ans, je me suis habituée
à elle mais elle est toujours dans la lune.

— À quoi passait-elle ses journées?

— Quand elle était plus jeune, elle jouait dans la
cour avec des petits cailloux ou avec sa poupée mais,
le plus souvent, elle restait des heures entières à rêver
devant la tapisserie du salon. Ah oui elle aimait aussi
moucher les chandelles et m'accompagner au marché.

— Ma foi, sortir de cette maison lugubre devait
être effectivement un vrai plaisir, maugréa le moine.

— Elle en avait peu l'occasion. Son père sortait peu
et, lorsqu'il le faisait c'était seul. Sa fille ne pouvait
donc que m'accompagner au marché ou pour quelques
menues courses mais parfois, elle se faufilait dehors
sans qu'on la voie. Elle est morte, c'est ça?

— Oui, répondit le commissaire aux morts étranges en observant ses réactions.

Il en fut pour ses frais. Cette femme était d'une rare insensibilité.

— Si c'est pas malheureux, maugréa-t-elle. Et de quoi est-elle morte que vous êtes donc tous ici ?

— Vous le saurez le moment venu, répondit froidement le policier. Ne quittez pas cette maison, nous aurons à vous interroger.

— Et où voulez-vous donc que j'aille, marmonna-t-elle. Je n'ai que ce toit sur ma tête même si je dors sur un mauvais grabat. Mieux vaut ça que rien du tout…

Et elle sortit tout en continuant à ronchonner. Le moine prit la parole en s'adressant à Hélène et à Volnay.

— En sortant, sur votre gauche et de l'autre côté de la rue, il y a une auberge. Vous n'avez pas faim ?

— Mais…

— Partez devant, fit le moine à voix basse, je vous rejoindrai.

Le commissaire aux morts étranges réprima sa surprise. Il jeta un coup d'œil incisif à son père puis se saisit du bras d'Hélène.

— Venez, lui fit-il d'une voix grave.

Resté seul, le moine reprit en main le livre qui avait retenu son attention et s'assit lourdement sur le lit. Était-ce un problème d'impression, le verso de chaque page était blanc mais la jeune fille y avait consigné son journal en une écriture serrée. Il fronça les sourcils et entreprit de lire.

C'était le journal d'une enfant qui n'avait personne à qui se confier et qui racontait là sa vie, ses tristesses et ses espérances. Ses journées étaient longues et grises, ses jeux pensifs. Le moine parcourut quelques pages, se laissant gagner par la mélancolie profonde qui s'en dégageait.

Quand elle était petite, une nourrice faisait déjeuner Sophia à la cuisine, lui portant la cuillère à la bouche. Le moine l'imagina, absorbant avec gravité les mets et surveillant du coin de l'œil la nourrice attentive. Plus tard, Sophia apprit à se nourrir toute seule mais même encore la nourrice restait à la surveiller pour vérifier qu'elle mange tout. La nourrice sembla s'attacher à elle et lui parla du reste du monde : les bois, les lacs, les montagnes, les animaux… À l'âge de six ans, Sophia se mit alors à retranscrire d'une écriture maladroite tout ce qu'elle entendait dans un livre qu'on lui avait offert mais qui comportait des pages blanches. Elle n'y parla jamais de son père.

Parfois, le soir, sa nourrice lui lisait la Bibliothèque bleue et Sophia émerveillée écoutait sans broncher des contes peuplés de voleurs et de revenants qui tourmentaient la nuit les vivants. Elle aimait aussi les histoires d'ogres qui mangent les enfants et frissonnait jusqu'à ce que le héros échappe à son terrible destin.

Le moine l'imagina, les yeux écarquillés, se mordillant les lèvres à l'approche du dénouement. Le soir de l'Avent, sa nourrice la régalait de deux histoires au lieu d'une. Elle les écoutait en grignotant des friandises avant d'aller se coucher et prolonger dans ses rêves les naïves aventures entendues à la veillée.

Le moine plissa son front, se souvenant de soirs où il lisait à son fils des contes remplis de nains, de gnomes et d'esprits malins. Un jour, lorsqu'il revint après un séjour de quelques mois en prison, son fils lisait désormais seul. Un frisson nostalgique le secoua. Le temps passait si vite, filant entre les doigts. Il soupira et reprit sa lecture.

À sept ans, l'âge de raison pour les enfants, son père décida que Sophia n'avait plus besoin de nourrice. Sept ans ! Elle n'était pas une demoiselle, rien qu'une enfant à qui on retirait le seul être cher. Sept ans ! Le moine savait qu'à cet âge on troublait l'âme des enfants en leur annonçant avec gravité qu'ils se trouvaient désormais en âge de pécher et de perdre leur innocence.

De la paume de sa main, le moine se frotta le front, geste habituel lorsque quelque chose le tourmentait. Qu'avait-il dit lui-même à son fils à l'âge de sept ans ? Rien qu'un baiser sur le front et une pensée fugitive : *comme le temps passe vite !*

À sept ans, donc, on congédia la nourrice de Sophia. Peut-être s'attachait-elle trop à l'enfant. Désormais, Sophia déjeuna seule à la cuisine. Elle le nota dans son journal, avec gravité mais sans révolte car elle semblait douce et docile. Mais désormais, plus personne ne s'occuperait d'elle jusqu'à sa mort.

Le livre en main, le moine se releva et d'un pas fut à la fenêtre, scrutant le pauvre horizon offert à l'enfant. La cour ressemblait plus à la cellule d'une prison qu'à un espace de jeux et de liberté. Il appuya son front contre la vitre froide et s'amusa, comme elle avait dû le faire, à laisser se dessiner sous son souffle une buée fantomatique. Son jeu terminé, il retourna s'allonger sur le lit et contempla le plafond. Sophia passait-elle ainsi son temps lorsqu'elle ne lisait pas ? Imaginait-elle sur ce plafond des personnages de conte de fées qui viendrait la tirer de sa morne vie ? Comment trompait-elle son ennui dans ces journées interminables où personne ne lui adressait la parole ?

Il ferma les yeux et réfléchit. Sophia n'était pas une enfant maltraitée. Elle avait eu un toit et de quoi se nourrir. Son corps ne portait aucune trace de coups. C'était seulement une enfant ignorée.

Mais qui était-il pour juger les autres et qu'avait pensé de lui son fils lorsque, sous couvert de répandre les lumières de l'esprit dans son siècle, il avait laissé filer tous ces précieux instants que rien ne pourrait jamais faire revivre ?

Une pesante tristesse l'envahissait. Il aurait voulu rattraper le temps perdu mais n'y parvenait pas.

Il était plus de midi et tout un peuple d'artisans, ouvriers et maçons, portefaix ou journaliers cherchait sa pitance. De la table des plus riches parvenaient sur celles des bourgeois les restes des soupers. Et ce que ne mangeaient pas les bourgeois finissait dans les étals, pour les plus pauvres, en compagnie des fruits gâtés, des viandes décomposées et des poissons puants. Les deux jeunes gens n'avaient rien avalé depuis la veille. Une enseigne en fer forgé signalait la présence de l'auberge. Le givre avait tissé autour des guirlandes glacées. Ils poussèrent la porte avec soulagement, soulevant les récriminations des convives qu'un vent froid balaya. Ils découvrirent alors qu'ils se trouvaient dans un cabaret à bière empli d'une faune bruyante qui fumait de longues pipes en terre ou buvait un vin aux relents aigres. Quelques filles de petite vertu s'y pressaient. Le commissaire aux morts étranges insista pour choisir une table près d'une fenêtre et, sans souci d'Hélène, s'empara de la chaise qu'il souhaitait occuper. Ensuite, il regarda dans la rue et parut satisfait car il apercevait de là la maison de l'astrologue.

Hélène jeta un coup d'œil aux autres tables. On servait un ragoût noirâtre d'où émergeaient des os et des petits paquets de chair compacte. D'un commun accord, les deux convives jugèrent préférable de s'en tenir à une soupe et une omelette.

— Voulez-vous boire un peu de vin? demanda Volnay avec une politesse forcée.

— Pourquoi pas mais votre moine tarde à venir, remarqua la jeune femme. Que fait-il exactement?

Le policier haussa légèrement les épaules.

— Il s'imprègne des lieux.

— Pas vous?

— Moi, j'ai vu tout ce que j'avais à voir.

— Pas votre moine?

Le commissaire aux morts étranges eut un rire bref.

— Oh, lui, il voit les choses derrière les choses…

Elle le considéra attentivement. Le commissaire aux morts étranges soutint tranquillement son regard, dissimulant son trouble car il remarquait pour la première fois que les yeux d'Hélène semblaient recéler un fragment de nuit étoilée. Ses souvenirs le renvoyèrent à une autre femme, Chiara, qu'il avait connue l'année précédente et qui s'en était allée. Les femmes ne lui portaient pas chance.

— Comment en êtes-vous arrivée à travailler pour Sartine? demanda-t-il abruptement.

Elle ne parut pas s'offusquer d'une question aussi directe mais répondit par une autre question :

— En dehors du mariage, que laisse-t-on comme choix à la femme sinon le couvent ou le bordel? J'ai pour ma part emprunté une autre voie !

Elle a le même caractère que Chiara, pensa fugitivement Volnay, *mais en moins innocent et bien plus dangereux… Chiara a vécu dans un écrin de velours mais Hélène porte une dague sur elle !*

Il n'eut pas le temps de s'appesantir sur ses souvenirs. La porte du cabaret s'ouvrit et le moine apparut.

— Eh bien, fit-il gaiement, comment est le vin?

Son fils lui jeta un regard inquiet. Le faux entrain de son père ne le trompait pas et Dieu seul savait pourquoi il s'était attardé dans la chambre de cette enfant. Le moine s'assit et jeta autour d'eux un coup d'œil méfiant. Les mouches de Sartine pullulaient dans les tavernes, observant et écoutant tout. Volnay intercepta son regard et, d'un imperceptible signe du menton, lui désigna Hélène. Cela signifiait clairement:

Fais donc attention à tes propos devant elle!

Le moine resta imperturbable. Si la jeune femme demeurait pour lui un mystère, il ne pensait pas qu'elle était une mouche et rapporterait leurs conversations.

Le silence s'établit et l'on entendit le vent siffler à travers les carreaux. Une serveuse vint leur apporter leurs bols et une grosse miche de pain. Avec ses flancs étroits, elle ressemblait à un petit chat maigre mais son minois était piquant et son regard plein d'assurance.

— Voici la soupe de Ses Seigneuries, fit-elle.

Elle ne devait certes pas avoir souvent l'occasion de servir des gens de condition. Le commissaire aux morts étranges la questionna.

— Connaissez-vous les occupants de la maison à deux étages avec une tourelle que nous apercevons par cette fenêtre?

Elle se pencha légèrement pour regarder, lui dévoilant un peu d'une poitrine manifestement peu fournie.

— L'homme qui regarde les étoiles?

— C'est bien cela, fit le jeune homme en détournant les yeux et en lui glissant une pièce.

— Que voulez-vous savoir? demanda-t-elle en l'empochant prestement.

— Tout ce que vous savez d'eux.

Elle se renfrogna.

— Je n'en sais pas trop.

— Allons, allons, fit le commissaire aux morts étranges en dardant sur elle un regard pénétrant. Dans chaque quartier, tout le monde observe tout le monde, c'est même la principale occupation de chacun !

— C'est que leur servante passe sans s'arrêter devant l'auberge et elle est aussi peu bavarde qu'une pie.

Le moine intervint.

— Les pies sont très bavardes, jeune fille. En fait, elles peuvent parler comme vous et moi si on les éduque…

Hélène lui posa la main sur le bras pour l'empêcher de continuer. Déçu, le moine se concentra sur sa soupe, un bouillon dans lequel on avait ajouté des pois, des fèves et des morceaux de pain d'orge.

— La jeune enfant ? demanda Volnay.

— Oh, elle est bien mignonne et bien aimable même si elle paraît toujours triste. Mais elle sort peu, sinon accompagnée par la servante.

— Connaissez-vous la mère qui l'a couvée ? demanda le moine.

— Non, elle est morte alors qu'elle avait trois ou quatre ans je crois.

— Hum… et qui voit-elle ?

— Elle n'a pas d'amis dans le quartier, à part un chien.

— Un chien ?

— Oui, elle lui donne à manger quand elle sort, alors il la suit.

Elle darda sur Volnay un œil effronté en se campant en arrière pour tenter de faire ressortir sa poitrine.

— C'est comme cela la vie, non ? On suit celui qui vous fait du bien !

Le commissaire aux morts étranges jeta un regard bref à son père. Ils venaient tous deux de penser au chien qui hurlait à la mort devant le cimetière.

— À quoi ressemble ce chien ?

— Oh, il me va à la cuisse, plein de poils blancs quand il est propre avec des taches marron. Parfois, lorsque son père n'est pas là et la servante sortie, elle l'emmène chez elle pour le laver !

— Quelle gentille enfant, murmura le moine attendri.

Le policier se mordit les lèvres. Cela ressemblait bien au chien rencontré devant la maison de son père la nuit de la mort de Sophia puis de la sienne le lendemain matin. L'intelligent et fidèle animal avait pu suivre la carriole qui transportait le corps de sa petite maîtresse. Il soupira tristement et la servante lui jeta un regard curieux. Sentant son flottement, Hélène prit alors le relais.

— Parlez-nous du père. Sort-il parfois ou vient-on le visiter ?

La serveuse haussa les épaules.

— On ne le voit pas trop traîner dans le quartier et il ne vient jamais ici. On dit qu'il est si avare qu'il n'ose cracher de peur d'avoir soif. S'il sort parfois, c'est à la nuit tombée. Il reçoit aussi quelques visiteurs, plutôt entre chien et loup.

— À quoi ressemblent ces visiteurs ?

La servante fit une petite moue.

— Comment voulez-vous que je le sache ? Je suis moi-même plus souvent à servir les clients qu'à rôder dehors ou à regarder par la fenêtre. D'ailleurs, j'ai encore de la marmite à remuer. Je n'ai guère de temps naguère !

Volnay lui glissa une autre pièce.

— Vraiment pas une idée ?

Elle s'empara de la pièce qu'elle glissa dans son corsage, pointa en avant son petit nez retroussé et répondit insolemment :

— Vraiment pas !

Le commissaire aux morts étranges lui retint le poignet mais Hélène laissa fuser un rire amusé.

— Laissez voyons…

La serveuse lui jeta un regard complice et s'en fut prestement.

— M. Marly, notre astrologue, est un cul de plomb, commenta le moine, il ne bouge guère de son cabinet…

— Sauf la nuit, remarqua Volnay. Étrange pour un astrologue qui devrait la passer à observer les étoiles ! Je vais placer une mouche près de la maison pour observer les allées et venues…

Tous méditèrent quelques instants cette réflexion en nettoyant leur bol puis le commissaire aux morts étranges reprit, en s'adressant au moine :

— Nous devons dessiner le profil des personnes qui ont assisté à cette messe noire.

— Dessiner le profil ? répéta Hélène surprise.

— L'action de la police de Sartine se fonde sur l'espionnage et la délation, expliqua pompeusement le moine. Volnay et moi développons des théories nouvelles et plus subtiles en matière de crime. La vérité ne doit pas être simplement le résultat d'une intuition mais les conclusions de la raison par l'esprit d'observation, d'analyse et la déduction logique. Les certitudes sont toujours des obstacles à son apparition.

Il agita le doigt avec un sourire malicieux.

— Je suis un sceptique, je doute. Et mon esprit critique me permet de me remettre sans cesse en cause et de me préserver de l'erreur !

— C'est de la simple logique, le coupa le commissaire aux morts étranges peu porté sur l'emphase. Nous avons remarqué que chaque crime a sa propre signature, pas seulement sur un plan matériel. Les motivations et comportements des meurtriers diffèrent d'un individu à l'autre.

— L'étude des cas, renchérit le moine déterminé à briller aux yeux d'Hélène, démontre que la victime connaît en général son meurtrier et que celui-ci est souvent un proche. Je m'efforce de tenir les comptes. Sur dix affaires résolues par nos soins, huit des criminels connaissaient bien leur victime. Toujours sur dix affaires, trois sont le fruit d'adultères ou de rivalités amoureuses. Les autres relèvent d'intérêts pécuniaires ou d'hostilité de longue date. Quant à l'infanticide, nul ne risque plus d'être assassiné qu'un enfant !

Il nettoya du doigt le bord de son bol et reprit :

— Les enfants risquent avant tout d'être assassinés le jour de leur naissance ou dans le premier mois. Plus âgés, de mauvais traitements répétés peuvent également les tuer.

Un éclair de pitié traversa son regard.

— Nul n'est plus sans défense qu'un enfant et certains adultes en profitent. Ceux-là mêmes qui n'ont que le courage d'abuser des plus faibles qu'eux…

Il se pencha sur son verre qu'il vida d'un trait.

— Mais Sophia n'était pas une enfant maltraitée, murmura-t-il, simplement une enfant ignorée…

Un silence lourd sembla couler entre eux une chape de plomb. Volnay réagit le premier :

— Le meurtrier n'est pas forcément un gueux brutal, un vicieux borné ou un vicieux intelligent. Nous pouvons nous trouver face à des individus, qui, fous ou non, commettent leur crime dans un schéma de pensées ou de convictions bien précis. Dans notre affaire, le profil s'esquisse déjà car le crime s'est produit lors du rituel très particulier d'une messe noire.

Il marqua une pause et jeta un coup d'œil circulaire pour vérifier que personne ne les écoutait.

— Qui trouve-t-on dans les messes noires ? Des gens quémandant des faveurs terrestres de la part de Satan. Risquer son salut éternel en invoquant *le Très Bas* dénote généralement un goût avide du pouvoir et des biens matériels.

— Cela peut être aussi une certaine forme de désespérance, hasarda Hélène.

— Ou de la simple perversité, murmura lugubrement le moine. Et Dieu sait comme la nature humaine peut être perverse !

— Ne sois pas trop catégorique, conseilla Volnay. Nous vivons dans un siècle où beaucoup de gens contestent l'ordre établi quel qu'il soit. Ils assimilent à tort le sacrilège à une forme de liberté.

— Dire non à Dieu pour dire oui à Satan, c'est seulement changer de maître, remarqua le moine sarcastique.

On revint pour les débarrasser de leurs bols. Les convives se turent et observèrent avec amusement la jeune servante se déhancher devant le commissaire aux morts étranges pour attirer en vain son attention.

— Quand je parle de perversité, reprit plus tard le moine, c'est que les messes noires peuvent se terminer aussi bien par les plus honteuses débauches que par des sacrifices de nourrissons !

— Oui, et comme l'Église proscrit le meurtre et le péché de chair, on s'y livre ! conclut le commissaire aux morts étranges. Le satanisme se construit uniquement en opposition et dans le déni de toute dignité humaine.

Hélène intervint.

— Si vous voulez insinuer par là que les participants à des messes noires sont des libertins, des pervers ou encore des opposants à l'ordre social, nous avons affaire à beaucoup de monde !

— Certes, en convint le policier, mais toutes les formes de sacrilège sont systématiquement observées pendant les messes noires. Derrière cela, il y a l'horreur, l'horreur absolue. Nous affinerons progressivement le profil de ces êtres pervers avec chaque élément glané.

La serveuse revint avec une omelette baveuse à souhait et l'on se tut, le temps de lui faire honneur. Cela fut rapide car les portions n'étaient pas copieuses.

— Ma foi, ils nous font chier petite crotte, remarqua le moine dépité.

Il continua néanmoins à manger en racontant avec entrain des anecdotes amusantes sur sa vie passée, s'évertuant à faire rire Hélène sous le regard impassible de Volnay qui dit finalement :

— Il est temps. Retournez chez l'astrologue et amenez-le reconnaître formellement le cadavre de sa fille. Pour ma part, j'ai à faire au Châtelet puis en un certain lieu.

Et en disant cela, il jeta un regard appuyé à son père qui approuva d'un imperceptible mouvement de tête.

Dehors, le policier suivit longuement du regard son père et Hélène. Malgré leur différence d'âge, ils formaient un duo harmonieux qui s'en allait en devisant gaiement. Volnay pensa que son père suivait une mauvaise pente.

V

LE CHIEN, LE BROUILLARD
ET AUTRES DIABLERIES

Saturé d'humidité, un brouillard épais se formait dans la ruelle de l'Or. L'après-midi était avancée lorsque le commissaire aux morts étranges y pénétra après un tour au Châtelet pour y laisser un rapport à Sartine. Ici, chaque maison semblait bâtie sans tenir compte de la position de la maison suivante et, par moments, la ruelle devenait si étroite que deux personnes s'y croisaient avec peine. Suivant les indications de son père, Volnay se dirigea vers la maison de la dame qui lisait l'avenir dans l'eau. La sensation d'être suivi le saisit de nouveau. C'était une présence furtive, à peine perceptible. Quelque chose qui n'avait rien d'humain et se manifestait par moments avant de se projeter dans une autre dimension. Cette fois-ci pourtant, il surprit ce qui l'avait pris en chasse.

— Ah te voilà, toi! Décidément, tu as tout d'un chien policier! Veux-tu donc entrer au service de M. de Sartine?

Il s'approcha de l'animal qui demeura immobile. Seule sa queue remuait comme s'il venait de retrouver une vieille connaissance. Volnay lui caressa la tête.

— J'ai pensé à toi dans cette auberge et j'ai emporté ce bout de pain au cas où je te retrouverais devant chez moi. Je ne pensais pas que tu me suivrais, mon discret compagnon. Tu es plus doué qu'une mouche pour cela! Il faudra que je te trouve quelque emploi au Châtelet!

— Quel tableau touchant! fit une voix ironique. Notre commissaire aux morts étrange n'est donc pas si insensible que ça!

Volnay releva vivement la tête pour se retrouver face au moine, hilare.

— Que fais-tu là? Tu devais faire reconnaître le corps par le père puis occuper Hélène… euh, l'espionne de Sartine pour éviter qu'elle ne me suive.

— Ne t'inquiète pas! Elle s'est rendue chez le commissaire de quartier pour découvrir s'il est fait mention de notre astrologue dans quelque dossier.

— Elle a accès aux dossiers d'un commissaire du Châtelet? s'étonna le commissaire aux morts étranges.

— Apparemment! Quant à moi, j'avais compris, à ton regard à l'auberge, où tu te rendrais après le Châtelet…

Il s'interrompit et sembla découvrir la présence du chien.

— Oh le bon *chien-chien*!

Il le flatta vigoureusement avant de le gratter derrière les oreilles.

— Mais c'est un bon *chien-chien* ça!

Son fils poussa un soupir exaspéré.

— Pour l'amour de Dieu, parle normalement et arrête d'appeler cette bête *chien-chien*!

Son père prit un air vexé.

— Mais dis-moi, serait-ce donc là le chien de Sophia dont nous a parlé la servante de l'auberge?

— C'est fort possible. Il correspond à la description et il me suit depuis la nuit du drame.

Le moine s'émerveilla.

— Intelligent animal ! On raconte qu'il y a trois ou quatre siècles, rue des Marmousets à Paris, un barbier tuait parfois un client de passage puis faisait basculer son corps dans la cave de son voisin pâtissier qui le transformait en excellent pâté ! Les aboiements du chien d'une victime, qui resta jour et nuit à hurler à la mort devant la boutique du barbier, attirèrent l'attention et permirent de découvrir les procédés criminels de ces deux mauvais commerçants !

Son fils hocha la tête.

— Il y a dans la fidélité de certains de ces animaux quelque chose de troublant. Allez viens !

Volnay tapa sur sa cuisse et le chien suivit.

— L'astrologue a bien reconnu sa fille ?

— Oui, répondit le moine, et ce fut pénible. Nous l'avons ensuite reconduit chez lui. Il voulait emporter le corps mais j'ai refusé. Je ferai d'abord venir un cercueil chez moi.

— Oui, il vaut mieux qu'il ne voie pas le corps de sa fille ouvert.

Le moine baissa la tête comme un enfant pris en faute.

— Je ne l'ai pas autopsiée. À quoi bon ? Cela ne nous apprendra rien et j'aurai bien d'autres cadavres pour continuer à me faire la main !

Son fils le considéra comme s'il était devenu fou.

— C'est toi qui décides, dit-il finalement d'un ton neutre.

Décidément, son père ne se comportait en rien comme à l'ordinaire. Le moine releva vivement la tête.

— Eh oui, c'est moi qui décide !

Le policier eut un hochement de tête pensif.

— Je n'ai pas voulu te demander devant Hélène pourquoi tu restais dans cette chambre chez l'astrologue mais, te connaissant, il devait bien exister une raison.

— J'avais remarqué que notre victime tenait un journal dans le livre que je feuilletais. Je voulais le dérober pour le lire plus attentivement mais pas sous les yeux de notre nouvelle amie !

Son fils parut rassuré. Le comportement de son père lui semblait de nouveau logique.

— Qu'as-tu appris dans son journal ?

— Rien qu'une enfance grise et solitaire.

Son ton lugubre alerta de nouveau Volnay.

— Eh bien, lança ce dernier pour dérider son père, que penses-tu de notre astrologue et de sa servante revêche ?

Le moine ne répondit pas directement mais lui désigna une bâtisse au toit biscornu.

— Ici, tu trouveras un augure qui se livre à l'examen du foie et des entrailles. Les Mésopotamiens se livraient à ce type d'augure ainsi que les Grecs qui en codifièrent l'étude sur des tablettes d'argile. En Mésopotamie encore, on étudiait l'aspect que prenait le mélange de l'eau et de l'huile…

— L'eau ? Comme ton amie ?

— Oui. Elle étudiait également la fumée en faisant brûler de l'encens mais elle a abandonné cette pratique car cela la faisait tousser !

Il glissa sur le sol verglacé, se rattrapa miraculeusement à la manche de son fils et poursuivit sa savante péroraison comme si de rien n'était :

— En Grèce, on étudiait les bruissements des feuillages d'un chêne. Dans la Rome antique, on interprétait tous les signes comme autant de messages des dieux. Tonnerre, éclairs, tout leur parlait ! Les augures interprétaient le vol des oiseaux, l'appétit des poulets sacrés et déchiffraient également dans leurs entrailles. Certains s'avisèrent même de lire l'avenir dans les viscères humains. Rome s'en émut et condamna ces pratiques en instituant la loi des Douze Tables proscrivant l'usage de la magie.

— Et désormais, on se tourne toujours vers le ciel mais la nuit et pour observer les étoiles !

Le moine lui jeta un regard satisfait.

— Tu as bien compris où je voulais en venir : à notre astrologue ! C'est un augure ! L'astrologie a pris le pas de nos jours sur toutes ces anciennes formes de divination. La connaissance sans cesse approfondie des mouvements cycliques des planètes et des étoiles leur a donné un sentiment de puissance. Sentiment éphémère ! Voici un homme qui lit dans les étoiles le destin des hommes mais n'est même pas capable de prédire la mort dramatique de sa fille ! Quant à sa servante, elle n'a pas paru plus étonnée que ça d'apprendre cette dramatique nouvelle. Voilà une femme sans cœur !

Il claqua des doigts en l'air.

— Au fait, as-tu remarqué le thème astral que notre astrologue s'est empressé de dissimuler lorsque je l'ai remarqué ?

— Oui, répondit nonchalamment Volnay, j'ai jeté un coup d'œil lorsque vous étiez en conversation et j'ai noté la date de naissance du thème.

— Digne fils de ton père ! Puis-je la voir ? Où l'as-tu écrite ?

— Là, fit le commissaire aux morts étranges en pointant son index sur sa tempe.

Son père lui jeta un regard fier et admiratif.

— Et alors ?

— C'est une date de naissance que nombre de personnes connaissent en ce royaume de France puisque c'est celle du roi !

Le moine sautilla avec excitation sur le sol gelé.

— Oh… Je comprends pourquoi il l'a dissimulé. Faire le thème astral du roi est un délit passible de prison. Un crime de lèse-majesté ! L'astrologie est sanctionnée par la mort dès lors qu'elle touche au destin du roi ou de ses enfants.

— Surtout s'il prétend prévoir la date de la fin de leur règne !

Le moine s'arrêta devant une maison dont l'entrée, plus étroite que le reste du bâtiment, laissait penser à la proue d'un bateau fendant le brouillard.

— Ah, c'est là où je me suis rendu suite aux conseils de ma belle amie, maîtresse des eaux. Je t'accompagne. Comme il m'en a vendu hier, il ne pourra nier en posséder. Pour lui faire raconter qui sont ses clients, je compte sur ton pouvoir de persuasion ! D'autant plus qu'il possède dans un vase des fleurs de chanvre et de coquelicots, des racines d'ellébore et des graines de tournesol…

— Et alors ?

— Alors, mêlées à de la mandragore et de la graisse d'humain non baptisé, on en fabrique l'onguent des sorcières !

Le commissaire de quartier était grand et corpulent mais tout son corps semblait disproportionné tant sa tête était petite, ses jambes démesurément longues et ses bras trop courts. D'épaisses paupières voilaient par moments ses yeux mais ses lèvres remontant aux commissures suggéraient une perpétuelle bonne humeur.

Il se présenta à Hélène sous le nom de Cornevin et lut avec soin le papier que lui tendit la jeune femme. Lorsqu'il releva la tête, son regard était devenu respectueux.

— Diable, madame, une introduction du lieutenant général de police lui-même ! Je suis bien entendu à votre entière disposition. Que puis-je pour votre service ?

— Je m'intéresse à la rue des Canettes.

— Oh, cette rue est plutôt calme. Il y a bien quelques voleurs de mouchoirs dans les appartements ou des voleurs de boucles de chaussures dans l'église Saint-Sulpice…

— Des voleurs de boucles de chaussures ?

— Oui, elles ont un certain prix parfois et lorsque les gens sont agenouillés, il est assez aisé de les leur dérober.

Il marqua une pause.

— Nous connaissons peu de violence dans ce quartier. Bien entendu, quelques maris frappent durement leurs femmes ou des artisans leurs apprentis mais cela ne va jamais bien loin.

La jeune femme pinça délicatement l'arête fine et étroite de son nez.

— Connaissez-vous un astrologue du nom de Marly ?

— Marly, dites-vous ? Un astrologue…

Le commissaire de quartier se leva pesamment et alla jusqu'à une pile de registres sur une table près de la fenêtre.

— J'ai eu affaire à la fille de l'astrologue, une enfant d'une douzaine d'années, très aimable même si un brin mélancolique. Elle est venue de son propre chef pour se plaindre que quelqu'un frappait un chien. Vous rendez-vous compte ?

Il eut un petit rire grinçant.

— Je lui ai demandé si la personne était propriétaire dudit chien et elle m'a répondu que oui mais qu'il ne lui donnait pas à manger et se bornait à le cogner du poing et du pied !

— Et qu'avez-vous fait ? demanda Hélène intéressée.

Cornevin se tourna vers elle, un registre dans les mains, l'air désabusé.

— Que voulez-vous que je fisse ? Deux jours après un homme est venu se plaindre qu'on avait tenté de lui voler son chien. Il avait appelé un sergent de guet qui l'accompagnait avec la jeune fille en question, la fille de l'astrologue. Comment se nommait-elle déjà ?

— Sophia, fit doucement Hélène en jetant un coup d'œil par la fenêtre.

Elle constata que l'ombre commençait à envahir les rues.

— C'est cela, oui. Un bien charmant nom mais qui ne lui correspondait pas trop. Voyons mes registres.

Le policier se mit à tourner des pages, les sourcils froncés.

— Ah, voici ! Peut-être ne connaissez-vous pas la procédure. Mon greffier enregistre toutes les plaintes. Je vais vous lire leurs déclarations.

Hélène se pencha, attentive. L'autre commença sa lecture, son doigt soulignant chaque ligne à lire au fur et à mesure.

— "Le 7 mars 1758 à deux heures de l'après-midi, en notre hôtel par-devant moi, conseiller du Roy commissaire au Châtelet, est comparu Legrand, sergent du guet de poste près de l'église Saint-Sulpice, lequel nous dit avoir été requis par un particulier maintenant une jeune fille d'environ treize ans qui l'aurait rudoyé et poussé dans le ruisseau. Pourquoi on les a conduits en notre hôtel. Interrogé, le particulier dénommé Berger-Rabot a dit qu'aujourd'hui, il était occupé à cercler un tonneau dans sa cour lorsque ladite Sophia s'est approchée de lui pour lui crier d'un ton très insolent : Allez-vous finir de frapper votre chien. Il n'est pas méchant mais vous si ! A répondu que ce n'était pas son affaire et ordonné de s'en aller. A refusé et entrepris de détacher la corde qui maintenait le chien. Lui a alors arraché ladite corde des mains. En réponse, ladite jeune fille l'a poussé et fait choir lourdement, lui faisant mal au dos. A crié alors : Au guet ! À la garde ! Que, ayant été entendu, un sergent du guet en poste non loin d'ici est venu le secourir."

Le commissaire porta un doigt à la bouche, le lécha et tourna une page.

— "Ayant examiné la dénommée Sophia et trouvant qu'elle portait des traces de coups au visage, moi, commissaire au Châtelet, lui a demandé s'il ne l'avait pas frappée. Le dénommé Berger-Rabot ayant reconnu l'avoir poussée à son tour, j'ai ordonné l'élargissement de la jeune fille et les ai renvoyés tous deux chez eux après admonestation et remontrance sur leur conduite mutuelle."

Il joignit les mains et adressa à la jeune femme un sourire aimable.

— Voilà toute l'affaire ! Vous voyez que c'est bien peu de chose. Pourquoi vous intéressez-vous à cette charmante enfant ?

— Parce qu'elle est morte.

Lorsque le moine et le commissaire aux morts étranges sortirent de chez le marchand grec, le brouillard voilait peu à peu les ombres grisées du crépuscule. À leur vue, le chien remua la queue.

— Brave *chien-chien*, fit le moine.

Son fils eut un soupir excédé et claqua des doigts à l'intention de l'animal.

— Viens !

Le chien s'exécuta docilement.

— J'ai déjà rencontré des gens peu loquaces mais notre marchand grec vient en tête de ceux-ci, dit Volnay.

— Toujours est-il, rétorqua le moine, qu'une fois la menace de la question agitée, il a parlé *celerius quam asparagi cocuntur*. "En moins de temps qu'il n'en faut pour cuire les asperges !"

— Et il nous a avoué avoir vendu sa potion à une prostituée du faubourg Saint-Marcel, renchérit Volnay, connaissant même le cabaret où elle exerce l'hiver ! Nous nous y rendrons demain.

— Espérons que ces prostituées ne soient pas trop nombreuses, soupira son père, je ne me vois pas toutes les soumettre à confesse !

En quittant la ruelle de l'Or, ils remarquèrent des ombres difformes glisser rapidement sur les pavés glacés. Ces longues silhouettes emmitouflées de noir et coiffés de chapeaux à larges rebords marchaient l'une derrière l'autre dans un ordre parfait. Une brève plainte s'échappa de la gueule du chien.

— Ces gens-là s'en reviennent de la ruelle de l'Or, remarqua le commissaire aux morts étranges. Je me demande ce qu'un tel groupe y fabriquait… Suivons-le !

La nuit envahissait tout. Les artisans se hâtaient d'installer des barres de bois pour bloquer les volets de leurs boutiques. Dans les boutiques, les commis préparaient leurs lits à même les tables sur lesquels ils travaillaient le jour. Lentement la brume s'épaississait. Le moine et le policier suivaient toujours à distance l'étrange procession.

— Il fait un temps à ne pas mettre un assassin dehors! grommela le moine. Qu'avons-nous donc à suivre ces gens que nous ne connaissons pas? Sans doute, vont-ils à quelque fête…

Le commissaire aux morts étranges hésita. Son instinct de policier l'avait poussé à emboîter le pas aux hommes en noir. Malgré son peu d'habitude de la ruelle de l'Or, surtout fréquentée par son père, il savait qu'il était rare d'y croiser un groupe de personnes. Des gens seuls et méfiants s'y glissaient discrètement pour y accomplir leurs achats ou acheter quelque prestation inavouable. On se gardait bien d'être accompagné.

— Ces gens-là m'intriguent, s'entêta-t-il, suivons-les un instant et voyons où ils se rendent.

Jugeant que son fils était devenu fou, le moine grommela :

— Toi, tu as bien des chambres à louer dans ta tête !

Mais, comme d'habitude, il s'exécuta, s'assurant discrètement que le chien les accompagnait toujours. Ce lien animal et familier avec la jeune Sophia lui plaisait et, sans trop de raisons, il appréciait de le conserver.

Ils marchèrent en silence à la suite de l'étrange procession, traversant d'étroites rues tortueuses bordées de maisons aux rez-de-chaussée de pierre et aux étages de bois en saillie. Le brouillard et l'obscurité rendaient la filature difficile et les contraignaient à se rapprocher afin de ne pas perdre de vue les hommes en noir. Au fil du temps, la bourre grisâtre qui flottait dans l'air sembla se solidifier, estompant toutes formes. Aussi, au détour d'une rue, le commissaire aux morts étranges ne fut pas trop surpris de constater la disparition des suspects, happés d'un coup par la nuit.

— Nom de Dieu ! fit le moine.

— Ne blasphème pas, le gronda Volnay. Il est interdit de jurer le nom de Dieu ou celui du roi. N'oublie pas que cela est puni de mort !

Il ne manquait jamais une occasion de donner la leçon à son père tant, des deux, c'était lui qui semblait parfois faire l'enfant.

— Tiens, remarqua-t-il. Il y a un cimetière là-bas, allons voir.

— Nous ne savons pas qui sont ces gens, protesta le moine. Tu sais comme moi qu'il est recommandé de ne pas traverser les cimetières pendant les heures noires.

— Allons voir quand même !

Ils pénétrèrent sans bruit dans le lieu funèbre et se faufilèrent à travers les tombes. Le brouillard semblait s'exhaler de la terre, l'âme des morts sourdre d'entre les pierres. Peu impressionné par l'atmosphère, le chien errait de droite et de gauche, reniflant et levant la patte par endroits sous le regard désapprobateur de Volnay. Les deux hommes plissèrent les yeux pour scruter les environs. Plus loin, la nuit semblait parcourue de mouvements furtifs et, bientôt, le bruit mat d'une pioche qui mord la terre glacée les aiguilla. Des silhouettes sombres se regroupaient autour d'une tombe fraîchement creusée. Le commissaire aux morts étranges les rejoignit à grands pas. Ses bottes écrasaient la neige fraîche avec un bruit sourd, faisant voler une poudre blanche à chaque enjambée. Il pointait résolument son pistolet et sa main ne tremblait pas. De son côté, le moine avait dégainé sa dague. Les hommes en noir ne bougèrent pas, figés par la surprise.

— Je suis commissaire au Châtelet, s'écria Volnay, et je vous décrète de prise de corps ! Savez-vous qu'à la nuit tombée, les peines sont doubles pour les délits ? Vous risquez la corde pour cela !

Le grand homme qui semblait commander la petite troupe fit un pas en avant. Il émanait de lui une autorité tranquille.

— Monsieur, je suis un anatomiste. Je ne déterre pas les cadavres comme certains pour en prélever la cervelle en vue de fabriquer des potions magiques mais afin de pousser plus loin les limites de la science.

— Vos buts ne m'intéressent pas, répondit Volnay avec une rectitude glaçante, je ne retiens que les faits !

Le moine lui saisit vivement le bras.

— Tu as perdu une roue ou quoi ? Ce sont des scientifiques !

L'anatomiste approuva et désigna du doigt trois jeunes gens échevelés.

— Ceux-là sont mes étudiants. Eux deux…

Il pointa du doigt vers deux hommes à la mine plus farouche.

— Ceux-là sont moins portés vers la science que nous. J'ai bien peur qu'ils ne soient plus intéressés par le profit que par les progrès de la médecine. Il faut dire que les cadavres se paient trente livres pièce. Néanmoins, ils me sont loyaux…

Le moine posa une main sur l'épaule de son fils.

— Mon garçon, il ne nous appartient pas de nous mettre sur le chemin de la science.

L'anatomiste fit un pas hésitant en direction du moine.

— Vous ! Seriez-vous qui je pense ?

Il s'approcha plus près pour le scruter.

— Mon Dieu, c'est vous! Je vous croyais mort! Alors ce que l'on dit est vrai? Vous travaillez pour la police, messire Guillaume de…

— Pas de nom, mon ami, pas de nom! Je travaille à découvrir les coupables de crimes horribles et j'emploie pour cela toute ma science. Pour le reste, j'estime toujours que le roi et sa cour sont des jean-foutre!

L'anatomiste rit.

— Vous n'avez pas changé, me semble-t-il, et c'est tant mieux!

Il réfléchit un instant puis appela près de lui un homme court et râblé.

— Nous sommes, lui dit-il, dans une situation complexe. Il nous faut donner preuve de notre sincérité envers ce policier sinon il nous mènera en prison. Je sais que tu répugnes à livrer le nom de tes clients mais il le faut, c'est pour notre bien à tous. En dehors bien entendu des médecins ou professeurs comme moi…

L'autre hésita.

— Eh bien, insista l'anatomiste, n'as-tu donc pas livré, en dehors de gens de science comme moi, des clients récemment, ces deux dernières semaines?

— Cela ne se passe pas comme cela, grommela l'homme. On me donne rendez-vous à un endroit et l'on y charge le cadavre dans une voiture. Après, je ne sais pas ce qu'ils en font. On dit que certains mages utilisent le cœur ou la cervelle pour des potions ou des sorts. Mais la plupart du temps, ce sont des étudiants de médecine qui préfèrent s'exercer sur les morts plutôt que sur les vivants! Ils jettent ensuite les restes dans la Seine et gardent la graisse des corps pour se chauffer l'hiver.

— Eh bien, constata l'anatomiste d'un ton égal, vous avez l'information que vous souhaitez. Nous allons prendre congé les uns des autres.

Mais Volnay n'avait pas baissé le canon de son arme.

— Tout doux, monsieur, les réponses me laissent insatisfait. Et il y a toujours entre nous le cadavre d'un gardien de cimetière !

— Quel gardien de cimetière ? Oh ! Cette histoire-là ?

L'anatomiste se tourna de nouveau vers le déterreur de cadavres.

— N'est-ce pas celle que tu nous as racontée tout à l'heure à la taverne ?

L'autre hocha lugubrement la tête.

— C'est que j'aimerais mieux ne pas la répéter !

L'anatomiste soupira.

— Je crains que nous n'ayons guère le choix et puis tu n'es pas obligé de citer les noms !

Le déterreur de cadavres prit un air buté mais, devant le regard résolu du commissaire aux morts étranges, s'exécuta.

— Nous, les déterreurs de cadavres, nous nous retrouvons parfois pour boire quelques pintes ensemble. Hier soir, j'ai vidé des chopines avec un collègue à moi. Je ne savais pas s'il était ivre mais il m'a raconté une drôle d'histoire.

Il fit tourbillonner machinalement sa pioche en l'air.

— Or donc, dans la nuit de dimanche à lundi, il s'est rendu à son travail avec ses aides dans un grand cimetière. Ils déterrent un client sans bruit puis vont plus loin mais ne voilà-t-il pas que lui et ses hommes butent sur un cadavre pas du tout enterré ! Ils veulent rebrousser chemin mais d'autres personnes sont près de là et les ont vus. Croyant avoir affaire à la police, mes collègues se mettent en garde avec leurs pelles et leurs pioches. Mais les autres sont aussi surpris et effrayés qu'eux d'autant plus que des feux multicolores s'échappent de là où ils ont creusé! Au bout du compte, tout le monde se sauve prestement de son côté!

Le commissaire aux morts étranges réfléchit. L'histoire paraissait vraisemblable et expliquait en tout cas l'interruption de la messe noire et l'abandon des deux cadavres dans le cimetière. Après tout, cette explication payait bien le déplacement! Il abaissa le canon de son arme.

— Filez, dit-il.

L'anatomiste le salua de son chapeau.

— Monsieur, merci de votre contribution à la science!

Le moine et son fils regardèrent les hommes en noir détaler sans plus de commentaire.

— Ils vont probablement aller ailleurs, fit le moine amusé.

— Probablement, répondit sèchement son fils.

Le chien sur leurs talons, ils sortirent discrètement du cimetière. Plus épais qu'à leur entrée, le brouillard semblait prendre une consistance plus dense, avalant les maisons de la rue les unes après les autres.

— Par où prendrais-tu? demanda le policier.

— À droite.

— Nous prendrons donc à gauche, fit Volnay qui n'avait qu'une confiance limitée dans le sens de l'orientation de son père.

Le moine marmonna quelque chose d'inintelligible dans sa barbe mais suivit son fils. Il sentit alors comme un souffle chaud sur sa cuisse et s'aperçut que, pour ne pas le perdre, le chien marchait pratiquement sur ses talons.

— De nos jours, reprit le moine pour combler le silence de la nuit, de plus en plus de monde s'intéresse à l'anatomie. Même les femmes s'en passionnent ! La comtesse de Coigny ne voyage jamais sans un cadavre dans son coffre !

— À droite ?

— Non, à gauche.

— À droite !

Ils empruntèrent de sordides venelles, incapables de se repérer dans la ouate épaisse qui les entourait. Une dizaine de minutes plus tard, le commissaire aux morts étranges s'immobilisa, les narines frémissantes.

— Je sens l'odeur des quais, murmura-t-il.

— J'avais dit : à gauche !

Les deux hommes se regardèrent silencieusement. Leurs sens atrophiés par la nuit et le brouillard, ils ignoraient exactement où ils se trouvaient et retrouver leur chemin ne serait pas chose aisée.

— Rentrons vite chez nous, dit le moine en frissonnant. Nous allons attraper la mort.

D'un geste, son fils le fit taire.

— Écoute !

Quelques instants auparavant opaque et silencieuse, la nuit semblait soudain s'éveiller et fourmiller d'une vie inquiétante.

— Il y a du monde derrière nous, chuchota le commissaire aux morts étranges, et je doute qu'il s'agisse d'une patrouille du guet. Prenons rapidement les quais de Seine et mettons de la distance entre eux et nous !

En trébuchant dans la rue non pavée, ils rejoignirent le quai, serrant au plus loin du fleuve. Soudain le bruit d'une course les fit sursauter. Le policier porta la main à son pistolet mais n'eut pas le temps d'achever son mouvement. Une forme noire s'écrasa contre lui dans un soupir inarticulé et, avec un juron qui ne lui était pas habituel, Volnay chuta lourdement.

Avec une vivacité surprenante, le moine se jeta sur l'agresseur et le cloua au sol. Lorsqu'ils se penchèrent sur lui, le policier et son père découvrirent un petit homme replet, aux bajoues tremblotantes, habillé comme un bon bourgeois. Il semblait en nage, comme au terme d'une longue course, et dégageait une forte odeur de singe.

— Non, non ! Ne me tuez pas ! geignit-il.

Le moine et le commissaire aux morts étranges s'entreregardèrent.

— Je suis commissaire du Châtelet, fit Volnay. Vous n'avez rien à craindre de nous. Qui êtes-vous ?

— Je m'appelle Lefranc, je suis maître rôtisseur rue des Postes.

— Que fuyez-vous ?

L'autre leur jeta un regard hagard.

— Ils m'ont pris en chasse et m'ont forcé à aller sur les quais !

Par-delà le souffle haletant de l'homme, Volnay perçut un nouveau bruit, une sorte de piétinements étouffés et le bruit de bâtons heurtant le sol avec une régularité de métronome.

— Ils sont nombreux, constata le policier. Peut-être une centaine…

On commençait à distinguer des silhouettes fantomatiques qui avançaient en une ligne serrée. D'affreux nez de papier déformés ornaient leurs visages.

— Avec leurs bâtons, ils battent à mort ceux qu'ils trouvent sur leur passage, souffla Lefranc.

— Cela ne se peut, souffla le policier en baissant néanmoins la voix. Ce groupe porte des masques de Carême et des femmes en font partie !

— Existe-t-il encore un quelconque bon sens aujourd'hui ? Ces débordements font gémir toutes les âmes pieuses, se plaignit le bourgeois.

— Je vais leur parler, décréta Volnay en sortant son pistolet. Je suis policier.

À cet instant, un hurlement éclata dans la nuit. Un bruit de coups sourds se fit entendre et une longue plainte s'éleva dans l'air froid avant de s'éteindre dans un dernier râle.

— Policier ou pas, à ta place je ne bougerais pas ! fit le moine.

Son fils hocha sèchement la tête.

— Tu as raison, nous n'avons pas affaire à un groupe d'étudiants qui jouent à effrayer le bourgeois mais à des tueurs !

Il plissa les yeux, essayant de percer nuit et brouillard.

— Ils doivent sortir les nuits de mauvais temps, lorsque les patrouilles des archers du guet se font rares. Ils s'affublent de masques de Carnaval au cas toutefois où ils en rencontreraient une…

— Ils arrivent ! Sauve qui peut ! cria le rôtisseur en prenant ses jambes à son cou.

— Attendez, restons ensemble ! fit le policier.

L'autre ne ralentit même pas. Le bruit de la course du bourgeois se perdit dans la nuit, derrière eux la troupe avançait.

— Ne restons pas là, fit le moine. Imitons notre peu courageux compagnon ! Comme le disait Démosthène : "Tel qui fuit peut combattre encore !"

— Je me demande si c'est vraiment la meilleure solution, rétorqua Volnay.

Il se leva toutefois et suivit son père.

— Ils connaissent l'endroit, ils vont plus vite que nous, remarqua le moine. Ventrebleu ! Le chien n'est plus là !

— Rassure-toi, je pense qu'il est nettement plus malin que nous ! Allons-y !

Ils se mirent à courir en aveugle. Ils n'entendaient plus que le bruit incertain de leur course et leur respiration haletante, trébuchant parfois sur des obstacles inattendus. Il leur semblait toutefois plus logique de risquer de se rompre le cou que de s'offrir aux bâtons de leurs poursuivants. Le moine pesta car il venait de perdre sa peau de loup. Devant eux retentirent un hurlement horrible puis le bruit mat mais distinct de coups étouffés. Ils stoppèrent net. Le moine gratta son collier de barbe.

— Nous venons de perdre notre maître rôtisseur. Il en vient par-devant.

— C'est ce que je craignais, murmura Volnay d'un ton lugubre. Comme à la chasse, on rabat le gibier sur les autres chasseurs. Ils doivent se disposer de part et d'autre des quais pour chasser leurs proies. S'ils n'en trouvent pas, ils démarrent leur battue dans les rues adjacentes.

— Et personne ne survit pour raconter quoi que ce soit, termina le moine. Remontons dans les rues.

— Si des complices y sont embusqués, c'est notre fin assurée.

Des bruits de voix étouffées se firent entendre devant eux. Derrière, les silhouettes fantomatiques se rapprochaient.

— Voilà qui n'est pas bon du tout ! constata le policier sans perdre son sang-froid.

— L'eau ! Sautons dans le fleuve, c'est le seul endroit où ils ne nous suivront pas.

— Nous n'y survivrons pas ! À tout prendre, je préfère essayer de remonter des quais mais la pente est raide et avec la neige cela ne sera pas facile.

— Essayons de trouver un endroit où il y a des anneaux.

Volnay s'appuya dos au mur et joignit ses mains pour que le moine y pose un pied.

— Trouves-tu une prise ?

— Non et je n'y vois goutte ! Cela glisse trop. Nous aurions dû choisir l'eau.

Le bruit de pas martelés se rapprochait. Une écorce de glace semblait raidir les muscles du moine alors que ses pieds cherchaient une fente où se placer.

— Il est trop tard, père. Trouve quelque chose ou ils vont nous réduire en purée !

— Non, je ne… un anneau ! Décale-toi un peu à droite sans me lâcher ! Voilà !

— Dépêche-toi !

Les assassins se rapprochaient. Ils avaient amorcé un mouvement d'encerclement en entendant les deux hommes. Déjà, leurs bâtons fouettaient l'air.

— Prends ma main, vite !

Volnay fit quelques pas en arrière. Un bref regard lui permit de voir à quelques mètres de lui les sinistres silhouettes au regard aveugle, affublées de leur horrible masque de papier au nez démesuré.

Le policier se précipita en avant et sauta, la main de son père se referma sur la sienne.

— Saisis l'anneau, vite !

Alors qu'il s'en emparait, un coup porté à sa jambe par un bâton le fit hurler de douleur.

— Je vais me mettre debout sur l'anneau, fit le moine. Si je tombe, je suis mort. Donc, adieu peut-être…

Volnay jura et, de sa main libre, sortit son pistolet.

— Je vais faire un peu d'air en dessous de nous, haleta-t-il. Attention, je tire !

Le coup de feu troua l'air. Un cri d'agonie traversa la nuit. Les bâtons cessèrent de s'agiter et les poursuivants reculèrent. Ils n'avaient pas l'habitude d'une si forte résistance. Volnay lâcha son arme et, les deux mains tenant l'anneau, il tenta de grimper jusqu'à celui-ci. Au-dessus de lui, le moine poussa un cri de triomphe.

— Les pierres dépassent, on peut s'y appuyer. Voilà ! Je suis arrivé. À toi. J'enlève ma bure et je te la lance.

À son tour, Volnay se dressa sur l'anneau, s'écorchant les mains sur de mauvaises prises gelées. Il sentit le bout de la bure effleurer sa tête et leva les mains pour l'attraper. Au-dessous de lui, le sifflement des bâtons avait repris.

— Tu tiens bien ? demanda-t-il.

— Penses-tu ! Je suis vieux et faible !

Tout en pestant, le moine entreprit de le hisser tandis que Volnay s'efforçait de faire reposer le poids de son corps sur l'arête des pierres sous ses pieds. Haletant, il s'effondra enfin près de son père.

— Je suis mort, dit celui-ci en claquant des dents. Mort de froid.

Volnay l'aida à remettre sa bure.

— Quelle folie !

Derrière eux, ils entendirent leurs poursuivants s'efforcer de se hisser à leur tour.

— Filons d'ici, fit le moine, je n'ai pas envie de voir leur sale tronche sous leurs masques de papier !

Après une course éperdue, ils se retrouvèrent devant la porte de la maison du moine. Sur ses épaules, la bure de celui-ci semblait être devenue une armure de glace. À leur grande surprise, la porte n'était pas fermée à clé. Les deux hommes entrèrent prudemment et découvrirent une Hélène souriante, assise près d'un bon feu.

— Que faites-vous là ?

Elle se leva.

— Je vous attendais…

— Comment êtes-vous rentrée ?

— Je vous ai dérobé une clé !

— Vous avez osé ?!

— Vous m'avez bien droguée pour me faire dormir !

— Oh, ça… murmura le moine gêné. Ce n'était qu'une petite décoction…

Une longue toux caverneuse s'échappa de la gorge du moine. Hélène se tourna vers lui, inquiète.

— Stoppons là nos querelles, vous avez pris la mort. Ôtez tous deux vos habits et mettez-vous près du feu, je vais vous apporter des couvertures.

Tremblants et frissonnants, les deux hommes s'exécutèrent piteusement.

— Qu'est-ce que ceci ? demanda Hélène.

On venait de gratter à la porte.

— Incroyable ! s'exclama le moine. Il est revenu.

Volnay se hâta d'ouvrir et le chien se faufila sans gêne entre eux pour se coucher avec un soupir de satisfaction devant l'âtre après s'être ébroué.

— Un compagnon à quatre pattes, commenta le moine, nous vous expliquerons plus tard.

— Ne serait-ce pas le chien que Sophia voulait protéger ? demanda Hélène. Son propriétaire a porté plainte contre elle et j'ai pu entendre toute l'affaire…

— Oui, admit Volnay. C'est sans doute lui qui hurlait à la mort à la porte du cimetière. Il nous suit depuis que nous avons porté le corps de sa maîtresse mais apparemment il a plus un faible pour moi que pour le moine !

— Pas du tout ! rétorqua l'autre, c'est juste que…

— Taisez-vous et ne gardez rien sur vous ! décréta avec autorité la jeune femme. Je vais chercher des couvertures.

Le moine tourna la tête vers son fils.

— J'ai bien entendu ? Elle nous a bien dit de ne rien garder sur nous ?

Une minute plus tard, comme si elle connaissait par cœur la maison, Hélène revint et marqua un temps d'arrêt devant les deux hommes qui ne conservaient que leur haut-de-chausses et se frottaient mutuellement à la chaleur des flammes. D'un œil exercé, elle apprécia la carrure de leurs épaules, leur torse musclé et leur ventre plat. S'en apercevant, le moine bomba avantageusement la poitrine. En souriant, Hélène leur tendit à chacun une chaude couverture de laine. Gênés, le moine et le policier s'en couvrirent avant d'enlever leur dernier vêtement. Alors, Hélène se mit à les étriller comme des chevaux, en commençant par le plus âgé. Elle ne tarda toutefois pas à marquer un temps d'arrêt.

— Oh pardon, fit joyeusement le moine, vous réveillez la nature qui est en moi !

Hélène le considéra un instant.

— Trop honorée, terminez donc seul de vous sécher !

Elle se tourna vers le policier.

— À vous !

À sa surprise, Volnay se laissa faire, semblant même prendre plaisir au passage vigoureux des mains sur son corps. Instruite par son expérience, Hélène se borna à lui frotter le dos et les épaules, s'attardant pourtant sur lui peut-être plus que de raison. On décida ensuite que la jeune femme prendrait la chambre et que les deux hommes dormiraient, gorgés de tisanes et enveloppés de couvertures, près du feu qui fut alimenté avec soin.

— Que nul maléfice ou mauvais rêve ne vienne troubler votre sommeil, fit Hélène en les contemplant d'un air doux. Bonne nuit et dormez !

VI

LA VORACE ET AUTRES DIABLERIES

Lorsque Volnay ouvrit un œil, ce fut pour découvrir Hélène s'affairant auprès du feu. Éveillé, le moine la contemplait avec ravissement.

— Je ne me sens pas très bien. J'ai une fièvre de veau ! Jeune fille, voulez-vous bien m'apporter la carafe que vous voyez là-bas ?

Une quinte de toux lui déchira les poumons. Le moine soupira puis reprit :

— L'eau de Paris est putrescible, je ne bois de l'eau de fontaine qu'après l'avoir fait bouillir avec une racine de réglisse et laissée reposer.

Il s'interrompit pour éternuer.

— Je passe ensuite mon eau par un entonnoir bouché avec un bouquet de thym séché.

Une autre série d'éternuements le secoua tout entier.

— J'y ajoute un peu de vinaigre et d'eau-de-vie, ajouta-t-il dans un souffle. Cela donne meilleur goût.

Interdite, Hélène se tourna vers Volnay qui s'était redressé sur son séant.

— Il délire ?

— Je ne crois pas, non. Il fait vraiment tout cela !

— Installons-le dans sa chambre, fit-elle.

Celle-ci était meublée d'un lit bas avec un matelas de plumes recouvert de couvertures de laine blanches, d'un poêle en faïence, d'un secrétaire en noyer et d'un siège de travail. Sur une étagère se côtoyaient des bronzes féminins couchés et des volumes in-folio reliés en veau du *Dictionnaire encyclopédique*. Une haute fenêtre était occultée par de lourds rideaux de velours rouge qui réchauffaient la pièce.

— Il est très malade, insista Hélène après avoir aidé le moine à se coucher. Il va falloir appeler un médecin.

Le commissaire aux morts étranges leva les yeux au ciel.

— Il n'acceptera jamais d'en voir approcher un de son lit.

— Il n'est pas en état de le rosser ! Dépêchez-vous !

En maugréant, Volnay se hâta de s'habiller et, en milieu de matinée, revint avec un médecin du quartier qui n'avait pas trop mauvaise réputation. Celui-ci, sec comme une trique, vêtu d'une robe longue à grandes manches et le crâne surmonté d'une belle perruque poudrée, se hâta de brosser un tableau d'ensemble de la situation.

— Tout Paris est malade, c'est l'action conjointe des brouillards, de la neige et du mauvais air. Il n'y a guère de maisons dans le quartier où l'on ne saigne ou fasse prendre des lavements.

— Purgez ceux-là, saignez ceux-ci, se moqua le moine entre deux quintes de toux.

— Monsieur mon consultant ferait mieux de garder ses forces. Gardez-vous la nourriture que vous ingurgitez ?

— Ma foi oui, si elle est bonne.

— *Sus ad vomitum !*

Il pointa un doigt accusateur vers le moine.

— J'espère que vous n'êtes pas de ces gens qui s'empiffrent ! Respect au malade innocent mais honte au malade qui sacrifie sa santé à ses vices.

138

— L'indigestion du riche venge la diète forcée du pauvre, remarqua le moine, mais en l'occurrence, j'ai simplement pris froid.

— Bien, bien… Si l'on en juge par l'état de monsieur mon consultant qui me paraît d'un âge avancé…

Le moine eut un cri de protestation.

— Monsieur mon consultant, reprit le médecin en s'adressant désormais à Volnay qu'il semblait juger seul digne de l'entendre, souffre visiblement d'une forte fièvre et ses poumons sont encombrés comme le démontre suffisamment sa toux. Son sang doit être trop épais, voire acrimonieux. Une bonne saignée le délivrera de ses humeurs âcres. Mais, pour parfaire mon diagnostic, je dois goûter à ses urines…

— Ne vous gênez pas ! dit le moine.

— D'abord, toussez puis crachez dans ce mouchoir, je vous prie. Hum…

Il se tourna vers Volnay, l'air peiné.

— Crachats d'écume sanguinolente, il y a lieu de le saigner abondamment.

— Pas de saignée, cela l'affaiblirait.

Le médecin jeta au policier un regard peu amène.

— Remettre en question la Faculté, c'est dénier la raison ! *Per scientiam ad salutem aegroti* : "Le salut du malade passe par la science !" D'abord, il faut aligner le lit parallèlement aux poutres pour hâter la guérison puis aérer cette chambre à coucher tous les matins afin de la débarrasser du produit de la respiration de la nuit. Faites de même le soir pour évacuer celle de la journée. En effet, il s'agit de deux principes contraires qui s'opposent, exposant l'occupant des lieux à cette lutte malsaine dont il sera la principale victime. Et commençons tout de suite !

Il alla jusqu'à la fenêtre qu'il ouvrit bien grande. Un vent glacé s'engouffra dans la pièce, arrachant un hoquet de stupéfaction à Hélène.

— Le sommeil, s'exclama le docteur avec enthousiasme, le sommeil !

Il leva les bras en l'air pour ânonner :

— *"Lever à cinq, dîner à neuf,*
Souper à cinq, coucher à neuf
Font vivre d'ans nonante et neuf."

— Votre malade sera mort de froid sous peu, dit le commissaire aux morts étranges qui referma la fenêtre d'un geste sec. Monsieur, merci de vos services, je vous reconduis.

L'autre ouvrit la bouche pour protester mais le commissaire aux morts étranges lui saisit le bras avec fermeté pour le conduire à la porte. Avant que celle-ci ne se referme, les deux hommes entendirent clairement le moine crier de sa chambre :

— Dehors le médecin d'eau douce !

Volnay n'attendit pas la prochaine saillie pour pousser le battant de la porte mais le moine hurlait assez fort pour qu'on l'entende de dehors :

— Estropié de la cervelle ! Sot à triple étage !

Restée seule avec le malade, Hélène se pencha sur lui et lui caressa la joue.

— Arrêtez de crier comme cela, vous allez vous briser la voix.

Le moine éternua et répondit :

— J'ai cette engeance en horreur. En France, en dehors des soldats, les médecins sont les seules personnes habilitées à tuer ! Certains d'entre eux ne voient même pas leurs patients et se contentent de répondre en latin à leurs courriers où ils décrivent leurs symptômes ! Il ne viendrait pas à l'esprit de cette bogue de châtaigne qui m'a visité de me prendre le pouls, la température ou de faire la percussion des poumons !

Il s'interrompit pour tousser et reprit d'une voix éraillée :

— Son seul remède est d'ouvrir les fenêtres et saigner son patient. Si j'avais survécu, il m'aurait ensuite prescrit de la purgation suivie de la prise de bouillon et de lait d'ânesse tous les matins. C'est très à la mode…

— Ne vous agitez pas comme cela, lui reprocha Hélène compatissante. Reposez-vous plutôt.

— Allez me chercher mes herbes à la cuisine, répondit faiblement le moine. Je vous expliquerai quoi faire.

Il pointa le menton vers son fils qui se tenait coi sur le pas de la porte et les observait.

— Bourre ce poêle jusqu'à la gueule et ajoute-moi une couverture. Il me faut bien suer. Quand ce sera fait, tu calfeutreras la fenêtre de linge de manière à ce que je ne prenne pas un mauvais courant d'air.

La jeune femme apporta dans un torchon une poignée d'herbes. Le moine se redressa pour les contempler.

— Prenez celle-ci, un brin de celle-là, une feuille ici. Voilà, ajoutez ceci et deux feuilles de celle-là effritées entre vos mains. Tout est là ? Faites bouillir une grande casserole d'eau et plongez-y tout cela quelques instants.

Il toussa puis reprit.

— Vous passerez au tamis d'un linge le liquide et m'apporterez deux bols bien pleins avec du miel. Vous mettrez le reste en carafe que vous poserez près de mon lit. Avant de partir, mettez de grosses bûches dans la cheminée. Il est important que toute la maison soit bien tiède.

— Je vais chercher quelqu'un pour veiller sur toi, décida son fils. À deux pas de là, il y a une ouvrière en linge qui s'occupe de nos vêtements. Elle a peu d'ouvrage actuellement et sera heureuse de passer la journée au chaud et bien rémunérée.

Restée seule avec le moine, Hélène chercha un tissu vierge et se mit à écrire dessus *ABRACADABRA*. Elle répéta ce mot à la ligne d'après en enlevant la dernière lettre et ainsi de suite jusqu'à ce qu'il ne subsiste plus que le "A" initial, formant un triangle inversé, une espèce d'entonnoir par lequel s'écoulerait le mal en se réduisant.

— C'est amusant, dit le moine s'intéressant à l'ouvrage. Savez-vous que cette célèbre formule magique *ABRACADABRA* provient d'une contraction des mots hébreux *abreq ad hâbra*, ce qui signifie…

— Envoie ta foudre jusqu'à la mort.

— Oh…

Le moine lui jeta un regard respectueux.

— J'oublie toujours que vous êtes presque aussi savante que moi! Qui donc vous a enseigné cela?

— Ma mère.

Elle n'en dit pas plus mais lui noua le tissu autour du cou.

— Vous serez vite guéri, ajouta-t-elle. C'est un triangle magique!

Volnay revint bientôt avec une femme d'une quarantaine d'années à la nature joviale et au large sourire édenté. Hélène leur apprit que le moine s'était endormi.

— Très bien, fit son fils soulagé.

Il se tourna vers l'ouvrière.

— Veillez-le jusqu'à notre retour.

Il lui tendit quelques pièces.

— Voici pour votre peine, vous aurez le double à notre retour. S'il se réveille, faites tout ce qu'il vous demandera même si cela vous étonne!

Il était plus de midi lorsque le commissaire aux morts étranges et la jeune femme quittèrent le domicile du moine, laissant celui-ci à la garde du chien et de l'ouvrière en linge. La neige s'était mise doucement à tomber et leur piquait les yeux.

— La prostituée que nous recherchons est surnommée la Vorace, expliqua Volnay. Je n'ose imaginer ce que traduit ce terme dans ce métier-là !

Hélène lui jeta un regard amusé. Le ton léger du policier était nouveau pour elle. Était-il capable de drôlerie comme le moine ? Elle jugeait Volnay sévère et rigide mais, aujourd'hui, il semblait se détendre avec elle. Il lui conta d'un ton badin quelques anecdotes pittoresques sur le quartier qu'ils traversaient, allant même jusqu'à la faire rire, et lui tint galamment le bras lors des passages difficiles.

À mi-chemin, le vent se leva pour les cingler. Mordus par le froid, Hélène et Volnay se rapprochèrent instinctivement pour s'en protéger. Forte de cette nouvelle complicité, la jeune femme s'appuya sur son bras plus que de nécessité. Ils empruntèrent des rues étroites et malodorantes, bordées d'immeubles aux façades lépreuses et de petits commerces d'où s'élevaient des clameurs bruyantes. Une population bigarrée s'y pressait, toujours en mouvement. Des portefaix se tuaient à la tâche en portant des colis presque aussi lourds qu'eux. Chiffonniers, crocheteurs, colporteurs et petits ramoneurs savoyards au visage ravagé par la suie des cheminées se bousculaient sur la chaussée glacée. Dans les échoppes, on vendait l'arlequin, une mosaïque des mets dont plus personne ne voulait. Les traiteurs quant à eux proposaient des ragoûts, les tripiers des abats. Même en l'état peu appétissant, tout restait cher pour les habitants des environs.

À un coin de rue, ils croisèrent un fourgon où des archers du guet chargeaient un colosse au regard abruti et un vieillard épouvanté. Des lèvres du colosse hagard s'échappait comme une mélopée.

— Que se passe-t-il ? demanda doucement Hélène qui s'était arrêtée.

Volnay la considéra calmement. Même la neige ne pouvait faire oublier les lueurs mordorées dans ses grands yeux verts.

— On enfourne pêle-mêle, pour l'hôpital de Bicêtre, les fous, les vagabonds, les épileptiques et les vieillards, expliqua-t-il.

— Dans ce mouroir ?

— Remerciez-en le roi et son zélé serviteur, M. de Sartine !

Elle lui jeta un regard triste mais ne répondit pas. Il avait cru la mettre en colère mais, au contraire, elle se rapprocha plus encore, comme cherchant auprès de lui un soutien qu'elle ne pouvait espérer trouver ailleurs.

Lorsqu'ils arrivèrent faubourg Saint-Marcel, la neige avait cessé de tomber et un soleil anémié tentait de réchauffer quelque peu le monde à ses pieds. Ici, la pauvreté se lisait aussi bien sur les visages maigres qu'à travers le mouvement des corps, immensément douloureux, brisés par la fatigue. On y sentait tant le manque de nourriture que la brièveté du sommeil et les mains rendues calleuses par les travaux les plus pénibles. Les gens ne portaient pas de souliers mais des sabots. Leurs vêtements étaient dépareillés, boutons et poches arrachés. La rudesse de leur vie n'empêchait pas le recours au vice. Ils virent deux jeunes hommes qui commettaient sous un porche des indécences avec une prostituée. Malgré le froid, le plaisir se prenait aussi toujours dans la rue, rapidement et brutalement. Hélène jeta un rapide coup d'œil à Volnay qui détourna le regard.

Dans le cabaret décrit par le marchand grec à Volnay, se trouvaient trois grandes tables. L'une d'elles était jonchée de débris de nourriture et, tels des rats affamés, hommes, femmes et enfants aux vêtements rapiécés se chargeaient de la nettoyer, mangeant avidement. Leurs ventres maigres, leur teint blanc et leurs yeux brillants dévoilaient tout de leur misère. Dieu seul savait où ils passeraient ensuite la nuit.

À une autre table, des ouvriers tentaient d'oublier leur fatigue à coups de vin servis dans des vases de grès et la fumée de leur pipe ajoutait une note boisée à l'odeur rance de leur boisson.

À la dernière table, l'atmosphère était plus tendue. On jouait aux cartes en buvant et en s'apostrophant. Auprès des joueurs chanceux s'agglutinaient des femmes qui se voulaient aguicheuses. Parfois des éclats de voix jaillissaient et des chopes ou des poings cognaient lourdement la table. On sentait qu'il suffisait d'un geste ou d'une parole pour que tout s'embrase et qu'une rixe éclate.

Volnay prit le bras de la jeune femme et l'entraîna dans un coin où un demi-tonneau servait de table.

— Sacrée garce, dit bruyamment un joueur en lorgnant effrontément Hélène.

Le commissaire aux morts étranges coula vers lui un regard glacial et s'assit en soulevant son manteau, laissant dépasser la pointe de son épée. Les rires se turent et l'on se mit à chuchoter tout en les observant de biais. Leurs vêtements trahissaient leur condition et seuls les gentilshommes ou les militaires étaient autorisés à porter l'épée. On se demandait bien ce qu'un tel couple fabriquait par ici. Le policier commanda et on leur servit pour huit sols deux pintes de vin et pour vingt sols un morceau de salé.

Pendant qu'il mangeait, Volnay observa du coin de l'œil les personnes à la table de jeu. Plusieurs prostituées se trouvaient manifestement parmi elles et lui adressaient des œillades coquines. Aucune d'elles ne semblait assez âgée pour être la Vorace que le marchand grec dépeignait comme une femme d'une quarantaine d'années. Le policier repéra une fille aux manières plus soignées que celles de ses collègues. Son visage, parsemé de taches de rousseur sur le nez et les pommettes, était encadré d'une courte chevelure rousse. Sa vivacité, ses yeux noisette, deux jolies fossettes et un ravissant petit menton en pointe faisaient penser à un écureuil. D'un geste discret, le commissaire aux morts étranges l'invita à sa table.

La prostituée eut un imperceptible mouvement de surprise et, après un court moment d'hésitation, les rejoignit sous les quolibets des joueurs. Les mots de *putain* et de *coquine* revenaient maintenant dans les conversations sur le couple. La fille se tint devant eux, les mains dans le dos, en se mordillant les lèvres. Volnay la considéra. De près, elle semblait très jeune, presque fragile, dans ses vêtements de mauvaise qualité : un casaquin de toile violette, des jupons à raies rouges et des bas de laine grise. Des bijoux de pacotille tintaient faiblement à ses poignets. Ses yeux laissaient filtrer une lueur inquiète que n'arrivait pas à atténuer son sourire engageant.

— Asseyez-vous, dit gentiment Hélène. Quel est votre nom ?

— Ici, on m'appelle l'Écureuil, répondit-elle en froissant nerveusement ses jupons aux couleurs défraîchies.

— Asseyez-vous, fit Volnay. Nous ne vous voulons aucun mal. Je cherche une de vos compagnes, une dénommée la Vorace. La connaissez-vous ?

L'autre prit une expression rusée.

— Pourquoi la voulez-vous elle plus qu'une autre ? Elle n'est pas de première jeunesse !

— Mais elle a bien d'autres qualités, répondit Volnay en clignant de l'œil.

L'Écureuil le considéra avec méfiance.

— C'est pour vous deux ?

Cela ne semblait guère avoir de sens pour elle qu'un couple aussi distingué soit à la recherche de cette femme. Volnay sentit la faiblesse de son argument sans trouver pour autant la bonne répartie. Ce fut Hélène qui vint à son secours.

— Mon mari a l'aiguillette nouée et n'est donc plus en mesure de me faire du bien au lit.

Si l'aiguillette était le lacet ferré à ses extrémités qui permettait de fermer les vêtements, c'était aussi le surnom du sexe des hommes. L'Écureuil prit un air soucieux.

— Oh ! Est-ce qu'on lui a jeté un sort ?

— Je l'ignore mais il m'a avoué que la Vorace est la dernière femme avec qui il a pu mener à bien son affaire.

Elle jeta un coup d'œil espiègle à Volnay.

— Mon mari a l'air sérieux comme cela mais en vérité c'est un homme à femmes !

Le policier ne broncha pas.

— Nous espérons tous deux, reprit Hélène, qu'en retrouvant la Vorace, elle puisse lui dénouer l'aiguillette.

La compréhension se fit jour sur le visage de la jeune fille.

147

— Mais, dit-elle encore méfiante, il n'a pas besoin de vous pour cela.

— C'est que, avoua Hélène en baissant les yeux d'un air gêné, j'aimerais bien voir comment elle s'y prend avec lui. Je pourrais reproduire ce qu'elle lui fait…

La prostituée hocha la tête. L'explication lui paraissait claire maintenant. Elle côtoyait le vice depuis assez longtemps pour ne plus être étonnée de rien.

— Je peux vous conduire jusqu'à elle mais cela vous coûtera quelques pièces car pendant ce temps c'est autant de clients que je ne prends pas.

— Vous serez bien rétribuée, intervint Volnay, mais dehors car je ne tiens pas à attirer l'attention sur ma bourse dans ce cabaret.

— Vous êtes un homme avisé, approuva-t-elle en le contemplant songeusement. Si madame votre épouse le permet, après que vous serez passé sur la Vorace, je pourrai lui montrer comment on ranime la flamme d'un homme avant de la moucher à nouveau.

Son regard s'attarda sur le beau visage du commissaire aux morts étranges.

— Vous seriez surpris de ce que je peux lui apprendre, ajouta-t-elle en se passant la langue sur les lèvres.

Le policier se leva, imité par Hélène.

— J'en suis persuadé ! Allez chercher votre manteau et sortons retrouver la Vorace.

Le temps s'était gâté mais, sous la clarté de la lune, les flocons de neige semblaient de la poudre d'argent. Volnay regarda Hélène et la trouva belle. À côté d'elle, la prostituée vacillait légèrement comme si la boisson et le froid la saisissaient soudain. Le policier leur prit le bras à toutes deux pour les aider à marcher sur le sol glacé. Étonnée par tant de délicatesse, l'Écureuil lui jeta un regard surpris.

L'immeuble sale et délabré dans lequel ils pénétrèrent exhalait des odeurs de fange fortes et prenantes. Des immondices formaient un tas puant à son entrée. Au rez-de-chaussée, se trouvait un atelier de menuiserie bruissant de vie.

— Garce à soldats ! marmonna un apprenti en les bousculant, une serpette à la main.

— Je ne connais pas cet homme, murmura l'Écureuil la tête baissée.

Derrière une porte, ils entendirent la querelle d'un couple suivi de quelques claques bien senties et des hurlements. Sans mot dire, ils empruntèrent un escalier aussi raide qu'une échelle, se tenant aux murs tant les marches craquaient, menaçant de se rompre à tout moment sous leur poids. Hélène lui prit naturellement la main et, un instant, le policier sentit son parfum l'envahir. Au second étage, à peine essoufflée, l'Écureuil désigna une porte sous laquelle filtrait une faible lueur. Tout à son rôle, Hélène se blottit contre Volnay. Tendant l'oreille, le policier distingua des bruits sourds et des halètements significatifs.

— Ah, fit la jeune prostituée, elle est en affaire. Il va falloir attendre. Avec les hommes, ce n'est jamais très long !

Volnay haussa légèrement les épaules. Hélène sourit, s'écarta de lui et croisa les bras sur sa poitrine, les yeux fixés sur le plancher. Soudain on entendit des cris :

— Garce ! Savate de tripière !

— Il ne la ménage pas, commenta sobrement l'Écureuil.

Des coups sourds se mirent à pleuvoir suivis d'exclamations :

— Gueuse ! Puante ! Prends ça !

Hélène tressaillit violemment comme si c'était elle qu'on venait de frapper. D'un geste instinctif, Volnay porta la main à son épée.

— Laissez, fit l'Écureuil d'un ton neutre, les hommes aiment à battre les femmes. Cela les aide à se croire plus forts que nous.

La porte ne tarda pas à s'ouvrir sur une face de rat d'un âge indéterminé. Surpris de trouver tant de monde sur le palier, l'homme les examina en écarquillant les yeux.

— Quelle foutue drôlesse ! dit-il dans un souffle avant de s'élancer dans l'escalier en se cognant l'épaule contre le mur.

— Au suivant ! cria une voix aigre. Et fermez la porte ou je vais attraper la mort !

Le commissaire aux morts étranges entra, suivi des deux femmes.

— Êtes-vous la Vorace ?

Celle-ci les fixa un instant. Elle avait dû être belle avant que la dureté des temps n'altère et ne durcisse ses traits. Ses paupières à demi baissées laissaient filtrer une lueur rusée, presque sournoise.

— À qui dois-je frotter le cul ? demanda-t-elle finalement.

Volnay réprima un sourire. À ses côtés, Hélène prit un air détaché. Le policier tira la pièce promise de sa bourse et la tendit à l'Écureuil.

— Merci, fit celle-ci en singeant une révérence. Si vous avez encore besoin de mes services, vous savez où me trouver quand je ne suis pas occupée.

— Je m'en souviendrai, répondit poliment Volnay.

Il la poussa doucement dehors et ferma la porte derrière elle.

— À nous deux, fit-il en se tournant vers la Vorace.

— À nous trois plutôt, remarqua la prostituée.

— Ce n'est pas ce que vous croyez. Je suis commissaire au Châtelet et je viens vous interroger sur votre participation à une messe noire qui a conduit au meurtre d'une enfant dans un cimetière.

Son ton était assuré, le policier préférant commencer par la conclusion plutôt que par la question. Le coup porta. Le visage fripé de la Vorace devint tout blanc comme si on venait de la vider de tout son sang. Elle ouvrit la bouche, la referma comiquement puis coassa dans un murmure :

— Quoi ? Que dites-vous ? Non, non ! Jamais je n'ai fait ça !

Volnay planta durement son regard dans le sien.

— Allons, je sais tout ! Comment vous avez acheté ce produit au marchand grec dans la ruelle de l'Or et comment vous avez administré la communion dans ce cimetière ! Vos complices ont parlé. Si vous ne voulez pas être accusée de meurtre, il faut tout me dire.

— Ce n'est pas moi ! Pas moi ! C'est ce damné curé !

— Comment se nomme-t-il ?

— Je ne sais pas ! On l'appelle le curé dansant. C'est un diable, il ne tient pas en place !

— Et les autres ? demanda Hélène. Il y avait trois hommes et deux femmes en plus de la victime dans ce cimetière…

— Je ne les avais jamais vus !

Le ton de sa voix était désespéré.

— Cela suffit ! fit Volnay en saisissant le coude de la femme. Vous allez me suivre au Châtelet.

Il la traîna jusqu'à la porte mais, arrivée là, elle cessa toute résistance et se projeta soudain en avant, déséquilibrant le policier. Avec l'énergie du désespoir, elle s'engouffra dans l'escalier. On entendit soudain un cri suivi du bruit sourd d'un corps qui roule. Volnay et Hélène se précipitèrent. La Vorace gisait sur le palier du premier, le corps désarticulé comme un pantin. Le policier s'agenouilla auprès de la prostituée.

— Elle s'est brisé la nuque, murmura-t-il lugubrement.

La jeune femme s'accroupit près de lui. Derrière eux, des portes s'entrouvraient et des visages hagards apparaissaient, contemplant le spectacle d'un air effaré. Volnay fixa curieusement Hélène.

— Le prêtre récite la messe à l'envers, la prostituée donne l'eucharistie et nous avons retrouvé les autres traces des pieds de deux hommes et d'une femme qui assistaient à cette messe. Cela dit, comment le saviez-vous puisque nous ne vous en avons jamais parlé?

— Sartine me l'a indiqué, vous lui avez fait un rapport, souvenez-vous…

Cette fois, Volnay ne détourna pas les yeux, plongeant dans ses immenses yeux verts aux reflets mouchetés de doré. Silencieusement, ils s'affrontèrent, aucun d'eux ne voulant céder le premier.

— C'est juste, dit enfin le policier d'un ton neutre.

Il lui prit la main et l'aida à se relever.

— Venez, nous allons prévenir le guet. Ensuite, nous rentrerons. La nuit tombe et je n'aime guère laisser le moine seul et malade.

Baignés par la lueur grisâtre d'un crépuscule précoce, les deux jeunes gens quittèrent le quartier populeux du faubourg Saint-Marcel et regagnèrent la demeure du moine.

— Il a dormi quelques heures, expliqua l'ouvrière en linge lorsqu'ils prirent des nouvelles du malade. Lorsqu'il s'est réveillé, il m'a demandé de lui préparer de nouveau une tisane et de lui appliquer sur les tempes un onguent pour faire tomber la fièvre. Ensuite, il s'est rendormi. J'ai dû le réveiller toutefois lorsque les messieurs sont venus pour le corps.

— Le corps?

Volnay se souvint tout à coup des embaumeurs qui devaient venir faire la toilette de Sophia et la mettre en bière.

— Ah oui, ceux-là… je les avais oubliés.

— Après, il a dormi de nouveau, continua l'ouvrière en linge.

Elle se mordilla les lèvres.

— Il faut que je vous dise, pendant qu'il dormait, j'entendais comme le bruit d'une conversation mais, lorsque je suis entrée dans la chambre, elle avait cessé et votre père se trouvait seul, l'air extasié…

— La fièvre devait le faire délirer, risqua Hélène.

La brave femme se tourna vers elle.

— C'est étrange pourtant, on aurait dit deux voix, la sienne et une voix féminine. À la porte, je l'ai entendu l'appeler Sophia. Le chien est devenu comme fou. J'ai été obligée de le sortir dans la cour. Mais même là, il continuait à gratter contre la porte…

Le commissaire aux morts étranges prit un air soucieux et tira de sa bourse quelques pièces.

— Je vous remercie. Peut-être aurai-je encore besoin de vos services demain.

— Vous savez où me trouver!

Elle empocha l'argent en remerciant et sortit. Une toux déchirante s'éleva de la chambre. Hélène se précipita et, lorsque Volnay la rejoignit, la jeune femme était assise sur le lit, caressant la main du moine.

— Voilà exactement le genre de soins que mon père adore! commenta sans réfléchir le policier.

— Votre père ?!

Hélène le contemplait, les yeux écarquillés de surprise. Volnay se rembrunit. Cela lui avait échappé.

— Je ne pensais pas Sartine aussi discret, murmura le moine.

— Il l'est, fulmina Volnay. C'est moi qui suis un âne bâté !

Un sourire illumina le visage d'Hélène.

— Votre père ?! répéta-t-elle.

Elle rit.

— Cela explique bien des choses !

— Sartine est seul au courant de notre parenté, fit sèchement Volnay. Je compte sur vous pour conserver ce secret.

— Mais pourquoi ? demanda Hélène.

— Cela vaut mieux pour nous deux, intervint le moine. Dans ma jeunesse, j'ai dit et fait bien des bêtises !

— Si c'était seulement dans ta jeunesse ! soupira son fils.

À nouveau, le rire clair d'Hélène emplit la pièce, résonnant joyeusement entre les murs froids. La jeune femme se leva, rejeta sa splendide chevelure en arrière et les contempla d'un air amusé.

— Jamais le proverbe tel père tel fils ne s'est révélé aussi faux ! commenta-t-elle avant de sortir de la pièce. En tout cas, vous vous êtes bien joué de moi, endormeurs de mulots ! Bon, je vais vous chercher à manger.

Elle sortit. Le moine l'accompagna du regard jusqu'à la porte. Volnay agacé secoua la tête mais son père sourit.

— Cette jeune femme est admirable, j'aimerais l'avoir pour fille !

— Il est vrai que tu n'as cure de ton fils, marmonna Volnay.

Le moine le considéra avec effarement.

— Mais pourquoi donc dis-tu ça?

— T'es-tu jamais soucié de moi quand j'étais enfant?

Le moine étouffa une quinte de toux sèche.

— C'est faux!

— Tu me disais que tu allais venir jouer avec moi et moi je te croyais bêtement, attendant des heures que tu lèves la tête de tes maudits bouquins.

— Mais je venais! Et puis je t'ai appris à écrire et à lire…

— Tu ne m'as appris à lire que pour te débarrasser de moi en me mettant dans les mains un de tes foutus bouquins!

Son père prit une expression attristée.

— Tu me fais de la peine, mon fils!

Il s'interrompit car Hélène revenait, une miche dans les mains.

— Nous avons acheté cela sur le chemin du retour, expliqua-t-elle. C'est un bon pain blanc à la farine de froment. Il vous faut reprendre des forces.

— Il me reste des noix, dit faiblement le moine. J'en mangerais bien quelques-unes trempées dans du bon sel blanc.

— Je vous les apporte tout de suite!

Le moine cligna de l'œil en direction de son fils.

— Je découvre tous les plaisirs d'être malade avec une jeune et jolie femme pour s'occuper de moi…

— N'en abuse pas! Et maintenant raconte-moi en détail ton rêve…

— Mon rêve? Mais est-ce bien un rêve?

VII

LE RÊVE DU MOINE
ET AUTRES DIABLERIES

Ce fut d'abord comme une présence invisible mais insistante qui lui fit ouvrir les yeux. Il s'efforça de garder son calme pour distinguer l'imaginaire du réel. Au bord du lit, fragile et pâle, les mains sagement posées sur ses genoux, Sophia assise le contemplait d'un air grave. Il nota qu'elle avait un petit air perdu mais rien de sa beauté subtile n'en était occulté et ses cheveux blonds lui ceignaient la tête comme un casque doré. Ses yeux bleus avaient la pureté des glaciers. Si, à son âge, il avait été son camarade de jeux, le moine pensa qu'il en serait tombé follement amoureux.

— Vous êtes bien malade et vous avez de la fièvre, dit-elle.

Le moine ne bougea pas comme si la jeune fille était un oiseau qu'un seul mouvement, même furtif, pouvait faire s'envoler.

— Dormez-vous ? demanda-t-elle.

— Non, je ne dors pas. Je ferme simplement les yeux pour me reposer de la vie.

— Vous devriez dormir, reprit-elle d'un ton très sérieux. Vous n'avez pas l'air bien du tout…

— Ce siècle est trop dur pour me permettre de dormir, répondit le moine.

Un gémissement se fit entendre derrière la porte.

— Qu'est-ce que c'est ?

— Votre chien. Il nous a adoptés moi et mon fils.

Elle battit des mains, ravie.

— Oh que je suis contente. Je peux lui ouvrir ?

— Il ne vaut mieux pas, il y a une dame dans l'autre pièce. Il ne faut pas qu'elle vous voie !

Il se redressa sur son séant. Sophia était habillée d'une robe de velours bleu pâle qui lui allait bien malgré la pâleur de sa mine. Un manteau couvrait ses épaules.

— N'avez-vous pas froid ?

— J'ai trouvé ces vêtements dans votre armoire. Ils étaient bien pliés, j'espère que cela ne vous contrarie pas.

— Ils appartenaient à ma femme, personne ne les porte plus aujourd'hui.

— Oh, j'en suis désolée.

— C'est ainsi.

— Enfin, ils sont un peu grands pour moi mais ils me tiennent chauds, surtout le manteau. J'ai eu si froid dans votre cave.

— J'en suis navré, je vous croyais morte.

— Mais vous avez posé cette grosse couverture sur moi, remarqua-t-elle. C'était gentil. Je vous entendais, vous savez ? Vous paraissiez tellement triste de me voir morte. Qui êtes-vous donc ?

Le moine plissa les yeux pour réfléchir.

— Disons que je suis une sorte de philosophe en avance sur son temps et de savant un peu fou. J'aide mon fils qui est policier. Il est chargé d'enquêter sur votre mort.

— Oh ! Alors, je suis morte ? Vraiment morte ?

Elle avait pris un air désemparé, presque apeurée.

— Que va-t-il m'arriver ?

Le moine tenta de la rassurer.

— J'imagine que vous allez gagner la lumière. C'est notre but à tous.

Sans un mot, Sophia se leva et alla à la fenêtre.

— Le ciel est si gris, murmura-t-elle. Serai-je encore là demain ? Passerai-je l'hiver et sentirai-je de nouveau les lilas et la rose ?

— Vous serez toujours en moi, répondit gravement le moine. *Macte animo ! Generose puer, sic itur ad astra.*

Et il traduisit pour être certain qu'elle comprenne :

— "Courage noble enfant ! C'est ainsi qu'on s'élève vers les étoiles."

Elle se tourna vers lui, son sourire flottait dans l'air, teinté de mélancolie.

— Je n'ai rien eu le temps d'apprendre, murmura-t-elle, et j'avais tant de choses à donner…

Pensive, elle se mordilla les lèvres avant de revenir vers lui à pas lents, les mains dans le dos.

— Avez-vous d'autres enfants que votre fils ?

Le moine se troubla.

— Non mais c'est la fierté de mes vieux jours même s'il l'ignore.

— L'important est qu'il sache que vous l'aimez !

À cet instant, le soleil sembla la frapper d'un de ses rayons anémiés. Le moine lui trouva une pâleur qui lui rappela la nuit au cimetière.

— Qui donc vous a tuée ? demanda-t-il.

Sophia se troubla.

— Tant de gens, chuchota-t-elle. Si vous saviez… À cet instant on entendit un bruit de pas puis une voix inquiète :

— Monsieur ? Tout va bien ?

Sophia posa un doigt sur ses lèvres pour lui intimer de se taire.

— Il faut que je disparaisse. Rendormez-vous ! Non, en fait, vous dormez déjà et moi je suis morte !

VIII

LE CURÉ DANSANT
ET AUTRES DIABLERIES

Le moine termina ainsi son récit, trônant comme un roi dans son fauteuil près de l'âtre. Il portait une magnifique robe de chambre d'indienne aux couleurs vives et aux motifs orientaux qui lui donnait l'apparence d'un monarque d'un pays exotique. Hélène et son fils l'écoutaient à ses pieds comme de fidèles sujets.

— Et c'est tout? demanda Volnay.

— Diable, fit le moine, oui. Je me suis rendormi mais sa présence était bien réelle, je te l'assure. Tiens, regarde, même le chien en a encore le poil tout hérissé!

Le policier jeta un coup d'œil à l'intelligent animal. Celui-ci haleta brièvement, la langue pendante avant de jeter un bref aboiement.

— Que veux-tu me dire? demanda le commissaire aux morts étranges avec un grand sérieux.

Les oreilles du chien bougèrent dans sa direction.

— Je vois, ma pie est plus explicite que toi…

Il contempla de nouveau le chien. Son poil était blanc mais parsemé par endroits de touffes rousses.

— Cet animal n'était-il pas d'une autre couleur lorsque je t'ai quitté?

— La bonne dame qui m'a gardé l'a jugé trop sale et l'a frotté. Cela l'a mis dans un état proche de la folie!

Volnay grogna quelque chose et s'approcha du feu, prenant plaisir à réchauffer ses doigts gourds au-dessus des flammes.

— Tout ceci est bien mystérieux mais je ne suis pas certain d'être le mieux placé pour interpréter tes rêves !

— Les rêves viennent à l'homme par des voies bien étranges, remarqua Hélène, et je ne pense pas que ceux-ci doivent quelque chose à la disposition des étoiles. Il me semble que c'est plutôt une voix extérieure, mais pourtant pas étrangère à nous-mêmes, qui nous parle sans que nous voulions l'entendre.

— Je tiens pour très intéressante votre approche des rêves, ma chère, fit le moine. Moi-même, il y a peu, j'ai rêvé d'abeilles. Vous savez ce que cela signifie ? Profit pour les pauvres, rien pour les riches ! Mais attention, si elle vous pique dans votre rêve, cela révèle un prochain échec !

Il étouffa une toux sèche.

— Enfin, pour en revenir à notre sujet, je ne suis pas certain que l'apparition de cette enfant puisse être qualifiée de rêve. J'ai plutôt l'impression que Sophia me parlait depuis l'au-delà.

Volnay et Hélène se jetèrent un coup d'œil entendu.

— Cette petite me hante, reprit le moine sans paraître remarquer leur inquiétude. J'ignore pourquoi mais elle m'a parlé, j'en suis certain !

— C'est sans doute parce qu'on l'enterre demain, hasarda Hélène, tout cela vous trouble.

Le commissaire aux morts étranges soupira puis tenta de changer de sujet de conversation.

— Il est bien de s'intéresser à la victime d'un meurtre mais il est plus important de porter son attention sur ses assassins. Tu es tellement fasciné par cette petite Sophia que tu ne nous as même pas interrogés sur notre enquête!

Il lui raconta alors l'épisode de la Vorace et le moine, les yeux brillants, poussa des exclamations.

— Eh bien, conclut-il, la justice a frappé. La prostituée a payé sa participation à cette sinistre messe noire, au tour de ce curé dansant!

Volnay se rembrunit. Il ne parvenait pas à s'habituer au comportement inhabituel de son père, d'habitude si posé, logique et réfléchi dans une enquête.

— Nous nous en occuperons plus tard, la nuit tombe tôt et je suis fatigué. J'aurais d'ailleurs peut-être besoin de quelques mouches pour m'occuper du curé dansant. Et puis demain matin, c'est l'enterrement de Sophia. Son père nous en a finalement laissé la charge. Il ne s'en occupe pas plus dans la mort que dans la vie! On viendra chercher le cercueil dans la cave demain vers dix heures.

Il jeta un coup d'œil à Hélène.

— Je vais rester veiller mon père. Si vous le souhaitez, vous pouvez passer la nuit chez moi puisque c'est à deux pas de là.

Il réalisa soudain qu'il ignorait où logeait la jeune femme, celle-ci ayant toujours couché chez son père jusqu'à présent!

— Je préfère rester là, un fauteuil me suffira. Allez prendre du repos, vous êtes fatigué, je le veillerai.

Volnay se figea.

— Ce n'est pas la peine, il n'est pas à l'article de la mort.

— Il est malade et encore faible, il faut que quelqu'un reste près de lui.

— Certes et je resterai.

Ils se défièrent du regard.

— C'est mon père, articula doucement Volnay avec une nuance dangereuse dans le ton. Je demeurerai près de lui.

Le moine intervint doucement.

— Non mon fils, rentre chez toi. Tu as besoin de repos car tu as beaucoup de sommeil en retard. Hélène restera près de moi. Et puis, ta pie a besoin de ta présence !

Le jeune homme se raidit.

— Père, je ne pense pas…

— Au contraire, tu penses trop. Rentre vite te reposer et dis bonsoir à la pie pour moi !

D'habitude impassible, le visage de Volnay sembla exprimer toute une série d'émotions contraires puis, comme sonné par un coup porté trop violemment, il se dirigea vers la porte en titubant légèrement. Avant de sortir, il se retourna comme s'il venait de se souvenir de quelque chose.

— Viens ici, toi ! ordonna-t-il au chien.

Celui-ci le regarda puis se retourna pour fixer le moine. Il semblait perplexe. Finalement, il choisit de se coucher aux pieds du propriétaire des lieux. Volnay sortit en claquant sèchement la porte derrière lui.

— Pourquoi avez-vous renvoyé votre fils ? demanda Hélène.

Le moine prit un air contrit.

— Quand je suis malade, je préfère la compagnie féminine.

— Vous avez déjà eu Sophia, lui fit-elle remarquer ingénument.

— Oui mais vous, vous êtes bien réelle !

Volnay était sorti furieux de chez son père. Il rentra chez lui, alluma du feu puis ôta la chaude couverture sur la cage de sa pie avec laquelle il engagea sa conversation habituelle.

— Ce vieil égoïste n'en a plus que pour cette Hélène! Ah, j'enrage! Elle est en train de lui mettre la main dessus. Et lui ne se rend compte de rien, trop heureux de pavaner devant elle qui l'écoute étaler sa science!

Cette fois, la pie resta silencieuse.

J'aurais dû tenter de l'embrasser, songea Volnay mais il n'en dit rien à la pie.

Il tourna encore en rond un moment avant de se décider à sortir. Ses pas rageurs le ramenèrent au cabaret où il avait fait la connaissance de l'Écureuil. La Vorace connaissant le curé dansant, peut-être en serait-il de même de la jeune prostituée. L'entrée du commissaire aux morts étranges suscita un regain de curiosité et les réflexions fusèrent. L'Écureuil se trouvait là, agrippée aux épaules d'un joueur chanceux. Le commissaire aux morts étranges commanda à boire et s'efforça d'avaler la piquette sans grimacer. Après un instant d'hésitation, la jeune prostituée le rejoignit et se tint près de lui, les mains dans le dos, se balançant d'un pied sur l'autre.

— On parle beaucoup dans le quartier, chuchota-t-elle. On raconte qu'un policier brutal a rendu visite à la Vorace et qu'elle en est morte.

— Elle s'est précipitée la tête la première dans l'escalier en voulant s'enfuir, se brisant la nuque contre les marches.

L'Écureuil déglutit péniblement.

— N'importe! Je ne veux pas avoir affaire à vous. Je tiens à ma réputation dans le quartier.

Volnay hocha la tête. Il savait que tout le monde connaissait tout le monde dans un quartier et qu'une réputation perdue pouvait dresser contre soi toute une communauté, rendant la vie impossible.

— Si l'on savait que c'est moi qui vous ai conduit à elle… reprit l'Écureuil en frissonnant.

— Que diriez-vous d'un louis d'or? demanda Volnay qui savait toujours trouver les bons arguments.

Une lueur d'envie voila le regard de l'Écureuil.

— Deux! fit-elle précipitamment. Congédiez-moi violemment comme si je vous agaçais puis sortez et rejoignez-moi à ma chambre dans une heure. La seconde rue à votre droite en remontant vers le maître bonnetier. Comptez trois portes et montez au dernier étage. J'ai dessiné un oiseau sur ma porte pour que les clients trouvent plus facilement.

— Un oiseau? Savez-vous que j'ai une pie chez moi? Elle sait parler…

— Vous m'en direz tant! Vous verrez que mon oiseau à moi est des plus ordinaires. Maintenant repoussez-moi, traitez-moi de gueuse et dites-moi de fiche le camp!

Le policier haussa les épaules, lui donna une bourrade et la repoussa brutalement en l'insultant, déclenchant des quolibets et des menaces à la table des joueurs. Volnay jeta ensuite son manteau sur ses épaules et se leva, toisant la tablée d'un air glacial, la main sur la garde de son épée. Cet avertissement muet éviterait qu'on ne le suive dans la rue.

Dehors, la nuit semblait porter tout le poids de la neige. Le vent jouait à projeter dans le ciel des gerbes d'écume blanche. Volnay cligna des yeux et, à travers les bourrasques, s'efforça de trouver l'adresse indiquée qu'il dépassa. Au coin de la rue, il s'embusqua pour vérifier que personne ne le suivait. Puis il revint prudemment sur ses pas, tous ses sens aux aguets. Il entra dans l'immeuble de l'Écureuil et gravit silencieusement les marches jusqu'à la porte de la jeune fille, reconnaissant le dessin grossier annoncé de l'oiseau.

Il s'emmitoufla dans son manteau et s'assit sur la dernière marche de l'escalier, les mains serrées autour de son corps pour se réchauffer, essayant d'oublier les effluves nauséabonds qui emplissaient les lieux. Au bout d'une petite heure qui lui parut interminable, un pas léger lui fit dresser l'oreille. Il se pencha avec précaution au-dessus de la balustrade et aperçut dans la pénombre une ombre menue. Bientôt se précisa la silhouette de l'Écureuil. Elle montait lentement, économisant son souffle en marquant une pause à chaque étage. Personne ne la suivait. Lorsqu'elle fut devant lui, les yeux brillants, Volnay craqua une allumette.

— Vous voilà…

La neige avait laissé son empreinte blanche dans ses cheveux. Volnay se retint de les épousseter même si l'envie lui en prit. L'Écureuil fourragea dans sa poche et en sortit une grosse clé qu'elle introduisit dans la serrure.

— Je vais faire de la lumière, dit-elle en passant devant lui.

Bientôt, la maigre lueur d'une chandelle se refléta contre le mur, révélant un réduit si étroit que Volnay eut la sensation qu'en écartant les deux bras il toucherait les murs de chaque côté. L'unique fenêtre était garnie de papier huilé et un froid atroce régnait dans la pièce. Hormis une paillasse recouverte de deux couvertures de laine, seuls un coffre pour les affaires, une petite table et une chaise meublaient l'appartement. Le commissaire aux morts étranges entra. En souriant, la jeune fille referma à clé derrière lui.

— Est-ce bien utile ? demanda Volnay étonné. Je ne compte pas rester.

— Monseigneur sera plus rassuré qu'on ne puisse pénétrer ici, remarqua-t-elle finement.

Le policier hocha la tête pour marquer son approbation mais conserva ses distances lorsque la jeune fille s'assit sur son grabat. Elle était si maigre qu'elle semblait avoir les flancs cousus. Ses jupons relevés laissaient entrevoir une paire de bottines noires et des bas de laine gris rapiécés. Elle tendit la main.

— Mes deux louis, s'il vous plaît.

Volnay lui en glissa un dans la paume et tira la chaise à lui.

— Vous aurez l'autre si vous me renseignez bien.

— Ce n'était pas convenu ainsi, se plaignit-elle.

— C'est ainsi. Je cherche un curé, sans doute défroqué. On le surnomme le curé dansant. Avez-vous entendu parler de lui ?

Elle rit.

— C'était un bon ami de la Vorace mais il n'est pas plus curé que vous et moi. Il était bedeau mais on l'a chassé car il buvait trop, surtout le vin de messe ! C'est un mauvais homme. Il rôde dans le quartier et l'on raconte qu'il travaille avec les voleurs de cadavres.

— A-t-il des amis ?

L'Écureuil eut un bref haussement d'épaules.

— Personne ne peut le supporter. Il vous regarde avec le mauvais œil et vous lance des sorts ! Ici, on craint cela. Savez-vous que le démon est déjà passé par la taverne d'où nous venons il y a dix ans de cela ?

— Vraiment ? fit Volnay sceptique mais amusé.

— Oui, on raconte qu'un soir de grand orage un homme vêtu de noir entra dans la taverne et offrit à boire à tous les clients jusque tard dans la nuit. Sa bourse était bien pleine. Le tavernier alla dormir en cachant celle-ci sous son oreiller. Au matin, lorsqu'il l'ouvrit, elle ne contenait plus que du charbon et du fumier !

— Et il en déduisit que c'était le diable qui l'avait payé !

Volnay songea qu'on avait surtout habilement détroussé le tavernier mais il n'en dit rien.

— Revenons à notre curé dansant, savez-vous où il demeure ?

Elle secoua la tête.

— Je n'en ai aucune idée.

— Alors, vous n'aurez pas ce second louis.

— Attendez !

Elle fronça comiquement les sourcils et tordit sa jolie bouche en une moue désabusée.

— Comme vous êtes dur avec moi ! Ne vous êtes-vous jamais demandé pourquoi on le nomme le *curé dansant* ?

Vexé, Volnay dut reconnaître que non.

— Eh bien, triompha l'Écureuil, parce qu'il danse ! Je connais un cabaret où l'on joue de la musique pour danser. Chaque fois que j'y suis allée, je l'ai aperçu. Je peux vous y conduire. Nous y serons une heure avant minuit.

Elle tendit la main.

— Ma pièce !

— Je vous la donnerai lorsque nous verrons notre homme. Vous avez fort bien pu inventer cette histoire de cabaret !

Elle fit semblant de bouder.

— Méchant policier !

Mais Volnay n'était pas d'humeur à plaisanter.

— Allons-y, la pressa-t-il en se levant.

L'Écureuil ne bougea pas. Sa main froissait et défroissait nerveusement les plis de son jupon. Un instant, le bas qui couvrait sa cheville luit faiblement à la clarté de la chandelle.

— D'accord! fit-elle précipitamment en sautant sur ses pieds.

Et elle trébucha pour tomber dans les bras de Volnay. Le jeune homme la retint instinctivement, les bras autour de sa taille. Elle en profita pour plaquer ses lèvres sur les siennes. Volnay la repoussa doucement, sa bouche encore fraîche du baiser déposé. Son cœur était ailleurs, à soupirer après Chiara qui s'en était allée après le lui avoir brisé.

— Je ne suis pas assez bien pour vous, c'est cela? regretta l'Écureuil.

— Cela n'a rien à voir, la rassura-t-il.

Et cela était vrai tant Volnay n'éprouvait aucune fierté particulière à tenir son rang et ne portait en lui que des idées d'égalité et de fraternité.

— Mettez votre manteau, reprit-il, nous sortons.

La jeune fille recula d'un pas et, levant la main, effleura du bout des doigts la fine cicatrice qui courait du coin de son œil droit à sa tempe.

— On a été bien méchant avec vous, j'espère que celui qui vous a fait cela subira le feu de la justice divine…

Le commissaire aux morts étranges la considéra soudain avec attention.

— Vous parlez bien pour une fille des rues, remarqua-t-il. Vous avez dû recevoir de l'éducation. D'où venez-vous donc?

Charmée que le policier s'intéresse enfin à elle, la jeune prostituée se montra bavarde.

— Mon grand-père était fabricant de bas et mon père maître tailleur. Il épousa ma mère qui était étalante au marché Saint-Martin. Mes parents étaient très sévères avec moi, un peu moins avec mes deux frères. Ils nous firent apprendre à lire et à écrire, à compter et quelques petites autres choses qui peuvent servir.

Elle regarda autour d'elle, hésita puis se rassit sur son grabat.

— Pour mon malheur, lorsque j'eus quatorze ans, je rencontrai un beau garçon aux manières très honnêtes et qui me paraissait sincère. Il était garçon parfumeur et me fit la cour avec suffisamment de sentiment et de conviction pour toucher mon cœur. Il vint à bout de toutes mes réticences jusqu'à jouir de moi et prendre mon pucelage. Il s'en vanta ensuite dans le quartier, ce qui fut vite rapporté à mes parents.

Le policier hocha la tête. Dans un quartier tout se savait et la rumeur allait parfois aussi vite qu'un cheval au galop, souillant et dévastant les réputations.

— Je fus jetée à la rue sans procès. Mon amoureux m'installa avec lui dans sa mansarde mais se lassa de moi et prit l'habitude de me partager avec un de ses camarades. Je n'osais dire non, de peur d'être jetée dehors, seule et sans travail, et de finir en prison. Un soir, ce garçon amena deux amis à lui avec un pâté et un tonnelet de vin. On but, on mangea puis on abusa de moi. On me frappa tellement fort que les voisins vinrent s'en plaindre et menacer d'appeler le sergent du guet. Cette fois, on me jeta dehors et je finis la nuit sur le parvis d'une église. À partir de là, je me jurai qu'on ne me prendrait plus mon corps sans m'en payer le prix.

Elle baissa la tête.

— Même s'il n'est pas très élevé…

Un frisson la saisit. L'Écureuil frotta ses mains l'une contre l'autre pour se réchauffer. Volnay ôta son manteau pour lui couvrir les épaules et s'assit à côté d'elle.

— Vous valez plus que tout l'or du monde, dit-il gentiment.

Elle ouvrit grande la bouche et oublia de la refermer, surprise de tant d'attention désintéressée à son égard. Pour sa part, le commissaire aux morts étranges savait qu'en ville une jeune fille sans famille ni protection courait facilement le risque de tomber dans la prostitution. Les plus chanceuses parvenaient à se faire embaucher dans l'industrie où les ouvrières se trouvaient bien payées, même si elles occupaient les plus bas emplois, mais pour cela des connaissances étaient nécessaires. Les autres, si elles ne vendaient pas leur corps, se retrouvaient dans les petits métiers de rue, à vendre des vêtements usagés sur les marchés, des bottes d'épingles sur les trottoirs ou à colporter du charbon ou du bois. D'autres enfin arrivaient parfois à coudre et repriser lorsqu'elles trouvaient un compagnon qui connaissait suffisamment de monde pour obtenir de l'ouvrage.

— Allons, racontez-moi la suite, l'encouragea Volnay.

— Au petit matin, reprit l'Écureuil enhardie en se serrant contre lui, j'allai mendier un quignon de pain dans une boulangerie. Le boulanger me proposa de me donner chaque jour une miche de pain contre mes faveurs. Dans la nuit, il quittait quelques instants son fourneau pour me promener dans les rues et me prendre rapidement sous un porche ou dans une cour dès qu'il en avait l'occasion. Je fis cela avec plusieurs commerçants du quartier, le temps d'avoir de quoi louer une petite chambre.

Du regard, elle parcourut les tristes lieux.

— Ici, c'est tout petit. Je ne possède presque rien et mon logement sent mauvais mais j'ai un toit pour dormir chaque nuit et j'arrive à manger deux fois par jour. C'est bien mieux que rien !

Elle ouvrit sa paume et contempla avec ravissement le louis d'or qui scintillait faiblement.

— C'est la première fois que j'ai quelques économies. Je vais aller m'acheter des vêtements plus chauds, une bonne couverture et payer quelques mois de loyer d'avance. Peut-être pourrai-je même faire mettre une vraie fenêtre !

Ému malgré lui, Volnay la questionna.

— Quel âge avez-vous ?

— Seize ans. Et vous ?

Ses yeux noisette le fixaient avec curiosité.

— Presque dix de plus !

— Oh ! Vous faites plus vieux que cela !

Un mince sourire éclaira le visage pâle du commissaire aux morts étranges. Embarrassée, elle rougit.

— Ce n'est pas ce que je voulais dire. Vous ne faites pas vieux, c'est juste que vous êtes un peu… sérieux !

Elle s'arrêta stupéfaite. Volnay riait aux éclats, surpris et charmé par tant de fraîcheur. Elle jugea qu'il paraissait bien plus jeune lorsqu'il se laissait ainsi aller et se prit à espérer toucher son cœur car il lui plaisait bien.

Le commissaire aux morts étranges baissa la tête et sembla s'absorber dans la contemplation des bottines de l'Écureuil. La distance qu'il maintenait par rapport aux autres ne le privait ni d'émotions, ni de sentiments. Ému par l'histoire de la jeune fille, il n'en voulait toutefois rien laisser paraître.

— Venez, petit Écureuil, dit-il d'un ton très doux. Il faut nous en aller. Couvrez-vous bien ! Je ne veux pas que vous preniez froid.

Ils sortirent sous la voûte étoilée, silhouettes solitaires dans la nuit glaciale, marchant prudemment côte à côte à travers les rues enneigées. La rue Bordelles se prolongeait au-delà de l'enceinte de Philippe Auguste et des eaux putrides de la Bièvre par la rue Mouffetard traversant le bourg Saint-Médard. L'odeur des tanneurs, écorcheurs et tripiers qui la bordait souleva le cœur de Volnay mais ne sembla pas incommoder sa compagne.

La foule s'amassait dans une sorte de grange auberge au fond de laquelle se dressait une estrade. Des violonistes échevelés y tiraient l'archet, arrachant de leur instrument un son triomphant. Sous les lampions dansait, sautait et hurlait une foule bigarrée. Les danseurs portaient de mauvais habits, souvent rapiécés. Leurs chaussures ou sabots frappaient le sol de terre battue, provoquant un nuage de poussière, dans un rythme sourd qui reproduisait celui d'un cœur battant follement.

— Cela vous prend dès que l'on entre, n'est-ce pas ? fit l'Écureuil.

— Quoi donc ?

— L'envie de danser et de se serrer l'un contre l'autre !

Et elle accompagna cette déclaration d'un regard brûlant. Volnay haussa les épaules. Il ne suffisait pas d'une œillade pour enflammer le cœur du commissaire aux morts étranges.

— Faisons ensemble le tour de la salle pour tenter d'apercevoir notre homme.

— Sans danser ?

— Oui, sans danser.

— Alors, tenez-moi par la main comme si nous étions ensemble et souriez. Vous ressemblez trop à un policier !

Il lui prit donc la main, elle était toute menue dans la sienne. On jouait maintenant une gavotte à deux temps, assez enlevée, et les danseurs formaient une ligne pour suivre le mouvement vif et gai. Il fut alors plus aisé de dévisager les hommes présents et l'Écureuil secoua la tête.

— Il n'est pas là.

— Vous êtes sûre ? Regardez encore, s'il vous plaît. Prenez votre temps.

— Il n'est pas là, vous dis-je.

— Et parmi ceux-là ?

Il désigna du menton des hommes qui ne dansaient pas. Les yeux assombris de désir, ils fixaient durement les plus mignonnes des filles qui se déhanchaient.

— Non, confirma-t-elle. Et je vous l'ai dit, le curé dansant danse ! Nous pouvons peut-être l'attendre en mangeant quelque chose ?

Elle désignait dans un coin de la salle une table qui venait de se libérer. Volnay considéra un instant ses flancs maigres et approuva. Pour dix sols chacun, ils eurent droit à une soupe, un bouilli, un petit morceau de fromage et un demi-verre d'un vin aigre à déchausser les dents. L'Écureuil mangea gaiement et avec appétit. Elle semblait satisfaite de sa soirée et glissait de temps à autre un regard langoureux en direction du commissaire aux morts étranges, fort beau garçon au demeurant. Mais lorsqu'une femme aux sourcils peints frôlait son compagnon, elle fronçait les sourcils en guise d'avertissement, indiquant clairement qu'il était sa propriété.

Volnay se détendit et raconta une anecdote qui courait en ville. Un médecin bien connu se pavanait à l'Opéra avant une représentation, accompagné de deux danseuses. Par jeu, l'une d'elles lui ôta sa perruque et l'autre s'exclama :

— Oh, qu'as-tu fait ? Tu viens de lui ôter sa réputation !

Un rire irrépressible gagna l'Écureuil et Volnay charmé l'accompagna jusqu'à ce que la main de la jeune fille couvre la sienne. Il tressaillit et la retira avant de jeter un coup d'œil autour de lui.

— Il n'est toujours pas là ?

Dépitée, l'Écureuil secoua la tête.

— Attendons-nous encore ?

— Il se fait tard.

— Vous ne voulez toujours pas danser ?

— Non.

— Je suis sûre que vous n'avez jamais essayé !

Sans répondre, il donna le signal du départ en se levant et en lui tendant la main. Debout face à face, ils se considérèrent en silence. L'Écureuil trouvait difficile de se plonger dans le regard sans fond du commissaire aux morts étranges. Et puis, celui-ci se détourna et leur fraya avec assurance un chemin dans la foule.

En sortant, ils rencontrèrent un groupe masqué qui semblait pris de boisson. Des quolibets fusèrent à l'intention de la jeune fille. D'une main, Volnay saisit le bras de l'Écureuil et de l'autre caressa la poignée de son épée, geste qui ne passa pas inaperçu et refroidit l'ardeur des moqueurs.

— Les rues ne sont pas sûres. Je vais vous raccompagner chez vous.

Elle le considéra songeusement avant de répondre d'un ton neutre :

— Si vous le désirez.

Ils marchèrent l'un contre l'autre dans la rue pour se protéger du froid et de la bise sifflante. Arrivés en bas de l'immeuble de l'Écureuil, Volnay s'arrêta.

— Vous ne montez pas ? demanda la jeune fille.

— Non.

Elle se mordit les lèvres.

— Je ne vous plais pas ?

— Ce n'est pas cela.

— C'est parce que je suis une prostituée alors ?

— À la cour de Versailles, on se prostitue beaucoup plus que dans les rues de Paris !

Il ôta son gant et caressa du bout des doigts la joue rosie par le froid de la jeune fille qui frémit.

— Vous valez beaucoup mieux que vous ne le pensez.

— Alors pourquoi ne pas monter quelques instants avec moi, je prendrai soin de vous, fit-elle d'un ton plein d'espoir.

— Le frottement de deux épidermes l'un contre l'autre ne résout pas tout ! Que reste-t-il après cela ?

— Il n'y a pas que les corps, fit-elle d'un ton plein d'espoir. Il y a aussi l'amour…

Volnay recula d'un pas, désabusé.

— L'amour est un jeu de dupes, pourquoi y jouerions-nous ?

Il se saisit de sa main et y déposa le second louis d'or. Puis, mû par une étrange impulsion, il se recula pour baiser cette main en effleurant le bout des doigts de ses lèvres comme il aurait fait avec une marquise.

— Mais nous n'avons pas trouvé le curé dansant, s'étonna-t-elle en rougissant.

— Vous n'y êtes pour rien.

— Vous reverrai-je ? demanda-t-elle d'une voix soudain fluette.

— Oui. Je reviendrai chez vous demain soir, à neuf heures. Nous retenterons notre chance. D'ici là, renseignez-vous mais discrètement. N'éveillez pas l'attention. Si nous trouvons notre curé dansant, vous aurez droit à deux autres louis d'or.

— Oh, s'exclama-t-elle. Je serai riche !

Elle se haussa sur la pointe des pieds et, avant qu'il ne puisse réagir, déposa sur ses lèvres un baiser glacé.

— À demain alors ! fit-elle.

Il la contempla s'éloigner et, alors même que la porte de l'immeuble s'était refermée derrière elle, resta un long moment immobile, songeur sous la neige qui tombait et recouvrait toute chose.

IX

SARTINE ET AUTRES DIABLERIES

Au petit matin, Volnay prit le chemin du Châtelet. Il devait signaler les assassins des quais et en profiterait pour visiter Sartine. Le lieutenant général de police était un personnage considérable dans le royaume et il n'était pas de bonne politique de le négliger.

Malgré le froid dans la pièce, Sartine se trouvait en gilet sans manches. Pour une fois, il reçut cordialement son collaborateur et sembla satisfait des premières explications de son commissaire aux morts étranges.

— Alors, vous avez pu identifier la victime. Sophia, vous dites ?

À sa grande surprise, Volnay le vit aller à son bureau et se saisir du croquis de la jeune victime qu'il lui avait laissé. Ainsi Sartine le gardait à portée de main ?

— Voici donc son nom, murmura le lieutenant général de police en contemplant songeusement le portrait. Sophia...

— Ce n'est pas tout, reprit le commissaire aux morts étranges en cachant son étonnement devant l'attitude inhabituelle de Sartine. J'ai pu retrouver la prostituée qui donnait l'eucharistie au cours de cette messe noire.

Et il raconta toute l'histoire.

— Comment avez-vous fait pour laisser échapper cette femme ? tempêta Sartine à la fin du récit. La prochaine fois, prenez avec vous des archers du guet! Cette histoire pourrait déjà être terminée sans votre maladresse!

Le commissaire aux morts étranges encaissa sans broncher ces injustes reproches et parla du second suspect, sans toutefois mentionner la piste de l'Écureuil.

— *Le curé dansant?* répéta Sartine. Quel drôle de surnom! Il dansera encore mieux au bout d'une corde! Je vais mettre mes agents sur ses talons. De votre côté, ne vous en mêlez pas et concentrez tous vos efforts à rechercher l'identité des trois autres participants. Deux hommes et une femme, c'est cela?

Le commissaire aux morts étranges acquiesça. Sartine s'assit sur son bureau, une jambe balançant dans le vide et le fixant d'un air pensif.

— Dites-moi, cet astrologue traitait-il bien sa fille?

Volnay haussa un sourcil interrogateur.

— Était-il un bon père? La battait-il? insista le lieutenant général de police.

— Je ne pense pas. Il ne s'en occupait pas tout simplement. Comme bien des gens de nos jours.

— Ah oui, je comprends.

Sartine hésita.

— Néanmoins, possédait-elle une chambre à elle, prenait-elle trois repas par jour?

— Oui, elle avait un toit et de quoi manger, répondit Volnay de plus en plus étonné par l'insistance de son supérieur et l'étrangeté de ses questions.

Le lieutenant général de police lui tourna le dos et alla se planter devant la fenêtre, les mains dans le dos. Volnay l'observa à la dérobée, remarquant que le teint vieil ivoire de Sartine avait fait place à une pâleur extrême. D'habitude vif, une espèce de langueur semblait aujourd'hui accompagner tous ses mouvements.

— J'ai rêvé d'elle.

— Pardon ? fit Volnay abasourdi.

— Cette nuit, j'ai rêvé de Sophia, dit Sartine d'une voix basse. Elle venait me parler.

Il se retourna vers Volnay, l'air gêné, attitude également peu fréquente chez lui.

— Ce n'est qu'un rêve me direz-vous mais elle semblait si réelle. Comment était-elle habillée dans le cimetière ?

— Vous savez bien que nous l'avons retrouvée nue.

Sartine parut embarrassé.

— Certes, certes ! C'était curieux, dans mon rêve, elle portait des vêtements qui convenaient plus à une femme qu'à une enfant de son âge.

— Que vous a-t-elle dit ? demanda le commissaire aux morts étranges en entrant dans son jeu.

— Elle m'a raconté qu'elle était à la recherche de son chien.

Malgré la fraîcheur de la température dans la pièce, Volnay sentit une sueur glaciale lui couler dans le dos. Sartine ne manqua pas de remarquer qu'il se raidissait.

— Ah, je vois que cette histoire de chien éveille quelque chose en vous ! Dites-moi tout ! Ne me cachez rien !

Le commissaire aux morts étranges lui rappela alors les plaintes et gémissements du chien devant le cimetière le soir du meurtre.

— Oui, je me souviens, fit Sartine. Vous m'aviez très bien restitué l'ambiance de cette nuit-là.

Et pour cause ! Le policier savait que son supérieur allait raconter chaque semaine au roi tout ce qui se passait et qu'il aimait mettre un peu de piquant dans ses récits pour mieux capter l'attention de Louis XV.

— Cet intelligent animal m'a ensuite suivi.

— Quoi ?!

Volnay développa toute l'histoire ainsi que les découvertes d'Hélène chez le commissaire de quartier. Sartine parcourait la pièce de long en large, étrangement agité, ne s'arrêtant que pour prendre une prise qu'il s'envoya directement dans les narines avant d'éternuer.

— On me cache des choses !

— Ce n'était qu'un chien ! Ce n'est pas lui qui nous conduira aux assassins !

— N'importe !

Sartine froissa nerveusement son mouchoir de dentelle.

— Je veux tout savoir sur cette affaire, vous m'entendez ? Tout !

Il réprima un frémissement et s'approcha du feu qui brûlait joyeusement dans la cheminée. Le commissaire aux morts étranges fit de même, tendant avec lui les mains vers les flammes pour les réchauffer. Ainsi côte à côte, Sartine prit le ton de la confidence.

— Ce qui est très curieux, c'est que j'ignorais cette histoire de chien. Je n'ai pas donc pu l'inventer.

— L'esprit nous joue souvent des tours, fit Volnay. Mon père a ses théories là-dessus et affirme qu'une certaine voix, étrangère et familière à la fois, tente de nous parler dans notre sommeil.

— Votre père est un fou ! Je ne parle pas de cela, moi !

Il hésita et jeta un coup d'œil derrière son épaule comme s'il avait peur d'être espionné et chuchota d'une voix basse :

— On dit que l'âme des défunts erre quarante jours…

Un instant, la raison de Volnay vacilla, saisie d'une peur subite. Après son père, Sartine…

— Je n'y crois pas, murmura-t-il.

Le lieutenant général de police lui jeta un regard acerbe.

— Vous et votre père ne croyez en rien d'autre que ce que vous pouvez prouver !

Le commissaire aux morts étranges hocha sèchement la tête.

— C'est juste !

Sartine s'abîma dans la contemplation des flammes claires qui jaillissaient de l'âtre.

— C'est votre force, Volnay, mais aussi votre faiblesse. Votre esprit manque de spiritualité. Vous n'êtes pas ouvert comme moi à l'invisible et à l'inattendu !

Le commissaire aux morts étranges se mordilla pensivement les lèvres. La conversation avec son supérieur prenait une tournure surprenante. Elle aurait même pu être dangereuse avec quelqu'un d'autre que lui mais Volnay savait pertinemment que Sartine n'entretenait plus aucun doute sur son impiété et celle de son père. Le lieutenant général de police se tourna brusquement vers lui, l'air effrayé.

— Volnay, et si l'âme de Sophia était revenue pour se venger de ses meurtriers ?

X

L'ENTERREMENT
ET AUTRES DIABLERIES

La lumière pâle du jour perçait à travers les volets lorsque le moine ouvrit les yeux. Ses médications semblaient lui avoir vidé la poitrine des humeurs mauvaises qui l'habitaient. Le lait chaud et le miel enveloppaient encore son palais d'une gangue douceâtre. Pour apaiser sa soif, il prit un verre de la tisane de sa composition qui ne quittait plus son chevet. Ensuite, il alluma la chandelle et, ne percevant aucun bruit dans la maison, quitta son lit tiède pour alimenter son poêle et rapporter avec lui le livre de Sophia sous les couvertures.

Avec impatience, il tourna les pages. La jeune enfant consignait ses rêves lorsqu'elle s'en rappelait au matin. Connaissant les saintes Écritures, le moine savait qu'elles enseignent que *Dieu se sert des rêves afin que l'homme puisse voir à travers les ténèbres.* Ce n'était pas le cas de Sophia. Les récits de sa nourrice et les histoires dont elle s'était nourrie avaient gravé dans son imaginaire l'ombre effrayante d'ogres qui s'en prenaient aux enfants pour les dévorer ou pire encore. La tombée de la nuit l'effrayait car, selon les récits à la veillée, elle annonçait la sortie des spectres de leurs tombeaux et leur errance jusqu'au chant du coq à l'aube. Le moine fronça les sourcils, attentif à déceler dans ces pages le réel de l'imaginaire afin d'y découvrir des faits qui auraient secrètement imprégné son esprit.

La tour dans laquelle vivait en reclus son père, l'astrologue, lui inspirait les plus vives terreurs. Sans trop savoir pourquoi, Sophia la considérait comme un endroit dangereux, fermé sur d'horribles vérités. Le moine essaya de débrouiller les temps de rêve des temps de réalité. Seule subsistait une pénible impression de peur de l'inconnu et le désagréable sentiment que la tour de son père recélait un danger innommable. Il lui était d'ailleurs formellement interdit d'y pénétrer.

Le passage suivant était plus pénible. Âgée de onze ans, Sophia accompagna son père à la boutique d'un graveur. Pendant que les deux hommes discutaient entre eux sans lui prêter la moindre attention, l'enfant s'aventura jusqu'à l'atelier où travaillait un jeune apprenti. Celui-ci leva les yeux sur elle avant de l'inviter à voir de plus près son ouvrage. Tandis qu'elle admirait la gravure, l'apprenti s'empara de sa main pour la porter jusqu'à son entrecuisse. Sous les doigts de Sophia, quelque chose d'extrêmement dur se contracta et se rétracta comme un monstrueux serpent. Troublée et mal à l'aise, Sophia retira vivement sa main. Malgré son ignorance de la vie, elle sentait confusément que le jeune garçon cherchait à abuser d'elle.

— Oh, ce doit être très mal! chuchota-t-elle.

L'autre eut un rire dur.

— Votre père fait bien de même avec votre mère, se moqua-t-il.

À la pensée de sa pauvre maman, les larmes vinrent aux yeux de Sophia et elle s'enfuit. Plus tard, elle consigna son émoi dans son journal. Cette incursion inattendue dans le monde des adultes n'éveilla en elle aucun désir, simplement une certaine révulsion et une aversion profonde pour les hommes qui abusaient de son jeune âge pour des choses malhonnêtes.

Le moine reposa le livre pour essuyer ses yeux. Dans la promiscuité des immeubles, des boutiques et des ateliers, sans surveillance des parents qui laissaient errer leurs enfants pendant qu'ils travaillaient, ce genre de choses était monnaie courante. Il plissa les narines avec dégoût. Par moments, la nature humaine le révulsait si fortement qu'il en était prêt à oublier sa fraternité pour elle.

Il tourna une page. Heureusement, la très sérieuse Sophia laissait parfois place à la fantaisie, ainsi lorsqu'elle racontait avoir versé une bouteille d'encre dans le bénitier de l'église !

Le moine rit puis subitement la réalité le glaça. C'était ce matin qu'on enterrerait la jeune fille. Un coup discret se fit entendre contre la porte qui s'entrebâilla lorsqu'il y répondit. Les beaux yeux mouchetés d'or d'Hélène brillèrent dans la demi-pénombre.

— Vous êtes réveillé ? Je vous ai apporté du pain frais et du lait. Je n'aurai pas le temps de vous le chauffer.

Il laissa son regard traîner nonchalamment sur elle.

— Où allez-vous donc, ma chère ?

Elle hésita.

— À l'enterrement de Sophia.

Le moine rejeta brusquement ses couvertures.

— Je vous accompagne !

La jeune femme le gourmanda.

— Est-ce bien raisonnable ?

Le moine ne prit même pas la peine de répondre et commença à se déshabiller. Hélène émit un petit cri de désapprobation et referma vivement la porte. Une fois chaudement vêtu, le moine tourna en rond dans la maison.

— Je ne retrouve plus ma clé ! Pourtant, je la laisse toujours dans la serrure, c'est le meilleur moyen de ne pas la perdre. Ah, les clés ! Les clés !

Il toucha son trousseau à sa ceinture.

— N'importe, j'en ai une autre. Je chercherai plus tard !

Dehors, ses pieds mordirent dans une couche de neige fraîche. Un vent cinglant le frappa au visage, lui tirant les larmes des yeux. Il s'immobilisa, les narines frémissantes.

— Quel est le jean-foutre qui vient pisser devant ma porte ?

Hélène le rejoignit et passa sur ses épaules un chaud manteau de laine.

— Ce n'est pas moi, je vous l'assure !

Le moine étouffa une toux sèche.

— Diable ! C'est que je ne vous accusais pas mais regardez vous-même cette tache dans la neige.

— Le chien ?

— Non, je suis sorti en même temps que lui et il a directement filé plus loin pour gambader sans même daigner lever la patte ! Bah, n'en parlons plus ! Où sont donc les employés pour emporter le cercueil ? Ah, les voici ! Je crois que je vais aller boire ma potion pour me protéger du froid.

Elle le regarda avec malice.

— Celle à base d'eau-de-vie ?

L'enterrement avait lieu en fin de matinée dans le petit cimetière Saint-Sulpice. Le cercueil était parti de la demeure du moine pour marquer une première étape à la demeure de l'astronome afin qu'il se recueille une dernière fois dans l'intimité devant la dépouille de sa fille. Pour sa part, le commissaire aux morts étranges était venu un peu à l'avance pour mieux observer les gens assistant à l'enterrement et noter leur ordre d'arrivée. On en apprenait parfois plus devant un cercueil que dans une conversation.

Un attroupement se pressait devant la grille et Volnay accéléra le pas pour en connaître la cause. Lorsqu'il en vit la raison, un grand froid l'envahit et les paroles de Sartine à propos de Sophia revinrent à sa mémoire. Sur un panneau était inscrite cette simple phrase : *Interdit à Dieu d'entrer dans ce lieu.*

Volnay sentit une fois de plus sa raison attaquée par l'irrationnel. Les propos de Sartine l'avaient surpris et ébranlé. Et voici qu'une main inconnue venait d'inscrire cet avertissement qui résonnait comme une provocation.

Interdit à Dieu d'entrer dans ce lieu… Les satanistes étant gens discrets, aucun d'eux ne s'amuserait à une telle provocation. Cette interdiction planait plutôt comme une menace insensée et désespérée. Le commissaire aux morts étranges contempla avec attention les visages des badauds attroupés. Leurs expressions étaient outrées et indignées. Personne parmi eux ne souriait. On ne plaisantait pas avec la mort.

Volnay se décida rapidement, fendit la foule et, sortant sa dague, décrocha le panneau. Ceci fait, il se tourna et, sans rien dire, fixa de ses yeux bleu pâle et gris les gens autour de lui. Cela sentait le policier. Les gens baissèrent la tête et s'éparpillèrent en grommelant.

À ce moment-là, une procession approcha et l'on se signa avec respect devant elle. M. Marly et sa servante marchaient en avant, suivis d'une vieille parente et de quelques voisins. Malgré sa faiblesse, le moine avait tenu à venir et Hélène lui tenait le bras. Volnay vit la jeune femme saluer un grand homme au maintien compassé et devina qu'il s'agissait du commissaire de quartier. Ainsi, lui aussi avait-il tenu à rendre hommage à la petite Sophia. Le commissaire aux morts étranges connaissait de réputation cet homme, plus enclin à la conciliation qu'à la répression. Avec intérêt, il nota également la présence de la servante de l'auberge.

Le commissaire aux morts étranges examina tous les participants, les uns après les autres, marquant leurs traits dans sa mémoire. Son attention fut tout à coup attirée par l'attitude étrange d'un homme qui priait devant une tombe à cinquante pas de là. Le commissaire aux morts étranges remarqua qu'en réalité celui-ci semblait suivre la cérémonie du coin de l'œil. L'homme était grand, les épaules larges et un air brutal se lisait sur ses traits marqués par la petite vérole. Une longue épée pendait à ses côtés. Lorsque le prêtre bénit le cercueil, il se signa discrètement.

Un sourire froid illumina le commissaire aux morts étrange. Cela s'était déroulé rapidement mais pas assez pour échapper à l'attention acérée du policier. Le signe de croix catholique allait d'abord vers le ciel puis vers la terre avant de toucher l'épaule gauche puis la droite, celle de *Celui qui bénit du haut de sa croix*. L'homme près de la tombe s'était signé par l'horizontale avant de monter au ciel et de terminer par une plongée en direction de l'enfer. Le signe de croix inversé des satanistes…

Volnay se déplaça lentement dans une allée adjacente, s'appliquant à garder de vue l'homme au visage vérolé. Lorsque celui-ci se détourna afin de quitter le cimetière, le policier le suivit discrètement avant de gagner la rue. Il conserva une distance prudente avec son suspect, jouant avec les piliers des maisons pour esquiver un éventuel regard en arrière.

Au détour d'une rue, il se précipita pour ne pas perdre son homme mais glissa malencontreusement sur une plaque de verglas. Jurant, il se releva prestement et se précipita. La réverbération du soleil sur la neige l'éblouit. Il plissa les yeux et fit quelques pas hésitants avant de se rendre à l'évidence : le sataniste avait disparu !

Le soleil frappait les lieux de rayons gris et ternes.

— *Sit tibi terra levis*, murmura le moine en jetant une poignée de terre dans la tombe. "Que la terre te soit légère."

Avec Hélène, il quitta le cimetière parmi les derniers. Plantée entre deux tombes, la servante du cabaret le regardait à la dérobée. Le moine le remarqua et alla la rejoindre après avoir échangé quelques mots avec Hélène. Celle-ci hésita à les rejoindre avant que Cornevin, le commissaire de quartier, ne lui propose de se réchauffer devant un bon feu à une auberge près de là.

— J'ai à vous parler, ajouta-t-il pour la convaincre.

Ceci décida Hélène. Le commissaire de quartier la conduisit alors à travers un dédale de rues qu'il semblait connaître comme sa poche. La neige piétinée et foulée par les passants, les chevaux et les voitures était devenue une boue noirâtre qui, mélangée aux excréments qu'on continuait à vider dans la rue, crottait les bas. Avec un soupir de soulagement, Cornevin poussa la lourde porte d'une auberge qui se révéla accueillante. D'un œil approbateur, il contempla un gigot de mouton entrelardé d'ail qui tournait à la broche tandis que le rôtisseur l'arrosait régulièrement de son jus.

Une petite femme volubile les conduisit à une table, pas loin de la cheminée où brûlait un feu d'enfer, avant de leur apporter un pichet d'un vin clair et parfumé.

— Cet endroit est bien agréable, fit le commissaire de quartier. On y sert ce petit vin de Suresnes qui chatouille la gorge…

— Vous désiriez me parler, rappela Hélène avec un léger sourire.

L'autre soupira et se frotta le visage avec les mains. Il semblait soudain abattu.

— Eh bien, pour tout vous dire, cette petite Sophia n'arrête pas de me hanter. J'ai même rêvé d'elle…

La jeune femme prêta aussitôt l'oreille. Après le moine, voici donc que Sophia venait d'entrer dans les songes nocturnes d'une autre personne. La jeune fille semblait avoir marqué de son empreinte tous ceux qu'elle avait croisés, vivante ou morte.

— Pourquoi?

L'autre plissa les yeux et les rides de son front s'accentuèrent.

— Vous vous souvenez de l'affaire du chien qui m'a donné l'occasion par deux fois de la rencontrer. Chaque fois, je l'ai écoutée et traitée avec bienveillance. Je pense donc que, dans une certaine mesure, elle avait confiance en moi, voire même que je lui inspirais quelque sympathie. Ce n'était pas une enfant ordinaire, vous savez…

Hélène se pencha un peu plus vers lui. L'émotion se lisait sur son visage et elle se souvenait à quel point l'annonce de la mort de la jeune fille l'avait bouleversé.

Elle posa doucement sa main sur la sienne et, d'un sourire, l'invita à poursuivre.

— Ce que je ne vous ai pas raconté, c'est que je l'ai revue une troisième fois.

Il fit une pause pour s'humecter les lèvres.

— Je ne vous en ai pas parlé car, sur le moment, cela m'a semblé insignifiant.

— Elle est venue vous demander quelque chose ?

— Pas exactement. Elle paraissait effrayée et m'a parlé d'un homme qui semblait la suivre ou la surveiller lorsqu'elle sortait.

On les servit et le commissaire de quartier commença à manger sa volaille avec les doigts, rompant les os avec dextérité. Bientôt des taches de graisse ornèrent ses vêtements.

— Que lui avez-vous répondu ? demanda Hélène qui ne toucha pas à son assiette.

Cornevin jeta un regard à la broche puis reporta son attention sur la jeune femme, s'attardant un instant sur la courbe de ses lèvres avant de se ressaisir.

— Je lui ai conseillé de ne pas sortir seule. Je suis même allé flâner près de sa maison à l'heure où elle sortait pour aller au marché. Je n'ai pas remarqué cet homme.

Il suça pensivement un os puis scruta attentivement Hélène.

— Ceci peut-il vous aider dans votre enquête ?

La jeune femme secoua la tête et sa belle chevelure brune aux reflets roux s'éparpilla sur ses épaules.

— Malheureusement, non.

Le commissaire de quartier jeta son os d'un air dépité.

— Dommage, j'aurais pu vous aider. Je reste néanmoins votre serviteur.

Il la couva d'un regard paternel.

— Prenez garde à vous toutefois, toute cette histoire ne me dit rien qui vaille. Quel dommage ! Saint-Sulpice était un quartier si tranquille…

Le moine et la serveuse marchaient lentement dans les allées du cimetière bordées d'herbes figées par le givre. Le moine avait proposé son bras que la jeune femme accepta après quelques instants d'hésitation, peu habituée à la galanterie des hommes.

— Désirez-vous que nous allions boire un verre ou manger quelque chose dans un endroit où il fait plus chaud ? proposa le moine en réprimant une quinte de toux.

— Merci mais je n'ai pas le temps. Il faut que je retourne vite à mon travail. Et puis ici, c'est calme et personne ne peut nous voir.

— Vous aviez quelque chose à me dire ?

La serveuse hocha la tête.

— Serai-je payée si je vous donne quelques informations intéressantes ?

— Comment savez-vous ce qui pourrait m'intéresser ou pas ?

Elle prit un air rusé.

— J'ai bien compris que vous travaillez pour la police. Vous recherchez le meurtrier de la petite Sophia, n'est-ce pas ?

— C'est vrai, reconnut le moine. Qu'avez-vous à me dire ?

La jeune femme frissonna. Ils marchaient à travers les tombes glacées et jamais la mort n'avait trouvé un pareil écrin blanc.

— Hier, j'ai vu Sophia !

Le moine tressaillit.

— Vous dormiez ?

— Non, j'allais travailler à l'auberge et, en passant devant la maison de l'astronome, je l'ai vue, assise sur le perron, son chien à ses pieds.

— Son chien ?

— Oui, cet animal sale qui la suivait tout le temps. Il était couché devant elle. Sophia a levé la tête et m'a jeté un regard triste.

— Qu'avez-vous fait ?

— Je me suis signée avant de m'enfuir. J'ai couru sans me retourner jusqu'à l'auberge. Quand j'ai regardé par la fenêtre, elle n'était plus là.

Elle se mordit les lèvres.

— J'avais peur qu'elle vienne me hanter, mais pourquoi moi ?

Le moine ne répondit pas. Il fixait droit devant lui un point imaginaire, le regard sombre. Enfin, comme avec effort, il détourna son attention de ce point et se tourna à demi pour la regarder.

— Peut-être était-ce une jeune fille qui lui ressemblait, hasarda-t-il sans conviction.

— Non, répondit la serveuse dans un souffle, c'était bien elle.

Elle esquissa un rapide signe de croix et chuchota :

— Pauvre enfant ! Le repos éternel lui est refusé et voilà qu'elle erre comme une âme en peine !

— Nous sommes tous des âmes en peine, murmura le moine.

Pensif, le moine rentra à sa demeure. Le chien lui fit fête et lui tendit la patte. Le moine s'en saisit et la secoua gravement puis le caressa et lui gratta la tête derrière les oreilles. Il s'absorba ensuite dans la préparation d'une savante décoction à base d'eau-de-vie, de noix de muscade et de safran. Sa gorge lui faisait encore mal et, parfois, ses poumons le brûlaient. Il cracha pour les vider puis bourra la cheminée de bûches bien sèches et s'assit pour contempler les flammes. De sombres pensées le tourmentaient. Il se prit le front entre les mains. La chaleur dégagée par l'âtre n'était pas sans lui rappeler messes noires et flammes de l'enfer mais la glace qui entourait son cœur et recouvrait les rues l'amenait à penser à Sophia. Il songea à son petit corps frêle et raide dans ce cercueil trop grand et à son âme qui errait maintenant à travers les rues dans une immense solitude.

Un courant d'air glacé courut dans la pièce. Il frissonna mais ne se retourna pas, son oreille désormais habituée au pas léger, presque glissant, d'Hélène.

— Vous voilà, fit-il.

Et son ton n'exprimait rien d'autre que cette simple constatation.

— Comment vous sentez-vous? demanda-t-elle d'une voix inquiète. Ce n'était pas très raisonnable de sortir même si vous vous sentez mieux.

— La nuit m'a redonné calme et vigueur. Je vais bien.

Il s'obstinait à fixer le feu sans la regarder.

— Que se passe-t-il? demanda-t-elle.

— Ce matin, à mon réveil, le chien était couché près de la cheminée et n'a pas exprimé le besoin de sortir. Je vous ai demandé si vous lui aviez ouvert pour ses besoins et vous m'avez répondu que non.

— Oui, nous l'avons fait sortir dans la cour.

— Et il n'a ni uriné ni déféqué, remarqua le moine. Étrange non, puisqu'il n'était pas sorti depuis la veille au soir?

— Effectivement, car la maison était propre. Il s'est retenu…

— Ou bien, il était déjà sorti mais alors qui lui a ouvert?

Hélène hésita.

— Votre fils est peut-être passé?

Le moine lui jeta un regard froid.

— Je ne vois pas pourquoi…

Il s'enfonça dans une rumination silencieuse.

— N'avez-vous pas faim? lui demanda-t-elle au bout de quelques longues minutes.

Le moine sursauta.

— Diable, maintenant que vous m'en parlez!

Il alla jusqu'à la cuisine.

— Par la queue de Neptune, fit-il, il ne reste déjà plus de ce beau pain blanc?

— Vous aviez faim, c'est bien normal.

Le moine jeta un regard soupçonneux en direction du chien.

— Je n'ai pas souvenir d'en avoir mangé beaucoup.

Hélène rit.

— Après avoir soupçonné le chien, ne me mettez pas en cause s'il vous plaît. Je n'y ai tout simplement pas touché!

— Alors, c'est cet intelligent animal, fit gaiement le moine. Mon fils se vante de sa pie bavarde mais moi j'ai un chien qui sait tourner la clé dans la serrure, ouvrir la porte et trancher le pain!

— J'ai une autre explication, se moqua Hélène. Pendant la nuit, les lutins pillent volontiers les garde-manger des maisons où ils vivent!

— Des lutins?

— Oui mais rassurez-vous, ils ne sont jamais bien méchants! Sortons donc pour acheter de quoi vous sustenter.

Hélène avait acheté un collier de cuivre pour le chien. Elle le lui attacha sans problème mais, étonnamment, l'animal refusa de sortir. Ils durent littéralement le traîner dehors.

— Ce chien a un comportement de plus en plus étrange, constata le moine intrigué. J'espère que sa maîtresse ne vient pas aussi le visiter en rêve.

L'animal eut un bref glapissement puis se mit à hurler. Tout son corps semblait pris de tremblements. Il fallut toute la patience d'Hélène pour le calmer. Enfin, il les suivit docilement, non sans jeter de fréquents regards derrière lui.

Au marché Saint-Jacques, des vendeurs échangeaient des coups de poing avec de petits revendeurs qui usurpaient leur place. Le moine les ignora et entraîna sa compagne devant les étals des commerçants transis jusqu'à la devanture d'un boucher. Celui-ci achetait le regrat, c'est-à-dire le reste des plats des maisons riches de la veille pour en remplir de vastes terrines et revendre le tout le lendemain. Mais il commerçait aussi de beaux quartiers de viande. Hélène choisit un rôti de porc. Rentré dans leur chaude demeure, le moine s'empressa de l'entrelacer adroitement de thym et de feuilles de laurier. Hélène revint de la cuisine avec un plat de fèves.

— Hum, des fèves ! fit gaiement le moine. Quelle bonne idée ! Pour Pythagore, le poisson est phosphorescent et donc aphrodisiaque, quant aux fèves, elles sont échauffantes !

Elle lui jeta un regard entendu.

— Grand bien nous fasse !

Une fois le rôti et les fèves disposés à cuire, Hélène s'assit et tapa légèrement du talon sur le sol en arquant les sourcils.

— Quelle est la date de naissance de Sophia? demanda-t-elle abruptement.

Il le lui dit. Elle le considéra avec surprise.

— Comment savez-vous cela?

Il le tenait du journal de Sophia qui était tombé dans ses mains. Celui-ci commençait par: "Je m'appelle Sophia et je suis née…"

— Je sais parce que je suis! répondit-il laconiquement.

Hélène arqua délicatement un sourcil.

— Et moi, je sais que vous l'avez lu dans le livre que vous avez subrepticement rapporté chez vous et qui tenait lieu de journal à Sophia.

— Diable, vous possédez le troisième œil!

Elle allongea les jambes près de l'âtre et, nonchalamment, les yeux du moine suivirent ce mouvement, épousant les plis de sa robe. Ils restèrent ainsi sans parler, gagnés par la douce chaleur du feu. Il la regarda feindre ne pas sentir ses regards sur elle. Des pensées sans nom s'agitaient chez le moine. Et le soir n'arrêtait pas de tomber et elle se tenait là, rêveuse au coin du feu, tandis que son âme à lui se troublait. Surpris d'entendre une voix au fond de son cœur, le moine écoutait.

Que se passe-t-il dans mon âme?

Il se leva et vint sans bruit derrière le fauteuil où Hélène rêvassait. Comme hypnotisé par sa nuque blanche, il se pencha vers elle. Une volupté plus chaude encore que l'enfer le fit frissonner des pieds à la tête.

Je suis un fou, pensa-t-il en se redressant. *Me voici à bander comme un carme auprès d'une jeune femme qui a la moitié de mon âge!*

Mais il savait bien qu'il ne s'agissait pas de cela. Un sentiment plus profond mûrissait en lui, le rapprochant inexorablement d'Hélène. Même consciente de l'agitation dans son dos, la jeune femme n'avait pas bougé.

— Qu'avez-vous, mon ami ? demanda-t-elle.

Il se corrigea de son affolement en décidant d'affronter l'air glacé de la nuit.

— Rien, j'ai besoin de prendre l'air. Je vais amener le chien avec moi.

— Ce n'est pas très prudent, vous n'êtes pas encore guéri.

— Je vais bien me couvrir…

Dehors, le froid était si vif que le sang lui monta au visage, rosissant ses joues comme une paire de gifles. Il se morigéna.

Quelle vacuité de mes pensées ! Je la regarde avec des yeux de jeune fou !

Le vent s'était levé et rabattait les pans de sa bure derrière lui. Près de lui, le chien s'était mis à gronder sourdement.

— Rentrez tout de suite !

La silhouette fine d'Hélène s'était encadrée dans la lumière. Docilement, le moine revint à l'intérieur.

— Quel temps du diable, murmura-t-il avant de se courber en deux pour éternuer.

— Un temps à ne pas mettre un moine hérétique dehors !

Elle lui tendit son mouchoir.

— Tenez…

— Grand merci ! L'air est si frais !

Il se retourna pour se cacher pendant qu'il se mouchait mais elle perçut son souffle irrégulier et lut la tension qui habitait ses épaules.

— Venez près du feu, insista-t-elle. Voulez-vous que je réchauffe pour vous un peu de cette potion contre la toux ? Le rôti sera bientôt cuit.

Elle virevoltait soudain dans l'espace, emplissant la maison de bruits et de mouvements comme pour en chasser les mauvais souvenirs ou les pensées trop étroites.

— Comment êtes-vous devenu moine ? lui demanda-t-elle plus tard alors qu'il buvait à petites lampées son remède brûlant, le chien couché à ses pieds.

Les yeux de son interlocuteur brillèrent.

— On a voulu faire de moi un membre du clergé parce que j'étais le second des garçons de ma famille et que, selon l'usage, l'aîné est destiné au métier des armes. Je n'avais à l'égard de la religion qu'une simple curiosité intellectuelle. Lorsque je découvris la diversité des religions dans le monde et le mal qui régnait sur terre, mon scepticisme s'accrut. Certes, je tenais l'homme comme seul responsable de ses propres maux puisque c'est lui qui sciemment crée et entretient l'enfer sur terre. Mais, comme vous l'entendez, j'étais moins sensible au catéchisme enseigné qu'à la hardiesse de pensée de nos philosophes. En fait, je brûlais d'un feu réformateur bien avant l'heure !

Il trépigna sur place et reprit d'un ton plus exalté :

— Mon aîné mourut au combat, le pauvre, lui qui était si doux de nature. Je courus le venger, abandonnant l'habit pour l'uniforme. Vous n'imaginez pas dans quel état de délabrement se trouvait l'armée ! On recrutait les plus pauvres et désespérés de la société par force ou supercherie. Les grades s'achetaient et ce sont les plus sots qui commandaient nos troupes. De fait, rien n'a changé aujourd'hui. Sous Louis XIV, de bons officiers roturiers parvenaient à s'extraire du lot. C'est maintenant chose impossible. À part l'excellent maréchal de Saxe, tous nos généraux et maréchaux sont des sots et des estropiés de la cervelle.

Avec eux, on ne fait jamais retraite mais on recule toujours! Bref, à l'armée, je me lassai des combats et un médecin m'enseigna. Rentré à Paris, je me passionnai pour l'anatomie, disséquant le plus possible de cadavres pour me former.

Il s'interrompit pour ajouter un peu de miel dans sa tasse.

— Je rejoignis ensuite Padoue où enseignait Giovanni Battista Morgagni qui pratiquait très régulièrement des autopsies. Il est âgé aujourd'hui de soixante-dix-huit ans! Il a découvert que toute maladie que nous observons du vivant des personnes, à travers les signes habituels de celle-ci, laisse des lésions dans les organismes. Dès lors, les lésions cadavériques peuvent nous permettre de connaître les causes de la mort par maladie des personnes. C'est ce que je dis toujours : ouvrez les cadavres et vous en saurez plus!

Les étranges yeux verts d'Hélène étincelèrent joyeusement.

— Comment avez-vous fait pour devenir si savant? demanda-t-elle en caressant affectueusement sa main.

Le moine reposa sa tasse.

— J'ai étudié sans trêve jusqu'à dompter les sciences. C'est à la lueur des lampes que l'on travaille le mieux. Je ne connais plus belle récompense qu'une nouvelle découverte après une âpre nuit sans sommeil!

— Vous avez été une lumière dans ce siècle où demeure tant d'obscurité…

— J'en ai trop fait! Je ne sais pas m'arrêter! Tous mes ennuis sont venus de là!

— Racontez-moi!

— Un jour, je commençai à écrire sur le ridicule des prééminences, remettant en cause la distinction des fonctions et la supériorité des uns et des autres. Je partais du principe que ce qui est petit peut être grand. Par prudence, je maniais l'ironie, la seule arme possible face à la monarchie policière. Donner de soi une image plus sotte que celle de l'autre, faire d'une apparente maladresse le comble de l'adresse et paraître louer ce que l'on blâme alors qu'en vérité l'on s'en moque, voilà ce qu'est l'ironie. J'acquis ainsi beaucoup de prestige et d'ennemis. Des femmes m'aimèrent. Elles s'en allèrent aussi, lassées par la vacuité de mes pensées. L'une d'elles resta. Je l'épousai et elle mit bientôt mon fils au monde. Hélas, hélas…

Il fourragea dans sa barbe comme pour y chercher ses mots.

— Elle prit une fluxion de poitrine et mourut alors que notre enfant avait quatre ans. Il me revint la douleur de pleurer ma chère femme et la lourde tâche d'éduquer mon fils.

— Vous avez été très certainement un bon père.

— N'en soyez pas si sûre, regretta-t-il, j'ai éparpillé mon âme aux quatre coins de l'Europe alors que j'avais un fils merveilleux qui m'attendait.

Il baissa la tête.

— J'ai manqué à mes devoirs de père et il m'en veut toujours pour cela.

— Voyons, remarqua Hélène, il est aujourd'hui à vos côtés.

— Oui mais avec lui j'ai l'impression de ne pas pouvoir rattraper le temps perdu. C'est comme si le sable me coulait des doigts.

La jeune femme s'assit sur l'accoudoir de son fauteuil et, à la manière d'une petite fille, entoura son cou de ses longs bras. Son corps était aussi souple que celui d'un chat et, comme cet animal, ses grands yeux le fixaient avec des reflets mordorés dans les prunelles.

— Pourquoi être revenu en France travailler avec lui ?

Il soupira.

— J'étais tel Ulysse un voyageur fatigué et je n'avais nulle Ithaque à regagner.

— Et puis vous songiez à vous rapprocher de votre fils…

— Il me manquait tant.

— Et bien sûr, vous ne lui disiez pas !

— Vous me comprenez si bien, ma chère…

Il porta une de ses mains à sa bouche. Ses lèvres esquissèrent une moue clémente et elle le laissa baiser délicatement le bout de ses doigts. À cet instant, une bourrasque s'engouffra en hurlant par la porte. Le commissaire aux morts étranges entra et s'immobilisa en découvrant la scène.

— Je ne vous dérange pas ? demanda-t-il sèchement.

Les mains d'Hélène quittèrent le cou du moine.

— Que vous arrive-t-il ? demanda tranquillement la jeune femme.

Volnay lui jeta un regard couleur de glace.

— Je trouve votre conduite envers mon père inconvenante.

Hélène se leva tranquillement et lui tourna le dos sans répondre.

— Oh, mon fils, protesta le moine, tu fais erreur. Nous évoquions juste les sentiments filiaux.

— Je ne les avais jamais vus aussi tendrement évoqués ! persifla Volnay. Certainement pas avec moi en tout cas !

204

— Tu es injuste !

— Je suis consterné de te voir jouer les jolis cœurs avec une intrigante qui pourrait être ta fille !

— Mon fils, tu vois Padoue à la place de Pise et tu fais des montagnes d'un rien. Avec toi, autant chie un bœuf que mille moucherons !

De nouveau, la porte s'ouvrit brusquement. Le commissaire aux morts étranges et son père échangèrent un regard surpris. C'était la seconde fois de leur vie que Sartine faisait irruption chez le moine, et cela en l'espace de quelques jours !

— Ah ! Je vous trouve tous ensemble, s'écria le lieutenant général de police. C'est bien ! Je suis allé chez vous Volnay mais vous n'y étiez pas !

— Que se passe-t-il ? s'étonna le commissaire aux morts étranges.

Il était encore tout pâle de son altercation avec son père et Hélène. Un peu surpris, Sartine le jaugea du regard puis eut un sourire sarcastique.

— Nous avons retrouvé votre curé dansant. Il danse toujours mais, comme je l'avais prédit, au bout d'une corde !

XI

UN PROCUREUR
ET AUTRES DIABLERIES

Volnay grimpa dans la voiture derrière Sartine. Il y trouva un troisième passager.

— Je vous présente le procureur Siltieri, fit sobrement le lieutenant général de police. C'est lui qui instruit notre affaire avec… euh… toute la discrétion voulue.

Le procureur était un grand homme efflanqué, aux joues creuses, au menton proéminent et au regard brûlant. Il déplut tout de suite au commissaire aux morts étranges par ses manières sèches et hautaines.

— Il était temps de nous rencontrer, dit-il à Volnay d'un ton acerbe. M. de Sartine m'a raconté comment vous avez laissé échapper la prostituée qui participait à cette messe noire.

— Il m'a d'abord fallu la trouver, répondit froidement le commissaire aux morts étranges. Je n'avais au départ pour indice qu'un cadavre dans un cimetière. Cette femme s'est ensuite rompu le cou dans un escalier mais je n'ai pas perdu pour autant le fil de cette enquête puisque je recherchais le curé dansant.

— Malheureusement, il ne vous a pas attendu pour se pendre, ricana Siltieri. Il est grand temps que j'intervienne !

— Nul doute que vous sachiez faire mieux que moi !

Siltieri lui jeta un regard noir.

— J'ai une certaine expérience en la matière, voyez-vous. J'instruis des dossiers de sorcellerie depuis dix ans. J'ai eu affaire à ces maîtres en perversité, pères du mensonge et serviteurs du démon qui prient le diable à la place de Dieu. Ces boucs fornicateurs singent l'eucharistie et rendent un culte fébrile à Satan. Ils récitent l'introït à rebours pour dénier la virginité et appeler à la débauche. Tout chez eux est grotesque. Leurs flatulences remplacent l'encens. Ils chantent *Gloria in profundis Satani* au lieu de *Gloria in excelsis Deo*. L'*Ite missa est* étant remplacé par un *laus Satani*.

Il se signa fiévreusement.

— Dieu m'est témoin qu'en d'autres temps, la répression aurait été plus sévère avec les tribunaux de l'Inquisition !

Sartine s'agita, mal à l'aise.

— Il appartient à la justice du roi de rendre celle-ci et non aux tribunaux de l'Église.

— Certes mais il fut un temps où ils collaboraient ensemble ! Rappelons-nous que feu notre bon roi Louis XIV a sommé sorciers et sorcières de quitter son royaume sans délai et ordonné de punir exemplairement ceux qui ont pratiqué la magie.

— Ma police s'y emploie, rétorqua Sartine d'un ton aigre.

— Pas assez ! Pas assez ! Ils sont toujours là à tenter de nous faire prendre une paille pour une poutre !

Volnay frémit intérieurement. Chargé par la justice d'instruire l'enquête, Siltieri était un nostalgique des tribunaux de la très sainte Inquisition ! Cela le situait certainement dans le camp du parti des dévots contre celui de la marquise de Pompadour, ces deux camps se livrant à une lutte féroce dans les coulisses du pouvoir. Les deux policiers gardèrent le silence durant le reste du trajet, laissant le procureur continuer un monologue fébrile sur la nécessité de purifier l'hérésie par le feu.

Leur voiture suivit un lacis de ruelles ténébreuses dans le faubourg Saint-Marcel avant de s'arrêter dans un cahot devant un immeuble mal entretenu, rue du Puits-de-l'Ermite. Des archers du guet les attendaient et les conduisirent dans un appartement haut de plafond où régnait un froid glacial.

Le curé dansant avait été un grand gaillard dégingandé, long et maigre, sec comme une trique. Vêtu d'un mauvais gilet de serge noir et d'une culotte de peau rapiécée, il se balançait maintenant au bout d'une corde, la langue hors de la bouche. Le commissaire aux morts étranges le contempla un instant en silence puis se mit à arpenter la pièce, notant du regard chaque objet ou meuble qui s'y trouvait : une mauvaise tapisserie, un coffre pour les affaires, une table et quatre chaises...

Le spectacle qui s'offrait à eux dans ce qui semblait être la cuisine était assez édifiant.

— Que pensez-vous de tout cela ? lui demanda Sartine.

Volnay n'eut pas le temps de répondre car le procureur se planta au milieu de la pièce et prit la parole d'une voix forte.

— Mon avis est fait. J'ai déjà vu par le passé tant de signes de ce type ! Voyez par vous-même : hosties noires, cadavre de chat noir, cierges noirs. Quant à la présence de ce crucifix, n'ayez crainte, il sera probablement piétiné au cours de quelque séance. Il n'est pas possible que l'on ne l'ait pas entendu psalmodier ses diableries. Il doit y avoir des complices dans cet immeuble. Que les archers du guet fouillent tout !

Sartine jeta un bref regard à Volnay puis fit un signe au sergent du guet. Des hommes sortirent précipitamment de l'appartement.

— Ah, dit Siltieri en se ruant dans un coin de la pièce, un bâton de sorcier ! "Bâton blanc, bâton noir, mène-moi là où tu dois, de par le diable !"

Le commissaire aux morts étranges s'approcha calmement.

— Il s'agit d'un bâton de marche. Voyez, il est ferré à son extrémité.

— Vous ignorez donc que ces maudits sorciers font poser à leur bâton une ferrure avec la lame d'acier grâce à laquelle ils ont égorgé une victime afin d'en accroître la puissance ?

Volnay préféra ne pas répondre.

— Que quelqu'un dépende cet homme ! ordonna le lieutenant général de police pour tenter d'être utile.

Le commissaire aux morts étranges intervint.

— Un instant ! Cette scène de crime a été assez tourmentée comme cela. Toutes les traces ont été piétinées par le guet. Il faut que je me fasse une idée des assassins, moi !

Il prit une chaise et monta dessus pour examiner le cou de la victime. En bas, le procureur Siltieri haussa les épaules.

— Il n'y a ni empreinte de pas, ni indices qui tiennent. Toutes les preuves sont là sous vos yeux, jusqu'à ces hosties noires et triangulaires ! Les hosties à trois pointes comme ces hérétiques les appellent ! Voici les premiers ingrédients pour se livrer à une parodie de messe où tout est inversé et perverti !

— Cela ne me dit pas qui a tué cet homme, remarqua tranquillement Volnay en tirant sur le crochet.

— Il s'est pendu tout seul par repentir ou bien ses acolytes ont probablement jugé qu'il leur fallait un autre sacrifice…

— Je pense surtout que ses complices ou commanditaires ont eu peur, osa le commissaire aux morts étranges. Ils ont dû apprendre que nous avions trouvé la prostituée qui assistait à la cérémonie et que nous étions sur les traces du curé dansant. M. de Sartine, ici présent, ayant mis tous ses agents à sa recherche, je suis certain que cela n'est pas passé inaperçu.

Le lieutenant général de police se rembrunit. Le commissaire aux morts étranges examina la poutre à laquelle était accroché le curé dansant.

— Le crochet est planté ici depuis longtemps, constata le commissaire aux morts étranges. Il ne l'a pas été pour l'occasion.

Il redescendit et se saisit des mains de l'homme.

— Pas de traces de lien. Elles n'ont pas été attachées puis détachées.

— Cela confirme l'hypothèse selon laquelle il s'est donné la mort, intervint Sartine. S'il se savait recherché…

Volnay secoua la tête.

— Pas forcément. Il pouvait être déjà mort étranglé avant la pendaison ou simplement assommé. Le moine nous le dira.

Il examina les ongles du mort.

— Hum, il y a de la peau sous certains ongles. Il a dû griffer ses agresseurs. Voyons pour la longueur de ses souliers.

Il sortit d'une poche une cordelette avec différents nœuds.

— Celle-ci correspond à une empreinte relevée sur les lieux du crime, tout comme celle de la Vorace. Et de deux ! Il m'en reste encore trois à trouver…

Redescendant de sa chaise, il jeta un coup d'œil aux souliers du curé dansant qui pendaient dans le vide.

— Tiens, un boiteux, remarqua-t-il machinalement.

— Que dites-vous ? s'enquit Siltieri.

— Voyez les talons de ses chaussures, l'un est complètement déformé sur la droite, signe qu'il s'y appuyait plus que sur l'autre.

— Voici encore une preuve ! s'exclama le procureur.

— Pardon ?

Siltieri eut un reniflement méprisant.

— Vous ignorez donc que ceux marqués par la lettre "B" sont plus prédisposés que les autres à devenir des agents du diable ? Bohémiens, boiteux, borgnes, bègues, bossus, bâfreurs ou buveurs !

— Et baveux, compléta Volnay sans rire.

Il se recula.

— Je vais faire un croquis de la scène.

Sortant d'une poche papier et fusain, il se mit à dessiner les lieux. Malgré lui, Sartine s'approcha pour admirer la sûreté et la justesse de la main de son commissaire aux morts étranges. Pendant ce temps, un archer du guet rapporta de la chambre du curé dansant un livre dont Siltieri s'empara avec un rugissement de triomphe.

— Nous sommes dans l'antre du démon ! Voyez plutôt !

Sartine s'approcha et jeta au livre un coup d'œil prudent avant de se reculer vivement.

— La liste des principaux démons a été établie il y a mille deux cents ans par l'Église au canon 7 du concile de Braga, expliqua Siltieri avec ferveur. Tous

ces noms abjects me sont malheureusement familiers :
Adramelech, grand chancelier des Enfers mais aussi
dieu du meurtre ! Il est ici représenté sous sa forme
de paon. Astaroth, démon et trésorier des Enfers qui
chevauche un dragon et tient dans sa main une vipère
car il aime se changer en serpent. Ayperos qui commande à trente-six légions et connaît le passé et l'avenir. Astarté à la tête de génisse, démon femelle de la
débauche. Béhémond, démon, sa force est dans ses
reins. Bélial, le meurtre et le vice réunis…

Sartine et les archers du guet se signèrent en frissonnant tandis que Siltieri poursuivait avec frénésie
son étrange litanie. Sans lui prêter attention, le commissaire aux morts étranges termina son croquis et
demanda qu'on emmène le corps du curé dansant
chez le moine. Le cadavre venait d'être descendu et
chargé dans une voiture lorsque les archers du guet
revinrent de leur fouille dans l'immeuble. Ils poussaient sans ménagement devant eux un couple terro-
risé. Des couches de saindoux superposées semblaient
tenir lieu de cou et de menton à l'homme, court et
mal bâti. Jamais deux personnes n'avaient été aussi
mal assorties car la femme était maigre comme une
brindille.

— Nous avons trouvé des cierges noirs chez eux,
dit le sergent du guet en brandissant triomphalement
la pièce à conviction.

— Sacrilège ! Hérésie ! s'écria le procureur. Qu'on
les emmène au Châtelet !

La femme se jeta à ses genoux.

— Pitié monseigneur ! Nous n'avons rien fait de
mal ! Nous sommes d'honnêtes fournisseurs en bougies pour un marchand du Marais.

— Et vous le fournissez aussi en cierges noirs ?!

— Non, ce sont des commandes de notre voisin. Il faut bien vivre…

— *Confessionem esse veram, non factam vi tormentorum !* s'écria Siltieri. "Les aveux ont été spontanés et non obtenus sous l'effet de la torture !"

La femme s'accrocha avec désespoir aux genoux du procureur.

— Pitié ! Nous ne faisons que fabriquer des cierges et des chandelles !

Le visage de Siltieri se fendit d'un sourire méchant.

— Vous chanterez un autre refrain lorsque l'on vous mettra les brodequins ! En attendant, nous visiterons demain cette échoppe que vous fournissez. Je suis curieux de savoir ce que nous allons y trouver ! Allons, au Châtelet ! Au Châtelet !

Il se tourna vers le commissaire aux morts étranges sans prendre garde aux cris effrayés poussés par le couple qu'on emmenait de force.

— Vous voyez que les choses sont simples : la mauvaise engeance s'assemble ! Ces blasphémateurs et agents sacrilèges du mal vont livrer leurs complices sous la question !

— À travers les messes noires, ce n'est pas seulement le goût pervers du sacrilège qui s'exprime, remarqua Volnay, mais toute la cruauté et l'inhumanité d'un monde pour lequel la vie de l'autre n'est rien. Ces gens-là n'en sont pas.

Le procureur haussa les épaules.

— Les choses sont moins complexes que vous ne le supposez : il s'agit d'hérésie.

Il lui tourna le dos, salua Sartine et sortit en ramenant le pan de sa cape derrière lui d'un geste sec. Le commissaire aux morts étranges demanda à monter chez les suspects arrêtés. Ceux-ci devaient dormir dans une grande armoire sans battants, sur un grabat posé sur la planche. L'appartement était sombre et sentait le renfermé. Une lucarne l'éclairait, fermée par une planche à coulisse. Dans les cendres du feu refroidissaient des oignons et des raves. Volnay fit le tour du misérable logis, ne trouvant que de quoi fabriquer des cierges noirs. Peu convaincu de sorcellerie, il rejoignit Sartine. À cet instant, un des archers du guet eut un hoquet de surprise.

— Que font-ils donc tous ceux-là ?!

Le commissaire aux morts étranges alla le rejoindre à la fenêtre et jeta un coup d'œil dans la rue où la population s'assemblait, le visage rouge de colère et l'invective aux lèvres.

— Les nouvelles vont vite dans un quartier, murmura-t-il. Ils ont l'air hostile. Il faut dire que la police embarque sans ménagement des gens qui sont leurs voisins ou leurs amis…

Sartine le rejoignit et jeta un bref coup d'œil avant de s'essuyer nerveusement le front avec son mouchoir de dentelle.

— Regardez-la, Volnay, cette foule canaille. Si nous n'avions pas vingt archers du guet avec nous, elle nous mettrait en charpie. De nos jours, nous ne pouvons plus faire d'exécution publique sans que l'on insulte le bourreau et nos hommes ne parviennent même plus à mettre un gueux au pilori sans qu'on leur jette des pierres !

Le commissaire aux morts étranges demeura silencieux. Il avait senti la peur de Sartine. Ce n'était pas un manque de courage car l'homme possédait un caractère bien trempé mais la crainte de ce que représentait la foule, les grandes masses incontrôlables. Sartine savait pertinemment que la loi du nombre appartenait au peuple. Celui-ci l'ignorait mais un jour il se compterait. Sartine haïssait la foule car il avait prise sur tout sauf sur elle.

La foule, songea Volnay, est comme l'eau. Rien ne l'arrête lorsque la digue cède. Et qu'est-ce que la digue au final ? Quelques milliers d'hommes en uniforme, eux-mêmes fils du peuple ? La foule n'était ni consciente de sa force, ni dirigée.

Un jour, moi ou quelqu'un d'autre, nous l'enflammerons comme une torche et la lancerons contre la monarchie.

— Ne restons pas là !

La voix sèche et coupante de Sartine ramena Volnay à la réalité. Déjà une pierre venait de briser une vitre et roulait dans la pièce. Le peuple avait aperçu la perruque et le visage poudré et fardé du lieutenant général de police.

Ils descendirent précipitamment les escaliers et s'engouffrèrent dans la voiture sous un jet de pierres. Les archers du guet débordés reculaient en désordre.

— Tenez vos positions ! cria le sergent du guet. Tenez vos positions !

Une pierre bien ajustée le fit taire. Ce fut la débandade. Des archers du guet tirèrent.

Volnay jura.

— Allez ! Allez ! cria Sartine au cocher.

Celui-ci claqua son fouet et, d'une voix brutale, hurla après ses chevaux. Des hurlements de peur et de rage jaillirent de la foule. La voiture eut un soubresaut avant d'être secouée de cahots. Volnay comprit qu'on venait de passer sur un corps humain. Des mains apparurent à la portière du carrosse puis un visage. Sartine frappa dans le front de l'homme qui lâcha prise. À sa portière, Volnay vit un assaillant entrer le buste dans la voiture. À la main, il tenait un couteau. Le commissaire aux morts étranges sortit son pistolet.

— Tirez! cria Sartine.

Le doigt de Volnay se crispa sur la détente.

— Tirez!

L'homme le contemplait stupidement, son couteau toujours pointé dans sa direction. À cet instant, la voiture prit de la vitesse et vira brusquement, l'homme déséquilibré chuta.

— À quoi vous sert de tenir une arme si vous ne vous en servez pas! cria Sartine mécontent.

Volnay rangea calmement son pistolet.

— Je n'en avais pas réellement besoin.

Le lieutenant général de police maugréa puis s'enferma dans un silence maussade dont il ne sortit qu'une fois quitté le quartier.

— Nos hommes vont regagner le Châtelet, espérons que la foule ne les accompagne pas.

Volnay eut un sourire sombre.

Un jour, le peuple ne se contentera pas de les reconduire jusqu'à leur caserne mais il marchera sur Versailles.

— Cela vous amuse, Volnay? gronda Sartine. Vous espérez un jour voir nos corps gigoter à un réverbère! Croyez-vous réellement que je ne connaisse vos convictions?

Le commissaire aux morts étranges ne répondit pas. Sartine savait trop de choses sur son passé pour le berner. Cela lui donnait d'ailleurs prise sur lui. Ceci et son efficacité dans les enquêtes expliquaient qu'un serviteur aussi zélé de l'État que Sartine conservât dans ses services un opposant secret au régime monarchique.

— Je ne souhaite la mort de personne, dit doucement Volnay. Et je voudrais bien résoudre cette enquête. La prostituée, le prêtre renégat… il nous manque encore trois participants et ceux-là j'aimerais les prendre vivants !

— Le procureur Siltieri ne va pas tarder à les identifier parmi tous les mécréants qu'il a fait embarquer.

Volnay secoua la tête.

— Je ne crois pas. Les trois personnes assistant à la messe noire devaient en être les commanditaires. Ce sont des gens d'un autre niveau et d'une autre condition que les malheureux qui vont subir la torture. J'ai parlé avec la Vorace et je peux vous assurer qu'elle n'avait ni l'imagination ni l'intelligence nécessaires à une telle chose. Mais voilà, le procureur Siltieri est un fanatique à l'esprit étroit. Il a déniché quelques pauvres bougres qui se trouvaient au mauvais endroit, au mauvais moment, et pense avoir tiré la fève du gâteau ! Il va les mettre à la question et leur faire avouer tous les crimes que l'on souhaite. *Postquam depositus fuit de tormento.* "Aveux déposés après retour de la torture", comme dirait le moine !

Sartine sortit une prise mais les cahots de la voiture sur les pavés l'empêchèrent d'enfourner sans dégât le tabac dans les narines. D'un geste agacé, il brossa ses habits parsemés de brins.

— Si vous étiez plus rapide, nous n'aurions pas Siltieri sur le dos, maugréa le lieutenant général de police. Qu'allons-nous faire maintenant ?

— Si nous passions chez le moine ? proposa Volnay.

À sa grande surprise, Sartine accepta.

Le moine les contempla d'un œil satisfait. Cabotin, il ne lui déplaisait pas d'avoir pour public une aussi haute autorité que le lieutenant général de police. Hélène absente, la présence inespérée de Sartine le remplissait d'aise.

— J'ai procédé au déshabillage du corps, commença-t-il d'un ton docte, et j'ai relevé la présence d'importantes ecchymoses. L'homme s'est défendu. Cela s'est passé récemment car la couleur des ecchymoses est rouge vif le premier jour.

Il fronça délicatement les sourcils et poursuivit.

— La pendaison produit une pression qui provoque une compression du cou, ce qui empêche les vaisseaux d'amener le sang au cerveau ou à la trachée. Enfin, les muscles du cou sont atteints par la chute mais la hauteur de celle-ci a été faible selon ce que m'ont dit les agents du guet. J'ai observé que les marques de strangulation existent bien mais qu'elles sont situées à un niveau beaucoup plus bas qu'en cas de pendaison. De plus, les marques ne sont pas celles d'une corde car elles sont plus larges, probablement un bas ou quelque chose de ce type... En tout cas, un matériau plus souple que la corde...

— N'a-t-il pas pu être étranglé à mains nues ? demanda Sartine.

Le moine se tourna vers lui, les yeux brillants.

— Question intéressante, monsieur le lieutenant général de police ! Mais la réponse est négative car l'étranglement par voie manuelle exige plus de pression et donc les marques en seraient beaucoup plus nettes et les dommages musculaires plus importants. Je ne vous parle même pas de l'état de la gorge...

— Cela suffira en effet, s'empressa de dire Sartine. Vous soutenez donc que notre curé dansant a été étranglé par un bas et pendu ensuite à un crochet pour laisser croire à un suicide ?

— Je ne soutiens pas : je prouve ! Tiens, qu'est-ce que ceci ?

Le moine ouvrit avec précaution le sachet que le curé dansant portait autour du cou.

— Du sel… On en porte autour du cou pour se prémunir du malin. Le curé dansant devait craindre que le diable ne l'emporte avec lui après l'invocation…

Le lieutenant général de police se tourna vers Volnay.

— Les participants tueraient leurs complices car ils les savent repérés ?

Le commissaire aux morts étranges haussa légèrement les épaules.

— Peut-être l'auraient-ils fait de toute façon. J'ai la conviction que la prostituée et le curé n'étaient que des pions dans leur jeu, de simples outils pour respecter un rituel. Une fois celui-ci accompli, ils n'en ont plus besoin.

— Pensez-vous que les commanditaires de la messe soient de plus noble condition ?

Volnay décrypta la question muette de Sartine : la cour pouvait-elle être impliquée ? Si c'était le cas, le parti des dévots s'en réjouirait car cela lui permettrait de porter des coups à tous ceux qui n'étaient pas du même bord.

— Je ne vois guère la cour de Versailles mêlée à ce meurtre, dit le commissaire aux morts étranges.

— Tu as tort, intervint le moine au grand désespoir de son fils. Les grands de ce monde courent les devineresses et les tireurs d'horoscopes. Ils achètent des potions magiques ou des runes. Et il est de notoriété publique que la vicomtesse de Polignac recourait à des chercheurs de trésor. Quant au duc de…

— Nous parlons de meurtre, le coupa sans ménagement Volnay. Et il existe suffisamment de chapelles privées dans les châteaux ou les hôtels particuliers pour éviter que les grands de ce monde viennent salir leurs bottes la nuit dans des cimetières glacés !

Il laissa échapper un sourire sarcastique.

— À moins que notre ami Siltieri ne découvre que le marchand de chandelles fournissait en cierges noirs quelque seigneur…

Sartine émit un soupir irrité mais son attention fut attirée par le moine.

— Voyons voir ce que tu as dans les poches, disait ce dernier en s'adressant au cadavre.

Le moine énuméra un à un les objets trouvés sur le corps.

— Un mouchoir, une clé, une tabatière en bois, oh…

Il tenait entre deux doigts un anneau dans lequel était enchâssé un œil.

— Quelle horreur, fit Sartine en plissant le nez de dégoût.

— N'ayez crainte, le rassura le moine, ce doit être un œil de belette. C'est une amulette pour empêcher que l'on vous jette un sort pour vous nouer l'aiguillette. Pour les hommes, c'est toujours gênant !

Il ricana avant de reprendre son énumération :

— Un almanach, une paire de dés, un couteau, un billet de loterie sur l'hôtel de ville et une inscription en latin sur un billet…

— Laissez-moi voir ! s'écria Sartine.

Sa mine s'allongea lorsqu'il lut :

— *Cintra me ad incarte cla, a filiia Eniol, Lieber, Bruya, Braguesca…* Qu'est-ce encore que ceci ?

— Une formule magique pour gagner aux dés, expliqua le moine. On en vendait déjà quand j'avais vingt ans et je vous confirme que cela ne marche pas du tout !

Une toux qui sembla lui déchirer la poitrine l'interrompit.

— Pardonnez-moi, dit-il au lieutenant général de police, voulez-vous avoir l'amabilité de me passer le verre d'eau derrière vous ?

Tandis que l'autre se retournait, le moine dissimula rapidement sous sa bure une feuille de papier pliée. Volnay le fixa intensément mais ne dit rien.

— Il n'y a aucun verre derrière moi, dit sèchement Sartine.

Il lui fit face de nouveau, l'air mécontent.

— Ah pardon, fit le moine, c'est ma maudite fièvre. La carafe est à côté de toi, mon fils. Si tu veux bien avoir la gentillesse…

Volnay lui servit un verre qu'il but goulûment.

— Nous disons donc, continua-t-il après s'être essuyé les lèvres d'un revers de sa manche, un couteau, une quittance de loyer et de l'argent.

Il compta minutieusement.

— Trois livres et douze sols très précisément.

Sartine croisa les bras et les contempla d'un œil sec.

— Tout ceci ne nous avance pas vraiment. De son côté, Siltieri va faire mettre à la question ce couple qui va leur livrer des noms…

— Qu'ils parlent sous la torture, j'en suis bien certain, fit Volnay d'un ton calme, mais je ne pense pas qu'ils sachent grand-chose. Ils fabriquaient des cierges noirs pour le curé dansant mais seul celui-ci savait où les livrer…

Il s'interrompit. Au-dessus de leur tête, un hurlement à glacer le sang se faisait entendre. Sartine frissonna.

— Qui crie ainsi à la mort ?

— Oh, ce n'est rien, s'empressa de répondre le moine. J'ai recueilli un chien mais parfois il semble devenir fou…

— C'est de vivre sous le même toit que vous ! répliqua Sartine.

Le moine se rembrunit mais, sagement, ne répondit rien.

— Il est vrai que nous sommes tous sur les nerfs, conclut Volnay conciliant.

Sartine regarda avec stupéfaction son commissaire aux morts étranges à l'impassibilité et au calme légendaires.

— Nous n'avons pas connu d'affaire aussi difficile depuis longtemps, ajouta le moine. Et la victime est ici la plus délicieuse des enfants, la plus triste aussi…

— Comment savez-vous cela ? demanda le lieutenant général de police.

— Parce qu'elle me l'a dit !

Sartine le considéra comme s'il était devenu fou.

— Cette Sophia vous a tourné la tête !

Le moine lui jeta un coup d'œil complice.

— Cette jeune fille nous hante tous. Elle n'aura de repos avant que l'on ne trouve son assassin !

— Votre fils vous a raconté notre conversation privée, constata Sartine en jetant un méchant regard à Volnay.

— Oh, il n'y a pas de mal à cela, intervint le moine. Pas plus qu'il n'y en a à rêver. Depuis l'Antiquité, les hommes tentent de trouver une explication à leurs rêves. Artémidore d'Éphèse racontait déjà des tas de choses très intéressantes à ce propos. À Babylone, les prêtres révéraient le Soleil, *seigneur de la vision*, et l'on se rendait au temple des songes pour y décrypter ceux-ci.

— Tout ceci n'en fait pas une science, remarqua le lieutenant général de police d'un ton acerbe.

— Détrompez-vous, l'oniromancie est la science de la divination à travers les rêves. Il nous revient à chacun de déchiffrer la révélation ambiguë de ceux-ci et de devenir les interprètes de nos songes.

Sartine le contempla d'un air sarcastique.

— Ne me dites pas qu'un esprit aussi rationnel que le vôtre s'emploie à ces fadaises.

— Mon esprit rationnel, comme vous dites, s'intéresse à tout ce qui est inexpliqué !

Une fois la porte de la maison refermée derrière le lieutenant général de police, Volnay s'empressa auprès de son père.

— Eh bien, qu'as-tu donc dissimulé aux yeux de Sartine ?

Le moine sourit finement.

— Tu as remarqué ma présence d'esprit ? Le verre d'eau, Sartine tourne la tête et hop !

On aurait dit un enfant se vantant d'une farce réussie. Volnay secoua la tête, atterré par les facéties de son père.

— Tu as pris un risque inconsidéré. Si Sartine s'en était rendu compte, je n'ose imaginer les conséquences... Tu sais qu'il ne nous apprécie guère et qu'avec lui nous sommes toujours sur le fil du rasoir...

— Peut-être mais bon je préfère que cette enquête progresse sans interférence extérieure. Ah oui, il reste du rôti de porc si tu en veux quelques tranches. Hélène et moi ne t'avons pas attendu pour lui faire honneur...

— Je n'ai pas faim.

— Bien, bien...

Le moine déplia soigneusement la feuille et l'approcha près du feu.

— Ma vue n'est plus ce qu'elle était mon fils, peux-tu me donner cette loupe sur la table à écrire ?

Volnay s'exécuta.

— Ah ! fit le moine d'un ton triomphant. Quelques adresses de livraison pour les cierges avec le nom des rues et des dates. J'aime les gens ordonnés !

Son fils s'approcha et lut par-dessus son épaule.

— Trois adresses seulement ces dernières semaines, observa-t-il. Le commerce n'est plus aussi lucratif qu'autrefois !

— Et le premier nom de rue qui apparaît est la rue des Canettes où réside notre astrologue ! Mon Dieu, le curé dansant livrait en cierges noirs le père de notre victime !

— La coïncidence est troublante mais ne sautons pas à des conclusions hâtives, tempéra Volnay. Des centaines et des centaines de personnes habitent dans cette rue.

— La seconde adresse mentionne un quartier de Versailles. Sartine n'aimerait pas cela ! Sans indication pourtant, autant chercher une aiguille dans une meule de foin. Mais quand même : Versailles !

Il approcha encore son œil de sa loupe.

— La troisième adresse est le Palais-Royal, sans autre mention ! Sans doute un lieu de rendez-vous…

Le commissaire aux morts étranges examina le papier puis le rendit à son père. Il croisa ensuite les bras sur sa poitrine et laissa son esprit s'échapper des lieux. Lorsqu'il parla, son ton était ferme et décidé.

— Demain matin, nous irons interroger sans ménagement l'astrologue. Nous prendrons avec nous des archers du guet pour fouiller toute sa maison. Depuis le début de cette affaire, je ressens la pénible sensation de passer à côté de quelque chose d'évident !

— Cela arrive souvent ! expliqua son père. Une part de ton esprit a découvert une partie de la solution mais ton esprit conscient ne veut pas en entendre parler pour des raisons diverses et variées. Ainsi luttent en nous *ce* qui croit savoir et *ce* qui sait.

L'expression du commissaire aux morts étranges resta indéchiffrable mais un léger mouvement d'épaules marquait son incrédulité face aux thèses osées de son père. Un instant le silence régna puis une bûche en se consumant s'écroula dans l'âtre, ce qui les fit tous les deux sursauter. Le moine se baissa pour tisonner le feu et rajouter du bois. En se relevant, il se saisit du poignet de son fils et baissa furtivement la voix.

— Je n'en ai rien dit à notre supérieur mais un nouveau mystère a surgi.

Il s'humecta nerveusement les lèvres avant de continuer.

— Lorsqu'on a descendu dans la première cave le cadavre du curé dansant, je suis allé dans la seconde cave chercher mes instruments. Or, c'est dans cette seconde cave que j'avais transporté le corps du gardien du cimetière pour le saler afin qu'il ne sente pas. Ma maladie m'a empêché d'accomplir cette corvée. Bref, je vais dans ma seconde cave et là, surprise, plus de cadavre !

Volnay sursauta.

— Hélène sait tout cela ?

— Oui, je l'ai envoyée chez le commissaire de quartier déclarer le… euh… vol. Un cadavre cela ne passe pas forcément inaperçu.

Les mains dans le dos, le commissaire aux morts étranges se mit à marcher de long en large comme pour donner de l'ampleur à ses pensées.

— Pourquoi vole-t-on un cadavre? demanda-t-il.

Il s'apprêta à répondre lui-même à sa propre question.

— On le vole pour qu'on ne reconnaisse pas l'identité de la victime ou pour dissimuler la cause de sa mort. Or, toute personne sensée doit penser que ce cadavre dans la cave de l'assistant du commissaire aux morts étranges a été autopsié et identifié!

Le moine approuva.

— Bien entendu, on vole aussi des cadavres pour alimenter les médecins qui veulent progresser en matière d'anatomie. Ceux-là sont prêts à payer cher pour cela. Cependant, il y a des cimetières pour ça! Les déterreurs de cadavres n'oseraient pas s'introduire dans ma cave. Et d'ailleurs comment sauraient-ils que ce cadavre s'y trouve?

— Il y a bien les hommes qui sont venus chercher le cadavre de Sophia, remarqua Volnay. Ils ont pu remarquer l'autre corps mais ils n'auraient pas pu s'en emparer sous tes yeux.

Le moine baissa la tête.

— Tu ne les accompagnais pas? s'étonna son fils.

— Je n'avais pas le cœur de voir le corps de cette petite et puis tu sais bien que j'étais malade et alité. Ils se sont occupés de tout : nettoyage, habillage et mise en bière.

— Et tu les as laissés seuls dans ton laboratoire? Toi!

Son père haussa les épaules.

— Ils travaillent pour moi depuis deux ans. Ils connaissent mon laboratoire et se garderaient bien d'y toucher quoi que ce soit, me connaissant et me craignant!

— Étrange, fit le policier en plissant les yeux. Il doit pourtant exister une explication logique. Quelque chose auquel nous ne pensons pas!

— Peut-être n'a-t-on rien volé, murmura songeusement le moine. Tout cela pourrait être diablerie mais Sophia possédait un cœur pur. Il est possible après tout qu'elle soit devenue un ange et que son corps ait disparu.

Volnay lui jeta un regard soucieux mais se tut. Par habitude, il inspecta les lieux comme s'il s'agissait d'une scène de crime avant de secouer la tête.

— Une messe noire dans un cimetière est déjà inhabituelle en soi. Une enfant nue que l'on retrouve morte sur une dalle et qui hante les esprits des vivants, le gardien du cimetière que l'on assassine et dont le corps disparaît… tout cela sort décidément de l'ordinaire.

Le commissaire aux morts étranges réfléchit avant de reprendre :

— Le gardien du cimetière n'a pas vraiment été étranglé…

— Oui, répondit vivement le moine, comme je l'ai dit, on l'a privé d'air par compressions successives pour ne pas laisser de marques…

Le jeune homme fronça les sourcils.

— On n'a pas tué Sophia de cette façon. Les marques sur son cou étaient peu prononcées. Tu n'as d'ailleurs pas accompli toutes les recherches qu'il fallait en refusant de l'autopsier! On ne sait si elle est morte de froid ou de l'étranglement.

— Certes, fit le moine troublé. Certes…

— Et si l'assassin n'était pas le même? demanda Volnay.

Son père plissa les yeux, tentant de capter les pensées de son fils.

— Tu insinues que deux faits différents se sont produits cette nuit-là dans ce lieu ?

— Peut-être. N'oublie pas que la messe noire a probablement été interrompue. Mais par qui ? Qui donc peut bien se promener seul la nuit dans un cimetière ?

— Mais le gardien de celui-ci, fit le moine.

Volnay s'impatienta.

— Si ce gardien n'a pas été tué par les célébrants de la messe noire, qui, en dehors de tous ces gens-là, peut rôder dans un cimetière pendant les heures sombres ?

Le moine se frappa le front.

— Quelle bourrique je fais, moi qui suis si intelligent ! Bien sûr ! Les déterreurs de cadavres ! Mais, de ce que nous avons appris d'eux, ils n'ont tué personne !

— C'est ce qu'ils ont raconté aux hommes de main de ton anatomiste, à moins que ceux-ci n'aient inventé cette histoire afin que je les laisse filer.

Son père demanda :

— Veux-tu retourner de nuit dans le cimetière où nous avons retrouvé Sophia ?

— Sartine y a certainement posté des hommes à lui et, après ce qui s'est passé, je pense que l'endroit va être évité pendant quelques années !

Il hésita.

— Je suppose qu'Hélène va passer la nuit ici.

— Mon Dieu, si elle le souhaite…

— N'a-t-elle donc pas de logement ? s'agaça Volnay.

Le moine écarta les bras en un geste de désespoir comique.

— Nous ne sommes pas intimes…

— Mais vous n'êtes pas loin de le devenir ! Bonne nuit, père !

Volnay sortit. La neige tombait dans un silence magique. Dans l'impasse, il vit soudain Hélène s'avancer vers lui. Le vent semblait lutter avec les plis de sa longue robe, provoquant des frémissements de soie. Une certaine langueur paraissait affecter tous ses gestes. Elle sourit en le voyant.

— Hélène…

Elle s'arrêta, frémissante devant lui.

— Vous ne restez pas ?

— Non. Mon père vous racontera les derniers événements de la journée. Il faut que je rentre chez moi pour réfléchir en paix. Il me semble que je ne vois pas les évidences !

Elle le regarda avec curiosité.

— Voilà qui ne vous ressemble pas !

Des flocons de neige s'accrochaient à ses magnifiques cheveux. D'un geste doux, Volnay les cueillit comme autant de fleurs.

— Vous êtes très attentionné, remarqua-t-elle.

— Vous êtes très belle.

Il la saisit à la taille et l'attira à lui. L'haleine d'Hélène vint se briser contre son visage, réveillant en lui des souvenirs oubliés. Sa bouche trouva la sienne. Elle se laissa faire mais ne lui rendit pas son baiser.

— Pardonnez-moi, chuchota-t-elle, mais c'est votre père que je préfère !

Le policier sursauta et recula d'un pas comme s'il venait d'être giflé.

Lorsque Hélène rentra, elle trouva le moine le front appuyé contre la fenêtre qui donnait sur l'impasse.

— Que faites-vous devant votre fenêtre ?

— Je guette les âmes esseulées…

Volnay rentra chez lui à pas lents, accablé. Il raviva le feu et sortit son oiseau de la cage.

— Eh oui la pie, le croiras-tu ? J'ai essayé d'embrasser Hélène !

L'oiseau leva la tête.

— Et ce n'est pas par inclination pour elle, continua le policier. Je me méfie de cette espionne que Sartine m'a mise dans les pattes. Simplement, j'ai pensé que si elle était dans mes bras, elle cesserait ses familiarités avec mon père !

Il s'appliqua à lisser soigneusement le plumage de la pie.

— Eh bien mes craintes étaient fondées, elle en a bien après mon père. Et elle a eu le culot de me le dire !

La lueur des flammes se réfléchissait sur la tranche dorée des livres. Il la contempla un instant puis son attention se reporta sur l'oiseau.

— Toutefois, si cette femme est bien l'aventurière que je soupçonne, pourquoi m'avoir fait cet aveu ? Je ne comprends pas.

— Comprends pas, répéta la pie.

XII

LE FEU ET AUTRES DIABLERIES

La lune n'était plus qu'une coulée d'argent sur les toits. Cornevin, le commissaire de quartier, se planta devant Volnay. Il s'était trop approché du feu. Son visage avait pris une teinte de pierre cuite et ses cheveux une couleur de cendre.

— La maison a commencé à brûler après minuit. Je me suis rendu sur les lieux puis j'ai songé à vous prévenir.

— Vous avez bien fait, répondit Volnay.

L'autre se tourna vers les ruines fumantes.

— Les gens ont jeté des boules de neige sur le feu en attendant qu'on tracte par cheval des pompes à bras sur le lieu de l'incendie !

— Comment le feu a-t-il pris ?

— Peut-on savoir ? Il y a bien des incendies dans Paris. Une cheminée mal ramonée, le vent qui attise, les structures en bois de l'immeuble… La neige a empêché que le feu ne se communique aux autres maisons alentour.

Leur attention fut attirée par une carriole qui arrivait au pas prudent d'un cheval au poil gris, creusant de grandes balafres sur le sol enneigé.

— Oh, fit le commissaire de quartier. Il est déjà là…

— Oui, je l'ai prévenu avant de venir, dit Volnay.

Il se souvenait du baiser refusé par Hélène et de son aveu envers son père. Ses traits se durcirent. Le moine descendit tranquillement de sa voiture et avança vers eux en récitant :

— *"Hier, durant la nuit obscure*
Un grand feu s'éprit d'aventure
Mais avec soin et diligence
On amortit sa véhémence!"

— Tu m'en diras tant! fit son fils.

Ils contemplèrent en silence les ruines calcinées. Une douce chaleur s'en échappait.

— Il va me falloir un peu d'aide, dit enfin le moine. Je dois récupérer les corps dans la maison, si corps il y a.

— Pourquoi? s'étonna le commissaire de quartier.

Volnay et son père échangèrent un regard complice.

— Pour identifier les victimes, répondit le commissaire aux morts étranges, et connaître la cause de leur mort.

Le commissaire de quartier les regarda avec effarement.

— Mais s'il y a quelqu'un, il est mort brûlé, voyons!

Le moine eut un petit rire condescendant.

— Ah, si toute chose pouvait être aussi simple !

Et sans un mot de plus, il se dirigea vers les restes de la maison.

— Donnez-lui des hommes, fit le commissaire aux morts étranges, et allons un peu interroger le voisinage pour savoir s'ils ont vu quelque chose.

— Mais pourquoi?

Volnay le considéra d'un œil sévère.

— Mais pour faire notre métier !

À l'aube, Hélène entra dans le bureau de Sartine au Châtelet. Celui-ci se tenait frileusement devant le feu qui éclairait son visage de reflets incendiaires sous sa perruque poudrée et frisée. La jeune femme ôta nonchalamment son manteau de fourrure pour le confier à un domestique. Elle soignait ses apparitions chez le lieutenant général de police, s'étant vêtue pour l'occasion d'une belle robe de velours rouge. La pièce d'estomac triangulaire était décorée d'une échelle de rubans. La coupe et le tissu soulignaient la rondeur des seins moulés dans le corset. Des engageantes de la plus belle dentelle ornaient les poignets de sa robe toute couverte de rubans et de fleurs artificielles.

Une lueur intéressée brilla un instant dans l'œil de Sartine avant qu'il ne retrouve sa froideur habituelle.

— Aucun d'eux ne vous suspecte ? demanda-t-il abruptement.

— Le moine est on ne peut plus charmant mais Volnay se méfie de moi.

— Cela ne me surprend guère, rien n'a prise sur mon commissaire aux morts étranges.

Il dit cela avec un mélange de dépit et de fierté.

— Pour le moine, reprit-il avec une grimace, c'est un savant cabotin, toujours prêt à faire la roue comme un paon devant les jolies femmes. Mais ne le sous-estimez pas, son intelligence est remarquable. En revanche, et c'est sa faiblesse, son orgueil en ses capacités est incommensurable. Flattez-le toujours et il vous adorera.

— Je sais comment le manier, ne vous inquiétez pas !

Sartine hocha la tête, satisfait, puis son regard s'assombrit.

— Notre cheval de Troie est dans la place, tout cela est fort bien mais la prostituée et le curé dansant sont morts, le père de Sophia a sans doute brûlé dans sa maison… Que reste-t-il comme piste ?

— Un homme au comportement suspect pendant l'enterrement de Sophia…

— Oui, grogna Sartine, encore un que Volnay a laissé filer entre ses pattes. Il épuise une demi-douzaine de mes mouches à le chercher dans le quartier où il l'a perdu ! Je me demande s'il ne serait pas plus sensé de jeter mon filet dans la ruelle de l'Or ou dans quelques endroits de ce genre et de mettre à la question tous ces nécromanciens, alchimistes, jeteurs de sorts ou marchands de philtres ! Tant pis pour les honnêtes marchands, il se trouvera bien un ou deux coupables dans le lot !

— Le résultat n'est pas certain mais vous pourrez être sûr que tout Paris en parlera. Gardez vos enquêteurs. Ne vendez pas votre cheval pour acheter de l'avoine !

Le lieutenant général de police la considéra un instant en silence.

— Ce n'est pas mon intention, vous l'avez deviné. Hélène, vous n'êtes plus une enfant et vous connaissez les rouages du pouvoir. Le procureur Siltieri m'a été imposé. Il est proche de l'Église mais loin de Dieu ! C'est un homme du parti des dévots. Ce parti est soutenu par le Dauphin, fils du roi, et en lutte contre celui de la marquise de Pompadour, proche des encyclopédistes. Pour se conforter auprès du roi, les dévots ne rêvent que de l'effrayer avec un scandale sans précédent qui soit le fait d'hérétiques.

Sartine se tut. La personnalité tourmentée et morbide du roi l'effrayait secrètement. Persuadé d'être monarque de droit divin et ayant ancrée en lui une peur terrible de la mort et de la justice divine, il n'en était pas moins incapable de résister à ses pulsions et ses vices. Seule sa jouissance du moment l'intéressait. Une fois celle-ci passée, il devenait à nouveau un pantin sans âme aux mains de l'Église. Isolée et occupée à contrer les dévots avec le clan philosophique, la favorite, la marquise de Pompadour, s'éteignait doucement, rongée par la fatigue et la maladie.

— Ma situation est extrêmement compliquée, reprit le policier d'une voix tendue qui lui était inhabituelle. Je me vois dans la double obligation d'étouffer cette affaire et de la résoudre ! Le procureur Siltieri n'a, quant à lui, pour seul objectif que de faire le plus de bruit possible et d'envoyer à la potence quiconque sera pris la main dans le sac, coupable ou innocent !

Il s'assit sur le bord de son bureau et soupira.

— J'ai besoin d'une arrestation et Volnay ne me ramène que des corps !

— Il est parti de rien et il a déjà relevé plusieurs pistes, objecta Hélène.

Sartine darda sur elle un regard impérieux.

— N'allez pas succomber à son charme, ce n'est pas ce que je vous demande. Volnay a une conception de la justice bien particulière et le sens de la hiérarchie lui fait cruellement défaut. Vous êtes avec lui et le moine pour me rapporter tout ce qu'ils me dissimulent. Tenez, l'histoire de ce chien… Pourquoi me cacher cela ?

— Ils craignaient peut-être que vous ne le soumettiez à la question !

Devant l'impertinence de sa visiteuse, un rare sourire illumina le visage de Sartine avant de disparaître aussi vite, laissant même douter de son apparition.

— Des résultats, vous m'entendez ? Je veux des résultats et ceci par tous les moyens ! C'est peut-être le sort politique de la France qui se joue derrière tout cela !

Il alla s'asseoir à son bureau qu'il se mit à tambouriner avec ses doigts. Son œil avait pris une teinte vitreuse.

— Cette affaire est propre comme une écuelle de chats, murmura-t-il. Et dire qu'il faut que cela tombe justement sur Sophia !

La jeune femme le considéra attentivement.

— Savez-vous sur sa naissance quelque chose que j'ignore ?

Sartine la fixa sans mot dire. Son regard était dur et impitoyable.

— Ai-je dit quelque chose de tel ? Tenez-vous-en aux faits, répondit-il, et non à des hypothèses !

Le moine avait allumé les chandelles dans la cave et frottait ses mains pour les réchauffer. Devant lui, une masse informe noirâtre gisait sur une table.

— Alors ? demanda le commissaire aux morts étranges.

— Deux corps. Une femme et un homme. Ils sont complètement calcinés mais le corps féminin pourrait bien être celui de la servante, quant au corps masculin il a la même taille que notre astrologue. Et puis regarde sa main. J'ai remarqué cette énorme bague avec un rubis lors de notre première visite. Il la porte. C'est bien lui car c'est elle !

Volnay fronça les sourcils et contempla fixement le cadavre de l'astronome.

— Que se passe-t-il ?

Le commissaire aux morts étranges haussa les épaules.

— Je ne sais pas. J'éprouve une étrange impression mais je ne saurais dire quoi. Cette pierre…

— Elle est de grande valeur assurément. Chaque pierre a ses particularités. On dit que le rubis donne de la persévérance aux indécis…

Le commissaire aux morts étranges fit quelques pas dans la cave, caressant du bout du doigt un alambic, rangeant sans s'en rendre compte ce qu'il jugeait en désordre sur la table.

— Arrête de toucher à mes affaires, dit le moine, tu sais bien que j'ai horreur de ça !

— Toi et tes manies de rangement ! grogna son fils.

Il se tourna vers son père, perdu dans ses réflexions.

— Tout se complique, dit-il. Une enfant tuée, le gardien du cimetière étranglé, la prostituée qui se rompt le cou et notre curé dansant qui gigote au bout d'une corde, récapitula-t-il comme si cela était une comptine. Ajoutons deux cadavres brûlés… l'astrologue et sa servante…

— Je n'ai trouvé aucune trace de meurtre sur ces cadavres, dit son père. Enfin, vu l'état…

Il désigna d'un geste dégoûté les restes calcinés.

— J'ai l'habitude qu'ils soient moins… abîmés !

Devant la porte de l'église Saint-Sulpice, un tremblement saisit tout entier le corps d'Hélène. Elle se figea et le laissa passer, fermant les yeux pour calmer les battements désordonnés de son cœur. Une douce plainte la saisit pourtant lorsqu'elle pénétra dans les lieux sacrés. Ceux-ci ne lui étaient ni agréables, ni familiers. Elle n'appréciait pas plus le Christ qui se tortillait sur la croix que les saints des vitraux, agonisant dans d'atroces souffrances.

Ses pas résonnèrent lugubrement sur les dalles froides. À la lueur tremblotante des cierges qui se consumaient, elle se dirigea vers un coin de l'église où étaient placés en vis-à-vis des chaises et des bancs. Au milieu, sur un siège surélevé, trônait le curé qui faisait répéter le catéchisme à des enfants.

Hélène attendit patiemment qu'il termine. De plus en plus intrigué par sa présence, discrète mais attentive, le curé lui jetait des regards curieux. Lorsqu'il la vit se saisir d'une bourse qui semblait remplie de bonne monnaie sonnante et trébuchante, il termina rapidement et renvoya d'un geste les enfants qui l'écoutaient, l'air grave et recueilli. La mine onctueuse, le curé s'approcha d'elle. Il avait atteint cet âge intermédiaire où, faute d'exercice et d'hygiène de vie maîtrisée, les muscles laissent place à l'embonpoint avant de se transformer définitivement en graisse. L'homme était pourtant sagace et avisé. Hélène savait qu'il avait fait établir dans sa paroisse une fabrique de mousseline.

— Madame, je suis le curé de la paroisse, puis-je quelque chose pour vous ?

La visiteuse arbora son plus beau sourire, s'efforçant de ne pas le fixer de face car il avait des yeux rapprochés et elle ne savait trop comment porter son regard.

— Vous le pouvez. Puis-je vous entretenir en particulier ?

D'un geste, il l'invita à le suivre jusqu'à la sacristie. Là, elle lui montra la lettre de recommandation de Sartine, ce qui l'impressionna fort.

— Je vous remercie, mon père, de me recevoir à l'impromptu, dit-elle en rangeant la lettre.

— Dieu, madame, vous avez des titres de recommandation qui obligent... Pensez donc ! M. le lieutenant général de police en personne ! Il a beaucoup œuvré dans notre bonne ville pour son approvisionnement et le commerce des grains. Je ne parle même pas de la sécurité publique. Que puis-je pour votre service ?

Hélène dissimulait derrière un masque aimable d'étranges pensées. La remarque anodine de Sartine l'avait alertée.

Et dire qu'il faut que cela tombe justement sur Sophia !

L'agressivité du lieutenant général de police lorsqu'elle l'avait questionné sur la naissance de Sophia la confirmait dans son soupçon. On lui cachait quelque chose !

— Je souhaite quelques renseignements sur la famille Marly, fit-elle d'un ton neutre. Vous savez, l'astrologue de la rue des Canettes...

— M. Marly, je vois, oui. On parle un peu de lui dans le quartier...

Le curé eut un reniflement dédaigneux.

— Faire commerce des étoiles pour prédire l'avenir ! Vous pensez bien que je ne vois pas un tel homme à la messe !

— Est-il homme de mauvaise vie ?

L'autre haussa un sourcil.

— Pas à ma connaissance, il se tient à l'écart autant des récréations mondaines que de la messe ! Mais l'astrologie...

Il se signa.

— Voilà bien diablerie que de prétendre connaître le sort des mortels en contemplant les étoiles. Ceci est blasphème ! Notre sort est entre les seules mains de Dieu.

Sa bouche marqua un pli sarcastique.

— Mais hélas, nous vivons dans un siècle de superstition, il est encore des parents qui m'apportent leur enfant à baptiser avec un morceau de pain noir autour du cou pour éloigner le mauvais sort !

— C'est surtout à la fille de l'astrologue que je m'intéresse, précisa Hélène.

Elle prit un air enjôleur.

— Je sais combien les archives des paroisses sont admirablement tenues. M. Marly a toujours vécu dans le quartier et je connais la date de naissance de sa fille. Je voudrais vérifier qu'elle a bien été déclarée à votre paroisse à sa naissance ou à son baptême.

— Je ne peux rien vous refuser ! dit onctueusement l'ecclésiastique. Quelle est cette date de naissance ?

— Le 12 janvier 1747.

— Je vais vous chercher cela dans nos archives des registres paroissiaux.

— Je suis certaine que tout y est consigné.

Un sourire suffisant éclaira le visage du curé.

— Madame, avec les registres des commissariats de police, les archives paroissiales sont ce qu'il y a de mieux tenu en France. Vous verrez que dans trois siècles, on y lira encore toute l'histoire de France !

Le curé revint une vingtaine de minutes plus tard avec un ouvrage relié de cuir noir.

— Pardonnez-moi. Le recueil était parfaitement bien archivé mais difficile d'accès !

D'un revers de la manche, il fit voler la poussière.

— Hum, l'année 1747… Janvier, m'avez-vous dit. Elle n'avait donc pas douze ans lorsqu'elle est morte cette pauvre enfant !

— Comment savez-vous cela ?

L'ecclésiastique lui jeta un regard surpris.

— Ignorez-vous que tout se sait dans un quartier ?

Il mouilla son index et son pouce avant de tourner les pages.

— Janvier… voilà…

Il lut, avança encore, fronçant les sourcils.

— Non, elle n'y figure pas. Je vais regarder par sécurité le mois de février.

Hélène attendit patiemment, voyant la déception se peindre progressivement sur le visage de son interlocuteur.

— Non décidément mais peut-être a-t-elle été déclarée à une autre paroisse ? J'étais là à cette époque mais je n'ai pas souvenir d'elle.

Il se gratta pensivement la joue.

— À l'époque, ce Marly n'était pas astrologue. Étonnamment, il était maître joaillier.

Hélène fronça délicatement les sourcils. Elle se souvenait de l'énorme et inhabituel rubis monté sur bague au doigt de l'astrologue.

— Maître joaillier ? répéta-t-elle pour marquer son intérêt et l'inciter à continuer.

— Oui, il épousa une femme qui était la domestique d'une personne de qualité à la cour. Je crois que c'est à la mort de son épouse, deux ans après la venue au monde de leur fille, qu'il vendit son commerce pour se consacrer aux étoiles. Le chagrin probablement et sans doute un brin de folie…

— La petite a donc perdu sa mère très jeune.

— Certes.

— Et elle n'a pas été déclarée et baptisée à votre paroisse ?

— Non.

Hélène se pencha légèrement en avant et le regard du curé effleura sa poitrine avant de se réfugier dans ses yeux.

— Dites-moi mon père, savez-vous de quelle personne de qualité la mère de Sophia était la domestique ?

Son interlocuteur s'agita nerveusement.

— Dieu tout-puissant ! Pensez-vous donc que l'on sache dans les quartiers de Paris ce qui se passe à la cour de Versailles ?

La jeune femme haussa négligemment les épaules.

— Ma foi, oui !

Elle posa une bourse sur la table. Les écus tintèrent dans un bruit métallique qui fit sursauter le curé.

— J'aimerais faire un don aux pauvres de votre paroisse.

Mais elle garda ses doigts serrés autour de la bourse. Le curé se racla la gorge, embarrassé.

— Madame, vous me mettez dans une situation délicate…

— Dieu a confiance dans votre jugement !

L'homme se tortilla les mains. Malgré le froid de la pièce, une goutte de sueur coula le long de sa tempe. Hélène contempla le sillon humide qu'elle avait laissé. C'était celui de la peur.

— Tout ceci restera entre nous ?

— Je vous le jure sur le Christ, répondit-elle d'une voix égale.

— Ce n'étaient d'ailleurs que des rumeurs…

— Bien entendu.

Il baissa encore la voix et, lorsqu'il parla, celle-ci était devenue presque inaudible.

— C'était une danseuse de l'Opéra, à l'époque tout Paris était à ses pieds. On la surnommait Mlle Belle Ange.

Ils étaient remontés de la cave. Tandis que son fils bourrait la cheminée de grosses bûches, son père dépliait avec précaution une couverture qui recélait ses découvertes de la nuit.

— En fouillant dans les décombres avec le commissaire de quartier, j'ai trouvé ce livre. Il se trouvait dans une niche de pierre, ce qui l'a protégé. Seule la couverture a souffert.

Les yeux du moine brillaient de plaisir en effleurant les pages du bout des doigts.

— Ce livre n'a pas brûlé. Une chance car il propose quelques recettes pour enflammer les sens de sa belle !

Il commença à le feuilleter avec un plaisir évident.

— Cette recette-là est un peu compliquée puisqu'elle nécessite de réchauffer des excréments de crocodile et d'antilope, de la bile de bouc sauvage et je t'en passe. J'aurais un peu de mal à trouver tout cela ! Celle-ci me semble plus abordable mais elle nécessite quand même les cheveux d'un mort, des grains d'orge enterrés dans son tombeau, du sang de tique d'un chien noir... Non vraiment... Ah, voilà pour retrouver vigueur : "Frictionne ton membre d'écume de la bouche d'un étalon..."

Il releva la tête pour se retrouver sous l'œil inquisiteur de son fils.

— Naturellement, je n'ai pas besoin de tout ça, s'empressa-t-il d'ajouter. Je suis resté jeune et très vigoureux...

— J'espère que ce n'est pas Hélène qui te met ainsi en émoi, remarqua froidement Volnay.

Le moine cilla brièvement.

— Au cours de nos investigations dans les ruines, poursuivit-il rapidement, le commissaire de quartier a également découvert un second livre. Celui-ci était dans un coffret de fer, sans doute scellé dans un mur.

Pour le dissimuler ainsi, il devait posséder une certaine valeur.

— Qu'est-ce que ceci ? demanda son fils en pointant un doigt inquisitorial sur la couverture du livre.

— Des sceaux démoniaques : Lucifer, empereur, Belzébuth, prince, et Astaroth, grand-duc des Enfers… Et ce cavalier portant lance et sceptre se nomme Abigor. Il commande soixante légions de démons et est très prisé des chefs de guerre pour sa science militaire. Et voici Baël, chef de guerre aux trois têtes de chat, d'homme et de crapaud. Ici Ayperos, le lion à la tête et aux pattes d'oie avec une queue de lièvre et enfin là, épervier au poing, Balan, roi des Enfers qui connaît tout du passé comme de l'avenir…

— Tes connaissances de l'occulte me stupéfieront toujours, fit son fils d'un ton aigre-doux.

Gêné, le moine haussa négligemment les épaules.

— Tu sais, je m'intéresse à tout et à n'importe quoi !

Volnay lui jeta un regard impavide.

— Ainsi, notre astrologue s'intéresse aux forces de l'Enfer. Serait-ce lui l'instigateur de la messe noire dans laquelle a péri sa fille ?

— Pas forcément ! s'écria le moine. On peut aussi s'intéresser à Satan par curiosité intellectuelle ou encore pour mieux le combattre…

— Et la servante ? Non, je l'ai vue se signer lorsqu'elle a bâillé à notre arrivée. Or, l'on se signe pour empêcher que le diable entre par votre bouche et s'empare de votre âme. Mais l'astrologue… Il achetait peut-être des cierges noirs à un homme qui a participé au meurtre de sa fille et lisait des livres à la gloire des démons… À propos, que dit donc ce livre ?

— Il est en latin. Je le maîtrise bien mais c'est un ouvrage ésotérique et compliqué. J'aurai besoin de temps pour le lire et le comprendre. Tant mieux car, pour achever de me remettre, il me faut rester au chaud et boire des tisanes !

— Avec une jeune et jolie garde-malade ! compléta sans rire son fils.

La neige tombait en petits cristaux blancs et froids. Giflée par la bise, Hélène tenait sa tête rentrée dans les épaules. Elle ne releva la tête qu'avant de passer l'angle de la rue Saint-Jacques. Des passants la bousculèrent sans un mot d'excuse car elle s'était immobilisée sans avertissement. Le sentiment d'une présence derrière elle la tenaillait. La jeune femme résista à la tentation de se retourner comme elle l'avait déjà fait à plusieurs reprises sans résultat. La foule se pressait, anonyme, grelottante. Tous les visages se ressemblaient, beaucoup exprimant la même difficulté de vivre. Un instant, elle hésita. Ce n'était pas une personne qui la suivait, plutôt une ombre… quelque chose de fluide qui se faufilait à travers la masse compacte des gens dans la rue.

Hélène s'engagea rue de la Lanterne, retrouvant le calme et le silence ouaté procurés par la neige. Là, elle s'arrêta. Un regard pesait lourdement sur ses épaules. Lentement Hélène se retourna. Son cœur rata un battement. Une lueur laiteuse baignait maintenant la rue, estompant les formes d'une irréelle silhouette frêle. C'était Sophia ! Elle avait un petit air perdu dans ses vêtements trop amples et ses grands yeux tristes la fixaient, semblant lire au-dedans d'elle. Un instant le soleil perça les nuages et Hélène ferma les yeux, éblouie par la réverbération sur la neige. Lorsqu'elle les rouvrit, Sophia avait disparu.

Hélène rentra sans frapper. Volnay lui jeta un regard mécontent et allait se livrer à quelques réflexions mais il s'arrêta à la vue de son visage couleur de cendres.

— Qu'avez-vous? On dirait que vous venez de croiser un fantôme!

La jeune femme s'adossa à la porte, la poitrine frémissante.

— J'ai vu Sophia!

Le moine se précipita vers elle.

— Ah vous aussi!

Il se tourna vers son fils.

— Avec moi et la servante de l'auberge, cela fait trois maintenant? Persisteras-tu à me prendre pour un fou?

— Un instant, fit Volnay en saisissant le bras d'Hélène. Où l'avez-vous aperçue?

— Dans la rue, à deux pas de là.

Le policier se précipita dehors. Le moine soupira.

— La réaction de mon fils est parfaitement logique et rationnelle mais je sais qu'elle ne le mènera nulle part. On ne voit Sophia que lorsqu'elle le veut bien!

Une dizaine de minutes plus tard, le retour de Volnay lui donna raison.

— Personne en vue, fit-il. Vous avez rêvé!

Hélène jeta un regard entendu au moine. Elle avait appris à connaître les mécanismes intellectuels du commissaire aux morts étranges basés sur l'observation, la réflexion, l'analyse puis la synthèse. Il n'y avait pas place pour tout ce qui relevait du domaine de l'irréel. Pour lui, un fait irrationnel signifiait simplement que l'explication était plus difficile à trouver!

— Vous avez été longtemps absente, remarqua le policier. Où étiez-vous donc?

— Chez moi, j'avais besoin d'un bon bain!

Volnay renifla l'air comme s'il voulait vérifier et marqua son scepticisme d'un haussement de sourcils.

— Et où résidez-vous?

Une lueur de moquerie traversa le regard d'Hélène.

— Seriez-vous en train de mener un interrogatoire, commissaire? Dans notre cas, mon adresse ne vous regarde en aucune manière à moins que vous n'ayez en tête l'espoir de me rendre quelque visite…

Gêné, Volnay détourna la tête.

— Pas le moins du monde!

Le souvenir du baiser volé à Hélène le tourmentait tout autant que l'attitude de la jeune femme.

— Allons, fit le moine d'un ton conciliant, arrêtez de vous chamailler tous les deux!

On frappa à la porte. Un coup timide d'abord puis renouvelé avec un peu plus d'assurance.

— J'espère que ce n'est pas encore Sartine! se plaignit le moine.

Hélène arbora un sourire figé.

— Pour le savoir, le mieux est d'aller ouvrir! dit sèchement le commissaire aux morts étranges.

Un étrange individu fit son apparition sur le seuil de la maison. Il avait un visage rond et hilare, une bouche pleine de dents gâtées et une haleine à faire tomber par terre. D'un geste ample il salua Volnay et le moine puis se courba presque à terre devant Hélène en l'appelant *Votre Gracieuseté*.

— Ah, voilà une de mes mouches, constata le commissaire aux morts étranges. Venez donc Gaston vous réchauffer devant le feu avant de me conter ce qui vous amène.

L'autre ne se fit pas prier et, après avoir quitté ses gants, promena avec ravissement ses mains au-dessus des flammes.

— Oh, que faites-vous là? demanda-t-il en baissant la tête.

— Des œufs à la braise, répondit le moine. Je vous en donnerai un si vous nous avez rapporté de bonnes nouvelles!

— Avec plaisir, monsieur le moine!

Il sembla alors découvrir la présence de l'animal près du feu.

— Oh, vous avez un chien maintenant! Quelle belle bête!

Il se tourna vers Volnay.

— Je suis d'abord passé chez vous mais ne vous y trouvant point, j'ai couru jusqu'ici. J'ai de la chance que vous ne soyez pas au Châtelet!

— Qu'avez-vous à me dire? demanda le commissaire aux morts étranges en lui servant un petit verre d'eau-de-vie pour se réchauffer.

La mouche vida celui-ci d'une traite, s'essuya la bouche d'un revers de main et remercia aimablement.

— J'ai retrouvé la trace de votre homme, celui avec l'épée au côté. Grand, blond, les cheveux filasse, les épaules carrées, l'air brutal et le visage mangé par la petite vérole… Il se peut qu'il en existe d'autres mais celui-ci répond point par point à votre description.

— Avez-vous trouvé où il habite?

— Ah commissaire, hélas non. J'ai repéré l'homme dans une taverne mais ensuite il est reparti à cheval. J'ai eu beau courir, je l'ai vite perdu!

Le moine soupira.

— Je suis ensuite revenu interroger les gens à la taverne, reprit vivement la mouche. J'ai dû payer quelques tournées pour cela. D'ailleurs, monsieur le chevalier, si vous pouviez faire quelque chose pour mes frais… J'attends toujours des mois avant que l'on me rembourse !

Volnay hocha la tête et sortit sa bourse.

— Voici de la part de M. de Sartine.

— Oh, commissaire, vous êtes généreux. Grand merci !

Il empocha les pièces et reprit son récit.

— J'ai donc appris dans cette taverne que l'homme est un habitué. Il vient boire seul ou, parfois, avec quelque prostituée du quartier. Je me suis donc permis de poster une mouche dans cette taverne jour et nuit. D'ailleurs, si je pouvais avoir une petite avance car là-bas nous sommes obligés de consommer…

— Ce que je vous ai donné ne vous suffit pas ?

— Diable, commissaire, pour moi si mais je ne suis pas seul ! Nous allons nous relayer à quatre pour ne pas manquer votre homme !

De nouveau, la main de Volnay plongea dans sa bourse.

— Ne buvez pas trop, conseilla-t-il, mes petites mouches doivent garder tous leurs sens en éveil.

— Vos mouches, commissaire, ont leurs yeux et leurs oreilles bien ouverts et rien ne peut leur échapper ! s'exclama Gaston.

Il fit mine d'ouvrir ses ailes et de s'envoler.

— Avant de partir, puis-je avoir un de ces œufs à la braise ? demanda-t-il plein d'espoir.

XIII

ABBAYE ET AUTRES DIABLERIES

Une fois Gaston parti, ils se partagèrent avec plaisir les derniers œufs à la braise, se brûlant les doigts et les lèvres.

— La mouche s'est envolée mais nous avons encore beaucoup à faire, dit le moine en débouchant une bouteille. Vous allez me goûter celui-ci, c'est du vin de Bordeaux, il vient de mes amis libraires les Madison, à Livourne, des gens plein d'esprit. Que faites-vous cette après-midi, ma chère?

— Je vais poursuivre mon enquête.

— Très bien, fit le moine d'un ton un peu pincé, nous poursuivrons la nôtre également. Décidément, vous nous délaissez ces temps-ci. Je vais bouder!

En réponse à son caprice, elle lui adressa un sourire charmant.

— Mais pour le moment, rebondit-il gaiement, j'ai à vous soumettre une amusante petite énigme. Vous souvenez-vous qu'hier soir je vous ai raconté nos découvertes dans les poches du curé dansant?

Il but une lampée de vin et claqua la langue d'un air appréciateur.

— Par acquit de conscience, j'ai depuis fouillé la doublure de la veste du curé dansant, j'y ai trouvé un second papier, soigneusement dissimulé. Deux adresses y figurent: le quai de la Mégisserie, sans plus d'indication, et la seconde certainement un lieu connu de notre curé dansant mais pas de moi ! Voyez par vous-même : *la couche ou la louche de lensser...*

— Jamais entendu parler de ce lieu ! Montrez-moi donc ce papier.

Le moine alla le lui chercher tandis qu'elle portait son verre à ses lèvres. Elle but encore une gorgée en examinant le papier, ses jolis sourcils délicatement froncés.

— Je ne lis pas la même chose que vous, murmura-t-elle enfin. Les lettres sont mal tracées et je ne suis pas certaine que notre curé dansant maîtrise parfaitement l'écriture. Je lirais plutôt *la bouche de l'enfer* !

Le moine jaillit brusquement de son siège.

— La bouche de l'enfer ! Mais oui ! C'est ainsi qu'on surnomme une abbaye abandonnée à quelques lieues de Paris. Le père abbé était tellement intraitable qu'on raconte que des moines se jetèrent dans le puits par désespoir et revinrent ensuite hanter les vivants. Persécuté par les revenants, le père abbé se pendit. Les derniers moines s'empressèrent de déguerpir et plus personne n'osa reprendre possession des lieux car on entendait la nuit des cris et des gémissements. On imagina bien vite que les diables avaient pris possession de cet endroit et même les bergers des environs n'osèrent plus s'en approcher.

Il jeta à Hélène un regard complice.

— Les diables vous font-ils peur, ma chère ?

— Pas le moins du monde, répondit-elle, puisqu'il en existe un dans chaque homme !

Pour gagner l'endroit, ils avaient décidé de prendre la carriole du moine. Au pas prudent mais sûr de leur cheval, ils quittèrent Paris et gagnèrent les hauteurs du

Petit-Montrouge. Ils prirent ensuite, en direction de la Beauce, une route environnée de moulins à vent à la toiture en charpente couverte de bardeaux. Enchanté, le moine se fit lyrique et déclama :

— "En ce moment, ils découvrirent trente ou quarante moulins à vent et don Quichotte dit à son écuyer : La fortune conduit nos affaires mieux que ne pourrait y réussir notre désir même. Regarde ami Sancho ; voilà devant nous au moins trente démesurés géants auxquels je vais livrer bataille et ôter la vie à tous tant qu'ils sont. Avec leurs dépouilles, nous commencerons à nous enrichir car c'est prise de bonne guerre et c'est grandement servir Dieu que de faire disparaître si mauvaise engeance de la face de la terre !"

Hélène rit et se blottit près de lui pour échapper à la morsure du froid. Instinctivement, le bras du moine lui enserra les épaules. À une intersection, ils empruntèrent une voie sinueuse dont l'état se dégrada au fur et à mesure de leur avancée. Envahi de broussailles, le chemin qui menait à l'abbaye baignait dans la boue et la neige. Les ronces griffèrent les roues de la voiture et égratignèrent le flanc de leur cheval. Plus loin, couvertes d'une croûte de neige, les branches des arbres formaient une voûte immaculée sous laquelle ils s'engouffrèrent.

Au détour du chemin, ils découvrirent le sommet d'un colombier puis les ruines grises de l'abbaye, dévorées par les mauvaises herbes et recouvertes d'une nappe de lierre. Des fleurs de givre décoraient le bord du toit de l'église surmontée d'un modeste clocheton. Le moine se souleva de son siège pour examiner les environs.

— Eh bien, mon fils, toi non plus tu n'as pas peur des diables ?

Volnay haussa les épaules.

— Pas plus que des hommes !

Le moine rit puis fit silence lorsqu'ils franchirent le portail de l'abbaye.

— As-tu remarqué qu'il y a des carrières à côté ? demanda le policier à son père. Par temps de grand vent, cela doit faire un bruit impressionnant. De là viennent peut-être les bruits et gémissements que les gens croient entendre.

Le moine se tourna vers Hélène, un large sourire à la bouche.

— Vous voyez, c'est tout mon fils, il a une explication rationnelle à tout !

Volnay sauta à terre et tira son pistolet.

— Soyons prudents, nous pourrions tomber sur un repaire de brigands ou de contrebandiers.

Il lança un regard ironique à son père.

— Cela aussi peut être une explication à la réputation des lieux. Un endroit hanté est un endroit sûr pour qui se cache de l'ordre royal !

Le moine haussa les épaules et descendit à son tour. Il tendit ensuite les bras pour aider Hélène, recevant sans frémir son corps frais contre le sien et le conservant près de lui un instant de trop, les cheveux de la jeune femme au vent lui fouettant le visage.

— Où donc sont vos diables ? lui demanda-t-elle gaiement.

— Ils sont probablement allés traire les vaches !

L'abbaye était disposée en trois épis bas et trapus qui s'appuyaient comme un gros animal engourdi contre le flanc sud de l'église. Rongés par la mousse, les vantaux de la porte de l'église tenaient encore bon et leur livrèrent passage dans un geignement criard. Les pas des trois visiteurs résonnèrent lugubrement dans l'austère église au transept flanqué de part et d'autre d'une chapelle. Les vitraux ornant la façade éclairaient faiblement les lieux déserts. La nef voûtée comptait huit travées dont les voûtes reposaient sur des colonnes en faisceaux. Au plafond, des oiseaux avaient fait leurs nids, jonchant le sol de leurs immondices. Ils remontèrent jusqu'au maître-autel surélevé, impressionnés malgré eux par la solitude imposante des lieux.

Deux portes s'ouvraient sur le cloître dont l'une dans le haut de la nef. Ils s'avancèrent en silence, frappés par la froide beauté de la pierre dans la perspective enneigée. Entre les contreforts, deux arcs reposaient gracieusement sur des colonnettes sculptées. Dans une niche creusée, l'abbé des lieux devait pouvoir donner ses lectures publiques avant l'office de complies. La salle du chapitre ne leur révéla rien, aussi se dirigèrent-ils vers le réfectoire, le moine n'oubliant pas de donner la main à Hélène. Le battant de la porte pivota sans bruit comme s'il était bien huilé. Ils clignèrent des yeux, cherchant à accommoder leur vision à la semi-obscurité qui régnait. Le moine se saisit de son briquet et alluma la torche dont il s'était muni.

Ils firent quelques pas. Lorsque la porte se referma derrière eux, la flamme de la torche vacilla et le moine s'immobilisa. Un souffle contraire venait face à eux, du passe-plat creusé dans le mur attenant à la cuisine, et la fumée de la torche leur piquait les yeux, irritant leur gorge. Le moine leva haut sa torche, éclairant la charpente en châtaignier qui surplombait le réfectoire. C'est alors qu'ils aperçurent les peintures.

— Comment a-t-on pu faire des restes d'une abbaye un lieu aussi sacrilège ? murmura Volnay choqué.

— En matière de magie noire, rétorqua le moine, on utilise beaucoup de rituels chrétiens en les détournant de leur sens initial. Ici, c'est un lieu sacré que l'on détourne de son objet.

Il brandit sa torche devant lui.

— Pour savoir contre qui vous vous battez, il vous faut connaître votre adversaire car, comme vous le savez, Satan se nomme aussi l'Adversaire.

Satisfait de son jeu de mots, le moine fit une petite pause comme s'il s'attendait à des applaudissements. Déçu, il reprit :

— Comme Zeus contre les Titans, le grand Rê en Égypte contre les dragons et tant d'autres divinités, Dieu aussi dut combattre les siens en révolte. C'étaient des anges rongés d'orgueil ayant à leur tête Satan. Il les combattit avec ses anges restés fidèles et les précipita dans les profondeurs de la fosse, la géhenne.

"Te voilà tombé du ciel
Astre brillant, fils de l'aurore !"

Un long silence régna. Ils contemplaient tous comme hypnotisés les peintures démentes.

— Ce n'est pas tout, fit doucement le moine.

Ses doigts coururent le long des murs pendant qu'il se déplaçait, les amenant à une autre fresque.

— La chute, reprit-il, s'accompagne de la métamorphose. Voyez ces anges si beaux qui se couvrent d'écailles, de cornes et de queues fourchues. Quel châtiment pour ces splendides créatures qui ambitionnaient de s'élever et de siéger au-dessus des montagnes de Dieu.

— Des animaux… murmura Hélène d'une voix étranglée.

— Sept animaux, précisa le moine. Le lion pour son orgueil démesuré, le porc pour sa gloutonnerie, l'âne pour sa paresse, le singe pour son impudeur, le loup pour sa férocité, le rhinocéros pour sa colère et enfin le dragon rouge pour sa cupidité. *Benedicite omnes bestiae et pecore Domino* : "Bêtes sauvages et troupeaux, bénissez tous le Seigneur!"

La jeune femme était blême. Semblant ne pas s'en apercevoir, le moine les conduisit au mur suivant.

— Le diable a tous les vices… comme l'homme! commenta-t-il brièvement.

Hélène exhala une plainte à la vue des images représentant toutes les perversions de l'humanité dans leur horreur la plus crue.

— Voici l'œuvre de l'homme, conclut le moine. Cet enfer qu'on appelle le monde!

Et il ajouta d'un ton sec :

— Il est parfois plus aisé de dire qu'elle est celle du diable!

Il y eut un bruissement d'air et un choc contre terre. Hélène venait de s'évanouir.

Le rat se figea soudain dans le noir. Il tourna la tête. Le sol était rongé par une lueur orangée qui semblait envahir le monde, jetant pêle-mêle contre les murs des ombres monstrueuses. Avec un petit couinement, il s'empressa de disparaître dans un trou.

Portant un flambeau, le moine ouvrait la marche. Le commissaire aux morts étranges le suivit, portant dans ses bras Hélène comme si elle pesait moins qu'une plume. Volnay la déposa à l'entrée de l'église, près de la porte sous laquelle s'infiltrait un vent cinglant. Son manteau avait glissé pendant qu'il la portait, il l'emmitoufla dedans. Le moine l'examina et lui tapota les joues jusqu'à ce qu'elles reprennent un peu de couleur. Hélène ouvrit les yeux et les referma aussitôt. Le moine tendit une fiole à son fils.

— Je vais lui soulever la tête. Tâche de lui glisser quelques gouttes de ceci entre les lèvres. C'est de la liqueur de fleur d'oranger que je fabrique moi-même.

Son fils lui jeta un regard de reproche.

— C'est juste pour lutter contre le froid, ajouta précipitamment le moine.

Il saisit délicatement la nuque de la jeune femme. Hélène ouvrit de nouveau les paupières. Le moine la contempla gravement. Ange inconnu, il y avait dans ses yeux quelques éclats de la splendeur des cieux.

— Buvez, dit Volnay avec une douceur inattendue.

Elle but puis hoqueta et toussa.

— Vous allez mieux ? s'enquit le moine. Que vous est-il arrivé ?

Il hocha la tête et continua :

— Toutes ces diableries sont impressionnantes !

Du menton, il désigna l'extérieur à son fils.

— Peux-tu aller chercher une couverture dans la carriole ? Nous partirons lorsque Hélène sera remise de son malaise.

Il reporta son attention sur la jeune femme, inquiet de son teint diaphane.

— Je ne vous pensais pas si sensible, pardonnez-moi. Qu'est-ce qui vous a donc tant effrayée dans ces peintures ?

— Moi, répondit-elle d'une faible voix.

Elle se releva à demi pour lui saisir le poignet.

— Aidez-moi à prier Dieu.

— Je ne peux pas, répondit le moine, je ne crois plus en lui.

XIV

RITUEL ET AUTRES DIABLERIES

Depuis leur dernière venue, une chape blanche s'était abattue sur la maison de la Dame de l'Eau. Désorientés, le commissaire aux morts étranges et le moine contemplèrent les lieux, le chien sur leurs talons. Discrète de nature, la ruelle de l'Or sous la neige s'était enfoncée dans une ouate cotonneuse qui étouffait jusqu'aux respirations des rares passants. Le temps semblait s'être arrêté, figé dans une gangue de glace.

— C'est une bonne chose qu'Hélène n'ait pas manifesté l'intention de nous accompagner, déclara Volnay en s'approchant de l'entrée.

— De toute manière, dit le moine, je n'autorise que toi à rendre visite à ma bonne amie Dame de l'Eau! *Chien-chien* également, bien entendu!

La première remarque parut rasséréner Volnay. Manifestement, il lui savait gré de conserver quelque méfiance envers la jeune femme, notamment pour ses relations avec Sartine. Son père n'avait pas dû juger nécessaire que le lieutenant général de police apprenne l'existence des étranges et anciennes relations entre lui et la Dame de l'Eau. Satisfait, il poussa la porte.

Le plafond était haut et quelques chandelles sur le lustre jetaient des ombres lugubres sur le sol et contre les murs. La propriétaire des lieux et ses deux visiteurs se pressèrent près du feu pour se réchauffer car la température dans la pièce était glaciale.

— Oh, le joli chien ! s'exclama la Dame de l'Eau en découvrant qui les accompagnait. Je vais lui donner un os à ronger.

— En parlant d'os à ronger, fit le moine, nous avons quelque chose pour vous !

— Des livres magiques et des déterreurs de cadavres ? s'exclama leur hôtesse après les avoir écoutés. Que ne m'aurez-vous demandé mon cher moine !

— Tout cela est monnaie courante par ici, plaisanta celui-ci.

Il jeta un regard en coin vers son fils au masque impassible avant de plaider sa cause.

— Nous avons besoin d'aide. Comme je vous l'ai déjà expliqué, nous sommes ici aux lisières de la nuit. Nous avons besoin d'un guide !

— D'un guide ou d'un indicateur ? Une mouche, comme vous dites si élégamment…

Le moine lui prit le bras avec empressement.

— Sartine ne patientera pas indéfiniment. Si nous n'avançons pas dans notre enquête, le procureur Siltieri fera mettre à sac la ruelle de l'Or et ses hommes ne feront aucune distinction entre magie blanche et magie noire !

La Dame de l'Eau hésita. Elle jeta une poignée d'herbes sur les charbons ardents et une fumée âcre se dégagea de l'âtre.

— On dit que certains mages déterrent des cadavres pour fabriquer philtres ou potions, murmura-t-elle, mais je pense pour ma part qu'ils sont plus nombreux à s'en vanter pour donner du sérieux à leurs tours qu'à le faire réellement !

262

Elle jeta un bref regard aux deux livres que le moine avait posés sur une table basse près de là.

— Quant à ces ouvrages, fit-elle mal à l'aise, je ne sais si…

— Jetez donc un coup d'œil à celui-là, proposa le moine, il y a toutes sortes de recettes que les clients de la ruelle de l'Or doivent adorer !

D'un geste prudent, la Dame de l'Eau se saisit du premier livre que le moine lui tendait et le feuilleta avec méfiance. Rapidement, elle se détendit et un rictus ironique vint orner ses lèvres.

— Voyons voir, dit-elle avec indulgence, comment nouer l'aiguillette : "Prendre une verge de loup mort, appelez le nom de celui à qui vous voulez nouer l'aiguillette et liez ladite verge avec un fil blanc. L'homme sera alors aussi impuissant pour accomplir l'acte de Vénus que s'il était châtré !"

Elle jeta un regard aiguisé au moine.

— C'est amusant comme le monde entier semble parfois tourner autour de l'aiguillette des hommes !

Ses doigts longs et fins coururent le long des pages pour s'arrêter au hasard.

— Oh mais voilà comment réparer le pucelage perdu ou paillarder avec vigueur toute la nuit !

Elle leva les yeux au ciel et reprit sa lecture en secouant la tête d'un air consterné.

— Des recettes de grand-mère tout cela, propres à flatter la virilité de l'homme !

Avec un air moqueur, elle rendit l'ouvrage au moine.

— Est-ce là tout ce que vous avez à me montrer ? Des recettes pour déflorer les pucelles ?

Le moine alla reposer le livre en souriant puis lui apporta le second ouvrage.

— Savez-vous qu'il est extrêmement facile de connaître les passages préférés d'un livre de ce genre ? demanda-t-il. En effet, lorsqu'on l'ouvre toujours au même endroit, il en prend la marque. Regardez, je feuillette et il s'ouvre à cet endroit. Je le referme, je recommence et c'est la même page. Essayez…

D'un pas prudent, la Dame de l'Eau s'approcha. Elle tendit une main hésitante au-dessus du livre ouvert et la retira soudainement comme si on venait de la mordre.

— Magie noire ! fit-elle en reculant vivement.

Elle frissonna.

— Une magie très puissante…

Dans un coin de la pièce, les bras croisés sur sa poitrine, Volnay observait la scène en silence. Les traits de son visage restaient indéchiffrables. La Dame de l'Eau s'approcha à nouveau très lentement de l'ouvrage. Un instant, sa main sembla flotter dans l'air comme l'aile d'un ange, pure de toute ombre. Et puis, elle glissa jusqu'au livre et fut envahie par l'obscurité.

— Mon Dieu, chuchota-t-elle, où donc êtes-vous tombé ?

Surmontant sa répugnance, elle tourna les pages jusqu'à celle que lui désignait le moine.

— C'est un rituel d'envoûtement, chuchota-t-elle d'une voix oppressée. Un envoûtement de sang…

— Dites-nous-en plus ! la pressa le moine.

— Non ! Je ne lis pas ce genre de livres ! Pour rien au monde, je n'oserais prononcer ces formules même silencieusement ! Je ne sais pas où vous avez mis les pieds mais vous êtes face à…

Elle hésita avant de terminer dans un souffle :

— Satan…

Le moine lui effleura le bras.

— Comment procède-t-on au rituel d'envoûtement?

— Il faut une mèche de cheveux, répondit-elle à contrecœur, ou une rognure d'ongle de la personne qu'on désire envoûter. Pour les envoûtements de sang, plus puissant, une goutte du sang de la personne ou de celui de sa descendance est nécessaire. Une statuette de cire ou une poupée de chiffon représente l'envoûté. On la baptise et on lui donne parrain et marraine. Ensuite, on la pique avec une aiguille tout en récitant une certaine formule.

La Dame de l'Eau s'écarta du livre et revint au centre de la pièce, les contemplant d'un air soucieux. Elle tenait loin de son corps sa main qui avait touché le livre.

— Y a-t-il moyen de faire cesser l'envoûtement? s'enquit le moine.

— Le maléfice ne peut être levé que par le sorcier lui-même mais celui-ci doit obligatoirement le transférer à une autre personne. C'est une règle essentielle de la magie noire: ce qui a été formé ne peut être détruit, juste transmis. Dans le cas contraire, le maléfice retombera sur lui. C'est ce que l'on appelle le choc en retour.

La Dame de l'Eau se dirigea vers une grande vasque remplie d'une eau claire.

— J'ai besoin de me purifier au contact de l'eau. Venez, je la lirai pour vous.

Elle s'adressait au policier. Celui-ci ne bougea pas d'un pouce. Il se souvenait d'une séance précédente où il avait vu dans cette même eau un crime qui allait se commettre.

— Vous avez peur?

Cela décida à la rejoindre le commissaire aux morts étranges, dont la fierté ne tolérait pas une telle suspicion. Son hôtesse agita l'eau du bout de ses doigts et lui dit :

— Ne prononcez aucune parole inutile et surtout ne vous signez pas.

— Ces deux choses ne sont pas dans mes habitudes ! répondit froidement Volnay.

La cloche du couvent des Bénédictins sonnait quinze coups lorsque Hélène arriva chez l'ancien inspecteur de police qui lui servait à l'occasion d'informateur. Maintenant âgé de soixante ans, il résidait avec sa mère dans un appartement simple mais propre et bien entretenu où elle avait déjà eu l'occasion de se rendre. Si quarante-huit commissaires de police contrôlaient Paris sous l'autorité d'un lieutenant général de police, vingt inspecteurs assuraient des tâches plus spécialisées comme la censure du théâtre ou des livres, la pédérastie, les juifs, la voirie, les étrangers… Il avait été l'un d'eux.

À sa grande surprise, l'occupant des lieux lui ouvrit la porte, ses mains pleines de mousse de savon.

— Je lave les cheveux de ma mère, expliqua-t-il d'un air embarrassé, cela vous ennuie-t-il que je termine ? Elle adore ça. Elle a si peu de plaisir, la pauvre…

Hélène l'accompagna près du feu où, sur une chaise au dossier roide, se tenait une petite femme toute rabougrie qui ne se retourna même pas à son approche. Les yeux clos, elle était si raide et immobile qu'un instant la jeune femme craignit qu'elle ne fût morte. Et puis, elle vit la poitrine se soulever doucement et les lèvres s'entrouvrirent sur un refrain. La chose était douée de respiration et fredonnait une chanson !

— Vous pouvez parler devant elle, dit l'ancien inspecteur. Elle est sourde comme un pot et ne possède plus tous ses esprits.

Il entreprit de lui frotter avec vigueur la tête, faisant poindre le sang jusqu'à la racine des cheveux. Hélène expliqua brièvement son cas à son interlocuteur.

— Vous étiez chargé de la surveillance des prostituées et des mœurs des chanteuses ou danseuses des théâtres royaux…

— Tout comme le contrôle des écrivains, ce qui n'était pas moins passionnant. Mais bon, ce sont les enquêtes sur la vie amoureuse des grands de ce monde qui intéressent le pouvoir, si possible avec des anecdotes bien croustillantes. Notre bon M. de Sartine ne déroge pas à la règle. Il se fait bien voir du roi en le régalant chaque semaine des mœurs déplorables de son temps.

D'un geste, il fit voler des bulles de savon dans l'air. Hélène suivit des yeux l'étrange ballet de celles-ci jusqu'au sol.

— Et tout ça, pour quoi ? reprit l'homme. Qu'en font-ils là-haut de tous nos rapports ? Savoir que tel fermier général entretient une danseuse ou une comédienne et se rend tous les dimanches après la messe dans une certaine maison de plaisir du Louvre ? Entretenir toute une armée d'agents pour cela, c'est jeter les épaules de mouton rôties par la fenêtre !

Il haussa les épaules avec philosophie.

— Seulement, voilà : le pouvoir est fasciné par la chose, toujours !

Hélène jugea bon de reprendre en main le cours de la conversation.

— Vous avez connu la Vorace ?

Il fronça les sourcils.

— Oui, une prostituée aux plus bas instincts. Elle se faisait cogner mais cognait aussi durement les hommes qui le lui demandaient à l'occasion ! De riches négociants se faisaient ainsi fesser en soirée après avoir rossé leurs employés dans la journée ! Mais croyez-moi, les premiers y prenaient plus de plaisir que les derniers !

— Chacun trouve ses plaisirs où il peut ! dit la jeune femme d'un ton neutre. Connaissiez-vous ses fréquentations ?

L'ancien inspecteur haussa les épaules.

— Toute la racaille et quelques bons bourgeois qui aimaient à s'encanailler. Elle ne possédait pas de protecteur en particulier.

Les bracelets s'entrechoquèrent aux poignets d'Hélène alors qu'elle agitait la main pour stopper la discussion.

— N'en parlons plus. Parlez-moi plutôt de Mlle Belle Ange. Je sais qu'il y a douze ans, elle dansait à l'Opéra et tout Paris se traînait à ses pieds.

— C'est peu de le dire, ricana l'ancien policier. De tous les péchés, la luxure est celui auquel l'homme a le plus de mal à résister. Je ne connais pas un des grands de ce monde qui n'adore entretenir une jeune danseuse du corps de l'Opéra.

Ses yeux brillèrent.

— La beauté de Mlle Belle Ange surpassait sans fioriture celle des autres. On se battait pour déposer sa fortune à ses pieds. À vingt ans, elle roulait déjà en carrosse avec deux laquais à plumet derrière sa voiture.

— Comment se nommaient ses amants ?

L'autre eut un rire gras, imité niaisement par sa mère.

— Comment voulez-vous que je me souvienne ? Dans ce royaume, tout le monde fornique !

— Fornique ! Fornique ! brailla soudainement sa mère.

Hélène pensa fugitivement à la pie de Volnay qui aimait tant répéter la fin des phrases qu'elle entendait. Cette femme ressemblait à un petit oiseau blessé, faible et dépourvu d'esprit mais, quelque part, toujours à l'écoute du monde qui l'entourait.

— Il y a douze ans qui cela pouvait-il être ?

L'autre agita en l'air ses mains trempées.

— Elle les prenait puis les laissait. Vous savez bien comment sont les femmes ! Que voulez-vous que je vous réponde ?

Hélène hocha la tête. Elle s'était préparée à la réponse.

— Mlle Belle Ange a mis une petite fille au monde douze ans plus tôt. Savez-vous qui est le père ?

— Personne ne s'en est vanté à l'époque !

— Si vous ne savez pas, déclara Hélène, je passerai alors par l'accoucheuse. Dans ce milieu-là, il faut des femmes discrètes et compétentes et elles ne sont pas si nombreuses que cela. Donnez-moi des noms.

Devant sa ténacité, l'ancien inspecteur lui jeta un regard admiratif.

— Ah mais ça, c'est tout à fait possible !

Il jeta un coup d'œil à la bourse qu'elle venait de prendre en main.

— Vous avez les petites pièces en or qui ravivent la mémoire ?

Le commissaire aux morts étranges fixait sans ciller l'eau claire. Derrière lui, il entendit son hôtesse murmurer :

— Gardez bien les yeux ouverts et surtout ne devenez pas fou !

D'abord, Volnay ne vit rien. Il se pencha plus encore et soudain la terre sembla fuir sous ses pieds et un vertige le prit. Un gigantesque brasier se consumait au milieu d'une clairière et une ronde infernale s'était formée autour. Des crapauds à la bouche énorme s'épuisaient à souffler à contresens dans leurs flûtes, des scarabées boiteux battaient la mesure tandis que des écrevisses faisaient claquer leurs pinces.

Au son de cette musique horrible, chaque danseur entraînait en hurlant derrière lui une danseuse échevelée et débraillée. Puis le feu s'éteignit d'un coup et seule la lune éclaira la clairière enfumée. Les hommes se jetèrent sur le corps énervé des femmes. En un instant, chasubles et soutanes furent arrachées et les membres s'entremêlèrent dans la plus obscène des orgies. Des râles et des gémissements montèrent au ciel. Soudain le feu se ralluma et le silence se fit, craintif et respectueux. Les corps se détachèrent lentement les uns des autres. Les danseurs se relevèrent pour s'attrouper au pied du brasier devant lequel un trône noir était apparu. Sur celui-ci siégeait un prince au visage de bouc. Sur ses genoux se trémoussait l'une des danseuses, livrée à ses caresses lubriques. Lorsqu'il en eut fini avec elle, il la renvoya d'une chiquenaude. Alors la foule sembla se fendre en deux comme si elle venait de recevoir un coup d'épée. Pâle et glacée, une femme la traversa pour aller droit jusqu'au prince noir. Son corps luisait faiblement à la lune et ses yeux étincelaient d'une joie sauvage dans l'obscurité. Volnay la reconnut d'un coup : c'était Hélène !

Hélène déversa sur la table une bourse remplie de pièces et les étala devant elle jusqu'à ce qu'elles forment un éventail doré.

— Il y a douze ans, vous avez accouché une jeune danseuse de l'Opéra, Mlle Belle Ange. Son enfant a été confié à un maître joaillier nommé Marly et à son épouse. Vous souvenez-vous de tout cela?

La sage-femme contempla l'argent avec effarement.

— Dieu, madame, je suis tenue dans mon métier à la plus grande discrétion. Et croyez-vous qu'en me faisant venir pour accoucher quelqu'un de qualité, on me précise qu'elle était la maîtresse d'un tel ou un tel?

Hélène sourit ironiquement.

— Dans votre milieu, tout se sait! À Versailles tout se sait!

Elle soupira.

— C'en est même étonnant : on ne peut plus garder un seul secret de nos jours!

Et bien entendu, pensa-t-elle fugitivement, *M. de Sartine sait également. Seulement voilà, il sait mais ne veut pas dire, lui!*

— Marly… Mme Marly, oui… fit songeusement l'accoucheuse.

Ses doigts tremblants effleurèrent les pièces.

— Mlle Belle Ange avait dix-sept ans, dit-elle très vite, belle mais pas plus de cervelle qu'un joli oiseau. On m'a fait venir au soir alors que le travail commençait. L'affaire se présentait mal et j'y ai passé toute la nuit. Mais à l'aube…

Son regard se teinta de fierté.

— À l'aube, reprit-elle, je réussis à tirer le bébé de son embarras, une mignonne petite fille.

Elle hocha la tête.

— Mlle Belle Ange n'a pas voulu prendre son enfant dans ses bras. Cela arrive parfois… Elle m'a demandé si je connaissais quelqu'un d'honnête condition qui désirerait l'adopter. Je n'eus pas à répondre car la dame de compagnie de Mlle Belle Ange s'écria qu'elle voulait un enfant de tout son cœur mais que la nature ne lui en laissait pas la possibilité. Cette dame de compagnie s'appelait Mme Marly…

L'accoucheuse ramena d'une main avide les pièces vers elle tout en regardant Hélène avec crainte.

— Par la suite, j'ai ouï dire que Mme Marly avait quitté son travail, sans doute avec l'enfant et une pension. Vous savez comment cela se passe… Plus personne n'a reparlé de cette histoire.

Elle commença à compter les pièces.

— Un mot encore, intervint la jeune femme en plaquant sa main sur la sienne, donnez-moi le nom du père.

L'accoucheuse sursauta au contact de la main d'Hélène. Sous sa paume, elle sentait les pièces marquer leur empreinte dans sa chair. Prise de panique, elle ferma les yeux pour mieux se concentrer.

— Je vous jure que je l'ignore mais en sortant, je croisai deux hommes qui en étaient presque venus aux mains et que l'on tentait de séparer. L'un d'eux était M. de Sartine! Quant à l'autre, il s'agissait de messire Guillaume de…

Elle dit le nom et Hélène resta sans voix en reconnaissant le nom secret du moine.

La Dame de l'Eau tendit à Volnay un bol fumant.

— Tisane de toile d'araignée! annonça-t-elle.

Le policier eut un mouvement de recul.

— Je plaisantais, voyons !

Le moine éclata de rire. Le commissaire aux morts étranges prit un air boudeur.

— Très drôle !

Assis à califourchon sur une chaise, près du feu, le moine laissa reposer sa tête sur ses poignets.

— Ainsi tu as assisté à un sabbat et tu y as vu Hélène… fit-il songeusement.

— Comme je te vois !

— Hum, hum, étrange… Hélène avec le prince à tête de bouc…

Le moine leva le doigt en l'air pour réciter doctement :

— "Aimer un bouc puant ardemment, le caresser amoureusement, s'accointer et s'accoupler avec lui horriblement et impudemment !"

Un sourire naquit sur ses lèvres.

— Non, cela ne lui ressemble pas !

— Je me suis toujours méfié d'elle, maugréa Volnay.

— Tu crois maintenant à la divination, s'étonna son père. Lorsque cela t'arrange en fait !

Le moine secoua la tête.

— Il faut savoir interpréter les choses que l'on voit. Hélène est peut-être celle qui nous conduira jusqu'à la résolution de cette énigme. Quant au sabbat…

Il réfléchit.

— S'il y a sabbat, il y a adoration de Satan. Ceci confirme bien que nous sommes face à des satanistes. Dis-moi, tu n'as pas vu de sorcières sur des balais par hasard ?

Le commissaire aux morts étranges secoua la tête.

— Ah dommage, regretta le moine, j'aurais bien voulu savoir à quoi elles ressemblaient !

Il se gratta la barbe.

— J'ai lu quelque part que les balais qu'elles chevauchent figurent la verge de Moïse. C'est un puissant symbole phallique !

La Dame de l'Eau secoua la tête en souriant :

— Tout tourne autour de cela !

Le moine approuva vigoureusement et continua :

— Sais-tu que les sorcières n'ont pas besoin de cours pour chevaucher leur balai ? Il leur suffit d'accrocher une chandelle à son extrémité et de dire : "Bâton blanc, bâton noir, mène-moi là où tu dois, de par le diable."

— Tu as de drôles de lectures, remarqua sèchement Volnay.

La Dame de l'Eau et le moine échangèrent un fin sourire.

— Plus que tu ne l'imagines mon fils, rit le moine, plus que tu ne l'imagines !

Il eut encore un long rire silencieux, ses épaules se soulevant et s'affaissant. Une fois calmé, il expliqua :

— Dans *L'Âne d'or*, Apulée, un auteur latin du IIe siècle, raconte comment Pamphile se change en hibou pour se rendre au sabbat. Pour cela, elle se sert d'un onguent en s'en couvrant du plus petit orteil à la racine des cheveux ! C'est de cette lecture qu'enfant mon goût de l'insolite est né !

Il questionna de nouveau son fils.

— Tu n'as rien vu d'autre ?

— Non, la scène s'est brusquement évanouie.

— À l'aube, tout disparaît d'un coup, murmura la Dame de l'Eau.

Volnay ne releva pas. Il porta le bol fumant à ses lèvres et but une gorgée prudente.

— Messe noire ou envoûtement alors ? demanda-t-il en reposant le récipient d'un air gêné.

— Les deux, répondit son père.

— Mais nous n'avons retrouvé sur les lieux du crime ni poupée, ni statuette de cire !

— Si, elle était sous tes yeux !

Le commissaire aux morts étranges le considéra avec effarement. Le moine haussa les épaules.

— Non, mon fils, je ne suis ni vieux, ni fou, ni gâteux.

Et il ajouta avec un plaisir évident :

— D'ailleurs, si tu étais un peu plus concentré sur ton sujet et si tu gardais l'esprit plus ouvert, tu aurais déjà deviné de quoi il retourne !

Volnay ouvrit et referma la bouche sans prononcer un mot comme si on venait de lui jeter un sort. Enfin, il réussit à articuler :

— J'ai fouillé toute la scène du crime, en long, en large et en travers. Je te dis qu'il n'y avait nulle statuette de cire et nulle poupée !

Le moine lui jeta un regard triste.

— Ils n'en avaient pas besoin, la poupée c'était Sophia !

XV

NEIGE ET AUTRES DIABLERIES

Il s'était mis à neiger très doucement alors qu'ils remontaient la ruelle de l'Or. Les flocons de neige tombaient avec une grâce aérienne. Le moine releva la tête comme pour humer l'air du soir.

— La sorcellerie, dit-il, est née de l'ignorance et de la misère mais aussi d'une révolte contre l'ordre établi qui en était la cause. La messe noire n'est qu'une rébellion contre le culte de Dieu et son Église. Tout est inversé dans le satanisme et l'inversion, c'est la rébellion !

Il s'amusa à tendre la main pour y recueillir de la neige. Chaque flocon semblait posséder sa propre structure, merveille architecturale plus complexe qu'on ne l'imaginait.

— Une messe noire, chantonna-t-il comme s'il s'agissait d'une ritournelle, un flocon de neige, un rituel d'envoûtement par le sang, un flocon de neige, une vierge que l'on n'a pas profanée, un flocon de neige et autres vilaines diableries…

Le commissaire aux morts étranges haussa les épaules et dit :

— À mon avis, la clé de l'énigme réside dans le choix de Sophia comme poupée d'envoûtement. Lorsque nous en aurons découvert les raisons, nous trouverons les coupables.

— Et qu'est-ce qui pousserait un père à sacrifier sa propre fille ? C'est impensable !

Il sursauta soudain.

— Sauf s'il ne s'agissait pas de sa fille mais d'une enfant adultère… Mais comment savoir maintenant que notre astrologue est mort ?

Volnay réfléchit une seconde puis se décida.

— Je dois passer au Châtelet pour faire un point sur l'affaire avec Siltieri. Accompagne-moi.

Le moine sursauta.

— Moi ? Au Châtelet ? Tu veux ma mort !

Son fils haussa les épaules.

— Il ne t'est pas interdit d'y entrer et Siltieri ne te connaît pas.

Lorsque les deux hommes arrivèrent au Châtelet, le moine ne put s'empêcher de commenter.

— Les cachots sont abominables et l'air est difficile à respirer car il n'y a point d'ouverture extérieure et descend seulement d'en haut. Tout n'est que ténèbres et contagion.

Si le Châtelet comportait des prisons, il abritait aussi les affaires de police et celles de justice, aussi y croisèrent-ils conseillers, procureurs, notaires, gardes-notes, commis-greffiers ou huissiers à verge que le moine s'amusa à dévisager impudemment. Avant d'entrer chez Siltieri, Volnay confia le chien à un archer du guet de sa connaissance. Il hésita une seconde et jeta un regard en biais à son père.

— Siltieri n'est pas très commode. Certains le considèrent même comme assez buté alors ne va pas le provoquer ou te moquer de lui. Fais attention à ce que tu dis.

Il fit encore un pas et ajouta :

— Ne dis pas de mal du roi, du pape ou de l'Église, ne jure pas et ne parle pas de tes expériences de laboratoire.

Tout à coup, il s'arrêta net et se tourna vers son père.

— En fait, il vaudrait mieux que tu ne dises rien du tout !

On les introduisit dans le cabinet de travail de Siltieri, seulement éclairé par la chiche lumière d'une fenêtre et d'une chandelle. Celui-ci les salua sèchement. Volnay présenta le moine comme son assistant et s'enquit des suites de l'arrestation des voisins du curé dansant. D'un coup, le visage fermé de Siltieri se fit rayonnant.

— J'ai soumis à la question les gens que j'ai fait arrêter hier et ils ont donné le nom d'un boulanger.

— Magnifique ! dit le moine.

Le procureur ne releva pas l'ironie.

— Le maudit hérétique fabriquait des hosties avec de la farine, des herbes et de l'urine !

— J'espère bien que tous les boulangers ne font pas ça, murmura le moine sans se soucier des sourcils froncés de son fils.

Siltieri s'approcha de lui.

— Pardon ?

— Non, je disais que cela me rappelle que l'on réduit cette mixture en poudre pour empoisonner les puits.

Triomphant, le procureur se tourna vers le commissaire aux morts étranges.

— Vous entendez !

Volnay jeta un regard noir à son père.

— J'ai mis aussi le boulanger à la question, reprit Siltieri. Il ne parle pas, il chante !

Le procureur exultait.

— Les noms tombent les uns après les autres et vont nous permettre de remonter tout le réseau de ces diables.

Le commissaire aux morts étranges eut une moue dubitative.

— Tout cela est de la piétaille, de pauvres gens qui contribuent à alimenter les commerces de fausse magie des escrocs qui pullulent dans Paris. Vous savez bien que ceux-ci exploitent la crédulité du peuple comme des bourgeois et des nobles. Ils leur promettent l'immortalité ou la fortune, leur vendent des cartes au trésor, des formules ou des carrés magiques…

Siltieri le coupa.

— Faire acte de magie, c'est faire croire au peuple qu'il peut rivaliser avec Dieu et le roi !

Volnay contempla le procureur d'un œil neutre, notant son visage illuminé, brûlé de l'intérieur par une flamme noire. Son âme ardente semblait lui sortir par les yeux.

Un exalté au service de Dieu et du roi. La pire espèce.

— Si vous croyez que tout ceci ne concerne pas votre enquête, reprit Siltieri, vous vous trompez. Les mauvaises gens que vous cherchez sont plus près que vous ne le pensez. Des fabricants de cierges, je remonte au boulanger, du boulanger je vais au meunier puis, curieusement, je bifurque sur des mécréants se livrant à la vente de cadavres…

Son regard accrocha celui du moine.

— Cadavres souvent destinés à des hérétiques qui croient lire dans les corps des réponses qui n'y sont pas !

Impavide, le moine ne cilla pas. Volnay sentit la sueur lui glacer l'échine. Manifestement, il s'était fourvoyé en amenant son père au Châtelet. Siltieri savait parfaitement qui était son père.

— Sorts, maléfices, propos diaboliques, sabbats, gronda le procureur en se plantant devant le moine, je vais passer au fer rouge toute cette ville ! Puis je ferai brûler vifs sorciers et sorcières, au bois vert pour prolonger leur agonie. Seuls ceux qui se confesseront pourront être étranglés !

— Nom de Dieu ! siffla le moine.

— Attention ! gronda le procureur. Jurer le nom de Dieu, de Jésus ou du pape constitue un blasphème inspiré par le diable et en France on vous coupe la langue pour cela ! Les blasphèmes sont des indices du crime de sorcellerie et, en ce domaine, je peux poursuivre sur la simple clameur publique !

— Je n'ai voulu sacrifier personne sur une pierre tombale, fit doucement remarquer le moine, je suis ici pour trouver le coupable de ces crimes.

Siltieri resta un instant interdit.

— Certes, fit-il, certes…

Le moine renchérit :

— Nous soupçonnons le père de cette jeune victime d'être peut-être le coupable de ce crime.

— Vraiment ? Ce tireur d'horoscopes !

— Nous n'avons pas de preuve, d'autant plus qu'il est mort cette nuit dans l'incendie de sa maison.

— Mort ? Tout comme cette prostituée et ce curé dansant ? Voilà beaucoup de coïncidences…

Siltieri n'était pas l'idiot à triple étage que l'on pensait.

— Oui, renchérit le moine devant son fils interdit, et nous avons trouvé dans les ruines de sa maison des livres terribles et interdits.

Il les cita et se signa. Siltieri apprécia. Il revint à sa table de travail et trempa sa plume dans l'encre.

— Ainsi ce maudit bougre d'astrologue versait dans le satanisme ! Le châtiment de Dieu l'a rejoint, à moins que ses complices…

Avec application, il se mit à tracer des lettres serrées.

— J'ordonne qu'on enquête auprès de son entourage, fit-il.

— Il n'avait pas d'amis et sa servante est morte dans l'incendie, remarqua Volnay.

— Qu'importe ! dit Siltieri. Nous trouverons bien quelqu'un à qui brûler la plante des pieds pour l'inciter à parler !

Le commissaire aux morts étranges et son père s'entreregardèrent avec anxiété.

— Eh bien, nous allons vous laisser et continuer l'enquête de notre côté, conclut Volnay. Je ne manquerai pas de vous tenir informé de la suite.

— Faites, faites…

Siltieri ne releva pas la tête lorsqu'ils sortirent. Les deux hommes ne dirent pas un mot avant d'avoir quitté le Châtelet rempli de courants d'air glacé. Le chien trottinait auprès d'eux, tout à sa joie de les avoir retrouvés.

— Ton Siltieri a une tête à boire des infusions de queues de cerises ! remarqua gaiement le moine une fois à l'air libre.

— Pourquoi lui as-tu raconté toutes ces choses ? grommela Volnay.

— Pour me faire bien voir de lui ! Je croyais que c'était ce que tu désirais !

— Je t'avais demandé de te taire.

— C'est difficile pour moi !

Le commissaire aux morts étranges exhala profondément et un halo de brume sembla se dérouler de sa bouche.

— Était-il nécessaire de le mettre au courant pour l'astrologue ?

— Sartine le sait bien, lui. Et de toute façon, cela ne mènera Siltieri nulle part car je ne le juge pas plus intelligent que nous et sans doute beaucoup plus obtus. Par ailleurs, s'il ne sait rien sur l'astrologue, c'est qu'il ne dépense guère en espions.

Volnay opina du chef puis fit la moue.

— Quand même, j'aurais préféré que tu te taises. Sais-tu seulement ce qu'est le silence?

— Comme dit M. Pascal, le silence est la pire des persécutions : jamais un saint ne s'est tu!

Son fils leva les yeux au ciel.

— Tu es tout sauf un saint!

Une cohue encombrait le Pont-Neuf. Ils piétinèrent sur place avant de l'emprunter, observant autour d'eux comme à leur habitude. Ils virent un maître joaillier sortir avec son client de la boutique afin de lui montrer l'éclat d'une bague à la lueur du jour. Il la retira ensuite du majeur de sa main gauche pour l'enfiler au doigt de la main droite de son client. Volnay jeta un coup d'œil distrait au manège puis s'immobilisa brusquement comme si une idée venait de le frapper net. Son souffle resta suspendu une seconde alors qu'il comprenait enfin ce qui le tourmentait.

— Oh, mon Dieu! Pourquoi n'y ai-je pas pensé plus tôt! Que c'est bête de ma part!

Et, le regard dans le vague, il répéta encore dans un murmure accablé :

— Que c'est bête!

Hélène avait trouvé refuge dans le faubourg Saint-Jacques où, dans un morne silence, se bousculaient cloîtres, hôpitaux ou couvents. De temps à autre, on entendait une cloche sonner mais, hormis cela, la neige épaisse semblait étouffer tous bruits, venant encore ajouter à l'impression de solitude et de recueillement de l'endroit. La jeune femme n'aimait pas ce quartier mais il avait pour avantage que personne ne songerait à y chercher quelqu'un comme elle.

Alors qu'elle grimpait l'escalier de son immeuble, rue des Marionnettes, Hélène perçut dans son dos un pas léger et jeta un rapide coup d'œil par-delà la rambarde. Derrière elle, un homme montait avec prudence, se gardant de faire du bruit. Un chapeau rabattu sur ses yeux dissimulait son visage. Elle gagna rapidement un coin de son palier et s'immobilisa dans l'ombre. Sa main glissa sous sa robe et en ressortit armée d'une dague. L'homme passa devant elle sans la remarquer et s'arrêta devant sa porte. Hélène fit deux pas rapides et lui mit le fil de sa lame sous la gorge.

— Ce ne sera pas nécessaire, fit alors Sartine.

Le lieutenant général de police l'avait aidée à allumer du feu dans la cheminée et tendait ses mains aux flammes. Son expression était pensive.

— Pourquoi a-t-il fallu que vous alliez là-bas? demanda-t-il.

Il soupira et appuya son front sur le manteau de la cheminée.

— Qui vous a renseigné? demanda-t-elle.

Et elle pensa : *L'accoucheuse ou l'inspecteur?*

Un éclair de fierté traversa l'œil de Sartine qui s'était redressé.

— Ce sont vos sales petites mouches, c'est cela? fit dédaigneusement Hélène. Vous me faisiez suivre parce que vous n'aviez pas plus confiance que ça en moi!

— Ai-je eu tort? demanda-t-il d'un ton tranquille.
Et il ajouta d'une voix neutre, sans regret inutile :

— De toute façon, je n'ai confiance en personne.

Il remit en place une boucle de sa perruque.

— Mes mouches sont effectivement partout !

Et tout à coup, avec ses deux bras, il imita un vol désordonné tandis que sa bouche émettait un bourdonnement bizarre. Hélène frémit. Par moments, cet homme lui faisait peur.

— Vous avez connu cette femme, n'est-ce pas? demanda-t-elle.

— Elle était très belle, répondit-il d'une voix basse et sourde. Nous la voulions tous mais elle n'était à personne…

Et il ajouta dans un soupir :

— Sinon au plus offrant comme il se doit…

Elle attendit.

— Sophia lui ressemblait beaucoup, ajouta-t-il après un silence.

— Volnay m'a dit que vous aviez gardé son portrait, c'est pour cela?

Il lui jeta un regard vide.

— Décidément, mon commissaire aux morts étranges est bien bavard avec vous, à moi il n'en dit pas autant !

— Et pourtant, il est loyal.

Sartine secoua la tête.

— On ne peut rester loyal qu'à un idéal et je ne corresponds pas à celui du chevalier de Volnay.

Il sourit.

— Encore moins à celui du moine d'ailleurs !

Hélène se raidit.

— Il ne faut rien leur dire, reprit Sartine d'une voix basse et pressante. La chose doit rester discrète. Ce n'est pas tant Volnay qui m'inquiète que le moine. Je ne sais pas comment il pourrait réagir.

Il fixa la jeune femme dans les yeux.

— Soyez certaine que, de mes deux enquêteurs, le moine est le plus dangereux. C'est aussi un homme redoutable, les armes à la main. Vous ne devineriez jamais ce dont il est capable !

Hélène cilla brièvement. De découvrir que Sartine craignait le moine la remplissait de surprise et d'effroi.

— Qui de vous deux était le père de Sophia ? demanda-t-elle néanmoins.

XVI

LOGIQUE ET AUTRES DIABLERIES

Un vent violent soufflait, le moine repoussa avec difficulté la porte de sa demeure derrière lui.

— *Chien-chien* est content de rentrer chez lui ! constata-t-il en voyant l'animal filer vers la cheminée.

— Hum. Descendons à la cave, vite ! commanda son fils. Je veux revoir le cadavre de notre astrologue.

Tout en dévalant l'escalier, le commissaire aux morts étranges expliqua à son père :

— Quelque chose m'a troublé la première fois que j'ai vu le corps mais je ne parvenais pas à comprendre quoi. Il y avait, coincée dans mon esprit, comme une évidence, une vérité qui ne voulait pas se faire connaître. Et puis tout à coup, lorsque dans la rue j'ai vu ce joaillier, tout s'est éclairci. Quand je rencontre quelqu'un au cours d'une enquête, je ne me contente pas de le regarder, je l'observe et je m'imprègne de mille détails. Or, l'astrologue portait une chevalière d'un genre très particulier, à la main droite. Cette chevalière nous a permis entre autres d'identifier le cadavre.

Ils étaient arrivés devant le corps calciné. Le commissaire aux morts étranges le considéra un instant, un sourire de satisfaction aux lèvres.

— Voilà ! Sur ce corps affreusement brûlé et méconnaissable, la chevalière ne se trouve pas à la bonne main !

Il hocha la tête.

— Lorsque nous répétons sur quelqu'un en face de nous le même geste que pour notre propre personne, la gauche et la droite s'embrouillent. Ce n'est pas l'astrologue qui est mort. Il a voulu nous le faire croire en mettant sa bague à la main d'un cadavre mais il s'est saisi de sa main gauche et non de la droite !

Le moine se figea.

— Mais tu as parfaitement raison, il la portait à l'autre main. Je m'en souviens car c'est de celle-ci qu'il nous a ouvert la porte !

Ses yeux brillèrent d'excitation.

— On a incendié cette maison après y avoir introduit un cadavre de la même taille que l'astrologue. La chevalière à son doigt avait donc pour but de nous permettre de l'identifier comme étant M. Marly, l'astrologue.

— Et d'échapper ainsi à nos soupçons. Avec la découverte de la Vorace, l'astrologue a dû sentir l'étau se resserrer autour de lui et a choisi de disparaître.

Ils regagnèrent pensivement le rez-de-chaussée de la maison, s'épuisant en hypothèses. Soudain, le commissaire aux morts étranges s'immobilisa. Ses yeux s'étrécirent en regardant le sol.

— Des miettes de biscuits par terre… cela vient de la cuisine.

Le moine le rejoignit et s'exclama :

— Mes biscuits secs ! On m'a mangé tous mes biscuits secs ! Ce doit être Hélène…

— Qu'ai-je fait ? demanda une voix enjouée derrière eux.

Hélène s'arc-boutait pour refermer la porte.

— Euh, ce n'est rien ma chère, fit le moine. Nous nous demandions qui a mangé les biscuits secs…

— Ce n'est pas moi, je vous assure, dit-elle tranquillement en époussetant son manteau recouvert de neige.

Le commissaire aux morts étranges la scruta attentivement. Elle avait l'air pâle et fatiguée. Finalement, il se retourna vers son père.

— Tu as normalement quatre clés de cette maison. Tu en portes une sur toi, moi également et…

Il jeta un coup d'œil incisif à la jeune femme qui ne broncha pas.

— Si j'ai bien compris tu en as confié une à Hélène…

— Certes, fit le moine qui avait compris où son fils voulait en venir. Et la quatrième clé est pendue ici…

Il désigna un clou au mur de la cuisine.

— Mon Dieu, elle a disparu !

Volnay se tourna vers Hélène.

— Est-ce vous ?

— Non.

— Bien sûr… et pourtant, il existe toujours une explication rationnelle !

Le commissaire aux morts étranges sembla s'absenter en lui-même. Il était immobile mais ses pensées prenaient une tournure vertigineuse. Hélène et le moine virent le bleu de ses yeux se teinter d'un gris aux textures d'acier trempé. Ses paupières se fermèrent et plus rien en lui ne bougea. Le moine retint Hélène de parler car il savait comment procédait son fils. Lorsque celui-ci ouvrit les yeux, le bleu avait de nouveau envahit ses yeux.

— Père, peux-tu prendre le livre de Sophia, là où elle a consigné son journal ? Ensuite, suis-moi.

Le moine s'exécuta en silence et, bien qu'elle ne fût pas formellement invitée, Hélène les accompagna jusque chez Volnay. La pie les accueillit dans un torrent de jurons à l'adresse de la jeune femme.

Manifestement, l'oiseau tenait Hélène comme responsable des absences répétées de son maître, à moins que celui-ci n'ait prononcé devant la pie des mots qui visaient la jeune femme.

— Calme-toi, gentil oiseau, fit la jeune femme en grattant les barreaux de la cage. Je suis Hélène…

— Hé… lè… ne, fit la pie, gaar… ce…

Hélène se tourna vers Volnay.

— Monsieur, que dit votre pie ? demanda-t-elle froidement.

Sans répondre, le commissaire aux morts étranges alla droit à son cabinet de travail et ouvrit un tiroir en bois de rose.

— Vous vous souvenez du panneau qu'on a placé sur la porte du cimetière et sur lequel était inscrit…

— *Interdit à Dieu d'entrer*, compléta le moine.

— Le voici !

Il le posa sèchement devant eux, près de la cage de la pie.

— Et maintenant, père, ouvre le livre dans lequel Sophia a consigné son journal et compare les deux écritures.

Le moine s'exécuta et se figea instantanément sur place. Tout le sang semblait s'être retiré de son visage.

— Mon Dieu, fit-il au bord de la panique, celle qui a écrit ce journal et celle qui a inscrit ces mots sur le panneau à l'entrée du cimetière sont une seule et même personne : Sophia !

Tandis que la pie jacassait, Volnay arpentait rageusement son salon.

— Tout était pourtant logique : toi, Hélène et la servante de l'auberge voyez Sophia après sa mort.

Son chien devient fou à certains moments comme s'il sentait sa présence. Le cadavre du gardien de cimetière disparaît. Vous avez tous voulu mettre cela sur le compte des esprits, soit !

Il se planta devant son père.

— Mais ne pouvais-tu pas te rendre compte que quelqu'un vivait dans ta maison ? De la nourriture disparaît dans ta cuisine. On urine devant ta porte. On sort le chien pendant que tu dors, on t'emprunte une clé…

Pour la première fois de sa vie, le moine resta muet car son esprit avait du mal à accepter la vérité. Sans pitié, le commissaire aux morts étranges reprit sa diatribe contre son père :

— On vit chez toi et il faut encore que ce soit moi qui aie l'idée de comparer l'écriteau du cimetière au journal de Sophia !

— Mais…

— Pour moi, cela signifie une chose : Sophia n'est pas morte !

— Mais on l'a enterrée ! protesta le moine.

— Enterrée ? Tu ne l'as ni autopsiée, ni mise en bière !

— Les embaumeurs l'ont mise en cercueil !

— Qu'en sais-tu ? explosa son fils. Tu n'y étais pas ! Sophia avait quitté la cave quand les embaumeurs sont venus. Tu leur as demandé de s'occuper du cadavre dans la première cave mais sans préciser qu'il s'agissait de celui d'une jeune fille, n'est-ce pas ?

Le moine essaya de se souvenir.

— C'est ma foi vrai, murmura-t-il.

— Tu as pour excuse ta maladie, bougonna son fils. Les embaumeurs se sont donc rendus dans la première cave, ne trouvant pas le cadavre, ils ont regardé dans la seconde. Au vu de ton état, ils ont dû penser que tu avais confondu le lieu et se sont donc occupés du corps du gardien du cimetière, le mettant en bière. Comme, pas plus que toi, le père de Sophia n'a voulu la contempler une dernière fois, les embaumeurs ont cloué le cercueil. Ainsi, il est naturel que l'erreur n'ait pas été réparée. Voilà ce que c'est que de devenir gâteux !

Pour la première fois depuis qu'elle les avait suivis, Hélène intervint d'une voix dure.

— Vous ne devriez pas parler ainsi à votre père.

Volnay se figea. Le noir de ses prunelles sembla grandir démesurément, signe d'une intense colère.

— Qui êtes-vous, intrigante, pour vous permettre de me juger ? gronda-t-il d'une voix basse et rauque. Que savez-vous de nous et de quel droit vous mêlez-vous de nos affaires ?

— Vos affaires ? ironisa-t-elle.

Elle balaya la pièce d'un vaste geste de la main.

— Des livres, un oiseau savant et quelques cadavres, voilà à quoi se réduisent et vos affaires et votre vision du monde ! Respectez donc votre père, entendez-le et écoutez-le pour changer.

— Mon père est un vieux fou !

Hélène le gifla. La claque résonna sèchement dans toute la pièce. La joue marbrée de rouge, Volnay la fixa d'un air abasourdi. Le moine ouvrit la bouche et la referma comiquement. Les mains le long du corps, légèrement cambrée en avant, Hélène défia du regard le commissaire aux morts étranges. Puis, elle passa très lentement devant lui et recula jusqu'à la porte, sans le quitter un instant de ses étranges yeux aux reflets dorés. Une bouffée d'air froid coucha les flammes des bougies lorsqu'elle sortit sans prononcer un mot. À son tour, le moine tourna les talons.

— Où vas-tu ? demanda son fils.

— Le vieux fou rentre chez lui.

— Père…

Le moine leva la main pour l'arrêter.

— N'en rajoute pas, tu en as assez dit pour aujourd'hui.

Demeuré seul, Volnay ralluma le feu et resta quelques instants à le contempler sombrement. Puis, comme s'il venait de prendre une résolution, il jeta un manteau sur ses épaules et sortit, ignorant les commentaires dépités de sa pie.

Sans surprise, le moine retrouva Hélène chez lui. Ce n'était pourtant pas la compagnie qu'il souhaitait. Les reproches de son fils l'avaient profondément blessé et il préférait rester seul pour ressasser ses pensées.

— Mais où est donc *chien-chien*? s'étonna-t-il. Je pensais qu'il allait me faire la fête.

C'est alors qu'il s'aperçut de l'émoi d'Hélène.

— Le chien a disparu! dit-elle. Je l'ai cherché dans toute la maison.

— Voyons, cela ne se peut! Nous l'avons laissé ici pour aller chez mon fils et nous avons refermé la porte à clé.

— Certes.

Le moine voulut descendre dans les caves puis gagna le cellier, sa chambre et le séjour, cherchant partout.

— Il n'est plus ici, quelqu'un nous l'a pris!

— C'est une chose certaine. Nous n'avons plus qu'à attendre qu'on nous le ramène.

Elle n'avait osé prononcer le prénom de Sophia. Sans mot dire, le moine gagna son fauteuil favori devant le feu qui flambait joyeusement et s'abandonna silencieusement à la contemplation des flammes.

Hélène hésita un instant. Elle savait que la détermination du commissaire aux morts étranges à mener ses enquêtes cachait une faillite personnelle intime. Son père en souffrait pour lui. Par amour pour son fils, il l'avait rejoint pour l'aider et le conseiller mais celui-ci n'était plus l'enfant qu'il avait connu. De se voir ainsi rejeter devait lui avoir brisé le cœur.

Elle vint près de lui et, très naturellement, s'assit sur ses genoux. Le moine ne réagit pas. Il grattait sa barbe d'un air pensif, évoquant des souvenirs de temps heureux ou en tout cas tels qu'il croyait avoir été.

— Il vous aime, dit Hélène, n'en doutez point.

Le moine hocha la tête sans rien dire. La jeune femme posa la main sur son épaule. Elle n'était pas sans ignorer que, tel le cheval de Troie, son intrusion dans le duo d'enquêteurs suscitait tension, désir et méfiance. Le couple père et fils se trouvait au bord de l'explosion et ce n'était pas ce qu'elle désirait.

— Quelle erreur épouvantable ai-je commise, murmura soudain le moine. Ma fierté intellectuelle ne s'en relèvera pas !

Hélène sourit. C'était tout lui !

— Voilà qui est mieux, chuchota-t-elle à son oreille. Il vous faut raisonner en homme de science. Une succession de faits vous a mené où vous en êtes : la présence d'une drogue inconnue, le corps d'une enfant que vous refusez d'ouvrir parce que tout votre être s'y oppose, votre maladie, la présence de deux corps dans votre cave… et une enquête bien compliquée.

— En verrons-nous jamais le bout ?

Les lèvres d'Hélène se pincèrent et elle le considéra avec une certaine sévérité.

— Il le faut ! Je termine toujours ce que j'ai commencé et je ne vous sens pas différent de moi.

La main du moine se posa sur son genou.

— Oui, je crois que nous nous ressemblons beaucoup !

Il eut un sourire d'excuse.

— Pour ce qui est de notre caractère, pour le reste, je ne vous ferai pas injure…

Comprenant ce qu'il voulait dire, elle eut un sourire indulgent.

— Vous êtes resté très bel homme et vous avez beaucoup de charme…

— Vous êtes bien aimable !

À cet instant, Volnay entra chez le moine et jeta un rapide regard circulaire dans la pièce, notant au passage la présence d'Hélène sur les genoux de son père, la main de celui-ci sur la jeune femme, et s'abstenant stoïquement de tout commentaire.

— D'où viens-tu, fils ? demanda le moine d'un ton neutre.

— Je reviens de chez les embaumeurs, répondit Volnay en lorgnant sur les mains que son père venait de poser sur les hanches d'Hélène comme pour le narguer.

Il détourna le regard.

— Pas de chance, poursuivit-il d'un ton neutre, nos bougres sont partis à cinquante lieues de Paris pour s'occuper de la tante de leur patron qui est morte. Ils ne reviendront pas d'ici trois jours. Avec ce temps affreux, envoyer un archer du guet à cheval leur poser la question ne nous aidera guère. Il nous faut déterrer le cercueil pour en avoir le cœur net.

— Mais…

— J'ai toute autorité par Sartine. Et puis, le père de Sophia étant mort, personne ne s'y opposera. Je vais aller de ce pas voir notre obligeant collègue commissaire de quartier. Il m'a paru assez compréhensif jusque-là.

Ses yeux se posèrent brièvement sur Hélène.

— Inutile pour l'instant d'en informer Sartine. Je peux m'être trompé et il peut y avoir une autre explication à la similitude d'écritures sur le panneau et dans le livre de Sophia.

Son ton n'était guère convaincant. Il hésita encore, contrairement à ses habitudes.

— Eh bien, je crois que je vais vous laisser…

Pour la première fois, Volnay ne semblait pas remettre en cause la présence d'Hélène dans la maison de son père. On ne lui répondit pas.

— Bonne nuit ! dit-il en tournant sèchement les talons.

— Bonne nuit, mon fils ! fit le moine en relevant la tête.

Lorsque la porte se referma, Hélène se leva pour aller ajouter une bûche dans le feu et resta un instant devant l'âtre, comme hésitant sur l'attitude à adopter. Le regard du moine coula de nouveau vers la jeune femme et il soupira.

— Mon fils me cause bien des soucis, mon amie.

— Ne vous inquiétez pas pour lui, il est allé raconter ses malheurs à sa pie !

Le moine ne dit rien. Il contempla songeusement Hélène et les rides autour de ses yeux s'accentuèrent. C'était un peu comme lorsqu'on découvre qu'un félin n'est pas qu'un bel animal mais aussi un tueur.

— Nous avons oublié de lui parler de la disparition du chien, constata-t-il, mais cela attendra bien demain.

Il fit une pause.

— Je vais me coucher dans mon lit, reprit-il en se levant lentement. Peut-être feriez-vous bien de rentrer chez vous… Il n'est pas tard et les rues sont encore sûres. Si vous le souhaitez, je vous raccompagnerai.

Elle secoua la tête.

— Ce n'est pas nécessaire mais, si vous me le permettez, je boirai une de vos tisanes avant de partir.

Il lui tourna le dos.

— Je vous en prie, faites. Bonne nuit. Fermez bien la porte à clé en partant même si cela n'a guère d'importance. On entre et l'on sort de cette maison comme dans un moulin !

Allongé sur son lit, le moine ferma les yeux, se laissant envahir par le chagrin et la mélancolie. La vie passait trop vite. Il n'avait pas vu son fils grandir et maintenant voilà que celui-ci le rejetait.

Le temps passe et nous emmène comme feuilles au vent.

Le bruit d'un loquet l'arracha à ses pensées. Un bref courant d'air balaya la pièce. Hélène tira la porte de la chambre derrière elle et annonça d'un ton définitif :

— Je viens dormir avec vous.

XVII

CERCUEIL ET AUTRES DIABLERIES

Volnay ne trouvait pas le sommeil. Il retira du tiroir de son secrétaire la lettre de Chiara qu'une fois de plus il lut et relut. La jeune femme lui donnait un an pour la rejoindre en Italie sans toutefois lui en promettre. Le cœur du jeune homme se serra. La trahison de Chiara avait encore valeur de fer rouge.

Il porta la lettre à ses narines pour en humer le parfum qui s'en était évaporé depuis longtemps. Par moments, il lui semblait retrouver quelques notes florales qui, effet de son esprit, lui remontaient en mémoire avec quelques souvenirs en lien comme ce jour où leurs lèvres s'étaient trouvées en un baiser profond et sensuel. Le souffle court, il reposa brutalement la lettre.

— Que croit-elle donc ? demanda-t-il à la pie.

Mais l'oiseau resta sage dans sa cage. Volnay se sentit ridicule. Au lieu de rester à raconter sa pauvre vie à sa pie, il se revêtit d'un chaud manteau et, armé de la tête aux pieds, se glissa parmi les ombres de la nuit. Pour quelques liards, il trouva un porteur de falot qui lui dénicha un fiacre qui le conduisit au faubourg Saint-Marcel. Là, il se rendit directement chez l'Écureuil. L'odeur des égouts et des immondices le saisit dès qu'il descendit de voiture. Il inspira l'air glacé et expira bruyamment comme pour nettoyer ses poumons de toute cette pestilence. Le voyant seul et bien de sa mise comme de sa personne, des prostituées s'accrochèrent à lui comme autant de sirènes abandonnées. La pénombre masquait à peine l'épaisse couche de fard rougissant leurs joues. Dans ce quartier, elles ne portaient pas de bas de soie mais de laine grossière et rapiécés recouvrant leurs longues jambes. Volnay écarta doucement de lui ces pathétiques appels à l'amour et poursuivit résolument son chemin vers l'immeuble où résidait la jeune prostituée.

Il trouva l'escalier aussi raide que dans son souvenir. Il le gravit sans faire de bruit, s'arrêtant à mi-chemin pour reprendre sa respiration. Devant la porte, il reconnut l'oiseau gravé d'une main malhabile et cela le fit sourire. Tendant l'oreille, il perçut les halètements d'un homme. Il n'entendit pas l'Écureuil. Volnay imagina son corps se tortillant dans la chambre et son cœur s'assombrit inexplicablement. Pensif, il redescendit l'escalier et affronta de nouveau le froid, se forçant à contourner le pâté de maisons à pas lents avant de revenir à son point de départ et remonter l'escalier. En haut, il colla l'oreille à la porte avant de frapper doucement. Un pas léger puis un verrou qu'on tire et la porte s'ouvrit, accompagnée d'une petite exclamation inquiète :

— Tu as oublié quelque chose ? Oh…

L'Écureuil considéra le commissaire aux morts étranges qui se tenait gêné dans l'embrasure de la porte et s'empourpra.

— Je vous dérange ? demanda-t-il.

Elle rougit violemment.

— Non, j'allais juste me coucher…

Sur la table se trouvaient un broc d'eau et une bassine. Les éclaboussures marquaient l'usage que l'on en avait fait. Le regard de l'Écureuil rattrapa le sien, allant avec lui jusqu'à la bassine puis vers le galetas en désordre. De nouveau, une rougeur envahit la jeune fille.

— Vous…

Elle hésita.

— Vous êtes venu pour…

— Pour parler, dit rapidement Volnay.

— Ah…

Imperceptiblement, elle se détendit et répéta comme pour mieux s'en convaincre :

— Me parler…

Et elle ajouta d'un ton espiègle :

— C'est vrai que vous n'êtes pas comme les autres hommes !

La jeune fille le fit asseoir sur son grabat et le rejoignit, calant son flanc contre le sien comme pour rechercher un peu de sa chaleur.

— Avez-vous toujours besoin de moi pour votre enquête ? s'enquit-elle avec curiosité.

Un instant il hésita et puis, sa raison reprenant le dessus, il lui décrivit très précisément l'homme croisé au cimetière.

— Cet homme est dangereux, la prévint-il. Si vous le voyez, suivez-le très discrètement pour connaître ses habitudes : un appartement où il se rend ou un endroit où il aime à se divertir, cabaret ou tripot. Venez ensuite m'en avertir.

Il lui donna son adresse ainsi que celle du moine, lui décrivant comment y aller pour le trouver ou lui laisser un message. Ceci dit, il retomba dans une pesante torpeur car il n'avait nulle idée de la conversation à tenir.

— Qui était la femme qui vous accompagnait ? demanda l'Écureuil d'un ton faussement innocent.

— Quelqu'un qu'on m'a imposé pour cette enquête.

— Ah donc, elle n'est pas… enfin… elle n'est pas votre…

— Dieu me garde, elle n'est rien pour moi ! dit sans hésitation Volnay.

La jeune fille remua d'aise.

— Et vous n'avez personne pour s'occuper de vous ?

Le commissaire aux morts étranges baissa la tête.

— Je suis seul, vous savez. J'ai cru connaître l'amour mais il m'a abandonné. Il me restait mon père mais il s'est perdu dans les jupons d'une aventurière et moi je suis comme un benêt à parler à ma pie qui ne sait que répéter mes dernières paroles…

L'Écureuil se pencha vers lui et son doigt suivit lentement la cicatrice qui courait du coin de son œil à sa tempe.

— Vous avez bien fait de venir, chuchota-t-elle. Je saurai comment chasser vos idées noires.

Il secoua la tête.

— Je ne suis pas venu pour cela, j'avais juste besoin de parler à un être humain, pas à une pie.

Les lèvres de l'Écureuil cherchèrent les siennes et, un moment, Volnay sentit son souffle tiède sur sa bouche. Il se laissa embrasser sans joie ni réaction. La jeune fille se recula comme s'il venait de la frapper.

— Pardonnez-moi, dit-elle.

Désorientée, elle le contempla. Sa connaissance des hommes ne lui était d'aucun secours face à celui-ci. Finalement, elle posa sa main sur son épaule.

— N'avez-vous donc personne chez qui aller ?

Il secoua la tête.

— Je n'ai pas d'amis…

Et il ajouta dans un murmure :

— À part vous…

L'Écureuil se pencha encore un peu plus sur lui. Ses doigts glissèrent sur ses joues, y recueillant avec surprise une larme amère qui laissa un sillon argenté sur son passage.

— Vous feriez mieux de rentrer chez vous, fit-elle d'une voix soudain paniquée, ce que vous attendez de moi, je ne puis vous le donner…

Au début, le moine pensait résister à la tentation. Et puis, il s'aperçut que ses mains soudain empressées couraient sur le corps d'Hélène comme prises de folie et voilà que, sur son ventre lisse et poli, il imprimait la marque de dizaines de baisers. Maintenant, la jeune femme se tenait couchée à ses côtés et il goûtait au bonheur de la savoir là, son jeune corps encore vibrant d'énergie auprès de lui. Ses lèvres chaudes et aimées, cette haleine de vie, faisaient frissonner l'âme du moine. Le parfum d'Hélène semblait être passé par son sang qui charriait désormais dans ses veines des parfums d'automne et de printemps mélangés. La jeune femme souffla doucement sur son visage et à ses narines puis dit :

— Par la vertu de mon souffle, je t'enflammerai d'amour.

Le moine rit.

— J'aime toujours à la folie, on s'ennuie quand on aime médiocrement !

Et il ajouta malicieusement :

— J'ai toujours su que vous fréquentiez les sorcières !

— Et moi que vous étiez un homme vigoureux !

Le rire du moine s'amplifia.

— Certes!

Il rejeta la couverture et se leva.

— Où allez-vous?

— Faire de la lumière!

Elle se redressa avec un sursaut et la couverture glissa de ses épaules.

— Non, n'y allez pas!

Son ton était paniqué. Surpris, le moine gratta une allumette et se retourna vivement avant de se figer. Sur l'épaule d'Hélène, il venait d'apercevoir fugitivement une fleur de lys marquée au fer rouge. Elle était donc flétrie! Pas avec un "V" pour voleur mais par l'emblème royal réservé aux crimes les plus graves!

Elle le considéra avec un mélange de haine et d'effroi saisissant avant de recouvrir vivement son épaule.

— Vous avez vu?

Le moine ne répondit pas. La flamme de l'allumette lui brûla soudain les doigts et il la lâcha avec un grognement de douleur.

— Qu'avez-vous fait pour mériter une telle infamie? demanda-t-il d'un ton douloureux.

— J'ai tué un homme, répondit-elle d'un ton tranquille et détaché.

— Oh, fit le moine en reculant d'un pas.

— Ne craignez rien, je ne vais pas recommencer ce soir!

Il revint près d'elle et s'assit au bord du lit, gardant néanmoins une distance prudente avec la forme allongée immobile.

— Vous deviez avoir une bonne raison, lâcha-t-il enfin, prêt à tout lui pardonner.

— Des tas! Si vous saviez…

Dans la pénombre, il sut qu'elle gardait les yeux fixés au plafond.

— Nous vivions à Paris où mon père était apothicaire. Ma mère l'aidait à préparer ses drogues, cuissons et distillations. Elle possédait un réel talent pour cela. Mon père mourut lorsque j'étais très jeune et ma mère, qui avait bonne réputation, parvint à faire survivre son commerce. Mais elle ne se contenta pas de composer. Elle avait l'esprit curieux…

Hélène s'interrompit pour tourner lentement la tête vers lui.

— Comme vous, remarqua-t-elle.

Le moine hocha la tête et vint se recoucher auprès d'elle, humant discrètement le parfum de sa chair tiède.

— Elle cherchait à comprendre la propriété des plantes, les actions entre elles, et les principes chimiques, reprit Hélène d'un ton neutre. Elle se mit en quête d'explications dans des livres anciens, dans l'observation de la nature et en interrogeant les plus savants.

Elle fit une pause.

— Peut-être même vous a-t-elle consulté? ajouta-t-elle.

Le moine perçut un mouvement dans le noir, le bruit de draps froissés et tout à coup la jeune femme posa sa tête sur sa poitrine.

— Comme votre cœur bat vite, remarqua-t-elle.

Il l'enveloppa de ses bras.

— Continuez votre récit, ma chérie.

Un léger soupir s'exhala des lèvres d'Hélène.

— Ma mère se trouvait en butte à la jalousie d'autres apothicaires de son quartier. Le travail en laboratoire est en effet exclusivement réservé aux médecins, aux professeurs de chimie et aux maîtres apothicaires. On lui en contesta le titre et on lui en fit procès mais, comme vous le savez, la justice est lente, aussi continua-t-elle à exercer. Ses recherches l'amenèrent à composer un élixir d'anti-vapeurs crâniennes puis elle composa un philtre de beauté, un philtre d'amour… Au fil du temps, la clientèle changea. Sa réputation grandit mais pas dans les bons milieux. Les gens ne venaient plus seulement pour se faire soigner mais aussi pour espérer. Elle voulut leur faire plaisir et se plongea dans les grimoires de Paracelse ou Agrippa. Elle inventa une potion de répulsion pour faire fuir les indésirables puis un philtre de jeunesse.

La jeune femme s'interrompit et darda sur lui un œil pénétrant.

— D'après les croyances populaires, on est sorcière de mère en fille. Je ne vous fais pas peur?

Le moine secoua la tête en silence.

— Vous avez tort, rétorqua-t-elle. Peut-être puis-je d'un souffle dessécher la moelle de vos os!

Sans réaction de son compagnon, Hélène fit une petite moue et reprit son récit.

— La police commença à s'intéresser à ma mère et, de nouveau, ses confrères la dénoncèrent. Les policiers envahirent son laboratoire. On y trouva, comme chez tout apothicaire, des plantes, poudres, pommades, liqueurs et drogues qu'un expert jugea *bonnes ou mauvaises suivant l'utilisation que l'on en fait et la dose utilisée*. Ses grimoires la trahirent toutefois car ils contenaient des formules magiques. Elle se retrouva donc en prison au Châtelet. On la fit croupir dans une cellule infestée de rats avec de l'eau jusqu'aux mollets. Sa santé se détériora rapidement. Elle n'y résista pas un mois.

D'un geste instinctif, le moine la serra contre elle. La chaleur de son jeune corps sembla se joindre à la sienne, l'engourdissant insidieusement.

— Lorsqu'elle mourut, reprit Hélène, elle me laissa seule et sans famille. Les amis de mon père s'étaient depuis longtemps détournés de nous et les nouveaux amis de ma mère me fuirent comme la peste, craignant d'avoir affaire à la police. On me jeta à l'hôpital des Enfants-Perdus, c'était un mouroir. Je crus y devenir folle.

Elle sentit la main du moine lui caresser les épaules et ferma les yeux. C'était une main rassurante, celle d'un homme droit et loyal qui ne faillit jamais.

— Un couple de maraîchers cherchait un enfant à adopter, murmura-t-elle d'une voix altérée par l'émotion. Le mari me choisit. Ce n'était pas par charité mais pour faire de moi leur bonne à tout faire. J'avais quatorze ans. Comme je possédais de l'éducation et qu'eux relevaient d'une ignorance crasse, ils aimaient à m'humilier comme si cela pouvait être une revanche sur leur pauvre vie. Le moindre prétexte était bon, une marmite mal récurée et le mari m'attachait pour me suspendre à la poutre maîtresse de la grande pièce, parfois par les pieds, la tête en bas. Sa femme se contentait de m'appliquer contre les aisselles des œufs à la coque bouillants ou de me planter des aiguilles dans la paume de la main. Leurs enfants contemplaient le spectacle en hurlant de joie.

Le moine se raidit et attendit la suite avec appréhension.

— Un an passa, mon corps se développa et ma poitrine affirma ses rondeurs. Un jour, ce qui était écrit arriva. L'homme m'amena avec lui, soi-disant pour l'aider à vendre les produits de sa ferme au marché. À l'aller, il arrêta sa carriole sur le bord de la route, m'attacha les mains dans le dos et me viola. Comme je me débattis, pour me punir, je fis le reste du chemin

307

à pied jusqu'au marché au bout d'une corde. Pendant la foire, je lui dérobai un couteau. De nouveau, au retour, il décida de me violer. Je comprenais désormais pourquoi son choix s'était porté sur moi à l'hôpital des Enfants-Perdus.

Elle jeta un regard farouche au moine. Dans la pénombre, celui-ci vit ses yeux briller comme ceux d'un chat en colère.

— Il ne revit plus jamais sa maison, fit-elle d'un ton glacial. Je le persuadai de me laisser faire pour qu'il ait plus de plaisir. Tout émoustillé, il accepta et je m'assis à califourchon sur lui avant de lui planter mon couteau dans le cœur. Je visai mal et il me fallut m'y reprendre à plusieurs reprises. Il criait plus fort que les cochons qu'il saignait à la ferme. Je l'ai frappé et frappé, ensuite, j'ai attendu qu'il se vide de son sang. Cela a été le plus heureux moment de ma vie.

Le moine sursauta. Il sentit plus qu'il ne vit Hélène poser sur lui un regard moqueur.

— Vous avez cru à mon histoire?

— Oui, fit-il doucement.

— Il ne faut pas, fit-elle sur un ton de doux reproche. Mais je vais quand même vous raconter la suite.

De nouveau, elle appuya la tête sur sa poitrine. Cette fois, le moine caressa ses cheveux comme pour l'apaiser.

— Je retournai à la maison où l'on m'avait tant maltraitée et j'y mis le feu. Je regardais la femme et ses enfants s'éparpiller dans les champs en hurlant, m'assurant qu'il n'en restait plus un dans la maison. Ma vengeance terminée, je marchai jusqu'à Paris en mendiant. Là-bas, je fus arrêtée pour vol et on m'amena devant le commissaire de quartier. Je sentis que je le troublais. Je lui lançai quelques œillades engageantes et il me proposa d'arranger mon affaire et de me prendre pour servante. Il vivait seul avec une cuisinière qui lui servait de bonne à tout faire. Il l'envoya dehors sous prétexte de courses et me prit, à moitié habillée, sur la table de la cuisine. Cela dut lui plaire car il me conserva avec lui.

— Quel porc! lança le moine d'un ton dégoûté. Un commissaire du Châtelet.

— Un homme, Guillaume, le reprit-elle d'un ton las. Seulement un homme…

Elle semblait fatiguée.

— Il n'était pas vraiment méchant d'ailleurs. Il ne me battait presque jamais et ses besoins étaient vite satisfaits. J'eus droit à une chambre sous les combles et à des livres. Il m'apprit à tirer au pistolet et à manier l'épée. Un jour, je proposai qu'il m'emploie pour une enquête. Je me fis marquer au fer rouge des criminels pour m'introduire dans une bande de voleurs et d'assassins que je lui permis d'arrêter. Tout cela l'impressionna fort. Dès lors, je lui devins indispensable et un jour, peu avant sa mort, il me présenta à Sartine… Vous pouvez deviner la suite…

Le silence tomba brutalement entre eux.

— Pour la fleur de lys, lui glissa-t-elle au bout d'un instant, ne dites rien à votre fils!

— M'avez-vous vraiment menti pour votre histoire?

— Bien sûr que je vous ai menti! Pourquoi irais-je donc raconter ma vie au premier venu?

À sa grande surprise, le moine approuva.

— Je comprends, moi-même je ferais de même! Néanmoins, votre histoire est en partie vraie pour ce que j'en sais.

Étonnée, elle le regarda.

— Votre mère m'a effectivement consulté à un moment de ma vie, expliqua le moine avec une douceur infinie. Je n'étais pas en France à l'époque où elle fut jetée en prison. Ce n'est qu'un an plus tard que j'appris cette affreuse nouvelle. Son corps avait été jeté à la fosse commune et je n'avais pas un endroit où me recueillir. Je savais qu'elle avait une fille et la recherchai pour m'assurer qu'elle allait bien mais personne ne put me renseigner sur votre sort.

Il soupira et ajouta d'un ton las :

— Je suis désolé.

Hélène se souleva sur un coude et le contempla songeusement.

— Ce n'est pas votre faute, dit-elle enfin. Je sais que si vous m'aviez retrouvée, vous vous seriez bien occupé de moi.

La main de la jeune femme se promena impudemment sur le corps fin, noueux et musculeux du moine, suivant les nombreuses cicatrices qui marquaient sa peau de l'empreinte indélébile d'une jeunesse tumultueuse.

— Mais peut-être pourrez-vous me renseigner? chuchota-t-elle.

— Quoi donc?

Elle lui mordilla légèrement le lobe de l'oreille et demanda d'un ton provocant :

— Est-ce que je fais l'amour mieux que ma mère?

XVIII

LEVÉE DE CORPS
ET AUTRES DIABLERIES

L'aube se levait à peine, baignant d'une faible lueur croix et angelots aux pieds glacés. Les rafales de vent faisaient tourbillonner la neige poudreuse entre les tombes. Telle la statue du commandeur, la haute et rigide silhouette du commissaire aux morts étranges se découpait comme une ombre spectrale. À ses pieds s'entassaient des pelletées de terre. Le soleil n'avait pas encore percé lorsqu'on ôta le couvercle du cercueil de Sophia. Volnay s'approcha d'une démarche raide et baissa les yeux. Impassible, il se retourna ensuite vers son père.

— Regarde par toi-même !

Le moine vint à pas lents, presque malgré lui. Il jeta un coup d'œil prudent au cercueil et son teint vira au gris.

— Je suis un âne bâté.

Il venait de constater qu'il s'agissait bien du cadavre du gardien du cimetière.

— C'est peu de le dire ! renchérit son fils.

Le commissaire de quartier, Cornevin, s'approcha à son tour. Volnay devait à son obligeance l'ouverture de la tombe.

— Mon Dieu, fit-il en blêmissant, ce n'est pas la petite Sophia.

Volnay se tourna vivement vers lui.

— Gardez cela secret ! Rien de tout ceci ne doit être révélé.

L'autre déglutit péniblement et acquiesça.

— D'accord mais m'expliquerez-vous enfin ce que signifie cette diablerie ?

— Plus tard, plus tard…

Volnay se saisit du bras de son père et l'entraîna loin de la tombe au bord de laquelle le commissaire de quartier et les fossoyeurs les observaient avec curiosité. Il jeta un coup d'œil pour s'assurer qu'ils se trouvaient assez éloignés du petit groupe.

— Père, il y a une chose que je ne m'explique pas, c'est que tu aies considéré cette enfant comme morte alors qu'elle ne l'était pas ! Comment as-tu pu ?

Le moine se tordit les mains de désespoir.

— C'est sans doute la propriété de la substance qu'elle a ingurgitée malgré elle. Avec une dose importante, celle-ci doit ralentir toutes les fonctions vitales, les battements du cœur et donc tout signe de vie. D'ailleurs, bien des personnes ne doivent pas s'en réveiller dans de telles circonstances car seule la dose fait le poison…

— Oui, et comme tu ne t'es pas livré sur elle à une autopsie…

— Dieu du ciel, heureusement que je n'ai pas eu envie de charcuter cette pauvre enfant !

Le moine se signa ce qui surprit fort son fils.

— Sophia était plongée dans un sommeil aux portes de la mort mais elle était bien vivante, déclara Volnay les yeux mi-clos. La cérémonie devait l'exiger. La mise à mort n'intervenait qu'à son terme. Mais le gardien du cimetière est arrivé. Il a fallu le tuer. On l'a étouffé avec beaucoup de sang-froid pour ne pas laisser de traces. Et puis les participants ont dû vouloir reprendre la cérémonie. Seulement, ce n'était pas leur jour : des déterreurs de cadavres sont arrivés ! Nos participants de la messe noire ont cédé à la panique et se sont enfuis en laissant Sophia sur la pierre tombale. La suite, tu la connais. Les assistants du gardien sont allés voir les feux follets, ont trouvé le cadavre de leur maître et alerté le guet.

Le moine respira un grand coup.

— J'étais très troublé ce soir-là, avoua-t-il. Le corps de Sophia était glacé et elle portait des marques à son cou. Cela, ajouté à la substance qui la mettait en état d'hibernation, m'a complètement trompé. Dans ma cave aussi il faisait froid. Et puis, je suis tombé malade.

Une vapeur s'exhala de ses poumons en même temps qu'une longue plainte. Celle-ci n'émut pas Volnay qui considéra son père avec colère.

— J'ai mis du temps mais je suis arrivé à comprendre que Sophia n'était pas morte, moi ! Toi-même serais arrivé aussi vite, sinon plus, à la même conclusion en temps normal. Seulement voilà tu n'es pas dans ton état normal. Cette jeune femme, Hélène, t'a fait tourner la tête !

Pour la première fois depuis longtemps, le moine se mit en colère.

— Mon fils, tu commences à me baver dans la cornemuse !

Surpris, Volnay ouvrit toute grande la bouche et la referma stupidement. Il contempla un instant son père et puis son attention fut attirée par l'irruption intempestive d'un homme dans son champ de vision. La perruque aux rouleaux de pigeon de Sartine semblait voler d'une tombe à l'autre. Le lieutenant général de police marchait à grands pas dans l'allée, le visage fermé. Avec appréhension, Volnay le regarda se diriger vers eux d'un air décidé, écrasant la neige fraîche sous ses talons.

— Qu'est-ce que ceci ? murmura le moine.

— Ça, fit son fils, ce sont les ennuis !

De loin, ils entendirent les imprécations de leur supérieur qui venait de les apercevoir.

— Tambour et cymbales, soupira le moine. Cet homme remplit le monde de bruit !

En arrivant devant eux, Sartine ne les salua même pas.

— Alors, est-ce vrai ?

— Oui, monsieur, fit Volnay d'un ton neutre. C'est le gardien du cimetière qui a été enterré à sa place. À mon avis, Sophia est bien vivante. Nous avons également découvert que M. Marly, son père, n'est pas mort et sans doute à l'origine de toute cette affaire…

Et le commissaire aux morts étranges raconta pourquoi il en était arrivé à cette évidence. Sartine le coupa sans ménagement.

— Décidément, vous êtes en dessous de tout ! Non seulement, vous laissez cette prostituée vous échapper mais vous perdez aussi le cadavre de la victime qui par ailleurs n'est même pas morte ! Pas plus que son père du reste, d'après vous ! En fait, dans cette affaire, personne n'est mort à part le gardien du cimetière ! Mais qu'est-ce que c'est que cette histoire abracadabrante ? De qui se moque-t-on ? De la police du roi ?

Il se tourna vers le moine et, se haussant sur la pointe des pieds, vint coller son visage à un fil du sien.

— Et vous, vous n'êtes même pas capable de voir qu'une personne est vivante ? Vieux fou !

— Je ne suis pas vieux, rétorqua le moine.

Puis il se retourna vers son fils :

— Décidément, c'est l'évangile en cours : je suis vieux !

Sartine recula et siffla entre ses dents comme un serpent. Jamais, Volnay ne l'avait vu dans cet état.

— Mes policiers, dit-il d'une voix où perçait une sourde menace, doivent être de bonnes vie et mœurs et de confession catholique lorsqu'ils me prêtent serment. Ce n'est pas votre cas, je le sais parfaitement. Je vous tolérais jusqu'à présent comme un élément étranger au sein d'un corps parfaitement sain pour votre efficacité mais force est de constater que celle-ci a disparu.

Il contempla un instant ses bottes souillées par la neige puis releva la tête.

— Je vous retire cette enquête et vous suspends de vos fonctions !

— Qui mènera l'enquête à votre place ? protesta Volnay. Ce sot de Siltieri ?

Sartine l'écrasa de son dédain.

— Vous me connaissez mal ! Ai-je la réputation de mettre tous mes œufs dans le même panier ?

— C'est Hélène qui va poursuivre l'enquête, constata le commissaire aux morts étranges avec amertume.

Le lieutenant général de police eut un geste agacé.

— Votre moine me l'a convertie ! Elle ne me servira plus à rien dans cette affaire. Non, j'ai un autre atout dans ma manche et il est temps pour moi de le jouer !

Dans un grand bruissement, il tourna les talons et s'éloigna. Soudain il s'arrêta et se retourna.

— Bien entendu, vous ne serez plus rémunéré et vous devrez me faire parvenir au Châtelet le solde de mes avances pour vos frais en me justifiant ceux-ci !

— Ça, c'est très mesquin, murmura le moine lorsque Sartine eut de nouveau tourné le dos. Il veut rogner notre écuelle pour étrangler l'affaire !

Et il ajouta pour lui-même :

— Heureusement que j'en mets un peu de côté à chaque enquête pour assurer nos arrières. Il n'est pas encore venu le temps où nous ne pourrons plus faire frire !

Volnay le considéra avec effarement.

— Quoi ?

Son père haussa les épaules avec fatalisme.

— Tu es trop honnête alors je suis prévoyant pour deux ! Sans le savoir, Sartine finance nos vieux jours !

Pour la première fois depuis longtemps, Volnay rit. Son rire s'éleva au-dessus des pierres, léger dans l'air immobile. C'était le rire clair d'un enfant qui retrouve son père. Il semblait soudain débarrassé d'une chape de glace. Sous les yeux des fossoyeurs, les deux hommes se livrèrent alors à un étrange manège en se tapant dans les mains, paumes retournées avant de se congratuler. Puis, leur gaieté exprimée, ils retournèrent à l'entrée du cimetière sous un soleil qui ne réchauffait rien.

— Père, qu'a voulu dire Sartine en disant que tu avais converti Hélène ?

Le moine eut l'air gêné.

— Je n'en ai pas la moindre idée, au fil du temps, Sartine devient de plus en plus difficile à comprendre !

— Toi et Hélène, vous n'avez pas… euh… tu vois ce que je veux dire ?

— Oh, mon fils, elle a vingt ans de moins que moi !

— Un peu plus, père, un peu plus…

Ils marchèrent en silence entre les tombes glacées, heureux de leur complicité retrouvée jusqu'à ce que le moine questionne Volnay.

— Mon fils, puis-je te poser une question?

— Oui, père.

Le moine humecta ses lèvres gercées par le froid. Sa mâchoire tremblait légèrement.

—Ai-je tant vieilli que ça que tout le monde me traite de vieux gâteux?

Sa voix était si tremblante que le cœur de Volnay se serra. Dans un geste instinctif, il s'arrêta et prit son père dans ses bras.

— Sartine et moi ne sommes que des imbéciles. Bien sûr que non, papa!

Le moine tressaillit, Volnay venait de prononcer le plus beau mot du monde pour son oreille. Naturellement, sa main prit celle de son fils et celui-ci qui, adolescent, avait horreur de cela, se laissa faire sans résistance. Ce fut ainsi qu'ils sortirent du cimetière.

XIX

SOPHIA ET AUTRES DIABLERIES

D'abord Sophia n'avait rien vu, rien entendu. Ce fut une voix grave et cuivrée qui la sortit de sa léthargie. De plus en plus réceptive, elle s'efforça de capter des sons, au début inaudibles, puis elle entrouvrit les yeux, s'efforçant d'accommoder sa vision. Une présence s'affairait dans la pièce froide. Elle guetta du coin de l'œil une ombre dans son champ de vision ou un changement de forme, s'efforçant de distinguer les couleurs mais le monde restait gris. Elle se rendormit.

Les heures passèrent et, lorsque Sophia s'éveilla véritablement le matin du second jour, ce fut pour constater qu'elle se trouvait dans une cave glaciale. Seule une lugubre lumière mouillée filtrait d'un lointain soupirail. Heureusement une épaisse couverture la recouvrait tout entière et, délicatesse suprême, on lui en avait étendu une autre sous elle. Dans sa compassion, le moine avait même glissé en cette occasion un coussin sous sa nuque.

Sophia essaya de bouger ses membres mais sans vraiment y parvenir. Évitant de céder à la panique, elle se concentra sur une de ses mains jusqu'à faire fonctionner ses doigts l'un après l'autre. Lorsqu'elle glissa un mollet hors de la couverture, le froid la mordit. Tous ses mouvements semblaient se ralentir. Frissonnante, elle réussit au bout d'une heure à s'asseoir, envelop-pée dans la chaude couverture.

Si l'enfer était un gigantesque laboratoire rempli de fourneaux, de fioles et de cornues, Sophia devait donc s'y trouver mais, en y réfléchissant, elle ne se souvint pas d'avoir commis quelque chose pour le mériter. Elle pensa alors au purgatoire car elle n'estimait pas avoir vécu suffisamment pour avoir mérité son para-dis. Mais pourquoi personne n'était-il là pour l'ac-cueillir? Perplexe, elle réfléchit. Il y avait bien eu une personne près d'elle. Il lui semblait se souvenir d'une bure comme celle d'un moine. Il lui parlait gentiment. Il fallait qu'elle retrouve cet homme ou cet esprit.

Sophia se laissa glisser à terre, étouffant un gémis-sement lorsque ses pieds nus prirent contact avec le sol glacé. Resserrant la couverture autour de son corps, elle entreprit d'explorer les lieux. Jamais, elle n'avait observé un tel endroit. On aurait dit qu'un savant fou avait entrepris de mettre le monde en éprouvettes ou en alambics. D'un pas mal assuré, elle tenta d'échap-per à ces lieux étranges mais la porte de la cave était fermée à clé.

C'est donc bien le purgatoire, se dit-elle. *On ne peut en sortir avant l'heure mais où donc sont les autres âmes en peine?*

Elle remarqua alors qu'on avait laissé un mor-ceau de pain blanc sur une table ainsi qu'une carafe d'eau. Elle avait faim et mangea donc le pain, s'éton-nant que dans la mort on dût ainsi continuer à s'ali-menter. Ensuite, elle eut soif et but. Ainsi rassasiée et désaltérée, elle fit de nouveau le tour du laboratoire et découvrit une seconde cave. Un frisson la secoua tout entière. Le cadavre d'un homme gisait là et nulle couverture ou drap ne le recouvrait.

Fébrilement, Sophia fit le tour des lieux, secouant en vain la lourde porte. Le cœur battant, elle revint ensuite dans la deuxième cave. Là, elle découvrit une autre porte, plus petite et plus basse. Elle tendit la main vers le loquet et découvrit qu'il jouait. Un escalier très raide la mena jusqu'à une chambre. Dans celle-ci, sur un lit à bas piliers, dormait un homme. Elle le contempla avec surprise puis pensa qu'il ressemblait à l'inconnu qui parlait souvent au-dessus d'elle pendant qu'elle dormait. Une certaine tiédeur régnait dans la pièce et elle se sentit mieux, s'enhardissant à ouvrir un coffre et y découvrant avec plaisir des robes et mantelets, des manchettes et coiffes ornées de dentelles, des bas et une paire de mules et des bottines. Elle se vêtit, choisissant la robe la plus chaude même si elle était trop grande pour elle, des bas de laine. Les bottines étaient en revanche à peu près à sa taille.

Une fois vêtue, Sophia regarda autour d'elle. Ses besoins primaires assouvis, boire et ne plus avoir froid, elle se sentait vide et inutile. Son attention fut alors attirée au chevet du dormeur par une belle couverture au cuir vieilli et marbré sur laquelle elle déchiffra un titre : *Éloge de la folie* d'Érasme. Elle le prit en main pour le feuilleter puis le reposa, le trouvant trop compliqué.

Ne sachant que faire, elle s'assit au bord du lit, savourant le confort de celui-ci, le plaisir de ses nouveaux vêtements et la douce quiétude de la pièce. Au bout d'un moment, l'homme ouvrit les yeux. Ils étaient remplis d'humanité. Il lui parla et elle lui répondit même si la conversation n'avait pas grand sens pour elle. Saisie d'une brusque impulsion, elle lui déclara avec beaucoup d'assurance qu'il rêvait. Elle en venait en effet à penser qu'elle était un ange et que nulle personne sur terre ne devait connaître sa présence.

L'homme ferma les yeux et, légère et silencieuse, elle se glissa de nouveau par la porte.

Sophia ne redescendit pas dans la cave. À mi-chemin de l'escalier, une porte donnait sur un minuscule cellier. En refermant la porte, elle avait tout juste la place pour y étendre ses deux couvertures et s'y enrouler. Il faisait moins froid ici que dans la cave. Après avoir vidé un pot de confiture, elle s'endormit, enroulée dans sa couverture, un goût de framboise dans la bouche.

Elle se réveilla d'un sommeil sans rêve qui parut lui avoir duré des années et gagna la chambre où elle avait rencontré le moine malade. Elle n'y trouva personne. La maison qu'elle traversa était vide et silencieuse mais soudain une masse de poil se précipita sur elle en glapissant de joie. Elle tomba à terre et une langue râpeuse courut sur son visage. Éperdue de joie, elle serra son chien dans ses bras.

— C'est donc vrai que tu es là?

Un long moment, elle le tint contre elle, réchauffant son corps à sa chaleur. Puis elle eut faim et trouva un reste de beau pain blanc qu'elle partagea avec le chien. Ainsi ragaillardie, elle s'enhardit et résolut de sortir pour voir à quoi ressemblait le monde après la mort.

La porte était fermée. Elle explora les lieux et trouva une clé suspendue à un clou dans la cuisine. Elle s'en saisit, la tourna dans la serrure et sortit. Ensuite, très naturellement, elle referma à clé derrière elle. Le monde était le même que dans la vraie vie. Dans la rue, elle fut assaillie par le bruit. Les commerçants vantaient leurs produits et, par moments, lui parvenait aux oreilles la voix reconnaissable des cochers, le timbre cassé d'avoir trop crié.

Elle avançait à pas lents dans la ville avec une liberté nouvellement acquise. La jeune enfant éprouvait désormais un sentiment de paix même si des souvenirs mélancoliques frémissaient encore en elle. Sophia entreprit de retourner à la maison qui l'avait vue grandir. Elle ne s'y sentait rattaché en rien. La vie y avait été des plus mornes et des plus ennuyeuses. Néanmoins, elle constituait un repère dans une existence, ou plutôt une non-existence, qui en manquait. Sans émotion, elle revit les pierres noires et la tour qui se dressait dans le ciel. Elle s'assit un instant sur les marches, perdue dans ses réflexions. Des souvenirs contraires la firent alors frissonner et elle se hâta de s'éloigner. Elle croisa la servante, lui jetant un regard vide qui parut la terroriser car elle se signa comme pour conjurer un mauvais sort. Sophia comprit alors qu'elle était morte et devenue une de ces revenantes dont sa nourrice lui parlait à la veillée.

Témoin fidèle de ses pèlerinages, le chien l'accompagnait, la queue frétillante. Son séjour chez le moine lui avait profité. On l'avait lavé et frotté, coupé le poil en trop, flatté et donné sans compter une nourriture abondante. De retrouver ensuite sa petite maîtresse, ou celle qu'il s'était choisie comme telle, semblait lui conférer une énergie débordante.

Ne sachant où se diriger, Sophia décida de suivre le chien qui semblait parfaitement savoir où aller. Il la conduisit non loin de la maison du moine, dans un curieux dédale de cours, chacune plus petite que l'autre au fur et à mesure qu'elle avançait. Dans la troisième de ces cours, se dressait un arbre. Elle s'amusa à en secouer les branches et la neige retomba en poudre sur elle. Le chien alla jusqu'à la porte de la maison sur laquelle donnait la cour et leva la patte pour uriner. Elle rit puis le gronda avant de l'imiter.

Lorsqu'elle jugea qu'il était temps de rentrer, Sophia s'agenouilla près de son chien et lui demanda de la ramener à ce qu'elle considérait désormais comme sa maison ou son lieu de transit vers une autre vie. Le chien haleta doucement entre les paumes de ses mains puis la conduisit non loin de là. Sophia sortit la clé de sa poche et ouvrit. Elle alla jusqu'à la cuisine et partagea un biscuit avec son ami à quatre pattes, près des cendres de l'âtre. Se sentant fatiguée, elle embrassa son animal et gagna la chambre du moine. Le chien geignit et gratta à la porte puis se tut. Sophia descendit jusqu'à la cave. Horrifiée, elle y découvrit un corps calciné et regagna vivement le cellier. Encore frissonnante, elle s'y réfugia. L'endroit était rassurant avec ses jambons pendus, ses pots de confitures, ses herbes odorantes et ses bouteilles cachetées soigneusement rangées. Elle trouva un panneau et un fusain près des bouteilles. Un autre panneau récapitulait les noms des vins et leurs années. Elle s'amusa à écrire sur celui qui était vierge : *Interdit à Dieu d'entrer* et songea à l'apposer sur la porte de son repaire avant de renoncer. Elle trouverait bien une autre manière de l'employer. Comme elle y songeait, la fatigue la gagna soudain. Elle ferma les yeux et sentit son esprit dériver avant de s'endormir au milieu de parfums de thym et de laurier.

XX

DANS LA TÊTE D'UN CHIEN
ET AUTRES DIABLERIES

Un blanc laiteux flottait dans les rues. Comme à leur habitude, au petit matin, les employés de la voirie ramassaient crottes et cadavres dans Paris. Les boulangers de Gonesse envahissaient les rues avec leurs petits pains. Par centaines, les porteurs d'eau se faufilaient dans les immeubles pour vendre l'eau de la Seine, désinfectée au vinaigre blanc. Dans l'aube glacée, les deux enquêteurs regagnèrent à grands pas le domicile du moine. Celui-ci ressassait toute l'affaire dans sa tête avant de la régurgiter en phrases hachées.

— Sophia entendait nos paroles dans son demi-sommeil ou sa demi-mort et puis elle s'est réveillée. Par chance pour elle, j'avais posé une chaude couverture sur son corps. Cela l'a empêchée de mourir définitivement de froid dans ma cave !

— Elle aurait pu mourir de froid dans le cimetière.

— Nous sommes venus très vite et l'avons apportée. De plus, la substance avait ralenti son métabolisme pour la faire entrer dans une sorte d'hibernation tout comme un ours.

— Mais quand elle s'est réveillée ?

— Elle s'est crue morte ! C'est une pauvre enfant de douze ans à qui on a parlé de l'enfer, du paradis et du purgatoire ! Elle est venue me visiter dans ma chambre car j'ai un accès direct à ma seconde cave.

Elle s'est habillée dans un coffre des vêtements de ta pauvre mère et elle m'a parlé. Fiévreux et croyant avoir affaire à un spectre, je ne l'ai pas détrompée sur son état. Plus tard, elle a navigué entre la cave et ma chambre, allant dans la cuisine pour se nourrir.

— Et c'est probablement ce faisant qu'elle a compris qu'elle n'était pas morte...

— C'est vraisemblable. Aussi s'est-elle rendue chez elle en amenant le chien mais elle s'est contentée de s'asseoir sur le perron de sa maison. Quelque chose l'a empêchée de rentrer.

— Est-ce elle qui a mis le feu à la maison de son père ?

Le moine fronça les sourcils.

— Tu m'en demandes trop !

Une fois arrivés, ils fouillèrent minutieusement toute la maison du moine, découvrant dans le petit cellier l'endroit où Sophia avait dormi et le pot de confiture vide.

— Où peut-elle bien être ? se lamenta le moine.

— Elle entre et elle sort à sa guise, remarqua Volnay. Toutefois cette nuit elle n'est pas rentrée puisque tu m'as raconté avoir mis une clochette à ta porte, côté intérieur pour te prévenir de son éventuel retour après la disparition du chien.

— Par un tel froid, elle est peut-être morte cette fois-ci.

— À moins que...

— À quoi penses-tu ?

— Le chien l'accompagne. Si elle ne sait où aller, elle peut suivre cet intelligent animal.

Le commissaire aux morts étranges croisa les bras, appuyant son poing sous son menton et fermant à demi les yeux, dans l'attitude qu'il adoptait parfois pour mieux réfléchir.

— Je ne sais pas entrer dans la tête de Sophia, avoua-t-il au bout d'un instant, aussi vais-je tenter de pénétrer dans celle de son chien !

— Tu as parfaitement raison, mon fils. Platon remarque que le chien sait distinguer un ennemi d'un ami, l'ennemi étant celui qu'il ne connaît pas, ce qui suppose, sinon un certain savoir, une certaine mémoire. Quant à Aristote, dans *De anima*, il attribue quelques qualités intellectuelles aux espèces animales, spécialement à celles qui ne se contentent pas de procréer mais nourrissent et élèvent leurs petits, allant même jusqu'à développer une forme de collaboration sociale. Note d'ailleurs que dans l'espèce humaine, certains ne vont pas si loin et, après avoir procréé, abandonnent femme et progéniture !

Les parenthèses du moine pouvant être interminables, Volnay le coupa gentiment.

— Le chien ne la conduira donc pas chez son ancien maître où il ne prenait que des coups.

— Quoique la fidélité de ces animaux soit parfois touchante, ils sont comme ces enfants que leurs pères frappent mais qui tentent désespérément de leur manifester de l'amour.

— Oui, bien. Le chien connaît son quartier. Il y a peut-être des endroits où il trouve plus facilement à se nourrir, dans les cours des auberges par exemple… Il a suivi aussi Sophia au cimetière où on l'avait entraînée pour la messe noire mais pourquoi y retournerait-il ? Il t'a enfin suivi chez toi mais aussi chez moi puis dans la ruelle de l'Or… Oui ! Il est entré avec nous chez la Dame de l'Eau et y a trouvé un bon feu ! Elle lui a même donné à manger !

— Tu crois donc que son estomac gouverne *chien-chien* ? s'exclama son père outré.

— Arrête de l'appeler ainsi et trouve-lui plutôt un nom !

Le moine plissa les yeux.

— Bonne idée, je vais l'appeler Aristote !

Volnay leva les yeux au ciel puis se décida rapidement.

— Couvre-toi, nous allons aller chez moi puis, si nous ne trouvons rien, nous nous rendrons à la ruelle de l'Or.

— Bien, je vais laisser un mot à l'intention d'Hélène pour qu'elle nous attende ici. Je ne sais pas où elle est passée après… euh… cette nuit.

Son fils lui jeta un bref coup d'œil mais se tut. Dehors, un ciel vitrifié les accueillit. Ils se rendirent chez Volnay puis gagnèrent ensuite la rue Saint-Jacques. Là, le commissaire aux morts étranges s'immobilisa. Face à eux, une silhouette sombre se découpait dans la blancheur immaculée. Les yeux du commissaire aux morts étranges s'étrécirent.

— Attends-moi, fit-il au moine.

Il traversa rapidement la rue et rejoignit la silhouette encapuchonnée. Les têtes des deux hommes s'inclinèrent l'une vers l'autre. Le moine observa attentivement. L'inconnu semblait murmurer à l'oreille de son fils. Celui-ci l'interrompit à plusieurs reprises pour le questionner. À la dernière réponse, le commissaire aux morts étranges leva la tête en l'air, son regard semblant se perdre dans les tourbillons frisés des fumées de cheminée. Puis il tira quelques pièces de sa bourse et les glissa dans la main de l'autre avant de rejoindre le moine.

— C'est une des mouches qui surveillent le quartier où a disparu l'homme à l'épée croisé au cimetière lors de l'enterrement de Sophia, expliqua Volnay. Les recherches n'ont rien donné mais je leur ai demandé de persévérer.

— Vraiment? fit le moine avec méfiance. Sartine nous a retiré l'enquête et donc tout pouvoir sur ses mouches.

Il s'arrêta devant une vieille femme qui, pour deux sols, vendait du café au lait dans un gobelet. Le visage rouge, l'œil sanglant et la respiration saccadée, elle portait sur le dos une fontaine en fer-blanc qui devait peser bien lourd.

— Les ordres du lieutenant général de police vont mettre un peu de temps à parvenir aux mouches, dit Volnay tandis que son père sirotait son café. Ce ne sont que des pions, des ombres dans la rue…

Son père acquiesça. Il prit une nouvelle tasse de café, autant pour soulager un peu la femme de son fardeau que pour doubler son obole. Ceci fait, ils reprirent leur route.

— Dans la *Métaphysique*, reprit gaiement le moine, Aristote écrit que les chiens sont pourvus de sensations, celles-ci générant la mémoire. Or la mémoire permet d'apprendre et donc de développer une forme d'intelligence. Il est plus aisé d'ailleurs de la développer lorsque l'on est doté de l'ouïe, ce qui n'est pas le cas de tous les animaux, les abeilles étant par exemple sourdes comme un pot!

Le commissaire aux morts étranges continua sa marche sans répondre, entièrement concentré sur les paroles de la mouche qui résonnaient encore à ses oreilles, ouvrant un abîme sous ses pieds. Sans s'apercevoir de ce manque d'attention, son père gazouillait tout en battant l'air des bras.

— Un philosophe stoïcien, Sextus Empiricus, démontre qu'un chien poursuivant un gibier qui peut avoir pris trois voies différentes, s'il renifle et ne sent rien pour les deux premières, ne reniflera pas la troisième car il en déduit qu'il l'a prise !

Le moine agita triomphalement un doigt en l'air.

— Il manifeste donc une capacité de réflexion !

Le moine pouvait être intarissable. Volnay subit en chemin, sans broncher, l'étude du philosophe Héraclite d'Éphèse, son père concluant par sa citation préférée de ce dernier : "Je gémis sur l'instabilité des choses ; tout y flotte comme dans un breuvage en mixture ; amalgame de plaisir et de peine, de science et d'ignorance, de grandeur et de petitesse : le haut et le bas s'y confondent et alternent dans le jeu du siècle."

Les deux hommes pénétrèrent enfin dans la ruelle de l'Or. L'étrangeté de l'endroit qu'ils connaissaient pourtant bien leur fit adopter spontanément l'attitude furtive et silencieuse des gens qui s'y glissaient. Le moine baissa sa capuche sur ses yeux et le commissaire aux morts étranges rentra le menton dans le col de son manteau. Ensemble, ils frappèrent à la porte de la Dame de l'Eau.

On leur ouvrit très rapidement et ils entrèrent avec reconnaissance dans la maison, découvrant du même coup le chien et un bon feu flambant dans la cheminée. L'animal se leva en glapissant et se jeta sur le moine, les deux pattes avant levées, cherchant à lui passer sa langue râpeuse sur le visage.

— Voilà *chien-chien*… euh… Aristote ! s'exclama le moine en lui ébouriffant le crâne. Remarque comme il a le sens du juste puisqu'il remue la queue de contentement en nous voyant ! Ce qu'il fallait démontrer !

La Dame de l'Eau le regarda avec stupéfaction. Volnay haussa les épaules.

— Une démonstration de l'intelligence animale, expliqua-t-il brièvement. Sophia est-elle là?

— Oui. J'ai entendu gratter à la porte cette nuit. C'était le chien et je l'ai tout de suite reconnu. Il était accompagné de cette jeune fille. Elle semblait épuisée et transie. Je l'ai fait entrer puis lui ai donné à manger. Elle a répondu à mes questions par des réponses sans queue ni tête et s'est endormie à table. Il a fallu que je la réveille pour l'amener à ma chambre. Cela fait bien douze heures qu'elle dort! Je pensais l'accompagner chez vous une fois debout.

Elle les conduisit à sa chambre où dormait Sophia. À leur entrée, le chien agita joyeusement la queue, fit le tour du lit, renifla les draps puis se coucha pesamment en poussant un profond soupir.

Les deux hommes contemplèrent Sophia dans un silence émerveillé. Bien que pâle, son visage n'avait plus la teinte livide de la nuit dans le cimetière. Sur l'oreiller, il était auréolé d'un casque de cheveux d'or filé. Les deux hommes admirèrent la finesse de ses traits, la moue charmante de ses lèvres abandonnées au sommeil et ses petits poings crispés sur les draps.

Le moine sembla en tomber amoureux à l'instant même. Aussi son fils crut-il plus prudent de le raisonner d'emblée.

— Nous ne pouvons pas la ramener chez nous, dit-il. Sartine nous a retiré l'affaire et il serait immédiatement informé par ses mouches de l'arrivée de Sophia.

Il s'interrompit et fronça les sourcils, l'air tendu.

— Je pense également que Sartine nous cache bien des choses dans cette affaire.

Couché au pied du lit, le chien releva la tête avant de la reposer sur ses deux pattes avant, l'air désolé. À cet instant, Sophia ouvrit les yeux et les fixa. Son regard semblait être le miroir de son âme. Le moine la contempla, extasié.

— Sophia !

Un long frémissement saisit l'enfant.

— Suis-je morte ? demanda-t-elle angoissée.

— Non, ma jeune amie, vous êtes bien vivante !

Elle coula vers lui un doux regard de reproche.

— Alors pourquoi ne pas m'avoir détrompée lorsque nous avons parlé ?

Le moine soupira.

— J'étais dévoré par la fièvre et je croyais rêver…

Il baissa la tête et murmura :

— Où donc peut-on rencontrer des êtres tels que vous sinon dans nos rêves ?

Elle ne sembla pas comprendre. Aussi le commissaire aux morts étranges intervint avec peu de ménagement.

— Qui donc a voulu vous tuer ?

Sophia se troubla.

— Je ne sais pas, je ne sais plus… tant de monde…

Le policier se pencha vers elle.

— Avez-vous rencontré des gens effrayants ou des inconnus qui n'auraient pas dû s'intéresser à vous ?

Elle ferma les yeux comme pour mieux réfléchir avant de les ouvrir tout grands, la mine effrayée.

— L'an dernier, je crois, un jour où je jouais aux cailloux sur les marches de ma maison, un carrosse s'est brusquement arrêté devant moi. Un homme a passé la tête par la portière. Il portait une très jolie perruque et de beaux habits. Il m'a demandé si je me nommais Sophia. Quand je lui ai répondu que oui, il m'a souri et m'a tendu une pièce en or pour que j'aille m'acheter une belle poupée.

— Cet homme a-t-il dit comment il s'appelait ? la questionna Volnay.

— Non mais lorsqu'il a ordonné au cocher d'aller de l'avant, celui-ci lui a répondu : Où désirez-vous aller monsieur le lieutenant général de police ?

Le moine laissa échapper un terrible blasphème.

— Enfer et damnation ! Ce fils de chien de Sartine !

La Dame de l'Eau et l'enfant le regardèrent avec effarement. Sophia semblait sur le point de pleurer.

— Où est mon père ? demanda-t-elle d'une voix faible.

Le moine lui prit alors la main et lui apprit prudemment que son père était mort. Cela ne sembla pas chagriner outre mesure Sophia mais le moine savait que les enfants n'associaient pas à la mort la même peur que les adultes. Mourir, c'était simplement partir. Parfois d'ailleurs, après avoir appris la mort d'un proche ou d'un parent, ils demandaient quand il allait revenir…

Avec beaucoup de délicatesse, le moine ne la détrompa pas.

Mal à l'aise, le commissaire aux morts étranges écoutait son père sans mot dire et son regard ne quittait pas la pointe de ses bottes. Il releva pourtant la tête lorsque le moine demanda à Sophia si elle se souvenait de qui l'avait enlevé.

Les souvenirs de l'enfant semblaient brouillons, ses impressions se chevauchaient. Elle avait échappé à la surveillance de la servante pour se glisser dans la rue afin de retrouver le chien. Une voiture, noire comme un corbillard, s'était arrêtée près d'elle. Une main gantée, tenant une fiole, sortit de la portière.

— Mon enfant, fit une voix masculine bien timbrée, bois cette potion et tu t'échapperas enfin de ce monde qui te tient prisonnière.

Sophia était restée immobile, à la fois fascinée et terrifiée. Soudain, un bras puissant avait emprisonné les siens tandis qu'un mouchoir humide s'écrasait sur ses narines. Ses muscles étaient devenus tout mous tandis qu'elle flageolait sur ses jambes et que sa vue se brouillait.

Le commissaire aux morts étranges hocha la tête, comprenant toute l'affaire. Tandis qu'un homme accaparait l'attention de l'enfant, un autre se glissait derrière elle pour l'endormir et la jeter dans la voiture.

Sophia pleurait maintenant, revivant ses peurs.

— Que me voulait cet homme qui m'appelait mon enfant ? sanglota-t-elle.

La Dame de l'Eau jeta un regard inquiet au moine mais celui-ci n'avait aucunement l'intention de lui raconter la messe noire dans le cimetière.

— Sophia, nous t'avons retrouvée inconsciente et comme morte. C'est pour cette raison que nous t'avons conduite dans ma cave. Tu t'es ensuite éveillée et tu as commencé à aller et venir dans ma maison. Tout cela est du passé. Aujourd'hui, tu es en sécurité ici. Néanmoins…

Il fit une pause et jeta un bref regard à son fils.

— Néanmoins, il nous paraît plus prudent que tu demeures ici jusqu'au moment où nous arrêterons les deux hommes qui t'ont enlevée.

— Vont-ils revenir ?

— Non, car ils ne savent pas où tu te trouves.

Sophia le regarda avec de grands yeux innocents.

— Pourquoi les adultes font-ils ainsi du mal aux enfants ?

Le moine secoua sombrement la tête.

— C'est une question que je n'ai pas fini de me poser…

Dans cette matinée laiteuse, les deux hommes se pressaient au milieu de la foule des portefaix, des colporteurs et des domestiques. Une armée de jeunes gens s'employait à décrotter bas et chaussures. À un coin de rue, malgré ses doigts gourds de froid, un escamoteur divertissait le public de ses tours de passe-passe. Le moine et son fils lui accordèrent un regard entendu.

— Voici Sartine ! gronda Volnay. Il agite une main vide devant nous et tiens la pleine dans son dos ! Depuis le début, il nous mène en bateau. Cet homme est d'une duplicité sans égale !

Il retrouva son calme, le temps que des pensées cohérentes s'ordonnent dans son esprit. Sartine l'avait intrigué en gardant pour lui son croquis de Sophia. Il s'était même enquis avec une espèce d'émotion de ses conditions de vie avant qu'elle ne trouve la mort. Il avait ensuite rêvé d'elle…

— Cela explique l'intérêt qu'il a toujours manifesté pour cette petite à partir du moment où il a vu le dessin, dit-il.

— Mais pourquoi ne rien nous dire tout en nous confiant cette enquête ? objecta le moine.

— À qui pouvait-il la confier à part nous ? rétorqua Volnay. Tout le monde aurait été étonné que le commissaire aux morts étranges ne soit pas en charge du plus mystérieux des crimes de Paris depuis…

— Depuis la femme sans visage, compléta le moine.

Le commissaire aux morts étranges ne répondit pas. Parler de cette affaire le ramenait à Chiara.

— Père, dit-il brusquement, promets-moi de ne dire à personne où se trouve Sophia.

— Bien entendu.

— Ni à Hélène… surtout pas à Hélène !

Songeuse auprès du feu, Hélène les attendait chez le moine. Elle releva la tête à leur entrée dans une interrogation muette.

— Nous avons retrouvé Sophia, lui apprit le moine d'un ton réjoui.

— Quoi? Comment?

— Grâce à Aristote!

Le commissaire aux morts étranges intervint.

— Ce serait un peu long à expliquer et cette information doit rester secrète. N'avez-vous rien à nous apprendre de votre côté?

— Non. Où se trouve Sophia?

— Cela ne vous regarde pas, décréta froidement le commissaire aux morts étranges. Je répète ma question : n'avez-vous rien à nous apprendre?

Hélène demeura impassible. Ses beaux yeux verts mouchetés d'étoiles étaient aussi peu expressifs qu'une pierre précieuse.

— Rien, répondit-elle.

Volnay se tourna théâtralement vers le moine.

— Père, la preuve en est donnée que nous ne pouvons faire confiance à Hélène puisqu'elle nous cache des informations de la plus haute importance.

La jeune femme ne broncha pas.

— Que voulez-vous dire?

Volnay se planta devant elle, irradiant d'une satisfaction mauvaise.

— Vous ne nous racontez pas vos visites à un ancien inspecteur de police à Paris ou à une accoucheuse? Ni celle de Sartine, ensuite, à votre domicile?

Hélène le contempla avec des yeux ronds. La surprise semblait l'avoir figée sur place.

— Comment savez-vous? murmura-t-elle.

Puis un éclair de colère traversa brutalement son regard.

— Les mouches ! s'exclama-t-elle horrifiée. Vous m'avez fait suivre par des mouches !

Le commissaire aux morts étranges eut un imperceptible haussement d'épaules.

— Pas exactement, c'est Sartine qui vous fait suivre par ses mouches. Moi, je me suis contenté d'acheter l'une d'elles !

Il se tourna vers son père et lâcha avec bonne humeur.

— Tu vois qu'il n'y a pas que toi qui utilises l'argent de Sartine à des fins qu'il ne soupçonne pas !

Un rare sourire illumina son visage et ses yeux pétillèrent de gaieté. Tout à coup, Hélène eut l'impression de voir en lui son père le moine tel qu'il avait pu être plus jeune.

— En l'occurrence, reprit Volnay, j'achète une mouche de Sartine avec l'argent de Sartine !

Cette fois, il rit comme si la chose le ravissait. Le moine et Hélène le contemplèrent avec effarement.

— J'oubliais de vous dire, précisa le commissaire aux morts étranges en reprenant son sérieux, que la mouche en question a cuisiné l'accoucheuse. Il lui a fait très peur, aussi lui a-t-elle avoué ce qu'elle vous avait confié. Pour la mouche, cela ne signifiait pas grand-chose, ces gens-là se contentent d'espionner, de faire parler puis de rapporter sans toujours comprendre.

Hélène chercha en vain à sonder le regard de Volnay pour savoir s'il mentait. Peine perdue. Qui donc pouvait se vanter de lire dans ce puits sans fond ? Elle se décida et dit très rapidement à l'attention du moine :

— Sartine m'a fait suivre par ses mouches. Il a su le résultat de mes découvertes et m'a interdit d'en parler à quiconque.

Aiguillonné par le serpent du doute, le moine fixa Hélène d'un œil étincelant.

— Je comprends. Néanmoins, fit-il d'un ton où perçait le regret, entre nous et Sartine, il vous faut choisir votre camp !

Impressionné par la fermeté de son ton, Volnay jeta un regard approbateur à son père.

— Cette accoucheuse, reprit Hélène d'un ton égal, a mis au monde le bébé d'une danseuse de l'Opéra il y a douze ans. La mère ne voulait pas de l'enfant qui a été confiée à sa dame de compagnie de l'époque : Mme Marly. Celle-ci a quitté son emploi contre sans doute une rente. Son mari était alors joaillier. À sa mort, deux ans plus tard, il a vendu son commerce pour se livrer à sa passion : l'astrologie.

Impavide, le moine acquiesça sans mot dire.

— Et comment se nommait cette jeune danseuse de l'Opéra ? s'enquit son fils.

C'était reconnaître qu'il l'ignorait. Hélène eut le sentiment d'avoir été jouée. La mouche de Volnay n'avait pas questionné l'accoucheuse. Cela dit, rien n'empêchait le redoutable commissaire aux morts étranges de le faire plus tard. Aussi, répondit-elle de bonne grâce, son regard accrochant au passage celui du moine dont elle guetta la réaction.

— Mlle Belle Ange.

Un frisson sembla ébranler tout entier le moine. Volnay s'en étonna.

— C'est le froid, je n'arrive pas à me réchauffer, expliqua son père.

Son expression restait indéchiffrable mais ses sentiments remontaient à fleur de peau.

— Intéressant, fit-il en se levant. Je te laisse réfléchir là-dessus, mon fils. Moi, je vais visiter mes pauvres, cela me changera les idées.

— Tu me laisses pour tes bonnes œuvres alors que

nous venons de découvrir que Sophia n'est pas morte et que nous avons un nouvel indice ? s'étonna le commissaire aux morts étranges.

— Tu n'es pas seul, répondit son père d'un ton sarcastique. Hélène est là. J'ai toute confiance en sa sagacité et en ton esprit logique !

Quittant la rue de l'Arbalète, il emprunta la rue des Postes puis la rue Sainte-Geneviève. Là, il entra chez une fripière qui, le reconnaissant, le conduisit sans mot dire à l'arrière de sa boutique. Elle lui porta des vêtements dignes d'un gentilhomme et l'aida à enfiler une chemise de soie, un gilet brodé et à nouer son jabot. Une culotte à pont d'un bleu éclatant souligna sa taille mince et une veste à velours de soie sa belle prestance. Ainsi paré, et après s'être complaisamment admiré dans une glace, le moine lui glissa quelques pièces dans la main et elle lui ouvrit une porte qui donnait sur une cour. Il s'inclina pour lui baiser galamment la main et l'appela *princesse des étoffes*, ce qui la fit rougir de plaisir.

— Attention, le prévint-elle, le sol est très glissant jusqu'à l'immeuble d'en face.

Il sortit donc d'un pas prudent en murmurant :

— Eh bien, je souhaite beaucoup de plaisir à la mouche qui m'attend devant cette friperie !

Une patache survint. Il se gara prudemment pour éviter d'être renversé ou de salir ses beaux vêtements contre les essieux de la voiture.

Restés seuls, Volnay et Hélène se regardèrent en chiens de faïence.

— Vous vous valez bien vous et Sartine, grogna enfin le policier. Dire qu'il nous lance sur une enquête sans nous apprendre ce qu'il sait, nous adjoint les services d'une femme pour nous aider et lui interdit de nous révéler ce qu'elle a trouvé !

La jeune femme soutint son regard avec une expression d'audace sur le visage.

— Vous avez raison sur un point : Sartine ne veut pas que cela se sache. Il était très fâché de ma découverte.

Elle réfléchit rapidement. Ce n'était pas à elle de révéler à Volnay que son père pouvait être aussi celui de Sophia.

— Votre père ne semblait pas intéressé à connaître le nom du géniteur de Sophia mais vous peut-être…

— J'allais vous poser la question, la coupa Volnay.

— L'accoucheuse ne connaissait pas le nom du père, dit-elle rapidement, mais le jour de l'enterrement, elle a aperçu dans le corridor M. de Sartine.

Le commissaire aux morts étranges se figea.

— Sartine encore… murmura-t-il.

Voici pourquoi le carrosse de Sartine s'était arrêté devant Sophia et que le lieutenant général de police lui avait demandé son nom, souri et tendu une pièce. Sophia était sa fille ! Volnay exhala profondément comme pour se vider d'une trop grande colère.

— Ce maudit bougre savait tout cela depuis le départ mais il n'en a rien dit !

Toute sa rancune envers son supérieur trouvait à s'exprimer en cette occasion.

— Je vais aller le voir !

Hélène se jeta à son bras, l'épouvante se lisait sur son visage.

— Non, il saura que j'ai parlé et sa rancune sera terrible envers moi ! À moins que vous ne lui racontiez que vous le faites espionner par une de ses propres mouches et alors sa vengeance s'abattra sur vous !

Volnay la dévisagea avec étonnement.

— Vous avez peur de lui?

— Terriblement!

Son visage était d'une pâleur diaphane.

— Pas vous? demanda-t-elle d'une petite voix.

— Mais… non…

Volnay réfléchit.

— Mais parfois pour mon père, oui…

— Et l'inverse doit être vrai, remarqua Hélène.

Le commissaire aux morts étranges la contempla pensivement puis alla prendre son manteau.

— Rassurez-vous, je vais simplement le voir pour le convaincre de nous confier de nouveau l'enquête. Je lui dirai que je suis sur les traces de Sophia et que je me fais fort de la retrouver sous deux jours.

— Vous allez lui livrer cette petite?

— Lui livrer?

Il s'était planté devant elle et l'affrontait.

— Lui livrer? répéta-t-il d'un ton offusqué. Vous oubliez que cet homme, si impitoyable qu'il paraisse, pense être son père. Et de toute façon, nous ne pourrons lui cacher bien longtemps Sophia. Que voulez-vous donc que nous fassions d'elle? La dissimuler et l'élever dans la clandestinité?

Il se dirigea vers la porte et, lorsqu'il l'ouvrit, se retourna une dernière fois.

— Je ne le crains pas mais j'ai appris une chose ces dernières années, c'est que l'on ne peut pas avoir sur terre pire ennemi que Sartine!

L'hiver aidant, de grands braseros brûlaient dans les cours des hôtels particuliers de la rue Saint-Honoré, délicate attention pour les invités lorsqu'ils descendaient de leurs carrosses. Pendant ce temps, dans les rues, on mourait de froid.

Sans hésiter, le moine se dirigea vers l'entrée et se fit annoncer sous son nom. Il savait que Mlle Belle Ange était devenue Mme de Morange. À l'époque, les mauvaises langues insinuèrent qu'elle avait conservé ainsi son ange. Son mari était riche mais réputé pour être fort bête. Pour se moquer de lui, des amis de la nouvelle Mme de Morange lui prêtèrent un livre, chose fort nouvelle pour lui, puis un second du même auteur qui était en fait le même. "Tout ceci est très intéressant, avait dit le mari, mais l'auteur se répète un peu…"

Dans l'antichambre, un valet somnolent se redressa en sursaut. Il portait une livrée rouge garnie de galons tissés aux couleurs et armoiries de sa maîtresse.

Mme de Morange était encore à sa toilette du matin, la toilette légère, et, comme toutes les dames de la bonne société, elle y recevait. Celle plus sérieuse du soir s'y accompagnait d'un bain de modestie. Il s'agissait d'un bain moussant qui préservait l'intimité de l'hôtesse à ses visiteurs.

La maîtresse des lieux se trouvait entre les mains de son coiffeur. Autour d'elle trônaient dans un joyeux désordre des boîtes à poudre, des boîtes à mouches, des pots à pommade et des flacons de parfum. De jolis bronzes et d'exquises porcelaines décoraient des consoles et des tables de marbre. Deux petits marquis occupaient des fauteuils de noyer sculpté, ornés de tapisseries de soie au petit point. Le moine dissimula sa contrariété et, d'un regard, jaugea les importuns. De jeunes prétentieux à la langue bien pendue qui savaient tout sans avoir jamais rien fait, s'étant donné comme seul labeur celui de naître.

Le moine fut accueilli dans ce lieu exquis par la maîtresse de maison avec une surprise ravie. Du moins, c'est ce qu'elle laissa paraître. Mme de Morange dardait sur le monde des yeux de poupée de faïence. Son visage était fin, sa bouche vermeille se découpait en un arc gracieux et elle présentait une gorge bien blanche. Elle possédait les mille et une manières de plaire de ces femmes éduquées pour cela ou ayant tout compris de la vanité des hommes.

Malgré lui, le moine ressentit un frisson nostalgique. Il se souvenait d'une époque où les baisers coulaient de ses lèvres. Il observa les plis rouges de celles-ci tandis qu'elle parlait d'une voix fraîche et sucrée. Son regard glissa ensuite le long de son corps, admirant la robe en fil de soie bleu, aux broderies au point de chaînette et aux boutons recouverts de taffetas doré. À la naissance de ses seins, sa poitrine semblait jaillir en globes de l'échancrure de sa robe. Sagement posées sur ses genoux, il lui trouva également les plus belles mains du monde, blanches et délicates, perdues dans un flot de dentelles, et le lui dit. Cela fit rire les petits courtisans.

— Monsieur est d'une galanterie d'une autre époque, remarqua l'un d'eux.

Le sourire du moine vacilla.

— Vous avez l'esprit en écharpe, leur répondit-il, je ne vous comprends guère !

Le coiffeur frisa les cheveux de Mme de Morange avec des papillotes et des fers chauds. Pendant ce temps, la conversation allait bon train. On faisait assaut d'esprit tout en se moquant des absents. Le moine jouait son rôle avec une indifférence étudiée, l'air vaguement ennuyé par la conversation des deux petits marquis. L'acuité de son regard démentait toutefois cette fausse nonchalance. Il était prompt à relever leurs erreurs, à redresser un propos ou se moquer d'eux sans y paraître. Comme leurs habits étaient surchargés de dorure, il leur dit humblement :

— Je fais pâle figure à côté de vous qui êtes dorés comme un calice !

Ils froncèrent les sourcils et décidèrent de se liguer contre lui, faisant allusion à son âge avancé et l'appelant grand-père des sages.

— Décidément, marmonna le moine, c'est l'évangile du jour !

— Madame, fit soudain le plus jeune des petits marquis à la maîtresse de maison. On ne voit plus à vos dîners ce monsieur toujours assis en bout de table, qui ne parle jamais et a l'air un peu bête…

— Il s'agit de mon mari, répondit-elle aimablement, et il est mort l'année dernière.

Cette fois, le moine éclata et dit aux jeunes marquis :

— Vous avez la bouche trop près des oreilles, vous vous écoutez parler comme de jeunes sots que vous êtes ! Sortez donc avant que je ne vous embroche sur mon épée !

Ils sortirent en se bousculant comme des gazelles et l'on entendit nettement l'un d'eux dire à l'autre d'un ton offusqué :

— Cet homme est grossier et sans industrie !

Le sourire du moine s'accentua et il se tourna vers la maîtresse de maison.

— Vos petits marquis ont des cervelles de colibri.

— Ne me les abîmez pas, ils sont de très bonne famille !

— Oh, ne vous inquiétez pas, la rassura le moine, je ne sors désormais mon épée que pour les affaires sérieuses.

Et il ajouta après réflexion :

— Je suis désolé d'apprendre la mort de votre mari…

Mme de Morange haussa les épaules d'un air indifférent.

— Ne le soyez pas, c'est vrai qu'il était bête et son seul mérite est d'avoir fait de moi une veuve très convenable.

— Je qualifierais en d'autres termes que *convenable* une veuve de trente-deux ans, si je ne m'abuse, aussi fraîche et belle que vous !

Flattée, elle hocha modestement la tête.

— Quel beau parleur !

— Oh, la langue est une des rares choses qui ne rouille pas avec l'âge !

Elle sourit.

— Mais que me vaut le plaisir de vous voir après tant d'années ? Comment se fait-il que vous ayez tout à coup trouvé le chemin de ma demeure ?

Le front du moine se plissa de rides profondes.

— Une fâcheuse affaire, madame, très fâcheuse.

— Mon Dieu, vous m'effrayez…

Il posa sur elle un regard triste.

— Madame, pardonnez-moi de raviver peut-être de mauvais souvenirs mais il y a douze ans, vous avez donné naissance à une enfant que vous abandonnâtes le jour d'après.

Mme de Morange chancela et porta la main à son cœur.

— Mon Dieu, pourquoi me parler de cela ? Pourquoi remuer ainsi le passé ? Que vous prend-il ?

— Cette jeune fille est aujourd'hui au cœur d'une enquête policière. Vous ne le savez peut-être pas mais j'assiste le commissaire aux morts étranges de Paris.

Mme de Morange agita frénétiquement son éventail.

— Lui est-il arrivé quelque chose ?

Le moine la contempla un instant sans rien dire puis secoua doucement la tête.

— Non madame, n'ayez crainte.

— Alors, je ne comprends pas.

— Il n'y a rien à comprendre, fit-il, une enquête de police a lieu sur ses parents adoptifs. J'ai besoin de renseignements sur Sophia.

— La vérité est que je n'en ai malheureusement aucun à vous donner, regretta-t-elle.

— La vérité est que vous n'avez rien à faire de cette enfant, corrigea le moine.

— Que voulez-vous, mon cher, répondit-elle négligemment, je n'ai pas l'instinct maternel. D'autres l'ont pour moi !

Le moine la considéra gravement.

— Vous pouvez, certes, ne pas me répondre. C'est votre droit le plus strict, comme est mon droit d'aller poser la question à mon supérieur, M. de Sartine.

Mme de Morange se troubla.

— Que vient faire là M. de Sartine ?

— C'est un homme que j'apprécie beaucoup, dit sans rire le moine. Et sans doute, le personnage le mieux renseigné de tout notre royaume.

Son hôtesse prit un ton enjôleur :

— Déranger le lieutenant général de police pour cela alors que je pourrais tout vous révéler…

— Me direz-vous enfin qui est le père de cet enfant ?

Le moine perdait patience mais sans hausser le ton et il accompagna cette question d'une gracieuse révérence comme pour s'excuser d'insister. Mme de Morange cilla nerveusement.

— Soit, je vous le dirai mais ce soir, après le souper que je donne et à la condition que vous l'animiez suffisamment de votre brillant esprit.

Devant ce caprice de femme du monde, le moine conserva son sang-froid. Mme de Morange était charmante mais son cerveau ne pesait pas plus lourd que celui d'un moineau. Il s'inclina devant elle.

— Il en sera fait selon vos désirs…

Dans son bureau du Châtelet, Sartine se retourna vivement et s'empressa de réajuster sa perruque. Un valet était en train de la poudrer à l'aide d'une grosse houppe emplie d'un mélange de farine et de racine réduite. Pour se protéger de la poudre qui volait, le lieutenant général de police portait un cône sur le visage qui lui donnait l'apparence d'un grand échassier. Il l'ôta brusquement et toussa. Volnay réprima un sourire. Lorsque Sartine se poudrait, il devait y en avoir pour une journée de pain !

— Pour qui donc vous prenez-vous à forcer ainsi ma porte ? gronda ce dernier.

— Je suis sur le point de retrouver Sophia !

Avec satisfaction, Volnay vit Sartine se troubler. D'un geste sec, il congédia son laquais.

— Sophia ? s'écria-t-il. Elle est donc toujours en vie ?

— Toujours, oui.

Sartine ferma les yeux un bref instant.

— Ramenez-la-moi et il vous sera beaucoup pardonné, dit-il très rapidement.

— Je n'avais pas le sentiment d'avoir trop de choses à me faire pardonner, remarqua froidement le commissaire aux morts étranges. Mais n'êtes-vous pas désireux que je vous ramène également le criminel derrière tout cela?

Le regard du lieutenant général de police se fit calculateur.

— Son père, l'astrologue? Peut-être auriez-vous meilleur marché de me le ramener avec une balle entre les deux yeux! Cela éviterait beaucoup d'explications…

— Évidemment!

— Oh, ne prenez pas vos airs supérieurs, Volnay! Je m'efforce de maintenir l'ordre royal et il est menacé. La messe noire, la mort du curé dansant et les arrestations de Siltieri ne sont pas passées inaperçues et c'était sans doute l'intention de ce dernier. L'imagination fait le reste! J'ai ici un rapport selon lequel, dans un cabaret où l'on s'ivrognait, une femme de mauvaise vie prise de boisson a évoqué le diable. Aussitôt, au dire des témoins, celui-ci est apparu, l'a soulevée dans les airs avant de la projeter contre un mur, comme un fétu de paille, lui brisant le crâne!

— Ce sont les autres convives qui ont dû la tuer.

— Sans doute mais j'ai encore trois rapports de police où le guet a dû s'introduire dans des maisons car l'esprit malin frappait dans les murs ou détruisait tout sur son passage. Un gendre a même été tué par son beau-père qui l'avait pris dans la nuit pour Satan en personne alors qu'il se rendait à la cuisine pour calmer une petite faim!

— Quelqu'un alimente ces rumeurs et colporte des ragots!

— Et qui donc croyez-vous que ce soit, sinon le parti des dévots? hurla Sartine.

Il se calma et réajusta sa perruque.

— Vous les connaissez pourtant et les conclusions de Siltieri vont dans leur sens. Plus on craint le diable, plus on craint Dieu et plus ils ont d'influence !

Volnay hocha la tête, toutes ces considérations politiques ne lui avaient pas échappé mais son affaire à lui était simplement de trouver des meurtriers. À chacun ses préoccupations !

— Puis-je reprendre mon enquête et vous ramener Sophia ? demanda-t-il tranquillement.

Le lieutenant général de police le considéra attentivement, cherchant sans succès à percer le masque impénétrable de son collaborateur.

— Quarante-huit heures à partir de maintenant, siffla-t-il. Pas une minute de plus. À vous et vous seul !

— J'ai besoin de mon père pour réussir !

— Votre père décline. Il croit qu'il a toujours vingt ans mais ce n'est pas le cas.

— Où voulez-vous en venir ?

Sartine lui jeta un regard glacé.

— À ceci : votre père a jugé morte Sophia lorsqu'elle était vivante. Il est dépassé. Je ne peux plus l'employer dans ma police.

Il leva la main en l'air pour interrompre les protestations du commissaire aux morts étranges.

— Il y a pire ! Votre père se livre à l'exercice de la chimie qui conduit inévitablement à des agissements plus dangereux comme la transmutation des métaux en or. Des arrêts ont été rendus par le Parlement de Paris en matière de sortilèges et de maléfices. L'enrichissement par l'alchimie ou la recherche de trésors par conjuration d'esprits sont interdits et punissables !

Volnay l'arrêta d'un geste.

— Vous savez bien que mon père est un scientifique et que seule le pousse sa curiosité intellectuelle.

Sartine coupa court à sa défense.

— Votre père est un danger pour moi comme pour vous. Oh, je ne suis pas un ingrat. En récompense de ses bons services, je lui ferai attribuer une jolie pension et il pourra se retirer à la campagne. Pourquoi pas en Bourgogne ? C'est une terre si riante…

Il se campa devant son subordonné, les pieds écartés et les mains dans le dos, adoptant un ton d'une rondeur enjouée.

— Là-bas, il pourra se livrer à toutes les expériences qu'il souhaite dans un beau laboratoire que nous lui ferons installer…

Un sourire rusé s'afficha sur ses lèvres.

— Qui sait, peut-être qu'une fois le poids de ses enquêtes enlevé de ses épaules il trouvera le secret de l'élixir de longue vie et nous enterrera tous !

La fausse bonne humeur de Sartine inquiéta Volnay.

— Et si mon père trouvait la solution de notre énigme, le réintégreriez-vous dans votre police ?

— Cela n'arrivera pas ! répondit Sartine. Cela ne peut arriver !

On frappa. D'un ton impatient, le lieutenant général de police ordonna d'entrer. Un valet lui remit un pli après moult courbettes. Sartine fronça les sourcils en voyant le sceau et le déplia d'une main fébrile. Sans qu'il sût pourquoi, Volnay vit la figure de son supérieur devenir mortellement pâle. Finalement, le lieutenant général de police congédia le laquais et se tourna vers Volnay.

— Le roi, dit-il. Il veut nous voir tous les deux.

Dire que Sartine parut contrarié aurait été un euphémisme. Jamais, le commissaire aux morts étranges n'avait observé son supérieur dans un tel état d'agitation. Comme s'il en était conscient, Sartine expira doucement, ferma brièvement les yeux et les rouvrit pour les poser sur Volnay.

— Nous allons nous mettre d'accord sur l'histoire à raconter au roi, dit-il.

Le moine se dirigea vers l'Observatoire. Lui et son fils avaient déjà discuté de la nécessité de cette visite mais les événements qui se succédaient à un rythme frénétique l'avaient toujours repoussée à demain.

Construit au siècle dernier sous Louis XIV, l'Observatoire royal était une construction rectangulaire flanquée de deux tours octogonales à ses angles méridionaux. Une troisième tour carrée servait d'entrée au nord. Haut de vingt-six mètres, le bâtiment était imposant et l'atmosphère à l'intérieur confortait l'impression que ceux qui y demeuraient se sentaient investis d'une mission suprême. Le moine avait bien connu l'un des astronomes qui y travaillait, un certain Jean de Foy. Il s'enquit de lui et bientôt un homme au profil énergique et aux yeux de charbon le rejoignit. Sous sa veste, il portait un gilet de taffetas agrémenté de broderies de soie. Le moine le salua comme s'ils s'étaient quittés la veille. L'autre le considéra avec attention, ses yeux pleins d'une prudence visible, avant de le reconnaître.

— Messire Guillaume de…

— Pas de nom, pas de nom! le coupa vivement le moine. Ma situation n'est pas officielle même si j'aide à mener des enquêtes qui le sont!

Jean de Foy approuva d'un mouvement sec du menton.

— Je comprends, dit-il.

Il tira de sa poche une longue bouffarde de terre blanche puis, sortant sa tabatière, entreprit de découper une carotte de tabac.

— *Nicotiana tabacum*, murmura le moine en plissant les yeux.

— Je préfère la pipe à la prise, précisa l'astronome comme s'il fallait s'en excuser.

— Éternuer est réservé aux gens de la bonne société, dit gaiement le moine en pensant à Sartine.

L'autre, décontenancé, haussa un sourcil.

— Que puis-je pour vous ?

— Je m'intéresse à M. Marly. Il a trouvé la mort dans l'incendie de sa maison, le saviez-vous ?

— Oui, les nouvelles circulent vite à Paris !

— L'avez-vous connu ? questionna le moine.

Jean de Foy jeta un regard circulaire autour de lui.

— Ne préférez-vous pas faire quelques pas dans le jardin ?

— Certes, dit le moine en souriant.

— Je vais chercher mon manteau.

Leurs pas crissèrent bientôt sur la neige tassée qui recouvrait l'allée.

— M. Marly, n'est-ce pas ? fit l'astronome en soufflant la fumée entre ses dents serrées sur le tuyau de sa bouffarde. Oui, il venait parfois lorsqu'il se posait des questions et comme sa connaissance des étoiles était extrêmement pointue et précise, nous avions toujours plaisir à discuter avec lui, même s'il n'était pas des nôtres.

— Que savez-vous de lui ?

Jean de Foy se gratta la tête.

— Je crois que son père était officier de marine.

Il baissa le ton pour qu'on ne l'entende pas.

— Il s'est fait tuer loin des siens au cours d'une guerre inutile, laissant seule sa femme élever son fils…

— Parlez-moi de lui. Il s'intéressait à des choses bien étranges…

— Vous parlez des étoiles?

— Des étoiles et de ce que l'on peut en faire…

Jean de Foy réfléchit une seconde et hocha la tête.

— Il est vrai que M. Marly développait des idées peu conformes à celles du pouvoir royal. À vous je peux le dire. Même si la science d'aujourd'hui nous fait tout passer au crible de la raison, il n'en reste pas moins que les sciences humaines ont observé maintes choses merveilleuses et inexplicables.

Il posa une main fraternelle sur l'épaule du moine.

— Mais nous sommes des scientifiques, vous comprenez cela? Aux yeux de la police, la limite est floue entre astrologie et magie. Nous autres, astronomes, nous observons les étoiles. Les astrologues, eux, les font parler.

— Que croyait Marly?

L'autre soupira.

— Que tout était écrit dans la voûte étoilée. La géomancie astronomique pour connaître les choses passées, présentes et celles futures.

Il fit une pause, regardant autour de lui et formant sans en être vraiment conscient un globe de ses mains.

— Vous savez, l'astronomie a pour but l'observation et la découverte des étoiles, nous ne tirons pas de conclusion autre que scientifique dans cet Observatoire. L'astrologie, elle, s'est développée à partir de croyances puisant dans des civilisations aussi riches que variées, en Perse, à Babylone ou en Égypte, le tout saupoudré de philosophie grecque. Aujourd'hui, les astrologues observent le mouvement des planètes et, à partir d'une date de naissance, révèlent le caractère

et le destin de cette personne. Mais d'autres s'intéressent à quelque chose de plus grand.

— La divination, suggéra le moine.

— Oui. En Chine comme dans les Amériques, on
dresse depuis longtemps des calendriers prophétiques.
Cela fascinait Marly. Que ce ne soit pas que les des-
tins individuels qui soient prédéterminés mais aussi
le sort des civilisations.

Il marqua une pause et ajouta :

— Et aussi que l'on puisse influencer la destinée sur
terre en s'appuyant sur le secret des étoiles.

— Le secret ?

Jean de Foy haussa les épaules.

— Dieu me garde de le connaître, je serais le plus
savant des hommes ! Mais Marly estimait que si l'on
accomplissait telle chose, avec la bonne conjonction
des étoiles, on possédait plus de chance pour que tout
se passe parfaitement.

Le moine hocha la tête.

— C'est le principe même de l'astrologie ! Mais
dites-moi, je me souviens d'avoir vu sur son bureau
un livre sur l'Apocalypse. Bien étrange lecture pour
un admirateur des étoiles.

Jean de Foy se troubla.

— Dites-moi tout mon ami, fit doucement le moine,
vous savez bien que nous sommes du même bord.

L'astronome écarta la bouffarde de ses lèvres et se
racla la gorge.

— Il existe une tradition selon laquelle le Christ
serait descendu trois jours aux Enfers après sa mort
et avant sa résurrection. Nul ne sait ce qui s'est passé
durant ce séjour mais l'on dit qu'aux Enfers le Christ
aurait remis à Lucifer une étoile à cinq branches. Pourquoi ? Cette question tourmentait bizarrement Marly.

— Je comprends, murmura le moine. Selon l'Apocalypse, le mal doit être racheté à la fin des temps. Lucifer donnera alors aux justes l'*Étoile du matin* et recouvrera son état angélique.

Il inspira profondément.

— Serait-ce l'Étoile du matin que le Christ a remise à Lucifer ?

Jean de Foy s'arrêta de marcher et toussota. Une écharde de brume semblait plantée dans sa gorge.

— Ce n'est pas quelque chose dont on peut discuter avec tout le monde car cela signifierait que Lucifer est en fait le serviteur du Christ.

Les yeux du moine s'étrécirent.

— Étoile tombée du ciel, il aurait volontairement accepté de tomber dans le mal pour servir les desseins de Dieu, tout comme Judas, la rage au cœur, trahit Jésus pour accomplir sa mission et achever l'œuvre…

Il se tourna vers Jean de Foy.

— Savez-vous ce qu'il avait en tête ?

— Je l'ignore mais…

L'astronome s'arrêta net, sous le coup d'une pensée.

— Il citait souvent Shakespeare, un auteur anglais.

— Je connais. Que disait-il ?

Jean de Foy plissa les yeux puis, les mains théâtralement levées, récita :

— *"Lorsque les mendiants meurent, on ne voit aucune comète ;*

Mais les cieux s'enflamment d'eux-mêmes à la mort des princes !"

XXI

VERSAILLES ET AUTRES DIABLERIES

Figés sous le givre, les jardins de Versailles déga-geaient une impression féerique. Volnay ne leur accorda pourtant qu'un regard éteint. Tous ces carrés de verdure glacés, ces allées rectilignes et ces angles droits ne reflétaient pour lui qu'une société trop sur-veillée et en coupe réglée. Son esprit aspirait à plus de courbes, de souplesse et de liberté.

Un nuage de poudre annonça le passage d'un cour-tisan aussi immaculé que le mont Blanc tellement il s'était poudré à la toilette. La rencontre des dames de la cour, transies dans leurs beaux atours au milieu de leurs promenades, le laissa de marbre. Les perruques des hommes lui semblaient trop poudrées, les coiffures des femmes de véritables pièces montées et leurs joues trop colorées par les rouges pour rehausser le teint. La mine superbe et la gorge blanche, ces femmes ne le faisaient pas rêver. Elles nourrissaient à leur façon l'atmosphère de fin de partie d'une cour décadente, arc-boutée sur son arrogance et ses privilèges.

Volnay regarda du coin de l'œil les courtisans regroupés dans les couloirs glacés du château. Si son expression demeurait indéchiffrable, répulsion et dégoût s'agitaient en lui. Non contents de posséder la majorité des terres de France, tous les courtisans grouillant autour du monarque s'accaparaient encore rentes et pensions. Du matin au soir, ces inutiles gravitaient autour d'un seul point fixe : le roi. Dès l'aube, gagnés par l'unique obsession d'être vus de celui-ci, ils s'affolaient dans les escaliers et les corridors pour se trouver sur son passage. Leur journée se passait ainsi dans une course éperdue après leur astre pour parvenir peut-être à assister à son coucher. Un duc racontait que le plus beau jour de sa vie était celui où il avait porté la lumière pour le coucher du roi !

La vie des courtisans était une vie d'esclaves. Il leur fallait faire des grâces pour être admis à dîner par quelqu'un en vue qui leur permettrait de rencontrer un proche du roi. Ensuite, ils devraient manœuvrer auprès de celui-ci pour être conviés à un des soupers royaux. Les plus chanceux parviendraient à se faire inviter à la chasse du roi qui forçait le cerf trois à quatre fois par semaine pour oublier ses idées noires. La récompense de cette interminable partie de chasse se manifestait parfois sous la forme d'une invitation à l'un de ces petits voyages qu'affectionnait le roi à Choisy, La Celle ou Marly. Arrivés dans un de ces châteaux, les courtisans se retrouvaient soit dans le camp des "Polissons" qui repartaient au soir dans de grandes voitures inconfortables, soit dans celui des "Logeasses" qui restaient coucher. Le cœur battant, ces derniers se regroupaient alors en bas d'un escalier, attendant qu'un huissier vienne lire la liste des participants au souper.

Telle était la vie à la cour de Versailles.

Volnay jeta un coup d'œil à la dérobée à Sartine. Celui-ci dénotait assurément dans le lot : plus intelligent que la moyenne, plus dangereux... Il accomplissait un dur labeur au service de son roi et en était raisonnablement récompensé. Mais, comme les autres, pour conserver l'estime du monarque, il devait en permanence éviter les pièges de ses concurrents, les chausse-trapes des envieux, flatter la favorite pour rester dans ses bonnes grâces, soigner ses relations avec le Dauphin, se méfier du parti des dévots et se garder des jésuites… toute une vie d'équilibre.

Pour conserver ses privilèges, Volnay savait Sartine prêt à tout. Serviteur sans état d'âme, il avait fait persécuter M. de Tiercelin, qui tentait de préserver la vertu de sa fille des faveurs royales. Celle-ci finit dans une maison du roi, avenue Saint-Cloud. Une fois lassé par la jeune fille, comme par toutes les autres, le monarque se rendit à Saint-Cloud pour jouer une dernière fois son rôle d'amant attentionné avant de les faire embastiller le lendemain, elle et son père. Il la fit libérer plusieurs années plus tard pour qu'elle finisse sa vie au couvent.

Si Volnay avait la patience des chats, Sartine, lui, n'aimait pas attendre. Il soupirait bruyamment, pianotait sur l'accoudoir de son fauteuil et fixait d'un œil courroucé l'huissier impassible comme s'il le rendait responsable de son attente.

Enfin, on les introduisit dans le cabinet de travail du roi qui donnait sur la magnifique cour de Marbre. Le monarque revenait de la chasse et avait offert le pied du cerf tué à une marquise dont il convoitait les faveurs. Maintenant, il tournait en rond car, une fois l'animal tué, il lui fallait un autre gibier.

Louis XV, qui approchait de la cinquantaine, conservait une belle prestance et il portait fort majestueusement son habit et son gilet richement brodés de fils d'or et d'argent. Cependant, tous les excès de sa vie dissolue lui donnaient un teint de plomb et une bouche aux commissures crapuleuses. Cet écart entre majesté et canaillerie devenait frappant selon les sujets qu'il abordait dans la conversation.

— Sire, fit cérémonieusement Sartine en s'inclinant, voici le chevalier de Volnay que vous avez demandé à voir. Notre fameux commissaire aux morts étranges…

Un instant, le roi sembla s'évader du sombre cachot de ses pensées et regarda Volnay avec curiosité.

— J'ai appris que vous retourniez les tombes ?

Le jeune homme cilla brièvement. Il connaissait le caractère morbide du monarque. Celui-ci aimait à s'enquérir de qui était mort ou qui allait bientôt l'être. Une histoire de tombe ouverte devait le fasciner. Mais cela suffisait-il pour le recevoir en particulier ?

— Votre Majesté est bien informée.

— Je suis au courant de tout ce qui se passe dans mon royaume, répondit le roi d'un ton condescendant.

Et il ajouta avec un brin d'ironie :

— Quand ce n'est pas mon bon Sartine qui me le raconte, c'est quelqu'un d'autre qui le fait…

Du coin de l'œil, Volnay vit le lieutenant général de police pâlir imperceptiblement. Il savait qu'avec ce roi la disgrâce frappait sans prévenir. Un soir, il vous parlait aimablement et vous félicitait, le lendemain, vous étiez démis de vos fonctions sans rien comprendre.

— Alors, cette tombe ? s'impatienta Louis XV.

Le commissaire aux morts étranges sentit tout le poids du regard de Sartine sur lui et répondit comme convenu :

— Sire, j'ai pris sur moi de faire ouvrir une tombe car je soupçonnais que la bonne personne ne s'y trouvait pas.

Une lueur d'intérêt traversa l'œil du roi.

— Racontez-moi ça.

Volnay jeta un coup d'œil de côté. Sartine fixait un point du mur devant lui avec une indifférence affectée.

— Sire, expliqua le commissaire aux morts étranges, par un incroyable concours de circonstances les cadavres de deux victimes d'un meurtre ont été inversés.

— Voyez-vous donc ! Mais comment est-ce possible ?

Sartine jugea opportun d'intervenir.

— Sire, lui rappela-t-il, il s'agit de cette affaire de messe noire dans un cimetière.

Le roi pâlit.

— Messe noire, murmura-t-il d'un ton atone. Il n'y a jamais rien eu de tel sous mon règne.

Sartine s'agita à côté de Volnay.

— Monsieur le lieutenant général de police, lui dit le roi, il est important que vous disiez à vos policiers de ma part tout ce que des gens de bien comme eux doivent faire pour déconcerter ceux qui, de quelque qualité qu'ils soient, sont mêlés à un si vilain commerce.

Il avait parlé d'un ton ferme, inhabituel. Tout ce qu'il y avait d'adulte et de responsable en lui s'était concentré dans cette phrase. Un instant, Volnay le vit comme il aurait pu être s'il avait pris son devoir de roi au sérieux et considéré l'étendue des obligations de sa charge envers ses sujets. Puis sa curiosité malsaine reprit le dessus et l'impression passa :

— Dans quel état se trouvait le cadavre lorsque vous avez fait ouvrir le cercueil ?

Sartine lui avait soufflé préalablement sa réponse, aussi Volnay fit comme son supérieur attendait de lui. Pour amuser le roi, Sartine prit le relais, racontant que les embaumeurs devaient être saouls pour avoir inversé les deux cadavres et qu'il était très difficile de creuser la terre dans les cimetières par ce froid avec la couche de neige qui recouvrait la terre.

Le roi se lassa vite. C'était Louis XV. Trop éphémère, tout plaisir le laissait sans joie une fois l'instant passé. L'anecdote l'avait amusé quelques secondes avant qu'il ne retombe dans son mortel ennui.

— Cette enquête avance-t-elle? demanda-t-il soudain.

Son regard glacé pesait lourdement sur eux. Sartine se raidit.

— Oui, sauf erreur de sa part, le chevalier de Volnay est en passe de remonter une piste jusqu'au commanditaire.

C'était là faire peser sur le commissaire aux morts étranges tout le poids de l'échec si l'enquête échouait. Volnay comprit en un quart de seconde l'habileté du lieutenant général de police. L'attention du roi attirée sur cette affaire, il se devait de fournir un coupable. Cela dit, Sartine se montrait rusé en évitant de parler des soupçons pesant sur l'astrologue mort. Cela pouvait constituer une porte de sortie honorable. Trois coupables : la prostituée, le curé renégat et le père de Sophia. Une bonne histoire pour régaler le roi.

Volnay se détendit légèrement. Louis XV se pencha vers son lieutenant général de police.

— Pensez-vous que des gens de ma cour se livrent à de telles choses?

Le ton était coupant.

— Non, sire, s'empressa de le rassurer Sartine. L'enquête du chevalier de Volnay démontre bien qu'il s'agit de gens du peuple, de petits-bourgeois.

Le roi se rejeta en arrière, arborant une moue satisfaite.

— Tant mieux, tant mieux… je ne supporterais pas que des gens de haute naissance sacrifient des êtres humains pour acquérir gloire, richesse et puissance.

C'est pourtant ce que vous faites à longueur d'années, pensa Volnay. *Sacrifier des gens sans autre raison et résultat que satisfaire à votre grandeur et votre gloire… Quant à vos gens de haute naissance, qu'ont-ils de plus que les autres, à part d'être nés dans un berceau doré ?*

— Votre Majesté, fit Sartine en aiguillant de nouveau la conversation dans la direction qu'il souhaitait, dans ce type de messe noire, il est plus souvent question de débauches que de sacrifices.

— Vraiment ? fit Louis XV de nouveau intéressé.

— Sire, généralement la cérémonie sacrilège a lieu dans une cave. On étend un matelas sur des sièges avec des tabourets à chaque bout. Une jeune fille nue s'y couche. Elle est vierge mais ne le demeure pas longtemps !

Le roi s'esclaffa malgré lui.

— Son corps sert d'autel vivant au célébrant, continua Sartine impavide. Il place un calice entre les seins de la vierge et, sur son ventre blanc, un crucifix posé à l'envers. Après avoir chanté la messe à rebours, au moment de l'Offertoire, lorsque les fumées d'encens contenant des parfums capiteux envahissent la pièce, l'assistance arrache ses vêtements et se livre à des luxures éperdues. Le célébrant, quant à lui, s'occupe de son autel…

Volnay jeta un coup d'œil étonné au lieutenant général de police. Celui-ci semblait bien renseigné sur ces pratiques. Le roi, convenablement émoustillé, attendait la suite avec intérêt.

— Ainsi, continua Sartine d'un ton ennuyeux pour bien montrer que le sujet ne l'excitait pas, l'acte accompli, les hommes s'échangent… que dis-je, s'arrachent leurs partenaires et se livrent avec elles à tous

363

les transports possibles, y compris ceux que Dieu comme la Nature réprouvent…

Volnay songea avec tendresse à son père. Celui-ci aurait simplement dit que, le péché de chair se trouvant au centre des préoccupations du monde chrétien, le culte de Satan permettait bien évidemment de s'en libérer dans le délire de la débauche.

— Je peux néanmoins affirmer, reprit le lieutenant général de police, que ces pratiques, existant depuis des siècles, sont fort rares sous le règne de Votre Majesté. L'affaire de cette messe noire dans un cimetière nous a conduits d'ailleurs à nous livrer à des arrestations qui permettront, dans la plus grande discrétion, de mettre totalement fin à ce type de pratiques exécrables.

— Je n'en attendais pas moins de vous. Dites-moi mon bon Sartine, est-il vrai que la duchesse de…

Il jeta un bref regard à Volnay et reporta son attention sur son lieutenant général de police.

— Vous voyez qui je veux dire ?

Sartine hocha la tête.

— Est-il vrai, reprit le roi, qu'elle paillarde avec un garçon d'écurie et ceci aux pieds de ses chevaux ?

— Certes, fit Sartine vaguement gêné par la présence du commissaire aux morts étranges.

— Et est-il exact qu'elle se fasse également monter par les chevaux ?

S'enfermant dans son monde, Volnay n'écouta plus la conversation entre les deux hommes. Le roi y révélait une fois de plus que le seul intérêt qu'il portait aux autres était d'ordre nauséeux. Isolé dans son château glacé de Versailles, à des lieues de l'humanité, il n'aimait personne, pas plus lui que ses proches. Personne.

Le jeune homme se mit à le considérer d'un œil perçant, l'imaginant courir nu autour du lit auprès de toutes jeunes filles. Dans cette nudité, dépouillé de son faste, le roi devait apparaître comme un homme comme les autres.

Sa naissance a placé son destin plus haut que tous, son comportement le fait redescendre plus bas que nous tous, songea-t-il.

Il dut supporter encore quelques minutes le croassement du roi et de son lieutenant général de police. Quand l'audience fut terminée, il suivit Sartine, familier des lieux, pour sortir au plus vite de cet endroit.

Ils empruntèrent la galerie des Glaces et Volnay se questionna à propos de ce détour inutile. Mais sans doute le lieutenant général de police aimait-il à se montrer lorsqu'il revenait de visiter le roi. Peut-être, plus subtilement, désirait-il rappeler à son insolent collaborateur toute la majesté du roi dans le miroir de sa splendeur.

Les miroirs… Reflet des vanités, trois cent cinquante-sept miroirs au mercure apportaient une transparence et une luminosité un peu trouble. Mais l'essentiel se trouvait ailleurs. Quand on parcourait la galerie des Glaces sur ses soixante-treize mètres de longueur, il était inévitable de porter les yeux au plafond pour se perdre dans des cieux d'un bleu unique traversés par mille mètres carrés d'histoire en allégories ou trompe-l'œil.

Se reprenant pour ne pas céder à l'admiration, il baissa la tête et remarqua alors la femme de loin, reconnaissant son port altier mais fatigué. Son beau visage intelligent affichait une grâce tranquille et le charme particulier de ses yeux subjuguait ceux qui croisaient son regard. Une dame de compagnie et plusieurs courtisans marchaient derrière elle. A son passage, on s'empressait de lui faire place et de la saluer avec déférence.

C'était la marquise de Pompadour. Souriant, Volnay s'apprêta à la saluer mais elle détourna la tête en passant près de lui.

— Eh oui, ricana Sartine ravi de sa déconvenue, les amitiés tournent vite avec les grands de ce monde. Vous leur servez un jour, ils vous en récompensent parfois. Et lorsque vous les croisez de nouveau, ils ne vous reconnaissent même pas ou font semblant de ne pas vous remettre !

Comme si une idée nouvelle venait de lui traverser l'esprit, il jeta un regard froid au jeune policier.

— Il me semble tout à coup, chevalier de Volnay, que vous n'avez plus de protecteur en ce beau royaume de France !

Le commissaire aux morts étranges rentra directement de Versailles jusque chez lui, ruminant sombrement l'inexplicable comportement de la marquise de Pompadour. Elle lui devait pourtant beaucoup pour avoir résolu au printemps dernier une affaire dans laquelle elle était impliquée. À sa grande surprise, il trouva son père chez lui, s'adonnant à la conversation avec son amie la pie. Un grand feu flambait dans la cheminée et réchauffait quelque peu la pièce sans que la température atteigne toutefois une quelconque tiédeur.

— Toi ici et seul ! voulut plaisanter Volnay.

Le moine ne releva pas l'allusion à Hélène.

— Je ne suis pas seul puisque j'instruis ta jolie pie ! Elle s'ennuie, tu sais ? Tu la délaisses…

— Et Hélène ?

— J'ignore où elle se trouve depuis ce matin puisque je suis passé à l'Observatoire après avoir rendu visite à Mme de Morange.

— Mme de Morange ?

Le moine fit signe à son fils de s'asseoir près de lui.

— Mlle Belle Ange, jeune danseuse de l'Opéra il y a encore douze ans, a trouvé un riche benêt pour l'épouser il y a une dizaine d'années et est devenue Mme de Morange. Tu devrais un peu plus t'intéresser aux commentaires des gazettes !

Volnay haussa les épaules.

— Et tu ne m'as rien dit !

Le moine eut une moue d'excuse.

— Je ne tenais pas à en parler avec Hélène. Sans les révélations de ta mouche, elle ne nous aurait rien dit de ce qu'elle venait d'apprendre. En conséquence, j'ai revu ma position. Jusqu'à ce que j'aie la preuve qu'elle soit fiable, je me considérerai en droit de lui dissimuler certaines informations. Qui plus est si ce froid au cul de Sartine rôde dans les parages !

Rien ne pouvait faire plus plaisir à son fils.

— D'autant plus, renchérit celui-ci, qu'Hélène nous a été imposée par Sartine lui-même !

— Oui, fit le moine dubitatif.

Il marqua un temps et plissa les yeux. Les rides de curiosité de son front se creusèrent.

— Néanmoins, fit-il, cela ne ressemble pas à Sartine d'employer des femmes, encore moins de nous en lancer dans les pattes.

— Tu sais, remarqua Volnay soucieux, je me suis moi aussi demandé pourquoi Sartine avait introduit Hélène dans notre enquête et notre intimité. J'ai pensé à Hélène de Troie et au cheval de Troie. Le but de Sartine, par l'intermédiaire d'Hélène, n'était-il pas de nous séparer ? Tout ce jeu de la séduction qu'elle a joué avec toi…

Le moine resta impavide. Le souvenir de la jeune femme lorsqu'elle était venue s'allonger près de lui, tout son corps rayonnant d'énergie, le poursuivait encore.

— "Elle a terriblement l'air, quand on l'a devant soi, des déesses immortelles", dit-il en récitant un vers d'Homère sur la vraie Hélène de Troie.

— Celle-là a aidé à déclencher la guerre de Troie, remarqua Volnay, mais j'ai aussi pensé à Hélène de Tyr…

Son père lui jeta un regard noir.

— La prostituée ?

— La compagne de Simon le Magicien, le concurrent de Jésus à l'époque ! Était-elle un ange déchu dans un bordel de Tyr ?

Le regard du moine sembla s'éparpiller autour d'une nuit passée, d'une fleur de lys gravée comme un joyau brûlant sur une épaule lisse.

— Les anges déchus… murmura-t-il. "Elle fut la lune, l'accord parfait, puis un jour, les anges, ses fils, se révoltant contre elle, de son empire la chassèrent et, dans un corps de femme, l'enfermèrent."

Il se tut. Ses regrets étaient autant d'éclats de verre plantés dans son cœur. Son fils l'examina avec curiosité.

— Père, es-tu attaché à cette jeune femme ?

Le moine hésita. À nouveau, son cœur s'affolait mais il n'en montrait rien.

Plus que je ne saurais le dire…

— Je l'apprécie certes beaucoup mais elle a semé le doute dans mon esprit en nous dissimulant des démarches et des informations cruciales.

— Ses relations avec Sartine sont fort troubles, renchérit son fils, elle me paraît assez le craindre pour bien le servir.

Le moine ferma un instant les yeux, lorsqu'il les rouvrit, son regard était de nouveau serein.

— Ne la condamnons pas trop vite comme d'autres l'ont fait pour nous car je la tiens en haute estime. Revenons plutôt au cœur de notre affaire. Après toutes nos découvertes, il semble certain que notre astrologue a voulu sacrifier au diable la fille qu'il avait adoptée, en échange de quelque chose. Le portrait que l'on me fit de M. Marly à l'Observatoire est révélateur. C'est celui d'un illuminé, un illuminé qui s'intéresse autant à l'Apocalypse qu'au roi dont il a tiré l'horoscope, souviens-toi.

— Mais quelle est la raison qui l'a poussé à sacrifier Sophia?

Le moine réfléchit.

— Tu te souviens de l'affaire des Poisons? Nous en avons suffisamment discuté. Lors de son arrestation, on a retrouvé dans les papiers de la marquise de Brinvilliers des lettres de confession dans lesquelles elle s'accusait de ses crimes commis. Elle y racontait aussi son viol, à l'âge de sept ans, par un de ses frères. Le passé n'excuse rien mais explique tout!

— C'est-à-dire?

— Cet homme en veut beaucoup au roi parce que celui-ci a envoyé son père officier se faire tuer sur les mers, laissant sa mère élever seul son fils.

Il s'interrompit et leva les bras d'un geste ample pour réciter:

— *"Lorsque les mendiants meurent, on ne voit aucune comète;*
Mais les cieux s'enflamment d'eux-mêmes à la mort des princes!"

— Qu'est-ce? demanda Volnay.

— Shakespeare! Et lorsque M. Marly le récite, ce n'est à mon avis pas anodin. Il en veut au roi pour avoir bridé les libertés de son peuple et assez peut-être pour le tuer.

— Et ceci en assassinant Sophia…

— Envoûtement de sang. Je te l'ai dit, Sophia est la poupée que l'on sacrifie !

Un silence pensif s'ensuivit, seulement rompu par les jacassements de la pie qui s'affolait en tourbillonnant dans la cage, son plumage reflétant des lueurs métalliques. L'évocation du diable et de ses anges déchus semblait imprégner l'atmosphère de la maison d'une menace impalpable.

— Où étais-tu de ton côté ? s'enquit enfin le moine.

— Au Châtelet, faire la paix avec Sartine. Et de là à Versailles…

— Versailles !

Le commissaire aux morts étranges lui narra sa rencontre avec le roi tandis que son père secouait doucement la tête, un sourire ironique aux lèvres.

— Pour Sartine, conclut le policier, la situation n'est pas aussi désespérée que je le pensais mais elle est néanmoins préoccupante.

Volnay considéra son père d'un œil attentif.

— Sartine ne nous aime pas mais toi il te craint.

Un silence.

— Aurais-tu une quelconque prise sur lui ?

— Non.

— Attention, l'avertit son fils. Tu sais qu'on peut vite se faire égorger au coin d'une rue.

Le moine eut une moue indulgente.

— Un homme menacé peut avoir mis en sécurité certains papiers qui, à sa mort ou sa disparition, peuvent être remis à la bonne personne au bon moment. C'est pour cela que cet homme ne craint pas de se faire égorger au coin d'une rue.

— Tu disposes de moyens de pression sur Sartine? s'étonna Volnay.

— Je ne dis ni oui ni non. Reste à l'écart de tout ça! Moins tu en sauras, mieux cela sera!

Le commissaire aux morts étranges considéra longuement son père. Il le savait homme ouvert mais rempli de secrets accumulés tout au long de son existence.

— Sartine veut t'écarter de moi et donc de son chemin, avoua Volnay mal à l'aise. Il te verrait bien couler de vieux jours paisibles en Bourgogne devant les fourneaux de ton laboratoire.

— Pour que je puisse couler *de vieux jours*, répliqua avec humeur le moine, il faudrait d'abord que je sois vieux et ce n'est pas le cas!

Il se leva vivement et ajouta d'un ton rageur:

— Quant à mes fourneaux, Sartine peut toujours aller se cuire un œuf dessus!

Un coup discret à la porte interrompit le moine.

— Si c'est Sartine, fit-il, son cul va lui en cuire!

Il bondit à la porte.

— Mais ce peut être Hélène, ajouta-t-il en s'apaisant. Ah non, elle ne frappe pas, elle!

Il ouvrit la porte et baissa la tête, surpris de l'apparition d'une frêle jeune fille de seize ans aux vêtements rapiécés et au visage couvert de taches de rousseur.

— Mademoiselle? Vous cherchez quelqu'un?

Elle parut intimidée à sa vue et une légère rougeur envahit son visage. Le moine lui sourit pour la rassurer.

— Ne vous êtes-vous pas trompée de porte?

Prenant son courage à deux mains, elle releva la tête avec plus d'assurance.

— Monsieur, pardonnez-moi mais je cherche M. le commissaire aux morts étranges…

— Oh…

Volnay avait rejoint son père et découvert la visiteuse.

— Entrez, fit-il précipitamment, il fait si froid dehors…

Elle pénétra dans la pièce comme à contrecœur, regardant timidement autour d'elle. Son regard trahit son admiration pour la belle bibliothèque qui regorgeait de livres aux belles enluminures. Elle eut un petit cri de surprise en découvrant la pie.

— Oh, le bel oiseau ! s'exclama-t-elle.

— Elle parle plusieurs langues, intervint le moine avec orgueil. C'est moi qui les lui enseigne !

— Elle est à moi, intervint le commissaire aux morts étranges, en bousculant légèrement son père pour arriver à la cage avant lui. Tenez, ajouta-t-il en se saisissant d'une main de la jeune fille, vous pouvez la caresser, elle y est habituée…

L'Écureuil se laissa faire, partagée entre la crainte et le ravissement, enchantée de la présence de la main de Volnay autour de la sienne. Le moine s'émerveilla de voir son fils sourire et rire en présentant sa maison, fier des rangées bien alignées de ses livres et de sa merveilleuse pie parlante. De son côté, la jeune fille semblait consciente que derrière la sécheresse feinte du commissaire aux morts étranges se dissimulait une sensibilité exacerbée, et les regards qu'elle lui lançait dénotaient plus qu'un simple calcul.

Son tendre intérêt pour le beau commissaire aux morts étranges l'avait conduite à un achat dont elle n'était pas coutumière. Dans son quartier, on parlait d'une vieille femme qui vendait des philtres d'amour à base de sang de mouton noir mêlé à du sang menstruel. Le garçon qui l'absorbait tombait inévitablement sous votre charme. Seule une infusion de nénuphar pouvait rompre le sortilège. Néanmoins, la composition du philtre lui déplaisant, elle avait opté pour un sachet de poudre de chauve-souris.

Vous en jetez une pincée par-dessus l'épaule du jeune homme et il ne pourra plus se détacher de vous.

Encore fallait-il en avoir l'occasion sous le regard d'un témoin et alors que l'œil de son commissaire aux morts étranges semblait toujours aux aguets.

La visite de sa demeure accomplie, Volnay fit asseoir la jeune fille dans son meilleur fauteuil et ajouta deux bûches dans le feu, lui proposant ensuite une boisson qu'elle déclina. Surpris de tant de sociabilité de la part de son fils, le moine hochait la tête d'un air approbateur. Enfin, lorsqu'ils furent tous assis près de l'âtre, gagnés par une douce tiédeur, Volnay s'enquit des raisons de la visite de l'Écureuil.

— J'ai retrouvé l'homme dont vous m'avez parlé dans une taverne, expliqua-t-elle. J'ai fait en sorte qu'il me remarque et très vite je…

Elle baissa les yeux gênés.

— Je lui ai plu… Il voulait… enfin… je lui ai dit que ce n'était pas possible car j'avais un autre rendez-vous. Il n'était pas très content de ce contretemps mais je lui ai proposé de le revoir le lendemain. Il m'a donné rendez-vous devant le jardin des Tuileries demain matin, dimanche, à neuf heures.

— Vous êtes très habile, apprécia le moine.

— Merci, dit Volnay. Merci !

Il alla à son cabinet de travail et en sortit une bourse. L'Écureuil le rejoignit vivement et posa la main sur son poignet.

— Je ne veux pas d'argent pour cela.

Elle hésita.

— Ce que j'ai accompli, c'est pour vous…

Dans un coin de la pièce, le moine eut un sourire entendu.

— Je serai chez vous demain à huit heures, dit-elle doucement.

— Plutôt sept, si vous le permettez, j'aime arriver à l'avance.

— Comme vous le désirez…

Elle se haussa sur la pointe des pieds pour lui donner un baiser sur la joue. Alors il se passa une chose étonnante, loin de la repousser, Volnay se pencha sur elle pour chercher ses lèvres et accompagna tendrement son baiser tout en la serrant contre lui.

Oh, se dit le moine, *mon fils s'humanise!*

Oh, pensa l'Écureuil, *je n'ai même pas eu à jeter ma poudre de chauve-souris!*

Hélène avait parcouru la ruelle de l'Or dans la journée, observant et posant des questions, la bourse à la main pour délier les langues. Finalement, elle s'arrêta devant la maison de la Dame de l'Eau. La neige recouvrait tout mais des traces fraîches ornaient celle-ci. Un animal était sorti de la maison pour se soulager et avait gaiement gambadé sur l'étendue blanche. Hélène observa un instant les empreintes, cligna des yeux sous la luminosité trop forte puis se détourna et reprit le chemin de sa maison.

Entrée dans son appartement du faubourg Saint-Jacques, Hélène fit le tour de la pièce après avoir allumé les bougies. La clarté de celles-ci jeta des lueurs incendiaires sur le cercle qu'elle traçait en disposant autour d'elle les chandeliers. Les lueurs dorées dans ses beaux yeux verts semblèrent lutter contre le noir des prunelles. Une plainte sourde, presque un gémissement, s'exhala de la poitrine de la jeune femme.

Lorsqu'elle était enfant, le soir, Hélène rejoignait sa mère apothicaire dans la salle de préparation où elle la trouvait devant ses balances, une balance avec scrupule et une balance à trébuchet. Elle y pesait minutieusement ses préparations car si une dose guérissait, une infime proportion supplémentaire pouvait aussi tuer. Hélène se promenait alors au milieu des bassines et des chaudrons, admirant au passage les moules à pilules ou les alambics dans lesquels sa mère préparait les eaux distillées.

Sa mère lui racontait parfois des légendes d'un autre temps. L'homme est un dieu fourvoyé qui ne se souvient plus des cieux car son œil a mesuré tout l'abîme de la nuit. Mais, si l'homme est tombé, la rassurait-elle, il conserve sans le savoir certaines des facultés que Dieu lui a données. Ce pouvoir endormi, pour d'obscures raisons, quelques-uns encore savent le réveiller…

Quelques-uns…

Assise en tailleur, les mains reposant sur ses genoux, paumes ouvertes, Hélène cligna des paupières. Ses yeux semblèrent alors se révulser et elle se mit à psalmodier d'une voix caverneuse et dans une langue qui ne ressemblait à nulle autre sur cette terre :

— *Atha Gabor Leonam Adonaï !*

XXII

DÎNER D'ESPRIT
ET AUTRES DIABLERIES

Dans les bureaux d'esprit des salons de la bourgeoisie, régnait une légèreté qui n'existait pas à Versailles. La cour fascinait encore mais n'attirait plus. Beaucoup de grands de ce monde qui n'avaient plus rien à obtenir du roi préféraient habiter à Paris et s'y divertir. La capitale dictait désormais le ton en matière de bon goût et d'art de vivre.

À une cour rigidifiée par l'étiquette, se substituait ici la plaisante réunion d'une bonne société. Le snobisme n'en était pas absent mais sans affectation outrée et le ton de la conversation restait badin. L'hôtesse y recevait toutes les attentions galantes propres à la contenter et un public divers s'y pressait : poètes ou hommes d'affaires, comédiens ou négociants, gens de lettres, danseuses et demi-mondaines. La seule obligation était de laisser tous ses soucis à l'entrée du salon. On ne tolérait ni les gens frustes, ni les esprits chagrins. La vie se résumait au jeu, à l'art de la conversation, au rire et au plaisir de faire la cour et d'aimer.

À son époque, et sous son propre nom, le moine avait fait fureur dans ce type de soirées, dispensant bons mots et saillies drolatiques, inventant des charades et poussant le couplet en chantant fort juste. Parmi les plus anciens, on l'accueillit donc avec curiosité mais le vrai centre d'intérêt restait Mme de Morange, mélange fascinant de jeunesse à demi éteinte et de grâce espiègle.

Elle portait une robe de soie bleue rayée d'argent avec des motifs de ruban floral et des manches pagodes à double volant. Un collier de perles fines ornait sa gorge. Le haut du corset replié à la naissance des seins laissait apercevoir deux globes d'un blanc laiteux. Sa main agitait nonchalamment un éventail brodé.

Le souper était un ambigu. Tous les mets se trouvaient sur la table de manière à exciter l'appétit par la vue et le sentiment du beau. La salle se parait de lumières qui se réfléchissaient dans la porcelaine délicatement ouvragée et jusqu'à la pointe des couverts. Dans leurs flacons du cristal le plus pur, vins et liqueurs brillaient de mille éclats. Pâtisseries et confitures sèches ornaient le milieu du jour de table. Les colonnades de sucre des gâteaux miroitaient de couleurs roses ou jaunes sous les girandoles de lumière. Viandes, poissons, tourtes et chartreuses entouraient les desserts en cercles concentriques, entremêlés de sauces ou de crèmes de toutes les couleurs. Les corbeilles débordaient de pain blanc en forme de cygne ou de tourterelle. L'image de ces mets se projetait en même temps que les flammes des chandelles dans une succession de miroirs vénitiens des plus exquis.

L'hiver étant là, d'exquises guirlandes de fleurs en papier remplaçaient les plantes. Elles ornaient vases et urnes, serpentant auprès des chandeliers tandis que des lierres se trémoussaient autour des lustres de Murano. On avait même poussé la délicatesse à figer dans de la gelée des herbes et des piments de couleur.

On passa bientôt à table et le moine nota la ronde parfaite des valets débarrassant par la droite, dans un seul mouvement semi-circulaire, l'assiette usagée tout en introduisant la nouvelle par la droite.

De nos jours, apprécia-t-il, *le bon service se perd. Voilà une maison où l'on sait tenir son rang !*

Après le bon dîner de quatorze heures, il se contenta des plats les plus proches de lui, à savoir des écrevisses cuites à l'eau et farcies de laitance de carpe avant d'être rôties au beurre et panées à la mie de pain. Il goûta aussi par distraction à un saucisson royal à base de chair de perdrix et de chapon crue, assaisonnée d'épices, de champignons et de truffes. Il ne s'en soucia pas plus que cela car il mangeait maigre le premier jour de la semaine et soumettait son corps au jeune le second.

La conversation ne l'intéressa guère car sa venue avait pour seul but de questionner Mme de Morange. Néanmoins, il lui fallait justifier sa place et le moine n'était pas homme à passer pour un cul pincé ou un sot d'esprit même si l'assemblée cherchait surtout le bon mot qui ferait rire l'hôtesse ou la flèche qui percerait le cœur d'un rival. Les convives prenaient des airs fins et entendus, adressant à leur interlocuteur de fades sourires. On développait, dans ce qui se prenait pour la bonne société, la raillerie au rang d'un art. Avec une politesse extrême, on amenait sournoisement la victime dans le ridicule en approuvant tout ce qu'elle disait, en l'exagérant même à l'extrême.

— Dieu a décidé qui naîtrait pauvre ou riche, il n'y a rien à redire là-dessus, lançait justement un nobliau qui, de notoriété publique, devait son titre à l'enrichissement de son père dans le commerce des esclaves.

— Dieu a très certainement pourvu aux quartiers de noblesse de chacun et décidé quelles familles participeraient ou non aux saintes croisades, répliqua vertement le moine.

L'autre rougit. C'était lui faire subtilement remarquer sa position de parvenu.

— Les croisades n'ont pas été la seule façon de servir Dieu, remarqua-t-il.

— Certes, il n'y a pas de sots métiers, admit le moine. Les petits Savoyards sont bien utiles pour ramoner les cheminées et permettre à la fumée de celles-ci de grimper haut vers le ciel.

— Je ne vous parle pas des petites gens ! s'emporta le nobliau.

Le moine se rafraîchit avec une douce plombières avant de répliquer :

— Il n'y a pas de petites gens, simplement des petites personnes ! Tenez, prenez les marchands d'esclaves…

Des rires moqueurs fusèrent autour de la table. Les regards se portèrent vers le fils du marchand d'esclaves. Sans bonne répartie, son sort était scellé dans la bonne société.

— Et moi, je vous réponds que petites gens et petits métiers sont une seule et même chose car Dieu l'a ainsi décidé ! lança le parvenu.

— Vous prêtez sans savoir à Dieu beaucoup d'intentions, répondit le moine d'un ton mordant. A-t-il voulu que des enfants meurent de faim ou de froid tandis que vous vous gorgez de carpes bien grasses ou de cochon de lait ?

— Dieu pourvoira au bien-être des méritants dans l'au-delà ! Je doute que vous en soyez avec votre esprit hérétique et séditieux.

Le moine lui jeta un regard glacial.

— On dit que les choses qui mènent l'homme en enfer sont au nombre de trois : la calomnie, l'endurcissement et la haine. Ce chiffre de trois vous désignera-t-il pour les flammes éternelles ?

Le nobliau se leva écarlate, jeta sa serviette par terre et sortit après avoir salué la maîtresse de maison. Un silence gêné tomba dans la pièce. Le moine fut le premier à le rompre.

— Cette plombières, dit-il en agitant nonchalamment sa cuillère, est à damner le saint que je ne suis pas.

Des rires coururent le long de la table et la conversation reprit son cours. Le souper terminé, on passa dans un salon pour organiser des parties de pharaon. Les invités s'éparpillèrent autour des tables, sortant leur bourse pour miser. Un joueur représentait la banque et possédait les cinquante-deux cartes, les deux autres, nommés *les pontes*, misaient sur une nappe de velours de soie.

Le moine rejoignit Mme de Morange dans son boudoir, une ravissante pièce aux lambris imprimés d'un rose tendre. La pièce sentait le jasmin comme si l'on venait d'y brûler un parfum. Dans une niche peinte couleur lilas, une ottomane reposait sur un parquet de marqueterie. La maîtresse de maison s'y allongea voluptueusement et darda sur lui un regard flamboyant.

— Vous avez manqué ruiner ma soirée, lui reprocha-t-elle vertement.

— Ce grand singe n'a eu que ce qu'il méritait !

— Quand même, vous êtes bien prompt à offusquer mes invités, ces petits marquis ce matin et ce soir…

— Un fils de marchand de viande humaine.

— Sont-ce vraiment des hommes que l'on envoie travailler dans les îles ?

— Oui, madame, je vous l'assure, répondit gravement le moine, et ils ont une âme et des sentiments comme vous et moi.

Enfin, surtout moi, pensa-t-il fugitivement, en contemplant Mme de Morange.

Il la jugeait désormais sans plus de cœur que les hommes et les femmes de son époque, sa seule conscience, légère, semblant née de la jambe gauche.

— Vos idées nous amèneraient tout droit à… à une révolution ! s'exclama-t-elle. Et d'abord, pourquoi s'appesantir sur une idée ? On peut bien disserter sans raisonner !

— Parler pour ne rien dire me fatigue !

— Allons, mon bon Guillaume, lui dit-elle en lui pressant affectueusement la main, laissez tomber vos bonnes causes et parlons plutôt de vous.

Le moine ne se laissa pas enrober par son sourire sucré.

— Madame, je me suis plié à toutes vos exigences. J'ai participé à votre souper, j'ai donné la réplique à vos caniches, j'ai aboyé avec eux contre les gens qu'on peut se permettre de moquer mais il est tard et je suis fatigué. J'ai une enquête à mener et besoin de réponses. Mon ami Sartine n'apprécierait pas de me voir perdre mon temps dans les soupers.

— Oh, Sartine…

Elle semblait soudain en avoir moins peur. Le moine lui jeta un regard aigu et ajouta :

— Le procureur Siltieri s'occupe également de cette question et il n'est pas homme facile !

À la mention de Siltieri, Mme de Morange s'agita, mal à l'aise.

— Que venez-vous me menacer ? gémit-elle. J'étais si tranquille dans mon hôtel à recevoir mes amis et à jouir de la vie. J'en avais même oublié jusqu'à…

— Jusqu'à l'existence de votre fille, termina sèchement le moine. J'avais bien compris !

Il la considéra d'un œil neuf, conscient d'avoir devant lui les restes d'une enfant gâtée, une poupée de porcelaine dans une maison de marbre, une femme qui se nourrissait du regard que les autres portaient sur elle, une personne qui recevait mais ne donnait rien.

On est parfois bien surpris de retrouver plus tard qui l'on a aimé, pensa tristement le moine.

— Ma question est simple, reprit-il d'une voix glaçante, à l'époque vous fréquentiez plusieurs hommes à la fois. J'en étais. Sartine, de même. Peut-être d'autres… Et puis, le roi vous avait remarquée… Qui est le père de Sophia?

Mme de Morange froissa nerveusement les plis de sa robe et releva la tête, les larmes aux yeux.

— Vous me pressez de questions sur mon enfant, que se passe-t-il donc? Lui est-il arrivé quelque malheur?

Le moine secoua la tête d'un air désapprobateur.

— Madame, vous n'avez pas vu votre enfant depuis sa naissance. Me trompé-je? Non! Alors, ne parlons pas de sentiment ou d'émotion et gardez au sec vos jolis yeux.

Elle ravala ses larmes.

— Que savez-vous donc de l'instinct maternel, moine du diable? J'avais dix-sept ans lorsque je la mis au monde. Dix-sept ans!

Il lui renvoya un sourire dur.

— Madame, vos remords et vos regrets sont tardifs et je ne peux qu'y compatir mais, encore une fois, j'ai à faire. Je mène une enquête pour laquelle je dois trouver des réponses. Je vous repose donc une dernière fois ma question: qui est le père de Sophia?

Mme de Morange le fixa, le regard vide.

— Après tout… dit-elle simplement.

Malgré lui, le moine contempla ses lèvres pleines et rouges, suspendu à celles-ci comme si le reste de sa vie en dépendait.

— Le père de Sophia… commença-t-elle.

Il se pencha en avant, son cœur cognant durement contre sa poitrine.

— C'est le roi, termina-t-elle.

Comme frappé d'apoplexie, le moine chancela.

— Le roi, répéta-t-il. Bien sûr, que je suis bête…

Le moine fit quelques pas dans la rue déserte et, frissonnant, ramena son manteau au plus près de son corps. Le vin cognait trop dans son crâne, il trébucha sur le sol glacé. Dans la rue de lourdes masses d'ombre semblaient se précipiter sur lui. Il se releva et fit quelques pas en expirant doucement, laissant la brise caresser ses tempes et rafraîchir son front, abandonnant au vent ses idées noires. Ardemment, il avait souhaité que Sophia fût de lui mais il n'en était rien. C'était l'enfant d'une crapule royale. Sur terre, le mal régnait et la justice n'existait pas. Seules subsistaient quelques âmes de bonne volonté.

Peut-être que les satanistes ont raison : le diable tient Dieu prisonnier de son ciel !

En faisant le tour de l'hôtel particulier, il surprit le manège du cuisinier et de l'intendant, revendant déjà à quelques traiteurs les restes du dîner dont les invités s'étaient régalés.

Sophia… Accablé de chagrin, le moine prit le chemin du retour et bientôt la nuit l'avala. Les rues obscures de Paris semblaient étrangement calmes par rapport au brouhaha de la journée. Il passa devant le Palais-Royal. On y jouait ou on soupait en caressant les filles. Il obliqua rue du Coq en direction du Vieux Louvre. Des cabarets italiens s'échappaient déjà des mélopées avinées et il se mit à chantonner à l'unisson.

Alors la nuit fut trouée d'éclats métalliques et l'enfer se rua sur lui.

— Tue ! Tue !

C'était le cri des assassins qu'ils poussaient autant pour se donner de l'audace et de la rage que pour impressionner leur victime. Brutalement dégrisé, le moine dégaina son épée et se mit souplement en garde. Une lueur froide et affûtée brillait maintenant dans son regard. Tirant sa dague de la main gauche, il para les coups d'épée de chacun de ses assaillants. Le moine en compta quatre, armés de lourdes rapières et conduits par un grand roux malingre au visage balafré de la joue au menton.

— Tue ! Tue !

À chaque attaque, le moine encaissait sans broncher cette détermination à l'assassiner. Il parait au plus pressé, défendait, attaquait sans se départir de son calme et la sueur coulait le long de son visage buriné. À un moment, une lame lui entailla le dessus de la main qui tenait la dague.

Ils sont trop nombreux, je n'y arriverai pas.

— À l'assassin, cria-t-il d'abord sans conviction puis d'une voix de plus en plus forte.

Il para de justesse un coup au ventre et, du revers de sa dague, ouvrit la gorge de son adversaire qui s'était trop fendu pour lui porter le coup.

Trois ! fit intérieurement le moine. Il avait cessé de crier "À l'assassin !". Personne ne viendrait et les gens restaient peureusement derrière leurs fenêtres, s'efforçant de distinguer dans le noir le féroce combat engagé dans la rue. Le moine ne s'en formalisa pas. Il avait appris de la vie à ne pas trop attendre le secours des autres lorsqu'il se trouvait dans le besoin.

De nouveau, une pluie de coups s'abattit sur lui mais de manière trop désordonnée. Avec un calme hallucinant, le moine bloqua l'attaque de ses adversaires et riposta aussitôt. Comme l'un de ses agresseurs se ruait seul sur lui, il dégagea et, glissant sa lame sous le bras de l'autre, le blessa profondément.

Les assassins hésitèrent. Le moine était un homme terrible les armes à la main. Rares étaient ceux qui possédaient comme lui le sentiment du fer, cette faculté de sentir en une fraction de seconde, au contact de la lame de l'adversaire, si celle-ci s'engageait par-dessous ou par-dessus et si l'autre s'apprêtait à attaquer, croiser, retourner ou dégager. Avec une adresse diabolique, il para un coup porté à son cœur et repoussa ses assaillants en claquant leur fer. Une détermination effrayante irradiait de toute sa personne. L'agresseur blessé à l'épaule recula, vacillant sur le sol glacé. Le moine se rua sur lui et l'embrocha sans un battement de cils. C'en était trop pour l'un des spadassins qui tout à coup fit volte-face malgré les imprécations de son chef. Le rouquin se retrouva seul face au moine et là celui-ci sut que cela allait être une autre affaire. C'est alors qu'un cri jaillit dans la nuit.

— Halte-là, le guet !

Le rouquin recula de plusieurs pas avant de tourner les talons et s'enfuir dans la nuit. Le moine fit de même mais dans une direction opposée. Manifestement, aucun des deux combattants ne se fiait aux archers du guet.

La pie jacassa lorsque la porte s'ouvrit, heureuse de revoir autour d'elle son petit monde. Volnay jeta un regard épouvanté au sang qui gouttait par terre.

— Que s'est-il passé ? Tu es blessé ?

— Un simple bobo, fit le moine avec une mâle assurance. On a essayé de m'assassiner au sortir de l'hôtel de Mme de Morange. Peux-tu m'aider à bander ma main ?

Son fils se précipita. Le moine lui indiqua comment nettoyer la blessure avant de la bander.

— Des spadassins de bas étage, gronda-t-il, ce n'est pas faire honneur à un escrimeur de ma qualité qui en a refroidi cent en duel !

— Huit, père.

— Huit en duel officiel avec témoins mais bien plus en réalité ! Enfin, seul le rouquin tirait correctement mais des rouquins Siltieri nous dirait que leurs cheveux ont été brûlés par les flammes de l'enfer !

Volnay étouffa un sourire.

— Hélène n'est toujours pas revenue ? s'inquiéta le moine.

— Es-tu seulement passé chez toi ?

— Oui et elle n'y est pas.

Le commissaire aux morts étranges haussa les épaules.

— Qu'as-tu appris là-bas ? s'enquit-il enfin.

Pour une fois, le moine fut bref.

— Que Sophia est la fille du roi !

Volnay tressaillit. L'affaire commençait dans un cimetière et le menait maintenant tout près du roi, dans sa propre descendance ! Mais où donc étaient-ils encore tombés ?

— Notre maître joaillier est marié à une femme qui ne peut avoir d'enfant, récapitula-t-il. Celle-ci lui demande d'adopter un jour la fille de Belle Ange, elle-même maîtresse du roi. Recevant pour cela une pension, et après la mort de sa femme, il vend son commerce et abandonne son métier pour se consacrer à sa passion : les étoiles. Puis il laisse sa fille adoptive s'élever toute seule…

— Peut-être en voulait-il au monarque pour avoir introduit sans le vouloir son propre enfant dans son foyer, le privant de l'affection de sa femme ? hasarda le moine.

— En tout cas, ce père adoptif s'intéresse à la sorcellerie et au roi ! Souviens-toi que, lorsque nous avons visité l'astrologue, il nous a caché qu'il établissait le thème astral de Louis XV ! Ce n'est donc pas un hasard si l'on retrouve cette fille de roi allongée nue sur une tombe ! Et pour une messe noire !

— Pour un rituel d'envoûtement, le corrigea le moine. Souviens-toi du livre de l'astrologue. Le rituel nécessite une conjonction bien précise d'étoiles, la célébration d'une messe noire et le sacrifice d'une victime. Mais attention, il s'agit d'un envoûtement par le sang. La personne à envoûter doit être du même sang que la victime.

— Et Sophia est la fille de Louis XV !

Ils se regardèrent stupéfaits.

— C'est le roi que l'on veut envoûter ! s'exclama Volnay.

XXIII

CHEVALIER SATANISTE
ET AUTRES DIABLERIES

Comme une pointe en diamant, les rayons du soleil vinrent se poser avec délicatesse sur l'Écureuil lorsque le commissaire aux morts étranges lui ouvrit la porte. Elle eut un sourire céleste quand Volnay l'invita à boire un café. Le moine arriva bientôt et lui baisa galamment la main.

— Je suis de plus en plus inquiet, Hélène n'est pas rentrée de la nuit, glissa-t-il à son fils.

Volnay lui jeta un regard moqueur.

— Et pourquoi donc cette jeune femme rentrerait-elle chez toi tous les soirs ?

— Mon Dieu, c'est ce qu'elle fait depuis le début de cette enquête. Je n'ai aucune nouvelle d'elle et je ne sais où et comment la joindre.

— C'est elle qui en a décidé ainsi ! Pour ma part, je l'ai quittée hier matin avant de partir voir Sartine. Elle ne m'a rien confié de ce qu'elle comptait faire.

Le moine refusa le café qu'on lui proposait et s'appliqua à lisser sa barbe d'un air pensif. Enfin Volnay donna le signal du départ pour le jardin des Tuileries. Deux statues représentant Mercure et la Renommée chevauchant un cheval ailé flanquaient l'entrée principale. Haut lieu de promenades mondaines, les entrées en étaient toujours gardées et n'importe qui n'était pas admis. L'Écureuil eut un sursaut en lisant l'écriteau à l'entrée du jardin *"Interdit aux chiens, aux filles, aux laquais et aux soldats"*. Remarquant son trouble, le policier lui tendit son bras et entra avec assurance avec elle et son père, passant sans un regard pour le factionnaire de service.

— Comme c'est beau, chuchota l'Écureuil à l'oreille de son compagnon. Je ne suis jamais venue ici.

Le moine observa avec désapprobation le maintien raide de Volnay alors que la jeune fille à son bras n'attendait de toute évidence que compliments et badinage.

Pourquoi lorsqu'il est avec une femme mon fils donne toujours l'impression de marcher sur des épines ?

— Nous sommes en avance d'une heure, reprit l'Écureuil pour meubler la conversation.

— C'est mieux ainsi. Mon père et moi avons l'habitude d'arriver toujours au moment où l'on ne nous attend pas. Cela nous a parfois appris des choses intéressantes !

Jardins de galanterie aux beaux jours, les jardins sous la neige étaient presque déserts. Volnay observa l'allée centrale percée dans l'axe du palais des Tuileries et délimitée à l'est par un bassin rond, à l'ouest par un bassin octogonal. Louis XIV avait fait redessiner les jardins par André Le Nôtre qui avait introduit des terrasses dotées de rampes en courbe pour y accéder. Le commissaire aux morts étranges remarqua une silhouette connue emprunter l'une d'elles. Il s'immobilisa comme un chien en arrêt, les narines frémissantes.

— Je connais cet homme, murmura-t-il.

— Mon Dieu, dit le moine, n'est-ce pas Sartine qui vient ?

— C'est bien lui, confirma son fils.

— Étonnant ! Mais alors…

— Alors, cachons-nous !

Ils quittèrent précipitamment l'allée centrale, contournèrent les parterres qui refleuriraient au printemps et trouvèrent derrière un bosquet de sapins un bon point d'observation. Leur attention fut alors attirée par un homme à la large carrure marchant à grands pas entre des haies de buis. Ses bottes écrasaient la neige, faisant voler autour de lui des nuages d'une fine poudre blanche. L'Écureuil laissa échapper une exclamation :

— C'est lui !

— L'homme du cimetière ! s'exclama le moine. Voici donc l'atout dans la manche de Sartine : un sataniste !

— Mieux vaut qu'il ne sache pas que nous savons ! murmura son fils. Restons dissimulés à leurs yeux.

Ils observèrent en silence les deux hommes qui parlaient vivement. Sartine s'agitait nerveusement et ses gestes étaient de plus en plus brusques. Finalement, le lieutenant général de police tourna les talons et s'en fut à grands pas, fort mécontent.

— Les voilà qui se séparent ! s'exclama le moine. Que faisons-nous maintenant ?

— Laissons Sartine repartir, il doit avoir sa voiture non loin de là. Je vais suivre le sataniste avec Gaston et cette fois je lui mettrai la main dessus.

— Il m'a l'air dangereux, je viens avec toi.

— Tu es très repérable avec ta bure et je préfère que tu raccompagnes mon amie jusqu'à une voiture.

— Certes ton épée n'est pas pucelle mais je serais plus rassuré si…

— Ne t'inquiète pas, le coupa Volnay, je te rejoindrai chez moi. Restez là quelques instants avant de quitter les jardins.

L'Écureuil eut une moue attristée.

— Ne puis-je aller avec vous?

Le moine intervint.

— Mon enfant, vous n'avez pas idée de l'affaire où vous mettez les pieds.

Mais elle ne l'écoutait pas et s'accrochait au bras de Volnay.

— Vous reverrai-je?

Le policier la contempla un instant et dit :

— Oui.

Il reçut comme une offrande son corps mince contre le sien, la serrant à son tour avec ferveur contre lui puis il s'arracha à son étreinte et, à pas souples, prit la direction de la sortie du jardin.

— Eh bien eh bien… murmura le moine. Mon fils m'étonnera toujours.

Il le suivit des yeux alors qu'il s'éloignait avant de reporter son attention sur l'Écureuil.

— Je vois que vous vous entendez bien avec mon… euh… avec le commissaire aux morts étranges.

Elle rougit pudiquement.

— Oui, enfin je crois. Il n'est pas toujours facile à cerner.

Le moine approuva, amusé. Vive et éveillée, la jeune fille lui plaisait.

— Voyez-vous, fit-il en lui prenant le bras et en l'entraînant hors du jardin, dans l'exercice de son métier Volnay est un homme froid et rationnel. Mais en compagnie des femmes, il est capable de se montrer tout à fait ridicule !

— Pourquoi donc?

Le moine haussa les sourcils.

— Mon… euh… Volnay aimerait pouvoir tout maîtriser dans sa vie, y compris ses sentiments.

Il soupira.

— Pour ma part, j'y ai renoncé depuis fort long-temps !

Le commissaire aux morts étranges se glissa hors des jardins des Tuileries. Déjà, l'épaisse silhouette du sataniste disparaissait à l'angle d'une rue. L'homme marchait très vite. Volnay courut pour le rattraper mais, lorsqu'il arriva au carrefour, l'autre avait disparu.

— Psitt !

Le commissaire aux morts étranges repéra une silhouette qui semblait changée en statue de glace. L'homme grelottait, dissimulé à moitié dans une porte cochère.

— Ah, les mouches de Sartine sont parfois bien utiles ! souffla Volnay.

Il le rejoignit rapidement.

— Alors, la mouche, dis-nous ce que tu as vu ! lança gaiement le policier.

— Il a pris la première rue à droite et va traverser la place Louis-le-Grand, dit Gaston en battant des bras pour se réchauffer. Venez ! Il va très vite !

Ils le retrouvèrent rue des Capucins, marchant lour-dement botté et éperonné, l'épée aux côtés, comme un condottiere. Deux yeux de prédateur brillaient dans son visage anguleux d'où saillaient deux pommettes sèches. Volnay le suivit jusqu'à une enseigne repré-sentant un bras tenant une épée. L'homme entra au rez-de-chaussée de la maison. Le commissaire aux morts étranges échangea un signe discret avec Gas-ton pour lui indiquer de l'attendre avant de se glisser à son tour dans les lieux.

Il se retrouva dans une salle d'armes où résonnait le bruit des fleurets entrechoqués. Le sol était parqueté mais patiné et usé par les semelles des combattants. Tout un pan de mur était couvert de glaces dans lesquelles se reflétaient les fleurets accrochés dans un râtelier. De grandes fenêtres dispensaient la lumière terne du jour. Dans un coin de la salle, trônait un cheval de bois pour apprendre l'escrime à cheval.

Maigre et nerveux, le maître d'armes portait une ample chemise de batiste aux manches larges, les poignets à boutonnière rentrés dans les gants. Il discutait avec le sataniste lorsqu'il aperçut Volnay. Il interrompit sa conversation pour s'approcher de lui.

— Monsieur, désirez-vous une leçon ? Mes deux élèves terminent leur engagement et je devrai m'occuper de monsieur qui vient d'arriver, à moins que tous deux vous ne souhaitiez croiser le fer ensemble ?

— J'en serai ravi, fit Volnay en s'inclinant légèrement.

Le maître d'armes revint vers le sataniste qui feignait l'indifférence. Celui-ci l'écouta et hocha brièvement la tête en signe d'assentiment. Il jeta ensuite un regard lourd sur Volnay avant de s'incliner pour le saluer. Le policier lui rendit son salut. Puis les deux hommes attendirent, les yeux fixés sur l'échange en cours, évitant de s'observer.

Les combattants s'affrontaient, vêtus d'un plastron bourré d'une laine épaisse maintenue entre deux grosses toiles recouvertes d'une épaisseur de cuir. Au centre du plastron, un cœur de cuir rouge était dessiné. Les fleurettistes battaient souvent l'air de leur fer, peinant à se trouver tant ils faisaient preuve de prudence, ne se risquant que pour esquiver des bottes maladroites sans les mener à leur terme. L'assaut achevé, le maître d'armes donna quelques conseils aux combattants. Une fois ceux-ci sortis, il revint vers Volnay et le sataniste, tenant à la main deux fleurets moucheté par une bourre de tissu enveloppée de cuir, maintenue par une cordelette à l'extrémité de l'arme.

— Messieurs, dit-il, je ne vous connais pas, aussi vais-je vous observer dans un premier temps. Désirez-vous un plastron pour amortir les coups ?

— Pour moi, ce n'est pas la peine, dit le sataniste. Je ne crois pas que monsieur puisse me toucher.

— C'est drôle, fit Volnay, j'allais dire la même chose !

L'autre le considéra pensivement et fendit l'air de son épée avec une nonchalance affectée.

— Je pense que je peux vous donner une petite leçon…

Le maître d'armes intervint.

— Messieurs, ce n'est qu'un échange d'observation. Pas de touche au visage ou de bousculade. N'oubliez pas que l'escrime se résume en cinq points : le sentiment du fer, le coup d'œil, le jugement, la vitesse et la précision.

Il leva le bras.

— Messieurs, saluez ! En garde ! Allez !

Les fers teintèrent et s'entrechoquèrent. La garde du sataniste était parfaite. Tout de suite, le commissaire aux morts étranges comprit que son adversaire était redoutable. Combattant expérimenté, il alternait avec vivacité attaque et contre-attaque. Volnay tenta de prendre l'offensive mais se vit stoppé. L'autre battit alors brusquement sa lame et tenta un coup d'estoc avant de se fendre. Le policier recula prudemment, tenant sa garde en prime. Son adversaire attaqua de nouveau, tenta une botte, avançant toujours. Volnay porta sa garde en prime et se cantonna prudemment à une position défensive dans l'attente d'une ouverture.

Le maître d'armes approuva ce choix tactique d'un bref hochement de tête.

Le sataniste attaquait maintenant sans relâche, le pressant de plus en plus. Volnay reculait tout en tentant de se préserver. D'un geste vif, son adversaire arracha la mouche de son épée et bondit en avant. Ses yeux avaient pris une teinte farouche.

— Monsieur ! cria le maître d'armes.

Il n'eut pas le temps d'intervenir. Après un mouvement d'une rapidité inouïe, l'épée du sataniste se posa sur la gorge de Volnay.

— Monsieur, fit son adversaire, vous êtes mort !

Le commissaire aux morts étranges ne cilla pas. Son heure n'était pas venue et il le savait. D'un coup d'épée sec, le maître d'armes écarta la lame du sataniste.

— Monsieur, votre attitude est inqualifiable !

L'autre eut un rictus sardonique et, sans quitter Volnay des yeux, répondit :

— Pardonnez-moi, maître, c'était pour donner un peu de piquant à l'exercice !

Le policier fit un pas en avant, empêchant ainsi son adversaire de brandir son fleuret.

— Monsieur, dit-il, je suis commissaire au Châtelet et je vous déclare de prise de corps.

Un grand rire ébranla le sataniste pour se terminer dans ce qui ressemblait au hennissement d'un cheval.

— Vous voulez me faire prisonnier ? Eh bien attrapez-moi d'abord !

Il se jeta sur son adversaire pour lui asséner au menton un coup de la garde de son épée puis bouscula le maître d'armes et se précipita hors de la salle. Pendant ce temps, à terre, Volnay comptait les étoiles. Le maître d'armes alla chercher un flacon de sel et aida le policier à se mettre debout.

— Cet homme est fou, grommela-t-il.

— Est-ce un de vos clients ? demanda le commissaire aux morts étranges.

— C'est la première et dernière fois que je le vois, répondit fermement l'autre.

Il hésita et ajouta :

— En tout cas, c'est un redoutable bretteur. Je vous conseille de l'éviter car la prochaine fois, il pourrait bien vous tuer !

Volnay ignora le conseil et sortit rapidement. Dans la rue, il repéra Gaston qui revenait, tout essoufflé.

— Tu l'as perdu ?

— Diable commissaire, il court plus vite qu'un chien. Quand il s'est élancé dehors, j'ai… j'ai couru à sa poursuite mais il… il était trop rapide pour moi !

Il se cassa en deux les mains sur les genoux, soufflant bruyamment.

— Tu manges trop, fit Volnay. Cela t'alourdit. Jamais chat emmitouflé ne prit souris !

— Commissaire, les mouches n'ont pas pour fonction de courir mais de suivre ! Pas besoin d'être maigre pour espionner.

Le policier ne répondit pas. Sur ses épaules pesait le poids d'échecs répétés : la Vorace d'abord, Sophia puis le sataniste par deux fois. Ce dernier était un adversaire tout bonnement redoutable. Son assurance incroyable le disputait à son arrogance. Il semblait ne rien craindre de personne. Au cimetière, lors de l'enterrement de Sophia, il s'était sans vergogne signé à l'envers, révélant son identité de sataniste. Quelques minutes auparavant, il avait choisi d'affronter Volnay en combat singulier, s'offrant même le luxe de lui faire grâce de la vie.

Il virevolte trop, songea le policier. Un peu comme s'il voulait que l'on s'attache à ses pas plutôt qu'à ceux de son complice l'astrologue. À moins que son assurance ne provienne de la haute protection de quelqu'un.

— Dis-moi Gaston, dit-il, tu es seul?

— Oui, commissaire.

— Et la mouche qui me suit?

— Lorsque vous êtes entré dans la salle d'armes, je l'ai envoyée chercher du renfort.

Le commissaire aux morts étranges posa une main ferme sur l'épaule de Gaston.

— Dis-moi, mouche mon amie, que dirais-tu d'oublier ce qui vient d'arriver? Ce ne serait bon ni pour toi ni pour moi que Sartine apprenne que nous avons laissé filer un suspect!

— Je n'osais pas vous le proposer commissaire. Rien n'est advenu, tout est à advenir!

Un sourire éclaira brièvement le visage de Volnay.

— Nous nous comprenons!

Gaston soupira de soulagement.

— Nous sommes des hommes de terrain, commissaire. Dans leurs bureaux du Châtelet, au coin du feu, ils ne se rendent pas compte des difficultés de nos professions!

Pour remercier la mouche de garder le secret sur leur malheureuse aventure, Volnay décida de lui offrir le meilleur repas de sa vie. Aussi, après être allés chercher le moine, les trois hommes s'attablèrent chez un traiteur non loin de là.

C'était un des rares traiteurs où l'on pouvait emporter les plats mais également manger sur place, en arrière-salle *et à sa propre table*, pour ne pas concurrencer les aubergistes. Le premier plat bouleversa Gaston : des yeux de veau farcis au gratin dont les prunelles avaient été avantageusement remplacées par des truffes noires entières. La mouche n'utilisait pas de fourchette mais mangeait en utilisant le pouce, l'index et le médius car, disait-il, les deux autres doigts servaient au diable lorsqu'il mangeait. Le moine lui remplit de nouveau sa flûte en remarquant :

— Tu avais soif mon ami la mouche !

— Ah, soupira Gaston, j'aime le champagne mais le coût m'en a fait perdre le goût !

Après les entremets, les larmes vinrent aux yeux de la mouche à la vue du canard aux huîtres, cuit à la braise et servi baignant dans une sauce liée au coulis de veau et de jambon, avec un peu de lard fondu, des truffes et de petits champignons parfumés.

— Ah, ce doit être très onéreux ! commenta Gaston impressionné. Vous jetez la maison par les fenêtres pour moi !

Le commissaire aux morts étranges mangea peu mais les deux autres convives dévorèrent pour lui. Des pots de confitures sèches furent amenés pour dessert car Volnay, qui n'avait pas l'habitude de passer beaucoup de temps à table, estima que l'on pouvait se passer de fromage. La mouche pleura de bonheur en voyant les pots de mûres, framboises, prunes, pommes et poires glisser dans son assiette.

— Pourquoi pleures-tu ? s'étonna Volnay.

— Vous êtes si bons avec moi alors que je vous cache tant de choses !

Le moine se moqua.

— Ne voilà-t-il pas que notre mouche devient sentimentale devant des pots de confitures…

— Sans oublier ce merveilleux veau et ce splendide canard aux huîtres, s'écria Gaston, le tout arrosé de cet excellent vin de Champagne !

Il essuya ses doigts poisseux sur sa manche. Volnay lui tapota le bras.

— C'est pour te remercier de ne rien dire au sujet de notre poursuite si mal engagée…

La mouche se frotta le nez avec sa manche.

— Oh pour ça, je suis plus fautif que vous ! Non ce qui me peine, c'est cet homme après qui nous avons couru. Aujourd'hui, je l'ai bien vu à la lumière du jour et cette fois plus de doute possible, je l'ai reconnu !

— Alors ?

— Il s'appelle Fauve et c'est un inspecteur de police !

Le commissaire aux morts étranges empila les bûches dans la cheminée tandis que son père tirait d'une boîte en noyer une petite fiche. Il la lut avec application après s'être pourvu d'une paire de bésicles.

— Inspecteur Fauve, dit *le chevalier de Fauve* car c'est le nom qu'il prend pour s'introduire officieusement dans certains cercles aisés. C'est d'ailleurs un spécialiste des états civils et des actes de naissance. Le faux en écriture est sa spécialité ! Son secteur d'activité est les filles et les salles de jeu. Lorsque Sartine a mis en coupe réglée les maisons de jeu, le chevalier de Fauve lui a été bien utile. L'homme vit sur un certain pied. On dit que plusieurs femmes travaillent pour lui.

Il leva les yeux vers son fils pour apporter un commentaire éclairé.

— Ce n'est pas un cas rare, de nos jours, la probité des policiers laisse à désirer.

Un silence et le moine ajouta d'un ton dramatique :

— Le seul problème est que le chevalier de Fauve est mort, il y a deux ans, assassiné par un condamné qu'il convoyait et qui lui a brisé le crâne à coups de pierre.

— Difficile dans ces conditions de reconnaître un cadavre ! remarqua Volnay.

— Le coup a dû être monté pour lui permettre de disparaître officiellement et de travailler dans l'ombre pour Sartine.

— Réfléchissons ! décréta le commissaire aux morts étranges en se levant et en commençant à arpenter la pièce.

Cette nouvelle information permettait à son esprit de rebondir, d'échafauder d'autres hypothèses.

— Deux femmes à la messe noire : la Vorace et une inconnue. Trois hommes : l'astrologue, le curé dansant et… le chevalier de Fauve ou Sartine ? Comme à son habitude, Sartine sait tout. Il a suivi la trace de cette enfant dès sa naissance sachant qu'elle provenait de la couche du roi. Une bâtarde peut toujours servir… De plus, il semble remarquablement informé des pratiques de messes noires !

— Sartine… murmura le moine. Comme tu y vas, mon fils ! Disons plutôt le chevalier de Fauve, cela me semble plus plausible.

À cet instant, la porte s'ouvrit brutalement et toute une troupe d'archers du guet envahit la pièce, suivie du lieutenant général de police. Sous son manteau bordé d'hermine, celui-ci portait un habit de velours noir.

— Encore vous ! s'exclama le moine. Décidément, vous n'en finissez plus d'envahir ma maison ! Peut-être désirez-vous y prendre une chambre ?

— Vous ne croyez pas si bien dire ! Dites-moi où se trouve Sophia et je vous tiendrai pour quitte !

— Vous m'avez donné quarante-huit heures pour la retrouver, rappela Volnay indigné.

— Et moi, je crois que vous l'avez déjà ! répondit Sartine en se plantant devant lui.

— Vous vous trompez.

Le lieutenant général de police essaya de sonder le regard de son commissaire aux morts étranges mais, comme tant d'autres, il se perdit dans la profondeur de celui-ci, puits sans fond.

— Fouillez partout ! cria Sartine dépité. Ouvrez les coffres, les armoires, regardez dessous les lits, sondez les planchers et les murs !

Il y eut un vacarme dans toute la maison, ponctué par les cris du moine :

— Ne touchez pas à ce clavecin avec vos gros doigts, vous allez me le désaccorder. Reposez immédiatement ce vase ! Vous, laissez mes plantes tranquilles ou vous vous gratterez le cul toute la nuit !

On rapporta à Sartine des livres reliés en maroquin.

— Qu'est-ce que ceci ?

Le lieutenant général de police lut avec application le titre du livre :

— *Dissertation sur les apparitions des anges, des démons et des esprits et sur les revenants et vampires de Hongrie, de Bohême, de Moravie et de Silésie.*

Il releva la tête et fixa le moine avec ahurissement.

— Je m'attendais à tout, y compris à des facéties scatologiques, mais qu'est-ce donc que ces lectures ? Et qui est son auteur ?

— Dom Augustin Calmet est mort il y a deux ans, répondit le moine. Désolé, vous ne pourrez pas lui passer les brodequins et le livrer au bûcher ! Je le lis par curiosité mais j'avoue que ce n'est pas très sérieux…

— Et celui-ci ? reprit Sartine. *Caractères de magie tracés* de l'abbé de Rocheblanche !

— C'est un saint homme ! dit le moine sans rire.

— *Secrets merveilleux de la magie naturelle et cabalistique du Petit Albert*, continua Sartine impavide.

— Oh, de nos jours tout le monde sait que les salamandres habitent la région du feu, les sylphes celle de l'air, les gnomes le cœur de la terre et les ondins le fond de nos eaux !

— Et encore un autre ! s'exclama le lieutenant général de police. *Cosmopolite ou Nouvelle Lumière chimique pour servir d'éclaircissement aux trois principes de la nature exactement décrits dans les trois traités suivants...*

— *Le Traité du mercure, Le Traité du soufre* et *Le Traité du vrai sel des philosophes*, compléta le moine.

— Belle lecture ! commenta Sartine d'un ton sévère. Je vous félicite !

— Le contenu des livres permet d'en savoir plus sur le monde, expliqua le moine imperturbable. Bien sûr, on pourrait manger les livres pour mieux les digérer mais le plus sûr moyen de s'instruire est encore de les lire !

— Pas ces livres-là ! gronda Sartine.

Le moine secoua la tête.

— Je dénie toute forme de superstition ou d'obscurantisme. Je ne vois ni lutin, ni fée autour de moi. J'estime simplement que la nature recèle d'admirables secrets qu'il nous convient de percer.

— Vouloir percer les secrets de la nature est un outrage au ciel car si celui-ci désirait nous les révéler, il l'aurait fait !

— Je ne vois pas les choses comme vous, répondit paisiblement le moine. La nature me lance un défi, j'y réponds !

— Vous feriez mieux de cesser de lire toutes ces diableries et de demeurer à la place que Dieu vous a assignée !

— Sartine, gronda le moine, cinquante entrées différentes conduisent à la connaissance générale des mystères et vous n'en connaissez pas une seule !

Le lieutenant général de police eut un grognement exaspéré et se tourna vers Volnay.

— Dites-moi où est Sophia et nous en resterons là. Je sais que parfois vous agissez bizarrement mais, pour cette fois, je ne vous en tiendrai pas rigueur !

— Monsieur de Sartine, fit calmement Volnay, je vous ai dit que j'avais besoin d'un peu de temps pour la trouver. Pourquoi remettre en cause notre arrangement ?

— Mais parce que je n'ai aucune confiance en vous !

— Je ne peux vous répondre pour l'instant, s'entêta le commissaire aux morts étranges.

— Très bien, fit Sartine en se tournant vers les archers du guet. Tous à la maison du commissaire !

Il toisa Volnay d'un air menaçant.

— Vous nous accompagnez ou préférez-vous que l'on défonce votre porte ?

— Je préfère vous ouvrir, les voisins ne comprendraient pas !

Sous les quolibets de la pie, les hommes de Sartine envahirent la maison du commissaire aux morts étranges qu'ils se mirent en devoir de dévaster. Volnay eut un pincement au cœur en voyant les archers du guet saisir ses livres avec leurs grosses mains malhabiles.

— Sartine ! Qu'ils ne touchent pas à mes livres ! Sophia ne se cache pas entre les pages !

Le lieutenant général de police eut un grognement exaspéré.

— Vous, votre père et vos fichus livres ! Vous feriez mieux de vous intéresser aux gens !

XXIV

ENLÈVEMENT DE SOPHIA
ET AUTRES DIABLERIES

La tempête passée, Volnay et son père entreprirent de ranger la maison du commissaire aux morts étranges. La pie jacassait à qui mieux mieux mais les deux hommes gardaient un silence renfrogné. La matinée s'achevait mal. Ils avaient surpris leur supérieur avec un inspecteur de police officiellement mort et suspecté de satanisme, Volnay avait perdu l'homme et Sartine venait de faire fouiller de fond en comble leurs maisons par ses hommes afin de retrouver Sophia. Quant à Hélène, ils en étaient sans nouvelles depuis la veille au matin. Le moine remettait en place une grande glace dans un cadre en bois sculpté et doré lorsque l'on cogna contre la porte.

— Je crois que pour cette enquête le monde entier gravite autour de nos deux maisons ! se plaignit le moine. Si seulement, cela pouvait être Hélène...

— Je vais ouvrir, soupira son fils.

La porte ouverte, il se retrouva devant la gueule menaçante du pistolet du chevalier de Fauve !

— Puis-je entrer cher confrère ?

Volnay recula. Il jeta un bref coup d'œil derrière lui, apercevant le moine glisser sa main sous sa bure, sans doute pour se saisir de sa dague. Comme devinant les mauvaises intentions des occupants de ces lieux, le chevalier de Fauve leva une main en l'air.

— Tout doux, messieurs, je suis venu ici de mon plein gré et je ne suis pas animé de mauvaises intentions. Bien au contraire !

— Prouvez-le, dit calmement Volnay.

— Mais tout de suite !

Le visage illuminé d'un large sourire, le chevalier de Fauve tendit son pistolet à Volnay qui s'empressa de le pointer sur lui.

— Amusant ! commenta le moine en sortant sa dague. Mais est-il chargé ?

— Il l'est, le rassura son fils.

Le chevalier de Fauve prit un air vaguement ennuyé.

— Puis-je m'asseoir ?

Sans attendre de réponse, il ôta son manteau. Dessous, il portait un habit galonné et des manchettes en dentelles. Avec un soupir d'aise, il s'assit sur un fauteuil près du feu et se frotta les mains.

— Quel bonheur de se réchauffer !

Il jeta un regard circulaire à la pièce.

— Une charmante demeure, vraiment. Un peu en désordre toutefois… Ah, voici votre fameuse pie qui parle ! On dit qu'elle est très impolie !

— Comment savez-vous où j'habite ? le questionna Volnay.

— Oh, je suis un inspecteur de police et votre résidence n'est pas secrète.

— Pourquoi avoir fui ce matin ?

Le chevalier de Fauve haussa les épaules.

— Parce que vous vouliez me prendre et que je ne le voulais pas. J'avais à vous parler mais, pour prouver ma bonne foi, il me fallait me livrer à vous de mon plein gré. J'aurais pu vous tuer ce matin, convenez-en. Et j'aurais pu faire de même à l'instant.

— Cela peut aussi constituer une manœuvre, remarqua le moine.

De Fauve porta un regard nonchalant sur lui.

— Vous vivez dans un monde de soupçon. Il vous faut apprendre à faire confiance. Surtout entre collègues…

— Un collègue mort, ironisa Volnay.

L'autre hocha la tête.

— Il y a deux ans, Sartine m'a demandé de mourir pour mieux infiltrer les milieux les plus noirs de la capitale. Pour cette raison, je le rencontre de temps à autre mais jamais au Châtelet, toujours dans un endroit public à Paris et brièvement.

Il avait l'accent de la vérité. Impressionnés, Volnay et son père échangèrent un regard surpris.

— Pourquoi cette mission ? demanda le commissaire aux morts étranges.

— Croyez-vous qu'il ne se passe rien derrière les murs des hôtels particuliers de Paris ou même chez le bourgeois ? Il y a dix ans, la comtesse de Montboissier et son amant, le duc d'Olonne avec sa maîtresse ainsi que le duc de La Tour d'Auvergne ont traité avec le diable par l'intermédiaire d'un certain Dubuisson, peintre en bâtiment. Celui-ci traça même le cercle dans lequel il allait faire apparaître le diable avec la pointe de l'épée du duc d'Olonne !

Ses yeux s'étrécirent.

— Paris est une ville remplie de secrets, de secrets magiques souvent et cela déplaît à M. le lieutenant général de police. Il veut purger cette ville de ses sorciers ou faux mages. C'est même devenu une obsession chez lui.

Sa grande carcasse se plia en avant et il baissa la voix.

— Il faut dire qu'il s'en passe de belles et que Sartine a raison d'être inquiet. Vous seriez surpris des noms de certaines personnes de haut rang qui se livrent à des pactes démoniques.

Il s'interrompit pour froncer les sourcils comme s'il se souvenait de quelque chose de déplaisant.

— Sartine m'a semblé prendre goût à mes rapports, reprit-il d'une voix soucieuse. Il m'en demande toujours davantage. Mais au fur et à mesure de nos rencontres, il me paraît de plus en plus renseigné sur tout ce qui relève de la magie noire comme si…

— Comme si, dans un même temps, il lisait des ouvrages interdits, acheva le moine.

L'inspecteur hocha la tête.

— C'est cela, oui. Ses questions sont de plus en plus précises et surtout il me questionne sur certains livres très particuliers et me demande comment se les procurer. Il y a deux semaines, il voulait savoir si la main d'un pendu tenant une bougie allumée formait une main de gloire avec de vrais pouvoirs et si la mèche de la bougie devait bien être tressée avec les cheveux du propriétaire de la main ! Les notes et manuscrits que je parviens à subtiliser l'intéressent au plus haut point. Il se met aussi à me demander des adresses…

Le moine hocha la tête.

— À trop vouloir sonder l'abîme, on peut s'y perdre…

Le chevalier de Fauve soupira.

— Ne m'en parlez pas ! Ces derniers temps, Sartine m'a inquiété. Il ne m'a pas chargé d'enquêter sur l'affaire du cimetière. N'y voyez aucune envie ou jalousie, je n'ai pas pour habitude de mettre ma faucille dans le champ du voisin mais, du fait de mon implication dans le milieu, j'étais le mieux placé pour mener celle-ci, même parallèlement à la vôtre. Au lieu de cela, Sartine m'a occupé à des broutilles.

— Pourquoi alors vous êtes-vous rendu à l'enterrement de Sophia ?

— J'ai pris sur moi. Je me disais que peut-être j'y retrouverais des figures connues…

— Vous vous êtes signé à l'envers…

— Pour m'en faire reconnaître au cas où…

— Et Sartine ne vous a jamais demandé d'enquêter ?

— Non, il me gardait comme atout dans sa manche, comme il disait, mais en fait, lorsqu'il a daigné se souvenir de moi, c'était pour Sophia.

Le moine tressaillit.

— Oui, dit le chevalier de Fauve, il m'a parlé d'elle. Il voulait que je la retrouve à tout prix. Il ne comprenait pas comment elle pouvait être encore vivante. Je devais découvrir où elle se cachait car elle aurait, m'a-t-il dit, échappé miraculeusement à la mort.

Il se pencha vers eux, l'air grave.

— Sartine cherche cette enfant, elle occupe toutes ses pensées. Il veut la retrouver coûte que coûte !

Le moine s'appliquait à lisser le plumage de la pie à travers les barreaux de sa cage.

— Je me demande si nous avons bien fait de le laisser repartir, soupira-t-il. Que penses-tu de lui ?

— Je ne suis pas certain de vouloir lui confier ma pie à garder mais son histoire me paraît crédible, répondit son fils qui arpentait la pièce.

— Oui, tout ceci ne m'étonne guère. La police se soucie fort peu de la noblesse ou des bourgeois, son but est de défendre le régime contre tous. Les faux sorciers sont une injure à son autorité comme tout ce qui peut influencer les esprits faibles et Dieu sait qu'ils sont légion ici-bas !

— Sartine nous aurait donc manipulés ?

— Il l'a fait en nous taisant l'ascendance de Sophia alors qu'il la connaissait.

— Mais de là à commanditer une messe noire !

— Sartine est droit comme une faucille, se moqua le moine. Avec lui, rien ne m'étonne plus. Le chevalier de Fauve dit vrai au moins sur une chose. Sartine envoie ses inspecteurs et ses mouches provoquer les faux sorciers pour les démasquer puis il les fait arrêter discrètement par des lettres de cachet. Pour l'interrogatoire, un commissaire du Châtelet utilise une grille de questions…

Le commissaire aux morts étranges le coupa.

— Je redoute que l'on ne découvre Sophia. Tu as entendu le chevalier de Fauve à son sujet ? Sartine est reparti il y a deux heures avec ses hommes. Il connaît l'existence de la ruelle de l'Or et a pu s'y rendre après être revenu bredouille de chez nous. Ses mouches ont dû nous suivre bien souvent chez la Dame de l'Eau. Je crains le pire !

Le moine sursauta.

— Tu as raison ! Je vais ôter ma bure et ceindre mon épée. Va de l'avant, je te rejoindrai !

Enfouie sous la neige, la maison semblait abandonnée. Le commissaire aux morts étranges sortit son pistolet et poussa la porte. Du haut de l'escalier, il embrassa d'un coup d'œil la scène. En bas, près de la cheminée, la Dame de l'Eau gisait à terre. Des chaises étaient renversées, un vase brisé. Derrière une porte, on entendait les jappements rageurs du chien.

412

Volnay descendit précipitamment l'escalier. Il ranima la Dame de l'Eau en lui faisant respirer des sels.

— Que s'est-il passé ? haleta le moine. Qu'avez-vous, ma Dame ? Ont-ils enlevé Sophia ?

Le commissaire aux morts étranges répéta la dernière question.

— Ils étaient deux hommes masqués, geignit la Dame de l'Eau en se tenant la tête. L'un en habit de velours rouge, l'autre en habit de velours noir avec une perruque poudrée.

— Sartine ! s'exclama le moine.

Volnay devint pâle.

— Cela explique son étrange comportement et ses propos lorsqu'il m'a dit : *Vous n'êtes pas ouvert comme moi à l'invisible et à l'inattendu !* Il semblait effrayé à l'idée que Sophia soit un fantôme venu se venger de ses meurtriers !

— J'ai également vu le visage d'une femme à la fenêtre de leur voiture, ajouta la Dame de l'Eau.

— Comment était-elle ? la pressa le commissaire aux morts étranges.

— Jeune et belle, des cheveux bruns tirant sur le roux, de beaux yeux verts…

— Hélène ! s'écria Volnay. La complice de Sartine !

Le visage du moine devint d'une pâleur extrême.

— Non, je ne le crois pas ! Pas elle ! Pas elle !

C'était presque un cri désespéré. Le commissaire aux morts étranges lui posa la main sur l'épaule.

— Père, pour la première fois je commence à y voir vraiment clair dans cette histoire ! Les choses prennent enfin un sens pour moi. Nous n'écoutons plus ce que les gens nous disent ! Souviens-toi du jour où nous avons rencontré Hélène. Elle nous a dit qu'elle parlait l'araméen et était un peu sorcière.

"D'après les croyances populaires, on est sorcière de mère en fille."

— Et nous avons ri, se souvint le moine avec amertume.

— Toi, surtout !

— Hum…

Le moine se rembrunit.

— Qui plus est, et tu ne le sais pas, elle porte une fleur de lys à l'épaule.

— Quoi ! Et tu ne m'en avais rien dit ? Et d'abord comment l'as-tu vue ?

Son père écarta les doigts de la main.

— Euh… cela fait beaucoup de questions.

— Comment l'as-tu vue ? demanda froidement Volnay.

— Euh, par hasard, à la toilette…

— Et tu n'as pas jugé bon de m'en parler ?

— Elle m'a raconté une histoire à faire pleurer et puis je crois qu'elle m'a un peu ensorcelé, je l'avoue.

Il pointa un doigt en l'air pour citer Cornelius Agrippa :

— *"La femme ensorcelle l'homme quand, par un regard fort fréquent, elle dirige la pointe de celui-ci vers la pointe de l'autre et que ses yeux s'attachent fort, portant au cœur de l'autre une vapeur du plus pur sang engendré par la chaleur de son propre cœur."*

— On appelle cela l'amour, fit remarquer la Dame de l'Eau.

Le moine s'empourpra.

— Évitez-moi ces imbécillités ! trancha le commissaire aux morts étranges.

L'éclat de son œil était dur comme le diamant.

— Comme je l'ai dit, reprit-il, j'y vois désormais clair. Revenons en arrière, une nuit dans un cimetière. Sophia est allongée, inerte, sur la dalle froide. Cinq monstres l'entourent. Trois hommes, deux femmes. Ces trois hommes sont Sartine, le commanditaire, l'astrologue, le complice, et le curé dansant, l'exécutant. La prostituée donnant l'eucharistie, c'est la Vorace. La seconde femme participant à cette messe, sorcière à ses heures et agent de Sartine, s'appelle Hélène !

— Sartine, à la limite, je veux bien, murmura le moine, mais Hélène !

— Elle les a menés droit vers Sophia !

Le moine baissa la tête, accablé.

— Réfléchis ! insista Volnay. C'est Sartine qui, dès le premier jour, nous a mis Hélène dans les pattes pour l'aider à prendre le contrôle de cette enquête, Sartine qui ne quitte pas Sophia des yeux depuis des années. Tu l'as toi-même reconnu dans la description de l'homme qui lui a donné un louis d'or. Et comme tu as pu le constater, Sartine cherche Sophia. Il a fait fouiller nos maisons et il s'est ensuite rendu à la ruelle de l'Or car ses mouches l'ont assez renseigné sur nos fréquentations là-bas.

— Et Sartine portait aujourd'hui un habit de velours noir…

— Tout se tient ! renchérit Volnay. Lorsque j'ai voulu arrêter la Vorace et qu'elle s'est enfuie, Hélène n'a pas cherché à la retenir. Elle a dû ensuite avertir Sartine que nous étions sur la piste du curé dansant, ce qui a entraîné sa mort immédiate !

— Allons chez elle, décida le moine.

— Connais-tu son adresse ? s'étonna son fils.

Une lueur moqueuse brilla dans les yeux du moine.

— Moi non mais sais-tu quelque chose qui échappe aux mouches ?

Un sourire froid illumina le visage du commissaire aux morts étranges.

— Certes non ! Suis-moi !

Ils sortirent de la maison et marchèrent en ligne droite vers Gaston qui recula, épouvanté par l'expression de leurs regards.

— Conduis-nous chez Hélène !

— Hélène ? Mais je ne sais pas…

Volnay le saisit brutalement au col.

— Fini de jouer, mouche, oh ma mouche ! Sous tes dehors de benêt, je sais que tu es le plus rusé de tous ! Et tu dois parfaitement savoir où demeure cette jeune femme !

— Vous n'allez pas me faire du mal après m'avoir invité à votre repas, balbutia Gaston tout congestionné sous la poigne de fer du policier. Nous avons goûté aux mêmes plats…

— Mais nous n'avons pas partagé avec toi le pain de l'Eucharistie ! remarqua finement le moine.

— Et je ne vous jetterai pas la pomme du péché ! conclut la mouche résignée.

Il contempla le moine et le commissaire aux morts étranges. Une lueur farouche brillait dans leurs yeux. Rarement, il avait vu hommes aussi déterminés.

— Allons, murmura Volnay d'une voix rauque, hâte-toi de nous conduire.

Et dans sa voix perçait une sourde menace. La mouche n'hésita plus.

— Venez avec moi !

Ils le suivirent jusqu'à l'appartement d'Hélène, s'étonnant au passage du choix du faubourg Saint-Jacques et de la proximité des couvents.

— Siltieri aurait adoré habiter ici, commenta sans rire le moine. Je m'étonne qu'il n'ait pas encore visité cet endroit !

Rue des Marionnettes, ils s'engouffrèrent dans l'immeuble de la jeune femme et gravirent quatre à quatre les marches de l'escalier.

— Attends-nous à la porte et veille à ce que personne ne nous dérange, décréta le commissaire aux morts étranges.

L'appartement était meublé avec sobriété mais goût. Les meubles en acajou semblaient de ligne classique, avec peu de bronzes ou de dorures. Un rideau de vieux taffetas cramoisi masquait la grande fenêtre du salon. Volnay émit un petit cri étranglé en découvrant la table de la cuisine tout ensanglantée. Le moine s'empressa de le rejoindre.

— Chats noirs, crêtes de coq et rognons de bélier… murmura-t-il atterré devant l'étrange étalage.

— Voilà qui commence bien mal, constata le commissaire aux morts étranges.

— On lui donnerait le bon Dieu mais non sans confession, dit son père choqué.

Volnay alla jusqu'à la chambre et l'appela.

— Vois-tu ces livres ?

Le moine mit ses bésicles et se pencha pour lire les titres.

— *De la vray magie noire vel Sigillum Salomonis*, *Agrippa*, *Clavicula Salomonis*… hum… tout cela sent le soufre !

Il baissa la tête, atterré. Son monde s'écroulait.

— C'était donc ça ! Elle est allée à l'école du diable et en a appris la malice.

Son fils s'empara sur le bureau d'un cahier griffonné de figures et de chiffres.

— Des sorts, des formules, des conjurations, déchiffra le moine par-dessus son épaule. Où va se nicher le mal ? Décidément, toujours là où on l'attend le moins !

Volnay eut une moue dubitative.

— Inutile d'aller plus loin, nous savons maintenant à qui nous avons affaire ! Heureusement que tu n'as pas... enfin, tu vois ce que je veux dire...

— Comment ? Euh, oui...

Son fils lui jeta un regard soupçonneux.

— Dis-moi, père, avec Hélène, tu n'as quand même pas...

— Qu'est-ce qui peut te faire penser ça ! s'exclama trop vite le moine.

— Je ne sais pas, parfois il me semble que tu refuses d'accepter ton âge...

— Mais je n'ai aucune envie de vieillir, fils ! s'écria le moine.

— Oui, dit Volnay, c'est bien ça le problème !

XXV

MESSE NOIRE
ET UNE DERNIÈRE DIABLERIE

L'obscurité régnait partout en maîtresse mais était-ce la nuit pour autant ? se demandait avec inquiétude Sophia. Sa nourrice lui racontait que la lune rappelait à la vie des vampires dans leurs tombeaux, éveillant leur soif de sang. Alors, afin d'exorciser sa peur, Sophia ne cessait de parler à Hélène comme si seuls les mots pouvaient la maintenir loin de la folie et de la mort :

— Ma nourrice me disait que les monstres n'existaient pas et que ce n'était que des histoires auxquelles il ne fallait pas croire.

Dans le noir, les yeux vert et doré d'Hélène semblèrent se rétrécir pour n'être plus qu'une fente.

— Ta nourrice avait tort, Sophia, les monstres existent bien. Ils sont partout autour de nous et on ne sait même pas les distinguer des autres.

Elle se tourna à demi pour tenter de réduire la morsure des liens à ses poignets et ses pieds.

— Et dis-toi bien qu'ils prennent toujours l'apparence la plus aimable pour que tu ne te doutes de rien. Ils sont là pourtant, tout autour de nous...

Un sourire adoucit son visage.

— Heureusement, l'espoir demeure. Au mal s'oppose toujours le bien. C'est une question d'équilibre. Ils viendront...

— Qui cela ? demanda Sophia. Le commissaire et son gentil moine ?

— Oui, car ils sont braves et intelligents.

Hélène se tourna contre le mur et murmura.

— Du moins je le crois !

— Que croyez-vous donc ?

L'homme entrait, habillé de velours rouge. Avec lui, un pan de lumière se glissa jusqu'aux deux prisonnières avant de disparaître lorsque la porte claqua. Le nouvel arrivant alluma une lanterne qui jeta des reflets tremblotants sur les murs froids.

— Toi d'abord, fit-il en s'agenouillant près de Sophia.

Il lui fit ingurgiter de force le contenu d'une petite fiole. Curieusement, l'enfant ne se débattit qu'une fois enlevée la fiole de ses lèvres. Il se contenta de la maintenir au sol, sous les imprécations d'Hélène, jusqu'à ce qu'elle s'endorme. Alors seulement, il se tourna vers la jeune femme et sa bouche dévoila un sourire de loup.

— Vous ensuite…

Il montra une certaine familiarité avec Hélène, comme s'il la connaissait depuis toujours, car, après avoir soigneusement vérifié les attaches de ses mains dans son dos, il retroussa sa robe d'une main experte et lui caressa les cuisses.

— Belle bête ! apprécia-t-il.

Il rit et ajouta :

— Une fois, je n'ai pas vérifié l'état des liens d'une prisonnière et j'ai failli me faire arracher les yeux par cette femme. Cela a été la surprise de ma vie.

— Une fois, un homme m'a violée, rétorqua Hélène, cela ne m'a pas du tout surprise !

Il la regarda avec un froid détachement.

— Ne vous inquiétez pas, je m'occuperai plus tard à calmer vos ardeurs mais j'ai promis la primeur à un de mes amis qui a un gros sentiment pour vous.

Et il ajouta d'un ton tranquille :

— Nous vous tuerons ensuite.

Elle le suivit des yeux alors qu'il sortait de sa besace une coupe et un goupillon noir. Sans mot dire, il dénoua le lacet qui retenait ses chausses et urina dans la coupe. Il y ajouta du sel et ce qui semblait être du soufre. Ensuite, il trempa son goupillon dans la coupe et s'approcha de la jeune femme qui se contorsionna pour échapper à son étreinte. D'une main ferme, il la saisit par le cou et traça sur son front avec le goupillon le signe de croix à l'envers.

— Hélène, dit-il, je te rebaptise.

Dans un souffle, la jeune femme cracha :

— Je n'ai jamais été baptisée !

Surpris, l'autre la contempla avant d'éclater de rire.

Ils avaient fouillé sans succès l'appartement d'Hélène à la recherche d'indices pour les diriger dans leur quête désespérée.

— Ils n'ont pas amené Sophia chez Hélène et la maison de l'astrologue a brûlé, récapitula Volnay. Est-elle chez Sartine ? Ce serait prendre un risque énorme dans sa position et la chose se remarquerait…

Il médita un instant.

— Allons à l'abbaye en ruine !

— Mais pourquoi ?

— C'est le seul lieu où ils puissent se trouver, je n'en connais pas d'autre !

Le moine gémit de désespoir.

— Nous sommes complètement démunis !

Il claqua des doigts.

— Mais j'y pense, Hélène était avec nous lorsque nous sommes allés dans cette abbaye. Sachant que nous connaissons les lieux, ils n'y amèneront pas Sophia.

Son fils lui jeta un regard sombre.

— Je sais bien mais encore une fois je ne sais où aller et surtout n'oublie pas qu'ils ignorent que nous avons découvert l'enlèvement de Sophia.

— Voilà un sacré coup de dé! conclut le moine atterré.

Le second homme s'approcha d'Hélène à pas lents, le sourire aux lèvres. Il était vêtu d'un costume de velours noir et portait une perruque poudrée.

— Vous! souffla la jeune femme. Vous!

Son sourire s'effaça lentement et sa noirceur se dévoila. Il s'agenouilla et lui flatta la croupe.

— Mon compagnon a raison : belle bête! Depuis le temps que je pense à vous et que je vous espère! Soyez flattée d'avoir retenu l'attention d'un homme qui tient une si belle place dans la société. Que ferai-je de vous ensuite, Hélène? Peut-être mon cheval! J'ai lu que si je vous passais au cou des lanières de peau arrachées à des cadavres écorchés, je vous transformerai en une monture infatigable!

Et sans plus de commentaires, il commença à défaire son haut-de-chausses. Hélène ferma les yeux et ne les rouvrit que lorsqu'on la força à ouvrir la bouche.

— Non, balbutia-t-elle en montrant les dents.

Elle reçut une gifle qui lui ébranla une canine mais, par prudence, son agresseur changea d'avis et lui écarta les cuisses.

— Tu as raison, décida-t-il, nous nous passerons des préliminaires.

Il l'enfila d'un coup et s'activa en elle avec vigueur.

— Bouge un peu ! haleta-t-il.

— Je vous laisse faire, répondit-elle d'un ton glacial. Vous remuez beaucoup mais la nature vous a peu doté, je ne sens rien !

Il la gifla.

— Bouge je te dis ! Bouge femme !

Hélène resta inerte.

— Tu me tiens tête, hurla-t-il, aussi vais-je te corriger, impudente catin !

Il la frappa encore, lui fendant la lèvre et entaillant ses pommettes sans qu'elle laisse passer un son entre ses dents serrées. Comme émoustillé par le spectacle de la femme battue, l'homme s'activa en elle avec des petits cris de bête et éjacula dans un grognement satisfait.

Il resta allongé sur elle un instant puis, en soupirant, se leva et ajusta ses chausses. Il s'aperçut alors que la jeune femme ne l'avait pas quitté du regard.

— Vous serez le premier à mourir, lui annonça froidement Hélène.

Ils avaient réquisitionné trois chevaux à la première écurie venue et commencé une cavalcade folle à travers Paris puis la campagne enneigée. Le pauvre Gaston peinait à garder son équilibre sur sa pourtant placide monture et souffrait le martyre. À l'abbaye abandonnée, dans le vent glacial, ils se précipitèrent vers le réfectoire aux diaboliques peintures. Le commissaire aux morts étranges alluma son briquet et confectionna une torche improvisée.

— Rien, fit-il en examinant les lieux.

Ils passèrent à la cuisine puis cherchèrent le dortoir des moines avant de retourner à l'église. Dans le bras du transept, côté sud, s'ouvrait la sacristie. Ils poussèrent la porte puis décidèrent de revenir au cloître, explorant cette fois le côté ouest. Soudain, le commissaire aux morts étranges poussa une exclamation.

— Des traces de pas !

Il s'agenouilla dans la neige fraîche et les examina avec attention.

— Deux hommes qui portent un fardeau, déclara-t-il. Non ! Que dis-je ! Deux fardeaux car ils ont fait deux voyages.

Le moine leva les yeux, découvrant la double cheminée du chauffoir où l'on graissait les chaussures et où, à une lointaine époque, réchauffait l'encre tandis que les moines se faisaient tondre.

— S'il y a bien un lieu où amener une prisonnière et éviter qu'elle ne meure de froid, remarqua-t-il, c'est ici.

Son fils se releva souplement et, dans un même mouvement fluide, tira son pistolet et tourna doucement le loquet de la porte. La tiédeur relative de la pièce les saisit d'entrée. Dans l'âtre d'une cheminée refroidissaient des cendres.

— Bien vu ! fit le moine en clignant des yeux pour accommoder à la demi-pénombre. Ils l'ont amenée là, ligotée et recouverte d'une couverture. Vois les traces d'un corps d'enfant dans la poussière et cette longue corde qui devait la tenir sans doute pieds et poings liés.

— Attends, père ! s'écria soudain Volnay en désignant du doigt une autre corde et une seconde couverture. Regarde ! Cela change tout !

Il se pencha et examina les traces.

— Là se trouvait un second corps allongé. Le corps d'un adulte. On tenait ici deux personnes prisonnières !

— Mais qui…

— Qui accompagnait Sophia ?

— Hélène ! Mais…

— La Dame de l'Eau l'a aperçue dans la voiture mais on la menaçait peut-être d'une arme.

— Mon Dieu, oui, s'écria le moine. Tu as raison comme de bien entendu ! Ce n'est pas ce que nous pensions. Oh mon Dieu…

— Quoi ?

La lumière de la torche venait de jeter un éclat doré au sol. Le moine se saisit délicatement de l'objet.

— Un anneau ! Et il y a une inscription à l'intérieur !

Il chaussa ses bésicles et le porta à ses yeux tandis que son fils l'éclairait.

— *AGLA*, lut-il avec application. Il s'agit d'une formule cabalistique formée de la première lettre des quatre mots hébreux *Atha Gabor Leonam Adonaï* : "Vous êtes puissant et éternel Seigneur."

D'un soupir, il exhala l'air de ses poumons.

— Il ne peut appartenir qu'à Hélène ! C'est elle qui s'en est dessaisie pour nous laisser une indication. Cela confirme bien qu'on la tenait prisonnière !

Il lança une longue imprécation et se frappa la tête.

— On nous manipule !

— C'est aussi mon impression.

— Le tableau chez Hélène était un peu chargé : toute cette charcuterie sanglante et ces livres blasphématoires ! Siltieri n'aurait pas mieux fait comme mise en scène. Nous avions envie d'y croire et nous y avons cru. Pauvre enfant ! Oh, mon Dieu !

— Arrête d'en appeler à Dieu, remarqua son fils, il ne peut rien pour nous.

— C'est vrai ! Nous sommes partis comme des benêts en nous disant : si c'est comme ci, ça ne peut être comme ça ! En vérité, même une souris de laboratoire irait plus vite que nous dans ses réflexions !

Le moine tourna sur lui-même comme si ses pensées s'affolaient.

— Nous avons décrété que le but de cette messe noire était de tuer le roi. C'est ce que l'on a voulu nous faire croire. Brisons là toutes nos hypothèses ! Une enquête est comme un jeu d'emboîtement de pièces en bois. Éparpillons les pièces, recomposons-les différemment et posons-nous de nouvelles questions. La personne visée par l'envoûtement d'une messe noire peut littéralement sécher et dépérir jusqu'à passer à trépas et nul docteur ne pourra la sauver. Seule une contre-messe a ce pouvoir en faisant à son tour sécher et mourir le célébrant et ses commanditaires.

Il agita théâtralement les bras en l'air.

— Seulement, une messe noire peut avoir d'autres desseins que ceux de tuer... Pense à la Montespan, fils, pense à la Montespan ! L'histoire est là pour nous montrer le chemin de l'humanité et nous n'en tenons aucun compte !

Volnay le regarda avec effarement.

— Je vois où tu veux en venir : on peut ne pas chercher à tuer le roi mais à l'influencer dans son jugement et sa volonté ! Mais es-tu bien sûr de toi ?

— Oui car nous avons été manipulés de bout en bout, je me ruine le gosier à te le dire !

— Dieu ! Si tu devines bien, nos déductions sont tardives. Prions le ciel pour qu'il ne soit pas trop tard !

— Ne prions pas, fit le moine, armons-nous et courons !

426

— Et où courir ? l'arrêta son fils.

— Je crois le savoir et j'espère pour une fois ne pas me tromper !

Ils coururent enfourcher leurs chevaux et le moine indiqua brièvement à son fils où il fallait se rendre. Une fois sur leurs montures, ils les talonnèrent sans pitié.

— Et moi ! cria Gaston essoufflé qui débouchait à l'air libre. Attendez-moi !

Les deux cavaliers ne se retournèrent même pas.

Les ombres grisées du crépuscule les rattrapèrent une heure après, lorsqu'ils aperçurent la silhouette menaçante du château. Au-dessus de leurs têtes roulaient de gros nuages noirs, un orage menaçait d'éclater. Le commissaire aux morts étranges se dressa sur ses étriers.

— Ce château a l'air désert, remarqua-t-il, mais ce n'est pas une ruine en dehors de la partie nord qui aurait besoin de quelques travaux !

— Comment allons-nous entrer ?

— En sonnant à la grille comme des gens bien élevés !

Ils menèrent leurs chevaux écumants jusqu'à l'entrée. La foudre s'abattit tout près d'eux alors qu'ils arrivaient devant la grille du château.

— Fâcheux signe, murmura le moine, un Romain aurait rebroussé chemin !

— Mais pas nous ! répondit Volnay la main crispée sur son épée.

Le murmure de la pluie et l'odeur de pierre mouillée et de végétation pourrissante les saisirent lorsqu'ils descendirent de monture. Le commissaire aux morts étranges héla le gardien. Une face de rat d'âge indéterminé s'encadra dans la lucarne de la tourelle qui jouxtait l'entrée du château.

— Laisse-moi faire, fils, murmura le moine.

— Que voulez-vous? cria l'homme.

— Entrer pardi, se moqua le moine, nous sommes des invités. Veuillez avoir l'amabilité de vous approcher pour le vérifier.

Le visage disparut dans un grognement. Ils attendirent. Bientôt la porte de la tourelle s'ouvrit. Le gardien descendit le petit escalier qui la desservait et s'approcha, le visage chafouin et l'air méfiant.

— Je ne vous annoncerai pas, déclara-t-il avec hauteur, car il n'y a personne d'autre que moi ici ce soir. Tous les domestiques ont reçu leur congé pour la journée.

— Ne soyez pas si prompt à décréter que nous n'entrerons pas, répliqua le moine, et regardez d'abord ceci.

Il fit mine de fouiller ses poches et jeta une bourse entre les barreaux de la grille. L'autre fit encore quelques pas en avant et se pencha pour la ramasser en marmonnant.

— Votre argent ne change rien à tout cela…

Mais lorsqu'il releva la tête, il se retrouva face au canon d'un pistolet et à l'œil féroce du moine.

— Il me tarde de tuer quelqu'un aujourd'hui, annonça celui-ci d'un ton rauque, alors ne me tente pas! Ouvre cette grille et laisse-nous entrer!

Le gardien bredouilla quelque chose mais se hâta d'ouvrir la grille. Une fois à l'intérieur, le moine lui colla son pistolet sur la tempe, le doigt crispé sur la détente.

— Combien d'hommes de main à l'intérieur?

— Deux, monseigneur.

— Et les autres?

— Trois.

— Merci !

Il frappa d'un coup sec et l'homme s'écroula à terre. Volnay eut une exclamation étouffée et lui jeta un regard froid.

— Comment faire maintenant pour l'interroger ? Sais-tu où se déroule la cérémonie ?

Le moine cilla brièvement.

— Euh... Une chapelle ! Il doit bien y avoir une chapelle ici !

— Je l'espère pour toi ! La prochaine fois que tu as envie de frapper quelqu'un, demande-moi d'abord !

Ils se ruèrent à l'intérieur du château. Les nuages noirs voilèrent les derniers reflets du jour et, d'un coup, le château se remplit de ténèbres. Les portes tremblèrent, les boiseries craquèrent et les charnières grincèrent. Des tentures masquaient les fenêtres. Ils avançaient dans une pénombre oppressante au rythme de leur cœur battant, heurtant parfois dans le noir des meubles dressés sur leur chemin comme autant d'obstacles. Ils débouchèrent sur un salon dont les rideaux tirés laissaient percevoir l'éclat des éclairs au-dehors. Ceux-ci illuminèrent brièvement des porcelaines à l'effigie du roi.

— Ah, notre bon roi est là aussi, marmonna le moine sarcastique.

Son fils lui fit signe de se taire et ils continuèrent leur progression en silence. Soudain, le moine s'arrêta net. Dans cette pièce les fenêtres n'étaient pas masquées. Derrière de lourds meubles, un bruit de respiration compressée et étouffée lui parvenait, accompagné de frémissements diaboliques. Une présence maléfique les attendait dans le noir. Le moine recula jusqu'à se trouver dos au mur et posa la main sur la garde de son épée en criant :

— Venez, mes petits chéris !

Un rouquin se rua vers eux, l'épée à la main.

— Tue !

Son cri se répercuta en écho, ses yeux étincelaient d'une haine brûlante.

— Ah, une vieille connaissance ! gronda le moine en parant le coup. J'espère que tu as fait quelques progrès depuis notre dernière rencontre sinon va-t'en tenir l'écheveau à ta femme !

De son côté, Volnay croisait le fer avec un farouche spadassin. Il esquiva une série d'attaques poussives par de souples mouvements et tenta une botte audacieuse qui toucha son adversaire au flanc. Sans pitié, le commissaire aux morts étranges l'acheva sur place.

Le rouquin était d'un autre acabit. Il bloquait avec facilité les attaques du moine et se montrait redoutable en riposte. S'enhardissant, il tenta de presser son adversaire mais manqua sa contre-attaque. Aussitôt comme s'il avait attendu cela toute sa vie, le moine redoubla puis se fendit droit au cœur.

— Plus de morts, moins d'ennemis ! conclut-il en essuyant son épée sur le corps de son adversaire.

— Nous devons être dans la bonne direction, constata Volnay en reprenant son souffle, sinon ils n'auraient pas été postés ici.

— Il faut toujours aller dans le sens du combat, dit judicieusement le moine. Plus il y a de monde, mieux c'est !

L'éclair au-dehors zébra le ciel, une lumière intense auréola l'autel. L'homme avait quitté son habit de velours rouge et abandonné le goupillon avec lequel il avait baptisé Hélène. Il portait désormais une chasuble blanche bordée de pives noires. Ses poignets s'ornaient de bracelets de perles noires et, à sa ceinture, scintillait la lame luisante d'un couteau. Ainsi paré, le chevalier de Fauve avait belle allure. À l'aide d'une sanguine, il traça un triangle sur le sol et plaça des cierges noirs des deux côtés du triangle. À la base de celui-ci, il inscrivit les lettres sacrées IHS accompagnées de deux croix.

Ceci fait, Mme de Morange entra, drapée dans un manteau de laine rouge mais les pieds nus. À l'invitation du chevalier de Fauve, elle ouvrit son manteau et se coucha nue et frissonnante sur les dalles froides de la chapelle, les bras en croix, un cierge noir dans chacune de ses mains. Son compère lui couvrit le ventre d'un napperon brodé sur lequel il disposa un crucifix, la tête du Christ à l'envers.

— Heureux les forts! clama-t-il. Heureux les méchants, les violents et les blasphémateurs, le royaume de Satan est à eux!

Le chevalier de Fauve prit ensuite un calice sur l'autel et s'approcha du corps inerte de Sophia. Il se saisit d'un de ses poignets qu'il tint au-dessus du récipient. Mme de Morange brailla d'une voix de tête :

— Lucifer, maître des esprits rebelles, je te prie de m'être favorable!

Les éclairs au-dehors jetaient des reflets incendiaires sur les corps nus de la mère et de sa fille. Bleue de froid, Mme de Morange geignit faiblement. La foudre tomba non loin de là.

— C'est un signe, cria le chevalier de Fauve d'une voix exaltée, un signe très encourageant! Continuons!

Il leva son couteau vers le ciel et se mit à psalmodier :

— Astaroth, Asmodée, princes d'amour, je vous conjure d'accepter le sacrifice de cette enfant! En échange, je voudrais que reviennent à sa mère l'affection du roi, la faveur des princes et des princesses de la cour et la satisfaction de tous ses désirs. Voilà, en témoignage de son respect, la vie et le sang de sa propre fille et de celle du roi. Puisse-t-il l'aimer jusqu'à la fin de ses jours !

Le chevalier de Fauve allait ouvrir les veines de l'enfant lorsque la porte s'ouvrit violemment. L'arme au poing, Volnay et le moine apparurent. D'un coup d'œil, le policier embrassa la scène : Mme de Morange étendue nue auprès de Sophia, inerte, Hélène recroquevillée dans un coin de la chapelle, le visage tuméfié, pieds et poings liés, et le chevalier de Fauve, le poignard à la main. Le sataniste contempla les deux arrivants d'un œil joyeux.

— Un moine défroqué ! Voilà le participant qu'il nous manquait même si le policier est de trop !

Mme de Morange poussa un cri effrayé et se releva vivement pour courir se couvrir de son manteau.

— Eh, madame, ne courez pas si vite, se moqua le moine, ce n'est pas la première fois que je vous vois nue ! Quant à mon fils, les femmes comme vous le laissent de marbre !

D'agacement, Volnay siffla doucement entre ses dents et agita son arme en direction du chevalier de Fauve.

— Lâchez ce poignard !

Un sourire torve envahit la face du chevalier de Fauve.

— Que croyez-vous donc qu'il puisse m'arriver ? Les lois physiques n'existent plus, je suis à l'abri de vos balles dans le cercle sacré. Ici, il n'y a plus que vous, moi et le diable !

— Bougre de fou, dit le moine en levant son pistolet, je vais te montrer ce qui est sacré ici-bas, moi !

Vivement, le chevalier de Fauve souleva le corps de Sophia et posa la lame effilée de son poignard sur sa gorge.

— Lâchez vos armes ou, par l'Enfer, je vous jure bien que je l'égorge d'un coup !

Avec un geste léger, presque indétectable, Volnay fit signe à son père. De concert, les deux hommes se baissèrent lentement et posèrent leur pistolet à terre.

— Poussez-les loin de vous, fit le sataniste.

Le commissaire aux morts étranges devança son père et donna un coup de pied dans le premier pistolet. Celui-ci acheva sa course dans les pieds du chevalier de Fauve qui, satisfait, le ramassa. Le second coup de pied, plus violent sous le coup de la colère, fit glisser plus loin le second pistolet, à deux mètres à peine d'Hélène. Celle-ci jeta un regard inexpressif à l'arme puis à Volnay. Ses paupières cillèrent une fois, rapidement.

Pendant ce temps, le moine s'était nonchalamment écarté de son fils qui, lui-même, avait fait un pas de côté. Il devenait difficile au sataniste de les tenir ensemble dans sa ligne de mire.

— À votre place, je ne ferais pas cela !

Entré derrière eux, un homme grand et corpulent pointait deux pistolets chargés sur eux. Avec stupéfaction, Volnay reconnut Cornevin, le commissaire de quartier, vêtu d'un habit de velours noir.

— Vous !

— À mon avis, dit Cornevin au sataniste et à Mme de Morange, ils ont d'autres armes sur eux. Messieurs, couchez-vous sur le sol, je vous prie, les bras en croix.

Il s'approcha le premier de Volnay et trouva un petit pistolet à l'intérieur de sa botte droite. Il l'en ôta et s'approcha du moine. Celui-ci tenta de lui faucher les jambes mais l'autre évita le coup en traître.

— Tiens-toi tranquille, moine du diable ! fit-il en lui appuyant méchamment son pied dans les reins.

Sur celui-ci, il trouva une dague dans la ceinture et un poignard tenu au creux des omoplates.

— En voilà des façons de se promener ainsi armé pour un homme de Dieu, plaisanta-t-il.

— J'en suis désolé, en convint le moine, mais l'on rencontre tant de mauvaises gens au-dehors !

— Tu n'avais qu'à rester chez toi !

Il pointa son pistolet en direction de la tête du moine. Mme de Morange fit un pas dans leur direction. Elle frissonnait de froid et de peur.

— Un instant, fit-elle, qu'allez-vous faire ?

Le commissaire de quartier lui jeta un regard étonné.

— Le tuer, madame, lui et le commissaire aux morts étranges. Que voulez-vous que nous fassions d'autre ?

Elle s'agita nerveusement.

— On risque d'entendre le coup de feu.

— Madame, il n'y a personne d'autre que des gens à nous dans votre hôtel particulier ou plutôt ce qu'il en reste. C'est sans danger mais pour vous rassurer, je peux les égorger.

— Oh oui, égorgez-moi ! s'écria le moine. J'ai toujours rêvé de savoir ce que l'on ressentait en sentant son sang s'écouler hors de soi !

Le chevalier de Fauve émit un rire bruyant et contempla le moine non sans admiration.

— Il préfère cela à une balle dans la tête parce qu'il tentera sa chance quand vous vous pencherez sur lui pour le saisir au cou. Ce genre d'homme est plein de ressources et ne s'avoue jamais vaincu !

Son regard coula en direction de Volnay, toujours allongé, le souffle court.

— Quant à l'autre, reprit-il, regardez-le ! Tous ses muscles sont bandés, il est prêt à se jeter sur vous !

— Une balle dans la tête alors, décida le commissaire de quartier. C'est plus prudent ! Lequel d'abord, madame ?

Le moine releva la tête et dit à Mme de Morange :

— Moi d'abord, s'il vous plaît, vous me devez bien cette grâce !

— Si vous étiez resté tranquille, rien de tout cela ne serait arrivé ! lui cria-t-elle d'une voix aiguë. Vieux fou !

— Je ne suis pas vieux ! se récria le moine.

Il tourna rapidement la tête vers son fils.

— Allez, on se retrouve de l'autre côté, s'il y a quelque chose. Sinon, sache que je t'aime !

Et il se rua dans les pieds du commissaire de quartier mais celui-ci avait prévu une tentative désespérée et il bondit de côté. Lorsqu'il leva ses deux pistolets, Volnay et le moine s'étaient relevés mais pas assez vite. Tranquillement, l'autre les ajusta et visa.

Le commissaire de quartier mourut sur le coup. Un nuage de fumée envahissait la chapelle et lorsqu'il commença à se dissiper, Volnay et son père virent Hélène abaisser très lentement son pistolet, le visage dépourvu de toute expression.

— Je vous avais dit que vous seriez le premier à mourir, dit-elle à Cornevin d'un ton atone.

Le chevalier de Fauve ne l'avait pas vue se saisir de l'arme que Volnay d'un coup de pied avait envoyée dans sa direction. Il poussa violemment Mme de Morange sur les deux intrus avant de se précipiter à l'extérieur. La dame alla atterrir sur le moine qui trébucha et tomba sur le sol.

— Madame, arrêtez de me mettre votre poitrine sous le nez, maugréa le moine en se relevant et en la repoussant.

Déjà son fils s'était lancé à la poursuite du chevalier de Fauve le long du corridor. Soudain, celui-ci s'arrêta et commença à reculer, laissant place à Sartine et à quatre archers du guet qui s'avançaient sur lui.

— Vous ? balbutia Volnay essoufflé.

Sartine eut un sourire froid.

— Il semble que Gaston la mouche ait bien jugé de la situation en courant me prévenir au Châtelet après que vous avez déboulé hors de cette abbaye en criant qu'il fallait vous rendre au château de Mme de Morange ! Nous avons crevé nos chevaux pour arriver à temps.

Quelques mètres derrière lui, Gaston apparut et adressa à Volnay un timide signe de la main.

— Où sont les autres ? demanda sèchement le lieutenant général de police.

— À la chapelle, suivez-moi.

Sartine s'arrêta net en entrant dans le lieu sacré et en contemplant le spectacle qui s'offrait à ses yeux. Pieds et poings liés, Hélène à genoux tenait en joue Mme de Morange. Sophia gisait inerte sur le sol glacé.

— Dieu du ciel ! jura Sartine.

— Pouvez-vous tenir Mme de Morange en joue ? demanda calmement Hélène. Elle ne s'est pas encore rendu compte que mon arme n'est plus chargée mais la raison peut lui revenir ! Et si vous vouliez bien demander qu'on me délie…

Sartine fit un geste de la main et un archer du guet alla libérer la prisonnière. Une fois debout, Hélène s'approcha lentement du corps du commissaire de quartier en inspirant doucement. Les yeux dans le vague, elle leva le pied et d'un geste sec lui écrasa les parties génitales du talon.

— Belle bête ! murmura-t-elle d'un ton las.

Sartine eut un raclement de gorge gêné.

— Eh bien, eh bien…

Il ôta son manteau et en enveloppa maladroitement le corps de Sophia.

— Est-elle ? demanda-t-il d'une voix hésitante.

— Elle est plongée dans le sommeil, le rassura le moine, comme la première fois. Mais je sais comment la réveiller.

Sartine se releva lentement, un éclair de haine dans les yeux. Il s'approcha doucement de Mme de Morange pétrifiée.

— Ainsi c'était vous ! Vous !

Il tourna autour d'elle comme s'il allait la mordre et d'un geste brusque lui arracha son manteau. Mme de Morange eut une exclamation étouffée et couvrit sa poitrine de ses bras.

Le moine cracha de dégoût :

— Vous iriez jusqu'à sacrifier votre propre fille pour les hypothétiques faveurs du roi !

Elle se tourna vers lui, la rage aux lèvres. Un rictus la défigura un instant.

— Mieux vaut viser haut que voler bas par peur des branches ! Que savez-vous des honneurs et de la gloire ? Oui, que pouvez-vous donc savoir de tout ça, vous qui êtes tombé de si haut pour ne jamais vous en relever ?

Le moine secoua la tête en souriant.

— Vous n'y comprenez rien : je ne suis pas tombé, je suis monté plus haut que je ne l'ai jamais été !

Son regard glissa vers le corps de Sophia inerte.

— Qu'est-ce qui vous a fait croire qu'en sacrifiant votre enfant vous retrouveriez les faveurs du roi ? Comment une telle folie vous a-t-elle paru possible ? Et comment passer de l'espérance à la bêtise la plus noire ?

Sans attendre la réponse, le commissaire aux morts étranges fit un signe discret au sergent du guet qui entraîna Mme de Morange, encadrée de deux archers. Le moine se tourna vers lui :

— Tu as remarqué comme l'envie et la jalousie rendent les femmes laides ?

Son fils haussa nonchalamment les épaules. Il préférait conserver pour lui son jugement sur les femmes. Sartine tourna alors sa hargne vers le dernier prisonnier.

— Vous qui m'avez trahi, vos affaires sont faites !

Les fers au poignet, le chevalier de Fauve conservait toute sa superbe. Grand seigneur, il s'avança vers son supérieur, lui tendant la main :

— Allons Sartine, ne soyez pas fâché ! Une poignée de main…

Le lieutenant général de police recula d'un bond comme si un serpent menaçait de le piquer. Le moine comprit sa réaction et se moqua :

— Ne craignez rien, Sartine, le pouvoir d'un sorcier et sa damnation ne se transfèrent lors d'une poignée de main qu'à la mort du sorcier !

Dehors la foudre tonna et le chevalier de Fauve tendit l'oreille.

— Oui, murmura-t-il, c'est le moment… Satan, mon véritable maître, est là et demande audience !

Ses yeux se teintèrent d'obscurité. Il étendit les mains vers les policiers, comme pour les saisir, les doigts bien écartés à la manière des ensorceleurs. Sa voix semblait s'être retirée dans quelque caverne obscure d'où elle résonna sinistrement :

438

— Le jeu n'est pas terminé! J'ai beaucoup appris ces deux dernières années et vous ignorez encore l'étendue de mes pouvoirs. J'ai renoncé à Dieu et à Jésus-Christ, aux saints et saintes, à l'Église apostolique et romaine, à tous les sacrements d'icelle, et à toutes les prières et oraisons qu'on pourrait faire pour moi. J'ai vu l'abîme et je m'y suis englouti. J'ai vu l'abîme et je suis devenu un dieu déchu!

Sa voix monta pour couvrir le bruit de la foudre au-dehors.

— Croyez-vous donc qu'on puisse gagner contre le diable en personne? Vous allez mourir! Vous allez tous mourir!

Une grimace sardonique dévora tout son visage et l'écume coula de sa bouche. Les archers du guet reculèrent et se signèrent vivement. Le sataniste rit et leva les bras en l'air comme s'il allait briser ses chaînes, s'écriant d'une voix terrible :

— J'en appelle à Asmodée, Kobal, Nergal, Ukobach, Bélial et Astaroth, grand-duc très puissant aux Enfers!

— Tu leur donneras le bonjour de ma part! fit le moine en lui envoyant son poing dans la figure.

Sartine avait pris place dans un des fauteuils du grand salon, le visage dans l'ombre. Sophia était couchée, endormie sur une bergère, enveloppée de couvertures. On attendait la mouche et un archer du guet, envoyés à la demeure du moine afin d'en rapporter un certain nombre de plantes pour la tirer de sa léthargie.

Le regard du moine courait alternativement de Sophia, qu'il considérait avec tendresse, à Hélène avec, pour celle-ci, un brin de compassion, de respect voire de fierté. Il lui semblait toutefois que, comme un ange tombé, la jeune femme paraissait secouer ses ailes sans pouvoir s'envoler.

— La mouche a volé vite jusqu'à moi ! constata Sartine qui n'avait cure de ce drame muet. Sans elle, je ne suis pas certain que vous vous en sortiez indemnes.

— La situation était sous contrôle, fit Volnay, et j'allais rattraper le dernier lascar.

— Mouiii, fit Sartine.

Il jeta un regard aiguisé à Hélène assise près de lui, l'arme toujours à la main. Personne n'avait osé la lui reprendre.

— Je constate également que mon auxiliaire vous a été d'une précieuse utilité !

— Monsieur, fit Hélène d'une voix atone, je ne suis pour rien dans ce dénouement. J'étais prisonnière de ces mauvaises gens. Ce sont le commissaire aux morts étranges et son moine qui m'ont permis de retourner le cours des choses.

— Mais vous tirez sans ôter vos liens, commenta joyeusement Sartine. Cela est fort utile…

— Vous savez bien qu'il est difficile de m'attacher…

Le lieutenant général de police la regarda, quelque peu désorienté de cette réponse. Finalement, il se tourna vers son commissaire aux morts étranges.

— Voici venu le temps des explications, Volnay. Et peut-être me raconterez-vous comment un de mes inspecteurs s'est trouvé mêlé à toute cette histoire ?

Le commissaire aux morts étranges eut un sourire froid.

— Votre inspecteur a depuis bien longtemps basculé dans l'obscur ! L'avez-vous vraiment chargé de pénétrer les milieux de la magie noire de Paris ?

Sartine hocha sombrement la tête.

— Le service du roi le commandait. Nous œuvrons pour renforcer l'attachement au roi de ses sujets. La croyance dans le diable les en détourne. L'imagination échauffée du peuple lui fait voir le malin à la place de son monarque ! Je ne crois pas en la sorcellerie mais le peuple y croit, de même que des gens de plus haute condition. De simples va-nu-pieds de prétendus sorciers leur conseillent de planter leur argent dans leurs jardins pour le faire pousser et leur font prendre des feuilles séchées pour des rouleaux d'or ! Rendez-vous compte qu'on a même vu la marquise de Pompadour entrer déguisée chez une dame Bontemps qui vous dit l'avenir !

Il s'interrompit pour jeter un regard circulaire aux lieux enténébrés.

— J'aimerais bien comprendre comment vous en êtes arrivés d'un cimetière enneigé à la sinistre chapelle de ce château !

Volnay se racla la gorge et fit un pas en avant. Contrairement à son père, il était sobre et concis.

— Une nuit dans un cimetière, rappela-t-il, nous découvrons le corps d'une enfant de douze ans. Très vite, nous établissons son identité. Sophia Marly, fille d'un astrologue de la rue des Canettes, paroisse Saint-Sulpice.

Il jeta un regard peu amène à Sartine.

— Bien sûr, une autre personne aurait pu nous apprendre beaucoup plus vite son identité mais elle avait ses raisons pour ne pas le faire.

Sartine se rembrunit mais se garda de tout commentaire.

— Sophia était une fille naturelle du roi, nous l'ignorions. Il nous fallait mener une enquête pour trouver ses meurtriers mais sans savoir qui était vraiment la victime.

Son regard croisa celui d'Hélène et s'adoucit.

— Notre partenaire nous a permis de découvrir ce secret et cela a tout changé. Même bâtarde, Sophia restait une enfant de sang royal. Mme de Morange gardait sans doute un œil sur elle par l'intermédiaire du commissaire de quartier. Tout comme une autre personne pour des raisons tant politiques que personnelles...

Sartine blêmit et fit signe de poursuivre. Volnay reprit :

— Je ne sais quand l'idée est venue à Mme de Morange de se livrer à un envoûtement par le sang en sacrifiant sa propre fille. Après un beau mariage, elle était devenue une riche veuve mais, pour une ancienne maîtresse du roi, ce n'était décidément pas assez. Patience, cela nous le découvrirons plus tard. Revenons au début de notre histoire. Nous sommes sur les traces de la prostituée qui donnait la communion lors de la messe noire. Grâce à mon père, nous la retrouvons.

Le commissaire aux morts étranges joignit les mains et fronça les sourcils.

— Même si la Vorace se tue, l'inquiétude gagne les commanditaires de la messe noire. Le curé dansant reste un point faible pour eux. N'importe qui peut l'acheter et il peut prendre peur. On le pend donc et on met dans sa poche une liste de rues dont celle où habitait l'astrologue. C'est le désigner comme coupable du meurtre de sa fille.

Il fit un aparté.

— Ces assassins ignorent toutefois que le curé dansant porte sur lui la liste véritable de ses adresses de livraison, cousue à l'intérieur d'une doublure. Mon père retrouve celle-ci plus tard et l'une de ces adresses nous amène avec Hélène à une vieille abbaye abandonnée où vraisemblablement se tiennent d'abominables cérémonies.

— Heureux de l'apprendre ! marmonna le lieutenant général de police.

— Nous rentrons bredouilles de l'abbaye, reprit Volnay, mais la découverte de ce lieu nous servira bien par la suite ! Revenons pour l'instant à nos trois complices. Ils ont orienté nos soupçons sur l'astrologue. Toutefois, il ne faut pas le laisser tomber vivant entre nos mains car jamais il n'avouera ce meurtre et nos présomptions pourraient alors se porter sur d'autres. On incendie donc sa maison, brûlant du même coup la servante et son maître. On change de main la magnifique chevalière sertie d'un rubis que nous ne pouvions qu'avoir remarquée sur la personne de l'astrologue. Ruse brillante pour nous faire croire que l'astrologue est encore en vie et a mis en scène sa propre mort. C'est sans doute votre inspecteur de police, le chevalier de Fauve, qui a cette idée. Le plan est diabolique. Il repose également sur notre sens de l'observation.

Il eut un sourire bref qui n'atteignit pas ses yeux.

— J'avoue que celui-ci faillit être pris en défaut car ce détail m'échappa dans un premier temps. Sans doute pour renforcer nos soupçons, on dissimule deux livres dans la maison, dans des endroits où ils sont épargnés par les flammes. Ces livres horribles ne peuvent que désigner l'astrologue comme sataniste et donc commanditaire de la messe noire. Le moine met la main sur un de ces livres et, fort obligeamment, l'insoupçonnable commissaire de quartier trouve le second ! Son visage est à moitié cuit. Je pense maintenant que c'est lui qui mit le feu à la maison de Marly.

— Il ne vous soutiendra pas le contraire, murmura Hélène. C'était un acompte, maintenant, il brûle en enfer.

Il y eut un silence lourd que rompit Volnay.

— Nos trois complices se sentent désormais en sécurité. Ils ont raison de l'être car nous sommes sur une fausse piste. Heureusement pour nous, Hélène va débloquer la situation en identifiant la véritable filiation de Sophia, nous permettant de remonter à sa mère, Mme de Morange. Coup de tonnerre dans le plan idéal de nos compères, le moine rend visite à Mme de Morange. Celle-ci panique et, pour gagner du temps, lui demande de revenir souper. Pendant ce laps de temps, avec ses complices, la décision est prise de le faire assassiner. L'assassinat échoue. Les complices doivent craindre le pire et puis… rien n'arrive. Nos comploteurs comprennent soudain que rien ne relie dans nos esprits Mme de Morange, la propre mère, à la tentative de meurtre de Sophia. Le trio reprend de l'assurance. La découverte de Sophia en vie les fait sans doute même exulter. Ils s'attachent alors à la récupérer. Eh oui, j'ai sauté cet épisode, c'est le commissaire de quartier en personne à qui je m'adresse pour déterrer le cercueil de l'enfant !

Son regard se fixa avec tendresse sur son père.

— En refusant d'autopsier Sophia, le moine est passé à côté d'une vérité flagrante mais lui a également sauvé la vie ! Une fois sortie de sa léthargie, Sophia commence une double vie à l'intérieur et en dehors de sa maison jusqu'à ce que, enfin, nous comprenions la vérité, confirmée par l'ouverture du cercueil.

Il agita les mains en l'air en signe d'excuse.

— J'ai oublié de parler de la scène de l'enterrement et de ma première rencontre avec le chevalier de Fauve.

— Pourquoi le chevalier de Fauve s'est-il rendu dans ce cimetière ? le questionna Sartine.

— Qui sait ? La mort de Sophia était son œuvre, il a sans doute voulu contempler son achèvement. Que se passe-t-il dans la tête d'un criminel ? Toujours est-il qu'il ne prenait pas beaucoup de risques en s'y rendant. Il ne s'est pas mêlé aux participants à l'enterrement. Seul ce malheureux signe de croix à l'envers l'a trahi…

— Grâce à ton sens de l'observation ! renchérit son père.

— Merci ! Reprenons le cours de notre enquête. Nous retrouvons Sophia grâce à son chien…

— Comment ! s'exclama Sartine. Vous m'avez menti !

— Oui. Il faut vous avouer que nous n'étions plus très sûrs de vous à ce moment-là de l'histoire !

— Quoi ?

— Diable, intervint le moine, mensonge, dissimulation de preuves et, plus tard, nous vous surprenons avec un de nos suspects, le sataniste que mon fils a aperçu dans le cimetière…

Sartine se rembrunit mais, au prix d'un immense effort, se contint.

— À cet instant, reprit Volnay, nos soupçons se portent toujours sur l'astrologue et nous vous y associons bien volontiers ainsi que…

Il lui jeta un bref coup d'œil.

— Hélène…

La jeune femme ne réagit pas. Elle semblait s'être absentée à l'intérieur d'elle-même.

— Il faut dire que, spontanément, le chevalier de Fauve, avec une immense audace, est venu se constituer prisonnier pour nous faire part de ses soupçons à votre encontre. Nous nous inquiétons alors du sort de

Sophia que vous cherchez avec tant de rage et malheureusement nous arrivons trop tard à sa cachette. Là, on nous y fait la description d'agresseurs masqués mais dont l'un peut vous ressembler, monsieur le lieutenant général de police, et d'Hélène.

Volnay se tourna vers son père.

— Et c'est là que le moine intervient.

Le moine hocha modestement la tête. Volnay reprit sa respiration avant de continuer, remarquant que les yeux verts d'Hélène semblaient reprendre vie, envahis de lueurs mordorées.

— Une fois Sophia enlevée, nous décidons de nous rendre dans l'appartement d'Hélène.

Celle-ci tressaillit.

— Là encore, on l'a préalablement arrangé pour nous faire croire à sa culpabilité. Et nous nous laissons prendre même si, à réfléchir froidement, la mise en scène est un peu chargée! Mais où chercher Sophia? Nous hésitons entre chez vous, M. de Sartine, ou l'abbaye.

Le lieutenant général de police eut un sourire pincé.

— Nous allons à l'abbaye, reprit Volnay. C'est effectivement là que Sophia a été menée dans un premier temps, sans doute pour laisser le temps de vider le château de Mme de Morange de ses domestiques.

Hélène cilla brièvement.

— À l'abbaye, nous découvrons qu'on a gardé deux prisonnières, une enfant et un adulte. Qui donc peut être l'adulte sinon Hélène? Nous retrouvons d'ailleurs un anneau que mon père, toujours aussi observateur, reconnaît comme le sien.

Le moine rougit imperceptiblement. La main de Volnay plongea dans sa poche et il s'approcha de la jeune femme pour lui tendre l'anneau.

446

— Merci, fit-elle d'un ton neutre.

Elle garda quelques secondes l'anneau dans la paume de sa main avant de se décider à le remettre à son doigt.

— Et comment en êtes-vous arrivés au château de Mme de Morange ? demanda Sartine intrigué.

— À une déduction logique de ma part sur l'identité des deux prisonnières, Sophia et Hélène, suit une déduction foudroyante de mon père !

C'était afficher que le duo d'enquêteurs qu'ils formaient était inséparable. Sartine le comprit et se renfrogna.

— J'en vins à la conclusion, intervint le moine, que nous nous étions fourvoyés. On nous a tellement manipulés dans cette affaire que cela nous a tourné le cerveau à l'envers ! Et pourtant, nous détenions tous la solution du problème dès les premières pages, si j'ose dire, de notre enquête !

Sartine eut une moue interloquée.

— Comment ça ?

Le moine eut un fin sourire.

— L'affaire des Poisons ! La Montespan… Nous en avons tous parlé dès le début de notre énigme. Cela remonte au siècle dernier mais la nature humaine n'a pas changé. Le commanditaire de la messe noire de Sophia désirait la même chose que les courtisans participant aux messes noires sous Louis XIV. Quels que soient l'époque, leur pays, leur race ou position dans la société, nombre de gens n'ont soif que de pouvoir et de reconnaissance. Or, dans l'enquête sur les messes noires, sous Louis XIV, à deux reprises au moins, on parla de mère sacrifiant l'enfant dont elle venait d'accoucher ! Mme de Morange, ancienne maîtresse du roi et mère de l'enfant, aura attendu plus longtemps…

Quels benêts nous sommes de ne pas avoir trouvé plus tôt ce lien! Décidément, l'homme n'apprend jamais rien de l'histoire!

Il laissa planer un silence songeur puis ses yeux brillèrent de nouveau.

— Mais dès que j'eus compris, je comparais mes choix : courir avec mon fils à l'hôtel particulier de Mme de Morange ou au château de celle-ci. Comment je connaissais l'existence de ce dernier? Il faut vous dire que l'on parle beaucoup dans les dîners de Mme de Morange et c'est ainsi que j'appris son existence.

D'un geste en l'air, le moine esquissa un point d'interrogation.

— Alors, hôtel particulier ou château? La logique conduisait à choisir l'endroit le plus discret et isolé.

Il s'approcha d'Hélène qui le fixa sans mot dire.

— Là, nous sommes entrés en force mais nous nous sommes laissé surprendre par le commissaire de quartier et sans Hélène nous serions morts.

Le moine eut un sourire affectueux et sa main effleura l'épaule de la jeune femme qui ne réagit pas.

— Et voilà, conclut-il à regret, comment nous sommes partis du corps d'une enfant sur une pierre tombale à ce sombre château, démasquant une mère indigne, un inspecteur de police devenu fou et un commissaire de quartier vénal. Décidément, M. de Sartine, votre police n'est plus ce qu'elle était!

Le lieutenant général de police bondit sur ses pieds.

— Vous aimez faire pirouette mais je n'oublie pas tous vos tours et détours en cette enquête, c'est miracle que vous soyez encore vivant et les coupables arrêtés!

— Toute notre habileté consiste à retomber sur nos pieds, répliqua le moine en s'étirant nonchalamment.

Mais dites-moi maintenant, que va-t-il arriver à Mme de Morange et le chevalier de Fauve ? Seront-ils bien jugés ?

Sartine eut une grimace sarcastique.

— Deux lettres de cachet feront le nécessaire. Quant au commissaire de quartier Cornevin, officiellement il est mort en héros au détour d'une sombre ruelle dans l'exercice de ses fonctions.

Le moine explosa.

— Vous ne changerez donc jamais, vous les serviteurs zélés de l'ordre royal ! La vérité vous fera toujours peur !

Le lieutenant général de police le toisa de haut.

— La vérité, nous la connaissons, nous, et c'est déjà amplement suffisant. Quelle utilité de raconter toute cette histoire devant un tribunal ? Je ne désire pas divulguer en public qu'on a essayé d'asservir la volonté du roi en sacrifiant une de ses bâtardes au cours d'une messe noire ! Et encore moins que le commanditaire de tout ceci est une ancienne maîtresse de notre monarque, le cerveau de l'affaire un de mes inspecteurs de police et l'exécutant un commissaire de quartier !

Le moine se leva, le visage pâle.

— La vérité est la dignité de l'homme et se doit d'être connue de lui, même si cela heurte quelques intérêts privés. La vérité montre à tous que ni le monde, ni nous-mêmes ne sommes ce que nous devrions être !

— C'est raisonner en philosophe, c'est-à-dire inutilement !

— Sartine, dit le moine, vous faites du mal à l'idée que je me fais du genre humain.

— C'est votre faute, répliqua le lieutenant général de police agacé, pourquoi parlez-vous tant ?

— Parce que les mots veulent dire des choses, répondit paisiblement le moine.

Malgré les protestations du moine, Sartine avait amené Sophia avec lui, une fois celle-ci éveillée. Il parlait de l'adopter. Prenant le moine à part, Hélène s'était longuement entretenue avec lui puis elle avait embrassé le père et le fils avant de s'en aller sans un mot de plus.

Séparés par le corps, demeurons indissolublement unis par nos âmes, pensa fugitivement le moine.

— Reverrons-nous un jour Hélène? s'interrogea Volnay à haute voix après son départ.

— Qui sait? Mais ceci est une autre histoire!

Au milieu de la nuit, Volnay et son père arrivèrent chez le commissaire aux morts étranges, accueillis par une pie plus bavarde que jamais. Le moine soupira. Il cherchait à exprimer la conclusion de toute cette histoire mais ne la trouvait point. Après un verre ou deux, il dit enfin :

— Notre planète tourne autour du soleil mais nous, pauvres humains, le seul axe autour duquel nous gravitons est nous-mêmes afin de tenter de mieux nous connaître.

— Est-ce là ton mot de la fin? se moqua son fils.

— Non, en fait je le cherche en vain mais si tu me donnes quelques minutes, j'aurai bien une idée!

Pour une fois, son fils ne lui laissa pas le dernier mot.

— Père, je suis curieux de savoir ce qu'Hélène t'a dit. Vous vous êtes longtemps entretenus ensemble. On aurait dit deux amants qui se séparent…

— Que vas-tu imaginer, mon fils, j'ai vécu et tiré assez de leçons de la vie pour que celle-ci m'incite à la prudence…

— Tant mieux, dit Volnay, cela n'aurait pas été très malin au vu de votre différence d'âge…

— Je ne suis pas vieux ! le coupa le moine.

— Ce n'est pas ce que j'ai dit !

Son père l'arrêta. Il tenait sa fin.

— Quelle histoire merveilleuse digne des contes des *Mille et Une Nuits* ! s'exclama-t-il. *Si on la gravait à l'aiguille au coin de l'œil, elle servirait d'avertissement à quiconque peut apprendre par l'exemple !*

Hélène fit une petite révérence et on l'invita d'un sourire à se relever pour s'asseoir près du feu. Les deux fauteuils se trouvaient côte à côte, face à la cheminée, mais Hélène s'appliqua à garder le regard obstinément fixé sur les flammes. Assise à ses côtés, l'autre personne restait silencieuse, occupée à se remémorer tous les événements depuis la découverte du corps de Sophia dans le cimetière.

Après la venue du commissaire aux morts étranges, Sartine était accouru hors d'haleine à son hôtel particulier, le portrait de Sophia entre ses mains. Il lui avait appris qu'il s'agissait d'une des filles naturelles du roi que l'on venait de sacrifier lors d'une messe noire. L'affaire semblait d'une gravité exceptionnelle. Bien entendu, le commissaire aux morts étranges s'était saisi de l'affaire mais on savait l'homme tout aussi secret et incontrôlable que son collaborateur, le moine hérétique. Elle avait écouté en silence le lieutenant général de police affolé, prenant la mesure de la situation. Manifestement, la présence de sa meilleure et plus dévouée agente, Hélène, s'imposait. Aussi, en fin d'après-midi, Sartine s'était-il vu dans l'obligation d'amener Hélène avec lui chez Volnay et le moine, les obligeant à accepter sa présence pour cette enquête.

Sur un signe de tête de son hôte, Hélène commença le récit des derniers événements. Puis elle se tut, le regard toujours droit devant elle. Elle savait qu'elle aussi avait été manipulée au cours de cette enquête car ni Sartine ni la personne qui l'employait ne lui avait révélé ce qu'ils savaient au départ.

— Vous m'avez bien servi, dit finalement l'autre personne.

Plongée dans une demi-torpeur, Hélène ne répondit pas. Les flammes dansaient dans ses étranges prunelles, créant d'inquiétantes lueurs. Le feu lui remémorait des pensées que sa mère avait implantées dans sa tête avant de mourir pour un jour la venger.

Tout ceci n'est pas fini, pas encore...

Soudain, la fleur de lys sur son épaule la brûla.

— Je suis contente de vos services, ajouta encore la voix mélodieuse.

Hélène s'inclina.

— Madame la marquise de Pompadour est trop bonne.

TABLE

Retrouvez les enquêtes
du commissaire aux morts étranges
dans les collections Babel noirs et Actes noirs.

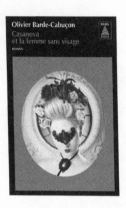

CASANOVA ET LA FEMME SANS VISAGE

*1759. Une femme sans visage est retrouvée dans Paris.
Volnay, le "commissaire aux morts étranges", se charge
de l'enquête. Surveillé de près par Sartine, qui voit d'un
mauvais œil ce policier hors normes, Volnay, secondé
par un moine étrange et Casanova lui-même, remonte
la piste d'un crime qui pourrait impliquer la Pompadour et Louis XV en personne. L'épisode inaugural
d'une formidable série policière historique.*

Grand prix Sang d'encre de la ville de Vienne 2012.

TUEZ QUI VOUS VOULEZ !

À Paris, peu avant Noël, trois hommes sont retrouvés égorgés, la langue arrachée. Au même moment, des inconnus veulent ressusciter la fête des Fous, des convulsionnaires se roulent sur le sol des églises et une jeune fille pousse des cris d'oiseau. Mais que vient faire là-dedans le mystérieux chevalier d'Éon, peut-être membre du Secret du roi ? En quelques jours, l'ordre social paraît s'inverser et le moine semble gagné par la folie ambiante. Le commissaire aux morts étranges, lui, garde la tête froide et mène l'enquête.

BABEL NOIR

Extrait du catalogue

OUVRAGE RÉALISÉ
PAR L'ATELIER GRAPHIQUE ACTES SUD
REPRODUIT ET ACHEVÉ D'IMPRIMER
EN DÉCEMBRE 2013
PAR NORMANDIE ROTO IMPRESSION S.A.S.
À LONRAI
POUR LE COMPTE DES ÉDITIONS
ACTES SUD
LE MÉJAN
PLACE NINA-BERBEROVA
13200 ARLES

DÉPÔT LÉGAL
1re ÉDITION : JANVIER 2014
N° impr. : 134721
(Imprimé en France)